THE
# ARCHITECT'S HANDBOOK
OF
# PROFESSIONAL PRACTICE
## STUDENT EDITION

The American Institute of Architects

# THE ARCHITECT'S HANDBOOK

## OF

## PROFESSIONAL PRACTICE

### STUDENT EDITION

### THIRTEENTH EDITION

JOSEPH A. DEMKIN, AIA, EXECUTIVE EDITOR

JOHN WILEY & SONS, INC.

*Book design by H. Roberts Design*

This book is printed on acid-free paper. ∞

Copyright © 2002 by The American Institute of Architects. All rights reserved.

Published by John Wiley & Sons, Inc.

Published simultaneously in Canada.

This publication is designed to provide accurate and authoritative information in regard to the subject matter covered. It is sold with the understanding that the publisher is not engaged in rendering professional services. If professional advice or other expert assistance is required, the services of a competent professional person should be sought.

**Library of Congress Cataloging-in-Publication Data:**
The architect's handbook of professional practice / Joseph A. Demkin, executive editor.—
Student ed., 13th ed.
       p. cm.
     Includes index
     ISBN 0-471-176-72-9 (pbk.: alk. paper)
       1. Architectural practice—United States—Handbooks, manuals, etc. 2. Architectural services marketing—United States—Handbooks, manual, etc. I. Demkin, Joseph A. II. American Institute of Architects.

NA1996 .A726 2001b
720'.68—dc21                                                                                            2001046973

Printed in the United States of America

10 9 8 7 6 5 4

# Contents

# AIA Documents on CD-ROM

**DOCUMENT SYNOPSES**

**COMMENTARIES**

A2O1 Commentary

B141 Commentary

**A SERIES DOCUMENTS**

A1O1 Standard Form of Agreement Between Owner and Contractor—Stipulated Sum

A101/CMa Standard Form of Agreement Between Owner and Contractor—Stipulated Sum, Construction Manager-Adviser Edition

A105 Standard Form of Agreement Between Owner and Contractor for a Small Project—Stipulated Sum

A205 General Conditions of the Contract for Construction of a Small Project

A107 Abbreviated Standard Form of Agreement Between Owner and Contractor for Construction Projects of Limited Scope—Stipulated Sum

A111 Standard Form of Agreement Between Owner and Contractor—Cost of the Work Plus a Fee, Guaranteed Maximum Price

A121/CMc Standard Form of Agreement Between Owner and Construction Manager Where the Construction Manager Is Also the Constructor (AGC Document 565)

A121/CMc-a Amendment to A121/CMc

A131/CMc Standard Form of Agreement Between Owner and Construction Manager Where the Construction Manager Is Also the Constructor—Cost Plus a Fee, No Guarantee of Cost (AGC Document 566)

A131/CMc-a Amendment to Al3l/CMc

A171 Standard Form of Agreement Between Owner and Contractor for Furniture, Furnishings, and Equipment—Stipulated Sum

A177 Abbreviated Form of Agreement Between Owner and Contractor for Furniture, Furnishings, and Equipment—Stipulated Sum

A191 Standard Form of Agreements Between Owner and Design/Builder

A201 General Conditions of the Contract for Construction

A201/CMa General Conditions of the Contract for Construction Where the Construction Manager Is Not a Constructor, Construction Manager–Adviser Edition

A201/SC Federal Supplementary Conditions of the Contract for Construction

A271 General Conditions of the Contract for Furniture, Furnishings, and Equipment

A305 Contractor's Qualification Statement

A310 Bid Bond

A312 Performance Bond and Payment Bond

A401 Standard Form of Agreement Between Contractor and Subcontractor

A491 Standard Form of Agreements Between Design/Builder and Contractor

A501 Recommended Guide for Competitive Bidding Procedures and Contract Awards for Building Construction

A511 Guide for Supplementary Conditions

**A511/CMa** Guide for Supplementary Conditions, Construction Manager–Adviser Edition

**A521** Uniform Location of Subject Matter

**A571** Guide for Interiors Supplementary Conditions

**A701** Instructions to Bidders

**A771** Instructions to Interiors Bidders

## B SERIES DOCUMENTS

**B141** Standard Form of Agreement Between Owner and Architect with Standard Form of Architect's Services

**B141/CMa** Standard Form of Agreement Between Owner and Architect Where the Construction Manager Is Not a Constructor, Construction Manager–Adviser Edition

**B144/ARCH-CM** Standard Form of Amendment for the Agreement Between Owner and Architect Where the Architect Provides Construction Management Services as an Adviser to the Owner

**B151** Abbreviated Standard Form of Agreement Between Owner and Architect

**B155** Standard Form of Agreement Between Owner and Architect for a Small Project

**B163** Standard Form of Agreement Between Owner and Architect with Descriptions of Designated Services and Terms and Conditions

**B171** Standard Form of Agreement for Interior Design Services

**B177** Abbreviated Form of Agreement for Interior Design Services

**B181** Standard Form of Agreement Between Owner and Architect for Housing Services

**B188** Standard Form of Agreement Between Owner and Architect for Limited Architectural Services for Housing Projects

**B352** Duties, Responsibilities and Limitations of Authority of the Architect's Project Representative

**B431** Architect's Qualification Statement

**B511** Guide for Amendments to AIA Owner–Architect Agreements

**B727** Standard Form of Agreement Between Owner and Architect for Special Services

**B801/CMa** Standard Form of Agreement Between Owner and Construction Manager Where the Construction Manager Is Not a Constructor

**B901** Standard Form of Agreement Between Design/Builder and Architect

## C SERIES DOCUMENTS

**C141** Standard Form of Agreement Between Architect and Consultant

**C142** Abbreviated Standard Form of Agreement Between Architect and Consultant to Be Used in Conjunction with Standard Form of Agreement Between Owner and Architect

**C727** Standard Form of Agreement Between Architect and Consultant for Special Services

**C801** Joint Venture Agreement for Professional Services

## D SERIES DOCUMENTS

**D101** The Architectural Area and Volume of Buildings

**D200** Project Checklist

## G SERIES DOCUMENTS

**G601** Request for Proposal–Land Survey

**G602** Request for Proposal–Geotechnical Services

**G605** Notification of Amendment to the Professional Services Agreement

**G606** Amendment to the Professional Services Agreement

**G607** Amendment to the Consultant Services Agreement

**G701** Change Order

**G701/CMa** Change Order, Construction Manager–Adviser Edition

**G702** Application and Certificate for Payment

**G702/CMa** Application and Certificate for Payment, Construction Manager–Adviser Edition

**G703** Continuation Sheet

**G704** Certificate of Substantial Completion

**G704/CMa** Certificate of Substantial Completion, Construction Manager–Adviser Edition

**G706** Contractor's Affidavit of Payment of Debts and Claims

**G706A** Contractor's Affidavit of Release of Liens

**G707** Consent of Surety to Final Payment

**G707A** Consent of Surety to Reduction in or Partial Release of Retainage

**G709** Proposal Request

**G710** Architect's Supplemental Instructions

**G711** Architect's Field Report

**G712** Shop Drawing and Sample Record

**G714** Construction Change Directive

**G714/CMa** Construction Change Directive, Construction Manager–Adviser Edition

**G715** Supplemental Attachment for ACORD Certificate of Insurance

**G722/CMa** Project Application and Project Certificate for Payment

**G723/CMa** Project Application Summary

**G805** List of Subcontractors

# Preface to the Student Edition

The *Architect's Handbook of Professional Practice* was first published in 1918, providing the still-emerging profession with a comprehensive guide to practice-related issues. Presenting fundamental practice concepts and procedures, the *Handbook* helped define the role of the architect and served as a useful tool in shaping a collective understanding of the structure of the profession.

Over the past 80 years, the *Handbook* has been periodically updated to reflect changes in the profession, in the industry, and in society, so it is perhaps no surprise that early in the 21st century a major new edition has been prepared. This comprehensive overhaul of the *Handbook*—departing markedly from its predecessors—creates a text that seeks to address the major challenges confronting today's architects, specifically "advancing technology, the explosive growth of information, increasingly sophisticated clients seeking greater value, an expanding global economy, and more intense competition from within and outside the profession." In a sense, it seeks to reinforce a redefinition of the profession by demonstrating how practices are shifting from product-based to knowledge-driven models.

The 13th edition of the *Handbook* focuses on the client as a key participant in the practice equation, the changing business functions of the office of the 21st century, and the enlarged realm of architectural services that expands the architect's role in the building world. As such, it represents an important new perspective on the continued evolution of the profession and a useful road map to its practical application.

Of course, the usefulness of the *Handbook* is not limited to practice alone. Comprehensive education in professional practice has not always been a staple in the now 130 or so schools of architecture in North America. However, the National Architectural Accreditation Board currently requires all students in accredited degree programs to gain a healthy exposure to practical matters, and material in the *Handbook* becomes required reading in many schools throughout the country. Given the importance of the educational role of the *Handbook*, a student edition of the 12th edition was published for use in the classroom.

With the production of the 13th edition, a new student edition was again considered necessary to serve the needs of the schools. A process of concentrating the most useful material into a compact (and therefore more economical) format was devised to best reflect the perspectives of those likely to be involved in its application as a teaching tool.

Academics experienced in the teaching of professional practice reviewed the material in the 13th edition to assess its potential for inclusion in the student edition. The members of the review board, drawn from architectural programs across the country, provided a collective viewpoint on the relative weight of the *Handbook*'s contents, which was then studied and discussed by the editorial board. After careful review, the editorial board chose the best possible cross section of information from the larger text of the professional 13th edition.

My thanks are due to the members of the review board, who labored over the summer to provide their invaluable input. They are David Haviland, Russell Groves, Greg Palermo, George Elvin, Bruce Dilg, and Barry Yatt.

I am also indebted to the members of the advisory board for their careful assessment of the reviewers' work and the contents of the *Handbook*. They too worked on a demanding timetable on the arduous task of whittling the contents of the 13th edition down to a manageable, yet extremely useful, student publication. Board members include Dana Cuff, Madlen Simon, Brian Schermer, and Marvin Malecha.

Thanks go to both Amanda Miller and Jennifer Ackerman of John Wiley and Sons for their assistance in preparing the student edition, and to the publisher itself for taking on such an important project on behalf of the American Institute of Architects and the architectural profession.

ROBERT GREENSTREET
Student Edition Editor
Chair, School of Architecture and Urban Planning
University of Wisconsin-Milwaukee

# Foreword to the Professional Edition

The chairman of the steering committee that guided the writing of the *Handbook* characterizes this, the 13th edition, as a "departure." That is something of an understatement. This latest edition of the *Handbook* is animated by a fresh approach to a time-honored profession. It creatively addresses the major tectonic shifts transforming the marketplace for architectural services and, in the process, returns the favor by being itself an agent of transformation.

To be sure, much of what readers will find in this new edition will not be alien territory. The accumulated wisdom of the profession that has stood the test of time remains. It is clearly laid out in these pages to inform today's architects and a new generation eager to take their place. Nevertheless, even a cursory glance at the table of contents reveals something new is afoot; the first entries, for example, boldly shift the focus from the architect to the client.

The boldness of this departure is not without precedent. Consider the world in which The American Institute of Architects first took shape. The year was 1857. This nation's economy and society were being radically reconstructed by the Industrial Revolution. One major consequence was a push for standardization. In the economy that was emerging just before the Civil War, cast-iron pipes fabricated in Pittsburgh had to mesh with fittings manufactured in New England or, for that matter, Manchester, England. Architects and the construction industry were not immune to these powerful winds of change.

In the years preceding Lincoln's election to the White House, anyone who wanted to call himself an architect could. There were few if any standards. No schools of architecture, no licensing laws, no widely accepted contract documents. Strictly speaking, there was no *profession*. The 12 men who met in the Manhattan office of architect Richard Upjohn back in 1857 were responding to the forces set in motion by the Industrial Revolution. In a marketplace that increasingly demanded predictability and consistency, they had to define a profession. Somehow an architect coined in Boston had to have the same value (in the abstract at least) as an architect coined in San Francisco.

The strategy for achieving this goal was to create a professional society. Through the power of collective action the AIA and its members would manage the change from an unstructured craft to a respected profession. Both the vision of its first leaders and the needs of the marketplace worked for success. In the years that followed its founding, the AIA and its members were responsible for establishing the schools, curricula, documents, and practice legislation that organized the profession.

Nearly a century and a half later the profession and the AIA once again stand on the shifting ground of a major reconfiguration of the marketplace. The magnitude of the challenge is similar, but the forces are driving society and the profession in new directions. If the task in 1857 was to define a profession, the challenge in the opening decade of the 21st century is to break down and erase the old boundaries while redefining what it means to be an architect.

What are the forces driving change? One way to answer that question is to compare where we have been to where we find ourselves today. The 19th century was about horsepower; the 21st is about the power of the brain. The centripetal forces driving standardization are being replaced by the centrifugal urge of customization. It is unity vs. diversity, product vs. process or service, mass vs. speed.

These pairs of opposites are offered as a shorthand way of thinking about the world architects are waking up to. How ironic, then, and how appropriate as well, that the *Handbook,* one of the AIA's oldest products, which first appeared in 1918, is once again being offered as a resource to manage change! Conceived nearly a century ago as a tool to give the profession greater definition or structure, the *Handbook* in this, its latest edition, places the emphasis not on formulas or setting boundaries, but on flexibility, nimbleness, and innovation. In fact, this edition begins with the client as a sort of first cause and then moves to the relationship between architect and client as a consequence.

This is different—and the difference is energizing.

To effect a departure as bold as this called for visionary leadership. The Institute and its members owe a great debt of gratitude to the Handbook Steering Group, so ably chaired by Robin Ellerthorpe, FAIA, and to the executive editor, Joseph A. Demkin, AIA. Gratitude is likewise owed to the many contributors whose knowledge and insights inform every chapter. Their individual contributions and the contributions of those responsible for the production of this edition of the *Handbook* are specifically acknowledged elsewhere.

But I cannot leave this all-too-brief tribute to those who had some role in bringing the 13th edition to light without recognizing the great contribution made by our publisher, John Wiley & Sons, Inc. This edition of the *Handbook* represents the first fruit of a new alliance between the AIA and Wiley. The fact that this alliance accommodated a publication so strikingly different from past editions exhibits a level of support and trust that bodes well for the future. As I suggested above, the opportunities for the future of the profession in the 21st century lie in knowledge- and service-based practice in which the relationship between client and architect plays a key role. How appropriate, then, that the 13th edition of the *Handbook* is itself the product of a relationship that prizes knowledge and service.

NORMAN L. KOONCE, FAIA
Executive Vice President/CEO
The American Institute of Architects
Washington, D.C.

# An Overview
# of the *Handbook*

The American Institute of Architects has published the *Architect's Handbook of Professional Practice* for more than 80 years to provide a comprehensive practice manual for the architecture profession. With this edition—the 13th—the AIA has reinforced its long-standing commitment to the *Handbook* by entering into a publishing partnership with John Wiley & Sons, Inc. This alliance expands the resources available to develop, produce, and deliver the *Handbook* by merging AIA's wealth of practice knowledge with Wiley's publishing expertise.

## REDEFINING THE *HANDBOOK*

The 12th edition of the *Handbook* was published in 1994. Since then new challenges have emerged to confront practicing architects. These challenges—and the opportunities that go with them—are inextricably linked to rapidly advancing technology, the explosive growth of information, increasingly sophisticated clients seeking greater value, an expanding global economy, and more intense competition from within and outside the profession.

During the latter half of the 1990s, the AIA "Redefinition of the Profession" initiative stressed that attitudinal shifts about architecture practice would be needed to meet the challenges and demands of the emerging knowledge-based economy. Those shifts involve a transition from practices that are product-based to those that are knowledge-driven. Within this context, the 13th edition:

- Explores the realm of the client to show how clients are motivated, how they think, what they value, and how architects can build stronger client-architect relationships
- Addresses business functions that are vital to the support and operation of an architecture practice
- Presents processes that define, obligate, and deliver professional services
- Profiles a spectrum of core and expanded services with which architects can respond to a wide range of facility needs beyond the design and creation of physical space

## MAJOR DIFFERENCES BETWEEN THE 12TH AND 13TH EDITIONS

This edition of the *Handbook* differs from the 12th edition in format, organization, and content. The single hardback volume of the 13th edition (with a CD-ROM containing sample AIA

Documents) replaces the four-volume loose-leaf format of the 12th edition. While having a new look and feel, the 13th edition retains features of the 12th edition, including the structure that organizes chapters, topics, and backgrounders within major divisions.

About half of the material in the 13th edition is new. The other half consists of updated topics from the 12th edition. Because of its strong focus on practice issues, the 13th edition leaves subjects such as professional life and intern development to be more appropriately addressed in a student edition of the *Handbook*.

## STRUCTURE AND CONTENT OF THE 13TH EDITION

The *Handbook* is divided into four parts: Client, Business, Delivery, and Services. Each part consists of chapters about areas of practice such as firm planning, marketing and outreach, and financial operations. In turn, each chapter contains two or more topics that address specific aspects of the chapter's focus. For example, the chapter Understanding Clients includes topics on The Nature of the Client and Understanding Client Values. The chapter Risk Management includes topics on Risk Management Strategies, Insurance Coverage, and Managing Disputes.

Some topics contain backgrounders that elaborate on some portion or aspect of the material covered by the topic. For example, the topic Financial Systems in the Financial Operations chapter contains a backgrounder on Computerized Financial Systems. The topic Project Team Agreements contains a backgrounder on Joint Venture Agreements.

The Appendix section contains a list of useful information sources, including organizations relevant to the design and construction industry; a list of architecture practice terms and definitions; and a finder for locating AIA contract documents. The information in each of these sections has been updated.

The CD-ROM included with the 13th edition contains samples of all the AIA Contract Documents in PDF format. Users may print copies of the documents for reference purposes only.

## USING THE *HANDBOOK*

The *Handbook* has multiple entry points. Topics can be read individually and in any order. An exception is the material in Part 1 on clients. These topics are best read sequentially because of interrelationships between them.

Information in the margins of each topic helps the reader navigate the *Handbook* and provides additional perspectives about the subject matter. For example, margin elements

- Lead the reader to related *Handbook* topics or backgrounders
- Refer to relevant AIA programs, services, and documents
- Provide capsules of information and data from the 2000 AIA Firm Survey
- Amplify ideas in short side commentaries
- Show how others have perceived or viewed some aspect of the topic through selected quotations

At the end of some topics, For More Information identifies organizations, books, and other information about subjects addressed in the topic.

## THE *HANDBOOK* AUDIENCE

The target audience of this edition is the licensed architect with at least five to ten years of practice experience. Nonetheless, architects not yet licensed, students of architecture, consultants to architects, and others will find the *Handbook* a valuable information source. Following are some examples of who may find the *Handbook* useful:

- Principals and associates of architecture firms seeking to identify new markets, acquire new firm capabilities and skills, develop strategic business plans, and negotiate and prepare contacts with clients or consultants
- Firm architects in need of communicating an aspect of practice to a client or consultant, including such issues as risk management, project management, or regulatory requirements
- Architects seeking to start their own firms who want to obtain a basis for defining the business and delivery systems needed to conduct a practice
- Staff architects with corporations, institutions, and public agencies working on projects involving architectural services
- Architecture students looking to become informed about the general and detailed dimensions of practice
- Attorneys needing information about architecture practice in their work for architects, contractors, and building owners
- Clients or their representatives involved in or about to be involved in architectural services

## HOW THE *HANDBOOK* WAS PREPARED

The AIA Handbook Steering Group guided the overall development of the *Handbook*. In the initial planning phase, members of the steering group worked closely with the *Handbook* executive editor to create a comprehensive framework for the *Handbook*'s content and to develop a program to guide content development. After an editorial program was in hand, contributing authors consisting of AIA members and others were engaged to prepare new topics and to bring selected ones up to date from the 12th edition.

Individuals knowledgeable about specific practice subjects were asked to review draft material—often several times. Constructive comments, advice, and suggestions were forwarded to the authors for consideration in the preparation of final manuscripts. In this process, the editorial staff helped to resolve differing opinions and varying points of view.

## PEOPLE WHO WORKED ON THE *HANDBOOK*

The AIA extends its deepest appreciation to everyone who helped bring the *Handbook* to realization. The accompanying list gives the names of those who participated. There are too many to thank individually; however, several participants merit special recognition.

Collectively and individually, members of the Handbook Steering Group played an important role in the editorial planning process. The vision and leadership of Robin Ellerthorpe, FAIA, chairman of the steering group—reinforced by the critical thinking of Gordon Chong, FAIA—helped to identify "redefinition themes" for infusion into the *Handbook*. In sharing his personal experience with the development the 12th edition, David L. Hoffman, FAIA, brought valuable knowledge to the planning process. With their perspectives from a large and a small firm, respectively, C. Richard Meyers, FAIA, and Morris Hancock, AIA, helped to keep "practical" practice considerations in the forefront. As the group's liaison with the AIA Documents Committee, Allan Sclater, FAIA, provided insight about the direction of the documents program; and from a legal perspective, David Perdue, Esq., Hon. AIA, furnished advice on addressing matters of law and ethics.

Appreciation is also extended to AIA staff members who participated in the deliberations of the steering group. Richard Hobbs, FAIA, provided a wealth of ideas and information on leading-edge practices and methodologies, and John R. Hoke, Jr., FAIA, made many helpful suggestions on editorial and publishing matters.

Special recognition goes to Kevin W. C. Green for his able effort in preparing the Client material in Part 1. This collection of topics represents a significant addition to the *Handbook*'s body of practice information and knowledge.

A note of thanks is extended to Frank D. Musica, Esq., Assoc. AIA, of the Victor O. Schinnerer Company. His insights and assistance on developing insurance and risk management subjects were extremely valuable.

The AIA is indebted to Elena Marcheso Moreno for preparing several business and delivery topics and for editing the work of contributing authors for these parts of the *Handbook*. Consulting editor Karen Haas-Martin merits a thank-you for coordinating and editing many of the service topics. In the editorial realm, Pamela James Blumgart was of immeasurable help with content editing and other related chores.

Among the AIA headquarters staff, a hearty thank-you goes to Jay Stephens, Esq., the Institute's general counsel, for his review of the *Handbook* through a legal lens. Other current and former AIA staff deserving thanks include Stan Bowman; David C. Bullen, AIA; Pradeep Dalal; Laura Eide; Dale Ellickson, Esq., FAIA; Douglas H. Gordon, Hon. AIA; Christopher Gribbs, Assoc. AIA; Richard Hayes, Ph.D., AIA; Joseph Jones, Esq., AIA; C. D. Pangallo, Ed.D.; Janet Rumbarger; Michael Tardif, Assoc. AIA; and Gina Yegerlehner. Their help was useful in identifying resources, offering guidance, reviewing selected material, and contributing to the development of topics.

The *Handbook* editorial staff made numerous research requests which were cheerfully accommodated by Maureen Booth, Art Levine, and other staff of the AIA Knowledge Center. The editorial assistance provided by Michelle Evans and Cheryl Burlingame is also appreciated.

Lastly, the AIA is indebted to the staff at John Wiley & Sons who helped bring the *Handbook* into its final physical form. Especially appreciated are the efforts of Amanda Miller, who coordinated the numerous exchanges between Wiley and the AIA during the publishing process. And a well-deserved thank-you goes to Maury Botton for his management of the design and production workflow.

The 13th edition of the *Handbook* strives to provide a picture of architecture practice today by describing its varied components within a comprehensive and coherent framework. It is hoped that the *Handbook* content and messages will serve in some measure to help architects refine—or redefine—their existing practices and to build new ones to meet the demands and capture the opportunities of the emerging knowledge-based economy.

JOSEPH A. DEMKIN, AIA
The American Institute of Architects
Washington, D.C.

# 13TH EDITION HANDBOOK PARTICIPANTS

## Steering Group
Robin Ellerthorpe, FAIA, Chairman
Gordon Chong, FAIA
David L. Hoffman, FAIA
Morris Hancock, AIA
C. Richard Meyer, FAIA
Alan Sclater, FAIA
David Perdue, Esq., Hon. AIA

## Contributing Authors
Gretchen E. Addi, Assoc. AIA
Mark Appel
Christopher C. Arnold, FAIA
Phillip G. Bernstein, FAIA
Gary Betts, FCSI, CCS, AIA
Gregory D. Boothe, CIH
Brian Bowen, FRICS
Ann Marie Boyden, Hon. AIA
Howard Brandston, LC, FIES, Hon.
   FCIBSE, FIALD
Robert Burley, FAIA
Marvin J. Cantor, FAIA
William C. Charvat, AIA, CSI
Russell A. Cooper
Kenneth C. Crocco, FAIA
Philip R. Croessmann, Esq., AIA
Clark S. Davis, FAIA
Joseph A. Demkin, AIA
Paul Doherty, AIA
Laurie Dreyer-Hadley
John P. Eberhard, FAIA
Charles N. Eley, FAIA
Robin M. Ellerthorpe, FAIA
Dale R. Ellickson, Esq., FAIA
Katherine Davitt Enos, Esq., Assoc. AIA
Kristine K. Fallon, FAIA
Ellen Flynn-Heapes
Richard B. Garber, ASLA
Ralph D. Gerdes, AIA
Lowell V. Getz, CPA
Ronald V. Gobbell, FAIA
Howard Goldberg, Esq.
Douglas E. Gordon, Hon. AIA
Kevin W. C. Green
Susan Greenwald, FAIA, CSI
Ernest L. Grigsby, AIA
Ron S. Gupta, AIA
Morris C. Hancock, AIA
Patricia Henriques
Robert G. Hershberger, Ph.D., FAIA
Charles R. Heuer, Esq., FAIA
Hugh M. Hochberg
David L. Hoffman, FAIA

Christopher Jaffe, Ph.D., Hon. AIA
Joseph H. Jones, Esq., AIA
Susan L. Kennedy
Eugene Kremer, FAIA
Larry Lord, FAIA
Jacqueline Lytle, IIDA, Assoc. AIA
Muscoe Martin, AIA
John Mason
Kathleen C. Maurel, Assoc. AIA
Patrick C. Mays, AIA
Richard L. McElhiney, AIA
C. Richard Meyer, FAIA
Elena Marcheso Moreno
Thomas O. McCune, AIA
Robert C. Mutchler, FAIA
Frank D. Musica, Esq., Assoc. AIA
Charles Nelson, AIA, FRAIA
James O'Brien, Esq.
Lorna Parsons
Dan L. Peterson, AIA
Roger Pickar
Peter A. Piven, FAIA
William M. Polk, FAIA
Donald Prowler, FAIA
John P. S. Salmen, AIA
Margaret Serrato, AIA, ASID
Frank A. Stasiowski, FAIA
Harris M. Steinberg, AIA
Ralph Steinglass, FAIA
Doug Stelling, AIA
John (Jack) C. Stevenson, Jr., AIA
William W. Stewart, FAIA
Michael Tardif, Assoc. AIA
Jennifer Taylor
Edward T. M. Tsoi, FAIA
Timothy R. Twomey, Esq., AIA
Christopher Widener, AIA
Roger B. Williams, FAIA, JIA
Howard J. Wolff
Floyd Zimmerman, FASLA

## Reviewers
Jerome Albenberg, AIA
Gregg D. Ander, AIA
Lee H. Askew III, FAIA
Ellen Berky, AIA
Anthony N. Bernheim, FAIA
Phillip G. Bernstein, AIA
Scott W. Braley, FAIA
Michael Brill
Bradley S. Buchanan, AIA
James W. Buchanan, PE, AIA
John W. Busby, FAIA

William Cavanaugh
George Christodoulo
Edith Cherry, FAIA
Jonathan W. Cohen, AIA
Philip Crompton
Carolyn Dasher
Robert J. Erikson, AIA
Scott R. Fazekas, AIA
Edward A. Feiner, FAIA
Benjamin P. Fisher, AIA
Sofia Fonseca, AIA
Harry T. Gordon, FAIA
Alex Grinnell
Robert Gutman, Hon. AIA
Barbara Golter Heller, AIA
Stephen J. Kirk, FAIA
John M. Laping, FAIA
Robert D. Loversidge, AIA
Lucinda Ludwig, AIA
Lauren Mallas, AIA
William Mandel, Esq.
Laurin McCracken
Thomas W. McHugh, AIA
Herbert P. McLaughlin Jr., AIA
James Mitchell, AIA, RIBA
Elizabeth Mossop
Paul R. Neel, FAIA
James O'Brien, Esq.
Arthur F. O'Leary, FAIA
Robert A. Odermatt, FAIA
Wendy Ornelas, AIA
Ennis Parker, FAIA
Dan L. Peterson, AIA
G. William Quatman, AIA
Paula Reese
Ennis Parker, FAIA
Carolyn Richman Peart
Carroll L. Pruitt, AIA
Judith L. Rowe, FAIA
Robert P. Smith, AIA
Charles Alfred Spitz, AIA
Jay Stephens, Esq.
David A. Stone, Assoc. AIA
Lawrence L. Strain, AIA
Stephanie Vierra, Assoc. AIA
Christopher R. Widener, AIA
Steve L. Wintner, AIA

## Editorial Staff
Joseph A. Demkin, AIA, Executive Editor
Pamela James Blumgart, Project Editor
Karen Haas-Martin, Consulting Editor
Elena Marcheso Moreno, Consulting

# THE ARCHITECT'S HANDBOOK OF PROFESSIONAL PRACTICE, STUDENT EDITION PARTICIPANTS

**Editor**

Robert Greenstreet
School of Architecture and Urban
    Planning
University of Wisconsin–Milwaukee

**Advisory Board**

Dana Cuff
Department of Architecture
University of California Los Angeles

Madlen Simon
Department of Architecture
Kansas State University

Marvin Malecha
North Carolina State University
School of Design

Brian K. Schermer
Department of Architecture
University of Wisconsin Milwaukee

**Review Board**

Russell Groves
Department of Architecture
University of Kentucky

George Elvin
Department of Architecture
    University of Illinois at Urbana-
Champaign

David Haviland
Department of Architecture
Rensselaer Polytechnic Institute

Gregory Palermo
Department of Architecture
Iowa State University

Bruce Dilg
Department of Architecture
Ferris State University

Barry Yatt
Department of Architecture
Catholic University of America

# Architecture as a Profession

## Dana Cuff, Ph.D.

Architecture is in the family of vocations called professions, all of which share certain qualities and collectively occupy a special position in society. Architects' status as professionals provides them with an underlying structure for their everyday activities.

### A PROFESSION DEFINED

To be a professional means many things today. One can be a professional athlete, student, or electrician. Each of these occupations uses the term in ways distinct from what we mean by the professional who is a doctor, lawyer, or architect.

Typically, we distinguish professionals who do certain work for a living from amateurs who work without compensation. The term *amateur* connotes a dabbler, or someone having less training and expertise than a professional.

We also differentiate between professions and other occupations. Expertise, training, and skill help define those vocations that "profess" to have a specialized territory of knowledge for practice. While many occupations require expertise, training, and skill, professions are based specifically on fields of higher learning. Such learning takes place primarily in institutions of higher education rather than in vocational schools or on the job. Universities introduce prospective professionals to the body of theory or knowledge in their field. Later, this introduction is augmented by some form of internship in which practical skills and techniques are mastered.

A high level of education is expected of professionals because their judgments benefit—or, if incompetently exercised, endanger—the public good. Thus, people who are attracted to the professions usually have altruistic concerns for their society.

The status of professions, their internal characteristics, and their relationship to society are constantly, if not always perceptibly, changing. The professions have grown dramatically in recent years, in keeping with the rise of the postindustrial, service economy. Growth in professional employment has accompanied expansion of the service sector of the economy, estimated today to be 70 percent of the labor force. In a service economy, information and knowledge industries become dominant, creating the context in which professions can rise among occupations.

**DANA CUFF, PH.D.,** *is a professor and cochair of the School of Architecture and Urban Design at the University of California, Los Angeles. She has conducted extensive research and published widely on the subject of architectural practice, including the book* Architecture: The Story of Practice.

# CHARACTERISTICS OF A PROFESSION

Professions are dynamic entities that reflect our society, our economy, and, generally, our times. There is no widely accepted definition or list of features that covers all professions. Nevertheless, they have some characteristics in common, which have appeared throughout history.

## Lengthy and Arduous Education

Perhaps the most frequently cited characteristic of a profession is a lengthy and sometimes arduous education. A professional must learn a body of technical knowledge and also develop an ability to exercise judgment in the use of that knowledge. Thus, all established professions incorporate long periods of high-level education.

Professional education is also a form of socialization. Like a rite of passage for initiates, architecture, medical, and law schools are places where future practitioners are introduced to the knowledge, values, and skills of their profession. Students undergo tests of their commitment and ability. In architecture schools, a good example is the charrette (often involving all-nighters), during which students concentrate all their efforts to finish a project. These experiences instill tacit beliefs about the significance of architecture, the work effort required to do a good job, and the commitment needed to become an architect. Through selective admissions, carefully designed curricula, and rigorous graduation standards, schools guide the formation of their professional progeny. Professional schools play a key role in developing the shared worldview that characterizes a professional community.

## Expertise and Judgment

Professions traffic in ideas and services rather than goods or products. Rather than marketing a better widget, professionals sell their expertise. They have knowledge outside the ken of the layperson. Professions are based upon a balance of technical knowledge, reasoned judgment in applying such knowledge, and inexplicable, even mysterious talents that some call artistry. Thus, while doctors need a high degree of scientifically based knowledge, they also need diagnostic ability and a good bedside manner.

Expertise begins with theoretical knowledge taught in universities, but being a competent professional also means knowing how to apply this knowledge. Among practitioners, both expertise and experience contribute to quality performance. While initial skills are taught in school, a large share of professional training comes from the practicum or internship; it then continues in lifelong learning through the gathering of experience and the application of new concepts and technologies.

## Registration

Because professional judgments affect the public good, professionals generally are required to be licensed in order to practice. This serves as a means of protecting the public health, safety, and welfare. Professions require sophisticated relationships with people and information. To become licensed, professionals are usually required to meet education and experience standards and to pass a compulsory comprehensive examination.

## Relative Autonomy

Because professionals exercise considerable judgment and discretion, professional work is intended to be more autonomous and self-determined than work controlled by owner-managers as in the production of goods.

## Other Traits

In addition to these primary characteristics, a number of other traits are typical of professions:

- Because they are well trained to perform complex services, professionals generally command relatively high incomes and high prestige in their communities.
- As a group, professionals attach a large part of their identity to their careers, rarely changing vocations.
- Within each profession, members usually hold a set of common values; they often speak what amounts to a dialect that is not easily understood by outsiders.
- Professionals understand the importance and value of lifetime learning.
- Professions are relatively well organized, and a significant proportion of their members belong to a national professional organization such as the American Medical Association, the American Bar Association, or the American Institute of Architects.

These characteristics are in constant evolution. For example, the prestige of a given profession may suffer under consumer dissatisfaction or be enhanced by significant developments in the field that have positive social repercussions. The professional degree that was once optional becomes a necessity. Professional organizations are periodically strengthened by programs that capture practitioners' attention. Such evolution depends in part upon the participation of professionals themselves—in their schools, professional associations, and communities.

## ARCHITECTURE AMONG THE PROFESSIONS

Many of the trends influencing architectural practice have parallels in other professions. For example, the tensions created by complexity and specialization, consumer influences, and divergence of goals among practices can also be seen in the professions of law and medicine.

These common influences notwithstanding, each profession introduces its own variations and idiosyncrasies. Looking at architecture among the professions, we observe these features:

### Relationships with the Arts

The qualities that most clearly set architecture apart from other established professions are its close ties to the arts and its similarities to artistic endeavors. Creativity is crucial to all professions, but for the architect it is of the highest priority. Moreover, architects produce objects that are fixed in space, highly public, and generally long-lasting.

### Importance of Design

Although all professions are based on a balance of technical and indeterminate knowledge, some stress one over the other. Architecture emphasizes an artistic, relatively inexplicable domain of expertise—design—as the core of the practitioner's identity. Design requires rational knowledge of how buildings are put together, how they will function, historical models for building types, materials, mechanical systems, structures, and so on. But being a good architect also presumes that the professional possesses something extra—aesthetic sensibility, talent, or creative ability, whatever we choose to call it.

### Place in the Social Structure

According to one study that compared a number of professions on a variety of dimensions, architecture ranked high in terms of prestige but in the middle range in average years of education, average income, and proportion of members belonging to professional organizations. This suggests that architecture's respected place in the social structure has been granted by society rather than defined through numbers, dollars, or professional control.

The profession's position in the social structure has been changing. Historically, the church, the state, and powerful individuals were the primary patrons for architectural services. Now, industrial and commercial enterprises have become major clients as well. During the 1960s, when community design emerged as a subdiscipline, architects sought and secured a role in housing and neighborhood revitalization; this activity has evolved into a growing presence in community and urban design.

Architectural practice is developing in new ways that allow architects to intermingle with a broader population. One recent study argues that architecture is more closely connected to a large, relatively affluent middle class than to a small group of the very rich. In a similar vein, the composition of the profession is changing, particularly as more women and ethnic minorities become architects.

## Place in the Economic Structure

The well-being of the architectural profession depends upon ties to a healthy building industry. The level of construction activity both nationally and internationally significantly determines the amount and type of services architects will render.

As the United States urbanized and industrialized, the demand for buildings was great and the architectural profession grew rapidly. In more recent times, however, construction has declined proportionally in the national economy. With the evolution from a goods-producing economy to a service economy, there are fewer major new building projects.

At the same time, the demand for architectural services has increased—especially in the predesign and postconstruction phases. This suggests a repositioning of the profession, along with other professions, as part of the service economy. New roles and markets for services have been created. In addition, new roles and specializations mean that more professionals are doing what was once one individual's job.

## Internal Social Structure

Within any profession, there are social divisions that complement and compete with one another. Those who study professions call these divisions the rank and file, the administrators, and the intelligentsia.

In the architectural profession, the rank and file might be considered to include drafters and junior design and production people; the administrators to include principals, senior designers, and project managers; and the intelligentsia to include academicians, critics, practitioner-theorists, and those architects who push the parameters of architecture outward and whose work often establishes precedents for others to follow.

The values and objectives of each group are likely to conflict with those of other groups at times. The first two groups have very different convictions, agendas, and knowledge of the way practice operates. These differences become important in a profession where, even though a majority of architecture firms are small, the provision of architectural services has been heavily influenced by larger firms in which many of the architects are wage-earning employees who work not for clients but for their architect-employers. Data from the 2000 AIA Firm Survey confirm this: While only 24 percent of the firms owned by AIA members had ten or more employees in them, these firms accounted for 83 percent of the operating revenues earned by all AIA member-owned firms.

Initially, an increase in intraprofessional stratification brought a greater need to formalize professional control. Firms created organization charts, personnel policies, and manuals governing project procedures. Many professionals became organizational men and women. As firms grew, they dealt with these phenomena in different ways. Compare, for example, the large law firm, which is a collection of relative coequals (the main distinction being seniority among partners), and the hospital, which has a stricter hierarchy of medical administrators, senior physicians, residents, and interns. In recent years, however, there seems to be a general trend away from stratification in architecture firms—even in large firms.

## PROFESSIONS AND SOCIETY

Professionals possess knowledge and ability not accessible to the public. As a result, the public establishes a special relationship with professional groups, essentially granting each a monopoly in its area of practice. Society thus grants members of professional groups certain rights and privileges:

- A certain level of prestige and respect
- A certain amount of autonomy and authority
- A relatively high level of compensation
- A standard of reasonable care with which to judge the appropriateness of professional actions

In return for these rights and privileges, society expects a profession to assume certain obligations:

- Establishing and maintaining standards for admission and practice
- Protecting public health, safety, and welfare
- Considering the public good when working for an individual client
- Respecting public welfare over personal gain

Every profession participates in a coordinated body of tasks necessary to fulfill its obligations to the public and to manage the profession. These tasks include establishing a body of professional knowledge, regulating entry to the profession, and maintaining standards for practice. Each profession develops mechanisms for accrediting educational programs, licensing professionals to practice, encouraging continuing education, and regulating professional ethics and conduct.

By and large, these mechanisms are designed, staffed, and implemented by professionals. Architects have the major voice in where and how new architects are educated. They sit on registration boards, write and grade the licensing examination, and recommend laws and administrative guidelines for registration. Architects conduct disciplinary hearings and, through the AIA, establish and enforce codes of ethical behavior. Like all professionals, architects have substantial voices in establishing their own destiny.

# Intern Development Program Guidelines

## National Council of Architectural Registration Boards

An architect's education typically begins in a school of architecture, but it does not end there. Training in architecture firms, continuing education, and professional practice furthers the educational process. Schools and firms offer many opportunities for acquiring knowledge and skills; however, each architect is ultimately responsible for developing his or her competencies to the fullest.

State registration requirements establish the minimum criteria for legally practicing architecture. The most broadly accepted requirements are encompassed in the Intern Development Program (IDP). An individual's participation in IDP reflects a commitment to acquiring the comprehensive training that is essential for competent practice. (Throughout this topic, the term *intern* refers to any individual in the process of satisfying a registration board's training requirement. This includes graduates from recognized architecture programs, architecture students who acquire acceptable training prior to graduation, and other qualified individuals identified by a registration board.)

IDP responds to the professional development needs of the intern by providing a wide range of resources that enhance day-to-day experience. The IDP training requirement establishes levels of training in important areas of architectural practice. Through the IDP mentorship system, interns receive advice and guidance from practitioners. The IDP record-keeping system facilitates documentation of internship activities, while the IDP supplementary education system provides a variety of learning resources designed to enrich training.

The creation of core competencies for each IDP training area is another major program enhancement. The IDP core competencies give interns and employers a tool for assessing the actual *quality* of day-to-day experience against recognized performance standards. Two distinct kinds of activities have been identified for each training area. Awareness and understanding activities are designed for interns needing basic information, while skills and application activities include actual tasks that, when successfully accomplished, result in a core competency.

The shift from school to office is not a transition from theory to pragmatism. It is a period when theory merges with pragmatism. Internship is, in many ways, the most significant developmental period in an architect's career. It's a time when formal education is applied to the daily realities of architectural practice, comprehensive experience is acquired in basic practice areas, specialized areas of practice are explored, professional judgment is developed, formal education in architecture is continued, and career goals are refined.

Participation in the Intern Development Program prepares the intern for both the Architect Registration Examination and the wide range of career opportunities that lie beyond registration.

# THE INTERN DEVELOPMENT PROGRAM: AN OVERVIEW

Historically, most interns were trained by mentors. A daily working relationship allowed the experienced practitioner to transfer knowledge and skills to the apprentice. However, such a sustained learning environment became less attainable as the practice of architecture grew more complex. With the decline of mentorship, interns lacked a structured transition between formal education and architectural registration. A deficiency emerged in the preparation of competent architects. The Intern Development Program (IDP) was created to remedy this deficiency.

## IDP Purpose and Objectives

IDP is a profession-wide, comprehensive program that contributes to the development of competent architects who can provide exemplary architectural services. A comprehensive internship program is necessary to encourage and reinforce the discipline, integrity, judgment, skills, knowledge, and quest for learning that must serve the registered architect for a lifetime. IDP has five objectives:

- Define areas of architectural practice in which interns should acquire basic knowledge and skills
- Encourage additional training in the broad aspects of architectural practice
- Provide the highest-quality information and advice about education, internship, and professional issues and opportunities
- Provide a uniform system for documentation and periodic assessment of internship activity
- Provide easily accessible educational opportunities designed to enrich training

## IDP Organization

The program's policies are established by the IDP Coordinating Committee, which is composed of representatives of the American Institute of Architects (AIA), the American Institute of Architecture Students (AIAS), the Association of Collegiate Schools of Architecture (ACSA), and the National Council of Architectural Registration Boards (NCARB). The Council of Architectural Component Executives (CACE) and the Society of Design Administration (SDA) maintain liaisons with the Coordinating Committee.

- The **AIA,** as the professional society, has primary responsibility, through its state and local components, for identifying, organizing, and educating IDP supervisors and mentors. The AIA also develops supplementary education resources and a system to deliver them to interns.
- The **AIAS** collaborates with the IDP Coordinating Committee on matters related to student concerns about internship and registration. Through its publications and network of student chapters, AIAS keeps students advised on IDP and related issues.
- **ACSA** is the organization of the architecture schools. ACSA's role in IDP is to present the program to students and educators, keep them advised of new developments, and assist educator coordinators in their activities.
- **NCARB,** as a federation of all registration boards of the United States, sets national standards for architectural registration. NCARB interprets these standards, maintains records, and acts as the central clearinghouse and contact point for all interns, architects, and registration boards in matters dealing with the registration and professional conduct of architects. NCARB is responsible for establishing, interpreting, and enforcing the IDP training requirement.
- **CACE** represents the executive staff who support IDP activities in AIA state and local components.
- **SDA** represents architecture office administrators who support IDP activities in firms and organizations.
- The **Coordinating Committee** monitors IDP through input from program par-

ticipants. IDP is organized by state coordinators, local coordinators, and educator coordinators.

- The **state coordinator** is appointed by the state AIA component or the state registration board. State coordinators monitor IDP progress and undertake group presentations and statewide communication efforts to help participants understand the program.
- **Local coordinators** assist the state coordinator through local AIA components.
- **Educator coordinators** are faculty members appointed by schools of architecture. These individuals provide faculty and students with information about internship opportunities and registration requirements.

The IDP Coordinating Committee has developed and identified several resources for facilitating IDP activities in offices, AIA components, and architecture schools. These resources are available at http://www.ncarb.org/idp/resources.htm.

## ARCHITECTURAL REGISTRATION AND IDP

Regulation of the profession of architecture, including registration of practitioners, is a function of each state exercising its power to protect the health, safety, and welfare of the people. Registration is an administrative process resulting in the granting of a license to practice architecture within a state (The term *licensure* is often used to denote the issuance and maintenance of an architecture license. To avoid confusion, and since licensure is part of the registration process, the terms *registration* and *registered* are used in lieu of *licensure* and *licensed* in this topic.)

All fifty states, the District of Columbia, Guam, the Northern Mariana Islands, Puerto Rico, and the Virgin Islands have established architectural registration boards to regulate the profession. These boards constitute NCARB's membership. Each board has established a set of registration requirements that, when satisfied, results in the granting of an architecture license.

Although registration laws vary among states, all boards require satisfaction of an education requirement, a training requirement, and an examination requirement. NCARB publishes a document listing each board's registration requirements; this is available at www.ncarb.org/stateboards/index.html. More detailed information regarding specific state requirements is available from each state board.

### Education Requirement

Historically, individuals seeking a license to practice architecture could qualify for a registration examination after apprenticing in an architect's office for a specified number of years. In addition to apprenticeship, or training, the majority of NCARB member boards now require postsecondary education in architecture to qualify for examination.

Approximately 70 percent of the boards have established as their education requirement a professional degree in architecture from a program accredited by the National Architectural Accrediting Board (NAAB) or a professional degree in architecture from a Canadian university accredited by the Canadian Architectural Certification Board (CACB). NAAB- and CACB-accredited professional degree programs include bachelor of architecture programs and master of architecture programs. These programs typically require between five and eight years of postsecondary education. NAAB and CACB do not accredit four-year preprofessional degree programs in architecture (e.g., bachelor of arts in architecture, bachelor of science in architecture, bachelor of environmental design, etc.). Most preprofessional degree programs are components of bachelor of architecture and master of architecture programs. Some schools have established master of architecture programs for those whose undergraduate degrees were in other disciplines. A list of NAAB-accredited programs can be found at www.naab.org.

Some registration boards requiring a professional degree in architecture from an NAAB-accredited program also accept other education assessed as equivalent (e.g., a professional degree in architecture from a foreign institution). For a guide to equivalency requirements, refer to NCARB's education standard, available at www.ncarb.org/forms/educstand.pdf.

With respect to applicants with a degree in architecture granted by an academic institution outside the United States and Canada, an EESA-NCARB Evaluation Report is required from Educational Credential Evaluators, Inc., stating that the applicant has met the NCARB education requirement.

However, not all boards require a professional degree from an NAAB-accredited program (or equivalent education) to satisfy their education requirement. Some boards have alternative paths to registration that require less education but more training. For more detailed information regarding a specific state's requirements, contact that state registration board directly.

## Training Requirement

Every NCARB member board requires that interns acquire experience under a registered architect's direct supervision. Many boards also accept experience acquired under the direct supervision of other professionals (e.g., a professional engineer, interior designer, landscape architect, planner, or general contractor). The specific amount and quality of experience are specified by a board's training requirement.

All boards require a minimum period of training. Most boards that require the intern to have a professional degree from an NAAB-accredited program (or equivalent education) require three years of training. For boards with different education requirements, the training period varies considerably, from 2 to 13 years, depending upon the type and extent of previous education. For details on a particular state's requirements, contact the state board directly.

A specified training period has existed since the first architectural registration laws were enacted. More recently, boards began requiring training in specific areas of architectural practice.

Most boards have adopted the training requirement established for IDP as their training requirement for registration. It is advisable for an intern to compare his or her board's training requirement with the IDP training requirement. Any differences should be carefully noted. Where differences exist, the state's requirement should be complied with first; however, satisfaction of the IDP training requirement is required to facilitate future registration in other states.

## Examination Requirement

Every NCARB member board requires interns to pass the NCARB Architect Registration Examination (ARE) to satisfy its examination requirement. The ARE is administered on a year-round basis and covers

- Predesign
- Site planning
- Building planning
- Building technology
- General structures
- Lateral forces
- Mechanical and electrical systems
- Materials and methods
- Construction documents and services

The content of the ARE is based on the knowledge and skills required of a newly registered architect, practicing *independently,* to provide architectural services. The ARE evaluates an applicant's competence in the provision of architectural services in order to protect the public health, safety, and welfare.

For more information concerning the ARE, refer to NCARB's ARE Guidelines, available on the Web at www.ncarb.org/forms/areguide.pdf.

## Registration in Other States

Uniformity of requirements among registration boards is important primarily because of the mobility inherent in the architectural profession. Architects customarily work not only in the state where they live, but also in several other states.

Once an architect has been granted an initial license, he or she may acquire licenses in other states by complying with those states' education, training, and examination requirements. Since many boards have uniform requirements, a number of agreements have been developed that allow licenses to be granted without additional qualification. One way boards facilitate this process is by recognizing architects who hold an NCARB certificate. In most cases, architects holding an NCARB certificate are qualified to receive a license without satisfying additional education, training, or examination requirements.

NCARB grants a certificate to qualified architects through an administrative process called certification. Qualifications for an NCARB certificate include a current license issued by an NCARB member board and satisfaction of NCARB's education, training, and examination requirements. These requirements are described in NCARB's *Handbook for Interns and Architects*. This publication is available at www.ncarb.org/forms/handbook.pdf.

Because many boards have adopted NCARB's education, training, and examination requirements as their registration requirements, NCARB certification is often confused with registration. The two processes serve similar purposes, but with respect to practicing architecture, they are significantly different.

An NCARB certificate is not a license to practice architecture. As explained earlier, one must acquire an architecture license to practice within a state. After an initial license has been granted, the NCARB certificate facilitates registration in other states. Many boards will register out-of-state architects only if they have an NCARB certificate. See www.ncarb.org/stateboards/index.html for more information.

## HOW IDP WORKS

IDP helps interns achieve comprehensive exposure to architectural practice. To understand how IDP works, one must first become familiar with those resources designed to fulfill each of the program's objectives.

### IDP Training Requirement

The IDP training requirement is the program's foundation. To satisfy this requirement, the intern must complete specific periods of training in four major categories: design and construction documents, construction administration, management, and related activities (professional and community service). Training in areas beyond the traditional scope of architectural practice is encouraged but not required.

Each of the IDP training categories is subdivided into training areas. In order to satisfy the IDP training requirement, a specific period of training must be completed in each training area.

In IDP, training is measured in training units. One training unit equals eight hours of acceptable experience. The required training units for each IDP training category and area can be found at http://www.ncarb.org/idp/idptraining.htm.

Training units are earned for training acquired under the direct supervision of a qualified professional in one of two ways. Through participation, experience is acquired by performing a particular task. This is the best way to satisfy the program's training objective. Experience through observation occurs when working with a professional who is performing the task.

A description of each IDP training area and recommended intern activities are found at http://www.ncarb.org/idp/idpdescrip.htm. Conditions governing satisfaction of the IDP training requirement can be found at http://www.ncarb.org/idp/trainingsettings.htm.

It is important to remember that differences may exist between the IDP training requirement and related conditions presented in this document and those established by a particular registration board. Interns must first comply with their own board's training requirement; however, compliance with the IDP training requirement is required to facilitate future registration in other states.

### IDP Mentorship System

The architectural profession has a responsibility to provide interns with the best possible advice relating to day-to-day training and long-range career plans. In IDP, two key individuals share this responsibility: the supervisor and the mentor.

The **supervisor** is the individual within the firm or organization who supervises the intern on a daily basis, regularly assesses the quality of the intern's work, and periodically certifies the intern's documentation of training activity. The intern and supervisor must both work in the same office in circumstances where personal contact is routine.

Supervisors are usually registered architects; however, in certain cases others experienced in the tasks the intern is performing may serve as supervisors (e.g., engineers, landscape architects, interior designers, planners, or contractors). The impact of such circumstances on satisfying the IDP training requirement can be found at http://www.ncarb.org/idp/trainingsettings.htm.

The supervisor is responsible for

- Providing reasonable opportunities for the intern to gain adequate experience in each IDP training area
- Meeting regularly with the intern to review progress and verify the intern's IDP training report
- Encouraging the intern to participate in seminars and utilize other supplementary education resources
- Conferring, if needed, with the intern's mentor

The **mentor** is a registered architect, usually outside the intern's firm, with whom the intern meets periodically to review training progress and discuss career objectives. In many respects, the mentor has a traditional role that is as old as the profession itself. An intern's supervisor may also serve as a mentor. NCARB publishes the *IDP Mentor Guidelines* as a reference tool for mentors. The guidelines are available at www.ncarb.org/forms/mentor.pdf.

The mentor is responsible for

- Meeting regularly with the intern to review training progress and signing the intern's IDP training report
- Suggesting additional training and supplementary education activities
- Providing guidance to enhance the intern's professional growth
- Conferring, if needed, with the intern's supervisor

Criteria for selecting a supervisor and mentor are reviewed at http://www.ncarb.org/idp/gettingstarted.htm.

## IDP Record-Keeping System

The intern is responsible for maintaining a continuous record of training and supplementary education activities during participation in IDP. This record has several functions. For the intern, it identifies areas where training is being acquired and areas where deficiencies exist; for supervisors, it is an assessment and personnel management tool; and for registration boards, it is verified evidence of compliance with the IDP training requirement.

Interns may develop their own daily record-keeping resources or use NCARB's downloadable Excel spreadsheet, available at www.ncarb.org/idp/idpworkbook.html. Many firms have time management systems that can accommodate the IDP training categories and areas.

NCARB has developed a nationally recognized record-tracking system that involves establishing an NCARB Council Record. This record is a detailed, verified record of your education, training, and character. Maintained at the NCARB office in Washington, D.C., the Council Record is used to compile qualifications for examination, registration, and NCARB certification.

Most registration boards require the Council Record to verify an intern's qualifications for examination and/or registration. Interns should contact their individual boards regarding acceptable record-keeping procedures.

## IDP Supplementary Education

Supplementary education serves two primary functions: (1) to expand upon knowledge and skills acquired through training and (2) to keep abreast of new information affecting architectural practice. Supplementary education is not designed to substitute for required training in each IDP training area, but rather to enrich day-to-day experience.

Training units for a postprofessional degree in architecture may be earned if the degree follows receipt of a professional degree in architecture from a program accredited by

**Week One: 3/26/00—4/1/00**

| DESIGN & CONSTRUCTION | SUN | MON | TUES | WED | THURS | FRI | SAT | Total Hours for Week | Units for Week | Total Units in Workbook |
|---|---|---|---|---|---|---|---|---|---|---|
| Programming | | | | | | | | 0.00 | 0.00 | 0.00 |
| Site and Environment Analysis | | | | | | | | 0.00 | 0.00 | 0.00 |
| Schematic Design | | | | | | | | 0.00 | 0.00 | 0.00 |
| Engineering Systems Coordination | | | | | | | | 0.00 | 0.00 | 0.00 |
| Building Cost Analysis | | | | | | | | 0.00 | 0.00 | 0.00 |
| Code Research | | | | | | | | 0.00 | 0.00 | 0.00 |
| Design Development | | | | | 3.00 | | | 3.00 | 0.38 | 0.38 |
| Construction Documents | | | | | | | | 0.00 | 0.00 | 0.00 |
| Specifications and Materials Research | | | | | | | | 0.00 | 0.00 | 0.00 |
| Document Checking and Coordination | | | | | | | | 0.00 | 0.00 | 0.00 |
| | | | | | | | | 3.00 | 0.38 | 0.38 |
| | | | | | | | | | | |
| **CONSTRUCTION ADMINISTRATION** | | | | | | | | | | |
| Bidding and Contract Negotiation | | | | | | | | 0.00 | 0.00 | 0.00 |
| Construction Phase —Office | | 4.00 | | 3.00 | | | | 7.00 | 0.88 | 0.88 |
| Construction Phase —Observation | | | | | | | | 0.00 | 0.00 | 0.00 |
| | | | | | | | | 7.00 | 0.88 | 0.88 |
| | | | | | | | | | | |
| **MANAGEMENT** | | | | | | | | | | |
| Project Mamagement | | | 3.00 | | | | | 3.00 | 0.38 | 0.38 |
| Office Management | | | | | | | | 0.00 | 0.00 | 0.00 |
| | | | | | | | | 3.00 | 0.38 | 0.38 |
| | | | | | | | | | | |
| **RELATED ACTIVITIES** | | | | | | | | | | |
| Professional & Community Service | | | | | | | | 0.00 | 0.00 | 0.00 |
| Landscape Arch. | | | | | | 4.00 | | 4.00 | 0.50 | 0.50 |
| Select | | | | | | | | 0.00 | 0.00 | 0.00 |
| Select | | | | | | | | 0.00 | 0.00 | 0.00 |
| Other/Please Specify | | | | | | | | 0.00 | 0.00 | 0.00 |
| | | | | | | | | 4.00 | 0.50 | 0.50 |
| Hours Logged Per Day | 0.00 | 4.00 | 3.00 | 3.00 | 3.00 | 4.00 | 0.00 | 17.00 | 2.13 | 2.13 |

NAAB or CACB (e.g., bachelor of architecture or master of architecture degree). A postprofessional degree can be at the master's or doctoral level.

Training units may also be earned by completing supplementary education resources recognized by an individual registration board. The AIA offers a wide range of continuing education programs at the national, regional, state, and local levels. The AIA also approves programs offered by other professional organizations, educational institutions, or private consultants.

Training units may be earned for AIA-approved continuing education programs by multiplying the number of AIA learning unit hours by a factor of 0.15. An AIA transcript must accompany IDP training reports to document completion of AIA-approved programs.

Refer to http://www.ncarb.org/idp/supplementary.htm for the NCARB conditions affecting supplementary education. Interns should compare their board's conditions governing supplementary education with those presented. Where differences exist, interns must first comply with their board's conditions.

This Excel spreadsheet can be downloaded from the NCARB Web site for interns to use in tracking hours needed to fulfill their education requirement.

## THE IDP PROCESS: GETTING STARTED

To benefit most from IDP, participation should begin at the beginning of the intern's first acceptable employment. This point is determined by the level of education that must be achieved before experience can count toward satisfying the intern's registration board's training requirement.

*What is the Intern Development Program?*

The Intern Development Program (IDP) is a set of resources that, when used in a systematic manner throughout the internship period, contributes to the development of skilled architects. IDP is not a series of registration requirements and conditions, nor is it a study program for passing the Architect Registration Examination (ARE). The program's major objectives are listed at http://www.ncarb.org/idp/overview.htm.

*How do I enroll in the program? What does it cost to participate?*

Interns may begin participation in IDP by taking the following steps:

- Request an IDP Information Package from NCARB by visiting http://www.ncarb.org/Forms/req_idp.html. This package includes a Council Record application.
- Identify an IDP supervisor and select an IDP mentor. Refer to http://www.ncarb.org/idp/gettingstarted.htm for general selection criteria.
- Develop a personal record-keeping system for documenting training on a daily, weekly, and monthly basis, or use NCARB's IDP Workbook at http://www.ncarb.org/idp/idpworkbook.html.
- Submit the application to NCARB to establish an NCARB Council Record for documentation purposes.
- Document all previous acceptable training in accordance with your state registration board's training requirement and conditions.

The cost of participating in IDP varies, depending on which resources are used. Refer to http://www.ncarb.org/idp/councilrecord.htm for specific information.

*Do I need an accredited professional degree in architecture to participate?*

The level of postsecondary education required to begin earning IDP training units varies from state to state. Most registration boards will only accept training units earned after completion of the first three years in an NAAB-accredited professional degree program, or the first year of a master of architecture program for those whose undergraduate degrees were not in architecture. For more information, refer to the IDP Entry Points at http://www.ncarb.org/idp/idpentrypoints.htm.

*Can I defer repayment of my student loans by participating in IDP?*

Most lending institutions will defer repayment of federally and state-insured student loans granted prior to July 1, 1993, if you comply with certain criteria. Check with your lending institution, and refer to http://www.ncarb.org/idp/maintpart.htm#loans for further information.

*Why should I begin documenting my training when my internship starts? Why not wait until I've completed the IDP training requirements?*

To derive the maximum benefits from IDP, you should begin documenting your training and supplementary education at the beginning of your first acceptable employment. Retroactive documentation is discouraged for several reasons:

- Previous employers often cannot verify training units earned, resulting in a loss of training credit toward admission to the examination.
- Retroactive record keeping usually delays the examination application process, resulting in postponement of examination and registration.
- Several registration boards place limits on the amount of previous experience that can be retroactively documented.

For further information on examination application procedures, refer to the guidelines at http://www.ncarb.org/idp/applyexam.htm.

*I'm having trouble getting the minimum training units required in several areas. Can I use supplementary education to satisfy these requirements?*

No. Supplementary education can be used to supplement minimum levels of required training but cannot serve as a substitute for such experience. More specifically, supplementary education cannot be used to satisfy the minimum training units required in IDP Training Areas 1–16.

The AIA has developed many excellent educational resources. You are encouraged to use them to augment required training and to explore the broader aspects of architectural practice. You should also discuss means of acquiring training with your mentor and refer to IDP training area descriptions and recommended core competencies for possible activities. Refer to the Supplementary Education Conditions at http://www.ncarb.org/idp/supplementary.htm.

The level of education varies from state to state. Some boards accept experience after graduation from high school; however, others accept only experience acquired after receiving a professional degree in architecture from an NAAB-accredited program.

To participate in IDP, an intern must (1) identify a supervisor, (2) select a mentor, and (3) develop a system for documenting training activities.

## Identifying a Supervisor

Architects who serve as supervisors must hold a current license in the state where they are practicing architecture. Supervisors are expected to have a general understanding of the IDP objectives and training requirement. Although supervisors are not responsible for documenting the intern's activities, they must be familiar with documentation procedures. The IDP supervisor verifies and signs the intern's NCARB Employment Verification/IDP Training Unit Report forms.

## Selecting a Mentor

An IDP mentor should demonstrate a long-term commitment to the intern's professional growth. The intern-mentor relationship personifies the architectural profession's historical mentorship system.

The mentor meets with the intern at least once every four months to review training progress and discuss career objectives. Mentors must hold a current architecture license; however, they do not have to be registered in the state where the intern's firm or organization is located.

Since the mentor provides guidance from an independent perspective and is not required to certify training activities, most interns select a mentor from outside their own office; however, interns are free to select a mentor from within their own office. For all training occurring after July 1, 2000, IDP mentors must sign an acknowledgement of their intern's IDP Training Unit Reports.

A mentor may be selected by

- Asking a personal acquaintance (e.g., faculty member, previous employer)
- Asking an employer or fellow interns for recommendations
- Contacting local AIA components—many AIA members volunteer to serve as mentors
- Contacting an individual state or local IDP coordinator (see AIA Resources at http://www.ncarb.org/idp/resources.htm)

## Establishing a Record of IDP Activity

Each intern should establish a verified record of IDP training as early as possible. Continuous documentation

- Ensures accurate verification
- Guides the supervisor in providing training opportunities
- Identifies areas where supplementary education may enhance training
- Provides prospective employers with a verified record of experience
- Saves considerable time when applying for examination

Most registration boards require the Council Record in order to verify qualifications for examination and registration. In addition to facilitating registration, the Council Record serves as an application for NCARB certification.

A Council Record contains the applicant's academic transcript(s) and verification of previous and current employment, which includes verification of activity in the IDP training areas.

Council Records are confidential documents. NCARB will not make their contents available to anyone other than registration boards.

The procedure for establishing an NCARB Council Record is explained at http://www.ncarb.org/idp/councilrecord.htm. A Council Record should be initiated at least one year prior to the applicant's anticipated examination date. Delays in verifying education and training can result in financial penalties and/or postponement of examination and registration.

The intern is the primary beneficiary of IDP. However, to gain the greatest benefit from participation, interns should pursue it as a cooperative arrangement with their employers. Because employers cannot charge IDP training costs to clients, a commitment of time apart from normal working hours is often necessary to ensure that project schedules are maintained while training is being acquired.

Although firms are responsible for providing training opportunities, the intern is responsible for documenting training, scheduling meetings with supervisor and mentor, and using supplementary education resources. These activities typically involve at least two hours (beyond normal working hours) each month.

The periodic documentation of training is a fundamental program activity. Most architecture firms use daily logs for recording time spent in various project phases. These logs can easily be adapted to encompass the IDP training areas. Many interns use computer spreadsheets to display weekly and monthly activity. NCARB provides an Excel spreadsheet that may be downloaded from www.ncarb.org/idp/idpworkbook.html.

Interns should prepare employment verification/IDP training reports approximately every four months until all training requirements are satisfied. NCARB recommends that these reports be submitted to the Council office on or about January 1, May 1, and September 1, if employment is continuous.

To maintain IDP participation, interns must meet periodically with their supervisor and mentor to review the quality of their work, verify employment and IDP training reports, identify weak training areas, plan for future involvement, and refine career objectives.

## Changing Employment

During the course of IDP participation, personal circumstances or external factors can result in new employment opportunities. If an intern changes employers, the following procedures apply:

- Identify a new supervisor.
- Select a new mentor if the ability to maintain adequate contact with the original mentor is impaired.
- Record all activity occurring prior to the change on an employment verification form and an IDP Training Unit Report form. The report must be signed by the intern's previous supervisor.
- Indicate employment termination in the diary section of the report form.
- Record the next reporting period at the new employer (after minimum duration— see http://www.ncarb.org/idp/trainingsettings.htm#duration) on a new IDP Training Unit Report form. This report must be signed by the intern's new supervisor.

## Deferring Repayment of Student Loans

Repayment of federally insured student loans granted prior to July 1, 1993, may be deferred through participation in IDP. Eligibility criteria and deferment forms are available from individual lending institutions. Most deferment forms require two certifications. The intern's supervisor ("program official") must certify that the intern is employed in an acceptable training setting, and a registration board official must certify (1) that an internship is required for architectural registration, (2) the required length of the internship period, and (3) that a baccalaureate degree is required before entering the internship program.

Questions regarding loan repayment and deferments should be directed to the lending institution(s) or to the agency that has guaranteed the loan(s). The American Institute of Architects and the National Council of Architectural Registration Boards are not authorized to sign deferment forms.

Participation in a required professional internship program does not qualify for deferred repayment of most federally insured student loans granted after July 1, 1993, except in cases where significant economic hardship can be demonstrated. Questions regarding alternative loan repayment options must be directed to the individual lending institutions.

# THE IDP PROCESS:
## APPLYING FOR EXAMINATION

As discussed previously, architectural registration is an administrative process resulting in the granting of a license to practice architecture within a state. Each registration board establishes its own application procedures for examination.

A few boards allow interns to take the registration examination upon satisfaction of their education requirement (e.g., earning a professional degree from an NAAB-accredited program); however, most boards require satisfaction of education and training requirements before examination. The information given here applies primarily to those who have satisfied (or will soon satisfy) the IDP training requirement and are seeking admission to the examination.

Interns should request application materials from their board at least one year prior to their anticipated examination date. Each board's training requirement and conditions (and related application procedures) must be reviewed. Find out answers to the following questions:

- What is the board's required training period? Can this period be reduced if the IDP training requirement is satisfied in less time?
- How many years are required in the office of a registered architect after satisfaction of the board's education requirement?
- Must the board's education and training requirement be satisfied prior to the examination? after the examination?
- Will an NCARB Council Record be accepted in lieu of the board's verification documents? Is an NCARB Council Record required?
- Are references required?
- Who can be used as a reference?

All application procedures must be strictly adhered to. Failure to comply with the procedures in a timely manner can result in postponement of examination and registration.

Applicants with an NCARB Council Record must provide NCARB with written notice of their intent to apply for examination at least 90 days prior to their anticipated completion date. This request can be made at www.ncarb.org/forms/req_idptran.html.

NCARB will review the Council Record and request (if necessary) additional employment or education information. Upon receipt of all information and the appropriate fee, NCARB will send a complete copy of the applicant's Council Record to the relevant board. If the NCARB education and training requirements have been fulfilled, the transmittal will include NCARB's recommendation for admission to the examination. The board will review the applicant's record and make the final decision on admission.

## EPILOGUE

The processes of education, training, and examination culminate in receipt of an architecture license, a significant achievement in the architect's career. Professional development, however, does not end here. Today's architects must continue to build upon their knowledge and skills. This involves keeping abreast of new trends and changes while refining and expanding basic competencies.

Some registration boards require continuing education for maintaining an architecture license. NCARB assists its member boards through the Professional Development Program, a national program that assures the public and registration authorities that architects are continually expanding their knowledge base.

Continuing education is also required for maintaining AIA membership. The AIA Continuing Education System assists members in maintaining their competence and achieving their professional goals.

While schools of architecture and firms share the responsibility for preparing interns for productive careers, the profession itself must continue to provide opportunities for architects to reinforce and extend their competencies. Only through such a sustained commitment to lifelong learning can architects meet the public's high expectation for quality service.

# Introduction:
# Practice in Transition

## Robin M. Ellerthorpe, FAIA

In today's business world, architects encounter more demanding clients and face competitors from both within and outside the architecture profession. To help architects deal with these challenges, the 13th edition of the *Architect's Handbook of Professional Practice* departs from the viewpoint of earlier editions. It does so by redefining its audience, its content, and—at times—the fundamental concept of the *Handbook* itself. This edition also introduces ideas and concepts that can help architects become proactive leaders in creating a better built environment, even though some of these ideas have not yet become industry standards.

The outlook for architects appears bright. With the U.S. and world economies in long-term expansion, there is a growing demand for housing, office, health care, worship, educational, and entertainment facilities. The combination of this expansion and the preceding recession helped to spawn the emergence of what the profession indelicately calls "architects in nontraditional practice." Stewart Brand has called them "hyphenated architects." Educator-architects, public-architects, corporate-architects, city-architects, and scores of others have proliferated across the practice landscape.

What appeared as a stopgap measure for architects who were hungry and perhaps less oriented toward design became institutionalized as architects began to build practices and careers around what some termed "bookend services." This trend is reflected in the AIA Professional Interest Areas (PIAs), which support knowledge development in such areas as practice management, documents, risk management, international practice, construction management, design-build, and facility management, among others.

During the deep building recession of the early 1990s architects sought to regain a leadership position in the design-and-construction industry—a position that had been eroded during the litigious '60s, '70s, and '80s. Project delivery was a rallying point, and new approaches were introduced that called for architects to participate in construction management, design-build, facility management, and other services. While design-related PIAs were still thriving, membership in the newly ascribed expanded-practice areas increased substantially.

During the maelstrom of project delivery forums put on during the first half of the '90s, architects began to adapt their practices, refining and improving their project delivery methods. Some ventured into areas of expanded practice that were being supported by industry insurers. During this maturing process, it became clear that discussions about expanded ser-

---

**ROBIN ELLERTHORPE** *is with the Chicago-based firm of OWP&P Architects, Inc. and directs the firm's facilities consulting group, which he started in 1997. Ellerthorpe chaired the steering committee for the development of the 13th edition of the* Handbook.

## REDEFINITION OF THE PROFESSION: FROM PRODUCT-BASED PRACTICE TO KNOWLEDGE- AND SERVICE-BASED PRACTICE

|  | PRODUCT-BASED PRACTICE | KNOWLEDGE- AND SERVICE-BASED PRACTICE |
|---|---|---|
| **Basic strategy** | Uses core knowledge and skills in responding to long-recognized client needs that focus on physical and regulatory considerations. Design professionals generally view the completed building as an end in itself. | Expands the knowledge base and skill sets to address a wider range of building needs beyond physical and mandated considerations. Design professionals view the completed building as a means to help clients achieve other ends. |
| **Beyond projects** | Projects encompass services required to design and prepare documentation for the creation of physical space. | A project is defined as a planned undertaking in which the architect provides services to achieve desired client objectives. A project may or may not result in the creation of physical space. |
| **A broad range of services** | Services are largely aligned with the design-construction axis for the creation of new space or the modification of existing space. | An expanded range of services is applied to bring together knowledge, skills, and resources beyond those used for design and construction. |
| **Client-architect relationship** | Architects normally have long-term relationships with consultants, contractors, and other team members. Client-architect relationships, however, are frequently aligned with the timeline of a single project. | The architect fosters interaction with the client to build stronger relationships beyond the project timeline. In the process, the architect works toward a consultative role to become a trusted advisor. |
| **Facility life cycle** | The life cycle vista focuses on the design and construction stages. | The vista is widened—upstream and downstream of design and construction—to embrace the entire facility life cycle. |
| **Facilitator and integrator** | The architect applies design thinking and uses facilitative and integrative skills to design and create physical space. | The architect uses design thinking and leverages facilitative and integrative skills to address a broad range of needs beyond the creation of physical space. |

vices all pointed to the same component of practice. This component, it was realized, offers the most significant opportunity for the future of the architectural profession. It is the client.

The Institute began focusing on and listening more intently to clients at a watershed event in 1995 called the AIA Summit on Expanding Architectural Services. To be sure, the AIA had a history of assembling client focus groups to address issues such as contracts, advertising, and liability. The summit event, however, permitted a broad level of input from clients such as Quorum Healthcare and the Bank of America. Some of the client participants were emotional in their appreciation for being listened to; others were indignant and insisted that they be understood. They spoke about architects in terms of needing to do the following:

- Going beyond projects
- Offering a broad range of services
- Developing long-term architect-client relationships
- Considering the facility life cycle
- Emphasizing the role of facilitator and integrator

In short, these client voices created the platform for the Institute's Practice & Prosperity program, which eventually evolved into the Redefinition of the Profession initiative. Both efforts focused on long-term institutionalization of the five concepts listed above through involvement of the PIAs, realignment of Institute programs, and the rewriting of AIA Document B141, Standard Form of Agreement Between Owner and Architect. In the latter, the basic services embodying building design remain. However, a new modular format enables discrete service descriptions to supplement or wholly supplant the basic services. In this approach, the client can better understand the scope and importance of any array of services along with the compensation for providing them.

Pressure to continue redefining the profession increased during the late 1990s, partially from the push of membership but more from the vacuum created by clients. A combination of economic expansion and more sophisticated clients in most markets resulted in demand for services that ranged beyond the traditional design-bid-build approach.

Thus began a fundamental shift in architecture, one that struck at the strategy of firms as it played out against the building blocks of core competencies, service processes, and the skill sets housed within them. The shift was driven by recognition that building life cycle services required more than traditional architectural, engineering, and interior design skills. Coupling additional skills with new processes to meet the service requirements became the key for future growth and opportunities. The code word for enabling an increase in the tolerance of diverse skill sets within architecture firms is *inclusiveness*.

This 13th edition of the *Handbook* is another step in the delivery of redefined knowledge and tools to architectural practitioners. It is written for journeyman architects seeking to introduce new services into their firms, to gain information about clients (including who they are and what motivates them), and to obtain information about best business practices. As a result, the organization of the *Handbook* has changed from an introspective architect-firm-project view to a more embracing client-business-delivery-services orientation.

Taking its cue from visionary business strategists, the *Handbook* is intended to move the profession from an either/or mentality—where architects provide a narrow set of services—to a position in which core competencies *and* extended capabilities are combined to deliver a comprehensive array of facility services. In this transformation, architects have the opportunity to provide greater value to their clients and to reestablish themselves as leaders in the design and construction arena.

# part 1
# CLIENT

*Client satisfaction is a prime determinant in measuring*

*success in architecture practice. The path to client satisfaction*

*begins when the architect chooses clients whose values*

*resonate with his or her own. Rooted in understanding,*

*commitment, and effective communication, strong client-*

*architect relationships serve to reinforce client satisfaction.*

*As architects address a wider spectrum of facility needs for*

*their clients, they have the opportunity to achieve the role*

*of a trusted advisor.*

# 1 Understanding Clients

## 1.1 The Nature of the Client

### Kevin W. C. Green

*Clients today look for architects who can be part of their team, understand their perspective, and support their goals.*

Once there were no clients and no call for architecture or architects as we define any of these terms today. The earliest people simply designed and built their own shelter. Nonetheless, understanding as we do the instinctive human drive toward specialization, we can imagine that soon after the dawn of civilization there evolved specialists in shelter—people who designed and built better than, and thus for, their neighbors. So arose *builders*. And so arose *clients*.

At some point the landed gentry began to aspire to shelter that was especially impressive. Wealthy clients desiring grand personal villas or great public or religious buildings searched for particularly skilled builders and commissioned particularly magnificent structures. So arose the *patron,* a client with expectations outside the norm and the funds to achieve them. And so arose the *master builder,* an archetype—though still not an architect in any modern sense. The notion of master builder traces its antecedents to mythical Daedalus but has endured so long, it embraces figures ranging from the erectors of the pyramids to those who influenced our own architecture as much as Leonardo da Vinci and Michelangelo Buonarrati, Gian Lorenzo Bernini and Sir Christopher Wren, Thomas Jefferson and Benjamin Henry Latrobe.

The work of these historic designers is not representative of common design and construction practices in their eras, however. Until recently, most buildings were designed and built by carpenters and masons rather than by the master builders whose names and plans we know from the pages of architectural history. Most of the work of tradesmen was done not for patrons but for average user-owners whose names are as long forgotten as their projects.

Not until the late nineteenth century, at least in the United States, did the artists, artisans, and amateur architects who had designed and built for centuries without special legal standing become *architects,* with the unique legal standing that defines the profession today, or with the educational infrastructure on which that standing largely rests. It was 1868 before the United States saw its first dedicated school of architecture—established at the Massachusetts Institute of Technology with a first-year roster of four students—and well past 1900 before any school of architecture existed west of the Mississippi.

> **"The ordinary *Builder* may construct the edifice required: you apply to an *Architect* for the superadded graces of correct design and suitable decoration."**
>
> *Letter to prospective clients from George Wightwick, c. 1825, as quoted in Barrington Kaye,* The Development of the Architectural Profession in Britain, *1960*

KEVIN W. C. GREEN *heads Green & Associates, Inc., Alexandria, Virginia–based marketing and strategic planning consultants to architecture and engineering firms. He was director of marketing for Leo A. Daly from 1988 to 1998 in the firm's Washington, D.C. office.*

Accompanying and perhaps even driving this late-nineteenth-century evolution toward professionalism was the simultaneous emergence of a raft of new regulations governing buildings and those responsible for their construction. These regulations were necessary, arguably, to keep pace with fast-advancing technologies and materials as well as with the nation's rising interest in protecting both life itself and the quality of people's lives.

Within this evolving legal, technical, and social environment arose the modern architect, a specialist in building design and technology. Increasingly trained through formalized professional education, architects were for the first time licensed by the state with the charge to protect human life by ensuring compliance with the laws, codes, and standards that govern virtually all forms of building construction.

The rise of the professional architect affected clients dramatically. Originally free to commission construction however they chose, clients throughout the Western world faced more constraints over the centuries as village, town, shire, county, city, state, and national governments began to control structure size, street-front setback, sanitary systems, and more. By the mid-twentieth century, the participation of a licensed design professional—architect, engineer, or both—was widely mandated by law for all but minor residential projects.

The evolution of architects as prerequisites to construction went hand in hand with the evolution of clients of an equally novel stripe. Clients who had once initiated, without benefit of architect, the design and construction of the lion's share of the built environment—including buildings and bridges, parks and gardens, homes and offices, banks and warehouses—were now *required* to hire an architect.

We live and work today in a world shaped by this relatively recent and remarkably rapid evolution. The architect is a licensed professional with a specifically defined legal standing and, typically, a mandated role to play in construction. Ours is a better world for the contributions of architects properly educated and ordained, to be sure. Nonetheless, it is a world in which the vast majority of clients bring not much more (or less) architectural appreciation to their projects than the average citizen with a yen to build or renovate in Jefferson's Virginia, Wren's London, or Bernini's Rome. The question is, would these clients hire an architect if they weren't required to?

Today's client population includes the usual number of patrons—a precious few—and a host of clients who as recently as 100 years ago would have built without hiring an architect and would do the same today if they could. Between these two extremes is a broad spectrum of clients who care to varying degrees about the uniquely valuable contributions an architect might make. Some of these clients want to build, some to rebuild, some to renovate, and some simply to move desks around. This client population is probably as heterogeneous as it has always been—in which sense little has changed over the centuries.

But this much *has* changed: All architects practicing in the United States today are state-licensed participants in a building delivery process so closely regulated by government that their formal participation is typically mandated by law and serves as the primary regulatory device by which government ensures the safety of building projects. As a result, virtually all clients in the United States today are either directly required or carefully advised by their attorneys and liability insurers to hire an architect whenever they wish to do *anything* with or to a building or other structure.

> **"Americans don't care much about architecture. They perceive it merely as a product, a form of shelter, or an indication of status, rather than as art or an expression of culture."**
> *Andrea Oppenheimer Dean,* Architectural Record, *January 1999*

The legal requirement that an architect participate in virtually all building development has generated immeasurably more work for the profession. It is reasonable to assume that much if not all of that work would have gone, in the old days, to the master and lesser builders for whom building designers worked or, more commonly, who themselves designed what they built.

Although the transition to mandatory architect involvement has been a boon to the profession, it has carried a price, as most boons do: Today's architects are forced to deal with clients far more varied—in class, taste, character, sophistication, aspiration, and willingness to involve an architect in the first place—than the remarkably patronlike clients we envision when we think of the great and famous architects of the past. Yesterday's clients, too, were a wildly diverse assortment of people seeking to build and maintain an equally diverse assortment of buildings. The difference is that few of yesterday's clients ever hired or even met a Bernini, a Wren, or a Latrobe. Today the range of clients seeking architectural consultation has grown to include not only the patrons who commissioned those master designer/builders but also—and here's the crux—the vast middle sector of commercial and residential user-owners who, in centuries past, were entirely satisfied with the crudely sketched plans of masons and carpenters. Which means—because the middle is always where the numbers get big—that today's architects primarily serve clients whose similarly engaged ancestors wouldn't have hired an architect at all.

With the vastly broadened spectrum of clients come two concerns. One is the strong likelihood that a young architect who expects to work much as Bernini, Wren, and Latrobe did—in the contemporary vernacular, of course—is going to be disappointed with most of the clients he or she meets. The other is that, even for an architect aware of the nature of the modern client population, today's clients present a wide range of challenges in project, practice, and client management.

These challenges include those posed by clients who don't share an architect's interest in or commitment to design or who are concerned with cost above all else. Special challenges also come from clients who opt, when they can, to procure design from a competitor engaged in design-build or construction management or some other emerging discipline, rather than from an architect engaged in traditional architectural practice—meaning architecture as it has been practiced since about 1900.

## THE CLIENT DEFINED

A client is never a what but a who, never a thing but a person. A client may represent a thing—a corporation, for example, or an institution. A client may be delegated to lead or represent a group of people—a board of directors, perhaps, or a building committee, the members of which may also be, or become, clients who act and decide matters consensually.

Thus, as one defining element, a client is at least one person with whom at least one architect will deal on what is often a remarkably intimate basis. That personal relationship is almost invariably the single most important determinant of project success and, ultimately, of success in practice.

The second defining characteristic of a client, at least in architecture, is that the client has something to do with some aspect of a built environment. Architecture encompasses many fields of knowledge and understanding—so many, in fact, that architects frequently disagree about which fields fall within the core competencies of the profession. For the moment, suffice it to say that fields of knowledge with no direct connection to the built environment are, if nothing else, usually better understood by someone in another line of work. Even some fields that *are* directly connected to the built environment—acoustical engineering, for example—are generally better understood by other, specialized professionals. Nevertheless, for the sake of a definition specifically relevant to architecture, let us agree that a client is someone responsible for some aspects of facility planning, design, construction, and operation.

The third defining characteristic of an architecture client? A client always faces the need to deal with change. Stasis is not a condition conducive to architectural practice. But stasis rarely exists, especially not in a built environment and certainly not in one with people in it. Things change constantly, and as they do, the buildings in which people live, work, pray, and play must be adapted to meet their changing needs, wants, and preferences.

The fourth defining characteristic of a client hinges on the third, for not all change impels environmental adaptation. Sometimes people make do. A client must be in need of an architect's services in order for an ethical professional to provide them. If, ethically, that need must exist in order for an architect to perform his or her function, then what can an architect do with people who have such a need but don't recognize it? Make them aware—and turn them into clients.

**client . . . 1. formerly, a person dependent on another, as for protection or patronage 2. a person or company for whom a lawyer, accountant, advertising agency, etc. is acting 3. a customer . . .**

Webster's New World Dictionary of the American Language, *1986*

**client . . . 1. *Rom. Antiq.* A plebeian under the patronage of a patrician, in this relation called a patron . . . , who was bound, in return for certain services, to protect his client's life and interests . . . 2. *gen.* One who is under the protection or patronage of another, a dependent . . . 3. *spec.* One who employs the services of a legal adviser . . . ; he whose cause an advocate pleads . . . 4. *gen.* A person who employs the services of a professional or business man in any branch of business, or for whom the latter acts in his professional capacity; a customer . . .**

Oxford English Dictionary, *1977*

> ▶ **"Unlike architects, who view the design and construction of a building as 'an end,' the majority of our clients see buildings as 'a means' to satisfying a wider set of requirements . . . One of the most important challenges facing us as architects is to ensure that we fully understand our clients and their motivations."**
>
> *Gordon Chong, FAIA, June 1998*

The definition of an architecture client, then: a person or group of people dealing with the effects of change on and in the built environment and in need of professional assistance.

Only three kinds of people fit this definition. The first—and best—is the client who is already a client of yours, for a client in hand is the single most valuable commodity in the business of architecture. The second—a distant second—is the client aware of the need for, and actively seeking, professional assistance, which may or may not come from you. The third—always a long shot, but surprisingly often a winner—is the client who needs help but simply hasn't recognized it yet.

## CLIENT VS. CUSTOMER

Semanticists who work hard to differentiate between *client* and *customer* protest too much, for client and customer are essentially identical. Each has a problem that needs

---

### Customer vs. Client

#### CUSTOMER

*Customer enters process here, after product is manufactured*

**CUSTOMER**

**MANUFACTURING PROCESS**
**(manufacturer is product provider)**

**PRODUCT**

*Product is predesigned, preproduced, manufactured in quantity (no or minimal customization)*

**CHARACTERISTICS:**
1. Customer follows extensive promotion to find seller at convenient place
2. Usually there is an array of competing or complementary products from which to choose
3. People for guidance or future service are available at point of sale
4. Prices are commensurate with high availability (and less differentiation) of product

#### CLIENT

*Client starts at beginning, since product is always customized*

**CLIENT**

*Client first interacts with product*

**CLIENT**

**DESIGN + CONSTRUCTION PROCESS = CUSTOMIZATION PROCESS**
**(architect is customizer and service provider; contractor is manufacturer)**

**PRODUCT**

*Product is customized to client's needs*

**CHARACTERISTICS:**
1. Client interacts with the architect during the customization process of design and construction and with the building itself during its operation and use
2. Client decides, based on value to him/her, what the criteria are for choosing an architect (and thus the end product)—promotion, type of product, people, place, and price (compensation + construction costs)

---

to be solved. Each has choices, not only among competing means of solving that problem but also among competing sources for those means.

Clients and customers alike are searching for solutions to their problems. But if *solution* is defined as an end result—the problem solved—then solutions aren't for sale. It is the means to a solution that a client or a customer buys. The means is virtually always embodied in a good, a thing, a deliverable that, through its use or application, solves a problem. Rarely, and especially in architecture, is the means embodied in a service. If that seems counterintuitive, consider the suggestion of marketer Theodore Levitt: "Customers do not buy a ¾-inch drill; they buy a ¼-inch hole." The solution to the problem faced by Levitt's customers—the thing they actually *need*—isn't a drill; it's a hole. The drill is merely the means by which a customer may decide to achieve that solution.

Virtually all products (and services) sold to customers (and clients) are means to an end. Business, whether the business of architecture or some other, is simply a matter of matching problem-burdened clients or customers with the right means to achieve the ends they desire. Business becomes complex in the attempt to increase the odds that those customers or clients will give their business to you.

> **"Value is not determined by a firm's principals. It is determined by the client, and the only way the firm will know is if they ask the client. . . . Design and construction firms have to find out what the client wants and fulfill his/her needs. That's how you take project selections out of a price-driven competition and create a value-based selection."**
> *Steve Polk of the American Consulting Engineers Council,* A/E Marketing Journal, *March 1994*

## The Five Ps

Many marketers use a mnemonic device called the five Ps to break down the structure of a client's decision-making process. The Ps stand for *promotion, product, people, place,* and *price.* The breakdown goes like this: Given a problem to solve, a client or customer will begin to pay attention to *promotion* (advice from friends, advertising, a story in the news) in an effort to find the right *product* or service (means to a solution) available from helpful *people* (one aspect of source) at a convenient *place* (another aspect of source) and at an acceptable *price.* Simple as that.

Or almost that simple. What makes business a horse race is the fact that, given an identical problem, different clients or customers quite often choose different means—from different sources—to attain identical solutions. Why? Because clients and customers rarely buy on the basis of product alone. They consider all five of the Ps. And different clients and customers place different values on each one.

## Using the Five Ps to Evaluate Client Values

Promotion, product, people, place, and price are variables in an equation. The equa-

### Sample Client Values and How They Influence Choosing an Architect

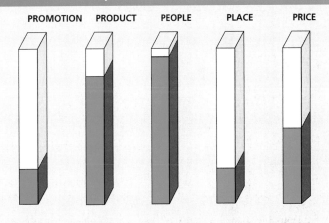

**CLIENT A**
While ignoring advertisements or recommendations *(promotion),* Client A is willing to travel great distances *(place)* and to pay top dollar *(price)* for great service and a good product *(product).* Client A values the end product—a good building— and the relationship with the architect *(people).* The building itself is a source of pride, and the process of getting it built, that is, working with people, is important. For these reasons, Client A chooses Architect #1.

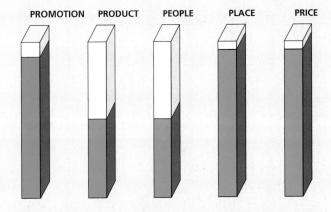

**CLIENT B**
Client B is highly swayed by recommendations from friends and advertising *(promotion)* but also wants to work with someone local *(place)* and to pay a relatively inexpensive fee *(price).* Client B doesn't care much about high quality *(product)* or working with people *(people).* The building is a commodity, and Client B wants a simple program fulfilled with little expenditure of time, energy, or money on the client's part. For these reasons, Client B chooses Architect #2.

## Home Depot vs. Mom and Pop

Hardware store customers have traditionally valued the advice and guidance of the friendly people who work in small neighborhood hardware stores. Yet the rise of regional and national hardware superstores, such as Lowe's and Home Depot, suggests that many of today's hardware customers value low price and a wide selection of product more highly than the aid of the congenial staff traditionally found at neighborhood hardware stores.

Interestingly enough, Home Depot's recent national advertising campaign emphasizes its friendly, helpful salespeople rather than its discounts and selection. Why? Home Depot believes it will expand its sales if it can attract the old-line hardware store customers who most value people in addition to the customers who most value low price and product selection.

tion yields a different result whenever the value of even a single variable is changed.

For example, a client who hears a colleague praise a particular design firm's collaborative skills hires that firm for an upcoming project. The client has valued both the colleague's opinion (promotion) and architects who collaborate well (people). Another client doesn't like the look of the firm's last building and chooses a competing firm instead. In this case, product was valued more highly than people or promotion—or perhaps one kind of promotion (past work on public display) was valued more highly than another (free advice).

In another example, a customer values a bargain above all else and willingly travels miles to find a better deal. Another customer, valuing place more highly than price, happily pays a premium for the convenience of buying the same product just around the corner.

The five Ps focus attention on the values that clients and customers place on different variables in the decision-making equation. Those values change constantly. And they're full of surprises. Few in architecture, for example, forecast that St. Louis–based HOK would roughly triple its revenues in the 1990s, largely on the strength of its design of a charmingly retro downtown baseball stadium in Baltimore. It did just that when dozens of American cities decided they, too, needed a product—an indigenously influenced center-city stadium just like HOK's Oriole Park at Camden Yards—that no other firm seemed able to produce.

The five Ps can be likened to the graphic equalizer on a stereo amplifier—five sliding scales, each with a range of values, each assigned a particular value by the client or customer. The value assigned to promotion—of any sort, or of one kind over another—may be high or low. The value assigned to price may be higher or lower than the values assigned to place and people. Almost always valued most highly is product—hence customers who will heed ungainly promotion, shop in an inconvenient place, pay a ridiculously high price, and endure rude salespeople if running that gauntlet nets the only product out there that promises to solve a tough problem.

Conversely, the value assigned to product can fall well below the values assigned to other Ps if the product in question (whether a good or service) has little to differentiate it from competing means to similar solutions. Such undifferentiated products typically are called *commodities,* and the P most highly valued by their purchasers is typically price.

A sale takes place when the values a client or customer assigns to the five Ps most closely mirror the values he or she perceives across the counter. In other words, clients or customers decide to purchase from sellers whose graphic equalizer looks most like theirs.

Though client and customer values change regularly and frequently yield surprises, the variables themselves—the five Ps—seldom if ever change. Promotion, product, people, place, and price form an equation that runs through the mind—consciously or unconsciously—of everyone who intends to buy something. The set of values a client assigns to the Ps may differ from moment to moment, problem to problem, product to product, and product to service. But that's par for the course; every buyer assigns different values to different things, and every buyer has different reasons for buying or not buying those things.

# 2 Clients and Change

## 2.1 Clients and the Forces of Change

### Kevin W. C. Green

*There is irony in the fact that architecture, the most permanent of the arts, can prove its validity only over time, for it is change—time's chief and implacable vicissitude—that brings about the need for architecture in the first place.*

Clients and their architects both respond to change continually, whether in their businesses specifically or in the economy at large. With the advent of the twenty-first century and the upheaval caused by the shift from a product-driven economy to a service-driven one, clients are looking for partners who can help them face change and adapt their buildings to help them survive.

### RECOGNIZING EVOLUTIONARY CHANGE

Philosophers—most famously represented by the Frenchman Alphonse Karr, source of the observation that the more things change, the more they stay the same—have long recognized that change is constant, perhaps the only constant. It was Karr's English contemporary Charles Darwin who promulgated the notion that internal (genetic) and external (environmental) changes could conspire in perfect ignorance to yield evolution, a concept so important that biologists have done little since publication of Darwin's *Origin of Species* but explore its ramifications for organisms on every scale from the cellular to the societal.

Biology's current take on evolution can be seen as a river moving along in its timeworn course, rising and falling as momentary conditions change, until something really catastrophic happens, such as a hundred-year flood. Then, as the river's rain-swollen torrent smashes against a riverbank once strengthened by cottonwood tree roots but now held in place by no more than the soybean rows planted last spring by Farmer Jones, something dramatic happens: The weakened riverbank gives way, and the river violently carves for itself a new course—right through Farmer Jones's barnyard. The river may occupy that new course forever or just until the next unforeseen concatenation of changes—some made by nature (the rain, the flood) and some, perhaps, by man (the clearing of the cottonwoods)—converges thoughtlessly to change the river's course again.

The concept of evolution not as a steady, gradual process but as a series of long, quiet plateaus studded with sudden bursts of massive evolutionary redirection is called *punctuated equilibrium.* It is today the closest thing to a prevailing view of evolution's modus operandi. Its best-known example is probably the asteroid that scientists now

> **"The only thing that we can predict with certainty is change."**
> *Jayne Spain*

KEVIN W. C. GREEN *heads Green & Associates, Inc., Alexandria, Virginia–based marketing and strategic planning consultants to architecture and engineering firms. He was director of marketing for Leo A. Daly from 1988 to 1998 in the firm's Washington, D.C. office.*

believe struck the Yucatán peninsula some 65 million years ago, unexpectedly launching a climatic shift that eliminated the dinosaurs and cleared the way for Earth's domination by our own favorite species, us.

Punctuated equilibrium is relevant here because architecture deals with both evolution and change and does so both internally (in terms of practice) and externally (in terms of client needs and expectations). Internally, architectural practice today is the product of its own evolution—the sum of the myriad advances, adaptations, innovations, styles, and standards developed since the dawn of design and construction but inculcated far more rapidly since the advent of modern architectural practice and education in the mid-nineteenth century. Many of these changes have been touted as evolutionary—which is to say they've punctuated the equilibrium of practice and become permanent in their impact—and yet have faded as circumstances have changed once again. For example, the importance of energy efficiency as a design goal has risen and fallen in cadence with the price of oil since the energy crisis of 1973–74. It's not easy to know when, or to what extent, a change amounts to a true, evolutionary shift that moves things to a new plateau.

Like architects, clients endure change in their lives, businesses, and industries, as well as in their aspirations for the buildings in which they live and operate (and in their expectations of the consultants who help them achieve these goals). When do such changes amount to evolutionary punctuations of equilibria? Hard to tell. However, the pace of change today—whether global, societal, or regional, in the home or at work—is so rapid that there may be a greater likelihood that the seeds of actual evolution are embedded in it.

## CHANGE AT THE GLOBAL LEVEL

The most broadly felt change of the more than thirty years since Apollo 11 went to the moon "in peace for all mankind" has been the actual realization of the global village that Marshall McLuhan forecast exactly that long ago. Planet Earth is now a village of more than 5 billion people linked by a worldwide wireless (if not yet seamless) communications network, through which virtually all peoples worldwide share increasingly equal access to the same entertainment, political thought, and opportunities to trade in the same goods, services, stocks, bonds, and currencies.

The barely controlled chaos of this first stage of globalization is reminiscent of earlier frontier eras in all but its planetary scale. It is rich in both opportunity and danger for the developed nations and multinational corporations that seek to profit at the global table and which bring most of the competitive advantage to it. And since multinationals often take their architects with them, existing client relationships are the single most traveled route to overseas projects for American firms.

The overseas desire for goods and services that bear distinctive Western brand names—from beverages by Coca-Cola (maker of 50 percent of all soft drinks sold worldwide) to scarves from Hermès and gold jewelry from Gucci—goes for architecture, too. European, Middle Eastern, and Asian clients (and their clients) have hungered for decades for American design as well as for the American technology it so often reflects and (in architecture and engineering) encompasses. In response, they have imported many of the best-known high-design names in the business—from SOM and KPF to Gehry, Pelli, Stern, and Graves—principally to satisfy global consumers' strong desire for Western brands.

At the same time, companies in developed nations have taken it on the chin from globalization. Since 1997, the staggering Asian economy has sent sales there tumbling for several U.S.-based multinational manufacturers. Such setbacks are reflected in reduced earnings, lower stock valuations on Wall Street, job cuts, and a host of other injuries induced at home by overseas hits. Coca-Cola and Eastman Kodak, among others, know just how much that can hurt.

Opportunity will keep companies in developed nations engaged and

---

### Globalization Arrives

Writing in the Ivey Business Journal *(winter 1997)*, John McCallum sees two facets to globalization.

*First:* In an increasing number of industries, globalization is rapidly creating a single, worldwide marketplace. Being the best in a city or region is no longer sufficient to ensure success; when everyone . . . everywhere is a competitor, world-class is the only standard that matters.

The more aggressive the competition, the faster the pace of change and the more serious the consequences of standing still.

*Second:* Electronic money, globally interconnected financial markets, 24-hour-a-day worldwide trading, a spectacular debt binge, derivatives, and mutual funds have ushered in a new era in finance. Risk management has become a specialty in its own right.

McCallum agrees with MIT economist Lester Thurow that the prime mover of globalization is technology, which is "driving a third industrial revolution every bit as impressive and all-encompassing as the first two," according to McCallum. "Microelectronics, molecular biology, particle physics, and optics are turning manufacturing, finance, transportation, communications, and personal services upside down in the same way that steam and spinning technology did in the eighteenth century, and electricity, internal combustion, and the telephone did in the nineteenth century."

investing in markets in developing nations, to be sure. That's what makes globalization an evolutionary event. Huge, untapped markets await; China alone, with 40 percent of the world's population, is irresistible despite its many barriers. Production efficiencies await as well; Disney's 1999 animated feature film *Tarzan* was the result of three years of worldwide, round-the-clock production. Several architecture and engineering firms have taken a similar approach to their overseas projects.

But dangers lurk along the vast new global business frontier. Cross-border trade agreements such as NAFTA and GATT, for example, and the currently low wage expectations of workers in Asia and Central and South America will sooner or later disrupt standing job patterns in both the United States and Europe. A wider economic world makes, by definition, for a wider range of potential problems. As Paul Blustein recently wrote in a *Washington Post* op-ed piece, it's "just a matter of time before some new trouble spot erupts and threatens to destabilize the global economy."

> **"Change always involves work. Work is not at the top of many agendas. Comfortable old ways must be discarded, new things must be learned, and new skills must be acquired. . . . People often have genuine trouble understanding why change is necessary. . . . [T]he issues are complicated, nothing is for sure, and people are afraid."**
>
> *John McCallum, "The Face Behind Change,"* Ivey Business Quarterly, *winter 1997*

## CHANGE AT THE SOCIETAL LEVEL

Demographic change is clearly the driver of change in American society at the turn of the twenty-first century, but it's difficult to say whether that phenomenon will have long-term, evolutionary impacts. Still, even the short-term effects on architecture clients have been and continue to be significant.

Since the advent of the baby boom generation (those born between 1946 and 1964), demographic change has done more to shape American architecture than any other single factor. Beginning in the 1950s, the swelling population propelled the construction of millions of new "starter" homes in new suburbs nationwide, followed by thousands of new K-12 schools, then thousands of college and university campus expansions. The list goes on to include the new office buildings in which today's overwhelmingly white-collar boomers work and the "move-up" homes into which they've moved as they've grown wealthier. And coming off the drawing boards for the past decade are the new suburban schools currently attended by the even more numerous "echo boom" children (there were more American children between the ages of 1 and 6 in 1996 than in 1960, the baby boom's peak year for that age range) and the new retirement-living centers to which boomers will be reporting in droves by roughly 2016, when the first boomers hit 70.

## CHANGE AT REGIONAL, URBAN, AND COMMUNITY LEVELS

The millennial shift "toward self-reliance, free markets, prudent government finance, tax cuts, fewer services, reduced subsidies, privatization, and free trade," says John McCallum, is likely to strengthen the hand of the private, client-controlled economic forces that have always chiefly shaped urban, regional, and community development. Those same economic forces have driven the largely unplanned development of the "edge cities" that, since roughly 1960, have been enormously successful at enabling business to follow its workforce out of the cities and into the other great success story of late-twentieth-century America, the suburbs themselves.

For all of the valid criticism aimed at the nation's suburbs—targeting their white-bread character, cookie-cutter housing, and "there's no there there" sprawl—the suburban living concept that first proved immensely popular in the postwar years clearly remains so today. The fact is that the nation's first generation of born-and-bred suburbanites

### Three Information-Age Megatrends

The first seismic shift in the way we live is mobility. . . . [M]ore than 25 percent of Americans move on a yearly basis. Mobility has become so ingrained in our lives that home is no longer a location but a concept. . . . The architectural profession will have to come to grips with the ability of people to "take" their home with them as they go about their journeys and adventures.

The second great influence will be homophyly. This term, borrowed from the life sciences, connotes the tendency of things that touch to resemble each other. In the same way that two people who have been married for forty years begin to look, speak, and think alike, humankind is becoming more similar, not more different. . . . [W]hile humanity hurtles toward the haven of sameness, we will at the same time put an even greater premium on things that stand out. Frank Gehry's Guggenheim Museum Bilbao is an important new "signature" building in the homophylized world. And cities and corporations will go to even greater lengths to present unusual, stand-out design like Gehry's over the next 25 years. . . .

The third great influence on future architecture will be information technology. . . . If the 1980s was the era of the personal computer and the 1990s that of microprocessors, the hallmark of the new age will be microelectronic mechanical systems [that] sense their environment and react, continually altering a building's conditions to accommodate the structure itself and the people inside it. In the future, every new building will be "smart"—with an increasing capacity for smartness.

*Watts Wacker,* Architectural Record, *March 1998*

has stayed put in the 'burbs to raise the second. The "new civics" movement, which rejects old-school, curvilinear suburban patterns in favor of gridded plans that replicate America's traditional small towns (complete with Main Street), is powerful evidence that suburban thinking—refreshed and reinvigorated—is here to stay, sprawl and all. That's evolution.

If John McCallum is right, then sprawl will continue to be the primary problem with suburban and edge-city development and its eventual redevelopment. The fact is, economic forces don't care much about quality-of-life issues until the traffic gets so bad that people can't get to the office on time. However, if and when clients do—for economic reasons—become concerned about the quality of urban, regional, and community planning, they'll be wide open to new ideas that address the irregular street layouts, ill-considered landscaping, and miserable traffic characteristics of so many suburban strips and edge cities.

## CHANGE AT THE HOUSEHOLD LEVEL

The size of the average American family is shrinking, *Time* magazine reported in June 1999, because of improved contraception and the increase in the number of women working outside the home. And yet the size of the average new American house increased by 20 percent in the 1990s. Experts pin responsibility for that on the distaff side, too. Builders report that women—now said by researchers to make most large as well as small goods purchase decisions in American households—are the ones insisting that kitchens and master baths (traditionally female-controlled spaces) be made larger.

New roles for women translate into higher household incomes, rising expectations, and new demands on time already split between child rearing and work. A July 1999 report that the nation's marriage rate has dropped by 43 percent since 1960 explains much of the increase in single-parent households over the same period. What these stats will mean for home design—beyond more space at home and less time to enjoy it—few experts seem willing to predict.

Technology promises to reshape home infrastructure as thoroughly as it has office (and home office) infrastructure. Clients in both settings are expected to continue to demand infrastructural flexibility in design as new technologies—from flat-screen high-definition TV to wireless communication and TV/PC/Internet/telephone/fax hybridization—create new programmatic requirements.

For the short term—the next thirty years or so—the other driving force behind home design is likely to be the aging of the baby boom generation, which will send the number of Americans over the age of 65 skyrocketing from roughly 35 million (13 percent of the population) today to nearly 70 million (21 percent) in 2030.

The vast majority of Americans—as many as 80 percent—opt to stay put in retirement, remaining in their own communities rather than moving to sunnier climes or nursing care environments (until they have to, that is). Still, the increasing number of aging boomers will continue to feed the nation's population shifts to the South and West, the construction of a wide range of facilities for retirement living, and the construction and reconstruction of homes to accommodate the diminishing physical abilities of the aging.

## CORPORATE CHANGE

The corporate world is a particularly compelling place to examine changing client influences because it is a prima facie example of evolution in action. Business exemplifies the struggle for survival.

Unlike nations, societies, communities, and families, corporations ultimately have the self-interest of only a single class—ownership—to worry about and only a single goal—maximized value of ownership's equity—to strive for. The result is an aggressive quest for competitive advantage and profitability in the marketplace.

As survival often does, the quest for profitability boils down to relatively few important issues. Competitive advantage can be achieved in many ways, but in one way or another all of them hinge on the values a corporate client believes its customers assign to the five Ps (promotion, product, people, place, and price). Profitability—the achievement of revenues

> **"Change is a process, not an event."**
> *Tom Eherenfeld,* Harvard Business Review, *January-February 1992*

## Change, Ready or Not

*In 1996 David Carr, Kevin Hard, and William Trahant of Coopers & Lybrand's (now PricewaterhouseCoopers's) Center of Excellence for Change Management listed the forces driving that accounting and consulting firm's corporate clients to adapt. Their list and its accompanying commentaries remain valid and worth quoting at length.*

Today, four types of forces are driving organizations to change, ready or not:

1. Market forces. These include global competition, new market opportunities, and changing customer needs and preferences. Noel Goutard of France's Valeo, a large vehicle parts maker, sums up the situation his company and others are facing: "I've never seen changes take place without strong incentive. The incentives are here now: erratic markets, Japanese competition, intense job pressure. They are forcing change."

"What are we going to do," asks Jack Welch, CEO of General Electric, "when a restructured and hungry Europe and a lean, low-cost Japan, with improved economies, come roaring back—show them our press clippings?" Welch [says] the international dynamics of today's marketplace leave no country room for complacency. Welch also [talks] about market opportunities that are driving change, stating that "Asia is the greatest growth market we will see in our careers. It is our future."

2. Rapidly changing technologies. Technology today changes almost as quickly as the weather, and long-term forecasts have similar reliability. . . . Edward McCracken, CEO of Silicon Graphics, says [that] in his industry, cutting edge innovation is the only real source of competitive advantage. "No one can plan the future," he explains. "Three years is long-term [for strategic planning]. Even two years may be. Five years is laughable." The rapid pace of technological change is also relevant to organizations that use technologies. They offer the potential for competitive advantage or parity, but only when an organization changes to create new ways of doing business using the high-tech tools.

The days of gaining lasting advantage from simply automating current processes are over.

3. Changing political institutions and societies. Putting businesses and services in private hands has long been a factor of increased activity and productivity. Over the past decades, European socialist governments, in the first flush of political victory, nationalized or kept nationalized major manufacturing and services industries. But when they realized it was harming the economy, they soon started reversing the policy. In the U.S., deregulation, added to foreign competition, has helped raise service-sector productivity to a 1.6 percent annual rate in the 1990s, double its .8 percent in the 1980s.

The two most significant trends are the privatization of organizations that were once government- or monopoly-run and the need for government organizations to become more efficient and less costly to operate.

4. Internal need to improve performance and competitive situation. While the external world creates many compelling needs for change, the internal one is the everyday reality for many organizations. Shareholder dissatisfaction, falling profits or market share, and threats to corporate survival itself command the most immediate attention. In Italy, for example, Pirelli Tire Company was facing bankruptcy in the 1990s because acquisitions in the 1980s had increased its debt to 1.5 times its equity. This "edge of destruction" scenario prompted changes that would otherwise have been unimaginable in the European climate, such as closing 12 plants, selling off a large division, leaving a swank corporate headquarters for a spare one, and downsizing 170 senior managers.

The factors compelling change today have one more thing in common: They aren't going away. In fact, the majority of U.S. executives polled . . . think the pace of change will accelerate from today's "rapid or extremely rapid" speed.

---

greater than costs—must grow, and it can grow in only three ways: by increasing revenues, by decreasing costs, or by doing both through the achievement of more efficient production.

At the end of the day, the issues affecting profitability are the only issues on any corporate client's mind, and change is the context in which the corporate client thinks about them. Why? Because change is the natural order of things, in terms of both competitive advantage and profitability. A corporate client's customers constantly vary the values they place on the elements in the mix of promotion, product, people, place, and price, in part because their own circumstances are constantly changing and in part because the corporate client's competitors are constantly adjusting their value-based appeals to the same customers. Thus a company's competitive advantage in the marketplace changes from day to day. As for profitability, revenues must always be increased and/or costs reduced because inflation never sleeps. The costs of a company's raw materials overwhelmingly tend to rise over time, as do the wages and salaries sought by the company's employees.

There is one other thing on every corporate client's mind, and that is ownership's relentless demand for rising equity value. Without this, ownership will simply take its money and invest it elsewhere at a higher rate of return. In theory, rising equity value naturally follows the achievement of superior competitive advantage and maximized profitability, keeping ownership's constantly implied threat from the front of a corporate client's mind—and leaving room for the development of strategies for achieving competitive advantage and more efficient production. Nonetheless, the threat of having the plug pulled is never far away.

# 3 How Clients Choose Architects

## 3.1 How Client Values Affect Architect Selection

Kevin W. C. Green

*Clients want what they value. Discovering what a particular client values is a research problem, and the five Ps—product, people, place, promotion, and price—offer a methodology for finding the answer.*

The *Handbook* topic The Nature of the Client (1.1) discusses the five Ps—*promotion, product, people, place,* and *price*—as mnemonic tags assigned to the principal values that customers and clients bring to their purchase decisions. The topic Understanding Client Values (1.2) discusses other values in which clients of architecture might universally be interested: Vitruvius's *firmness, commodity,* and *delight* form one set, David Maister's *delivery, service,* and *idea* another.

It is important to understand the different ways in which clients classify these values and how this affects their purchases. All clients buy on the basis of unique equations, in which they have assigned different weights to each value according to how important they perceive those values to be. Perhaps because they know instinctively that they can't afford it all, or—more likely—because they simply consider some things more important than others, clients and customers shop by looking for particular attributes and buy when they find those attributes present to the greatest degree.

### CLIENT VALUES

To achieve client satisfaction, it is critical for architects to ascertain what the client really wants. Architects can use the five Ps to discover the answer.

*Promotion* in architecture was traditionally frowned upon until about 25 years ago. In overt forms such as advertising, it was actually forbidden to AIA members until the U.S. Supreme Court and others issued a series of rulings beginning in the mid-1970s, affecting the Institute and other professional associations (including the American Bar Association) that similarly maintained certain mandatory standards of conduct. Prohibitions on advertising, the production of free sketches for clients, the "supplanting" of one architect by another without the former's permission, and similar competitive efforts were found to be unreasonable restraints of free trade. Today's architects are, like today's lawyers, free to promote themselves in any and all legal ways and venues within the bounds of taste—which, of course, knows no bounds.

> "[F]or the most part, the firms we work with are equal in their technical abilities, [so] we go to more subjective factors, such as their presentation, the way they handle themselves and address our issues, as well as their ability to deal with our questions."
>
> *Vice president of planning and development Mark Brenchly, A/E Marketing Journal, February 1996*

---

**KEVIN W. C. GREEN** *heads Green & Associates, Inc., Alexandria, Virginia–based marketing and strategic planning consultants to architecture and engineering firms. He was director of marketing for Leo A. Daly from 1988 to 1998 in the firm's Washington, D.C. office.*

Clients seek architects who reflect their own values, and promotion is anything in which they see that reflection. The profession's old archetype of promotion was the genteel architect whose membership in one or two exclusive men's clubs exposed him (architecture was a male bastion in those days) to his likeliest potential clients—other men of wealth, taste, and substantial business interests likely to offer an architect commercial and industrial jobs as well as town and country house commissions.

An architect's clientele nowadays is far more democratic, as is architecture itself. For the past two decades architects have begun—though only just—to explore correspondingly wide-band ways of promoting the values that characterize their work. The useful width of any band, however, is limited by the notion that each client views the five Ps differently and is receptive to value-related messages only if they relate to something the client values.

*Product,* in architecture, focuses squarely on the Vitruvian virtues of firmness, commodity, and delight. Even when the product of an architect's services is not a physical structure—in the case of a facility management plan, a due diligence study, or just a few words of advice—the subject generally deals with a physical environment (if not several), and the client is generally focused on one or more aspects of its solidity (firmness), efficacy for human occupation (commodity), and inducement of general client satisfaction (delight).

Clients with a strong product orientation are generally interested in past products that have taken the same form—buildings, plans, reports, studies, databases, advice—and are similar in use, objective, or application to their own. How similar? Product-oriented clients are likely to be interested in past projects that resemble theirs closely in

- *scale,* because larger projects pose different challenges than small projects
- *use and complexity,* because requirements can vary hugely and many clients see certain building types as highly specialized in their user requirements
- *cost,* because cost containment always matters
- *schedule,* because time is always money
- *delivery method,* because it drives cost and schedule
- *location,* because local familiarity can make a difference
- *design,* because it demonstrates talent, which, like history, tends to repeat itself
- *client,* because similar clients tend to handle projects in similar ways, and past projects with similar clients are powerful builders of trust

*People,* in architecture, focuses on delivery, service, and idea. Whatever the product of an architect's services will be, the client wants to know that the people who propose to provide them have completed similar efforts in the past. This assurance allows the client to trust that the architect has the knowledge and talent to provide such services. The notion that a firm has done the same kind of work before enhances its reliability as an organization specialized, in Maister's terms, in project delivery, client service, or the generation of bright ideas in similar situations.

Clients who value relationships are generally interested in meeting and learning about the people proposed for their projects. At a minimum, they want to know

- whether the same people whose past projects are described by the firm will work on theirs, in the same capacities
- whether the firm's most senior people will be involved—or, alternatively, whether a project-appropriate balance of senior (expensive) and less senior (inexpensive) people will be cost-effectively maintained
- whether the number of people involved will be sufficient to meet the project's technical and schedule demands

*Place,* in architecture, focuses on geographic area. The physical locations of client, architect, and project form a triangle that is golden to some clients and meaningless to others. Each client's valuation of place may vary depending on the services the client is looking to buy.

"We look at [firms'] experience, their background in dealing with schools, and their understanding of education-related issues. One of the biggest questions that we have is what these firms have done for other districts and how this work has helped and is helping [their schools]."
*School facility management director Mike White,*
A/E Marketing Journal, *February 1996*

"We rate . . . firms in terms of their experience, the qualifications of the staff, and who the 'number-one person' on the project will be. We also rate firms on how well they can maintain their commitment to the project after the design phase of the project has been finished."
*California State University, Sacramento, facility planning manager Ron Richardson,*
A/E Marketing Journal, *February 1996*

Some clients recognize the advantages of a consultant's proximity to a project or to the client's offices. However, many factors can outweigh the importance of proximity. If, for example, a client sees only a few firms nationwide as capable of handling a particular technical complexity, the client will search far and wide for the most qualified firm and may hire one neither near the client nor near the project. For many building types—large airport terminals are one—the short supply of firms perceived as qualified drives clients' selection equations. If, on the other hand, a dozen firms in a client's immediate neighborhood are similarly qualified for a job, why hire an out-of-towner?

This is how place raises the issue of the exportability of a firm's services. Exportability is one of the ratios driven (as all selection criteria are to one degree or another) on the X-axis by a client's specific values and on the Y-axis by the scarcity of firms capable of delivering those values.

Exportability often finds its most dramatic expression in clients who value design excellence so highly that they will disregard place altogether as an issue in selection. A classic example is Irwin Miller, the Cummins Engine Corporation CEO who saw design excellence as a magnet that would attract talented executives to Columbus, Indiana, the village in which Cummins was (and is) headquartered. Miller underwrote the design of virtually all of the small town's public buildings by an international roster of star architects that is unmatched worldwide.

The Walt Disney Company has done much the same thing to draw residents to Celebration, its "new civics" experiment in central Florida, offering row houses designed by (New Yorker) Robert A. M. Stern, a town hall by (New Jersey's) Michael Graves, and an art deco movie theater by (Connecticut-based) Cesar Pelli, among others. Historically, of course, it was design-based exportability *in extremis* that took Wisconsin's Frank Lloyd Wright to Tokyo in the 1920s, Philadelphia's Louis Kahn to Chandigarh in the 1960s, and Santa Monica's Frank Gehry to Bilbao in the 1990s.

The particular attribute a client values enough to pump up a project's exportability ratio can be anything from star-quality design to technical complexity, understanding of a rare project type, or familiarity with a particular locale. What matters is that the client values the architect's experience sufficiently to care not at all about the location of the architect's office.

The architecture firm itself, though, can be an important place issue to a client. Its size, staffing, facilities, equipment, and technologies can be qualifiers as important as location(s) to clients who care about such things. Some clients—the U.S. Department of State and other federal agencies with secure-room requirements, for example—bring specific workplace criteria that can rapidly narrow a field of otherwise evenly qualified firms down to a select few.

The fact that client values change over time in response to competitive pressures (in their own businesses as well as in architecture) is illustrated well by the evolution of the importance of office technologies as a factor in architect selection. Computer-aided design and drafting (CAD)1 in the 1970s and '80s was something unusual, an innovation marketed (and priced) as a strong differentiator by relatively few firms and highly valued by a small client set. By the mid-1990s CAD was commonplace in firm offices and a baseline requirement among most clients. Its value as a differentiator is now vastly diminished (unless you lack it) and its specific costs are not even called out in project pricing.

*Price,* in architecture, governs virtually every selection issue and focuses closely on the law of supply and demand. How much a client is willing to pay—for design, construction, or other services—reflects that client's values and the relative scarcity (in the client's perception) of firms capable of delivering on those values.

A product or service in any market goes through a life cycle with predictable stages of maturation. When first introduced, a product—the digital video disk (DVD) player, for example—is typically purchased by only a few innovators willing to experiment with an altogether new technology. As the product's popularity spreads to slightly less daring "early adopters," its sales increase. When the masses discover it, its sales enter a period of steep annual growth. Ultimately—assuming the product becomes, like the television, a staple that most people own—its market will become saturated or "mature." At that point, its annual sales growth will effectively cease, although unit sales will continue and hold steady at an annual replacement rate usually equal to the annual growth of the market's population or the overall economy as measured by gross domestic product (GDP).

The basic phases of a product or service life cycle—introduction, growth, and maturity—have typical competitive and price characteristics. For example, competing manufacturers are usually nonexistent when a new product or service is introduced, but they tend to jump into the market when growing sales persuade them to copy it. By the time the sales growth flattens, in maturity, many makers or providers will be competing for shares in a market crowded with virtually identical products or services. Typically, because their products are undifferentiated, those makers or providers will be competing on price. They will vie to draw customers with discounts and profit only if they were wise enough earlier to use the revenues from the high-growth stage to fund process improvements that reduce their production costs to the lowest possible point.

A product or service undifferentiated from nearly identical competitors and marketed to customers or clients who chiefly value price fits the definition of a mature-market commodity. Typically, a commodity generates paltry profit now and promises little future growth—unless, through innovation and innovation-based marketing differentiation, it can become (in buyers' eyes) a "new" product or service and thus be reborn at the beginning of a new life cycle.

All clients are interested in price. It's the intensity of their interest that reflects the point in the project life cycle at which they peg the services they seek. Firms whose qualifications for a particular project or service type are seen by clients as rare and unusual can command commensurately high fees, generous hourly rates, and comfortable contracts. Those whose services aren't so perceived generally can't, because they are selling a commodity.

## PERCEPTIONS OF VALUE

We have established that clients want what they value and choose architects who reflect their values. It is therefore incumbent on the architect to work hard to ascertain the values of potential clients. How? The obvious answer—ask them—is rarely the right one. While talking to clients is the direct route to unearthing their perceptions of value, asking them directly doesn't usually work for two reasons.

The first reason is that innovation—change—is the only route to competitive advantage and productive efficiency in business. Evolution—cumulative change—amounts in business to a constantly rising floor of customer (and client) expectations, which is propelled by the aggregation of past innovations in competitive advantage and productive efficiency offered by providers of goods and services.

The evolution of CAD from a differentiating innovation to a baseline requirement is only one demonstration of this natural law, the net effect of which is that client expectations are virtually always for a state of the art product, or very near to it. Even clients who profess a distrust for innovation's legendary "bleeding edge" will inevitably be dissatisfied if a firm delivers products of (in their view) lesser value than alternatives attainable at the same price from someone else.

The second reason a direct inquiry usually doesn't work? Clients are among those *least* likely to accurately portray their own values—we have human nature to thank for that. To the rising floor of innovation-based client expectations, add clients' belief that they must actively seek maximization of all values in order to avoid being shortchanged. Purchasers of goods and services know it isn't possible to maximize all values, but they are afraid they'll get less than full value if they don't demand maximization. This defeat of common sense by the forces of greed is a daily event. It is why humorously cartooned signs in gas station waiting rooms and other customer gathering points nationwide regularly remind us, "You can get it good, fast, or cheap. Pick two."

Only the most sophisticated clients will freely admit aspiring to anything less than the highest levels of the five Ps—and they're probably not being truthful. In fact, that quest for more, more, more is the force that drives innovation and constantly lifts the level at which businesses must compete. Few customers will happily make a purchase that doesn't reflect the sum total of past innovation related to that product or service. Yet all products and all services are not created equal, nor are all selected and purchased. Perhaps the greatest value of the five Ps is that, as a tool, they offer a way of gauging client-perceived valuations of specific product and service attributes that is not overburdened by human nature, which always aspires to achieve the greatest possible combination of values at the lowest possible price.

**"[W]ith left-brained, business-minded executives on one side and right-brained interior architects and designers on the other . . . the American Society of Interior Designers released [a study] . . . aimed at showing how far apart business and designers can be even when they are using the same language. . . .**

**"Barbara Nugent, one of the team members at Benson Hlavaty & Paret Architects in Dallas, said it's invaluable. 'So often, we're all using the same terms and phrases, but we are worlds apart in what we think each word means,' Nugent said. 'It may sound elementary, but from the study we have learned that a client wants to know what the effect of an office design will be, not what the design is. . . . One of the biggest areas of difference comes when we talk about words like cost controls or value,' Nugent said."**

DesignIntelligence, *August 15, 1998*

# 3.2 Client Approaches to Architect Selection

## Kevin W. C. Green

*Product, place, people, price, and promotion aren't simply categories of client-held values. They're the dimensions of the playing field on which all architects compete, even when things appear otherwise.*

The way in which clients approach their business decisions stems from their basic understanding of what is important for the survival and prosperity of their companies. The five Ps serve as a means of broadly defining the factors at play in business decision making. Architects who can determine how much weight a particular client places on each of the five Ps will know how good the match is between their firm and a potential client. The more closely a firm's values are aligned with those of its clients, the better the relationships—and the more repeat business—it is likely to have.

### SELECTION APPROACHES

Clients can view competing architecture firms in one of several ways. The most common ways of comparing firms are by looking at their qualifications and their cost. Some clients, most often government agencies, hold design competitions when they must choose an architect.

***Qualification-based selection.*** The federal government's Standard Forms 254 and 255 ask all architects chasing all federal design commissions to describe their relevant Ps: the similar products they've designed and built, the people directly responsible, and the places in which those products were produced, all framed in a common format enabling the client's even-handed review of all promotion—everything but price, which gets negotiated later with the selected firm.

Most clients today, public and private, select architects on the basis of a list of criteria that closely resembles the one embodied in the SF 254 and 255. That model—complete with its refusal to share information about the client's values generally or for the specific project at hand—is replicated in requests for qualifications (RFQs) and requests for proposal (RFPs) issued daily from coast to coast by clients large and small. The language varies, but the Ps rarely do, except perhaps price, which—particularly in cases calling for commodity services—receives more and earlier attention in private projects than in government ones.

Those RFQs and RFPs ought to be called RFVs (requests for values), for they focus on firm and, by extension, client values. Architects who have done enough homework to understand something about a client's values for a particular project are usually smart enough to shape their qualifications—to the extent they can—to reflect those values.

***Cost-based selection.*** Price is always a client value. *Price elasticity* is economic jargon for the willingness of buyers in a market to pay higher or lower prices for a product in limited supply, based—of course—on the other ways in which they value that particular product. All of us will pay more for something we want when it's hard to come by, just as all of us will pay as little as we can for something when all other values are equal.

Cost-based competition among the providers of a good or service tests the lower limits of price elasticity. It affects products and services so common and undifferentiated in the marketplace that price alone determines their sale: In this situation cus-

KEVIN W. C. GREEN *heads Green & Associates, Inc., Alexandria, Virginia-based consultants in A/E-firm marketing and strategic planning. He was director of marketing for Leo A. Daly from 1988 to 1998 in the firm's Washington, D.C. office.*

## Federal Architect Selection

The federal government's Standard Forms 254 and 255 were developed roughly thirty years ago by an interagency team of clients. Mostly trained as architects and engineers, these individuals were determined to rid themselves of the mountains of wildly varying (in size, cost, and quality) proposals dumped on their desks whenever they invited architects to compete for a federal design opportunity.

Unable to compare such heterogeneous qualifications statements fairly—and driven by Texas representative Jack Brooks's bill requiring that only firm qualifications, not prices, be evaluated in federal architect selection—the team came up with a remarkably elegant solution in Standard Forms 254 and 255. For three decades, despite architects' occasional complaints that the forms don't do justice to their design achievements, SF 254 and 255 have served as the universal selection-process tool throughout the federal government, which is the nation's single largest A/E contracting client. For all intents and purposes, they remain in use at all A/E contracting agencies today.

SF 254 asks for information about a firm that is submitting a proposal to produce a project as lead architectural contractor—its office location(s), staffing, most common project types, and so on. SF 255 focuses on the project at hand, asking for detailed information about the team formed for this project and detailed resumes of the personnel proposed for it. It also gives the submitting team an opportunity to describe and show, at length, ten projects (preferably constructed) that it feels are closely comparable to the project on which it is bidding.

In the mid-1990s the U.S. General Services Administration (GSA)—which not only runs design and construction for the federal government in general but often manages A/E selection and projects for individual agencies as well—came up with a selection process that focuses almost exclusively on what it calls "design excellence." The process is used only when a project is deemed large enough, costly enough, or "public" enough to warrant design by one of the nation's best architects. Other architect selections at GSA still rely on Standard Forms 254 and 255.

tomers can set prices unilaterally, driving out of business any provider incapable of profiting at that price. That is the awful risk faced by competitors in a commodity market.

Value-based competitors face the identical risk: They, too, can cost themselves out of business, that is, operate at a level of productive efficiency that is costlier than the market will profitably bear. But value-based competitors enjoy the grace of greater distance from disaster; their operating costs are less tightly strapped to late-learning-curve efficiencies. In addition, they don't rely on price as the *only* differentiator between competing products.

Cost-based competition allows clients to place unilateral limits on firms, limits on both freedom and integrity of action as well as on price. Value-based competition assumes an even balance of power between client and firm—the marketplace operating in ideal form, ensuring a fair exchange of goods or services for commensurate remuneration.

Still, if value-based competition is the marketplace in ideal form, cost-based competition is the marketplace in *natural* form: It operates—ruthlessly, as in Hobbes's state of nature—to drive inefficient, unprofitable providers out, thus diminishing supply, decreasing competition, and restoring a more even balance of power in which price is only one of several values that clients use to select services.

In the meantime, architects in commodity markets—or architects offering run-of-the-mill services that clients believe have no other, sufficiently differentiated virtues to redeem price—are either bemoaning their markets or bailing out of them.

***Design competitions.*** From the viewpoint of the client—our interest here—design competitions have many attractions.

In theory, and often in reality, a client's interest in a design competition represents a frank admission of the high value the client places on seeing a design solution as a selection factor. Indeed, an open competition, inviting all comers, establishes design as the primary (if not only) attribute of value to the client. There are projects for which open design competitions are clearly appropriate; the competition for the Vietnam Veterans Memorial in Washington, D.C., won

**Commodity-based firms**
- **Solve problems through design**
- **Try to control people and results**
- **Practice a mysterious process**
- **Provide experts with answers**
- **Grow presentation skills**
- **Educate the client**
- **Take all the design risks**
- **Listen and interpret**
- **Provide what clients say they want**
- **Overcome opposition or compromise**

**Value-based firms**
- **Work through problems with the client**
- **Sacrifice control to gain influence**
- **Practice an "in-your-face" process**
- **Provide trusted advisors**
- **Grow facilitation skills**
- **Share the path of discovery**
- **Share the responsibility**
- **Question and interpret**
- **Define and manage expectations**
- **Weigh disagreements against project goals**

*Modified from Vander Kaay & Co.,*
DesignIntelligence, *March 31, 1998*

## How to Compete

*Research the client's business thoroughly.* Read all the stories that discuss the company's current business and its strategies for procuring new business so that you can speak articulately about what challenges the client's executives must address for a successful project. . . .

*Develop a financial profile of the client.* Through your stockbroker, secure copies of the prospective client's past three annual financial statements. . . . Search the Internet for government filings and other business reports on the client, then compare this image with the one reflected in the [financials] . . . to sound like an insider with specific insight into your client's game plan. . . .

*Identify whether the client has a strong interest in design issues.* If a corporation has always hired star designers for showcase offices and buildings, you can be certain that there will be a heavy emphasis on design experience at your interview. . . .

*Show how your firm can provide services that are part of the client's larger goals.* Highlight your ability to be part of a problem-solving team prepared to integrate its services with clients who are operating on a global perspective. . . .

*Tell clients what they want to hear—and be ready to deliver*

*what you tell them.* Show that you are sensitive to business problems and willing to meet your client's budget-setting goals in cooperation with contractors, construction managers, and lenders. . . .

*Ask questions before the interview.* Preliminary sessions should be scheduled for inquiries addressing the client's special concerns. . . .

*Show that you've been there before.* Cite examples of how you were confronted with a thorny problem by a prior client and helped develop a cost-effective solution. . . .

*Project your expertise in a friendly manner.* Nobody wants to work with someone, regardless of talent, who is a social snob, a bore, or who makes them feel uncomfortable. Be friendly from the outset. . . .

*Convey a hands-on concern for the client's business goals.* Make it clear that you will be personally involved in every aspect of the project. . . .

*Make the client look good.* Let your client or client team know from the outset that you will make them shine in the eyes of their superiors, their lenders, their stockholders.

**Barry LePatner,** Architecture, **February 1996**

by Maya Ying Lin, then an architecture student at Yale, is a well-known example of the type. And there are steps that can be taken to address the potential inexperience of an open-competition winner. The most common is the involvement of an experienced associated architect, as Washington's Cooper-Lecky Architects was involved with the Vietnam Veterans Memorial.

Having established that design competitions can have merit, it must also be said that competitions are open to witting and unwitting abuses by clients. Because they often replace a thoughtful, collaborative programming process, competitions are vulnerable to the tardy emergence of important client issues and objectives. Competitions almost always coax architects into spending more time and money on their competitive efforts than they anticipate—more, as a rule, than even compensated competitions fund. And competitions can sometimes veil the preordained selection of a particular firm or firm type, to the costly chagrin of unwired competitors.

Stated or unstated, paid or unpaid, legitimate or stacked, conducted privately or out in the open, under public scrutiny and with public pressure for outcomes that may or may not be seen by the client as the best, competitions are often problematic. Yet they are continually dangled before hungry architects by clients who either highly value the one aspect of architecture that is least subject to objective analysis—the achievement of high design—or cannot envision what they want until they've seen a number of design solutions.

**"[Dissatisfied clients] are invaluable in several ways. . . .**

**"*They alert you to problems.* Clients leave for many reasons. . . . If the [reasons they leave] concern your business, it probably is a signal of adjustments that need to be made. . . . Making changes now can prevent further erosion of your client base.**

**"*They alert you to competitors' offerings.* If clients are defecting because of real or perceived benefits from competitors, you . . . may want to offer similar promotions or pricing, or you may need to educate your clients about the value of your services compared to the competitors' apparent value."**

DesignIntelligence, *July 15, 1998*

## CLIENT SELECTION OF A KNOWN QUANTITY (GETTING REPEAT BUSINESS)

The best argument for diligently researching client values and competing only for work from clients whose values closely mirror your own is this: Eighty percent or more of any successful firm's work is repeat business or referrals from existing clients. So it's not only important to do a good job for one's clients—it's crucial. In fact, it is the single most critical aspect of marketing, which is no more nor less than competing for work on the basis of perceived and actual value. And the easiest way to do a good job is to figure out in advance precisely how the client defines value.

Any firm that understands a client's *values* will know how to deliver what that client will define as value; the relationship between those intangibles is as simple, direct, and proportional as relationships get. The fact that the client has selected the firm assumes that its qualifications equip it to follow through in delivery. And follow through it must, or the client's expectations will be shorted.

Imagine a firm that isn't delivering on its clients' expectations. As a piece in the marketing newsletter *DesignIntelligence* (July 15, 1998) put it, "Clients have a very effective way of telling you that they are unhappy with your services—they go somewhere else." The way to "prevent lost clients and . . . recover those who . . . [are lost is to] constantly interview all of your clients—not just the ones" who seem dissatisfied, the author opines. "Clients who leave obviously hurt business. . . . Major repercussions can be avoided by determining early on that something is changing."

Keep your ears open; it's much cheaper to keep your existing clients than to find replacements for them. The opportunity cost of a client lost is steep. It includes not only the dollars in evaporated future earnings (EFEs) from that client alone but also the many, many dollars in EFEs from other present and potential clients who end up with an earful about you.

Deliver the spirit and the letter of the value you promise, or you'll play the client-retention game—a game so popular that most marketing consultants say *every* firm needs a game plan.

The first rule in that game plan: Don't give up. "Call or write every client who leaves you within two weeks," *DesignIntelligence* advises. "Ask them what you can do to get them back. . . . A significant percentage of lost customers can be recovered by communicating with them."

If that doesn't work, go to the second rule: *Learn from your mistakes.* Failing with a client is far too important a marketing misstep to not gain something from it.

Finally, console yourself with this, from Kent Grayson and Tim Ambler in the *Journal of Marketing Research* (February 1999):

> Moorman, Zaltman, and Deshpande [suggest] that long-term relationships foster relational dynamics that dampen the positive impact of trust, commitment, and involvement on [a client's] use [of a consulting services firm] . . . clients in long-term . . . services relationships may come to perceive that their service providers "have become stale or too similar to them in their thinking and therefore have less value to add." . . . Finally . . . clients may come to believe that service providers in long-term relationships are taking advantage of the trust between the two parties and acting opportunistically.

If you do find your relationship with a client getting stale, you can try what Grayson and Ambler suggest: "[Switch the client] to a new [internal] team, thus starting a relationship anew." Nobody wins 'em all.

# 4  Working with Clients

## 4.1  Focusing on Service
### Kevin W. C. Green

*Service is a powerful business strategy and the key to working in a broad market. Clients and potential clients share certain values and expectations to which firms can successfully respond with focused marketing tactics and practice standards.*

Service is a big deal for one very simple reason: It's a great form of insurance. A firm capable of delivering outstanding design is still a hostage to style, since subjective preferences come and go and clients come and go with them. By the same token, a firm capable of skillfully delivering specific project types is a hostage to demand, since project types fall in and out of market favor, too. Only by earning clients' trust can a firm insure itself—not entirely but to an extent—against the ebbing tides of style and demand. Why? Because clients who trust a firm believe the firm understands their values so well that it will learn whatever it needs to know to deliver work that responds specifically to their needs. And a firm earns that trust through good service.

> ▶ **"Many will . . . remember with fondness a time when architects, interior designers, contractors, engineers, builders, construction managers, and in-house corporate architects did not all compete for the same work. Today, no service provider dares to dictate terms to a quality client. Attentiveness and the clear willingness to bend over backward to a client's needs are the norm."**
>
> *Barry LePatner, Architecture, February 1996*

### SERVICE AS A STRATEGY

In *Success Strategies for Design Professionals* (1987)—a short, brilliant book that recommends "superpositioning" strategies for firms whose clients have specific sets of values—David Maister and the Coxe Group suggest that the rising client demand for specialized skills and the sheer difficulty of managing overgeneralized firms combine to dictate that firms focus on only one client type. They narrow client types to three:

- Clients who value cost-effective project *delivery* most highly
- Clients who value the *ideas* embodied in great design most highly
- Clients, those squarely in the center, who value *service* most highly

According to Maister and the Coxe Group, more firms work this middle ground, sometimes by default (lacking the competitive advantages needed to compete against firms specializing in specific project types or high design) and sometimes by intent (refusing to commit their eggs to a specialized-market basket). They note, too, that more clients tend to dwell in the center, moving into the other sectors as their project or business needs change—and taking evolving firms with them—but generally gravitating again toward the middle.

---

**KEVIN W. C. GREEN** *heads Green & Associates, Inc., Alexandria, Virginia–based marketing and strategic planning consultants to architecture and engineering firms. He was director of marketing for Leo A. Daly from 1988 to 1998 in the firm's Washington, D.C. office.*

## Quality Service for Competitive Edge

The need to adapt to changing market conditions puts enormous pressure on service organizations to change both processes and values. . . . Front-line workers are being put under pressure to get more done at higher standards with greater accountability. Without some conscious relief from the pressure, the outcomes will be predictable: dissatisfaction, stress-related symptoms, and turnover will compromise the productivity and service quality goals.

Many organizations have formal definitions of service standards, either as a mission statement or as an operational rule. Generally, these take the form of global imperatives. "The client is always right" or "Excellence is creating client satisfaction" are typical examples we encountered. At the other end of the spectrum are definitions that are focused on the client, the product, or the transaction. Two examples are "Meet the client's expectations" and "The only difference between firms is how they treat clients."

### What People Are Doing

1. Soft-sell: Sales skills are taught to client-contact employees to increase the amount of each sale by cross-selling services. The better programs achieve increased client satisfaction by demonstrating awareness of needs beyond the successful completion of a single transaction. If the desired result of improved service quality is short-term increased business from existing clients, this kind of training is appropriate.

2. Positive thinking: Motivational programs are particularly popular for non-exempt contact people. Often run by outside consultants, these sessions are designed to change the attitudes of front-line workers [with an] emotional "shot in the arm" [that] rejuvenates employee attitudes toward their jobs, the company, and clients. However, the good feeling dissipates. A potential result may be more cynical employees who become desensitized to motivational programs as hype and management duplicity.

3. Telephone and courtesy skills: Skills for handling telephone interactions, ranging from listening and probing to handling complaints, are combined with courtesy skills. The programs are designed to increase client-service representa-

tives' efficiency and to present a positive, upbeat image. A courteous and helpful front-line employee does make for greater client satisfaction. Aerotek, for example, calls each receptionist "Director of First Impressions." These employees must also, however, take responsibility for resolving issues and assuring action. If the organization as a whole is not prepared to be responsive, then the employee will have to deliver service in spite of the company, creating employee stress and frustration.

4. Problem-handling and listening: Rarely described as handling customers' problems but rather as handling problem customers, these programs focus on managing personalities and identifying problems before they flare up. As with courtesy skills, problem-handling and listening skills are critical. When an external client presents a problem, the employee may have to resolve that issue by requesting help, clearly communicate the issue to others, figure out ways to prevent similar situations from occurring, and keep his or her boss informed along the way.

### Common Needs to be Addressed

1. Universal application: everyone needs to be involved in service quality.

2. Management participation: managers must lead by example.

3. Internal customer—the employee: Each employee should understand his or her contribution to the client's ultimate satisfaction, the importance of listening to immediate client wants and needs, the value of using one set of performance standards throughout the firm, the value of helping vendors meet client needs, and a rule that helps employees separate productive from unproductive activity.

4. Effective training: Service quality values expressed in company slogans must be put into place and followed through.

5. Integration: integrate service quality with product quality.

*Nancy Cushing, Carol Laughlin, and Roland Dum, DesignIntelligence, June 30, 1998*

For Maister and colleagues, *service* is a strategy. It defines a market—a very broad market—whose clients share certain values and expectations. Firms can successfully respond to these values and expectations with relevant marketing tactics and practice standards.

But service is more than that. If the floor of client expectations has risen as the practice of architecture has evolved, it has risen most in the center, driving up client expectations for service from all firms in all markets.

"It is no longer acceptable," Barry LePatner wrote in *Architecture* (February 1996), "to tell clients, 'This is the way we've always provided this type of service' or 'Nobody ever asked us to do it that way.'" No matter what a firm's area of specialization, it must be sensitive and responsive to its clients' demands for service.

*A/E Marketing Journal* (February 1998) reflected this new level of client expectation when it said, "The foundation to every marketing program is strong client service." Speaking to client retention as well as to new-client pursuit, the journal recommended five ways of using service "to turn sound professional practices into sales opportunities":

*Understand your client.* Develop a thorough understanding of your client's business, his goals and objectives, organizational characteristics, and the impact of this current project on that business. . . .

*Generate ideas.* Brainstorm with team members on ways to help the client succeed through this project. Speculate on what opportunities you may suggest to be of greater service through value engineering, strategic partnering, or through the use of alternative [delivery] methods. . . .

*Assure timeliness.* Manage the plan to ensure that you meet all deliverables and milestones on schedule. Be sure that your team and the client share a common understanding of the plan and what constitutes on-time performance. . . .

*Initiate client contact.* Have frequent contact with your client. Demonstrate your interest in how the current project status impacts the client's larger organizational goals [and look] for opportunities to meet with your client concerning non-routine subjects [in a setting] that encourages reflection. . . .

*Gain performance feedback.* Involve all team members [including the client] in [a] Project Evaluation at closeout. Consider how well the client's objectives were met and to what degree the project was executed within time, cost, and profitability goals.

*A/E Marketing Journal* (November 1994) has also noted that a firm's leaders must set the firm on a service-focused course. It simply won't happen if the firm's CEO doesn't demonstrate these three principles of service:

1. *Foster a service-oriented culture.* . . . [The] CEO must live and breathe service by demonstrating how he or she provides it to clients every day. Back up slogans with actions and programs. [Create] an open-door policy to all staff and [hold] weekly meetings to inform, inspire, and solve service problems. . . .

2. *Make client service everyone's business.* The CEO must make staff feel like they own the firm so they will care about its relative success or failure. . . .

3. *Eliminate bureaucracy* . . . the number one killer of providing excellent service. CEOs must minimize formal control mechanisms and rely on cultural climate for control and re-educate staff to completely support the front-line staff who interact with clients on a daily basis.

*The Nordstrom example.* These lessons in the importance of service are far from exclusive to architecture, the design professions, or even professional services. Nordstrom, the Seattle-based clothing retailer, has revolutionized both its industry and the specific geographic markets it has entered (and promptly conquered) solely on the strength of its service to customers. The key to its success? Nordstrom takes service seriously as an overall market strategy, aligning all of its interconnected tactics in support thereof.

Each new Nordstrom store opens with the following already in place:

- An inventory distribution system that guarantees the availability of the goods customers want and offers them twice the inventory offered by competing stores
- A commission-based compensation system that encourages and rewards the productivity and efficiency of individual salespeople
- An operations system that allows salespeople to maximize their individual sales by taking customers from department to department, rather than handing them off to other salespeople (or into thin air)
- A human resources system that brings new hires in only at the bottom (on the sales floor) and promotes department managers and buyers only from within, on performance

Nordstrom's is a hotly competitive, up-or-out culture, but it succeeds in delivering product- and people-focused customer service in defiance of price (virtually no discounts), place (few locations), and promotion (advertising at or near industry averages).

*The value-chain concept.* Harvard's Michael Porter is often credited with codifying the service-as-a-strategy movement in the early 1980s with a pair of books arguing

| CLIENT VALUES VS. FIRM'S INTERNAL ORGANIZATION | |
|---|---|
| **CLIENT FOCUS** | **ARCHITECTURE FIRM'S INTERNAL ORGANIZATION** |
| Product | Design values and methodologies |
| Place | Workplace operations |
| People | Human resources |
| Promotion | Marketing |
| Price | Pricing, contracting, and billing (financial accounting approaches) |

that a firm's competitive advantages in product, people, place, promotion, and price are a function of the values embodied in its internal structure. In effect, Porter correlated the five Ps (which we've discussed primarily as client values) with a firm's internal organizational dimensions. In an architecture firm, for example, a client's valuation of product corresponds to the firm's design values and methodologies; a client's interest in place corresponds to the firm's workplace operations; a client's interest in people corresponds to the firm's human resources; a client's interest in promotion corresponds to the firm's marketing; and a client's interest in price corresponds to the firm's pricing, contracting, billing, and financial accounting approaches.

Every large company or firm has divisions, departments, or managers in charge of marketing, finance, operations, human resources, and product quality/R&D. All play a role in the firm's delivery of service to its clients (as opposed to its product-focused services). Porter's contribution to business theory is his notion that a *value chain* links all departmental activities together in the delivery of one big, cumulative thing called value, to which every department, every employee, and every activity—not just those in direct project interface with the client—can add value. Nordstrom does just that by aligning all of the facets of its organization to maximize value in the service it delivers to its customers.

Architecture firms have the same all-encompassing opportunity.

## SERVICE MODELS

The ways in which a firm can work with its clients—in approach, rather than professional services provided—may be manifold, but three broad models capture, at rising levels, the potential value inherent in the firm-client relationship irrespective of services provided or project delivery method employed. They are the partnership/collaboration, team builder, and trusted-advisor models.

*The partnership/collaboration model.* This is the baseline model, which is premised on the notion that a firm and its clients approach every project with common values, shared goals, and mutually understood expectations. Underlying it is the recognition that firm and client play different roles and carry different responsibilities but do so in partnership. The best interests of the client and the professional aspirations of the firm are unified and delineated in the first priorities of a project—the achievement of goals and the satisfaction of expectations. The result, ideally, is a collaborative process that comfortably accommodates the different roles of the players (including, when relevant, the contractor) but focuses attention on the quality of the product rather than on the process.

"Partnering" is a formalized reflection of this model. In an approach reminiscent of design-build project delivery (which it can accompany but most often is an alternative to), partnering typically engages architect, owner, and preselected contractor in a series of project-start meetings. These are intended to square away potentially differing perspectives on goals and, in so doing, transform the project's individual players into committed members of a unified project team.

*The team builder model.* This model builds on the baseline, envisioning expansion of a firm's role and responsibilities for projects with expanded requirements without fundamental changes in the firm's structure, services, or overall strategy in its markets.

As projects grow more complex—as even small projects do—areas of expertise beyond those encompassed by a firm are inevitably required. For firms practicing archi-

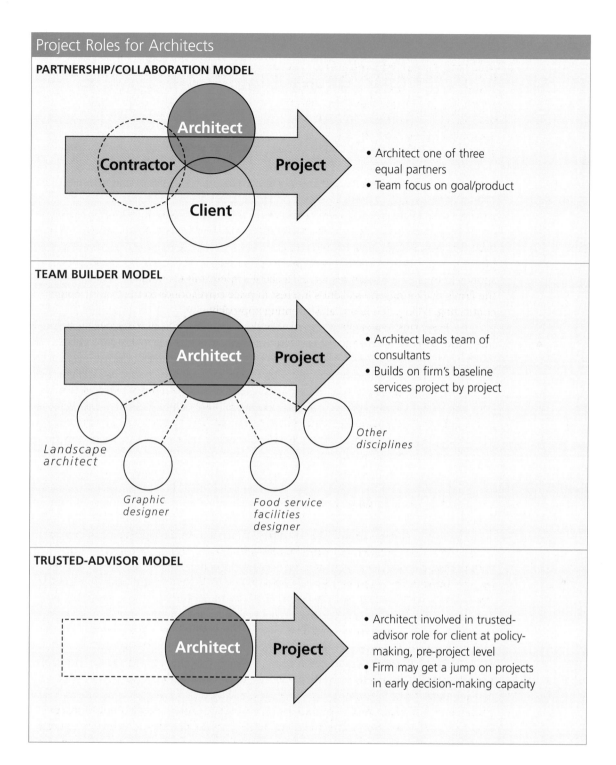

## Project Roles for Architects

### PARTNERSHIP/COLLABORATION MODEL

Contractor
Architect
Client
Project

- Architect one of three equal partners
- Team focus on goal/product

### TEAM BUILDER MODEL

Architect
Project

Landscape architect
Graphic designer
Food service facilities designer
Other disciplines

- Architect leads team of consultants
- Builds on firm's baseline services project by project

### TRUSTED-ADVISOR MODEL

Architect
Project

- Architect involved in trusted-advisor role for client at policy-making, pre-project level
- Firm may get a jump on projects in early decision-making capacity

tecture only, the obvious, common examples are civil, structural, mechanical, and electrical engineering. The list can expand, however, to include scores of specialized environmental design disciplines, from landscape architecture to food service facilities design, as well as disciplines not tied directly to building design, such as graphic design and public relations. At some point, depending on the regular demands of clients in its markets, a firm draws a line on adding specialized disciplines to its own staff. Instead, it builds teams to meet specific project needs (more precisely, specific client needs).

Teaming well can be a field of study in itself. Many firms team frequently enough to maintain lists of favored consultants who specialize in disciplines and specific project types. The idea is to build teams that are competent, capable, and reliable and whose members demonstrate a level of commitment comparable to the firm's. That commitment—which can lead to longer-term strategic alliances among regular team members—is vital, because the performance of a team built by a firm is always judged by the client as the performance of the firm itself.

Being able to serve a client beyond the narrow constraints imposed by a firm's limited expertise, expanding into the broad confines delineated by client needs, is an enormous step up, for three reasons:

First, it demonstrates a firm's recognition that client needs, not professional limitations, drive the business equation.

Second, it captures revenues for managing services as well as for providing services.

Third, it forces a firm to expand its scope of abilities beyond the provision of its professional services to the management of a broader array of services defined by actual client requirements. That better serves the client and sets the stage for future firm evolution without immediately affecting core services. Thus the way is opened for the development of new markets or new products that, ideally, will be younger on the product life cycle than the firm's current services.

> **"We do not always realize how important we are to our clients and client organizations when we thoroughly research and understand the challenges they face in the marketplace. We must place a new emphasis on the client side of the professional practice of architecture in order to achieve a dramatic improvement in the relationship between architects and clients.**
>
> **"Architects must move from a commissioned-service mentality to a client-service culture. . . . Architects must develop a new attitude about who we are and what we can do. We need to think, act, and live in the world of the client. We need to think about what we can do for the client, not just what we can build for the client. Participating as a trusted partner in a client's strategic thinking and planning should be our primary goal."**
>
> *Paul Neel, FAIA*

In other words, teaming can do more than lead a firm to larger projects; it can make it possible for a firm to access new opportunities for developing new kinds of competitive advantage, productive efficiency, and profitability.

*The trusted-advisor model.* As discussed above, team building can be seen as a form of horizontal integration, through which a firm broadens the array of services it can provide. Its underlying assumption is that, although the scope of services has expanded, the services themselves remain project-driven. In other words, a firm is not involved with the client until a project has been identified.

Most professional services firms aspire to a higher station—which is to say, to a call from the client not only prior to the emergence of a particular project but prior to the emergence of the problem that may lead to that project. Every architect wishes for clients who won't take a step into the facilities minefield without calling him or her first.

Firms that have punctuated the equilibrium of conventional practice and reached that station have achieved a form of vertical integration. They have left behind the blinders that come (necessarily, and for the good) with a focus on facilities alone to adopt a wider view that encompasses—as the client's own view does—all of the issues that drive facility development, from tax analysis, financial accounting, and capital budgeting to operations analysis, work-process engineering, and human dynamics. These issues aren't *horizontally* related to building planning and design, as are acoustical engineering and even public relations. Because they precede most (if not all) client decision making with regard to facility development, they are *vertically* related to facility planning and design and have—quite literally—precedence over it.

A firm that aspires to trusted-advisor status seeks to be involved in facility decision making above the project level, at the client policy-making level. In so doing, knowingly or unknowingly, it competes with the Booz-Allens and Arthur Andersens of the world, who in delivering their traditional core competencies at the higher levels of management and financial consulting have also managed to capture some of the more basic services—for example, contract documents production—traditionally delivered to the same clients by consulting design professionals.

Can those tables be turned? Perhaps. According to the conventional wisdom, such a design firm risks more than the Booz-Allens or Arthur Andersens in that competition because of the vertical relationship between competing core competencies. The conventional view is that to compete in this arena, architecture's core competency—design—must be less highly valued than the financial and management competencies brought by the consulting titans. This view stems from the simple fact that facility decisions are driven by financial and management decisions.

In other words, Booz-Allen and Andersen can foul up the workplace design aspects of a job and still, in all likelihood, retain a client without diminished estimation of their core financial and management competencies. A facilities-focused firm that fouls up the financial management aspects of the same job puts at risk not only its expanded services but its core competencies as well—and its relationship with the client.

Still, not every design firm aspires to operate as a trusted advisor at the same level as the corporate world's preferred financial and management consultants. Some are successfully carving niches a notch or two below the Booz-Allens and the Andersens, while others, such as Detroit's Smith Group, seem to be giving the Big Six a real run for their money—and dropping the words *architecture* and *engineering* from their marketing lexicons to do so.

In the meantime, firms such as BSW International are earning their clients' trust by concentrating on the quick, cost-effective delivery of business environments precisely crafted to meet their clients' needs—needs their clients have calculated with equal precision. Other firms, among them Cesar Pelli & Associates, Frank Gehry & Associates, Tod Williams Billie Tsien & Associates, and many others best known for award-winning work, are earning their clients' trust by delivering precisely the values those clients—the patrons of the late twentieth and early twenty-first centuries—hold most dear.

And what do all of these firms have in common? Not much with each other, perhaps. But a great deal with their clients because they deliver service.

# part 2
# BUSINESS

*The business component of architecture practice comprises an array of support activities for the entire firm. These activities collectively provide a platform that supports the delivery of the firm's professional services. Business operations define the firm's mission, set and guide its strategic direction, acquire the kinds and quantity of work that will fulfill the firm's goals and objectives, and ensure that financial and human resources are adequate along the way so the firm's mission can be achieved.*

# 5 Firm Planning

## 5.1 Firm Identity and Expertise

### Ellen Flynn-Heapes

*Clients in all markets seek value from their architects. Design your firm's distinctive expertise to match what your ideal clients value most.*

When all is said and done, the rewards of the profession accrue to value-producing experts. Rather than defining value the lazy way, as low cost, a deeper look reveals that value is, of course, in the eye of the beholder. Some clients value Sir Norman Foster, while others value the firm that can get things done in town. Some value BSW and its talent for rollouts, while others value Heery International for its program management expertise.

Large or small, experts build value. In fact, they are the only ones who build sustainable value rather than take advantage of lucky breaks. Just being a responsive and flexible firm that provides service can be a passive approach. Instead, think of your firm in terms of its leadership, mastery, innovation, and contribution.

The new millennium, marked by global choice, will be the era of the expert. So the only important questions are "In what will you build expertise?" and "How will you choose to lead your market?"

The highest responsibility of firm principals is to answer these questions. The answers bring rewards—a successful practice, with good clients, good projects, good people, and a good level of compensation. The answers can evolve for a while, but at some point you must make a commitment—to a clear, well-crafted identity, a consciously conceived business design, and a profit model that works. Then you can rivet your attention on being the best you can be.

### ABOUT COMPANY DESIGN

Every company is already designed to some extent. However, it takes a steadfast commitment to keep focused and stand for something special.

Like a visit to the doctor, thinking about company design begins with this question: "Where does it hurt?" The answers are where we find both ideas and energy for forward motion. For a comprehensive study of motivation, see *Cradles of Eminence,* by Victor Goertzel and Mildred Goertzel, which is a study of 400 eminent individuals and the childhood motivations that sparked them to greatness.

What frustrates people in the design profession the most? The top headaches are competing on price, trying to meet unreasonable client expectations for schedules

ELLEN FLYNN-HEAPES *is president of SPARKS: The Center for Strategic Planning, located in Alexandria, Virginia. Focused on the special issues of design practices, her firm counsels architects on company growth and transition strategies. She has written more than a hundred articles and four books and has lectured widely on strategic business planning.*

and budgets, not making the profit deserved, not hiring and keeping talented people, and lacking leadership, along with handling leadership transition. Most of this pain stems directly from poor business design. In their planning, many firms still default to hackneyed mission statements and vague wishes to be "the premier firm in (fill in the blank), providing excellence in service and quality, and meeting or exceeding the client's expectations." In other words, company leaders plod along as nice people doing good work but are unable to stand for something special in which to excel.

So what would help firms begin to design their businesses well, not just tweak their efficiencies or, worse, just go along blindly? Good examples abound, but until now no real synthesis was available for reference. The Sparks Framework addresses this need. It is a strategy-mapping tool that aids architecture firm leaders in business design decisions. It is a detailed road map of the major choices—a new tool to help principals decide their best direction, choose the right investments, and build their firm for the future.

## THE SPARKS FRAMEWORK: SIX ARCHETYPES

At its core, the framework helps firms choose to be great. It offers a simple yet breakthrough concept: You must become masterful at something—a building type, a client type, a locale, a process—that you build to a high level of worth. Only then is the firm in a position to create true value.

The personality structures of Swiss psychologist Carl Jung's six heroic archetypes have been adapted through the Sparks Framework to correspond to six archetypes for the design professions:

- The Einsteins
- The Niche Experts
- The Market Partners
- The Community Leaders
- The Orchestrators
- The Efficiency Experts

Each archetype has a personality. When you get to know them, you can say, "An Einstein would never do *this*," or "Of course they did *that*—they're Orchestrators." In fact, each archetype is a full portrait that includes the underlying driving forces and core values that comprise its identity, a set of best practices that comprise its operating model, and a model for optimizing profit.

See if you can find your firm among the following archetypes. Is it steadfastly seated in one? Is it a well-designed hybrid of two? Or is it straddling the fence—a little of this, a little of that?

***The Einstein archetype.*** Einstein firms generate original ideas and new technologies. In architecture, they are the high-profile design firms with original styles or philosophies. In engineering, they're the Ph.D.-owned firms with a strong commitment to research and development. This type of firm often receives research grants or endowments, and its staff members love to experiment as well as teach and publish. Pritzker Prize winner Renzo Piano even hosts an online design workshop (www.rpwf.org).

Norman Foster, Frank Gehry, Michel Virlogeux, Santiago Calatrava, and Buckminster Fuller are all Einstein-type firms. They are known for their distinctive set of original ideas, which they can apply across building types and around the world. Their philosophy, however, is singularly focused.

***The Niche Expert archetype.*** Niche Experts are specialists, dedicated to a specific type of project or service within a broader market. They watch the experiments of the Einsteins and adapt them to create state-of-the-art work. They frequently team through a network of other firms to provide full services for a given project, and are often national or international in scope.

HOK Sport fits in this category. Besides the firm's highly successful focus on sports facilities, it enjoys a unique reputation relative to its parent company, HOK. Yet it also benefits from a separate, descriptive name, separate location, and separate management.

Duany Plater-Zyberk has a service niche that focuses on "new urbanism" master planning. Andres Duany and Elizabeth Plater-Zyberk have built a marketplace power-house, commanding some of the highest fees in the profession.

Beyer Blinder Bell distinguishes itself through its work in historic preservation, the Croxton Collaborative in sustainable design, and Allan Greenberg in neoclassical architecture. Some firms' niches center around an ethnic background, such as Douglas Cardinal, of American Indian descent.

**The Market Partner archetype.** A Market Partner leads in one or a few major markets, such as health care, higher education, the food and beverage industry, or airports. One of the first practicing Market Partners was Einhorn Yaffee Prescott. When they formed the firm, the principals targeted three markets and created an organization around them: academic, corporate, and government. ADP Marshall is committed to the technology and research-and-development market. Wimberly Allison Tong & Goo is renowned for its hotel and resort designs. Fanning Howey competes nationally for—and wins—school projects.

Market Partners are strong advocates for their clients and their clients' industries, often leading lobbying efforts and crusading at client trade meetings. They share goals and values with their clients, creating a base of personal friendships. Market Partners typically serve multiple segments within their industry and benefit from offering a broad range of services to support their chosen market (and keep their clients coming back for more).

It is characteristic of the Market Partner to incorporate former client-side staff members into the firm. AI, an architecture, engineering, and interior design firm focused on the corporate market, gains legitimacy with big business from Rusty Meadows's AT&T background. Many firms keyed to the federal markets have former employees of the targeted agencies in high-level marketing and project management positions. This represents real commitment to the market of choice.

**The Community Leaders archetype.** These firms will aim for a leadership role in their town. They set deep roots into the community, developing close relationships on both social and political levels. They seek premier local project work, which ranges across the board in size and type, including public buildings, police and fire stations, recreation centers, schools, shelters, public works, and other municipal facilities. For projects requiring significant technical knowledge, they team with a network of Niche Experts around the country.

Many design professionals begin with a small, local practice. The difference between being a high-performing Community Leader and an underperforming generalist is that Community Leaders are so woven into the fabric of the community that they open doors that are closed to outsiders. They can expedite decision making by virtue of their professional and personal relationships in the community.

One of the best examples of a Community Leader is Carde Ten Architects in Santa Monica, California. Focused on community projects, the firm scouts for funding, arranges real estate opportunities, and organizes the entire project for the potential client. This packaging process takes the firm out of the realm of competition and fee-for-time. Besides a healthy design fee, the firm also takes part of the development and construction management fees.

Community Leaders invest heavily in their local networks. Freidl Bohm, president of NBBJ, established his infrastructure in Columbus, Ohio, with the Young Presidents' Organization (YPO), local board involvement, and ownership of a successful chain of restaurants in town. Harvey Gantt served as mayor of Charlotte, North Carolina, again illustrating a depth of commitment to the community.

**The Orchestrator archetype.** Orchestrator firms focus on outstanding project management, bringing their skills to bear on large, complex projects, including the best design/build jobs. Emphasis is on speed, coordination, and control. Many Orchestrators are known for their project management and construction management expertise.

Bechtel, Fluor-Daniel, and some of the other large engineer-contractors are classic Orchestrators. The leading program managers, such as Heery International, 3D-International, and CRS Constructors, are Orchestrators.

In some design circles, practitioners bemoan the fact that the big accounting

> **Public Service and Community Involvement (6.3) presents several ways that architects can become involved in public and community-based endeavors.**

> **Project Operations (13.2) covers the facets of project management that represent the expertise of Orchestrators.**

and management firms, including Ernst & Young and Andersen Consulting, are moving into our industry. They are taking advantage of a high-demand Orchestrator role. You won't see them active in the other archetype configurations.

Askew Nixon Ferguson Architects (ANFA) is an example of a smaller firm operating as an Orchestrator. Early in its history, ANFA started out working for Federal Express, by definition a speed- and logistics-oriented client. ANFA developed a culture to match, full of high-energy people concerned with project management. Today it is still working for Federal Express but has added casinos, another fast-paced project type, to its expertise.

Privatization is the realm of the Orchestrator. Because Orchestrators know their work, know their process, and enjoy time and cost challenges, they are effective with these financial/technical behemoths. Of all the design firm archetypes, this one has the most MBAs.

***The Efficiency Expert archetype.*** These firms have the real cost advantage, focusing on prototypes, site adaptations, and multisite project rollouts for retail stores, health maintenance organizations, branch banks, service stations, telecommunications towers, U.S. Job Corps centers, and large government office projects.

Volume rollouts, a fast and inexpensive way for client organizations to expand into multiple geographic markets, save the costs of individually developed and designed units. Tulsa-based BSW International is a leader here, specializing in multiple-facility building programs for clients such as Wal-Mart, Circuit City, and Marriott. BSW is unabashedly dedicated to improving its clients' financial success, and even casts itself as a real estate development services company that offers program management, real estate, and site development services as well as design and construction. BSW has been featured in the *Wall Street Journal, Business Week, Inc.,* and *Fortune* not only as a thriving design firm but as a leader among American service firms.

Efficiency Experts have been successful with total quality management, unlike other firms in the profession that view speed and cost leadership as unprofessional. Because Efficiency Experts are such an integral part of their clients' financial success, they move very quickly. If you are committed to besting time and money challenges, you need a serious program that ensures quality—just like the ones your clients have.

## A CLEAR IDENTITY FOCUSES BUSINESS DESIGN

The typology outlined above is based on some major principles. Each of the six archetypes has a bold, clear identity driven by internal goals and values and matched to complementary client groups. Each has a cohesive, integrated business design—a scaffold of best practices that comprise its operating model. Although not discussed here, it is worth noting that each of the six archetypes also has a specific profit model that optimizes its financial performance.

Setting company direction begins with the question of identity. This is especially true for organizations in the knowledge industry, with no tangible product until after the fact. Can you answer the following questions?

- What are the firm's most deeply held values?
- What are its driving forces?
- How is it distinctive?
- How is it expert?
- What is its greatest value to the client?
- What does it hope to accomplish in the next twenty years?

It's not easy to uncover and articulate the unique ingredients that make up the essence of a firm. It is particularly difficult for architects, who in school are trained against this kind of thinking—rather, virtue lies in the ability to design anything. Doctors, by contrast, are trained with the explicit expectation of further choice: to focus on a specialty or to focus on a general practice.

Certainly, creating wealth is a good thing, but like King Midas, if you haven't got your values and purpose right first, you can run into trouble. According to management guru Peter Drucker, defining your purpose is especially critical today. Since the best and most dedicated people are ultimately volunteers, they have many lucrative opportunities from which to choose. They have multiple job offers and pick a firm because it's doing something that they consider important. In order to attract, motivate, and retain outstanding people, companies need to have a clear understanding of their own identities. This goes double for attracting the best clients.

"Tell us about your firm" is a directive that frequently meets with the following set of answers: "We were established in 1909/1949/1979. We have 30/300/3,000 people and 3/7/15 offices. We offer these services (laundry list), and work in a wide variety of project types (another laundry list)." Next in the formula is a discussion of their great service and quality.

"Understand my problems and deliver to my needs efficiently," project owners tell us over and over again. In our research, 96 percent of the clients we interview for design firms want the experts, the firms that know what they're doing. Many of the larger firms know that cross-selling services is tough; clients today do not want a wide variety of project types. They only want to hear about how you relate to their problem. And they don't care about one-stop shopping unless the package gets their current job done most efficiently.

A representative from SmithKline said recently, "Please tell us how you're different. We want to hire you. But we can't if you won't tell us how you're the best. Give us real reasons! Give us meat!"

## The Source of Identity: The Driving Force

Although many firms operate expediently and reactively, most have a favorite place where they live—or at least aspire to. They have an array of values, but a single special one reigns supreme. The firm's supreme business value is called its driving force, and if you can capture it, you're on your way to building the right business model.

For example, the driving force of the Orchestrator is a love of the logistics chess game. Project management, Orchestrators believe, is the greatest challenge in the world and the most worthwhile endeavor of all. They consider themselves an "elite cadre"—a SWAT team. As applied to their business design, we would see a very well organized and planned firm, corporate in feel. Its top staff are the best project managers. They have formal training curricula, and they make their highest profit on the most complex projects. All staff members understand what's really important.

> "All business proceeds on beliefs, or judgements of probabilities, and not on certainties."
>
> Charles W. Eliot

Specific driving forces characterize each of the archetypes. They are shared gut-level beliefs about what is most essential to accomplish together. More than any cultural value, such as integrity, collaboration, or "fun," agreement on these driving forces influences the success of the firm. Conflicts on this pivotal point can also destroy the firm.

When probing for the deepest elements of identity, we often encounter fearful protests: "We have to be flexible!" "We can't survive without having all these abilities!" "We have to keep looking for new opportunities!"

Flexibility, openness, and responsiveness to clients are always required. But reactivity at a firm's core shows that it has lost its way. Every firm needs a solid baseline of quality, efficiency, creativity, flexibility, openness, and client service in its work. The key is to keep your eye on where your real distinctive value is and build strength. The essential question is not how can you respond well but how can you lead well.

| WHAT IS YOUR FIRM'S DRIVING FORCE? | |
| --- | --- |
| **ARCHETYPE** | **DISTINCTIVE DRIVING FORCE** |
| Einstein | Cutting-edge innovation |
| Niche Expert | Perfecting the specialty |
| Market Partner | Customer partnership |
| Community Leader | Community connectivity |
| Orchestrator | Project management challenge |
| Efficiency Expert | Cost/quality challenge |

Driving forces tend to be discovered rather than invented. Through exercises and models, firms can learn what has been driving them to date. Most likely a hidden structure can be ferreted out that either facilitates or presents obstacles to the full expression of the driver. And if you can discover these structures, you can discover the driving forces that have been surreptitiously operating. Then you can work with them.

Rather than seeking simple discovery and refinement, some firms go well beyond this to revolutionize things with a brand-new driving force. Sienna Architecture, a midsize firm in Portland, Oregon, is a good example. Over the course of several years, through a well-designed

## What Makes Your Firm Distinctive?

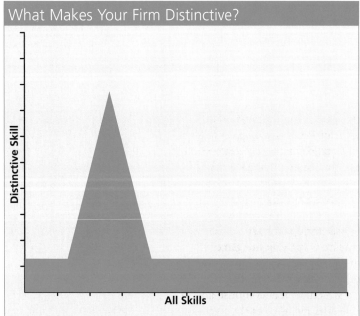

*Distinctive Skill* (vertical axis)

*All Skills* (horizontal axis)

Every firm needs a solid base of client service, quality, efficiency, and creativity in its work. However, it should choose one of these and hone it to a distinguishing characteristic that sets it apart in the marketplace.

©1998 Sparks: The Center for Strategic Planning

strategic planning process, the firm's owners successfully moved from being a cost/quality-driven firm to being a cutting-edge design leader in the Pacific Northwest.

When you uncover your driving force, you'll foster certain values and weed out others, using care and patience. You'll fine-tune your entire business model, including staffing, marketing, project systems, and perhaps your ownership structure. Once this model is in focus and consensus is built, you can't help but bring the more powerful vision into reality. It becomes so clear.

***Driving forces and the hidden client agenda.*** The beauty of an identity is that it acts like a magnet to attract clients seeking your kind of expertise. In other words, certain client groupings have typical agendas for which they need certain kinds of firms. Rarely do clients go outside their unspoken agendas, and if they do, they tend not to recognize value.

It's tricky to determine what the client views as most valuable; in fact, some don't consciously know themselves. Sure, they want and need everything it takes to do their project. But certain aspects will be more critical than others. Needless to say, it's wise to spend time on this question and get real answers. Go beyond what the client tells you first. Push beyond the shorthand clichés: "Be faster, be cheaper, and give us good service." Find out whether these are the most important needs or if they're just the outside layer of the onion. Whatever your chosen clients value most—and you find most worthwhile—make your firm the ultimate expert in it.

## WHAT IS YOUR CLIENT'S HIDDEN AGENDA?

| ARCHETYPE | DISTINCTIVE DRIVING FORCE | HIDDEN CLIENT AGENDA |
|---|---|---|
| Einstein | Innovation | Needs to gain prestige, improve image |
| Niche Expert | Cutting-edge method | Needs to overcome risky, adverse conditions |
| Market Partner | Customer partnership | Needs to augment client's own skills as full-service "partner" |
| Community Leader | Community contribution | Needs facilitation through community gatekeepers |
| Orchestrator | Project management challenge | Needs to control project complexity |
| Efficiency Expert | Cost/quality challenge | Needs to deliver the product, optimizing the budget |

***Driving forces and the sacred technology.*** Very specific technologies (defined here as methodologies for doing things rather than computer technologies) characterize each of the archetypes in the Sparks Framework. These are the true centers of excellence for which the firm is valued in the marketplace. They are links on the overall project value chain, and it's a rare customer that considers them all equally valuable. Ask yourself whether you are so busy getting the work in and out that you neglect to nurture the more difficult and risky technology that makes you special. When the firm's driving force is clear and its leaders understand what is most valuable to its clients, then its core or "sacred" technology also becomes clear.

## WHAT IS SPECIAL ABOUT YOUR WORK?

| ARCHETYPE | DISTINCTIVE DRIVING FORCE | SACRED TECHNOLOGY |
|---|---|---|
| Einstein | Innovation | Generating brand-new ideas and technologies |
| Niche Expert | Cutting-edge method | Transferring new knowledge to the target niche |
| Market Partner | Customer partnership | Expanding ways to help the sector-specific client |
| Community Leader | Community connectivity | Nurturing the network of relationships with local leaders |
| Orchestrator | Project management challenge | Pushing sophisticated logistics control on large projects |
| Efficiency Expert | Cost/quality challenge | Advancing brilliant new production technologies |

Firm identity (not corporate identity as an advertising statement) is nothing less than the wellspring of value creation. Determining what you are as a firm—and what you are not—is worth very serious consideration indeed. It requires experimentation, comparison, and, most of all, the courage to stand for something.

## BUSINESS DESIGN: THE WEB OF STRATEGY AND STRUCTURE

Curiously, many design firms are themselves not designed. They simply do their clients' bidding and react to whatever is needed at the time. Some firms inadvertently build a business design that is dysfunctional, with lots of structural obstacles in the way of success. Perhaps you know a firm that wanted to build deep community relationships, but the leaders were introverted technical folks. Some firms want to build their project management expertise but have a chronic fear of becoming "paper pushers." Some want to master a specialty service but feel they must be flexible.

Beyond choosing the firm's identity, the next essential element is a conscious design of the business so that it can play at its peak. When a firm is "playing the game" well, it's using a scaffold of practices that are both cohesive and aligned. Things aren't in conflict; they're in flow. Although we can't see what supports this desired state, the firm is working with a very specific web of internal strategies and structures that comprise an understood operating model or business design. In a healthy situation, they encourage the desired behaviors and inhibit the undesired behaviors fairly effortlessly. Business designs are largely intangible, reflecting culture, aspiration, and even policy—and they are powerful shapers of behavior.

Strategic planning, if done correctly, is the process that helps the firm think through its business design and make deliberate refinements. Some people think the end result of strategic planning is a sequential list of tasks to be implemented, but a list is ineffectual compared with business design.

In the Sparks Framework, each of the six archetypes relies on a characteristic business design. And each business design is organized into three distinct strands that form its structural elements:

1. Getting work: markets and marketing
2. Doing work: projects and people
3. Organizing work: money and leadership

The three strands are primary strategic systems that operate in every firm. And each archetype has characteristic strategies and activities that operate within the three systems. Broadly speaking, we can use a continuum to array these strategies and activities, ranging from the Einsteins and Niche Experts at one end to the Orchestrators and Efficiency Experts at the other. A macro view only, the following table illustrates the range of these basic practices. By emphasizing the strategies most aligned with their type, firms use their resources most effectively. They can also adopt the others as secondary tools if they choose.

For example, when the archetypes at the left seek higher visibility, they increase their writing, teaching, and speaking. When the archetypes at the right seek higher visibility, they benefit more from exhibits, direct mail, and advertising. When the archetypes at the left seek to improve their work, they try more experimentation and collaboration,

| DIFFERENT PERSPECTIVES OF THE ARCHETYPES | | | | | | |
|---|---|---|---|---|---|---|
| **BUSINESS ELEMENT** | **EINSTEINS** | **NICHE EXPERTS** | **MARKET PARTNERS** | **COMMUNITY LEADERS** | **ORCHESTRATORS** | **EFFICIENCY EXPERTS** |
| ***GETTING WORK*** | Writing, teaching, and speaking $\longleftrightarrow$ | | | | Exhibits, direct mail, and advertising | |
| ***DOING WORK*** | Experiment and collaboration $\longleftrightarrow$ | | | | High utilization and productivity | |
| ***ORGANIZING WORK*** | Design performance and statistics $\longleftrightarrow$ | | | | Budget and schedule statistics | |

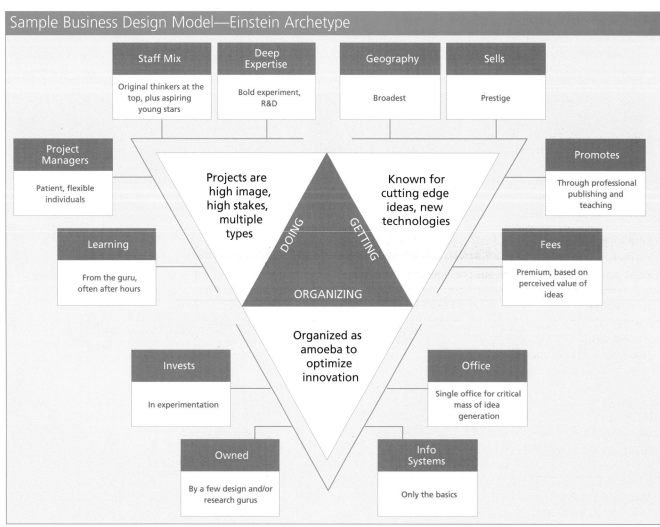

**Staff Mix**
Original thinkers at the top, plus aspiring young stars

**Deep Expertise**
Bold experiment, R&D

**Geography**
Broadest

**Sells**
Prestige

**Project Managers**
Patient, flexible individuals

**Promotes**
Through professional publishing and teaching

**Learning**
From the guru, often after hours

**Fees**
Premium, based on perceived value of ideas

Projects are high image, high stakes, multiple types

Known for cutting edge ideas, new technologies

DOING    GETTING

ORGANIZING

Organized as amoeba to optimize innovation

**Invests**
In experimentation

**Office**
Single office for critical mass of idea generation

**Owned**
By a few design and/or research gurus

**Info Systems**
Only the basics

©1998 Sparks: The Center for Strategic Planning

while their colleagues at the right focus on greater utilization and productivity. When the archetypes at the left seek to track their performance, they look for design-related statistics, while their colleagues at the right aim for budget and schedule statistics.

A graphic can be used to illustrate each business design in detail. Each corner of the business design model refers to one of the design strands.

Within each of the three strands is a set of subsystems. Of course, many other subsystems operate in any given organization, but these offer a short list of the most essential.

The business designs in the tables starting on the following page are based on extensive research and practical experience with successful design firms throughout the country. Our findings show that these organizations are most successful when their strategies are aligned with one model rather than a blend of various models.

That said, most firms find themselves practicing under several models. We see hybrids—for example, Market Partners using a Niche strategy, or Orchestrators using a Community Leader strategy. However, the best choice is to be firmly anchored in one archetype and then cross-fertilize in a deliberately designed way.

## BASIC ELEMENTS OF A BUSINESS DESIGN MODEL

| | |
|---|---|
| **Getting work:** <br> **Markets and marketing** | ***What is the firm known for?*** <br> • Sales message <br> • Promotional strategy <br> • Geographic reach <br> • Best fees |
| **Doing work:** <br> **Projects and people** | ***What are the firm's targets?*** <br> • Deep expertise <br> • Staff mix <br> • Project management <br> • Learning |
| **Organizing work:** <br> **Money and leadership** | ***How does the firm organize for business?*** <br> • Ownership <br> • Investments <br> • Offices <br> • Information systems |

part 2 BUSINESS

# CHALLENGE

Any firm can go along with conventional growth and diversification tactics, but as Lee Iacocca said, "My biggest mistake with Chrysler was to diversify beyond our expertise." Jack Welch, chairman of GE and one of the most distinguished leaders in business today, said, "We released half our staff and businesses, and focused on becoming number one or number two in each of our markets. It was remarkably successful." If you're still skeptical, consider this fact: In the past three years, spin-offs in industry have reached record numbers, and because of their focus, many are doing better than their parent companies.

The expert firms delight in seeking mastery. Their work is challenging, and their businesses make meaningful contributions to the world. To create firms of value, company leaders must be the executive designers of their firm's distinctive enterprise.

## THE EINSTEINS

| | |
|---|---|
| **Client agenda** | Needs prestige, improved image |
| **Client values** | Cutting-edge ideas or technologies |
| **Getting work**<br>*Known for cutting-edge ideas* | *Geography:* National, international<br>*Sells:* Prestige<br>*Promotes:* Teaching/publishing<br>*Fees:* Premium, perceived value of ideas |
| **Doing work**<br>*High image, high stakes, multiple types* | *Deep expertise:* Bold experiment, research and development<br>*Staff:* Original thinkers, aspiring stars<br>*Project management:* Patient, flexible<br>*Learning:* From guru, often after hours |
| **Organizing work**<br>*Organized as an ameba to optimize innovation* | *Invests in:* Experimentation<br>*Owned by:* One or few gurus<br>*Info systems:* Basics<br>*Office:* Single, critical mass of ideas |

## THE NICHE EXPERTS

| | |
|---|---|
| **Client agenda** | *Needs to overcome project risk, adverse conditions* |
| **Client value** | *Unsurpassed leadership in a specific area* |
| **Getting work**<br>*Known for deep expertise in project or service specialty* | *Geography:* National, international<br>*Sells:* Rare knowledge<br>*Promotes:* Speaking/writing to client groups<br>*Fees:* Premium, for documented results |
| **Doing work**<br>*Complex or high-risk, singular type* | *Deep expertise:* Latest approaches<br>*Staff:* Specialists at top, dedicated youngsters, and stabilizers in middle<br>*Project management:* Dedicated specialists who can also handle the realities of the management process.<br>*Learning:* Juniors initiate mentoring |
| **Organizing work**<br>*Organized around specialists to optimize advancement of the niche* | *Invests in:* New applications, depth of network<br>*Owned by:* Distinguished experts<br>*Info systems:* Service/design performance<br>*Office:* Single for critical mass, alliances |

They must treat this responsibility with all the care and passion that they bring to just one of their projects.

We challenge you to look at a fresh reality—the age of the expert:

- Devote your firm to what you care most about achieving.
- Seize the needed resources to fully fund your business design.
- Decisively assert leadership of your market.

### For More Information

Other books by the author on strategic business planning include *Creating Wealth: Principles and Practices for Design Firms; The Sparks Framework: A Handbook of*

| THE MARKET PARTNERS | |
|---|---|
| **Client agenda** | Needs a trusted partner, augment skills |
| **Client value** | Service depth within a market area |
| **Getting work** *Known for broad experience within an industry* | *Geography:* Regional or national<br>*Sells:* Market dedication, experience, access<br>*Promotes:* Industry connections, trend setters<br>*Fees:* Improved with patron clients |
| **Doing work** *Range of types within one or few markets* | *Deep expertise:* Industry operations, people<br>*Staff:* Stable array of professionals, some from within client industry<br>*Project management:* Well organized, experienced in market |
| **Organizing work** *Organized as practice groups to optimize market expertise* | *Learning:* Conventions, informal mentors<br>*Invests in:* Bench depth, like-firm acquisitions<br>*Owned by:* Known market players, select technicians<br>*Info systems:* Statistics by market, repeat clients<br>*Office:* Select regional offices |

| THE COMMUNITY LEADERS | |
|---|---|
| **Client agenda** | Needs access and service |
| **Client value** | Mutual commitment to community |
| **Getting work** *Known for contribution to the community* | *Geography:* Community-based<br>*Sells:* Access, service, connectedness<br>*Promotes:* Community events, PR, network<br>*Fees:* Improved when "wired in" |
| **Doing work** *Range of types, moderate complexity* | *Deep expertise:* Local relationships, issues<br>*Staff:* Multidisciplinary groups<br>*Project management:* Combined project management/discipline chiefs; if large, firm has strong work-sharing process<br>*Learning:* Networking locally, professionally |
| **Organizing work** *Organized around local leaders to optimize connectivity* | *Invests in:* Local visibility, niche partners, new offices<br>*Owned by:* Broad group, may be employee stock ownership plan<br>*Info systems:* Performance by local office<br>*Office:* One or multiple, for local access |

Value-Creation Strategies; and *Making It Real: A Strategic Planning Playbook for A/E Business Design and Transition.* All are available through SPARKS: The Center for Strategic Planning, www.forsparks.com.

Other recommended works on company strategy and business design include the following: James C. Collins and Jerry I. Porras, *Built to Last: Successful Habits of Visionary Companies,* 1997; Victor Goertzel and Mildred Goertzel, *Cradles of Eminence,* 1978; Tom Peters, *Say It and Live It,* 1997; Al Ries, *Focus: The Future of Your Company Depends on It,* 1996; Al Ries and Jack Trout, *Positioning: The Battle for Your Mind,* 1993; Adrian J. Slywotsky and David Morrison, *The Profit Zone: How Strategic Business Design Will Lead You to Tomorrow's Profits,* 1997; Michael Treacy and Fred Wiersema, *The Discipline of Market Leaders,* 1995; and Benjamin Tregoe and John W. Zimmerman, *Top Management Strategy: What It Is and How to Make It Work,* 1980.

## THE ORCHESTRATORS

| | |
|---|---|
| **Client agenda** | Needs logistical control |
| **Client Value** | Skilled project management for larger, complex projects |
| **Getting work**<br>*Known for great project management, organizational skills* | *Geography:* Regional or national<br>*Sells:* Speed, process control<br>*Promotes:* Through business press<br>*Fees:* Premium fees for project management/construction management |
| **Doing work**<br>*Highly complex logistically, larger scale, often design-build* | *Deep expertise:* In project management<br>*Staff:* Senior and junior project managers, MBAs<br>*PM:* Top project management systems, tools, resources<br>*Learning:* Formal training curriculum |
| **Organizing work**<br>*Organized around project managers to optimize systems and technologies* | *Invests in:* Elite corps of project managers, local firm alliances<br>*Owned by:* Current or former project managers, corporate<br>*Info systems:* Project-level statistics<br>*Office:* Corporate headquarters plus satellites; project managers travel |

## THE EFFICIENCY EXPERTS

| | |
|---|---|
| **Client agenda** | Needs product delivered, budget optimized |
| **Client value** | Cost, quality, and consistency |
| **Getting work**<br>*Known for quality work at a low cost* | *Geography:* Regional base, broad site alliances<br>*Sells:* Best quality for price, consistency<br>*Promotes:* Direct mail, ads, sales reps<br>*Fees:* Bid work, clever efficiencies |
| **Doing work**<br>*Mostly prototype/site adaptations* | *Deep expertise:* In replication efficiencies<br>*Staff:* Junior professionals and technicians<br>*Project management:* Accountability, standard procedures<br>*Learning:* Formal training classes |
| **Organizing work**<br>*Organized around production teams to optimize efficiency* | *Invests in:* Production capacity, technology<br>*Owned by:* One or few entrepreneurs, may be family-owned<br>*Info systems:* Production unit costs<br>*Office:* Production center, field offices |

# 5.2 Starting a Firm

## Elena Marcheso Moreno

*When you feel the time to start your own architecture practice is upon you, there are many pragmatic decisions to be made.*

Sometimes it is a long-held ambition for an architect to open his or her own firm. Sometimes the decision to start up on one's own is spurred by downsizing by an employer or frustration with the course of one's career path. While the reasons to start a new architecture firm can be as varied as the people who start them, architects of all ages and at most stages of their professional careers are setting up shop.

According to data collected by AIA, nearly 1,000 new architecture firms are started every year. Whatever their reason for starting a firm of their own, architects—indeed, all entrepreneurs—must make enough money to stay in business and prosper. The architect who starts a firm must have a clear set of goals, sufficient training, and enough capital to operate for some amount of time. Ideally, too, there will be a project waiting the day after the architect sets up his or her office space and equipment, although many architects start out with no work in hand.

Careful decisions when you first start your firm will pay dividends long into the future. Identify your goals, your business plan, your market, your capitalization, your marketing approach, and your delivery abilities as soon as possible. Thousands of new businesses start up every year, but experts estimate that only 25 percent of all architecture start-ups are still in business three years after their principals first hung out their shingles. Many fail for lack of capital to see them through slow times.

> **"Starting a business is like getting married. There is no good time and no bad time."**
>
> *Anonymous*

## WHAT IT TAKES TO SUCCEED

To run a firm, you—or a partner—will need to have or acquire some basic business skills. You will want to obtain work, which means you need to market your services, negotiate contracts, and reach agreements. Someone needs to build relationships with clients and maintain their trust. To grow, you must hire staff and consultants, and then work hard to build and keep their loyalty. You also need the skills to work effectively with contractors and consultants.

Ideally, someone at the new start-up will already have the skills and experience to run a design practice as a business, or will have to learn them. Finding loans and other financing, entering into leases, and managing cash flow and financial stability are all required skills. The sum of all these skills is a business that is operated profitably.

> **Thinking of leaving your current firm? Before deciding to start a new firm, you may want to ask:**
>
> - **Are there untapped possibilities in your current firm? Are its leaders aware of your needs? Can you propose a new alignment of responsibilities or some other change that might help both of you?**
> - **Are you looking for an alternative role in an architecture firm or are you really looking for an alternative setting in which to practice architecture?**

## DESIGNING THE FIRM

When architects open their own office, they generally have a mental image of what they want their firm to be—its size, its project types, its clients, and perhaps its structure. To turn this image into a reality, they need to meld these prospective compo-

**ELENA MARCHESO MORENO** *is a freelance writer and editor based in McLean, Virginia. The topic was adapted from "Firm Start-Up" by James R. Franklin, FAIA, in the* Architect's Handbook of Professional Practice, 12th Edition.

nents into a single whole that functions well. That means they need strategies for structuring the architecture practice, identifying markets, selecting types of projects, marketing to gain those projects, obtaining clients, pricing projects for profitability, executing projects on time, leading and managing the business, and finding, developing, and retaining staff.

***Legal forms of business.*** When first structuring your firm, you will decide on its legal form of business. The law recognizes various forms of business, but all are derived from just three basic structures: sole proprietorship, partnership, and corporation. There are tax and legal consequences associated with each form, and you should consult both an attorney and an accountant when making a decision about the form for your firm to take.

The business structure you adopt will be affected by many factors. Even if you elect a sole proprietorship—the simplest form of business—now, you may want to change the business form in the future as both your business and the complexity of its projects grow.

There is one variation on the corporate form, the subchapter S corporation, that many design firms ultimately elect to use. In this form, a small business can treat its income as if it were a partnership, avoiding the double taxing of corporate earnings and shareholder dividends typical of normal corporations. Shareholders can also offset business losses against their personal income with the subchapter S corporation. Other forms, such as limited liability partnerships or corporations, have been the preferred forms of other design firms. Before you set up your firm and its legal structure, talk about your specific needs with the appropriate legal and financial consultants.

***Organizational structure.*** The framework you design for your firm will be the underlying support for all your business activities. You will want to establish an identity for your firm and decide how to position it in the markets where you will operate.

Your identity can be anything you want—a focus on unique aesthetics, providing service and added value, or technological innovations are examples. Take stock of your targeted markets and be brutally honest with yourself as you evaluate their growth potential for architectural services. Then plan where you will concentrate—which building type, which range of services. Don't overextend your firm at this point; you cannot be all things to all people. Clients today are looking for *experts* who can serve not only as their designers but also as their consultants. Finding your own niche and specializing in a few areas or even a single one is likely to be more profitable than trying to be an architecture firm that can design any building type and offer any type of service connected to architecture.

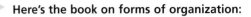

**Here's the book on forms of organization:**

***Sole proprietorship:*** **easiest to set up; only you limit its growth; okay until you need or want partners in owning the firm**

***Partnership:*** **great, provided you "marry well"; most often means finding the right partner early; many architects form corporations for business reasons but still think of themselves as partners**

***Corporation:*** **a separate legal entity that takes on a life of its own, with special laws, taxes, and documentation**

## IMAGE AND MARKETING

Your marketing efforts and your firm's image are so closely aligned, it is almost impossible to consider one without the other.

***Image.*** New firms rarely have an image that is readily recognized, so image alone will not be enough to bring in work. Rather, the firm's or principal's reputation combined with the firm's marketing efforts should help determine its success. The image you create for your firm should be closely aligned with the vision you have for your new firm. Without consistency between image and vision, you will have difficulty leading your organization to success. Your firm's image will be projected in everything you do in your firm's name from now on—the name you choose for your firm, your letterhead and business cards, your office and its location. Create an image that is realistic and attainable in the short term. As your firm grows, its image will grow also.

If your firm is small, it will probably be offered small projects. A small project can be just right for helping to set your firm's professional standards. Established early, these standards are easier to maintain and the resulting image can bring in good clients, and good projects, for years to come. Conversely, only one or two unprofessional actions can quickly set a precedent that will leave you and your firm open to manipulation by clients you might prefer not to have.

## FORMS OF ORGANIZATION

| FORM | ADVANTAGES | DISADVANTAGES |
|---|---|---|
| **Sole proprietorship**<br>This is the simplest form of business: You are the company. Your main legal burden is to pay taxes quarterly and retain all receipts and records of business expenses. | • Easy to form<br>• Few legal expenses to create<br>• Profits all go to one owner<br>• Easily sold or closed | • Unlimited personal liability<br>• More difficult to obtain financing from banks<br>• Limits on business deductions<br>• No shared decisions |
| **Partnership**<br>An agreement between two or more people to work together. Each partner contributes capital and services, and shares in profits or losses. Legally, all partners typically have an equal vote, and most decisions require a majority vote. Partners can typically withdraw from the business at any time. | • Easy to form<br>• Greater chance for profit with more people<br>• More available capital<br>• Few government controls and no special taxes | • Unlimited personal liability<br>• Potential conflict over partnership agreement<br>• Management conflicts<br>• Difficult to obtain bank financing<br>• Partnership interests hard to sell |
| **Corporation**<br>A separate legal entity that exists regardless of its shareholders | • Limited shareholder liability (but designers still often held personally liable)<br>• Flexible tax planning and management<br>• Ownership easily transferred | • More government regulation<br>• Ruled by charter and bylaws<br>• Potential majority shareholder control of voting<br>• Expenses for incorporating |

*Marketing.* Developing an effective marketing strategy is one of the most important activities for your start-up architecture practice. You might think that good work will speak for itself—and your firm—and bring in more work. Sometimes that is true. But active marketing is a much better approach to bringing in projects.

One way to start marketing is to send a simple letter to prospective clients, previous clients, consultants you have worked with in the past, local business groups, friends, relatives, and just about anyone who might provide a lead. This letter lets people know you are starting a firm and helps establish your identity.

You can develop lists of potential clients by checking business directories and company annual reports at your local library. There are references for associations by subject areas, and if you plan to specialize, say, in religious buildings, go through the book for those organizations that might have members who build these facilities. Go through the publications your potential clients will read, and see if you find leads. Talk with representatives of specific government agencies and find out what future building programs might be coming along in the near future.

Like image, marketing "happens" with everyday activities as well as those geared towards particular clients. Give a speech, offer a service to a community group, write an article, serve on community organizations, or offer story ideas to the press. The point is to get your name recognized and to build your image.

Start drafting a marketing strategy after you make yourself pin down a few points about the firm, where you want it to go, what are its likely strengths and weaknesses, and what types of projects you want to get. A good marketing plan is clear, to the point, and able to be measured. Your plan can target the steps you want to take to reach a particular market—the number of calls you will make each day, the meetings you will hold, the proposals you will submit.

Your marketing goals should rely on marketing data—which you can develop, find in local publications, garner from business publications, or pay a consultant to provide. Avoid committing to a tough marketing challenge unless you have the data that prove a need for your services in that market. Remember, statistics show it is common

> **Marketing Planning and Strategies (6.1) presents approaches and techniques for marketing your firm.**

for the typical design firm to win only one out of every ten jobs it goes after, so make sure you include the funds and time to go after these jobs in your business planning.

## CHOOSING YOUR CLIENTS

A financially sound architecture practice depends on building and maintaining strong, long-term relationships with clients. And that depends on having the right clients.

The idea of selecting your clients as a new start-up might seem ridiculous—who would have the luxury of not taking any work that comes along? But choosing clients is not a luxury; it is a sound business practice that will help you manage project risk and ultimately increase your firm's profitability.

In selecting clients, learn as much about them as you possibly can. While large, well-established corporations are likely to be dependable clients, there are many others in corporate and other areas who could represent greater risk to the small architecture firm. Find out about clients. Has this client commissioned buildings in the past? Does the client understand the process of design, construction, and development? If a client is new to the process, you will be spending a lot more time explaining things and petitioning for what you know will work.

Check into the client's reputation on the street. If they have worked on construction projects before, someone designed them and someone else built them. Ask about the process. Some questions to answer include: Was the client focused and decisive, or did they change their mind so often that work had to be redone? Did they pay on time?

It is important to know your client's management structure. At what level will you be interacting? Will you have personal access to the ultimate decision maker, or will you present your ideas to someone who has to work along a chain of command? The best scenario is where the person who hires you makes all decisions.

Know your client's financial status—is it a stable organization or individual? Ask for financial references. Check with the client's bankers. Check credit rating histories and find out if there are any judgments or liens filed against the client.

Finally, is the chemistry right? This is a significant factor if you are to work effectively with your client. If you don't like or understand each other, the relationship will be undermined.

By answering many of the questions above, you can make wise client choices. You will also be in a better position for contract negotiations. Just remember that a bad client and a bad project can have a negative impact on your fledgling firm's reputation. Even a few bad words on the street can have a domino effect just at the time when you need projects the most.

## THE BUSINESS SIDE OF ARCHITECTURE

Few architects say they enjoy the administrative side of running their businesses, but most will likely agree that without a smoothly functioning organization, there is little hope of conducting a flourishing design practice.

### Financial Considerations

While design could be your most appealing practice area, financial planning will be just as important. Successful design firms generally have an easily understood financial plan.

To begin a practice, you will need *start-up capital*. For most new design firms, especially those with an aggressive start-up approach, the sum required can be quite large. Unless you open your doors with a project in hand, your start-up capital will pay for office space (if you are not working from an office in your home), phone lines, computers, fax, e-mail, drafting supplies, furniture, and any other equipment you need to begin to design and manage projects. It will also cover the costs of stationery and business cards. Start-up capital also goes to paying yourself if you must have an income to survive. It can help with your marketing expenses. It can help you pay consultants while you wait for your own accounts receivable to be paid into your firm's coffers.

Where does start-up capital come from? The majority of practitioners receive bank loans during their firm's formative months and beyond. Lots of other designers use

## Tips for Emerging Firms

*Decide what kind of firm you want to be.* It's like riding a bike. You go in the direction you lean. In terms of client and project types, in scope and kind of services offered, lean where the going's been smooth and fast for you in the past. Then present yourself as a winner and describe the firm that won—yours—in terms of size, staff, resources, expertise. Hold on to and revisit that image, knowing all the time it's the real you. The world loves a winner; start out knowing you are one.

*Solicit only clients who can help you get there from here.* Choosing your direction well is the key to doing this task well. Appropriate goals allow you to go for the right targets of opportunity when they drift by—and they will. Everybody who socializes, works, plays, or joins in cultural or civic activities with your chosen client(s) is a valued and useful gatekeeper to your next project. Be the architect whose name springs to their lips because you are so sincerely interested in their welfare and success.

*Listen hard to your clients.* And don't just listen. Play back to them what they have just said to you until they signal that you have understood them correctly. The hard part is to keep yourself from making judgments, giving solutions, or solving problems until you have listened carefully. Success on projects comes when clients discover the best solution because you asked the right questions and kept them talking long enough.

*Collect quality risk management information and act reasonably on the basis of it.* Empower yourself out of a sense of capability, instead of limiting your practice by living in fear of liability. You already have access to the technical capability you need, so it's a matter of active listening. Be street-smart. Play "what if" about what could go wrong, who would be damaged if it did, and who can best keep it from happening. Then agree with your client on an equitable allocation of responsibilities and power to make things go right.

*Learn how to say no intelligently.* The best way to avoid having to say no is to employ active listening at the outset. Failing that, try readily agreeing to what clients want, provided *they* provide you with one or a series of quid pro quos in

forms such as time, independent tests or estimates, consultants, insurance, information—whatever would make it equitable. Through joint ventures, associations, and consulting agreements, team up with whomever it takes to overcome your own limits and to perform in the client's best interests. To do this successfully means knowing your own limits.

*Build your own database.* This is your best source of information when planning a new project, when preparing for negotiating, when educating your clients to have reasonable expectations, or when preparing an invoice. Logging a running total of time spent on a drawing on its margin is a good idea, as is the use of a time management system that includes pages for listing out-of-pocket expenses by project. But keep it simple enough to be neither a guilt trip nor a burden on your overhead.

*The rest is only money.* The primary reason young firms fail is undercapitalization. Start-ups report using some of the following strategies to combat this lack of capital:

- Understand that profit is a business expense. Working at break-even leaves nothing for unexpected expenses—and there will be some.
- Do not take loss leaders lightly. Consider the overall firm benefit and the likelihood of these benefits occurring.
- Ask for retainers. Many clients expect to pay them, but only if you ask.
- Work on the basis of hourly rates for all portions of the project services for which you can't set extent or duration.
- Bill early and often. Bill at least monthly. Writing small checks routinely is a lot easier than paying large sums less often. Many clients do not mind paying every two weeks if your cash flow requirements are explained to them in advance.
- Do not love your work so much that you fail to market. When a project is finished, do not overwork it because you have nothing else to do; go out and get another project.

*James R. Franklin, FAIA, and Ava J. Abramowitz, Esq.*

their own savings, borrow from relatives, or convince a new client to pay a hefty retainer.

Banks are in the business of lending money to make money. They like to invest in what they consider a good risk. Few start-up or newly formed design firms are recognized as good risks. So you must be well prepared when you approach a bank. Getting a loan is mostly a matter of selling yourself, since your firm does not have a track record. The better prepared you are, the greater your chances for success. It is your responsibility to explain your firm to the banker. To start the loan process, you must submit a loan proposal.

Typically, banks require that owners of a new firm invest 25 to 50 percent of their own savings into the business. Then the banks will consider the character and managerial abilities of the borrower and the firm's prospects for profits. Generally, a loan to a small business without much of a track record will require a personal guarantee by the owner. Even if the business doesn't generate the necessary income or fails, the loan will be repaid.

When you go to the bank, bring along a preliminary business plan, your current résumé, and some type of projection of your operating budget. Banks want to know where your income will come from, what your expenses will be, and how you plan to handle your new firm's cash flow.

Cash flow is difficult enough to manage in a thriving business; for a new design firm it can be completely unpredictable. Some new firms take the plunge and rent an office, buy equipment, and otherwise invest at a fairly heavy rate from the very beginning. But unless you have signed contracts for a significant amount of work, a more cautious approach would be to go slow: Set up an office in your house, lease a copier for a short period, and buy used but still useful equipment, until you have a better idea of your actual needs to perform actual work. This approach is probably the least risky, yet it is only one option. At this stage, it is a good idea to list the assets you think you need and also the expenses you expect to incur, along with specific dollar amounts. Then make the choices that will immediately help to shape the firm identity you have chosen.

The odds are that your clients will not be coming to your offices too frequently. You probably don't need an elaborate office. On the other hand, do invest in high-quality stationery and attractive business cards, and do prepare marketing materials you can give to prospective clients; just remember to keep your costs in line with your start-up budget.

Some designers start their own firms with only enough cash to last a month or two. Consultants strongly recommend enough savings to cover six months to a year of operations for practitioners who start a firm without projects.

When you start your own design firm, you are investing money—your own and that from other sources. You need the money your clients have promised to pay you for work you have performed— your accounts receivable—to continue to operate and fund your business. Design firm failures can result from inadequate management of accounts receivable. Without enough money in hand, firm owners cannot afford to hire good business advisors, pay good staff, or pay licensing and other government fees. For that matter, they can't even to do a good job marketing without cash on hand.

To solve this problem, first determine the operating cash needs for your new business. There are a few approaches to this, but one convenient way is to calculate your firm's average monthly budget. This is how much cash needs to come in from clients each month. Both designers who have opened their own firms and management consultants say not to wait until the end of the month to anticipate cash flow problems. Call clients soon after sending invoices to make sure they have been received, verify that the client plans to pay on time, and follow up on the day after the due date.

Financing your marketing time and activities with your operating budget means that you need to make a profit on the projects you complete. Profit is a normal component of any business endeavor, and design firms are no different.

▶ Acquiring Capital (7.4) tackles the important issue of start-up.

> ### The Components of a Loan Proposal
>
> When you approach a bank, be ready to sell them on the viability of your new firm. Your loan proposal should include the following:
>
> - *The amount of money you want to borrow, for how long, and how the loan will be used.* Banks like to collect their money on time, so be sure to mention how you plan to repay the loan, and list anything you can use as collateral.
> - *A description of your business.* Explain what you do, your own background and qualifications, and the nature of prospective clients.
> - *A current business plan.* Your plan should describe your market, your niche if you have one, your organizational structure, your marketing plans, your approach to financial management, and your profit objectives.
> - *Financial budgets and operation costs.* These should be organized by project, by month, by year, or by a longer term, as appropriate.
> - *Additional financial information.* This may include an income or profit-and-loss statement, a balance sheet, and personal finances.

▶ Insurance Coverage (11.2) provides a summary of insurance types and needs.

## Setting Fees

To make a profit, you must set your fees so that there is money left over after you pay all your bills. Place a value on your services that reflects what your time is worth to a client. This includes a salary expense for you, even if you do not plan to take any salary for a while. It also includes overhead.

When you start your own firm, the general idea is that your rates will be competitive because you do not have the kind of overhead with which larger organizations are saddled. You don't have expensive rent, your salary is not too big, your equipment isn't too costly. Running your new small operation will require much less overhead than was true for any of your former employers. As a result, your rates can, and should, be less.

▶ Risk Management Strategies (11.1) suggests a complete approach to accepting and handling the risks and opportunities each project presents.

Clients do not expect to be billed one rate for all of your activities, however. Clerical staff activities do not command the same level of expertise as do structural decisions. So identifying an average hourly rate is a popular approach to setting project rates. However, an argument can be made for pricing your services based on their value, not on a cost basis.

Still, architects tend to bill for their services on the cost basis. If you want to be paid what you were paid at your last position as an employee, take your hourly rate in salary, multiply it by the number of hours a day you will likely be working, and then multiply the whole thing by the number of your workdays in a year. This becomes the base salary rate, but there are additional costs to add. Your overhead needs to be included. And don't forget to include a percentage for profit.

Albert Rubeling Jr., in *How to Start and Operate Your own Design Firm,* explains that hourly rates should be burdened by overhead rates. To come up with your overhead factor, divide your indirect costs—those things you can't charge directly to a project—by your direct costs. Normal overhead ratios for medium-size firms could be 1:4, according to Rubeling. But a start-up, with its higher overhead, could have ratios in the 1:1 or 1:2 range. Now, to get the hourly rate you charge your clients, Rubeling uses the following formulas:

Salary rate + Overhead factor = Payroll burden
Salary rate + Payroll burden = Salary + Burden rate
(Salary + Burden rate) × Profit factor = Hourly rate

## Financial Management Systems and Taxes

Few architecture firm start-ups require a complicated or elaborate financial management system. Instead they need a simple one that works for them. The best rudimentary system will allow you to view the health of your business at a particular point in time and help you plan for and meet tax obligations. For many practitioners, their monthly bank statements, along with simple cash flow projections and periodic documentation required by bankers, the IRS, and some clients, seem to compose the bulk of their financial management system.

*Insurance.* Liability insurance has become an integral part of architecture practice. Construction and materials get more complicated and society more inclined to sue. Liability insurance can be very expensive for a small firm with no track record. Take time to evaluate all of your insurance options and weigh any potential risks against the costs.

Some small design firms whose projects are quite small and uncomplicated elect to skip liability insurance, but this is not recommended by the AIA. Before making any insurance decisions for your new firm, consult with the appropriate legal and insurance advisors. As your business grows, review your liability insurance and your risk avoidance strategies.

*When is the best time to start your own firm?* The answer is that it depends. There is no precise number of years an architect needs to work for another employer. While it doesn't make much sense to leave before your internship is complete,

## Financing Firm Start-Up: Expense Items

### What Will You Have to Pay For?

#### Initial Expenses
- Space rental and remodeling
- Furniture
- Telephone, fax, copier
- Computer equipment: office and CAD
- Initial legal and accounting fees
- Costs of any required licenses or permits
- Utilities deposits
- Insurance
- Stationery and business cards
- Unanticipated expenses

#### Monthly Expenses
- Your salary or "draw"
- Employee salaries and benefits
- Taxes, including Social Security
- Rent and utilities
- Marketing and public relations
- Telephone, copier, etc.
- Maintenance
- Legal and accounting fees
- Insurance
- Supplies
- Miscellaneous expenses

### Where Will You Get the Money?

#### Personal Resources
- Savings, stocks, and bonds
- Mortgage on real property
- Home mortgage refinancing
- Loan against surrender value of insurance
- Passbook, credit union, personal loan
- Cosigned loan
- Credit cards
- Family and friends

#### Other Possibilities
- Bank loans
- Finance companies
- Government small business or economic development loans
- Equity capital from partners (or stockholders if you form as a corporation)

*Adapted from Coopers & Lybrand,*
Growth Company Starter Kit, *1992*

your licensing requirements fulfilled, and (preferably) your license in hand, the time to leave the security of a paid position with another firm for your own start-up is when it feels right for you. If you believe you need more experience, wait. If you have the confidence to march out right now and access to the capital you need, then now might be the time.

### For More Information
For more in-depth information on firm start-ups, you might want to consult Frank Stasiowski, *Starting a New Design Firm, or Risking it All* (1994), and Albert W. Rubeling, *How to Start and Operate Your Own Design Firm* (1994). The Small Business Administration runs community mentoring programs, offering free advice on all aspects of business from retired entrepreneurs through its SCORE program. For the SCORE nearest you, call (800) 8ASK-SBA. For additional information about starting a business, as well as state-specific information on line, link to the Oasis Press/Oasis Business Network at www.psi-research.com/resource.htm.

### Strategies to Succeed

- Take to heart the idea that profit is a business expense. Don't work for break-even, or you will have nothing left for extraordinary expenses, which you can count on becoming an ordinary line item in your budget.
- Consider work as a loss leader with great care. You must weigh the likely overall benefit with the loss in income and still be able to justify the work as part of your overall business plan.
- Don't forget to include a retainer up front as part of your contract negotiations. Clients will pay retainers but rarely offer them.
- Bill on an hourly basis for work that cannot be clearly specified in terms of its outcome or time for execution.
- Bill early and often—at the very least, monthly. And follow up with clients to make sure they have your bill and plan to pay on time.
- Never stop marketing, no matter how busy you are right now.

# 5.3 Firm Legal Structure

## Philip R. Croessmann, AIA, Esq.

*Regardless of their size and orientation, firms are organized and behave according to some basic principles established in the law.*

An architecture firm may be established as a proprietorship, partnership, corporation, or limited liability company. There are several factors to consider when selecting the form of practice, and certain legal requirements apply to all forms.

### SOLE PROPRIETORSHIPS

From a legal standpoint, a sole proprietorship is the simplest form of practice. By definition, a sole proprietor is an individual conducting business in an unincorporated format. The sole proprietor makes no legal arrangements with other individuals in order to conduct the practice and has full, personal control of the firm. The individual and the (unincorporated) firm are one.

Some of the simplicity inherent in this form of practice will be lost unless the proprietor makes special efforts to isolate the activities of the architecture practice from personal and unrelated business endeavors. For example, although there is no legal requirement to maintain separate records for tax purposes, it is possible for an individual's financial matters to become entangled with the finances of the proprietorship. The Internal Revenue Service regards business expenses differently—and more favorably—than personal expenses. If tax deductions are to be taken for business expenses, they must be reported to the IRS, thus suggesting the need for separate bookkeeping.

Keeping business and personal finances separate is part of an important management discipline that can contribute to a financially successful practice. A sole proprietorship does not file a separate federal tax return; instead, relevant information is included with the proprietor's personal tax return.

In determining whether a sole proprietorship may be worth considering, two issues predominate: liability and the effect of death or retirement.

*Liability.* A sole proprietor's liability for professional errors and omissions, and for business debts, is unlimited. Both a professional liability claimant and a vendor of business services or products can reach all of the assets of the proprietor—except those that may be protected pursuant to state bankruptcy statutes. A professional liability insurance policy will protect the proprietor, to a certain extent, from the losses associated with professional liability claims, but the proprietor remains fully liable for all business claims.

▶ **Risk Management Strategies (11.1)** assesses the use of professional liability insurance as a part of a firm's risk management strategy.

*Death or retirement.* The death or retirement of the proprietor terminates the proprietorship. Unless a provision has been made for a successor to purchase the practice or take over the proprietor's projects, the only method for wrapping up a sole proprietorship is through an appropriate estate plan and contingency business plan. Because there are advantages in placing certain assets in trust, chief among them avoiding probate, a proprietor could consider the use of a trust instrument in conjunction with an estate plan.

▶ **Insurance Coverage (11.2)** provides details on professional liability coverage for design errors and omissions.

---

**PHILIP R. CROESSMANN** *is a member in the Washington, D.C., law firm of Bastianelli, Brown & Kelley, Chartered. He has extensive experience in construction litigation and contract law and has authored many articles on these and related subjects.*

# PARTNERSHIPS

A partnership is an unincorporated association of two or more persons or entities to operate a business with the intention of making a profit. The partnership, however, is not a separate legal entity that is distinct from the partners.

***The partnership agreement.*** Partnerships are more complex than proprietorships. A partnership agreement should be in writing and should address issues such as the following:

- Financial (capital) contributions of the partners
- Responsibility and authority of the partners
- Fiduciary duties of the partners
- Liabilities of the partners
- Operation and management of the partnership
- Distributions of profit and loss
- Transferability of interests
- Admission of new partners
- Resolution of disputes
- Dissolution of the partnership

> **"With partners, make sure you get along and you both know which one of you is boss."**
> *Courtland L. Logue, Texas entrepreneur, quoted in* Fortune, *July 10, 1996*

Nearly all states have enacted some variation of a model statute called the Uniform Partnership Act, which establishes certain legal requirements to govern relationships between or among the partners (unless the partners themselves have made other specific arrangements) and the partnership's relationships with third parties.

There are several reasons why it is preferable to establish a partnership with a specific written agreement instead of relying on a state's statutes to supply the terms of agreement between the partners. For example, partnership statutes presume that all partners share income and losses equally. These laws do not commonly take into account a partnership's intention that certain parties be treated differently from others with respect to income, losses, or both. Also, they do not take into account that certain assets or efforts contributed by the partners should be treated differently if the partnership succeeds—or fails. Furthermore, most state statutes do not recognize the contribution of effort in excess of other partners' efforts as the equivalent of making a cash contribution. Thus, should a partnership fail with some partners having contributed more effort and others more initial capital, the partners making the greater effort would still be responsible for their proportionate share of the capital lost.

***Partners' liabilities.*** Each partner has liability for all of the business and professional liability debts of the entire partnership jointly and severally. Therefore, should a business vendor or a professional liability claimant make a claim against the partnership, each partner's personal assets may be reached to satisfy the claim.

> An architect considering becoming a partner in a firm should carefully weigh the amount of liability to which he or she will become subject, and whether or not the capital contribution being made might soon be lost to existing creditors and claimants.

What liabilities does an incoming partner assume or an outgoing partner retain? In most states, incoming partners become responsible only for partnership debts incurred after they became partners—except that the new partner's capital is subject to claims by prior claimants or debtors. Departing partners remain liable for all partnership debts incurred by the partnership while they were partners. This is because, technically, when a partner retires or terminates the relationship with a partnership, the partnership is dissolved and a new partnership composed of the remaining partners automatically comes into being. Of course, a partnership agreement can overcome this result if it is clear on the subject.

Another consideration in deciding to join a partnership is whether the rules concerning death and disability make sense. Often a retiring or deceased partner may be entitled to compensation far beyond what the partnership can or should pay for the partner's contribution. Joining such an arrangement leaves the new partner at risk should the existing partners die or retire.

> Ownership Transition (5.4) looks at the intricacies of selling, buying, or closing a practice.

***Requirements for professional registration.*** Many states require that all partners be registered architects in the state where the firm is located. Some states specify

Architects involved in general contracting—as developers, designer-builders, or construction managers—may find it necessary to obtain a contractor's license in states where they intend to engage in construction.

Federal, state, and sometimes local income tax laws and regulations are complex. They change frequently and are reinterpreted constantly. The table included in this topic provides a summary of some provisions. Your accountant should keep you posted on changes that affect your practice.

Agreements with Clients (10.1) notes that partnerships and corporations need to be mindful of some legal issues when entering into project agreements—or, for that matter, any business agreement.

that a certain percentage of the partners must be registered architects if the firm is to be classified as an architecture partnership. If a partnership consists of practitioners of multiple disciplines, the registered partners must be identified with their respective disciplines—for example, "architects and engineers."

**Income taxes.** A partnership files a separate federal tax return (called an information return), but it does not pay federal income tax on profits. A schedule showing each partner's share of the profits or losses and other reportable tax information is filed with the partnership's tax return and is given to each partner. Partners must transfer the information to their individual income tax returns and pay taxes on their share of the partnership's profits, whether or not those profits are distributed. States and localities have different requirements related to partnership taxes and tax returns.

## CORPORATIONS

Corporations are separate legal entities that can conduct necessary business actions—including bringing suit and being sued—in their corporate name. Because corporations have "lives" of their own, they are the most complicated to establish and maintain. There are legal requirements for boards of directors, shareholders' meetings, and a variety of other organizational issues. On the other hand, a corporation can be much more stable (in a legal sense) than a sole proprietorship or a partnership because its existence transcends that of the individuals who own and manage it.

Many states have separate statutes for general business and professional corporations.

• *General business corporations* may be formed for any legal purpose and are subject to the requirements of the state's general corporation laws. Every state allows the establishment of general business corporations, although some states do not allow architecture to be the primary business of a general business corporation.

• *Professional corporations* are established specifically to provide professional services and are subject to restrictions enumerated in the professional corporation statute. Professional corporations normally must be owned or at least controlled by professionals licensed to practice in the state. Moreover, the corporate entity usually does not protect against professional liability. Professional corporations may be required to pay income taxes as general business corporations or may be subject to special tax considerations.

• *Practice in corporate form.* A few states do not permit architecture practice in a corporate form. Some states require architects who want to incorporate to do so as a professional corporation authorized and certified by the secretary of state for that state. Most states permit practice through either the professional corporation or the general business corporation; some permit both. The number of principals in the corporation who must be registered architects depends on the state in which the corporation conducts its practice.

A corporation seeking to practice in a state other than the one in which it is incorporated must register as a foreign corporation in the other state.

**Ownership and control.** Just because someone is a shareholder does not necessarily mean his or her compensation will be proportional to his or her ownership. Compensation in a corporation is based on the agreement between the corporation and the individual and may be set in relationship to the number of shares owned. This is also true for management and control. It is possible (though uncommon) for the ownership of the corporation and the control and management of the corporation to be in different hands. This is uncommon because the majority of shareholders elects the board of directors, which appoints the officers. Under most circumstances, the individual or group of individuals who owns the majority of the shares is able to elect directors who will appoint them or their designees as officers.

When shares of a corporation are offered, consider whether the costs of share purchase will be justified by an increase in compensation commensurate with the investment (or an increase in leverage within the firm). If owning shares does not increase the compensation to which an architect is entitled, there may be no value in purchasing the shares. This is particularly true if the number of shares being purchased is small compared with the holdings of others, in which case the new shareholder may have little, if anything, to say about the election of directors and the appointment of officers.

Liabilities. Unlike in a proprietorship or a partnership, the shareholders' personal assets cannot be reached to satisfy the corporation's business debts. If the corporation purchases services or goods in its own name and fails to pay for them, the vendor can look only to the corporation for payment, not to the individual shareholders.

Professional liability is a different question. In many states, an architect remains liable for his or her professional errors or omissions, even if they were committed while the architect was an employee of a corporation. Other states make design professionals jointly and severally liable for professional errors and omissions in the same way they would be liable as partners. In certain states the practice of architecture as a corporation shields the architect from personal liability for errors and omissions. An important question to ask in purchasing shares, therefore, is whether or not the corporation is adequately insured against professional errors and omissions, and what the state statutes provide with regard to the liability of the new shareholder for such errors and omissions.

**Ownership transition.** As with partnerships, a shareholder who retires or dies may have rights to compensation through his or her employment agreement. Before becoming a shareholder, it is essential to understand what liability the corporation will have to departing shareholders in order to determine whether the corporation will be sound and viable into the future. Similarly, provisions for the incoming shareholders' ultimate retirement or termination should be made in a way that fairly compensates the shareholders for the efforts they made during their tenure.

Ownership transition for the corporation is, in many respects, easier than for a partnership. Shares of more than one type and variety may be bought and sold under a large number of circumstances in order to provide orderly ownership transition and pay retiring shareholders.

The usual method for compensating departing shareholders is a buy/sell agreement. These agreements require departing shareholders to sell their shares back to the corporation or its shareholders in order to keep them in the "family" of shareholders. This arrangement may be mandated by a state registration statute that requires all shareholders to be licensed architects. The buy/sell agreement establishes a purchase price and method of sale for the departing shareholder's shares and may also determine the price to be paid by incoming shareholders. Because such devices affect the long-term viability of the corporation, a prospective shareholder should carefully review the buy/sell agreement to determine the corporation's prospects for viability after the other shareholders depart.

**Income taxes.** Unless an "S election" is made, a corporation is a separate taxable entity. Individual shareholders who are employees of the corporation are taxed on their salaries in the usual fashion. The corporation itself reports as gross income the professional fees received and deducts salaries and other business expenses. Any amounts remaining are taxable to the corporation at the corporate tax rate. The corporation has options with these remaining amounts; for example, it may pay bonuses or employ a profit-sharing plan. If these amounts are distributed to the shareholders as dividends, the amount will be subject to a double tax; first the corporation pays corporate taxes on the dividend and then individual shareholders pay taxes on the same dividend income. Under certain circumstances, if earnings are not distributed to shareholders, an accumulated earnings tax may be imposed on the corporation.

Upon sale or liquidation of the business aspects of its practice, a corporation will have to pay tax on the appreciation of its assets, and the shareholders will pay an additional tax when they receive the after-tax proceeds of the sale.

**Subchapter S corporations.** Provided certain technical requirements are met, a corporation may elect to be treated as an S corporation for federal income tax purposes. An S corporation is treated similarly to a partnership for tax purposes. That is, the shareholders of an S corporation are taxed on their pro rata share of the corporation's income, regardless of whether it is distributed. The S corporation itself, however, is subject to income tax only in special circumstances. The use of an S corporation status can thus avoid or mitigate the double tax that may otherwise be imposed on portions of corporate income.

▶ An architect who plans to establish a corporate form of practice should seek legal counsel and accounting advice to make sure the tax ramifications and conditions of practice in various states are thoroughly understood.

## Comparison of Legal Structures: Legal Attributes

| Legal Attributes | Sole Proprietorship | Partnership | S Corporation | Regular Corporation | Limited Liability Company |
|---|---|---|---|---|---|
| **Liability** | Individually liable for all liabilities of business | General partners individually liable on partnership's liabilities; limited partner liable only up to amount of his/her capital contribution | Same as regular corporation | Shareholder's liability in most cases is limited to capital contribution | Shareholders liability in most cases is limited to capital contribution |
| **Qualified Owners** | Single individual owner | No limitations; however, need at least two partners (including general partner) | Only individuals, estates, and certain trusts may be shareholders (limited to 75 shareholders) | No limitation | No limitation except in the case of professional limited liability companies, in which case the members must conform to the applicable licensing requirement |
| **Type of Ownership Interests** | Individual ownership | More than one class of partner permitted | Only one class of stock permitted | More than one class of stock permitted | One class of member |
| **Transfer of Ownership** | Assets of business transferable rather than business itself | New partnership may be created; consent of other partners normally required if partnership interest is to be transferred | Shares can only be transferred to individuals, certain types of trusts or estates; no consent to Subchapter S election is needed; restrictions may be imposed by shareholder agreement | Ready transfer of ownership through the use of stock certificates; restrictions may be imposed by shareholders' agreement | A new limited liability company may be created; consent of other members normally required if partnership interest is to be transferred |
| **Raising Capital** | Capital raised only by loan or increased contribution by the proprietor | Loans or contributions from partners | Loans or contributions by shareholders; "straight debt" avoids second class of stock | Met by sale of stocks or bonds or other corporate debt | Loans or contributions from members |
| **Business Action and Management** | Sole proprietor makes decisions and can act immediately. Proprietor responsible and receives all profits or losses | Action usually dependent upon the unanimous agreement of partners or, at least, general partners. Limited partner actively participating in management may lose limited liability | Same as regular corporation except unanimous consent is required to elect S status; more than 50% of shareholders needed to revoke Subchapter S status | Unity of action based on authority of board of directors | Managed by professional managers or the members |
| **Flexibility** | No restrictions | Partnership is contractual agreement, within which members can conduct business subject to the partnership agreement and applicable state laws | Same as regular corporation | Corporation is a legal entity created by the state, functioning within powers granted explicitly or implicitly and subject to judicial construction and decision | Great flexibility in management and ownership |

Firm Planning

# COMPARISON OF LEGAL STRUCTURES: TAX ATTRIBUTES

| TAX ATTRIBUTES | SOLE PROPRIETORSHIP | PARTNERSHIP | S CORPORATION | REGULAR CORPORATION | LIMITED LIABILITY COMPANY |
|---|---|---|---|---|---|
| **Taxable Year** | Usually calendar year | Generally a calendar year is required, unless §444 or a business purpose test is met | Generally a calendar year is required, unless §444 or a business purpose test is met | Any type of year available; however, personal service corporation has restrictions | Generally a calendar year is required, unless §444 or a business purpose test is met |
| **Ordinary Distributions to Owners** | Drawings from the business are not taxable; the net profits are taxable and the proprietor is subject to the tax on self-employment income | Generally not taxable; distribution in excess of basis is taxable as capital gain | Payment of salaries deductible by corporation and taxable to recipient; distributions generally not taxable; however, certain distributions can be taxable as dividends; distributions in excess of basis = capital gains | Payments of salaries are deductible by corporation and taxable to recipient; payments of dividends are not deductible by corporation and generally are taxable to recipient shareholders | Generally, not taxable; distribution in excess of basis is taxable as capital gain |
| **Limitation on Losses Deductible by Owners** | Subject to at-risk, hobby loss, and passive activity loss rules | Subject to basis limitation; partner's investment, plus his/her share of partnership liabilities; at-risk and passive activity loss rules may apply | Subject to the shareholder's basis, including loans to the corporation; at-risk and passive activity loss rules may apply | No losses allowed to individual except upon sale of stock or liquidation of corporation. Corporate carry back and carryover rules may apply. Closely held corporations limited by at-risk and modified passive activity rules | Deductible by owners subject to basis limitation; partners investment, plus his/her share of partnership liabilities at risk and passive active loss rules may apply |
| **Dividends Received** | Fully taxable | Conduit—fully taxable | Same as partnership | 70% to 100% dividend-received deduction | Conduit—fully taxable |
| **Former Election Required to Obtain Tax Status** | No | No | Yes | No | Yes |
| **Capital Gain** | Taxed at individual level | Conduit—taxed at individual level | Conduit—taxed at shareholder level; possible corporate built-in gains tax | Taxed at corporate level | Conduit—taxed at individual level |
| **Capital Losses** | Carried forward indefinitely; limited to $3,000 per year | Conduit—carried forward indefinitely at partner level; limited to $3,000 per year | Same as partnership | Carry back three years and carryover five years as short-term capital loss offsetting only capital gains | Conduit carried forward indefinitely at partner level; limited to $3,000 per year |
| **Section 1231 Gains and Losses** | Taxed at individual level—combined with other §1231 gains or losses of individual; net gains are capital gains for individual; net losses are ordinary losses for individual | Conduit | Conduit; possible corporate built-in gains tax | Taxable or deductible at the corporate level | Conduit |

| TAX ATTRIBUTES | SOLE PROPRIETORSHIP | PARTNERSHIP | S CORPORATION | REGULAR CORPORATION | LIMITED LIABILITY COMPANY |
|---|---|---|---|---|---|
| **Basis of Allocating Income to Owners** | All income is reported on owner's return | Profit and loss agreement may have "special allowances" of income and deductions, if they have substantial economic effect. | Pro rata portion of income based on per share, per day allocation | No income allocated to shareholder | Profit and loss agreement may have "special allowances" of income and deductions, if they have substantial economic effect |
| **Basis for Allocating a Net Operating Loss** | All losses flow through to owner's return | Profit and loss agreement may have "special allocation" of income and deductions, if they have substantial economic effect | Pro rata portion of income based on per share, per day allocation | No losses allocated to stockholders | Profit and loss agreement may have "special allowances" of income and deductions, if they have substantial economic effect |
| **Group Hospitalization and Life Insurance Premiums and Medical Reimbursement Plans** | 45% of self-employed person's health insurance premiums may be deducted from gross income; remainder subject to 7.5% AGI limitation for itemized medical expenses<br>45% becomes:<br>60% in 1999–2001<br>70% in 2002<br>100% in 2003 | Cost of partners' benefits is generally treated as compensation, deductible by the partnership and includable in the partner's income; 45% self-employment health insurance premiums available as a deduction<br>45% becomes:<br>60% in 1999–2001<br>70% in 2002<br>100% in 2003 | Cost of benefits to more than 2% of shareholders treated as compensation, deductible by the corporation and included in the shareholder's income; 45% of self-employed health insurance premiums available as a deduction<br>45% becomes:<br>60% in 1999–2001<br>70% in 2002<br>100% in 2003 | Cost of shareholder-employee's coverage is generally deductible as a business expense if plan is "for the benefit of employees"; normally excluded from employee's income | Cost of partners' benefits is generally treated as compensation, deductible by the company and includable in the partner's income; 45% self-employment health insurance premiums available as a deduction |
| **Retirement Benefits** | Limitations and restrictions basically same as regular corporations | Limitations and restrictions basically same as regular corporations | Limitations and restrictions basically same as regular corporations | Limitations on benefits from defined benefit plans and from defined contribution plans; special restrictions for top-heavy plans; 401(k) limitation began in 1992 | Limitations and restrictions basically same as regular corporations |
| **Organization Costs** | Not applicable | Amortizable over 60 months | Amortizable over 60 months | Amortizable over 60 months | Amortizable over 60 months |
| **Charitable Contributions** | Subject to limits for the individual; gifts for the use of private foundations, 20% of AGI; gifts to public charity, cash, 50% of AGI; appreciated property, 30% of AGI; other limitations for specific items contributed | Conduit | Conduit | Limited to 10% of taxable income before special deductions | Conduit |

part 2 BUSINESS

| TAX ATTRIBUTES | SOLE PROPRIETORSHIP | PARTNERSHIP | S CORPORATION | REGULAR CORPORATION | LIMITED LIABILITY COMPANY |
|---|---|---|---|---|---|
| **Tax Preferences (Alternative Minimum Tax)** | Graduated from 26% of the first $175,000 of AMTI, 28% of anything over that; applied to minimum taxable income, including tax preferences in excess of $20,000 ($40,000 for joint returns); payable to extent exceeds regular tax | Conduit | Conduit | Taxed at corporate level; 20% on preferences and adjustments in excess of $40,000 or regular tax liability, whichever is greater (does not apply to corp. with <7,500K gross rev. ave. 3 years) | Conduit |
| **Character of Income and Deductions** | Taxed at individual level; limitation on investment interest deductions | Conduit | Conduit | Taxed at corporate level | Conduit |
| **Self-Employment Tax** | Half of SE tax paid is deductible from gross income | Same as proprietorship | Not applicable | Not applicable | Same as proprietorship |

## TAX CONSIDERATIONS

As suggested so far, the various forms of legal organization are subject to different federal (and often state as well) income tax methods. Some additional income tax considerations follow.

*Tax rates.* Under current law, the maximum federal income tax rates imposed on individuals are lower than the maximum corporate income tax rate. Although the individual tax rates are higher than corporate rates at certain lower levels of individual income, architecture and other personal service corporations are not entitled to the benefit of these rates, and all of their income is taxed at the flat rate of 35 percent.

*Tax year.* Sole proprietorships, partnerships, and corporations are generally required to use a calendar taxable year (i.e., January 1 through December 31) unless sufficient business reasons can be established to adopt a fiscal year. A corporation engaged in architecture or other personal services, whether organized as a professional corporation or a regular business corporation, should consult with its accountant to see if it is entitled to use a fiscal year for tax planning purposes.

*Accounting method.* An architecture firm organized as a sole proprietorship, partnership, or S corporation is entitled to compute its taxable income under the cash method of accounting. Under this method, fees are reported as income only when actually received and not when billed. Similarly, expenses are deductible only when actually paid, not in the year in which they accrue. An architecture firm organized as a corporation that has not made an S election may use the cash method only if its gross receipts do not exceed certain amounts and if certain other requirements of the Internal Revenue Code are met.

*Pension and profit-sharing plans.* Regardless of their form of legal organization, architecture firms may establish pension and profit-sharing plans. If these plans satisfy the requirements of the Internal Revenue Code, contributions to the plans (up to certain limits) are deductible by the plan's sponsor. When the corporate form is used, the corporation is entitled to a deduction for such contributions, and when a partnership or sole proprietorship is used, the partners or the proprietor is entitled to the deduction. Withdrawals made before the individual participant reaches the age of fifty-nine may be subject to a penalty.

Substantial differences no longer exist between the qualified retirement plans that may be established by corporations and those established by partnerships and proprietorships. Corporations do, however, have some advantages over other forms of organization with respect to certain fringe benefits, such as group term life insurance and medical payment plans (which they may be offered on a more favorable tax basis).

*Other taxes.* Many states and some cities impose their own income taxes. Some impose professional services or gross receipts taxes as well. Other federal taxes to which architecture firms and architects may be subject include employer and employee Social Security taxes (and the comparable self-employment tax in the case of partnerships and sole proprietorships) and the unemployment tax on compensation paid to employees.

## LIMITED LIABILITY COMPANIES

Limited liability companies are hybrids of corporations and partnerships. They are separate entities that can conduct business in their own name, and they have many of the characteristics of a corporation. They are, however, classified as partnerships for federal tax purposes. This makes them particularly suitable for investments and businesses where individuals wish to pass through losses to their personal income while at the same time limiting their liability.

The use of limited liability companies for architectural practice varies greatly from state to state. In some states general limited liability companies can be used to practice architecture without any restrictions. Other states completely prohibit the use of general limited liability companies for the practice of architecture, and still other states have statutes creating professional limited liability companies.

*Ownership and control.* Limited liability companies (LLCs) are unique in that they do not have to be managed by the members of the company. The statutes generally provide that an LLC may be managed by professional managers. These managers are afforded limited liability for their acts on behalf of the company, yet they do not have to be members of the company. On the other hand, an LLC can be managed directly by its members or any group of members. This provides a great deal of flexibility in the management and ownership of an LLC and can offer some interesting opportunities for raising capital. To tailor management to the needs of the business, a detailed operating agreement should be developed. The operating agreement, like the bylaws of a corporation and the partnership agreement of a partnership, specifies the authority of the managers and members and how the organization will conduct its business.

*Liabilities.* Like a corporation, the members of an LLC have limited liability. In many states, however, architects will remain liable for their professional errors or omissions even if they were committed while the architect was an employee of the company. While the state's position on architects' liability varies from state to state, generally design professionals cannot avoid professional liability through the use of an LLC or a corporation.

*Ownership transition.* Like ownership of a corporation, memberships in an LLC may be transferred with the permission of the other members. Although many states have limitations on the transferability of membership, the authority to transfer the memberships may be specified in the operating agreement. This makes it possible to avoid the termination and creation of a new limited liability company under the state law when a membership is transferred. In addition to provisions in the operating agreement, the members should enter into buy/sell agreements that will establish the purchase price and methods of sale.

*Income taxes.* As previously mentioned, limited liability companies are generally treated as partnerships under the tax laws. It is also important, due to a recent statute concerning LLCs, to check with your tax consultant to be sure that the LLC meets the requirements for treatment as a partnership for tax purposes. Whether to organize as a corporation or an LLC will often depend on the treatment of these entities by local and state taxes as well as miscellaneous federal taxes and other tax factors. Therefore you should involve your tax consultant in the choice.

# 5.4 Ownership Transition

## Hugh Hochberg

*Every organization undergoes systemic changes that present both problems and opportunities. Some of these changes result from the transitions inherent in maturing businesses; others reflect changes in leadership and ownership.*

As an architecture firm evolves, it undergoes transitions in organization, management, and operation. For example, changing accounting procedures, experimenting with a new project management structure, expanding a computer system's capabilities, and revising a profit-sharing plan all require adjusting the firm's organization and management and/or its approaches to staffing, marketing, financial management, project delivery, and risk management.

Some transitions require fundamental changes in the firm. These transitions most often revolve around questions of growth: Does the firm need to add a partner? Does it need more division of labor and thus more structure? Should it spread the responsibility for design? Others focus on aging: How does the firm plan for the transition of ownership and leadership to others?

## GROWTH

Nearly all successful practices face the prospect of growth. In a perfect marketplace, quality work and strong professional service will, over time, create opportunities to do more and probably larger projects. Those who choose to grow are making certain commitments, both to an increasing need to make organization and management a more explicit activity and responsibility in the firm and to the prospect of additional passages as the firm grows from 10 to 15 people and then to 20 to 25 or more.

The existence of so many one-architect firms reveals that principals of many firms have chosen not to take the first step—navigating the first passage of adding another experienced architect or principal. Conversely, 80 percent of all AIA members work in firms with five or more employees, and 64 percent in firms of ten or more—firms that have chosen to grow. Firms that face (or target) rapidly changing markets will be more successful if they embrace an organizational philosophy and structure that encourages flexibility and responsiveness. Interestingly, a strong management infrastructure that conveys a sense of stability and security may well cover an underlying inability to reposition as market conditions and leaders' ambitions change.

***Passages in staff size.*** In firms that are growing, there are a series of staff sizes that have particular organizational impact. With a generous allowance for special conditions of personalities and abilities of principals and staff—as well as the mix of clients and project—these "impact points" are at staff sizes of 7, 12, 18, and 35.

It has been observed that when a carpenter hires his fourth assistant, he lays down his own tools; managing workers, overseeing quality, administering the business, and marketing services have

▶ **The percentage of large firms has almost doubled since 1990, whereas the percentage of midsize firms has remained relatively stable. There was a steady decrease in the percentage of two- to four- person firms from 1990 to 1996, but a 4 percent increase since 1996.**

| Number of Employees | Percent |
| --- | --- |
| 1 | 23 |
| 2 to 4 | 30 |
| 5 to 9 | 23 |
| 10 to 19 | 11 |
| 20 to 49 | 8 |
| 50+ | 3 |
| 100+ | 2 |

*AIA Firm Survey 2000*

▶ **It's difficult to know how many one-architect firms there are. Clearly the 23 percent of AIA firms that report themselves as sole practitioners are in this group. An additional 30 percent report two to four employees; many in this group have but one principal.**

---

**HUGH HOCHBERG** *is a partner with the Coxe Group in Seattle, Washington. He has consulted over twenty years to professional service firms on leadership, management, marketing, and ownership transition.*

## Symptoms

### "Joe Can't Do It All"

A 60- to 70-hour workweek for the principal, and there is still not enough time to get everything done. Too much time is spent putting out fires, and staff have trouble getting decisions from the principal. Clients are happy with personal attention but find they have to prod to get things done.

### "Why Does Everyone Have to Make Every Decision?"

The firm has grown to 15 or 20. There is a growing imbalance in workload and a sense that some principals are pulling more weight than others. It's not possible to make a decision without calling a meeting.

### "Joe Has Got to Stop Trying to Design Every Project"

A single designer is responsible for every project, and the firm is encountering difficulty in meeting schedules. Profitability, especially during the design phase, may be slipping. Depending on the size of projects, this may occur in firms as small as 10 people.

### "What's Going to Happen When I'm Gone?"

The firm's leadership is over 55, and anyone with potential is under 30. The firm has lost some good people to competitors over the years. The organization is beginning to lose old and loyal clients to younger firms.

### "How Come It's Not Working Like It Used To?"

Occurs shortly after the firm's founders have retired. The client base is eroding, and the firm is having difficulty attracting new clients. The staff is shrinking, and the younger talent is bailing out.

## Problem

The firm has outgrown the ability of one principal to be all things to all problems.

The firm is beginning to outgrow the ability of its leaders to juggle all the balls. All principals are obtaining and serving clients, and everyone has a voice in decision making.

The firm has focused design responsibility in a single person or team—to ensure quality control, to provide consistency, for pride of authorship, or for some combination of these reasons.

The principals have failed to plan for ownership transition. Younger staff were not given opportunities for management or ownership and have drifted away, taking vitality—and probably clients—with them. This can happen in a firm of any size.

This is the classic "second-team syndrome." The first generation of leaders were entrepreneurial and charismatic and surrounded themselves with competent support staff—staff not given the opportunity (and possibly without the ability) to lead once the founders retire.

## Solutions

- Remain a one-principal firm, limiting size to 4 or 5 people, enjoying fruits of a personal practice, and accepting the practical limitations on the number and size of projects you do.
- Delegate some of the design, technical, or management responsibility within the staff.
- Add another principal (there are limits to this; if you are still growing, you will either need to stop growing or begin to delegate).
- Stop growing and work within the limits you have set for yourself.
- Someone in the firm accepts a prime-time management role, becoming disengaged from the primary client/project responsibility. The other principals yield some of their authority to the managing principal.
- Stop growing and continue to have a single person's imprint on each job.
- The designer shifts into a quality-control role, overseeing the work of other designers without personally controlling all of it.
- Shut the doors and retire—if you have the financial resources and your ego will accept it.
- Begin turning over authority, responsibility, and a piece of the action to younger people in the firm—preferably long before you think they are ready.
- The second generation throttles the firm back, living off its reputation, fighting to keep overhead down, and, as they retire, hoping to sell the firm (and its good reputation).
- The second generation can swallow its pride, bring in new blood, hand them the reins, and go back to what they have always done best.

*Adapted from Weld Coxe,* Managing Architectural & Engineering Practice, *1980*

become a full-time job. The same phenomenon occurs in an architecture firm, although the "laying down of tools" begins at a slightly larger staff size. Adding partners and developing a new role to deal with some necessary nonproject issues can allow principals to remain substantially involved in projects even as the firm grows.

At a staff size of about 12, the purely administrative aspects of the practice, particularly the handling of finances, must be addressed. Some means of dealing with the transition to this size are instituting more effective administrative systems and procedures, adding an administrative role, or restructuring the organization into what are, in effect, two smaller firms (perhaps requiring an additional partner).

The same kinds of stresses that occur at a staff size of 12 occur again when the firm reaches a staff size of 18, although generally the stress is noticeably greater at one size or the other. The stress is not typically high at both sizes. Particularly if further growth is anticipated, an office administrator (or some other manager) frequently is hired and allows others in the firm to continue to concentrate on those things that provide the highest value to clients.

A different phenomenon occurs typically in the size range of 30 to 40. Firms frequently describe their cultures as a "family" in one way or another. But by the time a firm reaches this size, it is unlikely that all employees truly consider themselves to be members of the family. People who are new or junior are particularly out of touch with the people at the top of the firm; they are not connected with the history and heritage that coincide with being a family. Every person in the firm no longer knows every other person.

When those at the top—the principals who are leading the practice—are not accessible enough to everyone in the firm, and when their ideas about where the practice is going are not clearly evident to everyone in the firm, it is a strong signal that the firm has arrived at another passage. In this situation, strong management—people who serve as a middle layer between the firm's leaders and its doers—is necessary to keep things on track. And because management in this context is generally alien to architects, its addition to the firm can be traumatic.

The major contribution of management at this stage in a firm's life is to *interpret* for the staff what the leadership is trying to achieve. This interpretation comes in subjective ways, such as ensuring adequate dialogue about where the principals want the firm to be going and how it will get there. It can also come about in objective ways, such as defining marketing targets for appropriate client and project types, establishing targets for individual and group performance, maintaining a training and development program that encourages professional growth consistent with the firm's needs and goals, and monitoring performance and taking corrective steps as necessary.

> ### Partners
>
> In partnership as in marriage—and becoming partners is a form of marriage—it is hard to predict who will make a success of it or who is a suitable long-term mate. We all know of couples who, despite having the same interests and being equal in intellect or abilities, still end up in divorce court. Some of these couples, however, become strong and cohesive single entities; they become interchangeable, and each can stand in for the other no matter the situation.
>
> On the other hand, plenty of marriages in which the parties are wildly different from each other go through life fascinated by, and enjoying, the differences. What is important in any of these situations are shared values, mutual respect, and absolute trust in matters of intention, motivation, and integrity.
>
> Unless you have known each other for many years and worked together on a lot of projects, try to think of ways you can test the partnership. Do projects together as joint-venture partners. Work individually on projects and share results; that will give you insight into a potential professional life together. Look particularly at complementary strengths and weaknesses and at potential divisions of responsibilities.
>
> Remember these words from management consultant Carol McConochie: "A firm is only as strong—at any age—as the strength of the relationship among the partners."
>
> *James R. Franklin, FAIA*

**Typically larger firms are corporations. As the share of larger firms has grown over the past three years, so has the share of firms that are corporations. The share of corporations—whether private, professional, or professional services—has grown from 22 percent in 1996 to 25 percent in 1999.**

*AIA Firm Survey 2000*

## DOWNSIZING

The flip side of growth is shrinkage. Since the 1960s there have been about a half dozen periods of economic recession. Each of those recessions resulted in general shrinkage in the average size of architecture practices. In addition, such things as inadequate anticipation of market and competitive conditions and just plain bad luck can cause firms to shrink.

In other cases, leaders of firms target smaller size as a more desirable way for them to practice. Downsizing, like growth, triggers the need to examine organizational requirements—specifically, what does the firm need to do and provide organizationally to succeed in its primary mission and delivery of projects? The leadership and management that worked well at a staff size of 15 are likely to be ineffective at a staff size of 50; the reverse is also true.

Going backward through the transitions just outlined presents a distinct set of problems for the firm. For one thing, firms tend to grow an increment at a time, adding people steadily, or at least in clusters, during periods of expansion. Downsizing, on the other hand, may take larger cuts from the firm, with a substantial portion of the staff laid

*James R. Franklin, FAIA,* Current Practices in Small Firm Management *(AIA, 1990)*
*Contributed by H. Kennard Bussard, FAIA*

Here's one way of looking at firm growth and transition. The top graph shows the firm's view and the bottom graph the principal's view.

**FIRM GROWTH**

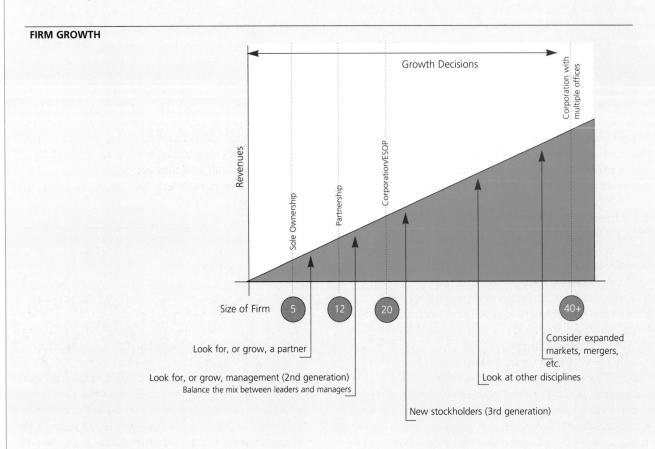

**PRINCIPAL'S CAREER**

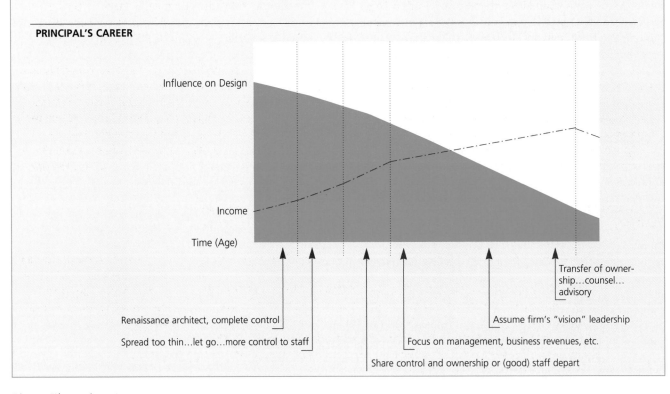

## Planned Downsizing: A Case in Point

After several years of success in meeting the needs of its clients and the marketplace, Firm A has grown to a staff of 55 people. The three partners have taken on the major aspects of management, marketing, and client maintenance. They have set up an administrative system and delegated to others the major project delivery functions. On reflection, however, they realized that they were no longer receiving the strong personal gratification that came from starting and growing the firm.

After examining the situation with input from within the firm and from their clients, the partners realized their strengths have brought them so much work that they are no longer as involved in projects as they would like to be. They identified many options and, after discussion, reduced them to three.

*Option one.* Delegate management responsibilities to a skilled manager, who would have authority for the nonproject activities of the firm, allowing the partners to focus more of their energy on projects. The partners saw several advantages. They would be able to maintain the firm's momentum, not have to turn away clients, stay profitable (once the management was in place and everyone had adjusted to their new roles), and give their staff opportunities for advancement. The biggest risk they saw was that they might never be comfortable being somewhat removed from the day-to-day management of the firm.

*Option two.* Become more selective about the clients and projects they undertake, with the assumption that such selectivity would lead to a smaller but more satisfying workload that allowed the partners to be involved in projects. For the firm to remain at its current level of profitability (on a percentage basis), the partners concluded that two things would have to happen: The firm would need to reduce its staff to 30 people, and it would need to shift emphasis from management by partners to administrative systems for such things as financial management, marketing, and office support. They saw the downside as the perception—and perhaps the reality—that staff advancement would be inhibited as the partners took on responsibilities others had been developing the skills to perform or were already performing. Over the long haul, many of those with the potential to lead the firm would leave.

*Option three.* Continue on the existing path. The partners expected that this would result in incremental growth for a

while but, as their professional satisfaction waned further, there would be a decline in morale and profitability. These trends would be exacerbated as the partners drifted away from everyday contact with clients and projects.

The partners concluded that their desire for project involvement was a driving force—and even a competitive requirement, as other firms were beginning to make inroads on Firm A's clients by promising heavy partner involvement with projects. As a result, the partners decided on option two. Their rationale was based on the philosophy that their highest responsibilities were to their clients, the firm, and themselves—a shift from placing the highest priorities on their clients, their staff, and their profitability.

With their commitment clear, the partners made these key moves:

- They developed and implemented a marketing strategy and public relations program emphasizing their renewed project and client focus.
- They identified the most suitable mix of staff, met individually with each person, clarified roles for those they wanted to remain, and offered outplacement assistance to those they did not think fit in with the long-term needs of the firm. In the latter group were a few people who were important in carrying current projects to completion; the partners offered generous compensation packages to these architects, recognizing that the firm might lose them anyway.
- They developed a new position, that of management coordinator, to oversee the administrative aspects of the firm, provide management information to the partners, keep the partners aware of issues requiring their attention, and make decisions within specified constraints (e.g., purchasing items up to $500 in value).

Regarding the firm's continuity, the new philosophy eliminated the sense of wholesale advancement of staff into the ranks of owners and partners. Instead it focused transition thinking on identifying and grooming a limited number of people whose skills, style, and commitment were perceived to be most important to the firm's future leadership.

*Hugh Hochberg*

off at once. When this happens, there is trauma—both for the individuals who leave and for those who remain ("Will I be next?" "Should I start looking?" "Should I become more defensive in protecting my position here?").

Some issues to consider when downsizing, whether it is planned or not:

- Take a careful look at overhead costs and cut them where appropriate. Some of the firm's overhead may have been intended to support a much larger organization.
- Do not be afraid to sever business relationships that no longer best serve the firm's interests. It may, for example, be less expensive to break a lease (breaching the contract) than to continue paying rent for space the firm no longer needs and cannot sublet.

**The distance between staff and leaders adds to the problems that larger firms often have when they are downsizing.**

- Take special care in deciding which employees will be laid off. Avoid discriminatory actions, however unintended they may be.
- Do everything you can to maintain the esprit de corps of those who remain; remember that trust is under siege during a time of downsizing.
- Safeguard the firm's corporate memory by making sure that research, project, and office information remains in the firm; this may require some documentation.
- Keep clients and key prospects involved, indicating how the resized firm will continue to serve their needs.
- Take the opportunity to rethink the firm's goals and position in the marketplace: Is the resized firm to become a smaller version of what it is or a new firm? Many firms believe that they have become leaner and meaner, more focused and effective, as a result of resizing.

Probably the best summary advice is, first, keep a close eye on the firm's people, and second, imagine the firm as it will appear once the downsizing is accomplished. Will it have the complement of people, expertise, and attitudes it needs to thrive as a smaller firm?

## LEADERSHIP AND MANAGEMENT TRANSITIONS

Some key firm transitions are a function of the interrelationships between leadership and management. In essence, a strong argument can be made that the most successful professional practice is one whose direction, goals, standards, and values are so clear and so reinforced by everything that goes on that people in the firm do what they are supposed to do with minimal supervision. In other words, such a firm is strongly led and minimally managed.

When the clarity of the basic parameters of a strongly led practice diminishes—in other words, when the firm is no longer as strongly led—the firm suffers to some degree. Symptoms include people working toward different overall goals, values that are not shared, disagreement as to what constitutes a suitable client and project, weakened position in the marketplace, and unstable financial performance. In this situation, the firm's doers are probably no longer as close to its leaders, because increased staff size means each person has less time with the leaders. With growth and turnover, newcomers have little sense of the firm's heritage, culture, and values. Increasing competition in the marketplace draws leaders to spend more time outside the firm than in it.

An obvious but difficult solution is to strengthen the firm's leadership. Another approach is to strengthen the firm's "followership," that is, to restaff as necessary with people who share goals and values. Both approaches make at least theoretical sense, but in practical terms the likely solution is another option: to strengthen the firm's management.

The passages that firms experience can be tracked by the primary characteristics of their most influential players at any time. Firms in the first generation of owner-

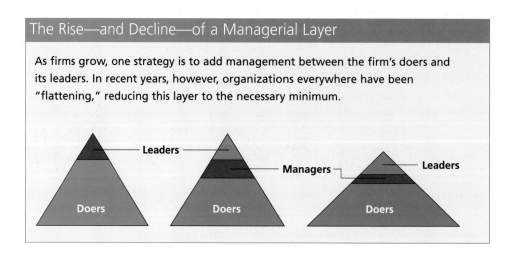

### The Rise—and Decline—of a Managerial Layer

As firms grow, one strategy is to add management between the firm's doers and its leaders. In recent years, however, organizations everywhere have been "flattening," reducing this layer to the necessary minimum.

ship are characterized by the entrepreneurial spirit of their founders, as demonstrated by their willingness to assume the risk of starting a new venture.

When new firms survive more than a few years, other characteristics are likely to have contributed: the ability to get work, serve clients, and attract, retain, and develop a capable staff. Quite noticeably, senior staff members who have grown with the firm complement rather than duplicate the major strengths of the key members of the firm who preceded them. Entrepreneurs in one generation are surrounded, and often eventually succeeded, by less entrepreneurial, more risk-averse, more technically oriented and project-oriented people. On a personal level, these individuals are strongly loyal and patient, willing to wait as long as two decades to gain an ownership position.

The balance the firm needs as this second generation assumes control typically comes from a younger, more entrepreneurial group, whose profile is not unlike that of the firm's founders. A major risk at this point in a firm's development, curiously compounded by their risk aversion and resistance to change, is that the second generation may expect those who follow them to exhibit the same loyalty that got them to ownership. The more entrepreneurial types, on the other hand, may feel that time is running out for them and that they need the opportunity to blossom sooner, in terms of both experience and age. If this need cannot be fulfilled, they may behave like the first generation and leave to found their own firms.

## OWNERSHIP TRANSITIONS

As time passes, two sets of forces are at work in most firms. First, the founding principals are aging and may be developing other interests and priorities. Second, some of the new or younger staff members are seeking to play an increasing part in the firm's leadership, management, and ownership. If maintaining the firm's continuity and keeping its best people are important, change in ownership is the most important transition of all.

Particularly since the founders of post–World War II firms began to approach retirement, transition of ownership has been a popular topic. The transfer process can be a gradual one, in which new and current owners are co-owners for a period of time. The transfer can be to insiders or outsiders; it can be for cash today or for deferred payment tomorrow.

Firm founders who anticipate a transition will likely want to develop successors in their own practice, and they would be well advised to begin developing these future buyers early. Some experienced industry professionals find that it can take five to ten years for a young architect to gain the experience to be an effective principal. They advise starting the transition process early, certainly by the time the time the founders are well into their forties. The rate of transition depends mostly on the founder's time frame to give up some responsibilities or to retire.

*Leaders* offer vision and inspiration; they are willing to state positions and take risks. *Managers* are skilled at pulling together people and systems and getting them to carry out the organization's mission.

However important its parts, a firm is a whole organism. It lives and breathes. It responds to changes in its environment, and its actions bring changes to that environment. It positions itself to accomplish its objectives. And it changes over time. The most significant idea here is that architects can design their firms and their practices to accomplish their professional and business goals.

part 2 BUSINESS

## Generational Succession

As firms grow, their leaders often hire and promote people with complementary strengths. When it is time for ownership transition, this "second generation" of leaders may find they need the complementary strengths of the next generation of staff, who often resemble the firm's founders.

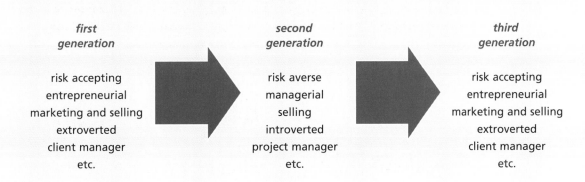

| first generation | second generation | third generation |
| --- | --- | --- |
| risk accepting | risk averse | risk accepting |
| entrepreneurial | managerial | entrepreneurial |
| marketing and selling | selling | marketing and selling |
| extroverted | introverted | extroverted |
| client manager | project manager | client manager |
| etc. | etc. | etc. |

*James R. Franklin, FAIA, Current Practices in Small Firm Management (AIA, 1990)*
*Contributed by H. Kennard Bussard, FAIA*

In this model two architecture firms form a holding company with an eye toward acquisition of additional firms by the holding company.

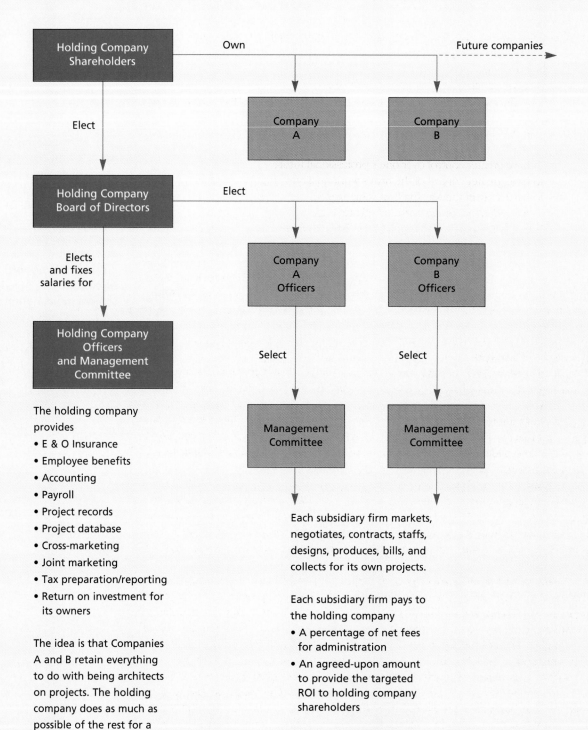

The holding company provides
- E & O Insurance
- Employee benefits
- Accounting
- Payroll
- Project records
- Project database
- Cross-marketing
- Joint marketing
- Tax preparation/reporting
- Return on investment for its owners

The idea is that Companies A and B retain everything to do with being architects on projects. The holding company does as much as possible of the rest for a profit.

Each subsidiary firm markets, negotiates, contracts, staffs, designs, produces, bills, and collects for its own projects.

Each subsidiary firm pays to the holding company
- A percentage of net fees for administration
- An agreed-upon amount to provide the targeted ROI to holding company shareholders

The idea is that Companies A and B decide on and achieve their own levels of profitability independently of each other.

Why sell? Architects have various reasons for selling their firms:

- To maintain the firm's continuity, which satisfies owners' egos and preserves client relationships
- To gain a financial return on the investment of energy, emotion, and money that has helped get the firm where it is
- To acknowledge the efforts of others toward that same result
- To induce key people to stay with the firm
- To attract new, talented people who can help with marketing, design, and sophisticated project management, or who have expertise in a particular building type
- To gain financial security during retirement
- To avoid the difficulty of closing down a multiclient, multiproject practice

Why buy? There are also various reasons for buying a firm:

- To have greater control over one's professional future
- To have greater control of the firm's work quality
- To have a say in the way the firm is managed
- To have greater clout in personal selling roles
- To gain an opportunity to expand the firm and penetrate new markets
- To acquire financial return

In theory, these two lists are not at odds, but the process of buying and selling a firm is rarely accomplished without some friction. Differences often arise about the firm's financial valuation, terms and conditions of payment, relative control of new owners vs. existing owners, and identification of prospective owners in the future. These differences can be negotiated and the details of a transition plan can be settled, but not without some hard work.

Having new partners means that an owner will have to share information and decision making with others. This can be an unsettling experience for some owners. The concept of full disclosure comes up when ownership is offered. The seller is required to give the buyer relevant information about all aspects of the business and its finances. This is a requirement that some sellers resist, and some even back out of the offer at this juncture.

Some guidelines to ease the process of ownership transition for both sellers and buyers are given below.

*Transition and positioning.* These two concepts are closely linked. A firm may be undergoing a transition because its position is changing; new approaches, new markets, and shifts in values inevitably require changes in the firm. The converse is also true: Firms undergoing transitions may find they need to reevaluate their position with respect to the markets they serve, their delivery approaches, and the values and goals of their owners.

*Mergers and acquisitions.* In an acquisition, one firm gains ownership and control of another, with the acquired firm's principals becoming employees of the acquiring firm. In a merger, two or more firms pool their combined resources and balance sheets to create a larger firm, and the owners of each become owners of the new entity. An interesting variation of the merger is the holding company, which provides an umbrella under which firms that choose to collaborate while maintaining a degree of independence—for ego, marketing, financial, or other reasons—can operate together.

There always seems to be at least a modest level of interest in the sale of firms to outsiders and in mergers of firms. The profession has seen phases in the past—often a function of Wall Street activity in the business community at large—in which design firms were bought and sold more as commodities than as professional practices. Most of these transactions have had disappointing results.

Mergers and acquisitions entered into for combined business and professional reasons have been far more successful, particularly when issues surrounding goal commonality and culture fit were adequately addressed beforehand. Mergers and acquisitions have led to noteworthy successes, often as a means toward such professionally

## Some Ownership Transition Guidelines

Every transition is different. Here are some general concepts to be considered in approaching a transition:

- Be clear about why owners are beginning the transition of ownership.
- Understand the firm's need for continuing success—and identify and develop prospective owners with this tenet in mind. As an added inducement, remember that most sales include a payout to sellers over a period of years; the firm's success during these years allows buyers to afford the purchase.
- Remember that buyers are usually short of cash, and a purchase plan with low after-tax payments can make a transfer both appealing and affordable.
- Have an ownership plan to document the rules of the game, including the structure and participation of decision making. The ownership plan can greatly enhance the relationship of new and existing owners—as long as the rules are not unilaterally changed.
- Recognize that those interested in buying the firm may not have the same approach to practice and management as those selling it. Realizing the differences in characteristics, strengths, and styles of individuals comprising the next group of owners is important to a successful transfer and the subsequent evolution of the firm.
- Clarify the expectations of buyers and sellers so that discussions and negotiations can result in commitment to a common set of objectives.
- Determine the value of the firm. Valuation can be problematic, because buyers and sellers may see the firm's value in different terms. At issue may be its accrued book value, the value of its plan files, and its goodwill value (the latter two factors are usually reflected in a multiple applied to the book value). It may be necessary to secure an outside opinion of the firm's value to facilitate the negotiation.
- Address issues of ownership and leadership separately to avoid problems during a transition of ownership.
- Buyers and sellers will want to agree on whether the divesting principals are to remain with the firm—and, if so, for how long—in order to ensure continuity, especially with clients and in marketing.
- Buyers and sellers will want to agree on how they will attribute projects done prior to the sale.
- Consider each prospective owner independently from others who might be joining ownership ranks, and then consider them collectively as well.

- Acknowledge that even in the most carefully planned ownership expansion, there may be situations in which the ownership "marriage" does not work. It is valuable to define procedures for "divorcing" owners with minimal effect on owners, staff, and clients. Emphasize creating a buy/sell agreement that establishes a process for the founders to repurchase ownership if the transition is not working. Valuation of the interest being repurchased and a schedule of repayment should be included.
- Obtain consultation and legal advice to prepare and document the ownership transition plan. This helps ensure that the legal and tax bases are covered. Using the services of someone familiar with professional firm ownership transitions provides an objective third-party view.

Valuation of architecture firms is always a subject of discussion. Valuations in internal transitions over the past decade have come closer and closer to an accrued book value or equivalent, rather than the multiple of book, averaging 1.5, that prevailed in the early to mid-1980s. The reason for the decline in value is simple: Internal buyers' ability to pay is a direct result of their share of the firm's profitability, and very few internal buyers have adequate funds and financing beyond their compensation from the firm. As profitability and consistency of financial performance have declined, so have valuations. However, different values can be placed on the firm for different buyers. The internal buyer may be offered something close to book value, but sellers need not be so generous with external buyers.

For the external sale, a better valuation method might be a multiple of earnings or discounted cash flow. Experience places the likely accrued book value, exclusive of the value of plan files and goodwill, which typically are not balance-sheet items, at about 25 percent of the annual accrued net revenue (gross revenue less pass-throughs to consultants and reimbursable expenses). Thus a firm valued at 1.0 times its accrued book value is worth 0.25 times its accrued annual net revenue. (*Warning:* Because only a very small number of architecture firms are publicly owned and traded, it is almost always inappropriate to apply ratios and to extrapolate "comparables" from such companies and apply them to privately held design firms. When such valuation techniques are employed, the resulting valuation is almost always far in excess of buyers' ability and willingness to pay.)

*Hugh Hochberg*

related goals as expanding markets, improving design and technical skills, expanding services, capitalizing on excess leadership capacity, expanding geographically, increasing capacity to take on larger or more specialized projects, and bringing in previously unavailable leadership capacity. The track record is not as good when the goals are more business-related, such as bailing out a firm in financial straits.

Regardless of the reason for selling or buying, each of the participants in an ownership transition will benefit from professional assistance. Attorneys, accountants, and management consultants can all provide valuable assistance in helping parties to the transition protect their own interests.

# 6 Marketing and Outreach

## 6.1 Marketing Planning and Strategies

### Roger L. Pickar

*A thriving architecture practice requires a steady flow of challenging projects. Marketing is a series of steps firms take to attract clients and gain the projects they need to maintain their practice.*

All firms market. They build relationships with their clients and seek a steady flow of projects in fulfillment of their practice goals. All firms engage in everyday marketing—paying attention to their clients' needs and finding ways to meet new prospects. Some also undertake carefully considered and highly focused marketing campaigns to acquire new clients and projects or to establish new services.

At the most general level, marketing activities can be grouped into four interrelated realms:

- *Marketing:* the total process of business development and developing clients, including planning, implementing, and evaluating sales support tools such as market research, public relations, and advertising
- *Public relations:* getting the firm known in support of its marketing goals
- *Sales:* the steps the firm takes to present itself and its services, to negotiate with potential clients, and to close contracts
- *Project performance:* attracting new projects from old clients by serving them well and following up on completed projects

Some architecture firms see these realms as distinct and develop specific plans, strategies, and everyday actions to build relationships, get the firm known, generate and follow up leads, and close projects. These firms may also see their project architects as part of their marketing effort, expecting them to build the working relationships and confidence intended to maintain the clients they work with. The secret to success lies in *focus* of the firm's efforts and *coordination* of the four realms.

Other firms—including most small firms—see all four realms as blending into one. They often work less formally, without careful research and written plans. They may even say they don't market at all, instead relying on one of the four realms—project performance—to bring them additional work. Despite this informality, the twin ideas of focus and coordination are just as important for these firms. Yet today more small firms

> ▶ **Before developing marketing plans and strategies, a firm should first make an assessment of its values and expertise and identify markets in which those values and expertise can be applied. See Firm Identity and Expertise (5.1)**

> ▶ **It may be helpful to think of marketing as planting and the steps in acquiring projects as harvesting. This topic addresses planting, and Seeking the Project (6.2) looks at harvesting.**

**ROGER PICKAR** *is president of I³ Intelli-Sys Info Inc. A nationally recognized lecturer and author, he concentrates on strategic market planning for design, contracting, and other professional service firms.*

> "It wasn't raining when Noah built the ark."
>
> *Howard Ruff*

understand that each of these activities is important on its own. They recognize that few firms, especially smaller ones, can afford to scatter their limited time and resources in ways that don't help the firm move forward.

For the past decade there has been increasing innovation in the area of marketing tactics. Architecture firms are dramatically increasing the sophistication of their marketing efforts by learning from other industries. Some architects are aggressively conducting direct mail programs and media advertising, as well as creating an Internet presence and participating in trade shows and conventions.

## PRINCIPLES

Some underlying principles work for most architecture firms in their search for focus and coordination.

> Over 40 percent of architecture firms use the Internet for marketing purposes. See Using the Internet in Practice (12.2) for more information on this versatile marketing tool.

*Think big picture.* What kind of firm are you, and what do you want to become? What is the added value that you offer to clients? What are your strengths, and how do you want to build on them? What kinds of clients and projects could you attract, and how can you gain access to them?

*Build relationships.* When surveyed, clients for design services talk about the need for trust. They recognize that the relationship is a professional one and that a great deal is at stake. Trustworthiness is not a product to buy and sell but rather a perception that grows over time. Firms that build long-term, mutually supportive, and beneficial relationships with their clients—both current and inactive—are in the best position to do projects for these clients. They realize that communicating with clients about what they need from the client, and what they believe the client needs from them, will go a long way toward building relationships.

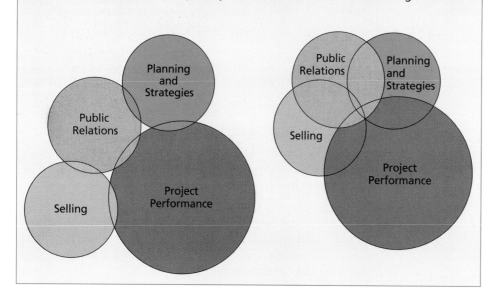

### The Four Realms of Marketing

Some architecture firms see these realms as distinct, developing plans, strategies, and tactics for each. Other firms, especially smaller ones, see them as blending into one.

Planning and Strategies

Public Relations

Selling

Project Performance

*Be there first.* Most architecture projects have an extended birthing process; they may be a gleam in the owner's eye long before they are announced projects. An architect involved early in the project formulation and definition process can be of real help to the client by offering key information and guidance. Building long-term relationships, of course, is the key to being there first. However, while being first is important, being qualified and experienced can often be just as important.

*Deliver more than you promise.* For most firms, this is added value. For some, it is outstanding design, and for others, it is exceptionally productive delivery of services. Whatever the firm offers, remember that service is now a commodity—providing it well and with full awareness of what the client is seeking is a key to getting repeat work.

> The largest single source of work for architectural firms comes from existing clients. In 1999 work acquired through noncompetitive selection accounted for 46 percent of all work done by firms.
>
> *AIA Firm Survey 2000*

Architecture firms implement these principles in a variety of ways. Some firms find they need not invest a great deal of obvious effort in marketing. They have an established base of repeat clients who are well satisfied with the firm and the added value of its services; they have competitors, but their markets are stable or growing. These firms *have* built relationships and *are* there first; clearly they have the trust of their clients. They enjoy the luxury of being able to react to project opportunities and possibilities as they arise. Yet it is a mistake for them to be lulled into complacency. All firms need to invest in new business development on a regular basis. Someone in the firm should be continually marketing, looking for projects three to four years in the future.

Most owners are not building all the time, and firms require a flow of new clients and projects. Most markets are highly competitive, and few are stable for long periods of time. Thus most architecture firms find themselves in a position of competing for clients and projects.

Competition is a complex phenomenon—one that architects approach in different ways. Some firms internalize it, competing with their own past experience to provide excellent design, service, or delivery of professional services. Others select a target—perhaps the best firm in the region—as their standard. Most, to some degree, orient themselves to the marketplace, recognizing that their competitors are other firms offering similar services to the same clients they wish to attract. These competitors can be engineers, interior designers, or consulting firms.

## Proactive Marketing

Whatever approach they may take, most firms find they need to be *proactive* in their competitive quest. That is, they must invest time and effort to reach the clients that can help take them where they want to go. In highly competitive markets this means reaching clients early in their decision-making process—at the "think phase"—and gaining their trust before formal architect selection occurs. A design firm marketing in this way seeks to provide data and insights about design issues of particular concern to its prospective clients. Accompanying this with information about the firm can provide a foot in the door. Following up the initial contact by continuing to make such information available develops the potential client's trust and increases the likelihood of bringing a project to contract.

Even proactive marketers find themselves reacting to unplanned project possibilities that arrive on the doorstep. They may decide to respond to a published request for qualifications from an unknown client. They may find that, despite their best efforts, they need to make cold calls to prospects they don't know in order to find projects. The point, however, is that proactive firms don't rely *only* on reactive marketing and its many uncertainties.

Firms that do rely on reactive marketing (responses to client-generated project announcements) may find themselves in difficulties on two fronts:

• They may operate more from a *sales* outlook than a *marketing* one. They become involved late in the prospective client's decision-making process, when the competition is greater. They depend on reacting to (often untargeted) leads, screening them, bringing in the team, and eventually bringing some prospects to contract. Their success depends almost totally on the ability of their principals—or marketing specialist—to identify, screen, and sell to large numbers of prospects.

• They may place themselves and their technical expertise at the center of their sales efforts. Because they spend so much time reacting to possibilities and selling their qualifications, these qualifications become central. In this situation, firms can lose touch with their markets—who the clients are, how *they* are expressing *their* needs, and what they want to hear from design firms.

Marketing in a negotiated environment takes time and interaction. The earlier an architecture firm can identify a prospect, the more time there is to demonstrate the elements of trustworthiness: dependability, honesty, integrity, consistency, and expertise. The stages involved in proactive marketing are

• Understanding and agreeing on the firm's goals and strengths
• Focusing on the markets and clients most likely to help the firm build its practice
• Researching these markets, identifying trends, generating leads, and networking to identify and screen prospects and their needs and attitudes

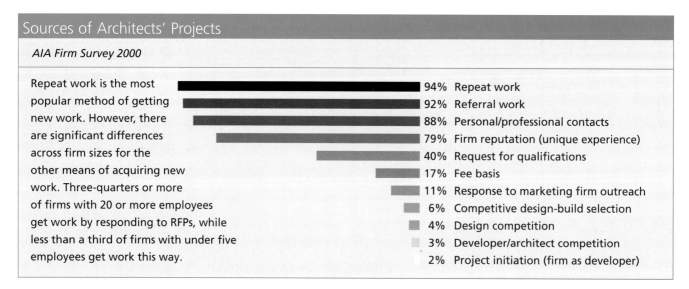

Repeat work is the most popular method of getting new work. However, there are significant differences across firm sizes for the other means of acquiring new work. Three-quarters or more of firms with 20 or more employees get work by responding to RFPs, while less than a third of firms with under five employees get work this way.

| | |
|---|---|
| 94% | Repeat work |
| 92% | Referral work |
| 88% | Personal/professional contacts |
| 79% | Firm reputation (unique experience) |
| 40% | Request for qualifications |
| 17% | Fee basis |
| 11% | Response to marketing firm outreach |
| 6% | Competitive design-build selection |
| 4% | Design competition |
| 3% | Developer/architect competition |
| 2% | Project initiation (firm as developer) |

- Determining what these prospects are seeking, developing promotional materials, and tailoring presentations accordingly
- Closing contracts through the development of trust and the establishment of a relationship as a competent provider of industry information

## Cross Selling

Cross-selling design expertise from one division of a firm to existing clients of another division can be effective, but there are hidden pitfalls. The design discipline is the real issue: It can be a problem when the landscape group markets architecture services to one of its clients. The reverse is true as well. The inherent danger is the client's expectation of the level of service it has received (and will continue to receive) from the firm. If a new project is more complex, it can require much more design time than anticipated by either client or architect, and it could ultimately cost too much for the client and not be profitable for the firm. Yet in today's market cross selling is becoming more common, particularly in mid- to large-size firms, which see an opportunity to build on the goodwill and good relationships the firm already has with its customers. But there is a learning curve for all new types of work—gaining new expertise demands time and dedication before you seek new project types.

## PLANNING

Some firms take the narrow view that marketing involves only calls on new prospects and old clients; contacts with unfocused networks of people who provide leads; and preparation and distribution of brochures, letters, and qualification statements. Although these are all part of the process, a marketing program is usually more effective if it includes a more comprehensive and less risky set of actions that are focused by the first step of the process—marketing planning.

Simply put, marketing planning is a series of steps that allows the firm to target particular markets and decision makers. It attempts to provide a means of addressing these markets better than the competition. A marketing plan answers these questions:

- Who are we?
- What and where do we want to be in the future?
- What rate of growth or profitability should we aim for?
- Which markets and potential clients should we target?
- Who are our competitors for those clients and how do we compare with them?
- What are the major strategies we could use to address these opportunities?
- How can we best implement our selected strategies?
- How can we sell to and close the targeted prospects?

- How can we best serve our clients?
- How are we doing, and can we do even better?

Marketing planning is a step-by-step process that charts the marketing course for the firm based on present and future, internal and external conditions. It begins with general firm planning and positioning; defines marketing goals, strategies, and tactics; and produces a flexible plan that specifically sets out what needs to be done over an interval ranging from several months to several years.

A key to success is participation by the firm's leaders and the staff who will implement the marketing plan. Because the firm's leadership develops the vision and sets the tone, one of the partners or the president should be involved in the planning process. In a larger firm, a marketing-oriented principal (in some cases an associate) may chair the overall effort, but the firm's leadership must buy in.

The next step is to select other participants. Where there are choices, the firm's leadership will want to consider factors such as these:

- *Motivation and involvement.* Because the staff involved in marketing will help move the firm into the future, it is important to have them identify with and participate in the planning process. This personal involvement creates a commitment to the plan.
- *Capabilities.* Those responsible for developing and carrying out the plan must be capable of actually doing so.
- *Resource knowledge.* The planners should know which resources—the time, money, and other commitments needed to implement a marketing plan—can and cannot be made available.

Marketing planning can offer significant benefits to a design firm. To be successful, though, it must overcome some obstacles:

- It takes time to develop and implement a plan.
- It takes discipline to move forward constantly, especially in areas of limited familiarity.
- It requires ongoing evaluation, which takes considerable objectivity.
- It sometimes appears restrictive, causing a firm to lose what might appear to be opportunities.
- It breaks the comfortable old pattern of reacting intuitively to new situations.

Financial Planning (7.2) illustrates how projections from the marketing plan factor into the firm's financial planning.

## *Proactive and Reactive Marketing*

### Proactive Marketing

*Advantages*
- Allows the firm to take a longer-term view of opportunities in the market
- Helps the firm penetrate its market by identifying potential clients earlier
- Allows the firm to establish its uniqueness
- Helps sell projects because the firm has a sense of the prospective client's potential problems
- Establishes a framework that allows a greater cross section of the firm to participate in marketing
- Helps focus the selection on quality and diminish the importance of price

*Disadvantages*
- Takes time and money to develop and implement; this may be substantial
- Takes discipline, commitment, and support from the firm's leaders
- Requires a considerable amount of research to understand each market
- Extends the time between initial contact and close of sale
- Requires extra effort on the first projects in a new market because of the firm's lack of experience in that market
- Does not guarantee success; despite considerable invested time, some projects will still not come to fruition

### Reactive Marketing

*Advantages*
- Requires little change or investment
- Keeps overhead expenses down, allowing maximum chargeable time to projects
- May enhance profitability—as long as there is a lot of work in the marketplace
- Works fast
- Feels simple and comfortable; no habits have to be broken
- Reduces the risk of investing time and money in a project that doesn't go

*Disadvantages*
- Requires the firm to react to the marketplace; the firm is not in touch with the long-term needs or problems of the market
- Places the firm at the mercy of the short- and intermediate-term ups and downs in the market
- Focuses time on clients and projects that may be too small (or too large), too competitive, or outside the firm's real capabilities
- May increase the number of estimates, presentations, and sales calls involved
- Sometimes makes it necessary to take any project that is available

## Steps in Marketing Planning

You may already have accomplished the first four or five steps in this process through an overall strategic planning effort.

1. *Determine the firm's mission.* The mission or purpose statement reflects why your firm is in business, gives basic guidelines for further planning, and establishes broad parameters for the future.

2. *Set company goals.* Goals define the overall results your firm wants to achieve. They guide the marketing plan and the strategies needed to implement it.

3. *Perform external analysis.* An external analysis examines trends in the marketplace: hot vs. cold markets, the local economic outlook, market types, available financing, and market needs.

4. *Perform internal analysis.* An internal analysis looks at your firm's strengths and weaknesses—what needs changing and what needs marketing emphasis. It is a good idea to include a client view of your firm's performance.

5. *Establish marketing goals.* Marketing goals should reflect what your firm thinks it can accomplish through marketing in the coming years—for example, the amount of new business vs. old, job and client profiles, and promotional and sales goals.

6. *Generate strategies to accomplish these goals.* Strategies are specific activities that can achieve stated marketing goals over the next two to three years. They range from pursuing a new type of client to expanding an existing market geographically or even adding or changing a specialty.

7. *Research and refine strategies.* It is important to focus as much as possible, selecting only those strategies that will make it possible to reach your goals.

8. *Create and refine promotional and sales tactics.* Tactics are short-term, immediate, planned actions undertaken to implement strategies. Tactics are specific reactions to research. Limit tactics to those necessary to accomplish marketing goals.

9. *Implement the plan.* Once the plan is put into action, good coordination and record keeping are critical to its success.

10. *Evaluate the plan in action.* Finally, the entire marketing planning process must be continuously evaluated and updated. Conduct regular evaluations of your efforts to achieve your marketing goals, studying both successes and problems.

# RESEARCH AND MARKETING GOALS

With the firm's mission in hand—that is, what the owners see as the reason their firm is in business—the next step is to analyze its situation and set marketing goals that will enable it to increase business in the markets that best match its interests and abilities.

A critical internal analysis of a firm's position in the market, strengths and weaknesses, and mission creates the foundation for the remainder of the marketing plan. It tells the firm what it has to work with and what it should beware of. Situation analysis includes both internal analysis and external analysis, which seeks to understand the competition, the market trends the company is facing, and where the emerging, declining, and steady needs are in the marketplace.

It is valuable to get an objective view of the firm from both its staff and its clients. Internal analysis may be approached in three stages: a client survey, a parallel evaluation by the firm and its staff, and a careful evaluation of the firm's projects, sales approaches, marketing, and profitability, including comparison of these to mission and goals.

External analysis step includes looking at trends in the marketplace—needs, sudden downturns, growth potential—and what the competition is doing or might do. Considering these two factors in combination with the firm's strengths and weaknesses should provide a solid base from which to make sound decisions about strategy and direction.

The following steps are commonly involved in external analysis:

- Determine the objectives of the analysis, especially the markets the firm is interested in addressing.
- Learn about these markets, including their extent, areas of growth, and how long the growth will last. Look beyond the immediate future: Where is a market heading? What do those who know something about the market believe its next evolutionary step or stage will be?
- Develop a network of people who understand the market and could provide more in-depth information when needed.
- If you find a trend or direction described by the experts, confirm it with other sources.
- Compile a list of who decides which design firm to hire, and identify the specific needs and concerns of those decision makers.

A sound marketing plan includes an assessment of your competitors in the same way you assess your own firm: What are their goals, strengths, and weaknesses? Where have they been most successful? A determination of the effects of old and new competition and of what these firms do well will affect your decision to push into a particular marketplace. Here are some ideas to consider:

- Include major current competitors as well as those who are likely to become competitors in the future.
- Explore competitors' internal weaknesses and determine whether particular markets and strategies make sense for you in light of these weaknesses.
- Ascertain what you must do to strengthen your firm so it will be an effective competitor.

Marketing goals help define which targets make sense. They answer questions of how much promotion, research, and sales the firm should engage in and what results should be expected. If, for example, the overall goal is to enter a new market, the marketing goals spell out which market and set specific targets for the level of penetration to be achieved. Viable marketing goals recognize the limitations of the firm's resources and the expectations of its principals. Goals can always be modified later, once more in-depth research and experience are added to the information gathered in the situation analysis.

Marketing goals can be broken down into three categories: research, public relations, and sales. Avoid laundry lists of goals, and limit the firm to a few achievable ones. It's better to add a new goal later than not to achieve any of those on the initial list. As with overall firm goals, effective marketing goals should be

- Motivational, achievable, and challenging
- Specific, well-thought-out ideas, rather than hopes
- Expressed clearly, so they can be understood by non-marketing people
- Limited in scope

## MARKETING STRATEGIES AND TACTICS

Marketing strategies can be defined as the planned use of the firm's resources to achieve its goals. Because marketing strategies determine where the firm will be in the short and long term, they often serve as the base for its operational, financial, and administrative strategies and plans.

The objective in selecting marketing strategies is to choose those the firm needs to achieve its goals, including profitability. Look at all the possibilities and then develop those with the best potential for achieving the stated marketing goals. Operating with too many choices dilutes resources and makes it harder to achieve any of the goals.

In descending order, it is generally easier to market

- Existing services to existing clients
- New services to existing clients
- Existing services to new clients
- New services to new clients

For a firm inexperienced in marketing, it is probably best to begin with a marketing program designed to bring more business into the firm's profitable core services. The goal is to get more business from new or existing clients without altering the service being offered. This approach is an obvious choice when your firm's marketing effort has not been competitive in the marketplace.

Moving beyond an improved marketing program suggests strategies such as

- Solidifying your client base
- Expanding your office geographically
- Introducing add-on services
- Adopting an innovation
- Introducing lead-in services
- Acquiring new project and client types
- Expanding your services geographically

---

### Goals, Strategies, and Tactics

Marketing planning, and planning in general, suggests that firms define goals, strategies, and tactics. Here are some brief definitions and examples.

*A goal is an end, a measurable state to be achieved within a specified time frame.* A sample marketing goal is

- "To increase our firm's revenues from private colleges and universities by 20 percent within three years."

*A strategy is a means by which a firm seeks to achieve one or more of its goals.* A sample strategy to achieve the sample goal is

- "To expand the services we offer existing university clients to include facilities management and project definition."

*A tactic is a specific short-term action aimed at implementing one or more of the firm's strategies.* Two sample tactics the firm might select to implement the sample strategy are

- "To develop a 'white paper' describing the benefits of postoccupancy evaluation projects. Obtain and publish testimonials from some of our past clients about what they have gained from these services."
- "To become active in newly formed educational facilities users group in our region: attend meetings, join our clients in offering tours of recently completed facilities, place this group on our newsletter mailing list."

However you define your goals, strategies, and tactics, avoid meaningless generalizations such as these:
"Our policy will be to lead the competition."
"We will offer a better product."
"We will get our image into the public eye."
"Our plan will increase sales."
"We are aiming to penetrate the high-class market."
"Our plan is to satisfy the client.

---

Seeking the Project (6.2) outlines tactics for acquiring specific projects.

## Some Marketing Strategies

### 1. Solidifying Your Existing Client Base

*When.* This is a conservative strategy that usually requires less marketing effort than other strategies. Based on existing profitable relationships, it is useful when your firm seeks increases in revenue and profitability with a minimum investment of marketing resources.

*Rationale.* Solidification is a comparatively simple strategy used to get more work without extending the base of clients. It is usually employed when

- Your existing base of clients is substantial.
- Client satisfaction is high.
- Your quality of work is not in danger of diminishing if more projects are added.
- Research shows your existing clients would be amenable to giving more work to your firm.

*Cautions.* Solidification can be a risky strategy if it means putting all your firm's eggs in a few baskets for an extended period. It can also make a small firm vulnerable to the demands of a single client. Although this strategy is appealing because little new business development is needed, the lack of effort required can lull you into a false sense of security that may make efforts to develop new business.

### 2. Introducing Add-on Services

*When.* An add-on service strategy can be launched to increase profitability and to maintain existing clients who might switch loyalties if your firm is slow or unimaginative in serving their needs. Add-ons can also be used to capture new clients who are frustrated with other firms that do not offer the service. One add-on service that should not be ignored is design-build.

*Rationale.* Instituting an add-on service makes sense when some of these conditions apply:

- The add-ons will solidify your existing client base.
- Client research has indicated a need or desire to see the add-on service or product, reducing the risk of failure.
- The firm has the expertise to offer the service.
- Your competition already provides the service and could significantly erode your client base if you do not.

*Cautions.* Make sure the add-on matches what clients need or have requested, and be sure that the quality of your service does not disappoint.

### 3. Introducing Lead-in Services

*When.* A lead-in service strategy can be introduced when you want to bring more business to your firm's profitable core services. It is used to preempt the competition by getting to the client first.

*Rationale.* Consider a lead-in service when some of these conditions apply:

- It will generate profitable clients without significantly altering the basic services you are offering.
- Existing services are profitable and more clients are wanted.
- The service can generate a significant amount of trust.
- A clear connection exists between the lead-in service and the follow-up core service.

*Cautions.* Initiating a lead-in service normally requires significant planning if you have not offered it before and it lies outside your existing capabilities. To serve its purpose, the service must be of obviously high caliber—and priced flexibly to accommodate different clients' expectations. You may need to add staff or other resources to build your capability.

### 4. Expanding Your Services Geographically

*When.* This strategy can be employed when your service is of such high quality or otherwise special enough to attract distant clients to buy expertise they feel is not available locally. But it is effective only when your firm truly has expertise not really available in the market you seek to penetrate.

*Rationale.* This approach to expansion works best under the following conditions:

- Your firm has a base of experience consistently deeper than that of potential competitors.
- It is clear to clients that they need your deeper expertise.
- A clear, broad need for this service exists in another geographic area.
- Your firm recognizes that it could implement a long-distance, narrowly defined market attack.

*Cautions.* Your firm must establish its ability and track record in servicing long-distance clients, particularly the willingness of key staff to travel to project sites. To offset the cost of long-distance selling, your marketing support functions for research/lead generation and public relations must be especially strong.

## 5. Expanding Your Offices Geographically

*When.* Consider geographic expansion when the potential for growth in your current market is limited by the following factors:

- The need for your particular services has leveled off.
- Your present location has seen an increase in competition beyond the market's growth rate.
- There is potential for a long-term downturn in the existing market.
- The local economy has proved too cyclical or too dependent on a limited market base.

Other reasons for choosing geographic expansion could be a client's demand for a local office (sustained by your projection of substantial additional work in that market) or the presence on your staff of managers with strong skills who want an opportunity for personal growth in a more independent atmosphere.

*Rationale.* Geographic expansion can be effective in the following situations:

- A long-term need for specialty experience in the design service you want to offer has been documented in the new area.
- Your firm has a unique depth of expertise in the services to be offered or a competitively superior commitment to service, quality, or pricing.
- The new market offers insurance against a downturn in a current situation. Occasionally, geographic expansion is undertaken in a defensive posture to prevent a strong local or national competitor from gaining a regional foothold.
- You are comfortable using techniques for attacking a marketplace as the "new kid on the block."

*Cautions.* To be successful in the new arena, your firm must offer a level of service and quality that is competitive or better and that can offer better added value. Offering services that local firms already provide will drain your resources while you search for a niche. Before you begin your expansion, research and identify the special needs and concerns of the market and match them to your firm's experience, strengths, and resources. Compare the costs and benefits of setting up a new office with those of serving clients from an established office, and determine the source of the recognized added value.

## 6. Adopting an Innovation

*When.* This strategy is advantageous when it offers the existing market a benefit that prospective clients clearly rec-

ognize in terms of value, price, speed, time, and longevity. The innovation must be powerful enough to motivate most potential clients to choose your firm.

*Rationale.* Innovations are best when:

- The market has confirmed the need for the innovation or its result.
- The innovation itself offers a means of reaching the firm's stated goals.
- The image and direct benefit created by the innovation reduce your prospects' sensitivity to price.

*Cautions.* An innovation is most effective as a marketing tool when your firm's proprietary interest in it can be maintained and the competition cannot readily copy or improve on it. Research your proposed innovation to determine whether you can clearly demonstrate its direct benefits to the buyer. Make sure you can easily produce it to meet market demand.

A decision to market a technological innovation works best if the change fits within the normal scope of your firm's services and reinforces existing markets without forcing you into new ones. Marketing new products and services to *new* markets creates not one but two stresses.

## 7. Acquiring New Project or Client Types

*When.* Searching for new client types (and, inevitably, new project types) is important if your existing client base is being competitively attacked, is saturated, or offers little promise for growth. New client types, the nature of the services they require, and their approaches to selecting and working with architecture firms may require significant changes in your services, capabilities, attitudes, and procedures.

*Rationale.* Adopting a new client type works best under the following conditions:

- You must expand or shift your efforts away from existing client and project types.
- Research proves that the new client type exhibits a significant need for the services you offer.

*Cautions.* This strategy may require a new kind of client relationship. Rarely can you do too much market research when trying to understand these new clients' attitudes. For this strategy to be successful, there must be a clearly perceived improvement in service, quality, or price to motivate clients to switch their loyalties to a new firm. Attacking the new market without testing the premise of unique benefits is a common mistake.

Each of these strategies offers potential gains to, and also requires something from, the firm. Each works best in certain situations and, as might be expected, produces risks that should be carefully assessed before moving ahead. Some of these strategies can produce growth for a firm that is seeking to grow; however, in a competitive marketplace it may be necessary to employ one or more of these strategies simply to stay even.

Another strategy is a more generic market attack—such as speedy project delivery—to address a variety of clients and markets. The assumption made in choosing this broad-brush approach is that the firm can create a perception of value that will be clearly and quickly understood in many markets. From the marketing perspective, this strategy is rarely applicable and particularly difficult to implement.

Tactics are short-term actions aimed at achieving long-term strategies. Depending on the specific strategies selected, tactics might include the following:

- Research projects and other activities that generate information and guidance that can be shared with current and prospective clients
- Public relations activities, including newsletters, brochures, news releases, advertising, and other media outreach
- Civic events, parties, or open houses organized at completed projects and other efforts focusing attention on the firm and its contributions
- Newsletters, bulletins, holiday cards, and other approaches to keeping in touch
- A lead-swapping network including key advisors (banker, realtor, insurance broker, accountant), consultants, contractors, and others
- A variety of other activities focused on acquiring specific clients and projects within the overall parameters set by the marketing plan and strategies

▶ **Public Service and Community Involvement (6.3) covers various opportunities for architects to apply their knowledge and skills in the public arena.**

## IMPLEMENTATION AND EVALUATION

With marketing goals, strategies, and tactics in hand, it is time to put all this work to the test.

***Responsibilities.*** Someone must direct the overall marketing effort and have final responsibility for ensuring that the whole firm participates in it responsibly. The assignment of responsibility depends on the size of the firm. In a small firm, the leaders are also the doers; a commitment by the leadership is a commitment to the doing.

In larger firms, leaders and doers may be distinct groups. There may be a marketing manager and a designated marketing staff. Marketing may be coordinated by a marketing committee composed of the participating principals, any marketing-oriented or business development associates, and key support staff. This committee can be responsible for directing the effort and getting results.

Implementing the marketing plan may be easier if all staff members understand the changes being made and know what their roles will be. Commitment and perseverance on the part of the firm's people, combined with a good system for monitoring results, will help a program succeed.

***Costs.*** The costs of marketing depend on how aggressively the firm seeks to develop new business. Few firms can prosper in the long term only by reacting to opportunities presented to them. Most find that they must consistently commit time and other resources to marketing, public relations, and sales to optimize their profits and opportunities. A firm that places itself in an aggressive mode, looking for significant growth and new clients each year, may need to commit extraordinary funds—perhaps up to 15 percent of its gross revenues—to marketing.

*Evaluation.* To function best, marketing strategies and tactics require constant evaluation. Some activities may be reviewed and assessed weekly, others monthly or quarterly. The plan itself should be reviewed periodically, perhaps quarterly. Each review should ask some fundamental questions about the effectiveness of marketing research, marketing strategies and tactics, sales and promotion efforts, and customer service. This vigilance allows the firm to get the most out of its plan by updating it to meet new circumstances as they arise.

### For More Information

The material in this topic is based on the author's perspective as a marketing researcher. Further detailed treatment as well as case studies for specific strategies is offered in the author's *Marketing Design Firms in the 1990s*, 1991.

Weld Coxe, Hon. AIA, *Marketing Architectural and Engineering Services,*

> ▶ **In 1999 AIA member-owned firms spent on average 7.5 percent of their total expenses for marketing purposes.**
> *AIA Firm Survey 2000*

---

## Sample Marketing Responsibilities

*Marketing Committee*
- Review goals (quarterly)
- Analyze all marketing efforts (monthly)
- Meet to consider operational issues and to monitor, evaluate, and develop the follow-up of day-to-day marketing efforts (biweekly)

*Principals*
- Lead in establishing marketing goals and motivating the firm's marketing effort
- Serve on the long-term marketing planning committee
- Recruit, train, organize, and motivate personnel involved in marketing and sales
- Help key staff refine their daily routines
- Recommend pricing policy for major contracts
- Close deals when a prospect is ready to make a decision
- Establish policies and controls that maintain total marketing expenses at satisfactory ratios
- Represent the firm in public relations ventures

*Sales Teams, Including Project Architects*
- Participate in the development of new contact forecasts, profit plans, and pertinent budgets
- Develop specific sales plans for key prospects
- Develop new project opportunities by contacting prospects, presenting the firm's capabilities, providing useful information that will establish the trustworthiness of the firm, answering inquiries, and bringing prospects to contract
- Coordinate client relations
- Maintain contact with past clients and follow up with those recently acquired

*Marketing Director*
- Supervise all of the firm's marketing efforts, except closing
- Direct the marketing committee
- Concentrate and develop the firm's sales management skills

- Identify and define sales opportunities
- Establish sales projections and ensure an orderly flow of sales to meet them
- Follow up on all jobs done to thank clients and ascertain their next work prospects (may be assigned to principals or project architects)
- Maintain regular contact with all major clients to determine if they are satisfied with the firm or, if not, what changes need to be made
- Maintain all documents and files pertaining to client contracts and sales statistics
- Collect data for market and competition analysis, comparative sales analysis, and forecasting
- Monitor all targeted trade associations, their seminars, periodicals, etc.
- Identify new markets, products, services, and opportunities and prepare definitive strategic plans to attack them, including sales (new market capture) and profit projections
- Define and do market research studies to identify new projects and clients
- Develop promotional literature and programs to support the sales effort, including advertising, trade shows, brochures, newsletters, etc.
- Supervise any marketing staff members who perform or help to perform any of the above tasks

*Marketing Support Staff*
- Maintain marketing files and sales reminder systems that centralize information about prospects, current clients, and past clients
- Maintain slide and photograph files of the firm's work
- Undertake market research/lead generation
- Assist with writing and coordinating proposals
- Help create public relations materials
- Maintain good relationships with the press

## MARKETING PROGRAM EVALUATION

*Roger L. Pickar,* Marketing for Design Firms in the 1990s, *(1991)*

Periodically, perhaps quarterly, you will want to evaluate your entire marketing program. Ask these questions about marketing information and research.

- Are there any indicators of change that would seriously affect the strategies we have chosen?
- Have we received enough information to make decisions about altering our strategies and tactics?
- Do we know whether our competitors are making significant changes in their approaches to our clients?
- Has our image changed with our clients?
- Do we know our potential clients' earliest decision-making points?
- Do our potential clients understand why we are special?
- Have we analyzed why we lost jobs in order to avoid similar situations in the future?

Ask these questions about strategies and tactics.

- Is this strategy or tactic precise, well communicated, and understood?
- Is this strategy or tactic based on evidence of the competition's strengths and weaknesses? Do we have a program to overcome the former and exploit the latter?

Ask these questions about promotion.

- Are our solutions and the information we share relevant to the client's needs?
- Do the letters and other communication tools we use reflect the best of what we are?
- Have we, in our approach, differentiated ourselves from our competitors?
- Are we perceived as the expert by clients and prospects?
- Are we applying enough resources to accomplish our task?
- Are there situations in which we could reduce our investments by focusing our efforts better?
- Are we wasting resources on nonessential image building when we could be more effective by targeting fewer clients and pouring more money into the effort of landing them?

Ask these questions about your sales effort.

- Are we making enough sales calls to reach our goal?
- How many sales calls are we making per potential client, and can we be more efficient?
- Is there any way to reduce the labor intensity of making sales calls to potential clients?
- Are we listening to the needs our clients express? Are these needs changing?
- Do our sales techniques reflect the type of client we are trying to close?
- Are we selling solutions or are we reactively selling ourselves?
- Do we know why we are winning—and losing—projects?

Finally, to check the effectiveness of your customer service, ask this question every quarter.

- Are our clients satisfied, and to what degree?

2d ed., 1990, remains a classic. Other books on basic marketing strategies along with tips for implementing the strategies include Dick Connor and Jeff Davidson, *Getting New Clients,* 1993; Rodney D. Stewart and Ann L. Stewart, *Proposal Preparation,* 2d ed., 1992; and David G. Cooper, *Finding and Signing Profitable Contracts: A Guide for Architects, Engineers and Contractors,* 1993.

Parts of more broad-based works—applicable to any professional design service firm—offer practical advice on many aspects of marketing. These include part three of David Maister's *True Professionalism,* 1997, and Barbara Geraghty's *Visionary Selling,* 1998. Two other important works are Harry Beckwith's *Selling the Invisible,* 1997, and Harvey Mackay's *Dig Your Well Before You're Thirsty,* 1997.

Firms can stay up to date by participating in marketing-related sessions at AIA meetings, seminars, and annual conventions. Visit www.aia.org for current announcements. Another source of information is the Society for Marketing Professional Services (SMPS), an organization dedicated to marketing professionals. For programs, events, and publications offered, call SMPS at (703) 549-6117 or visit www.smps.org.

# 6.2 Seeking the Project

## Howard J. Wolff

*More than one well-known architect has said the first job is to get the job. In a world of sophisticated owners and many qualified architecture firms, getting the job can be a challenge.*

More than an activity, seeking the project—sales—is a managed process. Typically, the selling process includes the following ten stages:

- Finding leads
- Screening prospects
- Making the go/no-go decision
- Expressing interest
- Developing strategy
- Courting prospects
- Writing proposals
- Making presentations
- Closing
- Debriefing

The ten stages are not necessarily linear; thus, they may not happen in the order listed. Courting may have begun months or even years earlier and will likely continue through all of the steps listed. Some clients don't require the submission of detailed qualifications until proposals for services are made. When a firm has a long-standing relationship with a client, the activities listed may happen all at once, in a single meeting or in a phone call confirming the architect's selection.

## FINDING LEADS

Sources of leads are all around you. The easiest and cheapest sources of leads—and often the most fruitful—are your current and recent clients. They know you, they know your firm, and they know your capabilities. Don't be afraid to ask these questions: "What else do you have coming up that we can help with?" "Who else should I be talking to?" "May I use you as a reference?"

These questions are an opportunity to think beyond a narrow definition of architectural services. As you discover a client's needs, think of yourself as a consultant who can help solve problems. By reframing how you view your business, you expand the ways you can help your client. For instance, architects can offer a range of expanded services, which might include facilities management, Americans with Disabilities Act assessments, site analyses, training of clients' staffs, and development consulting. Architects can also help clients make the business connections needed to expedite a project.

The other benefit of directly asking your clients about their needs is that the leads generated are usually yours and yours alone. You don't have dozens of competitors privy to the same information (as you have with leads you glean from publications, for instance).

You can also generate leads through your market research, public relations,

> **Here's a handy short list of lead sources:**
>
> **Attorneys**
> **Bankers**
> ***Commerce Business Daily***
> **Community service clubs**
> **Consultants**
> **Contractors**
> **Employees**
> **Existing clients**
> **Friends**
> **Lead-finding services**
> **Lead-swapping networks**
> **News media**
> **Other architects**
> **Past clients**
> **Realtors**
> **Receptionists**
> **Religious institutions**
> **Secretaries**
> **Services**
> **Trade associations**
> **Trade publications**
> **Vendors**

HOWARD J. WOLFF *is vice president and worldwide director of marketing for Wimberly Allison Tong & Goo, an international architecture, planning, design, and consulting practice with offices in Honolulu, Newport Beach, London, and Singapore. He is a frequent speaker and author on the subject of selling design services.*

and networking activities. For example, a large local company is reorganizing: Might there be a need for facilities studies? Your greatest success will come from those situations in which you can cultivate leads before others are alerted to the opportunity.

## SCREENING PROSPECTS

> **Risk Management Strategies (11.1) suggests that careful screening of prospective clients is a good risk management strategy, too.**

After uncovering a lead, the next step is to assess its viability. The objective at this stage is simply to screen the leads by determining the answer to two questions: "Is this a real project with a real client?" and "Is it right for us?" (For example, "How do the client and the project fit our marketingstrategy?")

If the answer to either question is no, move on to something more promising. (To help build your network, you might want to pass the lead along to a noncompeting firm.) If the answer to both is yes, you still need to decide whether or not to proceed. An interesting sidelight: If you adopt the approach of pursuing clients rather than projects, you may turn down (or be turned down for) a particular job but go on to have a long-term, fruitful relationship with that individual, organization, or institution.

Increasingly, the best and fastest way to conduct research on a prospective client is via the Internet. Often you can assess the individual's or company's home page as well as relevant citations that have appeared in news stories.

## MAKING THE GO/NO-GO DECISION

Saying yes is easy. Most architects, however, find it very difficult to "just say no," to decline an opportunity to submit a proposal—especially when a lead falls in their lap or they are asked out of the blue to submit a proposal.

As tough as it may be, saying no to certain opportunities is critical to staying focused and growing your firm. Pursuing work that does not meet the criteria defined in your marketing strategy can consume the time, money, and energy needed to obtain projects more suited to your goals.

Repeatedly pursuing projects for which your chances are slim—and continually losing them—can have a devastating effect on morale, not to mention the bottom line. Simply submitting proposals to the same client (this is particularly tempting with government clients) in the hopes that eventually it will be your turn won't work if you're not the right firm for the job. The right strategy is to clearly define your target and give it your very best shot.

Some firms make go/no-go decisions on the basis of gut instinct; others find it help-

*James R. Franklin, AIA,* Current Practices in Small Firm Management *(1990)*

**SHOTGUN**

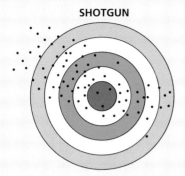

**RIFLE**

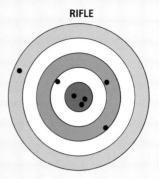

| |
|---|

• Requires a lot of resources over time to be successful

• Lets the market (and luck) control your destiny

• Can tempt you to undertake projects outside your area of competence

• Can lower your hit rate and eventually your self-esteem and credibility

• Requires tremendous energy and time

• Keeps your firm from ending up in "market niches" that may dry up

• May be the only choice in markets limited politically or demographically

• Is frequently the essential strategy for starting a practice

• Lets you act on the market—not just react

• Lets you build a body of work and a level of expertise in project types you are good at

• Encourages you to build relationships with clients and to manage projects in ways that keep your existing clients

• Allows better ability to size up and accept or reject clients

• When you lose, it hurts more

• Works against expanding your market—can lead to problems of unintended specialization

• May result in missed opportunities

• Requires a lot of nerve and will power

ful to develop a checklist of criteria with weighted numerical values assigned to each factor. You may want to design such a form for your firm to aid in the process of making decisions, while acknowledging that many of your responses will still be based on gut instinct.

A final go/no-go question revolves around the probable costs of pursuing the project. Substantial outlays may be necessary for principal time, team meetings, travel expenses, proposal writing, special printing, and graphics. If your firm is short-listed, there are the costs of preparing for and carrying out the interview as well as the ongoing commitment to continuous courting.

## EXPRESSING INTEREST

After you have decided to pursue a particular prospect, it's generally necessary to introduce your firm. Send enough information describing your capabilities to ensure that you will be in the running for the job.

A personalized cover letter addressing the client's needs and concerns can do wonders in setting you apart from the competition. A letter that focuses on the unique benefits you can offer the client will have more impact than one that simply states facts about your firm. There are some pitfalls to avoid at this stage:

• Don't send the client extraneous information. Send only what will position you as a firm especially well suited for the particular project you are pursuing. Less is more.

• Don't include every piece of printed material you have in your possession. Remember that you have several stages left in the selling process. Keep an ace or two up your sleeve.

• Don't send an informal expression of interest if the client has requested a formal submission of qualifications or even a proposal for professional services. (More on this later.)

*Source: Perkins & Will, used with permission*

Prospect _____     Raters _____

Location _____     Date _____

| | -5 | -4 | -3 | -2 | -1 | 0 | 1 | 2 | 3 | 4 | 5 | 6 | 7 | 8 | 9 | 10 |
|---|---|---|---|---|---|---|---|---|---|---|---|---|---|---|---|---|
| | < 10,000 | 10,000 | 25,000 | 50,000 | 75,000 | 100,000 | 200,000 | 300,000 | 400,000 | 500,000 | 750,000 | 1,000,000 | 1,250,000 | 1,500,000 | 1,750,000 | > 2,000,000 |

Fee _____

Need to associate    NEED    DON'T NEED    _____

Competition    WIRED    HEAVY    LIGHT    NONE    _____

Firm's relationship with client    POOR    NONE    EXCELLENT    _____

Likelihood of project proceeding    NOT LIKELY    UNCERTAIN    LIKELY    CERTAIN    _____

Firm's special qualifications    NO EXPERIENCE    AVERAGE    ABOVE AVERAGE    SPECIALIST    _____

Future potential with client    NONE    SOME    EXCELLENT    _____

Contributes to current or future market expertise    MINIMAL    CONSIDERABLE    _____

Marketing expense/effort    EXTRAORDINARY    HIGH    AVERAGE    LOW    _____

Technical leader available    NOT AVAILABLE    MARGINAL    AVAILABLE    _____

Marketing support available    NOT AVAILABLE    MARGINAL    AVAILABLE    _____

Likelihood of securing commission    NOT LIKELY    UNCERTAIN    LIKELY    VERY LIKELY    _____

TOTAL _____

part 2 BUSINESS

## DEVELOPING STRATEGY

After going on record as interested in a project, you generally have time to plan your approach to getting the job while the client is going through the discovery and qualification process. Not only will gathering information at this stage help you develop a strategy to win the business; it will also (if done well) position you as an expert consultant able to help clients articulate and define their needs and concerns.

Generally the firm that is best informed has the greatest chance to win. The best source of that information is usually a face-to-face meeting with the client. This may be more time-consuming and costly than a phone call, but it affords you the opportunity to (1) develop greater rapport and (2) record not only what is said but also how it is said (nonverbal clues).

Architects are trained to ask questions about the physical needs of the program, budget, and site (how big, how much, how tall, how many acres, and so on). Of even greater importance is gathering information about the client's environment, with answers to questions such as these:

- What is the history behind this project?
- What are your client's concerns and expectations?
- Who else is for or against this project?
- How does the client feel about other architects with whom they have worked?
- What time frames have been established?
- How is the project to be funded?
- With whom will you be competing?

You will also find it helpful to ask questions about the client's decision-making process:

- What will the decision-making process entail?
- Who will be assisting the client with this decision?

One word of caution: The answers to these questions may vary depending on who is supplying the information. In some client organizations, the architect selection process can get quite political. In these cases, you will be best equipped to develop your strategy for getting the job if you ask these questions not only of your primary contact but also of the technical decision maker, the financial decision maker, and the "big cheese."

## COURTING PROSPECTS

In most cases, the client considers the decision to buy an architect's services to be a relatively big investment. In addition, it is often perceived as a high-risk or high-visibility decision. The client's decision making process, therefore, is likely to be studied and thorough. The earlier you start the courtship process, the greater your chances of success. Those who wait to receive a request for proposal before trying to get to know the client are at a distinct disadvantage.

Often one factor that can help a client choose among several seemingly well-qualified firms is the level of comfort the client feels with the individual who will lead the project. It is a commonly held belief that friends buy from friends. The objective of the courting process, therefore, is to develop a business friendship with the prospective client. This need not entail attending social events together and becoming personally involved in each other's life. Rather, the emphasis should be on gaining an understanding of the client's business needs and concerns and then developing a helpful habit of providing assistance in a variety of ways.

> ▶ Like a good doctor, you need to diagnose before you can prescribe. The focus is on the client at this stage; effective listening skills are critical. Some helpful hints:
> - Ask thought-provoking, open-ended questions.
> - Take notes.
> - Summarize.

> ▶ "Market new clients with the changes of the seasons. Call on your existing clients with the cycles of the moon. Service your projects with the dependency of the tides. Anticipate the clouds. And soak up the sun you can grab hold of."
>
> *Lee Waldron, Grenald Associates Ltd., in Best Marketing Advice for the 1990s, 1993*

> ▶ "Knowing your customer means knowing what your customer really wants, maybe it's your product, but maybe there's something else too: recognition, respect, reliability, concern, service, a feeling of self-importance, friendship, help."
>
> *Harvey Mackay, Swim with the Sharks Without Being Eaten Alive, 1988*

Instead of being viewed as an adversary, you can position yourself as a valuable colleague. Here are just a few examples of what you can do to build a relationship with your clients:

- Send a useful article on a subject of interest to them.
- Point out a beneficial seminar they might attend.
- Feature them in your newsletter.
- Ask them to give a presentation to your firm.

As with other business relationships, it is helpful to know who your clients are as human beings—what their likes and dislikes are, what they feel strongly about, what their special interests are, what they are most proud of having achieved. Only then can you develop a strong bond.

Selection committees present a special challenge. Try to find out who is on the committee, what experience they have in projects like the one at hand, and whether certain individuals have special interests or agendas. Even when clients prohibit contact with members of the committee before the interview, it is possible to get to know these people by collecting as much information as you can about the client.

As in any relationship, chemistry counts for a lot. If you don't like a particular client, chances are he or she doesn't feel particularly comfortable with you, either. If you're more than a sole proprietor, maybe one of your partners would hit it off better with that client. If you don't have someone to whom you can hand off the client, then you may need to step out of your comfort zone and adjust your style to match the client's personality.

## WRITING PROPOSALS

The proposal stage of seeking the project presents you with an opportunity to prove how well you listen. An effective proposal states in clear and concise terms your understanding of the client's needs and what you hope is your unique ability to meet those needs.

Many firms make the mistake of viewing the proposal as a purely technical document rather than a sales tool. Clearly it is both. A good proposal supports your selling effort by enhancing the client's perceptions of your uniqueness and professionalism while at the same time, allowing you to clarify the terms and conditions of what you will do and what you expect others will do.

A well-written proposal benefits the recipient as well, because it

- Minimizes surprises
- Makes the decision-making process easier
- Helps the client justify why the winning firm was selected

Depending on the client and the circumstances, the type of proposal called for will vary considerably. Sometimes a letter proposal may be all that is required. In these situations, you may have a repeat client who simply wants to know, "How much will it cost and when can you start?"

Most firms find the bulk of their proposals are submitted in response to a request for qualifications (RFQ) or a request for proposals (RFP). These are generally highly competitive situations in which the clients have determined from whom to solicit proposals and what information they consider important to know.

To make it easier to compare apples with apples, many public and private sector clients ask that you fill out a questionnaire detailing your experience and qualifications. Standard Forms 254 and 255, used by the federal government as well as some state and local agencies, are examples of this type of submittal.

If you have identified a client's need, you may be in a position to provide an unsolicited proposal. In this case, you design and organize your proposal, and you determine when to submit it.

## Proposals: Strategies for Improving Your Odds

- Seek—on a proactive basis—opportunities to submit a proposal; it beats being just one of the pack responding to an RFQ or RFP.
- Make the proposal as client-focused as you can. Check your language: Use *you* and *yours* much more often than *I, me, my, we,* or *our.*
- If it's possible to do so, submit a draft of your proposal for the client to review in advance. Asking if the information is on target will save you from putting in days or weeks of effort only to be told, "It isn't really what we wanted."
- If you are responding to a formal RFP or RFQ, present your information in the order and format requested. This is not the place for artistic license.
- Hand-deliver your proposal whenever possible. This gives you one more chance to contact with the client and reinforces your interest in the project.
- Make sure your proposal is comprehensive and complete, yet still concise. Don't overwhelm the reader with extraneous information.

▶ **Architectural Services and Compensation (9.2) reviews project pricing and proposals.**

*Howard J. Wolff*

- *Cover letter.* Here is your first opportunity to sell yourself and your firm—and to tell the client why you should be selected.
- *Table of contents.* It is helpful to list the sections in the proposal and include page numbers.
- *Executive summary.* In client-focused language, the summary confirms your understanding of the current situation, provides an overview of what you are proposing, and stresses why your firm is uniquely suited for the job. (This is a very important section; it may be the *only* part of your proposal that certain decision makers will read.)
- *Scope and situation analysis.* Here is your opportunity to communicate your knowledge of the client's needs and the scope of the project.
- *Services.* Indicate the services included in your proposal. You may want to specifically list excluded services if they have been discussed but are not part of the proposal.
- *Approach and methodology.* Detail how you plan to provide your services. Highlight any areas in which you can distinguish yourself from the competition.
- *Project team.* Describe how you will be organized to provide the services. It is good advice to include cus-tomized resumes of key personnel to be assigned to the project.
- *Recent relevant experience.* List and/or illustrate examples of how you have solved similar problems for other clients.
- *Schedule.* This is a timetable for accomplishing the work. Because schedules can slip (often through no fault of the architect), it may be wise to indicate time frames in weeks or months rather than with specific calendar dates. Also, make sure to build in time for client reviews.
- *Compensation (fee).* If required, provide a fee proposal based on a clear delineation of the scope of services to be provided.
- *References.* Though not always requested by the client, strong references can greatly enhance your ability to get selected. List the contact person's name, title, company, and phone number, as well as a brief description of the services you provided. Be sure your references know you are using their names.
- *Additional information.* Certain materials, if considered helpful to the client and supportive of your sales effort, can be included here if not presented earlier: lists of awards, article reprints, brochure materials, etc.

The key components of almost any proposal (especially the longer ones) may include those in the accompanying list. Like all other aspects of marketing and selling, the proposal should be carefully tailored to the client and the project. A quick letter may be as inappropriate for a sophisticated client as a thick package may be for a client anxious to cut to the chase and get on with the work. Here are some tips for increasing the efficiency and effectiveness of your proposal production efforts:

- Approach the process as you would a design project: Define the scope of work, assign responsibilities for writing and production, and determine the amount of time and money to be devoted to the effort.
- Think about the messages you want to convey and get them up front. Where possible, put the meat—analysis of the client's needs, your approach, and fee proposal—at the beginning. A lengthy proposal may require an executive summary.
- Consider boilerplate copy for information you use again and again. Customize as necessary so it doesn't appear generic. Sections of a proposal that can be 80 percent boilerplate might include a description of your firm, your capabilities, philosophy, resumes of key personnel, relevant project descriptions, design process and methodology, and standard terms and conditions. Check your boilerplate for currency.
- Start early on those parts of a proposal that require extra lead time: a customized cover, special graphics (photos, charts, and other illustrations), and information from consultants who will be part of your team.
- Put yourself in the recipient's place and ask, "Does this proposal tell me what I need to know to select this firm?"
- Budget time for editing, revising, proofreading, printing, binding, and delivering the proposal. Find out in advance how many copies the client would like to have.
- Have someone else in the firm review the proposal before it goes out.
- Remember that the proposal represents the firm and its leaders, no matter who puts it together.

> **A fee proposal detailing the scope of your services may either accompany or follow the other types of proposals described.**

> **Some RFPs are very clear on what the proposal is to contain and how the information is to be presented. Don't run the risk of being nonresponsive by ignoring these requirements.**

*James R. Franklin, FAIA,* Current Practices in Small Firm Management *(1990)*

Depending on circumstances, the client may perceive you—or you may want the client to perceive you—as large or small, local or out-of-town, expert or novice at the project type. Working within the bounds of honesty, of course, here are some of the "messages" firms use to relate their capabilities to the circumstances at hand.

### SMALL FIRM

- Today's fast-breaking technology demands a generalist overview and one-point responsibility—that's me.
- We are not encumbered by in-house engineers who try to be expert for every project type. We assemble the best team we can from consultants who are truly expert for your unique project. Most of the nationally recognized designers agree with us—they don't have engineers in house.
- Your project is a big one to us. It means a lot and will merit our day-to-day attention at the top. It won't get relegated to lower echelons. In our firm the same architect [me] personally controls [design, specs, other elements of the process].
- Just as in your business, in architecture it all comes down to people. You want to deal with the people who make the professional judgments—not with computers or technicians.
- Your job means so much to us, you can be assured we won't be shifting personnel.
- We are a close-knit office—overview and coordination of all aspects of a project are automatic. Everybody in the office overhears everything—there is no compartmentalization. It's all one-on-one.
- Contractors—just like you—want to deal with and tend to pay more attention to the head of the firm.
- There is a limit to the number of people who can effectively work on a project. Regardless of firm size, it always comes down to the project team. We are just that—a team—and plenty big enough.

### LARGE FIRM

- To be a "master builder" is impossible in today's industry. A team of specialists is required.
- We have in-house capability and therefore have tested relationships and teamwork among well-qualified specialists. We stress coordination. We don't expect you to fund our experts' organizational learning curve. You'll get a dedicated team to see your project through.
- There is a reason we are the size we are—we have to pay attention to service and responsiveness. You'll get a project manager assigned 100 percent to your project, with oversight by a partner.
- Technology is moving so fast, it takes a firm our size to afford [CAD, quality control systems, continuing education, and so on—if true].
- We have staff depth and plenty of second opinions to ensure the quality of professional judgments.
- We can ride out stop-and-go on a project when necessary.
- We aren't dependent on outside consultants, so coordination is built in—it's automatic.
- [Construction administration, specs, design, project management, etc.] is a discipline all its own—it deserves an expert such as ours.

### LOCAL

- We are here for the long haul. We have a personal stake in the community as well as a professional one. We intend to live with the results just as you do.
- We are here every time we are needed—we are only [xx]minutes from you, [xx]minutes from the site. We'll know when to be on the job, without you or the contractor having to call us.
- Fees spent locally get respent seven times locally. Keep the money in our own town.
- Even if we end up with an out-of-town contractor, most of the actual work will be done by local people. If they screw you, they will have to work with us for years to come. We keep score—and they know it.

### OUT-OF-TOWN

- We are purely professional—no local bias or pressures to use anything or anybody on your project other than what's best for it. If it meets your needs and wishes, we will fight to get it for you. You wouldn't be talking to us if we weren't specially qualified.
- In an information society there's no such thing as "remote." Here is how we plan to manage project communication and coordination.
- The fee for architecture services is about one-tenth of 1 percent of the life cost of the project. Pick the best.
- We offer fresh eyes, new ideas, and objective evaluation of the performance of the contractor and all the subs. And we have a basis for comparing their work to the best work in other localities.

*(continued)*

**VERY LITTLE EXPERIENCE**

- William W. Caudill, FAIA, says, "An architect who claims to have done ten schools may really have only done one school ten times." We have no preconceptions. We'll be working to answer your needs as you define them.
- We'll be looking for breakthroughs. Your project and site offer unique opportunities. You deserve more than a cookbook solution.
- Let's talk about what's unique about your project and how we would approach the design.
- No assembly line with us. We work hard at staying generalists. Similar but different project types keep us from getting stale. Here are examples of different projects we have done that had similar concerns—and how doing them has given us the diverse experience to qualify us to do well with your project.
- We do lots of different project types to keep ourselves enthusiastic and growing professionally. Nothing is by rote or done without our full, professional attention. We *have* to pay attention.

**A LOT OF EXPERIENCE**

- Everybody likes a winner—which is why we keep being selected for projects like yours. You have a lot at stake here. We have a demonstrated track record.
- We have no learning curve on this and won't ask you to pay our tuition. Instead of our time being spent learning the project type, we can focus on what's unique about your specific needs.
- Let me show you all of the projects like yours that we have done. You'll want to talk to our other clients for this type of project. Here is a list of references.
- Because your project type is one we like and work with a lot, we naturally research it and continually stay abreast of the latest advances in design and technology relevant to it. We've got a head start on anybody else you'll talk to.
- Though we are proud of our design, it's still only 15–20 percent of the service we provide. You want experts on the technical aspects—people who've been there and have seen all the variations. We have a lot.

## MAKING PRESENTATIONS

Unless they know all the design firms well, clients will usually request a presentation by those that are short-listed. In some situations, this turns out to be the first and only chance in the selling process for the architect and client to meet face-to-face.

Having gone through an extensive screening process to get to this point, most clients consider all the firms being interviewed capable of doing the project. You now have the opportunity—however brief the presentation itself—to establish rapport and instill confidence. At this stage it is usually chemistry and your knowledge of the project, not past experience, that win the job.

There are many things you can do to carry the day. Careful preparation—including anticipating what's on the client's mind and responding to the client's immediate needs and concerns—is essential. The selection interview is a time to build trust and rapport, not to show off your wares.

## CLOSING

Although you may come away from the presentation a winner, you don't necessarily have the job—yet.

If price hasn't been an issue up to this point, it now becomes one. If you have done all you can in the other stages of the selling process to develop a strong relationship built on trust and to position yourself as the best architect for the job, then negotiating an appropriate fee for your services will be the natural outcome.

While it is helpful to know certain negotiating techniques, the emphasis need not be on learning "tricks" to get the prospect to sign on the dotted line. If the contractual relationship between you and the client is perceived as a win-win deal, you will be off to a good start.

So, congratulations. You have the job. Before turning your focus to technical issues and project management concerns, however, it is important to put yourself in your client's shoes. Here is where a little empathy will go a long way.

Psychological studies of consumers suggest that the most stressful stage of the buying process can be immediately after a decision has been made. Panic and doubt often set in. At this point your continued focus on the client's needs and concerns can be reinforced through your actions, confirming that the client made the correct decision in hiring you.

## DEBRIEFING

Though the term *closing* suggests that it is the last stage in the process of seeking the project, there is, in fact, a further step. Debriefing, or finding out why the winning firm was selected, is critical to ensuring your long-term marketing success. Many firms think of asking why they were not selected, but few do—and even fewer ask why they were selected. In both cases, an honest debriefing session with the client can yield valuable information.

*If you lose a job,* call to thank the client for having considered your firm. No sour grapes. Say that you're interested in the client's business in the long term. Ask if the client would be willing to share information that could help you do a better job next time. Listen to what the client has to say without offering explanations or justifications. If you come across as defensive, the client will stop offering honest feedback. Remember, too, that you may not always get the complete story.

*If you win a job,* while the process is fresh in the client's mind, ask these questions:

▶ **"Call a client once a month and ask: How are we doing? What could we be doing better? This will result in a more dynamic professional relationship, a friendship, and repeat business."**
*Steven L. Einhorn, FAIA, Einhorn Yaffee Prescott, P.C., in* Best Marketing Advice for the 1990s, *1993*

- What does the client like about you?
- What did you do right and what did your competitors do wrong?
- What could you have done better?
- What does the client see as your firm's uniqueness?
- What did the client see that differentiated the various firms?

With the information you glean from the debriefing, you are ready to start the process of seeking the next project. And the next one. And the next one.

## FOCUSING YOUR EFFORTS

▶ **"Professional attention is still the best sales tool."**
*Eugene Kohn, FAIA, RIBA, Kohn Pederson Fox Associates, P.C., in* Best Marketing Advice for the 1990s, *1993*

If we assume that, as the AIA firm survey has consistently indicated, at least eight out of ten times an architect's work comes from repeat clients, referrals, and reputation, then logically at least 80 percent of your selling effort should go toward building and strengthening long-term relationships with existing contacts.

Most firms, however, spend the majority of their marketing efforts on pursuing new clients—often at the expense of losing the very clients who helped make them successful. Taking clients for granted can be costly in terms of both lost business and damaged reputation. Conversely, the most cost-effective sales dollars you can spend will be on getting new work from old (or current) clients. Studies suggest that it costs five to six times as much to obtain a new client as it does to maintain an existing one.

▶ **Agreements with Clients (10.1) offers guidance on the continuing process of bringing expectations into line.**

Selling is part of marketing—a larger process that begins with building relationships, includes public relations and selling (seeking and closing specific projects), and continues throughout the project. Most of the resources listed in Marketing Planning and Strategies (7.1) address project acquisition.

# The Project Interview

*Howard J. Wolff*

The selection interview is a major opportunity. If it comes at the end of a long period of relationship building, it is your firm's final opportunity to instill confidence and establish rapport. If there has been no courtship, the interview may represent your only opportunity to acquire the project.

During the presentation, clients are looking for clues to help them gauge what they might experience if they select you for their project:

- If you run over your allotted time, clients may infer that you'll have trouble sticking to a schedule.
- If your presentation is not well orchestrated, it may be taken to mean that you'll have trouble managing the design team.
- If your projector bulb blows and you don't have a spare, clients may suspect that you are unable to plan ahead.
- If you engage the clients in the presentation, it will suggest that, once selected, you will continue to involve them in the design and decision-making process.
- If you demonstrate your listening and communication skills by clearly and accurately summarizing the clients' needs and concerns, it will instill confidence in your abilities as a professional.
- If you are comfortable enough with the content and delivery of your presentation to let your personality shine through, the odds are dramatically increased that the clients will feel, "That's somebody I'd like to work with."
- If you imagine that the interview is the first project team meeting, you can demonstrate (through actions, not just words) how you will work together to accomplish the project.

The secret to a successful presentation is planning and preparation. Some suggestions follow:

***Gather information on the client and the project.*** Information obtained earlier in the business development process can be verified and updated at this stage.

***Learn about the members of the selection committee.*** Know your audience. Find out who will be in attendance and learn as much as you can about their backgrounds, roles, interests, biases, and concerns.

***Obtain specifics about logistics.*** It's helpful to confirm the following in advance:

- The date, time, location, and duration of the presentation
- Client preferences regarding the agenda
- The physical characteristics of the presentation space: size and shape; seating configuration; location of electrical outlets, windows, and drapes; availability of props (projectors, computers, easels, flip charts, etc.)

***Uncover details about the selection process.*** You can revise and refine your message depending on the answers to such questions as these:

- How many other firms are being interviewed? Who are they?
- Where are you in the sequence of presentation (first, last, or in the middle)?
- What criteria will the client use to make the selection? (Is there a checklist or matrix, for instance?)
- How soon after the presentations will a decision be made? (Will there be an opportunity to follow up with any additional information?)

Admittedly, the answers to these questions are not always readily obtainable. Some clients are not as forthcoming as others, which underscores the benefits of developing a relationship with the client well in advance of being asked to deliver a formal presentation.

The architecture team with the most information is in the best position to design and deliver a winning presentation. But simply having the information is not enough; the planning and preparation work continues.

***Strategize your presentation.*** Based on the knowledge you now have, it's time to hone your message and determine who the players will be. You will need to demonstrate an understanding of how the client's problem is unique and how your approach to solving it is appropriate. Decide who will take part in the interview, remembering that most clients want to meet the "doers" with whom they will be working. Be sure that everyone at the interview has a role to play. Develop a script and choreograph the action.

***Prepare your visuals.*** Whether it is slides, boards, PowerPoint presentations, flip charts, videos, or overhead transparencies, much of your material can be prepared in advance. If you're good with a marker, you may want to sketch as you talk, using your visuals to enhance your presentation. Darkening a room to show slides—and losing eye contact with your audience for a prolonged period—can detract from your ability to establish rapport. If you are using presentation technologies (projectors, computers, etc.), be sure that everything is hooked up and working beforehand—and carry replacement parts (such as projector bulbs).

***Rehearse, rehearse, rehearse.*** Yes, there is such a thing as overrehearsing and having your presentation appear canned, but for most architects this is a very remote possibility. Under the guise of wanting to appear fresh and spontaneous, many presenters risk being unprepared and disorganized.

Rehearsing the choreography of the presentation is as important as rehearing the content. Don't leave these things to chance:

- Who will speak when and from where?
- How will introductions and handoffs be handled?
- Who will turn lights and projectors on and off? Close the blinds? Display the boards?
- How and by whom will questions be handled?

Time each part of the presentation to ensure that you can say everything that needs to be said and still leave an appropriate amount of time for interaction with the client. Videotaping can help you practice this.

Consider using a devil's advocate. Ask a colleague to take the owner's part, asking questions that are likely to come up and pressing until your answers are clear and crisp.

You may want to use video as a tool in reviewing your presentations. Training consultants Tim Allen and Peter Loeb suggest these guidelines to reduce people's fear of seeing themselves on video:

- Give the presenters a chance to say what they think after viewing themselves, before you offer your comments.
- Correcting something you see and don't like is more valuable and powerful than listening to others tell you what to do.
- Videotape the whole presentation to see how well it flows and to decide if it can be condensed or sharpened.
- Concentrate on only small portions—three minutes maximum—of a person's presentation. No one can absorb more than that at one time. Improve that one part and then apply the lessons to the rest of the presentation.
- Have the presenter do the same three minutes again, making the changes he or she wants to make. End on a positive note.

***Get the client to talk.*** The best interview is a dialogue, not a monologue.

In summary, the content and delivery of your message—and your ability to develop rapport with the clients while demonstrating an understanding of their needs and concerns—is much more important than being a wonderfully articulate, silver-tongued presenter. Clients generally don't expect their architects to have the skills of a polished public speaker, but if you are interested in increasing your comfort level in this arena, programs such as Toastmasters (offered in nearly every community) can work wonders.

**Presentation Tricks of the Trade**

Here are some stories from the battlefield that show how some firms delivered winning presentations by standing out from the crowd:

- After learning they were the eighth firm to present to the client on the same day, a design team showed empathy for the selection committee by bringing soda and popcorn to the interview.
- Having talked to the manufacturer of equipment that a hospital client was about to specify, an architect (with no previous health care design experience) discovered that the equipment wouldn't fit in the elevator and discussed alternatives at the presentation, showing an understanding of the problem greater than that of the client or the competition.
- When asked by the client if he would provide concepts at no charge, an architect stood up on the table and did a tap dance. "That's what I can offer for free," he said. "Everything else I need to get paid for."

*Howard J. Wolff is vice president and worldwide director of marketing for Wimberly Allison Tong & Goo, an international architecture, planning, design, and consulting practice with offices in Honolulu, Newport Beach, London, and Singapore. He is a frequent speaker and author on the subject of selling design services.*

# 6.3 Public Service and Community Involvement

## William M. Polk, FAIA

*By participating in public life, architects have the opportunity to improve the built environment and the lives of those who experience it. In this capacity, architects increase their exposure, make new contacts, learn how things get done in the public arena, and gain knowledge that can be helpful in serving their clients.*

Most architects, by virtue of their work, *are* in public life. They design buildings and places for the public. Its very nature makes their work highly visible and an integral part of any community. Some of the most successful architects have leveraged that visibility with their personal efforts as volunteers, community activists, public service appointees, and elected government leaders. And as citizens, architects participate in the public and political environment by supporting issues and voting for government officials who share their interests, values, and beliefs.

Being active in community service means an architect is in the public eye, even when not working on a high-profile commission. Although time away from the office can be costly, it can be time well spent. Public service can ultimately enhance the architect's image, keep the architect working side by side with potential future clients, and boost the firm's intangible goodwill assets.

Architects can participate in their communities and in public service in a variety of ways, including working as volunteers for various public entities such as community organizations or boards, serving as advocates to communicate the profession's views and positions, providing pro bono services for the public good, and serving as appointed or elected officials.

## VOLUNTEERING

Many architects find time to volunteer in their communities, despite busy work schedules and family or personal commitments. Examples of volunteer positions that licensed architects seek out or become appointed to include

- Zoning and planning boards
- Historic preservation commissions
- Architecture and design review boards and committees
- Building code commissions and variance review boards
- State registration boards
- Special committees and commissions to review and recommend public policy in housing, land use, environment, design, and construction
- Boards or committees of nonprofit organizations such as museums, housing coalitions, and conservation foundations

In these positions—as paid or unpaid volunteers—architects contribute their technical expertise and professional values to the day-to-day workings of government and community organizations. From a professional and business perspective, architects gain important knowledge and contacts in these positions. Recognizing that architects provide professional services on projects they administer or control, these entities have developed procedures for handling potential conflicts of interest.

> The Architect in the Political Process backgrounder (6.3) introduces the architect as an advocate for change in public policies and programs to improve the quality of the built environment.

> The AIA sponsors Regional/Urban Design Assistance Teams (R/UDATS) and other community service programs. Contact your AIA component or AIA headquarters for information on how you might become involved.

> Architects who participate on zoning, planning, and design boards usually find that you can legally and ethically excuse themselves from voting on projects in which they have an interest. If you serve in this way, you may find yourself avoiding projects that may create a conflict of interest in your role as a public servant.

WILLIAM M. POLK *heads the architecture firm of William Polk Associates in Seattle, Washington. He is a former speaker of the Washington State House of Representatives*

# PUBLIC ADVOCACY

Making public policy and developing the programs that carry out this policy are the work of government.

The policy-making process seeks to synthesize the needs and aspirations of the public while recognizing that the "public" is a collection of people and organizations with diverse interests and motivations. These people and organizations develop and advocate positions on current issues and form alliances with the intent of influencing policy. For their part, legislators and government officials responsible for shaping policy depend on the information and positions presented to them.

At any moment, government officials, legislatures, and even the courts are considering rules, initiatives, and cases in which architects may have knowledge or interest. Working as individuals, and especially as parts of coalitions, architects can have a significant effect on government action. As individual professionals and through their professional associations, architects can participate in the policy-making process by contributing technical expertise on important problems and questions in the public arena and—as advocates—articulating and communicating the profession's position on issues and initiatives. For example, it is not uncommon for an architect—usually as part of the AIA or state or local AIA components—to become involved in the process of contributing ideas and even language to executives and legislators, especially to their bill-drafting staffs. These architects may then commit time and energy to establishing and maintaining legislative interest in a bill, working toward its passage or defeat, and encouraging the chief executive to sign or veto it. Architects can also become involved in the judicial process as participants—plaintiffs and defendants—in individual litigation, which may test existing laws and provoke new judicial interpretations.

Effective advocacy requires continuity and steady involvement. This is most often done through local and state AIA components as well as the national professional organization. Many volunteers are needed to carry the message. The most effective lobbying is done by constituents who will be affected directly by a bill or other proposal being considered. In addition to individual visits with legislators and key government officials, many AIA components organize special events for legislators, lobbying days, and rapid-response programs to ensure contact between their members and those in the political arena.

The political action committee (PAC) provides another forum for advocacy. With the financial support of many individual members of an interest group, a PAC plays an important role in helping to elect legislators who share the goals and concerns of the interest group. The AIA's PAC—ArchiPAC—is an integral part of the Institute's efforts to increase congressional awareness of AIA policies and positions on national issues. Many AIA state components have PACs as well.

## PRO BONO PROFESSIONAL SERVICES

An increasing number of architects are providing professional services *pro bono publico*—literally, "for the public good." This may take many forms, including organizing community planning and design exercises; recommending solutions for community problems; and participating in projects for the homeless, AIDS shelters, and other situations where funds for needed professional services are limited or nonexistent. Some architects volunteer design services for community centers, churches, theaters, and other nonprofit organizations.

Yet many architects look askance at these pro bono activities, perhaps with good reason. The point is repeatedly made that many of these same organizations will raise funds for construction, so why not include design fees in those fund-raising endeavors? The argument is that architects and contractors should be paid for their work. But the biggest deterrent to many architects and firms is not the lack of payment for work but the legal ramifications. Regardless of whether they are paid for their services, in the majority of instances the licensed architect can be held fully responsible in the event of any problems. The architect's liability does not go away.

▶ **"I've always been fascinated by the fact that the architectural process, the approaches that are used in architecture, could so easily and effectively improve the public debate. The creative process of architecture allows for a broader examination of a problem and possible solutions—as opposed to the compartmentalization governed by the case history approach the legal profession has imposed on our legal system."**
*Richard N. Swett, FAIA, ambassador to Denmark, quoted in "Drawing Architects into Public Life," Boston Globe, October 5, 2000*

▶ **Architects report feelings of pride, even idealism, in working with fellow design professionals, articulating and communicating their values and positions, and serving the public good through political activity.**

There is usually one important exception to the liability issue, however. Architects volunteering as disaster service workers for building assessments are often deputized and indemnified for their disaster assistance by the appropriate governing body. It is a good idea to check into this *before* volunteering to help out with disaster relief.

Often pro bono services are focused on the front end, providing analysis, concepts, cost estimates, and presentation materials that can be used to attract funding. Sometimes, though, a firm may provide services through design documentation and construction.

Architects who make time for pro bono work find personal and professional satisfaction as well as opportunities to work on new kinds of problems. They also report receiving increased visibility in the community, which can lead to new clients and new projects for the firm.

## ARCHITECTS AS PUBLIC SERVANTS

Much of the architect's day-to-day practice is regulated by government in the form of zoning and planning ordinances, community design standards, landmark and environmental management standards, building codes and standards, and rules regulating professional practice and conduct. As outgrowths of administrative law, these regulations are often complex and require technical expertise in their administration, interpretation, and enforcement. Architects who choose careers in government serve as:

- Staff architects and administrators of public design and construction programs
- Specialists and researchers in design and construction agencies
- Code enforcement officials
- Staff to state registration boards
- Staff to legislators, legislative committees and commissions, and executive offices responsible for environmental, design, and construction policy

In addition, architects serve as elected public officials in various capacities and at several levels. Some serve full time. Others serve part time in addition to working as designers or running a firm.

Perhaps the aspect of pursuing a political career that is most appealing to architects is the challenge and capacity to achieve legislation or programs that will benefit large segments of the population in areas such as housing, health care, education, and urban development. The longevity of a political career is, of course, in the hands of the voters and in the structures they create to operate their governments. Nonetheless, the opportunity to bring about change while holding elected office may be unparalleled.

Regardless of the program or forum, the architect's participation in public life brings a specialized training and problem-solving focus to community activities and provides a great benefit to the people and groups involved. And for the architect, the professional and personal rewards of being recognized for your contributions can be just as great.

> **The standard of care for professional services is not reduced because the services are being provided pro bono.**

## The Architecture of Engagement

It is clear that the architecture profession has much to offer society at large. As planners, problem solvers, and holistic and optimistic generalists, architects have valuable skills to offer the community, the business world, and the political arena. Of signal importance are our professional attributes of civility, cooperation, and openness. Our professional training makes the architect well suited for engagement within the civic life of the country. How do we begin to define "civic engagement" and develop a framework for meaningful engagement?

In *A Call for Civil Society: A Report to the Nation from the Council on Civil Society,* published by the Institute for American Values in 1998, a bipartisan group of concerned citizens constructed a strategy for renewal of our democratic moral truths. The report identifies 12 "seedbeds of civic virtue," which include the arts and arts institutions among those aspects of our society that constitute "our foundational sources of competence, character and citizenship." Another seedbed of civic virtue identified is our voluntary civic organizations, which the report recognizes as a "hallmark of American excellence."

What does this mean for us as citizens and as architects today? What is the relationship between voluntary civil associations, political planning processes, the media and American civilization? What opportunities are there for architects to participate actively in the civic life of the country? What are the dangers? How might we begin to fully engage the profession in the civic life of America?

There are clearly ample opportunities for architects to maintain, bolster, and invigorate the quality of life within our communities. Who is better suited for that than architects, with our ability to reach consensus and complete complex projects, our vision and leadership ability? However, as we delve into the world of civic engagement, we must be mindful of the cautionary words of Lewis Mumford, written in 1924 in his groundbreaking work *Sticks and Stones.* In a chapter entitled "Architecture and Civilization," Mumford wrote:

*Our architectural development is bound up with the course of civilization: this is a truism. To the extent that we permit our institutions and organizations to function blindly, as our bed is made, so must we lie on it; and while we may nevertheless produce isolated buildings of great esthetic interest . . . the matrix of our physical community will not be effected by the existence of separate jewels.*

Mumford, in understanding the intrinsic relationship between architecture and civilization, tapped the essential need for architects to be engaged in the life of the community. As Mumford wrote:

*A city, properly speaking, does not exist by the accretion of houses, but by the association of human beings.*

Let's get to work.

*Harris M. Steinberg, AIA*

# The Architect in the Political Process

*William M. Polk, FAIA*

———

To be effective, government institutions require individual participation at every level. At the same time, the world of politics is a world of coalitions. Coalitions provide useful and effective frameworks through which individuals may participate in legislative affairs. This backgrounder is written for the individual architect, but it is meant to be taken in the context of some form of coalition—chapter, society, committee, task force, or just a loosely knit group with similar motivations. The principles work for all.

## Fundamentals

In legislative affairs, there are some fundamentals:

*Get to know your legislator.* Approach this task as if you were attempting to make the legislator a client. Look for occasions such as town, club, or organization meetings when the conversation can be light and you can become comfortable with each other. Find out what makes the legislator tick. On what committees does he or she serve? What issues are important to the district? As you develop this information, you develop a better understanding of how best to present your issue.

It is always easier to get the ear of a friend. As your friend, the legislator is not wondering who you are, where your interests lie, who your allies are, or what your political involvement may be. He or she already knows. You will be better able to explain your issue in terms the legislator can relate to—and to do it quickly, without a lot of get-acquainted small talk.

*Become involved in the legislative process.* It is far easier to change a bill before it becomes law than to change the law later. The dynamics of the legislative scene keep shifting—sometimes day by day and hour by hour. This compels many associations, including the AIA and its components, to lobby as an ongoing part of legislative activity.

*Limit your issues.* As all citizens do, architects have the right to speak out on any issue. Their effectiveness necessarily diminishes if they are vocal on too many issues or issues outside their professional expertise. As a result, most architects choose to limit the issues to the handful that are most important to the profession. Too many issues sap energy; they also provide legislators with a way to allow the profession minor victories while thwarting its main goals.

*Understand the separation of powers.* Recalling the separation of powers among the executive, legislative, and judicial branches of government focuses our professional concern on those who can actually help. Yet the separation of powers is not always clear. Some legislative functions are delegated to the executive branch. The executive veto is a form of legislative act. Likewise, the writing of administrative rules and procedures by departments, commissions, offices, or bureaus is a legislative activity. Many celebrations after a bill has passed a state legislature have been ruined by a gubernatorial veto. Many successful advocates of legislation have searched for what went wrong after the administrative rules were published. Conversely, many have

achieved their legislative goals through the writing of rules and the power of the veto.

*Learn how the system works.* The road from introduction of legislation to its passage can be long and rocky. Legislative leadership can assign a bill to a committee whose members may be philosophically opposed to it. Committee chairs can exert influence by not holding hearings soon enough to give a bill a reasonable chance of clearing all the hurdles. The rules committee chair may order the calendar to place a bill early or late for consideration. The continuing lobbyist is in a position to monitor these subtle but critical influences.

## Lobbying

The legislator's stock in trade is good information. Thus, information is the currency by which the legislative advocate, whether professional lobbyist or citizen lobbyist, gains the legislator's ear and confidence.

*Providing information.* Legislative staff provide research on general issues; the lobbyist provides information detailing the impact of a proposal on the lobbyist's own group. The information provided must be factual and well organized. It is recognized that the information is being delivered to support the lobbyist's point of view, but it is expected to be accurate and complete. Once an individual or group is known to provide worthwhile information, the system will seek that information.

Legislative staff members should be provided with extensive documentation supporting your view, while the legislator in most cases would appreciate a summary. Some legislators are satisfied only if they do their own staff work, and they must be supplied with copies ofdocumentation. Generally speaking, though, the press of time dictates accepting someone's evaluation of the facts surrounding a proposal.

*Testifying.* Testifying before a committee has the appeal of reaching committee members, staff, and news media at one time. You have no guarantee, however, that you will have the undivided attention of all those present. They may be preoccupied, still thinking about the last presentation, or discussing other issues among themselves. You will want to be alert to the personal dynamics of the committee, just as you would be if it were an architect selection committee. Always leave at least a written summary of your presentation with the members.

*Constituent contact.* Since constituents gain the attention of the legislator first—even if the legislator disagrees with the proposal—constituent contact is an essential ingredient in any lobbying effort. If a constituent is involved, the legislator is more likely to return the phone call, answer the letter, or make an appointment. Coalitions that focus constituent contact on individual legislators get things done.

Visit the legislators you know. Take them to lunch, make an appointment to see them in their offices, or, if necessary, wait at their office doors until they are available. Legislators are impressed by those who have determination—particularly if they are also constituents. When you are given time, make the most of it. Communicate what you have to say in an organized and straightforward way.

**Make it personal.** The most important information you can get across to a legislator is the impact the proposal in question will have upon you. Translate the issue into a concrete example. Personalize it. This is information that can come from no other source, giving the legislator a unique piece of information that no one else knows. This can be immensely valuable in arguing amendments as well as a gold mine to the legislator during debate on the floor.

**Offer your assistance.** Offer to be a resource for information on issues affecting architecture and the environment. This can be accomplished in many ways. As an example, the legislator's staff could send you copies of all legislation in which the profession is interested for your review and comment. This is another opportunity to personalize the issues and to maintain contact with your legislator.

**A final word.** No matter what the outcome, thank the legislators you called upon for their consideration, and thank the ones who voted with you. Give those who supported your cause credit in chapter newsletters and other public communications. While it is correct to inform chapter members of who opposed the AIA position, there is nothing to be gained by abrasive or antagonistic talk. Be graceful in victory or defeat, because there will be another occasion when you will be searching the legislature for friends.

## Elections

The best way to become known is to help a legislator become elected. Every candidate for office needs organizers, workers, information, and financing. Successful campaigns require planning; selection and articulation of issues; effective communication and advertising; newsletters, signs, and other graphics; and, most important, lots of one-on-one contact and conversation. Your decision to contribute time, talent, and/or funds is a personal one. You may decide to become involved through regular political party activities or through special committees and independent campaigns organized around specific candidates for office.

## Get Organized

Action through the AIA is essential to successful legislative efforts intended to benefit the profession. To coordinate your activities with the Institute's, participate in your chapter's government affairs program. (The AIA's *Component Operations Manual* has a section on how to organize one if none exists.) This program should be the focal point for discussion among chapter members who want to identify issues of concern and set chapter goals and priorities. The government affairs program should also be charged with liaison with other chapters and organizations such as engineers, landscape architects, interior designers, contractors, and real estate, preservation, and environmental groups—any organization with whom an effective alliance can be built.

*William M. Polk, FAIA, heads the architecture firm of William Polk Associates in Seattle, Washington. He is a former speaker of the Washington State House of Representatives.*

# 7 Financial Operations

## 7.1 Financial Systems

### Lowell Getz, CPA

*Managing your firm's finances and keeping track of its financial health are easy once the systems are in place.*

To stay in business, you need to mind the money. Most architects want to practice without tripping over mysterious financial concepts, reports, and accountants at every step. They do, however, want to be able to check the "financial temperature" of the firm and its projects at any time. And they want to have some idea of where the firm is going.

To track a firm's finances, it is necessary to have a financial management system. Firms require a straightforward, timely, and reasonably accurate way of monitoring financial performance of their projects and the firm as a whole in order to

- Know if the firm is meeting its financial needs and goals, including making a profit. To remain in practice, an architecture firm must earn a profit—an excess of revenue over expenses that sustains the firm and allows it to provide the level of professional service it aspires to offer.
- Know if there will be cash to cover payroll and other current expenses. Even a profitable firm will run into trouble if it does not maintain a positive cash flow—enough cash and other liquid assets to meet current payrolls and other expenses.
- Plan for capital, setting aside funds for acquiring equipment or meeting other needs. As computing and related technologies become more important, setting aside funds for acquiring equipment becomes a must for most firms.
- Price professional services at levels that not only best serve clients but also accomplish the firm's goal of staying in business and providing quality services.

This practice topic provides some basic information on financial systems in architecture firms, exploring the common sources and uses of funds, accounting methods and systems, and financial reports. The remaining topics in this chapter address financial planning (setting workable targets), temperature taking (to see how the firm is doing), and acquiring capital when it is needed. Some firms have elected to pursue associated business ventures, such as real estate development or contract interior furnishings, for the economic return they bring. These ventures increase the complexity of financial management.

> **Financial Planning (7.2)** addresses profit planning.

> **Financial Health (7.3)** suggests some indicators of financial well-being.

> Architects are in business to do architecture. If they are to have that opportunity, somebody in the firm needs to look after the money. If you are that person—or aspire to be that person—this topic and those that follow are for you. If not, these topics provide some basic insights into the finances of architecture firms and how they can be managed to accomplish the firm's goals.

**LOWELL V. GETZ** *is a financial consultant to architecture, engineering, planning, and environmental service firms. He has written, taught, and lectured widely on financial management. Getz is a certified public accountant and a certified management consultant.*

# SOURCES AND USES OF FUNDS

An architecture firm's basic financial calculus—where the money comes from and where it goes—is usually not very complicated.

**Revenues.** Revenues to operate the firm come largely from its projects; that is, with fees received from providing professional services. Additional sources of revenues may include the following:

**Acquiring Capital (7.4)** looks at capital requirements and ways to meet them.

- Capital infusions by the firm's founders at start-up and at key times in the firm's growth, as well as from additional owners if ownership is expanded over time
- Any associated business ventures the firm may have, such as software development, contract interiors, or real estate
- Income from interest, rents, royalties, honoraria, investments, sale of assets, or other miscellaneous sources

The backgrounder **Computerized Financial Systems (7.1)** offers guidance in selecting a computer-based system.

***Direct (project) expenses.*** Like revenues, a significant portion of the firm's expenses are incurred directly in the process of providing project services. These direct expenses can be identified with a specific project in the firm and can be placed into three categories: direct (in-house) salary expenses, expenses for outside (consultant) services, and other direct expenses.

The category of direct (in-house) salary expenses represents time charged by the firm's staff, both professional and support, to providing project services. It includes time spent on project activities as well as that involved in administering and coordinating the services of consultants working on projects.

Expenses for outside (consultant) services are for services provided by outside consultants working on a project. The architecture firm may mark up outside services to reflect the expenses it incurs in providing those services, including, for example, coordination, processing, accounting, financing, and risk.

In providing project services, a firm will likely incur travel, telephone, printing, and other nonsalary expenses. These other direct expenses may be nonreimbursable (included in the architect's fee) or reimbursable (paid separately by the client).

Reimbursable expenses are project-generated expenses that cannot be accurately quantified before the owner-architect agreement is signed and that are passed on to the client when they occur. Reimbursable expense categories are specified in the owner-architect agreement and may include travel, lodging and meals, telephone, reproduction expenses, specialty consultants, and similar project-related costs. Each charge is billed to the client, and the appropriate documentation (e.g., phone bills) would be provided at the client's request. Reimbursable expenses have associated in-house administration services and therefore are usually marked up when they are billed. Sometimes the client and architect negotiate a "not-to-exceed" limit on reimbursable expenses, taking care to develop a reasonable estimate that includes a contingency amount.

***Indirect expenses.*** Not all of the firm's expenses directly support project activities. Indirect expenses generally fall into two categories—payroll burden or general and administrative costs.

**Government agencies** may have their own definitions of what are considered to be direct and indirect expenses, and what indirect expenses are allowable within a firm's overhead rate or multiplier.

Payroll burden includes the costs of benefits provided to staff members, including the costs for health insurance, workers' compensation insurance, federal and state unemployment insurance, and payroll taxes.

All other costs are included in the category of general and administrative costs. These include both salaries and benefits for management, marketing, professional education and training, civic activities, and other efforts that are important to the firm but cannot be charged directly to a specific project. The costs of renting or owning space, office operations, taxes, business taxes, liability insurance, and depreciation also fall into this category, as do a variety of other business expenses that cannot be directly attributed to specific projects.

Taken together, these indirect expenses—often called overhead expenses—represent a significant portion of a firm's overall expenses. In making proposals for project services, it is common to include overhead either as a percentage of direct salary expense (for example, 150 percent) or as a multiplier applied to the direct salary expense (DSE) figure (in the same example, 2.5 times DSE). Some firms apply their overhead rates and multipliers to direct personnel expense (DPE). DPE includes direct salary expense and payroll burden; payroll burden thus is removed from the overhead category.

**Profit.** Defined as the difference between revenues and expenses, profit represents the funds required to sustain the practice, providing a cushion for lean times, a base for rewarding the risks taken on by the firm's owners and the performance of the staff, and a source of funds for extraordinary investments in the firm's people and equipment.

## ACCOUNTING SYSTEMS

Most of an architect's financial activity revolves around projects. Thus the financial management system handles individual projects (project accounting) as well as the firm as a whole (general accounting).

**Project accounting.** This keeps track of expenses directly assigned to projects. Time sheets assign labor expenses to projects. Other direct expenses are generally assigned by coding them to projects either when they are accrued or when they are paid. Overhead expenses are assigned to projects as a percentage of direct labor expense. For

The world of financial systems is replete with specialized terms. The following are defined in Appendix B.

| | | |
|---|---|---|
| Account | Deferred revenue | Margin |
| Account balance | Depreciation | Moving average |
| Accounting period | Direct expenses | Net |
| Accounts payable | Direct personnel expense | Net worth |
| Accounts receivable | (DPE) | Nonexpense items |
| Accrual accounting | Direct salary expense (DSE) | Organizational expense |
| Aged accounts receivable | Dividend | Outstanding stock |
| Asset | Double-entry bookkeeping | Overhead expense |
| Audit | DPE factor | Paid-in capital |
| Average collection period | Draw | Par value |
| Backlog | DSE factor | Payroll journal |
| Bad debt | Earned revenue | Payroll taxes |
| Balance sheet | Earned surplus | Pension plan |
| Bankruptcy | Earnings per share | Petty cash |
| Billable time | Equity | Profit |
| Billing rate | Equity capital | Profit margin |
| Bookkeeping | Expenditure | Profit-sharing plan |
| Book value | Expense | Profitability |
| Break even | Fee | Pro forma |
| Break-even multiplier | Fidelity bond | Pro rata |
| Budget | Fiscal year | Project gross margin |
| Budgeting | Fixed assets | Project revenues |
| Burden | General journal | Reimbursable expenses |
| Capital | General ledger | Retained earnings |
| Capital accounts | Goodwill | Revenue |
| Capital expenditure | Gross income from projects | Salary |
| Cash accounting | Income | Share |
| Cash budget | Income statement | Short-term |
| Cash cycle | Indirect expense | Solvency |
| Cash flow | Indirect expense allocation | Staff leveling |
| Cash flow statement | Indirect expense factor | Statement of account |
| Cash journals | Insolvency | Stock |
| Cash projection worksheet | Interest | Trial balance |
| Chart of accounts | Investment credit | Unbilled revenue |
| Compensation | Invoice | Unearned revenue |
| Contribution | Journal | Utilization ratio |
| Credit | Liabilities | Variance |
| Current asset | Line of credit | Vouchers |
| Current liability | Liquid assets | Working capital |
| Current ratio | Liquidity | Work in process |
| Debit | Long-term | Write off |
| Debt | Loss | |

example, overhead may be assigned at the rate of 150 percent of direct labor. Project accounting compares project labor spent with revenue earned to determine whether a profit or loss was incurred on the project. If the project fee includes expenses, then reimbursed expenses, marked up by a percentage when appropriate, are included in project revenue, and direct expenses are included in project expenses. Effective project control systems also routinely compare actual project expenses with budgeted expenses to determine whether the project is proceeding in accordance with the work plan.

Computerized accounting systems vary in complexity. Today there is a wide range of available computer software, and even the smallest firms can use it to obtain timely and accurate information for project accounting.

**General accounting.** This includes the activities concerned with keeping account books as well as preparing financial statements and tax returns. The general accounting system consists of payroll records, receipts and disbursements journals, accounts receivable, accounts payable, and the general ledger; the last is used to summarize transactions and prepare financial statements.

**Chart of accounts.** An accounting system includes a chart of accounts listing the accounting categories the firm uses. In a sense, it is a dictionary that evolves to meet the firm's needs. The chart of accounts often classifies accounts under the following headings:

- Assets: everything owned by the firm or owed to the firm by others
- Liabilities: claims of creditors against these assets; what the firm owes to others

---

## EXPENSES

### Direct Expenses

In addition to the expenses of salaries and outside services, architecture firms incur a variety of other expenses that can be charged directly to a specific project. These expenses, which may be nonreimbursable or reimbursable, often include costs for

- Printing, duplication, and plotting, including reproduction of drawings and specifications
- Photography
- Diskettes, tapes, and other electronic media requested by the client
- CAD and other computer services associated with the project
- Items purchased on the client's behalf, e.g., fees, permits, bid advertising, models, renderings
- Project meeting expenses
- Transportation, including expenses to and from the job site
- Lodging and meals
- Long-distance telephone, fax, telex, etc.
- Postage, courier, and overnight delivery
- Project professional liability insurance premiums
- Additional premiums for project professional liability insurance in excess of basic firm coverage• Other project-related insurance premiums
- Legal and accounting services related to the project
- Financing and carrying costs of professional services at the client's request

### General and Administrative Expenses

Indirect or overhead expenses—expenses that cannot easily be attributed to a specific project in the office—include salaries not charged to project, payroll burden (fringe benefits), and a wide variety of general and administrative expenses. These G&A expenses may include costs for the following items:

#### Current Operating Expenses

- Rent (or equivalent), utilities, operation and maintenance, and repair of buildings, equipment, and automobiles
- Printing, duplication, photographs, and similar items for marketing and other nonproject uses

- Printing of in-house check sets and consultant base sheets
- Computer hardware, software, and operating expenses
- Postage and messenger services
- Travel and entertainment for marketing and firm or staff development
- Office supplies
- Library materials, books, periodicals
- Telephone, facsimile, electronic mail, information services
- Taxes, e.g., real estate, personal property
- Professional dues and licensing fees
- Seminars, conventions, in-house training and professional development
- Marketing and proposal preparation
- Public relations
- Charitable and civic contributions
- Insurance, e.g., automobile, contents, building, principals' life, valuable papers, comprehensive general liability, equipment, professional liability
- Interest on loans and credit lines
- Bond premiums

#### Capital Expenditures

- Depreciation, e.g., furniture, equipment, automobiles, buildings
- Amortization on leasehold improvements

#### Losses

- Theft or casualty loss not covered by insurance
- Expenses to correct design errors and omissions, including deductibles on insurance payouts
- Uncollectable compensation and bad debts

#### Prepaid Expenses

Expenses that affect operations beyond the current fiscal year and that the Internal Revenue Service requires to be spread over more than one year, e.g., long-term insurance premiums, certain taxes, equipment leases, licenses/fees, organization expenses

- Net worth: claims of the firm's owner or owners against its assets; what the firm owes to its owners
- Revenue: value or money earned by a firm during an accounting period
- Expenses: what it costs the firm to produce its revenue
- Profit or loss: the difference between revenue and expenses.

***Accounting codes.*** A coding system is the "shorthand" used to record various entries into the proper accounts. Each project is assigned a number; in more complex systems, subcodes may be used for departments, phases and tasks, and additional services (perhaps including alternates and change orders). In addition, accounting codes (from the chart of accounts) permit identification of specific revenues, expenses, assets, and liabilities, categorized by subject or type. Accounting codes sharpen project control. They allow a firm to track revenues and expenses by project, by phase or task, or by object of expenditure to better control costs and to improve budgeting for future projects.

## ACCOUNTING METHODS

There are two primary methods for recording accounting transactions: the cash and accrual methods. The firm's accounting system may use one or, more likely, both methods.

*Cash method.* Cash accounting records entries at the time they involve cash. For example, revenue is recorded when checks are received from clients, and expenses are recorded when cash is paid out. Transactions that do not involve cash are not recorded until they do. When you send a bill to a client, it is not recorded as revenue until the check arrives.

Cash accounting is very straightforward. The problem is that it doesn't match revenue with expenses. Certain cash expenses, such as salaries to employees and bills from vendors, are generally paid shortly after the obligation for them is incurred. However, revenue for services provided is generally not received until much later. Therefore, because revenues aren't matched against expenses, an income statement based on cash accounting doesn't answer the basic question of whether the firm made or lost money in a given period. Cash accounting statements record only the excess or deficit of cash that occurred during the period.

*Accrual method.* The accrual system of accounting records revenue when it is earned and expenses when they are incurred. For example, if labor and expenses are charged to a project in January, the revenue earned to cover them is reported in January as well, even though the cash has not yet been received. This means that revenue is usually shown before it is received. The drawback, of course, is that the firm may not collect the cash for the reported revenue. The revenue must be written off when the bad debt is discovered—which may be several months after the revenue was shown on the books.

Similarly, expenses are recorded in the accounting period when they are incurred rather than when they are paid. For example, a vendor invoice for supplies provided to the firm in January is applied to January even though it may not be paid until later because the firm does not have the cash. The invoice is recorded both as an expense and as an account payable to match it against the corresponding revenue. Likewise, certain expenses such as annual insurance premiums that are paid in advance (prepaid) are spread over the entire period to which they apply.

Many firms prefer accrual accounting because it addresses the question of profitability by matching revenue and expense. Also, the firm's revenue earned but not yet billed (work in progress) and its billed revenue (accounts receivable) are recorded as assets on the balance sheet. By reporting these figures each month, a firm can see how much it is owed and can take steps to collect it. Similarly, unpaid expenses are recorded as liabilities, indicating how much the firm owes to others.

Using accrual accounting does not minimize the vital importance of cash and the need to closely monitor cash flow and the firm's cash position. The firm's reporting system needs to supply both cash and accrual information, but the fullest measurement of operating performance is accomplished by means of accrual accounting. Firms that

▶ For income tax purposes, most professional services firms pay taxes on a cash basis—few practitioners want to pay taxes on money that has not been collected. These firms keep accrual records for management purposes, which are then converted to a cash basis for tax purposes at year's end.

Accrual accounting provides an accurate picture of the firm's revenues and expenses within a given time frame—in the case of our example, the month of January. This picture is not skewed by cash coming in or going out that does not relate to the month's activities.

Look at this simple example. On a cash basis, this firm recorded a surplus of $12,000 in January. In reality, though, much of the revenue producing this surplus resulted from old invoices being paid by the firm's clients—perhaps as a result of a year-end effort to clean these up. In January the firm actually committed to spend $3,000 more than it earned.

**January—Cash Basis**

| | |
|---|---|
| Revenues received by the firm: | |
| October invoices | 6,000 |
| November invoices | 14,000 |
| December invoices | 22,000 |
| Total January revenues | $42,000 |
| Expenses dispersed for salaries, vendors, etc. | $30,000 |
| Net cash revenue for January | $12,000 |

**January—Accrual Basis**

| | |
|---|---|
| Revenues earned from clients | $27,000 |
| Expenses incurred in January: | |
| Billable to clients (project services) | 15,000 |
| Not billable (marketing) | 5,000 |
| Other expenses | 10,000 |
| Total January expenses | $30,000 |
| Net income (loss) for January | $(3,000) |

are organized as regular corporations generally are allowed to pay taxes on the cash basis. The accountant must convert the accrual income statements to the cash basis for the purpose of calculating corporate taxes owed.

# FINANCIAL REPORTS

Financial management systems produce reports that can be used to keep the firm and its projects on track.

*Income statements and balance sheets.* Two of the most common financial statements used to describe a firm's basic finances are the income statement and the balance sheet. Taken together, these complementary statements present a complete picture of the firm's current financial status. In essence, an income statement is a moving picture, whereas a balance sheet is a snapshot. The income statement is a summary of revenue, expenses, and profit for a particular accounting period, whether it is a month, quarter, or year. The income statement presents activities, operations, and their results over a specific period of time. The balance sheet, on the other hand, is a report of current condition or position, showing the status of the firm's assets, liabilities, and net worth at a particular time.

As a statement of operations, a well-prepared income statement can be used to monitor several key ratios, including profit margin, multipliers, utilization, revenue per employee, and indirect expense (overhead) factors. The balance sheet can be used to monitor working capital and average collection period of monies owed to the firm. These statements provide indicators of the firm's ability to manage debt (leverage), pay current debt (solvency), and convert assets to cash (liquidity).

*Management reports.* The computerized financial management system may produce invoices, summaries of monies owed to and owed by the firm (accounts receivable and accounts payable), reports for tax and regulatory agencies, and other information for use in general firm management. Project reports track expenses against budgets and/or the project architect's estimates of what it will take to complete the task, phase, or project. These reports may provide detail to help the project manager understand and manage the financial aspects of the firm's project services; they may also provide summary information on project performance to the firm's leadership.

*Frequency of reporting.* How often should financial statements be prepared?

▷ **Financial Health (7.3)** offers a number of ratios and illustrates flash reports that can help in assessing the firm's financial performance.

▷ **Project Controls (13.3)** discusses project status reports and provides status reports and examples.

Here are the income statement and balance sheet for a hypothetical nine-person firm for the year just ended.

As shown in the income statement, the firm took in $718,840 in revenues and incurred $659,651 in expenses, ending the year with a profit of $59,189. (This is labeled net profit before taxes because no federal, state, or local income taxes have been deducted.)

While the principals may have considered this profit level to be adequate, the firm missed its budgeted profit of $90,000.

An analysis of the income statement shows that revenues from fees were below estimates and that while the firm was able to keep direct labor and other direct expenses within budget, it was less successful with outside consultants and indirect (overhead) expenses.

In budgeting for the coming year, this firm will need to boost fees, control overhead expenses, or establish a more realistic profit target.

On the balance sheet, the firm ended the year with $240,868 in assets, $140,694 of which represents work billed but not yet paid by clients (accounts receivable), as well as another $46,182 in work in progress.

The firm's liabilities, including a few bills payable and a note to the bank, totaled $32,168. Subtracting this from assets produces a net worth (owners' equity) of $208,700.

Note that the balance sheet is only a snap-shot. It produces some valuable information (for example, the firm has only $4,182 in cash on hand—not enough to cover its accounts payable of $7,168) and flags significant problems (for example, the need to track and collect accounts receivable). To be most useful, however, it would be necessary to compare this balance sheet with one prepared at the end of the previous period to see if assets, liabilities, and owner's net worth are increasing or decreasing.

**INCOME STATEMENT** (for the period beginning January 1 and ending December 31)

| Revenues | BUDGET | ACTUAL | VARIANCE |
|---|---|---|---|
| Fees | $700,000 | $681,340 | ($18,660) |
| Reimbursable expenses | 37,500 | 37,500 | 0 |
| Total revenues | $737,500 | $718,840 | ($18,660) |

| Expenses | BUDGET | ACTUAL | VARIANCE |
|---|---|---|---|
| Direct expenses | | | |
| Direct personnel cost | $187,500 | $185,897 | $1,603 |
| Outside consultants | 124,000 | 128,500 | (4,500) |
| Other direct expenses | 18,500 | 16,483 | 2,017 |
| Total direct expenses | 330,000 | 330,880 | (880) |
| Indirect expenses | | | |
| Indirect personnel | 130,000 | 143,566 | (13,566) |
| Other indirect expenses | 150,000 | 147,705 | 2,295 |
| Total indirect expenses | 280,000 | 291,271 | (11,271) |
| Reimbursable expenses | 37,500 | 37,500 | 0 |
| Total expenses | 647,500 | 659,651 | ($12,151) |
| Net profit before taxes | $90,000 | $59,189 | ($30,811) |

**BALANCE SHEET** (as of December 31)

| Assets | BUDGET | ACTUAL | VARIANCE |
|---|---|---|---|
| Cash | $10,000 | $4,182 | ($5,818) |
| Accounts receivable | 150,000 | 140,694 | (9,306) |
| Work in progress | 50,000 | 46,182 | (3,818) |
| Fixed assets (less depreciation) | 50,000 | 49,810 | (190) |
| Total assets | $260,000 | $240,868 | ($19,132) |

| Liabilities and owners' equity | BUDGET | ACTUAL | VARIANCE |
|---|---|---|---|
| Accounts payable | $10,000 | $7,168 | ($2,832) |
| Notes payable | 25,000 | 25,000 | 0 |
| Total liabilities | 35,000 | 32,168 | (2,832) |
| Owner's equity | 225,000 | 208,700 | (16,300) |
| Total liabilities and equity | $260,000 | $240,868 | ($19,132) |

The answer is a function of the size and complexity of the firm and how often management needs to look at the financial performance. Many firms operate satisfactorily with semimonthly summaries of project hours spent and monthly financial statements. Others use computer programs that provide information whenever it is needed—sometimes in the form of "flash reports" or weekly summaries on topics such as accounts receivable and payable, project budget summaries, and cash on hand. Most firms have the ability to access the latest financial information from their computer systems. Firms also need to prepare reports for banks, insurance carriers, the government, and at times clients. Such requirements influence the frequency of reporting.

In several areas of the financial arena, it may be necessary or merely helpful to seek special advice.

*Accountants.* Public accountants and certified public accountants (CPAs) are expert in preparing financial statements, auditing, and preparing and filing tax returns. CPAs are required to undergo additional formal preparation and testing and are licensed by the state. They are experts in tax and audit matters. Accountants can help set up the firm's financial books and can direct the bookkeeping staff in proper procedures. Depending on their background and experience, accountants may be equipped to provide management advice to architects about their business operations.

*Lawyers.* Lawyers are knowledgeable in matters such as legal form of practice, business entity registrations, labor and employment, corporate bylaws, securities, pensions, contracts, liability, and litigation. In addition, some lawyers have become adept at various forms of business transactions, relationships, and regulations; such experience may be helpful to architects in areas affecting finances, such as contract and fee negotiations and collections.

*Management consultants.* Architecture practice management has emerged as a new and distinct discipline. Such capabilities can be provided by management consultants, some of whom have specialized in working with architects and who may be architects themselves.

*Personal financial advisors.* A new field has emerged for financial advisors, analysts, and planners who provide advice regarding personal financial matters, including personal income and expense budgeting, insurance, investments, and retirement. Although some of these individuals may represent insurance companies, stockbrokers, or retirement plan administrators, others are independent consultants who provide advice on a fee-for-service basis.

It is important that the consultant

- Have the appropriate credentials
- Have relevant experience, especially in situations similar to yours
- Be prepared to listen to and understand your problem, not just give pat answers or prescriptions
- Be someone with whom you feel personally comfortable and can work closely

*Peter Piven, FAIA*

## USING FINANCIAL REPORTS

Architects do not have to be accountants to be assertive managers of financial information. Architects need to understand the significance of financial information rather than the details of how reports are prepared. They are then in a position to ask questions, seek clarification, and have enough information to make the decisions necessary to maintain a healthy practice.

### For More Information

*An Architect's Guide to Financial Management* (1997), by Lowell V. Getz, updates *Financial Management for Architects* (1980), by Robert E. Mattox, FAIA. Getz's book builds upon principles in the Mattox work.

# Computerized Financial Systems

*Lowell Getz, CPA*

With the price of hardware and software within reach of even the smallest firms, virtually any architecture firm can use a computerized financial system. The task facing the architect is to identify and select the system that is most appropriate to the firm's current needs and for the foreseeable future.

### Getting Started
First-time buyers should begin by talking with colleagues to learn about their experiences with the various systems. Attending seminars, subscribing to newsletters, and talking with experienced consultants are other ways of getting the latest information in this fast-changing field. The point is that you should research the field before selecting a system. A casual visit to the computer store usually will not result in the most appropriate solution to your needs.

### Selecting the System
Concentrate on finding the most appropriate software for the computer platform you use in your office. In most cases, the system will be Windows-based. As you become familiar with what is available, the search will narrow to a few software vendors whose financial reports appear to meet your needs. Review the output reports in detail, and evaluate the system for its management aspects. Can you find the information you need without hunting through several reports? Are the summary reports valuable and the detail breakdowns in appropriate formats for your use? Try not to get bogged down in the technical aspects of the system, such as maximum capabilities and transaction speed.

These points will prove useful in finding the right system:

- Review your present system. Look for improvements that you would like incorporated into the new system.
- Solicit vendor responses. Develop a list of vendors whose systems interest you and request additional information from them.
- Determine finalists. Narrow your choices to two or three systems that best satisfy your needs. Obtain a demonstration disk and examine samples of the vendor's documentation.
- If possible, view a working demonstration, preferably in the office of a comparable firm, and check references.

### Accounting Functions
As you begin to examine the products available, you will be reviewing systems to accomplish various accounting functions:

*Accounts receivable.* The system prepares and keeps track of invoices that have been sent out but are not yet paid, as well as unbilled work in progress. Information is posted from time sheet records and reimbursable expense reports into the accounts receivable module.

*Accounts payable.* The system prepares checks and keeps track of the amount of payables owed by the firm. The accounts payable module ensures that materials and services have been charged either to the proper project or to the overhead account. Reimbursable expenses need to be controlled separately so that they can be properly billed to the client.

*Payroll.* The payroll module is set up to deduct federal, state, and local taxes, along with insurance payments and any other payroll deductions. Other reports are automatically prepared on a quarterly and year-end basis.

*General ledger.* This module collects all accounting transactions and creates summaries at the end of the month or the close of the accounting period. The summarized information is presented to the firm's principals in the form of financial statements.

*Project control.* The project control module collects and reports actual-against-budgeted information, which enables project managers to determine how projects are progressing. This module is the most important one to consider in making your selection. The other modules are basic to all businesses, but project control is unique. That is why it is important to select a system specifically designed for architecture firms rather than one adapted from some other source (e.g., a time-and-billing system for lawyers or accountants).

### Key System Characteristics
Keep the following points in mind when choosing a computer system:

*Integrated systems.* Integrated systems allow data to be entered once and automatically posted to all modules. For example, a time sheet entry would be processed in both the project control and payroll modules. Integrated systems are superior to stand-alone systems (which require that data be entered separately into each module) because fewer mistakes are likely to be made.

*Experience.* How long has the vendor been serving the architecture/engineering market, and what is its reputation in the industry? These points are very important because although many excellent systems have been developed, vendors that do not have staying power may not be around later to serve your needs.

*References.* What firms in your area are using the system? Can you visit them for an on-site demonstration? Checking references is a must before making a decision.

*Documentation and training.* What kind of documentation is available with the software, and how clearly is it written? What training is available with the system, and what kind of service is available after the sale (e.g., is there an 800 number for help)?

*System upgrades.* Good software vendors are constantly upgrading and improving their products to stay current with the state of the art. Inquire about the vendor's history of upgrades and on what terms they are made available to customers.

*Custom programming.* If the system does not meet your needs in all respects, what are the possibilities for customization? Does the system allow you to design your own reports?

Will the vendor provide custom programming services? Keep in mind that the latter may make the system unable to incorporate later upgrades.

*Local support.* Are there local support people who really know how to operate the system to help in troubleshooting, advise on upgrades, and customize the system if you need it?

*Contract terms.* Review contract terms with an attorney who is familiar with computer-service contracts. Try to negotiate some holdback payments until the system has been operated using your data; that is the ultimate test. Negotiate as much training time as you can get; this is one area in which the vendor has considerable leeway. Ask the attorney to investi-

### TYPICAL FINANCIAL MANAGEMENT PROGRAM MODULES

Today many software packages, most of which can run on personal computers, make computer-based financial management accessible to firms of all sizes. Typically these packages are divided into modules that handle various aspects of project and general accounting and provide the information and reports the firm needs to monitor projects, invoice clients, track accounts receivable and payable, produce payroll, and

provide necessary government reports. Some packages enter information into databases that can be manipulated by the user. Many include custom report-writing features.

The diagram here outlines the modules and reports for the Wind2 FMS, developed and distributed by Wind2 Software Inc., Fort Collins, Colorado.

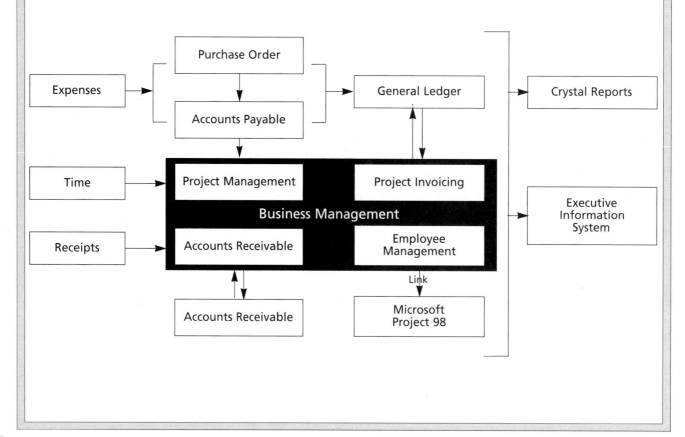

gate the contract provisions concerning what happens if the software vendor goes out of business.

*User group.* Determine whether a local user group exists for the system under investigation, and obtain information on the group's activities. Call members of the group and ask about their experience with the system. User groups are formed to help the vendor get feedback about desired system enhancements. Although not an overriding consideration, the existence of a user group is one more sign that the vendor is committed to the long-term development of the system.

*Overall service.* The vendor's attitude and responsiveness are often good clues about whether the product should be selected. Observe how easy it is to contact the vendor's rep-

resentatives and get answers to your questions. If the vendor is difficult to reach, the problem will only grow after you become a customer.

You will rarely find one system that clearly stands out among all others. Thus, when making the final decision, weigh the pros and cons and choose based on a few overriding characteristics. By making a careful study and comparing the various systems, you increase the chance of selecting one that meets your needs.

*Lowell V. Getz is a financial consultant to architecture, engineering, planning, and environmental service firms. He has written, taught, and lectured widely on financial management.*

---

Financial Management Software
for Large A/E Firms

**AXIUM**
XTS Software Corporation
5150 S.W. Griffith Drive
PO Box 2208
Beaverton, OR 97075-2208
(800) 637-2727
www.axiumae.com

**BST Enterprise**
BST Consultants, Inc.
5925 Benjamin Center Drive,
Suite 110
Tampa, FL 33626
(800) 726-3300
www.bstconsultants.com

---

Time Tracking Software

**Timeslips**
**Timesheet Professional**
**Carpe Diem Electronic Timesheet**
Sage U.S. Holdings, Inc.
17950 Preston Road, Suite 800
Dallas, TX 75252
(972) 818-3900
www.timeslips.com

---

Financial Management Software
for Medium to Large Firms (Ten or
More Employees)

**Advantage**
(formerly Harper and Shuman
CFMS)
Deltek Systems, Inc.
68 Moulton Street
Cambridge, MA 02138
(617) 492-4410
www.deltek.com

**Peachtree Software**
1505 Pavilion Place
Norcross, GA 30093
(800) 247-3224
www.peachtree.com

**Semaphore**
7320 S.W. Hunziker Street
Tigard, OR 97223
(888) SEMA411
www.sema4.com

**Wind2**
Wind2 Software, Inc.
1825 Sharp Point Drive
Ft. Collins, CO 80525
Phone: (970) 482-7145
Sales: (800) 779-4632
www.wind2.com

---

Financial Management Software
for Small Firms

**Quickbooks Pro\***
Intuit, Inc.
(800) 433-8810
www.quickbooks.com

*Architect's Guide to
QuickBooks Pro v.2000*
(bookwith CD)
by Karen Mitchell and Craig
Savage
Online Accounting
3144 Spring Street
Redwood City, CA 94063
(650) 361-1399

\* Quickbooks is a general small business accounting software program. Some customization is needed to adapt it to the accounting needs of an architectural practice. *Architect's Guide to Quickbooks* is a resource about the Quickbooks program. The CD with the book contains a sample architectural firm file, which significantly reduces the setup time. Many small firms find that that this program meets their accounting needs.

# 7.2 Financial Planning

## Lowell Getz, CPA

*Financial planning sets targets and provides essential information for pricing professional services and operating the practice.*

The principal task of a financial management system is to help the firm achieve its practice and business goals. Effective financial management requires guideposts—some ideas about where the firm is and wants to be next week, next month, next year, or even beyond. The guideposts come from the firm's own objectives: profit targets, staffing needs, and the costs of providing the level of service it deems appropriate.

### BUSINESS PLANNING

Business planning enables an architecture firm to chart and follow its course instead of reacting to situations and opportunities as they arise. Planning begins with "big-picture" strategic thinking and positioning. Goals and strategies are then translated into a business plan—a set of financial projections and operational plans that will support the principals in leading a firm.

Business plans may be prepared at all levels of formality, from a few ideas and numbers on a single sheet of paper to a carefully prepared instrument the firm can use to seek a line of credit, bank loan, or some other form of funding. Frequency of preparation varies, too, although a common approach is to prepare a plan before the start of each year. Annual financial plans typically include four components:

**Financial Systems (7.1) outlines basic financial management concepts and systems.**

- *A revenue projection,* which outlines anticipated revenues from projects under agreement and in the negotiation stages and estimates revenues from projects not yet secured
- *A staffing plan,* which defines the size and cost of the staff required to provide the services outlined in the revenue projection
- *An overhead expense budget,* which defines the indirect costs of supporting the staff and providing the services outlined in the revenue projection and staffing plans
- *A profit plan,* which establishes and budgets the profit required to sustain the firm and allow it to meet its goals

These four components are closely interrelated; decisions made about any one will affect the others, so it is necessary to develop them concurrently. With this said, the planning process can proceed along one of the two paths shown in the accompanying graphic, Paths to Profit Planning:

- Start with the workload you expect and determine the resources, including profit, needed to accomplish it (Path A).
- Start with the staff and other resources you have, add the profit you seek, and determine the workload you need to support them (Path B).

**The discussion in the text follows Path A. The discussion in The Minimalist Financial Manager follows Path B.**

As an alternative, it is possible to start with the profit you would like to have and determine the relationship of revenue and expenses needed to produce it. All of the approaches set profit goals, help in deciding billing rates, and provide yardsticks for monitoring progress and making course adjustments to keep the firm on track.

---

LOWELL V. GETZ *is a financial consultant to architecture, engineering, planning, and environmental service firms. He has written, taught, and lectured widely on financial management.*

| PATH A | PATH B |
|---|---|
| Start with the workload you expect and determine the resources needed to accomplish it: | Start with the resources you have and determine the revenues needed to support them: |
| 1 Project the firm's revenues. | 1 Calculate staff expenses. |
| 2 Establish staffing needs. | 2 Calculate overhead expenses. |
| 3 Determine overhead expenses. | 3 Set a profit target. |
| 4 Develop a profit plan. | 4 Develop a revenue goal. |

Either way, you are then in a position to
  5  Establish billing rates.
  6  Set project profit goals.

Then, after collecting some basic financial information, you can
  7  Monitor the firm's financial performance.
  8  Make the adjustments needed to keep the firm on course.

## REVENUE PROJECTION

The planning process can start with projected revenues, expenses, or profit. Most firms begin by projecting revenues. The revenue projection (i.e., what you realistically expect to gain in project fees and any other revenue) should be neither too optimistic nor too pessimistic but should reflect your best estimate of market conditions over the next twelve months. Beginning with projects in hand and projecting the possibilities of acquiring projects from outstanding proposals, this plan establishes marketing goals for the firm over the planning period. The revenue projection usually includes three sections, each covering one type of projected income:

*Existing projects to be completed.* Work to be accomplished on existing projects is budgeted by month for the balance of the year based on the amount of compensation yet to be earned. Work that extends beyond the plan year can be budgeted in total for the following year or years. The sum of these figures is the firm's backlog, or total amount to be earned on existing projects. The backlog figure is an important planning tool and needs to be monitored carefully. An early warning sign of impending problems is a shrinking backlog. If the backlog is not replenished at the rate it is being worked off, the firm will face a shortfall of work in the months ahead.

*Proposals outstanding.* This section of the revenue projection lists proposals and provides an estimate of the probability of converting them into projects. An estimate is also made regarding when this work is likely to be awarded. The revenue estimate is then made by month and entered into the plan.

> **At first glance preparing a monthly projection seems like extra effort. However, this will help you plan cash flow. It's just as important to know when cash is likely to arrive as to know how much is expected.**

*William H. Haire, AIA, Oklahoma State University*

Here is a quick-but-not-so-dirty approach to financial planning and management in six steps:

## Step 1: ESTABLISH A PROFIT PLAN.

Financial guideposts come from a profit plan—which is also an estimated operating budget. Here is a bare-bones method for profit planning for the small firm:

A. Estimate your expenses. Include salaries of principals and staff (include any planned adjustments), payroll taxes and benefits, and office expenses (use past history as a starting point and estimate anticipated changes over the next year). Do not include pass-throughs such as reimbursables and fees for project-related outside consultants.

B. Set a profit goal. Each firm sets its own profit goal. In the case illustrated here, the firm has established a goal of 20 percent of net revenues before any income taxes are paid.

C. Calculate the net revenue goal by adding estimated expenses and the profit goal. This is called net because you have omitted reimbursables and outside consultants' fees.

### Sample Profit Plan (excludes consultants and reimbursable expenses)

*Expenses*

| Salaries | | |
|---|---|---|
| Principal | (1 @ $75,000) | $75,000 |
| Registered architect | (1 @ $45,000) | 45,000 |
| Technical employees | (2 @ $30,000) | 60,000 |
| Secretary | (1 @ $20,000) | 20,000 |
| Total salaries | | $200,000 |
| Payroll taxes and benefits (@ 25%) | | 50,000 |

| Office expenses | |
|---|---|
| Rent | $12,300 |
| Utilities | 5,500 |
| Telephone | 2,500 |
| Equipment purchase, lease, maintenance | 8,000 |
| Postage, shipping | 1,500 |
| Publications | 1,000 |
| Insurance (auto, office, liability) | 16,000 |
| Office supplies | 2,500 |
| Travel | 5,000 |
| Printing | 3,500 |
| Marketing tools | 3,200 |
| Professional development: dues, training, etc. | 5,000 |
| Legal and accounting fees | 3,000 |
| Other expenses | 1,000 |
| Total office expenses | 70,000 |
| Total expenses | $320,000 |
| *Profit Goal @ 20% of net revenues* | 80,000 |
| *Net Revenue Goal* | $400,000 |

## Step 2: RESTATE THE PROFIT PLAN TO REFLECT EFFICIENCY.

In architecture firms, revenue (and profit) are generated by direct services labor—people working on projects. The most easily used common denominator for planning and measuring financial performance is direct salary expense:

*Direct salary expense (DSE) = Salary cost of hours charged to projects (billable time)*

Financial guideposts in the form of DSE multipliers can be easily calculated from a profit plan that has been restated to isolate expected DSE. This can be done by applying an expected utilization ratio to total salaries:

*Utilization ratio = Direct salary expense ÷ Total salary expense*

Stated another way:

*Direct salary expense = Total salary expense ÷ Utilization ratio*

Utilization ratios are different for different firms, but statistical surveys indicate that most achieve about 65 percent overall efficiency (averaging all principals and employees) to maintain reasonable profitability. The other 35 percent is spent on nonbillable (indirect) time such as that spent for marketing, staff development, general office administration, vacations, holidays, sick leave, and so on.

The utilization ratio should be monitored because it reflects the firm's ability to generate revenue. A low percentage means low revenue potential, and a high percentage means high revenue potential.

Using the utilization ratio just described, the firm's profit plan can be restated:

### Restated Profit Plan (using a 65% utilization ratio)

| *Direct Salaries* | ($200,000 × 0.65) | | $130,000 |
|---|---|---|---|
| *Indirect Expenses* | | | |
| Indirect salaries | ($200,000 × 0.35) | $70,000 | |
| Payroll taxes and benefits | | 50,000 | |
| Office expenses | | 70,000 | |
| Total indirect expenses | | 190,000 | |
| *Total Direct Salaries + Indirect Expenses* | | | $320,000 |
| *Profit Goal @ 20% of revenues* | | | 80,000 |
| *Net Revenue Goal* | | | $400,000 |

## Step 3: CALCULATE NET MULTIPLIERS.

The next step is to calculate the planned DSE multipliers for each major item in the restated profit plan. Divide each major item by the direct salary expense amount as shown. The results for the illustrated firm are shown:

| To pay for direct salary expenses | $130,000 ÷ $130,000 | 1.00 |
|---|---|---|
| To pay for indirect expenses | 190,000 ÷ $130,000 | 1.46 |
| Equals the firm's *break-even multiplier* | | 2.46 |
| To add profit | 80,000 ÷ $130,000 | 0.62 |
| Equals the planned *net multiplier* | | 3.08 |

A low utilization ratio increases the necessary break-even multiplier because there are more indirect hours and fewer direct hours, resulting in a lower profit margin.

## Step 4: USE THE NET MULTIPLIER TO SET MINIMUM HOURLY BILLING RATES.

Using the sample firm's 3.08 net multiplier yields these hourly billing rates (at 2,080 hours in a year, rounded to the nearest dollar):

Principal (@ $75,000)  $36.06 × 3.08 = $111/hour
Registered architect (@ $45,000)  $21.63 × 3.08 = $67/hour
Technical staff (@ $30,000)  $14.42 × 3.08 = $44/hour
Clerical/administrative staff
(@ $20,000)  $9.62 × 3.08 = $30/hour

These are the minimum rates needed to meet the profit plan. Actual rates charged may also reflect the value of the services and market considerations.

## Step 5: SET PROJECT PROFIT GOALS.

To meet its profit plan, this firm needs to set aside 20 percent of its net revenues. When a project comes in, 20 percent off the top of the net fee must be set aside as untouchable. The project must be done for the money left if the profit plan is to be met.

## Step 6: USE ACTUAL NET MULTIPLIER EARNED TO MONITOR FINANCIAL PERFORMANCE.

This can be done quickly, easily, with reasonable accuracy, and without accountants. The only information needed is

- Net revenue earned (derived from fees invoiced)
- Direct salary expense (project hours at hourly salary rate as recorded on time sheets)

### Sample Current Project Analysis

|  | (1)<br>Net revenue<br>earned | ÷ | (2)<br>Direct salary<br>expense (DSE) | = | (3)<br>Net multiplier<br>earned | − | (4)<br>Break-even<br>multiplier | = | (5)<br>Profit multiple<br>earned | (6)<br>Approximate profit<br>or (loss) ((2) × (5)) |
|---|---|---|---|---|---|---|---|---|---|---|
| Project **A** | $20,000 | | $6,800 | | 2.94 | | 2.46 | | 0.48 | $3,264 |
| Project **B** | 35,000 | | 11,000 | | 3.18 | | 2.46 | | 0.72 | 7,920 |
| Project **C** | 12,500 | | 6,000 | | 2.08 | | 2.46 | | (0.38) | (2,280) |
| Project **D** | 42,000 | | 17,500 | | 2.40 | | 2.46 | | (0.06) | (1,050) |
| | $109,500 | | $41,300 | | 2.65 | | 2.46 | | 0.19 | $7,854 |

The sample current project analysis uses the break-even multiplier established as this firm's goal in Step 3. All figures are rounded to the nearest $100.

The break-even multiplier is the only variable factor in this analysis. It should be recalculated periodically using accrual-based financial information (you will probably need your accountant for this). In the meantime, check your utilization ratio. If it is holding about as planned,

your break-even probably hasn't changed much—unless, of course, some large indirect expense has come up unexpectedly.

Although it is not completely accurate (due to possible variations in the breakeven multiplier), this method of monitoring provides a simple and timely means of staying abreast of financial performance—and determining if and on which projects corrective action is needed.

This commentary and the next three (Staffing Plan, Overhead Expense Budget, and Profit Plan) provide views of the business plan of a hypothetical firm as it appears at the beginning of the year just ended.

An analysis of the revenue projection shows that the firm undertakes many projects of short duration. On the date this version of the plan was prepared (January 1), the firm had a backlog of $280,000 in expected revenues over the next nine months. There were three outstanding proposals totaling $300,000 in fees. After applying probability factors for actually receiving these projects, the principal preparing the plan assumed the firm would realize $105,000 in revenues from these proposals beginning in March.

The firm estimates that it requires $40,000 to $45,000 in revenues each month to sustain its staff and meet its overall goals; this figure is derived from the staffing, overhead expense, and profit plans shown in the next three commentaries as well as an assessment of how much of the projected revenue will be passed through to consultants. The "unidentified future work" figures, taken from the firm's marketing plan, establish the revenue that must be raised to meet its revenue goals.

Given the nature of the firm's projects, its revenue projection is updated monthly. Both backlog and outstanding proposals are carefully tracked. At the same time, the firm has a clear idea of the marketing effort required if it is to meet its goals

| | Total | Jan | Feb | Mar | Apr | May | June | July | Aug | Sept | Oct | Nov | Dec |
|---|---|---|---|---|---|---|---|---|---|---|---|---|---|
| **Existing Projects** | | | | | | | | | | | | | |
| Project A | $200* | $15 | $15 | $30 | $30 | $30 | $30 | $20 | $10 | $10 | $10 | | |
| Project B | 60 | 15 | 15 | 10 | 10 | 5 | 5 | | | | | | |
| Project C | 20 | 10 | 10 | | | | | | | | | | |
| Total backlog | $280 | | | | | | | | | | | | |
| | | | | | | | | | | | | | |
| **Proposals Outstanding** | | | | | | | | | | | | | |
| Project X    60 @ 25% | 15 | | | 5 | 5 | 5 | | | | | | | |
| Project Y    120 @ 50% | 60 | | | | 5 | 10 | 20 | 20 | 5 | | | | |
| Project Z    120 @ 25% | 30 | | | | | | | 5 | 10 | 10 | $5 | | |
| Total proposals | $105 | | | | | | | | | | | | |
| | | | | | | | | | | | | | |
| **Unidentified Future Work** | | | | | | | | | | | | | |
| Institutional clients | $115 | | | | | | | | 15 | 20 | 20 | $30 | $30 |
| Planning studies | 25 | | | | | | | | | | 5 | 10 | 10 |
| Total      $140 | | | | | | | | | | | | | |
| Grand Totals | $525 | $40 | $40 | $45 | $50 | $50 | $55 | $45 | $40 | $40 | $40 | $40 | $40 |

*This firm includes outstanding proposals by applying a probability factor to each one. For example, Project Z has an expected fee of $120,000 and the firm estimates that it has a 25 percent chance of acquiring the project. Thus only $30,000 is included in the projection.*

*All figures are in thousands of dollars.

***Unidentified future work.*** If your firm is typical, some portion of next year's revenues will come from projects that have not yet been identified. Using past experience and projections of what is likely to happen, the planner estimates where this new work will come from. Continuing work from existing projects should also be included in this estimate.

> **Financial Health (7.3) describes utilization ratios and their importance in firm management.**

## STAFFING EXPENSES

The next step is to develop a staffing plan, starting with a profile of the firm's staff and anticipating salary increases over the next year. This plan may be modified (through new hires and attrition) to bring it into concert with the revenue projection.

Certain assumptions need to be made in developing the staffing plan. Specifically, the percentage of billable time (utilization ratio) for each individual or category of personnel should be realistically estimated. Vacations and holidays need to be considered, as do allowances for training new personnel and continuing professional development for the staff.

Staffing plans require development of billing rates, either for individuals or for categories of staff. This begins with direct labor costs (hourly salary) and adds payroll burden (payroll taxes, fringe benefits, and other costs associated with salaries, such as sick time), general and administrative expenses, and a target profit that the firm hopes to earn.

For example, assume that the firm has an architect whose salary is $30.00 per hour. The billing rate can be calculated as shown. The overhead and profit rates used in this calculation come from other aspects of the business plan. (See the next section, Overhead Expenses.) Using the figures shown in the example produces a billing rate that is 3.125 times the cost of direct salary; in other words, a multiplier of 3.125 covers the costs of direct labor and overhead and also yields the desired profit for the firm in the example. It is important for a firm to derive the multiplier it requires to meet its goals so that it can price its services accurately.

## OVERHEAD EXPENSES

The next step is to develop an estimate of overhead or indirect expenses for the coming year. Each element of indirect expense should be listed together with the actual expenses for the previous year. Then realistic assumptions need to be made about what is likely to happen in the planning year.

Known cost increases, such as an increase in rent or insurance expense, should

▶ **Calculating an hourly billing rate:**

| | |
|---|---|
| Architect's hourly rate | $30.00 |
| Indirect expense* | 45.00 |
| Subtotal | $75.00 |
| Profit @ 25% | 18.75 |
| Hourly billing rate | $93.75 |

*Includes payroll burden @ 150%

---

### STAFFING PLAN

The hypothetical firm has a staff of five. For each staff member, the planner first calculates an hourly rate for direct labor (by dividing the individual's annual base salary by the number of hours available to be worked over the year, assumed at 2,080—52 weeks at 40 hours per week—for a full-time person employed for a full year).

Since all staff hours cannot be billed directly to projects, a utilization ratio (percent chargeable)1 is projected for each staff member. The resulting chargeable hours are translated into direct salary expense (chargeable hours

times hourly rate) and then into total billable revenue (direct salary expense times the firm's multiplier). The last column shows the portion of each staff member's salary that is not expected to be charged to projects and that will become part of the overhead (indirect) expense budget.

This firm must bill approximately $400,000 during the year in net revenues (that is, exclusive of consultants and reimbursable expenses) to sustain the level of staffing shown, cover its overhead, and meet its profit goal.

| | Base Salary | Hours per Year | Hourly Rate | Percent Chargeable[1] | Chargeable Hours | Direct Salary[2] | Billable Revenue[3] | Indirect Salary[4] |
|---|---|---|---|---|---|---|---|---|
| Principal | $75,000 | 2,080 | $36.06 | 60% | 1,248 | $45,000 | $138,600 | $30,000 |
| Registered architect | 45,000 | 2,080 | 21.63 | 70% | 1,456 | 31,500 | 97,000 | 13,500 |
| Technical employee | 30,000 | 2,080 | 14.42 | 85% | 1,768 | 25,500 | 78,500 | 4,500 |
| Technical employee | 30,000 | 2,080 | 14.42 | 85% | 1,768 | 25,500 | 78,500 | 4,500 |
| Secretary | 20,000 | 2,080 | 9.62 | 12.5% | 260 | 2,500 | 7,700 | 17,500 |
| Totals | $200,000 | | | | $6,500 | $130,000 | $400,300 | $70,000 |

[1] It is important to recognize the distinction between the terms *billable* and *chargeable* and their implications. Time spent on projects is chargeable and may or may not be billable. If the project fee is anything other than an hourly fee (with or without a maximum), then none of the hours charged to the project are billed. Billing is a percentage of the fee for work completed. Therefore, billable hours are possible only on hourly fee projects.

[2] Direct salary is calculated by multiplying the chargeable hours by the staff member's hourly rate.

[3] Billable revenue is calculated by multiplying direct salary expense by the firm's DSE multiplier (3.08—see profit plan).

[4] Indirect salary is calculated by multiplying nonchargeable hours (available hours minus chargeable hours) by each staff member's hourly rate.

## OVERHEAD EXPENSE BUDGET

The hypothetical firm anticipates that its overhead expenses will total $190,000 for the planning year. Dividing this figure by the total projected direct salary expense ($130,000, from the staffing plan) yields an overhead rate of 1.46 or 146 percent of direct salary expense (DSE); this rate is used to determine multipliers (for hourly billing rates).

|  | Prior Year | Budget Year | Change |
|---|---|---|---|
| Indirect labor | $68,000 | $70,000 | $2,000 |
| Payroll burden (on total salary) | 45,000 | 50,000 | 5,000 |
| Rent | 12,300 | 12,300 | 0 |
| Utilities | 5,000 | 5,500 | 500 |
| Telephone | 2,200 | 2,500 | 300 |
| Equipment purchase/maintenance | 10,000 | 8,000 | (2,000) |
| Postage and shipping | 1,500 | 1,500 | 0 |
| Publications | 1,000 | 1,000 | 0 |
| Insurance | 17,500 | 16,000 | (1,500) |
| Office supplies | 2,800 | 2,500 | (300) |
| Travel | 4,800 | 5,000 | 200 |
| Printing | 4,500 | 3,500 | (1,000) |
| Marketing tools | 3,000 | 3,200 | 200 |
| Professional development | 4,000 | 5,000 | 1,000 |
| Legal and accounting expenses | 3,000 | 3,000 | 0 |
| Other general and administrative expenses | 1,000 | 1,000 | 0 |
| Totals | $185,600 | $190,000 | $4,400 |

**Calculation of Overhead Rate Based on Direct Salary Expense (DSE)**

| | | |
|---|---|---|
| Total overhead | $190,000 | |
| Divided by total salary expense (staffing plan) | 130,000 | |
| Yields overhead rate | 1.46 | or 46% |

**Calculation of DSE Break-Even Multiplier***

| | |
|---|---|
| Total direct salary expense + total overhead | $320,000 |
| Divided by total direct salary expense | 130,000 |
| Yields DSE break-even multiplier | 2.46 |

**Calculation of DPE Break-Even Multiplier***

| | |
|---|---|
| Total direct personnel expense | |
|    Total direct salary expense | $130,000 |
|    Payroll burden | 50,000 |
| Total personnel expense | $180,000 |
| Total overhead (without payroll burden) | $140,000 |
| Total direct personnel expense + total overhead | $320,000 |
| Divided by total direct personnel expense | $180,000 |
| Yields DPE break-even multiplier | 1.78 |

* These are called break-even multipliers because a profit target has yet to be considered.

be factored in at actual amounts. Other expense items should be examined and, where necessary, increased or decreased to account for inflation and historical trends. It is good advice to make realistic assumptions based on what is likely to occur rather than to increase all expenses by a flat percentage rate.

With the total overhead number in mind, it's possible to set the projected overhead rate for the coming year. Most architecture firms use the direct salary expense (DSE) approach, in which the total overhead (indirect expense) budget is divided by the total budgeted direct salary expense to arrive at an overhead rate.

The profit plan presented here includes the information developed above. To provide a complete picture, it adds the amount the firm expects to pay for outside consultants ($125,000) and for reimbursable expenses ($37,500). The plan shows a profit target of $80,000, or 20 percent of net revenues (gross revenues minus pass-throughs to consultants and reimbursable expenses).

This, and the previous three commentaries, all provide insights into the hypothetical firm's business plan and performance. The information shows how the firm's budget, revenue, staffing, overhead expense, and profit plans relate to and interact with each other.

There is, however, a great deal that we don't know about the hypothetical firm: What are its overall goals, and how is it positioning itself? Are its utilization rates going up or down? Are accounts receivable aging and collection periods lengthening? Is the firm financially healthy over the long run? Is the firm producing quality architecture? Business plans and financial reports can't answer the first and last questions on the list. As they are produced, updated, and compared with past performance, however, these financial plans and reports—and the judgments drawn from them—produce a picture of the firm and its ability to realize its financial goals.

**Profit target**

| | |
|---|---:|
| Projected revenues | $525,000 |
| Minus reimbursable expenses | (25,000) |
| Minus outside consultant expenses | (100,000) |
| Projected net fees | $400,000 |

Minus projected expenses:

| | | |
|---|---:|---:|
| Direct salary expense | $130,000 | |
| Indirect expenses | 90,000 | |
| Total | | $320,000 |
| Profit target (20% of projected net fees) | | $80,000 |

**Net DSE multiplier required to attain profit target**

| | |
|---|---:|
| Total projected net fees | $400,000 |
| Divided by direct salary expense | $130,000 |
| Yields net DSE multiplier (rounded) | 3.08 |

Other firms use a direct personnel expense (DPE) approach, in which payroll burden (payroll taxes, Social Security, workers' compensation, unemployment insurance, health and pension plans, holidays, sick days, and other fringe benefits) is removed from the overhead expense budget and included with salaries as part of direct personnel expense.

## THE PROFIT PLAN

Profit is budgeted in the same manner as any other financial item. That is, the firm should have an expected level of profit and should budget for it in the same way that it projects and budgets for staffing and overhead expenses.

Profits are required to compensate employees, to fund capital expansion and growth, and to reward the owners for their risk. Some profits are subsequently distributed to the firm's owner—and perhaps to others through bonuses or profit-sharing plan—and some may be reinvested in the firm. It may not be possible to earn the targeted profit on all projects, but the important point is to establish an expectation level.

The most common method of estimating profit in professional firms is to establish it as a percentage of revenue. Another approach to establishing a profit target is to consider the owners' investment in the firm, establish a reasonable return on that investment, and then calculate how much must be earned on the expected level of project activity both to achieve that return and to make any bonus or profit-sharing payments to non-owners.

However the profit target is set, each new project should be reviewed in light of this target. Projects produced at profits lower than the target reduce the overall profit.

## INDIVIDUAL PROJECT PLANNING

An architecture firm accomplishes its profit plan one project at a time. Each project is a building block that helps achieve—or detract from—the firm's practice goals. Here are some keys to meeting your firm's profit targets:

**Seeking the Project (6.2)** covers the bases: seeking the right projects, preparing the client, assessing risks and opportunities, and developing appropriate pricing proposals.

- The right clients and projects
- Project pricing that is appropriate to the firm and its profit goals as well as to the client and project
- Contracts that implement these intentions
- A staff (and, where appropriate, consultants) with the talent and experience to provide the services
- Good management of project services, relationships, and risks

The remaining implementation details revolve around the other aspects of the firm's financial management: acquiring and maintaining the cash required to operate the practice, staffing at expected levels, controlling overhead expenses, monitoring project activities against budgets, billing and collecting monies owed the firm, and generally keeping a steady hand on the financial tiller. These subjects are addressed in Financial Health (8.3) and Acquiring Capital (8.4).

# 7.3 Financial Health

## Peter Piven, FAIA

*Well-managed firms continually assess their financial health and take appropriate measures to stay on track.*

Architects aspire to financial health. The reason is simple: They cannot attain their practice goals unless they do. They must practice at whatever level of profitability is required to stay in business, to fulfill promises made to clients, and to fulfill their own practice goals, including providing appropriate rewards for performance, risk, and a reasonable return on the firm owners' investment.

## THREE FACTORS IN FINANCIAL PLANNING

Financial health requires understanding, planning, monitoring, and controlling three interrelated areas:

- Profitability—the ability to create an excess of revenue over expenses
- Liquidity—the ability to convert an asset to cash with relative speed and ease and without significant loss in value
- Solvency—the ability to meet financial obligations as they come due

▶ **Appendix B defines most of the financial terms used in this topic.**

### Profitability

Profitability is required at three levels:

- For the firm, generally in the form of retained or reinvested earnings, so it can provide for capital investment, endure downward economic cycles, and sustain growth
- For those who produce the profit, as a reward for having done so
- For the risk taken by the firm's owners and as a return on their investment in the firm

By attending to profitability, architects ensure that they will not incur more expense than revenue on a project or on a firm-wide basis. The normal project cycle includes three steps: performing services, invoicing, and collecting cash to cover the cost—both direct and indirect—of performing the services. If the architect manages successfully, this cycle not only yields sufficient cash to cover costs but also returns profit to the firm. Practicing at a loss means two things: There is no profit and, even worse, essential costs are not being covered. Regardless of whether the firm uses the cash method or the accrual method for its accounting, losses eventually result in a cash drain—more is expended than is taken in.

▶ **Financial Systems (7.1) describes architecture firms' revenues and expenses, as well as cash and accrual methods.**

### Liquidity

In operating their practices, architects acquire both fixed (long-term) and current (short-term) assets. *Fixed assets* are those, such as real estate, leasehold improvements, furniture, fixtures, equipment, and automobiles, that they do not intend to convert to cash in the foreseeable future. *Current assets* include both cash and other assets that must be converted to cash, especially *accounts receivable* (the value of services

---

**PETER PIVEN** *is the Philadelphia-based principal consultant of the Coxe Group, Inc., marketing and management consultants to design professionals. He has written and lectured widely on practice issues including compensation management.*

billed but not yet collected) and *work in progress* (the value of services performed but not yet billed).

To keep a practice financially viable, the architect must maintain the firm's liquidity by constantly converting work in progress to accounts receivable by invoicing regularly. Then accounts receivable must be converted to cash by assiduously maintaining collections.

**Project Controls (13.3) suggests strategies for invoicing and collecting payments.**

## Solvency

Solvency is where the architect feels the day-to-day effects of profitability and liquidity—the need and ability to pay bills to keep the practice running. Solvency and profitability are closely related; a firm that is unprofitable will, in the long run, not have enough money to pay its debts. In the extreme, the inability to pay debts when they come due leads to insolvency and bankruptcy.

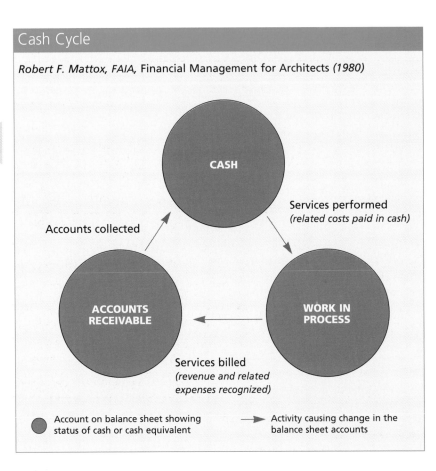

### Cash Cycle

*Robert F. Mattox, FAIA,* Financial Management for Architects *(1980)*

Accounts collected

CASH

Services performed
*(related costs paid in cash)*

ACCOUNTS RECEIVABLE

WORK IN PROCESS

Services billed
*(revenue and related expenses recognized)*

● Account on balance sheet showing status of cash or cash equivalent

→ Activity causing change in the balance sheet accounts

## MANAGING CASH

Keeping solvent requires sound cash management. Solvency is a cash problem: How much cash is needed? For what purposes? When? From what sources?

Cash management is a systematic procedure for forecasting and controlling the cash that flows through the firm. The objective of cash management is to ensure that adequate cash is always on hand and that cash surpluses, when they exist, are invested wisely.

***Cash flow projections.*** The best tool for addressing these questions and evaluating a firm's solvency is *cash budgeting.* This involves forecasting anticipated flows of cash into and out of the firm over time by gathering and reporting information about the amounts, timing, and certainty of the firm's future cash receipts and payments. The cash budget predicts cash flow. Its purpose is to provide a plan to indicate when cash receipts and disbursements can be expected. The forecast should indicate needs for short-term borrowing as well as surpluses available for short-term investing.

The steps in developing a cash budget are listed here:

- Forecast billings.
- Forecast amounts and timing of cash receipts (collections) from those billings.
- Forecast cash receipts from sources other than project revenues, such as investments, rents, and sale of assets.
- Forecast cash disbursements, including payroll, consultants, other direct (project) expenses, indirect (overhead) expenses, reimbursable expenses, and capital expenditures.
- Combine receipt and disbursement schedules and calculate net monthly cash increases or decreases.

**AIA Firm Survey 2000 reports these billings per employee:**

| Firm size | Billings |
| --- | --- |
| Sole architect | $85,000 |
| 2–4 employees | 93,000 |
| 5–9 employees | 87,800 |
| 10–19 employees | 91,000 |
| 20–49 employees | 95,000 |
| 50+ employees | 105,000 |

Monthly increase or decrease, when combined with the beginning cash balance, indicates the firm's cash position at the end of each month. The ending cash balance of one month is the beginning balance for the next month.

*Robert F. Mattox, FAIA,* Financial Management for Architects *(1980)*

This cash projection, made as of March 1, looks at anticipated revenues in terms of when the firm expects to be collect them. For example, a total of $36,000 was billed in January; of this, $9,000 was paid in January, an additional $21,600 in February, and the remaining $5,400 is projected for collection in March. Similarly, 25 percent of the anticipated billing for March ($8,250 of $33,000) is expected to be earned in March, another 60 percent ($19,800) in April, and the final 15 percent ($4,950) in May.

Adding receipts from sources other than billings (e.g., interest) provides the total cash figure for each month. Subtracting disbursements leaves the firm with an expected monthly cash gain or loss. Adding the cash balance at the end of each previous month produces the projected cash balance for each month. Adding the actual $1,500 cash balance from February to the projected $3,950 net cash gain from March brings the month-ending cash balance for March to the $5,450 shown.

| **Cash Flow Projection:** March 1 | January | February | March | April | May |
|---|---|---|---|---|---|
| Total billings | | | | | |
|   Actual | $36,000 | $34,000 | | | |
|   Projected | | | $33,000 | $38,000 | $40,000 |
| Collections on accounts receivable | | | | | |
|   First month (25%) | 9,000 | 8,500 | 8,250 | 9,500 | 10,000 |
|   Second month (60%) | | 21,600 | 20,400 | 19,800 | 22,800 |
|   Third month (15%) | | | 5,400 | 5,100 | 4,950 |
| Other (nonoperating) receipts | | | 1,000 | 1,000 | 1,000 |
| Total cash receipts (cash in) | | | $35,050 | $35,400 | $38,750 |
| Cash disbursements | | | | | |
|   Direct expenses | | | $14,900 | $15,500 | $17,000 |
|   Indirect expenses | | | 16,000 | 17,500 | 15,200 |
|   Other (nonoperating) disbursements | | | 200 | 0 | 6,000 |
| Total cash disbursements (cash out) | | | $31,100 | $33,000 | $38,200 |
| Net cash gain (loss) during month | | | $3,950 | $2,400 | $550 |
| Cash balance at beginning of month | | | 1,500 | 5,450 | 7,850 |
| Cash balance at end of month | | $1,500 | $5,450 | $7,850 | $8,400 |

***Cash flow controls.*** Cash budgeting is planning in advance for cash that will be required in the future. Controlling cash flow requires measuring actual performance against the budget and taking corrective action as needed. Techniques for managing cash include these:

- Sustaining backlog by developing a continuing flow of new projects and services
- Billing promptly and correctly, ensuring that clients are aware of the services provided
- Monitoring cash receipts and pursuing collections
- Controlling disbursements
- Preparing cash budgets on a regular basis and using them to monitor actual cash flow

▶ *Cash flow,* which is sometimes used interchangeably with *cash budgeting,* means simply the movement of cash into and out of the firm. *Positive cash flow* means that more cash flowed into the firm than out during a particular period.

Billing and collection are especially important in managing cash flow. From an overall practice perspective, clients who are slow to pay may be in the process of becoming less satisfied or even dissatisfied with the firm's professional service—or perhaps experiencing other problems that do not bode well for the project.

In managing cash flow, managing collections is only half the problem; the other

*Robert F. Mattox, FAIA, Financial Management for Architects (1980)*

| Beginning backlog | Less | Earned revenue | Plus | New contracts | Equals | Ending backlog |

half involves controlling disbursements. Careful timing of disbursements can be an effective way to control cash outflow. The firm has more ability to control when it will make a disbursement than when it will receive a cash payment. It can defer payment to vendors and other payees, reduce principals' draws or salaries, and, if necessary, borrow funds on a short-term basis.

If cash projections indicate a continuing deficit, longer-term financing may be needed, by such means as the following:

- Refinancing a major asset with a long-term note or mortgage
- Adding capital from existing partners, new partners, or shareholders
- Retaining additional corporate earnings rather than distributing all profits
- Deferring capital or other expenditures

## FINANCIAL STRENGTH

There are many indicators of financial performance and financial health. Often these are expressed as simple ratios of numbers created in everyday operations and reflected in the firm's income statement or balance sheet. These ratios can be useful in establishing the need for working capital, assessing productivity, managing overhead and project expenses, establishing fees, and seeking credit.

*Working capital.* The architect needs to know not only how much cash will be required to meet expenses in the near term but also what the firm's general requirements for working capital are. Working capital is the minimum amount of liquid capital needed to sustain the firm in business; more specifically, it is the minimum amount needed to maintain the flow from cash to work in progress to accounts receivable and again to cash. Practically, it is calculated in this way:

Working capital = Current assets − Current liabilities

Current assets include cash or other assets that are readily convertible into cash (such as work in progress and accounts or notes receivable). Current liabilities are those that come due within the next 12 months.

*Receivables.* An architecture firm's largest single current asset is usually its accounts receivable. The liquidity of this asset is extremely important to the firm's financial well being. It is critical to convert accounts receivable (receivables) to cash in a consistent and timely manner.

> **Acquiring Capital (7.4) explores sources of additional funds, both for financing short-term cash flow requirements and for longer-term growth.**

*Operating Statistics Survey (Harper and Shuman, 1998)*

A number of surveys report overall financial performance indicators for architecture firms. As an example, here are some 1998 data from respondents to Harper and Shuman's operating statistics survey. As in all such reports, these numbers reflect the experience of only the survey respondents (in this case, more than 200 of Harper and Shuman's clients) and only in the year surveyed. Each survey defines its own terms. And, of course, the survey group may not reflect *your* practice.

| By Firm Type | Effective Multiplier | Overhead Rate | Charge-ability Ratio | Pretax Profit* |
|---|---|---|---|---|
| Architecture | 2.98 | 144% | 64% | 4.6% |
| Architecture/engineering | 2.73 | 147 | 64 | 5.0 |
| Engineering/architecture | 2.74 | 155 | 65 | 2.1 |
| Engineering | 2.68 | 132 | 66 | 5.9 |
| Environmental | 3.35 | 196 | 56 | 3.6 |
| Interior design | 2.95 | 163 | 59 | 0.0 |
| Other | 2.86 | 160 | 65 | 0.4 |

| By Firm Size | Effective Multiplier | Overhead Rate | Charge-ability Ratio | Pretax Profit* |
|---|---|---|---|---|
| 1 to 5 | 2.44 | 144% | 59% | 2.3% |
| 6 to 10 | 2.88 | 161 | 62 | 4.8 |
| 11 to 15 | 2.70 | 142 | 63 | 4.8 |
| 16 to 20 | 2.84 | 154 | 62 | 3.7 |
| 21 to 30 | 2.92 | 146 | 64 | 3.3 |
| 31 to 50 | 2.87 | 136 | 64 | 5.2 |
| 51 to 100 | 2.91 | 144 | 64 | 3.1 |
| 101 to 200 | 2.75 | 141 | 63 | 2.7 |
| 200+ | 2.88 | 142 | 66 | 5.9 |

* On net revenue

If the firm invoices for services at the end of the month in which services are performed and collects two months later, it will need funds to cover three months' operations. This amount represents one-quarter of the firm's annual revenues. Therefore, working capital requirements are closely related to the cycle on which the firm collects its receivables—its average collection period.

Although it is advisable to keep track of individual invoices rendered for collection purposes, it is also valuable to know the rate at which *all* invoices are being collected. The calculation is

Average collection period (in days) = Accounts receivable ÷ Average revenue per day

To calculate the average revenue per day, divide gross revenues by the number of days in the period being considered. As a convention, most analysts use 30 days per month and 360 days per year.

Architects are well advised to keep the average collection period as close to 30 days as possible, although this will clearly be difficult with certain kinds of clients.

***Revenues per employee.*** Another measure of financial health is earned revenue per employee. This can be a gross figure before paying consultants or a net figure after. It can also be calculated per *technical* employee or for *all* employees. Probably gross revenue per total employees is more useful when analyzing the firm's overall volume of activity (such as dollars expended for marketing and business development), and net revenue per total employees is most useful when analyzing matters of operational productivity (such as the effectiveness of computer-aided design systems).

***Firm-wide profit.*** As a percentage of net revenue, profit is an important indicator. Average profitability in the profession has been low for many years, with some surveys reporting average profits, before taxes and discretionary distributions, in the 1 to 2 percent range. At the same time, many firms are performing well, some with profitability in the 25 percent range. A reasonably attainable profit for many firms might be in the 10 to 15 percent range.

## MANAGING OVERHEAD

To continue in practice, an architecture firm incurs indirect (overhead) expenses that are necessary to keep the firm in operation and that are not chargeable to any specific project. Indirect expenses can amount to 30 to 40 percent of revenues and 100 to 200 percent of direct salary expense (DSE).

Indirect expense must be managed. If it is too high, the firm will probably not be able to produce a profit, regardless of how efficiently projects are being produced. If it is too low, the firm may be spending too little on marketing, management, benefits, administrative services, or other important areas that ultimately affect the quality and/or quantity of its services.

> **Financial Planning (7.2) discusses the roles of overhead, DSE (direct salary expenses) and DPE (direct personnel expense), in firm-wide financial planning.**

*Indirect expense factor.* It is important to understand the relationship between indirect expenses and projects. Although there are many ways to view this relationship, the most useful is the indirect expense (or overhead) factor, which is the ratio of all indirect expenses (including payroll burden and general and administrative expenses) to DSE:

Indirect expense factor = Total indirect expense ÷ DSE

An indirect expense factor of 1.75, or 175 percent, indicates that the firm requires $1.75 in indirect expense to support each $1.00 of DSE; conversely, each $1.00 of DSE requires $1.75 in overhead. Although this ratio will fluctuate on a month-to-month basis, it is possible to plan for, monitor, and control overhead to keep the indirect expense factor appropriate for the firm.

## SAMPLE TIME ANALYSIS REPORT

*MICRO/CFMS, Harper and Shuman, Inc., Cambridge, Massachusetts*

This report looks at the time reported by firm members over the past month, breaks it into direct and indirect hours, indicates the use of indirect hours (vacation, sick time, etc.), and calculates three ratios: (A) direct hours divided by total hours charged, (B) direct hours divided by hours actually worked, and (C) target ratio, as negotiated with each employee and entered into the system.

**Time Analysis Report:** Apple and Bartlett

| | Total | Dir. | Ind. | A | B | C | Vac | Sick | Hol | B.Dv | Civc | Mgmt. | Actg. | P.Dv | Other |
|---|---|---|---|---|---|---|---|---|---|---|---|---|---|---|---|
| | | Hours Worked | | | Ratios | | | | | Indirect Time (hours) | | | | | |
| **00001 Apple, William** | | | | | | | | | | | | | | | |
| Current | 89 | 82 | 7 | 92 | 92 | 55 | | | | | | 4 | | | 3 |
| Year-to-date | 840 | 552 | 288 | 66 | 68 | 55 | 16 | | 16 | 3 | | 23 | | | 229 |
| **00002 Bartlett, James** | | | | | | | | | | | | | | | |
| Current | 110 | 103 | 7 | 94 | 94 | 65 | | | | | | 4 | | | 3 |
| Year-to-date | 859 | 561 | 299 | 65 | 69 | 65 | 27 | | 16 | 12 | | 31 | | | 214 |
| **00101 Gray, Brenda** | | | | | | | | | | | | | | | |
| Current | 86 | 62 | 24 | 72 | 100 | 85 | 24 | | | | | | | | |
| Year-to-date | 821 | 685 | 137 | 83 | 94 | 85 | 32 | 37 | 24 | 3 | | | | | 42 |
| **00201 Stone, Richard** | | | | | | | | | | | | | | | |
| Current | 101 | 101 | | 100 | 100 | 95 | | | | | | | | | |
| Year-to-date | 823 | 699 | 124 | 85 | 91 | 95 | 8 | 32 | 16 | 8 | | | | | 60 |
| **00202 Lambert, Roberta** | | | | | | | | | | | | | | | |
| Current | 114 | 114 | | 100 | 100 | 95 | | | | | | | | | |
| Year-to-date | 873 | 795 | 78 | 91 | 97 | 95 | 32 | 8 | 16 | | | | | | 22 |
| **00203 MacKenzie, Jonathan** | | | | | | | | | | | | | | | |
| Current | 108 | 108 | | 100 | 100 | 95 | | | | | | | | | |
| Year-to-date | 324 | 300 | 24 | 93 | 93 | 95 | | | | | | | | | 24 |
| **00301 Spencer, Wilbur** | | | | | | | | | | | | | | | |
| Current | 80 | 64 | 16 | 80 | 100 | 95 | | 16 | | | | | | | |
| Year-to-date | 823 | 744 | 78 | 90 | 99 | 95 | 8 | 45 | 16 | | | | | | 9 |

If the firm finds its indirect expense factor acceptable (that is, the firm is operating within its overhead budget), there may be no need to examine individual overhead items. If, on the other hand, the factor is higher than planned or desired, the architect should examine individual overhead items to identify areas of excess.

*Indirect salary expenses.* The most important category of indirect expense is likely to be indirect salaries—salaries paid for clerical services, firm management, marketing, education and training, civic activities, and downtime between project tasks.

Low payroll utilization frequently contributes to excessive overhead. Utilization is the ratio between DSE and total salary expense:

Time utilization ratio = Direct hours (charged to projects) ÷ Total hours
Payroll utilization ratio = DSE ÷ Total salary expense

The most important thing to understand about utilization ratios is this: As the amount of personnel time and expense charged to projects *decreases,* overhead time and expense *increases* (given a stable staff). Under normal circumstances, shifting staff from project assignments to overhead activities will result in reduced project effort and revenues and, at the same time, increased indirect salary expense and increased total overhead.

Two instruments can be used to monitor utilization:

- A time analysis that records individual and cumulative expenditures of staff time
- An income statement that records both direct and indirect salary expense

> **Architecture firms generally report utilization ratios ranging from 62 to 72 percent, with profitable firms having ratios over 65 percent. Within the office, utilization ratios may vary from 10 percent (clerical personnel) to 30–50 percent (principals) and 75–85 percent (production personnel). These ratios are based on time available: An employee working 2,080 hours a year, with two weeks of vacation, seven holidays, and two sick days, will be available in the office about 91 percent of the standard year. Thus, someone who charges all available time to projects would have a utilization ratio of 91 percent.**

Note, too, that utilization is a valid measure only to the extent that the firm is *actually paid* for the direct labor. Charged time is not always billable time. Charging time to projects without expectation of billing the client (as in the case of a fixed fee that is already spent) will result in a flawed view of utilization; the utilization ratio will be high, suggesting low overhead and efficient operations, but the profit will be reduced. On the other hand, it is important for staff to report their chargeable time so that the firm has an accurate idea for estimating future projects. Some firms report using a utilization ratio (UR) chart in combination with a project progress report, which compares actual to budgeted time, as an effective way of managing office efficiency.

*Other indirect expenses.* If overhead is excessive and indirect salary is not the cause, a review of the other items on the firm's indirect expense budget is in order.

These items can be budgeted by projecting prior-year expenses forward, by considering specific new needs, or by using a zero-based budgeting technique that requires thoughtful consideration and justification of any item to be included. Individual items (accounts), subtotals, and totals can be planned and monitored either absolutely (that is, the specific dollar amounts) or relative to other items, such as total payroll, total expenses, or total revenues. Exceptions or variances from budget should be noted and examined and corrective action taken as appropriate. If it is not possible to modify overhead expenses to bring them within the budget, it is usually necessary to revise the firm's overall financial plan.

## MANAGING PROJECT EXPENSES

Project expenses include DSE, consultants, and other direct expenses, such as project-related travel, reproductions, models and renderings, long-distance telephone calls, and similar expenses. Of these, the largest expense—and the one over which the architect has the most control—is DSE, the salaries of the staff engaged on projects. The two most important principles in managing DSE are these:

- Utilization—keeping the staff engaged on projects
- Productivity—the degree to which the direct efforts of the firm can generate revenue

*Askew, Nixon, Ferguson Architects, Inc., Memphis, Tennessee*

On this and the following page are copies of two reports used to plan and monitor staff utilization in a thirty-person firm. The first outlines a planned work schedule for each staff member in the upcoming week. The second plots actual utilization rate against a negotiated target for each employee in the current month and the past three. These reports are designed so they can be photoreduced and carried in a time management system binder for ready reference by the firm's principals. Weekly Work Schedule

## WEEKLY WORK SCHEDULE

Group headers: **P** = BF, BN, LA, SH · **CA** = GW · **CAD** = CS · **SM** = CW · **SPM** = BJ … mb · **T2** = BLa, JLW, JWs, WB

| No. | Project | BF | BN | LA | SH | GW | CS | CW | BJ | BJB | DG | DW | JHJ | JPW | LES | MH | MO | RC | SD | DC | DH | JFW | JWJ | KA | SB | mb | BLa | JLW | JWs | WB | Hrs |
|---|---|---|---|---|---|---|---|---|---|---|---|---|---|---|---|---|---|---|---|---|---|---|---|---|---|---|---|---|---|---|---|
| | | 3 | 2 | 1 | 3 | 1 | 2 | 3 | 2 | 1 | 2 | 1 | 1 | 2 | 2 | 2 | 3 | 3 | 1 | 1 | 1 | 2 | 1 | 1 | 3 | 3 | hourly | 1 | 2 | 3 | 1240 |
| 1093.00 | PATH Medical Jv | | | | | | | | | | | 36 | | | | | | | | | | | | | | | | | | | 36 |
| 26102.15 | UST Archibus | | | | | | | | | | | | | | | | | | | | | | | | | | | | | | |
| 87047.10 | FEC CTC FM | | | | | 1 | | | | | | | | | | | | | | | | | | | | | | | | | 1 |
| 87080.40 | Logistics Sup Fac | 6 | | | | | | | | | | | | | | | | | | | | | | | | | | | | 20 | | 26 |
| 89108.40 | TANG Aerial Port | | | | | | | | | | | | 2 | | | | | | | | | | | | | | | | | | | 2 |
| 90114.10 | IRS MSC | 2 | 32 | | 40 | 4 | 24 | | | | | | | | | | | | | | | | 44 | | | 36 | | 8 | | | 20 | 210 |
| 91064.30 | MCS SE Elem | 4 | | | | | | | | | | | | | | 22 | | | | | | | | | | | | | | | | 26 |
| 92009.20 | TVA Allen | | | | | 6 | | | | | | | | | | | | | | | | | | | | | | | | | | 6 |
| 92011.20 | TVA Turbine Mnt | | | | | | | | | | | | | | | | | | | | | | | | | | | | | | | |
| 92024.11 | Sprint Vienna | 12 | | | | | 8 | | | | | | | | | | | | | | | | | | | | | | | | | 20 |
| 92033.70 | Dobbs SanFran | | | | | | | | | | 4 | | | | | | | | | | | | | | | | | | | | | 4 |
| 92040.25 | MSCAA ALP | | | | | | | | | | | | | | | | | | | | | | | | | | | | | | | |
| 92051.25 | US Tobacco | | | | | | | | | | | | | | | 16 | | | | | | | | | | | | | | | | 16 |
| 92062.20 | Sharp Toner Bldg | | | | | | | | | | 4 | | | | | | | | | | | | | | | | | | | | | 4 |
| 92072.20 | TVA Wilson Ops | 2 | | | | | | | | | | | | | | | | | | | | | | | | | | | | | | 2 |
| 93004.25 | MSCAA #8 FM | | | | | | | | | | | | | | | | | | | | | | | | | | | | | | | |
| 93018.20 | Plough Print Plnt | 3 | | | | | | | | | 32 | | | | | | | | | 20 | | | | | | | | | | 18 | | 73 |
| 93035.20 | TVA Allen Portal | | | | | | | | | | 16 | | | | | | 16 | | | | | | | | | | | | | | | 32 |
| 93036.25 | Betz Contract | | | | | | | | | | | | | | | | | | | | | 36 | | | | | | | | | | 36 |
| 93037.80 | Hardin Hsp | | | | | 2 | | | | | | | | | | | | | | 20 | | | | | | | | | | | | 22 |
| 93040.70 | Dobbs San Ant | | | | | | | | | | 4 | | | | | | 9 | | | | | | | | | | | | | | | 13 |
| 93051.10 | Boatman's Bank | | | | | | | | | | 8 | | | | | | | | | | | | | | | | | 8 | | | | 16 |
| 93057.80 | Boyd Sam's Twn | | | 30 | | 16 | | | 36 | | | | | | | 22 | 16 | 13 | 36 | | | | | 36 | | | | | | | | 271 |
| 93066.10 | ATT Atlanta | | | | | | | | | | | | | | | | | | 20 | | | | | | | | | | | | | 20 |
| 93068.10 | TVA Allen Coal C | | | | | 6 | | | | | | | | | | | | | | | | | | | 10 | | | | | | | 16 |
| 93078.70 | UClub Grill | | | | | | | | | | | | | | | | | | | | | | | | | | | | | | | |
| 93079.35 | Baptist EAST POB | | | | | | | | | | | | | | | | | | | | | | | | | | | | | | | |
| 93082.25 | ATT Pittsburgh | | | | | | | 20 | | | | | | | | | | | | | | | | | | | | | | | | 20 |
| 93088.10 | FEC Indy Phase V | 9 | | | | | | | | | | | 30 | | 18 | | | | | | | | | | 10 | | | | | | | 67 |
| 20.00 | Marketing | 8 | 12 | 6 | | 1 | | | | | | | | 12 | 4 | | | | | | | | 36 | | | | | | | | | 85 |
| 40.00 | Training | 3 | | | | | 12 | 8 | | | | | | | 8 | | | | | | | | | 4 | | | | | 4 | 4 | | 43 |
| 60.01 | Committee Work | | | | | 8 | | | | | | | | | | | | | | | | | | | | | | | | | 5 | 13 |
| 80.00 | Computer | | | | | | | | | | | | | | | | | | | | | | | | | | | | | | | |
| | Vacat/Comp/Hol | | | | | | | 40 | | | | | | | | | | | 4 | | 36 | | | | | | | | | | | 80 |
| | **TOTAL** | 49 | 44 | 36 | 40 | 44 | 44 | 28 | 40 | 36 | 44 | 36 | 36 | 44 | 44 | 32 | 40 | 40 | 36 | 40 | 36 | 44 | 36 | 36 | 40 | 36 | 20 | 20 | 42 | 25 | 1160 |

| P | Principal | CAD | CAD manager | SPM | Sr. project manager | T1 | Tech level 1 | T3 | Tech level 3 |
|---|---|---|---|---|---|---|---|---|---|
| CA | Constr. admin. | SM | System manager | PM | 40 hour time record | T2 | Tech level 2 | | |

➤

---

**Financial Planning (7.2) describes methods for calculating net multipliers and break-even multipliers.**

The most common instrument for measuring productivity is the net multiplier, which measures the dollars of revenue generated by the firm (net revenue excludes consultants, reimbursable expenses, and any other pass-through expenses) as a ratio of each dollar of DSE:

$$\text{Net multiplier} = \text{Net revenues} \div \text{DSE}$$

The net multiplier is the best basis for measuring productivity because it eliminates all pass-through expenses, leaving as net revenue only those revenues produced by the firm's own forces. A net multiplier of 3.0, for example, indicates that each $1.00 of DSE is generating $3.00 of revenue for the firm.

# UTILIZATION RATIO (UR) CHART

| Personnel | Plan'd Weekly | MAY 5 | 12 | 19 | 26 | JUNE 2 | 9 | 16 | 23 | 30 | JULY 7 | 14 | 21 | 28 | AUGUST 4 | 11 | 18 | 25 | 1993 Plan'd Yearly | 1993 Actual YTD | 1992 Plan'd Yearly | 1992 Actual 1992 | 1991 Plan'd Yearly | 1991 Actual 1991 |
|---|---|---|---|---|---|---|---|---|---|---|---|---|---|---|---|---|---|---|---|---|---|---|---|---|
| PRIN: L. Askew | 62 | 70 | 87 | 82 | 87 | 52 | 22 | 97 | 55 | 99 | 87 | 57 | 31 | 52 | 56 | | | | 62 | 64.5 | 60 | 62.5 | 60 | 59 |
| B. Nixon | 70 | 67 | 79 | 74 | 84 | 63 | 42 | 75 | 87 | 87 | 73 | 82 | 88 | 84 | 79 | | | | 70 | 73.2 | 65 | 75.2 | 60 | 70 |
| B. Ferguson | 70 | 54 | 20 | 33 | 38 | 29 | 25 | 52 | 49 | 61 | 17 | 25 | 26 | 39 | 49 | | | | 70 | 40.8 | 65 | 67.4 | 60 | 56 |
| H. Wolfe | 62 | 85 | 85 | 79 | 59 | 60 | 55 | 74 | 87 | 70 | 34 | 34 | 34 | 34 | 12 | | | | 62 | 62.2 | 60 | 53.5 | 60 | 48 |
| S. Hill | 75 | 81 | 92 | 88 | 80 | 78 | 89 | 74 | 77 | 67 | 49 | 49 | 45 | 78 | 75 | | | | 75 | 77.1 | 80 | 72.0 | 70 | 75 |
| CA: G. Wagoner | 80 | 41 | 29 | 58 | 61 | 72 | 91 | 97 | | 57 | 3 | 54 | 76 | 96 | 79 | | | | 75 | 69.8 | 75 | 76.1 | 75 | 73 |
| C. Wagner | 40 | 14 | 52 | 62 | 59 | 40 | 91 | 8 | 20 | 40 | 18 | 45 | 23 | 28 | 52 | | | | 40 | 43.2 | 30 | 29.7 | | |
| SPM: B. Baggett | 85 | 100 | 100 | 100 | 100 | 100 | 51 | 0 | 33 | 98 | 74 | 97 | 92 | 97 | 100 | | | | 82 | 87.4 | 80 | 74.7 | 75 | 75 |
| D. Garrigan | 85 | 84 | 82 | 96 | 90 | 67 | 91 | 92 | 48 | 93 | 70 | 94 | 35 | 86 | 75 | | | | 82 | 78.9 | 80 | 85.3 | 70 | 79 |
| Les. Smith | 85 | 85 | 98 | 98 | 98 | 79 | 100 | 99 | 99 | 100 | 82 | 97 | 97 | 97 | 98 | | | | 82 | 77.5 | 80 | 85.7 | 75 | 77 |
| J. Wieronski | 85 | 89 | 98 | 85 | 94 | 77 | 99 | 11 | 66 | 99 | 73 | 95 | 1 | 38 | 20 | | | | 82 | 75.0 | 80 | 79.9 | 75 | 68 |
| PM: R. Conrad | 90 | 94 | 97 | 95 | 94 | 75 | 94 | 12 | 72 | 100 | 76 | 95 | 96 | 97 | 96 | | | | 85 | 83.8 | 80 | 85.6 | 80 | 82 |
| S. Dicus | 90 | 67 | 97 | 97 | 93 | 82 | 96 | 86 | 96 | 98 | 88 | 71 | 59 | 76 | 84 | | | | 85 | 79.9 | 80 | 86.0 | 80 | 76 |
| M. Ordoyne | 90 | 97 | 98 | 97 | 97 | 65 | 98 | 91 | 97 | 98 | 75 | 95 | 92 | 96 | 96 | | | | 85 | 90.3 | 80 | 84.7 | 80 | 81 |
| J. Safranek | 90 | 78 | 95 | 75 | 84 | 72 | 93 | 20 | 35 | 90 | 49 | 87 | 93 | 93 | 75 | | | | 85 | 76.4 | 80 | 85.6 | 80 | 78 |
| S. Bryant | 92 | 94 | 79 | 75 | 74 | 76 | 94 | 97 | 81 | 99 | 78 | 97 | 94 | 97 | 99 | | | | 87 | 82.7 | 87 | 69.0 | | |
| D. Choo | 92 | 99 | 100 | 40 | 60 | 80 | 91 | 84 | 100 | 94 | 84 | 99 | 96 | 99 | 99 | | | | 87 | 91.6 | 87 | 84.8 | 86 | 85 |
| J. James | 92 | 92 | 100 | 92 | 77 | 80 | 86 | 100 | 98 | 100 | 75 | 75 | 77 | 99 | 38 | | | | 87 | 86.2 | 87 | 88.7 | 86 | 87 |
| C. Smeltzer | 85 | 74 | 94 | 93 | 87 | 82 | 97 | 90 | 93 | 99 | 66 | 76 | 76 | 82 | 44 | | | | 80 | 76.9 | 75 | 75.5 | 86 | 80 |
| J. Wikins | 92 | 95 | 97 | 96 | 68 | 26 | 93 | 84 | 95 | 94 | 69 | 95 | 92 | 73 | 75 | | | | 87 | 87.4 | 87 | 78.7 | 86 | 84 |
| T2: W. Bower | 70 | 27 | 54 | 64 | 15 | 47 | 55 | 88 | 80 | 91 | 56 | 77 | 84 | 85 | 74 | | | | 65 | 58.6 | 70 | 59.1 | 70 | 45 |
| J. Wittichen | 92 | 100 | 87 | 91 | 87 | 69 | 86 | 77 | 97 | 93 | 67 | 97 | 93 | 94 | 66 | | | | 87 | 66.7 | 87 | 73.2 | 87 | 83 |
| John Williams | 92 | | | | | | | 67 | 87 | 93 | 77 | 94 | 89 | 91 | 70 | | | | 87 | 61.3 | 87 | 73.2 | 87 | 83 |
| MRT: B. Jones | 50 | 73 | 59 | 50 | 62 | 33 | 63 | 67 | 20 | 69 | 41 | 58 | 20 | 29 | 29 | | | | 50 | 54.9 | 40 | 53.3 | 15 | 18 |
| J. Jones | 60 | 9 | 75 | 10 | 25 | 60 | 40 | 57 | 56 | 22 | 53 | 78 | 53 | 44 | 49 | | | | 60 | 31.2 | | | | |
| K. Aquilini | 30 | | | | | | | | 0 | 18 | 11 | 20 | 27 | 1 | 0 | | | | 30 | 25.8 | 30 | 20.9 | 15 | 13 |
| SUPT: R. Fite | 20 | 25 | 20 | 12 | 10 | 10 | 7 | 12 | 9 | 16 | 15 | 46 | 15 | 7 | 6 | | | | 20 | 18.3 | 20 | 4.3 | 5 | 1 |
| L. Smith | 20 | 0 | 5 | 0 | 7 | 5 | 7 | 7 | 0 | 15 | 25 | 7 | 12 | 22 | 15 | | | | 20 | 14.9 | 20 | 16.2 | 5 | 7 |
| C. Whitaker | 20 | 4 | 0 | 0 | 0 | 5 | 0 | 0 | 0 | 9 | 42 | 34 | 15 | 0 | 0 | | | | 20 | 5.1 | | | | |
| AVERAGE | 74.5 | 70.5 | 76.9 | 68.7 | 69.0 | 60.1 | 68.5 | 64.0 | 67.4 | 77.5 | 58.7 | 70.5 | 60.6 | 67.0 | 60.2 | | | | 71.9 | 67.7 | 70.1 | 67.4 | 63.8 | 61.2 |

PRIN: Principal
CA: Const. admin.
CADD: CADD spec.
SPM: Sr. project manager
PM: 40 hour time record
T1: Tech level 1
T2: Tech level 2
T3: Tech level 3
MKT: Marketing
SUPT: Support

☐ Achieved planned weekly UR
■ Achieved 10% above planned weekly UR (5% for T1)
▨ Timesheet not turned in – amount shown is estimate

As suggested in Financial Planning (8.2), it is possible to look at an architecture firm as a series of DSE multipliers. For example,

| | | |
|---|---|---|
| To pay for DSE: | $1.00 ÷ $1.00 = | 1.00 |
| To pay for indirect expenses: | $1.50 ÷ $1.00 = | 1.50 |
| Break-even DSE multiplier: | | 2.50 |
| To add profit: | $0.50 ÷ $1.00 = | 0.50 |
| Net DSE multiplier: | | 3.00 |

Multipliers are useful in project pricing and in overall firm planning—especially in comparing your current multipliers with your own past performance and with those reported by other architecture firms. Architects commonly establish anticipated project expenses by determining the hours (and thus the DSE) needed to perform services and by using the firm's multipliers to be sure indirect expenses and profit are appropriately considered.

Generally speaking, your multipliers are not the business of your clients unless you choose to make them so. Some approaches to compensating architects, for example, involve multiples of DSE or DPE. (The latter approach includes the payroll burden associated with DSEs as part of the base rather than as an indirect expense.)

*MacArchitect, Arne T. Bystrom, FAIA, Seattle, Washington*

Some computer-based project and financial management systems have the ability to produce "flash reports"—executive summaries of project and firm performance. Some firms develop their own software or create spreadsheets using data in their financial management system. Two examples are shown here: a project budget summary that compares multipliers earned with the firm's target break-even multiplier (2.41 in this example) and a resume of financial indicators.

## Project Budget Summary

Breakeven Multiplier: 2.41    Planned Net Multiplier: 3.01    Earned Profit Multiplier goal: 0.60

| No | Active project abbrev | | 1. Net revenue earned | | 2. Direct Salary Expense | | 3. Net mult earned | | 4. Break-even mult | | 5. Profit Mult Earned | 6. Approx profit (loss) DSE x PME | Prj type |
|---|---|---|---|---|---|---|---|---|---|---|---|---|---|
| 19 | 9212 | $ | 4,320 | (÷) | $ 1,632 | (=) | 2.65 | (−) | 2.41 | (=) | 0.24 | $ 387 | hrly |
| 18 | 9211 | | 0 | | 0 | | 0.00 | | 2.41 | | 0.00 | 0 | phse |
| 16 | 9210 | | 11,640 | | 4,640 | | 2.51 | | 2.41 | | 0.10 | 458 | hmax |
| 15 | 9209 | | 10,000 | | 2,675 | | 3.74 | | 2.41 | | 1.33 | 3,553 | phse |
| 13 | 9207.F | | 2,395 | | 1.080 | | 2.22 | | 2.41 | | −0.19 | (208) | hmax |
| 12 | 9206 | | 57,529 | | 19,484 | | 2.95 | | 2.41 | | 0.54 | 10,573 | pcnt |
| 17 | 9205 | | 4,500 | | 1,250 | | 3.60 | | 2.41 | | 1.19 | 1,488 | phse |
| 7 | 9128a | | 105 | | 38 | | 2.80 | | 2.41 | | 0.39 | 15 | hmax |
| 6 | 9128 | | 65,126 | | 20,140 | | 3.23 | | 2.41 | | 0.82 | 16,589 | phse |
| Totals | | | $155,615 | (÷) | $50,938 | (=) | 2.96 | (−) | 2.41 | (=) | 0.55 | $32,854 | |

## Resume of Performance Finances

| | |
|---|---|
| Active Efficiency Utilization Ratio: | 69.21 |
| Total Efficiency Ratio: | 69.21 |
| Period Efficiency Ratio: | 68.59 |
| Date Efficiency Ratios Calculated: | 5.18.93 |
| Overhead Ratio: | 44.74% |
| Breakeven Multiplier: | 2.41 |
| Planned Net Multiplier: | 3.01 |
| Date Multipliers Calculated: | 8.16.93 |
| Financial Performance Profit/Loss (−): | $32,854 |
| Date Financial Performance Calculated: | 8.16.93 |
| Total Receivables: | $77,140 |
| Net Receivables: | $54,097 |
| Receivables over 30 Days: | $ 7,202 |
| Receivables over 60 Days: | $ 2,562 |
| Receivables over 90 Days: | $ 0 |
| Ratio Receivables over 90 Days | 0.00% |
| Date Receivables Calculated: | 6.15.93 |
| Total Active Office Salaries: | $12,267 |
| Total Active Proposal Salaries: | $ 1,084 |
| Cost per Proposal Win: | $ 1,084 |
| Ratio per Proposal Win: | 50.00% |
| Date Proposals Calculated: | 5.31.93 |

## Managing Indirect Costs

Following are some examples of indirect costs (overhead) and how they can be managed:

- *Indirect labor.* Each staff member should be expected to follow target guidelines for billable hours.
- *Professional liability insurance.* This is probably the second or third most expensive item of overhead, after indirect labor and perhaps space costs. This expense is established and controlled as part of the firm's overall risk management program. The decision to purchase professional liability insurance is explored in Insurance Coverage (12.2).
- *Comprehensive general liability insurance.* Use a knowledgeable insurance broker to write a complete insurance program, including fire, theft, liability, and automobile coverage. Make sure you include coverage of valuable papers.
- *Office space.* Plan space requirements well in advance of the expiration of leases, and try to tie up adjoining space with options covering the right of first refusal. When downsizing, consider the possibility of subletting unneeded space—or even breaking the lease if rental costs are onerous.
- *Equipment rental.* Analyze the difference between owning and leasing equipment, and review the tax implications with your accountant.
- *Accounting and legal expenses.* Ask other architects for referrals when selecting a lawyer and accountant, and make certain those you choose have experience working with professional services firms. Discuss fees; ask your attorney and accountant to suggest how you can control their costs.
- *Staff development.* Use experienced personnel in the firm to conduct in-house training sessions for other staff members.
- Office supplies. Shop around for the best prices; this business is very competitive.
- *Marketing costs.* Establish a marketing budget at the beginning of the year and keep track of expenses against this budget.
- *Support staff.* Make sure you are adequately staffed in this area. Use part-time, temporary, or loaned employees to handle temporary or peak workloads.
- *Fringe benefits.* Use salary surveys, other industry data, and discussions with other architects to make sure your costs for these benefits are competitive with what other firms are paying.

*Lowell Getz, CPA*

---

For architecture firms that do not provide engineering services in-house, consultant expenses may equal or exceed DSE, especially on large, complex projects. Other direct expenses, such as travel, reproductions, models, and renderings, are generally in the range of 20 to 25 percent of DSE.

Sound management of project expenses requires planning these expenses before they are incurred (creating a project budget and work plan), monitoring revenues and expenses as the project proceeds, and taking corrective action when actual performance varies from the plan.

**Financial Planning (7.2) describes planning and budgeting in general.**

### For More Information

In Chapter 4 of *An Architect's Guide to Financial Management* (1997), Lowell V. Getz describes financial ratios and analytical methods used to measure the financial health of a firm.

The AIA undertakes periodic firm surveys that include a number of statistics related to a firm's billings. The 2000 *AIA Firm Survey Report* contains data on billings by firm size and per employee. Other surveys are listed below. Contact the publishers for availability, coverage, and prices.

Operating Statistics Survey, published by Harper & Shuman, 68 Moulton Street, Cambridge, MA 02138, (617) 492-4410. The survey can be downloaded from www.harperandshuman.com.

*PSMJ Financial Statistics Survey,* published by PSMJ, is available from Practice Management Associates, 10 Midland Avenue, Newton, MA 02158, (617) 965-0055. PSMJ also publishes surveys on design fees, executive compensation, and human resources practices. Its Web site is at www.psmj.com.

Zweig White & Associates, Inc. (ZWA) publishes several surveys on financial performance, finance, and accounting for architects, engineers, and environmental consultants. For a complete list of surveys, contact ZWA at 600 Worcester Street, Natick, MA 01760, (800) 466-6275 or www.zwa.com/bookstore.

The Institute of Management and Administration (IOMA) publishes monthly newsletters and an extensive series of guides about cost management and control. Contact IOMA at (212) 244-0360 or www.ioma.com.

# 7.4 Acquiring Capital

## Peter Piven, FAIA

*At the outset, and then from time to time, it is necessary to add capital to help the firm achieve its practice goals.*

Like all businesses, architecture firms typically need capital infusions—at start-up and at various key points along the way.

### START-UP

Generally the need for capital is first recognized when the architect decides to set up in practice. There are two important questions at this juncture: "How much will I need?" and "Where will it come from?"

**Required amounts.** The answer to "How much capital will I need?" is a function of two things. First is the amount of money required to pay for start-up organizational expenses, including:

- Legal and accounting assistance
- Acquisition of office space and leasehold improvements
- Furniture, fixtures, and equipment
- Printed office materials, such as stationery, business cards, and business forms
- Marketing materials, such as announcements and brochures

Second is the amount of money required to fund operations until enough cash is generated as payment for services in the normal business cycle.

It is common for architects to start a practice after developing a business relationship and receiving commissions—or the promise of commissions—that enable them to leave their current firms and start practicing as proprietors or partners. If clients and projects are in hand and revenue is coming in, the cash cycle is under way. More likely the new firm will need to market services, secure commissions, perform services, send invoices, and—at last—receive the first payment to establish a cash flow. In this case, the amount of capital required is the amount necessary to cover all disbursements that must be made until the firm begins to collect for services.

> **Financial Health (7.3) describes and illustrates the cash cycle in architecture firms.**

Because it may take a few months' effort to generate new projects, architects initiating independent practices are usually advised to capitalize sufficiently to cover six months' expenses plus start-up costs. Under normal circumstances and with average collection rates, three months' cash is required—*if* work is already in hand.

**Sources.** Sources for initial capital include:

- Personal savings
- Personal credit cards
- Equity in personal real estate (mortgages and equity loans)
- Small Business Administration loans
- Loans from relatives and friends
- Commercial (i.e., bank) loans

Regarding commercial loans, it is important to understand that lenders do not

**PETER PIVEN** *is the Philadelphia-based principal consultant of the Coxe Group, Inc., marketing and management consultants to design professionals. He has written and lectured widely on practice issues including compensation management.*

want to be investors. Their business is based on the certainty of a return on capital in the form of interest on loaned funds, rather than the uncertainty of a return in the form of profit from successful operations (which would be the right of an investor and not a lender). Banks will want architects to invest some of their own capital—usually more than half the invested equity in the firm. Otherwise the bank would be the primary stakeholder, and risk taker, in the firm. As a result, architects are usually required to provide a substantial portion of the start-up capital from sources other than commercial loans.

## FINANCING GROWTH

Firms grow for many reasons, and a larger workload may require additional capital to pay for increases in key staff, equipment, and space.

*Financing space and equipment: lease or purchase?* The need for additional or enhanced space and equipment can be met financially through outright purchase or through leasing arrangements that reduce the amount of capital required. In these circumstances, the necessary capital is provided by the lessor and is paid for through the amount and terms of the lease.

*Financing staff and other needs.* The costs of funding the firm's general expansion can be substantial, and these costs cannot be met through leasing.

Consider this: If under normal circumstances the firm must fund three months' expenses—representing the month in which services are performed and the two before payment is received—then one-fourth of the firm's annual net revenues must be funded. For example, if the firm has maintained a practice at the level of $400,000 in annual net revenues, it requires $100,000 in working capital—composed primarily of cash and accounts receivable—to keep the firm solvent. If the firm grows, enjoying a 25 percent increase in net revenues to $500,000, it needs an *additional* $25,000 in capital (one-fourth of the additional $100,000 in net revenues) to meet its projected financial obligations—which are mostly in the form of payroll, benefits, and other current overhead expenses.

This condition prevails at every level of practice. As the firm grows in revenue and therefore staff, its need for capital will grow. Conversely, if the firm shrinks, it will find itself with excess capital—more than it needs to meet current obligations. In such circumstances, the principals can remove excess capital from the firm in the form of additional compensation or leave the capital in the firm for use at a later date.

Because the need for capital depends directly on the firm's ability to invoice and collect promptly—represented by work in progress and accounts receivable—a reduction in those assets will have the effect of producing cash, reducing the amount of other capital required. Conversely, increases in the amounts of work in progress and accounts receivable mean the firm is obtaining money more slowly and will need to *increase* the amount of other capital to sustain its operations.

**The need for capital is proportional to the firm's average collection period. If it takes a firm three months to be paid, instead of two, then it must finance four months, or one-third of its annual capital requirement.**

*Means of financing.* Architecture firms nearly always have needs for both increased short-term and long-term capital.

Short-term financial needs should be met through short-term means. Operationally, such means can include speeding up production, invoicing, and collecting; reducing proprietor's or partners' draws; and reducing or deferring cash disbursements. Alternatively, the firm can borrow funds on a short-term basis, generally through a line of credit.

**Project Controls (13.3) addresses invoicing and collections.**

Long-term financial needs should be met through long-term means. These may include retaining earnings, securing long-term loans, and infusing additional capital—by the current owner(s) or by new owners.

*Retained earnings.* Corporations are permitted to retain profits (rather than distribute them) after payment of a corporate income tax. Architects who practice in firms organized as corporations, and who do not choose to keep more capital in the firm than is required for current normal operations, typically distribute profits on a current basis, usually in the form of bonuses, rather than pay corporate income tax on undistributed profits.

In proprietorships and partnerships (and in limited liability corporations [LLCs], limited liability partnerships [LLPs], and S corporations) there are forms that allow shareholders to be treated as if they were partners for tax purposes. The firm's earnings are considered the

These pro forma financial statements depict the income statement and balance sheet that two principals of a new firm might have prepared to plan their first year's practice.

The two architects formed a corporation, each putting in $1,000 for stock plus another $4,000 for a total cash contribution of $10,000. They also borrowed $12,000 against personal assets to provide additional cash to improve their rented space, purchase furniture and a computer, and pay for operating expenses they expected to accrue pending collection of receivables.

They planned to take $40,000 each in salary. They assumed that 60 percent of their time would be billable, and planned to budget projects to return a multiple of three times their salary. They also assumed that consultants' expenses would come out of their fees (and not be directly reimbursable).

The statements are developed on an accrual basis and are shown before any distribution of year-end profit, for which cash would not likely have been produced by the end of the year.

### Income Statement

*for the first year of practice*

| | | |
|---|---:|---:|
| *Revenues* | | |
| Fees | $200,000 | 100.00% |
| Reimbursable expenses | 10,000 | 5.00 |
| Total revenues | 210,000 | 105.00 |
| | | |
| *Reimbursable expenses* | | |
| Reproductions, etc. | 10,000 | 5.00% |
| Total reimbursable expenses | 10,000 | 5.00 |
| | | |
| *Direct expenses* | | |
| Direct salary expense | 48,000 | 24.00% |
| Consultants | 56,000 | 28.00 |
| Other direct expense | 2,000 | 1.00 |
| Total direct expenses | 106,000 | 53.00 |
| | | |
| *Indirect expenses* | | |
| Indirect salary expense | 32,000 | 16.00% |
| Payroll taxes and benefits | 16,000 | 8.00 |
| General and administrative: | | |
| Occupancy | 10,000 | 5.00% |
| Telephone | 1,500 | .75 |
| Insurance | 8,000 | 4.00 |
| Postage and shipping | 500 | .25 |
| Supplies | 1,000 | .50 |
| Printing | 1,000 | .50 |
| Publications | 500 | .25 |
| Professional development | 500 | .25 |
| Legal and accounting | 1,000 | .50 |
| Total indirect expenses | 72,000 | 36.00 |
| | | |
| *Operating profit* | 22,000 | 11.00% |
| | | |
| *Indicators* | | |
| Utilization rate | | .60 |
| Overhead factor | | 1.50 |
| Net DSE multiplier | | 2.96 |

### Balance Sheet

*at the end of the first year of practice*

| | |
|---|---:|
| *Assets* | |
| Cash | $5,000 |
| Accounts receivable | 25,000 |
| Work in progress | 7,000 |
| Prepaid insurance | 3,000 |
| Total current assets | 40,000 |
| | |
| Leasehold improvements | 5,000 |
| Furniture | 4,000 |
| Computers | 5,000 |
| Depreciation | (2,000) |
| Total fixed assets | 12,000 |
| Total assets | 52,000 |
| | |
| *Liabilities* | |
| Note payable—bank | 12,000 |
| Accounts payable—consultants | 6,500 |
| Accounts payable—trade | 1,000 |
| Taxes payable | 500 |
| Total liabilities | 20,000 |
| | |
| *Net worth* | |
| Capital stock | 2,000 |
| Paid-in capital | 8,000 |
| Current year profit (loss) | 22,000 |
| Shareholders' equity | 32,000 |
| | |
| *Indicators* | |
| Current ratio | 2.0 |
| Debt-to-equity ratio | .375 |
| Average collection period | 45 days |

earnings of the owners, and the firm is not permitted to retain earnings. Architects who practice as proprietors or partners have to pay personal income tax on current earnings and then reinvest as required.

▶ Note that corporate earnings are taxed twice, once when the corporation pays its income taxes and again when stockholders pay income taxes on their earnings.

## LOANS AND CREDIT LINES

Architecture firms may seek credit lines to finance their short-term capital needs and possibly loans to finance longer-term requirements.

▶ Firm Legal Structure (5.3) addresses taxation of corporations, partnerships, and proprietorships.

*Lines of credit.* Lines of credit give the architect the opportunity to obtain short-term funds when they are needed to meet short-term cash shortfalls, which might result from an unexpectedly late payment of a large invoice. They are an important conventional source of short-term financing.

A credit line is a formal loan arrangement that permits borrowing funds at will, up to an agreed limit, at scheduled interest rates. The arrangement is documented in the form of a note provided by the lender (generally a bank) and executed by the borrower stipulating the amounts, terms, and conditions of the loan. The lender may require that the credit line or loan be paid down to zero at least once yearly, after which the agreed credit is generally made available again. Lenders may also require a personal guarantee by the borrower giving the lender the right to seek restitution from, and claim against, the borrower's personal assets in the event of a loan default. The lender usually requires the borrower to pledge certain assets, particularly accounts receivable, or to provide personal guarantees.

*Proposals for credit lines and loans.* Proposals require careful preparation. They must make the case for the firm and provide essential financial information. Lenders look carefully at two indicators in assessing the borrower's ability to repay and, therefore, the lender's interest in lending. The first is the current ratio, which measures solvency:

$$\text{Current ratio} = \text{Current assets} \div \text{Current liabilities}$$

▶ Current assets and liabilities are those that can be converted to cash, usually in less than a year's time.

In examining the firm's current ratio, bankers seek to ensure that current assets are sufficient to cover (pay for) the firm's current liabilities, plus a significant buffer. The current assets are usually in the form of cash, work in progress, and accounts receivable. Current liabilities usually include amounts owed to consultants, vendors, and other short-term creditors. The bank will want the current ratio to exceed 1:1 and will prefer a ratio closer to 2:1, indicating there are $2.00 of current assets for every $1.00 of current liabilities. The second performance indicator is the debt-to-equity ratio, which measures leverage:

$$\text{Debt-to-equity ratio} = \text{Total liabilities} \div \text{Owners' equity}$$

In considering the debt-to-equity ratio, bankers seek to ensure that the owners have an appropriate level of personal investment in the firm relative to outside lending. They commonly want the ratio to be at least 1:1.

## SPREADING OR CHANGING OWNERSHIP

Architects transfer ownership to others for several reasons, including retention of key people, firm continuity, realization of personal value in the firm, and retirement. The firm's owners may also consider expanding ownership to increase the firm's capital base. Ownership may be expanded by

- Bringing in other individuals
- Instituting an employee stock ownership plan (ESOP)
- Merging with or being acquired by another firm
- Issuing shares to the public

**Ownership Transition (5.4)** explores the reasons for, and implications of, ownership transition. This topic also addresses the valuation of architecture firms.

***Bringing in other individuals.*** Although specific criteria for new owners vary widely, individuals being considered for ownership should be able to provide what the firm needs from its owners. This usually includes some combination of capital, new clients and projects, management, quality assurance, and leadership. Regarding capital, however, few practicing architects own substantial amounts of capital other than what they can earn by practicing their profession. Therefore, architects buying into ownership look to the firm to provide, in one way or another, the capital needed to acquire ownership. If new owners have to use personal savings or borrow from sources outside the firm, then they will seek the return of such amounts through increased earnings. A firm seeking to increase its capital base by bringing in new owners therefore must understand that the firm—through the efforts of all its owners, including the new additions—will end up paying for the increase.

***Instituting an employee stock ownership plan (ESOP).*** To encourage businesses to expand ownership opportunities for rank-and-file employees, the U.S. Congress established the ESOP, which provides a benefit to owners in the form of access to cheaper money if they choose to offer an ESOP.

## Obtaining Bank Credit

Even if a firm does not need bank loans, it is good to establish a credit line. Unusual growth or unforeseen delays in receipt of funds can put a strain on cash resources. It will be easier to get the credit before, rather than after, a need arises; when a need does arise, the firm usually is not in the best position to negotiate favorable terms from the bank. If the firm is large or has more than one office, it is good practice to establish credit lines with more than one bank.

Preparing a good loan proposal shows you know what your financial requirements are and that you have carefully thought through your request. A good loan proposal includes these elements:

- A transmittal letter showing the amount to be borrowed, the purpose, and the expected date of final repayment. Include suggested terms, such as a revolving line of credit for one year on which interest will be paid quarterly.
- Year-end financial statements (i.e., balance sheet and income statement) and the most recent interim financial statements.
- Aging schedule for accounts receivable and work in progress.
- Cash flow projection showing the effects of borrowing and repaying the bank loan.
- List of major projects under contract by category of work (e.g., schools and churches). The intent is to show the firm's financial stability without giving so much information that the banker can call your clients for credit references (this can always be done later).

- List of major proposals outstanding by category of project (also identified only by general description).
- Firm brochure and resumes of principals.

Personal financial statements on the principals should be prepared but not included in the loan package sent to the banker before the meeting. Depending on lender requirements, personal statements may also include income tax returns. Present this information during the course of the meeting when asked, and ask the banker to make special note that it is highly confidential.

How much of a line of credit to ask for sometimes is a problem. What you need may differ from what you think you can get. Banks will generally lend a percentage (say 75 to 80 percent) of the accounts receivable that they are certain will be collected. The loan proposal, particularly the cash flow statement, will give you an idea of your requirements. Be careful not to ask for too little credit. Asking for too little shows the banker that you do not understand your requirements, and you risk a loss of credibility.

It's important to maintain personal contact with the banker—contact that extends beyond sending monthly or quarterly financial statements. A suggestion: Arrange a personal visit at least twice a year, more frequently if possible. Discuss the credit line with the banker and review your firm's prospects for the future. Such personal contact will result in fewer problems when it comes time to renew the credit line.

*Lowell Getz, CPA*

The normal arrangement is for the firm to create an employee stock ownership trust (ESOT), in which *all* employees of the firm are shareholders. The firm sells a percentage of the firm to the trust—generally less than half, and usually 30 percent. The trust borrows the money for the purchase from a bank at interest rates below the market rate, frequently 75 percent of the prime lending rate. The firm then contributes sufficient cash to the ESOT annually for the trust to retire the loan. In exchange, the bank becomes entitled to a tax credit on the amount lent to the ESOT, thereby permitting and encouraging it to lend at favorable rates.

Although ESOPs are a means of obtaining cash, they should not be considered a panacea. They require transferring ownership to all employees, not just those capable of running the firm successfully. They require formidable record keeping, annual valuations, and reporting to the government. They require an annual payment to the ESOT to permit retirement of the loan—regardless of the firm's financial means at the time. Finally, the firm may find itself in the position of having to buy itself back from the ESOT, which will have to be done at the full valuation amount with after-tax dollars.

**Merging with or being acquired by another firm.** There is a fine line between the definition of a merger and an acquisition. A merger describes the result of two firms joining to form a new one in which the stakeholders maintain relatively equal footing. An acquisition describes the result of two firms joining, with the stakeholders of one gaining effective control of the other through purchase.

Mergers are often accomplished without money changing hands. One typical way is for the owners of each firm to be assigned proportional amounts of ownership in the new firm based on the relative value of each firm. So although it is possible to consider merging with another firm as a vehicle for raising capital, this is achievable only if the firm being considered happens to own large cash reserves that it intends to leave in the merged entity.

Acquisitions, on the other hand, often are accomplished through a cash payment for some part of the value that changes hands. Valuation is defined as the amount an informed buyer would pay a willing seller in the absence of duress. Accordingly, in an acquisition, the acquiring firm and the firm being acquired would exchange a full range of financial and operational information, negotiate and agree on the worth of the acquired firm, and arrange the terms and conditions of payment. Although payment can be entirely in cash, a more common arrangement is for some portion of the value to be paid in cash at the time of settlement, with the balance paid in installments. The installments can be paid as an after-tax capital exchange, on which capital gains tax must be paid by the acquiree, or as pretax ordinary income paid as salary, consulting fee, or royalty, on which the recipient pays ordinary income tax.

**Issuing shares to the public.** Although rare, there are a few instances in which firms have offered shares to the public. When subscribed, those offerings may generate substantial sums, which can be used to reward individual owners and provide capital for ongoing operations and growth.

Ownership of virtually all architecture firms is closely held; there is no broad public market for their sale or purchase. In the past, successful candidates for public ownership were large, multidisciplinary, nationally recognized firms with records of stable, profitable practice.

Public ownership imposes significant legal and accounting obligations and scrutiny, especially regarding divulging what would otherwise be considered proprietary information. In most cases, the owners do not relinquish control of the firm, selling only a minority percentage of the total ownership. Sale to the public is rare, because outside owners are unlikely to have any control over the firm's future operations or success and therefore are likely to be uncertain about the probability of enjoying a return on their investment.

# 8 Human Resources

## 8.1 Managing People

### Kathleen C. Maurel, Assoc. AIA, and Laurie Dreyer-Hadley

*Your staff—the people who work for you—are your firm's most important asset. Effectively managing the human resources component of your firm can be an important strategy for success.*

Architecture may be the last renaissance profession. Architects must be facile with design and familiar with construction technology. Once in practice, they are confronted with issues of finance, law, marketing, and managing people. Of all these, managing human resources can be the most challenging. It is an issue for any professional practice, regardless of type or size.

Although architecture services usually lead to the construction and operation of buildings, an architecture firm's "product" is not the building. Rather, it is the design process and the production of technical ideas and information necessary to construct buildings. Architects are purveyors of knowledge. People, then, are an architecture firm's most valued resource. People, not capital investments, equipment, or computers, are the essence of an architecture firm.

There are other reasons to value the firm's people. Clients want to meet the individuals who will perform the services and to have some sense that they will guide the project through completion. How the firm relates to its people is reflected in the relationships its people have with the firm's clients.

As the profession's knowledge base grows in size and complexity, it becomes more costly to replace firm members who have acquired special skills. It is therefore in the firm's best interest to reduce turnover. Moreover, there are numerous benefits to nurturing staff from within. Individuals who are committed to the firm will perform with more enthusiasm and be more productive than those who are not. A committed staff is a firm's best marketing tool.

As firms of all sizes recognize the importance of staff development and management, they invest in their people. They focus on them, involve them in firm planning, pay attention to their working environment, and see the nurturing of staff as synonymous with building a practice.

> **Firms are shifting their marketing emphasis from acquiring *projects* to acquiring *clients*. Project architects and other staff with whom clients work become the keys to developing and maintaining good continuing relationships.**

---

KATHLEEN MAUREL *is the director of human resources for Callison Architecture, an international design firm based in Seattle. She has developed compensation, benefit, and performance review systems, and coordinates Callison's continuing education program.*
LAURIE DREYER-HADLEY *is vice president of human resources at Gensler, where she is responsible for all human resources functions. This topic was adapted from "Managing People" by Cynthia A. Woodward, AIA, in the 12th edition.*

Human resources (HR) functions address a broad spectrum of both formal and informal business needs in a design firm. There are many different facets to HR administration and many different ways to provide these services and related support to the organization. Certain core functions are part of HR activity required by all firms. Other functions vary according to the culture of the firm. These value-added HR functions can help make the firm attractive to employees and reduce staff turnover rates.

How HR functions are staffed is determined by the size and structure of the firm. Some firms hire a dedicated HR employee or employees. Other firms are small enough that responsibility for these functions can be spread among a number of people.

## Core Functions

Listed here are the key functions that must be carried out in all architecture firms, even the practice of a sole practitioner. Small firms may choose to divide these tasks up or to hire part-time employees or contractors to handle them.

- *Recruiting/hiring/orientation.* This includes developing ads, reviewing resumes, interviewing candidates, determining and extending job offers, and orienting new employees.
- *Benefits administration.* Functions include negotiating contracts; enrollment; additions, deletions, and changes; the Consolidated Omnibus Budget Reconciliation Act of 1986 (COBRA); billing; payroll deductions; and other benefits. Benefits can be either optional (medical, dental, and life insurance, vacation, etc.) or mandatory (workers' compensation, family care leave, etc.). Benefits programs overlap with applicable laws and policies.
- *Payroll.* Paying employees requires processing timesheets, payroll deductions, applicable taxes, and statutory payments; government reporting; and other such functions.
- *Laws/policies.* The HR staffer must understand and apply applicable federal, state, and local laws and benefit programs and communicate laws and policies to staff (e.g., use of paid time off, exempt vs. nonexempt status, affirmative action plan requirements, eligibility to work in the United States, etc.). A firm's policies must conform to applicable laws. Do not make policies or rules unless you need them.

**The backgrounder Architects as Employers: Legal Requirements (8.1) summarizes current federal laws relating to employment.**

## Value-Added Functions

When allied closely with the firm's business strategy, HR functions beyond the basic ones can directly and indirectly add value to the firm, resulting in superior individual and firm performance, reduced turnover, and ultimately, greater profitability. Firms may want to consider implementing any or all of the functions described:

- *Consultancy.* Consultancy includes being available to answer questions, reviewing what-if scenarios, counseling managers or staff members with conflicts or concerns, listening to complaints, conducting employee surveys, and assessing staff and firm needs and programs. This aspect of HR can take a great deal of time with no obvious tangible impact, yet it can constitute much of what a firm considers its "culture" or environment. Offering a sense of openness and communication, it helps establish trust between staff and the firm.
- *Learning programs.* Information gathered in the consultancy role can help the firm determine what kinds of learning will be most useful to the staff and to the business: Fee management classes? Public speaking classes? Orientation programs? Reward and recognition programs? Classes on the business of architecture? Diversity awareness?
- *Professional development opportunities.* People tend to continue working with an organization when they believe they grow professionally and advance their careers there. Identifying career paths for different positions, providing learning opportunities for skill building, and supporting managers as they coach their employees in development are essential for nurturing and maintaining the firm's human capital. Developing and coordinating an effective performance review program will reinforce a professional development emphasis that in turn enhances retention.
- *Reward and recognition.* Programs that recognize and reward behaviors, work

performance, and contributions supporting the firm's culture and values will reinforce and perpetuate the desired outcomes.

• *Compensation and benefits strategy.* The firm should develop a compensation and benefits philosophy that reinforces its mission statement and espoused values. Pay practices and benefits must be well planned, balancing the firm's goals to be profitable, attract and retain employees, comply with applicable laws and regulations, and reward desired performance. The firm's top leaders set the direction for these programs.

## HR Staffing

HR functions can be staffed in a variety of ways, as described below, but no matter how this is accomplished two points remain constant. First, human resources policies must be consistent and fairly administered. Second, human resources management is really a shared responsibility, not something assigned to only one or two selected individuals. For example, everyone in the firm can play a role in recruiting talent, and many individuals influence a particular employee's decision to stay with or leave a firm. Having everyone in the firm handling human resources effectively contributes to the firm's overall success.

In small and medium-size firms, planning and directing human resources activities is often the responsibility of a designated principal or senior design professional—a specific area of assignment, just as marketing and finance are. Others in the firm offer administrative support, and often accounting staff handle payroll and benefits administration.

Smaller firms may rely on the firm's lawyer, accountant, and insurance agent to handle specialized issues. Other consultants can help with tasks such as creating an employee manual or developing a performance appraisal system. Local colleges and universities frequently have seminars on these topics and sometimes provide consulting services. Numerous periodicals devoted to human resource issues provide good background information and stimulate thought.

Generally, when a firm reaches approximately 100 people, the employee-related issues are too numerous to handle on a part-time basis and too difficult to coordinate among a group of people. This is the time to consider adding or designating a full-time human resources person. An architect with experience in human resources or business might assume this nontraditional role, but often a human resources professional, particularly one with a background in professional service firms, is preferable. Such individuals will be familiar with employment laws, benefit regulations, equal employment opportunity regulations, recruitment and selection methods, and compensation plan design. An in-house HR staff member can work closely with firm principals to design and implement programs, freeing up design professionals to focus on clients and projects and reducing the firm's overall reliance on outside consultants.

The person directing the HR function must be someone who can assume authority and gain credibility with the entire staff. To make the position truly effective, this individual should report to a senior principal of the firm and have an active role in management. The individual's competence along with his or her relationship with top management should encourage employees to view the HR function as one that adds important business value to the firm.

> **Architects often are highly creative, and to thrive they require an environment conducive to creativity. Studies have consistently identified certain ways in which firms can foster creativity:**
> - **Accept the expression of new ideas and encourage their development**
> - **Encourage some risk-taking and be willing to accept occasional failure**
> - **Allow for individual efforts**
> - **Provide for professional growth and development**
> - **Recognize and reward working contributions**
> - **Constantly communicate the "big picture" to keep everyone on track**

## UNDERSTANDING TODAY'S WORKFORCE

From earliest times to the Industrial Revolution, architecture education and practice were gained through apprenticeship, with a high degree of loyalty on the part of the apprentice and a strong sense of familial responsibility on the part of the master. During the Industrial Revolution, architecture education became formalized in academic settings, separating those who could afford this option from those who could not. With

## Telecommuting

Many firms are considering flexible work schedules and "telework" or "telecommuting" arrangements under which employees work part or all of their regular schedule off-site. Because the work performed in architecture firms relies heavily on team synergy, sharing ideas, and collaborating, arrangements for full-time off-site work are rare. However, firms may find that productivity actually increases for some individuals who regularly work independently at an off-site location. If your firm decides to offer telecommuting opportunities, a policy should be developed and the program monitored for effectiveness. Firms should distinguish true telecommuting arrangements from those where an employee occasionally works at home. In bona fide telecommuting situations, the employee is prescheduled to work off-site (usually at home) on a regular basis; this arrangement differs from an occasional off-site day, or periodic additional hours beyond the normal schedule, when work may be performed at home.

In addition to a general policy on telecommuting, it is suggested that firms draw up individual agreements with each telecommuting employee to specify the terms of the arrangement, itemize firm supplies and equipment loaned to the employee for business use, and clarify other work issues. Following is a sample policy addressing key issues to be considered when establishing telecommuting work schedules.

### Telecommuting Policy Considerations

Telecommuting is a mutually agreed-upon work plan between an employee and manager in which the employee regularly works part or all of his or her work schedule off-site, usually at home. These arrangements are based on the needs of the job, work group, client, and firm.

A telecommuting arrangement may be changed or discontinued at any time by the manager. An employee may request modifications to or termination of the telecommuting arrangement, which will be reviewed by the manager.

*Eligibility.* Ordinarily employees will complete the orientation period before beginning a telecommuting arrangement. An employee's job performance must meet or exceed requirements in order for the employee to be considered for a telecommuting assignment.

Full-time and part-time salaried and hourly paid employees can be considered for telecommuting arrangements.

The employee's job must be one that can be effectively performed off-site all or part of the time, as determined by the manager.

*Work schedule and communication.* The telecommuting agreement will specify the work schedule, including which hours and days of the week the employee will be working. Specific hours of phone availability each day may also be established. Employees are expected to devote full effort to their work during the designated work hours. Telecommuters must maintain child care and other arrangements to permit them to concentrate on work.

The telecommuting employee is ordinarily required to be present at the firm at least one workday per week to interact with the manager, team members, or clients and attend any regular meetings. The agreement will specify which days and hours the employee will report to work.

In addition to a regular reporting schedule, the manager may require the employee to report to the office or another specific site as required for project work, training, performance review, meetings, or other functions. The manager will provide at least one day's notice of these reporting requirements when possible.

The employee and manager will determine the method and frequency of written communication and mail forwarding using U.S. mail, messenger service, e-mail, and other means of communication.

*Workplace.* The employee's off-site work location will usually be his or her home. The employee must establish and maintain a

developments in technology, buildings became more complex, demanding more information and effort to document the design. The working relationship in the firm shifted from master-apprentice to master-worker, with a larger number of draftsmen working for the architect.

After World War II this pattern shifted again. Today people in the average architecture office are highly educated and hold high expectations for their careers. Loyalty is more to the project and the profession than to an individual firm. At the same time, projects increasingly require the diversity of skills found only in teams.

Client demands have also changed over time. Typical design services in demand include "higher, faster, stronger, and cheaper." Clients have become more facile with architectural services, often using in-house attorneys to negotiate more services for smaller fees. We need to add this business and negotiation aspect to our in-house education, just to keep pace with our clients.

The tools used to provide design services also have changed. Computer-assisted design (CAD) is now the norm, and people just out of college in this profession have high capability in the technology yet may not understand what a good set of drawings looks like. Senior staff and management may know what a good set of drawings looks like but often are not fluent in the language of the technology production tool set. These trends create a whole new set of needs for us as businesspeople.

clean, safe, dedicated workspace; the manager or designee may visit and review the workplace for appropriateness initially and periodically thereafter. The employee is responsible for absorbing any costs related to remodeling and initial setup of the space in his or her home or other location. The employee is responsible for providing the furniture and telephone line(s) required to do the job.

The employee will be covered by workers' compensation for all job-related injuries that occur in the designated workspace during the defined work period. Since the workplace and home are the same, workers' compensation will not apply to non-job-related injuries that occur in the home.

The employer may inspect the workplace site, with reasonable advance notice, to ensure that the space is suitable for the work being performed, safe, and arranged correctly from an ergonomic perspective.

*Equipment and supplies.* The manager will determine what equipment and supplies will be provided to the employee. Any equipment loaned to the employee for use at home must be returned in good condition to the firm at the end of the telecommuting arrangement or employment with the firm. Employees will be responsible for reimbursing the firm for equipment not returned.

The employee will normally provide space, basic office furniture, and lines for telephones, fax, and modem as needed. The firm will reimburse the employee for job-related telephone charges based on submitted itemized telephone bills. The firm will provide computer equipment and software, or the employee may elect to use his or her own property. If the latter option is chosen, the employee may need to bring his or her computer into the firm to be evaluated by information services (IS) staff and loaded with standard company software. An approved surge protection device is required for all firm-owned equipment. Firm-owned equipment may be installed by IS staff at the telecommuting work site to ensure proper setup.

The firm will be responsible for the repair and maintenance of its equipment. The employee will be responsible for any intentional damage to the equipment or damage resulting from gross negligence by the employee, members of the employee's family, or others at the employee's home or workplace. The firm's equipment used off-site will be itemized and is normally covered under the firm's insurance policy unless damage is due to negligence.

*Intellectual property and confidentiality.* All company-related materials and information should be kept confidential as necessary. Sensitive material should be returned to the firm for disposal or destroyed by the employee. All work-related material is normally kept in the designated work area. Information or material should be shared only with those who have bona fide business reasons for receiving it.

*Supervision of work.* It is particularly important that the work to be performed be understood and agreed upon by the manager and employee. A position description and specific goals for telecommuting arrangements, with timetable and action plans, should be developed and updated periodically. A primary managerial contact and a backup contact must be designated for a telecommuting employee.

The employee's performance will be reviewed in accordance with the firm's program at least once annually. More-frequent reviews to confirm objectives and provide feedback may be appropriate for telecommuting employees.

Time sheets must be submitted regularly to the manager or payroll by the regular due date. The manager will review any questions regarding time and project numbers used with the employee.

*Tax issues.* The employee and his or her tax advisor are responsible for determining the deductibility and depreciation of business-related expenses for tax purposes. The firm will not provide advice on this issue.

*Applicability of firm policies and guidelines.* Unless modified by the telecommuting agreement, all existing policies and procedures are applicable to the telecommuting employee at the remote work site.

Technological, environmental, financial, and demographic trends will affect how we do business in the future, particularly how we manage the people who constitute our firms. At the same time, society has changed the nature of how we work, where we work, and who is available to work, as well as our societal expectations of employers.

People in today's highly educated workforce expect an opportunity to participate in decisions affecting their daily work. Participatory management styles are here to stay. Employees also want an equitable pay scale and a benefits package that suits their personal needs.

Today's workforce is becoming more diverse in every respect. There are more women, ethnic minorities, persons with disabilities, and openly gay employees in the workforce than ever before. There are more two-career couples juggling career demands with child care.

Architecture schools across the country are seeing a large increase in first-generation Americans—students from other countries and cultures. This fact affects diversity and cultural integration concerns, adds to the breadth of design ideas available, and creates new demands for firms to understand immigration and foreign work visa issues. To take advantage of the skills, new design talents, and global marketing contacts these various groups can offer, firms are responding with increasingly flexible hiring patterns, new employment arrangements, and new educational offerings.

In years past it was relatively easy for a firm to find new, young staff members who would work extraordinary hours for pay that was among the lowest of any of the professions. Employees today have higher expectations, are better educated, and are a more diverse group than ever before. Members of this new generation of workers have never been faced with a recession, their talents are in demand in more than one profession, and so their expectations are affecting what firms offer to prospective candidates. They have much to offer the profession, and today's firms must give thought to what they can offer in return.

To meet the needs of this increasingly diverse and multicultural workforce, employers are considering many new programs and benefits, including

- Flexible hours
- Part-time work
- Transportation alternatives
- Child care services or child care coordination
- Dry-cleaning services
- Dinner drop-off services
- Laptop computers that enable staff to work from anywhere
- Elder care assistance for baby boomers caught between the needs of children and those of elderly parents
- Working in teams
- Cultural diversity awareness
- English-language training
- Basic business etiquette (for host country)

Programs and benefits such as these help make the working environment more conducive to the needs of a diverse employee base. But it is the company's culture and approach to human resources that keep the employees at the firm.

### For More Information

Several organizations address HR and administration management issues. The Society of Design Administration (SDA) promotes the exchange of ideas and information in the related disciplines of design firm administration. Contact SDA at (803) 785-2512 or visit its Web site at www.sdadmin.org. The Society of Human Resource Management (SHRM) provides a voice for the human resources profession, and can be reached at (703) 548-3440 or www.shrm.org. The American Management Association International (AMA) addresses management development and training and provides information on human resources management. AMA's Web site is at www.amanet.org/start.htm.

# Architects as Employers: Legal Requirements

*James J. O'Brien, Esq.*

The employment relationship is governed by federal and state statutes, regulations, administrative orders, and case law. While most states still adhere to the basic rule that employment is "at-will"—a legal term meaning that in the absence of a contract providing otherwise, an employee's employment may be terminated at any time, for any reason, with or without notice—the modern-day reality is that there are many exceptions to the at-will concept. An overview of some of the laws governing employment follows. The body of law governing employment is complex and depends on individual circumstances. In addition, this brief overview does not come close to covering all the legal rules and potential pitfalls that apply to the employment relationship. For these reasons, this summary should not be considered a substitute for competent legal advice.

## Interviewing and Hiring

The *Fair Credit Reporting Act* (1971) requires employers who wish to use credit reports as part of their background checks of applicants or employees to follow certain rules governing the use of the information, and requires disclosure of the credit check to the affected applicant or employee.

The *Drug-Free Workplace Act* (1988) requires federal government contractors to have programs to ensure a drug-free workplace. The federal government also requires drug testing in some instances, for example, for certain employees of defense contractors. Many states and some local jurisdictions have their own laws addressing drug testing of employees or applicants for employment, and these vary widely.

The *Employee Polygraph Protection Act* (1988) restricts the use of lie detectors in most hiring and employment situations. Many states also regulate the use of polygraphs in employment.

The *Immigration Reform and Control Act* (1986) requires verification of authorization of new hires to lawfully accept employment in the United States and the maintenance of I-9 forms by the employer. The act also prohibits discrimination on the basis of national origin.

*Other background checks.* Checks concerning applicants and employees may be regulated by federal or state laws. They include criminal background checks, medical exams, and questions on an employer's application for employment.

## Wages and Benefits

The *Fair Labor Standards* Act (1938) governs minimum-wage and overtime requirements and defines classes of employees who may be exempted from these requirements. Paying an employee on a salary basis meets one of the standards for exempt treatment. However, even employees who are paid a salary may be entitled to overtime pay for time worked over 40 hours per week if their duties do not qualify as exempt. The

architectural intern is one position that must be carefully analyzed by the employer before it can safely be treated as exempt. Each state and many municipalities have analogous laws. Construction work of certain types on federal contracts may be subject to provisions of the Davis-Bacon Act, requiring payment of wages set at the local prevailing minimum wage.

The *Employee Retirement Income Securities Act* (1974) governs employers' duties and responsibilities regarding certain benefit plans, including retirement plans but potentially applying to many of an employer's benefits. It requires extensive disclosure to plan participants.

The *Family and Medical Leave Act* (1993) requires that employers of fifty or more persons provide employees with up to 12 weeks per year of unpaid leave due to a serious health condition of the employee; the arrival of a child, whether by birth, adoption, or through foster care; or the illness of an employee's spouse, parent, or child. The law provides this leave to employees who have worked for an employer for at least one year and for 1,250 hours over the previous 12 months. Some states also provide for family and medical leave, and the employee may be entitled to benefits under both federal and state provisions.

## Employment Taxes and Withholding

The *Internal Revenue Code* mandates withholding of taxes from employees' pay and forwarding the amounts withheld to the Internal Revenue Service. Employers are subject to various liabilities, including attachment, for failure to comply. States have analogous withholding requirements, as do many local jurisdictions.

The *Social Security Act* (1935) requires withholding contributions from employees' pay and forwarding these amounts, as well as employer contributions on behalf of employees, to the Social Security system.

*Unemployment insurance* requires employers to make payments for federal unemployment benefits. State statutes also govern payments to certain employees who have been terminated or laid off.

## Terms and Conditions of Employment

*Discrimination.* Title VII of the Civil Rights Act of 1964 applies to employers with 15 or more employees, and the Civil Rights Act of 1866 applies to all employers. These acts prohibit discrimination on the basis of race, color, sex, pregnancy, religion, and national origin. Executive Order 11246 applies to federal contractors and, depending on the dollar amount of a private employer's contract with the government, imposes certain requirements, such as implementing an affirmative action plan designed to improve employment opportunities for minorities and women. Most states and many local jurisdictions also prohibit discrimination.

*Sexual harassment* has been interpreted by the courts to be a form of sex discrimination prohibited by law. Recent court decisions on this issue have led to great potential liability for employers, and every employer should have a strict policy outlawing such discrimination and procedures in place to address any complaints of sexual harassment.

The *Americans with Disabilities Act* (1990) prohibits discrimination against persons with disabilities who can perform the essential functions of the job, and in some cases requires an employer to provide reasonable accommodations in order to permit the disabled person to perform those functions. Employers who have certain relationships with the federal government are required under the Rehabilitation Act of 1973 not to discriminate against handicapped individuals, and some employers are required to prepare affirmative action plans. Many states have analogous statutes applying to private employers.

The *Age Discrimination in Employment Act* (1967) prohibits discrimination on the basis of age by employers who employ 20 or more employees. Persons in this protected category are those age 40 and over. The act also governs certain aspects of the operation of retirement plans and sets standards for severance agreements in certain situations.

The *Equal Pay Act* (1963) prohibits most employers from engaging in wage discrimination based on gender for work involving equal skill, effort, and responsibility, unless the differential in pay is based on a lawful factor other than gender. Many states have analogous laws, and some have adopted the comparable-worth concept, applying to jobs that are similar but not identical.

*Veterans' employment rights.* These rights are governed by the Uniformed Service Employment and Reemployment Rights Act, which covers all private employers and prohibits discrimination because of application to or membership in a uniformed service. It requires reinstatement to the veteran's former position upon return from military training or service, and bars discrimination relative to hiring, retention, promotion, or other employment benefits. The Vietnam Veteran Readjustment Act applies to certain government contractors and prohibits discrimination against Vietnam-era veterans and disabled veterans.

The *National Labor Relations Act* (1935) protects the right of employees to organize and to form or join labor unions, the right to engage in concerted activity, and the right to bargain collectively.

*Workers' compensation laws.* These laws exist in almost all states and require employers to carry workers' compensation insurance (or to offer the option to employees), to provide benefits, and not to discriminate on the basis of claims. In some states an employer who fails to carry such insurance is liable for injuries to employees and is deprived of certain defenses normally recognized in comparable circumstances. Variations from state to state are often important.

The *Occupational Safety and Health Act* (1970) regulates employee health and safety and requires a safe workplace. The Department of Labor publishes specific regulations on certain workplace hazards, especially in construction. Under an approved state plan, states may regulate in this area. The act also regulates office workers as to fire protection and injury records.

The *Jury Service and Selection Act* (1968) bars an employer from discharging an employee for serving on a federal jury, and requires that leave be given for service. Nearly all states also require that employees be given time off to perform jury duty without being penalized.

*Employment contracts.* Contracts can be found to exist even when an employer did not intend to be contractually bound. In fact, all employment relationships are properly understood as contractual, with the objective of keeping the contract terminable at-will unless the employer intends otherwise. Thus care must be taken in drafting offer letters, employee policies, and handbooks to avoid creating an explicit or implied contractual commitment where none was intended. In addition, no-compete, no-solicit agreements with employees can be enforceable if properly drafted, helping architectural firms to protect their practices from unfair competition or raiding of employees or clients. It should be noted that case law in this sector is changing rapidly.

*Posting of notices.* Many federal and state statutes require that notices advising employees of their rights be posted so that employees can see them.

## Termination of Employment

The *Workers' Adjustment and Retraining Notification Act* (1988) requires that employers with 100 or more employees give 60 days' written notice to the employees and the local government in the event of a mass layoff (50 or more employees) or plant closing. Many states also have laws governing mass layoffs and plant closings.

The *Consolidated Omnibus Budget Reconciliation Act of 1986* (COBRA) requires that employees be given notice of the right to extend group health benefits coverage after termination and at the time of other qualifying events. COBRA applies to employers with 20 or more employees.

## Employment Records

*Retention.* Many federal and state laws require retention of employment-related records. The length of time these records must be kept can vary widely, from as few as 90 days to as many as 30 years beyond the termination of employment. Most statutes also require that all records be retained once a charge or claim has been filed, and kept until its final disposition. Employers should check with legal counsel regarding specific records.

*Access.* Third-party access to employment-related records is governed by statutory authority in the case of governmental agencies, and can be restricted by privacy rights granted to employees by state law in the case of disclosure to others. Various states require that employees and former employees be granted access to personnel files regarding their own employment, while other states continue to recognize that such files are the property of the employer and that the employee has no inherent right of access to them.

*James J. O'Brien is a partner in the Washington, D.C., law firm of Krupin, Greenbaum & O'Brien, LLC. His firm exclusively represents employers with respect to labor, employment, and business immigration issues.*

# 8.2 Recruiting and Hiring

## Laurie Dreyer-Hadley and Kathleen C. Maurel, Assoc. AIA

*The decision to hire is one of the most important an architecture firm makes. Each new person adds to the firm's capability and increases the possibility that it will achieve its practice goals.*

A firm hires for many reasons. It may be adding a new staff position or filling one that is currently vacant. Sometimes just finding an individual with desirable skills who is a good fit may cause a firm to create a new role or make staff changes that had been slated for a later date. Whatever the motivation, the decision to hire provides the opportunity to ask these questions:

- What does the firm need—now and in the future?
- Is there an opportunity to add someone who will make the firm "better and brighter" than it is now?
- How can this addition have the most positive impact on achieving the firm's practice goals?
- Should the firm take this opportunity to explore other changes in people and responsibilities?

The recruitment, interview, and selection process is merely the beginning. How an individual is oriented, trained, staffed on projects, supported, and managed ultimately determines the success of any hire.

## DETERMINING THE NEED

Anticipating current and long-range staff needs is not always simple. Many variables influence the projected workload and the type of staff needed—economic conditions, fluctuating project schedules, marketing effort results, and turnover are a few that come into play.

First, the firm should evaluate the current staff and project assignments to determine if everyone is working at his or her potential and that the distribution of work is optimal. It is often helpful to get input from current employees regarding their own aspirations, work assignments, and the need for new staff. The firm should avoid reactionary hiring—getting a body to fill the current gap without considering current employees' potential interest in taking on new responsibilities. This may be an opportunity to give someone a new role or promotion. Employees who perceive that they are denied growth opportunities in favor of new hires are likely to leave, resulting in yet another vacancy to fill. Retention is often tied to employees' perceptions of professional growth opportunities within the firm.

In deciding to add a new staff position, review past and projected billings and consider the work to be done, the skills needed, the appropriate billing rate, and the corresponding compensation. In addition to the direct payroll and benefits expenses, consider the expenses associated with providing space, furniture, equipment, software, support services, training, and orientation. Also consider the "learning curve" effect on project work and teams.

LAURIE DREYER-HADLEY *is vice president of human resources at Gensler, where she is responsible for all human resources functions.* KATHLEEN MAUREL *is the director of human resources for Callison Architecture, an international design firm based in Seattle. This piece is based on the 12th edition topic by Cynthia A. Woodward, AIA.*

part 2 BUSINESS

## *Staffing*

In any firm, one key business function is the proper staffing to ensure the best-quality product for clients, with an efficient use of staff time and, of course, business profitability. Staffing assessments also help determine who needs to be hired (for both immediate project needs and long-term strategic objectives), identify new skills needed for existing staff, and meet the professional development objectives of existing staff. When tied to billing projections, staffing tools help predict income and alert firms to the need to market for new projects.

David Maister's book *Managing the Professional Services Firm* (1997) has a chapter on the role of staffing in the design profession. He discusses the need to balance key business objectives when making staffing decisions: profitability, client satisfaction, professional development objectives, personal issues and desires of staff members, and promotion of existing staff. A new job role or assignment is one of the key methods to advance a person's career in the design profession. Staffing assignments are a major aspect of career advancement for any design professional.

Indeed, the volatile nature of staffing changes within the design profession has made clients ever more savvy, and they have started to ask for commitments as to availability of staff in the request for proposals process.

▶ **Avoid use of the term "permanent employees," since this implies a legal commitment to longevity that few firms can guarantee.**

After determining the responsibilities and the skill set needed, specify the parameters of the position. While most firms think in terms of full-time regular employees, there are other options. A position can be full- or part-time, temporary (for a specified period of time), or of an indefinite duration (commonly referred to as "regular" status). Part-time employment and flexible, alternative work schedules have become increasingly popular as people try to find new ways to mesh their lifestyles with their careers. Some firms are using "telework" arrangements under which employees work part or all of their schedule off-site, usually at home. When recruiting and retention are key issues, some firms are more inclined to develop innovative work schedules and arrangements. Usually a firm is looking for full- or part-time regular employees who have the potential to grow with the firm.

Sometimes firms hire students as paid employees, in many cases through co-op arrangements with colleges. Such students may be able to fill some short-term, entry-level needs, and may be able to fill regular positions in the future. Many firms develop an ongoing relationship with schools that have co-op programs and thus have a continual flow of junior-level employees. The schools seek participating firms of all sizes so that their students have access to a wide range of experiences. If students are paid, they are indeed employees and normally are subject to the same policies and regulations as other staff. Students may also receive academic credit for the work they do for a firm, or the experience may be required for graduation from some programs, or both.

Most firms adopt an "at-will" philosophy of employment, which means that the employment can be terminated by either party at any time. Thus it is best to avoid the term "permanent employment" or other language or policies implying a contractual commitment by either party.

In addition to employees who are paid through the firm's payroll, other types of personnel may be used.

***Contractual services.*** These services are provided by skilled people under contract, usually for a specified task and time period. These people are independent consultants or contractors, working at their own places of business, or under certain circumstances on-site, and are responsible for their own taxes, insurance, and other benefits. Alternatively, they may be provided by (or leased from) a contractual service agency that charges the firm an hourly rate, compensates the individual, and assumes responsibility for taxes, insurance, and other benefits. These individuals and agencies are usually paid at a higher-than-normal hourly rate because the firm is not carrying their indirect personnel expenses. It is important to note that specific legal and tax parameters define contractual services and differentiate independent contractors from employees. The distinction between employees and independent contractors is important, and firms are encouraged to obtain legal or tax advice to ensure that workers are properly classified and paid. Sometimes temps hired through an agency or other people working on a contractual basis may be candidates for longer-term employment, at which time the firm may pursue hiring them as employees.

***Loaned employees.*** Sometimes firms experiencing slack periods will "lend" employees to another firm. Such employees work at the office of the hiring firm but remain on the payroll of their original employer. The hiring firm reimburses the other firm, usually at an hourly rate that covers direct and indirect personnel expenses. Sometimes a small percentage fee is added to the hourly rate to cover the original firm's administrative cost. A legal review and letter of agreement between the firms involved is advisable in these situations.

# RECRUITING

Appropriate recruiting techniques vary with firm size, geographic location, and the kind of person being sought.

***Employee referrals.*** Surveys indicate that an effective method of finding good people who fit the firm's culture is referral from current staff members. Once a job description has been developed, a firm's employees should be informed, and their assistance in the search may be solicited. One caveat, however: Hiring people who have been referred by current employees may keep your firm from becoming as diverse as it could or should be. Firms seeking to broaden their workforce diversity may want to rely more heavily on other recruitment methods.

***Advertising.*** Depending on the position to be filled, firms may consider advertising in local, regional, or national newspapers, or professional publications or journals. Firms may also use AIA chapter newsletters that include a classified section, or post jobs with local AIA chapters that maintain listings (either online or in their offices) of vacancies in the area. A more recent and increasingly widespread practice is posting job openings on a firm's Web site. There are also a number of Web-based job posting services that can be used, ordinarily for a fee. As of this writing, www.mosaix.com and www.monsterboard.com are two sites architecture firms use. The decisions regarding where to advertise will be based on the type of opening, the time frame for recruiting, and the likelihood of appropriate candidates referring to that source. For senior or difficult-to-fill positions, firms may want to advertise in several regions as long as relocation costs are not an issue. Sometimes it is possible to attract qualified people from areas that have undergone economic reversal; such people may be willing to move at their own cost or for a small moving allowance in return for the job opportunity in a new locale.

Advertisements should be specific to the position, listing minimum educational and registration requirements, years and type of experience wanted, required skills, and desired project experience. A few succinct phrases about the firm (type of projects, staff size, values) can be included. Although blind ads (ads that generally describe the firm but do not list its name and address) may be used, some qualified people may be hesitant to respond to them. In most cases, firms list their name, e-mail address, telephone and fax numbers, and perhaps the name of a contact person. The advertisement should specify the materials and information wanted (resume, salary history or requirements, portfolio or work samples, etc.), the application methods preferred (mail, e-mail, in person, etc.), a deadline for application, and a statement regarding the firm's status as an equal opportunity employer or affirmative action employer.

***Universities.*** A proven method of recruiting is to look to regional university campuses with architecture programs, as well as the alma maters of current employees

## Employee or Independent Contractor?

Firms anxious to maintain flexibility often consider hiring temporary staff. To avoid making long-term commitments, withholding taxes, and paying for unemployment insurance, it may be tempting to consider temporary hires as independent contractors.

In recent years, however, the Internal Revenue Service (IRS) has been studying these arrangements closely. Penalties can be substantial for treating people as contractors when, in the eyes of the IRS, they are employed rather than serving as independent contractors.

At this writing, the IRS uses twenty common-law factors as a test. If any one of these factors applies, a worker is probably an employee rather than an independent contractor:

1. The worker is obligated to work full time for the business.
2. The worker is obligated to comply with the company's instructions regarding the work performed.
3. The worker receives training from, or at the direction of, the business.
4. The worker provides services that are integrated into the business operation of the company.
5. The worker provides services that must be rendered personally at the business.
6. The worker hires, supervises, and/or pays assistants for the business.
7. The worker has a continuing working relationship with the business.
8. The worker is obligated to observe set hours of work established by the business.
9. The worker does the work on the premises of the business.
10. The worker does the work in a sequence established by the business.
11. The worker is obligated to submit regular reports to the business.
12. The worker receives payments of regular amounts at set intervals from the business.
13. The worker receives payments for business and/or traveling expenses from the business.
14. The worker relies on the employer to furnish tools and materials.
15. The worker lacks a major investment in facilities used to perform the service.
16. The worker cannot make a profit or suffer a loss from the service.
17. The worker works for one business at a time.
18. The worker does not offer services to the general public.
19. The worker can be fired by the business.
20. The worker may quit at any time without incurring liability.

Given the consequences, this is a situation in which to consult an attorney—or to petition the IRS to classify the position before you fill it.

and other universities with reputable programs. Establishing some regular, ongoing contact with targeted university programs is a good way to identify strong candidates.

Part-time teaching, lecturing, jurying, and critiquing are ways a firm can support architecture education programs and identify some of the best students. Participation in these activities can also be a growth opportunity for staff at the firm, and ongoing communication with the dean and faculty members can benefit the firm as well as the university programs. If the school sponsors campus recruiting events, the firm can use this opportunity to share information about itself and screen a large number of candidates. College recruiting has short-term and long-range benefits. It may result in immediate, entry-level hires and, just as important, will provide exposure to other potential hires who may remember and contact the firm when they are ready for a job change later.

***Search firms and external recruiters.*** Sometimes firms turn to individuals or search agencies specializing in recruitment to assist them in filling jobs. At one time this practice was reserved for very senior, specialized jobs requiring regional or national searches. More recently, with the increased demand for talent, some firms have used outside resources to recruit locally or for entry- or middle-level professionals. One approach is to hire individual recruiters as temporary employees on an hourly basis to source candidates, screen resumes and portfolios, check references, and identify qualified candidates for consideration. Normally these recruiters have no financial stake in hiring decisions and allow the firm to leverage its own recruiting resources and talent.

Other external sources include search firms or independent contractors who specialize in recruiting, sometimes referred to as "headhunters." The fees and terms for this type of service can vary greatly, and it is important to understand the terms of the contract you are signing. The two main fee structures are *retained* and *contingency*.

A retained search involves a predetermined fee that does not vary regardless of the length of the search or whether a candidate is hired. A contingency search involves a fee that is paid in full when a candidate is hired and normally is based on the candidate's first-year cash compensation.

Regardless of the recruitment services used, many firms want to retain the exclusive right to make the job offer and negotiate the compensation package with the selected candidate. Last but not least, it is important that the recruiter understand the requirements of the position as well as the firm's culture and character.

***Employment agencies***. For administrative positions, the firm may want to consider the services of local employment agencies, which can often supply prescreened, pretested candidates for consideration. A number of these agencies are now offering computer-assisted design (CAD) temps. Typically the fees, like those for contingency search firms for professionals, are a percentage of the first year's salary. A short-term guarantee is usually provided, and the agency normally replaces unsatisfactory people during the guarantee period. Some agencies that place temporary employees stipulate specific terms if the firm wishes to hire them for a regular position. When working with search firms and agencies, carefully review the terms of the contract, and don't hesitate to get references from other firms for whom the recruiter or agency has worked.

***Ongoing recruiting.*** Filling a specific opening may be a one-time, pressing need, but preparing to fill that opening effectively can be part of a firm's ongoing public relations and marketing effort. The firm's completed work, press coverage, casual comments by current and past staff members, and the visibility level of the firm's principals all contribute to the image of the firm as a good place to work. Campus involvement, local AIA chapter involvement, effective client and consultant relationships, and open houses are all ways of bringing the firm to the attention of future job candidates. In a tight labor market in which firms compete for a limited number of qualified candidates, a good reputation and effective representatives who interact with the community, universities, clients, and others can have a positive, direct influence on the firm's recruitment and retention efforts. All employees should be encouraged to view recruitment as a process everyone is involved in all the time, not just a specific effort by "someone else" to fill a particular vacancy.

▶ **The AIA maintains a job bank at its Web site at www.aia.org.**

▶ **As part of their ongoing recruiting, some firms maintain "applicant banks," retaining applications from and following up with prospective employees even when no position is available. When an opening does arise, there is a ready pool of candidates.**

In larger firms, a human resources team may plan and coordinate the recruitment and selection process. In smaller firms, a partner or other senior member of the firm may do this. In any event, it is important to determine at the outset who will coordinate the process, who will have input into the selection, and who will be making the final selection decision.

## SCREENING AND INTERVIEWING

Screening applicants' resumes allows the firm to select the most promising candidates for interviews. Remember that not only will you be evaluating the candidate at the interview, but the candidate will also be evaluating you and your firm.

***Reviewing resumes and applications.*** Some firms may ask all applicants to complete a standard application form. The advantages of using such a form include having the same information in a consistent format to use when evaluating and comparing candidates: usually specific employment history and education credentials, and typically a statement certifying the accuracy of the information and a release for checking references. The disadvantages are that it takes more time to have all candidates complete and return the forms (and all applicants for a specific job, not just some, must be asked to complete the application if a firm elects to recruit this way) and that the longer process could result in desirable candidates getting jobs elsewhere. Candidates' perception of unnecessary paperwork and cumbersome processes compared with other firms also may be a drawback in a tight labor market.

After receiving the specified application materials, a person familiar with the job duties and skill requirements should review the information, keeping the following points in mind:

- Did the candidate supply the information requested, and do so on time?
- Is the cover letter, resume, or application well written and accurate?
- Are the candidate's experience in project types and level of responsibility consistent with the job's requirements?
- Does the employment history show progression through increasing levels of responsibility or complexity of work? Are there unexplained or frequent job changes?
- Do the personal goals and expectations (if stated) seem consistent with the job being filled?
- Do the work samples or portfolio (if submitted) reflect the type and quality of work you are seeking to add to the firm?
- Is the requested compensation or salary history consistent with the pay you anticipate for the position?

The next step may be a telephone screening. The applicant's information should be in front of the interviewer, with questions prepared in advance. If you are doing the screening, state at the outset that you are gathering more information from candidates over the phone and then will determine whom to contact for in-person interviews. Explain when and how the applicant will find out whether or not he or she is to be interviewed again. Sometimes you may ask applicants to provide more information or work samples for review before you decide who will be interviewed in person.

***Job interviews.*** The interview is a two-way process: The firm will be evaluating the candidate, and the candidate will be assessing the firm. Identify the individual(s) in the firm who will participate in the initial interview, ensure that they have reviewed the candidate's material in advance, and be sure they are trained in interviewing. When several firm representatives are interviewing the same candidate, consider scheduling small-group (two to four people) panel interviews or sequential one-on-one or small-group sessions. Provide an appropriate space for the interview and make sure scheduling and coordination are handled so that all involved perceive the process to be organized and efficient.

# Sample Interview Questions Checklist

## 1. Experience/education
- Why did you select architecture as your field of study?
- Please give me details on any internships in which you participated during school.
- How did your education prepare you for employment as an architect?
- Review your experience and education and detail any skills or responsibilities you think are particularly relevant to the position I have described.
- How many partners or managers do you support? How do you prioritize the range of requests?

## 2. Career goals/job satisfaction
- When you are considering different job opportunities, what do you look for?
- What were the challenges and satisfying elements in your last job? How did you meet the challenges?
- What elements of your last job did you find to be least satisfying?
- Give an example of an important goal that you have set in the past and tell me about your success in reaching it.
- What kind of management brings out the best in you?
- What career goals have you set for yourself? How do you feel working here will help you achieve those goals?
- What kind of time commitment could you give us as your employer? Be realistic.

## 3. Social skills
- Tell me about an experience from your former job(s) that illustrates your ability to interact effectively with a wide variety of people.
- Tell me about a situation that exemplifies your ability to handle the stress of a fast-paced, demanding job.
- What qualities would you identify in yourself that make you an effective coworker or team member? Give me an example of a situation that illustrates these qualities.
- Describe a difficult situation in which you successfully negotiated a win-win solution. Describe one in which you were unsuccessful.
- Give an example of a tough client situation.
- Give an example of something that is difficult to communicate to staff.
- What did you do in your last job to contribute toward a teamwork environment? Be specific.
- Describe the type of person you most prefer to work for or with, and the type of person you least prefer to work for or with.

## 4. Work style
- How do you organize and prioritize your work?
- What are the easiest decisions for you to make? What are the hardest?
- Give an example of a specific occasion in which you conformed to a policy with which you did not agree. How did you feel?
- Give an example of a time when you had to go above and beyond the call of duty in order to get the job done.
- What tasks do you delegate? What tasks do you do yourself?

- Describe your leadership style.
- How do you maintain an overall consistent image for your firm?
- What do you perceive your image to be within the firm? Outside the firm?

## 5. Management
- How would your staff evaluate your management style? Strengths and weaknesses?
- Give an example of a disciplinary problem in which you saved the employee, and one in which you terminated the employee. [Find out process and support given.]
- What methods do you use to determine individual staff members' workloads?
- How did you address contract negotiating, budgeting, scheduling, and staff organization?

## 6. Desire for the job
- What qualities do you have that would make you an asset to this firm?
- Why are you interested in this particular position/a position at this firm?

## 7. Physical qualifications
- This position requires heavy lifting of up to _____ pounds; or pushing and pulling up to _____ pounds; or sitting for extended periods of time. Are you able to meet these requirements? Would you need any assistance in order to do this?

## 8. Other questions
- What are some things you do particularly well? What are some of your greatest achievements? What are your strengths?
- What were some things you have found particularly difficult to do? How did you handle these situations? In what areas would you like to grow and develop? What skills would you like to acquire or improve?
- What frustrates you most about your current job, and how do you handle it? How do you feel about the progress you have made with your present company?
- How do you feel your present job or past jobs have developed you to take on more responsibilities?
- What are the reasons you left your last job? Why are you thinking of leaving your current job?
- Describe the types of deadlines or schedules you have worked under in the past. How did you meet them?
- What are your likes and dislikes?
- What are your strengths and weaknesses?
- What is important to you in a firm?
- Have you ever submitted suggestions to your manager on how to improve work flow or procedures? If so, what were they, and what happened to your suggestions?
- [Hypothetical questions] How would you handle [a studio-specific matter]? What would you do if [give a scenario]? What and how much experience have you had in _____? [Examples: dealing with a difficult client, coping with a delay in the acquisition of essential materials.]

The interview can follow several different patterns:

- A structured interview focuses on a series of prepared questions that are put to each candidate, theoretically allowing for easy and fair comparison.
- An unstructured interview is more conversational and free-flowing. This is an acceptable approach as long as the key job criteria and requirements are addressed in the discussion.
- Behavioral interviews are based on the notion that past performance is the best predictor of future performance. The candidate might be asked to relate highly specific examples from school or work that illustrate responses to a difficult situation or assignment. Sometimes questions about a hypothetical situation can be used to pose a problem or issue to the candidate and ask how he or she would handle it.

The most common approach involves using some prepared questions, including some hypothetical questions, along with some informal conversation. Regardless of the method used, it is useful to have a list of job-related criteria upon which all candidates will be evaluated, and some questions consistently asked of all the interviewees. In a more structured, formal approach, when many people are interviewing and providing input, numerical ratings may be assigned to the criteria and tallied or averaged. Sometimes one or two firm representatives conduct initial interviews, and the strongest candidates are brought back for second interviews with other firm members.

Evaluating a candidate's design or technical ability can be straightforward if the appropriate materials are provided and reviewed and the right questions are asked. Predicting a candidate's ability to adapt to the culture of a specific firm is not always as simple. In most cases you can make a good decision based on an assessment of the person's skills, style, and ability. To ensure that your hiring decision is sound, give the candidate accurate and complete information regarding the role and its responsibilities, professional growth opportunities, compensation, and benefits. Involve other firm members (peers, managers, and subordinates) in the interview and selection process, and always check references.

To check references, ask candidates for the names of individuals with whom they have worked in different capacities in the past, such as a former manager, peer, subordinate, or client. It is a courtesy to tell the candidate that you will be contacting references as part of the overall selection process. Work from a standard, prepared list of questions so that you can compare their responses. If you are not familiar with the reference-checking process, you may seek advice from your employment attorney regarding the liability issues associated with getting, giving, or sharing reference information.

Handling each applicant contact and job interview in a professional, courteous manner is always in the firm's best interests. This includes treating unqualified candidates and those who interview poorly with respect and courtesy. A firm's reputation as an employer and as a provider of architectural services can be damaged if job candidates perceive that they have been treated unfairly or inappropriately

## Giving Personal References

Providing personal references is often a no-win situation: If you give a glowing reference, it may be interpreted as hiding something. If a former employee had problems, you may not want to talk about them. It is also possible that you were at least part of the problem. A small but growing body of court cases has established an employer's potential liability for giving a less-than-favorable reference. To date, lawsuits have been filed on the basis of libel, slander, and discrimination. Negligence suits may also result from not giving honest references to potential employers.

Many architects feel that they must respond to requests for references. How much you say is a business decision. You need to decide how much of a risk you are prepared to take. If you have done your human resources homework and have been fair, consistent, and open throughout, a problem employee should know why he or she was terminated, and divulging this information might not create undue risk. Certainly you should not communicate any information not shared with the employee.

You may also choose an explanation like this: "John worked well when he had constant direction, and I just can't work that way." This conveys valuable information without blaming the employee.

There are other approaches to giving personal references:

- Some firms follow a policy of providing a written recommendation at the employee's request, perhaps at the time of departure.
- Some firms have an informal policy of giving willing and complete references for persons they can wholeheartedly recommend but giving only confirmation of employment dates and position for others. Such a policy, however, makes a firm vulnerable to claims from former employees of disparate treatment.
- Some firms establish a consistent policy of not giving references at all.

In the end, remember that your recommendations reflect on you and your honesty. Consider them carefully.

*Cynthia A. Woodward, AIA*

and share that perspective with others. Remember that recruiting is a form of marketing. A rejected applicant may have a good friend who is a potential client or candidate.

*Following up.* Everyone who submits a resume or comes in for an interview deserves a response within a reasonable time frame. A response could be a personal telephone call (not a voice mail message), a personal letter tailored to the situation, or a well-written form letter; in some cases, an electronic letter or e-mail message may be acceptable. When rejecting a candidate, you may simply want to explain that another candidate's experience or skill more closely matched the firm's needs, or that the candidate's background or qualifications lack something stated in the job qualifications. If asked, you may provide some factual information regarding the specific tasks or project experience that would have made the person a stronger candidate. Avoid detailed criticism of past work experience or interview style, or sharing unfavorable information received from references. The explanation should be brief and factual. Do *not* commit to considering candidates for future opportunities unless you plan to review their resumes for each future opportunity. You may want to encourage the candidate to check back with you at a later time.

Certain regulatory requirements apply to retaining job applicant files and tracking applicant information. Check with your legal advisor for the specific requirements for your firm.

*Equal opportunity.* The legal environment surrounding recruiting has become more complex in recent years, but it is not intended to prevent firms from hiring the person best suited for a given position. In fact, the farther you cast your net, the more likely it is you will find good people and attract a diverse applicant pool. A firm must consider all applicants without regard to race, religion, national or ethnic origin, gender, pregnancy, immigration status, age, marital status, physical or mental disability unrelated to job requirements, and, in some jurisdictions, sexual orientation.

The key to avoiding discrimination claims is simply to treat all applicants with consistency and fairness. Most upheld claims are based on the concept of "disparate treatment." An applicant, as well as a current or former employee, can initiate an investigation by the Equal Employment Opportunity Commission or a local human rights commission.

*Affirmative action.* Some firms that work for the federal government or work with clients that do may be required to submit an affirmative action plan to the federal government. This plan analyzes the current composition of a firm's staff vs. the availability of minorities and women in given job classifications in the pool from which the firm draws its employees. The plan identifies categories in which the number of minorities or women the firm employs is less than would be expected based on labor market data. Goals are established and procedures outlined for correcting the situation—for example, advertising in minority-oriented publications or recruiting at minority college campuses. If the firm is an affirmative action employer, legal advice or affirmative action plan consultants may be helpful.

> The backgrounder Architects as Employers: Legal Requirements (8.1) surveys the legal and regulatory landscape.

## SELECTION AND MAKING THE OFFER

After evaluating the candidates with respect to their skills and fit with the firm, you will identify the preferred candidate. If the applicant screening and interview process has been handled well and the decision maker has gathered necessary input from those involved in the process, the decision should be fairly straightforward. Sometimes there are two or three very strong contenders, and if the first-choice candidate declines the job, the job may be offered to one of the others. For this reason, it is advisable to extend the job offer first and confirm acceptance before notifying other candidates of the choice.

In formulating and extending the offer, consider compensation terms carefully. Pay for current employees with similar experience and responsibilities should be a guide for the pay rate offered. Perceived pay equity is a retention issue, and the firm must balance the need to offer a desirable pay rate to a new employee with the need to maintain some level of internal equity. (While discussion of pay among employees may be discouraged, information is frequently shared.) Some firms offer a one-time signing bonus upon hire to encourage acceptance of the job offer. For out-of-town candidates, the amount of reimbursement for moving expenses can be a negotiable item. The basic compensation terms must be determined before you extend the initial offer; however, some negotiation may take place after that.

A job offer, whether oral or written, constitutes an implied contract between the firm and the individual. A written job offer is preferable, but some firms may choose initially to extend the offer orally and follow up with a confirmation in writing, or confirm the offer and its acceptance after the applicant has agreed to take the position.

The letter should cover the terms of the agreement, such as job category, role, work schedule (full time or part time, and hours), pay rate, exempt vs. nonexempt status and overtime pay eligibility, relocation expense allowances or reimbursements, other bonus or compensation commitments, and designated manager. It is preferable to quote the pay rate on an hourly, weekly, or monthly basis, since quoting an annual figure could imply a one-year commitment. Some firms use a standard form to help them delineate pay and benefits information consistently. If you have not done so already, inform successful candidates of the requirement for new employees to provide proof of eligibility to work in the United States and complete the forms required by the Immigration Reform and Control Act (IRCA). In larger firms, an employee handbook typically discusses terms and conditions of employment, and a copy may be included with the offer letter.

## ORIENTATION

An individual's experiences during the initial few days or weeks in a new position will often determine whether he or she becomes a satisfied long-term employee or a turnover statistic. An employee's introduction to the firm is the beginning of the employment relationship, and as such, it should be carefully planned and executed. Many firms believe that the time spent up front acclimating new employees pays off through increased efficiency, collaboration, and employee satisfaction, which directly translates to higher profitability.

Before a new hire arrives, the hiring principal or manager should inform everyone who will be directly affected, giving a brief outline of the person's background and what his or her role in the firm will be. A workspace, with all the furniture and equipment normally supplied by the firm, should be set up. In larger firms, the support services teams also must be notified and will be involved in preparing for the new employee's first day.

A new employee must learn about many aspects of the firm —its culture, values, practice areas, high-profile projects, work processes, technology, and resource and support services, to name a few. The firm's size and organizational complexity will determine the scope of the orientation program. Firms ordinarily designate one individual or group of individuals to plan and coordinate this process to ensure that it is comprehensive and consistently administered. Principals, managing partners, human resources, and other professionals can participate in the orientation process, each handling different aspects of the program.

Recently firms have begun providing much of this information online and encouraging employees to access it on their own schedule. While certain items must be covered in the first few days, the entire orientation process takes weeks or months. Some of the items normally covered in an orientation program are outlined below.

*Mission, culture, values.* Firms often have formal statements outlining these items and publish them in marketing or recruitment materials and handbooks. Citing examples of firm activities that exemplify them can be very powerful in communicating the firm's character and values to new recruits.

*Markets and projects.* New employees need to know the firm's primary markets and service areas. Information on high-profile projects the firm has done is also helpful in making employees more effective representatives of the firm.

*Internal resource and support services.* Provide information regarding administrative and clerical support (telephone, fax, etc.), design support (specifications, illustration, model building, etc.), reprographics, photography, marketing, accounting, research centers or libraries, material libraries, supplies and purchasing, and human resources and other support services. Be specific about how to use these resources.

## Orientation Program

Each firm needs to develop orientation program activities to meet its needs. The following are some of the most common activities in the first few days:

- Review and completion of all necessary payroll, tax, and other forms (including federal and state income tax forms); verification of employment eligibility; emergency notification forms; and home address and telephone number records. This should occur on the employee's first day at work.
- Introduction to studio, project team, or other relevant work groups. The new employee's portfolio or work samples may be shared with coworkers.
- Tour of the firm, including introductions to the support services teams—reception, shipping, payroll, information services, etc.
- Review of all employee benefits and completion of enrollment and payroll deduction forms.
- Review of the employee handbook or employment policies; discussion of office policies and procedures, such as use of company cars, travel expense reimbursements, and meeting room scheduling; discussion of office safety policies and practices.
- Overview of telephone, messaging programs, computer equipment and software, e-mail, network, and CAD standards.

*Technology and special tools.* With the increased emphasis on the use of computers, information systems, sophisticated software, and electronic communication, there is an increased need to orient new employees to the firm's tools and resources so that they will be used appropriately.

*Employee policies, handbook (payroll, travel and expense guidelines, etc.).* Employees need to know where this information can be accessed, and usually sign an acknowledgment of receipt of this material as part of the orientation process.

*Compensation and employee benefits.* Pay rates, overtime, paid leave, and other pay policies must be communicated. Benefit packages are important to employees, are sometimes complex, and require the completion of forms.

*Job responsibilities, project team, studio structure.* All employees need to understand what they are expected to do and to whom they report. Job descriptions (if available) are often shared and performance objectives reviewed.

*Professional development and learning opportunities.* Review continuing education activities, training programs, and professional association affiliations the firm supports.

There are many different approaches to providing all this information, and there are limits to how much new information can be absorbed at one time. Some firms establish a "buddy" system whereby a coworker is designated to help acquaint the new employee with the firm. The firm may encourage or even pay for an informal lunch or after-work get-together to introduce the new employee. In larger firms, the arrival of newcomers can be announced via in-house newsletters, through e-mail, on bulletin boards, or through the intranet.

In any event, the components of the orientation program should be set up so that all new employees receive the same information within the first weeks on the job, and the hiring principal or manager should check back periodically to ensure that the new hire is successfully introduced and integrated into the firm. Employees who receive a thorough orientation to the firm and to their positions in the firm are more likely to be productive and successful from the outset.

In addition to general orientation, when hiring a new graduate into an entry-level position, it may be necessary to orient the individual to the business environment and to his or her responsibilities as a professional in the firm. Architects beginning their first job need to learn about what makes a firm profitable, how to manage their time, and how to work effectively in an environment that is very different from academia. Work processes, billable percentage targets, reporting and accounting systems, and role expectations may need to be explained to employees just entering the profession.

## INITIAL PERIOD

Most firms establish an initial time period—usually three to six months—during which the firm and the new employee can become familiar with each other and assess their mutual satisfaction with the employment relationship. Every effort should be made to give individuals frequent feedback during this period to ensure that they fully understand the expectations of the firm. At the conclusion of this initial period, a performance appraisal should be conducted, with the employee and firm exchanging views on how reality has met or failed their expectations.

To emphasize the end of this period, an employee whose performance has been satisfactory may become eligible for certain benefits previously withheld. A salary increase may or may not be granted at this time, depending on the firm's policy. If questions remain regarding the employee's skills and abilities or if the employee has not had the opportunity to demonstrate the full range of skills required, the initial period may be extended for a specific amount of time, usually one to three months depending on the situation. If performance has been unsatisfactory, new employees can be dismissed at this point, normally without extensive prior coaching or warnings.

# Compensation and Benefits

*Laurie Dreyer-Hadley and Kathleen C. Maurel, Assoc. AIA*

Recently compensation and benefits have come to be viewed together as "total compensation," representing the total labor expense to the firm. Also, benefits have become increasingly important to employees, who consider them along with salary when assessing their financial situation. In deciding whether to stay with a firm or accept an offer from another firm, employees evaluate the combined salary and benefits package.

Firms are advised to consider their total compensation strategy, including base pay, variable pay (bonuses, profit sharing, etc.), and benefits. A firm's philosophy and pay practices should reinforce its values and culture and support accomplishment of its business objectives. The firm's profitability and success are contingent upon having well-thought-out pay programs that attract and retain qualified staff.

Some items to consider when structuring the compensation and benefits program include the following:

- A formalized, structured approach versus a loosely defined, informal one
- An approach based on detailed job descriptions vs. broad job groups
- The decision to lead, match, or lag what other firms in the market are offering
- Perceived fairness/equity (employees do share information)
- Rewards/incentives for individual/team performance (merit), longevity, and skills
- The firm's culture—"family-friendly," egalitarian, offering a degree of employee involvement in planning and making benefit choices

There are many issues to consider in developing and maintaining sound pay and benefits programs. Workforce demographics must be considered, so that both recruits and employees view the program as competitive. The program must be reality-based (what the firm can afford and manage effectively), must comply with federal, state, and local laws, and must not be discriminatory with respect to protected classes of individuals (e.g., minorities, women, and individuals with disabilities). Firms should periodically communicate information about their programs to ensure that employees understand them.

## Compensation

To attract good people, a firm's pay structure needs to be competitive with that of similar jobs in the market within which the firm recruits. For example, if the firm recruits locally, rates must be attractive to local candidates. If it recruits regionally or nationally, compensation and benefit packages must be designed and explained so as to attract individuals from areas where average rates may differ. Information on pay rates according to firm size and region is available from national (and sometimes local) surveys; such information should be evaluated carefully since it may not fit a specific firm. Job titles used may vary, so it is necessary to compare experience level and duties for similarity when referring to surveys and matching data to your firm's jobs. When looking at market pay rates, consider base pay and bonuses, regional differences due to cost of living, local tax differences, and differences in

benefits offered in addition to the cash compensation. Because many employees will compare only base pay, a careful explanation of other variable compensation (bonuses, profit sharing, etc.) and the value of benefits is often necessary.

As a firm grows and acquires more staff members at all levels, perceived pay equity can become an issue, particularly if new, less experienced individuals are offered salaries higher than those of long-term staff members. Most medium-size and large firms adopt a more structured approach to setting pay rates and awarding increases based on job descriptions or years of experience plus education. A salary structure by no means implies that two individuals who each have a bachelor of architecture degree and five years' experience need be paid the same. It merely provides a framework to avoid inequities. Periodically a firm may want to verify that any pay differentials are either job- or performance-related.

Usually base pay rates are very close for recent graduates and interns. The pay ranges widen as individuals gain experience, develop particular areas of expertise, and make varying contributions to the firm's success. Base pay rates are closely aligned with assigned billing rates (the amount the firm can charge clients for the services the employee performs).

Most firms tie base pay to job performance, and many have instituted incentive pay programs to reward employees for meeting predetermined goals or for meeting or exceeding specific individual, project, team, or studio performance expectations. Some firms have bonus programs that allow for discretionary payouts based on job performance and/or firm profitability, often tied to role or level within the firm. There are many different ways to structure pay programs, and in a very competitive labor market, firms seek to be innovative in their pay practices to attract and reward top talent.

All pay practices must comply with federal, state, and local laws. Of particular importance is the distinction between hourly and salaried employees, which is based on definitions for nonexempt and exempt status. When overtime pay is required, there are specific guidelines for calculations. Firms must also follow laws and regulations governing pay deductions and timing of payments. It is advisable to get legal advice when developing your pay practices, and to have them periodically reviewed by an attorney or consultant.

Firms need to communicate the basis upon which pay increases are awarded and explain any incentive or bonus programs to all employees. Ongoing communication and effective administration are components of successful compensation programs.

## Benefits

Benefits, like handbook policies, evolve gradually, varying with the size and age of the firm. Benefit packages can grow quickly and add as much as 30 to 35 percent to base salaries. Once such packages are instituted, it is difficult to delete or reduce benefits without affecting employee morale. Therefore the firm should think through each addition carefully and perhaps seek advice from an independent consultant on expensive items.

The kind of benefit program the firm provides should also reflect the needs and desires of its workers. People tend to have divergent needs and priorities at different points in their lives, and when the workforce is diverse, developing programs can be a challenge. While individual preferences do vary, some general trends can influence benefit planning:

part 2 BUSINESS

# Architect's Compensation: Report From the Field

## Compensation by Position in the Firm

| | Mean | 1st Q* | Median | 3rd Q† |
|---|---|---|---|---|
| Associate | $71,900 | $60,000 | $69,000 | $80,000 |
| Manager | 63,300 | 53,100 | 60,200 | 70,000 |
| Architect III | 54,700 | 46,800 | 53,800 | 61,000 |
| Architect II | 48,100 | 42,000 | 47,000 | 54,300 |
| Architect I | 41,100 | 36,000 | 40,000 | 45,000 |
| Intern III | 40,700 | 36,000 | 40,000 | 45,000 |
| Intern II | 33,500 | 30,000 | 33,000 | 36,700 |
| Intern I | 28,300 | 25,000 | 28,000 | 31,300 |
| Engineer | 58,700 | 53,000 | 57,700 | 65,000 |
| Planner | 55,500 | 43,100 | 52,000 | 65,000 |
| Landscape Architect | 46,300 | 37,700 | 44,000 | 51,000 |
| Interior Designer | 43,600 | 36,000 | 44,400 | 50,000 |
| Construction Administrator | 51,500 | 42,500 | 50,000 | 60,000 |
| CAD Manager | 43,400 | 35,000 | 41,000 | 50,000 |
| Drafter | 32,600 | 28,000 | 32,000 | 37,500 |
| MIS Manager | 53,000 | 43,700 | 54,000 | 60,700 |
| Controller | 57,600 | 44,600 | 56,800 | 67,900 |
| Bookkeeper | 34,200 | 28,800 | 34,300 | 40,000 |
| Marketing Manager | 52,100 | 40,000 | 50,000 | 60,000 |
| Marketing Assistant | 34,000 | 29,100 | 33,000 | 38,000 |
| Office Manager | 37,600 | 29,000 | 35,000 | 44,000 |
| Administrative Assistant | 29,700 | 25,200 | 30,000 | 33,400 |

*First quartile. One-fourth of salaries fall under this figure
†Third quartile. Three-fourths of salaries fall under this figure, one-fourth above it.

The data in these tables provide three views of architects' compensation from the 1999 AIA compensation survey. The compensation figures include salaries, bonuses, and profit sharing.

These data represent a cross section response from 1,770 AIA member-owned architecture firms. The results are reported in *Compensation at U.S. Architecture Firms: 1999 AIA Report.* The purpose of the report is to provide information to AIA members and architecture firm management on prevailing salary scales within the profession. It is the policy of The American Institute of Architects that members are to make all decisions on matters of compensation and fees on an individual basis or within their own firms.

## Average Compensation by Position and Firm Size

| (selected positions only) | 5-9 | 10-19 | 20-49 | 50+ |
|---|---|---|---|---|
| Associate | $56,900 | $63,300 | $69,500 | $80,500 |
| Manager | 54,900 | 56,500 | 61,600 | 68,500 |
| Architect III | 49,100 | 48,800 | 51,300 | 58,700 |
| Architect II | 42,400 | 44,700 | 45,800 | 50,600 |
| Architect I | 37,600 | 39,900 | 40,000 | 42,300 |
| Intern III | 37,100 | 39,400 | 41,100 | 42,200 |
| Intern II | 31,100 | 32,800 | 33,700 | 34,700 |
| Intern I | 26,800 | 27,400 | 28,400 | 29,100 |

## Average Compensation by Position and Region

| (selected positions only) | New England | Middle Atlantic | East North Central | West North Central | South Atlantic | East South Central | West South Central | Pacific North-west | Pacific South-west |
|---|---|---|---|---|---|---|---|---|---|
| Associate | $73,500 | $75,700 | $71,700 | $71,800 | $69,900 | $68,400 | $69,800 | $59,800 | $76,400 |
| Manager | 62,800 | 63,400 | 64,100 | 64,900 | 62,900 | 59,000 | 64,100 | 54,400 | 65,600 |
| Architect III | 55,700 | 54,000 | 53,500 | 58,800 | 52,900 | 52,300 | 56,900 | 48,100 | 55,700 |
| Architect II | 50,100 | 47,100 | 47,300 | 51,700 | 46,100 | 46,100 | 49,900 | 42,500 | 48,900 |
| Architect I | 43,400 | 39,300 | 40,100 | 41,100 | 40,000 | 39,400 | 43,000 | 39,200 | 41,800 |
| Intern III | 42,800 | 41,900 | 39,700 | 38,500 | 41,000 | 37,500 | 39,800 | 37,800 | 42,700 |
| Intern II | 33,700 | 34,300 | 33,400 | 31,900 | 33,800 | 32,000 | 32,600 | 31,900 | 35,600 |
| Intern I | 29,000 | 28,000 | 28,300 | 26,900 | 28,700 | 27,500 | 27,700 | 26,700 | 29,600 |

- Young and unmarried members of the workforce are generally more interested in cash compensation, paid time off, and very basic benefits such as medical insurance. Benefit packages that focus on long-term savings and retirement programs may not be a priority. Their immediate need and interest is cash.
- As employees marry, have children, and buy their first home, cash, time off (or flexible schedules), and child care benefits (flexible spending accounts, referral services, etc.) may be most important.
- Those in the middle-aged group may be concerned with family needs and focus more on planning for retirement. Comprehensive health plans, dental plans, and life and disability insurance are more likely to be important to this group. Retirement and tax-deferred savings plans are desirable as well.
- Older staff members are even more interested in retirement benefits and other mechanisms for deferred savings that shelter money and help accumulate wealth.

There are several different benefits categories:

- *Required/statutory benefits* include FICA (Social Security), unemployment taxes, workers' compensation (state industrial) taxes, and any other payments or payroll taxes employers are required to make for employees. Employees do not always realize that the employer pays for these benefits, and they do add to the firm's overall labor expense.
- *Welfare benefits* are those that contribute to the well-being of employees and their families. They include medical, dental, and vision compensation, flexible spending accounts, long-term disability, and life insurance.
- *Retirement benefits* provide continuing income after the employee ceases to work. Many different programs fall into this category, including pension plans and tax-deferred savings plans such as 401(k) plans. Some retirement benefits may be structured to include a vesting schedule, requiring the employee to complete a certain number of years of service in order to receive the benefit and perhaps serving as a retention tool.
- In addition, firms typically provide some sort of paid-time-off benefits such as vacation, sick leave, and holidays.

Although they have no legal obligation to do so, most firms provide a core group of welfare, retirement, and paid-time-off benefits in order to attract and retain employees. A basic benefits package often includes some form of medical insurance, life insurance, paid time off, and retirement savings plan. The cost of these benefits can be paid in full by the employer or shared with the employee.

Some other benefits becoming more common in architecture firms include dental, vision, short- and long-term disability, pretax premium plans, health care and dependent (child) care reimbursement (flexible spending) accounts, and 401(k) plans. Firms may offer tuition reimbursement, commuter transportation subsidy, child care referral services, employee assistance programs (EAPs), and other benefits as well. A small number of firms have employee stock ownership plans (ESOPs), allowing staff to own shares of company stock that they can cash in at some point. Other firms may award stock bonuses or stock options to selected individuals at certain levels within the firm.

Paid-time-off benefits have continued to gain more attention in the past decade. With more two-wage-earner families and increasing interest in leisure activities, paid time away from work (as well as flexible schedules and telecommuting) is a key concern for many employees. Typical paid-leave benefits include vacation, sick leave, and holiday time. Jury duty, bereavement, and other types of paid leave may also be provided. Some firms offer a "paid-time-off bank" in which all paid leave benefits are bundled into one account and can be accessed for any reason. It is important to note that although paid-time-off benefits are not required by law, if a firm chooses to offer them, they must be administered in accordance with any local, state, or federal law that pertains to time off from the job. For example, the Family and Medical Leave Act (FMLA) does require some employers (of a certain size, under certain circumstances) to grant time off to employees and to allow them to use accrued paid leave if the employer provides it.

Some firms may choose to explore a flexible benefits approach, which is one way to address the diverse needs and interests of employees. Essentially employees are given an amount of benefit dollars with which they can "buy" additional benefits of their choice, such as additional vacation time, a better medical package, deferred-tax dollars, or child care expenses. Flexible options maximize the benefits' perceived value to employees. Because these programs are more complex to communicate and administer, they are more common in larger firms.

Other benefits include dues payments for memberships in professional organizations; continuing education opportunities provided in-house or from external resources; and fees, travel expenses, and/or paid time off to attend conferences and seminars.

Some firms inform their staff about the monetary value of their benefits. They may issue regular reports on the value of funds in savings, stock, or pension plans and the firm's out-of-pocket costs for benefits it pays for on the employee's behalf.

Employee benefits planning has become increasingly complex over the years as the number and type of benefits increase and as government regulations pertaining to benefits proliferate. There are a number of laws and regulations governing group benefit plans, some of which prevent discrimination in favor of highly paid employees or owners. When developing a benefits package for the first time or modifying a current one, it is a good idea to check benefits surveys, find out what similar local firms offer, and consider using a benefits attorney or consultant/broker for advice. Ongoing benefits administration and employee communication can be time-consuming, a fact that should be considered when planning benefits.

Once the programs are instituted, it is important to review them periodically to make sure they remain in compliance with changing regulations, continue to be consistent with the firm's philosophy and culture, and meet the needs of the majority of the employees.

*Laurie Dreyer-Hadley is vice president of human resources at Gensler, where she is responsible for all human resource functions. Kathleen Maurel is the director of human resources for Callison Architecture, an international design firm based in Seattle.*

# 8.3 Termination, Layoff, and Performance Issues

## Laurie Dreyer-Hadley, Kathleen C. Maurel, Assoc. AIA, and Jennifer L. Taylor

*Staff departures are a reality in all architecture firms. For whatever reason departures occur, handling these situations well—no matter which side of the desk you sit on—is a mark of professionalism.*

Despite all efforts at coaching and development, some individuals simply do not work out and their employment must be terminated. Others might decide to retire or leave for personal reasons, or the firm might decide to terminate someone's employment for other, non-performance-related business reasons. Long-term changes in the profession and building industry may cause fluctuations in staffing or cycles of expansion and contraction leading to layoffs. The reasons for employee terminations are numerous, and many are beyond a firm's control. But when a valued employee leaves the firm for any reason, the impact can be considerable.

### VOLUNTARY RESIGNATION

A valued employee's resignation can be disheartening. Every effort should be made to part on good terms. Even in large metropolitan areas, the architecture community is close-knit. Today's dissatisfied employee could be tomorrow's client representative.

It is common business practice to expect two weeks' notice from a resigning employee. Sometimes it is possible to negotiate a longer period with a senior employee whose absence will create significant gaps in project continuity. Usually it is best not to try to dissuade someone who has decided to leave. It is better to leave the door open for a possible future return. If the situation warrants, the firm can ask a dissatisfied employee to depart sooner than the resignation's effective date, and may choose to buy out the notice period. This may be appropriate to prevent dissatisfied employees from being disruptive or unproductive during the period before they leave.

Management should conduct an exit interview with the departing employee. The purpose of the interview should be to gain the employee's perspective on his or her employment experience with the firm. This interview should be conducted by a subjective individual who is not involved with the departing employee's day-to-day activities. The interviewer should listen carefully, remain impartial, and not try to defend the firm. A firm can learn a great deal from trends identified through exit interviews.

### TERMINATION

Terminating an employee is sometimes the only solution to a personnel problem. Except in the case of gross misconduct, termination should not come as a surprise to an employee, who should already have been given feedback and clear messages about consequences of failure to improve performance.

While there is no good way to terminate an employee, there should be planning before the meeting takes place. The meeting must take place in a private area with

> **A firm's investment in its people can be seen from both sides of the desk. If you are considering resigning, take a minute to think about the investment the firm has made in you—and you in it. Are you making the right decision?**

> **The percentage turnover rate is calculated by dividing the number of terminations each year by the average number of employees in that year and multiplying the result by 100.**

**LAURIE DREYER-HADLEY** *is vice president of human resources at Gensler, where she is responsible for all human resources functions.* **KATHLEEN MAUREL** *is director of human resources for Callison Architecture, an international design firm based in Seattle.* **JENNIFER L. TAYLOR** *is human resources manager at the Columbus, Ohio, office of NBBJ.*

only the employee, the direct supervisor, and another involved manager or human resources representative present. Review previous documentation and give succinct and objective reasons for the termination. While firms with "at-will" employment provisions are not required to provide justification for employment terminations, most do provide some explanation of the rationale supporting the termination decision. Reactions can vary from defensiveness to tears. The manager should remain calm and composed, even if the discharged employee becomes angry or distressed.

In most cases, the discharged employee should be asked to leave the office immediately. Have all necessary paperwork (e.g., insurance coordination forms, distribution of savings plan amounts, and verification of forwarding address) prepared for the employee to sign. Collect keys to the office, restrict access to software and archives, and change computer and other access codes. In some instances it may be wise to have someone accompany the discharged employee to collect personal possessions.

Some states have strict time limits for final payment. The Consolidated Omnibus Budget Reconciliation Act of 1986 (COBRA) requires that firms give employees and their family members the right to continue group health benefits at their own cost for a specified period.

Terminating partners or senior staff presents another kind of trauma. There is a strong tradition that public announcements of such events are characterized as resignations. This is a face-saving technique with a kernel of truth for the firm as well as the individual, because usually the firm and the individual have agreed that the best interests of both will be served by parting company. A mutual understanding should be reached about what reason will be given.

A clear-cut agreement should also be developed on transfer of ownership, liability, credits on work in progress, benefits, termination pay, and other buyout provisions. Some compromise obviously will be necessary; this may be facilitated by a knowledgeable third party. All separation agreements should be in writing, and legal review is advisable. This entire process is likely to take some time. Allow as much as three months or more to accomplish a smooth transition.

## LAYOFFS

Slow economic cycles are part of the architecture industry. In a design and construction market affected by ups and downs, firms will be faced with downsizing from time to time. A hard look at projected revenues can indicate the number of people or level of salaries the firm can support. Much more difficult are the decisions that follow. Here are some initial steps you may want to consider to avert layoffs:

- Allow natural attrition to occur without replacement.
- Eliminate paid overtime.
- Attempt to speed up start dates or project schedules.
- Encourage or require employees to use vacation time during a slow period; encourage voluntary schedule reductions, leaves of absence, etc.
- Refine project assignments to maximize billings.
- Review possible cost savings of subletting office space, temporarily reducing benefits, or tightening controls on overhead expenditures.

Communication with staff is critical during any economic downturn. When implementing cost-cutting measures, be honest and open with the staff about the goals of these tactics. Failure to do so may result in rumors and the appearance of keeping secrets. Thus the firm could lose good, talented employees it wishes to retain. Often the staff may have ideas to enhance cost-cutting efforts.

If these measures are not successful, a few intermediate steps can be taken to help retain all staff members. Contact other architecture firms to see whether arrangements can be made to lend employees for a specified period. Consider withholding pay

▷ **Recruiting and Hiring (8.2) provides a list of twenty tests that separate an independent contractor from an employee.**

▷ **Depending on the reason for termination, a former employee may be eligible for unemployment insurance benefits. Rules vary from state to state, but in general, employees are not eligible or must complete a substantial waiting period if they leave voluntarily without cause or are guilty of gross misconduct. Otherwise they are eligible, and each time a claim is filed against your firm, your contribution is increased.**

▷ **Ownership Transition (5.4) looks at downsizing from the firm's strategic perspective.**

increases and perhaps reducing salaries, starting first with the firm's owners, then senior staff members, and on down the line. Another alternative is to reduce work hours to a level consistent with project demands.

If layoffs are necessary, the firm leadership must develop a procedure for selecting the employees to be laid off. This can be done based on job function, seniority (last in, first out), or job performance. If performance is a selection criterion, the firm must proceed cautiously to make sure that all employees are compared equally. It is advisable to use documented performance appraisals or other evaluation criteria to make this determination. Using a specific procedure for selecting those to be laid off will aid the firm in the event of a wrongful-termination suit. When doing layoffs, firms, especially those with affirmative action plans, need to be aware of any adverse impact that layoffs will have on representation of individuals in protected classes, such as women or minorities.

## SEVERANCE PAY

Severance pay is not required under any circumstances; however, it is a common business practice when laying off staff. Firms vary in the amount of notice given or severance paid; sometimes this amount is determined based on years of service, such as one week's pay for every year of service. Severance pay can also be used when a firm comes to a mutual termination agreement with an employee. Many times this can defuse a tense situation and help a former employee move on. It is not recommended that firms have a formally stated severance pay policy; rather, such politicies should be determined on a case-by-case basis. Having a policy and standard severance payment practices would require filing it as a bona fide benefit plan under the Employment Retirement Income Security Act of 1974 (ERISA).

## RETIREMENT

In the early stages of one's career, retirement seems beyond a distant horizon. In time, that day approaches.

Retirement is for many a complicated decision. From the professional perspective, there are questions of motivation and fulfillment. From the personal perspective, there are issues of personal vitality and priorities. From the financial perspective, there are questions of costs and benefits. The needs and desires of the firm itself must be considered as well.

If an employee wants to retire, the firm should help smooth this major transition. It is good advice to allow plenty of time to calculate how much income will be available under any retirement plans and also to decide how to handle the transition of responsibility and expertise within the firm. For sole practitioners and those in small practices with only two or three principals, retirement may mean closing or selling the firm. These are, of course, major transitions and need to be considered long in advance of the actual day of retirement.

Many architects do not formally retire at all. They may form sole proprietorships and provide professional services in selected situations. Some take on small projects. Others seek specific roles or niches of interest to them: pro bono projects, public or professional service, expert witness work, or consulting in specialty areas.

## ADDRESSING PERFORMANCE PROBLEMS

Except in cases of gross misconduct, terminating an employee should be a last-step solution. Employees do not develop performance problems overnight, and there are usually opportunities to take corrective or disciplinary steps before termination becomes necessary.

Everyone has a natural tendency to avoid confrontation, but it is the responsibility of firm management to manage all performance—good and bad. Failing to address an obvious performance problem can send a message that substandard performance is tolerated and acceptable. Also, an employee may not know that there is a problem, and if it is brought to his or her attention, the issue may be easily corrected. This saves the firm the cost of turnover in the long run.

**The Age Discrimination in Employment Act forbids employers from dictating a specific retirement age.**

The first time a performance issue arises, the manager should have a fact-finding or coaching discussion with the employee. The manager can explain the issue, get the employee's view, and make sure that the employment expectations are clear. The manager should retain some type of documentation of the discussion. If the problem remains or recurs, another discussion should take place, followed by a confirming memo to the employee (with a copy to his or her personnel file) reiterating the problem and the expected change. This document should consist of the following: what performance standards are lacking, what has been done to assist the employee to date, dates of any previous performance discussions, what expectations must be met, a reasonable time frame within which change must occur, and the consequences of failure to meet the performance standard. Managers should be reminded to follow any coaching or disciplinary procedures outlined in the personnel manual. To ensure that all staff members are treated equally, everyone who is disciplined should have a record in their file, not merely individuals destined for termination. It is best to have the employee sign the written document, not to indicate agreement but to show that he or she has received it.

## COACHING FOR PERFORMANCE IMPROVEMENT

Five steps should be followed when coaching an individual to help improve his or her job performance:

- Explain the performance issue clearly.
- Ask for the employee's view of the situation or issue.
- Ask the employee for suggestions for a solution.
- Negotiate and agree on an action plan to resolve the problem and improve performance.
- Set up a time to review progress and follow up.

> **To avoid possible lawsuits, be sure you are fair and consistent. Especially be sure that your treatment of an employee in a protected class does not vary substantially from your treatment of those who are not. Relatively few discharged employees bring suits against their employers, but a substantial percentage of those who do are successful.**

### RESPONDING TO EMPLOYEE PROBLEMS

| PROBLEM IDENTIFICATION | POTENTIAL SOLUTIONS |
| --- | --- |
| Sudden downturn in job performance (sometimes due to outside forces such as divorce, sick child, etc.) | Informal discussion; refer to employee assistance program (EAP) or other outside counseling resources; change job duties temporarily; tolerate until it ends |
| Skill set or experience lacking | Refer to a book, class, or coach; teach them the skill or give them the experience (shadow) until they learn |
| Behavior, personality issues | Very difficult to change; refer to EAP; focus on business impacts; do not psychoanalyze |
| Motivation lacking | Change incentives; change job structure or assignment |
| Intellectual ability lacking | Change job assignment |

Remember, when something goes wrong, solve the problem and focus on doing better next time. Allocating blame is not the priority! The purpose of coaching is to solve problems, improve performance and results, improve working relationships, and support professional development—*not* to punish, chastise, denigrate, or vent.

***Coaching tips.*** Be courteous and respectful when you assume the coaching role. Use active listening techniques, communicate effectively, and attend to the nonverbal cues being used—both the employee's and your own. Avoid jumping to conclusions and instead focus on helping the employee solve the problem rather than solving it for him or her. Be open to new information, but negotiate when possible and be firm when necessary. It is always desirable to reach a consensus, although you may have to agree to disagree. Follow up on your commitments, set up a review for later time, and make sure it gets done. Document the exchange in notes or a memo to employee. Finally, it is up to you to acknowledge success or decisively address a continuing problem.

# DELIVERY

*The delivery of professional services encompasses processes that are tailored on a project-by-project basis. Project delivery process issues include organizational and contractual arrangements, compensation for services, management of project risk, application of appropriate technology and information systems, and management and control of resources. The activities and tasks involved in the delivery of professional services are carried out within a context that is bounded by legal, ethical, and regulatory considerations.*

# 9 Delivery Methods and Compensation

## 9.1 Project Delivery Options

### Philip G. Bernstein, FAIA

*The project delivery method chosen for a building project depends on two main considerations: What roles will the owner, architect, and contractor play during development and construction? Which variable factor(s)—cost, schedule, building quality, risk, and client capability—are driving the choice?*

A completed building results from a complex sequence of decisions made by the many participants in the design and construction process. Someone must define the key responsibilities and organize the work of these participants, as well as manage the delivery process. The architect, who is deeply involved in most projects from inception to completion, usually assumes this role. The owner relies on the architect's expertise about delivery decisions, often asking the architect to recommend the best delivery method for a project. Thus an understanding of delivery approach options is central to the successful practice of architecture.

Delivery methods have evolved primarily in response to different roles assumed by the entity that constructs a building. The roles and responsibilities of this player, variously known as the contractor, the GC, the construction manager, or the designer-builder, can vary greatly in different delivery methods. This wide variety in delivery approaches in the design and construction industry developed after the credit crunch of the late 1970s, during which the high cost of borrowed money required dramatic acceleration of typical construction schedules

Until the late '70s, most projects were built under what was then known as a traditional delivery approach. Now called design-bid-build, this approach assigned each player a clear and expected role. The owner hired and paid the architect to provide design services, a set of contract documents was developed and placed into the construction marketplace for competitive bid, general contractors assembled a collection of subtrades and submitted bids for the project, and the lowest bidder was awarded the project.

Today the design-bid-build approach—once almost the only way projects were built—has evolved into multiple variants with different designer, owner, and contractor roles and responsibilities. As interest rates in the late 1970s rose, speedier project schedules required not a single construction sequence but multiple

> **"Whether you are an owner/client, architect, engineer or contractor, we have all grown accustomed to the traditional design-bid-build process of designing and constructing projects. In recent years, however, we have seen evidence of growing dissatisfaction with the results of the process. Is the problem process? Is it the lack of participant professional knowledge? Changing client values and expectations? Changing demands of an external business environment? Or is it all of the above?"**
>
> *Gordon Chong, AIACC Handbook on Project Delivery (1996)*

PHILIP G. BERNSTEIN, FAIA, *is vice president of the Architecture/Engineering/Construction Market Group with Autodesk, Inc. He was formerly an associate principal with Cesar Pelli & Associates, Architects, of New Haven, Connecticut. Bernstein teaches professional practice at the Yale University School of Architecture and writes and lectures frequently on project management, technology, and practice issues.*

individual packages that were bid as their design was completed—resulting in the asynchronous construction of individual pieces of the project in the field. General contractors thus portrayed themselves as construction managers adept at controlling these complex projects.

The liability crisis of the 1980s pushed architects further from job site responsibilities and pressed new risks on contractors, who in most cases were willing to assume such responsibilities in exchange for ever-larger pieces of the overall design-construction fee. As projects became more complex and failures more dangerous, owners demanded in-depth construction advice during design that architects were unwilling or unable to provide. Frequent and acrimonious disputes, often fought out in court between architects and contractors, led owners to ask if design and construction responsibility could be consolidated under a single entity. Large construction projects such as renovation of hospitals and airports, which needed to operate during construction, required sophisticated management and construction planning beyond the capabilities or interests of architects and created new roles for professional program managers. All in all, projects built today are faster, entail more risk, and involve far more participants than those built even twenty years ago.

## PLAYERS IN THE PROJECT DELIVERY PROCESS

Regardless of how they are organized, all delivery methods involve three elemental parties: the owner, the architect, and the contractor. Their discrete roles, expertise, and expectations are described below.

The owner (or client) initiates a building enterprise and is usually the eventual owner or operator of the finished building. The owner can be an individual, organization, or other entity that has initiated a design project. For purposes of understanding delivery methods, the owner is the entity that holds one or more contracts with the architect and contractor and is responsible for payment of these participants. The owner is also responsible for paying for the construction of the building.

An owner's expertise in design and construction can vary widely, usually in proportion to the breadth and complexity of projects the individual or company has undertaken. Owners generally have similarly broad expectations of the other players in the process.

The architect is the licensed design professional who, acting as an agent for the owner by providing architectural expertise, generates a design concept for the project. While the specific role of the architect varies greatly according to delivery method, it is the architect who designs, documents, and administers the contract(s) for construction of the project. The "architect" could be an individual or a firm and could include consultants such as engineers who augment and support the design effort. In all delivery methods, the architect generates documents that describe design intent. These documents are used by the contractor to build the building.

The contractor is responsible for the actual construction of a building. Typically known as the contractor or general contractor, the contractor's team may include a variety of subcontractors, suppliers, and fabricators who together execute the design intent of the architect's documents. The contractor typically agrees at a prearranged point in the design process to construct the project for an agreed-upon sum. The determination of that moment and the resulting responsibilities of the contractor are the key components that distinguish the various delivery methods.

## VARIABLES

Once only the cost of construction drove the delivery approach of every project, and with little exception the contractor submitting the lowest bid was selected. Today, however, other key variables may affect the selection of a delivery approach. These include construction cost, schedule, level of quality, risk, and owner capabilities.

***Construction cost.*** As an owner's greatest financial obligation for a project, construction cost is frequently the central concern of design and construction. Buildings are very expensive, and owners rarely have infinite funds with which to pay for them. Fixed budgets create clear and definite obligations for the architect and the contractor.

**Risk Management Strategies (11.1)** describes strategies that architects may employ to limit risk.

**The Documents Finder (Appendix C)** describes the "families" of AIA documents. It also defines paths that can help lead owner and architect to the document family most likely to be appropriate for the project at hand.

***Schedule.*** Most projects include a schedule or time frame in which the project must be complete and ready to occupy. When a building program or function is critical to an owner's mission, meeting a precise schedule may be the most important consideration in determining how a project will be built. Typical of such situations are academic projects, which must be synchronized with the academic calendar. Schedule compliance (and acceleration) is critical when interest rates are very high and capital for building is scarce, as even small delays raise the cost of construction financing dramatically.

***Building quality.*** The demand for particular standards of performance in systems, finishes, enclosure, or other building elements is directly related to decisions about schedule and construction cost. The architect typically establishes a clear relationship between a project's level of quality, budget, and program, where an increase in one parameter implies a change in another. An owner may be willing to accept lower levels of quality to save construction cost or to allow a project to be completed in a shorter period of time. Conversely, projects with long anticipated life spans (e.g., civic or institutional buildings) may emphasize levels of quality, and construction costs and schedules must be calibrated accordingly.

***Risk.*** Perhaps the most intractable variable in the building process is risk. Each of the players in the process makes its best effort to reduce or transfer its exposure to liability as the project unfolds. Key risk considerations include the following:

- For the owner: Can the project accomplish its goals within the constraints of time and budget?
- For the architect: Can the project be accomplished within the standard of care at an acceptable level of quality, the owner's parameters, and the strictures of the fee?
- For the contractor: Is it possible to complete the project within the contractually stipulated time frame and/or cost?

***Client capabilities.*** The internal capabilities of a client organization can significantly affect the roles of the client, architect, and general contractor. The strengths, weaknesses, and preconceived notions of the owner can influence the degree to which design, documentation, construction administration, and management are outsourced and the relative importance of the role each team member plays.

## METHODS OF DELIVERY

The relationships and responsibilities of the players combine with an explicit approach to construction cost, schedule, level of quality, and resulting allocation of risk to define the project delivery method for a project. Answers to the following questions can help a firm select and implement a delivery method.

- Architect's role. What are the responsibilities of the architect, and how do these apply to each successive design and construction phase of the project?
- Contractor's role. What entity is responsible for building the project, and when in the process is that player selected?
- Establishment of construction cost. When is the actual cost of construction definitively established contractually between the owner and the contractor?
- Number and type of design and construction contracts. How many individual contracts for design and construction are necessary to accomplish the approach?

Many approaches are used in the design and construction market today, and new methods will no doubt continue to evolve. However, each can be categorized as a variation on one of three general types: design-bid-build, construction management, and design-build.

***Design-bid-build.*** Once known as the traditional approach, this involves a linear design sequence that results in a set of construction contract documents against which con-

▶ The backgrounder Project Scheduling (13.3) describes and compares various scheduling methods and techniques.

### Program Management

Some large, complex projects have multiple building elements and complicated sequencing. One example is construction of a new airport terminal, with associated roadways, garages, and airfield, adjacent to existing facilities that must be kept in continuous operation. For such projects, an owner may elect to hire a project manager to oversee and coordinate the project. Project managers support the owner's interests and for all practical purposes are the owner in these cases. Such services are usually provided by large construction management entities.

▶ The marketplace may suggest delivery options. It may be desirable to break large projects into smaller ones to stimulate local contractor competition. Critical shortages and items with long lead times may suggest fast-tracking so that orders can be placed early.

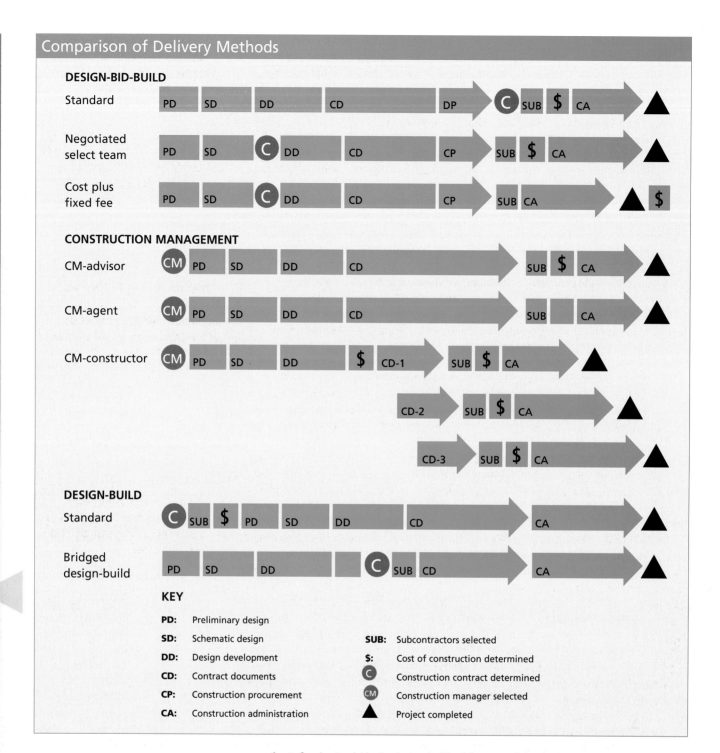

**DESIGN-BID-BUILD**

Standard: PD | SD | DD | CD | DP → C SUB $ CA ▲

Negotiated select team: PD | SD | C DD | CD | CP → SUB $ CA ▲

Cost plus fixed fee: PD | SD | C DD | CD | CP → SUB CA → ▲ $

**CONSTRUCTION MANAGEMENT**

CM-advisor: CM PD | SD | DD | CD → SUB $ CA ▲

CM-agent: CM PD | SD | DD | CD → SUB CA ▲

CM-constructor: CM PD | SD | DD | $ | CD-1 → SUB $ CA ▲

CD-2 → SUB $ CA ▲

CD-3 → SUB $ CA ▲

**DESIGN-BUILD**

Standard: C SUB $ PD | SD | DD | CD → CA ▲

Bridged design-build: PD | SD | DD | C SUB CD → CA ▲

**KEY**

**PD:** Preliminary design
**SD:** Schematic design
**DD:** Design development
**CD:** Contract documents
**CP:** Construction procurement
**CA:** Construction administration

**SUB:** Subcontractors selected
**$:** Cost of construction determined
**C** Construction contract determined
**CM** Construction manager selected
**▲** Project completed

tractors submit fixed price bids. In design-bid-build approaches, the lowest-bidding contractor whose proposal responds to the requirements of the contract documents is usually selected to build the project. Most projects in the United States are constructed under this approach.

A variation of design-bid-build is the negotiated select team approach, in which the contractor is selected early in the design process and certain of the firm's contract terms (such as overhead and profit multipliers) are determined prior to completion of the construction documents. Subcontractors are then selected and the final contractor team assembled once the documents are complete. Selected portions of the building that may be particularly difficult to fabricate or construct may be accelerated under negotiated select team.

Another approach is cost plus fixed fee. In this method the contractor is selected at the completion of contract documents, but the scope of construction is unpredictable (due in part

> **General contractors** offer construction goods and services under a single prime contract. **Specialty contractors** and **suppliers** provide specific products, trades, or other aspects of the project. Because they often subcontract to general contractors, specialty contractors are commonly referred to as "subs."

to unknown factors such as existing conditions). Under a cost-plus contract, the contractor is paid actual labor and material costs for construction plus a fee for coordination of trades on the site. Added incentives may be added to the fee if the project finishes early or under the original budget.

*Construction management.* This delivery approach is so named because of the participation of a contractor who acts in both advisory and technical roles during design and construction. Owners have increasingly demanded detailed construction and technical advice earlier and earlier in the design process, and the construction community has accommodated this need by creating the field of construction management. The construction manager (CM) can play one of three roles:

*CM-advisor.* The CM-advisor acts only as a constructability and cost management consultant during the design and construction process but will not build the building. CM-advisor projects can be delivered under any of the methods described in this section.

*CM-agent.* The CM-agent provides early consulting and may act on behalf of the owner in assembling and coordinating the construction trades prior to and during construction. CM-agents typically provide their services for a fixed fee and assume no risk for actual construction costs themselves but pass both savings and overruns directly on to the owner.

*CM-constructor.* The technical and cost advisor role of the contractor during the design phase of a project transitions at a predetermined moment to the role of contractor for the project itself. CM-constructor (CMc) methods of delivery frequently include the establishment of a guaranteed maximum price (GMP), which is a commitment by the CMc to build the project for a specified price based on early design documents (typically those available at the end of design development). An inherent difficulty in CMc arrangements stems from the CM's dual role as contractor and estimator, as decisions made early in design directly affect the CM's cost (and profitability) later in construction. Owners considering this approach should be aware of this issue.

In general, the construction management industry positions itself to owners as a central project participant when complexity, schedule, or commitment to budget objectives is critical. Because situations in which one or more of these issues is not important to a project's success are rare, construction managers are involved in many large building projects.

*Design-build.* This method has become increasingly popular when an owner is interested in single-point responsibility for both design and construction. The design-build approach stems from clients' growing dissatisfaction with the inherent tensions and conflicts of delivery approaches that place the architect and contractor in adversarial roles. Under design-build, a consolidated entity provides both design and construction services to the owner. A single contract is established between the owner and the architect-contractor or design-build entity. This contract typically includes a fixed price for both design services and construction cost. Design-build approaches require an explicit determination of the roles and responsibilities of the design-build team.

An interesting issue in design-build projects is the mechanism by which the owner establishes and enforces the performance and quality parameters of the project, a role typically assumed by the architect as an agent for the owner separate from the contractor. A variation on the consolidated approach of design-build is bridged design-build, which borrows a design approach from architect teams that include both a design architect (who establishes the design concept) and a production architect (who determines technical criteria and generates the construction contract documents).

Under a bridged approach, the owner will eventually hire two architects. The first is a design architect who prepares a preliminary design for a building and establishes, typically through a performance specification, detailed criteria to which the ultimate design must conform. The completed concept and criteria package (typically based on design development drawings and specifications) are then tendered to design-build teams that offer both technical architectural and construction capabilities.

The bridge between concept and technical design is the juncture at which design-build teams bid on a project, and a team is selected based on the consolidated costs of technical documents and construction. The design architect remains in an advisory role to the owner, reviewing and critiquing the evolving design and construction based on the criteria package. Detailed technical documents are provided by a technical architect who is part of the design-build team. This approach takes maximum advantage

▶ **Construction Management (17.6) describes reasons for using this delivery approach and the process involved.**

▶ **Construction Agreements (10.3) provides a more detailed discussion of GMPs and other approaches for compensating contractors.**

▶ **The AIA publishes a family of standard agreements for construction management projects, including forms for CM as advisor and forms for CM as constructor.**

▶ **Some design-build organizational possibilities may be prohibited by state or local law.**

▶ **Design-Build Services (17.9) looks at this delivery option and shows the productive roles that architects can play in it.**

| | TRADITIONAL DESIGN-BID-BUILD | CONSTRUCTION MGMT AGENCY APPROACH | CM, AT-RISK APPROACH MULTI-BID PACKS | DESIGN-BUILD | BRIDGING |
|---|---|---|---|---|---|
| **PROJECT CHARACTERISTICS** | | | | | |
| Complexity | Moderate to low | Medium to high | Probably high—may have multiple bid packages | May be driving factor in consolidating responsibility | Likely high, requires "bridged" spread, expertise |
| Schedule | Reasonable—not a key factor | Probably tight | Aggressive | Responsibility shifted to consolidated team | May be a driving factor |
| Budget | Normal importance | High priority—fixed | High priority, likely fixed, possible GMP | Likely fixed | Normal importance |
| Program resolution | Well resolved | Predesign likely | Not a driving factor | Not a driving factor | Not a driving factor, but agent firm resolves |
| Design quality | Not a driving factor | Complexity may drive higher quality | Complexity may drive higher quality | Not a driving factor | Likely needs to be high due to complexity |
| Construction quality | Normal | Complexity implies higher quality | Complexity implies higher quality | Normal | Complexity implies higher quality |
| **DEAL STRUCTURE** | | | | | |
| Compensation | Lump sum—all participants | Fee for service or lump sum | Standard fees to design team, GMP to CM | Lump sum to consolidated team; design quality likely | Both design firms get fees, so overlap possible |
| Contract agreement | Owner-architect and owner-contractor | Multiple design/GC; subs—bid or negotiated | B141CM or variant; bid or negotiate construction | fixed Single-point contact with team | Multiple design contracts |
| **DELIVERY TEAM STRUCTURE** | | | | | |
| Disciplines required | Typical project design and construction team | Standard design team plus CM | Standard design team plus CM | Contracting and design consolidated | Scope/design firm yields control to production firm |
| Experience needed | Moderate | Breadth required | Complex project: high degree of experience—all | Experience in design-build needed | Maintain clarity of roles, focus of design Design and agent: |
| Responsibility allocation | Onus on GC during construction | Unresolved—architect and CM must sort out | Ambiguous—CM at risk, therefore more aggressive | Single point to owner | design firm; technical: production |
| Communications | Traditional architect as agent | Architect as agent; CM as owner's rep.; GC as consultant | Architect as agent; CM as contractor— "open book" | Consolidated | Vision of project must be shared to production |
| **LEGAL/RISK MANAGEMENT** | | | | | |
| Liability | Standard | Standard, but does CM presence spread risk? | CM at risk, but design team further exposed | Single point: first line of defense—design team | Shifts to production architect |
| Dispute resolution | Typical ADR, mediation litigation (partnering) | Standard, but partnering likely | Standard, but partnering likely | External—standard; internal—good question | External—standard; internal—good question |
| Conflict of interest | None | With CM as preconstruction consultant, a conflict of interest? | With CM as preconstruction consultant, a conflict of interest? | Potential to design team | Possible, if production firm associated with GC |
| **PROJECT CONTROL** | | | | | |
| Schedule control | By contractor | By CM | By CM | The owner will look to consolidated design-build team leadership for guidance here; how responsibility within team distributed is internal issue | By GC |
| Cost control | Contractor/architect | By CM, in consultation with design team | By CM, in consultation with design team | By CM, in consultation with design team | Need accurate cost projections during scoping; control in CA |
| Quality control | Architect/contractor | By CM, in consultation with design team | By CM, in consultation with design team | By CM, in consultation with design team | Scope defined by design firm; technical by production |

## GMP Approaches to Construction Management

Until recently, the establishment of a guaranteed maximum price (GMP) suggested a commitment by owner and CM-contractor to a construction cost based on partially complete design documents. The price established was understood to account for the risk inherent in using these documents. Many CM-based projects now invoke the GMP at the same point in the design process but sustain it through the completion of construction to maintain flexibility with the owner about the final cost of a project. It might be argued that a GMP, carefully developed and refined based on construction documents, is actually a hard bid. Care should be taken to understand and define this term when it is used to describe construction cost commitments after design development.

of a traditional architect-owner relationship with the participation of the design architect and simplifies the contractual responsibilities of the design-build approach. It may not be suited, however, to projects that require extensive interaction between the architect and owner during the entire design and construction process, since a portion of the design team is contractually tied to the building contractor.

Like many professionals anticipating the challenges of practice today, architects face increasingly complex decisions that drive the very basis of how projects will be designed and built. Advising owners intelligently about delivery options requires an understanding of the players in the building process and their roles, the key variables that affect the choice of delivery method, and finally the range of choices available in the current design and construction marketplace. As design, quality, construction, financing, and schedule options develop, it is likely that new and unanticipated methods will evolve. In order to maintain a central role in the building enterprise, architects must strive to understand, master, and participate fully in all such methods.

### For More Information

*The Handbook on Project Delivery,* published by the AIA California Council and the Design Professionals Insurance Company in 1996, provides a comprehensive look at methods of project delivery. Section 2.2 of *Understanding and Managing Risk,* published by Victor O. Schinnerer & Company in 1998, discusses both the general aspects and the risk factors for alternative project delivery methods.

> The additional risks entailed in assuming the legal liability for actual contracting activities warrant a review of a firm's entire insurance program. Many of these problems can be addressed through special endorsements to the practice policy.

# 9.2 Architectural Services and Compensation

## Clark S. Davis, FAIA

*Clients are willing to compensate an architect in direct relation to the value they place on that architect's services. It is up to architects to make sure their clients understand the full range of their services and the benefits the clients can gain from them.*

Architects in all types of practice have a common challenge: identifying and then receiving appropriate compensation for services they provide their clients. This challenge continues to grow as the practice of architecture becomes more complex.

In the past, when architecture emerged as a distinct profession, architects and most of their works were commonly supported by the state. The church, the primary institution during the Middle Ages, employed many architects and craftspeople. During the Renaissance the concept of patronage of architecture extended to wealthy families and private businesses in leading European cities. In each of these historical settings the architect was an integral part of the enterprise, usually for the long term.

During the last two centuries the roles of architects, practitioners in new engineering disciplines, and construction contractors have become more separate, and project engagements have become the standard for everyone in the industry. Architects' early project-based fee structures were widely based on percentages of construction cost, and the AIA and other industry groups once promoted standard fee percentages.

## A FEE-BASED STRUCTURE OR . . .

The complexity, scale, and uniqueness of twentieth-century building projects led to the adoption of cost-based fees for design services. This approach emphasizes the recovery of costs—labor and expenses—incurred in performing the architect's services. It invites detailed negotiation of the projected effort, staff salaries, overhead rates, fee multipliers, and profit margin that the architect is allowed.

While the cost-based approach to architecture fees seems flexible, it has some serious limitations. It implies that the architect's value is equated only to hours of effort, not to ideas and results.

Several trends have emerged among firms working to realign themselves with new client needs and expectations.

• Many architects recognize the opportunity to make maintaining long-term client accounts (rather than individual project engagements) the fundamental unit of the architect's business. In this approach, flexible compensation terms are devised to cover many different services, individual projects, and locations.

• More projects today involve delivery methods beyond design-bid-build approaches. These may include third-party project management—usually by a developer, construction manager (CM), or program manager—or design-build responsibility. These approaches require new combinations of architectural services and fee considerations.

• Architects are increasingly sensitive to the business risks imposed by different service approaches, and they are seeking appropriate rewards in contract and compensation terms. For example, an architect who shares direct risk for construction cost might negotiate an incentive fee derived from savings under the client's project budget.

**CLARK S. DAVIS** *is senior vice president of Hellmuth, Obata + Kassabaum (HOK) and chief administrative officer of the firm's regional offices in St. Louis and Chicago. He is a past president of AIA St. Louis and AIA Missouri.*

> **"Not everything that can be counted counts, and not everything that counts can be counted."**
> *Alfred Einstein*

> **"There are two fools in every market. One asks too little, one asks too much."**
> *Russian proverb*

- Architects and clients are developing a clearer sense of value based on the contribution of architectural services to the success of a client's enterprise. Sophisticated clients realize that an architect's ideas can speed business processes, draw and delight customers, attract and retain key employees, and save money through wise choices among facility options.

## THE ARCHITECT'S SERVICES

Today, architecture encompasses much more than just design. As demonstrated by Part 4 of this *Handbook,* many architects have creatively expanded their service offerings to meet new client needs and market opportunities. We are thinking well beyond the isolated project that defined most practice tools in the past.

Specifically, we have realized that most clients' needs do not begin with programming and design and end with construction of a facility. Architects now address the entire facility life cycle that concerns our clients: planning, change management (including design and construction), and facility operation. This fact supports the idea that architects can serve their clients continuously in long-term relationships—sometimes with traditional design services, but often with operational needs and new facility strategies that anticipate future facility requirements.

This diversification of services has led to increased specialization among individual architects, firms, and consultants. The definition and pricing of services have therefore become more complex. More than ever before, architecture firm principals and project leaders must serve as integrators of ideas and information from a variety of team members with specialized expertise and experience.

### Options for Defining Services

The first step in structuring architectural services—and their appropriate compensation—is determining the scope and specificity of a client's service requirements. The services may be defined very precisely or very loosely, depending upon the clarity of the client's goals. There are three basic ways of understanding and communicating the scope of architectural services.

***Client-generated work scope.*** Some clients may provide very detailed service requirements as part of a request for proposals (RFP) soliciting architectural services. This approach is usually employed for repetitive or standard assignments, managed by the client's own personnel, for the purpose of comparing competing architectural service proposals on an apples-to-apples basis. Detailed RFPs may specify program requirements, site conditions, service expectations, required deliverables, and schedules.

***Owner-architect agreements.*** Standard service agreements are useful in defining architectural services, primarily for relatively traditional design and construction projects. This is particularly true of the current AIA standard forms of agreement (such as the B141-1997), which contain service definitions, checklists, instructions, and contract language based upon many years of practice experience by leaders in our profession.

***Customized work plans and scope descriptions.*** For a set of special services, it is up to the architect to create a customized definition, after extensive consultation with the client, as the basis for a service and compensation agreement. While customized scope documents vary considerably in level of detail, these common elements deserve consideration:

- Client goals and objectives for the architect's services
- Service tasks and expected work products
- Key review and decision milestones
- Schedules of tasks, phases, and milestone dates
- Requirements for information or services provided by others
- Allowances for changes or events outside the architect's control
- Exclusions and additional services available if needed

> **AIA Document B727, Special Services Agreement,** can be used to describe any scope of services—including services intended to help define services.

> **Agreements with Clients (10.1)** reviews the standard forms of agreement between owner and architect.

> *A prime contract* is one held directly with the owner. A prime contractor may subcontract with others for specific services or, in the case of construction, goals.

Before dealing with specific compensation options and pricing for the architectural services as defined, it is important to consider issues of value and risk related to the firm's strategy and a particular client and project assignment.

## THE VALUE POSITION

The traditional emphasis on cost-based project compensation has contributed to a low level of profitability among architecture firms as an industry. While there are exceptions, many architects have been conditioned to accept pretax profits of a few percent as a reasonable return for their businesses. In reality, this level of return is not sustainable over the long term.

The cyclical nature of design and construction investment has exacerbated this problem. During slow times in the industry, architects and other design professionals sometimes compete vigorously for work that is performed on a break-even or loss basis, just to retain staff and cover overhead costs. These projects and their low-margin fee precedents can hurt a firm's market position and financial performance for many years, in good times as well as bad.

Architects today have a new awareness of the value of their services in relation to those of other professionals and, more importantly, of the distinct benefits their clients derive from the architect's services. Although value is ultimately defined by client perceptions, architects recognize that they have the opportunity to develop business strategies and promote their services based on bottom-line client benefits.

***Relationship to firm market position and strategy.*** The most successful firms have adopted overall business strategies and market positions based on the value of architectural services as perceived by their clients. The principles are simple: Firms perceived as the best or offering something unique in serving client needs will be in demand and will be paid a premium for their services. Conversely, firms that are undifferentiated, that are perceived as being "just like everyone else," often will be evaluated on price alone.

Most architects have had experiences with potential clients who view several firms as equally capable of meeting their needs and who therefore seek to engage a firm on a commodity price basis. A practice built on this type of work will struggle to be profitable unless it becomes much more efficient than competing firms and can deliver its work profitably at a lower cost. In such a case, the ability to deliver a standard product at a lower cost may become a workable value proposition for a firm.

We all know architecture firms that have distinguished themselves as high-value (and generally high-profit) practices in one or more areas. There are a number of possible dimensions in which value may be perceived and delivered:

*Design preeminence.* Firms honored for the signature quality of their design work will be valued and well compensated for their work. This type of recognition can be regional, national, or international in scope and can apply to many different client and building types. In one recent case, a leading designer commanded an up-front fee of more than $250,000 just to have his name associated with a major public project, in addition to his fees for the actual design work.

*Building type expertise and experience.* Most clients seek architects with successful experience in the facility types that concern them. Many firms are recognized, locally or nationally, for their experience in particular building types, such as offices, schools, libraries, hospitals, or housing. In some building types—for example, stadiums or airports—the experience is so concentrated that four or five design firms dominate the entire industry.

---

### Another Perspective on the Value of Architectural Services

What is the value of the architect's services when

- A redesigned retail store increases its sales by $100 per square foot each year?
- A recommended facility reuse option saves the client's organization $5 million per year in occupancy costs?
- An office building is 100 percent preleased because of its unique siting and design features?
- An institution gains new 100 new members because of its new facility?
- A new research center brings top scientists together to develop a breakthrough medical product?

---

**Firm Identity and Expertise (5.1)** looks at the relationships between firms and their markets.

*Project leadership capability.* As clients seek simpler and more efficient ways to manage facility projects, firms that can lead the delivery process—through program management, construction management, or design-build services—are in demand. A number of architects have recognized the need to reclaim this industry leadership position, which has been substantially left to construction and engineering firms for the past two decades. Enhanced project management fees can approximate those paid for all of an architect's traditional design services, often with less business risk.

*Unique service methods and tools.* Some firms offer value through special services that improve quality, speed, and accountability in the planning, construction, and management of their clients' facilities. Today some design firms offer guarantees—usually putting their fees at risk—related to technical quality and schedule performance. Others offer unique computer-aided design (CAD) and computer-aided facility management (CAFM) capabilities. Innovations of this kind have limited product lives, however, as they become replicated by others. For example, facility programming was a distinctive service that has now become commonplace.

Every firm should know its own market strategy and value proposition and how they apply to the firm's individual clients and service assignments. The key is what Rackham and DeVincentis in *Rethinking the Sales Force: Redefining Selling to Create and Capture Customer Value* (1999) call "consultative selling"—knowing every client well enough to identify key needs and focusing the firm's capabilities to meet them in a way that no other firm can.

## RISK ASSESSMENT IN PRICING ARCHITECTURAL SERVICES

In addition to creating positive value opportunities, architects must be sensitive to the business risks they assume in providing their services. A risk is basically a potential financial loss outside one's control. Today's varied project delivery approaches present new combinations of risk for an architecture practice.

There are relatively few "typical" assignments; each one must be evaluated in terms of special risks as compensation and contract terms are proposed. In anticipating risks associated with a particular client or project, the goal is either to find ways to eliminate sources of risk or else to receive fair compensation for changing conditions that are outside the architect's control.

A fundamental risk, of course, is misunderstanding what is included in an architect's services, particularly under a fixed-fee contract structure. If two different clients were to hire an architect for two physically identical projects, they still might have very different expectations about the level of the architect's service, and one project might require twice the compensation level of the other. For this reason, successive editions of the AIA standard owner-architect agreements have become increasingly explicit about the architect's basic and optional responsibilities.

There are some specific risks that should be discussed with clients and considered in any architectural service proposal:

*Client decision making and approvals.* The architect should understand the structure and pace of the client's decision-making process. Will one or two representatives make decisions, or will the architect be required to review options with large groups of people? Can key decisions be reached in a few days, or will they take weeks because of the client's process?

*Scope changes.* If an assignment is expanded or substantially altered during the design and construction process, the change creates more work and cost for the entire project team. This is a particular issue in serving clients experiencing rapid growth or organizational change—facility change is constant and ultimately in the client's best interest, but it is an extra cost to facility service providers.

*Third-party project management.* If a client has engaged a third-party program manager or construction manager to lead a project's design and construction, the relationship can be more complex, as the architect responds to direction from two or more sources. This arrangement is typically more demanding of the architect's time than a project structure that has two parties.

*Fast-tracking and construction-driven delivery schedules.* Accelerated con-

▶ Owners who build often, or who are subject to many statutory constraints, usually employ a limited number of delivery approaches. These are honed over time, and from the owner's perspective there may be no reason to explore alternatives. In other instances the owner and architect are in a position to evaluate the possibilities and select the most appropriate delivery approach for the project at hand.

▶ The AIA Code of Ethics and Professional Conduct permits an AIA member to participate in construction or take a financial interest in a project. Rule 2.301 (1997 edition) calls for disclosure of the architect's financial interest to the owner.

struction schedules often drive the demand for design decisions and an architect's bidding and construction documents. An architect may begin a project expecting to produce one or two document packages but end up delivering many more to support a new construction schedule. Multiple document packages are inherently more costly, and more difficult in terms of technical coordination, than traditional deliverables.

*Construction cost responsibility and contingency structure.* Architects are usually held accountable for designing to a client's budget based on the architect's budget review and estimating services. This risk is compounded, however, when the architect is asked to rely on estimating by others (often third-party program or construction management firms) or when construction begins early based only on partial design and pricing information. At a minimum, the architect should retain parallel estimating capability and be confident that appropriate budget contingencies exist for program uncertainties, design completion, pricing variations, and unforeseen conditions during construction.

*Expected standard of care in design and technical coordination.* As instruments of service, architects' technical documents are never perfect or immune to differences in interpretation. A small percentage of the total cost of any construction project can be related to coordination issues or omissions in the technical documents that are exchanged. Some clients and contracts overlook this reality and expect architects to bear any additional construction costs attributable to normal coordination issues. This is a subject for serious contract negotiation—and higher fees to offset the architect's risk.

*Financial resources and payment terms.* Architects should confirm their clients' financial resources and intended payment practices related to any project assignment. The carrying costs of unpaid invoices and any at-risk design work can seriously reduce the profitability of an engagement and the entire firm.

> Some owners, particularly public owners, are precluded by law (or by their sources of construction financing) from beginning construction before the full construction cost is known and contracted for. Others have choices and will accept the risks inherent in overlapping design and construction.

> The backgrounder Intellectual Property and the Architect (10.4) explores the questions and issues surrounding the ownership of instruments of service.

## COMPENSATION OPTIONS

Several compensation methods can be considered when structuring a new client relationship or project assignment. They present different levels of flexibility, profit potential, and risk protection for the architecture firm.

*Fixed (stipulated sum) fees.* A fixed fee is a firm compensation amount related to a particular scope of service. Fixed fees are convenient and appropriate when services can be precisely defined, a client understands what is included, and the architect is confident the services can be managed within a fixed budget.

Fixed fee structures generally offer the greatest profit potential to the firm. Planned profitability is usually not revealed in negotiation, and the architect can increase profitability by completing the required services at less cost. There is an obvious risk, however, in the possibility that the actual cost of the services will exceed the budget on which the fixed fee is based. It is important to include a contingency within the fixed fee to cover the foreseeable risk.

When the entire scope of an assignment is unclear, or when the architect establishes an "umbrella agreement" to include a number of individual project assignments, it is reasonable to propose fixed fees for initial tasks and confirm follow-on fee amounts later. In any case, the owner-architect agreement should stipulate how fee adjustments can be made to respond to project changes beyond the architect's control.

*Hourly billing rates and fee multipliers.* Hourly billing is the most flexible fee option for architects and clients, and it is generally preferred when no exact service scope can be defined. For this reason, hourly billing is often used for the preliminary phases of project assignments that are later converted to fixed fees.

Hourly billing can utilize fixed dollar rates (e.g., $125 per hour) in which each rate is calculated to cover direct salary cost, fringe benefits, firm overhead, and profit. This option does not directly reveal actual salaries or the firm's overhead and profit markup. In addition, structuring rates by staff position, rather than by name, allows the architect flexibility in assigning people to roles within the project team.

Some clients prefer to negotiate a fee multiplier, which is applied to salary cost incurred by the project team. Two types of multipliers are commonly used: One is a multiple of direct salary expense (DSE), in which direct salary expenses incurred in performing services are multiplied by a factor that covers fringe benefits, firm overhead, and profit. The other is a multiple of direct personnel expense (DPE), in which staff fringe benefits are part of the DPE base and not part of the multiplier.

Hourly billing structures have the disadvantage of limited profit potential in that a planned profit percentage is earned only as staff effort and cost are applied to the work. This problem is made worse when a client wishes to impose a ceiling (or "not-to-exceed" or "upset" amount) on hourly service billings. In this case, the architect bears the risk of any fixed fee arrangement without the possibility of increasing profit through more efficient work effort. Hourly billings with limits are generally no-win options for architects and should be avoided.

*Cost plus fixed fee.* This is an hourly fee option in which a client is billed for the actual cost of an architect's effort—base salaries, fringe benefits, and firm overhead—on a rate or multiplier basis, and a fixed fee is negotiated as the firm's profit on the assignment.

This arrangement can be useful when a client does not want a completely open-ended fee arrangement but there are many unknowns and it is difficult to establish a stipulated sum at the outset. Clients often see the advantage of cost-plus approaches when the uncertainties would force any prudent architect to include substantial, and perhaps unnecessary, contingencies in a fixed-fee proposal. From the architect's perspective, cost-plus approaches limit profit potential but greatly reduce the risk of losses relative to a fixed-fee option.

*Unit cost methods.* In some cases, clients prefer to compensate professionals based on cost per square foot, room, store, building, or other unit. For example, office planning and interior design are often priced per square foot—the same unit used in lease rates and tenant allowances in commercial buildings. Hotel projects are often structured based on cost per room.

Unit cost estimating requires accurate and timely data on the cost of providing the services for each unit. It also recognizes that earlier units usually require more effort than those that follow.

*Percentage of construction cost.* This method ties compensation to the construction cost of the project and not to the scope or cost of the professional services provided. While it is useful to compare or budget fees as percentages based on experiences with other projects, this method is rarely used as a compensation basis today because of its inequities for clients and architects.

The fallacies of this approach include the assumption that construction cost is directly proportional to the architect's effort. It allows construction market conditions to benefit a client but penalize the architect, or hurt the client and benefit the architect, without any change in the architect's effort. It penalizes architects who invest extra effort in reducing construction costs. Finally, it can lead a client to believe that the architect has an incentive to increase construction costs, rather than keep them down, creating an adversarial architect-client relationship.

*Reimbursable and nonreimbursable direct costs.* While staff labor usually represents the majority of an architect's cost of service, it is also important to anticipate and budget other direct costs that are related to the work and not covered in the firm's overhead structure. These typically include travel, long-distance communications, mail and courier services, printing, photography, computer services and output, and materials or equipment dedicated to the architect's effort.

These direct costs may be reimbursable (billed directly to the client, at actual cost or with a markup) or nonreimbursable (covered by an architect's other fees for the assignment). Direct costs are almost always reimbursable under the hourly and cost-plus options described above.

**Calculations of fees as a percentage of actual construction cost provide a good reality check for compensation options such as lump sum fees, cost-plus fees, or fees established on some other basis.**

## PUTTING IT ALL TOGETHER: SERVICE AND PRICING STRATEGY.

Ultimately, all of these issues and options must be applied in proposing architectural services for a new client or project assignment. There is no single best strategy or compensation approach; the architect must apply professional judgment and experi-

There are benefits to mix-and-match compensation approaches. For example, hourly billing may be used for project definition, schematic design, and construction contract administration services (because the architect is not in direct control of the time required) with a stipulated sum used for design development and documentation services.

Project Team Agreements (10.2) looks at the specifics of contracting with consultants—and of working with owner-retained consultants.

The arguments for in-house staffing typically revolve around control ("We want to do things our way"), quality ("We are in the best position to do the right things for our needs"), and efficiency ("We can develop a process or system that helps us best accomplish our goals"). The arguments against usually focus on the cost versus the benefit of the investment.

ence in finding the terms that are appropriate to each new opportunity. The following process works well for many firms:

1. *Consult with the client about needs and priorities.* The most important step in forming any new business relationship is knowing the client—understanding a client's needs, expectations, style, and concerns. Architects can achieve this understanding by being good consultants in the acquisition of a contract, which means asking the right questions, listening well, and exploring options for serving the client's organization. Through this process we discover a client's "value drivers," paramount concerns that, if addressed properly, can ensure an architect's selection and a higher level of compensation.

This step may be more difficult when an architect is asked for service proposals through a formal RFP process. Opportunity for direct discussion of the client's goals may be limited. Unless the services are procured with a simple price comparison, however, the successful firm will find some way of understanding and responding to the client's special interests.

2. *Identify service strategy, team, and work scope.* Once the client's needs are understood, the architect should develop an overall service strategy to address them successfully. Consider questions like these:

- Is the effort limited to design and documentation services, or is it a long-term agreement under which multiple services can be authorized over time?
- Which of the firm's services and key people are appropriate for the assignment?
- What consultants and other outside resources are necessary to support the work?
- How will the architect relate to the client, facility users, public agencies, and other team members in terms of communication and decision making?

At this point, a description of the architect's services can be prepared using a standard form of agreement or customized work plan as described earlier in this chapter. Then the most favorable compensation approach should be apparent.

3. *Estimate the cost of providing the services.* Unless the architect is proposing an open-ended hourly billing arrangement, it is important to estimate the actual cost of providing the services (including the firm's staff, outside consultants, and direct costs) as the starting point for the compensation proposal. The compensation worksheet provided in the instructions to the latest AIA B141 Owner-Architect Agreement is an excellent template for this calculation on a fixed-fee assignment.

For an hourly compensation approach, the architect should determine the hourly rate or multiplier that will represent actual cost, including salaries, fringe benefits, and firm overhead. Specific hourly rates should include an allowance for escalation during multiyear contracts, unless the rates will be subject to annual adjustment.

4. *Evaluate risk factors and apply an appropriate contingency.* The architect should evaluate the potential risks described in this chapter and decide what additional compensation is appropriate to offset them. This may be a specific dollar amount added to the estimated actual cost for a fixed fee, a markup of hourly cost rates, or an increase in the base fee multiplier determined above.

This deliberate approach to potential risks and fee contingencies can be helpful in the negotiation of a final compensation agreement. This preparation allows the architect and client to discuss specific risks, and agree about their impact on the cost of services, without eroding the architect's basic profit expectations.

5. *Assess the firm's value position and add the appropriate profit terms.* Finally, the architect should assess the special value of the firm's services to a client and determine the most favorable fee and profit structure for each case. This involves three basic considerations:

- The firm's minimum profit targets. With few exceptions, the architect should plan to earn a base level of profit on every project to reward the team and support the firm's overall financial health.
- The value of the firm's services in the marketplace. As noted earlier, firms and services that clients perceive as unique or the best can eliminate competition and command higher fee and profit levels. An architect must know the firm's competitive position and price its services accordingly.

**COMPENSATION WORKSHEET** — DESIGN DEVELOPMENT

Project: FRANKLIN ELEMENTARY
Project #: 9501    Date: 6·30·93
Owner: ALTON SCHOOL DISTRICT
Architect: APPEL & BARTLETT

| NUMBER | 4.01 PROJECT ADMN | 4.02 COORDINATION | 4.05 SCHEDULE | 4.06 COST EST. | 4.23 ARCH. DESIGN | 4.25 MECH DESIGN | 4.26 ELECT. DESIGN | 4.31 RESEARCH/SPEC | 4.61 GRAPHICS | TOTAL HOURS | TOTAL DOLLARS | ITEM | LINE |
|---|---|---|---|---|---|---|---|---|---|---|---|---|---|
| Hrs. | 10 | 10 | 20 | 5 | 30 | | | 5 | 20 | 100 | 2000 | PRINCIPAL @ $20 | 1 |
| $ | 200 | 200 | 400 | 100 | 600 | | | 100 | 400 | | | | |
| Hrs. | 10 | 10 | 40 | 10 | 60 | | | 10 | 40 | 200 | 3000 | SUPERV. @ $15 | 2 |
| $ | 300 | 300 | 600 | 150 | 900 | | | 150 | 600 | | | | |
| Hrs. | 40 | 40 | 80 | 20 | 120 | | | 20 | 80 | 400 | 4000 | TECH. I @ $10 | 3 |
| $ | 400 | 400 | 800 | 200 | 1200 | | | 200 | 800 | | | | |
| Hrs. | 20 | 20 | — | — | 60 | | | 10 | 40 | 150 | 750 | TECH. II @ $5 | 4 |
| $ | 100 | 100 | — | — | 300 | | | 50 | 200 | | | | |
| Hrs. | 10 | — | — | — | 50 | | | 20 | — | 80 | 80 | TECH. III @ $1 | 5 |
| $ | 10 | — | — | — | 50 | | | 20 | — | | | | |
| **Sub-Total** Hrs. | 100 | 90 | 140 | 35 | 320 | | | 65 | 180 | 930 | 9830 | Direct In-house Salary Expense | 6 |
| $ | 1010 | 1000 | 1800 | 450 | 3050 | | | 320 | 2000 | | | | |

*(In-House Personnel)*

| | | ITEM | LINE |
|---|---|---|---|
| | — | Direct Personnel Expense [1] | 7 |
| | 14745 | Indirect Expense [2] @ 150% of #6 | 8 |
| | 1228 | Other Nonreimbursable Direct Expense [3] @ 5% of #6+8 | 9 |
| | 25803 | Total In-House Expense #6+8+9 | 10 |
| | 1500 | Outside Services Expense | 11 |
| | 30803 | Estimated Total Expense | 12 |
| | 5000 | Contingency | 13 |
| | 10000 | Profit | 14 |
| | 45803 | Proposed Compensation | 15 |
| | 1000 | Estimated Reimbursable Expense | 16 |

**Outside / Total Outside:**

ALTERNATIVE COMPUTATION

| | | |
|---|---|---|
| 9850 | Direct In-house Salary Expense | |
| 12287 | Direct 12.5% Personnel Expense | |
| 2458 | Indirect Expense @ 20% of #7 | |
| 1228 | Other Nonreimbursable Direct Expense | |
| 25803 | Total In-House | |

REMARKS:

---

[1] Direct personnel expense is defined as the direct salaries of the architect's personnel engaged in the project and the related portion of the cost of their mandatory and customary contributions and benefits (such as employment taxes and other statutory employee benefits, insurance, sick leave, holidays, employee retirement plans, and similar contributions and benefits).

[2] Indirect expense is defined as all expenses not directly allocated to specific projects and is synonymous with overhead.

[3] Other nonreimbursable direct expense covers the direct expenses not otherwise included in personnel and outside expenses, such as reproduction of documents for in-house use, unreimbursed travel, and items paid on behalf of the client without specific reimbursement.

*Note:* This sample is taken from AIA Document B141, Standard Form of Agreement between Owner and Architect with Standard Form of Architect's Services. The figures in it are not intended to reflect actual practice but simply to illustrate the procedure for performing calculations. A full set of instructions for completing the worksheet are included in the AIA B141 instruction pages.

---

- The value of the project to the firm. Occasionally an architect can justify reducing fee and profit levels to help the firm enter a new market, win a strategically important new client, or support the firm's staff and overhead structure during an economic downturn.

At a minimum, the target profit levels will determine the architect's fixed –fee, fully loaded hourly rates, or fee multiplier. It is also possible to increase compensation and profit by proposing incentive fees or bonuses to reflect high-value results from the architect's work. For example, an incentive amount might be related to a particularly aggressive schedule, tenant attraction and lease rates, or postoccupancy evaluation of building performance.

6. *Compare the proposal with the firm's past experience.* Throughout the pricing process, it is natural to compare a new client or project opportunity with the firm's past compensation experience. Most firms take an early educated guess about basic design service fees as a percentage of a project's estimated construction cost. A firm should track its history of fee earnings and profitability to support this process. Given the number of variables, however—even among related projects for the same client—it is wise to review proposed compensation terms with several firm principals or project leaders before completing the service proposal.

When the scope of service and compensation terms are finalized, they are normally included in a written proposal document presented to the client. Such proposals may take very different forms: letters with attachments, completed owner-architect agreements such as the AIA B141, or more elaborate formats prescribed by a client's RFP. Every firm develops its own preferences and standards for proposal documents.

At a minimum, the service proposal should contain the following elements:

- A description of the professional services covered by the proposal
- A time schedule for the services proposed
- Identification of the architect's key team members and their relationship to the client's own staff and other project participants
- The proposed compensation terms, including the basis for reimbursable expenses and any additional services required beyond the basic work scope
- Assumptions and qualifications upon which the proposal is based
- The proposed form of agreement for the client's review and approval

This information will provide a firm basis for negotiation of the architect's agreements with clients and consultants.

## TAKING IT TO THE BANK: BILLING AND COLLECTIONS

It is important to remember that these compensation options don't mean much without cash—the ability to collect payment on a timely basis. Some architects overlook the importance of collections in negotiating contracts and managing their projects and client relationships. Collection usually needs to be addressed by firm principals with their client counterparts. Even the best accounting staff cannot overcome high-level misunderstandings about payment obligations.

***Understanding a client's administrative and accounting practices.*** An architect should discuss preferred billing and payment terms in the earliest consultation with a client about goals, needs, and service scope. Most clients will appreciate this sign of good business practice. While the details are prescribed in any owner-architect agreement, a few basic questions should be asked and answered:

- We prefer to bill for services every [state number] weeks. Is that acceptable?
- Is there a particular schedule on which invoices should be submitted?
- What documentation is required with our invoices?
- Who will review our invoices and approve them for payment?
- How quickly will payments be processed once invoices are approved?

Unfavorable answers to any of these questions pose financial risks that should be addressed in structuring the architect's compensation agreement.

***Appropriate invoicing and payment terms for services.*** Most architects invoice their clients for services monthly or every four weeks, depending on their internal accounting practices. Collections can be enhanced if clients will accept more frequent billing, particularly on hourly fee arrangements.

While thirty days is a general standard for invoice payment, many architecture

There is no one way to establish the services to be performed and the compensation to be charged. Sometimes you make the proposal; other times you respond to the client's. In addition to contract terms and conditions, you may be in a position to negotiate services, compensation, or both. Sometimes you cannot.

firms experience average collection periods of sixty days or more. Long collection cycles require the architect to finance the staff and direct costs of providing services, at an increased carrying cost to the firm. Efforts should be made to negotiate a contract provision requiring interest to be paid to the architect on payments overdue by more than forty-five days.

**Special risks and responses.** There are some special concerns that should be addressed, if they exist, before finalizing a service agreement:

*Uncertain credit.* Like any provider of goods or services, the architect has a right to ask about a client's financial resources to support a specific project assignment. If financial capacity is in doubt, the architect should consider declining the engagement or requiring an up-front fee and an aggressive billing schedule to keep collections ahead of actual project costs.

*Fee retainage.* Contracts that allow retainage (amounts withheld from professional service fees until the completion of a project or work phase) dilute an architecture firm's financial performance and increase its risk. Retainage provisions should be eliminated from owner-architect agreements whenever possible.

*Slow payment.* Clients who describe a slow and complex payment process, or decline to commit to any specific process, present serious business risks for architects. This problem is best addressed by principals of the firm with their most senior client counterparts—and, if not resolved, by interest or prepayment provisions.

**Payment patterns as performance feedback.** A final word: As is the case with buyers of any goods or services, payments made by architecture clients often reflect their perceptions about the quality and value the firm is providing. Regular invoices provide a natural opportunity for the architect to ask—on paper or in person—for a client's assessment of the firm's performance. If payment patterns change, it's usually a sign that the perceived value of the service has changed and that it is an important time for firm principals to address the client's concerns.

### For More Information

Understanding the true needs and values of clients, including the forces that drive client values, is essential to receiving adequate professional compensation. Strategies for understanding and meeting the demands of today's sophisticated clients are presented by Neil Rackham and John DeVincentis in *Rethinking the Sales Force: Redefining Selling to Create and Capture Customer Value* (1999).

The Professional Pricing Society, a worldwide organization, provides full resource support for pricing professionals and executives seeking solutions to their pricing challenges. These resources—including numerous books and workbooks, a journal, a newsletter, and workshops—are listed on the PPS Web site at www.pricing-advisor.com.

# CHAPTER
# 10 Contracts and Agreements

## 10.1 Agreements with Clients

### Edward T. M. Tsoi, FAIA

*The architect's agreement with the client reflects the goals and expectations of each and sets the tone and conditions for the challenges ahead.*

Normally architects think of the contract as the primary legal document that records the promises that parties make to each other for specific purposes. It delineates services and compensation for those services. It allocates risk, helps the parties cope with change, and helps provide a method for resolving disputes.

All of these features are crucial. Yet the standard form of owner–architect agreement has become much more than just a legal document. The agreement should reflect how architects are able to serve a wide array of client types and provide an equally wide range of professional services that reach well beyond the conventional perception that architects only design buildings and interiors. The owner–architect agreement should deal with the drastic changes that have produced the building industry of today. It must clearly allocate responsibility between the owner, architect, and a host of design and construction specialists who are often part of a larger team.

In a survey done by a major professional liability insurance carrier, it was found that 55 percent of the claims against architects are made by owners. This statistic says that clients are too often dissatisfied with their architect or have unclear expectations of what it is the architect is really agreeing to deliver. It also indicates that some architects must be unclear about their own expectations of clients.

Contracts, when used in the right way, are a wonderful way to communicate. They can make explicit what might otherwise be unsaid. Unstated expectations can be time bombs, while clearly stated goals and assumptions are more likely to be mutually understood and confirmed as a basis for providing professional services. Think of a contract as a means of communicating explicitly and achieving a meeting of minds between the parties.

Contracts allocate rights and rewards, responsibilities and risk, aiding architects in managing their exposure to legal liability and business risks. Projects tend to run smoothly and parties tend to perform properly when they know what is expected of one another at the outset of the work. Architects must understand that every client represents a unique entity with specific project goals and constraints. It is the architect's responsibility to understand the client's overall mission as well as the nature of the client's functional requirements and financial resources.

Through contracts, architects can anticipate and prepare for future possibilities. Experience teaches us that circumstances change over time. For example, architects are commonly asked to perform services originally beyond those contemplated. When writing

**Edward T. M. Tsoi** *is a founding principal of Tsoi/Kobus & Associates, a ninety-person architecture, interior design, and planning firm in Cambridge, Massachusetts. Tsoi is chair of the Long-Range Planning Task Force of the AIA Documents Committee. This topic is adapted from Owner–Architect Agreements by Charles R. Heuer, Esq., FAIA, which appeared in the 12th edition of the* Architect's Handbook of Professional Practice.

part 3 DELIVERY

an agreement, parties to the contract can anticipate these events and settle on how to deal with them. Because the only certainty is the fact of change, contracts should address certain changes that are likely as well as types of changes that may occur but cannot be described in advance. It is important for contracts to establish ways of dealing with these changes.

Finally, contracts are useful as a means of resolving disputes. All contracts are based on the idea that parties intend to deal with each other in good faith, according to the terms of their agreements. However, misunderstandings or differences of opinion are often unavoidable. No contract can specify the resolution of every possible problem, but good contracts can specify a mechanism for resolving disputes and also for maintaining a working relationship between architect and owner while a resolution is found.

## PROPOSAL VS. CONTRACT AGREEMENTS

▶ **Architectural Services and Compensation (9.2)** looks at establishing fees for professional services and proposals.

Early in most owner–architect relationships, architects are asked to prepare a proposal to provide professional services. Sometimes architects are asked to propose the services they believe to be necessary, and other times they are asked to propose compensation for performing services requested by the owner. Whatever the circumstances, it is usually not enough simply to describe services and quote compensation. Such a response could be accepted by the owner as a basis for the key business terms, but such proposals do not represent a balanced, legal agreement between the owner and architect. The architect's proposal can be part marketing and part description of the business terms that will form the basis of a formal agreement. It may also include a project description, outline a project team, and propose a project schedule.

Every proposal for services and compensation should be based on a set of assumptions: what the architect will and will not do, what the owner will and will not do, the timing of services and payments, legal terms and conditions, and a host of other factors both implicit and explicit. Before the architect prepares a draft agreement there are two important questions to ask:

- Are the assumptions clearly defined? Are the project scope, program, site, budget, and schedule firm enough to serve as a basis for agreement with the owner? Should you propose a two-phase process in which the first step is a simple contract of short duration to establish the scope of the project?
- Are these assumptions clearly understood? What if the owner plans to pay only if the construction loan is closed? Might the project be fast-tracked? Will multiple contract document packages be required? Will a construction manager (CM) be involved? Who will engage special consultants, you or the owner? What if the budget is impossible to meet or the owner is proposing terms and conditions that require an unattainable (and uninsurable) level of performance on your part?

### Proposals as Offers

Your proposal is often your "offer," giving the owner the power to accept it and establish a basis for business terms. If the owner accepts the proposal with the terms offered, fine. If the owner does not accept the proposed terms or if circumstances develop that are not consistent with the assumptions in your proposal, you will have an objective basis for making modifications during negotiations. One effective way to do this—when very little has been specified and you are accustomed to working with AIA documents— is to say that your proposal contemplates the use of the terms and conditions "as in the current edition of AIA Document B141, Owner–Architect Agreement, modified if and as necessary." This does not cast anything in stone, yet it gives you negotiating room if counterproposals drift too far from what the B141 assumes and describes.

▶ **Unfortunately, some clients using nonstandard forms are unaware of the problems they can cause for everyone in the building process—including themselves.**

For example, many clients believe that programming is part of the architect's basic services. If that was true, it would be logical to assume that the proposed basic compensation covers programming services. By referring to the B141 in the proposal, the architect has an objective basis for saying that programming services are not intended to be covered by basic compensation, but instead may be included as an expanded service.

## Oral Agreements and Letters of Intent

Many times, regardless of how the proposal and negotiation stages have progressed, the formal agreement does not seem quite ready for signature when the owner wants the architect to begin performing services. Starting to perform services without a written agreement can be quite risky. If things do not proceed as planned, a court may find that the parties did not intend to be bound until the formal agreement was signed. In that case, the architect may be deemed a "volunteer" to whom no compensation is granted, or at best the architect may be compensated only on an "equitable" basis, that is, only for the services performed. Not only might there be less money than anticipated, but it may turn out that a carefully planned allocation of risk between parties is ignored, to the architect's detriment.

What about oral agreements? Are they valid? In general they are. It is not the validity of these agreements but the proof of terms that is a problem. What was agreed upon? Was there really an agreement at all? These questions are usually asked when each party has a vested interest in the answer. Unless you document decisions as you go, you may be accused of remembering what you want to remember—and that is likely to be different from what the other party wants to remember. So what can be done?

Assuming that you are unwilling or unable in these circumstances to withhold services until a formal written agreement is signed, consider using an interim agreement. Such an agreement would state that you begin to perform services on the basis outlined in your proposal (or according to your standard time charge arrangements, or some other arrangement) pending execution of the formal written agreement. The interim agreement might reference the proposed contract terms as forwarded to the owner by the architect. The architect should submit to the owner a draft of a preferred contract when no other form has been suggested by the owner, filling out as much of the terms of the contract as possible for the owner's review and comment. This represents the architect's best understanding of the terms and conditions of the engagement and, as such, would represent the architect's understanding until the owner or owner's lawyer requests changes to the draft agreement.

Once the architect is performing services, the owner is likely to feel no urgency to sign a formal agreement. To offset this, consider having the interim agreement and all services stop after a specified number of days or upon execution of the formal written agreement, whichever comes first. In most cases, 30 to 60 days is plenty of time to execute an agreement that essentially has already been negotiated in business terms. If the contract is not signed in this time, it may be a warning of underlying problems that would spur second thoughts about the successful outcome of this project.

## WHAT TYPE OF AGREEMENT MAKES SENSE?

Architects are generally faced with three types of owner–architect agreements. The first is an owner-generated contract. Often public agencies, large institutions, or major commercial clients that have repeated and ongoing building programs and many years of experience will create a highly specific owner–architect agreement that suits their particular needs and lessons learned. The second general source of owner–architect agreements will be from professional organizations other than the American Institute of Architects. The third and most often used form of agreement is one of the AIA standard form agreements.

The standard agreements prepared by the AIA have a history that goes back more than a hundred years and have earned a reputation for serving the building industry with a family of documents that represents the contractual link not only between owner and architect but also between owner and contractor and between architect and consultants. The AIA standard documents are updated periodically to reflect the broad changes that affect the building industry as a whole as well as specific changes in the practice of architecture. Updated documents require legal review on both sides, as well as careful review of new terms and conditions.

Project Team Agreements (10.2) reviews approaches for selecting consultants and other team members.

# Characteristics of the Owner

It would be best if we knew well the parties with whom we intend to deal, but it's unrealistic to think architects can know everything about their prospective clients. You can, however, know them by some general characteristics.

*Less experienced clients* may have unrealistic expectations of architects. They may expect perfection and be disappointed with anything less. They may require a lot of education during contract negotiations. It is particularly important in these cases to use the contract to communicate with the owners and to keep their expectations and goals in line with reality.

*Underfunded owners* require special attention during contract negotiations. They may want more building than they can afford, or they may not have the money to pay an architect until they have closed on a financial arrangement with their bank. In fact, an underfunded owner may not have the financial resources to do the project at all. Therefore it is important to establish a budget at the outset, especially if the contract requires the architect to design within it. Make every effort to communicate the importance of having a budget—and how it affects the project scope. Do not assume a client has unlimited funds, or any at all; you can always ask.

*Owners who are represented by boards or committees* also deserve special attention. School boards, church building committees, and condominium boards—as well as all groups using public monies or funds from members or foundations—operate under "sunshine laws." Everything they do is scrutinized by their constituents. It is sometimes difficult for these groups to develop, and maintain, consensus on goals, schedules, and budgets. It may take some time to develop the owner-architect agreement—an agreement that must be able to withstand close scrutiny.

It is usually important and helpful if the architect can insist that the owner designate a representative authorized to deal with the architect. This may be the board or committee chair, whose job it will be to synthesize the input from various sources and give the architect instructions on which the architect can rely.

*Litigious clients* pose special problems. Some people and organizations are simply more litigious than others. Whether it's a personality trait or a function of how they do business, it's a fact. Check with the local design community if you have any suspicions about the owner in this regard. You may want to consult with your lawyer or check into court records. The mere fact of past litigation should not prejudice you on a given client, but you will be better able to address potential problems and provide for their solution in your agreements if you are well informed.

How clients select their architects reveals something about their fundamental values and priorities. There is nothing wrong with owners investigating and comparing the scope and quality of services of different architects to determine what will be in their best interests. Nor is there anything wrong with the idea that price is a consideration when professionals compete for clients and projects. Nonetheless, ask yourself some basic questions about clients. Does a bidding requirement indicate the prospective client is inadequately funded and is trying to make up some of the shortfall by skimping on professional compensation? Does it indicate that the owner does not understand the nature of professional services?

Some owners believe that all architectural services are exactly the same (without regard to special expertise and factors such as the nature of the project and the scope of the required services). For them, price is the only difference. If that's the case, there may be problems ahead. Owners who see you as the provider of a product and not as a provider of professional services will likely be disappointed and dissatisfied if your "product" isn't perfect. A relationship is usually better if the owner and architect are able to negotiate a level of compensation that both of them feel reflects the owner's aspirations, the architect's qualifications, that nature of the project, and the type and extent of the services required.

*A program manager* may be hired by owners who find themselves either without the experience or without the staff to manage a building program. When such situations arise, owners have the ability to outsource to a program manager or a consultant, either a single individual or a company, to come in and act as an owner's representative to manage the project architect, construction manager, and contractor. Such program managers, who may also be architects, do not fully replace the owner, but they can help the owner make decisions needed by the project architect and contractor and make sure communications among the parties is timely and adequate for the decisions that need to be made.

## Negotiating the Agreement

It's said that good architecture requires good clients. To help your client become a better client, you may want to offer some advice and guidance on negotiating agreements for services. Here are some words you might want to share with your client.

The formal agreement between you and your architect is an opportunity to ensure that you both envision the same project, requirements, and expectations. Before committing these requirements and expectations to paper, use the five steps presented below to identify any items that may have been missed.

### Establish Project Requirements

Write down your project requirements as either a short statement or a very detailed compilation. Address these points:

- Project use: What is to be designed and built?
- Project site: Where will (might) it be built?
- Levels of quality and amenity
- Role of the project (in the owner's life, business, community, etc.)
- Schedule requirements or constraints
- Target date for completion
- Budget and sources of financing
- Anticipated key team members

### Describe Project Tasks and Assign Responsibility for Each

Owner and architect should identify the administrative, design, construction, and facility operation tasks that must be undertaken to achieve project objectives. Both parties should then identify the services required for the project and who will be responsible for each.

### Identify Your Schedule Requirements

Place the tasks and responsibilities necessary to accomplish your project on a time line, estimating duration for each task. (Be sure to include *all* tasks, even if they will be done by others, such as reviews by regulatory agencies.) Identify the tasks that if delayed for any reason will delay completion of the project—for example, obtaining financing or securing zoning approvals. Compare the time line with your target completion date and adjust one or both as appropriate.

Make sure the architect and other key team members who must live with the final project schedule are aware of these schedule requirements.

### Take a Critical Look at the Schedule You've Developed

Good project schedules allow enough time for decision making. Is your schedule reasonable, particularly given the project's requirements and budget? Have you allowed yourself enough time to review the architect's submissions, receive regulatory agency approvals, seek your own recommendations and approvals, and make your decisions?

### Use the Results of Your Planning as a Basis for the Architect's Compensation

Ask the architect to provide you with a compensation proposal that is based on the tasks and schedule requirements outlined above.

### The Owner-Architect Agreement

If you've done your homework, the written agreement should follow without difficulty. You and your architect should now be of common mind on the key issues of project scope, services, responsibilities, schedule, construction budget, and architect compensation. Following the advice below should help your project run smoothly

*Use a written contract.* A handshake or letter agreement is rarely sufficient to describe thoroughly all the roles, responsibilities, and obligations of the owner and architect.

*Use AIA documents.* These standard forms of agreement, first developed in the 1880s, have been carefully reviewed, court-tested, and modified over many years. Widely used by and accepted in the construction industry, they present a current consensus among organizations representing owners, lawyers, contractors, engineers, and architects. AIA documents are coordinated with one another—for example, the architect–consultant agreement serves as the subcontract for the owner–architect agreement, and the owner–contractor agreement, usually negotiated later, extends the architect's services into construction. These documents are readily available from most local AIA chapters or by calling (800) 365-ARCH (2724). You may need to modify the AIA documents to adapt them to your particular project. However, do so with great care. Since these documents form a cohesive system of contractual relationships, even simple revisions in one agreement may cause complications in another document.

*Understand that your architect cannot warrant or guarantee results.* As a provider of professional services, like your lawyer or doctor, an architect is required to perform to a professional standard. Courts recognize this, and so too must responsible clients.

*Consult both your legal and insurance counsels before signing any agreement.*

*Adapted from the AIA brochure "You and Your Architect" (2001)*

# Characteristics of the Project

Just as types of clients have characteristics that influence outside contractual matters, so do types of projects. Particularly important are the litigation history of a project type, jurisdictional factors, design and construction characteristics, and the adequacy of the construction and project budgets and the design and construction schedules.

*Litigation history.* Published claims data show that condominium projects, schools, and hospitals are involved in a relatively large amount of litigation. There are reasons for this. These projects are often undertaken by committee clients, and the owners are often not the users. Architects should recognize that the official client and the actual user may have different requirements and that it is usually impossible to respond to two voices at once. If the owner is not the end user and the end user is to be part of the process, then the latter's role should be outlined in the owner-architect agreement. In this way, all parties can clearly see who will give instructions and make decisions and on whose word the architect is to rely.

*Jurisdictional factors.* Different states place different requirements on agreements for professional services. The signing party must be legally competent to sign a contract, and the signature must be in a form recognized by the state. Some states place restrictions on the practice of architecture by partnerships and corporations. Some states allow corporations to practice but require the signature of a participating individual as a representative of the corporation. Business licenses are required in some jurisdictions.

Architects must be licensed to practice architecture in the jurisdiction in which the project is located. Sometimes *practice* is defined (it may even include offering to perform services), and most times the designation *architect* is restricted. When working in another state, you may have to form a new entity consisting of principals licensed in that state.

It's important to verify that you are properly licensed to practice where the project is located. Investigate this so that the owner-architect agreement can be prepared and executed properly. If you are not properly licensed, you may be subject to professional discipline, and frequently the law will deny you the right to use the courts of that state to collect fees or for other purposes related to unlicensed services.

> **Architects are frequently involved with construction budgets—evaluating them and sometimes providing professional services that help the owner set them**

*Design and construction characteristics.* When experimental design or construction techniques or unusual site conditions are to be part of the project, contracts should be flexible enough to reflect the possibility of design changes and a longer-than-normal design period. On the construction side, such conditions may increase construction problems, change order requests, delays, and construction costs. These are natural outgrowths of this type of project, and they are generally counterbalanced by other factors, which may save the owner time and money. The key is to use the contract to inform the owner of what to expect and to record the allocation of risks between owner and architect as well as between owner and contractor.

> **Construction Cost Management (13.4) discusses budgets and budgeting.**

*Budgets and schedules.* Perhaps the most unrealistic owner expectations are those related to budgets and schedules. For example, owners often confuse the construction budget with the project budget. In fact, there are many costs associated with delivering a project, and construction cost is only one of them. Owners should be informed about this and provide for other foreseeable costs, such as legal and accounting fees, cost of the land, surveys and geotechnical studies, financing charges, and costs of tests during construction, as well as furniture, furnishings, and equipment. It is critical to consider cost contingencies in preparing a budget because costs can be modified by market conditions, adjustments in scope, and refinements in design. Once a construction budget has been identified, the architect and client need to be realistic about what can be expected for a given amount of money and what the architect can and cannot do to help meet legitimate expectations.

It is also important for the architect to be realistic with the owners about schedule requirements. Projects are not designed and built overnight. Do not allow unrealistic expectations to go unchallenged. Consider making schedules part of the contracts. If you do, do so in a way that recognizes which elements of the schedule you, as the architect, can control. For example, if you expect municipal approval of something on June 1 and thereafter it will take 60 days to complete a phase of services, don't promise you will be finished on August 1. What if approval is not granted until July 15? Instead, say that services on the phase will be completed 60 days after municipal approval is granted. Owners whose projects are late are usually disappointed and unhappy. Therefore be realistic, and use the contract to communicate realistic expectations.

## Selecting the Delivery System

Generally the architect is the first, or one of the first, members of the eventual design-and-construction team to talk with the owner. As a result, architects have substantial influence on the selection of the project delivery method, the other types of professionals to be involved, the scope of others' services, and how these will mesh with what the architect will do.

Architects typically will suggest to the owner alternative methods for the owner to procure construction services and establish the basis for compensation for the cost of the work to the selected contractor. In today's building industry, there are an increasing number of delivery systems available to owners. Depending on whether the owner prefers design-bid-build, negotiated contract, design-build, turnkey, or one of several other hybrid methods of project delivery, the architect may not know the specifics of his or her obligation to prepare contract documents. Contract documents can be significantly influenced by choice of delivery system, and it is important for the owner and architect to make an early decision regarding delivery system. Many owners may rely on a tried-and-true delivery system without being aware of some of the advantages of using an alternative. The architect can play a valuable role in discussing the pros and cons of different delivery systems depending on whether the owner has a project that is well defined in scope or not, led by a fixed and unchangeable budget or not, or tied to a fixed timetable or not. Being involved early gives the architect an opportunity to provide the most comprehensive counsel to owners with respect to the process of both design and construction. This is a very important strategic service architects can provide to owners.

▶ **Project Delivery Options (9.1) describes the possible contracting methods for delivering design and construction services.**

## Understanding the Risk

Everything that has been discussed thus far contributes to a program for managing risk and exposure to professional liability. The two primary sources of risk and liability are (1) poor communication with the owner and (2) negligence in the performance of those professional services being provided to the owner.

Communication with the owner is vital. Starting with the proposal to provide services, continuing through the draft contract stage and the discussions and negotiations that culminate in a formal agreement, and then throughout the life of the contract, architects must strive to stay in close communications with the client. If the owner is informed of what is happening, has realistic expectations, and has participated in essential decision making, there is far less chance that problems will result in claims or a lawsuit.

The second source of risk and liability is perceived shortcomings in the provision of professional services. Examples that often arise include coordination of the architect's and engineer's construction documents, design details that must be modified for any one of a number of reasons, design documentation that when priced exceeds the owner's construction budget, delays in providing professional services when measured against an agreed-upon schedule, and features of the design that may be in conflict with the most current code or other relevant regulations.

Well-written contracts that include comprehensive descriptions of the services the architects will provide and the responsibilities of the owner are valuable risk-allocation devices. If the owner or anyone else claims the architect has been negligent, one element that must be proven is that the architect owed some duty to that person.

General duties are imposed by statute, case law, and professional licensing laws. Specific duties are created by contract and conduct. In other words, the owner-architect agreement is a principal source of the duties of an architect on any specific project. If there is no duty, there can be no negligence. Apart from the parties' responsibilities in their relationship with each other, the agreement between owner and architect can allocate the risks associated with professional liability. For example:

▶ **Competition puts pressure on architects; there is a temptation to sharpen pencils to minimize fees and to be overly optimistic about what can be accomplished within a given time frame and budget. Don't be your own worst enemy in this regard. The proposal and the contract that will be derived from it are not just nuisances to get past. In fact, they dictate the rules and become the "law" for your project. It's often necessary, though never easy, to be coldly analytical at a time when you are excited and enthusiastic.**

- Some owners—or their lenders—take an extreme position, asking architects to "guarantee" their work. Since architects have neither a legal nor a professional obligation to do perfect work, accepting such language is unwise at best and generally considered uninsurable.
- Some architects, on the other hand, take a position at the other extreme, asking their clients to hold them harmless from any liability claim that may arise. A client may reject this position, arguing that even though architects do not have to do perfect work, the client requires some protection should problems arise.

Experienced owners and architects understand what is meant by the level, or degree, of performance architects are obliged to meet. This degree of performance defines the level of written documentation and drawing documentation needed to communicate project requirements to others, particularly subcontractors. The level of documentation required for a particular project relates to the complexity of the project, the method of delivery selected by the owner, the timetable provided by the owner, and the compensation mutually agreed to by owner and architect. For example, an owner who may be building repetitive retail facilities in many different locations using the same contractor may request the architect to provide a less detailed set of construction documents compared to an owner who may be constructing a one-of-a-kind museum that requires extensive and detailed documentation for unique components within the building. The negotiation process between the owner and the architect is the primary opportunity to discuss the issue of performance levels and the allocation of risk should the owner choose a level of documentation insufficient for the building type.

***Indemnification (hold-harmless) provisions.*** Construction disputes are usually multiparty disputes. In the early stages of problem analysis, it is often not clear to disinterested parties whether, or to what extent, design defects, construction defects, or operation and maintenance defects have caused the problem. Therefore, all principals involved in a project—owner, architect, and contractor—are typically brought into any resulting claim or lawsuit. Even without a judgment against the architect, significant expense and effort may be incurred. In response, many architects have asked owners to indemnify and hold them harmless in cases where a third party has filed a claim in which the allegations are based on something other than the sole negligence of the architect. Some states have special requirements to make hold-harmless clauses valid; some prohibit them completely (see AIA Document A201, paragraph 3.18 for an example).

***Intellectual property.*** Experience has shown that some owners will attempt to treat drawings and specifications as products that are complete in and of themselves. They may then try to reuse those documents for other projects in other locations and circumstances—none of which was anticipated by the project architect. In fact, the drawings and specifications are instruments of the architect's services and are intended for use only on a specific project in specific circumstances; they are not suitable for use on any other projects or in any other circumstances. If someone misuses the documents prepared by the architect by changing them, misinterpreting them, or using them under changed circumstances, the architect could probably demonstrate this occurrence and would not be held responsible for resulting problems. But because proving this takes time and money, many architects make sure in their contracts that owners agree to hold them harmless when the documents are misused or used in unauthorized ways (e.g., see paragraph 1.3.2.3 in the B141).

## DEVELOPING THE AGREEMENT

Once these precontract issues have been resolved, it is possible to finalize the owner–architect agreement. The owner–architect agreement may be one of the standard forms of agreement published by the AIA, a standard form produced by an institutional or public client, or a form drafted specifically for the project.

### Standard Forms of Agreement

The goals of the AIA's documents program include producing useful documents that are fair to all parties and reflect a high measure of consensus within the construction industry. The AIA produces a series of standard owner–architect agreement forms. These cover the

## AIA Standard Forms of Owner–Architect Agreement

The American Institute of Architects has offered forms of agreement to the building enterprise since 1888. Its first standard form of owner–architect agreement—the first version of what is now AIA Document B141—was published in 1915.

The text describes the most commonly used of the forms of agreement available at the time this handbook topic was prepared:

- Standard form of owner–architect agreement (B141)
- Designated services (B163)
- Projects of limited scope (B151)
- Small projects (B155 )
- Special services (B727)

Other AIA owner–architect agreements have been developed for

- Interior services (B171; B177 for projects of limited scope)
- Single and multifamily dwellings, including those for government agencies (B181, which is accepted by the U.S. Department of Housing and Urban Development)
- Limited architecture services on projects for housing projects (B188)
- Architecture services on projects for which a construction manager acts as advisor to the owner (B141/CMa)
- Architecture services on projects for which the architect also provides construction management services (B144/ARCH-CM)
- Architecture services performed for a design-build entity (B901)

*Dale R. Ellickson, FAIA, Esq.*

range of essential contract issues and are periodically revised to reflect current practice. The AIA periodically produces a summary of all available AIA documents. This explains the various documents and suggests how they can be applied in varying circumstances.

The AIA publishes its standard documents in an electronic format. These electronic documents provide the full text of all agreements and the ability to edit that text. All changes made that are additions to the AIA text are shown underlined; all deletions from the AIA text are crossed out. Thus both the owner and the architect are able to see how a customized agreement relates to the original standard text published by the AIA.

AIA Document B141-1997, Owner–Architect Agreement, is the most commonly used agreement form published by the AIA. The B141, published in 1997, is very different from previous versions. The changes made to the document provide greater flexibility for architects to describe a range of project types and sizes, as well as a range of services and a host of expanded services that may be appropriate for a specific project. The essential terms and conditions in the B141 differ only in minor ways from the previous version.

AIA Document B151, Owner–Architect Agreement (Construction Projects of Limited Scope), is useful for less complex projects. The format has one part rather than the multiple parts that characterize the B141. The B151 resembles earlier versions of B141 except that it is simpler in the description of professional services and the terms and conditions are condensed as much as is generally prudent. There are two key points to remember:

- The limited scope mentioned in the title is not so much related to dollar value as to the complexity of the project and the relationships of the design-and-construction team members.
- Even uncomplicated projects can have major problems with significant liability exposure. Make sure the terms and conditions of the limited scope agreement form are appropriate for the project.

**The B141.** The B141 provides a comprehensive agreement between owner and architect that can be used for a wide variety of project types, client types, and delivery methods. The goal of the AIA in creating the multipart B141 was to make it more of a single standard, allowing the core agreement between owner and architect to be adapted to a larger variety of owners and projects.

There have been owners who were skeptical of using contracts with architects created by their own professional organization. Some have said that the B141 protects the architect more fully than the owner. The purpose of AIA documents is not to push away duties and responsibilities of the architect toward the owner, nor is there an attempt to push duties and responsibilities of the owner toward the architect. The major

> **AIA Documents (10.4) introduces the Institute's documents program.**

> **The Documents Finder (Appendix C) provides a description of the "families" of AIA documents and offers guidance in locating the documents most likely to respond to the needs of services being provided.**

> **The B141 Commentary included on the CD-ROM that accompanies the *Handbook* provides a paragraph-by-paragraph analysis and guide to this document.**

emphasis in the documents is to clarify the definition of initial assumptions for a project, which allows the architect to propose relevant professional services. The other emphasis of the B141 is to make clear to the owner exactly what services are being provided, especially those services that expand on the commonly used services of the architect (formerly known as "basic services"). The document has four key features:

*Initial information.* The B141 provides two pages to describe the initial information for a proposed project. This information allows the owner and architect to define the use, size, location, program, budget, and delivery method proposed for a specific project. It also identifies the key individuals who will represent the owner, the architect, and the architect's consultants.

*Changes in services.* The B141 makes the contract function as an adaptable document even after it has been signed. This allows changes in services, which so often arise as a project moves from design through construction. Changes in services by the architect may be initiated by changes in the initial information or assumptions described in article 1.1 or by changes in services similar to those described in former versions of B141. These are described under article 1.3.3. Changes in construction administration services that might be a result of quantifying such things as site visits are identified in Article 2.8.1. Other changes in construction administration services that might arise are described in Article 2.8.2.

The B141 attempts to clarify construction administration services by quantifying different aspects of the architect's services with regard to shop drawing reviews, visits to the site, punch-listing, final inspections, and postconstruction services.

*Division of responsibilities.* In Article 2.8.3 the B141 provides a simple matrix listing a series of expanded services, that is, services beyond basic services that an owner might choose depending on their applicability to a specific project. The architect identifies those expanded services, commenting on whether the architect or the owner is responsible. Assuming the architect is responsible for a particular expanded service, the specific description of those services may be described in an appendix or referenced paragraph that is not a part of the standard B141 description of services.

*Designing to the owner's budget for the cost of work.* The B141 contains language in Article 2.1.7.5 that describes the architect's obligation to match the design with the owner's budget for the cost of the work. If the architect's design does not come within the owner's agreed-upon budget, the architect shall redesign at his or her own cost—with, however, the flexibility to revise the project scope and/or quality as required. This obligation varies little from earlier versions of the B141 version. It is important to note that the architect is obligated to meet the budget of the owner if the architect agrees to this budget as identified in the initial information, which should have been done only if the architect felt the budget was realistic for achieving the owner's objectives. The combination of Article 1.1 and Article 2.1.7.5 imply that the architect must be cautious in agreeing to the owner's budget, because once the budget is accepted and deemed adequate for the program and quality as understood, the architect simultaneously accepts responsibility for designing within that budget.

**Dealing with changes.** It is expected that both the architect and the owner will modify the standard form of agreement, deleting clauses that are inapplicable or for any other reason undesirable and adding clauses to reflect concerns by either party not addressed by the standard agreement.

## Coping with Nonstandard Agreement Forms

Some owners, by choice or by regulatory requirement, draft their own agreement forms. These may have been custom-created to fit the owner's particular operational needs, or they may be extensive modifications of AIA documents. Architects are well advised to approach nonstandard agreement forms with care.

- Be sure you understand the services to be performed, the duties being created, and the compensation being offered.
- If the proposed agreement includes provisions that appear to redefine your liability, suggests exclusions from coverage under your liability insurance, or requires indemnification of the owner, then have your insurance advisor review it, too.
- Don't be afraid to modify AIA documents to use in the situation, but have your

## Entering into Contracts: The Legal Issues

Architects enter into myriad contractual agreements, some related to projects and others for general business purposes. Such contracts and agreements must be in the correct legal form. Before entering into project agreements, architects and their attorneys need to examine the provisions of the laws of the state where the project is to be constructed, as well as the states where the architect's and owner's offices are located.

*Black's Law Dictionary* defines a contract as "an agreement between two or more persons which creates an obligation to do or not to do a particular thing." The essentials of such an agreement are

- *Competent parties.* Just as it takes two to tango, it takes two to contract, although a contract may have more than two parties. The parties must be identified in the contract and must be competent, in the sense that they are of legal age and not mentally incapacitated. Legal entities, such as corporations, partnerships, and joint ventures, may be competent parties to a contract; in these cases, however, care must be taken to ensure that the person executing the agreement on behalf of the entity is authorized to do so.
- *Subject matter.* The agreement must have a subject. This is sometimes referred to as a "meeting of the minds" of the contracting parties in regard to the subject matter of their contract and their respective obligations pursuant to the contract.
- *Consideration.* Each party must provide and, in turn, receive something of value from the agreement. Legal consideration may or may not involve the payment of money. It may also involve the performance of an act the party is not already obligated to take or an agreement to forgo an act the party otherwise has a right to take.

*Partnerships.* Professional services contracts are usually entered into in the partnership's name and signed by at least one of the partners. The signing partner must be a licensed architect in the jurisdiction where the project is located. Contracts signed by one partner in the name of the partnership are nearly always binding on the partnership and all the partners. If the authority of a partner to bind the partnership is in doubt, the situation should be examined and resolved before the contract is signed.

*Corporations.* When a corporation enters into an agreement, the exact corporate name, including punctuation and abbreviations, should be used on both the front and signature pages.

The signature page should also include the name and title of the officer authorized to execute the contract, the corporation's seal, and attestation by the proper corporate officer. Inclusion of the officer's corporate title makes it clear the officer is signing for the corporation and not as an individual.

When engaging in a contract with a corporation, the following should also be established:

- That the corporation is authorized by its corporate charter and bylaws to make such a contract
- That it has made proper use of its authority, such as by a proper resolution at a meeting of its board of directors
- That the officer who executed the contract was authorized to do so

Failure to clarify these points may shift liability from the corporation to the individual signing the agreement, defeating one of the advantages of the corporate form of business.

*Public entities.* In the case of public agencies (such as school boards), the architect should establish that the public body making the contract has been authorized to do so. This can be done by requesting that a copy of the authorizing resolution be attached to the contract. The architect should also establish that funds to pay for the architect's services have been appropriated or are otherwise available.

*Witnesses.* Although witnesses are not legally necessary for the validity of a contract, it may be helpful to have someone present who can verify that the contract was signed by the contracting parties. A notary public serves this purpose.

*Legal seal.* The practice of sealing contracts can be traced to the English common-law tradition in which parties to an agreement impressed a wax seal of their coat of arms on a contract to signify its solemnity. Today this practice has been modified, and the word *seal* or the letters *L.S.* appear after signatures on a contract under seal. In many states, sealing contracts is merely a vestige of this custom. In nearly half the states, however, a contract under seal has increased significance, creating a binding obligation (even though no consideration or value is to be received in return for that obligation) and extending the time during which a legal action relating to the contract may be brought. In these jurisdictions, both parties should sign under seal. The seal referred to in this context is the firm's business seal (or the word *seal* written after a signature) and not the architect's professional seal or stamp.

*Howard G. Goldberg, Esq.*

attorney review the proposed agreement. To facilitate this review, you may want to carefully compare the proposed agreement against a checklist developed from AIA Documents B141, B163, or D200 (Project Checklist) or a checklist developed by your firm or your attorney.

- Be sure these documents are coordinated with the requirements of other project agreements (for example, architect-consultant and owner-contractor agreements).

> The architect needs to carefully review and evaluate the terms of client-prepared contracts. The backgrounder Responding to Owner-Developed Contracts (10.1) provides guidance on this matter.

Change is the only constant that may be relied upon as a project moves from inception to occupancy.

Initial definition of project scope, program site, schedule, and budget may change as time passes and as design gives shape and substance to the project. Regulatory and financing review may require design changes. The processes of bidding and negotiation may suggest or even require substitutions. Detailed design during construction—in the form of shop drawings and material and product submittals—will refine the project. Conditions encountered in the field may require changes. As time passes and technology improves, and as the owner experiences the building under construction, design changes are inevitable.

It is important, therefore, to think of the owner-architect agreement—and indeed all the project agreements—as having some flexibility. They will be interpreted and, if needed, modified as the project moves forward.

With this thought in mind, architects should recognize the importance of recording changes as they occur. Think of the descriptions, data, and arrangements initially included in the agreement as the baseline. As time passes, record and measure changes against that baseline. While some changes will not materially affect the scope, cost, or time of performance of the architect's services, most changes will. Owners frequently want to make changes, but only if they do not affect cost or time of completion. Therefore architects should promptly document changes and their effects and confirm their understanding with the owner and other affected parties.

> **AIA Document G604, Professional Services Supplemental Authorization, is suitable for use between owner and architect and also between architect and consultant. It provides for one party to authorize the other to furnish additional services, revise the initial scope of services, incur reimbursable expenses, or make some other change. Adjustments to compensation and time for performance can be described on this form.**

### For More Information

Most general law books addressing the practice of architecture include treatises and cases relating to owner-architect agreements.

To research or investigate legal rulings and interpretations about the applications of AIA documents, refer to the *AIA Legal Citator,* edited by Steven G. M. Stein and published by the Matthew Bender Company. The *Citator* contains charts and summaries of appellate court decisions that reference AIA A, B, and C series documents.

---

## B A C K G R O U N D E R

## Responding to Client-Developed Contracts

*Frank Musica, Esq., Assoc. AIA*

The U.S. civil justice system holds architects in a special place—it respects their exercise of judgment, acknowledges the uniqueness of their design services, and protects those who practice in a reasonable and prudent manner. U.S. law, however, also recognizes the freedom of parties to determine their own responsibilities and rights by contract. The tension that can exist between careful and rational services—services based on the standard of care expected of architects by the American legal system—and the ability of architects to modify their normal legal liabilities by contract sometimes results in an unintended, or at least unexpected, assumption of risks by the architect.

### Negotiating a Reasonable Professional Service Agreement

Most clients recognize the design process as only the first step toward a major capital investment. The design of a project usually is meant to result not just in the construction of a project but also in its use or sale. Except for the smallest of projects, clients consult lawyers, risk managers, and insurers from the start of the negotiation process for the design of a project.

There is often a temptation by advisors to clients to redefine the traditional professional client–architect relationship by creating documents with wording favorable to the client. This is not to say, however, that a client is likely to be represented by legal counsel experienced in the design and construction process. In fact, although a client's attorney or other advisor may influence the business relationship between client and architect by clarifying and documenting it, the attorney or advisor may do so without understanding the construction industry or appreciating the professional nature of design services.

Design and construction are dynamic processes. Even after agreements have been negotiated and signed, daily decision making is a constant. The tremendous amount of negotiation that occurs between client and architect throughout the life of a project makes open client–architect communication critical to project success. This continuous need for negotiation is one reason contracts drafted by lawyers unfamiliar with the construction process often produce disputes rather than prevent them.

Explaining the information contained in the consensus AIA documents to a client—or a client's attorney—should assist in the education and communication process and create realistic expectations that can be documented in a custom professional services agreement. As well, when a custom agreement is being created, it is important that the architect remember to include certain project-specific and general-condition terms and to limit onerous, unrealistic, or ambiguous terms. It is often useful, of course, to compare a proposed agreement with the comparable standard form AIA agreement.

### Contracts as a Productivity Tool

The contract negotiation process provides an opportunity to set the client–architect relationship on a firm and productive course. Both parties must have a full appreciation of the issues involved in the negotiation, their interrelationships, and their relative importance. According to the risk management specialists of the CNA/Schinnerer professional liability insurance program—the AIA's commended program—the outcome of the contract negotiation process can be considered successful if it results in a contract that satisfies the following criteria:

- The expectations of the parties are clearly articulated and reasonably integrated.
- The rights and obligations of the parties are clearly expressed.
- Risk and reward are addressed and fairly allocated.
- Each source of risk is allocated to the party in the best position to control or otherwise manage it.
- Insurance is available to support any common law or contractual indemnity obligation.
- Mechanisms exist to reasonably accommodate change during the course of the project.
- The mutual understanding of the parties is confirmed in writing.

A detailed, written agreement between the architect and the client can prevent confusion, uncertainty, and dissatisfaction. The contract establishes the scope of services, the overall relationship, the system of communication, the standard of care, and the rights and responsibilities of both parties. The likelihood of misunderstandings, disputes, and litigation decreases significantly if the contract is in writing and clearly represents the agreement of the parties.

### Basic Questions for Reviewing Client-Developed Contracts

Whenever you review a proposed contract, you should ask some basic questions:

- What does the language say? What does it mean?
- Why is this language better than the consensus language in the AIA standard documents?
- What problem is this language intended to solve?
- How does the language affect the architect's responsibilities?
- Will the language have an adverse impact on the working relationship between the client and the architect?

If, as a result of negotiation, you sign a contract that you think a court will throw out as unconscionable, think again. The purpose of contract law is to make commercial transactions predictable. Courts will enforce contracts unless they were made under duress or fraud or go against public policy. In other words, no matter how bad a deal you make, the courts will respect your ability to make a contract and they will enforce its terms.

### Onerous Transactional and Liability Terms

The business terms of any agreement—the general conditions and project-specific terms that define the services, delivery, and compensation—are usually accompanied by transactional and liability terms that structure the relationship. Often the structure becomes less of a victory for both parties than a trap for the unwary architect.

Few contractual provisions are deal breakers in that they alone should cause a prudent architect to reject a contractual relationship. That simplistic term implies that mere contract language—rather than the relationship created by the contract, the adequacy of the scope and compensation, and the ability of the architect to manage risk—should dominate the architect's decision to provide services. Some provisions, however, clearly go beyond the ability of the architect to manage risk. And since part of that management is the ability to transfer a portion of risk through insurance coverage, these provisions often exceed the scope of professional liability insurance and other insurance coverage.

In reviewing a contract, architects should be alert to the provisions described below. These contract provisions either significantly increase risk or create a situation in which the architect may not be able to manage it appropriately or insure against it.

*Indemnification or hold-harmless clauses.* These shift risk from one party to the other. Usually the shift is toward the architect. Frequently, indemnification clauses demand more of the architect than the law would otherwise require; if they do not, there is no reason for these provisions to be in a contract.

*Defense obligations.* These are rarely stated separately. Instead, they are usually hidden within an indemnification agreement. While it is reasonable for a client to ask for indemnification of defense costs if those costs are the result of the architect's negligence, the assumption of defense responsibilities by the architect is an entirely different matter. It is only in rare cases, for instance, that a professional liability insurer will defend the client as well as the architect. In most situations, the architect alone is responsible for the high costs of a legal defense of its client, even though there may be no allegation of active negligence by the architect.

*Express warranties or guarantees.* These impose liability in a manner that is neither realistic nor effective. They also can appear throughout a contract and often are cleverly disguised. While an architecture firm may feel comfortable providing a warranty of facts or situations within its control—

such as the existence of proper professional and business licenses in the state—providing a warranty of services is irrational. More important, guaranteeing the work of others—for instance, the work of the contractor—is irresponsible because the architect has no control over the contractor.

*Standard of care.* An improper or enlarged definition of the standard of care can create expectations that cannot be met. The law speaks for itself; without any statement of a standard of care, the architect must perform services with the usual and customary professional care and in accordance with generally accepted practices in effect at the time the services are rendered. While that standard can be restated—or even expanded to be based on the competence and qualifications of the firm—such changes must be carefully crafted.

*Cost estimates.* Any cost estimates provided by the architect should indicate the purpose of the estimate and the estimating technique used. For instance, initial estimates might be based on a conceptual estimating technique and subject to refinement during the design process based on the professional experience and judgment of the architect. Since an architect has no control over market conditions or bidding procedures, the client should realize that bids or ultimate construction costs may vary from cost estimates.

*Site visits.* The reason for site visits should be clearly identified. While architects can provide a wide range of services for evaluating the work of a contractor, the client must be aware of the scope, cost, and limitations of such services. It also is important that clients understand how often site visits will occur. They should be defined as either an agreed-upon number tied to specific construction events or a specific number conducted when the architect feels they are appropriate.

### Missing Provisions

Client-generated contracts may leave out statements of importance to architects. Of particular concern are those creating a "bright-line" separation between the services of the architect and the work of a contractor.

*Responsibility for the work.* A positive statement that the contractor should be responsible for the means, methods, techniques, sequences, and procedures of the construction work, and for the final project, should be included in any design contract leading to construction. Unless construction management or design-build services are being requested, the client should understand that while an architect can evaluate the work of the contractor during the project, that eval-

uation does not change the contractor's responsibility to accomplish the design.

*Worker safety.* Because the contractor has control of the site, the contractor alone should be responsible for the safety of the construction workers, the client, others on the site, and adjacent property owners. Liability may be created if a duty is assumed; the risk that liability will be implied because of imprecise language may be even more perilous.

*Agency status during construction.* A provision that helps deter the involvement of the architect in claims brought by the contractor is a clear statement that the architect is acting as the agent of the client.

*Dispute resolution.* A method of dispute resolution should be included in the agreement. A short statement of how any disputes are to be resolved is important, since nothing is worse than having a client threaten to take a dispute to litigation.

*Document control and ownership.* Agreements should clearly state the status of documents. The issue is not one of ownership or compensation; it is one of service and control. The service is professional judgment, not the production of documents, and the control is such that neither a direct client nor a client's consultant should feel it can make modifications without taking full responsibility for them.

### Focusing on Serving the Client by Managing Risk

The key, of course, is not to focus on liability but rather to focus on the various kinds and levels of risk and on risk management options. If a risk can be identified and its impact assessed, a strategy for addressing the risk in the contract and during the life of the project can be developed. Obviously, risks left unmanaged or inappropriately managed may cause problems for both parties to a contract and all those involved in a project.

The real issue is whether the client understands the role of the architect and clearly recognizes the duties and limitations placed on the architect by the constraints on the specific project. The initial communication effort and the continual reinforcement of the role of the architect are essential to a low-risk practice.

*As editor of the CNA/Schinnerer Guidelines for Improving Practice information service, Frank Musica advises professional liability insurance policyholders. He is also insurance counsel to the AIA Documents Committee and serves as a resource to AIA national and state components.*

# 10.2 Project Team Agreements

## Timothy R. Twomey, Esq., AIA

*When architects engage consultants or establish joint ventures with other firms, additional agreements result.*

The project design team may be a very small group—even a single architect who has the necessary expertise and performs all of the professional services required. Often, however, the team includes other firms with special expertise in building engineering systems, special design issues, a particular building type, or other aspects of the project.

Where design or construction consultants are required, it is common for architects to select them and add them to the project team. These consultants act as subcontractors to the architect, and the architect is responsible to the client for their professional services. The architect-consultant relationship may be established just for the project at hand, it may be a strategic alliance developed between the participants, or the two firms may have a long-standing working relationship.

Increasingly, owners are "unbundling" and structuring their own project teams. These teams are often led by third parties, typically referred to as either project managers or program managers, retained by the owner. In these circumstances, some consultants may hold independent prime contracts directly with the owner or with the owner's project or program manager. The owner (1) may provide overall coordination of the multiple prime contractors (including the architect) through in-house staff, (2) may assign this coordination to a project or program manager, or (3) may allocate this coordination to one of the contractors (perhaps the architect).

In each of the above cases, the liability and risk management implications to the architect are varied and different from what they would be in a traditionally structured project. For example, under scenarios 1 and 2, old habits and expectations may die hard for both owners and architects, each of whom may expect and act as if the architect will provide the typical coordination services. This expectation may become especially problematic should the owner's in-house staff or the owner-retained program or project manager prove ineffective at coordination. Pressure for the architect to step in may become tremendous.

> ▶ **Project Delivery Options (9.1)** addresses multiple prime contracts and other arrangements for delivering projects.

Under scenario 3, while the architect may perform in a traditional role, the architect may not have the clout with other contractors to effectively facilitate—let alone enforce—the needed coordination among the parties, since they are not contractually tied to the architect. In this case, the architect may have coordination responsibility but may lack the tools necessary to carry out this responsibility.

## ARCHITECT-CONSULTANT RELATIONSHIPS

> ▶ **Combine appropriate AIA standard forms of agreement to improve coordination of prime and consultant agreements.**

The architect may seek consulting arrangements with a wide variety of specialists—even with other architects. The most common interprofessional relationship is that between the architect and the professional engineer responsible for the detailed design and engineering of one or more of the building's systems. Most large, complex projects need special expertise in civil, structural, mechanical, and electrical design. Some architecture firms include one or more of these engineering disciplines in-house; many, however, do not.

TIMOTHY R. TWOMEY *is principal and chief administrative officer for Shepley Bulfinch Richardson and Abbott Incorporated. He is responsible for providing legal, management, and administrative support for the Boston-based architectural firm.*

## Consultant Services and Responsibilities

A consultant's services to the architect are outlined in the architect-consultant agreement. These services, and other contract terms and conditions, should be carefully coordinated with those in the architect-owner agreement.

***Services.*** As the architect and owner establish the services to be included in the architect's contract, both parties may consider the need for consultants. It is advisable to review the list of services required to accomplish the project and establish who will be responsible for each. Each professional service identified may be provided by

- The architecture firm, through its own staff
- A consultant subcontracted to the architecture firm. The consultant may be another architect, an alliance partner, or another firm acting as a subcontractor to the architect.
- A consultant to the owner. This arrangement may include a construction manager, a project or program manager, an independent design professional for another portion of the project, or another architecture firm performing a portion of the architecture services—with or without the architect's coordination.
- The owner. The owner's staff may provide services themselves or by some other arrangement—again, with or without coordination by the architect.

Clarifying responsibilities between owner and architect accomplishes at least two things: It helps the architect identify the services for which consultants will be sought, and it begins to allocate project risks among the owner, architect, and others on the project team.

***Role in project planning.*** When the architect-consultant relationship is formed early in the project—or before the project begins, in a strategic alliance or a team put together to acquire the project—the consultant can be involved in project planning and is in a position to commit to services, scope, schedule, and fee before the architect makes these commitments to the owner.

Often it is appropriate to assemble the project team as part of the marketing effort to acquire a project. Owners, especially those whose facilities require sophisticated engineering or other special expertise, are often acutely aware of the need for competent consultants and well-founded architect-consultant relationships. For these owners, consultants become an important part of the interview and selection process.

***The architect's responsibility.*** As the prime contractor, the architect assumes primary responsibility to the owner for the accuracy and completeness of the work of the architect's consultants. If something goes wrong, the architect can be held liable for the services performed by a consultant. As professionals, consultants are required to perform their services with reasonable care; their failure to do so, however, makes the architect liable.

This discussion underscores the importance of careful consultant selection and the need for clear agreement

### SPECIAL EXPERTISE AND CONSULTANTS

There is a wide range of special expertise that, depending on the project, owner, and capabilities of the architect, may be needed in providing professional services.

**Building Types**
Airports
Athletics/sports facilities
Computer facilities
Convention centers/public assembly facilities
Criminal justice/corrections facilities
Educational facilities
Healthcare facilities
Hotels
Laboratories
Libraries
Recreational facilities
Residential facilities
Theater/performing arts facilities

**Design/Practice Issues**
Accessibility
Acoustics
Audiovisual technology
Civil engineering
Cladding/curtain wall
Clean room
Construction
Construction management
Code interpretation
Communications
Computer technology
Concrete
Cost estimating
Demography
Display
Ecology
Economics
Editorial issues
Electrical engineering
Elevators/escalators
Energy systems
Environmental analysis
Equipment

Facilities management
Financial issues
Fire protection
Food service/kitchen
Graphic design
Historic preservation
Insurance
Interior design
Landscape architecture
Legal issues
Life safety
Lighting
Lightning
Management
Market analysis
Materials handling
Mechanical engineering
Power support systems
Process engineering
Programming
Psychology
Public relations
Radiation shielding
Real estate
Record retention
Reprographics
Safety
Sanitary engineering
Scheduling
Security
Sociology
Soils/foundations
Space planning
Specifications
Structural engineering
Telecommunications
Traffic/parking
Transportation
Urban planning
Value engineering

between architect and consultant. It is also important that the architect understand the impact of consultants' recommendations and that the architect be prepared to accept initial responsibility and liability for these recommendations. This, in turn, explains why insured architects increasingly seek to retain insured consultants and request a certificate of insurance from them.

▷ **"Education is when you read the fine print. Experience is what you get if you don't."**

*Pete Seeger*

## Architect-Consultant Agreements

Two major issues are covered in architect-consultant agreements: passing to the consultant the architect's rights and responsibilities to the owner and sharing risks and rewards. Once these key points have been worked out, it is not difficult to prepare an architect-consultant agreement that incorporates the decisions of and parallels the owner-architect agreement.

***Legal rights and responsibilities.*** Usually architects want to give consultants the same legal rights the architect has from the owner. At the same time, with respect to the consultant's professional discipline, a consultant should owe the same responsibilities to the architect that the architect owes to the owner.

Rather than restate all of these rights and responsibilities from the owner-architect agreement—and run the risk of error or omission—it is common to incorporate the owner-architect agreement (often without specifics of the architect's compensation) into the architect-consultant agreement, binding the consultant to provide all of the services in its discipline and to be subject to the same terms and conditions that the architect owes to the owner.

It may be prudent for the architect to clarify with its consultants what design services each consultant will provide and what design services, if any, each consultant will delegate to the contractor or others. These specifics should be coordinated with AIA Document B141, subparagraph 2.6.4.3, and AIA Document A201, subparagraph 3.12.10, reviewed and determined to be in accordance with applicable state law, and discussed by the architect with the owner.

***Risks and rewards.*** In assessing the risks associated with a project, the architect should assess how risks will be shared with consultants. The best advice is for the architect and the consultant to make each other aware of the risks associated with their aspects of the project. Providing a copy of the owner-architect agreement facilitates this process. With this information, the negotiation can proceed openly.

***Compensation issues.*** Consultant compensation is a matter for negotiation between the parties. Consultants who understand the risks and responsibilities they are assuming will be in a position to negotiate compensation with the architect. In considering compensation, architects will want to address two additional issues:

- What level of coordination is required for consultant services? Because consultant services must be fully integrated with those of the architect, coordination will not be casual. The architect will commit time and money to coordination, and these factors should be considered in establishing the architect's compensation. Some firms budget coordination services directly; others budget a multiple or markup of consultant costs to reflect the need for coordination as well as the costs of administration and liability.
- What will happen if the architect is not paid by the owner or if the project is delayed beyond reason? Consultant compensation can be a knotty problem for both architect and consultant.

### AIA Architect-Consultant Agreement Forms

AIA Document C141, Standard Form of Agreement between the Architect and Consultant, is intended to be used in conjunction with a prime agreement, such as AIA Document B141, Owner-Architect Agreement, or AIA Document B181, Standard Form of Agreement between Owner and Architect for Housing Services. C141 covers engineering services, such as structural, mechanical, or electrical engineering, that begin at the schematic design phase and parallel the architect's basic-services package throughout the course of the project. It also establishes the responsibilities the architect and engineer owe to each other and their mutual rights under the agreement. Although it is most applicable to engineers, C141 may also be used by consultants in the traditional five phases of basic services for owners under the provisions of B141. Its provisions are in accord with those of B141 and of AIA Document A201, General Conditions of the Contract for Construction.

AIA Document C142, Abbreviated Architect-Consultant Agreement, adopts the terms of a prime agreement between owner and architect by reference. It is intended that the prime agreement be based on AIA Document B141.

AIA Document C727, Standard Form of Agreement Between Architect and Consultant for Special Services, does not incorporate the terms of a prime agreement between the owner and the architect. It is suitable for use in situations in which other C series documents are not appropriate, such as when the consultant's services are limited in scope and do not extend into the construction phase. C727 requires a written description of the consultant's services, so each agreement can be tailored to a specific situation.

## Consultant Compensation

In most contracts, when the architect is not paid by the client, the consultant faces the risk of not being paid even when services are rendered. The consultant's protection against that risk rests in questioning the architect about the client's solvency and business practices before the project begins. If the answers are not satisfactory, the consultant can reject the commission. Later, should payments not materialize, the consultant's protection rests in the architect's making reasonable efforts to collect the money owed.

Therefore, when architects develop agreements with consultants, it is important to address this question: Will the consultant be paid if the architect is not paid by the owner? If nonpayment is caused by something that is the consultant's responsibility, the consultant understands when payment is not forthcoming. When this is not the case, however, the consultant may not be as understanding. It is a business risk that should be addressed by the parties in their contract.

Assuming the architect-consultant agreement is silent on what happens if the architect is not paid, the architect will have to explain that it is the custom in the design profession and construction industry for the consultant's compensation to be contingent on payment being made to the party hold-ing the prime agreement with the owner. This would be so even if the consultant was the prime contractor with the owner and the architect was the subcontracting consultant. The reasons for this custom are compelling:

- The prime contractor absorbs the costs—and risks—associated with project acquisition.
- The prime contractor will have to absorb the costs of collecting the fee should payment be tardy or otherwise not forthcoming.
- In the time between marketing and closeout, the prime contractor is directly responsible to the owner for the vagaries and tensions of the design process.

Architects need to understand that in most jurisdictions, if the agreement is silent on when the consultant is to be paid for satisfactory performance of its services, then the law requires payment within a reasonable period. The fact that the architect has not been paid by the client would be no defense unless the agreement between the architect and the consultant states that receipt of payment from the client is a condition precedent to the consultant's receipt of payment from the architect.

---

**"Can two walk together, except they be agreed?"**

*Holy Bible, Amos 3:3*

> Some state laws require that the architect coordinate owner-retained consultants. Check applicable law and take this into account in negotiating the owner-architect agreement.

***Forms of agreement.*** Architect-consultant agreement forms with major consultants such as engineers should parallel the owner-architect agreement. (This is normally less critical for consultants for limited purposes such as specifications, kitchens, elevators, security systems, etc.) Statements of service as well as terms and conditions should be carried consistently throughout the prime contract and subcontracts. Using the AIA standard forms does this; if they are modified, however, it is important to verify that the modification is reflected in all the documents. This is particularly important if the scope of services portion of the owner-architect agreement is changed; the consultant agreement should be modified accordingly.

## Owner-Retained Consultants

An owner may directly retain project consultants. The architect may or may not have any contractual responsibility for these consultants. If the architect is to have any contract responsibility, then the architect must be able to review and negotiate those responsibilities.

An owner may decide to write a prime contract with another consultant in addition to the architect for a number of reasons:

- Services may be substantially different and not overlapping. For example, the owner may retain a land surveyor to develop the information necessary to prepare for design services.
- The owner may have a long-standing relationship with the consultant.
- The owner may seek the benefit of direct and independent advice.
- The owner may prefer to structure the project team and then assume the responsibilities for its coordination, either through the owner's in-house staff or through a program manager.

On occasion, an owner may have motives that benefit the owner but not necessarily the project. For instance, the owner may want to save money by (usually unwisely) eliminating coordination services during design or construction, or the owner may want to keep total control of the project by retaining overall coordination responsibilities.

In some cases it is to the architect's advantage to have the owner directly retain a consultant. This is especially true when the architect must rely on a consultant's work but is not—and does not want to be—in a position to review that work independently and take responsibility for it. For this reason, AIA Document B141 specifies that it is the owner's responsibility to provide any necessary land surveying and geotechnical engineering data to the architect. These consultants are engaged by the owner, and the architect is entitled to rely on the survey and geotechnical information supplied by the owner.

Whatever motivations an owner has for directly retaining consultants, someone must coordinate the services of these professionals. The owner must either assume this responsibility and the risks associated with it or assign it to a program manager or to one of the prime professionals on the project.

Coordination is especially important from the architect's point of view. Because architects are the generalist design professionals on building projects, others on the project team may expect them to coordinate professional services even though they might not have contractual responsibility or authority to do so. An architect who acts on that expectation and coordinates other consultants' activities may be held responsible for the results of that coordination, even though the owner has engaged project consultants directly and has not made the architect responsible for them.

This situation poses unique dilemmas for the architect. As a generalist, the architect is usually in the best position to coordinate the activities of the other design professionals on the project. If the architect is not assigned these responsibilities and the owner is unable to provide them, the architect may want to negotiate to assume these responsibilities and to be compensated for them. When the architect is assigned coordination responsibilities, owner-retained consultants should be required, by contract, to coordinate their efforts with the architect, to submit to the architect's authority, and to look to the owner only if they have claims with respect to the architect as the owner's agent.

## JOINT VENTURES

A joint venture is a contractual union between two or more firms for one or more specific projects. The joint venture arrangement enables firms to combine key resources, expertise, and experience to perform professional services on a specific project while allowing each participating firm to pursue other projects outside the joint venture.

A joint venture functions essentially like a partnership. There is an agreement detailing who brings what to the venture, who will do what, and how the compensation or profit will be shared. The agreement also details how responsibilities and risks are allocated internally. Typically a joint venture retains no profits and pays no income taxes; it passes profits (or losses) and tax liabilities along to its participating members. Participating firms are individually and jointly liable to the client and others for the services offered by the joint venture.

Generally speaking, a joint venture is formed only for the purpose of seeking and executing a specific project. After a successful project, some firms feel there is enough value in the collaboration to seek further projects that require the unique talents represented in the venture. Some joint ventures have been so successful that they have resulted in permanent mergers of the participating firms.

There is always an element of risk in joint ventures. Every design and building project involves a temporary "multiorganization"—a condition that raises its own problems and adds to the risks inherent in the building enterprise. If the design entity itself is a joint venture (another such multiorganization), then it stands to reason there is added risk. The basic concept behind joint ventures, of course, is that the potential rewards outweigh the inherent risks.

It is imperative that the joint venture parties have and exhibit a high degree of trust and confidence in one another. The partnership-like relationship among the joint venture parties and the shared need to jointly address the many, varied, and complex professional and business issues that normally arise during the course of any joint venture project require a higher degree of candor and reliance among the parties than is typically the case in a more distant relationship.

It is also imperative that before the project moves forward, the joint venture parties clearly agree on a division of responsibilities for both the professional services the joint venture will provide to the client and the business responsibilities of managing the joint venture itself (e.g., who will handle the finances and banking arrangements, how will key decisions be made and by whom, how will risk for profit and loss be allocated). Leaving any of these key decisions to be resolved in "real time," when emotions may be running high and the consequences significant, creates an enormous risk that the parties' respective judgments will be heavily influenced by these factors and their ability to come to agreement severely compromised.

## Reasons for Forming the Venture

A successful joint venture begins with a clear understanding of why the venture has been formed in the first place. The initiative to form the joint venture is usually taken by the architect, although it may come from the owner. The reasons may be technical or political. For example, a national firm from outside the owner's geographic area may enter a joint venture with a respected local firm.

Some joint ventures are outstanding successes, and some are not. Each primary participant in the venture must make an independent decision that the venture makes sense, and the participants must make a similar decision collectively. A firm that discovers it is being used in some unexpected and undesired way—by the owner or by another firm—may have trouble remaining contented and performing at its best. Finally, it is important to understand that some owners are innately suspicious of joint ventures. They may see the advantages for the firms but may not want *their* project to be the testing ground for the relationship.

## Process

The process of forming a joint venture begins with asking these questions: What does the project require? What are your strengths and weaknesses relative to these requirements? Stated another way, what do you bring to the project, and what do you need to obtain through a joint venture? One approach is to examine these key issues:

- *Required skills.* What skills does the project require, and what does your firm have in-house (or through capable consultants)? Are other disciplines required? Is the owner expecting construction management, financing, or other specific services?
- *Background and knowledge.* What special requirements does the project have? How much expertise or experience does your firm have in accomplishing projects like the one under consideration?
- *Staffing.* Does your firm have the people with the right expertise and experience available to work on the project? If these people are committed to the project, can you meet your other commitments?
- *Geography.* Does the location of one or both of the venture partners bring an advantage to the project?
- *Financing.* If the joint venture needs resources your firm does not have (e.g., expanded computer-aided design capability), are you in a position to make the investment?
- *Insurance.* Is the scope of each firm's professional liability insurance acceptable to the others—and to the client?
- *Management.* Do you have the leadership and management capabilities to take on the project, service the client, and manage the people, processes, and risks involved?
- *Contacts.* Do you have the necessary contacts to secure the commission?

Alliance agreements should carefully spell out who is going to do what and how the fee will be allocated among the associated firms or within the joint venture. Here is one format for doing this.

SYMBOLS:  X Major responsibility   O Minor responsibility   *blank* No responsibility

## ARCHITECTURAL AND ENGINEERING SERVICES

| | Responsibility | | Fee split | |
|---|---|---|---|---|
| **Firms** | A | B | A | B |

### Schematic Design Phase

| | A | B | A | B |
|---|---|---|---|---|
| 1. Conferences with the owner | X | O | | |
| 2. Analysis of project requirements: program analysis and concepts, site analysis, space and cost analysis, climatic studies | X | O | | |
| 3. Building code information | O | X | | |
| 4. Diagram studies of space requirements | X | O | | |
| 5. Assembly of utility and survey data | O | X | | |
| 6. Schematic design studies and recommended solution | X | O | | |
| 7. Schematic design plans | X | O | | |
| 8. Sketches and study models | X | O | | |
| 9. General project description | X | O | | |
| 10. Engineering system concepts | X | O | | |
| 11. Preliminary cost estimate | X | O | | |
| 12. Presentation of SD documents to owner | X | O | 10% | 5% |

### Design Development Phase

| | A | B | A | B |
|---|---|---|---|---|
| 1. Conferences with the owner | X | O | | |
| 2. Refinement of project requirements | X | O | | |
| 3. Formulation of civil engineering systems | X | O | | |
| 4. Formulation of structural systems | X | O | | |
| 5. Formulation of mechanical and electrical systems | X | O | | |
| 6. Selection of major building materials | X | O | | |
| 7. Preparation of DD documents: plans; elevations; building profile sections; outline specifications; description of electrical, mechanical, civil, and structural systems | X | O | | |
| 8. Perspectives, sketches, or models | X | O | | |
| 9. Preliminary cost estimate | X | O | | |
| 10. Equipment schedule | X | O | | |
| 11. Reviewing plans with applicable agencies | O | X | | |
| 12. Presentation of DD documents to owner | X | O | 15% | 5% |

### Construction Documents Phase

| | A | B | A | B |
|---|---|---|---|---|
| 1. Conferences with the owner | O | X | | |
| 2. Development of major detail conditions | O | X | | |
| 3. Diagram study of major mechanical and electrical systems | O | X | | |
| 4. Diagram study of major civil and structural systems | O | X | | |
| 5. Architectural working drawings, specifications | O | X | | |
| 6. Civil working drawings, specifications | O | X | | |
| 7. Structural working drawings, specifications | O | X | | |
| 8. Mechanical working drawings, specifications | O | X | | |
| 9. Electrical working drawings, specifications | O | X | | |
| 10. Built-in equipment working drawings, specifications | O | X | | |
| 11. Cost of special consultants | O | X | | |
| 12. Update construction cost estimate | O | X | | |
| 13. Submission of construction documents to applicable agencies | O | X | | |
| 14. Presentation of CD documents to owner | O | X | 5% | 35% |

### Bidding/Negotiation Phase

| | A | B | A | B |
|---|---|---|---|---|
| 1. Conferences with the owner | O | X | | |
| 2. Advertising for bids | O | X | | |
| 3. Drafting of bid proposals | O | X | | |
| 4. Reproduction and distribution of plans and specifications | O | X | | |
| 5. Drafting of addenda | O | X | | |
| 6. Contractors' questions and information during bidding | O | X | | |
| 7. Bid opening procedure and forms | O | X | | |
| 8. Preparation of construction contracts | O | X | 1% | 4% |

### Construction Contract Administration

| | A | B | A | B |
|---|---|---|---|---|
| 1. Preconstruction conference | O | X | | |
| 2. Architectural construction administration | O | X | | |
| 3. Civil construction administration | O | X | | |
| 4. Structural construction administration | O | X | | |
| 5. Mechanical and electrical construction administration | O | X | | |
| 6. Equipment construction administration | O | X | | |
| 7. Shop drawing checking and approval | O | X | | |
| 8. Material substitutions, architectural | X | O | | |
| 9. Material substitutions, engineering systems | O | X | | |
| 10. Material color selection | X | O | | |
| 11. Change order procedure | O | X | | |
| 12. Verifying and approving periodic estimates | O | X | | |
| 13. Progress reports to owner | O | X | | |
| 14. Prefinal inspection | O | X | | |
| 15. Final acceptance procedure and reports | O | X | | |
| 16. Final inspection | O | X | | |
| 17. Postfinal guarantee period administration | O | X | 4% | 16% |

A careful and honest appraisal of what you bring to the project does two things: It helps you decide whether to pursue the opportunity, and it creates a profile of characteristics to seek in your joint ventures.

## Joint Venture Agreements

There are many business issues, some related to the project and others related to the ways the two firms will work together, that must be addressed in forming a joint venture. The best advice is to be aware of the full range of issues and to negotiate them before the joint venture offers to provide professional services.

## Associated Professional Firms

Sometimes two professional firms choose to represent themselves as "associated" with each other to undertake a project. From a legal standpoint, these firms have two choices: They may form a joint venture, or they may establish a contractor-subcontractor relationship, with one of the firms acting as a prime contractor to the other.

Whatever arrangement is chosen, the issues discussed above are on the table. Roles, responsibilities, risks, and rewards should be defined and delineated in a written agreement between the parties. Once an agreement has been signed, the associating firms should act with that agreement in mind. For example, two architects with a prime contractor-subcontractor arrangement may act so that a third party sees them as participants in a joint venture, jointly and severally liable for any resulting problems.

While any design team agreement should be approached with care, the level of attention is no more nor less than the architect pays to the arrangements with the owner, and the purpose is the same: To put in place an outstanding design team and a framework of arrangements that serve the client and the project well.

### For More Information

Most general law books addressing the practice of architecture include treatises and cases about design team agreements. AIA C-series documents relate to the agreement between the architect and consultant for professional services. This series includes standard forms of agreement between the architect and engineer or other consultants, as well as a standard form that may be used for joint ventures among design professionals to provide professional services.

# Joint Venture Agreements

*Timothy R. Twomey, Esq., AIA*

A joint venture is a business proposition, and it is important that a good business relationship be developed among the joint venture partners. As the parties come to agreement on the various aspects of a joint venture, these should be written, perhaps first as a statement of principles and then later as an outline for the joint venture agreement. In this process trust can be developed and expectations clarified and mutually agreed to, making the drafting of a joint venture agreement less difficult.

Following these steps to reaching agreement will make it clear when discussions should break off—the point at which one or more of the parties do not see the reward as justifying its risk. It is sometimes easy to coast into agreement, or at least apparent agreement. Writing it down provides the first real test. The time to discover that a joint venture is not going to work is before contractual commitments have been made to the owner. An even better time is before you pitch the owner on the merits of your team.

## Essential Issues

A review of the AIA standard form of joint venture agreement (AIA Document C801) reveals the points to be considered in negotiating a formal agreement:

- Identification of the parties
- Name of the joint venture
- Identification of the project to be undertaken by the venture
- Responsibilities of the parties
- Management of the joint venture
- Capital and other contributions to the joint venture
- Property of the joint venture
- Accounting principles and responsibilities
- Preliminary expenses
- Compensation of the joint venture participants
- Ownership and use of documents
- Insurance
- Commencement and termination
- Dispute resolution
- Legal counsel for the joint venture
- Notices
- Extent of agreement
- Assignment of interest
- Successors and assigns

Overall management. A mechanism and a budget must be created to manage the joint venture. Under AIA Document C801, a policy board includes a representative and an alternate from each participating firm. The board's responsibilities include

- Management of the joint venture
- Management of the project, including client contact
- Appointment of a treasurer to maintain accounts and records
- Acquisition and disposition of joint venture property

While the written joint venture agreement establishes broad contours, the policy board is expected to develop more detailed policies, such as

- Qualifications of policy board members
- Appointment and replacement of board members
- Frequency of board meetings and distribution of minutes
- Compensation of board members for administrative and technical time spent on joint venture business
- Compensation and benefits of employees
- Overhead rates
- Bank accounts
- Insurance
- Financial management and accounting
- Operating policies, such as those for travel and entertainment

Project acquisition and management. If the project is not yet in hand, the joint venture participants need to establish procedures for marketing: what will be done, who will do it, who will manage the marketing effort, who will maintain client contact, and who will approve expenditures. The participants in the joint venture will want to set aside funds to manage this effort.

The joint venture parties will also need to establish a project management structure to plan, organize, staff, direct, and control the project. Similarly, human resources, financial management, and risk management/quality control systems will be developed. Because each joint venture participant is likely to approach these aspects of their practices in different ways, care must be taken when deciding how the joint venture will function in each of these areas. The participants will want to be open about their policies and procedures and the rationales behind them so that appropriate practices can be established for the joint venture.

Responsibilities for professional services. It is important to understand that all of the participants are jointly and severally liable to the client for the quality of the joint venture's efforts. Internally, however, responsibilities for tasks can be allocated to individual participants. Conceptually, the joint venture may take one of three approaches to doing this:

- Each firm assumes full responsibility for a portion of the work. The policy board allocates specific services to each of the participants. For example, Firm A may design the building shell and Firm B may be responsible for the building's interiors package.
- Responsibility for all services is shared by the joint venture participants. The work is apportioned to individual par-

ticipants based on (1) skills and experience and (2) cost and availability of resources. For example, Firm A may provide design services, Firm B may prepare the construction documents, and Firm C may administer the construction contract.

- One participant takes the lead in providing services, and the others provide support as needed.

When responsibility for providing professional services is shared by two or more firms, it is essential that the participants allocate responsibilities clearly. This will eliminate gaps or overlaps in professional services and minimize disputes among participants. The greater the effort joint venture participants put into breaking down and delineating general tasks into specific subtasks before project inception, the greater the likelihood that gaps and overlaps will be eliminated and disputes avoided.

One simple method to consider is replacing the "major responsibility" and "minor responsibility" distinctions in the format with the notation "responsible" or "not responsible" and breaking down general tasks into more specific subtasks that can be allocated entirely to one participant. For example, Firm A may be responsible for completing all schematic design phase services "except for those subtasks specifically assigned to the other participant(s)." Those subtasks would then be assigned to Firm B, Firm C, etc. AIA Document B163, Standard Form of Agreement Between Owner and Architect for Designated Services, is a good source to consult for assistance in this effort.

Financial arrangements. Of particular importance to any joint venture are the financial arrangements and especially the allocation of risks and rewards to the participants. AIA Document C801, Joint Venture Agreement for Professional Services, outlines two possible approaches to dividing rewards: the division of compensation method and the division of profit/loss method.

The division of compensation method assumes that the services provided and compensation received will be divided among the parties as they have agreed at the outset of the project. The specific division is a negotiated amount (or percentage of total compensation to the joint venture) based on (1) what each of the parties brings to the joint venture and (2) what each party does as part of the venture. Compensation to each participant is fixed at the outset; each firm's profit or loss depends on the efficiency with which it carries out its responsibilities.

The division of profit/loss method is based on each party performing work and billing the joint venture at cost plus a stated amount for overhead. The ultimate profit or loss of the joint venture is divided among the parties at the completion of the project. This approach ensures that the participants share in the good or ill fortunes of the joint venture, but to be successful it requires allocation of time and costs acceptable to each party at each step along the way.

Whichever approach is selected, it is essential to budget for managing the joint venture. Sometimes joint venture participants overlook the additional time and expense involved in this management.

Insurance. The agreement should address insurance coverage for the participants, especially professional liability insurance. Participants may agree to coordinate insurance so that coverage, limits, deductibles, and other key provisions are negotiated and included in the joint venture agreement. An individual joint venture firm may find it needs an endorsement to its professional liability policy to cover participation in the joint venture—or that the participation is not covered at all. Another approach is to seek a project insurance policy that insures all parties of the joint venture.

**The Resulting Agreement**

Agreement on the essential business issues places all participants in a joint venture in a position to finalize the written agreement. At this point, each participant may want to involve its attorney.

While it is possible to draft an agreement from scratch, it often makes sense to use AIA Document C801, Joint Venture Agreement for Professional Services. This document is intended to provide for the mutual rights and obligations of two or more parties who, once they have established a joint venture, will enter into a project agreement with the owner to provide professional services. The parties may be all architects, all engineers, or a combination of professionals. Among other terms and conditions, AIA Document C801

- Allows joint venture participants to select either the division of compensation or division of profit/loss approach
- Allows the participants to specify who will be responsible for which professional services (especially important if the division of compensation approach is used)
- Allows the parties to identify capital, property, and other contributions to the joint venture
- Allows the parties to specify insurance coverage
- Sets up a policy board to transact the business of the joint venture
- Establishes conditions for ownership and use of the documents produced by the joint venture
- Limits the relationship among the parties to the performance of the project
- Remains in force until the project agreement is terminated or the parties agree to terminate the joint venture

*Timothy R. Twomey is principal and chief administrative officer for Shepley Bulfinch Richardson and Abbott Incorporated. He is responsible for providing legal, management, and administrative support for the Boston-based architectural firm.*

*Adapted from the backgrounder Joint Venture Agreements, by John N. Cryer III, AIA, in the 12th edition of* Architect's Handbook of Professional Practice.

# 10.3 Construction Agreements

## Dale R. Ellickson, Esq., FAIA

*No substantial construction should be undertaken without a written contract. Each party must understand the structure and purpose of all parts of such a contract, as well as the role each plays in creating it.*

When construction is under an architect's administration, it is commonly accomplished through written contracts between the owner and one or more construction contractors. These contracts are composed of several documents, including an agreement form with general, supplementary, and special conditions to cover the legal allocation of rights and responsibilities among the parties. They also include materials to cover the technical scope of the construction work, which is typically defined by the drawings and specifications prepared by the architect and other professional consultants. Although the architect is not a party to these contracts, the architect plays a critical role in their creation and administration during construction.

> ▶ **Project Team Agreements (10.2) outlines some features common to all project agreements.**

Most owners look to the architect for guidance in preparing the construction agreement and general conditions, and most architects respond by suggesting and completing standard AIA forms. That is fine; architects have substantial technical, practical, and administrative experience to contribute to the process. The critical factor, however, is that the architect should not unilaterally select and prepare owner-contractor agreements and include them in the project manual. They must be reviewed by the owner and, at the owner's election, the owner's legal counsel.

## STRUCTURE OF THE CONSTRUCTION CONTRACT

The contract between the owner and contractor is commonly composed of a number of documents. The structure of that contract is essentially the same for conventional project delivery methods where the owner has separate contracts with the architect and builder. Use of a particular document will depend on a number of factors, such as whether the project is bid or negotiated, the method for compensating the contractor, and so on. The present structure is a relatively recent phenomenon that was given form by industry-wide agreement in the mid-1960s with the publication of a guide for supplementary conditions (AIA Document A511) and a uniform location of subject matter (AIA Document A521). Today, the construction contract includes the following:

> ▶ **AIA Document A201, General Conditions of the Contract for Construction, states that the contract documents do not include bidding requirements. Therefore, if bidding requirements are to be included in the contract documents, they must be referenced specifically in the agreement.**

- *An owner-contractor agreement* (which the parties actually sign) incorporates by reference a number of other documents and makes them part of the contract. It also identifies the legal nature of the parties, states the contract sum and its basis, describes the work, specifies the time of commencement and completion, and provides a process for payments to the contractor.
- *General conditions* set forth the legal rights and responsibilities of the parties to the contract. This document establishes the baseline for the legal ground rules of the contract. It tends to be largely the same from project to project and from owner to owner, and if it is an AIA document, it will be national in application.

**Dale R. Ellickson, Esq., FAIA,** *is a consultant on special construction contracts. He was formerly the counsel for the AIA Contracts Documents Program. As an architect and an attorney, he writes and lectures widely on legal matters for the construction industry. This topic was adapted from the twelfth edition topic by Charles R. Heuer, Esq., FAIA.*

- *Supplementary conditions* modify and expand upon the general conditions in response to the special circumstances and requirements for a particular project and locality. They often include provisions relating to unique requirements for payments, retainage, insurance, and other contracted matters.
- *Special or other conditions* are used to modify or expand upon supplementary conditions that a corporate or institutional client has developed and adopted as its standard.
- The *drawings* provide a graphic representation of the quantity of work to be done with respect to measurements, configuration, materials, structure, systems, equipment, and siting.
- The *specifications* provide technical information about the quality of materials indicated on the drawings and other information not easily communicated graphically.
- *Addenda* are written or graphic modifications to or interpretations of the contract documents, issued before the agreement is signed.
- *Modifications* are similar to addenda except that they occur after the agreement has been signed. For example, a change order is a modification.

▶ **Construction Procurement (17.7) looks at the role of addenda within the bidding process.**

**While fixed-price compensation can simplify contracts, there usually are changes during construction; owners must recognize that the contract price may not be the final price.**

▶ **AIA Documents (10.4) reviews the documents program— including the availability of AIA documents in electronic form.**

## OWNER-CONTRACTOR AGREEMENT

Typically, the choice of owner-contractor agreement form begins with selection of the project delivery approach. AIA publishes several owner-contractor agreement forms within each of its document families:

- Conventional design-bid-build (A201 family)
- Construction management–advisor family and construction management–constructor family
- Design-build family
- Small project family
- Interiors family
- International family

While the issues covered in these various forms are similar, specifics depend on the delivery approach. The remainder of this section focuses on conventional design-award-build projects.

### Contractor Compensation

Within the various project delivery approaches, there are choices of how to compensate the contractor.

***Stipulated-sum contracts.*** Many contracts for construction are fixed-price, lump-sum agreements. The contractor agrees to do the work as outlined in the construction documents, and the owner agrees to pay the stipulated sum for satisfactory completion of the work.

A stipulated sum is almost always required for work that is competitively bid. There are two great advantages to this arrangement: This form of compensation is simple, and the owner knows the cost of the work at the time the contract is awarded.

Money saved (or lost) compared to what the contractor assumed in its bid increases (or decreases) the contractor's profit.

***Cost-plus-fee contracts.*** These contracts reimburse the contractor for its direct expenses plus the cost of subcontracts, labor, and materials used for the work. The contractor also receives a fixed or percentage fee for overhead and profit.

A cost-plus contract that includes a fixed, lump-sum fee encourages the contractor to be efficient because the contractor can reduce costs to the owner without reducing the contractor's profit. Owners choose cost-plus contracts under a variety of circumstances:

- The time for performance is short, and design criteria or construction cost is less critical than meeting the deadline for completion of the facility. For example, it may be critical to the owner that a new or remodeled facility be ready in time to take advantage of the high season in the market for the owner's products or services.
- Scope or timing of the work may be unknown at the start of the project. For example, the pace of building lot sales may dictate construction of the infrastructure of a new resort community.
- High quality is paramount. Defense projects, monumental buildings, and high-tech research facilities are examples.
- Construction expertise needs to be closely coordinated with design during the conceptualization of the project to save time for contingencies such as fast-track scheduling or weighing untested, unique materials or systems of building.

Cost-plus contracts carry an obvious disadvantage: the cost of the project is not determined in advance of contract signing. However, few cost-plus agreements are entirely open-ended. Limitations may include

- *Target price with or without an incentive.* Initially a target price, called a control estimate, is established based on preliminary construction documents, performance specifications, standard square footage costs, or some combination of these factors. A formula may be established for the contractor to share in savings if costs come in below the target price, or to absorb a portion of costs in excess of the target price.
- *Partial-cost guarantee.* Contractors can usually obtain fixed prices from some subcontractors and suppliers of equipment and materials even when construction documents are not complete. The contractor can then add a fixed allowance for general administrative work, plus overhead and profit, to get a partial fixed price. Such a partial guarantee reduces the risks to both the owner and the contractor.
- *Cost-plus-fee with a guaranteed maximum price (GMP).* Most of the cost-plus contracts used in the United States include a cap beyond which the contractor must absorb all costs (assuming there has been no change in the scope of the project). There may be a "shared savings" clause giving the contractor an incentive to reduce costs so that it can share in the savings below the GMP.

These limitations help to control risks associated with uncertainty about costs, but they have disadvantages, too. When target prices or GMPs are established, contractors will include contingencies and set the highest limit possible to reduce the risk of overrun. Further, if the limits are established before construction documents are complete, disagreement may arise over the scope of the work or the details of construction intended to be included within the GMP or target price.

**Federal and state government agencies frequently have their own forms of agreement and general conditions. So do many corporations and institutions with extensive construction programs. Invariably such documents have been drawn up by legal counsel employed by the agencies or corporations, and often they are based on the AIA documents.**

***Unit-price contracts.*** In the United States, unit-price contracts are often used for projects or portions of projects in which it is difficult or impossible to establish precise quantities of materials or equipment at the time the construction contract is bid or negotiated. In this system, contractors provide a price per unit (e.g., per cubic yard of rock to be excavated or square yard of carpet to be laid). When quantities are determined, the contract price is established by multiplying the unit price times the number of units. If unit prices are to be requested, it is important that the owner be informed about these points:

- The units should be carefully defined so that bids from competing bidders can be accurately compared.
- The number of different kinds of unit prices requested should be manageable, so that bidders can determine prices objectively and within the time frame allotted for the bidding process.

- The quantity of units likely to be required should be estimated as closely as possible. If the unit quantities originally contemplated are so changed during the course of construction that applying the stated unit prices would create a hardship on either the owner or contractor, the unit prices should be equitably adjusted. *Caution:* Sometimes contractors quote based on supplying only a few units, and the owner may pay a premium if a substantial number of units is actually required.

## Specific Terms and Conditions

Many agreement forms have a similar structure and address similar aspects of the owner-contractor relationship, because in all likelihood they follow the pattern established by AIA's standard form documents.

***Identity of the parties.*** The term owner is used consistently in AIA documents to designate the contractor's client. That individual or entity may be a tenant, however, and may not own the real property outright. It is good practice to use the full legal name of the entity that will be expected to pay for the work and that will be responsible for performing the owner's obligations as provided in the contract documents. The same is true for the entity that will be responsible for performing the contractor's obligations.

***Description of the project and the work.*** The project description helps to establish a baseline against which to measure or assess a change in the scope of the project. It should be as specific as possible. In many cases, the construction work to be performed under the agreement is all work on the project. In some cases, however, when the remaining portions are to be performed by the owner's own forces or by other prime contractors, only a portion of the project is included under the agreement.

One way the owner-contractor agreement describes the work is by identifying the contract documents and incorporating them into the agreement form by reference. If they exist at the time the agreement form is executed, all such contract documents should be specifically enumerated. Since the drawings and specifications can be extensive, an accurate index to the drawings and an accurate table of contents for the specifications can be labeled as an exhibit to the agreement, attached to it, or incorporated by reference.

***Date of commencement.*** For various reasons, both legal (e.g., authorization from a governing board is pending) and physical (e.g., there is not clear access to the site), the owner may want the contractor to delay commencement of the work until some time after the agreement form is executed. If a specific future date is known at the time the contract is executed, it may be specified in the agreement. If not, a notice to proceed may be used. Owners and architects should be aware that a delay of more than 30 days (or whatever period is specified in the bidding requirements) may affect the amount of the contractor's bid.

The owner needs to have a reasonable amount of time before the actual commencement of work on the site to record mortgages and other security interests. If a notice to proceed is used, the owner should set the date far enough in the future to allow time to accomplish these tasks.

***Substantial completion.*** The time limits in many construction contracts are "of the essence of the contract." Generally that means that timely performance is an express condition of the contract, and any delay in the owner's or contractor's performance may excuse the other party from its obligation to perform. Failure to abide by this condition may be treated as a material breach of contract. Because this can release the owner from payment obligations even when the contractor has substantially performed its obligations, courts have crafted an exception to this harsh rule by allowing the contractor to receive payment for work performed up to that point—provided, of course, that the contractor has substantially performed. This court-made exception comes with its own baggage, requiring a case-by-case determination by a court of whether or not the performance of the contractor or the owner has been timely. To simplify the administration of the contract and avoid unnecessary involvement of courts, the AIA adopted and defined the term "substantial completion," which is explained in detail in AIA

**Most agreements include what is commonly referred to as an "integration clause." One effect of such a clause is that everything that was said in negotiations but that was not, in fact, incorporated into the writing is not part of the contract. A court looking at the written contract will presume that it represents the end result of all discussion.**

**If the time for completion is based on a number of days from the commencement date, the owner and architect should recognize that AIA Document A201 defines "day" to mean a calendar day.**

Document A201, General Conditions of the Contract for Construction. The determination of substantial completion is made either by certification from the architect or, if no certification is forthcoming, by mutual agreement between the parties. Thus establishing the date or time period when substantial completion is to be achieved is critically important to both parties.

*Liquidated damages.* An owner may feel sure that late completion of construction will cause damages but be unsure of how to quantify these damages in order to prove them in court or before an arbitration panel. In those cases, the owner often includes a liquidated damage clause in the contract, fixing (liquidating) potential damages. Such contractually specified amounts are then used in lieu of actual damages, if any.

> **Courts distinguish liquidated-damages clauses from penalty clauses. The former are intended to compensate one party for the damages they will suffer due to breach of contract (late performance) by the other party. Penalty clauses are meant to punish late performance without regard to compensation for damages. It is nearly universally true that penalty clauses are unenforceable, even if tied to bonus clauses, which purport to reward early performance of the contract.**

Before including liquidated damages provisions in a contract, the owner and its legal counsel should consider the advantages and disadvantages of doing so. The advantages are clear, but the owner often overlooks the disadvantages: Contractors may focus too much attention on such a clause and may add something to their bid to cover the contingency that such damages may be assessed. Furthermore, they may spend an inordinate amount of time and effort during construction trying to document excuses for delays. Their attempts to avoid the impact of the liquidated damages provision may turn out to be expensive and may also spoil the relationships among the major project participants.

Liquidated damages, if any, may properly be included in both the agreement form and the supplementary conditions for the benefit of subcontractors and others who should be aware of them but who may not be privy to the owner-contractor agreement itself.

*The contract sum.* The contract sum is the amount the owner agrees to pay the contractor. The initial amount for the sum is entered in the agreement and may take one of the following formats:

- The accepted lump-sum bid or negotiated amount
- The lump-sum base bid adjusted by the owner's selection of acceptable alternate bid packages
- The lump-sum bid adjusted by minor changes negotiated after receiving bids

The AIA documents stipulate that the contract sum is to be paid in "current funds," in other words, something easily converted into cash. An owner could not pay, for example, with notes that are not negotiable.

Remember that the contract sum as stated in the agreement is not unchangeable, even in a stipulated-sum contract. The owner has the right under AIA Document A201 to order extra work, make changes, or delete parts of the work without invalidating the contract. Such changes require appropriate adjustments in the contract sum. Similarly, the contractor has the right, before such work begins, to claim that adjustments are necessary to the contract sum because of changes to the work and for concealed or unknown conditions.

*Payment provisions.* Under common-law principles the contractor could not demand payment from the owner until the contractor removed the uncertainty from the bargain by first properly performing its more time-consuming work. Today that is not a practical condition, considering the relatively great expense of construction compared with most other commercial transactions. The typical construction agreement provides for interim payments and stipulates the timing and other conditions for such payments. Typically each application for payment covers one month, running from the first through the last day of the calendar month. If the owner or contractor has a particular reason to adjust this provision by specifying either a different period (e.g., two months) or different starting and ending dates (e.g., from the 15th through the 14th), this can be included in the agreement form.

> **It is generally impractical to establish a payment period substantially less than one month in length because of the various reviews contemplated before the contractor's application for payment is approved and paid.**

The standard form required for the contractor's payment application and the type and level of detail required in the supporting data should be described in Division 1 of the specifications. In cost-plus-fee agreements the supporting data are normally extensive, since the contractor must document the expenses incurred. According to AIA documents, the owner must provide the accounting services it deems necessary to verify or audit such documentation. These accounting services normally are not part of the architect's function.

In stipulated-sum agreements there is normally a schedule of values for the various elements of the work, with specific dollar amounts associated with each item. One reason the architect may want to see such a schedule is to verify that it is not being "front-loaded," with the contractor assigning unjustifiably high values to work that will be done early in the construction process. Front-loading accelerates cash flow to the contractor and may cause the contractor to be overpaid at any given moment; this would be especially troublesome in the event of default by the contractor.

If the agreement is for a stipulated sum, the actual cost paid by the contractor for the work by subcontractors and others is not necessarily equivalent to the schedule of values for that work, since the contractor, not the owner, has the risk of profit or loss on it. The owner is committed to paying for the proper performance of the work and is not directly reimbursing the contractor for costs. However, the initial schedule of values and the estimated costs upon which the schedule is based should have some rational connection to a responsible contractor's likely actual costs. Percentage of completion utilizing a schedule of values, therefore, is the proper gauge for progress payments.

*Interest rates.* If payment is not made when due, interest may be added to compensate the contractor for the owner's use of money that is due for payment to the contractor. These rates are usually decided by the parties at the outset and written into the agreement. The parties should be aware, however, that usury laws and other federal and state requirements might affect the validity of their agreement.

*Retainage.* Whenever payments to a contractor are considered, the subject of retainage comes up. The purpose of retainage is to protect the owner, and there are many ways of going about it. Conventional practice has been to retain (hold back) a set percentage of the value of work completed to ensure faithful performance of the contract. This percentage may vary with circumstances and local custom. An alternative is to place a percentage of the funds due to the contractor into an interest-bearing escrow account. The terms of the escrow would make the money available to the owner upon default of the contractor under the contract, but the interest would accrue to the contractor and subcontractors. The owner and its legal counsel should determine the most appropriate method of retainage, if any.

The percentage retained from payment for delivered or stored materials and equipment need not be the same as that applied to work in place on the project. Since these items are not yet actually incorporated into the construction, there is inherently higher risk associated with them (e.g., risk of theft, vandalism, or damage in transit). Such risk may justify higher retainage than typical for work in place.

If the owner agrees to reduce retainage at some point during construction, that should be reflected in the contract. For example, an owner may decide to do so if confident that surety bonds will provide the required protection—and in the belief that bid prices will be lower if contractors know they will not to have to add the significant cost of financing to their bid prices. A common method is to retain a set percentage of the contract sum until the project is 50 percent complete and then to cease further retainage.

If a surety (bonding company) is involved in the project, the surety's consent should be obtained prior to release of all or any part of the retainage to the contractor. Otherwise the surety may have grounds to make claims against the owner and architect and thereby avoid obligations it would otherwise have under applicable bonds. The owner's legal counsel should verify that there are no statutory prohibitions related to reducing retainage.

*Final payment.* Final payment is a very significant event. AIA Document A201 provides that by making final payment, the owner waives all but specifically enumerated claims against the contractor. Similarly, the contractor, by accepting final payment, waives all claims against the owner that have not been previously made in writing and identified as still open and unsettled. Again, if a performance or payment bond has been issued for the project, the surety's consent to final payment is required so that the surety does not have grounds to avoid obligations it would otherwise have under applicable bonds.

> **Frequently at the end of a construction project the retainage is approximately equivalent to the profit on the project, and the contractor is particularly anxious to receive it in a timely manner.**

> **Construction Procurement (17.7) services touches upon payment and performance bonds, sometimes called surety bonds.**

# GENERAL CONDITIONS OF THE CONTRACT

According to common practice, and as reflected in the AIA system of documents, the owner-contractor agreement form has a companion document containing general conditions. The rights and responsibilities of the owner and contractor—and to some extent those of the architect, subcontractors, and others—are set forth in the general conditions.

Whereas the owner-contractor agreement contains project-specific provisions, the general conditions contain provisions mainly of a contractual (versus procedural) nature that are usable from project to project. The parties need a fair and comprehensive set of nationwide guidelines for their relationship, and the AIA general conditions provide them.

Although only the owner and contractor are parties to the construction contract, the general conditions are a part of that contract as well and are incorporated by reference into many of the subsidiary contracts on the project, including the architect's agreement with the owner and the contractor's agreements with the various subcontractors. During the construction phase, the architect has specific duties and responsibilities according to its contract with the owner. Those duties and responsibilities are restated in the general conditions to the contract for construction so that the contractor is informed about the architect's role and the obligations the architect has been engaged to undertake.

The provisions in the various forms of general conditions are also consistent with the provisions in AIA's forms of owner-architect agreement. Therefore, when properly selected AIA documents are used together on a project, the terms will be consistently used and the rights and responsibilities of the parties properly coordinated. This consistency is an important reason for selecting AIA documents.

Because the general conditions are intentionally somewhat generic, there must be a way to tailor them to reflect the specific requirements of the owner, the project, and local law. This is accomplished via *supplementary, special,* or *other conditions,* which modify or extend the general conditions. They are often used to modify the ground rules and relationships under the following conditions:

- Multiple prime contractors are involved
- The project is being fast-tracked
- The contractor is being compensated on a cost-plus basis

Supplementary conditions can contain provisions relating to payments, retainage, insurance, and other project-specific matters. AIA Document 511, Guide for Supplementary Conditions, contains additional and alternative language that is very helpful when preparing supplementary conditions.

AIA also publishes a form of supplementary conditions (A201/SC) for use on federally funded projects. It contains provisions required by federal contracting procedures and is often used on government projects at the federal, state, and local levels.

Supplementary conditions generally follow the format and numbering system of the general conditions. Matters not addressed at all in the general conditions are usually handled in "other conditions." "Other conditions" often contain federal, state, local, or private requirements prescribed by the owner.

## SUBCONTRACTS

Subcontractors are people or entities that have a contractual relationship with the general (prime) contractor to perform some of the construction work. The prime contractor has a contract with the owner, but subcontractors do not.

Some subcontractors are trade contractors. They are skilled in a particular type of construction work, such as plumbing or carpentry, and they tend to work exclusively

> The AIA's flagship form of general conditions, AIA Document A201, General Conditions of the Contract for Construction, is the result of more than a century of use, review, and testing, both in practice and in the courts. In fact, most forms of general conditions currently used in the construction industry in the United States stem directly from editions of AIA Document A201.

> AIA Document B141 assumes that A201 will be used as the general conditions of the contract for construction. If A201 is not to be used, find out what owner-contractor agreement and general conditions will be used—and what they will require of you as construction administrator—before estimating your costs and developing your compensation proposal.

> The AIA Documents List provides an enumeration of current documents, the latest versions, and prices. A list of authorized local distributors is available from the AIA, (800) 242-3837.

> The designation "subcontractor" is applied because a certain relationship exists, not because of the work or services being performed or provided.

The AIA publishes several owner-contractor agreements. The owner and architect can choose among them depending on the project delivery approach and other factors, principally the size and complexity of the project and the method of compensation to the contractor. The abbreviated forms may be used when the project is small or uncomplicated. The general conditions for the agreement for construction are usually a separate but coordinated form; sometimes, however, they are incorporated directly into the owner-contractor agreement.

| Owner-Contractor Agreement Forms | General Conditions Forms |
| --- | --- |
| **Design-Bid-Build** | |
| • Stipulated Sum Agreement (A101) | • A201 |
| • Abbreviated Stipulated Sum Agreement (A107) | • Combined with the agreement form |
| • Cost-Plus-Fee Agreement (A111) | • A201 |
| **Construction Management—Advisor** | |
| • Stipulated Sum Agreement/CM in which the CM is an advisor to the owner (A101/CMa) | • A101/CMa |
| **Construction Management—Constructor** | |
| • Stipulated Sum Agreement/CM in which the CM is the constructor (A101/CMc) | • A101/CMc |
| **Design-Build** | |
| Design-Build Agreement (A491) | • Combined with the agreement form |
| **Small Project** | |
| • Small Project Agreement (A105/A205) | • Combined with the agreement form |
| **Interior Design** | |
| • Furniture, Furnishings, and Equipment Agreement (A171) | • A271 |
| • Abbreviated Furniture, Furnishings, and Equipment Agreement (A177) | • Combined with the agreement form |

in that trade. By contrast, a supplier generally furnishes equipment or materials but does not normally perform any construction work at the site. At times both trade contractors and suppliers may be sub-subcontractors in that they contract with a subcontractor rather than the general contractor.

Subcontracting is a way of life in the construction industry. Some estimates are that 80 percent or more of construction work is performed by subcontractors. From the owner's perspective, an advantage of subcontracting is that the actual construction work is performed by people with specialized skills and equipment. They tend to be very productive in their trade and often do higher-quality work than generalists. Disadvantages include the risk that the general contractor will not properly coordinate and manage a multitude of subcontractors, that there will be jurisdictional disputes about which subcontractor is responsible for specific work, and that the subcontractors may have mechanics' lien rights against the owner's property if they have not been paid by the general contractor (even if the owner has paid all bills in full).

Subcontractors face their own harsh realities. They must invest in equipment and staff and pay for labor and materials, usually long before they are paid by the general contractor. This arrangement helps general contractors get work without having to finance everything themselves, but it leaves subcontractors at substantial risk of delayed payment or even nonpayment. Generally subcontractors have no input into the terms of the owner-contractor agreement but find themselves bound by many of its terms. And when one subcontractor has problems, financial or otherwise, they tend to ripple through the project, affecting the general contractor and many of the other subcontractors as well.

***Qualifications.*** Because subcontractors play such key roles in the success of a construction project, it is important to select good ones. AIA Document A201 requires the general

> **The AIA publishes a form of subcontract (AIA Document A401) for use with other AIA documents**

contractor to submit a list of the principal subcontractors and suppliers proposed for the project. This requirement gives the owner and architect an opportunity to object to the use of a particular subcontractor. Everyone should recognize, however, that the general contractor's bid is based in part on a specific subcontractor's sub-bid. If that subcontractor is to be replaced, the owner needs to understand that the bid price of an acceptable subcontractor may be higher than that of the original subcontractor—requiring the general contractor to raise its price in turn.

**Contract terms.** It is important that the subcontractors' work be governed by the same rules that apply to the general contractor. Since the owner has no direct contract with subcontractors, provisions in the general conditions of the contract for construction usually require that the subcontractor shall be granted all of the rights against the contractor that the contractor has against the owner. Similarly, the subcontractor shall owe to the contractor all of the duties (within its discipline) that the contractor owes to the owner under the prime (owner-contractor) agreement. The clauses that accomplish this are usually referred to as *pass-through clauses,* and the prime contract is usually incorporated into the subcontract by reference so the subcontractor has the opportunity to know the terms by which it is being bound.

If AIA Document A401 is used, there is consistency of terminology and the necessary pass-through is properly accomplished. Nothing in the AIA General Conditions or in other AIA documents mandates the use of A401, however. In fact, contractors and subcontractors tend to have different opinions about it. A401 includes payment provisions specifying that the subcontractor may require payment from the contractor at a specified time for subcontract work properly performed *whether or not* the contractor has been paid for such work by the owner. Clearly subcontractors tend to favor this kind of pay-when-due clause. General contractors, however, tend to favor pay-when-paid clauses, according to which they are not obligated to pay the subcontractor until the owner has paid them for the work in question. In general, this issue must be resolved between individual contractors and subcontractors.

Many owners require contractors to submit mechanics' lien waivers from all subcontractors with each payment application. These waivers provide assurance that the contractor is paying the subcontractors with the money paid by the owner and that the subcontractors are giving up their rights to mechanics' liens against the owner's property (to the extent they are paid). Some owners even provide for direct disbursement of funds to subcontractors, so they know the subcontractors actually receive the money they pay. The AIA documents allow for such provisions but do not include them per se. If the owner and the owner's legal counsel want to include such provisions in the owner-contractor agreement, they should include them in the supplementary conditions. These are essentially legal matters, and the architect is normally involved only peripherally in drafting and administering them.

Last, owners are concerned about their relationship—or, more precisely, the lack thereof—with the subcontractors in the event that the general contractor defaults or is otherwise unable to complete the project. In most cases, the owner would prefer to have the subcontractors continue to work and to complete their parts of the project as originally planned. However, since the owner has no contracts with the subcontractors, there is a risk that one or more of the subcontractors might refuse to continue or might want to renegotiate. To prevent the disruption that such action would create, the AIA general conditions require the general contractor to assign the subcontracts to the owner (that is, to allow the owner to replace the contractor in the relationship with the subcontractor) contingent upon (1) default by the contractor and (2) agreement by the owner to accept the assignment. Such clauses can substantially minimize the disruption and damage that default by the general contractor could cause.

Subcontractors tend to see themselves at the bottom of the construction food chain with respect to their legal situation. In any event, subcontractors perform a substantial amount of construction work on every project, and owners must be alert to the subcontractors' interests.

### For More Information

Most general law books addressing the practice of architecture include treatises and cases about construction agreements. Some books on construction contract documents provide a good overview of construction agreements as well. For example, consider Waller S. Poage, *The Building Professional's Guide to Contract Documents* (1990).

# 10.4 The AIA Documents

## Dale R. Ellickson, Esq., FAIA

*The AIA documents are powerful tools for capturing and conveying the complex expectations, relationships, responsibilities, and rules that tie together the parties to design and construction.*

Construction is a complicated undertaking. Unlike other commercial transactions, such as buying a car or office equipment, in construction, owners are buying professional services to create a unique product—a building. Even the smallest building projects require the involvement of many people: owners, architects, engineers, general and specialty contractors, suppliers, and perhaps others. Each entity has its own interests and goals.

As construction has become more complex, the industry has come to rely heavily on standardized form contracts. These forms help spell out who does what, when, how, and for how much. They also seek to assign responsibilities and risks fairly to those who are best able to assume them.

## THE DOCUMENTS PROGRAM

For well over a hundred years the AIA has been publishing documents that serve as forms of agreement among the various parties involved in building design and construction.

During this time the diligent efforts and experience of owners, architects, contractors, attorneys, insurance experts, and many others have contributed to the development and revision of the AIA documents. New documents have been added as conditions have changed. Some documents have been developed with, and endorsed by, other industry groups. The AIA documents enjoy a wide reputation for fairness to all parties and are accepted by the construction industry as bases for use in writing and administering project agreements.

The competitive low-bid process heavily influences construction in the United States. Its effect is so sweeping that even when other methods of procurement are used, this open-market approach is reflected in a changing mix—from project to project—of contractors, subcontractors, sub-subcontractors, trades, and so on, down through multiple tiers of participants and their relationships. Often no single person knows all the participants; for instance, it is quite common for off-site fabricators to use intermediary installers and never visit the project premises. This situation introduces more complications into an already complicated process. In addition, confusion and conflict are too often the result when oral or other inadequate agreements are used in isolation from related transactions. An obvious solution is to seek ways to simplify the process. In other countries, regulatory schemes have been introduced to do just that, with the result of limiting and controlling the marketplace. This approach is not well suited to our country's basic philosophies, which stress individual freedom.

The AIA's leadership realized that a systematic solution was needed to coordinate and tie all the parts and participants together. After the initial efforts in the 1800s with the Uniform Contracts proved to be marginally successful, the AIA adopted an approach at its 1906 convention to develop standard documents linked together by a single document for general conditions.

The AIA's rationale for adopting standard documents was based on several ben-

> **"The old idea of a good bargain was a transaction in which one man got the better of another. The new idea of a good contract is a transaction which is good for both parties to it."**
> *Louis Brandeis*

> **The AIA has developed commentaries on AIA documents A201 and B141. These are included on the CD-ROM that accompanies the *Handbook* and may be consulted for detailed explanation and guidance.**

**DALE R. ELLICKSON, ESQ.,** *is a consultant on special construction contracts. He was formerly the counsel for the AIA Contracts Documents Program. As an architect and an attorney, he writes and lectures widely on legal matters for the construction industry.*

## Benefits of the AIA Documents

The AIA documents reflect the collective experience and wisdom of many people and therefore go far beyond what a single mind might, even in good faith, be able to conceive. They are used and emulated more than any other construction industry documents. They have been acclaimed as one of the AIA's most significant long-term contributions to the profession and to the construction industry. AIA documents bring nationwide consistency and predictability to the construction process. They can be easily modified to accommodate individual project demands. Such changes are easily distinguished from the original, printed language. This reduces transactional time and cost.

AIA documents strive to be fair. The AIA seeks to create consensus-based documents that reflect advice from practicing architects, contractors, and engineers, as well as owners, surety bond producers, insurers, and attorneys. AIA documents are written with the specific goal of balancing the interests of all the parties, so that no one interest—including that of architects—is overrepresented.

AIA documents reflect and coordinate industry practice. They present a balanced resolution of interests to keep the project on track. The AIA documents provide "families" of contract forms for practitioners to use in setting up project contract relationships.

AIA documents reflect changing construction practices and technology. They are revised regularly to accommodate changes in professional and industry practices, insurance, and technology.

AIA documents reflect the law. The documents are revised and updated to incorporate changes resulting from court interpretations and rulings, legal precedent, and nuances.

AIA documents are easy to interpret. They use the common meaning of words and phrases. Industry and legal jargon is avoided whenever possible.

*The American Institute of Architects*

---

efits that could be derived from their use. First and foremost, the standard AIA documents bring nationwide consistency and predictability to the construction process. This is achieved by requiring the initial user (that is, the drafter) to restrict its method of completion or modification to one that clearly indicates the changes and differentiates those changes from the standard baseline. Today the most common methods used are (1) filling in blanks or supplements to the paper formats and (2) underlining and strikeover in the electronic formats of AIA documents.

The net result is that the secondary user (that is, the party on the receiving end of the draft) can quickly understand the nature of the changes. Commercial exchanges are simplified and expedited, good-faith dealing is encouraged, and otherwise latent clauses are exposed for scrutiny. This builds trust in the system, which is especially valued by construction contractors who have been given limited time to submit their bids.

A second benefit of standard AIA documents comes from a drafting method that links contract forms to create a family of documents. Again, consistency is enhanced, but in this situation the enhancement is across the various standard contracts that govern the multiple relationships from the highest to lowest tiers. Each participant is expected to act in concert with all others, and no relationship is treated in isolation. Communication and coordination among the many participants on all tiers are encouraged, making it possible to manage the otherwise confusing array of participants.

A third benefit concerns time and money. Over the years, people who use the AIA documents from project to project have gained a great familiarity with them. Many people in the construction industry know the AIA documents so well that all they have to do is look for the changes to understand the essence of a proposed bargain. This group includes people such as lenders, insurers, and sureties, who, although laterally related to the process, have a significant impact on a project's economics. They rely upon the AIA documents to set the standard baselines for their expectations. Based upon this time-tested reliance, the participants use the AIA documents to speed up their transactions.

Users of the AIA documents also save money by reducing their transactional costs. The savings can be as much as a thousandfold when compared with the cost of drafting and negotiating custom-made contracts. Additional transactional savings are achievable with standard AIA documents because the pricing of services and construction work is made more rational. Often when contractors and vendors receive custom-

> ▶ The AIA Documents Program continues to add new families of documents. The C series of interprofessional (architect-consultant and joint venture) agreements was inaugurated in 1963. Construction management and design-build families were added in 1974 and 1985, respectively. A family of small project documents was added in 1993. The electronic version of the AIA documents was also inaugurated by the AIA in 1993.

> ▶ Many organizations and associations are invited to contribute to the documents program, including owners, contractors, lenders, lawyers, insurers, and surety companies. Specific endorsements of individual AIA documents are noted in the documents themselves.

made contracts that may have hidden obligations, they will increase their prices to create contingency funds to deal with the unforeseeable consequences of such contracts. On the other hand, when they encounter a time-tested standard AIA document, such contingencies are often unnecessary. Ultimately the U.S. construction industry benefits from the use of standard AIA documents because of built-in efficiencies fostered by a coordinated and widely recognized system of documentation.

## BASIC DRAFTING RULES

The AIA and its Documents Committee follow several basic axioms in drafting standard agreements among the parties to design and construction projects:

- The AIA documents are intended to reflect the normal, reasonable expectations and actions of the parties to design and construction. To determine these expectations and actions, the AIA considers the customs and practices of the construction industry, gathered on a nationwide basis.
- Risks are allocated to the party that has direct control over that portion of the process. Where no party has direct control, the risks are allocated to the party that is best able to protect against an unexpected loss. When no party has control, the risks are the owner's—the party that started the project and is the ultimate beneficiary of the results.
- Risks are allocated along the lines drawn by case law. When the law is not definite enough, the AIA attempts to provide a solution in the standard forms and model contracts.
- Most AIA documents are standard forms; modifications to them are typically shown in a manner that allows all parties to see clearly the additions to and deletions from the standard provisions. This approach calls any reallocation of duties, responsibilities, and risks to the attention of all parties using the document.

A review of changes in the AIA documents over the years reveals the shifts that have occurred in the conditions under which design and construction take place. One example is the liability climate, and the accompanying sidebar examines some of the conditions leading to the AIA's redefinition of the terms used to describe the architect's role during the construction phase. The process of redefinition continues today.

Drafting and revising documents is a collaborative effort involving the AIA Documents Committee, the AIA staff, outside legal counsel, owners, representatives of other construction industry associations, insurance counsel, and attorneys with special expertise in matters pertaining to the design and construction process.

In addition to legal, liability, and other external influences, much of the intelligence feeding the revision process comes from those who use the documents daily. This information is gained at local, state, and national AIA meetings and from workshops on contracts and liability sponsored by the AIA and by legal, insurance, and construction industry organizations.

Project delivery involves a number of key participants. AIA documents, therefore, are often drafted or revised in collaboration with industry associations such as these:

American Arbitration Association
American Consulting Engineers Council
American Society of Interior Designers
American Specialty Contractors
American Subcontractors Association
Associated General Contractors of America
Construction Specifications Institute
National Society of Professional Engineers
National Association of Surety Bond Producers
Surety Association of America

## Going Beyond Substituting Observation for Supervision: An Example of Change in the AIA Documents

Until 1945 the liability climate within which the architect worked was fairly stable. Under the common-law rule known as "privity of contract," the client was the only party likely to gain a court's permission to sue an architect, because only the client had a sufficient contractual relationship with the architect.

Privity of contract, a nineteenth-century legal concept, was first invoked against plaintiffs to protect a contracting party against remote and unforeseen liability. It was feared that such third-party suits (suits by someone not a party to the contract) would unduly burden commercial transactions. As a result of this rule, architects were generally immune from third-party suits because, by definition, those parties lacked the privity-of-contract relationship with the architect.

With the maturing of the Industrial Age, however, the courts saw less and less need for maintaining the privity rule. It was first put aside in the area of mass-produced manufactured goods, specifically automobiles.

The trend against the rule slowly reached the architectural profession; in the 1950s several landmark cases opened the gates for third-party suits against architects. The privity of contract rule has not fallen entirely by the wayside, but third parties, especially those who have suffered bodily injury, have generally overcome the barrier of this rule.

With the possibility of third-party bodily injury claims against the architect, the AIA started to scrutinize its standard forms of agreement for injudicious language. The first warning of a potential problem came in 1958 from a Louisiana case involving the death of a worker caused by the explosion of a prematurely activated boiler. In that case, known as *Day* v. *National U.S. Radiator,* 241 La. 288, 128 So.2d 660 (1961), the worker's widow claimed the architect was liable because the owner-architect agreement and the general conditions of the contract for construction stipulated that the architect was to provide "supervision of the work" of the contractor.

The plaintiff argued that the word *supervision* meant the architect had a duty to manage, direct, and control the construction work, even though the contract documents clearly impose the duty of superintending the means and methods of construction on the construction contractor. Thus it was argued that Mr.

Day's bodily injury and death were caused by the architect's failure to direct and control the construction in a safe manner pursuant to the contract requirements. The lower appeals court agreed with this argument and found against the architect, but on further appeal to the Louisiana Supreme Court that decision was reversed in favor of the architect.

*Day* alerted the AIA to a potentially serious liability problem. In the 1961 revisions of the owner-architect and general conditions documents, the words *observation* and *observe* were substituted for *supervision* and *supervise* when describing the architect's construction phase services.

The *Day* case proved to be prophetic. In 1967 the Illinois Supreme Court, in *Miller* v. *DeWitt,* 37 Ill. 2d 272, 226 N.E.2d 630 (1967), found an architect negligently liable for failing to "supervise" the work, resulting in bodily injury to several workers when they were caught in a scaffolding collapse.

Some viewed the substitution of *observation* for *supervision* as a retreat from the architect's traditional role, tending to weaken the architect's services during this crucial project phase. However, interpretations of supervision by the courts had begun to broaden that role beyond anything intended by the parties. By avoiding its use, the AIA documents brought the role back to the limits customarily expected by architects (and contractors) during construction.

The story does not end with the *Day* and *Miller* cases. Ironically, the substitution of the term *observation* continued to be misinterpreted by some people, and it became a public relations issue. In 1997, to cure any misimpressions, especially those coming from clients who might think the term *observation* was a reaction against them and was too weak, the AIA dropped the word entirely from its most commonly used documents, A201 and B141. The AIA realized that no single word could adequately substitute for the detailed descriptions of the architect's services during construction administration already found in those documents. Furthermore, architects' services are evolving beyond a narrow, single package of services that assume that one size fits all. Today architects provide a broad range of services during the construction process that are tailored to each client's project.

## PARALLEL STRUCTURE OF THE DOCUMENTS

It is possible to classify the AIA documents into both series and families. Series divide the documents by type (owner-architect, owner-contractor, architect-consultant, etc.). Families, on the other hand, select from each series those documents that have been drafted using linking devices, such as general conditions or parallel phrasing, to support a particular arrangement of contractual relationships.

**AIA documents, especially those that serve as standard forms of agreement, have important legal consequences. They should be used in consultation with an attorney. It is especially important to remember that only attorneys are permitted to prepare contracts to which they are not a party. The owner and the owner's attorney, for example, are responsible for the owner-contractor agreement, the general conditions of the contract for construction, and any supplementary conditions. Agreements that substantially change or reallocate project risks should also be reviewed by the architect's insurance carrier.**

## Document Series

In the first instance, the AIA documents are divided into a number of letter-designated series.

*A series* documents relate to the agreement between the owner and general contractor.

*B series* documents relate to the agreement between the owner and the architect for professional services.

*C series* documents relate to the agreement between the architect and consultants for professional services.

*D series* documents are architect-industry documents.

*G series* documents are contract and office administration forms.

## Document Families

The Documents Finder (Appendix C) lists the documents in each family and helps in selecting the most appropriate family of AIA documents for the project at hand.

When using the documents, it makes sense to see them as groups of families. The choice of delivery approach—the specific allocation of roles, responsibilities, risks, and rewards—for each project influences the family of project agreements needed to carry out the project: What approach will be used to define architecture services? Is there a construction manager? How will the construction contractor be compensated? Is the project for the federal government?

The AIA documents are somewhat unusual, even among standard forms, because groups of documents—families—are drafted using common definitions, general conditions, and parallel phrasing, forming a consistent structure to support all the major relationships on a construction project. For example, consider the following provisions from AIA documents A201 and B141. AIA Document A201-1997, General Conditions of the Contract for Construction, 4.2.2, reads:

> The Architect, as a representative of the Owner, will visit the site at intervals appropriate to the stage of the Contractor's operations (1) to become generally familiar with and to keep the Owner informed about the progress and quality of the portion of the Work completed, (2) to endeavor to guard the Owner against defects and deficiencies in the Work, and (3) to determine in general if the Work is being performed in a manner indicating that the Work, when fully completed, will be in accordance with the Contract Documents.

Document B141-1997, Standard Form of Agreement Between Owner and Architect, 2.6.2.1, reads:

> The Architect, as a representative of the Owner, shall visit the site at intervals appropriate to the stage of the Contractor's operations, or as otherwise agreed by the Owner and Architect in Article 2.8, (1) to become generally familiar with and to keep the Owner informed about the progress and quality of the portion of the Work completed, (2) to endeavor to guard the Owner against defects and deficiencies in the Work, and (3) to determine in general if the Work is being performed in a manner indicating that the Work, when fully completed, will be in accordance with the Contract Documents.

Although the provisions are not identical, the similar phrasing is intentional. Also, the capitalized terms are intended to have the same meaning in both documents. Use of similar phrasing and defined terms is one of two drafting methods that provide linkage and consistency among the various contracts entered into by the players on the construction team. Another method is the use of general conditions for adoption by reference into each of the primary contracts (e.g., owner-contractor, contractor-subcontractor, owner-architect, and architect-consultant agreements).

Of the two methods, parallel drafting is more difficult, but when done well it makes the AIA documents stand head and shoulders above other documents, even custom-made agreements. The A201 family of documents, for instance, currently includes at

**A Series**

Documents relating to the agreement between the owner and general contractor, including:
- Owner-contractor agreements
- General conditions and supplementary conditions for these agreements
- Owner–designer-builder agreements
- Contractor-subcontractor agreements
- Guidance for bidding procedures
- Documents for use in bidding and negotiations, including contractors' prequalification statements, instructions for bidders, and forms for bid, performance, labor, and material bonds

**B Series**

Documents relating to the agreement between the owner and the architect for professional services, including:
- Owner-architect agreements
- Owner–construction manager (CM) agreements
- Designer-builder–architect agreements
- Special-purpose documents, such as the Architect's Qualification Statement and Duties, Responsibilities, and Limitations of Authority of the Architect's Project Representative (a document that specifies the representative's role at the construction site)

**C Series**

Documents relating to the agreement between the architect and consultant for professional services, including standard forms of agreement between the architect and engineer and other consultants, as well as a standard form that may be used for joint ventures among design professionals to provide professional services.

**D Series**

Architect-industry documents, including the industry standard for calculating the architectural area and volume of buildings (AIA Document D101)—essential, for example, for "square foot" budgets or cost estimates—and a detailed project checklist (AIA Document D200) for office project planning and management.

**G Series**

Contract and office administration forms, including:
- Standard forms for use in securing goods and services and administering and closing out project agreements, such as requisitions for land surveys and geotechnical services, changes to design and construction contracts, contractor payment requisitions and approvals, bonds and insurance forms, certificates of substantial completion, and a variety of affidavit, consent, and release forms
- Standard forms for office administration, including project transmittals, various project directories and lists, and employment applications and records

least thirteen documents, all of which need to be drafted fairly close together in time so that users receive a coordinated family when a new edition of A201 is issued.

In addition to the A201 family, the other AIA documents families are

- Interiors family
- Construction management–advisor family
- Construction management–constructor family
- Design-Build family
- Small Project family
- International family

## Mixing Documents

Generally, the instruction sheets to AIA documents warn the user against mixing AIA documents with non-AIA documents. This warning is given because the parallelism found among AIA documents can no longer be relied upon for coordination when these documents are combined with non-AIA agreement forms.

Likewise, if you have been in practice since 1970, you cannot assume that any AIA document can be combined with any other AIA document. For instance, the AIA documents in the CM-advisor family should not be combined with those in the CM-constructor family. While there are some similarities among all AIA documents, the separate families are often based on subtly different assumptions.

Parallel drafting is a great benefit to those using AIA documents, but it can also be a constraint. Changes can be made in the AIA documents, but they should be made cautiously. Never make changes based on purely personal preference for different phrasing. Change for its own sake is dangerous, and you risk losing case law precedents interpreting the AIA phrasing. If you think an AIA document is not clear, it is generally better to modify it as described below rather than to make substitutions.

## USING THE DOCUMENTS

The AIA documents are intended for use as the basis for project agreements and for project and office administration.

### Types of Documents Available

Most of the AIA documents are standard forms (i.e., they are intended to be used as originals for the written contract between the parties), but a few are models for adaptation by the user. All the AIA documents are continually reviewed and revised. Thus, it is essential to secure the current version of each document. AIA documents may be purchased from authorized local distributors of AIA contracts and forms.

***Standard forms of agreement.*** Standard form contracts are widely used in many industries. They save time and money by eliminating the need to draft a new document for every transaction. They can be used as is or modified to accommodate local business and construction practices as well as different project needs.

Modifications to the AIA standard forms must be made very carefully. It is especially important that changes in one agreement be carefully coordinated with all other relevant project agreements within the same family of documents. To modify standard forms:

- Attach supplementary conditions, special conditions, or amendments. For example, AIA Document A201, General Conditions of the Contract for Construction, may be amended by attaching provisions drawn from AIA Document A511, Guide for Supplementary Conditions.
- Write, type, or strike out language directly on the original forms. Take care in making these kinds of changes. Handwritten changes should be initialed by both parties to the contract. Under no circumstances should the original printed language be struck out in any way that renders it illegible; this may raise suspicions of fraudulent concealment or suggest that the completed and signed document has been tampered with.
- Do not retype standard form documents. Not only is retyping a violation of copyright, but it may introduce typographical errors and cloud the legal interpretation of a standard clause. Retyping also eliminates one of the principal advantages of standard form documents: By merely reviewing the modifications to the standard form, persons familiar with the document can quickly understand the nature of the changes. Contracting parties can more confidently and fairly measure their risks.

***Model forms.*** A few of the AIA documents are model forms—that is, they are reservoirs of suggested language the drafting party may or may not choose to include in a final written contract. Unlike standard forms of agreement (in which the user fills in the blanks and modifications are clearly evident), language selected from a model form is integrated into a contract being drafted by the user.

### Copying the AIA Documents

Most AIA documents are copyrighted under the name of the AIA national organization. As owner of the copyright, the national AIA has the exclusive right to make copies,

At this writing the AIA publishes more than 75 standard and model documents. Samples of the A, B, C, D, and G series of those documents are included in the CD-ROM provided with the *Handbook.*

AIA Document A511, Guide for Supplementary Conditions, is a model form. It includes suggested language for use in modifying AIA Document A201, General Conditions of the Contract for Construction.

Contact the AIA at (800) 242-3837 for information on AIA Contracts Documents: Electronic Format.

authorize the making of copies by others, prepare derivative works, and distribute copies, except as limited under the laws of the United States. The AIA grants licenses to reproduce the documents under the conditions specified.

The purpose of protecting the language of the AIA documents is multifold: to permit those who use the documents to rely upon their standardized content, to protect the user from the consequences of unauthorized reproduction, and to protect the good name and reputation of the AIA (as well as its interest in its work product).

The consequences of unauthorized reproduction may be minor ones arising from errors in transcription, or they may be major ones arising from an intent to deceive. Either way, it is in the interest of both the party offering the document as the basis for an agreement and the party considering that offer to use the original AIA standard form documents. Both parties are thus assured that the terms are accurately represented and fair, and they are spared the expense of exhaustively researching the document.

## Electronic Documents

In 1993 the AIA started licensing subscribers to use its documents in an electronic format. Designed to work with standard office equipment in the design and construction industry, the electronic format of the AIA contract documents allows users to call up the AIA documents, fill in project-specific data, and modify the standard text as required for each project. Inserted text is underlined or printed in a special font, and deletions are indicated by lining through the standard text. This approach shows clearly the changes to the standard text and preserves the commercial benefits of the standard documents.

# Intellectual Property and the Architect

*Dale R. Ellickson, Esq., FAIA*

Ideas are an architect's stock-in-trade. Traditionally they have been expressed through drawings and other documentation. According to the AIA standard forms of agreement, drawings, specifications, and other documentation are "instruments of the architect's service" and thus belong to the architect. The copyright laws also protect intellectual works generated by an architect's practice, such as written reports and specifications, models, artistic renderings, computer programs, and electronically recorded or produced documents.

In addition to the right to own the physical drawings or other intellectual works, the architect holds the copyright to them. The copyright gives the architect the exclusive right to authorize the reproduction of the copyrighted work, the preparation of derivative works, and the public display of the copyrighted work. The copyright remains with the architect (i.e., author) unless it is transferred by written agreement to another party. However, if the work is created "within the scope of employment" (i.e., an employer-employee relationship) or under a contract that specifies it is a "work made for hire," the copyright belongs to the employer or other party to the contract, respectively.

In 1990 Congress passed the Architectural Works Copyright Protection Act. This statute amended the U.S. Copyright Act and took effect on December 1, 1990. It expanded the copyrights available to architects to include the protection of the architectural design as expressed in the building itself. An architect may now claim copyrights based upon several categories of intellectual works found in the Copyright Act. Works that can be copyrighted include:

- Drawings (under the graphics works and architectural works categories)
- Specifications and written reports (under the literature category)
- Models (under the sculptural works category)
- Presentation renderings when made for limited distribution (under the artistic works category)
- Electronic software (under the computer software category)
- Building design (under the architectural works category)

The AIA often receives inquiries about copyrights. Some of the most frequently asked questions include the following.

**Q.** *Must an architect have a written agreement with the client to retain the ownership or copyright of the drawings and other documentation?*

**A.** It is best to state the architect's ownership in the written agreement. Some courts still confuse the right to ownership of the documents with the right to copy them even though Congress has clearly established that these are two separate rights under the U.S. copyright laws. Also, some court cases have concluded erroneously that the architect was selling a product (the drawings) rather than a service. Placing the architect's right to ownership in the agreement for services removes any ambiguity.

**Q.** *When does the copyright come into being?*

**A.** A copyright exists in an intellectual work at the moment of its creation. Drawings are created on the date they are completed. A building is probably created on the date of substantial completion; a precise definition is not included in the 1990 act.

**Q.** *How do I indicate the copyright?*

**A.** It is good practice to place an appropriate copyright notice on all design and construction documents that leave the office. Three forms of correct copyright notice are:

© 1994 John Doe

Copyright 1994, JD, Inc.

Copyr. 1994 JDI

If the firm's initials are used, they should be readily recognizable to the public as identifying the business. (Irving B. Mills, architect, should not use his initials!) Including the notice in the body of a document may be good practice, since a title block can easily be stripped away.

**Q.** *Do I need to register the copyright?*

**A.** To obtain full protection under the copyright laws, an architect must give adequate notice to other parties that copyright is claimed—hence the copyright notice just discussed—and apply for and obtain registration with the U.S. Copyright Office. Failing to do this does not forfeit the right to the copyright but can put the architect at a disadvantage, if all procedures are followed correctly. The copyright law grants more remedies, including your attorney's fees and statutory damages up to $20,000 for ordinary infringement, which requires only evidence of infringement to justify their award.

**Q.** *How do I register the copyright?*

**A.** It requires completing a form and submitting copies of the materials to be copyrighted along with a filing fee. (For copyrighting a built architectural work, photographs of the building are required.) Separate applications for each category of copyright are required. Request the appropriate forms and instructional materials (such as Circular 41 and Information Packet 115) from the U.S. Copyright Office, Library of Congress, Washington, DC 20559-6000, or call (202) 479-0700 or go to its Web site at http://lcweb.loc.gov/copyright/.

**Q.** *When is it too late to register my copyright?*

**A.** The copyright law requires registration within five years after publication of the work. (In the case of architecture "publication" means public presentation of the work.) To obtain full protection under the copyright law, including your attorney's fees and statutory damages, file within three months of publication.

**Q.** *Once I have registered the copyright, what rights do I have?*

**A.** When an architect registers a copyrighted work, he or she generally has the exclusive right to make copies or derivative versions of that work. If the copyright remains with the original author, the life of the copyright spans the author's life plus 50 years. If the copyright is transferred as a "work made for hire," it has a 75-year duration from the date of first publication.

Q. *How does the Architectural Works Copyright Act of 1990 protect a building design?*

A. The act protects "the overall form as well as the arrangement and composition of spaces and elements." The legislative history of the act indicates that Congress intended to focus on the "poetic language" of architecture. The language of the act is so sweeping that it could extend to otherwise unprotected elements that are selected, coordinated, and arranged in an original way; new design elements incorporated into otherwise standard building features; and interior elements of architecture. On the other hand, Congress did not intend to protect elements that are "intrinsic to the building in its most basic form—determined by pragmatic, constructional, and technical requirements." Thus an exception is made for "standard feature" building components such as stock doors and windows. Also, "generally, functional elements whose placement is dictated by utilitarian concerns are not included and neither are bridges, cloverleafs, dams, or walkways."

The act places two other limitations on an exclusive architectural copyright. First, photographs and other representations may be made without prior permission from the architect (i.e., author) as long as the built work is within public view (i.e., on a public right-of-way). Second, the owner of the building has the right to alter or destroy the building without the architect's permission.

Q. *What if someone takes one of my copyrighted drawings and makes a small change in it?*

A. If it is apparent to a reasonable person that the altered work was derived from the initial, copyrighted work and the alleged infringement was by someone having prior knowledge of the copyrighted work, the copyright protection is unchanged. The architect whose copyright is infringed may take legal action against the other party for infringement.

Q. *If I sell my drawings, do I also sell the copyright?*

A. Assuming that you have taken the appropriate steps to protect your copyright, the selling of the physical work does not necessarily transfer with it the right to copy that work. The Copyright Act of 1976 clearly makes a copyright a separate claim from that of ownership. It is important to note that as long as you retain the copyright, you retain control over the licensing of copies or derivatives of that work. You can assign limited rights through a licensing agreement, not only to the number of copies but also to the purpose for which they may be made. For instance, in AIA Document B141-1997, Standard Form of Agreement Between Owner and Architect, the architect grants the owner a limited license to use the copyrightable drawings and specifications in construction and maintenance of the project so long as the owner is not in breach of the contract. Furthermore, the architect is required to obtain simi-

larly limited licenses from the architect's consultants for use of their intellectual works.

Q. *Can I sell or otherwise transfer my copyright?*

A. Of course you can. That is a business decision. Be sure to scrutinize your owner-architect agreement before signing any copyright transfers. If the client requests or demands a transfer of ownership and copyrights for the documents and the design, be sure the firm will not be hindered in using derivatives of those materials on subsequent projects for other clients.

An architect's stock-in-trade is often displayed in the style he or she has adopted in drawings and building design. Since style is embodied in copyrighted works, be careful about any blanket transfers of copyright that might prohibit you from continued use of a style. Also, do not agree to transfer any copyright of your consultants until you check your architect-consultant agreements to verify your right to do so.

Q. *What happens if I take over from another architect?*

A. If the client and the first architect signed an AIA standard form of owner-architect agreement, that architect owns the drawings even if they are not protected through copyright registration. It is important that you get permission to use the drawings from the first architect.

Q. *If I am the first architect, do I have any liability exposure if I sell my drawings or license use of them to another architect who completes the project?*

A. You may. You created the initial work, and you may be held liable for any latent or patent errors in that work, even though you might have discovered them if you had been retained for the entire project. It is possible to obtain contractual limitations of liability from the owner, but it is best do this before you transfer the right to use your drawings.

Q. *If I am the second architect, do I have any potential liability exposure?*

A. Yes. The second architect has adopted and blended the first architect's work into his or her own work and has the same responsibility for it as would have been the case had it been produced in his or her own office—unless there is a clear demarcation between the two works, such as when the first architect's work deals with the building shell and the second architect's work deals with the interiors. If the two works are clearly separate efforts, the drawings and credits, as well as their title and seals, should reflect this separation.

Q. *What is the best way to administer the copyright process in the firm?*

A. Consider appointing one person in the office to handle all copyright matters. A log should be maintained showing registration dates and distributions made of any published or unpublished work.

*Dale R. Ellickson, Esq., FAIA, is a consultant on special construction contracts. He was formerly the counsel for the AIA Contracts Documents Program. As an architect and an attorney, he writes and lectures widely on legal matters for the construction industry.*

# 11 Risk Management

## 11.1 Risk Management Strategies

### Richard B. Garber, ASLA, and Charles R. Heuer, Esq., FAIA

*The early identification and appropriate allocation of risk among informed project participants can contribute significantly to the success of a project.*

Risk, the probability of an unfavorable outcome, is inherent in all business endeavors. However, design projects leading to construction are particularly risky. Even though an architect can transfer some risk through insurance, he or she will still face a significant threat to the firm's financial viability from disputes, claims, and write-offs. Thus for each project an architect will need to implement strategies that minimize the probability and severity of an unfavorable outcome at the lowest long-term cost to the firm.

### INITIAL RISK ASSESSMENT

Cost-effective risk management begins before an architect initiates services for a particular project. Architects who conduct reasonable evaluations of potential projects and clients and then prepare carefully thought-out, well-written proposals should have few problems. Even though risk cannot be avoided, it can usually be managed and mitigated successfully when addressed in a timely and appropriate manner.

All projects should pass through an initial triage phase during which an architect considers whether the project meets the firm's essential practice goals, profitability objectives, and risk tolerance. This initial activity is sometimes overlooked because of the euphoria accompanying an opportunity or because of the architect's real or perceived inability to challenge unreasonable or unrealistic requirements.

Risk is generated or influenced by the interplay of a variety of client, firm, and project characteristics, as well as the environment in which the services will be performed. At a minimum, firms should always examine:

- *The nature of the project.* This includes scope, site, budget, and schedule; community sensitivity or opposition; unusual regulatory requirements; or a history of repetitive litigation.
- *The firm's capabilities and experience.* Does the firm have the appropriate design expertise and time available for the project?
- *Specific client attributes.* Look at the client's attitude, funding, understanding of the nature of professional services, and sophistication.

RICHARD V. GARBER *is vice president for AEC risk management services at Victor O. Schinnerer & Company, Inc., and underwriting manager for the AIA's commended program of professional liability insurance.* CHARLES R. HEUER *is principal of the Heuer Law Group and principal of Covenants, a design and construction management consulting firm.*

- *Construction industry factors.* Consider influences on project delivery such as contractor selection process, the involvement of other parties during design and construction, and the state of the local construction economy.
- *Constraints on time and cost.* This includes compensation for design services, project budget, and scheduling constraints.
- *Forces external to design and construction.* Take into account the general economic climate, the attitude of the community and the government to new projects, the overall political climate, and laws, rules, and regulations that might be forthcoming.

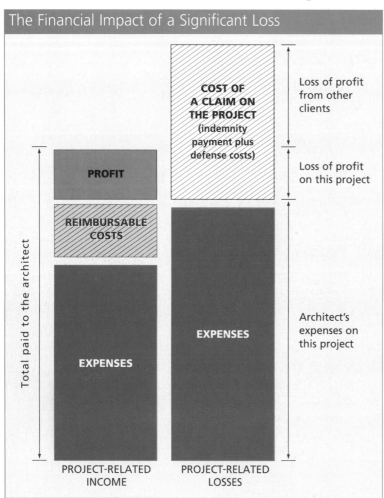

## The Financial Impact of a Significant Loss

**COST OF A CLAIM ON THE PROJECT** (indemnity payment plus defense costs)

Loss of profit from other clients

Loss of profit on this project

**PROFIT**

**REIMBURSABLE COSTS**

**EXPENSES**

Total paid to the architect

PROJECT-RELATED INCOME

**EXPENSES**

Architect's expenses on this project

PROJECT-RELATED LOSSES

Once an architect has completed an initial risk identification and assessment, he or she will be in a better position to determine the firm's interest in pursuing the project further and identify prospective team members and other project stakeholders who can contribute to a complete assessment of risk and the development of risk-response strategies. This more complete assessment is referred to here as the preproposal evaluation.

## PREPROPOSAL EVALUATION OF THE PROJECT

The preproposal evaluation is best conducted through the combined efforts of those who will be involved with the project—the staff who will interact with the client, consultants, and construction contractors. Their combined experience offers the best source of guidance on both known sources of risk and situations that might present unusual or new problems. Generally, the following issues should be addressed as part of the firm's preproposal evaluation:

**Type of project.** Historically, some building project types have a relatively high incidence of claims. Condominiums are a typical example. The architect's client and the ultimate user of the condominium project are typically not the same persons or entities. The users sometimes have distinctly different goals and requirements than do the clients. The architect may satisfy the client and then be sued by the users. Some architects might decide to avoid these types of projects altogether. Others are willing to accept the risk, partly because they have learned how to manage it and partly because the rewards are perceived as outweighing the risk, including the cost of mitigation.

The key is to identify the source of risk and respond to it with an affirmative risk management strategy. A common strategy used by architects experienced in serving condominium clients is to systematically document the recommendations made to the client. The client's instructions and decisions to accept or reject these recommendations should be recorded. While claims may not be completely avoided, architects are in a far better position to defend themselves against a claim and therefore are a much less attractive target for a potential claimant.

**Type of construction contract.** Claims statistics indicate that there is greater potential for disputes on projects with competitively bid construction contracts, rather than negotiated or cost-plus-fee contracts. A contractor who is awarded a fixed-price contract based on a competitive bid has an interest in doing the work inexpensively and in doing the least amount of work that will meet the owner's and the architect's requirements. The owner and architect, however, are interested in obtaining the designed and specified work without reduction in quantity or quality and without additional work.

The difference in interests creates an inherent tension in the relationship that often results in dispute. These disputes frequently involve the content of the construction contract documents or the quality of the construction contract administration services of the architect. Therefore these owner-contractor disputes tend to embroil the architect. This situation is often made worse because it can frequently be difficult to limit the bidding to contractors who are appropriately prequalified; thus it is harder to predict the contractor's abilities and experience. Obviously, architects are not going to avoid all projects that are to be competitively bid. Knowing the increased risk profile, however, will permit the architect to adjust, as he or she sees fit, the amount of detail in the drawings and specifications to minimize questions and disputes during bidding and construction. Also, the architect should communicate and document the fair and objective administration of the construction contract.

*Track record.* It is often advisable to investigate the track record of a potential new client. This is probably more of a factor with developers or corporate clients with continuing building programs, but it is even wise to do so with infrequent corporate or institutional clients. Colleagues and contractors may have worked with the potential client in the past and can provide personal insight about the quality of the professional relationship, whether or not bills were paid in a timely manner, and the client's attitude toward risk allocation.

Architects should also be alert to the "naive" client. Clients that have never been involved in a construction project before are more prone to be involved in disputes than more experienced clients. They may have unrealistic expectations of the architect and of the design and construction process. In addition, such clients may not have financial resources commensurate with their dreams. These types of clients tend to be easily disappointed, which can lead to disputes. Architects should frequently verify that a client understands the implications of the various decisions and approvals that a client must make during the design and construction process, as an uninformed consent may not really be consent at all.

The antithesis of the naive client is the "sharp" client. These clients may insist on a form of agreement that is substantially and unreasonably weighted in their favor. Such an agreement often includes a variety of broad-form warranties as well as indemnification clauses and provisions that raise the standard of professional skill and care by which the architect will be evaluated. Many of these types of problems or concerns can be mitigated during contract negotiation if they have been previously flagged for attention.

*Financial capability and integrity.* In commercial transactions, credit checks and financial investigation in conjunction with sales are commonplace. After all, in most cases architects effectively extend credit to clients when they begin work. Even if an advance payment is received, effort and expenses are normally performed or incurred prior to the time when the first invoice is due for payment. Governmental clients whose projects are publicly funded present a different challenge. Generally it is the architect's responsibility to verify that money has been appropriated to pay for the contemplated design services and that related matters are completed so that money is actually on hand.

*Claims history.* Just as certain types of projects have a history of claims associated with them, so do specific clients. Some clients are more litigious than others. It is possible to investigate the court records in your area or in the client's home area to determine the incidence of litigation to which the potential client was a party. Although arbitration cases are not a matter of public record, the architect's attorney may know or be able to informally determine the reputation of the client is in this regard. Word of mouth among colleagues is also valuable.

*Approach to professional compensation.* Some clients solicit bids for design services. Other clients negotiate compensation with the architect on the basis of professional qualifications, the nature of the project, the extent and type of services that will be required, and costs. The latter approach, sometimes referred to as qualification-based selection, is the superior method. In fact, architects are not fungible commodities (goods or services that will be exactly the same whether purchased from one firm or another, with selection based only on price). Each brings to the table unique experiences and abilities. When one considers that clients for professional services are, essentially, buying the skill and judgment of the architect, there can be little doubt that a system focusing on qualifications is more likely to produce a suitable matching of client, project, and architect. As the cost of an architect's services are such a small fraction of the life cycle costs of a project, a principal focus on the cost of services is generally not justified, even in economic terms.

Clients who do solicit bids for services could be raising warning flags for architects. It should be a red flag to the architect, for example, if a client solicits bids because he or she is short of funds and is trying to get the project "on the cheap." It may also indicate that the potential client does not understand the essential nature of professional services. If the potential client sees the services as fungible items, there may be tension in the relationship. Sometimes these concerns can be eliminated or mitigated by frank discussion

## Identifying, Assessing, and Managing Project Risk

Project risk management is a four-part process: identifying, assessing, responding to, and controlling the risk so that a project can be undertaken successfully and profitably. This list of questions is based on the CNA/Schinnerer Guidelines for Improving Practice risk management matrix that was developed from an analysis of claims data and surveys of practitioners. This list of questions can help you identify and quantify risk and then find techniques to manage it. When properly implemented, this approach can help individual members of the same firm address risk management from a common perspective.

### Client

- Will the client be able to afford your firm's services? The project? You may be able to obtain a financial report on your client to help you assess its financial strength.
- Are the client's objectives for the project clear? It may be prudent to first assist the client in defining objectives in order to avoid shooting at a moving target later.
- Is the client familiar with the construction process in general? This type of project specifically? You have probably already found that some clients require more attention than others do.
- Is this a repeat client with whom you've had an opportunity to establish a general rapport and a comfort level regarding the construction process?
- Does this client have a reputation for being difficult to work with or for making claims against design professionals? Investigating how the client has handled other projects or business disputes can give you a feel for how cooperative the client may be.
- Does this client comprise a committee (school boards, homeowners associations, civic or religious groups, or even a couple) that could be troublesome unless a single decisive decision maker is appointed?
- Are the client's expectations realistic? Do you have a good feeling about the client? Are there open lines of communications between you?

### Project

- Does this project type have more risk than others? Residential (particularly condominium) projects, large public use centers, and land/site development projects have the highest number of claims.
- Do the size and/or duration of the project pose additional risks? In general, the larger the project or the longer its duration, the greater the risk will be.
- Does the client have adequate funding or is it attainable? How does the client anticipate managing cash flow? If the client is a governmental entity, has funding been authorized and appropriated?
- Will your fee be adequate for the services required? Will it cover costs and provide a profit?
- Are there fee provisions for changed circumstances and additional services?
- Does the proposed professional service agreement provide a clear and sufficiently detailed scope of services?
- Is your firm capable of managing the required complexity of the design?
- Is the project team capable of managing the complexity of the construction?
- Are there unique project requirements that could pose more risk? For example, is it a new or state-of-the-art type of project?
- Will you be hired to provide the full scope of services you think is needed for the project? Will you be providing at least some construction phase services so that your presence at the construction site can help to mitigate potential problems or losses?
- Are there particular scheduling issues—such as meeting a developer's projections for selling the property—that may increase the risk? Is the overall project time frame adequate?
- Will new products or technologies be required or expected in the design and construction of the project? Have these products or technologies been adequately researched and tested?
- Are you comfortable with the mode of project delivery (design-bid-build, design-build, etc.)? Have the roles and responsibilities of the parties been adequately defined?

with the potential client or through terms in the professional service agreement that will eventually be executed. However, the architect should be cautious if the client's concern for cost overshadows such considerations as scope, quality, and time.

## YOUR RISK MANAGEMENT PLAN

The development of a project-specific risk management plan proceeds hand in glove with the firm's preproposal project evaluation. Essentially, the risk management plan articulates the affirmative actions the firm believes necessary to respond effectively to sources of risk identified, assessed, and short-listed for response during the preproposal project evaluation. Once the firm has gone through the process of identifying risk factors and assessing their impact, it must explore the options available for managing the

- Are there geographic considerations (e.g., earthquakes, hurricanes, mud slides, freezing temperatures) that may increase the risk?
- Are there environmental issues that you know or suspect may arise in the course of the project? Is the project team prepared to address them?
- Is there any perceived opposition or sensitivity in the community that could pose problems?

### Your Firm

- Does your firm have the capacity to undertake the project? If you do not have a sufficient number of qualified employees, can you supplement your existing staff by hiring additional employees or consultants?
- Does your firm—and do the available project team members—have sufficient positive experience with this project type? Under similar conditions?

### Consultants

- Are there qualified consultants with strong, positive reputations?
- Does your firm have experience with these consultants? If not, do you think you can develop compatible working relationships?
- Are these consultants adequately insured? The gap created by an uninsured or underinsured consultant will most likely have to be filled by your firm's insurance or assets.
- Do these consultants have capacity to provide services for this project at this time?
- Are your firm's systems compatible with those of your consultants?
- Do your consultants share the same values as your firm? How much time will you have to devote to team building?
- Are any special/high-risk consultants required? To the best of your knowledge, are these consultants capable? Are you accepting any vicarious liability for these consultants, and if so, are you appropriately compensated and protected?

### Contractor

- Will there be a construction manager? Has the construction manager's role been adequately defined? Is the construction manager sufficiently qualified to undertake this role?
- Will some contractors be prequalified? If so, in your professional opinion, are there acceptable considerations in formulating the list of prequalified firms?
- How will the bidding process be undertaken, and how will the bids be awarded?
- Do you believe you will have sufficient input in assisting the owner in reviewing the bids and selecting the contractor?
- Is the contractor bidding responsibly?
- Has the contractor demonstrated adequate financial strength to procure the necessary bonds and to complete the project?
- Does the contractor have sufficient experience with this project type and the anticipated site conditions?

### Contract

- Do all of the proposed contract forms (e.g., owner-architect, architect-consultant, owner-contractor) establish clear and distinct responsibilities balanced by the authority to carry out those responsibilities?
- Are the payment terms clearly delineated, including those for additional services and reimbursable expenses?
- Is there a provision that establishes fair terms for terminating the contract should that become necessary?
- Does the contract contain a dispute resolution provision (e.g., good-faith negotiation, mediation, or arbitration) that is fair and balanced?
- Does the overall contract fairly allocate risks and rewards? In some cases, imbalances may be addressed by negotiating well-drafted indemnification or limitation-of-liability clauses.
- Are there provisions that create insurance coverage questions or uninsurable exposures? You may wish to ask a representative of your insurance carrier to review any questionable provisions.

*Katherine Davitt Enos, Assoc. AIA, Esq.,*
*Victor O. Schinnerer & Company, Inc.*

risk. The basic options should be well understood within firm management and in many cases should be a matter of discussion and perhaps negotiation with the client.

Risk management is not a reactive process that is employed once a problem has surfaced; it is a proactive effort to identify the best method to control the risk environment in which a design professional practices. The prudent management of risk, as reflected in a project-specific risk management plan, allows a firm to pursue its practice objectives and not ignore professional opportunities because of unfounded concerns. The key in accepting risk is understanding the risk, securing authority to deal with the risk, and obtaining the compensation that makes accepting the risk a sound business decision.

## CONFIRMATION DURING THE PROPOSAL PHASE

After evaluating the type of project and the potential client and deciding to pursue them, other aspects come to the forefront for consideration and review. The proposal stage is really the unofficial commencement of contract negotiations. Frequently, the essential elements of the eventual professional service agreement are established at this time, and that should not happen without adequate thought. Consideration of the following is essential.

***Compatibility with staff size and experience.*** When considering and preparing a proposal for a new project, objectively evaluate whether your present staff is large enough to handle the added responsibilities. Rapid growth, which can stretch trained supervisory and coordination personnel to the limit, frequently contributes to quality problems. This is not to say that slow and incremental growth is the only alternative. An objective analysis may indicate that more time and money will have to be allocated to help compensate for the introduction of new staff members and the increased load on the firm's management systems. The same considerations apply to a prime professional's consultants because a troubled consultant is a threat to the success of the project's entire design team.

***Scope and nature of services.*** Clearly, the scope and nature of the services being requested or proposed are extremely important parts of any proposal. The easiest part of preparing the proposal from a risk management perspective is the description of services. Principals and managers know what the firm is willing to do and what they feel comfortable doing. But they should be cautious. Rules of professional practice in most states mandate that a professional not take on services that are not within his or her sphere of professional competence. That sphere can be enlarged considerably, however, through the use of consultants.

***Adequacy of project information.*** On most projects it is assumed that a client will provide certain types of information about the project and the proposed site. That information usually includes a program that sets forth a client's objectives, schedule, constraints, and design criteria. Under the consensus AIA contracts, a client is expected to furnish surveys describing the physical characteristics, legal limitations, and utility locations for the site, as well as geotechnical engineering services. When project information is comprehensive, well coordinated, and available early, the client and the architect can obtain a better mutual understanding of their goals and expectations, as well of as the attendant risk. A proposal structured to reflect that understanding is more likely to lead to a mutually rewarding project. In many ways that is the essence of risk management. When project scope, schedule, and budget are appropriately related and are determined early in the project, claims and disputes are minimized.

***Adequacy of professional compensation.*** In general, architects strive to do a proper professional job on all commissions, regardless of the amount of compensation involved. However, it would be unrealistic to expect that a firm can provide proper services without obtaining adequate payment. Too little compensation or a lack of coordination and communication with consultants, clients, and contractors can lead to mistakes. Before accepting proposed compensation, architects should make sure that it is adequate for the services to be rendered and that additional compensation will be received if additional services are required.

***Adequacy of the construction budget and project budget.*** Many owner expectations about a design and construction project are revealed by the budget for the project. If an owner's budget expectations are not met, several undesirable results are possible, including the possible abandonment of the project, incomplete payment to the architect, or litigation. Architects should strive to satisfy themselves at the proposal stage that (1)

## Client-Selected Consultants

When an architect agrees to provide services for a client, that architect takes the same level of responsibility for the service whether the service is performed directly by the architect or by a subconsultant. The legal concept of vicarious liability is the imposition of liability on one party, in this case the prime architect, for the conduct of another party, the subconsultant, based solely on the relationship between the two parties.

The legal system strives for efficiency; holding one party vicariously responsible for the acts of another eliminates the need to apportion fault. The most common vicarious liability situation is the responsibility of an employer for the acts of its employees committed in the scope of employment. This concept extends to the negligence of a subconsultant providing services through a prime consultant.

For various reasons, a client may want specific consultants as part of the professional service team. A prudent architect may contract directly with the consultants or arrange for them to contract directly with the client so that the architect is not vicariously liable for the actions of the consultants.

The latter arrangement may necessitate greater coordination of the independent services of the client-selected consultants. The prime architect's coordination of the documentation requires careful attention, and this service should be appropriately compensated. Because the architect does not have authority over the independent consultants' services,

the architect should not be held responsible for their accuracy. In an arrangement where the client is contracting directly with individual consultants, each of them should be acknowledged as being able to rely on the technical sufficiency and timely delivery of documents and services furnished by the others.

Clients can select specific consultants if they wish to contract separately for the services of consultants. In the case of having separate contracts for different design and engineering disciplines, the client must have a carefully developed multiple prime agreement. In such cases, the independent architects or other service providers should be required to coordinate their instruments of service through a designated prime consultant. The scope of review by the coordinating entity should be carefully described.

Moreover, it would be appropriate for the client to agree to indemnify the architect for any costs resulting from the negligence of the independent consultants. In addition, it may be prudent to require the client to indemnify and hold the individual consultants harmless from claims, costs, losses, or damages to them resulting from the negligence of the client's other consultants, since they have no independent capability to evaluate the accuracy of the results, services, and other consultants or the responsibility for such services.

*Frank Musica, Assoc. AIA, Esq.,*
*Victor O. Schinnerer & Company, Inc*

they understand the proposed construction budget, (2) they do not confuse the *construction* budget with the *project* budget, and (3) the budget is reasonable for the scope and nature of the project under consideration. If the budget is not adequate, there is the possibility that disputes will result and that the client will fail to pay for services rendered.

**Adequacy of time allowed for design and construction**. Rushing to comply with an unrealistically short design deadline will increase the likelihood of design errors and omissions, which may lead to construction defects and deficiencies. Moreover, a compressed time schedule can actually result in slowing down some of the work as trades overlap in congested areas and efficiency is diminished.

**Extent of construction phase services**. Some architects feel that cutting back on construction phase services decreases their professional liability exposure. Today that theory is not widely supported. Rather, there is more risk of professional liability claims and disputes if the architect is not engaged to perform construction phase services, is engaged to perform some of the services, or if a separate entity altogether is engaged to perform construction phase services.

If the architect is not performing construction administration services substantially similar to those described in the AIA agreement forms, there are a number of likely results:

• First, the drawings and specifications prepared by the architect might not be used as intended or substantially adhered to by the contractor. If problems subsequently occur with the construction, the architect may be embroiled in allegations that the documents were negligently prepared. The architect will have to conduct a defense without the benefit of having observed the construction. If the documents were not properly followed, the architect will generally not have any liability but will still have had to incur legal fees and expend the time and effort associated with defending against the charges.

• Second, there will be no opportunity before construction to find and correct possible errors or omissions in the construction documents. Clearly, correcting problems with an eraser is much cheaper, faster, and easier than correcting them with a jackhammer in the field. If the architect is not involved in the construction contract administration, the chance to avoid or mitigate the effects of any problems with the construction documents is lost.

• Third, if the architect does not evaluate the work of the contractor as it progresses, he or she loses the opportunity to have construction defects and deficiencies corrected before it is too late. Without this opportunity, the architect will be forced to try to prove in subsequent litigation that the problem was the result of construction deficiencies and not design. That may be possible, but the effort and expense might well have been avoided in the first place if the architect had performed usual construction contract administration services.

## ADDRESSING CONTRACT TERMS AND CONDITIONS

Many requests for proposals include proposed terms and conditions and ask an architect to indicate any provisions to which he or she takes exception. Frequently this poses a dilemma for the architect since the rules of the selection process may downgrade those who state any exceptions. Further, not all exceptions are equal: Some require only innocuous semantic changes, while others are deal breakers unless the original provisions can be substantially modified. Rarely would one want to be eliminated from consideration because of objections to precise terms and conditions without the opportunity to discuss and negotiate changes directly with the client.

Generally it is helpful to cite as few provisions as possible and then to explain what is objectionable. It is not productive to suggest specific changes at that point. Often it is sufficient simply for the architect to say that he or she feels confident that differences can be worked out in personal negotiation after being selected for the project. However, if a client proposes terms and conditions on a take-it-or-leave-it basis, it may raise substantial concerns about the client's approach to business. In particular, architects should be alert for the following provisions.

***Indemnification or hold-harmless clauses.*** These are essentially clauses that shift risk from one party to another. Frequently they demand more of the architect than the law would otherwise require. For example, the common law requires architects to be responsible for damages caused by his or her own negligence. Such damages are covered by normal professional liability insurance. If the architect is asked to indemnify for more than that, the indemnification obligation is broader than required under the common law and the contractual liability coverage afforded by professional liability insurance.

***Express guarantees or warranties.*** These kinds of clauses can impose liability on the architect even if services were performed in accordance with normal professional skill and care and were not negligently done or otherwise faulty. Generally, under the common law, there is no implied warranty associated with professional services other than that they will not be negligently performed. This is largely because such services are based on judgment, expertise, skill, and reasoning applied to a specific project. Accordingly, a warranty or guarantee is neither realistic nor effective. For those reasons, express warranties or guarantees are excluded from coverage under professional liability policies.

***Time limitations.*** Many clients attempt to force specific time limitations on architects or to impose late-performance penalties. Of course, timing issues are very important to clients, but schedules must be reasonable and adjustable to account for events beyond the architect's control. Arbitrary attention to interim deadlines may only translate into more adjustments later. Additionally, time-is-of-the-essence clauses convert any delay into a material breach of contract that might justify termination by a client. Clients should understand the necessary balance between adhering to a schedule and exercising sound professional judgment.

***Standard of care.*** The normal, legally mandated standard of care requires architects not to be negligent. If a client expects the "highest professional standard" or "perfect" services, that expectation may inspire the architect, but it will probably not be achievable. Objective and measurable standards are generally not appropriate for professional services, which require judgments unique to the circumstances of each project.

***Verification of owner-supplied information.*** Often a client will supply information but not allow the architect to rely on its accuracy or completeness. If the information is outdated or otherwise suspect, it may be prudent for the client to pay to have the information updated or verified. The client may or may not choose to do so, but the architect should not be required to accept responsibility for the accuracy or completeness of information that he or she did not generate or was not paid to verify. The client should assume the risks associated with deficiencies in the information it provides.

## CONTRACT NEGOTIATIONS

If the architect remembers that the proposal stage is the beginning of contract negotiations and responds with the appropriate level of detail to proposed terms and conditions, it will stand a better chance of not being eliminated from consideration and yet not prejudicing future specific contract negotiations. The proposal stage, therefore, is an opportunity to address any known client terms and conditions that are objectionable. If accepted by the client, the proposal may be considered the basis of the contract between the parties. Whether or not that is the case, clients sometimes require that the architect's proposal be incorporated into the professional service agreement that is subsequently prepared. Once the contract negotiation stage is reached, the risk management plan enters a new level.

For a contract to represent the agreement of the parties, it must be understood by them. Contract negotiation, therefore, is the prime opportunity to communicate with the client. That communication should include a discussion of guiding principles in establishing contract language that appropriately allocates risk. For instance, it doesn't make sense to assign a responsibility to a party that is not in a position to meet the contractual requirements, nor is it reasonable to ignore the fact that *authority* to act is a concomitant of the *responsibility* to act. It is important that one party is clearly responsible for each recognized assignment and that this party is given the authority to carry out the assignment.

Standard contract forms—such as the consensus documents published by the AIA—attempt to establish contracted liability within common-law standards of professional care, skill, and diligence. Unique or custom-drafted agreements may greatly enlarge the business risk to a design professional through the inclusion of contract provisions that exceed normal duties and responsibilities. Certainly a basic element of implementing a risk management process is to be familiar with the consensus agreement forms and to be able to explain the terms and conditions to a client in a clear and positive manner. Although there is an ever-increasing number of AIA documents that address specific project delivery methods, no AIA document should be seen as suitable off the shelf. The AIA documents, like other standard form documents, need to be tailored to the needs of each project.

## PERFORMING SERVICES WITHOUT A WRITTEN AGREEMENT

Financial and risk management considerations suggest that it is not a good policy to perform services in the absence of a written professional service agreement. For one reason or another, however, firms frequently decide to provide services prior to execution of a formal written agreement. In those cases, firms should keep a record of the arrangements they have made with the client. This can take the form of a so-called commitment letter, sometimes referred to as a letter of intent. The content may vary somewhat depending on the stage and content of prior communication with the client. If the client has serious reservations about either the proposed scope of services or the proposed compensation, it would be wise to refrain from performing services until these reservations can be further addressed and resolved.

On the other hand, if the scope of services and the basis of compensation have been proposed and essentially agreed upon, pending negotiation of the terms and conditions, a letter authorizing the architect to begin with services on that basis for a limited period of time could be executed. If only a few terms and conditions are controversial, those might be expressly identified as open for further discussion while all others are deemed to apply to the services performed under the letter agreement.

If the proposal only includes the scope of services and does not comprehensively address compensation, it may be possible to obtain authorization to proceed whereby compensation would be based on time expended at the firm's normal billing rates, at a multiple of salary, or on some other basis. In either event, it is advisable to include a time limit for the authorization contained in the commitment letter. That provides an incentive to negotiate and execute the formal agreement promptly. If no specific scope of services has ever been proposed, it may still be possible to begin with compensation on a time-and-expense basis.

Design professionals often think of risk as a professional liability issue and believe that the solution to dealing with risk is professional liability insurance. Risk management, however, as noted earlier, is not a reactive process. It is a proactive one that plays an important part in whether or not a firm succeeds. Managing risk is how firms profit. Risks that are ignored or mismanaged generate disputes and claims. All disputes have a negative impact on a design firm; those that result in demands for remedial services or money can destroy a firm's profitability.

The ability of a professional service firm to determine its own future and to remain viable as a professional practice is greatly influenced by the ability of its participants to understand risk management theories and to apply them to the challenges faced on a daily basis.

## OPTIONS FOR LIMITING LIABILITY

Risk can be limited to the reperformance of services; to a specific dollar amount; to professional compensation; to insurance proceeds; to direct rather than special, incidental, indirect, or consequential damages; or to costs resulting from negligence above a set contingency for change orders. AIA B141 has included the first of these forms of limitation of liability for almost four decades, and the 1997 version attempts to limit exposure for consequential damages. The AIA B511 addresses some of the other options; standard form language, however, does not replace the need for competent local counsel to evaluate the state-specific issues affecting the limitation of liability.

These types of limitation-of-liability clauses should be explored as alternatives since risk allocation provisions that limit an architect's liability do not always have to be tied to a monetary amount. Using the limitation on types of damages, the architect could negotiate a limitation for a particular situation based on his or her understanding of the nature of the project or specific circumstances.

A limitation of the architect's liability on a comparative negligence basis is logical in those jurisdictions where the architect may be held jointly and severally liable to the owner. The liability would not exceed the architect's percentage share of the total negligence of all entities and individuals.

***Limiting liability for change orders.*** An additional risk allocation provision that can be effective in minimizing claims and claims expenses is an agreement by the owner not to claim for the cost of certain change orders. This is often called a "safe harbor" provision. In it the owner recognizes and expects that certain change orders may be required as the result, in whole or in part, of deficiencies in the drawings, specifications and other design documentation, or other services performed by the architect. Whether these change orders are caused by negligence or imperfections that are within professional standards, the owner agrees not to make a claim unless the aggregate cost exceeds a contingency amount stated in advance. It is important that any responsibility for costs above the contingency is determined on the basis of applicable contractual obligations and professional liability standards.

***Limiting liability to insurance coverage.*** Insurers often suggest possible language to limit liability. The AIA commended program of professional liability insurance, the CNA program administered by Victor O. Schinnerer & Company, Inc., has suggested that insured firms include language such as the following in order to limit their liability for negligence to the amount of insurance:

> The liability of the Architect to the Client, for any actions, damages, claims, demands, judgments, losses, costs, and expenses arising out of or resulting from the Architect's or its consultants' negligent acts, errors, or omissions is limited to the amount of professional liability insurance maintained by the Architect and available at the time of determination of liability.

The following longer provision attempts to limit the architect's risk from all causes of action the owner may have:

Architect shall procure and maintain insurance coverage in amounts stated in the Agreement for such a period of time as Architect deems appropriate, as required by law, or as stated in this Agreement. Client agrees that to the fullest extent permitted by law, the total liability of Architect, Architect's employees or consultants to Client or anyone claiming through Client, for any and all claims, costs, losses or damages arising out of, in connection with, or in any way related to this Project or this Agreement from any cause of action including but not limited to negligence, error, omission, breach of contract, breach of warranty or strict liability shall not exceed the total amount paid to, or on behalf of, the Architect by Architect's insurers in settlement or satisfaction of Client's claims under the terms and conditions of Architect's insurance policies excluding any fees, defense costs or costs of settlement. If, at the time of any claim by Client, no insurance coverage is in force and available, then the total liability of Architect, Architect's employees or consultants to Client or anyone claiming through Client for any such uncovered claim shall not exceed the total compensation actually paid by Client to Architect under this Agreement.

While courts generally look with disfavor on parties attempting to exculpate themselves from liability for their own mistakes, there is still significant latitude in the contracting process. Generally, for a limitation-of-liability clause to be effective and enforceable, it should meet the following criteria:

- The contractual language allocating risk must be unambiguous.
- The types of risk being allocated must be clearly defined, such as risks associated

## The Allocation of Risk: Limitations of Liability

For architects, the threshold under tort law at which liability generally will be imposed is higher than it would be for a nonprofessional, but with professional liability, the indemnity obligation is typically unlimited. Limitation-of-liability provisions are one form of contractual language that allocates a risk or transfers the obligation to correct damage caused by a party to another party. These agreements with a client or other party can be useful and equitable where the risks faced are inordinate, especially in light of the scope of services being performed by the architect, the architect's limited fee, and the client's needs or potential for profit. Efforts to limit the architect's liability to reperformance of defective services, the amount of the professional services fee, amount of available insurance coverage, or direct damages caused by the services are logically related to the relative value of the benefits received by the architect and the client.

Any form of limitation-of-liability clause will probably be the most controversial provision that an architect can seek to incorporate into an agreement. Many architects are now attempting, by contract, to clearly share at least part of the professional liability risks of a project with the project owner, and at times even broader risks are being limited and thus placed on the other party to the contract. In most cases, architects point out that the project owner receives the princi-

pal reward and the long-term benefits from the project and is in the better position to assume and spread the costs of the liability risks over the life of the completed project. The architect, on the other hand, may be exposed to substantial risk even though the scope of services and the fee are limited.

Particularly where the risk greatly exceeds the scope of services and concomitant fee, it should be considered reasonable and professional for the architect's liability exposure to be limited to an extent that is more fairly commensurate with the scope of the project and the fee. One solution to this risk-reward discrepancy is to have the client agree to limit the architect's liability exposure to a degree that bears a reasonable relation to the reward received by the architect. On this approach the architect stands behind the professional service, but the liability would not unreasonably jeopardize the architect's financial capacity to stay in business and would not bear an unreasonable relation to the compensation received for the services rendered. The architect, however, should not routinely insert a limitation-of-liability clause into every agreement. Rather, each project must be evaluated to determine whether a logical basis for such a clause exists.

*Katherine Davitt Enos, Assoc. AIA, Esq.,*
*Victor O. Schinnerer & Company, Inc.*

with negligence, breach of contract, or breach of warranty. Limiting risk for one cause of action may leave an exposure under a separate cause of action.

- The parties must have bargained freely concerning the sharing of risk and must have had relatively equal bargaining strengths.
- The limitation must clearly indicate both a release from direct claims and an assumption of the risk from third-party suits.
- The retained risk must bear some logical relation to the scope of services being performed and the fee being paid.
- The client must have been advised of and afforded the opportunity to increase the scope of services, to negotiate a fee that acknowledges the significant risk that the architect may have to bear, or to insure its portion of the risk (for example, by agreeing to project insurance).

As we have seen, developing and implementing a risk management process requires analyzing and understanding the dynamics of your business and the clients for whom you work, rather than creating an overarching policy that can be applied to all situations. Use the foregoing strategies and concepts as guides, not as gospel. By sticking to the basics, you will protect yourself, your firm, the integrity of your work, and ultimately your clients, and ensure the successful and profitable completion of the projects you undertake.

### For More Information

Some professional liability insurers offer tools and resources for policyholders to manage the sources of risk inherent in professional practice. The CNA/Schinnerer program of professional liability insurance, as the AIA's commended program, provides risk management information for policyholders and design professionals generally. For information on risk management strategies, visit the Web site of Victor O. Schinnerer & Company, Inc., at www.schinnerer.com. In addition to selections from Schinnerer's *A/E Legal Reporter* and *Guidelines for Improving Practice,* the Web site includes papers from Schinnerer's Annual Meeting of Invited Attorneys and Management Advisories on a variety of risk management topics. Information on subscriptions to Schinnerer's publications is available to architects who are not policyholders.

The AIA Web page at www.aia.org includes risk management information from the CNA/Schinnerer program and other sources, including the Institute's Architects Risk Management Committee.

# 11.2 Insurance Coverage

## Lorna Parsons and Ann Marie Boyden, Hon. AIA

*Architecture firms use insurance as an instrument to help them manage the inherent risks of business and the specific risks associated with projects.*

As a participant in the highly complex design and construction process, the architect encounters a variety of risks that can result in financial losses for numerous people. Insurance is a means of managing those risks by transferring them to an insurance company in return for a premium payment.

In operating a private business as licensed professionals, architects purchase insurance to cover certain risks, including professional liability, risk of property loss, and risk of personal loss. As firms grow and consider providing benefits for their staff, they may participate in health insurance, life insurance, and pension plans. Sole proprietors may acquire insurance to protect themselves and their families from injury.

## PROFESSIONAL LIABILITY

For architects, a key set of professional and business risks arises from the possibility of causing harm by their negligence in performing professional services. These negligent acts, errors, or omissions may cause damage to owners, contractors, or other third parties, and the firm may be found liable for these damages. In buying a professional liability insurance policy (sometimes inappropriately called errors-and-omissions or E&O insurance), the firm is asking the insurance company to absorb a portion of the costs of claims in exchange for a premium paid to the insurance company.

Not all firms purchase professional liability insurance. This business decision is part of the firm's overall approach to managing its practices and risks. Even firms that do buy professional liability insurance retain the risk for expenses that fall under their deductible, exceed their policy's limits of liability, or are excluded from the scope of coverage.

> ▶ **Architects may be held liable for design errors and omissions that fall below the professional standard of reasonable care.**

### Sources of Professional Liability Insurance

Most architects purchasing professional liability insurance coverage do so through independent brokers. These brokers represent the interests of their client and not those of the insurer. By contacting a broker experienced in architects' professional liability insurance, a firm can shop around for insurance, obtain access to many insurance carriers, and, with the professional advice of the broker, decide which carrier best fits its needs.

Some insurance companies are represented by agents who are authorized to place policies on behalf of those companies in a certain territory. These agents represent the interests of a particular insurance company and may not have access to the entire insurance marketplace.

Regardless of whether a firm chooses an independent broker or an exclusive agent, the firm will want to select its broker or agent in much the same way it selects its lawyer and accountant—with careful scrutiny of qualifications, services available, cost, chemistry, and commitment.

In evaluating insurance options, architects will find that each professional liability insurance policy is different from all the others in some respects. The architect must reconcile coverage and cost, but the variety of coverages available through endorsements, exclu-

> ▶ **Risk Management Strategies (11.1) reviews the risk management framework, including the possibility of "going bare"—that is, not carrying professional liability insurance.**

**Lorna Parsons** *oversees the architecture, engineering, and construction industry insurance and risk management programs for the CNA/Schinnerer professional liability insurance programs.* **Ann Marie Boyden** *is executive director of the AIA Trust.*

part 3 DELIVERY

## Selecting and Working with an Insurance Broker and an Insurance Company

### The Value of an Independent Broker

Buying insurance is a major business decision. An architecture firm therefore will want to select its broker in much the same way it selects its lawyer and accountant—with care and scrutiny as to the broker's qualifications, independent judgment, services available, cost, understanding of the profession, and ability to work with the firm.

An independent broker—rather than an agent for a specific carrier—will examine the insurance market to obtain various quotes of premiums for specific levels of coverage and service, evaluate the quotes, and provide a professional opinion to the architect on which policies fit the firm's needs. An architect pays for this expertise and service; while some brokers work on a fee basis, most receive a commission—essentially the architect's money—paid to them by the insurance carrier out of the premium. Commission rates vary, and the architect has a right to know the commission level for each quoted premium. In some cases, a broker actually is an agent of a specific company, and while the agent may be able to offer coverage from other carriers, the agent may have a financial incentive to direct the architect to that company. Again, architects have a right to know whether a broker has an agency relationship with a specific company.

A broker can do more than advise in the selection of insurance carriers and policies. A firm also may rely on a broker to help with the following:

- Evaluation of the firm's range of liability exposures and identification of various forms of insurance available to protect it from financial loss
- Communication with insurance markets regarding all aspects of the firm's insurance needs
- Application of criteria used in evaluating and recommending a specific insurance program, such as the company's stability and financial strength; premium cost, limit, and deductible programs; coverage terms; claims management; and risk and practice management techniques
- Understand insurability implications of changes in the organizational structure or nature of the practice
- Review proposed contractual provisions affecting insurability while the professional services contract is being drafted
- Monitor claims administration

### Attributes of an Insurer and Policy

Once premium quotes are obtained, the decision about which policy to accept should not be made on price alone. Several factors should be scrutinized in considering which carrier best meets a firm's needs:

- What is the scope of coverage being offered, what endorsements are available to expand coverage, and what is being excluded from coverage?
- What is the proposed cost of the basic policy and any endorsements?
- Is the firm buying insurance to meet a coverage requirement or as a key component of its financial management program?
- How extensive is the insurance company's experience in underwriting professional liability for architects? In particular, what is its track record during hard markets, when few carriers offer insurance?
- How flexible is the company in meeting the firm's needs? Does it offer project insurance and coverage for design-build, prior acts, and retirement?
- How strong is the company? A. M. Best Company rates an insurance company's relative financial strength and ability to meet its contractual obligations based on its profit, cash liquidity, reinsurance quality, adequacy of reserves, and management strength. Standard & Poor's rates a company's ability to pay claims over time. Moody's and Duff and Phelps also rate aspects of insurers' financial strength.
- Is the company an admitted carrier? An admitted carrier subjects itself to all of a state's insurance rules and regulations, and in many states a state commission reviews and approves company rates, policies, and procedures before they can be implemented. In all states, having an admitted carrier means the insured is covered by guarantee funds, which provide coverage should the company fail. Nonadmitted (or excess-and-surplus) carriers are not subject to the same regulation and oversight. The state neither guarantees their coverage nor evaluates their rates. This translates into extra flexibility for the carrier, which historically in soft markets has produced low premiums and in hard markets has produced less available insurance.
- How extensive is the company's experience in the management of professional liability claims against architects? What claims services will it provide that will benefit the firm?
- How will the legal defense of claims be handled? Against what criteria are the company's defense attorneys evaluated and appointed? How much say will the architect have in the selection of counsel and in the conduct of a legal defense, a mediation, or an arbitration, or in settlement decisions?
- What professional liability risk management services will the insurance company offer? Does it offer reference publications, contract review services, educational programs, and risk management updates?

sions, and the core policies themselves makes reasonable cost comparisons very difficult. It is important to carefully evaluate endorsement options, coverage limits, and deductibles. The extra costs for some of these add-ons, including increased limits, can be minimal.

In addition, the service and stability of the insurance carrier must be considered. Services provided by professional liability insurance companies range from extensive educational and management assistance programs, such as those offered by AIA's commended program, to little or no information, advice, or guidance. The true value of a professional insurance policy probably is best defined by its claims handling process. The specialized expertise of a claims manager familiar with architectural practice and the knowledge, interest, and sensitivity of defense counsel may be the most critical factor for selecting an insurer.

While it is often difficult to rank competence and service above the cost of coverage, a low-cost insurer may be quite like a low-bid contractor. Certainly the attraction of a lower initial premium cost should be weighed against the potential of future significant rate increases and the risk that the carrier might not continue to offer professional liability insurance. Insurance carriers enter and leave the professional liability arena as business conditions change. In some past "hard" insurance markets, the number of carriers offering insurance on an admitted basis in a given state dropped to a single provider—the CNA/Schinnerer program that is the AIA's commended program.

***Admitted companies.*** States permit insurance companies to sell their products on either an admitted or non-admitted (usually called excess-and-surplus or E&S) basis. Companies that sell insurance on an admitted basis subject themselves fully to the oversight of the state and must have their rates, coverages, and policy forms reviewed (and, in many states, approved) by the state. In addition, each admitted company must contribute to a state-guarantee fund to be drawn upon to pay claims should the company be declared insolvent and lack the financial wherewithal to pay the claim itself. This process protects the consumer.

Nonadmitted carriers are not subjected to such scrutiny. Nor are they included in the state guarantee fund. Accordingly, they have an easier time moving into—and out of—the insurance market. For these reasons, many states require brokers to seek coverage from admitted carriers first, placing coverage in an E&S market only when admitted-carrier coverage is not available for the specific firm. Some states even require brokers to warn the insured person or firm that they are placing their coverage with a nonadmitted carrier by stamping the policy to that effect.

***Claims-made basis.*** The possibility of finding only a limited number of admitted insurance carriers might leave the architect in a difficult position owing to the traditional claims-made nature of many professional liability insurance policies. "Claims-made" means the policy must be in effect at the time the claim is made against the architect—even though this can be years after completion of construction. Claims-made policies are common to professional liability

▶ In "soft" insurance markets many insurance companies seek new policyholders, as they look to improve their cash flow by placing less emphasis on risk-based underwriting. In "hard" markets fewer insurance companies are actively seeking new business, and it may be more difficult to find the coverage you seek. Regardless of the market, you should always feel free to ask your broker to explain options to you.

## *The AIA-Commended Professional Liability Insurance Program*

Since 1957, the AIA has commended the professional liability insurance program available from Continental Casualty Company, one of the CNA Insurance Companies. The CNA program is administered by the underwriting management firm of Victor O. Schinnerer & Company, Inc. The CNA/Schinnerer program was developed at the request of the AIA and is continually reviewed by the AIA's oversight committee. The AIA commends the CNA/Schinnerer program because it is national in scope and meets the six commendation criteria established by the AIA Board of Directors:

- That the insurance company be able to provide coverage and local claim service anywhere in the country
- That the reinsurers of the insurance company be of satisfactory financial strength
- That the insurance company possess the highest possible rating in the A. M. Best financial ratings
- That the insurance company make no changes in the terms or rate of the policy without prior consultation with the AIA
- That the AIA has the right to examine the books of the insurance company and the administrator as these books pertain to this program
- That the insurance company be available to all AIA members with satisfactory experience or performance records

The commendation allows the AIA to set the standard of what a good insurance program is for architects. Further, it affords the AIA the platform to advocate for new and expanded coverage and services as member needs evolve. For example, project insurance, design-build coverage, and asbestos and pollution coverage all were developed with the assistance of the AIA Risk Management Committee.

In addition, COMMITMENT PLUS, CNA/Schinnerer's universal profit-sharing program coverage, was designed by CNA/Schinnerer with the help of the AIA as a way to stabilize insurance costs and prevent windfall profits. Under this program, CNA's underwriting profit is capped at 3 percent so that premium not needed to pay claims and claim expenses is returned to CNA/Schinnerer's insured firms with interest. The program, first put into place in 1980, returned approximately $300 million to CNA/Schinnerer-insured firms between 1989 and 1999.

The power and leverage of the AIA over the Commended Program is unique in the world of professional liability insurance. And because the AIA's commended program is the benchmark for the industry, its influence extends to the entire insurance marketplace.

insurance and should not be confused with the occurrence policies common to general liability insurance.

This distinction is important to understand. Under a claims-made policy, all coverage ceases when the policy is canceled or not renewed (by either the firm or the insurer), even though the architect may have been insured when the services were rendered. Under an occurrence policy, a claim filed after policy cancellation or renewal will be covered if the policy was in force when the incident that caused the claim occurred, regardless of whether the insured was still covered when the claim was made.

The claims-made basis is used for professional liability insurance coverage because it makes it easier to predict the costs to the insurer. If coverage for professional liability risks were offered on an occurrence basis, the cost of such coverage would be prohibitive, because the insurers would have to include contingencies for many more unknowns. This distinction, however, means that firms that buy insurance as a risk management tool have to keep it in force on a continuing basis for continuing protection. When a firm remains with one carrier, the claims-made nature of the policy is not an issue. When a firm first becomes insured or switches carriers, it should evaluate the availability and cost of prior-acts coverage to cover the risks from the earlier period.

Individuals practicing in firms may or may not be affected by this attribute of claims-made coverage after they leave their firms. If the firm retains coverage, former partners and employees who were listed as "named insureds" on the policy will enjoy coverage for services they rendered during the course of their partnership or employment. If the firm drops coverage or ceases to exist, they will lose coverage.

The claims-made feature raises the question of protection upon retirement or withdrawal from practice. A few programs offer professional liability coverage to continue the protection needed by architects who withdraw from active practice. Usually this "tail" coverage is arranged by endorsing the basic policy. Some states require admitted carriers to provide some level of tail coverage at an extra cost to the insured.

As one example, the CNA/Schinnerer program has coverage available to architects who have been insured for three consecutive years prior to retirement; the policy then covers the retired architect for prior acts. Coverage is similarly available to protect the estates of deceased architects if this is warranted.

***Prior acts.*** Firms can buy coverage for professional acts and services that took place before they first became insured or when they were insured by another carrier. The scope and availability of this prior-acts coverage varies from insurer to insurer. Often prior-acts coverage (perhaps to the day the firm started practice) is available to eligible firms after they have been covered by a carrier for some specified amount of time.

## Coverage

Generally a professional liability insurance policy covers the insured firm's liability for negligent acts, errors, or omissions arising out of the performance of professional services as an architect, provided these services are performed within the territory defined in the policy. All policies cover the United States, and many offer worldwide coverage in the basic policy or by specific endorsement.

A basic policy provides legal defense of claims covered by the policy and pays defense costs subject to the policy limit and deductible. Most insurance companies retain attorneys who are experienced in the defense of professional liability claims. When a defense attorney is selected and appointed to defend the policyholder, the policyholder—not the insurance company—is the defense attorney's client. Some companies, however, allow firms to choose their own defense counsel.

Broad policies insure not only the firm but also any partner, executive officer, director, stockholder, or employee of the insured firm when that individual is acting within the scope of professional duties. Some lower-cost policies may not automatically provide such broad coverage.

***Endorsements and exclusions.*** Policyholders and insurance companies can modify coverage through endorsements and exclusions. Exclusions are sometimes added to specifically preclude coverage for identifiable risks. This can be done to reduce the cost of the policy or to allow coverage in situations where risks cannot be determined.

From time to time, new issues surface that call for specialized risk management techniques including insurance coverage. Environmental hazards are an example. The AIA Risk Management Committee, with the help of the AIA membership, stays abreast of these issues and works with the commended program to create coverage for new exposures. The committee also reviews coverage available elsewhere in the insurance market so that AIA members know what their choices are.

Managing Disputes (11.3) describes the process of initiating and resolving claims.

*Victor O. Schinnerer & Company, Inc., Chevy Chase, Maryland*

Clients understand that a firm's practice policy covers the firm for negligence in providing services during the life of the policy. They also understand that professional liability claims from all projects can draw on that one policy or on the firm's own resources for indemnification. As a result, owners sometimes ask firms to find additional insurance that would not be eroded by other projects' claims. The CNA/Schinnerer program offers firms three choices: project insurance, additional liability limits, and split limits.

*Project insurance.* A separate policy can be purchased for a specific project that covers the entire design team's negligence for that project. Neither the claims nor the billings of the project policy have any effect on a firm's practice policy. The policy can last up to ten years.

*Additional liability limits.* This arrangement allows firms to purchase an endorsement that can provide up to $5 million of coverage for a specific project in conjunction with their practice policy limit.

*Split limits.* This choice allows a firm to secure a per-claim limit of liability and a larger term aggregate limit of liability. Although the coverage is not dedicated to any single project, an owner who wants a $1 million dedicated limit might find it acceptable for the firm to have a practice policy with a $1 million limit per claim and a $2 million aggregate limit.

Of course, a firm may always increase its overall practice policy limits. Again, while not dedicated in any way to an owner's project, higher limits give a firm more courage with which to pay all claims on all projects should the need arise.

The chart below highlights the various forms of coverage.

| Project Insurance | Additional Liability Limits | Split Limits |
|---|---|---|
| • Guaranteed term | • Annual renewal option | • Annual or multiyear term option |
| • Guaranteed rate | • Annual rate (not guaranteed) | • Term rate (not guaranteed) |
| • Unlimited number of policies | • Only two endorsements per policy | • Per-claim limit available to all projects |
| • Costs easily identifiable to owner | • Costs easily identifiable to owner | • Must estimate cost for project owner |
| • Limits up to $30 million available | • Limits up to $5 million available | • Claims can affect practice policy |
| • Claims do not affect practice policy | • Claims can affect practice policy | • Project billings affect practice policy |
| • Project billings do not affect practice policy | • Project billings affect practice policy | • Covers only the insured firm's negligence |
| • Covers entire design team's negligence | • Covers only the insured firm's negligence | • Aggregate limit sharing during policy term |
| • Dedicated limits | • Limits may be shared | |

Sometimes endorsements that expand coverage have an additional premium cost; sometimes they are included automatically at no extra cost. Firms should be aggressive about having their broker, or the insurance company's agent, check into those expansions of coverage that they need to practice or that fit into their practice management goals. Endorsements can include first-dollar defense, special project additional limits, expanded equity interest, and design-build coverage. In other words, a firm can negotiate its coverage based on its practice needs. The architecture firm should review these sections annually; practice needs change over time, as do the demands of the firm's clients.

**Limits of liability.** How much insurance a firm buys is a function of its financial needs (including those of its principals), its tolerance for risk, its risk management abilities, and the demands of its clients. Minimum annual and aggregate limits of liability for errors and omissions insurance are usually set at $100,000, with maximum limits running as high as $15 million (even higher limits can be arranged for special circumstances).

Annual and aggregate limits of liability are available to pay for claims and associated legal expenses in a policy year. The firm must absorb the costs of claims and legal expenses that exceed the limits. With most policies, the firm receives a new limit each policy year. Some insurance programs permit their policyholders to buy excess limits for specific projects or to buy "split limits," with one limit per claim and another for the aggregate in a year. The insurance company can determine the cost of these variations for the insured to consider.

**Deductibles.** To encourage risk management, insurance companies require a deductible amount that a firm must pay to defend each claim or after each determination of negligence. Deductibles as low as $1,000 are available, but many firms increase

# Establishing Professional Liability Insurance Premiums

Insurance seems like a simple business. Companies have to collect enough premiums to cover costs, make enough money to stay in business, and keep investors happy. Insurance company costs are many, and most are not apparent to the buyer. They include funds to cover administrative costs, costs of buying reinsurance, broker commission costs, state and federal government taxes, costs associated with insurance commission funds, stockholder dividends, and the investigation, defense, and payment of claims. Insurers live on the "law of large numbers," so pooled premiums can offset individual losses. Over ten years or so, the combined premium collected should approximate these combined costs. In any given year, however, either the insurance company or the insured individuals or firms may benefit more than the other.

The simplicity of insurance, however, often is influenced by the complexity of the financial markets. When interests rates are high, insurance companies try to bring in as much premium as possible to invest. Because there is a lag time between premium payment and the cost of claims, some insurers enter the market, collect premiums for investment, and leave the market before claims mature. When stock prices are increasing, some insurers enter the market offering low premiums to show an increase in their value to stockholders because of the influx of cash. After their stock prices rise and their investments in other stocks increase, they then can abandon the market before claims are brought against their policyholders and enter another venture on a short-term basis.

How does the insurance company calculate the precise premium a firm will pay? Sound underwriting management suggests that the insurer should actually measure the risk posed by the practice. As an example, a company might consider these factors:

- *Billing volume.* Basically, the more services a firm provides, the greater its exposure to claims. This exposure is influenced by the number of projects making up the annual billings. For instance, on an equal-dollar basis, in 1999 small firms were fourteen times more likely to have a claim paid by an insurer than very large firms. Part of this is simply the number of clients and size of each project. The severity (the cost of each claim paid) for small firms, however, was only one-sixth as high as each claim paid on behalf of large firms.
- *Types of services.* On a properly underwritten risk, premium levels mirror claims data. Firms should separate billings for types of services as carefully as possible. If an insurer has less information, the premium will include an "ambiguity cost" to cover the potential effects of unknown risks.
- *Project types.* Firms that do lower-risk projects may pay lower premiums. Some types of projects, because of complexity or clients, generate more claims than others.
- *Firm experience.* Premium levels also mirror the firm's own claims history. Firms with claims-free histories can get as much as a 25 percent credit off the standard rate charged for similar firms. (State insurance commission regulations generally permit no greater credit.) Firms with bad histories can pay 100 percent higher rates than similar firms with average claims histories; firms with very bad histories may be uninsurable. Each insurance company has its own definition of "bad" and "very bad." In soft markets, when insurers want to write business to bring in cash, the definition loosens. In hard markets, it tightens.
- *Geographic location.* Firms in low-risk states pay lower premiums than those in high-risk states. Again, claims data define high-risk states. In 1999, for example, firms practicing in California or Florida paid significantly higher rates for insurance than firms practicing in Vermont or Kansas.
- *Continuity.* The longer a firm is with a professional liability insurer, the more comfortable the insurer feels in accepting the firm's risk. These clients receive not only better consideration (that is, lower premiums) during tight markets but also the benefit of the doubt should they suffer a series of claims. The value of this "longevity credit" can be substantial.
- *Competition.* The professional liability insurance market is highly competitive. Companies enter and leave the market all the time. Company premium quotes, by and large, are price-sensitive, but the architect should be wary of a quote that looks too good. The history of the industry is that some companies undersell their policies to bring in premiums and then disappear when the claims roll in, leaving the architect with no coverage. Disappearing or underfunded insurance companies are a key problem with claims-made policies.
- *Coverage.* Based on its assessment of firm risk, an insurer calculates various coverage-deductible-endorsement-exclusion combinations and their premium costs. Firms can exercise some control over their premiums by negotiating these four factors through their broker. For example, agreeing to a higher deductible reduces the insurer's exposure and hence the cost of the insurance premium. Small firms with low deductibles and many small projects create a higher risk of paid claims than firms with higher deductibles. Higher deductibles increase a firm's exposure to claims payments but also provide a greater incentive for careful client selection and practice management.

If you are working with an independent broker who is being paid to represent your interests, give that broker as much information as possible. Your application should accurately reflect your practice. If you have a claim that needs explaining, insist that your broker attach the explanation to your application. If you institute new quality management programs, tell the company about them. If you have continuing clients, make sure that fact is recognized. Anything you and your broker think would help the company evaluate your firm as a risk will be welcomed by insurance companies following sound underwriting procedures. And if you do not understand your premium, have your broker call the insurance company for an explanation.

their deductibles to lower their premium costs. As with most insurance, the higher the level of risk retained by the insured—that is, the higher the deductible—the lower the premium cost. Determining the balance between the deductible, the premium, and the coverage basically requires weighing probabilities and finances and is best carried out by the firm with the advice of its broker. In making this decision, the firm should remember that there is a new deductible obligation with each claim.

**Costs of insurance.** Each firm's premium is calculated individually, based on such factors as the firm's practice, project mix, claims experience, coverage needs, and resulting risks to the insurer. This makes comparing premiums of different firms difficult at best. Thus a firm should pay attention to its application and work with a broker who can present the firm well to the insurance company. Prudent insurers must increase the cost of insurance if risks cannot be clearly delineated. The more specific and unambiguous the information a firm can provide, the lower the premium will be. A prospective policyholder should also feel free to call the company (through its broker) to ask how its premium will be determined.

**Contractual liability.** Professional liability insurance companies provide coverage only for the insured firm's negligence in performing or furnishing professional services. Most policies exclude coverage for express warranties and guarantees—separate contractual promises. Certificates that have the effect of warranties—for example, those that do not state a known fact or express a qualified professional opinion—are also excluded. Promises to absorb costs of errors and omissions, absent negligence, are excluded, too, because such promises have the effect of a warranty.

Insurability problems also arise when owners ask architects to contract to hold them harmless or otherwise indemnify them. An extension of coverage is needed when an architect agrees by contract, in writing or orally, to indemnify and hold harmless some other person such as the owner or contractor—unless the architect is indemnifying the other person for the architect's own negligence, at which point under many policies coverage is automatic. In most contractual liability situations such coverage may not be possible.

A hold-harmless (or indemnification) clause essentially is a contractual assumption of another's legal liability. Under many circumstances, use of a hold-harmless clause is an acceptable practice as long as the contractual transfer of liabilities is not against public policy and can be covered by insurance or available assets. For instance, in AIA Document A201, General Conditions of the Contract for Construction, a clause is included to require the contractor to indemnify and hold harmless the owner and the architect for bodily injury or property damage claims arising out of the contractor's negligent performance of the work. Many states have "anti-indemnity" statutes to regulate the use of indemnification clauses in construction contracts; some states prohibit these clauses completely.

The architect should look for hold-harmless provisions before signing any contract for professional services. A clause that otherwise appears innocuous might contain such a provision. An architect who finds or suspects such a clause should submit the provision to the architect's attorney and insurance advisor. A promise to indemnify may fall within the scope of professional liability insurance coverage, but broad wording may mean that the promise is a contractual obligation that cannot be covered by insurance.

**Interprofessional relationships.** Architects routinely retain consultants. This relationship means that the architect also has vicarious liability for any damage caused by the consultant's negligence. Insured architects will want to review their consultant's insurance status, as they, for all intents and purposes, will serve as their consultant's insurer if that status is inadequate. Similarly, if an architect agrees by contract to limit the liability of a consultant, the architect may find that the risk of the consultant's negligence has been shifted to the architect and the architect's insurer. At times architects are subconsultants to other professionals or subcontractors to construction contractors. Examining the prime design professional's coverage—or the professional liability coverage of a construction contractor through which the architect is providing services to a client—can alert the subconsultant professional to gaps in coverage that could result in the subconsultant becoming the only target of a claim.

**Joint ventures.** From a legal standpoint, a joint venture is quite similar to a partnership; the main difference is that a joint venture normally has a more limited scope or purpose. If a professional liability claim is filed against a joint venture, one or all of the members can be held liable for any judgment rendered against it. Broad policies—such as AIA's commended program—provide automatic joint venture coverage. Some insurers exclude joint ventures from the basic policy; coverage for joint ventures may be available by special endorsement for specific situations. The endorsement extends the coverage under the basic policy to provide for the insured firm's legal liability arising out of professional services performed on behalf of the named joint venture. However, the endorsement does not cover other participating firms in the joint venture. Special care should be taken when firms do not formally create a joint venture but present themselves to a client as an association or a team. Such alliances usually will be seen as joint ventures, and each party may be held liable for the negligence of the other(s).

Each member of a joint venture should obtain evidence from the other joint venture partner(s) that their policies have been properly endorsed, if necessary, to cover participation in the joint venture. This usually can be accomplished by obtaining a certificate of insurance and a copy of the joint venture endorsement.

***Project professional liability insurance.*** Project insurance covers the design team participants—even those who are uninsured. The policy covers the architect and named professional consultants for the term of the project plus a predetermined discovery period after completion of construction. Depending on the insurance carriers of the firms covered by a project policy, coverage may then revert to the individual firms' professional liability policies.

Project insurance is intended to cover only one project and is usually paid for by an owner who wants coverage beyond that normally carried by the firms. Such insurance is also useful when the project is of such increased scope that it drastically affects the cost of basic coverage and as a way to get coverage for underinsured or uninsured consultants. From the architect's standpoint, the billings associated with a project-insured project (and the cost of any claims) do not affect the premium for the firm's practice policy. A broker is necessary to compare coverage.

***Expanded project delivery approaches.*** Insurance companies have begun to provide coverage for architects practicing in roles such as designer-builder, construction manager, and land developer. While some companies offer endorsements for these services to the basic policy, potential gaps should be investigated to prevent uninsured liability. For example, a construction manager (as advisor to the owner) is covered under most professional liability policies; the at-risk construction manager—one acting as a general contractor—is not.

## Claims

In the world of professional liability insurance, there are two common ways to define claims. The first is objective: a demand for money or services with an allegation of a wrongful act. This definition produces a clear reference point indicating when the insured and the insurance company should intervene. It also is broad enough to cover not only a lawsuit but also angry calls from clients demanding that the architect "fix it." The second definition is subjective: It requires alerting the insurance company to a potential problem. Such a problem may become not necessarily a formal claim, but rather the threat of an action—or just a very troubling circumstance. A careful review of these policy terms is important, as failure to report a claim in a timely manner may jeopardize coverage.

Most policies require the insurance company to have the consent of the insured before settling claims. In cases involving a disagreement between the insured and the insurance carrier on settlement, the insured may be liable for the cost of any judgment above the amount for which the insurance company could have settled the claim. Similarly, the insurance company may be liable for the cost of any judgment above the amount that the insured asked the company to settle for. This check-and-balance approach encourages the insurer and the insured to work together to manage claims.

## GENERAL LIABILITY

Liability exposures can arise from an architect's office operations and nonprofessional activities at the job site. To cover such exposures, architects should carry a general liability policy. The following are elements of protection provided by a general liability policy.

***Coverage.*** A general liability policy provides coverage for claims arising against the insured involving third-party legal liability, but it does not cover professional, automobile, and workers' compensation exposures. The basic general liability policy covers only the insured; it does not protect employees unless specifically endorsed to provide for such an extension of coverage.

***Liability limits.*** General liability policies usually set definite dollar limits on the amounts an insurance company is obligated to pay. These limits relate to the type of claim (i.e., bodily injury, property damage, or personal injury) and to the total dollar amount of all claims, sometimes called the aggregate limits. For bodily injury and property damage, there are two limits: on the dollar amount of the claim for each occurrence or accident and on the aggregate dollar amount for all claims. For personal injury— claims involving libel, slander, defamation of character, false arrest, and the like—the limit of liability is a single aggregate amount for all claims.

***Contractual liability.*** In addition to professional service contracts, the architect can encounter a variety of business contracts, including office leases, purchase orders, service agreements, and the like, any of which may contain a hold-harmless provision that will contractually transfer another's legal liability to the architect. The architect must check all contracts, agreements, leases, and purchase orders for hold-harmless agreements. When these are found, the architect should obtain a coverage extension if the general liability policy does not already have one.

Other extensions of the general liability policy may be necessary to reflect the individual needs of the firm. A careful review of the liability situation should be made with insurance counsel to be certain the required coverage is being provided.

***Automobile (aircraft, watercraft) liability.*** Comprehensive automobile liability protection is an essential part of the architect's insurance program. The insurance should be written with adequate limits of liability to cover the use of automobiles by the policyholder, by employees, or by others. The policy should name, as insured persons, the individual architect, all partners in a partnership, and all officers and directors of the corporation. Coverage should include owned, leased, hired, and newly acquired automobiles. Personal automobiles of the individual architects also should be insured with adequate limits of liability to provide protection for possible business use. Similar liability coverage is needed for aircraft and watercraft if their use is part of the architect's practice.

***Employers' liability.*** As an employer, the architect can be subjected to claims by employees for job-related injuries. In most instances these claims are covered by workers' compensation rather than being treated as common-law actions. In some situations an employee's injury may not be covered under workers' compensation and the employee may attempt to sue the employer. Employee suits are excluded under both general liability and workers' compensation policies, and a potential coverage gap exists. To bridge this gap, the workers' compensation policy is generally extended to cover what is called employer's liability.

***Coordination of liability insurance.*** Professional, general, automobile, and other liability policies are interrelated. The architect should seek insurance counsel to avoid gaps in protection or duplication of coverage and to correlate limits. Umbrella or excess liability policies may sometimes be needed to provide higher limits than those the basic liability coverage offers.

***Excess (umbrella) liability policies.*** When higher limits of liability are required, certain underlying policy limits can be increased through the purchase of one additional policy—an excess or umbrella liability policy. This policy will provide higher limits in conjunction with underlying general liability, automobile, and employer's liability policies. Additional limits are provided in increments of $1 million; professional liability is not commonly included. Coverage generally will be the same as the underlying policies when coverage is broader. Claims are subject to a self-insured retention level (for example, $10,000), similar to a deductible.

## EMPLOYMENT PRACTICES LIABILITY INSURANCE

No one likes to think that their employees may sue them one day, but, unfortunately, employment practices claims are becoming an increasingly common basis of civil litigation. Recent changes in the laws related to employment have dramatically magnified both the complexity and the potential legal dangers inherent in any professional service firm's personnel management function. The number of employee harassment, discrimination, and wrongful termination charges filed has increased correspondingly.

Sound management practices will help deter claims and lawsuits—and will help provide a strong defense when allegations are made against a firm. But management practices are only one way to respond to employee claims. Employment practices liability insurance is another. While most design firms try to provide a workplace free of discrimination and harassment, mistakes can be made. While some commercial general liability policies can be endorsed to add employment practices liability coverage, most firms purchase a more comprehensive coverage through a stand-alone policy.

## OTHER BUSINESS INSURANCE

In addition to liability insurance, the architecture firm may choose to purchase insurance for other business risks.

***Architect's property insurance***. The architect's office building or the leasehold improvements where the architect is a tenant should be insured by a standard policy or by a broader all-physical-loss form. Careful attention should be given to establishing an accurate insurable value for the building or improvements. The amount of insurance always should be adequate to meet the requirements of any coinsurance clause (that is, any required fractional payment by the insured in case of a loss). Otherwise, the architect could end up paying for a substantially larger part of any loss. Consideration should be given to purchasing insurance for the building improvements on a replacement cost basis rather than on a depreciated cash value basis. All leases and mortgages should be reviewed, as they frequently stipulate coverage requirements.

Package policies are generally available. These policies may combine several types of coverage, such as insurance on the building or improvements, on office contents, and for public liability—possibly at a lower premium cost than if the policies were purchased separately. The package policy should be carefully examined to make certain it fits the architect's needs.

***Office contents.*** The architect's office contents can be insured by a standard policy covering fire, windstorm, and other extended coverage perils. Separate burglary and theft insurance also can be written to cover office contents. However, broader coverage of office contents is generally available to insure them against all risks of direct physical loss except as excluded in the policy.

Such insurance covers drawings that are damaged, but only to the extent of the cost of labor and materials to produce them. It does not cover the cost of the research that went into their preparation, although such coverage may be obtained by purchasing valuable-documents insurance.

Portable equipment that may be used outside the office can be insured under an all-risk floater policy. Money, securities, checks, travel tickets, and other negotiable instruments can be insured under a blanket crime or similar policy.

***Business interruption.*** Business interruption insurance reimburses the architect for continuing fixed expenses and for loss of profits in the event fire or other insured casualty interrupts normal business operations. This insurance can be written to cover fire, windstorm, computer crashes, and other hazards.

Coverage is available for an agreed sum or for actual gross earnings based on the firm's history. Options are available to reimburse the architect for the expenses of continuing business at another location while the damaged premises are being repaired.

***Valuable documents.*** This insurance coverage is one of the most important for architects' property. It covers the total value of documents lost or destroyed by any of the means described in the policy and is generally an all-risk coverage. It is available on a scheduled form, a blanket coverage form, or a reporting form indicating periodic changes in value. Documents in storage as well as work in progress can be insured. Coverage also is available for clients' documents in the custody of the architect.

***Fidelity bonds and criminal loss insurance.*** Usually all persons involved with the custody or disbursement of funds, management of firm finances (receivables and disbursements), authorization of payments to contractors or others, purchasing, and other activities requiring the use of funds or liability for the misuse of funds of others should be bonded. A blanket form of bond covering all employees is typically recommended.

Money, securities, checks, and other negotiable paper may be insured both inside and outside the firm's premises under a broad-form money and securities policy to include loss by robbery, burglary, theft, or disappearance and destruction by fire or other causes.

Comprehensive bonds or blanket crime policies are available. They combine coverage for loss of money, securities, and other property under a blanket fidelity bond and a check forgery bond. The architect's professional liability policy does not cover claims and losses stemming from the dishonest acts of associates or employees.

## EMPLOYER-RELATED INSURANCE

Architects with employees must face the prospect of additional insurance coverage for their employees. Some of this coverage is mandated by statute; some is at the firm's choice.

### Workers' Compensation

By statute, an employer is required to carry workers' compensation insurance. Sold by commercial insurance companies (or, in some states, available through state-run facilities), workers' compensation policies provide protection for work-related injuries. Benefits are prescribed by statute and include medical expenses, lost wages, and death benefits. These benefits are provided regardless of employer or employee negligence. Employees are precluded from suing their employers for injuries covered by workers' compensation.

A workers' compensation policy is rated, based on the firm's payroll, to cover various classes of employees. A full-time field architect performing construction contract administration services will have a higher rate than an architect who does not perform these services. Care should be exercised in the classification of employees to ensure proper coverage and rates applicable to the hazards involved. Improper classifications can result in much higher premiums.

### Disability Benefits

State disability benefit laws provide benefits for employees who are disabled due to non-work-related injury or illness. Not all states require this coverage, but in those that do, minimum benefits are fixed and prescribed by statute. For states where disability benefits are not mandated, or in situations where the architect wishes to increase mandated coverage, voluntary disability coverage is available through a number of commercial insurance companies as well as through the AIA Trust.

### Health Insurance

Health care is a major but costly consideration for both employees, the beneficiaries of the coverage, and employers, whose professional livelihood, to a great extent, depends on a productive and healthy staff.

The cost of health insurance has been increasing at a rate far higher than that of

---

## The AIA Trust

The AIA Trust was established in 1952 to develop life, health care, disability, and other insurance programs as well as benefit and financial planning programs of the greatest possible value, and to make them available to all AIA members.

Today the trust offers comprehensive benefits, affordable rates, and outstanding service to AIA members. The following plans are available to AIA members and their employees:

- Major medical insurance
- Major medical insurance for members living abroad
- Accidental death and dismemberment insurance for business travel
- Life insurance
- Business overhead insurance
- AIA Flex premium-only flexible spending account
- Association Members Retirement Program
- Small firm professional liability insurance program

The following plans are available to AIA members and their families:

- Major medical insurance
- Major medical insurance for members living abroad
- Accidental death and dismemberment insurance
- Life insurance
- Disability insurance
- Medicare supplement plan

The services the AIA Trust offers AIA members have evolved over the past forty-plus years and will continue to evolve to meet the future needs and practice requirements of members.

*Ann Marie Boyden, Hon. AIA*

inflation and wages for the past four decades. In 1997 the total cost of health care in the United States was nearly $4,000 per person, according to a 1999 report in the *New England Journal of Medicine.* As a result of spiraling health care costs, health insurance plans and health care delivery systems have undergone significant changes in recent years, and employers have had to develop strategies to control the increases in their benefits costs.

***Medical insurance.*** There are essentially two forms of delivering health care to employees: traditional indemnity plans, which pay a basic level of benefits for services provided, usually subject to features such as deductibles and required copayments from patients, and health maintenance organizations (HMOs), which restrict a participant's choice of health care providers, usually in exchange for broader coverage than is provided under traditional indemnity plans

There are numerous variations on both plan forms, and often the features of each are blended. For example, the AIA Trust plan is a traditional indemnity plan that uses a pre-ferred provider organization (PPO) arrangement in many locations to provide more favor-able benefits if the participant chooses designated hospitals and doctors. The AIA Trust also offers an HMO program in certain geographic areas.

For the small employer, a key consideration is the staying power of the insuring organization in the marketplace. Traditionally, small firms are at risk as to both the avail-ability of coverage and price. Selecting a stable organization with a track record has been the only effective way of ameliorating those risks.

***Dental insurance.*** Benefits for dental care required as a result of illness or injury are generally provided under the medical insurance plan. Insurance to cover regu-lar dental care can be obtained through either an indemnity plan or a dental HMO or PPO. Traditional dental plans typically provide benefits on the basis of a fee schedule, for example, paying a specific dollar amount for each scheduled treatment.

***Vision care.*** Vision care plans typically provide benefits on the basis of a schedule, paying a flat dollar amount toward the cost of one routine eye examination and a set of appropriate lenses, frames, and contact lenses every 12 to 24 months.

***Catastrophic medical care.*** For employees who have no chronic medical problem and who have reasonable financial resources, medical plans that protect only against catastrophic medical expenses may be cost-effective. One strategy that employers also find useful is to offer a flexible spending account arrangement in conjunction with a catastrophic medical plan.

***Flexible health care spending accounts.*** These plans, authorized under Section 129 of federal tax laws, allow participants to make pretax contributions to a spe-cial employer-managed account and then to be reimbursed from this account for out-of-pocket health care costs. Contributions are exempt from FICA (Social Security), federal, and, in most states, state income taxes. Commonly such plans are combined with a dependent care spending account, which permits an employee to pay for work-related child care expenses with pretax dollars. Regulation of such accounts is an especially fast-moving field; advice from the firm's accountants is essential.

## Income Protection and Replacement Benefits

In addition to health benefits, a firm may offer life insurance and long-term dis-ability protection.

***Life insurance.*** These plans, which provide benefits in the event of the death of the insured, should be thought of as income protection for the spouse or other employee beneficiaries and also as a potential source of protection for the firm in the event of the death of the owner or a principal. Group term life insurance (such as the product marketed by the AIA Trust) is commonly provided to all employees as a fixed-dollar amount per employee or as a multiple of salary.

***Disability benefits.*** These are provided in several forms. Short-term disability benefits protect against absence from work of short duration, typically three to six months. Both small and large employers often self-insure against the risk of short-term disabilities through a sick leave program, although it is possible to buy insurance for this purpose.

▶ **It is important to keep up-to-date in this fast-moving arena. The national emphasis on health care reform is likely to produce substantial changes and requirements for both employers and employees. Contact the AIA Trust for current information at (800) 552-1093.**

▶ **More substantial amounts of life insur-ance associated with buy/sell arrangements or key-person arrangements are generally purchased on an individual basis. The AIA Trust makes such a product available to AIA members.**

Long-term disability benefits protect against extended disabilities, often until the employee recovers or reaches age 65. The cost of this insurance is quite modest, and long-term disability insurance provides greater assurance that the financial resources to pay the claim will be available indefinitely. A third party is often needed to determine the continuance of disability; for architects, it is important that the test of disability be their ability to practice their chosen profession. This is the test used in the AIA Trust's policy.

***Business overhead expense (BOE).*** BOE disability benefits are similar to long-term disability benefits except that BOE protects business-related expenses in the event of total disability of a business owner. Benefit periods range from 12 to 24 months, and this low-cost insurance helps a business owner cover ongoing business expenses (e.g., rent, mortgage interest, utilities, and employee salaries). This valuable insurance coverage allows a disabled owner to maintain the business viability or avoid a forced sale of the business should the disability condition be long-term or permanent.

***Retirement benefits.*** In times of increased life expectancy, retirement plans take on added significance. These plans can take different forms and offer many variations and options.

Defined contribution plans start with an annual contribution based on earnings. The amount received at retirement is based on total contributions made and the investment strategies employed. Firms have a choice of several types of defined contribution arrangements:

- *Pension plans* require a fixed annual contribution, usually a specified percentage of income up to a specified cap. The Internal Revenue Service (IRS) limits contributions to 25 percent of compensation or $30,000, whichever is less. Pension plans are recommended for well-established firms with steady incomes because contributions are mandatory each year.
- *Profit-sharing plans* allow a variable contribution of an annually specified amount. Changes in law will affect the percentage contributed and maximum amount allowed. In 1999, for example contributions could range from 0 to 15 percent of an individual's income up to $160,000, with an annual cap of $24,000. Each year the amount of contribution is totally flexible, and it may be zero.
- *Paired plans* require a base fixed contribution and allow additional contributions from profits. This is accomplished by maintaining a pension plan for a relatively low annual fixed contribution and a profit-sharing plan to which additional, flexible contributions may be made.
- *Traditional 401(k) plans* allow individuals to defer a part of their salary over and above contributions the firm may make. Employee contributions are on a before-tax basis, and such plans are a good way to have employees share in the cost of saving for retirement. Of course, the IRS sets limits on how much employees may contribute a 401(k) plan. The firm must satisfy IRS 401(k) nondiscrimination testing and top-heavy rule requirements in order for highly compensated employees to defer salary into the plan.
- *Simple 401(k) plans* allow employees to defer a part of their salary, which is matched dollar-for-dollar by the firm up to 3 percent of compensation. The firm can adopt a simple 401(k) without being subject to discrimination testing or top-heavy rule requirements. Although the maximum salary deferral limit is lower in a simple 401(k), the additional flexibility is attractive to many firms.
- *Safe harbor 401(k) plans* allow employees to defer a part of their salary. The firm chooses one of two contribution requirements—either a nonelective contribution or a matching contribution.

Defined benefit plans specify, at the outset, the annual benefit at retirement for each participant. Actuaries then calculate the annual contribution required to reach this goal. These plans can be expensive to maintain but usually allow for larger contributions for older employees than defined contribution plans do. They are not often well suited for sole owners with younger employees, but they can be used to accumulate more retirement savings faster for partners and employees nearing retirement age.

A simplified employee pension plan (SEP) is a type of retirement plan in which

▶ **The AIA has commended the Association Members Retirement Program offered and administered by the Equitable Life Assurance Society of the United States. This program makes available a variety of defined contribution and defined benefit arrangements—as well as IRAs, SEPs, and safe harbors—to assist architects and firms in meeting their retirement savings needs. Call (800) 523-1125 for information.**

the firm sets up individual retirement accounts (IRAs) for its employees. The contributions to the SEP have limits similar to a profit-sharing plan. Firms must cover more employees than in a defined contribution or defined benefit plan, and therefore the SEP may be more costly. However, administration of a SEP may be simpler than defined contribution or defined benefit plans.

Individual retirement accounts (IRAs) are set up by individuals on their own behalf. Individuals can make relatively low annual contributions ($2,000) to an IRA. These contributions may not be tax-deductible, depending on income and whether the individual participates in a pension plan. Earnings on the IRA accumulate on a tax-deferred basis until withdrawal at age 59½ or later. Withdrawals at an earlier age carry a penalty.

***Plan details.*** Working within IRS and federal pension plan requirements—the IRS has rules relating to qualified plans, SEPs, simple IRAs, Roth IRAs, and IRAs—firms with retirement plans commonly establish eligibility criteria, vesting schedules, contribution levels, and integration with Social Security benefits.

However the program is designed, the key for firms as well as for individuals is to start early. Demographics (increases in the retirement age) and political necessity (taxing benefits for a growing number of people) have already caused major reductions in Social Security benefits.

The practice of architecture, like other businesses, requires leaders who can manage risk. Insurance is just a part of that risk management. Yet it is an important vehicle for transferring the risk of financial loss.

### For More Information

The AIA Trust offers a series of AIA-commended insurance programs for AIA members and their employees. Call (800) 343-2972 for information.

For professional liability insurance information, the AIA Trust can provide information on the Small Firm Program, a program administered by Victor O. Schinnerer & Company, Inc., for the CNA Insurance Companies. You can contact Victor O. Schinnerer & Company, Inc., directly at (301) 961-9800 for information on the AIA's commended program, which can accommodate firms of all sizes and in all practice areas.

AIA's risk management program publishes information on selecting professional liability insurance and managing professional liability risks. Publications can be ordered from (800) 365-2724. As a consequence of program commendation by the AIA, the Schinnerer/CNA operation supports the work of the AIA's risk management program and provides information to architects in AIA publications, online, and through seminars such as those provided at the AIA national convention and through components. Schinnerer also offers a voluntary educational program (72 learning units) to policyholders in the AIA commended program.

Information on insurance and risk management also can be obtained from the AIA Trust Web site, www.teleport.com/~aiatrust, or from CNA/Schinnerer, www.schinnerer.com.

# 11.3 Managing Disputes

## Frank Musica, Esq., Assoc. AIA

*A key to effective project management and successful projects lies in how conflict is managed—how differences are resolved before they become disputes, how disputes are managed before they become claims, and how any claims are resolved in the best interests of the project stakeholders. Success in preventing and mitigating disputes requires both a knowledge of the circumstances that could lead to a dispute and the knowledge and ability to take appropriate action when a dispute occurs.*

In recent years it has become apparent to many in the construction industry that managing the risk and consequences of disputes at the lowest long-term cost to the participants in a project requires the implementation of three essential strategies:

- Preventing disputes from happening in the first place
- Resolving those disputes that cannot be prevented quickly and at the lowest level possible within the project organization
- Resorting to binding adjudication only when voluntary, nonadjudicative procedures fail

Many risk management techniques focus on the strategy of preventing disputes from happening. However, some of these techniques also recognize that disputes arise and should be anticipated and reasonably addressed as part of the project delivery process. This realization is clearly reflected, for example, in the contract forms published by the AIA, which, while designed to prevent disputes, contain mechanisms to deal with disputes and minimize their impact on project progress.

Implicit in the second strategy—to resolve disputes quickly and at the lowest level possible within the project organization—is an emphasis on a continuum of nonadversarial, nonadjudicative methods of dispute resolution, sometimes referred to as alternative dispute resolution (ADR) methods. The term *ADR*, which became popular in the 1970s, refers to alternatives to litigation, such as mediation and arbitration. Arbitration is truly an alternative to litigation and is typically faster and less expensive. However, like litigation, arbitration is basically adversarial in nature and results in a binding decision imposed by a third party. Other ADR techniques, including negotiation, various project-site dispute resolution techniques, and mediation, are nonadjudicative—a resolution of the dispute is not imposed but voluntarily agreed to by the parties. Therefore the third strategy—resort to binding adjudication only when voluntary, nonadjudicative procedures fail—generally views both arbitration and litigation as dispute resolution methods of last resort.

## DISPUTE ANTICIPATION AND PREVENTION

Clearly, the process of anticipating and preventing disputes begins at the outset of the architect's relationship with the client. However, success in preventing disputes, and success in mitigating unavoidable disputes, requires both a knowledge of the circumstances that could lead to a dispute and the ability to take appropriate action when a dispute occurs.

***Common Danger Signals.*** Disputes with clients are by far the greatest source of professional liability claims against architects. Certain problems form the root of many

> **Agreements with Clients (10.1)** sets the stage for this topic by exploring how parties with disparate interests but a common goal can negotiate effective working arrangements.

> **Change is the only certainty the firm can guarantee in the design process. Chemistry will get a firm and its client through the first unexpected change. How well the architect handles that change will color the firm's effectiveness in managing future change.**

*As editor of the CNA/Schinnerer Guidelines for Improving Practice information service,* **Frank Musica** *advises professional liability insurance policyholders. He is also insurance counsel to the AIA Documents Committee and serves as a resource to AIA national and state components.*

types of client disputes and professional liability claims. Before becoming a dispute or claim, these problems send signals. Risk management depends on the quick identification of, and effective response to, these signals. Some common and all-too-familiar problems that may give rise to disputes and claims include the following situations:

**Insurance Coverage (11.2)** notes that professional liability insurers have their own definitions of claims.

- The client refuses to accept the architect's advice concerning a recommended scope of services or the necessary level of effort required to accomplish the project.
- The client is unwilling to negotiate fair terms and compensation for the architect's services.
- The client insists on holding the architect to a standard of performance that reasonably may be construed as requiring perfection (e.g., using superlatives such as "best," "highest," "most economical").
- The client demands an indemnification agreement under which the architect is obligated to indemnify the client for all loss or damage even if the client or some third party causes or contributes to the loss or damage.
- The client mandates that the architect perform services within a certain time frame when the architect's ability to meet that schedule is not entirely within the architect's control.
- The client refuses to consider conscientiously the advice of the architect concerning aspects of the contractor's performance.
- The client arbitrarily refuses to pay the architect, particularly when services are complete.

Although these problems and others like them are the basis of many disputes and liability claims, they may often be avoided through client education. To facilitate the education process, the architect must establish an effective method for timely communication with the client early in their professional relationship. Many professional liability claims arise, to some degree, from communication failure between the architect and the client. In the absence of effective communication, the client may develop unrealistic expectations.

**Risk Management Strategies (11.1)** offers some precepts that should be clearly communicated to clients.

***Managing client expectations.*** Internal management and administration play a critical role in the client education and contracting process, as well as in the process of educating personnel on risk management and dispute prevention principles. The effective performance of that role requires the dedication of time and effort. Management at all levels should encourage identification of potential problems or concerns, both general and project-specific. In addition, management should establish standard contract terms and restrict the contract negotiation/execution role to key personnel.

Firm employees involved in the actual performance of services should be trained in the importance of educating the client about realistic expectations of the architect's performance and the fair allocation of risk between the owner and contractor in the preparation of the construction general conditions. In addition, these employees should be trained to promptly identify and respond to problems that arise in the field during construction or as a result of other client contacts. Because field personnel are likely to learn of such problems first, they are in the best position, after consultation with management or supervisors, to address the problems in a timely and low-key manner.

**Keeping the client informed in writing offers many advantages. It shows that you care and are focused on the project's success. It says that you are listening and acting on the client's behalf. Such correspondence, written affirmatively, should show that you acted reasonably and with attention to the client's needs and decisions. It can help if you become part of a dispute. This correspondence also builds trust—and thus can be seen as good marketing.**

Once aware of an actual or potential problem, management should monitor developments and take a proactive role in mitigating the problem. Management can explore possible avenues of resolution or lay the foundation for an effective defense should a claim eventually materialize.

Most architects in senior management positions have had some experience in dealing with client problems and claims situations. They are in a position to give valuable advice to less experienced project staff handling problems on a day-to-day basis. Maintaining a low profile may be appropriate in some situations, but it is rarely advisable to avoid or ignore a client problem. The interaction between management and professional staff directly involved in the client problem serves to introduce some objectivity into the evaluation and potential resolution of the dispute.

***Thinking ahead.*** On some projects there are early indications of potential problems, such as on a publicly bid project when the winning contractor has a reputation for "lowball" bids and claims. In such a situation, it is important that the architect not adopt a fatalistic attitude.

Recognizing the enhanced potential for disputes, the architect should assign an experienced, skilled project manager to educate and prepare the client for the possibility of contractor claims. The architect should also clearly articulate project requirements at the preconstruction conference. The preconstruction conference, like the prebid conference and preaward conference (if any) that preceded it, represents an important opportunity to influence and refine owner and contractor expectations.

During project execution, the architect should be proactive in checking the contractor's compliance with all general condition requirements and should completely document in a timely manner all pertinent developments and communications with the contractor. Timely responses to the contractor's inquiries or other communications often avoid or reduce the potential for disputes. Finally, the architect should consult with experienced legal counsel as necessary to obtain timely, preventative advice. The key is to be proactive in anticipating and addressing potential or actual problems.

▷ **The process of responding to a claim is the same regardless of the claimant. There is not one set of procedures to respond to client-initiated claims, another for contractor-initiated claims, and a third for third-party claims.**

***Partnering.*** In recent years the concept of "partnering" has been promoted as a new method of dispute prevention for design and construction projects. Partnering works to create an environment that enhances communication, trust, and teamwork to the benefit of all project participants. It is a process, not a single event such as a preconstruction conference. The partnering process usually involves a structured, ongoing effort to develop and maintain communications and working relationships among the various project participants. It typically includes an initial workshop to outline mutual goals and the elements or procedures that will be used to implement the program. Usually a project-specific goals statement is prepared and executed by the project participants, including the owner, architect, contractor, and often various subcontractors and consultants. The initial workshop is followed by regularly scheduled team-building sessions to monitor progress and resolve potential disputes.

The partnering process is usually managed by a facilitator who coordinates the activities of the partners. The facilitator evaluates several key issues during the partnering process:

- Whether enough follow-through is taking place
- Whether the right number of team-building sessions is being scheduled
- Whether the proper mix of management and project staff are actually attending the team-building sessions
- Whether the partner participants have the proper skills to address potential disputes adequately and bring about mutually satisfactory resolutions

When measured by a reduction in the number of disputes requiring adjudicative resolution, the construction industry's experience with partnering has been very favorable. However, it is important to note that partnering is not a substitute for formal contractual arrangements that fairly allocate risk and reward among project participants.

## NONADJUDICATIVE DISPUTE RESOLUTION

▷ **"Agree, for the law is costly."**
*William Camden (1551–1623)*

Just as there are various ways to reduce the probability of disputes, there are various approaches that allow and encourage the parties to resolve disputes without resorting to an adjudicative process in which a resolution is imposed by a third party. For instance, if direct negotiation between the parties is unsuccessful, the next step may be one of several project-site dispute resolution techniques. Beyond that, mediation may be an appropriate option or may even be required as a precondition to arbitration or litigation. Each step along the continuum generally represents not only an escalation of the dispute but an escalation in the time and cost necessary to resolve it.

▷ **Project Teams (13.1) suggests, as one possibility, a "three-alternative rule" for presenting options.**

***Negotiation.*** Most construction industry disputes are settled, sooner or later, through negotiation. However, because construction industry disputes are often dynamic and involve the interests of many parties, and negotiation is not a purely standardized process, it is often hard to know when and how to get started. First, negotiation is a consensual process. Success depends on voluntary, good-faith efforts by all parties to reach a settlement. Second, a negotiated settlement must result in some adjustment in the relationship between the parties that effectively addresses the issues in dispute. Finally, the new relationship must represent an overall bettering of the position of each party given their respective bargaining positions (i.e., each party must perceive that it is better off settling than not settling).

With adequate preparation and the confidence and objectivity supported by that preparation, negotiation will have a good chance of succeeding. However, success will ultimately depend on a negotiation process that encourages good-faith efforts by, and mutual trust among, the disputing parties.

**Project-site dispute resolution techniques.** Three common methods of project-site dispute resolution are setting up the architect as the initial decision maker, employing a standing neutral, and establishing a dispute review board. These methods are typically built into the project delivery process and are designed to facilitate dispute resolution in a manner that is contemporaneous with the actual activities on the project. Project-site techniques are often used when initial attempts at direct negotiation fail to resolve a dispute. Their use avoids the need for more formal methods that may require weeks or months to bring about a resolution.

**Architect as initial decision maker.** Under the AIA standard documents, the architect serves as the owner's representative during construction. However, the architect also serves as an impartial interpreter of the requirements of the contract documents and initial arbitrator of disputes between the owner and contractor. When such a dispute arises, the architect's rendering of an initial decision in a quasi-judicial capacity is a condition precedent to the owner's or contractor's recourse to any other rights or remedies provided under the contract documents, such as mediation, arbitration, or litigation.

Some have criticized this project-site technique because the architect is not really neutral, given the architect's conflicting roles as not only owner's representative and initial arbitrator of disputes during construction but, typically, designer of record as well. These conflicts are often pointed out by advocates of other project-site techniques, such as the standing neutral and dispute review board. Notwithstanding these concerns, the architect's decisions under the AIA documents are commonly accepted by contractors and owners as the final resolutions to their disputes.

**Standing neutral.** A standing neutral is a third party, appointed by the parties to a particular contract, who stands ready to resolve disputes on short notice. This standing neutral should be well versed in design and construction issues and involved in the project from the start of construction. The most important attribute of the standing neutral, as well as of the dispute review board, is the ability to engender the respect of the parties. Demonstrated competence, experience, open-mindedness, and ethical integrity are key considerations.

At the outset of the project the standing neutral is provided copies of the various contract documents and other project documentation as needed. In addition, this individual may attend project meetings to maintain a current understanding of the issues at hand. Opinions issued by the standing neutral may be either binding or non-binding, depending on the wishes of the parties, but are most often nonbinding. Usually when the standing neutral issues an advisory opinion it is admissible in any subsequent litigation or arbitration concerning that particular issue. The expenses of the standing neutral are typically shared equally by the owner and contractor.

**Dispute review board.** Beginning with its application on tunneling contracts in the 1970s, the dispute review board has proven to be one of the most successful applications of nonadjudicative dispute resolution, particularly on larger projects. Like the standing neutral, the dispute review board is established before construction starts, convenes regularly during the project, usually has firsthand and contemporaneous knowledge of the events giving rise to the disputes or claims later submitted to it, and has specialized experience in a particular type of construction. These factors have contributed greatly to the success of this method.

As is the case with the standing neutral, the expenses of a dispute review board are normally shared equally between the owner and contractor.

**Mediation.** Mediation is a nonbinding, facilitative process in which an impartial

Since 1957 the AIA has commended the Professional Liability Insurance Program available from Continental Casualty Company, one of the CNA Insurance Companies. The CNA program is administered by the underwriting management firm of Victor O. Schinnerer & Company, Inc. The AIA commends the CNA/Schinnerer Program because it is national in scope and meets the commendation criteria established by the AIA Board of Directors.

About 20,000 architecture, engineering, landscape architecture, and land surveying firms were covered by the CNA/Schinnerer program in 1999. Almost 50 percent of these were architecture firms.

Collectively, almost 2,000 claims were filed against CNA/Schinnerer-insured architects in 1998. About 60 percent of these claims were brought by project owners who experienced some cost, loss, or damage or were simply dissatisfied and angry. More than 70 percent of all claims against architects were brought by parties to the design and construction contracts.

Over three-quarters of the claims against architects involved property damage or economic loss; the rest involved bodily injury to building users or construction workers. While injury claims are relatively frequent, very few result in any payment to the injured party by the insured architect or by the insurance company on the architect's behalf.

Spreading all the claims over all the firms in the program, a total of 22.4 claims were reported for each 100 firms in 1998. Small firms had fewer claims on the average—about 10 per 100 firms—while very large firms averaged about 180 per 100 firms. Most claims are resolved without payment. In fact, only about one in five claims ever requires the CNA/Schinnerer program to make a payment on the policyholder's behalf. Still, any dispute increases the cost to architects of providing their services.

Because larger firms retain higher deductible obligations, they tend to have fewer claims that require insurance indemnity payments. Smaller firms, in fact, are about twelve times more likely to have a claim that requires an indemnity payment than larger firms if the comparison is made on the basis of equal billings. The severity of paid claims (the cost of defense and indemnity above the deductible obligation), however, shows the other side of the claims story. The payments made by the CNA/Schinnerer program on behalf of large firms are, on average, about six times as high as the payments on behalf of small firms.

A thirty-year view of claims frequency shows that claims against architects and engineers grew substantially after 1972, reaching a high of about 44 claims per 100 firms in 1983. Since then, firms have been managing their practices—and selecting their clients—more carefully and with a greater appreciation of the risk management programs developed by the CNA/Schinnerer program. The

frequency of claims has stabilized at about half the 1983 level, and no major rise is anticipated.

As could be expected with property damage and economic loss situations, claims tend to closely follow substantial completion. Some Schinnerer studies suggest that about two-thirds of all claims are filed within three years of substantial completion, 85 percent within six years, and 95 percent within ten years. While the CNA/Schinnerer program and the AIA have pursued tort reform initiatives such as the requirement of a certificate of merit before a claim can be filed, the elimination of joint and several liability, and realistic statutes of repose to cut off claims after a specific number of years, such legislation seems to have little effect on the frequency or severity of claims against architects. Proper contract language—such as the use of AIA forms—and the careful management of projects through quality controls, communications, and documents seem to have the greatest impact on reducing the risk of professional liability claims.

Over a ten-year study period, three-quarters of all claims brought against architecture and consulting engineering firms were based on property damage or economic loss. Less than a quarter involved an allegation of bodily injury. In examining the disposition of claims, it is clear that very few bodily injury claims result in anything more than the expenditure of time and defense costs. Using indemnity payments (payments made by the insurance company on behalf of the insured to remedy a harm) as the measure, only 11.8 percent of injury claims result in a payment in compensation for the injury. Of all claims brought against architecture and consulting engineering firms, claims in which personal injury results in an indemnity payment amount to only 2.9 percent of closed claims.

The clients of architecture and consulting engineering firms bring most claims against these design professionals. The sources of claims during the period of study are in the following categories:

| | |
|---|---|
| Project Owner/Client | 57.3% |
| Contractor/Subcontractor | 10.8% |
| Other Property Damage | 7.4% |
| Nonworker Injury | 16.8% |
| Worker Injury | 7.7% |

Bodily Injury vs. Property Damage Claims

Bodily Injury Claims 24.6%

Property Damage Claims 75.4%

Injured Worker—Indemnity Payment Made by Insurer (3.0% of Injury Claims; **0.7% of All Claims**)

Non-Worker Injury—Indemnity Payment Made (8.8% of Injury Claims; **2.2% of All Claims**)

Injured Worker—No Indemnity Payment Made (29.4% of Injury Claims; **7.2% of All Claims**)

Non-Worker Injury—No Indemnity Payment Made (58.8% of Injury Claims; **14.5% of All Claims**)

mediator actively assists the parties in identifying and clarifying issues of concern and in designing and agreeing to solutions for those issues. For mediation to work effectively, it is important that the mediator be carefully selected on the basis of qualification, reputation, and knowledge of the design and construction process. Further, the parties' representatives who participate must have the authority to resolve the dispute directly and personally participate in the mediation process. Moreover, they must be willing to participate in good faith in the process and maintain open minds with respect to the issues in question.

Mediation can proceed under the rules or guidelines of a particular organization, such as the Construction Mediation Rules of the American Arbitration Association (AAA) or the Model Mediation Procedures of the CPR Institute for Dispute Resolution, and the mediator can be selected from that organization's panel of mediators. Alternatively, the parties may simply agree to engage a particular mediator who may establish any necessary ground rules. However the parties choose to proceed, mediation is a relatively informal process. Typically the mediator will conduct joint meetings with the parties and separate meetings or caucuses with each party to gain an understanding of the facts and issues involved in the dispute and the underlying concerns and priorities of each of the parties. During the course of these sessions, the mediator's objective will be to help the parties identify, clarify, narrow, and ultimately remove the barriers to a mutually satisfactory settlement. Often this requires the mediator to serve as an "agent of reality" by encouraging the parties to consider more realistically their individual views and demands as well as the uncertainty and expense associated with the alternatives to a negotiated settlement—arbitration or litigation.

Use of mediation can be promoted by including a contract provision requiring the parties to submit disputes to mediation before resorting to arbitration or litigation. The 1997 editions of AIA Document A201 and AIA Document B141 require mediation as a condition precedent to arbitration or litigation. The AIA documents further provide that mediation is to be conducted in accordance with AAA's Construction Industry Mediation Rules, with the fees to be split equally between the contracting parties unless they agree otherwise.

As a practical matter, the idea of making mediation mandatory is somewhat contrary to its purposes. However, it provides a valuable opportunity to resolve a dispute in a relatively relaxed, low-key environment. Even when the parties fail to reach a complete resolution of the dispute, they often succeed in sufficiently narrowing it so that it can be dealt with more expeditiously in any subsequent adjudicative proceeding. For that very reason, many local courts across the country include a mandatory "mediation track" for certain categories of civil litigation.

## ADJUDICATION PROCESSES

Despite the best efforts of both parties to anticipate situations and accommodate disputes, some disputes simply will not be resolved through nonadjudicative procedures. In this unfortunate event, the dispute will typically move into one of two principal forms of binding adjudication—litigation or binding arbitration.

Perhaps in no other area of our culture does a lack of familiarity breed more apprehension than in the processes, terminology, and institutions associated with the law. The following overview will not, and should not, relieve the architect of all apprehension concerning litigation or arbitration. However, familiarity should allow for more informed decision making in selecting a method of adjudication and more confident and knowledgeable participation in the proceedings.

### Arbitration

Arbitration is an alternative to litigation for the resolution of disputes. In this method the parties agree to have an arbitrator or panel of arbitrators familiar with the activity to which the dispute relates rule on the merits of their claims. Because an arbitration proceeding takes place outside (although not completely independently) of the judicial process, the parties must agree on rules for selection of arbitrators and on rules for the arbitration process. Organizations such as AAA have been created to provide stan-

The backgrounder Mediation (11.3) describes the process in more detail.

> "When angry, count to four . . . when very angry, swear."
>
> *Mark Twain*

The backgrounder Arbitration (11.3) describes the process in more detail.

dardized rules, a panel of prequalified construction industry arbitrators, and administration of the arbitration process. Alternatively, the parties can choose their own arbitrators and devise their own arbitration procedures. In many states, when an agreement to arbitrate disputes fails to define the rules and procedures for the arbitration, the Uniform Arbitration Act, which was adopted by the National Conference of Commissioners on Uniform State Laws in the 1950s and serves as the model for most state arbitration acts, will govern the selection of arbitrators and the procedures to be used.

Whereas plaintiffs, in litigation, can join multiple defendants and those defendants can join still other parties as third-party defendants, arbitration is strictly a creature of contract. In the absence of an agreement, no third party can be compelled, through joinder, to become a party to an arbitration proceeding. Also, the arbitration clauses in many contracts prohibit joinder of third parties and consolidation of separate arbitration cases (e.g., owner-contractor and owner-architect) unless mutually agreed to by the several parties. As a result, it is not unusual for one or more arbitration cases or for arbitration and litigation to proceed concurrently or serially in disputes involving several parties. In the interest of economy, a few states have adapted consolidation statutes. Courts in some other states have claimed inherent authority to consolidate separate arbitration cases arising out of the same facts or questions of law; however, they generally honor contractual prohibitions against consolidation.

The arbitration hearing process is quite similar to a trial, though less formal. Although there is no requirement for parties to be represented by counsel in arbitration, most parties choose to be represented. Each side explains its position and intended evidence in an opening statement. First the claimant's and then the respondent's witnesses testify and are cross-examined. Documents and other types of exhibits are introduced during the testimony. A party may object to certain evidence, but the courtroom rules of evidence are relaxed in arbitration. The hearings can last from a few hours to many months, depending on the complexity of the matters involved and the amount of money in controversy. At the conclusion of the hearing, the arbitrator or arbitration panel frequently asks each party for an oral or written closing statement. This gives each party the opportunity to restate its position and explain how the evidence supports that position. The hearings are then closed.

The essence of arbitration is finality. Unlike litigation, in which a verdict may be subject to appeal on the basis of various issues of law, an arbitration award may not generally be set aside or vacated because of an error in law. Rather, because arbitration is based on broad concepts of justice and equity, an award will normally be vacated only if the award was procured by corruption or fraud; there was evident arbitrator bias, corruption, or misconduct; or the arbitrators exceeded their authority. In addition, virtually all states have adopted laws that enforce the obligation to arbitrate and the award resulting from arbitration when the arbitration is required by contract. Finally, the Federal Arbitration Act, originated in 1925 and updated several times (most recently in 1990), reinforces the mandatory and binding nature of arbitration, because the act generally preempts state laws that may otherwise prevent enforcement of arbitration provisions in contracts involving interstate commerce. Courts have uniformly held that the design and construction of facilities require the movement of goods and personnel across state lines and therefore constitute interstate commerce.

That arbitration does not provide the procedural and legal safeguards afforded by litigation is a frequent criticism that merits careful consideration. Although arbitrators must act in good faith and without partiality, they are not bound to follow the rules of evidence or legal precedent, and their decisions are subject to very limited judicial review. Clearly, substituting arbitration for litigation involves trade-offs. The traditional objectives of this substitution—to avoid the delay, cost, and uninformed decisions associated with litigation—must be balanced against the more extensive protections afforded by the judicial system.

> "Anger is just one letter short of danger."
> *Anonymous*

> Traditionally the concept of privity of contract limited legal actions against the architect to those parties with whom the architect had a contract. The erosion of the privity concept opened architects to suits from third parties who had no contractual relationship.

## Litigation

Two of the more important contractual issues in connection with selecting litigation as the method for adjudication are venue (i.e., the place of the trial) and whether a jury trial or bench trial is preferable. The following paragraphs briefly address these issues.

***Venue.*** The parties to a contract can designate the geographical area in which a court with jurisdiction may hear and determine a case. In many instances the court for the state in which the project is situated may be selected. This can serve as a "choice of law" provision so that the agreement is governed by, and is construed in accordance with, the laws of the selected state. For instance, like earlier editions, AIA B141-1997 provides that the law governing the contract and services is the law of the principal place of business of the architect. With the advice of legal counsel, architects should be sensitive to differences in state laws on issues such as statutes of limitation and repose; concepts of negligence, including the accepted standard of care and causation; interpretations of common law and statutory indemnification; and judicial scrutiny of any limitations on tort or contract liability.

***Jury or bench trial.*** It is not uncommon for an architect's client, particularly a large corporate client, to propose contract language whereby the parties waive trial by jury. While this is rarely a critical question in contract negotiations, architects should be aware of some of the issues in play. Also, if the contract is silent on this matter, a decision may have to be made in the event of a claim.

A jury trial may not always be to the advantage of the architect. For example, a bench trial is usually shorter and less expensive then a jury trial. Also, some trial lawyers believe that judges are easier to educate and more patient, particularly when receiving expert witness testimony. On the other hand, some trial lawyers believe that a jury trial forces the judge to make legal and evidentiary rulings more precisely and earlier during the course of the trial. Also, some trial lawyers believe that juries are able to comprehend the evidence, including expert witness testimony, and make factual decisions as well as a judge.

There also may be a number of considerations that work to the advantage or disadvantage of the architect, depending on the case specifics. For example, a judge's individual bias or prejudice may work for or against the architect. Some trial lawyers believe that judges are more likely than juries to uphold technical defenses, such as a contractor's or architect's failure to serve timely notice of a claim. Local politics, particularly in jurisdictions where judges are elected, and community sentiment concerning a given project can have a bearing on the outcome of a case. Needless to say, when choosing between a jury trial and bench trial the architect and legal counsel should carefully consider these and other relevant issues.

## CONTRACTUAL ISSUES IN SELECTING ARBITRATION OR LITIGATION

The following contractual issues should be also be considered regardless of which method of adjudication is selected.

***Legal fees and expenses.*** Under the so-called American rule, attorney's fees are not generally awardable to the prevailing party in litigation unless the opponent acted in bad faith or the award of attorney fees is contractually authorized. Although the AAA rules allow an arbitrator to "grant any remedy or relief which is just and equitable and within the terms of the agreement of the parties," state arbitration laws modeled on the Uniform Arbitration Act follow the American rule's prohibition on the award of attorney fees in the absence of express contractual authorization. The AIA documents are silent on the issue, implying that each party should bear its own attorney's fees. Therefore, if the award of attorney's fees is desirable, an express provision should be inserted into the contract.

Many architects feel that requiring the nonprevailing party to pay the prevailing party's attorney's fees and related expenses is both fair and has a chilling effect on non-meritorious claims. However, such provisions can also inhibit a weaker economic party—often the architect—from asserting a meritorious claim, due to the uncertainty of the adjudicated outcome and fear of being held responsible for the stronger party's investment in legal fees. Thus a prevailing-party provision can work to the detriment, rather than advantage, of an architect.

***Limitation periods for assertion of claims.*** Most states allow parties to include a provision that specifically defines both the time within which either party may assert a claim against the other party and the start or trigger date for the running of that contractual limitation period.

The trigger date should be defined by reference to an objectively ascertainable date or occurrence, such as the date of substantial completion of the project, rather than a subjective or less clearly discernible or provable event, such as the date when the complainant actually discovered the basis for a claim against the architect. As to the length of the limitation period itself, the laws of some states require that the period not be unreasonably short. The AIA documents reference the applicable statute of limitations as the limitation period. However, because not all states have statutes of limitation or repose applicable to architect services and because the parties may agree to shorten the period covered by applicable statutes, the architect should consult with knowledgeable legal counsel in the jurisdiction.

## Settlement During Litigation or Arbitration

In principle, an unmeritorious claim should be vigorously contested. Frivolous or nuisance claims that result in profitable return to plaintiffs or claimants provide incentive for more such claims to be made. As a case unfolds, however, it may become evident that there is considerable risk of an unfavorable outcome. In that event, it is important to recognize the business component in evaluating the settlement alternative. Defense of a claim through a final, adjudicated outcome is an investment. The probable return on that investment should be evaluated as dispassionately as any other business investment.

There are a number of reasons why the insurer or defense counsel might recommend settlement. When a settlement is recommended, the defense team should clearly articulate the rationale for the settlement and alternatives so that the architect can make an informed decision. Many insurers, including the AIA's CNA/Schinnerer program, will not settle a claim without the informed consent of the insured party.

A settlement is not an admission of guilt or liability. Rather, it is a compromise among the parties in dispute whereby they agree among themselves on their respective rights and obligations. When a settlement is reached, it is important that the terms of the settlement be properly documented. The defense counsel will take the lead in formalizing the settlement agreement and in terminating the judicial or arbitration proceedings. In coordination with the defense counsel, the claims representative will arrange for any payments to be made by the architect or the insurer under the terms of the policy.

### For More Information

For information on managing disputes from a professional liability insurance perspective, visit the Web site of Victor O. Schinnerer & Company, Inc., www.schinnerer.com. For information on the construction industry dispute resolution procedures, AAA dispute avoidance and resolution services, and the full range of AAA services, contact the nearest AAA office or visit www.adr.org.

---

## Managing Claims or Incidents

Timely communication is critical to managing a claim. The sooner you contact your insurance broker or carrier, the more effectively your insurer can respond to your needs and help your claim reach a satisfactory conclusion. Different professional liability insurance carriers have their own procedures. Following are those used in the AIA-commended CNA/Schinnerer program. If you are not insured, or if your insurer will not provide the assistance you need, it is good advice to contact your lawyer. You might want to use the procedures outlined here as a checklist.

### What You Should Do

Under the CNA/Schinnerer policy, you have the option to report an incident (a situation in which you are concerned that a claim may occur) and are encouraged to do so. By reporting an incident, you can often avoid a claim altogether or resolve it favorably. To ensure the fastest possible response to your incident or claim, follow these steps:

1. When you are notified of a claim or become aware of an incident and you need immediate advice or assistance, call your local CNA claims specialist or (800) CNA-ASST.
2. Report an incident or claim as soon as possible by writing the CNA Insurance Companies in care of Victor O. Schinnerer & Company, Two Wisconsin Circle, Chevy Chase, MD 20815-7003 or as directed by your local CNA claims specialist.
3. With respect to claims, all principals and staff members involved in the claim should be prepared to document the circumstances surrounding the allegation. Include this preliminary information in your written report to CNA:

   - Your firm's name and address
   - Your policy number
   - Date, time, and location of the situation
   - Brief narrative description of the allegation against you (do not address the merits or your opinion of the claim)

*Andrew Shapiro, Esq., vice president for AEC claims, CNA Insurance Companies*

# Mediation

*Mark Appel*

If quality management, client education, and good practice can reduce claims, the next step is to reduce transaction costs—the costs of preparing and defending lawsuits and, more broadly, the human and emotional toll taken by litigation. Mediation may provide one, and ultimately the preferred, solution. The growing caseloads of mediators suggest that the public is willing to try mediation. The number of success stories resulting from mediation suggest that the time and minimal expense incurred by the participants are worth the effort.

## Why Mediate?

Mediators concur that there are several points during the development or prosecution of most claims when the claim becomes "mediatable." Parties may not notice those possibilities, though, and may need encouragement to consider mediation. Indeed, mediators invariably report that getting the parties to the mediation table is the hardest part of their job. Once mediation begins, mediators routinely report that 70 to 80 percent or more of claims are resolved.

Why do parties ultimately choose to mediate? The reasons are many. Litigation is financially prohibitive and emotionally exhausting. Mediation is cheaper, faster, and takes less of an emotional toll. In our cluttered courts, with civil backlogs of up to six years in some jurisdictions, mediation may be the best, if not the only, way to get a case resolved expeditiously. In many jurisdictions, courts themselves recognize this benefit and have established their own mediation capabilities to combat rising caseloads.

Mediation is not characterized with the formalities and rules of the courts. It is conducted in layman's terms, easily understood by the parties. More important, in a well-conducted mediation, everyone can win. No party may get everything it wants, but no party should leave feeling it was victimized by the process. Mediation also differs from arbitration and litigation in that it involves only stakeholders (and their key legal and insurance advisors). Witnesses are not necessary, as the strength of a case is often only one of many factors parties take into account in deciding how to resolve the case. Moreover, mediation is private, so all the parties share a sense of personal control and an understanding of the importance of the case.

Mediation is usually voluntary, although courts increasingly are requiring parties to try mediation before going to trial. There are two significant advantages to early voluntary mediation. According to Linda R. Singer, principal in ADR Associates, a leading Washington, D.C., mediation firm, "Sitting down with the other parties early, before positions harden, may avoid both unnecessary hard feelings and additional transaction costs. Coming to the table voluntarily without waiting for a court's encouragement or order also allows the parties to select their own mediator and thus retain more control over the process."

## Why Not Mediate?

If the reasons favoring mediation are so compelling, why aren't all cases mediated? Some claims do not come into mediation because they turn on legal issues that only a court can resolve and because parties need, if not want, that ruling. Some continue in court because parties without liability refuse to "pay up" solely to make the case disappear. Others are not resolved because parties and their counsel need to "know more" before they can secure their mediation stances; discovery must continue for those claims to be resolved. (Even these cases can be resolved more quickly if a creative mediator and cooperative parties devise a limited discovery schedule.) Still others are not resolved because of grossly uneven bargaining power among the parties that the mediator cannot undo or manage effectively. (Here again, a little creative mediation might succeed in negotiating an effective resolution once the mediator has brought the parties together.) Finally, some cases remain pending due as much to the incompetence of a poor mediator as to the reluctance of the parties.

## How to Decide

The fact remains that the very inducements to mediate can also be seen as reasons to avoid the process—namely, it is hidden and without rules and formalities. How, then, can you decide whether to mediate?

- *Evaluate your own case.* Will your success turn on a legal issue, particularly one that will free the firm without a trial? The solution may then rest in court, unless the firm has a reason not to take the chance of an unfavorable ruling. Alternatively, if some wrongdoing can be laid at the firm's door—because of the law, evidence, or equities—then mediation may prove the better route.
- *Evaluate the mediator.* There are no formal standards, training, or licensing procedures with which one must comply to wear the label "mediator." Anyone can enter the fray with minimal or no training. Therefore, before you agree to mediation, you should ask the mediators about their philosophy on mediation, how they view their role, and about their training, experience, and references. Only when you are certain that the mediators are the trained neutrals they are supposed to be should you agree to proceed.
- *Determine your stance before you begin.* As informal as mediation may appear, it has most of the attributes of a well-run settlement conference. The firm will need to determine negotiating strategies and best- and worst-case alternatives ahead of time. In particular, the firm will need to know where it will bend and where it will break and how to use those insights to its best advantage. Most important, you will have to be prepared to settle the case.
- *Make sure you have the authority you need to settle.* All sides should know that coming to the table with settlement authority is a prerequisite for attendance. Mediators often ask in confidence about the scope and nature of the authority already granted. Good mediators keep that information confidential. If asked, though, they may use its implications to test the settlement waters and to encourage the parties to get settlement authority more appropriate for the case, when necessary.

Mediators also recognize that during the course of mediation settlement ideas and restructuring options may surface that no one could have anticipated. A good mediator can help the parties develop ways to present those options to their respective management if that would help speed case resolution.

*Mark Appel is a senior vice president at the American Arbitration Association (AAA), a global provider of private dispute resolution services, education, and training to corporations, individuals, and governments. As an experienced mediator and mediator trainer, he oversees AAA's mediation outreach and education efforts.*

B A C K G R O U N D E R

## Arbitration

*Howard G. Goldberg, Esq.*

Why arbitrate? Because arbitration is designed to be faster and cheaper than litigation. If the parties and their attorneys enter and engage in the process with the appropriate attitude, and realize that arbitration is not litigation, it usually will achieve these goals.

One of the most common methods of resolving disputes, other than litigation, is arbitration. In fact, commercial arbitration has been the principal method of dispute resolution in some industries, such as the shipping industry, for centuries. It has been used in the construction industry since early in the twentieth century. Almost all AIA documents contain very broad arbitration clauses requiring all disputes "arising out of or related to" the agreement between the parties to be arbitrated after first attempting mediation.

Arbitration involves the submission of a dispute between two or more parties to a neutral, impartial person or panel who is empowered by the parties to resolve all and only those matters and questions submitted for arbitration. Resolution may be in the form of a monetary award from one party to the other or an order directing one party to either take or refrain from taking a particular action. With very limited exceptions, the award of an arbitrator or arbitration panel is binding on the parties as to all matters within the scope of the submission.

Arbitration is a dispute resolution system wholly apart from the judicial branch of government. Generally a court cannot interfere with the arbitration process. It can, however, order parties who previously signed a contract that requires the resolution of disputes by arbitration to arbitrate rather than resort to the judicial system. It can enforce an arbitration award by giving it the same effect as a judgment entered by a court. It can strike or modify an award only on very limited grounds, such as fraud or partiality on the part of an arbitrator or when an arbitrator has ruled on an issue not covered by the agreement to arbitrate.

Other than in these very limited circumstances, neither party has the right to appeal an adverse arbitration award to a court of law. In many jurisdictions, a court cannot overturn an arbitration award even when the decision of the arbitrator is factually mistaken, when the arbitrator misinterprets the law, or when the arbitrator ignores or misinterprets the terms of the contract between the parties. Thus arbitration is generally binding and final. If appeals to the judicial process were permitted, arbitration would become nothing more than a preliminary to litigation.

Since arbitration takes place outside the judicial process, organizations have been created to administer it. One such organization is the American Arbitration Association (AAA), a private, nonprofit organization endorsed by various construction industry groups, including the American Institute of Architects. The parties can, if they mutually choose, bypass the formality of an organization such as AAA and select their own arbitrator or panel of arbitrators and arrange their own procedure. In fact, in many states a statute called the Uniform Arbitration Act governs the selection of arbitrators and procedures to be used in arbitration (when the parties have not agreed to have their arbitration administered by AAA or a similar organization).

In many instances, parties to a contract have agreed to submit to arbitration possible future disputes relating to the contract. Having agreed in a contract to use arbitration, one party cannot later unilaterally decide that litigation would be preferable. On the other hand, parties to a dispute may elect to resolve their dispute by arbitration even when they are under no contractual obligation to do so.

The advantage of using an organization such as AAA to administer the arbitration is that specific rules govern the process. The disadvantage is that there are filing and administrative fees to be borne by the parties, often submitted to the arbitrator(s) for allocation.

*Initiating an arbitration.* When arbitration has been selected as the method of dispute resolution, the parties can jointly or individually prepare a submission for arbitration. The submission outlines the nature and extent of the dispute. When parties have previously agreed to arbitrate disputes, a party may demand arbitration by sending a copy of the demand to the other party and, if applicable, to AAA. No specific format or formal language is required for a submission or a demand for arbitration.

*AAA format.* AAA has adopted three different formats for the administration of arbitration, based upon the amount of money in controversy:

- *Fast track.* Claims under $50,000 are separately administered. Typically, they are to be fully resolved within sixty days by a single arbitrator appointed by AAA. A one-day hearing (within thirty days of filing) is usually permitted unless the parties agree to submission of only written materials.
- *Regular track.* Claims above $50,000 and less than $1,000,000 are handled as outlined below.
- *Large, complex case track.* Claims classified by the parties as unusually complex or involving more than $1,000,000 are handled under the Complex Case Procedures. They are handled in much the same way as regular track claims, except that three arbitrators from a separate list of highly trained neutrals are always selected; at the discretion of the arbitrator, discovery, including the taking of depositions, is permitted; and somewhat more formality is typical.

part 3   DELIVERY

*Selection of arbitrators.* Two methods are generally used to select arbitrators. If AAA administers the arbitration under its regular or complex case rules, it will, upon receiving the submission or demand and response, issue to the parties a list of names and short biographical sketches of potential arbitrators who have experience in the construction industry. The parties then independently strike those persons to whom they object and number the remaining persons as to preference. AAA compares the list of strikes and selects from the remaining names either one or three persons (depending on the complexity of the issues or the amount claimed) as arbitrators. If there are no mutually agreeable names, AAA will appoint an arbitrator or a panel. A party may remove an arbitrator selected by AAA only for cause (e.g., some reason to believe the person may not be impartial). In the alternative method, under the Uniform Arbitration Act, the parties each independently select one arbitrator, and the two arbitrators then jointly select a third. Under either procedure, none of the arbitrators needs to be an attorney or to have legal training or judicial experience.

*Schedule of hearings.* Along with the names of potential arbitrators, AAA distributes calendars, normally ranging from two to five months following the date of the demand. The parties then strike the dates on which they, their counsel, or important witnesses are unavailable. The arbitrator(s) schedule the first hearing.

*Prehearing activity.* Unlike litigation, in which the pretrial period is filled with the exchange of interrogatories (answers to written questions) and the taking of depositions (sworn testimony) of witnesses or potential witnesses, there is no formal discovery process in arbitration. Often, upon request, the arbitrators will allow an exchange of documents or may require disclosures of documents that a party will introduce as exhibits at the hearings and the name of persons who will be called as witnesses.

The lack of discovery is intended to reduce the cost and the length of the process but sometimes leads to surprises at the hearings. When surprise testimony occurs, arbitrators frequently allow the other party time to respond. In complex cases, greater latitude in allowing discovery is generally permitted.

*Hearings.* The arbitration process is completely controlled and directed by the arbitrator(s). Hearings are conducted in much the same manner as trials, but without the formality.

The atmosphere is orderly and dignified but relaxed. Typically, each side gives an opening statement describing its position and evidence. The claimant calls its witnesses first and the respondent second. Witnesses testify and are cross-examined. Documents and other types of exhibits, such as drawings, specifications, models, and memoranda, are introduced when each witness testifies. Although a party may object to certain evidence, the rules of evidence as would be applied by a court do not apply. The hearings can last from a few hours to many months, depending on the complexity of the matters involved and the amount of money in controversy.

Parties may be, and frequently are, represented by counsel; however, representation is not required. Normally when the sums in controversy are significant to a party, it will choose to be represented by counsel, since many of the attributes of a court hearing—presentation of evidence, cross-examination, argument over interpretation of a contract or legal document, and so on—apply.

The oral testimony frequently concludes with an oral or written closing statement. In these final arguments, each party can restate its position and explain why or how the evidence supports its position. The hearings are then closed.

*Award.* The arbitrator or arbitration panel reviews the testimony, analyzes and weighs it, and then issues an award. If AAA is used, the award must be issued within thirty days of the close of the hearings. The award is generally brief, with a statement as to which party prevailed on each of the issues presented and in what amount. Unless the parties, in their contract or submission, provide that the arbitrator issue a reasoned award, which requires an explanation for the decision, no explanation is generally given. The arbitrators have the authority to assess arbitration fees in a manner other than equally between the parties. They may also award legal fees.

The decision is submitted in writing and is final and binding. If a party fails to comply with the award of an arbitrator, the other party may apply for a court order enforcing the award.

*Howard G. Goldberg is a principal in the law firm of Goldberg, Pike & Besche, P.C. He is an honorary member of the American Institute of Architects and is legal counsel to the AIA Contract Documents Committee..*

# Litigation

*Katherine Davitt Enos, Esq., Associate AIA*

Under the current AIA contract documents, parties to the contract agree to use alternative dispute resolution procedures of mediation and arbitration. These provisions offer those involved an opportunity to avoid time-consuming, complex, and often costly litigation. Unless there are modifications to the AIA contract documents that interfere with the process, the parties involved should be able to complete their projects while avoiding actual litigation of most construction disputes.

However, the threat of litigation is a major phenomenon in the life of a professional. An architect who is sued feels the effects of what is perceived as an attack on his or her professional skills and personal integrity. To minimize the cost and aggravation of a lawsuit, architects need to understand the American civil justice system and their rights under it.

## Understanding the System

Most architects who have had a lawsuit filed against them say they would have felt less anxious if they had known what to expect during the litigation process. By familiarizing yourself with the sequence of events in a typical lawsuit, you can reduce the feeling of being caught up in a confusing swirl of activity. The greater your sense of control, the less litigation stress will affect your ability to function in your professional and private life. What's more, understanding the logic of the legal process will make you a better witness.

Civil litigation procedures vary by jurisdiction; this article is not intended as a comprehensive guide to litigation nor as a substitute for personal contact with your attorney.

### The Formal Process

Arrival of an official summons and complaint marks the beginning of an architect's formal involvement in a lawsuit, although this is rarely the first indication that a claim will be made, especially a claim of professional negligence. Before a complaint is sent, there are often warning signs that litigation may occur. Some professional liability insurance programs—such as the AIA's commended program—attempt to head off litigation through early investigation and early resolution of disputes. Certainly when you expect a dispute, you should check your professional liability insurance policy for notification requirements and claims assistance programs.

Once a summons and complaint is received, a response is required, usually within twenty or thirty days. Remember to look at the complaint for what it is—simply unproven allegations. Just because it is a formal, legal document does not make its allegations true. Keep in mind the following:

- It is a complaint, not proof of any wrongdoing.
- It may be the result of a misunderstanding or unreasonable expectations.
- The language in the complaint is based on established legal terminology and precedents. The harsh and accusatory terms used reflect the elements that must be established to prove negligence or breach of contract.
- The attorney may allege unsubstantiated claims in order to preserve the opportunity to sue on the basis of that allegation being supported by new evidence at a later date.
- The tone, language, and number of allegations may reflect posturing by the plaintiff's attorney in an attempt to induce quick settlement.
- It could be a nuisance suit—a nonmeritorious claim that is little more than an attempt by the plaintiff or the plaintiff's attorney to make money.

### Acting to Resolve the Dispute

Once you are formally notified of a lawsuit, your first step should be to contact your lawyer or your professional liability insurer. If you have not already notified your insurer of a circumstance that could lead to a formal claim, now is the time to do it. The real value of a professional liability insurance company is its knowledgeable, experienced claims specialists and attorneys who you can have on your side. Your insurer or lawyer might ask you to do the following:

- Gather all client records, including office notes, correspondence about the project, other project records, and financial records such as bills submitted for services.
- Preserve the records so that nothing is altered or destroyed.
- Establish a separate file pertaining to the lawsuit.

- Meet with your legal counsel as soon as possible. Most insurance policies give insurers the right to choose counsel so that an experienced attorney can be assigned, but remember, the attorney is ethically and legally bound to defend your interests—not those of the insurance company.
- Give your attorney everything you know, feel, and believe about the incident or events that led to the claim, regardless of whether the information supports or damages your case. With this information your attorney can provide the right advice and an adequate defense.
- Refrain from discussing the case with anyone other than members of your family, your insurance representative, and your attorney.

### Recognizing the Elements of the Process

Few claims against architects end in a trial. In the CNA/Schinnerer program, AIA's Commended Program, less than 3 percent of all claims are actually litigated. The U.S. legal system allows anyone to file a lawsuit as long as they pay the required filing fee, but few suits have both the substantive factual disputes and adversarial intensity to endure the cost and complexity of a trial. However, as you proceed toward the trial, you should understand the following elements:

*Discovery.* This is the period when each party to the lawsuit gathers information to support or defend their case. It begins shortly after receipt of the summons and complaint and continues until trial. Discovery allows attorneys from both sides to investigate the facts, the opinions of the parties, the opinions of experts, and the existence and contents of relevant documents.

Discovery often includes interrogatories (written sets of questions submitted to the opposing party that must be answered in writing and under oath) and production requests (demands for documents or other tangible evidence relevant to the case).

*Deposition.* This is a formal proceeding in which the deponent is required, in person and under oath, to answer questions relevant to the lawsuit. A deposition serves two purposes: It allows parties to the suit to obtain information that will assist in the preparation of the case for trial, and it serves to "freeze" deponents' testimony so that the deposition can be used to discredit (impeach) deponents as witnesses at trial if they attempt to alter their statements.

The deposition is also used to gather evidence not otherwise available through the discovery process. It gives the parties an opportunity to verify the accuracy of evidence and statements; to determine the credibility, knowledge, and demeanor of a witness; and to identity additional witnesses, defendants, or experts. As a written record of oral testimony given under oath, the deposition can often be read to a jury and given the same weight as live testimony.

As a named defendant, you have the right to attend all depositions. Although depositions can be emotionally and physically demanding—and time-consuming—they are necessary to move the litigation toward a conclusion. Your deposition takes preparation and practice. Moreover, your mere presence at the deposition of another party may encourage truthful responses and soften any critical opinions by expert witnesses.

Selection of an expert witness is a very important aspect of the discovery process. The expert witness provides an informed opinion on the standard of care that was required of the design professional. Expert testimony offers a reliable, objective determination of what is reasonable, rather than allowing a jury to make a subjective decision about how an architect should have performed.

In addition, design professionals might benefit from a certificate of merit in the early stages of the lawsuit. This is a statutory requirement for an affidavit (the certificate of merit) stating that in a professional's opinion, the possibility exists that the party against whom the claim is made could logically be responsible for the harm. Some states require that such a certificate accompany the complaint in order to avoid frivolous lawsuits. In effect, the certificate of merit is an early form of expert witness testimony. Some contracts even make this a condition to filing a claim between the parties, regardless of the statutory requirements.

### Pretrial Resolution by Motion

At any time prior to trial, attempts can be made to resolve a lawsuit by a motion of the plaintiff, the defendant, or the court. These motions may take the form of a voluntary dismissal by the plaintiff if expert testimony to support the case is insufficient, a defense motion such as a motion to dismiss or a motion for summary judgment (a procedural device used when no genuine issues are in dispute, or only a question of law is involved that can be answered by a judge without a trial), or settlement of the case to avoid litigation.

Settlement is not an admission of guilt or liability. While in principle an unjustified claim should be thoroughly contested, it may become evident that there is considerable risk in seeking a jury or bench decision. Settlement may quantify an unpredictable loss, avoid the expenditure of more time, and reduce the emotional turmoil of a claim. If your attorney recommends settlement, do not be offended and dismiss the idea outright. The reasons for such a recommendation may include the following:

- Your attorney may feel that your case is not defensible because of poor documentation or lack of evidence or witnesses in your favor.
- Your attorney may feel that you will not be a strong witness, particularly if you are uncomfortable with, or easily intimidated by, the process of litigation.
- Your attorney may believe that some degree of your negligence or fault is provable.

A settlement is not a decision on the merits of the case. A stipulation of dismissal that accompanies a settlement is a voluntary dismissal by the plaintiff. In other words, you may have been sued, but you were not found liable.

### The Trial

If a case does go to trial, it is likely that a jury will be empaneled to hear the case. The steps of a trial are fairly standard and include the following:

- *Jury selection.* The effort to select fair jurors varies, but usually both parties have the right to reject a number of potential jurors for cause or on peremptory challenges.
- *Opening statements.* Both parties have an opportunity to present an overview of the case and outline the charges, evidence, and defenses to the allegations.

- *Presentation of the plaintiff's case in chief.* The plaintiff presents evidence to create a claim against the defendant. This presentation of oral testimony, documentary, and evidence supporting the plaintiff's case includes the right of cross-examination of witnesses by defense counsel.
- *Motion for a directed verdict.* The defendant attempts to shorten the process by asking the judge to direct the jury that the evidence presented by the plaintiff is inadequate to meet the legal standards required to support the plaintiff's claim.
- *Presentation of the defendant's case in chief.* The defendant is given an opportunity to refute the plaintiff's allegations. The plaintiff's attorney may cross-examine witnesses for the defense.
- *Closing arguments.* Both parties summarize their cases. After the closing argument for the defendant, the plaintiff's attorney may be allowed to present rebuttal evidence that the defense then can attempt to disprove.
- *Jury instructions.* When all the evidence has been presented, the judge reads the court's instructions to the jury, providing rules to follow when deliberating its decision. For instance, the elements of professional negligence may be outlined and the legal standard of "by a preponderance of the evidence" explained.
- *Jury deliberation.* The jury retires to discuss the factual basis of the case and make its decision in accord with the judge's instructions.
- *Return of a verdict.* When the jury verdict is returned, the judge signs a judgment "on the verdict," which articulates the jury's findings, and the trial is concluded. If the verdict is appealed, an appeals court can only determine issues that are legal in nature, and therefore your involvement will be minimal. This stage involves mostly written legal briefs compiled by the parties' attorneys.

### Be Prepared

Involvement in a professional liability lawsuit or any other litigation can be frustrating and stressful. The best antidote is to be aware of what is expected throughout the entire process. Recognize that the process can be unpredictable. Accept this and take positive action to reduce that unpredictability. Remember the following:

- Familiarize yourself with the process. Learn all you can about it through reading and discussions with your attorney.
- Participate in choosing your experts, including giving your attorney names of potential expert witnesses who can testify on your behalf.
- Do not let yourself be overwhelmed by the legal system. You must be actively involved in the defense of your case.

Realize that the litigation process can be expensive. One benefit of professional liability insurance is the assistance claims managers will provide to help you manage and minimize the financial impacts. They can also help anticipate costs so that you can be prepared to make informed decisions about claims and litigations.

*Katherine Enos combines her architectural practice experience and training in law in her role as a risk management consultant for Victor O. Schinnerer & Company, Inc. She is also the managing editor of Schinnerer's* AE Legal Reporter.

part 3 DELIVERY

# 12 Technology and Information Systems

## Computer Technology in Architectural Practice

Michael Tardif, Assoc. AIA

*Computer technologies offer architects powerful tools that allow them to carry out their everyday tasks with greater effectiveness and efficiency. Emerging digital technology also permits architects to leverage their talents and expand their sphere of practice.*

### THE FUTURE OF COMPUTER TECHNOLOGY IN ARCHITECTURE

Computer technology, including that specific to the construction industry, is continually evolving. Architects who want to stay on top of the latest developments may be interested in some of the improvements in compatibility and standards that are currently under way, including developments in vertical integration, interoperability, aecXML, and CAD standards.

**Vertical integration.** Off-the-shelf computer-based tools designed to automate previously manual tasks are commonly used even in small architecture firms for project management, communications, financial management, contract document preparation, specification writing, bidding, construction contract administration, graphic design, publishing, and marketing. This type of computer software performs distinct tasks, but the proliferation of such technologies has given rise to an intriguing idea—vertical integration.

Vertically integrated applications share data along a continuum, eliminating repetitive reentry of data and allowing data entered for one purpose to be used for another. Vertical integration prompts architects to reconsider and redesign their business and design processes. For example, a project management application, which is designed to forecast the time needed to complete a project, could feed that data directly into a financial management application, which would then produce a project budget. Properly linked, a change in the project time line would automatically update the project budget and vice versa.

**Interoperability.** The benefits of vertical integration are apparent even to computer novices. Indeed, novices often *expect* this type of commonsense intelligence from their computer systems and are sorely disappointed to discover otherwise. In order for vertical integration to be realized, a new technological breakthrough is necessary. Interoperability, the ability to exchange electronic information seamlessly and predictably from one software application to another, is this breakthrough. Several industry-wide efforts to achieve interoperability in architecture applications are under way. Two address the matter at the level of electronic data formats, while a third addresses the development of nomenclature standards for users. The first two efforts, the development of a comprehensive building information model and the development of an organization and classification system to support the exchange of building design information over the World Wide Web, are proceeding under the auspices of the International Alliance for Interoperability (IAI). The third effort, a publication of the U.S.

MICHAEL TARDIF *is director of the AIA Center for Technology and Practice Management.*

National CAD Standard, is a joint effort led by the National Institute of Building Sciences.

The IAI has developed an open electronic data format, a comprehensive building information model collectively known as Industry Foundation Classes (IFCs). The IFCs are intended to define all conceivable attributes of a building facility. Software applications that are IFC-compatible are able to seamlessly and reliably transfer all or a portion of the building information model to other similarly IFC-compatible applications. Architects generally think in terms of being able to transfer data from one CAD application to another. IFC compatibility, on the other hand, is designed and intended to encompass all building-design-related applications—CAD, specification, construction cost estimating, energy analysis, building performance, project management, financial management, and facility management applications. The mission of the IAI, and the purpose of the IFCs, is to support the free exchange and preservation of electronic building design data throughout the life cycle of a building facility.

*aecXML.* The IAI is also spearheading the development of aecXML, an AEC industry subset of XML, which is an acronym for eXtensible Markup Language. XML is a standard promulgated by the World Wide Web Consortium (W3C) to support the exchange of data for electronic commerce on the Web. Information on the Web is currently presented in HyperText Markup Language (HTML). HTML is simply a format standard that instructs the Web browser how to display the text of a Web page, for example, in Times New Roman font, red, 14 point, bold. HTML is not capable of classifying or organizing the data presented. Search tools designed for the Web thus have to examine every word (character string) of an HTML document to determine whether or not the character string matches a given search criteria. This is a computationally intensive process that yields poor results for even the simplest searches. In XML the data are tagged, or classified, much the way books are classified in libraries. This allows XML search engines to perform highly accurate searches of large data sets quickly and accurately. XML is, in a very real sense, the Dewey Decimal Classification of the World Wide Web. AecXML, therefore, is that subset of the classification system that defines data for the architecture, engineering, and construction industry.

While XML and aecXML are intended to organize and classify data on the Web, it is possible to similarly tag data created by desktop applications. Data created by such applications are said to be "aecXML-enabled." This allows the application to export the data in aecXML format for import by other applications that are also aecXML-enabled. Because this is a worldwide, open data classification and organization system that exists as a subset of an accepted Web-based technology, the likelihood that aecXML will become an industry standard for data exchange is very high.

AecXML differs from the IFCs in one important respect: Where IFCs are designed to transfer the complete electronic building information model, aecXML is capable of transferring discrete subsets of data in response to narrowly defined queries. A subcontractor bidding on a project, for example, need only query an electronic building information file using aecXML for that subset of information needed to prepare a bid. The successful bidder, on the other hand, may need the entire data set, or IFC model, for construction purposes and to create a complete data set for the building owner when construction is complete. The two technologies are compatible and can coexist. Indeed, architects and related design professionals would be acting in their own best interest by insisting that all future software applications (or upgrades) they purchase be both IFC-compatible and aecXML-enabled.

*CAD standards.* The need for standard organization and classification of building design data extends all the way to the user level. Many aspects of electronic data classification are user-definable, and a common language to support data exchange is essential.

The National Institute of Building Sciences (NIBS) leads a coalition of industry organizations in the development of the U.S. National CAD Standard (NCS). The NCS defines standards for such things as file names, layer names, terms and abbreviations, symbols, and notations in order to achieve a consistent format. It also includes standards for the format of printed output, including ways of organizing drawing sets, drawing sheets, and schedules. *AIA CAD Layer Guidelines* is a key component of the U.S. National CAD Standard, as is CSI's *Uniform Drawing System.*

Taken together, Industry Foundation Classes, aecXML, and the U.S. National CAD Standard will help free electronic building design data from the applications that created them. This will open the door to a new technological environment in which software developers compete on the basis of the tools they create to manipulate data, rather than on their percentage of total market share. Architects and other consumers of building design technology can help speed the process by demanding that the software or upgrades they purchase be IFC-compatible, aecXML-enabled, and NCS-compliant.

### For More Information

Although it is five years old (an eon in computer technology circles), Ken Sanders's *The Digital Architect: A Common-Sense Guide to Using Computer Technology in Design Practice* (1995) still offers much valuable information about choosing technology for and integrating it into an architectural practice. In particular, the author discusses the strengths and weaknesses of commonly used tools such as Windows and AutoCAD and provides information about managing the digital office. Online, multimedia, and virtual reality resources are also addressed.

The AIA Technology in Practice Professional Interest Area (PIA) offers conferences, workshops, and publications on the subject of computer technology in architectural practice. For information about upcoming events and reports on past ones, check the American Institute of Architects Web site at www.aia.org.

Those interested in keeping up on the latest developments in creating standards for the architectural profession can access the Web sites of these leading edge groups: the International Alliance for Interoperability (www.iai-na.org) and the U.S. National CAD Standard (www.nationalcadstandard.org).

# 12.2 Using the Internet in Practice

## Paul Doherty, AIA, with Michael Tardif, Assoc. AIA

*With so much media hype centered on the Internet, it's little wonder some architects are confused about how this powerful information and communications tool can make their jobs easier. What is clear is that the Internet offers both quick, easy access to information and a reliable communications network.*

To survive in the current economic climate, architects must be prepared for constant change and ready to respond to it. One powerful tool that can help architecture firms keep up with change is the Internet. Constantly evolving, yet easily adapted and molded to fit your needs, the Internet is a perfect vehicle for the Information Age. It is a part of the information revolution that can benefit all businesses.

The initial design for the Internet was developed by a small firm with a specialty in architectural acoustics. According to the book *Where Wizards Stay Up Late: The Origins of the Internet,* by Katie Hanford and Matthew Lyon, engineers Bolt Baranek and Newman (BBN), of Cambridge, Massachusetts, beat out some of the biggest conglomerates of the 1960s for the project. Research scientists were asked to conceptualize a means of connecting government computers so that military personnel, federal employees, and contractors could quickly communicate information regardless of their location or time zone. A child of the Cold War, the Internet was conceived to be invulnerable to nuclear attack: If one area of the Internet is destroyed, the system reroutes information to another area that is still working.

Few people called themselves computer scientists in the 1960s, but those involved in a wide range of research activities were bent on developing a means to connect distant computers and allow them to communicate with one another. Some of these scientists were involved in acoustics research. BBN employed a few of the nation's foremost acoustics scientists, who were known to the Advanced Research Projects Agency (ARPA). BBN was awarded the contract to design and construct ARPANET, which later evolved into the Internet. BBN eventually wound up designing, building, expanding, and maintaining ARPANET for several years.

Today the Internet has a life of its own. With more than 100 million users online and millions of new ones connecting every month, it is no longer the domain of a technical elite. Thanks to its rapidly expanding collection of information resources and increasing ease of use, the Internet has become a central part of daily life. People form relationships, conduct business, and perform transactions using a communications medium in which traditional boundaries and concepts of communication are transcended.

Architects must develop the requisite skills and learn how to harness the Internet for business and design purposes. Those who neglect to master information technology (IT) will be at a severe competitive disadvantage in the twenty-first century. The challenge is not just for individuals but for the entire profession—those who do not understand and master the Internet will lose out to those who do.

Positioning your firm in the Information Age means looking beyond the technology of the day. As a first step, firm owners and managers must analyze their firms' business and design processes, both internal and external, and then make strategic decisions regarding the deployment of information technology for the next one, three, and five years. Many firms have created marketing "portfolio" Web sites and use e-mail for correspondence. Perhaps your firm manages internal communication through an intranet. You may even be using the collaborative environment of an extranet to facilitate project management. Whatever you choose, your business needs and functions should drive your technology decisions, not the other way around. A firm can organize its Internet technology strategy

> **"Being a sole practitioner, I depend on an online forum of people who exchange problems and solutions over the Internet, and a monthly newsletter of shared tips."**
>
> *Peter Wronsky, AIA*

**PAUL DOHERTY** *is the principal partner of the Digit Group, a company of the Greenway Group, an international management consulting and information technology services firm. Doherty has written and lectured widely about applying digital technology in architecture practice.*
**MICHAEL TARDIF** *is director of the AIA Center for Technology and Practice Management.*

in three broad categories: communication, information sharing and retrieval, and collaboration.

## INTERNET COMMUNICATION VIA ELECTRONIC MAIL

Just as fax machines became standard office equipment twenty years ago, e-mail is considered essential to business communication today. E-mail is a personal, direct connection to the Internet. You can send messages, attach drawings or other documents, and communicate instantly across the globe or across town with a few clicks of a mouse.

E-mail is much like regular mail. You send mail to people at their particular addresses, and they write to you at yours. Through e-mail you can even subscribe to the electronic equivalent of magazines and newspapers. E-mail has two distinct advantages over regular mail. The most obvious is speed. Instead of several days, your message can reach the other side of the world in hours, minutes, or even seconds. The other advantage is that once you master the basics, e-mail will enable you to send and receive graphics, CAD drawings, and other electronic data.

E-mail has some advantages that improve on communication over the telephone. You send your message at your convenience, and your recipients respond at their convenience. This is known in the lexicon as "asynchronous communication." And while a phone call across the country or around the world can quickly result in huge phone bills, e-mail lets you exchange vast amounts of information for about the price of a local phone call, even if the other person is on the other side of the world.

The speed of e-mail communication can create an unreasonable expectation of instantaneous response. Together with the volume of messages instant communication makes possible, this tool designed to speed communication can become time-consuming to manage. You can help foster e-mail rules of etiquette by allowing people a reasonable amount of time to reply to your messages. You may also want to monitor the volume of your incoming mail and respond judiciously. Periodically assess whether the amount of time you spend on e-mail communication is facilitating or hindering your business processes.

Haste can also make waste; too many e-mail messages are written in a hurry. Take the time to write as you would a business letter. E-mailing misspelled words reflects directly on your professional competence. Built-in spell-checkers are available in most e-mail packages; use them. When typing an e-mail, don't use all capital letters. On the Internet, ALL CAPS MEANS YOU ARE YELLING. Good e-mail includes a meaningful subject line and a brief message. Keep the subject line between five and eight words. There are times when more formal styles of communication, such as letter writing or face-to-face meetings, are preferable to e-mail. Use your judgment. It is wise to limit the size of your e-mail attachments to less than 50KB. Sending a 900KB CAD attachment with an overly long message is an inefficient use of e-mail.

Although using e-mail is relatively simple, procedures and guidelines should be in place before a firm rolls out an e-mail system. Personnel guidelines can be similar to a firm's policy on telephone use. Limits on personal use, restricted information communications, and other logical issues should be spelled out clearly for all employees. Most important, employees should be trained to understand the legal aspects of e-mail communication.

Although often regarded as a replacement for telephone conversations, and thus informal in nature, e-mail is a form of written communication that can be entered into evidence in a court of law. For this reason, employees should be trained to regard it as formal, professional communication. A firm may be liable for e-mail messages to the same extent as for written project-record correspondence such as field reports, project meeting minutes, letters, transmittals, change orders, and responses to requests for information (RFIs).

## INFORMATION SHARING AND RETRIEVAL

At its simplest, the Internet allows you to share information by automating traditional communication methods. It is now possible to create, at a reasonable cost, electronic marketing brochures or portfolios as Web sites. This makes marketing and public relations

> "The Internet helps minimize travel time on projects. It's also a nice way to convey project archive material to clients and a useful method for sending information to the job site since the image quality is superior to that of a fax."
>
> *Donald R. Wardlaw, AIA*

information about your firm available to a worldwide audience rather than to the limited number of prospective clients on a contact list. Job openings can be posted to a much wider audience of prospective employees than the local newspaper allows, giving you greater access to the best and brightest in the industry. The latest information from product manufacturers can be retrieved instantly when you click on their Web sites. But these are only first steps. The available technology creates opportunities to go beyond simply automating existing business processes to fundamentally change the way you do business.

*The World Wide Web.* The concept behind the World Wide Web, generally referred to as the Web, is transparent access to cross-referenced information. Transparency means that users do not have to know where or how the information is coming to them, although they can find out if they choose. To allow this transparency, Web sites employ a hotlink or hyperlink reference system for retrieving information. To move from one information resource to another, a user clicks on any highlighted picture, word, or phrase that will reference another electronic file. This file can be anywhere on the Internet, thus creating a "web" of cross-referenced information.

Information on the World Wide Web can be viewed with a Web browser, an interface that translates the Web's language—HyperText Markup Language (HTML)—into usable graphic information. The two most popular Web browsers are AOL/Netscape Navigator (www.netscape.com) and Microsoft Internet Explorer (www.microsoft.com/ie). The Web now allows sophisticated information to be viewed and processed through these browsers, which have become standard platforms for business information.

When connected to a browser, users view a screen of information called a Web page. Multiple pages form a Web site. The first page of a Web site is its home page. The home page is the most important element of a site because it shows the navigation plan of what will be presented and introduces users to the information. There are six phases in developing and maintaining a Web site: planning, content, graphic design, programming and technical help, marketing and promotion, and maintenance.

Depending on your own areas of expertise, you might bring in consultants on some or all phases of Web site development. Approach it like a construction project. First develop a good blueprint, perhaps with the help of an "information architect." Next hire individual contractors for the various tasks or perhaps a general contractor (Webmaster) who will take care of building all the pieces for you.

*Product manufacturers' information on the Internet.* Architects can use the Internet to locate product manufacturers' information quickly. Manufacturer Web sites are similar in style to electronic brochures, but the Web is capable of more than reproducing printed advertising. Manufacturers also use it as an efficient means of interacting with people who specify and purchase products. By posting a product's specifications and CAD details for download, a manufacturer can save millions of dollars on printing and postage costs and make the information resources instantly available to designers and specifiers. Although manufacturers' Web sites will not replace the traditional brochures and binders, they do make it possible for designers to get the most accurate and up-to-date information possible. That means no more wondering if the product and its specifications and details are still available or if the binder in your office has been updated recently.

The most useful product manufacturer Web content will include

- CAD and image details ready to be copied and pasted in any format (.dwg, .dxf, .gif)
- Specifications in CSI 16-division format for the specific product chosen
- A user-friendly keyword search interface
- Photographs to either download or copy and paste into client presentations or onto cut sheets
- Specification data sheets for code and standards compliance
- Contact information with toll-free telephone numbers and postal mail and e-mail addresses
- Quick access to local representatives, not just corporate offices

It is crucial that design professionals and specifiers have unhindered access to building product information early in the planning and project initiation phases. Formatted information—which means information that can be retrieved with one or two

## Searching the Internet

With all the information offered on the Internet, it is often difficult to find what you seek. Searching the Internet is as easy as typing in keywords and clicking a mouse a couple of times. The type of information that you want comes flowing down the phone line to your computer. The keys to searching the Internet are knowing which tools to use and developing the skills of "drilling down" to the information you need. Search tools provide instant links to thousands of information areas of the Internet, including the popular World Wide Web. Most search engines allow you to input a word, whereupon the engine will supply links to a wide variety of Web sites that include that word. The sheer volume of responses to your query can be overwhelming.

A number of tools are available to help with the hunt. Certain search tools, such as indices or directories, can search for your subject. Other tools, such as search engines, can search all the contents of a document, not just the site's name. Search results are usually ranked in descending order by the number of times the word appears in a document or by how closely the document appears to match a concept you have entered. This is a much more precise way of locating what you want. But not all search tools are created equal. In general, they fall into two categories:

- Indexes/directories such as Yahoo! (www.yahoo.com) and Magellan (www.magellan.com) search by indexing the titles of Web sites that have registered with that particular index. They are good for searching by broad subject areas. Your search will show sites that generally cover the subject you specified.
- Search engines such as AltaVista (www.altavista.com), Excite (www.excite.com), Lycos (www.lycos.com), and

InfoSeek (www.infoseek.com) will all find individual documents on individual pages of a Web site that match your search request even if the site itself is not specifically relevant. This is a very comprehensive way to search the Internet, often providing unexpected gems of information. But you must be prepared to wade through a lot of garbage if you have not learned certain search skills.

The easiest way to search is by typing a word or phrase into a form on a search engine Web site and then pressing Enter. The search results that come up in response to your query are organized with a relevance rating; usually the sites that best match your query appear at the top of the list. The results are indexed in a hyperlinked format, which allows you to explore the individual results by clicking on the word or phrase found. This click transports you to the site, where you can review the information and check its usefulness to you. The problem, you will find more often than not, is that your request brings you too much information. The key is to filter out what you don't need and quickly and accurately find what you do. To accomplish this, you can use what is often called a Boolean search.

"Boolean" refers to the way you type a word or sequence of words into the search form so the search results will be more focused. Boolean search tools, found in virtually every available Web search engine, rely on syntax, certain characters (such as commas and quotation marks), and certain words (such as AND, OR, or NOT) to define the search criteria more precisely. The resulting words or phrases are called a "search string." It can take as little as thirty minutes to master the syntax of a typical search engine. The time is well worth the investment.

---

clicks of the mouse—allows architects to make better decisions and prepare more precise bid packages.

Attempts to compile and consolidate information from many manufacturers in a single location on the Internet can be seen on industry-specific content-provider Web sites. The major sites that fall into this category for building design and construction include these examples:

- Architects' First Source (www.afsonl.com)
- Sweet's (www.sweets.com)
- Bricsnet.com (www.bricsnet.com)
- ARCAT.com (www.arcat.com)
- Pierpoint (www.pierpoint.com)

Each site has its own strengths and weaknesses, so be sure to visit them all to see which site best suits your needs and expectations.

***Technology convergence.*** Where is all of this Web-based product information leading? The Web allows you to link information together in an easy and understandable way. Its ability to link formatted product information to a design document, be it a digital sketch or a CAD drawing, is a technical boon to the designer as well as to the contractor and facility owner. This convergence of information is leading to a new type of compound document and a new way of communicating building design information. The ability to easily link objects with data in a meaningful way will add value to design services and result in a competitive advantage in the marketplace.

The technology that can link data and objects in a drawing—variously referred to as "virtual building modeling," "building information modeling," or "object-oriented modeling"—is under development. Conceptually, the idea is that each individual component of the geometric representation of a building (the object) is inextricably linked to a database of information about that object. The information can include not only design and construction specification data but also construction cost data, energy consumption data (both for product manufacture and operations), energy performance data, maintenance and operations data, and even recycling data for use when the building component is replaced.

For this vision of connectivity to become a reality, cooperation on a massive scale must take place in the AEC industry. Software developers, building product manufacturers, product information publishers, building design professionals, contractors, and facility owners must work together. Standards development efforts are being led by the International Alliance for Interoperability (IAI) and the National Institute of Building Sciences (NIBS). The AIA and its members are actively involved in these efforts.

The efforts under way to develop industry standards are mutually compatible, and a high level of cooperation and coordination exists among the IAI, NIBS, and the AIA. Theirs and others' efforts will culminate in a technology convergence that will render the distinction between the Internet and individual desktop computers artificial. Moreover, it will enable the AEC industry to streamline building design, construction, and operations methods.

## COORDINATION VIA INTRANET

In its simplest form, an intranet is nothing more than a private Web site to which individual employees are granted access by means of a password. Because most computers are shipped with Web browser software, you need only organize information in the proper format to take advantage of the browser's graphical display and hyperlinking capabilities.

**Computer Technology in Architectural Practice (12.1)** examines various applications of digital technology in architectural practice, including the Internet.

For firms with offices in multiple locations, intranets are an easy way to distribute information to all employees from a single source that can easily be kept up-to-date. Even firms with only one location and no Internet access can deploy an intranet, provided every employee's computer is connected to a local area network. In this configuration, the Web browser searches the network server, rather than remote Web servers, for the pertinent information. Everything needed to implement this type of intranet is already installed on your office computers or is available at little or no cost.

An intranet automates information distribution processes previously performed manually. Soon, however, the technology spurs rethinking and redesign of those processes. For example, online forms can be created for typical, routine communications and data transferred directly to databases or the applications that use it. The type of information that can be managed includes human resources, project management, time management, resource management, knowledge management, and employee training data.

An intranet can allow employees to share information, set up applications easily, participate in electronic discussions, and access images and databases, using the same technologies that make the worldwide Internet work so well. An intranet can enable a design firm to leverage years of computer investment into a more productive environment. Intranets can be used to distribute firm-wide information such as news, human resources policies, employee information, internal job postings, bulletin boards, staff directories, press releases, office standards, and computing policies. A few design firms use an intranet as a central information repository to augment building product sample and catalog libraries.

An intranet offers a friendly environment in which people can create their own information pages. If there are alternative ways to perform certain tasks, ask your employees to provide intranet links to the appropriate resources to save time for other employees. If a useful information resource for your business is found on the Web, ask the person who found it to create a link on the office intranet so that others can access it quickly.

All intranets have some key components:

- *A computer network.* Use your office's local area network (LAN) to provide intranet access to all users in your firm.
- *Web server software.* Simple, free software, such as Microsoft's Internet Information Server (IIS), can satisfy your firm's initial intranet needs.
- *Publication software.* The market leader, Microsoft's FrontPage98, is easy to use and empowers people to publish information on an intranet.
- *Web browsers.* This software creates a standard format for intranet information. With a Web browser used as a front end on your desktops and laptops, you and your employees have point-and-click access to company knowledge across all hardware platforms and office locations. You should standardize on the latest version of either Netscape Navigator or Microsoft Internet Explorer.
- *Web manager software.* Web manager software is essential to any intranet. Even if your intranet is small today, it has the potential to explode in size. Web manager software available today can represent your intranet's Web pages in a graphic format. Again, Microsoft's IIS is a good starter program for this purpose.

Leading design firms are adopting intranet technologies because they deliver an unprecedented and powerful combination of information accessibility and security. Since intranets use a Web browser as their main means of communication, highly graphic information is easy to access and use intuitively, without learning esoteric software programs. However, intranets must be continually updated and expanded to maintain their value.

## INTERNET COLLABORATION VIA PROJECT EXTRANET

The ability to communicate and coordinate information has been a major factor in the growth of applied Internet technology and use. But the potential to alter the way we share information through collaboration is the key to the Internet's greatest productivity gains. Internet collaboration can allow you to focus on your core competency rather than on the production of information. Internet collaboration may include external communications, hyperlinked project records, collaborative workspace, a shared design team knowledge base, and online conferencing.

Project-specific Web sites, sometimes called extranets, are an Internet-related phenomenon in architectural practice. Burgeoning digital information in the design and construction process has accelerated the need for information management and project control. Extranets allow authorized people to access specific project information on a secure Web site. This may sound very technical, but extranets are fairly easy to use and operate. The business reasons for creating and operating an extranet are many:

> "Extranets are personalized Web sites that can work for you both in managing the flow of your project documents and in communicating to all interested project participants."
>
> *Eugene M. Hollander, AIA*

- To reduce errors in communication between project team members
- To capture the collective intelligence of project decisions and information
- To lower costs for couriers, messengers, copies, and blueprints
- To customize a format for each project and team member
- To provide access to everyone who needs it
- To increase security

The most important reason for architects to implement this technology is that the entity that administers the project Web site controls the project information and therefore controls the project. Architects can choose to host an extranet system internally on their own computer systems, outsource system maintenance to a commercial extranet service provider, or upload project information into a client's extranet.

Although a few of the large design firms run their own extranets as a value-added service, most designers do not have the technical, financial, or human resources available to operate them internally. To respond to this market, two trends are emerging: use of project extranet products and use of project extranet services. Commercial providers have emerged to offer architects outsourced, Web-based project management services that can be charged back to the client as a reimbursable expense. An increasing number of clients are hosting

> Almost 50 percent of architecture firms use Web-based software to collaborate online. The most frequent online collaboration involves the exchange of information and the transfer of drawings with consultants.
>
> *AIA Firm Survey 2000*

extranets for their projects. Off-the-shelf project extranet products are also available. A firm can install and manage this software on its own equipment or purchase it and have it installed on the equipment of an Internet service provider (ISP). In the latter case, the firm would pay the ISP a fee for hosting and managing the firm's extranet.

No matter who supports it, a project extranet has certain universal components: a project directory, an electronic "file cabinet" of documents (CAD, specifications, etc.), online forms and logs (requests for information, revisions, etc.), discussion threads for topics, project progress information (photos, reports, etc.), and an easy-to-use front end (screen).

Most project extranet services operate in similar ways. You subscribe on a per project basis for a fixed monthly fee, running anywhere from $139 to $1,500 per month, based on your anticipated use of disk space. You are given limited customization alternatives that allow you to name the project, input contact information for each project team member, and upload information to your project's Web site. All services keep backup copies of your project information, so it will always be available on the Internet no matter when or where you need it.

Project extranet products are purchased on a licensing basis, with the cost usually determined by the number of anticipated users. Project extranet services are generally more cost-effective for smaller firms with limited internal IT staff. Larger firms with substantial internal IT staff find project extranet products more cost-effective since they can amortize the expense over a large number of projects. Firm size, however, should not be the sole criteria used to select a project extranet solution.

No matter how a designer implements an extranet, one thing is certain—owners are adopting these technologies at a rapid pace within their own businesses and expect them to be used on their construction projects. The computer hardware giant 3Com Corporation has $450 million worth of global construction projects being run on the World Wide Web through the company's own extranet. It requires all team members to have Internet access and use basic Information Age communication tools, such as e-mail. Why does 3Com require these skills and tools? Because it saves them an enormous amount of time and money during the design and construction of their buildings and, more importantly, this captured information can be reused to operate and maintain the buildings throughout their life cycle.

## VIRTUAL PRIVATE NETWORKS

A VPN uses World Wide Web technology and software to distribute information in a secure and stable environment, using the Internet as the roadway to send information back and forth. A VPN is a flexible extension to your private network that can include partners, suppliers, remote workers, customers, clients, and others. A VPN provides an alternative environment for secure and efficient transmission of mission-critical information. VPNs will be successful in a construction environment because of their efficiency in terms of cost and time; ease of use; universal open standards for data creation, distribution, and management; inexpensive tools for creation; and secure transactions and storage of data.

By linking remote sites securely over the Internet, VPNs can forge secure private tunnels through the very public Internet. Firms with high security needs and strict budget constraints carve out their own piece of the Internet (the "tunnel") and secure it with firewalls. The tunnel creates an encapsulated, secure path from one computer to another or from one intranet to another. In the past, remote communications meant hefty monthly telecommunications bills for private leased lines, frame-relay services, or cellular connections. Firms are reducing these costs with VPN technology, either by setting up their own service through tools such as Windows NT and Windows2000 or by outsourcing their VPN service. A growing number of telecommunications carriers and ISPs are offering VPN services. PSInet (www.psi.net) and UUnet (www.uu.net) are popular VPN service providers.

VPN technologies are widely available, selected, and integrated, rather than developed from scratch. Use of a VPN requires project team members to have access to an internal intranet or an individual computer setup. The linked intranets have a dedicated server, called a proxy, running as a firewall and tunneling system to send and receive information via the Internet. The VPN can be set up with domain and real Internet protocol (IP) addresses like "ProjectX.com." A VPN does allow communications to go out to the Internet, but only the specific traffic that needs to go on the Internet actually goes there, such as an e-mail to someone outside the VPN.

For overall security, draft a firm-wide security policy of steps employees should take to protect information. Implement an orientation and training program on information security for new employees. Create an emergency response team that can immediately address network intrusions and viruses, and track attack patterns to close security holes. Create a security awareness campaign that alerts employees to security risks and reminds them to take precautions that will prevent break-ins. Finally, never let employees store critical data on portable computers unless the information is encrypted.

## THE NEXT GENERATION IS HERE

In the Information Age, architects are being redefined by the IT tools they use. Traditionally, architects have been the source and managers of construction project information. If architects fail to understand and master IT, the control of digital information will shift to others, and architects will be relegated to a position as subcontractors of design services. By exploiting Internet technology, the architect can make project information accessible and understandable to more team members, improve the efficiency of the design and construction process, and maintain the traditional role of information manager. Internet technology should be considered an integral part of any firm's strategic business plan. No matter how large or small your firm, by correctly applying Internet technology, you can compete in the global marketplace.

Beyond construction project information, a firm that uses Internet tools can create a knowledge base that remains valuable after a building is built. A firm with the ability to manage digital building information on behalf of a client will be able to offer their clients valuable services beyond the deliverables of plans and specifications.

**"The Internet is like Darwinism on steroids. You evolve or get eliminated."**
*Raul Fernandez, quoted in the* Wall Street Journal, *September 8, 1997*

### For More Information

The PIA for Technology in Architectural Practice (TAP) addresses a range of technology issues, including the use of the Internet in practice. TAP maintains a Web page on the AIA Web site at www.aia.org.

In *Cyberplaces: The Internet Guide for Architects, Engineers and Contractors.* (1997), Paul Doherty describes how professionals can apply and use intranets, extranets, and other Internet technologies in practice. This publication has three parts: a book, a CD-ROM, and access to continuous updates online through the publisher's home page at www.cyberplaces.com.

# 12.3 Construction Documents Production

## Susan Greenwald, FAIA, CSI; Kenneth C. Crocco, FAIA; and Kristine K. Fallon, FAIA

*Construction documents describe what is to be built, how contractors are to be selected, and how the contracts for construction will be written and administered. The process of producing the construction documents strives for efficiency, comprehensiveness, and quality.*

Once a design has been developed and approved, the architect prepares the drawings and specifications that set forth the requirements for construction. The development of the construction documents is an extension of the design process. Decisions on details, materials, products, and finishes all serve to reinforce the design concept—and begin the process of translating the concept into reality. Of all project phases, the preparation of the construction documents typically takes the most time and resources.

## ORGANIZATION AND CONTENT

The construction documents are the written and graphic documentation used to communicate the design and administer the project. Typically, the construction documents include the following:

- Bidding requirements (the invitation to bid, or advertisement; information and instructions to bidders; bid forms; and requirements for bid security)
- Contract forms (the form of agreement to be used between owner and contractor; forms for bonds and certificates)
- Contract conditions (the general conditions of the contract for construction, which outline the rights, responsibilities, and duties of owner and contractor as well as others involved in the construction process, including the architect; supplementary conditions particular to the project)
- Drawings (includes architectural, structural, mechanical, electrical, civil, landscape, interior design, and other specialty drawings)
- Specifications (outlines the levels of quality and the standards to be met in the construction of the project)
- Addenda (additions to any of these documents issued by the architect during the bidding or negotiation process)
- Contract modification (orders for minor changes in the work, construction change directives, and change orders)

The construction documents serve multiple purposes:

- They communicate to the owner, in detail, what a project involves.
- They establish the contractual obligations the owner and contractor owe each other during a project, and they lay out the responsibilities of the architect or any other party administering or managing construction contracts for the owner.
- They communicate to the contractor the quantities, qualities, and configuration of the elements required to construct a project. The contractor, in turn, uses the documents to solicit bids or quotations from subcontractors and suppliers.

> "One of the nobler professional goals of every architect should be that every project is completed, closed-out, and delivered with the same verve, intensity, anticipation, interest, effort, attention to detail, dedication, enthusiasm, skill, poise, and concern for the project, as were present and employed when the project first came into the office, all to the client's complete satisfaction and pleasure."
>
> *Ralph W. Liebing,* Architectural Working Drawings *(1999)*

SUSAN GREENWALD *and* KENNETH C. CROCCO *are principals of ArchiText Consulting, Inc, a Chicago firm specializing in building specifications and information management.* KRISTINE K. FALLON *is a Chicago-based consultant for computer applications in the design profession.*

- They may be the basis for obtaining regulatory and financial approvals needed to proceed with construction.

▶ **Construction Agreements (10.3) addresses contract forms and conditions.**

To serve the above purposes, the construction documents include three basic types of information:

- Legal and contractual information (generally bound into a project manual in front of the specifications)
- Procedural and administrative information (generally Division 1 of the specifications and portions of Part 1 of each specifications section)
- Architectural and construction information (generally found in Divisions 2 through 16 of the specifications and in the drawings)

▶ **Contract Administration (17.8) discusses contract modifications.**

It is important that all parties understand that construction documents are not intended to be a complete set of instructions on how to construct a building. Construction means, methods, techniques, sequences, procedures, and site safety precautions are customarily assigned as responsibilities of the contractor to give the contractor full latitude in preparing bids and carrying out the construction phase. The contractor determines the assignment of work to specific trades and subcontractors. The contractor also manages logistical matters such as sequence of operations, scheduling, design of temporary supports and facilities, selection of appropriate equipment, and project safety.

▶ **Construction Procurement (17.7) reviews bidding requirements and addenda.**

## Legal and Contractual Information

The contract forms and conditions establish the legal framework of a project by setting forth the rights, duties, and responsibilities of the owner and contractor.

On larger projects, it has been customary to separate the contract form from the contract conditions. The former is the agreement between owner and contractor enumerating the contract documents, specifying the time of performance, and stating the contractor's compensation. The conditions set forth the rights, duties, and responsibilities of owner and contractor and other parties to the construction process (the architect, subcontractors, and possibly the construction manager, the owner's project representative, etc.). Separating the form from the conditions allows the contractor to disclose the contract conditions to subcontractors and suppliers without revealing the contract sum or other items in the agreement that may be privately held between the owner, architect, and contractor.

*The architect's responsibility.* The standard AIA owner-architect agreement forms state that the architect shall "assist the Owner in the development and preparation of (1) bidding and procurement information which describes the time, place and conditions of bidding; bidding or proposal form; and the form of agreement between the Owner and the Contractor; and (2) the Conditions of the Contract for Construction (General, Supplementary and other Conditions)." The architect is not required to prepare legal and contractual information but only to assist in its preparation. The architect is not in the practice of law and is not professionally qualified to give the owner legal or insurance counsel. It is common, however, for architects to assemble the bidding and contractual documents, providing them for review and approval by the owner.

*The owner's responsibility.* The owner is responsible for furnishing the necessary legal, accounting, and insurance services to accomplish a project. Therefore the owner, with the advice of the owner's legal counsel, approves the bidding requirements, contract forms, and conditions.

If the owner has little experience with construction projects and contracts, it may help to provide the owner with the following information:

- AIA Document A501, Recommended Guide for Competitive Bidding Procedures and Contract Awards for Building Construction. Jointly published with the Associated General Contractors of America, this document is most valuable when the design-award-build delivery approach is being used and when construction contracts will be awarded by competitive bid.

- AIA Document G612, Owner's Instructions Regarding the Construction Contract, Insurance and Bonds, and Bidding Procedures
- "You and Your Architect." This AIA brochure offers advice to clients on how the owner and architect can work together to keep a project on track throughout the design and construction process.

▶ **The backgrounder Responding to Client-Developed Contracts (10.1) provides guidance for dealing with the challenges that special forms of agreement offer all involved in the design and construction process.**

If used, these documents should be submitted to the owner at or prior to the beginning of construction document development because basic decisions about the handling of the construction contract affect all aspects of the project.

Some owners propose or mandate their own bidding requirements, contract forms, and conditions. Since the contractual agreements for construction are so closely related to the owner-architect contract (and any other contracts the owner may have written with a construction manager or other consultants), and since these agreements are usually already in place, it is essential that all of these agreements be carefully coordinated. It is often worthwhile for the architect's legal counsel to review owner-prepared documents with specific regard to the architect's rights, duties, and responsibilities as well as to review clauses covering indemnification of the architect, role of the architect during construction, ownership of documents, dispute resolution, and similar provisions.

## Procedural and Administrative Information

This information is typically found in three places in the construction documents: in the conditions of the contract, in Division 1 of the specifications, and in the opening articles (Part 1) of Divisions 2 through 16 of the specifications.

The general conditions of the contract for construction contain provisions common to the majority of projects. In addition to the legal and contractual information, the general conditions include requirements for a variety of contract administration activities, including submission of shop drawings and samples, contractor payment requests, changes in the work, procedures for uncovering construction for examination by the architect or for recommending that work be stopped, contractor's responsibility for job site safety, and final contract closeout. AIA Document A201, General Conditions of the Contract for Construction, is widely recognized for establishing common general conditions practices.

▶ **Most contracts also include supplementary conditions that pertain uniquely to the project at hand.**

Division 1 of the specifications expands on information in the general conditions and often includes:

- Standard office procedures, such as required format for shop drawing submittals, numbers of sets of submittals required, and procedures for certification of substantial completion
- Procedures required by owners, such as forms for payment requests and waivers of lien
- Procedures that govern the specific project, such as applicable codes, requirements for record documents, temporary facilities, and testing laboratory methods

Division 1 section titles include the following:

| | | | |
|---|---|---|---|
| 01035 | Modification Procedures | 01500 | Temporary Facilities and Controls |
| 01100 | Summary | 01600 | Project Requirements |
| 01200 | Price and Payment Procedures | 01700 | Execution Requirements |
| 01300 | Administrative Requirements | 01800 | Facility Operation |
| 01400 | Quality Requirements | 01900 | Facility Decommissioning |

Part 1 of each of the sections in Divisions 2 through 16 presents administrative and procedural information relating to the elements covered in that section including, for example:

- Definitions
- Delivery, storage, and handling requirements

part 3 DELIVERY

- Allowance and unit price items
- Alternates
- Site condition requirements
- Submittal requirements
- Warranty requirements
- Quality assurance requirements
- Maintenance requirements

It is worthwhile to develop a consistent approach to placement of procedural and administrative requirements in the documents.

## Architectural and Construction Information

This encompasses the quantities, qualities, and configuration of the elements required for the project. Quantities and relationships are usually best indicated on the drawings; qualities and standards of workmanship are best placed in the specifications.

The level of detail provided in the drawings and specifications responds to the needs of the project and of those who will own, regulate, and—most important—build it.

## CSI Format For Construction Documents

*Construction Specifications Institute,* Manual of Practice *(1992)*

The Construction Specifications Institute (CSI), a society of architects, engineers, specifiers, and manufacturers' representatives, has brought standardization and organization to construction documents. CSI's overall organization of the documents, and the names given to various assemblages of documents, are shown.

- *Construction documents* are all of the written and graphic documents prepared or assembled by the architect/engineer for communicating the design and administering the project.

- *Bidding documents* are all of the documents required to bid or negotiate the construction contract. They are the construction documents with two exceptions: The bid and contract forms are included but not yet executed and, of course, there are no contract modifications.

- *Contract documents* form the legal agreement between the owner and contractor. They include all of the construction documents except the bidding requirements.

- The *project manual* includes the documents that can be easily bound into book format, including the bidding requirements, contract forms and conditions, and specifications.

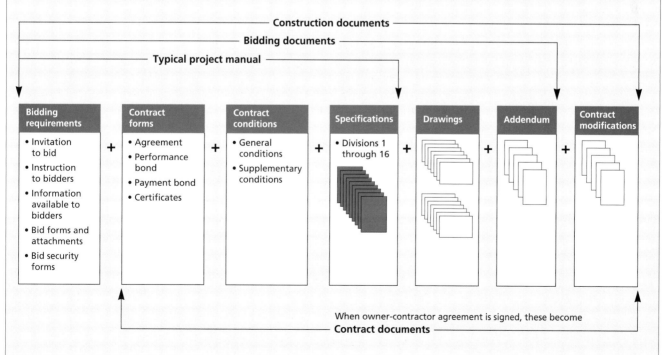

# DRAWINGS

The construction drawings show, in graphic and quantitative form, the extent, configuration, location, relationships, and dimensions of the work to be done. They generally contain site and building plans, elevations, sections, details, diagrams, and schedules. In addition to drawn information, they may include photographs, other imported graphics, and printed schedules.

## Sequence and Sheet Formats

A set of drawings is an organized presentation of the project. To the extent possible, the drawings are organized in the sequence of construction.

### Sample Construction Drawing

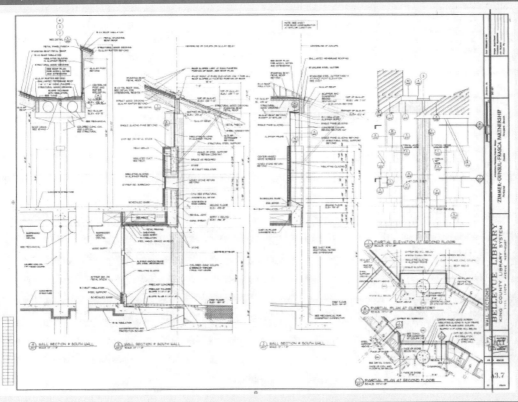

Construction drawings encompass many types of information used for bidding and construction of building projects. This detail drawing provides specific information for selected building elements.

*Zimmer Grunsul Frasca Partnership, Portland, Oregon*

### MASTERSPEC® DIVISION 1 OUTLINE

*MASTERSPEC Consolidated Table of Contents, AIA Master Systems (1992)*

This outline is based on the MasterFormat developed by the Construction Specifications Institute.

#### Division 1—GENERAL REQUIREMENTS

| | | | |
|---|---|---|---|
| 01010 | Summary of work | 01310 | Schedules and reports |
| 01020 | Allowances | 01340 | Shop drawings, product data, and samples |
| 01026 | Unit prices | 01380 | Construction photographs |
| 01027 | Applications for payment | 01400 | Quality control services |
| 01030 | Alternates | 01500 | Temporary facilities |
| 01035 | Modification procedures | 01600 | Materials and equipment |
| 01040 | Project coordination | 01631 | Product substitutions |
| 01045 | Cutting and patching | 01700 | Project closeout |
| 01050 | Field engineering | 01710 | Final cleaning |
| 01095 | Reference standards and definitions | 01720 | Project record documents |
| 01200 | Project meetings | 01730 | Operating and maintenance data |
| 01300 | Submittals | 01740 | Warranties and bonds |

## Project Delivery Options and Construction Documents

The project delivery option selected will affect the content, level of development, and packaging of the construction documents.

*Negotiated contract.* If the construction contact is to be negotiated, the contractor may be selected on the basis of early pricing documents, which include items the contractor needs to develop a price.

*Multiple prime contracts.* When the construction contract is divided into multiple prime contracts, there may be multiple construction documents sets or volumes, one for each prime contract. Alternatively, carefully delineated separate contracts of work may be made within a single set of documents. Each prime contract set clearly spells out requirements for that portion of the work, including relationships with other project prime contracts. The summary of work and the article on related work (in Part 1 of each specification section) are the major vehicles for clarifying the relationships between prime contracts. Related prime contracts should be available to all contractors for reference.

*Fast-track projects.* Fast-track projects are issued in phases, with separate bid packages prepared for each phase. Fast-tracking may be used with single or multiple prime contracts and with bid or negotiated contracts. The early construction packages are issued and bid (or negotiated) while the later phases continue in design. Because of this overlap of bid packages with design, careful coordination of packages is particularly important.

*Construction management.* While the drawings for a CM project may correspond to those for traditionally contracted work, the other construction documents must reflect administrative and contractual differences. The bidding requirements, conditions of the contract, and Division 1 of the specifications may vary substantially from those otherwise used.

Projects involving construction management are often fast-tracked. They may also involve scope documents, prepared before all construction documents are fully developed, as a basis for providing the owner with a guaranteed maximum price (GMP) for construction. Even though they are incomplete, scope documents are contract documents because they form the basis for defining work covered by the GMP. Thus they must be sufficiently developed to indicate material qualities and to provide both owner and CM with reasonable assurance that the CM's price will be accurate. Since a price based on incomplete documents always leaves room for interpretation, a strong working relationship between owner, CM, and architect is required for successful operation of this delivery system.

*Design-build.* When the owner contracts with a single design-build entity, the commitment to construct the project may be based on a performance specification with no design or the project may be based on a schematic design. The owner prepares a set of documents to describe the project, secure initial code approvals, and procure design-build services. The design-build entity's construction documents, depending on the provisions of the design-build agreement, may or may not serve as a method of legally defining the finished product for the owner.

Most firms develop office standards for sheet size, layout, and title blocks. Some clients, however, might dictate their own format requirements. In addition to the name, address, and phone number of the architecture firm, the title block may include the following:

- Project title and address, frequently including owner's name and address
- Drawing title and sheet number
- Names and addresses of consultants
- Notation of who worked on the drawing, including checking
- Dates drawings were issued (such as for bid, permit, and construction)
- Dates of revisions
- Architect's seal and, if required, signature
- Engineer's seal and, if required, signature
- Copyright information

The CSI Uniform Drawing System organizes this information according to the following categories:

- Designer identification block
- Project identification block
- Issue block
- Management block
- Sheet title block
- Sheet identification block

Each drawing should include the basic information required to orient the user, such as key plans showing location of partial plans, north arrows, and scales for drawings. Graphic scales are included in the event drawings are reduced. Most firms lay out the drawings early in the project. A cartooning or storyboard process may be used to determine how many and what kinds of plans, sections, elevations, details, schedules, and other graphic elements will be prepared; their scale (and thus size on the sheets); their sequence; and any interrelationships. This helps the architect conceptualize the project and understand what will be involved in developing and communicating it to the owner, regulators, and contractors.

## Drawing Scale, Dimensions, and Targets

Appropriate scale, dimensions, and targets (or "keys") are essential communication elements of the drawings. It is common for a firm to establish standard procedures and symbols for dimensions and targets, as well as for lettering size and style. The project manager usually determines the drawing scales to be used, as well as any variations from office standards.

*Scale.* The smallest scale that clearly presents the required information is chosen for a drawing. The selection of scales and lettering sizes must also take into account whether the drawings will be reduced for distribution.

*Dimensions.* Necessary dimensions should be numerically indicated on the drawings. Because the contractor is not permitted to scale the drawings for dimensions, drawings should contain sufficient numerical dimensions to construct the building elements shown. The system of dimensioning used in the drawings relates to horizontal and vertical reference planes (such as the structural grid) that, in turn, can be tied to one or more benchmarks established as permanent data points for the project. It is logical to establish a hierarchy of dimensions in the order of construction, using building elements that will be constructed early as dimensional benchmarks for elements constructed later. For example, it is common to first denote the dimensions of structural elements such as a column grid, and then measure distances from the columns to nonstructural elements, such as interior partitions.

Dimensions are laid out in lines called strings. It is necessary to develop several strings to properly locate a sequence of related building elements. These sets of strings are drawn in a hierarchy of detail, with overall dimensions shown in the outermost string and detailed dimensions shown in the innermost string. To ensure that numbers indicated on the dimension strings correspond to the intended built reality, contractors and others using the drawings will add up strings of dimensions and cross-check them against one another. In some cases the level of detail of the drawing or the construction method employed makes comprehensive strings, in which every dimension is determined, undesirable. In such cases the critical dimensions are noted and a noncritical dimension is noted with a plus-or-minus value. This gives the contractor an idea of the desired dimension, and further indicates that discrepancies during construction are to be resolved by adjusting this dimension.

> ▶ **Many architects will have cartooned the drawings as part of the project pricing and proposal process.**

---

### DRAWING SEQUENCE: THE CONDOC® SYSTEM

Most architects—and some owners—develop their own preferences for sequencing and numbering drawings. The ConDoc system offers the following format. Each discipline is subdivided into groups (only architecture is illustrated).

**G** General project requirements

*Sitework*
**TS** Topographic survey
**SB** Soil borings data
**SD** Site demolition
**C** Civil
**L** Landscaping

*Major disciplines*

| | |
|---|---|
| **A** Architecture A000, A001, etc. | Schedules, master keynote legend, general notes |
| A100, A101, etc. | Plans |
| A200, A201, etc. | Exterior elevations, transverse building sections |
| A300, A301, etc. | Vertical circulation, core plan and details |
| A400, A401, etc. | Reflected ceiling plans, details |
| A500, A501, etc. | Exterior envelope, details |
| A600, A601, etc. | Architecture interiors |

**S** Structural
**M** Mechanical
**P** Plumbing
**FP** Fire protection
**E** Electrical

*Special elements*
**ID** Interior design
**FS** Food service
**SG** Signage/graphics
**FF** Furniture/furnishings
**AA** Asbestos abatement
Etc.

Automatic dimensioning in computer-aided design and drawing (CAD) systems produces accurate dimension annotation. This reduces the need for manual cross-checking of dimensions and has the added benefit of highlighting dimensional discrepancies as the drawings are being completed. When establishing CAD standards and procedures for dimensioning, it is important for firms to thoughtfully select the display precision for their dimensioning—$\frac{1}{32}$", $\frac{1}{16}$" or $\frac{1}{8}$"—and to include that parameter in their CAD template or seed file. In the interest of accuracy and coordination, CAD users should not manually override automatically generated dimensions even though CAD systems do permit it.

The drawings should call attention to critical areas where standard construction tolerances are not sufficient or dimensions are tied to specific dimensions of manufactured assemblies. At the same time, the experienced architect recognizes that materials and construction tolerances in the field rarely approach those that can be achieved in manufacturing. For example, some architects regard field-created tolerances of less than 1/8" (1:100 in SI units) or even 1/4" (1:50) as unrealistic.

***Targets.*** Sometimes referred to as "keys," targets are one of the primary methods of establishing the relationships among the drawings. Floor plans use standard symbols to locate (or target) building sections, column grids, door designations, wall types and sections, details, interior elevations, enlarged plans, and similar information. Elevations target building sections, windows, and details. It is also helpful to target details on wall sections and building sections.

## Other Drawing Elements

The drawings often include the following:

***Symbols and abbreviations.*** The need to communicate a large amount of information in a limited space commonly dictates the use of symbols and abbreviations. Good practice suggests that these be defined early and used consistently.

***Drawing/specification coordination.*** Designations on the drawings should be coordinated with those used in the specifications. If, for example, only one type of elastomeric sealant is used in the project, the term "elastomeric sealant" is sufficient on the drawings. If more than one sealant type is involved, however, it is necessary to develop and use terminology that clearly differentiates among the various sealants.

***Notes.*** When drawings and specifications are separate, statements on quality and workmanship are made in the specifications. Notes on the drawings should be limited to the minimum needed to convey design intent clearly.

***Schedules.*** Information best presented in tabular form is most commonly shown in a schedule. There may be schedules for doors, windows, hardware, room finishes, paint selections, fixtures and equipment, repetitive structural elements (such as columns footings, or lintels), and similar items. Schedule formats vary according to office or project requirements. Many schedules can be developed and revised using

---

## SAMPLE DIMENSIONING GUIDELINES

*Booth/Hansen & Associates, Chicago*

Some offices develop standards for dimensioning drawings. Here is one firm's set:

Dimensioning requires an understanding of the sequence of construction, for new assemblies can only be located relative to assemblies already in place. Dimension only from a fixed reference point.

Begin with a work point, usually one that marks a corner of the foundation. From this point, locate all foundations, footings, and column centerlines. Show the dimensions on the foundation plan.

The outside face and top surface of the foundation walls and column centerlines now provide fixed reference for subsequent construction. Outside walls usually are first, followed by mechanical and electrical equipment spaces, interior walls, and finish work.

The following rules apply to all dimensioning in this office:
1. Dimension only those things that really matter.
2. Do not repeat dimensions, either within a drawing or on more than one drawing.
3. In general, do not close dimension strings. In a string of dimensions, leave tolerance by omitting the dimension for a noncritical space or assembly. When the dimension is omitted, delete the dimension line as well. Final decisions concerning the method of dimensioning reside with the project architect.
4. The thicknesses of tile, wood base, wainscoting, trim, and similar applied finishes are not included in room dimensions.
5. Vertical dimensioning appears on elevations or wall sections. Dimensions should be to the top of significant structural elements and to window and door heads (rather than sills), and should be from the top of the foundation, finish floor level, or similar fixed reference. Masonry is dimensioned to the top of the masonry unit, not to the joint centerline.
6. Ends of dimensions are indicated by short, bold, diagonal slashes. No dots, arrows, or crosses.
7. Specific dimensions are not always the best choice. The simple notes "ALIGN" and "4 EQUAL SPACES" are often more appropriate, if they relate clearly to information already present.
8. Dimensioning and its checking are the responsibility of the job captain alone. The work should not be delegated. All dimensions are to be double checked.

---

*Architectural Graphic* **Standards** (2000) presents conventions for symbols and abbreviations.

spreadsheet or word processing software programs. The Uniform Drawing System (UDS) and the U.S. National CAD Standard include a module on schedules. UDS establishes guidelines for creating schedules and complete illustrations of commonly used schedules. The UDS companion CD-ROM includes these schedules in a word processing format.

## Drawing Production Methods

For hundreds of years architectural drawings have been produced manually, making their production one of the most labor-intensive and time-consuming phases of professional service. Technological advances—especially in CAD—have enabled high-level professional time to be replaced with lower-level drafting and clerical time. This change has also blurred the distinction between the design development and construction documents phases.

***Manual drafting.*** Many firms continue with manual drafting as the production method of choice. A number of approaches and specific techniques can be used to reduce time and increase the accuracy and utility of manual drafting:

- Standard items such as sheet borders, title blocks, symbols, and common details may be produced ahead of time and incorporated into the drawings as needed. Some firms bind reference information and standard details into the project manual.
- Schedules and other highly organized data sets may be produced using computers and spreadsheet or database programs and incorporated into the drawings or bound into the project manual.
- Photographs of existing conditions may be reproduced directly onto drawing media. Planned renovations can then be drawn directly onto the photographs.
- Individual drawing sheets may be overlays or photographic composites of individual drawings, details, schedules, and notes, allowing flexibility in formatting.

***Computer-aided drafting.*** CAD systems promise the advantages of clarity, easy representation of elements (especially repetitive elements), fast changes, accurate dimensioning, and improved coordination among drawings as well as between drawings and specifications. Computer-produced drawings can be easy to read, with lettering and dimensioning consistent throughout. CAD software packages increasingly incorporate useful ancillary functions such as automatic area and material quantity takeoffs and concurrent development of door, window, and other schedules.

Managing drawing revisions is entirely different in the CAD environment. Telltale erasures, changes in lettering, and other marks that signal changes and revisions to manually drafted drawings are absent. The exchange of computer data files among collaborating design professionals via the Internet has underscored the need for controlling and verifying the integrity of electronically transmitted drawings. Electronic data management (EDM) systems prevent multiple persons from accessing the same drawing simultaneously, track drawing modifications, ensure that changes are not incorporated into the record copy of the drawing until properly approved, and automatically route the pending changes to the party responsible for approvals. However, EDM technology can be too costly and time-consuming to implement in multifirm environments except on large, long-duration projects.

Another CAD approach is for each firm on the project team to manage its own drawing controls internally and post new and revised documents on secure computer bulletin boards or project Web sites called project extranets.

## Drawing Standards

Reference was previously made to the value of establishing standards or conventions for the uniform production of construction documents. There are a few different approaches to establishing standards for your firm.

## Implications of Computer Technology on Documents Production

Today an experienced and computer-literate architect using automated methods can produce as much work as an architect and one or two drafters using manual methods. The improvement in productivity brought about by computer technology is partly offset by the demands of that technology. The maintenance of computer hardware, software, and networks requires a new type of technical staff within the firm. Midsize firms are finding they need a full-time technology support person for every 50 computer users.

With standardization, large firms may be able to gain economies of scale and support as many as 100 computer users per support staff. The rapid evolution of computer technology creates a need for continual technology skills training. Finally, there is the overhead cost of providing the hardware, software, networks, and Internet connections. The pervasive presence of computer technology in architectural practice has changed the economics of practice, requiring firms to rethink their fee basis, overhead rates, and utilization ratios.

Recent advances in computer hardware and software bring the concept of an intelligent building model within the realm of possibility. This technology is sometimes referred to as "parametric modeling" (meaning that the CAD software is capable of storing detailed parameters of the building elements, rather than simple graphic representation of those elements) or "object-oriented modeling" (meaning that the building information is created and defined as a collection of objects, not unlike the building itself, rather than a series of lines and planes).

This technology should be distinguished from first-generation 3-D computer modeling used for animation and rendering. The data in this type of modeling are created and stored as lines, planes and surfaces, with no other knowledge about the objects represented. Intelligent building models go beyond basic 3-D geometry to include material designations, product specifications building systems, and even performance data. They can be used to check interferences and to extract bills of materials for estimating or procurement purposes. It is conceivable that the production of working drawings could be bypassed altogether and a building could eventually be constructed directly from an intelligent 3-D model, with the required two-dimensional drawings—plans, sections, elevations, details—being extracted from the model as needed. If as-built conditions are documented in the model during the construction process, the model can then be used for operations and maintenance activities.

This technology has broad implications for work processes and sequencing, team composition, contractual relationships, and professional liability. It is unlikely that the building design and construction industry will adopt this approach quickly. Nevertheless, the technological tools now exist to reorder the entire building design and delivery process. Architects, as the original creators of the information used in the process, are uniquely positioned to assert a leadership role in a process that encompasses the entire life cycle of buildings, from conception, design, and construction through facilities management and retirement or reuse.

---

In the absence of comprehensive industry drawing standards, nearly all firms have developed their own standards as a way of ensuring quality, consistency, and thoroughness in this critical phase of service in which the architect's design intent is communicated to those who will construct the project.

The advent of CAD technology introduces a new level of complexity for construction drawing standards. The manner in which data is created and stored is not readily apparent to the viewer without a detailed examination of the data file. The laborious task of deciphering the organizational system of another person can easily negate any gain in productivity achieved by the use of CAD technology.

The ability to reuse design elements from previous projects is one of the principal benefits of CAD. However, if projects are developed with different layer names, line weights and colors, text fonts and dimension styles, the reuse of design elements may require extensive editing. This prevents reaping the anticipated productivity benefits of CAD. In a CAD environment, graphic standards for drawing organization must be supplemented by CAD standards for data organization. At a minimum, these standards should address the following subjects:

- Drawing sheet sizes, layout, scales, sequence, and numbering
- Targeting and other references within the documents
- Notes, abbreviations, and graphic conventions
- Dimensioning
- Organizational, informational, and procedural standards for use of CAD systems

# Chronology of Standards Development for Construction Drawings

The development of office standards is a time-consuming overhead task, and the quality of office drawing standards varies greatly from one firm to another. Consequently, even the best of efforts can prove futile if clients and consultants do not share and use the same standards. This situation has prompted a number of independent efforts aimed at bringing industry-wide order to the production of construction documents. The following profiles several of these efforts.

## ConDoc

ConDoc, developed by Onkal "Duke" Guzey, AIA, and James Freehof, AIA, was the first system for organizing construction documents. Based on a simple, uniform arrangement of drawings, a standard sheet format, a sheet identification system, and a keynote system that links drawings and specifications, ConDoc improved quality control, information management, productivity, and bidding results.

*Organization of drawings.* A uniform arrangement is established for locating project data within a set of drawings and for identifying individual sheets. Drawing sets are divided by disciplines, with each discipline assigned a discipline letter prefix. Discipline drawings are subdivided into groups of like information, with each group assigned a group number. Finally, each sheet within a group is assigned a sequential number. For example, A101 represents the architecture discipline (A), group plan (1), and sheet number (01).

*Standard sheet format.* Sheets are composed using a standard, modular format that may be subdivided into module blocks. The standard sheet has three zones. The first zone, on the right side of the sheet, contains the sheet title block and drawing keynote legend. Zone 2 is the graphics zone and contains a non-printing modular grid. Zone 3 is the perimeter or border, with alphanumeric grid coordinates.

*Keynote system.* This process establishes a connecting link between graphic information shown on the drawings and the related text in the specifications. Keynotes minimize the amount of text needed on drawings without restricting the notation process. Drawing notations are identified by keynote symbols. In general, notations with their respective keynote symbols are located on each sheet in a keynote legend, while only the keynote symbols are placed in the drawing. Each note may be repeated in the drawing as often as needed by simply repeating the symbol.

## The Uniform Drawing System

The creators of ConDoc shared their system widely through seminars and other events, and produced a detailed workshop handbook. In 1994, recognizing the need for a more detailed system fully described in a self-contained publication, the Construction Specifications Institute embarked on a project to create the Uniform Drawing System (UDS).

The first three UDS modules, published in 1997, build upon ConDoc's organizational concepts. The Drawing Set Organization Module (Module 1) establishes consistency between disciplines through the use of standard discipline designators, sheet types, and file names. The Sheet Organization Module (Module 2) establishes graphic layout standards delineating drawing area, title block area, and production data area, as well as a grid system of blocks or modules for organizing drawings and related information on a sheet. The Schedules Module (Module 3) defines a standard format for numerous schedules used in con-

struction documents. In 1999 the UDS was expanded to include Drafting Conventions (Module 4), Terms and Abbreviations (Module 5), and Symbols (Module 6). In 2000 the UDS was completed with the publication of Notations (Module 7) and Code Conventions (Module 8).

## CAD Layer Guidelines

Developed and first published by the AIA in 1990, the layer list in *CAD Layer Guidelines* is the only comprehensive system for the standard naming of CAD data file layers. The second edition, published in 1997, contains enhancements and refinements of the original edition. *CAD Layer Guidelines* offers a consistent, comprehensive yet flexible layer naming system that can be adapted to particular needs while maintaining the integrity of the system.

In 2001 the publication was completely revised and updated and given a new name, AIA CAD *Layer Guidelines: U.S. National CAD Standard Version 2.* The original layer naming system has been amended to enable U.S. design firms to conform to ISO Standard 13567, Organization and Naming of Layers for CAD, while largely preserving the integrity of data located according to earlier editions. The layer list has also been expanded for disciplines such as civil, civil works, structural, mechanical, plumbing, telecommunications, survey/mapping, geotechnical, process, and operations.

## The U.S. National CAD Standard

The National Institute of Building Sciences (NIBS) recognized a need for a single, comprehensive national standard for electronically produced construction documents. A single standard supports the seamless transfer of building design and construction information among a broad array of users throughout the building life cycle, including architects, planners, engineers, contractors, product manufacturers, building owners, and facility managers.

The NIBS Facility Information Council (formerly the CADD Council) provides an industry-wide forum for the standardization of computer-aided design and drafting (CAD). Membership in the council is open to all individuals and organizations with an interest in the subject matter. Components of the CAD standard include the following:

- CAD layering
- Drawing set organization
- Sheet organization
- Schedules
- Drafting conventions
- Terms and abbreviations
- Symbols
- Notations
- Code conventions
- Plotting guidelines

The U.S. National CAD Standard Version 2, published in 2001, is made up of four constituent documents: *AIA CAD Layer Guidelines,* published by the AIA; *The Uniform Drawing System,* Modules 1 through 8, published by CSI; "Plotting Guidelines" of the U.S. Coast Guard, as promulgated by the U.S. Department of Defense Tri-Service CADD/GIS Technology Center; and "Report of the National CAD Standard Project Committee," published by the National Institute of Building Sciences. The latter document amends the constituent documents to resolve minor discrepancies between them.

# SPECIFICATIONS

The specifications present written requirements for materials, equipment, and construction systems as well as standards for products, workmanship, and the construction services required to produce the work. The specifications are often presented in the project manual, along with the bidding requirements, contract forms, and conditions of the contract.

## Organization

In its *Manual of Practice,* CSI publishes a series of widely used conventions for specifications organization, format, and development. Especially important is the MasterFormat, which establishes a master list of section titles and numbers as well as a format for the organization of individual specification sections. This widely used format is incorporated into many industry standards and products, including AIA MASTERSPEC, which includes sixteen divisions:

| | |
|---|---|
| Division 1: | General Requirements |
| Division 2: | Site Construction |
| Division 3: | Concrete |
| Division 4: | Masonry |
| Division 5: | Metals |
| Division 6: | Wood and Plastics |
| Division 7: | Thermal and Moisture Protection |
| Division 8: | Doors and Windows |
| Division 9: | Finishes |
| Division 10: | Specialties |
| Division 11: | Equipment |
| Division 12: | Furnishings |
| Division 13: | Special Construction |
| Division 14: | Conveying Systems |
| Division 15: | Mechanical |
| Division 16: | Electrical |

Division 1 of the MasterFormat presents a series of general procedural and administrative requirements applicable to all portions of the work. The remaining divisions, each related to distinct portions of work, contain sections designated by five-digit numbers. Each of these sections is organized according to a three-part format: general, products, and execution. Each MasterFormat division contains sections designated by five-digit numbers. Each section, in turn, is organized according to the three-part format: general, products, and execution.

## Methods of Specifying

For each specifications section, the architect selects the method of specifying. These methods include descriptive specifying, performance specifying (listing required performance qualities of products and assemblies), specifying by reference standards, and proprietary specifying (listing products and assemblies by one or more manufacturers and trade names). In addition, the architect may use allowances and unit prices for parts of the work that cannot be accurately quantified or qualified at the time of bidding.

**Descriptive specifying.** Many architects use descriptive specifications, describing exact characteristics of materials and products without listing proprietary names.

**Performance specifying.** Some architects feel that performance specifications are best in principle because they specify the end result required and allow contractors, manufacturers, and fabricators the most flexibility and creativity in meeting the requirements. In practice, however, performance specifying is complicated by the vast number of qualities that affect the finished result.

**Specifying with reference standards.** Specifications may also incorporate references to standards published by industry associations and testing organizations. This allows designers, contractors, and suppliers to use industry-accepted standards of practice and perfor-

> **The backgrounder AIA MASTERSPEC (12.3) provides an overview of MASTERSPEC and related products.**

*Master Outline Specifications Table of Contents, AIA Master Systems (1999)*

This outline, based on the MasterFormat developed by the Construction Specifications Institute, is used by AIA Master Systems for its Master Outline Specifications.

**Division 1—GENERAL REQUIREMENTS**
01000 General requirements
01013 Summary of work (FF&E)

**Division 2—SITE CONSTRUCTION**
02060 Building demolition
02230 Site clearing
02240 Dewatering
02260 Excavation support and protection
02300 Earthwork
02361 Termite control
02455 Driven piles
02511 Hot-mix asphalt paving
02630 Storm drainage
02751 Cement concrete pavement
02780 Unit pavers
02900 Landscaping
02930 Lawns and grasses

**Division 3—CONCRETE**
03300 Cast-in-place concrete
03331 Cast-in-place architectural concrete
03410 Plant-precast structural concrete
03450 Plant-precast architectural concrete
03511 Cementitious wood-fiber deck
03532 Concrete floor topping
03542 Cement-based underlayment

**Division 4—MASONRY**
04410 Stone masonry veneer
04720 Cast stone
04810 Unit masonry assemblies
04851 Dimension stone cladding

**Division 5—METALS**
05120 Structural steel
05210 Steel joists
05310 Steel deck
05400 Cold-formed metal framing
05500 Metal fabrications
05511 Metal stairs
05521 Pipe and tube railings
05700 Ornamental metal
05720 Ornamental handrails and railings
05811 Architectural joint systems

**Division 6—WOOD AND PLASTICS**
06100 Rough carpentry
06130 Heavy timber construction
06130 Wood decking
06185 Structural glued-laminated timber
06192 Metal-plate-connected wood trusses
06200 Finish carpentry
06401 Exterior architectural woodwork
06402 Interior architectural woodwork
06420 Paneling

**Division 7—THERMAL AND MOISTURE PROTECTION**
07131 Self-adhering sheet waterproofing
07132 Elastomeric sheet waterproofing
07190 Water repellents
07210 Building insulation
07241 Exterior insulation and finish systems—class PB
07242 Exterior insulation and finish systems—class PM
07311 Asphalt shingles
07313 Metal shingles
07315 Slate shingles
07317 Wood shingles and shakes
07460 Siding
07511 Built-up asphalt roofing
07512 Built-up coal-tar roofing
07531 EPDM single-ply membrane roofing
07532 CSPE single-ply membrane roofing
07610 Sheet metal roofing
07620 Sheet metal flashing and trim
07720 Roof accessories
07810 Plastic unit skylights
07920 Joint sealants

**Division 8—DOORS AND WINDOWS**
08110 Steel doors and frames
08114 Custom steel doors and frames
08163 Sliding aluminum-framed glass doors
08211 Flush wood doors
08212 Stile and rail wood doors
08263 Sliding wood-frame glass doors
08305 Access doors
08314 Sliding metal fire doors
08331 Overhead coiling doors
08410 Aluminum entrances and storefronts
08460 Automatic entrance doors
08510 Steel windows
08520 Aluminum windows
08550 Wood windows
08610 Roof windows
08710 Door hardware
08800 Glazing
08840 Plastic glazing

**Division 9—FINISHES**
09210 Gypsum plaster
09251 Factory-finished gypsum board
09253 Gypsum sheathing
09260 Gypsum board assemblies
09310 Ceramic tile
09385 Dimension stone tile
09400 Terrazzo
09511 Acoustical panel ceilings
09513 Acoustical snap-in metal pan ceilings
09600 Stone paving and flooring
09640 Wood flooring
09651 Resilient tile flooring
09652 Sheet vinyl floor coverings
09653 Resilient wall base and accessories
09654 Linoleum floor coverings
09680 Carpet
09681 Carpet tile
09900 Painting
09920 Interior painting
09931 Exterior wood stains
09950 Wall coverings
09967 Intumescent paints
09981 Cementitious coatings

**Division 10—SPECIALTIES**
10100 Visual display boards
10155 Toilet compartments
10200 Louvers and vents
10270 Access flooring
10350 Flagpoles
10416 Directories and bulletin boards
10425 Signs
10505 Metal lockers
10520 Fire-protection specialties
10550 Postal specialties
10605 Wire mesh partitions
10615 Demountable partitions
10655 Accordion folding partitions
10671 Metal storage shelving
10750 Telephone specialties
10801 Toilet and bath accessories

**Division 11—EQUIPMENT**
11054 Library stack systems
11062 Folding and portable stages
11063 Stage curtains
11132 Projection screens
11150 Parking control equipment
11160 Loading dock equipment
11170 Waste compactors
11307 Packaged sewage pump stations
11400 Food service equipment
11451 Residential appliances
11460 Unit kitchens
11610 Laboratory fume hoods
11695 Mailroom equipment

**Division 12—FURNISHINGS**
12311 Metal file cabinets
12320 Restaurant and cafeteria casework
12347 Metal laboratory casework
12348 Wood laboratory casework
12353 Display casework
12356 Kitchen casework
12510 Office furniture
12567 Library furniture

**Division 13—SPECIAL CONSTRUCTION**
13052 Saunas
13090 Radiation protection
13100 Lightning protection
13110 Cathodic protection
13125 Metal building systems
13720 Intrusion detection

**Division 14—CONVEYING SYSTEMS**
14100 Dumbwaiters
14210 Electric traction elevators
14240 Hydraulic elevators
14310 Escalators
14320 Moving walks
14420 Wheelchair lifts
14560 Chutes

**Division 15—MECHANICAL**

**Division 16—ELECTRICAL**
Not included in Master Outline Specifications

*Construction Specifications Institute,* Manual of Practice *(1996)*

Each specification section is presented in these three parts:

## Part 1—General
SUMMARY
*Section includes:*
Products supplied but not installed
under this section
Products installed but not supplied
under this section
Related sections
Allowances
Unit prices
Measurement procedures
Payment procedures
Alternates

REFERENCES

DEFINITIONS

SYSTEM DESCRIPTION
Design requirements
Performance requirements

SUBMITTALS
Product data
Shop drawings
Samples
Quality assurance/control submittals
Design data
Test reports
Certificates
Manufacturer's instructions
Manufacturer's field reports
Qualification statements
Closeout submittals

QUALITY ASSURANCE
Qualifications
Regulatory requirements
Certifications
Field samples
Mockups
Preinstallation meetings

DELIVERY, STORAGE, AND HANDLING
Packing, shipping, handling, and
unloading
Acceptance at site
Storage and protection
Waste management and disposal

PROJECT/ SITE CONDITIONS
Environmental requirements
Existing conditions

SEQUENCING

SCHEDULING

WARRANTY
Special warranty

SYSTEM STARTUP

OWNER'S INSTRUCTIONS

COMMISSIONING

MAINTENANCE
Extra materials
Maintenance service

## Part 2—Products
MANUFACTURERS

EXISTING PRODUCTS

MATERIALS

MANUFACTURED UNITS

EQUIPMENT

COMPONENTS

ACCESSORIES

MIXES

FABRICATION
Shop assembly
Fabrication tolerances

FINISHES
Shop priming
Shop finishing

SOURCE QUALITY CONTROL
Fabrication tolerances
Tests
Inspection
Verification of performance

## Part 3—Execution
EXAMINATION
Site verification of conditions

PREPARATION
Protection
Surface preparation

ERECTION

INSTALLATION

APPLICATION

CONSTRUCTION
Special techniques
Interface with other work
Sequences of operation
Site tolerances

REPAIR/RESTORATION

REINSTALLATION

FIELD QUALITY CONTROL
Site tests
Inspection
Manufacturer's field services

ADJUSTING

CLEANING

DEMONSTRATION

PROTECTION

SCHEDULES

mance. The most widely known standards associations are the American National Standards Institute (ANSI), American Society for Testing and Materials (ASTM), and Underwriters Laboratories (UL). These groups either develop and organize performance standards or test material products and assemblies for compliance with published standards.

*Proprietary specifying.* Many architects use proprietary specifications for their brevity and simplicity and because they are familiar with the qualities of the specific products being specified. These specifications are frequently augmented with reference to standards, narrative descriptions of materials' qualities, and performance requirements.

Some standards, such as those published by the American Society of Heating, Refrigerating, and Air Conditioning Engineers (ASHRAE), the National Fire Protection Association (NFPA), and the Illuminating Engineering Society (IES), focus on specific aspects of building performance. Industry associations, such as the American Iron and Steel Institute (AISI) and the American Architectural Manufacturers Association (AAMA), write standards for the products and systems produced by their members. For example, AAMA publishes test methods, standards, and guide specifications for aluminum fabrications such as storefronts, curtain walls, and windows.

*Restrictive specifying.* The architect also determines how restrictive the specifications are to be—whether they will permit only one manufacturer's product, several products, or any product that meets specified criteria. Publicly funded projects require full and open competition. Therefore several brands of products are specified under the theory that qualified manufacturers should be able to compete equitably for the work. In private work the architect will typically specify restrictively, unless the owner prefers competition. When there is a choice, the architect should determine which approach best serves the client's interests.

## Master Specifications

Most firms employ some form of master specification that is modified for each project. A master specification covers an entire topic, including a range of options. The specifications editor then fills in blanks, deletes options that don't apply, and incorporates special requirements not included in the master. Computers are widely used to produce specifications, with the specifier editing text directly on the screen.

The most commonly used commercially available master specification is MASTERSPEC, developed by the AIA and available through ARCOM MasterSystems. It is available on electronic media for a variety of computers and is regularly updated by professional staff. MASTERSPEC is well suited for use in a variety of architecture offices. It covers most types of projects and is closely coordinated with AIA standard documents and procedures. MASTERSPEC also acts as a specifications writing tutorial, including overview and reference materials, editorial and drawings, and specifications coordination notes. Other commercially available master specifications include SpecsIntact, an automated specification system developed by NASA, and SpecText, maintained by Construction Sciences Research Foundation. Master specifications are also available from some government agencies such as the Navy Facilities Engineering Command and the Army Corps of Engineers.

## Specification Production Methods

Most specifications are produced using word processing. Much of the information is repeated from project to project (as the firm finds products and procedures that work well). Moreover, specifications typically evolve through multiple drafts, and, as in CAD drawings, tracking revisions is increasingly important.

Sixty-six percent of the firms responding to the 1997 AIA firm survey indicated that they used master specification software to develop, edit, and present project specifications. Systems such as MASTERSPEC employ a master specification that covers a series of topics and offers a range of options. Master specification may be done on paper or on the computer screen.

Well-coordinated drawings and specifications are essential in any set of construction documents. In particular, the architect is challenged to ensure that materials and products shown on the drawings are described in the specifications and that the language used is consistent and unambiguous. For small projects, the architect often develops the specifications concurrently with the drawings and may include them directly on the drawings (perhaps using photocopies attached to the drawings or importing a word processing file into CAD). For larger projects, however, it is common to include the specifications in a separate project manual. CAD and other automation tools can help architects achieve coordination, and in some cases they provide new techniques to create more tightly integrated drawings and specifications.

One important goal is maintaining consistency between the language used in drawing notations and the language used in the specifications. Inconsistency can be a major source of requests for interpretation and change orders during construction.

In addition to careful review of drawings and specifications, several production techniques are available to help architects achieve this consistency. Numerical keynoting offers one example. Instead of attaching a descriptive note, such as "batt insulation," to a component of a drawing or detail, the architect attaches a keynote number. This number is cross-referenced to a standardized keynote list, which is included on each drawing. It remains the responsibility of the architect to coordinate the keynote list and the specifications, but this technique generally makes it easier to revise drawing notations, and the notations are better coordinated. If a standard material notation changes, for example, only the keynote list needs to be updated—not every plan, section, elevation, or detail in which the material appears.

Keynote-based drawings lend themselves to automation. CAD systems allow the same information to be shared between multiple drawings using reference files. The keynote list, when attached as a reference file to many drawings, can be updated for all drawings simply by changing the master list.

ConDoc takes the concept of keynotes further by using the 16-division MasterFormat as the keynote numbering convention. Each material or product notation on a drawing essentially becomes a direct reference to the appropriate specifications section. At any point in the drawing process, the program can scan the drawing and print a keynote legend listing all of the materials on the drawing. Similarly, the user can locate all occurrences of a specific material within the drawings. The keynote list can be used to link drawings and specifications, helping to ensure that each building component drawn is described in the specifications.

CAD provides another mechanism to integrate drawings and specifications by allowing architects to add specifications data directly to the drawing in the form of database attributes. Predrawn standard components in the drawings (e.g., metal studs, furring channels, insulation, plumbing fixtures, etc.) can include specifications attributes. Some CAD systems can generate reports based on this information, so the architect can double-check that each component in the drawings is described in the specifications and vice versa. In addition, some systems quantify this information, producing bills of materials. Such systems require that the CAD operator know enough about the specifications data to make use of it.

The next step in CAD is the use of 3-D modeling systems and CAD systems based on object technology. These systems more tightly integrate specifications attributes and permit them to be assigned to assemblies of objects—an insulated masonry wall, for example—as well as to the components of that wall. This allows complete and highly accurate extraction of bills of materials. In addition, these advanced CAD systems incorporate design rules. In other words, knowledge about how buildings are designed and constructed is programmed into the software. An example might be a rule that a door inserted into a fire-rated wall must be a fire-rated door. The CAD system would prevent the insertion of a nonrated door object into a fire-rated wall. Although these systems are in their infancy, they hold great promise.

## OTHER CONSTRUCTION DOCUMENTS

In addition to drawings and specifications, construction documents usually include

- Bidding requirements, including bid invitation, information and instructions for bidders, bid forms, and bid bonds
- Contract forms, including proposed owner-contractor agreement, certificates, and performance and payment bonds
- General and supplementary conditions of the contract for construction
- Addenda issued during bidding
- Modifications made after the construction agreements are signed

Increasingly, the contract documents also include a code compliance summary (sometimes on the first sheet of documents) for use by the code enforcement official in reviewing the project and issuing the building permit.

These other construction documents are usually presented as a combination of documents generated in the architect's office and standard forms supplied by the AIA, the owner, or other sources. AIA documents, with or without modifications, are included in the project manual in their original form; others are commonly developed as word-processed forms that can be used, with appropriate modifications, on future projects.

## PRODUCTION MANAGEMENT

Production planning includes thinking through the documentation required (usually very early in a project, frequently as part of the proposal to acquire the project in the first place), selecting appropriate production methods, planning the production process, and managing this process to achieve the desired results.

Effective production management of construction documents is important to meeting both a firm's project goals and its practice goals. Good production management includes these major features:

- Careful production planning, scheduling, and oversight
- Documentation standards
- A library of construction information and technical references
- Effective coordination with consultants and others on the project team
- Thorough review and checking procedures
- The resources and the desire to produce high-quality construction documents
- Approval of the construction documents by the owner (sometimes at various stages of production)

Firms seeking continuous quality improvement usually consider construction documents a prime candidate for attention. Creation of the documents translates design intent into the information needed for approvals and construction. Errors and omissions in the construction documents inevitably require reworking later and may, in fact, degrade the quality of the service provided and reduce customer satisfaction with that service.

Construction documentation is what its name implies—documentation of decisions made and agreed to in the design development phase. While changes during the construction documents phase are inevitable, a complete set of design development documents, carefully coordinated by the design team and approved by the owner, provides a sound foundation for preparing the construction documents.

It may be necessary to impress upon owners that most design decisions are interrelated. Adding a new door, for example, may require changes in several drawings (floor plans, interior elevations, sections, details, and door and hollow metal schedules). It may also require a new specification section as well as changes in the electrical, mechanical, or structural work. Computers are helpful in coordinating design changes, but professional judgment is involved in even the smallest design decision.

### Production Planning

Considering the many interrelationships among the construction documents, most offices identify a single production coordinator. For many projects, this person is the project architect or project manager. For larger projects, production coordination may be delegated to a technical architect, a job captain, or another specially designated individual.

With CAD systems offering the possibility of simultaneous design and production as well as integrated specifications, firms are finding that their project architects and key project staff are doing production as well as design. The traditional distinction between designers and drafters is blurring and, in some offices, disappearing entirely.

As the construction documents phase approaches, the project manager determines, in detail, the time, staffing, and other resources required to produce the documents. Usually this involves cartooning the drawings, blocking out the specifications (which by now are in outline form), and outlining the remaining content of the project manual. Some, perhaps all, of these decisions may have been made earlier; some firms prepare design development documents in the formats planned for the construction documents.

***Production scheduling and budgeting.*** Many architects have found that the amount of time required to produce working drawings varies greatly, depending on project complexity and the level of detail required. It is good practice to allocate time (based on the previously prepared budget) for each sheet so that each person working on the drawings knows what is expected. Data from past projects will help sharpen these estimates. The time required to produce specifications varies widely due to a number of factors:

- The project delivery approach
- Size and complexity of the project
- Competitive bidding requirements
- Specification scope (broad to narrow)
- The specifier's experience with the specified products and systems
- The level of detail already achieved in the design development phase

Construction documents are prepared most efficiently if the decision-making process is well structured. With modern production techniques, more time can be spent researching systems and coordinating decisions than producing documents. As might be expected, the time required increases substantially if unfamiliar construction systems are used.

***Selection of production methods.*** As suggested above, each approach to production exerts a discipline on the process. The firm may use the same production approach for all of its projects or mix and match them according to the needs of the project at hand. In a similar vein, the firm must decide how specifications are to be produced, whether separate systems will be used for outline and final specifications, and to what extent specifications are to be integrated with the drawings.

If CAD systems are used, it is especially important that the project manager or production coordinator think through the organization of the CAD data as well as the number of drawings, scales, and sheet layouts. CAD issues include whether a single CAD file or multiple files will be created; the CAD layers to be used; how drawings will be created from the CAD data; and how the data will be presented in drawings of different scales in terms of line weights, text heights, and so forth.

Typically the firm's CAD standards provide guidance on these topics, but almost every project will present some unique requirements. Sharing CAD data with outside consultants or with the client requires additional planning to ensure that all parties can use the data without extensive editing. This highlights the usefulness of industry-wide standards, such as the National CAD Standard discussed above.

If CAD data will be exchanged between different organizations, the team must address the following questions:

- Which organizations are exchanging data?
- What information does each organization need from the other(s)?
- What format data is required (AutoCAD native, .dxf)?
- What are the project drafting and CAD standards?
- What is the frequency of data exchange?
- How will the data be exchanged (project Web site, bulletin board, e-mail, CD)?
- How much data preparation is required for each exchange and how long does the transfer take?
- Who is the person in each organization responsible for sending and receiving data?
- Who is authorized to request and release electronic data?
- How will data transfers be logged?

Archiving procedures are also important and frequently overlooked. Archiving is distinguished from data backup in that it is a complete copy of the project

▷ **Project Delivery Options (9.1) outlines the possible methods for delivering services.**

▷ **The Documents Finder (Appendix C) helps in locating the family of AIA documents likely to be most appropriate to the delivery option selected.**

▷ **Different delivery approaches allocate responsibilities, risks, and rewards in different ways. It is important that the contract forms and conditions included within the construction documents be consistent and coordinated with the other project agreements.**

## Elements of Production Planning

Sound production planning reflects the following:

- *The firm's experience.* Most firms accumulate historical information on which to plan projects and base compensation proposals. Past and present time records are readily adaptable to computerization using spreadsheet programs.
- *The production budget.* A large fraction of the architect's cost is budgeted for the construction documents; it is particularly important that scope, services, and compensation be in balance during this phase of services.
- *Project consultants.* On projects of any size or complexity, the consultants will prepare much of the documentation. It is essential that the architect and consultants agree on both production schedules and documentation standards.
- *Project technology.* CAD systems require careful planning and management if their potential benefits are to be realized.

Here is one firm's production sequence.

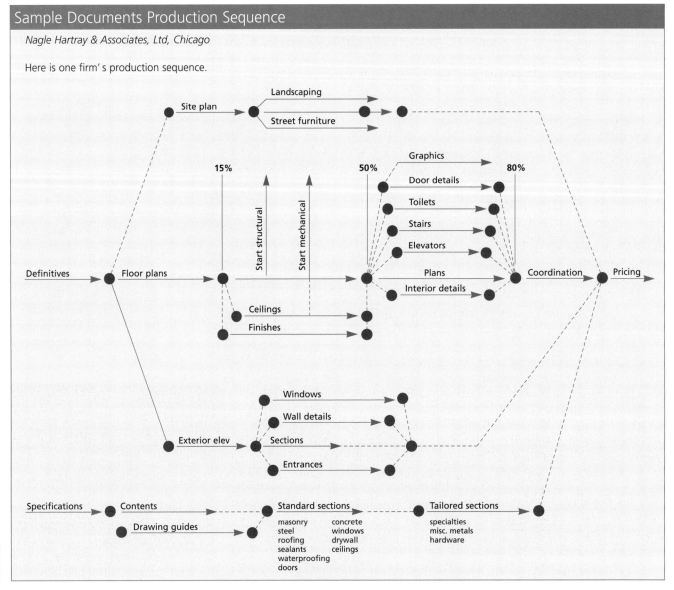

data at a defined point in time, typically a project milestone. Also, deciding what and when to archive is a project management responsibility, whereas data backup is typically a system management responsibility.

A key aspect of production planning is the search for bottlenecks that may slow down the project and endanger its schedule. Coordination points, where all drawings and specifications need to be brought to a common level of development for checking, are common candidates. Plotting CAD drawings and preparing, translating, and transferring CAD files to outside consultants are other likely bottlenecks.

***Technical references.*** Architects increasingly recognize that before new details and construction techniques are formulated, standard approaches should be investigated and understood as part of the design process. To facilitate this research, many valuable references are available to the practitioner. These include

- The building codes and regulations applicable to the project
- Technical references and standards, such as those published by ASTM, ANSI, and professional and industry associations
- Standard references, such as Architectural Graphic Standards
- Journals and other publications of professional societies and industry associations
- Manufacturers' catalogs and trade literature

This material is generally available in books or pamphlets and increasingly in disk, online, or CD-ROM format. Some of the computerized sources are integrated with product

▶ **Computer Technology in Architectural Practice (12.1) addresses automated production methods.**

selection, analysis, and detailing routines. In addition to working with printed references, most firms find that technical representatives of industry associations, product representatives, consultants, and senior members of architecture firms are valuable resources. Most firms develop a library of technical and reference information. Information on materials and products is often filed by MasterFormat division or section number, making the library easily accessible to all members of the project team.

## Documents Coordination

A goal of the construction documents phase is a fully coordinated set of documents—documents that are internally consistent. Plans, sections, elevations, details, and schedules must agree with each other. Materials shown on the drawings must be specified, the mechanical and electrical systems must fit within the chases and plenums designed for them, and so on.

The coordination task is complicated by the reality that more than one person or firm, and usually several, will work on the construction documents of all but the smallest projects. Staff may be in different groups within the firm or in consultant organizations. For CAD systems, it is necessary to develop protocols for who has access to what layers or drawings, exchange of updated files, and backups for all of the work.

Progress prints or plots of drawings and drafts of project manuals are commonly shared within the project team. Coordination meetings and milestone reviews may be used to achieve ongoing coordination.

Design changes are particularly critical. One of the responsibilities of the project manager or production coordinator is to make sure that when changes occur they are reflected in all appropriate locations in the documents. This includes notification of all disciplines. When overlay drafting or CAD systems are being used, the project manager decides when a new or revised base sheet, layer, or file is created and distributed to each discipline.

As updates are issued, it is good practice to note the date and purpose of the revision on drawing title blocks or on the cover of the project manual. Thus a record of issue dates and purposes appears on the documents. Some firms note the issue date on each page in the project manual or use a different color paper or binding for subsequent issues. These measures provide effective means of determining whether documents are current.

Once drawings are issued for contract, it is good practice to number each set of changes, circle and label each change on the documents, and record a new issue date (e.g., "3.24.94, Revisions #1").

A number of firms have found that thoughtful organization of CAD data and automation of CAD background updates have yielded significant advantages, both in productivity and in drawing quality and coordination. The key to reaping these benefits is moving beyond the idea that a CAD file is a drawing. It is not—whether the graphics are 2-D or 3-D, a CAD file is a model from which many drawings, or "views," can be generated. The major operational issues in setting up a project CAD model are:

- Never draw anything twice.
- Create a primary CAD model and make sure as many drawings as possible reference that model. This is consistent with the sheet file/model file distinction made in the *AIA CAD Layer Guidelines*.
- Establish CAD standards that permit each drawing to view the appropriate subset of the model information and to plot that information in the correct graphic representation, line weights, and text heights. Consider the needs of all users and all disciplines when setting CAD standards.
- Consider how any irregular geometry or rotated plans will be handled. This may require additional software or customization.
- Consider how data will be transferred to and received from outside consultants. How can the architect ensure that all consultants are referencing the most current version of the model?

Setting up the project CAD model properly is both technically challenging and time-consuming. It requires experience with the construction documents process as well as knowledge of the CAD system capabilities and limitations. Properly conceived and executed,

## 1. PRELIMINARY REVIEW

a. Quickly make an overview of all sheets, spending no more than one minute per sheet to become familiar with the project.

## 2. SPECIFICATIONS CHECK

a. Check specs for bid items. Are they coordinated with the drawings?

b. Check specs for phasing of construction. Are the phases clear?

c. Compare architectural finish schedule to specification index. Ensure all finish materials are specified.

d. Check major items of equipment and verify that they are coordinated with contract drawings. Pay particular attention to horsepower ratings and voltage requirements.

e. Verify that items specified "as indicated" or "where indicated" are in fact indicated on contract drawings.

f. Verify that cross-referenced specification sections exist.

g. Try not to indicate thickness of materials or quantities of materials in specifications.

## 3. PLAN CHECK CIVIL

a. Verify that site plans with new underground utilities (power, telephone, water, sewer, gas, storm drainage, fuel lines, grease traps, fuel tanks) have been checked for interferences.

b. Verify that existing telephone poles, pole guys, street signs, drainage inlets, valve boxes, manhole castings, etc., do not interfere with new driveways, sidewalks, or other site improvements on architectural site plans.

c. Verify that limits of clearing, grading, sodding, grass, or mulch are shown and are consistent with architectural or landscaping plans.

d. Verify fire hydrant and street light pole locations against electrical and architectural.

e. Verify that profile sheets show other underground utilities and avoid conflicts.

f. Verify that horizontal distances between drainage structures and manholes match with respect to scaled dimensions and stated dimensions on both plan and profile sheets.

g. Verify that provisions have been included for adjusting valve box and manhole castings (sewer, power, telephone, drainage) to match final or finish grade of pavement, swales, or sidewalks.

h. Verify that all existing and proposed grades are shown.

## 4. PLAN CHECK STRUCTURAL

a. Verify column lines on structural and architectural.

b. Verify that all column locations are the same on structural and architectural.

c. Verify that perimeter slab on structural matches architectural.

d. Verify that all depressed or raised slabs are indicated.

e. Verify slab elevations against architectural.

f. Verify that all foundation piers are identified.

g. Verify that all foundation beams are identified.

h. Verify roof framing plan column lines and columns against foundation plan column lines and columns.

i. Verify perimeter roof line against architectural roof plan.

j. Verify that all columns and beams are listed in column and beam schedules.

k. Verify length of all columns in column schedule.

l. Verify that all sections are properly labeled.

m. Verify all expansion joint locations against architectural.

n. Verify dimensions.

o. Verify that drawing notes do not conflict with specifications.

## 5. PLAN CHECK ARCHITECTURAL

a. Verify property line dimensions on site survey plan against architecture.

b. Verify that building is located behind setback lines.

c. Verify all concrete columns and walls against structural.

d. Verify on site plans that all existing and new work is clearly identified.

e. Verify building elevations against floor plans. Check in particular roof lines, window and door openings, and expansion joints.

f. Verify building sections against elevations and plans. Check roof lines, windows, and door locations.

g. Verify wall sections against architectural building sections and structural.

h. Verify masonry openings for windows and doors.

i. Verify expansion joints through building.

j. Verify partial floor plans against small scale floor plans.

k. Verify reflected ceiling plan against architectural floor plan to ensure no variance with rooms. Check ceiling materials against finish schedule, check light fixture layout against electrical, check ceiling diffusers/registers against mechanical, check all soffits and locations of vents.

l. Verify all room finish schedule information including room numbers, names of rooms, finishes, and ceiling heights. Look for omissions, duplications, and inconsistencies.

m. Verify all door schedule information including sizes, types, labels, etc. Look for omissions, duplications, and inconsistencies.

n. Verify all rated walls.

o. Verify all cabinets will fit.

p. Verify dimensions.

## 6. PLAN CHECK MECHANICAL AND PLUMBING

a. Verify that all new electrical, gas, water, sewer, etc. lines connect to existing.

b. Verify all plumbing fixture locations against architectural. Verify all plumbing fixtures against fixture schedule and/or specs.

c. Verify storm drain system against architectural roof plan. Verify that pipes are sized and all drains are connected and do not interfere with foundations. Verify that wall chases are provided on architectural to conceal vertical piping.

d. Verify that sanitary drain system pipes are sized and all fixtures are connected.

e. Verify HVAC floor plans against architectural.

f. Verify sprinkler heads in all rooms.

g. Verify that all sections are identical to architectural/ structural.

h. Verify that adequate ceiling height exists at worst case duct intersection.

i. Verify that all structural supports required for mechanical equipment are indicated on structural drawings.

j. Verify that dampers are indicated at smoke and fire walls.

k. Verify diffusers against architectural reflected ceiling plan.

l. Verify that all roof penetrations (ducts, fans, etc.) are indicated on roof plans.

m. Verify all ductwork is sized.

n. Verify all notes.

o. Verify all air conditioning units, heaters, and exhaust fans against architectural roof plans and mechanical schedules.

p. Verify that all mechanical equipment will fit in spaces allocated.

## 7. PLAN CHECK ELECTRICAL

a. Verify that all plans are identical to architectural.

b. Verify all light fixtures against architectural reflected ceiling plan.

c. Verify that all major pieces of equipment have electrical connections.

d. Verify location of all panel boards and that they are indicated on the electrical riser diagram.

e. Verify all notes.

f. Verify that there is sufficient space for all electrical panels to fit.

g. Verify that electrical panels are not recessed in fire walls.

h. Verify that electrical equipment locations are coordinated with site paving and grading.

## 8. PLAN CHECK KITCHEN/DIETARY

a. Verify equipment layout against architectural plans.

© William T. Nigro. Reprinted with permission.

this CAD modeling approach has proven to reduce the time spent on coordination reviews and subsequent reworking of the documents, and also to substantially reduce the number of change orders during the construction phase.

***Review and checking.*** The importance of review and checking cannot be overemphasized, given the extreme time constraints under which construction documents are often produced. Documents may be produced by individuals who do not fully understand the larger context in which details fit. Therefore, checking goes hand in hand with the ongoing education process that characterizes any professional office.

Lists to help architects check documents are available from many sources. Many offices develop their own guides for document checking—checklists that may be used by the individual in developing the drawing and by the project manager in checking it. Checking plays a central role in any firm's quality assurance effort. Most firms establish protocols for document checking. Some examples:

- Documents are comprehensively checked at one or more milestones before they are completed.
- A senior person not associated with the project checks all documents before they are issued.
- One person checks all important dimensions.
- The person responsible for the drawings reviews the specifications, and the specifier reviews the drawings.
- Consultants review the documents produced by other contributors for coordination.
- The owner reviews and approves the documents before they are issued for bid or negotiation.

The last point is particularly important. The owner issues the construction documents for bidding or negotiation, and the owner signs the construction agreements with contractors, the construction manager, or the design-build entity. It is the owner's project, and it is important—and mandated in AIA forms of agreement—that the owner approve the construction documents.

Of all project phases, the preparation of the construction documents typically takes the most time and resources. New technologies, especially computing and computer graphics, are changing the nature of this work, shifting the emphasis from rote production to decision making, coordination, and communication. A firm grasp of design and construction documentation is increasingly central to successful architectural practice.

### For More Information

*Time-Saving Techniques for Architectural Construction Drawings* (1997) by Fred Nashed addresses the process of planning construction documentation and provides office standards for drawings. Richard M. Linde and Osamu A. Wakita cover the skills, concepts, and fundamentals for working drawings in *The Professional Practice of Architectural Working Drawings* (1994). Fred Stitt provides guidelines and checklists for documents production in the well-illustrated *Production Systems for Architects and Designers* (1997).

Several publications address construction drawing standards. *Uniform Drawing System* (1998) establishes standards for sheet types, sheet organization, and schedules. *AIA CAD Layer Guidelines* (2001), establishes standard naming of data file layers. Both of these documents have been incorporated into the U.S. National CAD Standard along with plotting standards. The National CAD Standard is available from the the AIA at (202) 626-7541; the Construction Specifications Institute at www.csinet.org; and the National Institute of Building Sciences (NIBS) at www.nationalcadstandard.org.

In-depth treatment on preparing specifications can be found in Harold J. Rosen's *Construction Specifications Writing: Principles and Procedures* (1998). Specification software is available from ARCOM, including MASTERSPEC master specification system and SPECWARE specification enhancement software. See AIA MASTERSPEC for further descriptions of these practice tools or contact ARCOM at www.masterspec.com.

Redicheck Associates publishes an overlay checking and interdisciplinary coordination manual as a means for achieving more accurate and thorough construction documents. For information, call (877) 733-4243.

▶ Be sure to document the owner's approval of legal and contractual information, or you may assume liability for it.

# The U.S. National CAD Standard

*Michael Tardif, Assoc. AIA*

Business software applications, including computer-aided design and drafting applications (CAD), allow a high degree of control over the organization and classification of data and the graphic composition of printed output. These user-defined variables allow individual authors to organize and classify CAD data according to their own needs and sense of logic, and to establish their own graphic standards for printed documents. While this freedom to customize is among the benefits of computer technology, the proliferation of customized user-defined settings in the production of CAD documents has eroded the common language for data organization, classification, and communication that evolved over hundreds of years of hand drafting. Even the simplest of CAD software applications can have as many as a hundred user-definable settings. The lack of standards in this arena inhibits the sharing of data even among small design teams. The overhead costs of translating settings between organizations or of developing and enforcing office standards cuts deeply into any productivity gains of computer-aided design and drafting.

Over the years a number of industry organizations have addressed various aspects of this issue. The AIA published the first edition of *CAD Layer Guidelines* in 1992 for the purpose of establishing a common system of nomenclature for CAD data files and layer names. The second edition, revised and updated, was published in 1997. That same year, the Construction Specifications Institute (CSI) published the first three modules of the Uniform Drawing System. This document was intended to serve as an industry standard for the organization of construction documents, whether they are prepared electronically or by hand.

Recognizing the potential for these publications to serve as the foundation of a consensus industry standard, the National Institute of Building Sciences (NIBS) convened a coalition of building design and construction industry organizations in 1997 to explore the development of a U.S. National CAD Standard (NCS). Under the auspices of NIBS' Facility Information Council, the AIA joined with the Construction Specifications Institute, the U.S. Coast Guard, the U.S. Department of Defense Tri-Service CADD/GIS Technology Center, the Sheet Metal and Air Conditioning Contractors National Association (SMACNA), and other construction and software industry organizations to prepare the joint publication of the standard. These groups have committed to supporting the evolution and development of the NCS to keep pace with evolving technology. Efforts are also under way to incorporate the NCS directly into CAD and related software applications.

The product of a historic and unprecedented cooperative effort, the NCS is an important step in streamlining the free flow of building construction and design data throughout the life cycle of buildings, from initial conceptual design through eventual retirement and reuse. It comprises the following items:

1. "The Uniform Drawing System," published by CSI (a system for the organization of building construction drawings)
2. "AIA CAD Layer Guidelines," published by the AIA (a system of nomenclature for CAD drawing file names and CAD layer names). The updated version includes new layer definitions for disciplines such as telecommunications and electronic building systems and modifications and has been revised to improve compatibility with ISO layer standards.
3. The Tri-Service "Plotting Guidelines," developed by the U.S. Coast Guard and promulgated by the U.S. Tri-Service CADD/GIS Technology Center of the U.S. Department of Defense (defines colors and line weight assignments for CAD drawings)
4. The "National CAD Standard Project Committee Report," published by NIBS (resolves minor discrepancies between the constituent documents)

## The Benefits of a National CAD Standard

A uniform electronic data classification format will establish a common language for preparing building design and construction documents. It will eliminate the need for developing and maintaining office standards. Newly hired employees will not have to be trained or retrained to learn file and layer naming conventions, pen assignments, line weights, drawing set organization, or sheet layout conventions. Project designers and project managers will be able to access design data more easily without having to learn the arcana of varying organizational systems.

The benefits are better project management, higher-quality construction documents, reduced errors and omissions, and ultimately a better building project. Most importantly, design firms can provide a higher quality of service to their clients by delivering data in an industry-standard format. Savvy design firms will seize the opportunity to let clients know that they use the National CAD Standard format.

## Opportunities to Participate

The NIBS/FIC National CAD Standard Project Committee will convene annually with a goal of publishing a new version of the NCS in the spring of each year. Membership is open to the public, and an open-enrollment period will take place each summer. Anyone with an interest in the work of the committee may participate. The committee's work is conducted via the Internet. Committee membership is available in two categories: document reviewer (no travel required) and active (some travel required). All committee members have an equal voice and ballot vote regardless of membership category. Visit the National CAD Standard Web site at www.nationalcadstandard.org for details.

The National CAD Standard can be ordered from the AIA Bookstore by calling (202) 626-7541 or (800) 242-3837 (press 4). It can also be purchasedfrom NIBS at www.nationalcadstandard.org and the Construction Specifications Institute at www.csinet.org. A substantial discount is available to AIA, CSI, and NIBS members.

*Michael Tardif is director of the AIA Center for Technology and Practice Management.*

# AIA MASTERSPEC

MASTERSPEC is a specification development tool popular with the building design and construction industry. The newest versions offer architects powerful tools for preparing project specifications. MASTERSPEC is a product of the AIA and is published and supported by ARCOM. It is available in ten versions, called libraries, which are organized by design discipline as follows:

| LIBRARY | ABBREVIATION |
| --- | --- |
| Architectural/Structural/Civil | A/S/C |
| Structural/Civil | S/C |
| Mechanical/Electrical | M/E |
| Electrical | E |
| Interior Construction | IC |
| Interior Construction Supplement to A/S/C | ICS |
| Landscape Architecture | LA |
| Roofing | RF |
| Security and Detention | SD |

MASTERSPEC libraries are available in three formats: full-length, short form, and outline. These formats are available in two versions: basic and supplemental.

- *Full-length* specifications are comprehensive master specifications that include a large range of materials, products, and applications. They include multiple methods of specifying.
- *Short form* specifications are condensed from and compatible with full-length sections. They include a limited range of products, streamlined material and quality-control requirements, and concise specifying methods.
- *Outline* format specifications provide a method for recording product and material decisions early in the documentation process. A checklist is provided to help the project team select products and methods during development of the project manual.
- *Basic version* sections are the most frequently used specification sections because they cover the most commonly found construction conditions for all project sizes and types.
- *Supplemental version* sections are limited to work that is more specialized or customized than that covered by basic version specifications.

## Section Naming Convention

MASTERSPEC sections are assigned numbers and titles according to the 1995 edition of CSI/CSC's MasterFormat. Each section number is five digits, organized in one of 16 CSI/CSC divisions. For example, Section 06402, Interior Architectural Woodwork, is listed under Division 6, Wood and Plastics. The MASTERSPEC table of contents lists all of the sections by division and section number and includes the issue date and a description of the section contents. MASTERSPEC CD-ROMs contain a table of contents that can be printed for reference.

## Supporting Documents

Each basic and supplemental MASTERSPEC section includes the following documents:

- *Cover.* This describes the content of the section text; related products and work, including products that could be inserted into the section if required; similar work normally specified elsewhere; and closely related work specified in other sections. It also includes a summary of changes in the last update.
- *Evaluation.* This describes characteristics and criteria for specifying the products and materials in the section. Included are editing instructions, which are referenced in editor's notes in the section text; the scope of the section; a description of product characteristics; special design and detailing considerations, if applicable; environmental considerations; referenced standards; suggested reference materials; and a list of manufacturers. The list of manufacturers includes addresses, telephone numbers, and Web addresses. Tables of comparative information on products and manufacturers are included in some of the sections.
- *Section text.* The section text is in three-part format with editor's notes, alternative text, in-line optional text, and insert notes.
- *Drawing coordination checklist.* The checklist consists of drawing requirements organized and related to the section content. It indicates items that should be shown on the drawings because they are not in the section text.
- *Specification coordination checklist.* The checklist includes a list of specification sections and requirements that relate to the section content. It also provides a location for indicating items that will be furnished by the owner; how to apply allowances, unit prices, and alternates to the section if applicable; and other specification sections that may have requirements applicable to the section.

## Other MASTERSPEC Specifications

MASTERSPEC is available in three abbreviated versions that are updated every two years. The Interior Design and Furnishings versions include a cover, evaluations, section text, and drawing coordination checklist. The Small Project version includes the section text only.

- MASTERSPEC FURNISHINGS is a short-form specification for procurement of furnishings.
- MASTERSPEC INTERIOR DESIGN is a short-form specification for commercial and residential interiors practice.
- MASTERSPEC SMALL PROJECT consists of very brief specifications for less complex projects.

## Editing Assistance

MASTERSPEC is the only complete master specification system available. The evaluations provide editing instructions for each specification section, as well as product comparisons, a list of national manufacturers, reference standards, references, and a discussion of the section topic and graphics when appropriate. Each section text includes editor's notes with instructions for editing and selecting alternative text, in-line optional text, and insert notes. All section text is displayed for review and editing. Editor's notes and units of measure appear on-screen in color. Editor's notes are defined as hidden text and may be toggled on or off in word processing software.

You can edit MASTERSPEC by using your word processing software. The capabilities of your software can be enhanced with MASTERWORKS or with the LINX automated specification editor. Instructions for editing with ARCOM's MASTERWORKS software are included in the MASTERWORKS user's guide, and instructions for editing with the LINX software are included in an online tutorial. LINX operates only with the basic and supplemental versions.

### SPECWARE

SPECWARE is the family of specification enhancement software provided to MASTERSPEC licensed users. SPECWARE includes the following:

- MASTERWORKS. This software enhances your word processor to simplify editing of alternative text, selection of options to keep or delete, insertion of required text, and addition of project notes. The multifiles task options automate spell checking, searching and replacing, reporting, creating headers and footers and tables of contents, formatting, and other text appearance functions. Specification output formats include project manual, sheet specification, drawing notes, and outline.

- LINX. This stand-alone automated editor for MASTERSPEC operates on standard full-length MASTERSPEC sections that are in the ARCOM Structured Text database format. Text elements in each section are linked together hierarchically and semantically. All linked text elements are marked for deletion when a parent text element is marked for deletion. If the project has no wood decking, for example, deletion of wood decking in Section 06150 would automatically delete all text related to wood decking that may appear in the section, regardless of location. This allows for easy removal of large quantities of text. LINX also includes an interactive question-and-answer edit and an on-screen edit (including manual editing and override of system edits, automatic edits, and translation to a word processor of choice).

*Information on MASTERSPEC and ARCOM SPECWARE software is available through ARCOM at (800) 424-5080, on their Web site at www.arcomnet.com, or by email to arcom@arcomnet.com.*

# 13 Project Management

## 13.1 Project Teams

### Frank A. Stasiowski, FAIA

*Project teams function most effectively when the members work together to meet the client's project objectives.*

Even the smallest project requires a team of two: an architect and a client. Relationships expand as teams become larger and include office colleagues, consultants, contractors, and possibly others. Some type of plan is needed to organize the project on paper. Central to the plan and the agreement is a project team. This team's ability to work together is critical to the project's success.

### THE PROJECT MANAGER

> The project manager may also be involved in marketing the project, preparing the project plan, and negotiating the project agreements.

The central figure on a project team is the project manager (PM)—the person in the architecture firm who is responsible for managing a team of diverse people and interests and for balancing design, schedule, and budget concerns to meet client expectations.

Those with project management responsibilities may be called project managers, project architects, or project directors, or in some cases they may be principals or associates in firm without added titles. Whatever their titles, effective PMs assume project leadership responsibilities, accept certain challenges, and bring certain traits and abilities to their work.

### Historical Responsibilities

Although specific responsibilities may vary, the PM is generally responsible for managing the project's progress toward its time, cost, and quality goals. Project managers have these key challenges:

- *Client expectations.* The first responsibility of the project manager is to identify the client's expectations—what the client considers to be a successful project. Communication skills, especially listening, are essential.
- *Accomplishment.* The next most important responsibility of the project manager is to get things done. Projects are complex enterprises and present difficulties. The successful PM views difficulties as challenges and gains the respect of clients, supervisors, and peers by accomplishing objectives in spite of problems.
- *Taking charge.* It is the PM's responsibility to take charge. A project team requires sensitive guidance and direction. An effective manager allows each

**FRANK STASIOWSKI,** *is founder and president of PSMJ Resources. Stasiowski is a consultant to the building and design industry and the author of numerous books and publications about management.*

▶ **Project Team Agreements (10.2)** looks at owner-architect, design team, and construction agreements.

member of the team to exercise judgment and creativity within the constraints of the project.

- *Service.* The ability to manage client relationships successfully is one of the most important skills a PM can develop. The challenge is to serve without being servile. The PM must sometimes tell a client something the client does not want to believe—for instance, that the construction budget and a owner's project scope are not in balance.

- *Meeting contractual obligations.* A key responsibility is to meet a firm's obligations as outlined in the agreement for professional services with the client. This means doing everything reasonable to carry out the project within the scope, services, schedule, and construction budget established in that agreement.

## Innovative Roles

In addition to the roles architects have always assumed, most firms now expect the PM to take on additional roles involving marketing and financial matters.

***Marketing.*** It is often said that the best way to secure additional work is to do good work. Good work results in repeat business, which often serves as the lifeblood of a firm—75 percent of backlog as repeat business is typical of most architectural firms. The more successful firms expect PMs to assume an active role in securing even more new business.

Repeat business involves maintaining and building relationships with past clients, even without an active project. Actively securing referrals from past clients contributes to fostering this relationship. Securing new business requires the PM to close the deal. This means the PM leads the proposal effort, develops the strategy to win the project, and links the firm's direct experience to meeting or exceeding the client's needs.

***Financial.*** In the current business climate, the PM needs to lead the effort to secure payment from the client.

All projects start with a defined budget or at least an expectation of cost. It is up to the PM to define the client's budget and establish a clear financial baseline before the project begins. Profit must be included in the budget.

▶ **Tips for Leaders:**
- Don't be afraid to admit ignorance.
- Know when to intervene.
- Learn to truly share power.
- Worry about what you take on, not what you give up.
- Get used to learning on the job.

Fortune, *February 20, 1995*

The idea of profit confuses many professionals. Let's look at an example that involves a $20,000 service fee. The PM and the firm principal have agreed to earn a profit of 10 percent of the fee, or $2,000. If the PM exceeds the project budget by $500, for a total of $20,500, one could suggest that the PM made a profit of $1,500. However, the profit was established as part of the project baseline to be $2,000, so in actuality this PM *lost* $500 of the firm's profit.

Securing payment from the client has traditionally been considered the responsibility of the accounting department. But in the more successful firms PMs tend to lead this effort. No one is suggesting that the PM become a bill collector, only that he or she take proactive steps to ensure that billing the client and securing the payment are completed in a timely and expeditious manner. The PM can ensure that billing requirements are clearly understood and communicated to the accounting department. The PM can also expedite review of invoices prepared by the firm's accounting department to speed their issue to the client. To secure payment, the PM can inform the client that the invoice has been sent and that he or she would be happy to answer any questions the client may have. Regular follow-up with the client, while discussing other project-related matters, would also be appropriate. If payments are late, the PM may request a contact in the client's accounting department who could be called for an update.

## Place in the Firm

In smaller firms, the principals and the PMs are synonymous. The principals' styles dictate the ways in which both the firm and its projects are managed.

Even in larger firms, the principals typically manage projects. When the principal is too busy to provide all of the necessary project management services—or when the firm delegates day-to-day project management responsibilities to someone who is not a principal—it is common to have a principal-in-charge. Delegating project management responsibilities offers another advantage: It allows the firm to recognize the management skills of some of its people, and it helps in training the next generation of firm management.

Whenever there is a principal-in-charge and a PM, the two need to build a strong relationship. Any delegation of management responsibility should be clear, consistent, and devoid of second-guessing. As the PM learns—and makes mistakes—it is difficult but necessary for the principal-in-charge to resist the temptation to step in and take over. From the PM's standpoint, it is important to remember that the principal is likely to be an owner in the firm, has probably acquired the project, and will assume responsibility and liability for the services being performed. The PM must therefore be willing to learn and work with the principal's operating style.

Their relationship should be built as a partnership devoted to meeting project objectives. Project managers need to be invested with both authority and responsibility, but the principal cannot fully abdicate these functions. Both professionals can work together to prepare a winning proposal with a fee that meets the firm's financial objectives. As the project progresses, it is a good management practice to hold regular assessments of the client's satisfaction and the project's financial performance.

Sometimes a PM may not be experienced in important technical aspects of a project. In such a case it could be appropriate to delegate some project management responsibilities to a job captain, technical director, or assistant PM.

## Traits and Abilities

Effective PMs are usually characterized by their ability to organize a design project and to deliver high-quality, on-time, and within-budget performance. Accomplishing these objectives requires both technical competence and assertive leadership. The effective PM will have some combination of the traits and abilities outlined here:

- Is organized; directs and controls all key aspects of the project
- Is enthusiastic about achieving high standards
- Communicates well, both within the team and to those outside of it
- Motivates the project team to meet the project's goals
- Delegates when appropriate
- Listens well and can interpret clearly team members' issues and opinions
- Attacks aggressively every problem important to the project's success
- Is persuasive in a pleasing and nonbelligerent manner
- Has a conscious sense of time, knows what it takes to accomplish a task, and is aware of how much time is left to finish a task
- Knows where to find the answers for technical and managerial problems
- Knows that it takes a team to accomplish outstanding results, and gives credit to the group
- Is results-oriented, always keeping the final outcome of the project in mind

## MANAGING STAFF AND CONSULTANTS

In addition to the project architect, most architecture projects involve at least one other person. For a small project, the team may include a part-time draftsperson, a consultant, the contractor, and, of course, the client. Larger projects require expanded teams, including additional staff from within the firm and perhaps several consultants, associated firms, or other alliance members.

## Selecting In-House Staff

The architecture firm's staff forms the core of the project team. As long as a firm has more than one staff member or more than one project, in-house staffing involves establishing the specific skills and the level of effort (usually measured in hours) needed to perform the services, identifying the people to work on the project, and balancing the needs of the project with those of the firm and its other projects.

Assuming there are choices, it is natural for each project to compete for staff within

Project Operations (13.2) provides a closer view of project and team operations, including start-up, communications, decision making, documentation, and closeout.

the firm. PMs in this position need to recognize that the firm's leaders must make personnel assignments that are best for the entire office, not just for one of its projects. PMs can, however, encourage people to work on their projects by creating positive and supportive working conditions; even busy people seem to make time for what they want to do. It is wise to obtain tentative commitments from key personnel—including estimates of time and availability—during the proposal stage and to involve them in proposal preparation.

Few firms work on only one project at a time. The coordination of labor requirements for all projects in the office becomes a general firm management task. The key is regular dialogue among principals and PMs. Most firms schedule regular weekly meetings (often on Monday mornings) to work out the details of labor requirements for the week's work. Each PM prepares a work-to-be-done schedule and brings it to the meeting. With principals and PMs present, project personnel requirements can be discussed and decided.

> **Project Controls (13.3) looks at approaches to monitoring progress and making course corrections.**

## How to Delegate

This checklist may help you perform this most difficult of all project management tasks.

1. Define what only you can do.
2. Define the rest of the job in terms of

   - *What:* the mission, what must be done to succeed, upper goals and lower limits—and why it is important
   - *Who:* who's responsible, who's accountable, who must be checked with, who must be informed, and who supports
   - *When:* start, finish, how many hours to spend, what comes first, and what can slide
   - *Intended outcome:* how we will know we've done it

3. Encourage early feedback. Schedule the first time.
4. Define the level (and limits) of both resources and authority.
5. Define information sources and requirements. What needs to be recorded and saved?
6. Check understanding.
7. Ask for commitment.

*James R. Franklin, FAIA*

## Delegating to Others

One of the most difficult tasks for project managers is to delegate responsibility properly. Most project managers begin their careers on the boards (or on computer screens) performing design and technical services. The best professionals are often given project management responsibilities. This leads to a natural tendency for PMs to resist assigning work to others for fear it will not be performed as well as they would do it. The key to overcoming this reluctance is to establish acceptable levels of performance and resolve that these standards will be met.

Delegation spreads the workload, encourages initiative, and helps train additional staff. When an assignment is delegated, the first step is to define the task clearly. For each task delegated, it is wise to

- Identify the team member most capable of doing it
- Give that person the responsibility and authority he or she needs to complete the task
- Establish the level of performance required
- Define the completed activity or results
- Agree on the level of effort and time required
- Establish a suitable completion date
- Establish interim milestones or other approaches for checking progress

## When You Are Overloaded

Before hiring additional firm employees, you may want to consider these strategies:

*Work overtime.* Although this is an obvious solution to short-term needs, it can be counterproductive in the long run. Studies have shown that generally working 20 percent or more overtime for a sustained period (a month or more) can result in a significant drop in productivity.

*Control the timing of discretionary time off.* A regular personnel planning process can help predict workload bulges and slack periods, allowing appropriate scheduling of discretionary time such as vacations and elective surgery.

*Use short-term staff.* Many firms hire some staff on a project or other short-term basis. This approach fulfills immediate needs, can add expertise to the firm without long-term commitments, and allows short-term people to plan ahead.

*Subcontract work to other firms.* During very busy periods it may be possible to shift some effort to other firms with similar expertise and standards. This may be particularly advantageous for preparation of construction documents.

*Howard G. Birnberg*

Another important step in delegation is checking progress. The effective project manager encourages the project team to operate with a high degree of freedom but at the same time effectively monitors performance. On large projects, this may mean project managers spend most of their time monitoring work delegated to others, supporting their efforts, and helping them succeed.

The level of checking is a function of the importance of the task and the confidence a PM has in the person doing the work. Control mechanisms include identification and tracking of milestones as well as periodic reviews. One such mechanism is simply to walk through the office once or twice a day, stopping to see what each member of the project team has been doing—what's called "management by walking around."

***Task assignments.*** Assigning work to in-house staff colleagues affords the PM an opportunity to plan at a more detailed level. Discussion of the task being assigned, including the staff member's views on the time and resources needed to accomplish it, can encourage buy-in. The PM may want to write down assignments or ask staff and consultants to take notes and furnish copies. This helps maintain documentation of delegated work so the PM can follow it up properly.

***Consultants and other design team members.*** The PM is responsible for the performance of project consultants and will want them to share the firm's commitment to meeting the project's objectives. Depending on the delivery option taken and on the firm's strategy for acquiring the project, the team may include other firms such as joint venture partners, associated design firms, construction managers, PMs, or others with special expertise.

Commitment can be heightened by involving consultants and other design team members in project planning and by applying many of the same ideas about motivation and recognition used with in-house staff. The most important form of recognition for most firms is professional respect for their competence and their contribution to the quality of the project.

## MANAGING THE CLIENT

A PM's ability to work with clients will, to a large extent, determine the firm's ability to meet project objectives.

### Delegating by Using R-Charting

*James R. Franklin, FAIA*

R-charting (responsibility charting) involves publicly negotiated verbal contracts within a group. Agreements are especially binding when they are negotiated in a group and recorded on a large flip chart or poster paper for all to approve.

**STEP 1**
The team discusses the process or system that is at issue and agrees on an intended outcome—the goal.

**STEP 2**
Members develop the R-chart by agreeing on actions and decision making necessary to carry out the process successfully. These are listed down the vertical axis of a matrix in sequential order.

**STEP 3**
Each team member's name is listed across the top. Intended roles and responsibility for each task are agreed to, using these rules:

- There can be only one person responsible for a given task. In cases of disagreement there are two options:
  - Split the task into smaller tasks, each the responsibility of a different person.
  - Kick the original task upstairs to a person to whom those disagreeing all report.
- Minimize the A/V role—more than one team member has the responsibility when reporting to multiple bosses is involved.

| | Name | Name | Name | Name | Name | Name | Name | Name | Name | Name |
|---|---|---|---|---|---|---|---|---|---|---|
| Task | R | S | S | | | | I | | | S |
| Task | A/V | I | S | R | | S | I | | S | |
| Task | I | A/V | R | | S | S | I | | S | |
| Task | I | A/V | | S | S | S | S | R | | S | S |
| Task | I | A/V | S | S | R | I | S | | S | | I |
| Task | R | | | | | | I | | | S |
| Task | A/V | A/V | S | | | | I | | S | R |
| Task | I | | | A/V | | R | S | | | S |
| Task | A/V | A/V | | R | | | I | | S | S |

**R**—Is responsible
**A/V**—Must approve or veto
**I**—Must be informed
**S**—To furnish support

► **Project Team Agreements (10.2)** provides details on consultant, joint venture, and association agreements.

The first step in working successfully with clients is to learn as much as you can about them and their organization. To start, ask these questions:

- Who makes—and influences—project decisions?
- Who is responsible for scope, quality, schedule, and budget?
- Who has the authority to modify the contract?
- Who will approve the firm's services and evaluate the firm's performance?

In the case of a small project, only one person may be involved with the project. In a large public agency, there may be a large technical staff, numerous department heads, and elected officials, all of whom possess varying levels of authority and involvement in different aspects of the project.

## Uncovering the Client's Agenda

The mayor of Denver was speaking of the new Denver airport at a meeting of the American Society of Consulting Engineers. He made the point very clearly that meeting the client's needs is the true agenda. There were many levels of satisfaction to be considered in this project. In addition to issues of quality, budget, and schedule, he had his own concerns with getting the project finished on time, since he was up for reelection the year it was to be completed. He was very disturbed by the thought of having to go back to the city's building committee with any news of delaying the project. As mayor, he wanted to make this project the gem of his administration. The true job of the architects and engineers on the project, then, was to realize this goal: create a fabulous gem of an airport, on time, before election season.

How do you determine the client's true agenda? Bone up on listening techniques. If you don't know how to listen, it will be hard for you to get to the crux of the client's needs and wants. If you don't get to the heart of the client's issues, you won't understand how the client measures project success. Without this information, it is unlikely you will be hired again or recommended to other prospective clients.

Don't be bound by what we traditionally believe is the way to run a design practice. The client should feel as if he or she is the only client your firm is dealing with. Instead of telling clients how great you are, show them how great you feel they are. This attitude speaks for itself!

*Frank A. Stasiowski, FAIA*

***Client personalities.*** Like everyone else, clients have personality types, work styles, and behavioral traits. The client's needs, priorities, and operating style may be quite different from the architect's. The successful project manager develops methods of dealing with each client in order to be responsive to that client's needs.

Here is an example: Peter Drucker, a well-known management consultant, has divided supervisors into readers and listeners. If your client is a reader, like Dwight Eisenhower or John F. Kennedy, Drucker advises, don't just call or visit to talk about a problem or suggestion; write it up first to make sure the client has something to read. If your client is a listener, like Franklin Roosevelt or Harry Truman, don't send a memorandum; talk about it first and then summarize with a memo or letter.

***Client relationships.*** Relationships between architects and clients can take many forms. Toward one end of the range are relationships in which the architect has a good deal of autonomy and is a highly influential advisor. Many decisions are made jointly by architect and client, and the architect is viewed as an integral member of the client's team. At another extreme are relationships in which the firm has been hired to do a particular job within rigidly defined constraints. Here the architect may be required to make decisions within a narrow scope of work and to obtain formal direction for anything else.

Clients differ on the level of involvement they seek in their projects. For example, an architecture firm may be working with the chief executive of a small corporation on the design of a new corporate headquarters, in which case the client will probably wish to participate in making day-to-day project decisions. On the other hand, a client who is the chairman of the board for a small community museum may believe that no single board member is individually accountable for the project and the architect should make design decisions so long as the final product satisfies the community. Determine who is your client. The best project managers ask themselves, "What can I do to make my client look good to his or her supervisors and customers?"

## Making Good Clients: Keeping the Project on Track

It's said that good architecture requires good clients. To help your clients become better clients, you may want to offer some advice and guidance on how to keep the project on track. Here are some words you might want to share with a client.

Project scope, quality, and cost are inextricably related. Any two of these variables can be fixed and controlled in design; the marketplace takes care of the third. You will need to establish priorities among them and set acceptable ranges for each one.

A good architect challenges the program, schedule, and budget. Even when these have been developed through painstaking effort, it is in the client's best interest to encourage this challenge. In this way, the architect comes to understand project requirements. The analysis may also reveal existing or potential problem areas.

As design proceeds, important issues will surface. The architect's services bring increased client understanding of the project. As a result, the project changes. Each milestone, usually the end-of-phase submissions written into the owner-architect agreement, should be used to ensure continuing consensus on project scope, levels of quality, construction cost, and budget. It may also be necessary to adjust the services required from the architect at these points.

The secret to successful projects is effective project management by both owner and architect. A summary of what the owner can do to keep the project running smoothly through design and construction is presented here:

*Project plan.* Insist on a project plan, preferably as part of the process of negotiating project agreements. Ask that the plan be updated on a regular basis and after any major change in scope, services, or schedule.

*Project team.* Be part of the project-planning process and all project meetings. Be sure that your own deadlines, as well as your own decision processes, are reflected in the project plan.

*Client representative.* Identify a single person to represent you and to speak for you at planning sessions and project meetings. The scope of the client representative's authority should be understood by all involved.

*Internal coordination.* If yours is an organization in which several people or departments must be involved in the project work, make it clear that the client representative speaks as the boss. Conflicting advice or requirements inevitably cause problems later.

*Meetings.* Plan on regular meetings of the project team and participate in them. Meetings should have clear agendas. Persons with assigned tasks should have them done in time for meetings. Be sure the architect prepares minutes that clearly identify what was decided, what items now require decision making, and who is responsible for the next steps. Minutes should be circulated to all team members.

*Documentation.* Require that contacts between architect and client (for example, phone conversations, data-gathering sessions) be documented and the results shared with appropriate members of the project team. This system keeps everyone informed of what's being discussed and decided outside of formal project meetings and presentations.

*Milestones.* Your owner-architect agreement designates one or more design phases and submissions by the architect. Use these milestones to review what has been done and to approve it as the basis for moving forward.

*Decision process.* Be sure both you and your architect understand the process by which you will make decisions—who requires what information, who requires whose approval before deciding, how much should be allocated for review of submissions.

*Decisions.* Make decisions when they are called for. If you are stuck, talk it out and find out why. Keeping the project on hold while you decide increases the possibility of changes in conditions that may upset the delicate balance between project time, cost, and quality. Long or indefinite delays may force the architect to assign key team members to other projects.

*Agreement modifications.* Keep the owner-architect agreement up-to-date. Modify it when project scope or services are changed.

*Questions.* When you have questions, ask them. Pay particular attention to design submissions, for the work of each phase is further developed in the next. Look at these submissions carefully and ask about anything that is unclear or incorrect. Questions should be cleared up before the construction contract documents phase begins; changes after this point will most likely cost you time and money.

*Problems.* Address problems as they arise and before small ones become large ones. Regular project meetings offer a natural opportunity for doing this.

---

**Client decisions.** The effective PM realizes that the client has engaged the firm to employ its professional skill and judgment; thus the PM is not a "yes person" who goes along with everything the client says, regardless of the consequences. In writing a professional-services agreement with the owner, an architect is assuming many obligations, and it is wise to be assertive in fulfilling these obligations. The wise PM proposes and discusses possibilities. In developing and analyzing options, you are showing the client how you exercise your professional judgment. Documenting the final choice mitigates future questions or problems.

One of the most damaging things a PM can do is to lead a client into believing a project is in better shape than it actually is. If it becomes apparent that meeting the schedule or budget is becoming a problem, an effective manager informs the client as soon as possible. In addition, sharing this information often enables the PM to enlist the client's support in solving the problem. On one hand, joint problem solving can enhance the architect-client relationship. On the other, it is rarely appropriate to involve the client in every problem or decision.

***Agency coordination.*** As part of responsibilities to the client and the project, the PM will likely assist the owner in coordinating with government agencies and regulatory bodies. Building departments, environmental regulators, and others can cause schedule delays and budget overruns even if their reviews and approvals are well prepared for and carefully monitored. For some projects the PM may need to meet with outside agencies on a regular basis to establish rapport and to keep abreast of regulations and procedures. In extreme cases, representatives from key financial or regulatory agencies become part of the project team.

## EFFECTIVE TEAMS

Self-motivation tends to be an inherent characteristic of people in architecture firms and other professional organizations. The PM's task, then, is to create an environment in which individuals and groups of people working on a project can achieve their own goals so they remain self-motivated.

***Individuals and personalities.*** Fortunately, we know and are learning a great deal more about individual effectiveness. Often this process begins with understanding the individuals involved in the project—the project manager, principal-in-charge (if there is one), key team members, and the client's representatives—and how they gather information, process it to

make decisions, and relate to others. There is a growing body of research in personality typing and management styles; PMs—and everyone else, for that matter—can use this information to improve their effectiveness.

***Team building.*** An effective team is much more than the sum of the individuals who populate it. One of the PM's challenges is to build the team—actually, help the team build itself—into an effective working group. Characteristics of effective teams include the following:

- They are small enough to convene and communicate easily and frequently.
- They foster discussions that are interactive and open to all members.
- Team members have a mutual understanding of each other's roles and skills.
- The team members offer an appropriate combination of functional/technical, problem-solving, and interpersonal skills.
- The team has a truly meaningful purpose—clearly articulated, understood, and advocated for by all members.
- A specific set of team goals exists in addition to individual and organizational goals.
- The team has realistic, ambitious goals that are clear and important to all team members.
- The group plans for a specific set of team work products.
- Team members have a sense of mutual accountability, with members feeling individually and jointly responsible for the team's purpose, goals, approach, and work products.
- The team is able to measure progress against specific goals.
- All team members have a sense that "only the team can fail."

Moreover, effective teams have a working approach that

- Is understood and agreed to by everybody
- Capitalizes on (and enhances) the skills of those on the team
- Provides for open interaction, fact-based problem solving, and results-based evaluation
- Can be modified and improved over time

In the final analysis, projects are advanced and architecture is designed by a team. Team management is a—perhaps *the*—key to project success.

### For More Information

The publications in the AIA's *Managing Architecture Projects* series, written by David Haviland, Hon. AIA, outline the many facets of project planning, organizing, staffing, directing, controlling, and evaluating in architects' offices. The series includes *Managing Architectural Projects: The Process* (1981), *Managing Architectural Projects: The Effective Project Manager* (1981), *Managing Architectural Projects: The Project Management Manual* (1984), and *Managing Architectural Projects: Three Case Studies* (1981).

David Burstein and Frank Stasiowski, FAIA, in *The Ultimate Project Management Manual* (1999), provide a great many practical tips for improving project management. *Total Quality Project Management for the Design Firm,* by Frank A. Stasiowski, AIA, and David Burstein (1994), and *The Wild Card of Design: A Perspective on Architecture in a Project Management Environment,* by Kenneth Allinson (1993), provide additional perspectives on project management.

*Current Practices in Small Firm Management: An Architect's Notebook,* by James R. Franklin, FAIA (1990), and *Project Management for Small Design Firms,* by Howard G. Birnberg (1992), focus on smaller projects and practices.

Ruth Sizemore House, *The Human Side of Project Management* (1988), focuses on the human problems involved in building teams and accomplishing projects. The author also synthesizes a wide range of behavioral theory into practical advice for project managers.

You can do a self-assessment audit to evaluate your knowledge of successful practice approaches in project administration. The audit includes a self-assessment questionnaire, results report, and customized resource list. To participate in the AIA Self-Assessment Audit Program, call (800) 365-2724.

## On Design Teams

AIA Gold Medalist William Caudill, FAIA, a founder of CRS Architects, believed in and promoted the importance of the team concept. When *Life* magazine did a story on one of Caudill's projects, he asked to be pictured with his entire team. The editor objected, "Bill, everyone knows the MGM lion, but no one thinks he made the movie all by himself."

Of course, the editor was right about the public's view of movies, but not about architecture. The film industry is careful to identify and publicize the many different talents that go into the complex task of making a great movie. It is important to recognize and deal effectively with the many participants who play a role in the even more complex art of building design. Walter Gropius, a founder of the Architects Collaborative, described the importance of a coordinated team effort this way: "The essence . . . [is] to emphasize individual freedom of initiative instead of authoritative direction by a boss. Synchronizing all individual efforts by a continuous give and take of its members, a team can raise its integrated work to a higher potential than the sum of the work of just as many individuals."

*Bradford Perkins, FAIA, AICP*

# 13.2 Project Operations

## Frank A. Stasiowski, FAIA

*Day-to-day project events such as meetings, communications, and decisions require careful management by those in charge.*

Project planning and team building put the resources needed to execute a project in place. The next step, what some call the hard part, is making it all work—orchestrating and integrating these plans and resources to produce a successful project.

People are the key resource of an architecture firm. Thus much of everyday project management is directed to the project team—helping it work and keeping it on track. Project management also involves collecting, processing, and communicating information; making decisions; responding to project changes; and, in the end, closing out the project.

**Project Teams (13.1)**, which addresses project teams and the individuals who form them, should be read as a complementary topic.

## START-UP

If the project is typical, it has been "starting up" for some time—all through the processes of project definition, acquisition, planning, and contract negotiation. At this point, however, everything is ready to go, and it's time to start performing the contracted professional services.

***Team briefing and kickoff.*** One of the first steps is to be sure the team members are on board and up-to-date with current project requirements and plans, which may have changed in the negotiation process. One way to accomplish this is to hold a formal team briefing and kickoff meeting, which may include the following elements:

- Reviewing project requirements as developed with the client and by the firm. This may cover project goals, scope, quality, schedule, budget, codes and regulations, key design and construction standards, and other project information.
- Reviewing the project work plan. Critical tasks, responsibilities, uncertainties, and potential problem areas are discussed.
- Reviewing the schedule and milestone dates.
- Reviewing project policies. These include (as relevant) project responsibilities and authorities, client structure and relationships, approaches to identifying and resolving problems, team meetings and communications, project charges and reports, and other key management issues.

Some firms include a group reading of the contract so that all responsibilities and conditions are understood. As for all meetings, it is good advice to practice active listening, ask open-ended questions (to encourage participation), and leave ample time to help establish group chemistry.

***Project authorization.*** It is important to get internal mechanisms in place. Once a proposal becomes a project, for example, time charges are no longer considered part of overhead (marketing costs) but are charged to the project. Some firms use a formal project authorization form for the following functions:

**Project Controls (13.3)** notes that a project authorization form often is used to kick off the project charging, monitoring, and reporting cycle.

- Establishing the necessary project accounts
- Providing information on what can be charged to the project and what cannot, especially reimbursable (and non-reimbursable) expenses

---

**FRANK STASIOWSKI, FAIA,** *is founder and president of PSMJ Resources. Stasiowski is a consultant to the building and design industry and the author of numerous books and publications about management.*

- Identifying the internal project reports that will be prepared and distributed
- Providing the accounting department—or the bookkeeper or, in small firms, the principal—with information about project milestones, deliverables, and billing details

***Project files.*** It is common to establish a separate file (or set of files) for each project in the office. The most effective project filing system is one that can be easily understood and used by everyone in the firm. Avoid the temptation to invent a new or unique filing system for each project. Should a project manager be unavailable or leave the firm, everyone should be able to locate and use a project's files.

***Key project information.*** Most firms assemble the key information needed to inform project decisions at the outset of the project. Some of this may be placed in the project file; some may be located on a project shelf so it is accessible to all participants. This collection may include:

- Project directory (lists of names, addresses, and phone and fax numbers of key participants)
- Project program and construction budget requirements
- Site information, including climatic, environmental, survey, and geotechnical data
- Applicable codes and regulations
- Project schedule, milestones, and list of deliverables
- List of project files, locations, and access guidelines

Some firms include copies of the project agreements and even internal project budgets on the project shelf. As the project progresses, the architect may add technical information supporting construction systems, materials, and product decisions.

## COMMUNICATIONS

Professional services involve a continuing exchange of information, including data, advice and opinions, proposals, and decisions.

***Talking and listening.*** The vast majority of information on project requirements, on proposals and possibilities, and ultimately on decisions is conveyed through direct personal interaction—talking and listening. Increasingly we are recognizing that listening is the key to dialogue. What's more, we can train ourselves to become "active listeners."

Many of the day-to-day decisions in an office are made at the boards or at computer workstations—in countless formal and especially informal interchanges between the project manager and others working on the project. Architects can train themselves to be better at providing such desk critiques, from both sides of the interchange.

Meetings provide opportunities for groups to exchange information and make, modify, or affirm project decisions. Management studies indicate that meetings are the single most time-consuming activity during the workdays of most project managers. Thus the effective project manager (PM) views a project meeting as an opportunity that is to be carefully designed and managed.

A first step in managing a busy meeting schedule is to minimize the number of meetings attended, particularly those at which the PM is not an active participant. Consider these suggestions:

- Before calling a meeting, consider other ways to reach the same objective—for instance, memos, telephone calls, faxes, e-mail, or letters.
- Prepare an agenda. If there are no substantial agenda items, there is probably no need for a meeting.
- Consider "stand-up" meetings. These are short sessions usually directed to a single subject or decision to be made or reviewed. Sometimes a conference call will accomplish the same purpose.

When meetings are necessary, it is good advice to

- Do your homework before going into the meeting. The first question to ask is: What are the objectives for the meeting? Are we seeking a decision, providing

*Askew, Nixon, Ferguson Architects, Inc., Memphis, Tennessee*

**FEE AND MAN-HOUR BUDGET**
***Askew, Nixon, Ferguson Architects, Inc.***

Date: 04/20/92     Revised: 04/27/92     Prepared by: Joe Wieronski

## PROJECT INFORMATION

| | | Consultants: | | |
|---|---|---|---|---|
| Project name: | MLGW ANNEX | | | |
| Project No: | 92004.10 | Structural: | Burr & Cole | B. Burr |
| Location: | Memphis | Civil: | Burr & Cole | B. Burr |
| Client Contact: | Frank Gheri | Mechanical: | OGCB | J. Pilgrim |
| A/E Proj. Mgr. | Joe Wieronski | Electrical: | OGCB | J. Pilgrim |
| A/E PIC: | Lee Askew | Landscape: | Jackson Pers | J. Jackson |
| Start Design: | 4.6.92 | Other: | Cabling, Inc. | W. Richard |
| Start Constr.: | | Other: | Kitchen, Inc. | M. Fisher |

## CONTRACT BASIS

| | Fee Amount |
|---|---|
| Hourly | |
| Hourly NTE | |
| Lump Sum | $580,200 |
| Cost + Fee | |
| % of Constr | |

## MAN-HOUR BUDGET

| | | | |
|---|---|---|---|
| Total base A/E fee: (w/o Additional Services) | $580,200 | | |
| Minus indirect reimbursables: | – | 5,665 | |
| Minus consultants fee if included: | – | 233,690 | |
| | = | $350,845 | Subtotal |
| Profit: 20% of total | – | 70,169 | |
| Subtotal minus profit: | = | $280,676 | Net Fee |

| | | | | |
|---|---|---|---|---|
| Net Fee: | $280,676 | = | 5,847 | Avail hours w/o add. services |
| Average rate/hour | $48.00 /hour | | | |

| PHASE | % | Fee | C.O.'s | Total hours |
|---|---|---|---|---|
| 1: Measuring/CAFM | 0 | 0 | | 0 |
| 2: Predesign/program | 5 | 14,034 | 2,466 | 344 |
| 3: Schematic design | 14 | 39,295 | 6,908 | 963 |
| 4: Design development | 18 | 50,522 | 8,882 | 1,238 |
| 5: Construction docs | 37 | 103,850 | 18,257 | 2,544 |
| 6: Bidding/negotiation | 3 | 8,420 | 1,480 | 206 |
| 7: Construction admin. | 23 | 64,555 | 11,349 | 1,580 |
| | | | | 0 |
| | | | | 0 |
| **TOTALS** | **100** | **$280,676** | **$49,342** | **6,875** |

## A/E FEE DISTRIBUTION

| | | |
|---|---|---|
| Structural | $63,000 | 11.0% |
| Civil | 6,000 | 1.0 |
| MPE | 140,000 | 24.4 |
| Landscape | 2,690 | 0.5 |
| Kitchen | 3,500 | 0.6 |
| Cabling | 8,500 | 1.5 |
| Subtotal | $223,690 | 39.0% |
| Architectural | $350,845 | 61.0% |
| **TOTAL** | **$574,535** | **100.0%** |

## ADDITIONAL SERVICES

| | | A/E |
|---|---|---|
| C.O. #1 | $6,000 | B&C |
| C.O. #2 | 3,998 | B&C |
| C.O. #3 | 29,000 | B&C |
| Subtotal | $38,998 | B&C |
| C.O. #1 | $1,850 | OGCB |
| C.O. #1 | $15,000 | ANFA |
| C.O. #2 | 6,600 | ANFA |
| C.O. #3 | 27,742 | ANFA |
| Subtotal | $49,342 | ANFA |
| **TOTAL** | **$90,190** | **A/E** |

## REIMBURSABLES

| | indirect–ANFA–direct | | consultants |
|---|---|---|---|
| Airfares, mileage, travel | | $1,500 | $1,500 |
| Lodging, subsistence, meals | | 2,000 | 2,000 |
| Printing, copies, reprographics | $4,000 | 8,000 | 2,000 |
| Federal Express, courier services | 500 | 1,000 | 200 |
| Fax, long distance telephone | 150 | 200 | 100 |
| Testing | | 40,000 | |
| Boundary and topo survey | | 5,400 | |
| Geotechnical services | | 7,000 | |
| Other misc. | 500 | 1,000 | 500 |
| Additional reimbursables: | | | |
| Total NTE reimbursables = | $85,305 | | |
| Multiplier: 1.10     Totals: | $5,665 | $72,710 | $6,930 |

## CONSTRUCTION COST (ESTIMATED)

| | |
|---|---|
| Initial bid | $8,683,219 |
| Seismic cost | 716,781 |
| C.O. #1 | 458,000 |
| C.O. #2 | 0 |
| C.O. #3 | 56,400 |
| C.O. #4 | 101,500 |
| C.O. #5 | 33,069 |
| C.O. #6 | 64,500 |
| **TOTAL** | **$10,113,469** |

information, looking for advice, or preparing the client for impending problems? Communicate these objectives to the client—in advance if possible.

- Formulate an agenda that will accomplish the objectives. The agenda can serve as an outline to identify work that must be done before the meeting; it also helps the participants achieve their objectives without spending too much time on peripheral issues.
- Call ahead to confirm meetings, and be there early.
- Follow up after the meeting. Get minutes out quickly, identifying decisions made, actions pending, and next steps to be taken. Some project managers produce a running log of decisions still pending with a list that parallels the one above: What decision needs to be made? By whom? When? With whose input, approval, and notification?

*Routine communications.* Information is often conveyed via formal transactions between individuals and within groups—telephone conversations, fax and e-mail messages, correspondence, transmittals of documents and reports, and memos. These transactions serve two purposes: They convey important information, and they become part of the project record. Some points to consider in your communication efforts:

- Work on a warm and responsive manner—in print and when speaking. Work with your staff and colleagues to be pleasant and inviting in answering phone calls. Make each client feel that he or she comes first, even when you have many clients.
- Cover transmittals of information and deliverables with a form that captures the date, names of sender and addressees, information transmitted, and project reference.
- Make sure your telephone and fax numbers are on all pieces of correspondence, to encourage contacts and queries.
- Make sure every paper that crosses your desk is dated, so you can provide an accurate record of transactions if this becomes important.
- Take notes from conversations, focusing on the action items (what was decided and what the next steps are).
- Discipline yourself to write only about facts—and to leave your opinions about those facts unwritten.
- Consider cell phones, pagers, and laptop computers for staff who are on the road a great deal. These devices can keep people accessible and productive when traveling.
- Respond quickly to letters and other materials. If you delegate the response, provide a specific time frame (one person's "immediately" may be another's "I'll get it done in a week").

## MANAGING TECHNOLOGY

The use of technology—voice mail, fax machine, and Internet—can be an overwhelming exercise. We tend to lose sight of how these tools should contribute to increasing our efficiency and productivity. Just because information comes to us via voice mail, fax, or e-mail does not mean it is important. Some suggestions from Barbara Garro in *Hard Hat News* includes ways to take full advantage of your technology tools:

- Use technology to speed contract completion. Receive contract drafts from the other party via electronic means, submit revisions, and finalize terms—all in the same day.
- If you want to discuss a letter or proposal but the other party can't find their copy, send them another via fax or e-mail to expedite discussions. Use the revision features available in many word processing software applications to track changes by each party.
- When people say their proposal is in the mail, ask them to fax or e-mail a copy to you.

## Project Leadership Through Desk Critiques

The traditional desk critique—or "crit," in the jargon of the profession—has long been the principal method of teaching architecture, but it is just as effective in creating architecture. The project leader who is not the designer, specifier, and producer of construction documents can find the desk crit to be an effective approach to managing those who are accomplishing these key project tasks.

*Premises.* We begin with this proposition: The project leader—in the role of the critic—wants the staff member or designer to succeed. Therefore, the critic wants to have a conversation that will help the staff member or designer perform better. For you as the critic, this means

- Assuming that the designer is giving his or her best and that the reasons for making decisions are valid. You will best learn these reasons through open discussion.
- Treating the crit as an opportunity to learn. Ask yourself questions such as "What can I learn about this design problem through the designer's view of the best solution?" "What questions can I raise, and what steps can I suggest?"
- Remembering that, in the end, it's your project and thus your decision. If you simply make the decision, though, the crit is ended. The designer is reduced to drawing up your decisions.

Crits can be short, frequent, incremental, and over the shoulder at the drawing board or computer screen. Alternatively, they may be less frequent and more comprehensive—say, at a Friday afternoon pinup session. There are advantages and disadvantages to both methods, depending on the person you are critiquing and the stage of the work.

Crits begin with active listening:

- *Encourage.* "Fill me in on . . ." "You know, I've always had trouble with . . ." "It looks [Richardsonian, interesting, formidable, etc.]." "Tell me about . . ."

- *Acknowledge.* Sometimes this is best done by paraphrasing: "If I read your sketch properly, you see this building as . . ." "Let me be sure I understand. You want the users to . . ."
- *Check out.* Use open-ended questions that can't be answered with a yes or no. "Tell me more about how this meets the program requirements [addresses the owner's concerns, meets or changes the project goals, recalls a specific concept, relates to the context, etc.]." "How do you feel about this?"
- *Interpret.* Ask yourself what the designer left out about what he or she thinks, feels, intends, or does. Fill in the blanks for them. Watch, listen, or ask for verification.

Here are some steps to consider in approaching the actual critique:

1. Summarize the project's five or six key goals.
2. Say what's good about the solution and why. Be specific. What does it recall in history or in your own experience? What do these references suggest that can help extend the design? Where could that lead? Piggyback on what's good.
3. Overlay, sketch, diagram, use metaphors, think out loud. Visit and inhabit the design. Imagine it being built.
4. Then decide what should be changed, improved, or deleted —and why. Suggest sources for alternatives—better ways to approach a part—that might help.
5. If a fresh start is needed, provide the designer with specific guidance for taking the next steps.
6. At the end of the session, summarize, confirm understandings, and agree on next steps.

The next steps will depend on the designer's performance and how you responded to his or her efforts. You may want to coach, encourage, delegate, or even direct.

*James R. Franklin, FAIA*

- Fax or e-mail purchase orders and invoices.
- Use the Internet to get information you need for the project. Most materials suppliers have secure Web sites you can subscribe to, allowing you to get up-to-date technical data—no more out-of-date catalogs.

The Internet also affords us an emerging technology in the form of Web-based project management tools. There are presently two emerging categories of these tools. The more mature products include Web-based tools developed to support the process of construction document control and communication. These products are generally geared toward the contractor's needs for bid support, project buyout, subcontract administration, and submittals management. These tools also provide communication support with project participants including the owner and the architect for such things as requests for information (RFIs).

The second category of emerging Web-based tools is geared more toward project management during the design and contract document preparation phase. These tools allow the PM to establish project Web sites for the project team, owner, consultants, and contractors. Typically, the Web site is established so that it requires a password to gain access. The PM or support staff can place correspondence and project documentation on the secure site for access by authorized users only. Interim copies of the construction documents, including drawings and specifications, could also be included in a read-only format. As part of placing a document on the Web site, the PM can initiate notification e-mails to authorized users, informing them that the document is available. The notification e-mail can also include a link to the document on the Web site, allowing users to access it with a single mouse click. The Web site could also include a red-line revision tool that allows visitors to mark up text or drawings without compromising the integrity of the original document.

## DECISIONS

The ultimate purpose of all this interchange is *making decisions*. Even the smallest project requires the architect and the project team to make an enormous number of decisions. If each decision produces a successful outcome, then it follows that the project, as the aggregate of these decisions, should be successful. The management of the decision-making process is a key project management task.

**Understand the decisions to be made.** The questions are easy:

- What are the most important project decisions?
- When must they be made?
- Who will make them?
- Who needs to contribute data, opinions, or advice?
- Who needs to approve the decision?
- Who needs to be informed?

The answers are more difficult. They lie, in the first instance, in the project plan and then in the predesign effort to fully understand the problem and the keys to its solution.

For many projects the most important decisions are made or affirmed in group meetings. Often these involve the client and are tied to key project milestones. One management technique is to develop an outline agenda for each of these meetings—and then go ahead and schedule them—as a way of understanding and communicating the key decisions that are to be made.

**Submittals and approvals.** Most projects include milestones—points at which project decisions are synthesized, presented, discussed, and affirmed. The project agreement provides the first list of milestone dates and deliverables. Often it makes sense to establish interim points to affirm the project team's understanding of directions to be taken and results to be produced, and the client's agreement to these. Some suggestions for approaching these "moments of truth" in every project:

- Everyone on the project team, including the client, should have a clear conception of what is being brought forward and what decisions need to be made.
- Plan the presentation, and do so as far ahead of the actual due date as possible. If the submittal is to be in writing, it is good advice to cartoon or otherwise mock up the report. If there is to be a meeting, create an agenda. These approaches help everyone understand what must be done—and sometimes they identify gaps in the effort.
- Rehearse. Some firms plan presubmission presentations to others in the firm who are not involved in the project. Someone may be challenged to take the role of the client, providing a sort of devil's advocacy to ensure that the project requirements are being addressed.
- Be sure you understand the client's decision process and timetable once the submission is received. (This should have been considered earlier in project planning and pricing.)
- If possible, get the client's approval to proceed with services as soon as possible. Downtime is rarely beneficial for a project (with staff attention turned elsewhere during the interim) or for the firm's profit objectives. Sometimes, however, these approval points result in changes in project scope, schedule, or budget.

To manage time successfully, you must firmly believe that every demand on your time is a request to give up the most valuable thing you possess. Unscheduled interruptions can be a major source of frustration and lost time.

The key to avoiding such interruptions is to control the contact. If clients call frequently, ask if they would like to schedule a regular time when you can call them. If clients know a call is forthcoming, they may be more reluctant to phone unless it is urgent. (The same approach can be used with a supervisor who constantly calls the PM into the office for routine discussions or with a new staff member who asks for your approval of every detail.)

Another common problem is caused by people stopping in the office as they walk by. The simplest way to avoid this problem, of course, is to close the door (if one exists). However, this can result in losing touch with the rest of the office. A more subtle approach is to arrange the furniture in your office so that you can work facing the door or away from it.

For many, a big time waster is the telephone. Furthermore, long distance charges for most architecture firms are substantial. Here are some tips for managing the phone:

*Make your own calls.* It usually takes no longer to place a call than to ask someone else to do it. With answering machines and voice mail, you can usually make your point or ask your question even if the other party is not available.

*Return calls in groups.* You may want to review message slips, note agenda items, and start making calls once or twice a day. Good times for returning calls are late morning and late afternoon. People are more likely to be in their offices then, and the approaching lunchtime or end of the day can discourage protracted conversation.

*Select your tone in answering the phone.* If you seek a long, friendly conversation, you might start by asking, "How are you these days?" On the other hand, you can respond to a vendor with whom you don't care to spend much time with, "This is Elizabeth. What can I do for you?" This sets a polite but terse tone that can discourage small talk.

*Know how to end a conversation.* If stuck on a long-winded call, you can recapture the conversation by asking, "Well, that's all I have. Do you have anything else?"

*Frank A. Stasiowski, FAIA*

## DOCUMENTATION

Even the smallest project generates a great deal of paper such as notes, meeting agendas and minutes, technical materials, and other documentation. Effective management of this paper is needed to

**Many firms develop various checklists as guides for making project decisions. AIA Document 200, Project Checklist, is a starting point.**

- Collect, analyze, and record the information used to make decisions
- Inform the project team, the client, and others who need to know what's going on
- Document key decisions and the rationale behind them in case these decisions need to be reviewed or are questioned later

The project manager is responsible for keeping track of project correspondence and for documenting significant developments on all projects. Good business practice suggests it is wise to document transactions that take place between the parties in the design team and the client. Doing so keeps the project on track, and in those few instances when a claim is filed, you have a record.

## CLOSEOUT

Project closeout is an important and sometimes overlooked key to success in project management. With the project winding down, and with other projects waiting in the wings, it is common (and economically necessary) to disband the project team and reassign the project manager. This should not distract from appropriate attention to the project during closeout.

To avoid dropping the ball at the end, firms will want to budget enough time for construction contract administration closeout tasks and any contracted postconstruction services. Failure to satisfy the client at the end could undermine or even destroy a good relationship. No one wants the last memory of a client to be that of an incomplete punch list or an ineffective closing out of the job.

It will be necessary to close out the project internally as well, collecting project information, providing any required documentation, finalizing billing and collections,

*Thomas C. Moreland, FORMA, Inc., Denver, Colorado*

Sometimes projects advance at a very rapid pace. If key decisions are to be made at meetings that will involve many people, it is good advice to establish these sessions at the outset and include them in the project schedule. Here is one firm's form, designed to capture key information about timing, attendees, agenda, and key decisions to be made.

**PROJECT:** Spectra Physics

**EVENT:** C-7
**DATE:** Week #19
**DESCRIPTION:** Review Meeting

**ATTENDANCE:** Owner project representative
Contractor representative
Jim Lewis, project manager
Interior architect
Program consultant

**REQUIRED INFORMATION OR PRODUCTS:**
1. Design development elevation studies
2. Schematic interior layout studies

**AGENDA:** Review elevation studies and interior layout

**KEY DECISIONS:**
1. Fix exterior opening locations
2. Approve interiors schematic—authorize design development
3. Approve beginning of construction documents for Bid Package B.

DELIVERY part 3

*James R. Franklin,* Current Practices in Small Firm Management *(AIA, 1990)*

Brainstorming is a structured problem-solving process that can be tremendously effective and quick with any small group. Proof from research and countless workshops demonstrates that groups make better decisions than individuals—provided the group decides on the basis of consensus.

Note: Consensus doesn't mean you all agree. It means (1) each of you is satisfied you've been heard and fully understood and (2) all of you are willing to go along with the decision. To get there, try "playing back the tape" of what you hear "holdouts" saying until they agree you've got their meaning to their satisfaction. A good shortcut is to write all positions on a flip chart. The best way to advance the process, however, is to brainstorm.

### 1. Explain the rules.

As leader/facilitator, your job is to

- Present the problem
- Explain the rules
- Record (use a flip chart)
- Keep time
- Keep energies high
- Keep the group focused
- Keep the participants "safe" from each other; help them hazard being open and forthcoming

This means you can't be a participant. Tell them this. Agree how much time to spend.

### 2. Describe the problem.

Explain the issue or problem, giving them the background. Record any immediate answers or recommendations. Do this in order to:

- Make sure the participants know they have been heard and taken seriously
- Get the "pat" answers out of the way of the creative process

### 3. State the problem.

Agree on the problem. Make it one simple statement starting "How can we…" Have them do the work—you record.

### 4. Brainstorm.

Give the group 1½ minutes to list as many answers as possible (you'll keep the time). Tell them to work for quantity and speed; forget quality or making good sense. At the end of the first minute tell them to "get crazy"—to list the funniest, most wild and improbable solutions they can—forget cost, scale, time—no restraints.

### 5. Record the results.

On the flip chart, have each member in turn call out only the ideas not already mentioned. Again, work for speed, not a pretty flip chart. The rules are

- No discussion
- No judgment
- No ridicule
- No questions (other than for clarification)
- No criticism

Tip: Enlist the help of two of the group to take turns recording each idea in bold felt-tip on "Post-it" memo pads. You just put them on the flip chart. Then ask for any further ideas that have occurred to members through listening to each other's lists; record.

### 6. Make a cluster diagram.

Synthesize, clarify through questions, categorize. Do this only if it seems obvious. Don't spend a lot of time. Don't try to be exact.

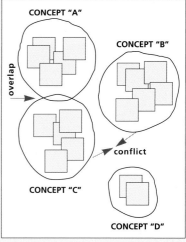

FLIP CHART

### 7. Prioritize.

To avoid peer or political pressure skewing the results, try giving each person three "votes" and polling them on each item—thumbs up or down. Then discuss the favorites and work for consensus.

If the decision is one that you, as boss, will make alone, you still can gain good information from this process. Stop with a sense of the group's priorities (no group decision). Thank them and tell them when you expect to decide.

## PROJECT MANAGEMENT EVALUATION

*Adapted from David Haviland,*
*Managing Architectural Projects: The Process (1981)*

Many firms find that undertaking a structured project management evaluation at the end of the project is a valuable learning tool—and, if the client is involved in an appropriate way, a marketing tool as well. Here are some of the questions you may want to explore:

### SCOPE AND SERVICES
- Did the project meet the owner's requirements? the firm's standards?
- Was quality adversely affected by scope, staff, schedule, or budget limitations? Could this have been avoided? Could the firm have been more responsive to these limitations?
- Were scope and services under control throughout the project?
- What did we learn that might improve the management of future projects?

### SCHEDULE
- Was the schedule met?
- Was the original schedule appropriate? How did it change?
- Was the schedule under control during the project?
- What did we learn that might improve the scheduling of future projects?

### BUDGET
- Was the original project, including the profit target, met?
- How does final financial performance compare to the original plan?
- What did we learn that might improve the budgeting of future projects?

### COMPENSATION
- Were owner invoices rendered and paid on time?
- Did the owner's payments provide an appropriate cash flow to the firm?
- What did we learn that might improve compensation planning, billing, and collections in future projects?

### PROJECT TEAM
- Were the right staff, consultants, and/or alliance members selected?
- Was the project team on track throughout the project?
- Were there any difficulties in managing the client, contractors, or other parties?
- What might have improved teamwork and team management?

### GENERAL MANAGEMENT
- Were there any difficulties in marketing, project planning, or negotiating?
- Were information flow and communications effective?
- Were there any difficulties in making, communicating, or securing approvals for decisions?
- Did the procedures for control and course corrections work as expected?
- What did we learn that might improve the management of future projects?

and closing out project files. In doing this, pay particular attention to establishing the project archive.

Finally, some firms undertake a project management evaluation at the completion of the project. This can be a way of gaining valuable information about the firm's overall effort, part of its process of continuous improvement, and a way of continuing to build the client relationship. A project postmortem—used to compare project actual costs to estimated baselines—can be a powerful tool for subsequent proposal efforts and to identify the areas of your firm's production process that need improvement.

▶ **Remember that repeat work, reputation, and referrals are responsible for about 90 percent of most firms' new projects.**

### *For More Information*

Most books and resources address many facets of project management—including project planning, team building, operations, and controls—as a unified whole.

Guidelines, Inc., publishes a number of checklists, forms, and operations manuals for projects and practices. Contact Guidelines at Box 456, Orinda, CA 94563, or call (510) 254-9393 for information and ordering.

# 13.3 Project Controls

## Lowell Getz, CPA, and Frank A. Stasiowski, FAIA

*As the project unfolds, progress is assessed against the project goals—scope, quality, schedule, and budget—as well as the firm's services and compensation requirements.*

Project control—tracking progress and comparing it with plans and objectives—is integral to effective project management. Without these activities, it's often not clear whether the project is on track, meeting the expectations—and requirements—established by the client and by the architect.

Project controls do not have to be elaborate, but there are some essentials:

- *Yardsticks.* A series of measuring sticks is necessary. These project objectives (services, scope, schedule, budget, and compensation) are expressed in the project agreements and work plan.
- *Measurements.* The firm periodically takes the pulse of the project, collecting vital signs—information in the form of time spent, costs incurred, and progress made.
- *Comparisons.* Comparing measured progress against the various yardsticks reveals whether expectations are being met.
- *Corrective action.* The will to address variances in progress compared to the plans is essential to keeping projects on track.

### SCOPE AND SERVICES CONTROL

The project manager (PM) will want to track a project's scope—both client-requested changes and changes that may be introduced as part of the design process—and the services being performed in order to evaluate what the architect is doing against the requirements of the owner-architect agreement. Often schedule, budget, and compensation problems are the results of unplanned variations or expansions in scope or services.

**Project scope.** Project scope embraces all of the owner's design requirements: program, site, area and volume, and levels of quality. During the course of design, scope can shift—and often grows—as possibilities unfold. Sometimes these shifts are clear and recognized by both owner and architect. More often, the scope of the project creeps under the pressure of owner interests or demands and the architect's enthusiasm for the evolving design.

Scope control involves asking—and answering—these questions:

- Is the scope of the project currently clear to you and the team?
- Do you and the client have the same view of the project?
- If the scope is changing, are you and the client formalizing those changes—including any impact on your agreement?
- If the scope is changing, are the budget and schedule also changing as needed? If the schedule and, especially, the budget are not changing, what steps can be taken to keep the project on track?

**Project services.** In the same vein, it is important to compare the services the

> **Construction Cost Management (13.4) addresses "scope creep," which can be a major problem when the construction budget is fixed.**

**LOWELL V. GETZ** *is a financial consultant to architecture, engineering, planning, and environmental service firms. He has written, taught, and lectured widely on financial management.* **FRANK STASIOWSKI,** *is founder and president of PSMJ Resources. Stasiowski is a consultant to the building and design industry and the author of numerous books and publications about management.*

PART 3 DELIVERY

project team is actually providing with those in the owner-architect agreement. There is a natural tendency to say yes to additional services in an effort to do the best job. It's also possible that increased scope or an extended schedule are forcing the team to provide more services than contemplated in the agreement. The best advice is to review your agreement and follow its requirements for initiating and seeking owner approval for additional services. This is not something to be left until after the fact.

*Milestone checks.* While scope and services review should be ongoing, project submittals provide a handy point for a careful look at both. Frequently the owner-architect agreement sets up design phases or milestones. If this is not the case, the architect may want to establish interim points to check scope and services. Approaches may include reviews and critiques by people not on the project team.

## SCHEDULE AND BUDGET CONTROL

Project schedules are developed to define target completion dates and major milestones. Schedules must be tracked and monitored to ensure that all activities and tasks proceed in an appropriate manner to reach target dates. Various scheduling techniques are used depending on the nature and complexity of the work.

Budget monitoring is usually periodic, with time and expenses charged against the project reviewed and compared to goals on a regular basis. Some firms establish a regular cycle for every project—say, every Monday. Many of these firms report separating these management meetings from design reviews—which may be scheduled on Fridays.

Sophisticated systems are not required to monitor schedules and budgets effectively. What is important is that it be done on a predictable basis so the PM knows how the project is progressing against expectations.

*Account codes.* A coding system is the shorthand used to record various entries into the proper accounts. The project is assigned a number; in more complex systems, vari-

---

### One Simple Monitoring Technique

One simple project monitoring technique is the Integrated Budget and Schedule Method (IBSM) developed by David Burstein, PE, and Frank Stasiowski, FAIA. The PM can practically and efficiently monitor the schedule and budget status of his or her project by using the proprietary IBSM system. It requires very little time and provides the PM with an early-warning system to identify schedule and budget problems while there is still time to deal with them. Here are the key points for IBSM:

- In order for this system to work, there must be a single task outline that describes the scope, schedule, and budget.
- The first step in the IBSM procedure—preparing an expenditure forecast—should be thought of as forecasting the rate of progress to be made, then expressing it in terms of expenditures. Progress of a task can be reported as earned value; that is, the task budget multiplied by the actual percent completion of that task. Determining this actual percent completion is the most difficult and important part of the IBSM system.
- Overall project progress can be computed by adding all the earned values for the various tasks, then dividing this sum by the project budget.
- To ascertain the actual costs expended, do not rely solely

on the information provided by the accounting department. Be sure to add costs that have been committed but not yet processed (such as subcontractor invoices, travel costs, etc.).
- Don't track actual vs. planned expenditures in an attempt to monitor budget or schedule status. Actual progress must also be tracked.
- Schedule status can be determined by comparing the forecast progress (or expenditures) with the actual progress (or earned value). If the actual progress is less than what was forecast, the schedule is in trouble.
- Budget status can be determined by comparing the actual expenditures with the earned value. If the earned value is less than the actual expenditures, the budget is in trouble.
- The IBSM system can be used for any project with a defined scope. For large projects, each task should be monitored, the results graphed, and trends followed. On small projects, a simple spreadsheet format is adequate.
- With the IBSM method it's easy to track the schedule status of each task, even for large projects.

*Additional details on the IBSM system are available in the* Ultimate Project Management Manual *(1999).*

ous subcodes are used for departments, disciplines, phases, tasks, and staff levels. In addition, account codes (from the chart of accounts) permit identification of specific expenses, categorized by type. Codes are also assigned to the various indirect expense (overhead) categories in the firm's budget.

Accounting codes fine-tune project control. They allow a firm to track its expenses by project, phase or task, or object of expenditure to control costs better and to improve budgeting for future projects. As with many management techniques, there is a trade-off: Detail improves accuracy but can become cumbersome and ineffective. Keep in mind that captured data for multiple account codes will only be as successful as the accuracy reflected on time sheets and expense reports.

**Financial Systems (7.1) looks at types of project expenses.**

***Project charges.*** Project control begins with recording time and expense charges against the various projects and other accounting codes in the office. Time accounting is the basis of a good reporting system. Most firms require weekly time sheets; to ensure greater accuracy and detail, some firms require them daily. Increasingly, time is entered directly into the firm's financial management software on a computer network.

The level of detail on time sheets should to some degree match the level used in project planning. It makes little sense to plan by project task if time is collected by project only. Remember, too, your time and expense records become part of the database you can use to price upcoming projects.

Employees need to have a clear explanation of how time sheets are used and why accuracy is important. If the staff believes the firm's management values lots of overtime, they may stretch their hours to accommodate. Another employee may believe that being under budget is most important and report fewer hours than worked—essentially putting in extra time for free. Even though such actions may be performed in good faith, both examples distort the project statistics and make them less useful for planning future projects.

Depending on the firm's policy, PMs may review time charges for their projects, either before the time sheets are submitted or after they are recorded. This provides the PM with an opportunity to make sure the proper accounting codes are charged and the results are commensurate with the work effort.

Nonchargeable or indirect time should also be monitored carefully. Indirect time can be charged to, for example, marketing, administration, new employee orientation, professional development, and civic and professional activities. In addition, time charges for vacation, holidays, and sick leave are generally recorded and monitored. In larger firms, the responsibility for monitoring indirect time generally rests with studio heads or the managing principal.

It is especially important that direct expenses the client will reimburse under the owner-architect agreement be charged to the project. These expenses are not in the firm's budget; failing to charge them to projects and then to bill clients is a direct assault on the firm's budget and profit targets.

***Project reports.*** Project accounting systems are intended to enable PMs to exercise proper control over their projects and to take corrective action to prevent unnecessary overruns. The project budget includes hours and dollars for various elements, including labor, consultants, other project expenses, and profits. The accounting system should enable the PM to compare actual time and expenses charged to the project with the budget to determine any variances.

Managers at various levels in the organization need different kinds of reports. PMs are likely to want frequent reports on the number of hours worked by individuals on their projects. The firm's management, however, is likely to be more interested in reports that summarize project and nonproject activities and flag variances from budgets. The purpose of these reports is to give brief but easy-to-obtain information on a frequent basis so that costs can be controlled accurately.

Increasingly, offices are using financial management software to facilitate timely collection and reporting of results. Sometimes the collecting and reporting cycle is reduced to hours or even real time, providing managers with an instantaneous look at progress and potential problems.

***Overruns.*** Project overruns occur when project expenses exceed their budgets and, ultimately, the amount that the client has agreed to pay. The project thus incurs a loss that must be recovered out of profits on other projects.

All firms use or develop some form of project progress reports. Computer -based financial management systems usually of fer an array of possibilities for consideration. Shown here are samples embodying a number of different approaches and prepared using both commercial software packages and in-house spreadsheets.

## SAMPLE PROJECT PROGRESS REPORT

MICRO/CFMS, *Harper and Shuman, Inc., Cambridge, Massachusetts*

| APPLE AND BARTLETT | | Project Progress Report | | | For the period 5/1/90 – 5/31/90 | |
|---|---|---|---|---|---|---|

Project: 09010.00     Principal: Bartlett     Client: SCDG
Name: Dance Center     Proj. Mgr: Stone     Type of Work: Educ
    Fee: 55,000     Office: Dtwn

| | Current | | Project-to-date | | Budget | | % | % | Balance | |
|---|---|---|---|---|---|---|---|---|---|---|
| Description | Hrs | Cost | Hrs | Cost | Hrs | Cost | Exp | Rpt | Hrs | Cost |
| **Architectural** | | | | | | | | | | |
| 01 Predesign | | | 21 | 569 | 25 | 455 | 125 | 100 | 4 | 114– |
| 02 Site analysis | | | 23 | 348 | 20 | 350 | 99 | 100 | 3– | 2 |
| 03 Schematic | | | 85 | 1961 | 80 | 1000 | 196 | 100 | 5– | 961– |
| 04 Design development | | | 47 | 1080 | 70 | 800 | 135 | 100 | 23 | 280– |
| 05 Construction docs | 56 | 1028 | 56 | 1028 | 205 | 3600 | 29 | | 149 | 2573 |
| 14 Design/plan | 37 | 615 | 8 | 731 | 80 | 1500 | 49 | 10 | 35 | 770 |
| 15 Bid/negotiation | | | | | 8 | 160 | | | 8 | 160 |
| 16 Construction | | | | | 15 | 350 | | | 15 | 350 |
| Total | 37 | 615 | 80 | 1313 | 138 | 2785 | 47 | 28 | 58 | 1473 |
| Total labor | 101 | 1763 | 368 | 7338 | 963 | 16605 | 44 | 26 | 595 | 9267 |
| Overhead allocation | | 2344 | | 9760 | | 26568 | 37 | 26 | | 16808 |
| **Direct Expenses** | | | | | | | | | | |
| 611.00 Structural const. | | | | 150 | | | | | | |
| 612.00 Mechanical const. | | | | 585 | | 1350 | 43 | 45 | | 765 |
| 613.00 Electrical const. | | | | 1100 | | 1100 | 100 | 100 | | 0 |
| 615.00 Other consultants | | 350 | | 350 | | 750 | 47 | | | 400 |
| 621.00 Travel and lodging | | | | 160 | | 500 | 32 | 32 | | 340 |
| 621.01 Meals | | | | 27 | | 200 | 14 | 30 | | 173 |
| 622.00 Reproductions | | | | 122 | | 100 | 122 | 90 | | 22– |
| 623.00 Models/renderings | | | | 19 | | 100 | 19 | 25 | | 81 |
| 624.00 Long distance | | | | 175 | | 100 | 175 | 100 | | 75– |
| 625.00 Fax expense | | | | 33 | | 50 | 66 | 75 | | 17 |
| 629.00 Misc. direct expenses | | | | 68 | | | | | | |
| Total direct expenses | | 350 | | 2789 | | 4250 | 66 | 51 | | 1461 |
| **Total labor-overhead-** | | | | | | | | | | |
| direct expenses | | 4457 | 368 | 19887 | 963 | 47423 | 42 | 29 | 595 | 27536 |
| **Reimbursable Expenses** | | | | | | | | | | |
| 512.00 Mechanical const. | | 190 | | 1340 | | 1350 | 99 | 85 | | 10 |
| 521.00 Travel and lodging | | | | 156 | | | | | | |
| 521.01 Meals | | | | 29 | | | | | | |
| 529.00 Misc. reimbursables | | | | 14 | | | | | | |
| Total reimbursement | | 190 | | 1538 | | 1350 | 114 | 85 | | 188– |
| **Project totals** | 101 | 4647 | 363 | 21425 | 963 | 48773 | 44 | 30 | 595 | 27348 |

## SAMPLE PROJECT PROGRESS REPORT

*MacArchitect, Inc., Arne Bystrom, FAIA, Seattle, Washington*

| | Project performance | ⬆ |
|---|---|---|

Enter project abbrev: [ ]   [ Find ]   [ New ]

Project abbrev  9206          No:   12          Active   yes          Type pcnt
Project name   Student Hall/U of D  % fee? no          Rate bill
Description    Student Hall North Addition, University of Designerville

| | | | | | |
|---|---|---|---|---|---|
| Total fee | $288,100.00 | Consultant fee | $160,400.00 | Net fee | $127,700.00 |
| Amt earned | $11,527.07 | Consult. earned | $6,417.71 | Net earned | $5,109.36 |
| Remaining fee | $158,310.95 | Remaining con | $88,139.80 | Remaining net | $70,171.15 |

### PROJECT FEE PERFORMANCE AT 45.05% COMPLETE

| PROJECT PHASE | Proj. phase rate (%) | Avg. hour rate ($) | Phase budget get amt ($) | Phase budget hours | Phase complete (%) | Amt earned to date ($) | Hours used to date | Amt used to date ($) | Hours needed to finish @ rate | Amt +/− ahead behind ($) | % +/− ahead behind (%) | Unused amt. to date | Remaining fee per phase |
|---|---|---|---|---|---|---|---|---|---|---|---|---|---|
| Schematic design | 12 | 50 | 15,324 | 305 | 100 | 15,324 | 208 | 10,445 | 0 | 4,879 | 32 | 4,879 | 0 |
| Design development | 18 | 54 | 22,986 | 422 | 100 | 22,986 | 330 | 17,928 | 0 | 5,059 | 22 | 5,058 | 0 |
| Construction docs | 43 | 39 | 54,911 | 1,418 | 35 | 19,219 | 617 | 23,900 | 1,146 | −4,681 | −24 | 31,011 | 35,692 |
| Bid/negotiation | 2 | 45 | 2,554 | 56 | 0 | 0 | 0 | 0 | | 0 | | 2,554 | 2,554 |
| Construction admin. | 25 | 45 | 31,925 | 705 | 0 | 0 | 0 | 0 | | 0 | | 31,925 | 31,925 |
| Rate/hour totals: | | 45 | | 2,820 | | | 1,154 | | 1,408 | | | | |
| %/amount totals: | 100 | | 127,700 | | 45 | 57,529 | | 52,272 | | 5,256 | 9 | 75,428 | 70,171 |
| Consultant fee: | | | 160,400 | | | 72,260 | | 14,404 | | 57,857 | 80 | 145,996 | 88,140 |
| Total fee: | | | 288,100 | | | 129,789 | | 66,676 | | 63,113 | 49 | 221,424 | 158,311 |

## SAMPLE PROJECT BUDGET SUMMARY REPORT

*Askew, Nixon, Ferguson Architects, Inc., Memphis, Tennessee*

| Project number | Project name | Current phase | | | | Total phase | | | | Project profit | | | |
|---|---|---|---|---|---|---|---|---|---|---|---|---|---|
| Number | Name | Phase | % Done | Phase budget | Budget to date | Actual to date | % Done | Total budget | Budget to date | Actual to date | Budget (%) | Proj'ed (%) | Last week(%) | Index |
| 90114 | IRS Comp. Change | 5 | 84 | 4,873 | 4,093 | 2,890 | 84 | 4,873 | 4,093 | 2,890 | 10 | **32.2** | 26.5 | 1,083 |
| 93057 | Sam's Town | 4 | 75 | 4,632 | 3,474 | 1,337 | 26 | 13,235 | 3,441 | 1,337 | 20 | **32.7** | 27.3 | 967 |
| 91064 | SE Elem. School | 7 | 70 | 1,302 | 911 | 826 | 90 | 4,481 | 4,033 | 3,226 | 15 | 30.3 | 31.4 | 686 |
| 92009 | TVA Allen Siding | 7 | 80 | 44 | 35 | 162 | 92 | 1,411 | 1,298 | 889 | 20 | 43.2 | 43.6 | 327 |
| 92011 | TVA Turbine | 7 | 10 | 176 | 18 | 7 | 90 | 912 | 821 | 681 | 25 | 36.5 | 45.2 | 105 |
| 93066 | AT&T Atlanta | 6 | 90 | 18 | 16 | 25 | 86 | 356 | 306 | 246 | 20 | 33.5 | 33.5 | 48 |
| 93035 | TVA Allen Portal | 3 | 30 | 46 | 14 | 12 | 20 | 293 | 59 | 60 | 20 | **19.6** | 16.1 | −1 |
| 92033 | Dobbs SF | 7 | 60 | 47 | 28 | 109 | 85 | 827 | 703 | 781 | 15 | 7.0 | 7.0 | −66 |
| 93051 | Boatmen's | 5 | 95 | 259 | 246 | 493 | 95 | 472 | 448 | 738 | 10 | −45.2 | −74.6 | −261 |
| 92062 | Sharp Toner | 7 | 85 | 291 | 247 | 265 | 96 | 1,164 | 1,117 | 1,479 | 20 | −4.8 | −4.2 | −289 |

Projects on hourly basis (without not to exceed) not shown
Hours shown do not include profit

Boldfaced numbers indicate profit increase of 1% or more
* Index= projected profit − budgeted profit x total budget hours

2 Predesign/programming
3 Schematic design
4 Design development
5 Construction docs
6 Bidding/negotiation
7 Construction admin.

Total rework hours this week:        14
Total rework hours year to date    567
Total rework hours last week          3

Project overruns occur for several reasons, including poor estimating, an unrealistic fee, scope creep, and inadequate project management. Sometimes the client delays providing approvals or requests changes that were not specified in the agreement as requiring additional compensation. When overruns are projected, it is prudent to examine the options:

- *Additional revenue.* Examine the project to determine whether, based on added services or changes in scope, there is justification to ask for additional revenue. If there is, the changes must be documented and a case made for the additional amount. Justifying the case for additional revenue will be easier if the request is made in advance (before the change is accomplished) and the client can see how much it will cost.
- *Overtime.* Staff members may work overtime to complete the project. It is important to account for overtime hours because the firm needs to know the true costs (in both hours and dollars) of all projects in order to price similar new projects correctly.
- *Review alternatives for completion.* Another way to overcome project budgeting problems is to reschedule and reassign the remaining portion of the work. People who can speed up the work might be assigned to the project; part-time people might help. Sometimes it is necessary to renegotiate contracts with clients or consultants.
- *Take the loss.* Occasionally it is necessary to absorb the loss and move on.

▶ **Decisions about reducing overruns must be checked against the terms and conditions of the owner-architect agreement.**

▶ **The backgrounder Architects as Employers: Legal Requirements (8.1) reminds us that a firm may be required by law to pay for overtime.**

## BILLING AND COMPENSATION CONTROL

Final project control steps involve billing clients and collecting accounts.

**Billing requirements.** Requirements for billing—how often invoices are prepared, what they include, the amount of time the owner has to pay them, interest rates on overdue

---

### Invoicing and Collecting: Some Advice from the Field

Practitioners have some advice to share. Here are some of their ideas collected at workshops and seminars:

- If possible, get a retainer up front to be credited to your final payment. If you don't ask for it, you won't get it. Architects wear many hats, and there's no point in taking up banking, too.
- Discuss invoicing and payment procedures with the client before submitting the first invoice. "What day of the month should we bill?" "Here's a sample of our invoice form; do you understand it, and is it okay?" "Is there some other form that works better for you?" "What's your payment review/approval process—and how long does it normally take?"
- Submit a projected invoicing schedule, and review it with the client. The point is to avoid surprising the client with invoices—but also to make sure the client understands what you expect to be paid and when. *Hint:* You can use this as a cash flow projection for the project.
- Consider billing more frequently than once a month. You are relying on this cash flow to pay your employees (who are usually paid weekly, biweekly, or monthly) as well as consultants and vendors.
- Bill promptly and completely. Use the agreed form, and check it thoroughly for errors—even misspellings. Fax

first, and follow up in the mail. If you don't ask for the money, you won't get it!

- A slow payment is often a danger signal. Meet with the client to find out if there is a problem with your services. If the client is satisfied but has cash flow problems, consider requesting a promissory note for overdue payments. One firm specifies the highest allowable interest rate for overdue payments in its owner-architect agreements and, if necessary, offers an interest rate on a promissory note that is close to its line-of-credit rate. This provides an incentive for the client to sign the note. In case of legal action, the note can be admitted as evidence the client was satisfied with the service and intended to pay you.
- Live up to the terms of your contract and keep the contract current. Amend it promptly when project conditions require changes in scope or duration of services. Don't give the client a good reason to delay, avoid, or dispute payment.
- Sometimes it is necessary to write off a bad debt after it has been owed for some time. Before doing this, you may want to tell the client you are planning to write off the amount owed and report it to the IRS.

*James R. Franklin, FAIA*

Sema4, *Sema 4, Inc., New York, New York, and Walnut Creek, California*

Invoices are often customized to meet the needs of the client and contract. Commercially available financial management systems offer a number of options (possibly including the ability to design your own). A few examples from a single software vendor are shown.

**SAMPLE PRE-BILLING WORKSHEET**

**Pre-Billing Worksheet** — Baxtor, Ryder & Associates, Inc.

| | |
|---|---|
| Gruber Advertising, Inc. | Invoice number : 44 |
| 304 West End Avenue | Project number : 9206 |
| 17th Floor | Period : 3.1.92 – 3.31.92 |
| New York, NY 10085 | Project type : 3 |
| Attn: Mr. Chuck Gruber | Invoice type : 101 |
| Project: GAI Lobby Renovation | Principal : TKB  Theodore K. Baxton |
| | Project manager : ACC  Alexander C. Chang |
| | Bill schedule : |

### A / E SERVICES

| Description | Title | Date | Rate | Hold hours | Actual hours | Bill hours | Write up write down | Billable amount | Adjustment |
|---|---|---|---|---|---|---|---|---|---|
| Alex Chang | architect | 2.15.92 | 70.00 | | 16.00 | 16.00 | | $1,120.00 | |
| Carla Rhodes | draftsperson | 2.15.92 | 52.00 | | 8.50 | 8.50 | | 442.00 | |
| Carla Rhodes | draftsperson | 2.13.92 | 52.00 | | 7.00 | 7.00 | | 364.00 | |
| Floyd Grant | draftsperson | 2.14.92 | 43.00 | | 6.00 | 6.00 | | 258.00 | |
| Floyd Grant | draftsperson | 2.15.92 | 43.00 | | 5.00 | 3.50 | S-64.50 | 150.00 | |
| | | | | | **42.50** | **41.00** | **S-64.50** | **$2,334.50** | |

### CONSULTANT EXPENSES

### REIMBURSABLE EXPENSES

| | Date | Hold quantity | Hold cost | Bill quantity | (Billable) cost | Write up write down | Billable amount | Adjustment |
|---|---|---|---|---|---|---|---|---|
| Bobbie L. Miller | 3.14.92 | 50.00 | 67.36 | | | | | |
| | | | **67.36** | | | | | |

| | |
|---|---|
| Total A/E services | $2,334.50 |
| Total consultant costs | 0.00 |
| Total reimbursables | 0.00 |
| **Invoice total** | **$2,334.50** |

### PROJECT SUMMARY

| | Budget | Previous billed | Current period | Budget left |
|---|---|---|---|---|
| A/E services | 150,000.00 | 21,435.00 | 2,334.50 | 126,230.50 |
| Consultants | 0.00 | 500.00 | 0.00 | −500.00 |
| Reimbursables | 0.00 | 1,432.96 | 0.00 | −1,432.96 |
| | **150,000.00** | **23,367.96** | **2,334.50** | **124,297.54** |

March 31, 1992

Share Associates, Inc.
1000 W. Foster Avenue
Chicago, Illinois 60640

Invoice number: 46
Project number: 9207

Attn: Sheri Morgenstern

For professional services rendered for the period March 1, 1992, through
March 31, 1992 for the referenced project.

The New Uptown Center Mixed Use Development

| Description | Contract amount | % work to date | Amount billed | Previous billed | This invoice billed |
|---|---|---|---|---|---|
| Concept study | 12,800 | 100 | 12,800 | 6,000 | 6,799 |
| Schematic design | 22,400 | 15 | 3,360 | 799 | 2,560 |
| Total | 35,200 | | 16,160 | 6,800 | 9,359 |
| Total fixed fee | | | | | 9,359.68 |
| | | | | | |
| HTR reprographics | | | | 35.59 | |
| In house copies | | | | 2.20 | |
| Mercury Messenger Service, Inc. | | | | 17.83 | |
| | | | | 55.62 | |
| | | | | | 55.62 |
| **Invoice total** | | | | | **9,415.30** |

## SAMPLE STIPULATED SUM— PERCENTAGE OF COMPLETION INVOICE

## SAMPLE HOURLY BILLING INVOICE
*(at the task level)*

March 31, 1992

Gruber Advertising, Inc.
304 West End Avenue
17th Floor
New York, NY 10085

Invoice Number: 44
Project number: 9206

Attn: Mr. Chuck Gruber

For professional A/E services rendered, for the design and renovation of the
lobby at the Gruber Advertising Building, 304 West End Avenue, New York,
NY, for the period March 1, 1992, through March 31, 1992.

| Description | Hours | Rate | Cost |
|---|---|---|---|
| Schematic design | | | |
|   Meeting | | | |
|     Floyd B. Grant | 3.50 | 43.00 | $150.00 |
| Design development | | | |
|   Concept evaluation | | | |
|     Carla A. Rhodes | 6.50 | 52.00 | $338.00 |
|   Drafting | | | |
|     Alexander C. Chang | 16.00 | 70.00 | 1,120.00 |
|     Carla A. Rhodes | 9.00 | 52.00 | 468.00 |
|     Floyd B. Grant | 6.00 | 43.00 | 258.00 |
|       Total labor | | | $2,334.50 |
| | | | |
| Reimbursables | | | |
|   3.12.92 In-house photocopy | 10 @ | .15 | 1.50 |
|   3.18.92 Mileage | 142 @ | .42 | 59.64 |
|     Total reimbursables | | | 61.41 |
| **Invoice total** | | | **$2,395.64** |

Wind2, *Wind2 Software, Inc., Fort Collins, Colorado*

USA Consultants, Inc.
P.O. Box 2010
412 East Parkway Drive
Denver, CO 80202-0000

A/R Aging Report—Full detail
Report date: 2.29.92

| Client/project | invoice# | billed | current | 31–60 | 61–90 | 91–120 | over 120 | Total A/R |
|---|---|---|---|---|---|---|---|---|
| ABC: ABC Corporation 303/489-6156 James T. Grant | | | | | | | | |
| 8850 | 10000 | 1.31.92 | 19.53 | 0.00 | 0.00 | 0.00 | 0.00 | |
| City Park development | 10005 | 2.5.92 | 5176.93 | 0.00 | 0.00 | 0.00 | 0.00 | |
| Phase II – children's playgrnd. | 10011 | 2.29.92 | 3353.44 | 0.00 | 0.00 | 0.00 | 0.00 | |
| | | | 8549.90 | 0.00 | 0.00 | 0.00 | 0.00 | 8549.90 |
| 8901 | 9989 | 12.15.92 | 0.00 | 0.00 | 509.87 | 0.00 | 0.00 | |
| City Park development | 9997 | 1.1.92 | 0.00 | 670.00 | 0.00 | 0.00 | 0.00 | |
| Phase III – Exercise course | retain. | | 484.84 | 0.00 | 0.00 | 0.00 | 0.00 | |
| | | | 484.84 | 670.00 | 509.87 | 0.00 | 0.00 | 1664.71 |
| 8903 | 10009 | 2.29.92 | 16900.69 | 0.00 | 0.00 | 0.00 | 0.00 | |
| City Park development | | | | | | | | |
| Phase IV – pool/ice rink compl. | | | 16900.69 | 0.00 | 0.00 | 0.00 | 0.00 | 16900.69 |
| Client total | | | 25935.43 | 670.00 | 509.87 | 0.00 | 0.00 | 27115.30 |
| | | | | | | | | |
| Case: Casebolt Corporation 303/332-6879 Henry Jones | | | | | | | | |
| 8902 | 10003 | 1.31.92 | 3600.00 | 0.00 | 0.00 | 0.00 | 0.00 | |
| TAV warehouse design | 10010 | 2.29.92 | 4728.56 | 0.00 | 0.00 | 0.00 | 0.00 | |
| | | | 8328.56 | 0.00 | 0.00 | 0.00 | 0.00 | 8328.56 |
| **Grand totals** | | | **34263.99** | **670.00** | **509.87** | **0.00** | **0.00** | **35443.86** |

*James R. Franklin, FAIA, Current Practices in Small Firm Management (AIA)*

Here's an approach suggested by Frank Stasiowski, AIA: Decide up front—either for a given project or as a matter of policy for all projects—how long you are willing to wait for your money before you suspend services on a project. As an example, you may decide on two months because your retainer actually pays for your costs for that long.

Then develop a follow-up tactic—and script it out—for every week in the two months. Put it in the form of a checklist to be followed. Here's an example:

| WHEN | MESSAGE | TONE | INITIATOR |
|---|---|---|---|
| Before it's sent | "I'm placing this month's invoice in the mail and want to explain why we had to place so many out-of-town phone calls (to the code variance bureau in the state capitol...)." | Informative | Project manager—normal client contact |
| Week 1 after it's due | "Did you get the invoice?" (This can be in the course of other discussion.) | Friendly, but don't use humor in any of this | PM |
| Week 2 | "About our invoice: Did you look it over? Is it OK?" | Solicitous, but this is a special call | PM |
| Week 3 | "Do you need additional information or clarification"? | (the same) | PM |
| Week 4 | "Can I come over and walk the invoice through?" | Concerned but still pleasant | PM |
| Week 5 | "When can we expect payment?" | Brisk and businesslike | Principal in charge (if not also the PM) |
| Week 6 | "Can I meet with you to collect payment?" | All business | Principal in charge (if not also the PM) |
| Week 7 | "Payment is overdue. Should we stop work?" | Deadpan | Preferably someone the client doesn't know |
| Week 8 | "We have stopped work. Should we notify our attorney?" | (the same) | Preferably someone the client doesn't know |

If the client hasn't paid at this point, you might have your lawyer send a letter—or draft one for your signature on your letterhead. The most effective collections are done in person, however. Go see the client. Nonpayment is usually a symptom of something else. Go prepared to listen and negotiate. If you receive a promise of payment, request a promissory note. If you need to sue for your fee later, you can do so on the basis of the note (which avoids the possibility of a counterclaim for negligence).

invoices, and related matters—are included in the owner-architect agreement. As indicated earlier, these are usually captured in some form of project authorization so that the PM (or whoever prepares invoices) has the necessary information on billing cycles, formats, allowable expenses, and other billing requirements.

**Invoices.** The firm will not be paid until the client receives an invoice. Therefore, full attention should be given to preparing and mailing invoices as soon as possible after the close of

## Preventing Fee Disputes

Avoiding fee disputes is important to addressing the fact that professional service fees do not always provide high profit margins and that firms are often strained for working capital. Moreover, the demand for fee payment by the architect often results in an allegation that fees were not paid because services were not authorized by the client or were negligently performed. How can you minimize the possibility of a fee dispute? Rely on the basics of good business practices such as the following:

*Use a client-evaluation checklist.* Before you sign a contract, use due diligence in evaluating the client and project. Businesses routinely check the financial strength and payment record of their business partners. Architects should ask similar questions, such as: Who are the principals involved in the project? What are their business reputations? Are they financially secure? What is their track record with other professionals on other projects? Is the project financially feasible and are scope, quality, schedule, and budget sound?

Answering these questions will inform your decision whether to work with the client on the project. The responses will also provide insight into special provisions you should build into the contract to protect your fee.

*Your contract needs to be specific as to scope and clear as to compensation.* AIA standard documents do just that. If you don't use the industry-consensus documents, make sure the contract you negotiate addresses the following issues:

- The manner, method, and form in which fees will be paid, including a schedule of payment dates and an up-front "mobilization" payment if appropriate. For instance, in AIA B141-1997 there is a provision for an initial payment that would be credited to the client's account at final payment.
- The right to suspend services until delayed payments are received and the right to terminate the contract and pursue legal remedies if the suspension is not effective. B141-1997 deems the failure by the client to make payments in accordance with the agreement to be "substantial nonperformance" and cause for termination or, at the architect's option, suspension of services.
- The ability of the parties to enforce the contract without spending extensive time or money in doing so. Some architects have been advised to use a prevailing-party provision that requires payment of the victorious party's legal fees by the party found to be at fault. While this may sound good when pursuing payment of a fee, it could be used by the stronger economic party (the owner) to coerce the weaker economic party (the architect) into a settlement that might not otherwise be justified.

- The services to be provided, the manner and method in which they are to be delivered, and the time frame for their execution.
- The specific responsibilities of the architect and client, including how the parties will handle any questions or problems that might arise during design and construction.

*Remember the rules of communication and documentation.* Clients risk the most on any project. They need to understand what is happening on their project and the value you add to the endeavor. Regular and prompt statements detailing the services provided (with appropriate references to contract clauses) should summarize the progress made since the last billing. By involving your clients in the design process, you make it easier to resolve problems and prevent an argument over fees.

Most disputes arise, in part, when clients become angry over misunderstandings that could have been avoided through good communication. Disputes over fees often become the unsatisfied client's final expression of discontent. However, the refusal to pay a fee—especially a final payment—may reflect an intentional strategy of fee avoidance or an evolution of a cost recovery scheme.

Ongoing communication also serves to keep you aware of your clients' situations. Are they still enthused about the project or have they been treating you differently? Is something about your services making them unhappy? Has a client's economic position changed? Delays in payment can also result from a client's internal problems. If your client is encountering financial difficulties, open architect-client communications may help detect these problems early.

*Think carefully before escalating a fee dispute into adjudication.* Any form of adjudication signals the end of the cooperative working relationship with a client. It probably also signals the end of your opportunity to provide future services to that client. Always consider mediation. While fee disputes are often easily resolved through arbitration, nonbinding mediation affords you and your client a nonthreatening opportunity to find a third party to help you resolve your dispute as soon as you both want it resolved.

Always consider the reasons you want to pursue payment. Are you no longer pleased with the client? Is the amount owed to you substantial? Are you confident that there is no potential liability on your part? Will any judgment you obtain be collectible? Remember, the collection of fees depends on the nature of the architect-client relationship, the soundness of the initial contractual arrangements, and the ability of the architect to reinforce the client's perception of the value of the services being provided.

*Frank Musica, Esq., Assoc. AIA*

the accounting period. It is good practice for the PM to review and approve invoices before they are sent to the client or, failing that, to establish a system for approving invoices in the absence of the PM. If the invoice requires explanation, it may make sense to call the client before it is sent.

Some firms customize their invoices to meet the needs of the client. Some send three invoices: one for regular services, one for any additional services, and one for reimbursable expenses. Some clients require that supporting documentation, such as copies of time records and expense reports, be included with all invoices.

***Collection.*** Once an invoice has been sent, the next step is to pursue collection in a timely manner. Many clients establish a payment cycle for invoices. For example, invoices received by the tenth of the month are paid in that month; otherwise invoices are held for thirty days. If your firm knows the client's payment cycle, it is important to comply with the dates established to avoid waiting an extra month for payment.

An aging schedule for accounts receivable helps a firm keep track of how long these accounts have been outstanding. If the firm does not regularly send out invoices at the end of the month for all work accomplished during the month, then the schedule should also include columns for work in progress. It is customary for the firm's principals to review the report periodically and take action on overdue accounts.

If invoices are not paid within thirty days, the PM may want to call the client to find out the reason for the delay. Sometimes a delayed payment is an indication of dissatisfaction with the architect's services or an indication of growing owner difficulties that may affect the health of the project, and these need to be addressed. This phone call can be followed by a reminder letter. *A note:* If the PM is not a principal in the firm, additional follow-up may be handled best by one of the firm's principals. A tickler file will help bring discipline to this process.

***Legal recourse.*** Sometimes it becomes necessary to engage the services of an attorney or collection agency when a client does not pay. This decision is usually reached when the firm no longer feels it has a relationship with the client and the firm's only interest is in getting paid for its completed services. The sooner this decision is reached, the more likely the overdue bill will be collected. *A caveat:* Statistics show that a claim against the architect often follows a demand for payment for professional services.

## VARIANCES AND COURSE CORRECTIONS

Periodic monitoring and progress reporting are meant to uncover variances from project plans. Scope and services may shift or expand. Tasks may take too long or cost too much. The client may not render approvals in a timely fashion or pay the bills. Consultants or contractors may not meet their obligations. Given the nature of design and construction and the temporary alliances required to advance projects, variances can occur in many ways.

Each variance represents a decision item for the firm and sometimes for the client. The decision may be to do nothing. Circumstances or actions already made are expected to correct the variance, but the firm may elect to accept the variance, even though it may reduce project profit. For example, a decision to sacrifice quality documents because the design budget is overspent is not taken lightly, and the firm may decide to bite the bullet and move forward.

In other instances the PM will need to take corrective action, directing a change in project activity or, in some cases, coordinating the revision of project plans. Actions involving changes in architect, consultant, or client responsibilities may result in amendments to the project agreements among these parties.

***Contract changes.*** Every project involves changes. The approach to be taken for proposing and approving changes in scope, services, schedule, and compensation should be established (and incorporated into the project agreement) at the outset. Usually the owner's specific authorization is required. Verbal authorizations are best confirmed in writing by the architect.

Some firms issue "zero change orders"—that is, proposals for scope changes without added compensation to the architect—for the first one or two small changes. These firms report that this procedure establishes a discipline and reduces surprises when the client authorizes changes that do require compensation adjustments.

***Documentation.*** The accounting department—or, depending on the firm, the bookkeeper or one of the principals acting in this capacity—maintains project files that contain copies of the project authorization, signed agreements, invoices, and other papers related to the financial aspects of the project. These files are separate from the technical files maintained by the PM. Whenever any changes are made to the contract, such as increases in project scope or authorizations for additional services, it is important that the accounting department receives a copy of the contract amendments. This can prevent accounting and billing errors.

***Suspending services.*** If a client is not paying invoices or meeting other contract requirements (such as supplying required information or approvals to the architect), it may

▶ **Project Operations (13.2) notes that most firms use some sort of project authorization to set up the necessary accounts and billing procedures.**

▶ **If interest charges for late payments have been negotiated into the contract, they should be invoiced whenever appropriate.**

▶ **Agreements with Clients (10.1) offers insights into contractual methods and how to anticipate and deal with disputes.**

## TQPM and the Project Notebook

Total quality project management (TQPM) presents an entirely new way of looking at quality in architecture, engineering, and other technical service firms. The word *quality* doesn't just mean how easily a design can be built, how functional the resulting facility will be, or how attractive it will look. The discussion of quality also includes such issues as how close the project came to its intended schedule and budget, how happy the client is, and how satisfied the firm's employees are. In short, quality embraces every aspect of how a professional service firm conducts its business.

TQPM—or, more generally, total quality management—is not new. The concept of controlling quality by using measurement techniques, targeting zero defects, and seeking continuous improvement was developed in the United States after World War II. After the war, General Douglas MacArthur sent W. Edwards Deming to Japan to help that nation rebuild its economy. Deming's approach was simple: Look for waste, measure its cost, determine what caused it, and get everyone involved to fix it so that it doesn't happen again. Japan's industry leaders heeded Deming's advice. The rest is history.

If you are like most design professionals, your first thought in setting up a TQPM program is marketing and beyond that is client satisfaction. Because the term *marketing* implies internal processes and actions, a better way to consider the process is as client-focused service. TQPM then becomes an integral part of your firm; the better the job you do at aiming for and providing client service, the better the firm will do for its current clients and in attracting additional projects and clients.

A quality management program requires a systemic response in every aspect of the firm's effort. More than anything, TQPM depends upon better-than-average project planning and monitoring. Here is a simple tool to help you with both: the client notebook.

For each project, set up and keep a three-ring binder with these tabs:

- *Tab 1: Client Expectations.* This is a written list of the client's expectations, reviewed and agreed to by the client. Clients seldom agree to these, but only because they are rarely asked. Make them concentrate, encourage them to let down their guard, and get them to tell you what they really want. Only then will you be prepared to deliver.
- *Tab 2: Schedule.* Place the schedule—and any updates—in this section.
- *Tab 3: Budget.* Break this section into three parts: up-front planning, ongoing project management, and postproject activity. Whenever a new report comes out on the budget, place it here.
- *Tab 4: Contract.* Describe the scope of services and other contract requirements.
- *Tab 5: Team.* Put in a complete list of people working on the project. For each staff member, consultant, contract worker, or other team member, include name, address, telephone, home telephone, fax, cell phone, and any other access number. The goal is to be able to reach everyone at any time of the day. Disasters inevitably happen at eight o'clock on Saturday morning or at nine o'clock at night.
- *Tab 6: Changes.* In this section describe precisely how you will handle design and/or construction changes throughout the project. The client should review and sign off on this section.
- *Tab 7: Communications.* This final section talks about how and when you will communicate with the client. Specify the purpose and frequency of telephone calls and meetings, your mail system, invoice system, and other communications. Get the client to sign off on this section as well.

This simple binder provides an at-a-glance view of project progress—for anyone on the project team.

*Frank A. Stasiowski, FAIA*

---

be appropriate to suspend services. This act can give the architect leverage and at the same time provide both owner and architect with an opportunity to resolve the problem before additional services (and expenses) pile up.

The possibility of suspending services should be part of the discussion with clients during negotiation of the owner-architect agreement. At that time the circumstances under which services could be stopped should be described and procedures incorporated into the owner-architect agreement. When negotiating a contract, no one enjoys considering how it might be stopped; yet it may be damaging to both client and architect to allow a project to continue beyond a certain point.

***An eye on quality.*** The overriding purpose of project controls is to help keep the project on track so the client's expectations and the firm's goals can be met. From an attitudinal perspective, architects can view the glass as half empty (projects sometimes veer out of control, and control helps reduce the possibility) or as half full (everyone wants a successful project, and controls provide another set of mechanisms for achieving that).

### For More Information

Most books on project management address project controls in conjunction with other management facets such as planning, team building, and operations. See books listed in the "For More Information" section of Project Operations (13.2).

# Project Scheduling

*Frank A. Stasiowski, FAIA*

Over the years, numerous systems have been devised to schedule projects. Each system has advantages and disadvantages, and each project should be scheduled using a method that best suits its scope and complexity. Also, a system must relate to the level of schedule control needed for the project. Using an overly complex scheduling method requires unnecessary effort and may, in fact, distract the project manager from the task of planning and, once the project begins, keeping things on track.

## Milestone Charts

Perhaps the simplest scheduling method is the milestone chart. In its most basic form, this method consists of identifying the target completion date for each activity in the task outline. The chart may also include the name of the person responsible for performing each task and, later, the actual completion date for each task. The two major advantages of milestone charts are their ease of preparation and emphasis on target completion dates.

The best applications for milestone charts are:

- Short design projects with few participants and little interrelationship between activities
- Preparation of presentations or proposals
- Summarizing complex schedules containing many tasks

When using milestone charts, list only key activities to avoid the excessive detail that can defeat the purpose of the chart.

A drawback of the milestone chart is that it only shows completion dates. For complex projects, this may result in uncertainty about when each activity should begin. Although the tasks are listed in the order in which they are to be undertaken, the completion dates may overlap. Furthermore, comparing actual completion dates with the target dates provides only a general indication of overall schedule status. Many projects are too complex to be adequately controlled using only a milestone chart.

## Bar Charts

Some of the drawbacks of milestone charts can be overcome by using a slightly more complex method—the bar chart, also known as the Gantt chart. Probably the most widely used planning tool among architects, the bar chart consists of a list of tasks along the left side of a page. Horizontal bars along the right side indicate the scheduled start and finish dates for each task. Today there are dozens of computer programs that make this scheduling method both accessible and easy to use.

Some firms create bar chart schedules in an interactive way. They will rough out a bar chart with spreadsheet or project man-

agement software before pinning it on the wall for critiques by other team members. During the scheduling meeting, the project manager can obtain commitments from all parties to accomplish their tasks on the schedule established by the group. Conflicts can be discussed and situations resolved while everyone is still in the room.

The principal drawbacks of bar charts are that they do not show interrelationships among various tasks, nor do they indicate which activities are most crucial for completing the entire project on schedule. Assigning equal importance to each activity (implicit in the bar chart method) may leave the project manager in a quandary when forced to decide which task should be delayed in the event of a labor shortage. This dilemma may result in assigning priorities to the wrong tasks. Despite these drawbacks, bar charts remain an effective method of controlling straightforward projects.

## Selecting a Scheduling Method

| Evaluation Criteria | Milestone Chart | Bar Chart | Interactive Bar Chart | CPM Schedule |
|---|---|---|---|---|
| Ease of communication | Good | Good | Excellent | Poor |
| Cost to prepare | Minimal | Minimal | Moderate | High |
| Cost to update | Minimal | Minimal | Moderate | High |
| Degree of control | Fair | Good | Good | Excellent |
| Applicability to small projects | Excellent | Good | Good | Poor |
| Applicability to large projects | Poor | Fair | Good | Excellent |
| Commitment from project team | Fair | Fair | Excellent | Fair |
| Client appeal | Fair | Good | Excellent | Excellent |

## Milestone Chart

| No. | Task | Responsibility | Target | Completed |
|---|---|---|---|---|
| 1 | Proposal cover | DB | 1/15/99 | x |
| 2 | Letter of transmittal | AWL | 1/22/99 | x |
| 3 | Introduction | AWL | 1/22/99 | x |
| 4 | Scope of services | MRH | 2/19/99 | x |
| 5 | Project schedule | MRH | 2/24/99 | |
| 6 | Project budget | MRH | 2/24/99 | x |
| 7 | Project organization | DB | 2/24/99 | |
| 8 | Appendix A: qualifications | DB | 2/25/99 | |
| 9 | Appendix B: biographical data | DB | 3/1/99 | |
| 10 | Typing and graphics | DB | 3/4/99 | |
| 11 | Final editing | AWL | 3/8/99 | |
| 12 | Printing, binding, mailing | DB | 3/10/99 | |

## BAR CHART

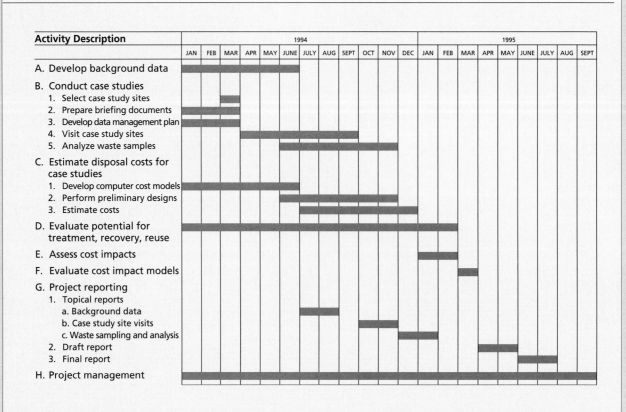

| Activity Description | 1994 | | | | | | | | | | | | 1995 | | | | | | | | |
|---|---|---|---|---|---|---|---|---|---|---|---|---|---|---|---|---|---|---|---|---|---|
| | JAN | FEB | MAR | APR | MAY | JUNE | JULY | AUG | SEPT | OCT | NOV | DEC | JAN | FEB | MAR | APR | MAY | JUNE | JULY | AUG | SEPT |

**A. Develop background data**

**B. Conduct case studies**
　1. Select case study sites
　2. Prepare briefing documents
　3. Develop data management plan
　4. Visit case study sites
　5. Analyze waste samples

**C. Estimate disposal costs for case studies**
　1. Develop computer cost models
　2. Perform preliminary designs
　3. Estimate costs

**D. Evaluate potential for treatment, recovery, reuse**

**E. Assess cost impacts**

**F. Evaluate cost impact models**

**G. Project reporting**
　1. Topical reports
　　a. Background data
　　b. Case study site visits
　　c. Waste sampling and analysis
　2. Draft report
　3. Final report

**H. Project management**

## Critical Path Method (CPM)

A highly mathematical system in which task interrelationships are defined and task schedules analyzed, critical path method scheduling is designed for use in very complex projects with many tasks and complicated logic. CPM is not often used to schedule design projects but is frequently used by contractors to schedule construction sequences and projects.

CPM diagrams graphically show the interrelationships among project tasks: which must be started first, which cannot be started until others are completed, and which can be accomplished in parallel. Through calculation, it is possible to develop an early and late starting date (and finish date) for each activity. It is also possible to plot one or more critical paths through the project—sequence(s) of tasks that, if delayed, would delay final completion of the project.

A number of CPM variations have been developed. They include project evaluation and review technique (PERT) and precedence diagramming. While the physical expression and some details vary, the concepts behind these systems are comparable to CPM. Developing a critical path schedule involves these steps:

*Step 1: Identify tasks and relationships.* The first step is to systematically identify all tasks and the relationships among them. There are three possible relationships between two tasks: task 1 must be completed before task 2 can begin; task 1 must be partially completed before task 2 can begin; or task 1 must be completed before task 2 can be completed.

*Step 2: Construct a precedence (task interface) diagram.* The precedence diagram illustrated shows the relationships described in the first step. Study this diagram to see which of the three types of interrelationships exists between each pair of tasks. Note that in this example there is more than one type of relationship between tasks. Look at tasks C2 and C3; task C3 (cost estimates) cannot begin until task C2 (preliminary design) is partially completed, and task C3 cannot be completed until task C2 has been completed. This double relationship is quite common.

*Step 3: Establish optimal task durations.* The next step is to establish the length of time required to complete this activity in the most efficient manner possible—assuming that all prerequisite tasks have been completed. A tabulation for the tasks in the sample project is shown in the accompanying task duration list.

*Step 4: Prepare the project schedule.* Using the precedence diagram and duration list, prepare the project schedule. This requires calculating the earliest each task can start (and finish). When the total duration of the project as depicted in the diagram is known, then work backward to establish the latest possible finish (and start) for each task.

## CPM TASK DURATION LIST

*Activity description*  |  *Calendar days*

| | | |
|---|---|---|
| A | Develop background data | 180 |
| B1 | Select case study sites | 30 |
| B2 | Prepare briefing documents | 30 |
| B3 | Develop data management plan | 90 |
| B4 | Visit case study sites | 180 |
| B5 | Analyze waste samples | 105 |
| C1 | Develop computer cost models | 90 |
| C2 | Perform preliminary case study site designs | 135 |
| D | Evaluate treatment, recovery, reuse | 90 |
| E | Assess cost impacts | 60 |
| F | Evaluate cost impact models | 30 |
| G1a | Prepare background data report | 60 |
| G1b | Prepare site data report | 60 |
| G2 | Prepare draft report | 60 |
| G3 | Prepare final report | 60 |
| H | Project management | (completed 60 days after the completion of all other tasks) |

*Step 5. Determine the critical path.* The last step is to determine which tasks are critical—that is, which tasks will affect the project completion date if any delay occurs. For these tasks, the early start and late start dates are identical (as are the early finish and late finish dates). There is no float time. These tasks are darkened in the CPM schedule shown.

Computer-based project management systems perform all these calculations quickly. They allow the scheduler to easily build, test, and modify various network schedules, and they can provide a series of analyses and reports for the project. Some software also allows the scheduler to allocate resources to each task (to help build budgets) or among multiple projects simultaneously. But use caution. Some software programs are easier to use than others, and some are designed for specific-size projects. These programs are continually evolving, with new ones being developed. It would be wise to carefully review what is currently available and consider these programs in light of your firm's needs before making a selection.

## CPM PROJECT SCHEDULE

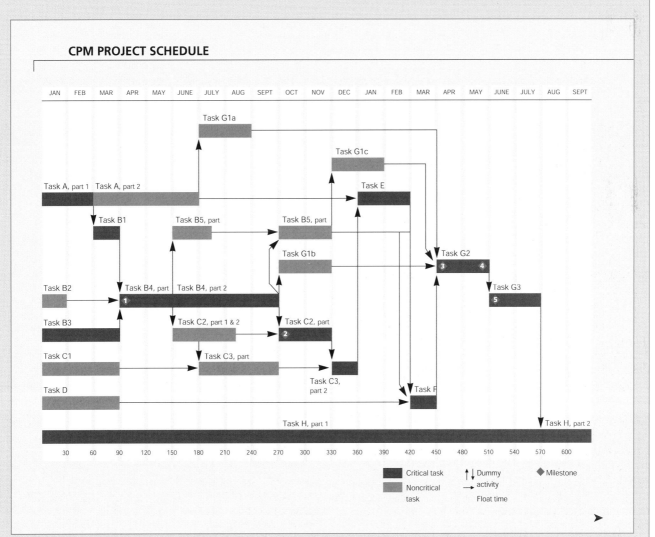

## PRECEDENCE DIAGRAM (CPM variation)

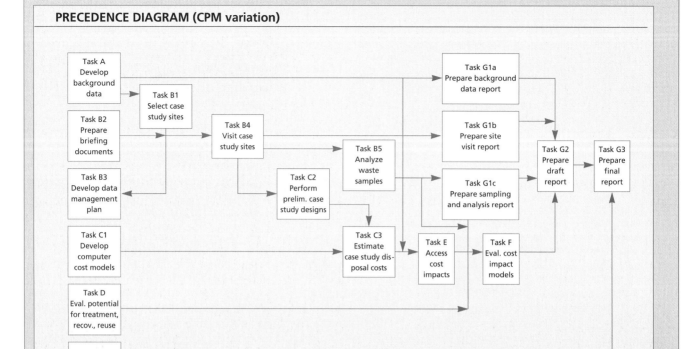

The principal advantage of a critical path method is that it shows task interrelationships clearly and highlights those activities that could create problems in meeting deadlines. It gives the project manager the most detailed control of a complex project. The major disadvantages are that CPM diagrams can be time-consuming to prepare, difficult to read, and tedious to update. Even with computers, the time and effort required to maintain a CPM chart can pose a problem for project managers with numerous project responsibilities. Moreover, most design tasks do not require such a precise level of control.

*Frank Stasiowski is founder and president of PSMJ Resources. He is a consultant to the building and design industry and the author of numerous books and publications about management.*

## Project Scheduling Software

### Microsoft Corporation
One Microsoft Way
Redmond, WA 98052
Tel: (425) 882-8080
www.microsoft.com

**Microsoft Project** is a high-end planning, scheduling, and tracking program for medium and large projects. Project 98 is compatible with Microsoft Office desktop applications and with ODBC-compliant databases. Output in PERT or Gantt formats. (Available for Windows; Project 4.0 available for Macintosh.)

### Primavera Systems, Inc.
3 Bala Plaza West, Suite 700
Bala Cynwyd, PA 19004
Tel: (610) 667-8600
www.primavera.com

**Primavera SureTrak Project Manager** is intended for use for planning and controlling small to medium-size projects. Streamlined analysis, reporting, and graphics. (Available for Windows 3.1, 95, NT, or OS/2.)

**Primavera Project Planner 3.0** is an industrial-strength program that provides planning, scheduling, and tracking capabilities for sophisticated and multifaceted projects. Allows access by multiple users. Output in PERT or Gantt formats. (Available for Windows 3.1, Windows 95 or Windows NT).

**Primavera TeamPlay** is intended for planning, controlling, and communicating on an enterprise-wide basis with multiuser, multi-project capabilities providing IT project portfolio management. Output in PERT or Gantt format. (Available for Windows 95, Windows 98, or Windows NT with a Windows NT or UNIX server.)

### AEC Software
22611-113 Markey Court
Sterling, VA 20166
Tel: (800) 346-9413
www.aecsoft.com

**FastTrack 6.0** is a scheduling and tracking program for projects requiring a low to moderate degree of control. Offers a rich array of graphical features with Gantt bar output. (Available for Windows 95, Windows 98, Windows NT, and Macintosh.)

# 13.4 Construction Cost Management

## Brian Bowen, FRICS

*Construction cost management is too important to be left to chance. Managing costs requires skill, effort, and continuing discipline throughout design and construction.*

Engaging in construction represents a substantial commitment for an owner. The costs of a project, coupled with the effort required to obtain financing, can be daunting. A project whose cost is estimated to exceed the amount borrowed or raised may have to be reevaluated or even abandoned. As a result, clients are very concerned that their projects remain within budget. Given the spotlight on construction cost in most projects, this is an area in which the architect can gain, or lose, credibility.

> "Architecture depends on order, arrangement, eurhythmy, symmetry, propriety, and economy . . . economy denotes the proper management of materials and of site, as well as a thrifty balancing of cost and common sense in the construction of works."
> *Vitruvius,* On Architecture, *Book 1 (25 b.c.)*

## THE ARCHITECT'S RESPONSIBILITIES

The architect's responsibilities for estimating and meeting construction costs are detailed in the owner-architect agreement.

***Professional services.*** If AIA standard forms of agreement are used, the architect's professional services include the following:

- Budget evaluation. Project scope, quality, schedule, and construction budget are interrelated, and design generally begins with an evaluation of (to quote AIA Document B141, Standard Form of Agreement Between Owner and Architect) each in terms of the other.
- Cost estimates. AIA Document B141 specifies that the architect provide a preliminary estimate of the cost of the work when the project requirements have been sufficiently identified. The owner must be advised of any adjustments to the previous estimates that result from updates and refinements of the preliminary design.
- Construction contract administration. As part of construction contract administration, the architect reviews and certifies amounts due the construction contractor when the contractor requests payment. Change orders are also evaluated and agreed upon.

Depending on the owner's needs and the architect's capabilities, the owner-architect agreement may include other professional services related to construction cost. The architect may agree to provide the following:

> Detailed construction cost estimates are a separate service that few architects undertake unless they also have specially developed estimating capabilities.

- Market research studies
- Economic feasibility studies
- Project financing studies
- Analysis of construction alternatives or substitutions
- Construction contract cost accounting
- Life cycle cost analysis
- Value analysis, engineering, or management
- Bills of materials
- Quality surveys
- Detailed cost estimating

**BRIAN BOWEN,** *a principal of Hanscomb, Inc., is a recognized expert in cost management who has written and spoken worldwide on the subject to numerous professional societies and technical organizations. He is a fellow of the Royal Institute of Chartered Surveyors, a certified cost engineer, and a certified value specialist.*

None of these services is included in the basic services package in AIA Document B141; however, they are listed on the menu of possible services in AIA Document B163. Owner and architect may also negotiate budgeting, budget evaluation, design analysis, or cost estimating services associated with site selection and development, planning and program options, energy or other special studies, tenant fit-up, and ongoing facilities management services.

▶ Architectural Services and Compensation (9.2) explores various approaches to selecting and packaging architecture services.

Not all architects are interested in or able to provide these additional services. Market research, financing, and economic feasibility studies require expertise in specific sales or leasing markets. Detailed construction cost estimating requires the firm to be in touch with the construction marketplace in which the project will be built. Some architecture firms develop these capabilities; others do not. Some firms include construction cost consultants, contractors, or construction managers (CMs) on their design teams.

**Budget for the cost of the work.** In addition to outlining cost-related services, the owner-architect agreement establishes a budget for the cost of the work as a condition of the architect's performance. That is, the agreement may include a statement (usually as part of the project description on the cover page) something like this: "New village town hall of 10,000 gross square feet floor area with a construction cost not to exceed $900,000."

Including such a budget in the owner-architect agreement establishes meeting the cost figure as a goal of the architect's performance. This immediately raises a number of questions that, in the interest of both owner and architect, should be addressed in the agreement:

- How is cost of the work defined? What is included and excluded? How will design and marketplace uncertainties be addressed?
- How will the architect achieve the flexibility needed to develop a design within budget?
- What options are available to the owner and architect if bids exceed the fixed limit?
- What happens if there are delays in awarding construction contracts?

These questions are addressed in AIA Document B141 in this way:

- The cost of the work includes the elements of the project designed or specified by the architect and the architect's consultants, excluding their compensation.
- The architect is permitted to include contingencies for design, bidding, and price escalation in statements of construction cost.
- The architect can determine the materials, equipment, components, and types of construction to be included in the project and is permitted to make reasonable adjustments in scope.
- The architect can include alternates that, if necessary, can be used to adjust the construction cost at the time of contract award.

---

### REQUIREMENTS FOR DESIGN COST ESTIMATES IN AIA DOCUMENT B141

*Standard Form of Agreement Between Owner and Architect, AIA Document B141, 1987 edition*

**SCHEMATIC DESIGN PHASE**

2.2.2 The Architect shall provide a preliminary evaluation of the Owner's program, schedule, and construction budget requirements, each in terms of the other, subject to the limitations set forth in Subparagraph 5.2.1.

2.2.5 The Architect shall submit to the Owner a preliminary estimate of Construction Cost based on current area, volume, or other unit costs.

**DESIGN DEVELOPMENT PHASE**

2.3.2 The Architect shall advise the Owner of any adjustments in the preliminary estimate of Construction Cost.

**CONSTRUCTION DOCUMENTS PHASE**

2.4.3 The Architect shall advise the Owner of any adjustments to previous preliminary estimates of Construction Cost indicated by changes in requirements or general market conditions.

---

▶ There is nothing absolute about construction prices—as sometimes evidenced by the wide spread among bids on a given project. Precontract estimating, therefore, is a hazardous business. An estimator who can bring 60 percent of the projects estimated within 5 percent of the low bid is probably doing better than expected, and it is statistically probable, on average, that one project in five will fall outside a 10 percent range. The architect can avoid some of this hazard by including adequate contingencies and by cooperating with the client in designing contingent features into plans to allow for additions or deletions depending on bid results.

- Several courses of action, including revising scope and quality at no additional cost to the owner but with the owner's cooperation, are listed if the lowest bid or proposal exceeds the budget.
- The budget is to be adjusted if bidding or negotiations have not commenced within 90 days after the architect submits the construction documents.

***The architect's performance standard.*** Unless they agree to a higher standard by contract, architects are expected to use reasonable care in performing all of their professional services, including meeting the owner's construction cost objectives.

It is worth discussing reasonable care here because neither the owner nor the architect can control actual construction cost—the price that one or more contractors will ultimately charge for building the project. That price is a product of competitive market influences associated not just with the bidding contractors but also with their suppliers of materials, products, labor, and construction equipment. Under the standard of reasonable care, professionals do not have to guarantee results; rather, they are obliged to use reasonable care in performing their services.

Many owners, of course, seek guarantees. Construction represents a substantial outlay of funds, and unplanned increases in cost may create very real problems for owners. Because they have no control over the contractor, architects guaranteeing construction cost should understand that this is their choice and that they are offering to perform at a level beyond the standard of reasonable care.

***Cost services and responsibilities of others.*** Some consultants and construction organizations specialize in cost estimating and management, and these specialists may be added to the project team by the owner or the architect. Specialists may include these:

- Cost consultants who provide estimates and advice on constructability, scheduling, and the construction cost implications of functional and design alternatives.
- Contractors and CMs who offer cost and constructability expertise during design. These firms may remain as advisors to the owner or architect without competing for the actual construction work, or at a predetermined time they may assume responsibility for construction, including construction cost. Some architects also offer construction management services.
- Design-build entities that assume construction cost responsibility.

> Some contractors may "force" higher construction costs by deluging architects with requests for information, substitutions, and proposed design changes. Architects' responses that go beyond the construction documents may be treated as "new" requirements and thus as candidates for renegotiating construction cost.

When construction cost is critical, both the owner and the architect may engage cost consultants, thus building in additional perspectives and problem-solving abilities. For small projects, the nominated contractor (or possibly a contractor engaged on an hourly basis) may provide advice on cost, constructability, and related issues. When responsibilities for providing construction cost services are divided, it is very important that responsibilities and risks be carefully spelled out, allocated among the parties, and incorporated into a series of coordinated project agreements.

## COST MANAGEMENT PRINCIPLES

Successful management of construction costs revolves around a set of basic cost management principles.

***Cost objectives.*** It is difficult to manage well without clear intentions and objectives. Depending on the circumstances, cost objectives may include some or all of the following:

- To complete the project within the capital expenditure limitations established by the owner. These limitations may be included in the owner-architect agreement, or they may be developed by the architect and owner together.
- To provide, within the budget limitations, an appropriate use of resources and value for the money.

- To optimize longer-term life cycle costs by examining alternatives that provide the best balance between initial capital expenditure and ongoing operating costs.
- To provide the owner, during the course of the project, with relevant cost information related to major owner decisions and the status of the construction budget.

▷ **Construction involves too many variables to establish generic cost objectives. These should be decided for each project.**

***Early attention.*** The most effective benefits of cost management are gained at the beginning of the project, in establishing scope and levels of quality, making schedule decisions, selecting delivery options, and translating requirements into design concepts. The project's big decisions are made up front, and they lay the groundwork for all the decisions that follow.

***Realistic budget.*** The most important estimate given during the course of a project's life is the first one, for this is the number everyone remembers. The budget may be prepared by the owner and evaluated by the architect, or developed jointly based on an analysis of the owner's statement of requirements.

The construction budget can arise in two fundamentally different ways. It may be a number built up from costing out the project's program and schedule requirements, or it may be a number derived from the financial pro forma or some other source (e.g., a public referendum). However the number is established, the design usually does not exist, so the budget is typically based on projected function, area, or some other general characteristics of the project. Alternatively, it may be based on the actual cost of another, similar project.

***Cost plan.*** Once a realistic and achievable budget has been drafted, the architect is in a position to assign cost targets to the major categories within the cost framework. The resulting cost plan provides guidance, as design begins, on the funds available for each part of the project. It may also include a cash flow projection to help the owner establish the financing schedule. A cost plan can help avoid the erosive designing/costing/redesigning that characterizes some projects.

A consistent framework for organizing cost data is an important part of the cost plan. This framework allows the architect to correlate data obtained at different stages of the project (reconciliation with original budgets and estimates is always required) and to compare data from different projects.

The most common classification in use within the industry is the 16-division MasterFormat, which is used for most specifications and construction documentation. The wide currency of this format makes it useful for cost control, but because it is oriented to construction materials and trade divisions, it is less suitable for cost management at conceptual and early design stages.

▷ **Construction Documents Production (12.3) describes the MasterFormat classification system.**

Recognizing this shortcoming, the AIA, in conjunction with the General Services Administration, developed the UniFormat for design cost management. This format uses functional subsystems—e.g., superstructure, exterior closure, interior construction—that parallel the way designers think about and ultimately select building components and assemblies. Design cost data are increasingly being published in the UniFormatcategories. During the 1990s an ASTM subcommittee undertook an extensive industry review of UniFormat, which resulted in several changes to the original; this was published as UniFormatII, and it is now ASTM Standard E-1557.

***Cost as a design objective.*** Controlling cost as a design objective requires an understanding of the factors that affect building costs. A list of geographic, design, and marketplace factors is included in the commentary, Factors Affecting Building Costs.

## The Benefits of Early Cost Control

This curve makes the point that early efforts to manage building costs offer, conceptually, the best opportunities to optimize the owner's investment in the project. "Program" decisions establishing the project's use, scope, quality, site, and scheduling have a large impact and set the stage for what can be done during design. Construction documents provide some opportunities for improvement, but most of the critical decisions have been made by this time. The percentages listed are conceptual.

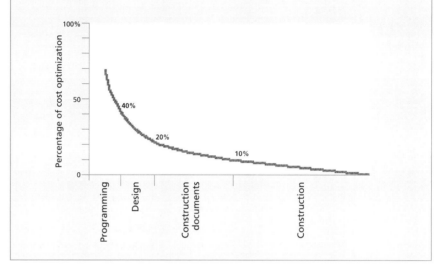

## Project Budgets

There is no easy method for establishing realistic and achievable budgets, because they are usually prepared before there is a definitive project design and before good information regarding construction costs is available. A realistic budget reflects the following:

*Project scope.* The gross built area and volume, together with occupancy type and numbers of occupants in the building, set the stage for construction cost. Establishing the scope requires accurate identification of the owner's functional space requirements and a reasonable translation of these into gross floor area, including allowances for circulation, mechanical and electrical equipment, custodial space, and other nonusable areas. The statement of project scope should also indicate what is included in the budget for such items as equipment, furnishings, or sitework.

*Quality and performance levels.* This is perhaps the most challenging set of factors because of the difficulty of adequately defining and describing quality and performance levels expected by the owner or achievable within a given budget limit. Diagrams, comparative projects, and published cost models may be helpful.

*Site.* The costs of developing the site and accommodating the building to it may be straightforward or very complicated.

*Schedule.* To fix the project in time, it is necessary to establish or assume construction bid and completion dates.

*Broad conceptual statement.* A statement of key design and budget assumptions (e.g., the number of stories, simple or articulated building form, single or multiple buildings, quantity of above- and below-grade construction, expected levels of renovation of existing structures) is usually helpful.

*Contingencies.* These may be built into the various budget items, or they may be separately identified. It is common to reduce contingencies as the project moves forward in design.

*Realistic figuring.* Avoid the temptation to highball the budget figure (protecting yourself but jeopardizing the project) or lowball it (creating what may be unreasonable expectations).

*Key assumptions.* Note these in the budget statement to reduce the possibility that they will be lost as the budget is communicated, used, and revised.

Remember that the construction budget sets the stage for the project's preliminary design. It provides a framework within which all design decisions will be made. Budgeting, incidentally, provides a good opportunity to help educate the client about scope, quality, time, and cost trade-offs.

Recall, too, that the budget is an estimate. Avoid language that would appear to guarantee or warrant the number. If the owner supplies the first number, do not accept it uncritically but evaluate it against program, site, schedule, and market conditions.

*Brian Bowen, FRICS*

---

**Project Controls (13.3) examines approaches to managing project scope.**

It is important to recognize that much of a project's cost is built into the project once its location, size, use type, and occupancy load are established; these decisions drive zoning, planning, and building code requirements. Geographic location and site set additional parameters for construction cost. The laws of supply and demand in the construction marketplace can exert great influence. Within these boundaries, the design team influences construction cost through its decisions about form, layout, systems, materials, and finishes.

**Scope control.** Clearly, a major cost driver is a project's scope: how much is to be constructed, and the levels of quality desired in the project. Increasing scope increases construction cost and may add design, financing, and operating costs as well. Thus scope control is an essential cost management discipline.

Many projects are subject to "scope creep," an enlargement of scope based on the many good ideas and solutions that arise during design. As the project becomes "real," owners may request changes in program requirements or levels of quality. Often these requests are small but numerous.

Most owners do not see their requests for changes as requiring changes in the budgets they have set. When budgets are fixed, scope creep forces reductions elsewhere: The chiller becomes several rooftop units. The granite facing becomes brick, then split-face block. The atrium becomes a corridor with a skylight (which ends up as an additive alternate).

An important challenge facing architects is to sit down with the owner and talk through changes, even (especially) the small ones. The objective is to secure the client's commitment to the change and its cost implications, or to determine what other owner requirements can be changed to keep the project within budget.

**Cost monitoring and reporting.** Construction cost should be carefully reviewed and, depending on the architect's contractual requirements, reported to the owner at each design submission or at agreed intervals. Cost reports should be reconciled to the cost plan and differences explained. This is a good time to review the status of project cost with the owner and obtain commitment to any budget updates that may be mutually agreed.

# DESIGN COST ESTIMATING

Successful cost management depends on sound estimating skills. Estimating involves two basic steps: quantifying the amount of work to be estimated and applying reasonable unit prices to these quantities.

There is a maxim among estimating professionals that the easier the measurement the more difficult the pricing, and vice versa. Thus it is more difficult to prepare accurate estimates at early project stages than later, when complete working drawings are available.

While there are many estimating approaches and systems, they generally fall into one of these basic categories:

- Area, volume, and other single-unit rate methods
- Elemental (assemblies and subsystems) methods
- Quantity survey methods

▷ **AIA Document B141** requires architects to provide preliminary construction cost estimates "based on current area, volume, and similar conceptual estimating techniques."

## Area, Volume, and Other Single-Unit Rate Methods

During predesign and even in preliminary design stages, it is usually necessary to develop construction cost estimates on the basis of one or more single units. Whether they are based on units of accommodation or on building area or volume, these estimating methods suffer from oversimplification and can produce widely varying estimates unless buildings of similar character, function, and location are being considered.

***Accommodation units.*** This approach involves counting the units of accommodation to be provided in the proposed building—the number of apartments or dormitory rooms, beds in a hospital or nursing home, parking spaces in a parking garage—and pricing these units at an overall inclusive rate. Selecting the appropriate unit price is usually difficult, even when a reasonable body of historical evidence exists. This is because there is wide variation in building forms and designs that contain the same units of accommodation.

***Area and volume methods.*** For preliminary estimates, architects often use computations based on the floor area (in square feet) or, less frequently, volume (in cubic feet) of construction. These methods require care in defining and counting area and volume. Basements, balconies, covered walkways, enclosed entries, interstitial spaces, and mechanical spaces may or may not require the same level of construction cost per square or cubic foot as more conventional enclosed and inhabited space. Also, care must be used in selecting the square or cubic foot unit cost factors to be applied. Finally, these methods require skill and experience in adjusting the unit costs to the special conditions of the project.

When using historical cost data for area or volume costs of construction, the architect should ensure that the project or group of projects selected for comparison is similar to the project being estimated. The projects

## Architectural Area and Volume of Buildings

*Document D101, 1995 edition*

AIA Document D101, Architectural Area and Volume of Buildings, provides a generally accepted set of definitions for establishing building area and volume. For example, an exterior balcony contributes one-half of its floor space to the total net assignable area, while an enclosed entrance is counted at its full floor area.

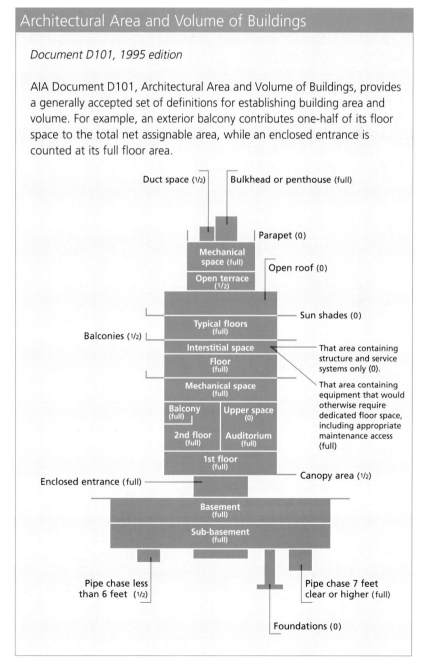

should be compared for similarity of use, size, site, type of construction, finishes, mechanical equipment, and economic climate during construction. The estimator can then compare characteristics and determine the modifications necessary to adjust the unit costs.

It should be noted that published single-rate unit cost figures customarily do not include the following:

- Site improvements and landscaping
- Utilities more than five feet from the building
- Unusual foundation conditions
- Furnishings and movable equipment not normally included in construction contracts
- Other items not normally included in a building of the type reported

***Functional area method.*** This refinement of the simple area method involves separately pricing each functional space type included in the project. Thus an estimate for a small school might include different square foot cost factors for its classroom, assembly, kitchen, and circulation spaces. This method assumes that the functions performed in the building will have a considerable bearing on its cost—a concept that holds true for interior construction but has less effect on the cost of the basic building shell. Using this method can be difficult because completed projects are rarely analyzed by the cost of individual areas, making it hard to find suitable cost data on which to base estimates.

## Elemental (Assemblies and Subsystems) Methods

An approach that falls between single-unit rate methods and the extremely detailed quantity survey method involves measuring basic building systems or elements. This approach subdivides the building into a series of functional subsystems, perhaps using the UNIFORMAT framework, and establishes a cost target for each subsystem.

The stage of design determines the degree of detail. In early stages, when no layouts have been designed, interior partitions can be priced on the basis of an allowance per square foot of finished area. Once layouts are done, these assemblies can be priced on a cost per linear foot of partition and, further along, on the basis of measured square foot area of the partitions, with doors, frames, and finishes priced separately.

The objective of using elemental methods is to produce an estimate by approaching a building as a sum of its systems and components. Construction cost is related to the configuration and construction of the building rather than just to its area, volume, or quantity of function. These methods do require a sophisticated database of information.

## Quantity Survey Method

This method involves detailed calculation of all the components necessary to construct the building, followed by the pricing of each component. For example, the elemental method may base plumbing costs on the number of fixtures, including roughing-in and water and waste connections. The quantity survey method measures each fixture separately, as well as the length of each piece of pipe and the quantities of fittings and trim. It applies prices to the materials involved in each construction operation, including allowances for waste, labor (crew sizes and makeup), installation time, equipment used, and for each trade, appropriate allowances for the contractor's overhead and profit.

Although such approaches to estimating are necessary for contractors, they are of limited value to architects. The designer might elect to do a careful quantity survey of alternative approaches for a given design decision or detail but is unlikely to undertake a quantity survey for an entire project.

## Contingencies and Reserves

All estimates should also include reasonable provisions for

- *Price escalation.* This generally is considered from the date of the estimate to the scheduled bidding or negotiation date (if the base estimate includes escalation during the construction period) or to the midpoint of construction (if the base estimate does not include any construction period escalation).

- *Design contingencies.* These may go as high as 20 percent for estimates based on area or volume. The completeness of the documents on which the estimate is based, the complexity of the project, and the accuracy of the information furnished by the owner all must be considered. As design progresses and estimating becomes more detailed, this contingency will be reduced.
- *Construction contingencies.* These generally allow up to 5 percent to provide for unforeseen changes during construction. This figure may be higher for renovation projects.

## Factors Affecting Building Costs

Fundamental to the development of sound cost management in design is an understanding of the basic factors that influence building costs. Some of these factors can be controlled in design, and others cannot.

### Location Factors

*Geographic location.* Costs will be influenced by such factors as climate and comfort requirements, building codes and regulations, ease of access, distances from sources of labor and materials, degree of union influence, and productivity of workers in the area.

*Condition of the site.* The bearing capacity of the soil, presence of rock, location of groundwater, slope, and existing conditions (such as old foundations or buried hazardous wastes) influence substructure costs and basic building design. Urban sites may require underpinning, extraordinary security, and limitations on access and maneuverability.

*Regulations.* Building design and construction are affected by a wide range of building codes and standards as well as planning, zoning, environmental protection, construction labor, and site safety laws and regulations. These requirements, and the regulatory fees the owner must pay, may vary considerably from locality to locality.

*Marketplace.* Construction prices are subject to change according to the laws of supply and demand. Overstressed and understressed construction markets will affect the level and quality of competition as well as the prices charged.

### Design Factors

*Plan shape.* The plan dictates the amount and complexity of the perimeter required to enclose a given space. Generally, the higher the perimeter-to-floor area ratio, the greater the unit cost. Exterior closure is a high-cost item (often 10 to 20 percent of total cost) and has a secondary effect on lighting and heating, ventilation, and air-conditioning (HVAC) system capacities and operating costs.

*Size.* As buildings increase in size, unit costs tend to decrease. This is due to more efficient perimeter ratios, better utilization of high-cost service elements (e.g., elevators, toilets, HVAC plant) and the effect of greater quantities on the contractor's purchasing power. As a rule of thumb (and, like all rules of thumb, unworkable in extreme cases), an increase or decrease in size by a given percentage is likely to lead to an increase or decrease in cost of roughly half that percentage.

*Building height.* Above six or eight stories, unit costs per square foot tend to increase due to the costs of increased loads, wind bracing, elevators, and fire code requirements. Taller buildings also become less efficient in their use of space, requiring more built area to house the same functions.

*Story height.* The greater the floor-to-floor height, the greater the cost. The vertical elements in a building may account for 25 to 35 percent of the total cost; thus a 10 percent reduction in story height might save 2.5 to 3.5 percent overall.

*Space utilization and efficiency.* To arrive at the gross building area, circulation, toilets, mechanical and electrical space, custodial, and other nonusable spaces must be added to the owner's stated net usable square feet requirements. The design task, which may be made more complicated by site or program adjacency requirements, is to minimize these nonusable areas and keep the net-to-gross floor area ratio as high as possible.

### Qualitative Factors

There is a direct correlation between qualitative factors, as stated in performance terms, and cost. The more demanding the performance requirements, the higher the cost. Some owners may have specific performance concerns or aesthetic preferences. Better quality and performance may need to be justified on a life cycle basis to optimize higher costs over a longer term.

### Construction Factors

In a marketplace with many available qualified constructors, competitively bid lump-sum contracts are generally expected to produce the best prices. Negotiated lump sums, all things considered, are often most appropriate for smaller projects, and cost-plus contracts may be useful when time or complexity of construction is a factor. Clear and complete documents reduce uncertainties (and possible contingencies) in competitive bidding.

### Time Factors

Accelerated schedules often increase construction costs because they require overtime, extra shifts, or other requirements. Construction during winter may have higher costs because of extra heating and protection requirements and the influences of bad weather. Time must be considered on a case-by-case basis. As an example, a winter start may ultimately make significant sums for a retail client if the project can be completed before the next major holiday shopping season.

*Brian Bowen, FRICS*

## Sources of Information

Architects providing construction estimates generally rely on published cost information and their own historical information.

A number of commercial sources publish cost information at three levels: area and units of accommodation; subsystems and assemblies; and individual components, products, and construction materials. The price levels in these guides represent the general market. Geographic and historical cost indexes may be used to help make the information time- and location-specific. Some guides present variations by building type, size, and general quality level. Some offer models with parameters that can be varied—within limits—to reflect the conditions the architect is facing; it may be possible, for example, to replace a masonry facade with precast concrete and calculate the resulting difference.

Construction cost guides are increasingly available in electronic form, allowing architects to enter cost information (and appropriate modifiers) into their own spreadsheets for what-if analyses and preparation of estimates.

Cost guides, of course, cannot reflect all the variations in the design or the marketplace. Intelligently used, they can help establish ballpark estimates and can assist in the choice of design features and building elements.

To supplement published cost information, many architects maintain cost data files in which their experience accumulated on completed projects is set up in a format that allows reuse on future projects. Project cost files generally include:

- Basic information (e.g., location, owner, names of consultants and contractors)
- Outline project description
- Project statistics (e.g., net and gross floor areas, number of stories above and below grade, story heights, perimeter lengths at each level, exterior closure area, foundation and roof footprint areas)
- Outline specifications and performance criteria
- Cost breakdown (e.g., in UNIFORMAT categories)
- Type and magnitude of change orders

## Computer Programs

A number of computer-based estimating programs are available. They range from simple spreadsheet versions to powerful programs linked to databases with plenty of flexibility. They may also have capabilities for interfacing with scheduling and computer-assisted design (CAD) programs. At this writing, very few programs are tailored to the architecture market, so it is wise to treat vendors' claims with caution.

## Presentation of Estimates

The method and information used in preparing estimates should be presented to the owner in a clear and concise manner. Depending on the circumstances and the architect's contractual requirements, the following information may be appropriate:

- Project title, location, and date of estimate
- Current project status (e.g., schematics, 50 percent construction documents)
- Estimate summary, with backup as appropriate
- Reconciliation of estimates with budget, previous estimates, or both
- Explanation of any variations and recommendations for action
- Estimating method used
- Assumed bidding and construction schedule
- Assumed delivery approach and procurement method
- Outline of items included and excluded from the estimate
- Assumptions about escalation and any escalation contingency included

---

### Cost Indexes

Construction cost indexes attempt to measure changes in price over a period of time and from place to place.

Like the Dow Jones or S&P 500 stock indexes, each cost index measures the cost of something specific; the *Engineering News Record Building Cost Index,* for example, is based on a hypothetical unit of construction requiring 1,088 board feet of 2-by-4 lumber, 2,500 pounds of standard structural steel shapes, 1.128 tons of Portland cement, and 68.38 hours of skilled labor.

Every index has a base, usually expressed as 100. This may be the value of the index in a given year (e.g., 1990 = 100) or at a given place (e.g., the 30-city index is 100).

Some indexes are segmented to provide additional information. For example, the R. S. Means city cost indexes are broken down by trade, revealing that while the overall city construction cost index for, say, Albany, New York, was 98.5 one year, the index for mechanical systems was 96.9 and the index for sitework 105.2.

Indexes are valuable because they facilitate comparisons. The year that Albany's index was 98.5, the index in New York City (150 miles away) was 126.6, while that in Charleston, South Carolina, was 79.8. Looking at the change in indexes from year to year provides information on inflation and other changes in the construction marketplace.

Most published construction indexes measure change in price of inputs to construction: labor, materials, equipment, and the like. Very few attempt to modify indexes for changes in productivity, technology, design, or market conditions. So take care when you use an index.

*Brian Bowen, FRICS*

- Design and construction contingencies included
- Outline specifications, and assumed performance and quality levels
- List of possible alternates or other considerations
- Comments on special conditions that might affect the accuracy of the estimate

## COST MANAGEMENT DURING CONSTRUCTION

### Cost Issues During Procurement

Even the most assiduous design cost management cannot ensure that the marketplace will respond with quotations or bids that exactly match the construction budget. Thus effective cost management builds in some flexibility at construction contract award time by incorporating an appropriate combination of allowances, alternates, and unit prices into the bidding or negotiation process.

***Allowances.*** Allowances are fixed sums determined by the owner and architect before bidding takes place, and bidders are instructed to include these sums in their bids. Allowances aim to cover the costs of items whose exact character or level of quality cannot be specified at the time of bidding and therefore cannot be accurately bid. Artwork for later selection, special hardware, ornamental lighting, kitchen cabinets, custom carpeting, and similar items may be carried as allowances if the owner or bidding authority permits. If the actual cost exceeds the allowance, the contractor is entitled to additional payment; if the cost is less, the owner receives credit.

Allowances should be priced, identified, and defined in the construction documents. It also should be clear whether allowance figures include overhead, profit, delivery, and sales taxes.

***Alternates.*** The construction documents may require the contractor to provide alternate bids. Alternates may delete work shown, require additional work, or change the level of quality specified. Alternates provide the owner with an opportunity to modify the project to ensure that construction costs fall within a fixed budget. In some cases alternates are intended to give the owner the opportunity to select specific materials or design features after the actual cost is known. Like changes in construction cost, alternates may increase or decrease the time required for construction.

While deductive alternates are occasionally appropriate, better prices will generally be obtained for additive alternates. It is good practice not to mix the two types of alternates on bid forms. Alternates require extra work by the architect, and especially by bidders, and should be used judiciously.

Decisions about which alternates to accept are usually made by the owner on the architect's recommendation. The base bid plus selected alternates is used to determine the low bid, but the selection of alternates should not be manipulated to favor one bidder over another.

***Unit prices.*** Unit prices are used to provide a cost basis for changes to the contract, usually to cover unknown conditions and variables that cannot be quantified exactly at the time of bidding. Rock removal, additional excavation, additional concrete for foundations or paving, and additional piping or wiring may be identified as units to be priced by bidders. Unit prices should be specified only when reasonably necessary and when they can be accurately described and estimated. Prices for additional quantities usually exceed credits for reduced quantities, and provision should be made for this fact in the bid form. It is good advice to review unit prices carefully before recommending contract awards.

### Cost Control During Construction

There are many opportunities to lose control of construction costs once a project is under way. Assuming the architect is engaged to provide construction contract administration services under the terms of AIA Document A201, here are some key areas to watch:

- *Schedule of values.* At the beginning of construction, the contractor submits a schedule of values that lists the various parts of the work and the quantities

This format may be useful for capturing construction cost information, as in a schedule of values, and setting up a cost data file. It is based on the 16-division MASTERFORMAT. The numbers in parentheses refernce the UNIFORMAT II.

| 1 | GENERAL REQUIREMENTS | |
|---|---|---|
| a. | Mobilization & initial expenses | (Total) |
| b. | Site overhead & fee | (Total) |

| 2 | SITEWORK | |
|---|---|---|
| a. | Building elements demolition | (G10) |
| b. | Site & building demolition | (G10) |
| c. | Building elements demolition | (F20) |
| d. | Grading & earthwork (site) | (G10) |
| e. | Excavation & backfill (foundations) | (A1010) |
| f. | Excavation & backfill (basement) | (A2010) |
| g. | Fill below grad slab | (A1030) |
| h. | Rock excavation | (A1020) |
| I. | Pile foundations & caissons | (A1020) |
| j. | Shoring | (A2010) |
| k. | Underpinning | (A1020) |
| l. | Site drainage & utilities | (G30) |
| m. | Foundation & underslab drainage | (A1030) |
| n. | Dewatering | (A1020) |
| o. | Paving, landscaping & site improvements | (G20) |
| p. | Off-site work | (G50) |
| q. | Railroad, marine work & tunnels | (G50) |

| 3 | CONCRETE | |
|---|---|---|
| a. | Conc. forms & reinf. (foundations) | (A1010) |
| b. | Conc. forms & reinf. (slab on grade) | (A1030) |
| c. | Conc. forms & reinf. (basement walls) | (A2020) |
| d. | Conc. forms & reinf. (superstructure) | (B10) |
| e. | Conc. forms & reinf. (exterior wall) | (B2010) |
| f. | Conc. forms & reinf. (site work) | (G20) |
| g. | Concrete finishes (exterior walls) | (B2010) |
| h. | Concrete finishes (interiors) | (C30) |
| I. | Concrete stairs | (C20) |
| j. | Concrete finishes (site work) | (G20) |
| k. | Precast concrete (exterior wall panels) | (B2010) |
| l. | Precast concrete (structural components) | (B10) |
| m. | Precast co crete (site work components) | (G20) |
| n. | Cementitious decks | (B10) |

| 4 | MASONRY | |
|---|---|---|
| a. | Masonry foundations | (A1010) |
| b. | Masonry basement walls | (A2020) |
| c. | Masonry exterior walls | (B2010) |
| d. | Masonry interior partitions | (C1010) |
| e. | Interior paving & finish | (C30) |
| f. | Exterior paving & masonry (site work) | (G20) |

| 5 | METALS | |
|---|---|---|
| a. | Structural steel in foundations | (A1020) |
| b. | Structural steel framing | (B10) |
| c. | Metal joists & decking | (B10) |
| d. | Metal stairs | (C20) |
| e. | Misc. & omamental metal (building) | (C1030) |
| f. | Misc. & omamental metal (site work) | (G20) |

| 6 | WOOD & PLASTICS | |
|---|---|---|
| a. | Rough carpentry (framing & decking) | (B10) |
| b. | Rough carpentry (interior wall) | (B2010) |
| c. | Rough carpentry (partitions) | (C1010) |
| d. | Rough carpentry (roof, other than framing & deciding) | (B30) |
| e. | Heavy timber & prefab. Structural wood | (B10) |
| f. | Exterior wood siding & trim | (B2010) |
| g. | Fin. carpentry, milwork & cabinet work | (C1030) |
| h. | Wood paneling | (C30) |
| I. | Wood stairs | (C20) |
| j. | Plastic fabrications | (C1030) |

| 7 | THERMAL & MOISTURE PROTECTION | |
|---|---|---|
| a. | Water & dampproofing (slab on grade) | (A1030) |
| b. | Water & dampproofing (basement walls) | (A2020) |
| c. | Water & dampproofing (exterior walls) | (B2010) |
| d. | Thermal insulation (foundation & slab) | (A1030) |
| e. | Thermal insulation (exterior walls) | (B2010) |
| f. | Thermal insulation (roof) | (B30) |
| g. | Roofing shingles & tiles | (B30) |
| h. | Shingles on exterior walls | (B2010) |
| I. | Preformed siding & panels | (B2010) |
| j. | Preformed roofing | (B30) |
| k. | Membrane roofing traffic topping | (B30) |
| l. | Sheet metal and roof accessories | (B30) |
| m. | Sealants & caulking | (B2010) |

| 8 | DOORS & WINDOWS | |
|---|---|---|
| a. | Exterior doors & frames | (B2030) |
| b. | Exterior window & curtain walls | (B2020) |
| c. | Interior doors & frames | (C1020) |
| d. | Exterior glass & glazing | (B2020) |
| e. | Interior glass & glazing | (C1010) |
| f. | Hardware & specialties (exterior) | (B2030) |
| g. | Hardware & specialties (interior) | (C1030) |

| 9 | FINISHES | |
|---|---|---|
| a. | Lath & plaster (exterior) | (B2010) |
| b. | Lath & plaster (interior) | (C30) |
| c. | Gypsum wallboard partitions | (C1010) |
| d. | Gypsum wallboard finishes | (C3010) |
| e. | Tile & terrazzo | (C30) |
| f. | Acoustical ceilings & treatment | (C3030) |
| g. | Wood flooring | (C3020) |
| h. | Resilient flooring | (C3020) |
| I. | Carpeting | (C3020) |
| j. | Exterior coatings | (B2010) |
| k. | Interior special flooring & coatings | (C3020) |
| l. | Interior painting & wall covering | (C3010) |

| 10 | SPECIALTIES | |
|---|---|---|
| a. | Chalkboards & tackboards | (C1030) |
| b | Compartments & Cubicles | (C1010) |
| c. | Signs & supergraphics | (C1030) |
| d. | Partitions | (C1010) |
| e. | Lockers | (E20) |
| f. | Toilet, bath, wardrobe accessories | (C1030) |
| g. | Sun control devices | (B2010) |
| h. | Access flooring | (C3020) |
| I. | Miscellaneous specialties | (C1030) |
| j. | Flagpoles | (G20) |

| 11 | EQUIPMENT (specify) | (E10) |
|---|---|---|

| 12 | FURNISHINGS (specify) | (E20) |
|---|---|---|

| 13 | SPECIAL CONSTRUCTION (specify) | (F10) |
|---|---|---|

| 14 | CONVEYING SYSTEMS | |
|---|---|---|
| a. | Elevators, dumbwaiters & lifts | (D10) |
| b. | Moving stairs & walks | (D10) |
| c. | Conveyors, hoists, etc. | (D10) |
| d. | Pneumatic tube systems | (D10) |

| 15 | MECHANICAL | |
|---|---|---|
| a. | Exterior mechanical (to 5ft. Of bldg.) | (G30) |
| b. | Water supply & treatment | (D20) |
| c. | Waste water disposal & treatment | (D20) |
| d. | Plumbing fixtures | (D20) |
| e. | Fire protection systems & equipment | (D40) |
| f. | Heat generation equipment | (D30) |
| g. | Refrigeration | (D30) |
| h. | HVAC piping, ductwork & terminal units | (D30) |
| I. | Controls & instrumentation | (D30) |
| j. | Insulation (plumbing) | (D20) |
| k. | Insulation (HVAC) | (D30) |
| l. | Special mechanical systems | (D2050) |

| 16 | ELECTRICAL | |
|---|---|---|
| a. | Utilities & serv. ent. To 5 ft. of bldg | (G40) |
| b. | Substations & transformers | (D5010) |
| c. | Distribution & panel boards | (D5010) |
| d. | Lighting fixtures | (D5020) |
| e. | Branch wiring & devices | (D5020) |
| f. | Special electrical systems | (D5040) |
| g. | Communications | (D5030) |
| h. | Electric heating | (D5040) |

TOTAL $

involved. This information helps the architect assess contractor payment requests and provides feedback for cost data files. It is recommended that a standard schedule of values be specified in the bidding documents that will enable translation between MasterFormat and UniFormat. The chart in Cost Breakdown Format would be a good place to start.

- *Construction progress payments.* Under AIA standard forms of general conditions, the architect reviews the contractor's requests for payment and certifies them to the owner. To ensure fair value to the owner and fair payment to the contractor, the amounts requested are checked against the schedule of values and actual progress in the field.
- *Change orders.* As changes take place, the contract sum may be increased (or, rarely, decreased). Each change order is, in effect, an opportunity to renegotiate the contract sum; thus cost control of changes is essential to effective cost management.

The use of unit prices (noted above) can help in the negotiation of fair cost adjustments, but more often than not, the basis of agreement is reached by negotiation based on estimated cost or actual time and material expended. One contentious item in change order negotiation is the markup for contractor overhead and profit. It is advisable to require bidding contractors to state on the bid form the percentages that will apply, or else to incorporate allowable markups into the specifications.

- *Claims and disputes.* Claims, too, can lead to higher construction costs. Careful administration of the construction contract, including management of conditions that might lead to disputes, is a key risk management strategy for the architect—on behalf of the project as well as the architect's practice.
- *Construction closeout.* The closeout process provides an opportunity to wrap up the project in an expeditious way. Cost control here revolves around making inspections and punch lists, handling releases of retainage, and accomplishing the final payments with attendant approvals and releases of liens.

## Postproject Review

Astute design professionals learn from their projects, gaining information and insight that helps them better plan and manage the next project. A postproject review can help the architect understand what it cost to construct a project, where the money went, and how the architect's design and project management decisions may have influenced these expenditures.

## SPECIAL ESTIMATING CHALLENGES

***Estimating renovations and alterations.*** This is a particularly challenging aspect of estimating, especially when project definition is just beginning. Renovations entail more unknowns than does new construction. Special issues will arise during renovations and will need to be accounted for with estimates. Some of these issues are:

- Availability of as-built drawings
- Condition assessment
- Impact of building codes and regulations (often upgrades not included in the program are necessary to meet code requirements in older buildings)
- Continued occupancy during alterations (complicating scheduling and staging)
- Need for unforeseen structural changes
- Extent of exterior envelope renovations and alterations
- Contractor access to space and staging areas

***Estimating international projects.*** The practice of architecture has become more global, and architects often need to estimate overseas construction costs. This adds to the challenge of estimating accurately.

Just as in the United States, construction prices vary from country to country according to competitive and economic factors. Sometimes exchange rates are distorted,

Contract Administration (17.8) discusses changes in the work, contractor payment applications, and project closeout issues.

"It ain't over till it's over."
*Yogi Berra*

and taxes and inflation may vary markedly from those prevailing in the United States. Availability of construction products and systems is different—air-conditioning might be uncommon and expensive at many locations in Europe. Drywall was not available until recently in Brazil, and at most locations the available choices are extremely limited. Yet it rarely pays to import materials. Design styles and preferences are not uniform—European factory managers prefer open areas and do not like interior columns. Building codes and regulations can be bewildering to navigate—in Germany no office can be placed further than 6.5 meters from a window, and the windows must be operable even in the presence of air-conditioning. Ultimately, construction resources and procedures will be different.

A common method of early estimating is to calculate the probable cost in the United States and then factor it to the overseas location. But this is not a good method. The owner should be asked to fund a proper market survey at the overseas location to ascertain costs and pricing levels and determine other factors likely to influence the cost of the work. Retention of a local cost consultant or contractor is advised.

## ORGANIZING FOR COST MANAGEMENT

In small practices responsibility for cost estimating and management typically falls on the principals and senior staff. Less experienced staff members often do not have the experience or feel for factors that influence construction prices or an appreciation of current and expected market conditions.

Some practices may develop sufficient volume (or sufficient depth in a specialty) to justify a cost estimator on staff. In recruiting for this role, preference is usually given to candidates with conceptual estimating abilities and all-around construction pricing experience, rather than estimators from a contractor's office who may be capable of estimating for only a few trades. Cost management personnel are most effective when they are fully integrated into the design team.

The alternative to an in-house cost estimator is an independent cost consultant. It is usually best to bring cost consultants in at an early stage so that their services can be established at the outset and included in the architect's compensation. The cost consultant can be useful at all stages and need not be relied on simply to provide a single estimate. As with all specialist firms, it is best to develop a working relationship over a period of years.

It is not unusual on construction management projects for the CM to have responsibility for estimating and control, although the architect is rarely entirely relieved of this duty. The architect must be satisfied that the CM's estimates are reasonable and that cost advice is received as expected.

However the architect arranges to manage construction costs, the challenge is to establish cost as a design discipline and to sustain that discipline from the beginning to the end of the project.

# Life Cycle Cost Analysis

*Brian Bowen, FRICS*

Life cycle cost analysis is a tool that can be used to evaluate the long-term economic merits of alternative design solutions. Sometimes different design alternatives have different effects on everyday operating costs, maintenance, energy consumption, and replacement cycles of components. To evaluate these alternatives by simply adding up all these costs—both first costs and long-term costs—is not sufficient because it ignores the effects of future inflation and the value of money, and may produce distorted results.

Life cycle cost analysis brings all of the costs being considered to their present value, allowing the architect and owner to judge the economic merits of design alternatives on an apples-to-apples basis, using comparative techniques such as net present value, payback period, or return on investment.

## Defining Design Alternatives for Study

Experienced architects focus on design alternatives when:

- Significant initial construction funds will be spent. There is no reason to do an analysis of skylights if there are only one or two small ones in the project.
- There are design choices to be made. There is no reason to do an analysis if there is only one real choice.
- The choices have significantly different in-use costs. There is no reason to do an analysis if two choices have identical in-use costs and one is initially less expensive than the other.

It should be no surprise that most of the big decisions are faced early in design, perhaps as early as the very decision to build (versus a decision to renovate or even to live with an inefficient existing facility). Studies of project scope (build now or later), flexibility (use demountable systems or simply demolish permanent construction later), and massing (long and low or high and thin) may include significant initial or continuing cost tradeoffs. As projects move into design, life cycle cost analysis usually focuses on systems and elements that will require varying costs for energy, equipment replacement, or continuing labor (of cleaning, building operation, security, and other personnel).

Because the primary beneficiary of these studies is the owner, and because life cycle cost analyses may influence the initial construction budget, sometimes it makes sense to pay more now to save more later. The owner plays an important role in establishing the alternatives for analysis and in making (or ratifying) the design decisions that result from these analyses.

## The Owner's Investment Criteria

The fundamental question is this one: Which design alternative represents the best investment for the owner? To address this question, it is essential that the owner provide some critical numbers:

- The *discount rate* that establishes the value of dollars to be spent in the future relative to dollars spent initially. The discount rate is the rate of interest, reflecting the investor's time value of money. It is usually the owner's cost of money, a minimum required rate of return, or the opportunity cost associated with using the money for this purpose. In the

analysis, the discount rate is used to convert benefits and costs occurring at different points of time to a common base (usually the present).

- The *time period* to be covered in the analysis. This is tied to the owner's occupancy, financing, and payback objectives; it may be as short as 5 years or as long as 20 to 25 years.
- Any information on *income tax* or *other economic consequences* to be considered in making design decisions.

## Costs to Be Included

To do the analysis, the architect must understand both the initial and the continuing costs of the design alternatives under examination. Typical cost categories include

- Initial capital costs
- Financing costs
- Operation and maintenance costs
- Repair and replacement costs
- Alteration and improvement costs
- Functional use costs (staff and other program operating costs)
- Salvage or enhancement of resale value

## The Analysis

Once design decisions to be analyzed have been identified, owner investment objectives and time frames set, and relevant costs estimated, the actual work of analysis is a matter of carefully and thoughtfully applying a series of financial formulas to the various alternatives under study. A life cycle cost analysis brings all of the relevant costs to a common measure—usually their present worth or present value—and compares them on an apples-to-apples basis. Computer programs and published financial tables are available to help the architect make the calculations.

## Presenting the Results

Calculating the *total net present worth cost* of each design alternative identifies the one with the lowest life cycle cost. Associated techniques allow the architect to calculate a *payback period* (the time required for the cumulative benefits from an investment to recover the investment cost and other accrued costs) or a *rate of return* on an investment (the owner's return for investing additional funds in a given design alternative).

## Interpreting the Results

It is important to remember that most of the costs included in the analysis are estimates. Moreover, many of the key parameters in the analysis (discount rates, time frames, tax rates, etc.) are assumptions. A *sensitivity analysis* can be used to test the outcome of the life cycle cost analysis by altering one or more parameters from their initial assumed values.

Because the analysis technique considers only those costs and benefits that can be measured in dollars, it is particularly important not to overlook the potential impact of noneconomic issues when analyzing the results and formulating recommendations for action.

*Brian Bowen, a principal of Hanscomb, Inc., is a recognized expert in cost management who has written and spoken worldwide on the subject to numerous professional societies and technical organizations. Bowen is a fellow of the Royal Institute of Chartered Surveyors, a certified cost engineer, and a certified value specialist.*

## Sample Life Cycle Cost Analysis

Here is an example that uses life cycle cost analysis to help determine whether to use paint or vinyl covering on partitions in an office building. Space has been rented on a twenty-year lease and a total of 20,000 square feet of partition surfaces is involved.

The analyst elects to consider the costs of initial installation, annual maintenance costs, and cyclical renewal costs for the two alternatives. The client has specified an 8 percent discount rate for the analysis (perhaps based on the cost of borrowing the money for the project) and a twenty-year time frame. Costs are expected to escalate at the rate of 4% per year.

In the analysis, all of the costs occurring in future years are converted to their present worth by using present worth factors (SPF for a single future cost, such as repainting in the fourth year, and CSPF for future costs occurring each year and escalating at the 4% rate). These factors can be found in standard investment tables as well as in books on life cycle cost analysis. In addition, serveral computer programs and hand-held calculators can be used to make the calculation.

The paint option has the lowest life cycle cost. The final decision, of course, will include other factors.

| | | | |
|---|---|---|---|
| **Design alternatives:** | A decision is required on whether to use paint or vinyl wall covering on partitions. A total of 20,000 square feet of partition surfaces is involved. | | |

| **Costs to be considered:** | **Paint** | **Vinyl Wall Covering** |
|---|---|---|
| Installation costs | $0.50/square foot | $1.40/square foot installed |
| Maintenance costs: cleaning, touch-up, and maintenance | $1,000/year | $500/year |
| Cyclical renewal costs: | $0.55/square foot every four years | $1.54/square foot every ten years |
| **Parameters:** | Discount rate: Escalation rate: Study period: 20 years Salvage value: nil | 8% 4%/year for maintenance and renewal costs |

### Analysis: Paint option

| | | | Present value |
|---|---|---|---|
| Installation cost | Base year | 20,000 sq ft x $0.50/sq ft | $ 10,000 |
| Maintenance cost | Every year | $1,000 x 13.778 (CSPF) | 13,778 |
| Cyclical renewals | Year 4 | $11,000 x .860 (SPF) | 9,460 |
| | Year 8 | $11,000 x .739 (SPF) | 8,129 |
| | Year 12 | $11,000 x .636 (SPF) | 6,996 |
| | Year 16 | $11,000 x .547 (SPF) | 6,017 |
| | | Total present value | $ 54,380 |

### Analysis: Vinyl wall covering

| | | | Present value |
|---|---|---|---|
| Installation cost | Base year | 20,000 sq ft x $1.40/sq ft | $ 28,000 |
| Maintenance cost | Every year | $500 x 13.778 (CSPF) | 6,889 |
| Cyclical renewals | Year 10 | $30,800 x .686 (SPF) | 21,129 |
| | | Total present value | $ 56,018 |

# Value-Enhanced Design

*Brian Bowen, FRICS*

Value management is a disciplined method of identifying areas for potential cost optimization, considering alternatives, analyzing them, and selecting preferred options. While terms such as "value analysis" and "value engineering" might have shades of meaning, they are considered synonymous with "value management" for the purpose of this discussion.

There is, of course, a lot of emphasis on value, and the value engineering process is helpful in defining just what this term means for the project under consideration. It helps identify where the conflicting criteria of minimum cost, maximum quality and performance, largest possible scope, and minimum time for delivery can be addressed and balanced.

All too often, however, value management is used as a blunt cost-cutting tool, and this is why it attracts the disfavor of many architects. Used sensibly, however, the approach brings considerable benefits to projects—especially when used at early design stages:

- All reasonable options and alternatives can be fairly evaluated and balanced against the client's value objectives.
- Urgent decisions are addressed up front.
- The budget and cost estimates are carefully examined and confirmed.
- Long-term life cycle cost issues and other operating considerations are addressed.

Value management in the early design stages is often delivered through the medium of a workshop coordinated by a value analyst and staffed by representatives of the owner, architect, engineers, and cost estimators. (Sometimes an independent peer group does the value management.) Workshops may be as short as a day or as long as a week. A formal value management plan can be followed:

- *Information phase.* All available information about the project is assembled and reviewed, including designs; cost estimates; operating, maintenance, and energy cost forecasts; building program; schedule; and proposed delivery strategy.
- *Function analysis phase.* The intended functions of the proposed facility are carefully analyzed and the cost of each function assigned and reviewed. Value criteria are defined.
- *Creative phase.* Ideas for alternatives that might improve value or save cost are identified through brainstorming or similar techniques. There are no judgments at this stage, just ideas.

- *Evaluation phase.* The ideas are evaluated against the value criteria, and those that have value engineering merit are carried forward.
- *Development phase.* The surviving ideas are further developed to test their feasibility. Some preliminary design analysis is done, and estimates for both initial capital cost and long-term life cycle costs are prepared.
- *Presentation phase.* The results of the workshop are summarized and presented.

At the end of the workshop, a value management report is produced and decisions made about implementation.

Approached in this way, value engineering can offer architects an opportunity to demonstrate that they produce value and to prove to owners that the best value, defined in the owner's terms and with the owner's participation, will be delivered.

Sometimes value management appears later in the project, particularly when the contractor or construction manager (CM) is brought on board. Some owners have value management programs that encourage builders to propose more economical approaches to achieving the specified performance and then to share in the savings that result. Or a construction organization might market its ability to squeeze costs out of already-designed projects as they head into construction.

Value management at this stage usually produces limited advantages for the owner. Value engineering proposals may have substantial impacts on design and may unintentionally affect other areas of building performance. Because savings in one area may increase costs in another, it is important that the architect be engaged to evaluate these proposals carefully.

*Brian Bowen, a principal of Hanscomb, Inc., is a recognized expert in cost management who has written and spoken worldwide on the subject to numerous professional societies and technical organizations. Bowen is a fellow of the Royal Institute of Chartered Surveyors, a certified cost engineer, and a certified value specialist.*

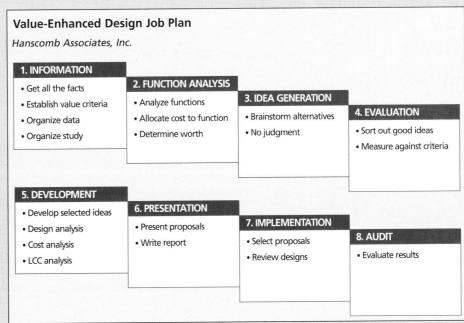

**Value-Enhanced Design Job Plan**

*Hanscomb Associates, Inc.*

**1. INFORMATION**
- Get all the facts
- Establish value criteria
- Organize data
- Organize study

**2. FUNCTION ANALYSIS**
- Analyze functions
- Allocate cost to function
- Determine worth

**3. IDEA GENERATION**
- Brainstorm alternatives
- No judgment

**4. EVALUATION**
- Sort out good ideas
- Measure against criteria

**5. DEVELOPMENT**
- Develop selected ideas
- Design analysis
- Cost analysis
- LCC analysis

**6. PRESENTATION**
- Present proposals
- Write report

**7. IMPLEMENTATION**
- Select proposals
- Review designs

**8. AUDIT**
- Evaluate results

# 14 Regulation

## 14.1 Legal Dimensions of Practice

### Joseph H. Jones, Esq., AIA

*The architectural profession functions within a matrix of laws intended to provide a level of consistency and predictability for all involved in design and construction.*

Architects are confronted on a daily basis with legal issues that pertain to many aspects of architectural practice. These issues are defined and governed by a body of laws, regulations, and judicial interpretations that establish requirements for entering the profession, forming firms, providing professional services, and operating in the business world. Unless architects have been educated in the law and admitted to the bar, they are not lawyers and cannot practice law. Nevertheless, a rudimentary understanding of a few basic legal concepts is essential to a successful architectural practice.

### LEGAL CONCEPTS

In our system of jurisprudence, law stems from several complementary but distinct sources:

> **"The powers not delegated to the United States by the Constitution, nor prohibited by it to the States, are reserved to the States respectively, or to the people."**
> *Tenth Amendment, United States Constitution*

- The Constitution of the United States and those of the states
- Statutes passed by federal, state, or local legislative bodies under their constitutional authority
- Administrative rules and regulations developed to implement these statutes
- Private legal arrangements based on contracts
- Interpretations of statutes, regulations, and contracts on a case-by-case basis by the courts and administrative agencies

Most of the legal issues involving the practice of architecture are civil rather than criminal matters. Civil laws are enacted by state and federal governments, but most civil law has evolved over the centuries. These laws work to adjudicate private rights, duties, and obligations. A lawsuit is a civil legal action brought by an individual against another individual, alleging violation of the rights of the party bringing the lawsuit. (Under the law, incidentally, an "individual" is broadly defined to include such entities as corporations and the state, as well as architecture firms.) Equity, or fairness to all involved, and damages, which involve compensation (usually monetary) for injury, are important civil law concepts.

Much of the architect's everyday exposure to the law is through administrative law—

**JOSEPH H. JONES** *is a senior risk consultant with Victor O. Schinnerer & Co., Inc., in Chevy Chase, Maryland. He was formerly assistant counsel for the AIA Contract Documents Program and has more than ten years of experience as a practicing architect. This topic is adapted from "Architects and the Law," by Ava J. Abramowitz, Esq., which appeared in the 12th edition of the* Architect's Handbook of Professional Practice.

the regulations developed to implement civil statutes. These statutes often establish only broad contours of public policy. Subsequently, public officials charged with carrying out these laws adopt regulations to address technical details.

Under their statutory authority, state registration boards, code officials, and other administrative agencies are given the power to develop, implement, and enforce regulations needed to do their jobs. Individuals and entities subject to regulation typically have opportunities to seek variances or appeal decisions through administrative channels (for example, zoning boards of appeal). When administrative avenues have been exhausted, it is possible to seek review of administrative decisions in the courts.

## THE ARCHITECT'S LEGAL RESPONSIBILITY

The law does not require perfection from an architect. As with any complicated human endeavor in which success depends on the exercise of reasoned judgment and skill, the law recognizes that perfection in architecture is a much-sought-after but rarely achieved end.

Accordingly, the law does not look to architects to guarantee, warrant, or otherwise insure the results of their efforts unless the architect agrees to do so by conduct or contract. Rather, the law grants architects the same latitude it provides lawyers, doctors, and other professionals: the freedom to exercise their judgment and skill reasonably and prudently, comfortably aware that as long as they act reasonably and prudently, the law will support their endeavors.

***The standard of reasonable care.*** Specifically, the law sets a standard of reasonable care for the performance of architects and, indeed, all professionals: The architect is required to do what a reasonably prudent architect would do in the same community and in the same time frame, given the same or similar facts and circumstances.

Although this standard can be specifically modified by contract or conduct, it establishes the law's underlying minimum expectation for the performance of professionals. The architect's legal responsibilities are examined in light of what reasonably prudent architects would have known and done at the time the services were performed.

The standard of reasonable care is the cornerstone of professional responsibility. For example, physicians are not required to guarantee a return to good health or lawyers an acquittal. Similarly, architects are not legally required, unless they contractually agree, to guarantee that a building will function perfectly or that its roof will not leak.

The professional standard of care is evolutionary in nature. For example, some jurisdictions now interpret "in the same community" to mean in the entire United States. These jurisdictions reason that communications technologies and the high degree of mobility in American society reduce the impact of regional variations. Stated another way, an architect should be aware of reasonable standards of practice nationally as well as locally. In rejecting a national standard, other jurisdictions reason that local services should mirror local needs and that only by enforcing a local standard of care can the jurisdiction ensure that its citizens' needs will be met.

Meeting this standard may not protect the architect from litigation; a suit can be brought by anyone, even a party with whom the architect has had no contractual relationship. The requirement to be reasonable, however, does provide a guidepost for the everyday practice of architecture.

***Expectations of project participants.*** Even though the law sets a standard of reasonable care for professionals, project participants often come to the table with different expectations. Many clients do not understand that architects are neither able nor required to perform perfectly. Such clients have high expectations for their projects and want their design professionals to provide guarantees.

Others in and out of the building enterprise may call for different standards of care. They may do so without understanding that architects, like lawyers and doctors, provide their clients with services, not products. They may also fail to realize that professional judgment is required at each step. Architects need to remind these participants that buildings, unlike automobiles, can't be pretested, and that no amount of effort, care, and conscientiousness on the architect's part can foresee every aspect of transforming a design on paper into reality.

***The architect's conduct.*** Even though the law requires only reasonable and prudent behavior, an architect can expand or raise the standard of care. This may be done either consciously or inadvertently. For example, the standard of care is altered by the architect's actions in the following:

- The architect agrees to contractual language "warranting" that the building will be constructed as designed or that it will perform according to the architect's design.
- The architect signs a financial institution's document "certifying" the project has met "all applicable codes and standards."
- To a client who has expressed concern about a damp basement, the architect writes an indignant letter stating, "I promise you that my basements do not and will not leak."
- The architect goes to the construction site and instructs the contractor on the means and methods of forming a complicated concrete wall.
- The architect assures the owner the construction contractors will complete their work by a specific date.

It is important to realize that raising the standard of care increases the architect's liability exposure by making the architect responsible for more than the professional standard requires. Sometimes design professionals—under pressure from clients or contractors, or propelled by their own drive for perfection—raise the standard of care that will be applied to their services without intending to do so.

Guidance provided in this handbook, as well as from the architect's legal counsel and insurance advisor, is based on the premise that it is inappropriate to raise the standard of care that will be applied to your services as a professional without first considering the consequences.

***Measuring the standard of care.*** Assuming the architect chooses to operate within the professional standard of care, the issue is not what is the standard of care, but rather what is prudent and reasonable given the facts and circumstances facing the architect in a given situation. Ultimately, what is reasonable is decided on a case-by-case basis. In a legal action involving a professional's liability, both sides present expert witnesses who testify whether the professional acted as another reasonably prudent architect would have in the same community and in the same time frame, given the same or similar facts and circumstances.

Most architects aren't sued. They must decide for themselves, before they act, what is reasonable and prudent given the circumstances facing them. As professionals, they look to themselves and to their colleagues' experiences for insights into these decisions, as well as to the rules and regulations controlling design and practice. Places to look for such information include other architects, state licensing laws, case law, codes and standards, the owner-architect agreement controlling the project, literature from AIA and other societies, insurance company publications, and the like.

## PROFESSIONAL LIABILITY

A professional who fails to meet the standard of reasonable care may be held negligent in the performance of professional duties if injury or damage results because of that failure.

***Negligence.*** For a successful negligence action against an architect, the law requires proof of four elements:

- Duty. The architect must owe a legal duty to the person making the claim; that is, there is a legal obligation to do something or to refrain from doing something.
- Breach. The architect fails to perform the duty or does something that should not have been done.
- Cause. The architect's breach of duty is the proximate cause of harm to the person making the claim.
- Damage. There must be actual harm or damage as a result of the breach.

When these elements are proven to exist, the architect may be held liable and made to pay monetary damages—or be unable to collect compensation for services rendered. It is important to note that *all four elements* must exist for a negligence claim to be successful. Sometimes an intervening event, rather than the alleged design error, is the actual cause of the damage.

Negligence actions can arise from either the architect's errors (acts of commission) or the architect's omissions (things that should have been done and were not). Examples of situations that can result in injury or damage, and hence in negligence actions, include the following:

- A building structure is inadequate for the wind loads encountered at the site.
- The architect fails to design in accordance with normally applicable statutes, ordinances, zoning regulations, or building codes.
- The architect fails to detect a readily discernible error in a contractor's application for payment or issues a change order without the owner's authorization.
- The architect follows an instruction from the owner knowing (or having reason to believe) that it will result in a code violation.

Thus an architect is responsible both for meeting contractual commitments and for performing professional services without negligence.

***Third-party actions.*** In addition to their direct contractual responsibilities, architects also can be held liable for negligent acts, errors, or omissions that physically injure or damage third parties with whom the architect has no contractual relationship. These third parties include construction workers, passersby, and occupants or users of projects.

Before 1956 the legal concept of *privity* would have barred third-party actions. Privity required the litigating parties to prove they were in a contractual relationship with each other and that the injury occurred in the course of that relationship. Since that time courts have—with regard to physical injury and in some cases property damage—extended the group of individuals to whom architects owe duties to include third parties whom architects can reasonably foresee as depending on them to provide services in a non-negligent manner.

***Statutes of limitations.*** The statute of limitations for professional liability actions isn't always clear. Moreover, the law relating to breach of contract and to negligence varies widely from jurisdiction to jurisdiction. The length of time within which a breach-of-contract action can be brought may be as short as one year. The length of time within which a negligence action can be brought may be as short as four years. Some jurisdictions, however, have no defined time limit.

The limitations period may begin at different times. In some jurisdictions the starting point is tied to completion of construction or occupancy of the project (these statutes are called *statutes of repose*). In other jurisdictions the limitations clock begins running only when the injury occurs or the defect is discovered, which may be many years after substantial completion (these are called *statutes of limitations*).

***Immunities.*** The architect is not normally liable for damages due to errors and omissions that are not deemed to be negligent in the eyes of the law. For example:

- Although the architect may feel obligated to correct a deficiency in the contract documents, the architect will not be liable for the cost of correcting the construction work itself unless there was a failure to meet the standard of reasonable care in the first place.
- Under AIA Document A201, General Conditions of the Contract for Construction, the architect administering the construction contract functions as the impartial interpreter of the contract requirements and as the judge of performance by owner and contractor. The courts have provided architects, while performing this role, a quasi-judicial immunity that protects them from professional liability for decisions made in good faith.

***An area of rapid change.*** Professional liability is a very active area of the law. Architects and other professionals therefore engage lawyers and insurance brokers to advise them in managing their professional affairs. With this advice, and with good training, experience, awareness of recent trends and developments, and plain common sense, architects can manage the inevitable risks in their practices and projects and reduce their exposure to adverse legal entanglements.

## AGENCY RELATIONSHIPS

In entering the contractual relationships necessary for professional practice, architects form several agency relationships that define their legal responsibility. As a legal concept, "agency" is the notion that a party, called a principal, may authorize another person or entity, called an agent, to act on that party's behalf. The concept permits principals to broaden their activities (and possible rewards) by having agents perform in their stead. Agency presents certain risks, especially as principals are bound by the acts of their agents as long as these agents are (or are believed to be) working within the scope of their authority as agents.

Agency relationships are common in everyday practice: An architect's employee may be acting as an agent of the architect. A corporate officer may be acting as an agent of a corporation in signing an agreement for professional services with the architect. Partners are agents and, under the law, also principals for each other. That is, partners are agents when they act for their other partners (principals) and principals when their other partners (as agents) act for them. Under an owner–architect agreement, the architect usually has an agency relationship with the owner for certain designated activities.

The central question in agency relationships is the scope of authority the agent has been granted to act on behalf of the principal. This is why architects, when acting as agents of the owner, need to know the limits of their authority in dealing with the contractor and other third parties. This is also why the firm will want every person who can be perceived as acting as the firm's agent to understand the limits of their agency authority. Staying within the limits of their authority is the best protection agents can give themselves and the principals they are serving.

**Owner–architect relationships.** Architects often act on behalf of the owners who retain them for professional services. As in all professional actions, the architect is legally required to employ reasonable care when acting in this capacity.

When AIA documents are used, the architect has a limited agency relationship with the owner during construction, in which the architect represents the owner's interests in dealing with the contractor. Under the terms of these documents, the architect also is called on to render impartial decisions affecting both the owner and the construction contractor, favoring neither party. To facilitate this, the AIA documents stipulate that the architect is not to be held liable for the results of interpretations of the contract documents or other decisions rendered in good faith—even if those interpretations go against the client.

It is also possible for architects to enter into agreements in which they are not in an agency relationship with the owner. Architect–construction managers and designer–builders who provide design and construction management services and who assume contractual responsibility for construction have moved away from a position in which they act as the owner's agent during the construction phase. In such roles, architects become more like vendors and may be subject to a commercial, rather than a professional, standard of care.

**Architect–employee relationships.** Under the agency concept, architects are responsible for the acts of their employees as well as of their partners and associates when they are acting—or are reasonably believed to be acting—within the scope of their relationships with the firm.

**Architect–consultant relationships.** Consultants who perform professional services on behalf of architects under the terms of an architect–consultant agreement are independent contractors and not agents of the architect.

While the law will hold these consultants, as professionals, to the standard of reasonable care applicable to their expertise, this does not mean the architect will be absolved from liability should something go wrong. Architects assume what the law labels vicarious liability for the actions of their consultants. Because the architect is delegating, to the consultant, duties the architect owes the owner, the architect is still responsible for the performance of those duties.

When the owner engages a consultant, the terms of engagement should be clearly stated in writing. Architects usually aren't responsible for project consultants hired directly by the owner—unless, of course, the architect agrees to this responsibility in the owner–architect agreement or acts in such a way to make the architect responsible. When the architect must coordinate or supervise consultant services for a project to succeed, the architect often retains these consultants.

**Joint ventures.** It is common for the courts to consider the parties to a joint venture to be jointly and severally responsible for the actions of the joint venture. That is, if an injury occurs because of the negligence of either party to the joint venture, the joint venture can be sued collectively or the parties to the joint venture can be sued individually. Therefore professional responsibility and liability should be carefully allocated in

If the architect's standard of care is to exercise reasonable judgment and skill such as another reasonably prudent architect would exercise facing the same or similar facts and circumstances, what is the contractor's standard of care?

Contractors generally guarantee they will perform strictly in conformance with the contract documents—even if those documents call for a building more complex than that which would be built by a reasonably competent contractor. In achieving the contracted result, the contractor must also perform the work in accordance with industry practices. The fact, however, that the contractor conforms its work to industry practices is not a defense for failing to provide what was called for by the contract documents and promised by the contractor in its agreement with the owner. Achieving that conformance is a requirement of contractor performance, and failure to do that may result in damages.

Contrast the contractor's responsibility with the professional standard of care. Architects and engineers undertake their services endeavoring to achieve a particular result, promising to use reasonable judgment and skill customary of their profession in that process. The law, however, recognizes the limitations inherent in design, and compliance with the profession's standard of care *is* an excuse for an architect's failure to achieve the desired result.

This table summarizes some of the key legal and contractual differences—in both substance and semantics—emanating from this logic and affecting architects and contractors:

| ARCHITECTS | CONTRACTORS |
|---|---|
| Act reasonably and prudently | Guarantee performance |
| Usually act as agents | Usually act as vendors |
| Legal focus is primarily on decision process | Legal focus is on results |
| Architects "endeavor to" | Contractors "will achieve" |
| Architects retain "consultants" | Contractors hire "subcontractors" |
| Architects provide "services" | Contractors do "work" |
| Performance is evaluated on standard of reasonable care | Performance is evaluated on a no-fault standard; the sole issue is conformance |

*Ava J. Abramowitz, Esq.*

contractual agreements between the parties to a joint venture. Because many states qualify how and under what circumstances professional responsibility may be shifted to another party, legal advice should be sought when preparing such agreements.

## THE LAW IN PRACTICE

Architects encounter the law in every aspect of daily practice—in conducting themselves as professionals, in operating their firms, and especially in developing, executing, and administering project agreements.

***Giving advice.*** Design professionals are constantly called upon to suggest and interpret project agreements with clients, consultants, and contractors. It is not practical or appropriate to bring every question to an attorney; many questions and interpretations involve technical rather than legal issues.

Architects may properly give technical information concerning building codes, zoning laws, and similar matters that do not require expert legal judgments. On the other hand, not every problem has a technical solution. When legal questions arise or waivers or exceptions need to be sought, clients may want to seek their own legal counsel.

Construction agreements are particularly complex in this regard. Both the architectural and legal professions are usually involved in preparing an agreement between owner and contractor. The architect typically suggests to the owner the form and content of the owner–contractor agreement and its general conditions. In this advisory role, the architect may provide the owner with sample agreement forms and other documentation. It should be clear to all involved, however, that the architect is only providing information, that the decisions are the owner's, and that these decisions should be made on the advice of the owner's legal counsel.

When legal counsel is needed on a contract or other project matter, one of the parties to the project may be tempted to seek legal advice from the other party's attorney. It is, however, unethical for lawyers to take more than one side in a controversy or represent more than one party when there are potentially opposing interests (unless all parties are so informed and give their consent). If lawyers are shared, it should be made clear at the outset that the interests of the parties may not coincide.

**Receiving counsel.** Architects have to decide for themselves when and how often to seek legal counsel. Lawyers who regularly represent architects say those who keep their lawyers up-to-date on their practices will spend less time and resources on legal expenses in the long run than those who call only when a serious problem arises and legal counsel cannot be avoided. There are, of course, times when legal counsel is essential. Access to the courts is a right under American law—and one that is frequently used today. Anyone, including architects, can sue anyone for any reason anywhere. This is merely a fact of modern living and conduct of business.

A final word: When receiving legal advice, question your lawyer until you understand what's being recommended and the reasons for that approach. This will help you understand the legal concepts involved in the situation and their effect on your practice.

### For More Information

A number of casebooks outline legal principles and provide excerpts from important or illustrative opinions handed down by our nation's appellate courts. Best-known is Justin Sweet, *Legal Aspects of Architecture, Engineering, and the Construction Process, 6th Ed.* (1999). Still other books focus on interpretations and cases associated with AIA standard forms of agreement. Examples include Werner Sabo, AIA, Esq., *A Legal Guide to AIA Documents, 4th Ed.* (1998), and Justin Sweet, *Sweet on Construction Industry Contracts: Major AIA Documents,* 2 vols., *4th Ed.* (1999). These casebooks can be instructive for architects' attorneys but are less helpful for an architect developing practice strategies.

Steven G. M. Stein, ed., *Construction Law* (1986, with thrice-yearly revisions and supplements), is the foremost treatise on the subject published in the United States. It consists of six volumes treating legal issues relating to the design and construction process. It contains the *AIA Legal Citator,* which identifies cases from all U.S. jurisdictions that interpret, are premised upon, or could assist in the interpretation of provisions of the AIA standard forms of agreement. Although written for lawyers, much of the information in this treatise and the *Citator* is accessible to design professionals.

The professional liability insurance industry offers ongoing practical guidance in understanding and managing risks and legal liabilities. For example, Victor O. Schinnerer & Company publishes the *A/E Legal Reporter* for attorneys serving architects and engineers. Call (301) 961-9800 or go to Schinnerer's Web site at www.schinnerer.com.

## Selecting Your Lawyer

When you choose to retain legal counsel, it is important to invest the time and education necessary to establish a continuing and healthy professional relationship.

Like architects, lawyers make choices in establishing their practices. Many choose general practices that offer a wide range of legal services. Others choose to specialize in particular aspects of the law, such as criminal law, negligence, labor relations, tax law, intellectual property, or antitrust law.

Most architects establish a business relationship with a lawyer in general practice who can handle a broad range of common concerns and can refer the architect to specialists when necessary. Because it may take time for a general lawyer to understand fully the technical aspects of architecture practice, a growing number of lawyers are now specializing in land use, design, and construction law. Some large architecture firms employ in-house legal counsel, as they have found it helps reduce claims and the legal fees associated with them.

Here's some advice about selecting a lawyer. We use the masculine pronouns for simplicity; in all cases, "she or he" is implied.

- Juxtapose the lawyer's specialties with your needs. If the lawyer is to review your contract documents, make sure he has a demonstrated knowledge of the industry and is familiar with construction law in your state.
- Ask the lawyer what makes architects suable. If you don't understand the answer (or you do, but he doesn't understand architects), keep looking.
- Ask a legal question. (For example: "What is negligence? How does it differ from breach of contract?") If he can't answer your question in plain English, find someone who can.
- Ask the lawyer how many architects and engineers he counsels. Ask for references, then check them out.
- Ask the lawyer what his limitations are. If he says he knows everything, find another lawyer.
- Ask the lawyer how he handles problems that arise in areas in which he has limitations. A good lawyer will tell you he will consult someone who does know that area of law. (He should also tell you that you will pay for that guidance.)
- Ask the lawyer what he expects of you, and listen for his expectations and his understanding of architecture and how he can help you.
- Talk about money. Ask him what his fees are, how he controls his costs, and how you can control his costs. If you're uncomfortable during this conversation, think twice about retaining him. If he's uncomfortable, walk out. Straight talk saves time and money.
- Trust your instincts. Even if everyone tells you the lawyer is the best, if you are uncomfortable with him, he's not the best for you.
- Remember: Lawyers have an expertise worthy of respect. So do you. Mutual respect and trust is necessary for the lawyer-architect relationship to succeed.

*Ava J. Abramowitz, Esq.*

# 14.2 Regulating Professional Practice

## Joseph Jones, Esq., AIA

*Professionals are granted certain rights by society, and in return they are obligated to meet accepted standards of professional behavior.*

A combination of laws, statutes, and codes regulate and influence the behavior of practicing architects. Some of these controls are publicly mandated, while others are voluntary. All are important, and often they act together simultaneously.

Mandated controls are included in state licensing statutes for the practice of architecture as well as in federal antitrust statutes that set rules for how businesses compete with one another. On the voluntary side, architects electing to join professional societies must subscribe to rules of conduct and ethics established and administered by those societies.

Architects can play important roles in establishing and administering some legal, professional, and ethical regulations. For example, architects often participate in professional degree program accreditation, serve on registration boards, examine candidates for registration, establish codes of ethics, and adjudicate professional misconduct cases. One of the obligations a profession accepts in striking its bargain with the larger society is that of setting and administering standards for professional behavior.

### REGISTRATION STATUTES AND REGULATIONS

In the American system of government, the authority to enact legislation protecting public health, safety, and welfare—including the authority to regulate the professions—is exercised primarily by the states and other jurisdictional authorities (specifically the District of Columbia and the U.S. territories). In our federal system, the Bill of Rights reserves to the states all powers not specifically granted by the Constitution to the federal government. Protecting the public health, safety, and welfare is one of these reserved powers. Thus the regulation of most aspects of design and construction falls to the states under the Bill of Rights.

Each jurisdiction has enacted legislation governing the registration of architects, legislation that is, in turn, implemented by a more detailed set of administrative rules and regulations. Statutes governing the registration of architects are usually broad in form and application. Typically, these laws

- Define the practice of architecture and limit it to those who are registered as architects within that jurisdiction
- Restrict the use of the title *architect* to those who are licensed as architects
- Establish, in broad terms, requirements for entry to the profession
- Empower a registration board to establish rules and regulations
- Indicate how architects registered in other jurisdictions may become registered to practice in the jurisdiction
- Define professional conduct and misconduct
- Outline penalties for those who practice architecture illegally within the jurisdiction

Registration laws may also exempt certain structures (say, farm buildings or small residential structures) from their requirements. They may give another professional group (e.g., professional engineers) the right to design buildings. They may also regulate corporate forms of architecture practice.

> **Legal Dimensions of Practice (15.1)** discusses basic legal concepts and the general requirements of laws that govern the practice of architecture.

> **Registration and conduct laws and regulations vary from jurisdiction to jurisdiction.** It is essential that architects become familiar with the requirements of each jurisdiction in which they seek to practice.

**JOSEPH H. JONES** *is a senior risk consultant with Victor O. Schinnerer & Co., Inc., in Chevy Chase, Maryland. He was formerly assistant counsel for the AIA Contract Documents Program and has more than ten years of experience as a practicing architect.*

The administrative regulations implementing a jurisdiction's registration law typically address issues such as acceptable internship activities; details of applying to take the registration examination; and specific requirements for the architect's seal, including its design, information content, and placement on drawings and other technical documents. An administrative regulation, for example, may require that the architect's signature as well as the seal be placed on each drawing. These regulations are usually developed and administered by the state registration board.

## PROFESSIONAL CONDUCT RULES

As part of their regulations governing architecture practice, the jurisdictions also promulgate rules of professional conduct. These rules deal with issues such as the use of the architect's seal, conflict of interest, disclosure of financial interests in projects, and other aspects of professional behavior.

Each jurisdiction's regulations include provisions for filing complaints, investigating the allegations made in these complaints, hearing both sides of the issue, and administering penalties for violation of the regulations. Usually anyone—a citizen, another architect, even the state itself—may file a complaint. Most violations of these regulations are handled as administrative infractions; they are investigated and adjudicated by an administrative agency that typically has the power to admonish, censure, or suspend or revoke an architect's registration to practice in the jurisdiction.

Architects in violation of a jurisdiction's rules of professional conduct may be in jeopardy on two other fronts as well. They may find themselves subject to civil suit; for example, an architect who falsely represents that a project is in full compliance with a building code may be the subject of a lawsuit alleging breach of contract, breach of warranty, or even negligence. If they are members of the AIA, architects also may find themselves in violation of the Institute's Code of Ethics. Failure to comply with applicable codes and standards, for example, is a violation of the AIA's Code of Ethics and Professional Conduct.

## AIA CODE OF ETHICS

The American Institute of Architects is the largest professional membership society of architects in the world. It and all of its members are "dedicated to the highest standards of professionalism, integrity, and competence." To assist them in meeting this goal, the AIA has established a Code of Ethics and

## Registration and Conduct Rules: Some Common Questions

Here are some commonly asked questions and some generalized answers. Every jurisdiction, however, promulgates and enforces its own rules for professional registration, conduct, and discipline. Therefore you must obtain specific answers from each jurisdiction in which you seek to practice.

Q. *What's the difference between a registered architect and a licensed architect?*

A. Registration is the act of granting the privilege to practice or offer to practice architecture. The license is a certificate or other official document indicating registration.

Q. *When can I use the title "architect"?*

A. This title is controlled by an individual jurisdiction's registration law. Generally the title "architect" or any form thereof may not be used without registration in that specific jurisdiction.

Q. *What does it mean when I stamp drawings and specifications with my architect's seal?*

A. The meaning varies among jurisdictions, but normally use of the seal indicates the architect's responsibility for the contents of the technical documents and that they have been prepared under his or her direct supervision.

Q. *Under what conditions can I stamp drawings prepared by others?*

A. An architect must exercise direct supervision of and responsibility for the preparation of the technical documents to avoid the act of "plan stamping" (stamping someone else's technical documents), which is a violation of jurisdictional laws and rules of conduct.

Q. *What is a corporate seal and when is it used?*

A. A corporate seal is an instrument reflecting how an architect's firm is organized—that it is some form of corporation. It is not a substitute for an architect's seal as required by most registration laws. Though an architect can practice in various organizational forms, including as a sole proprietorship, partnership, and general or professional corporation, an individual architect (and not the organization) is responsible for the contents of technical documents.

Q. *Does soliciting work constitute architectural practice?*

A. In most states, unregistered individuals are in violation of the law if they offer to provide services as defined in the laws regulating the practice of architecture.

Q. *Can I do a single project in a state in which I'm not licensed?*

A. Generally no, but some jurisdictions issue single-project or temporary registration—often referred to as a "fishing license."

Q. *Do the registration and conduct rules apply to me if I'm not licensed?*

A. Registration laws are written to define the practice of architecture, who is entitled to that privilege, and the penalties for violation thereof. In most jurisdictions violations of registration laws by unregistered individuals are prosecuted by the attorney general or other legal authority. Civil and criminal penalties can be invoked for unregistered practice and actions arising therefrom.

Q. *What do I do if a charge of professional misconduct is brought against me?*

A. The constitutional protections of due process establish the environment within which a charge of misconduct is adjudicated by a jurisdictional registration board. The preparation of a full response is required. Legal counsel during the preparation of the response and during all proceedings is advisable. The matter should be taken seriously because penalties could include suspension or revocation of the architect's registration, fines, censure, or admonition.

> The AIA Web site at www.aia.org contains the text for the current AIA Code of Ethics and Professional Conduct. Members and others with questions about the code, including available decisions and advisory opinions, may contact the general counsel's office at national AIA headquarters at (800) 242-3837.

Professional Conduct. This ethics code provides members with guidelines and rules for fulfilling their obligations to the public, clients and users of architecture, the profession, their professional colleagues, the building industry, and the bases of knowledge on which the practice of architecture rests.

Obligations under the AIA Code of Ethics exist in addition to those required by the rules of professional conduct promulgated by the states and other jurisdictions that regulate architecture practice. Each jurisdiction's code of professional conduct varies from the others and may vary from the AIA Code of Ethics and Professional Conduct. Architects will want to be familiar with the requirements of both types of codes.

The AIA Code of Ethics and Professional Conduct applies to all professional activities of AIA members. The code is arranged in three tiers:

- *Canons* are broad principles of conduct. The code's five canons are general statements that address professional responsibilities to the discipline, the public, the client, the profession, and professional colleagues.
- *Ethical standards* are specific goals toward which members should aspire in professional practice and conduct. For example, the first ethical standard (E.S. 3.1) under Canon III, Obligations to the Client, reads, "Members should serve their clients in a timely and competent manner."
- *Rules of conduct* implement the canons and ethical standards. The canons and ethical standards are stated in aspirational terms; the rules are mandatory and describe the floor below which a member's actions may not fall. Only a violation of a specific rule of conduct can be the basis for disciplinary action by the AIA. Continuing the example in the last paragraph, there are four rules under Ethical Standard 3.1, one of which (R. 3.103) states, "Members shall not materially alter the scope or objectives of a project without the client's consent."

The AIA's Code of Ethics and Professional Conduct covers a wide range of issues. A cursory reading of the code makes it clear that even the rules of conduct, when applied to specific practice issues, will not always result in a yes-or-no answer to the question "Is this activity ethical?" The canons, ethical standards, and rules of conduct illustrate a continuum along which each architect must measure contemplated activity. The AIA ethics code provides a framework to help the architect in that decision-making process.

## ANTITRUST CONCERNS

As with all business enterprises, architects are prohibited under federal law from combining with others to engage in activities that restrain trade or are otherwise anticompetitive. Understanding the basic principles of antitrust law is important to avoid engaging in illegal activities under these laws.

**Basic principles.** The most fundamental principle of the antitrust laws as they affect architects is that agreements or other joint conduct between two or more competitors that unreasonably restrain trade are illegal. In general, agreements among competitors risk being held unlawful if their purpose or their effect among others is to

- *Fix or maintain prices.* "Price fixing" broadly includes agreements that tend to raise, lower, or stabilize maximum or minimum prices that competitors charge for products or services or that fix other price-related terms and conditions of sale such as discounts, allowances, or credit terms. It is no defense that the prices set are reasonable or that there are socially worthy reasons why particular prices or terms should be fixed. A court can infer an agreement to fix prices from conduct even if no express agreement has been reached. Architects and firms must make independent decisions on fees for their products or services.
- *Boycott a competitor or customer.* An agreement or understanding among competing architects that they will not deal with another architect or a particular

client or category of clients is unlawful if the purpose or effect of such conduct is to limit customer choices without promoting better competition.

- *Allocate business or customers.* Architects or firms acting alone may decide to specialize their practices or to pursue any commission they choose, but an agreement among architects to divide or allocate customers or markets is unlawful. Even informal, unwritten understandings that architects will refrain from doing business with one another's clients violate the law.

**Common activities requiring review.** Certain subjects of recurring interest to architects—fees, competitive bidding, design competitions, and information surveys—nearly always have potential antitrust implications. It is therefore important for architects acting together to consider the antitrust implications of their actions in such areas.

- *Fees.* No professional organization or group of competing architects is permitted to have a mandatory fee schedule or to issue recommended fee guidelines. Setting fee schedules for competing professionals is price fixing. Subject to certain conditions, architects may collectively provide information about types of fee arrangements (e.g., stipulated sum, hourly rates, etc.). Actual fees, however, are a matter for negotiation between client and architect.
- *Competitive bidding.* The process by which a professional and his or her client agree on fees is subject to the antitrust laws. It is unlawful for architects collectively to decide not to submit price quotations for architecture services. They also may not collectively decide that bidding is unprofessional. Individual architects and firms may decide for themselves their policy toward bidding.
- *Design competitions.* For many years the AIA has made recommendations on how to conduct design competitions. The profession has much collective insight and experience on this subject that could benefit sponsors of design competitions. It is also appropriate for architects to learn how they can better decide for themselves whether to participate in a competition. However, if a group of architects encourages or organizes members to refuse to participate in a particular competition or type of competition, the group risks being challenged for sponsoring an illegal boycott.
- *Information surveys.* Professional societies often collect information from members about their practices. Collecting this information is lawful unless it is used to further a restraint of trade. Generally, surveys of competitively sensitive matters such as fees or costs should be confined to historical—not current or future—data and should be reported in an aggregated form that does not identify or permit the identification of individual contributors.

### For More Information

The definitive source for each jurisdiction's registration laws and regulations is its registration board. See Sources (Appendix A) for names and addresses of registration board in the United States and U.S. territories. For a summary of these registration laws, the AIA's government affairs group has published *Architectural Licensing Laws: Summary of Provisions* (1996). This publication summarizes key aspects of state licensing laws and regulations in a consistent format covering initial and reciprocal licensing requirements, scope of practice, exempt persons and projects, and enforcement. This publication is available from the AIA Bookstore at (800) 365-ARCH.

The National Council of Architectural Registration Boards (NCARB) manages services for interns and architects, including the Intern Development Program (IDP), the Architect Registration Examination (ARE), reciprocity issues, NCARB certification, and continuing-education initiatives. Information on these services can be obtained by writing to the NCARB at 1801 K Street, N.W., Suite 1100, Washington, DC 20006 or by calling (202) 783-6500. Services are also described on NCARB's Web site at www.ncarb.org.

# 14.3 Community Planning Controls

## Howard G. Goldberg, Esq.

*Architecture responds—and gives form—to community parameters that guide land use development to protect public welfare and conserve natural resources.*

Communities are generally very interested in land use, development, and design within their borders. They regulate planning, design, and construction in two ways:

- Incentives and controls stimulate, direct, or limit development.
- A series of regulations guides the use, layout, and design of specific properties and projects.

In terms of growth management, communities have a broad arsenal of approaches at their disposal. A comprehensive master plan often guides development by allocating land uses and locating the infrastructure to support those uses: roads, water and sewer systems, schools, and recreational facilities. Capital expenditures for infrastructure and public projects coupled with tax abatements for private projects further define growth and development. Localities may establish growth limits (perhaps capping the number of building or sewer permits) or even moratoriums on activity (usually for one to three years to allow study and development of solutions for growth problems).

As part of their constitutional ability to protect public health, safety, and welfare, states and localities regulate the development, use, and design of individual projects through a combination of the following:

- Local and regional master plans
- Zoning ordinances
- Planning and subdivision requirements
- Site plan review requirements
- Water, sewage, and waste disposal requirements
- Community fire protection requirements
- Historic district and landmark legislation
- Environmental conservation and management regulations
- Architectural and urban design review requirements
- Special environmental ordinances (for example, regulating air quality, noise, or billboards)

Regulatory vehicles vary significantly from state to state and sometimes from locality to locality—in coverage (what is regulated), approach to regulation (ranging from highly prescriptive requirements to performance standards that allow latitude in design), and the mechanisms used (one community's zoning code may regulate the size of building signage, a second may have a separate sign law, and a third may not regulate signage at all).

## ZONING

Zoning is a means of land use control exercised by governments to regulate the use and development of sites and buildings within designated districts. Its main purposes are to

HOWARD G. GOLDBERG *is a principal in the law firm of Goldberg, Pike & Besche, P.C. He is an honorary member of the American Institute of Architects and is legal counsel to the AIA Contract Documents Committee.*

▶ This topic provides general information on the use and enforcement of regulatory power. Due to the multiplicity of regulations and differing interpretations, you should obtain specific information from your state or local jurisdiction.

▶ "The history of land use law in the United States describes the working out of an uneasy and continuously evolving balance between the rights of local government to protect the public's health, safety, and general welfare and the rights of individuals to enjoyment of private property."

*Mike E. Miles et al.,* Real Estate Development: Principles and Process *(1996)*

▶ Building Codes and Regulations (14.4) expands this discussion to include building, plumbing, electrical, life safety, and other codes that directly influence the design and construction of buildings.

control the growth and development of a geographic or political subdivision in an organized manner and to mitigate the juxtaposition of incompatible land uses.

***Private controls.*** Before public regulations were used to control land use, private landowners used restrictive covenants running with the land to exclude uses and to designate height, bulk, setback, and design of buildings on the land.

Restrictive covenants are still used. While any landowner can establish a covenant, this is a common practice for owners and developers of larger-scale projects—such as residential neighborhoods and industrial research parks—where individual owners are expected to buy or lease parcels and build on them. In these cases, restrictive covenants may regulate design features such as

> ▶ **Restrictive covenants are restrictions in a deed that limit the use or prohibit certain uses of the property being conveyed.**

- The palette or "vocabulary" of materials, colors, and design features for individual buildings
- Rooflines and other massing features of buildings
- Visibility of structures and parking lots from neighboring properties and streets
- Landscaping, lighting, and signage

Some large-scale developments codify these restrictions into architectural or environmental guidelines. However these are presented, restrictive covenants included in property deeds or lease agreements have the force of law; breaking them requires judicial action.

***History of zoning.*** During the colonial period, the colonies passed ordinances that regulated the location of slaughterhouses, distilleries, and gunpowder mills. Regulations restricted building height, as exemplified by Philadelphia and Washington, D.C., and restricted the materials that could be used for building in order to guard against fires. The use of zoning to control growth began in the twentieth century; today few municipalities ignore zoning as a means of controlling development.

***Goals.*** Zoning is utilized to promote the health, safety, and general welfare of a municipality and its citizens. Specific goals often include separating industrial, commercial, and residential uses; providing safe and efficient transportation; satisfying recreational needs; promoting aesthetic values; and controlling density for safety and welfare reasons. Over time, zoning has increasingly been used to address concerns related to substandard housing, urban decay, the demands of a growing population, environmental issues, conservation of resources, and the preservation of land, wetlands, and coastal areas.

> ▶ **Like most building regulations, zoning is a power reserved to the states and not to the federal government. Most, though not all, states have passed enabling legislation that transfers the power to develop and enforce zoning to local municipalities (within rules established by the state).**

***Enactment.*** Zoning begins with the state governments, which generally pass enabling legislation granting municipalities the power to implement zoning regulations. Local officials normally adopt a zoning map, which divides their municipality into a series of districts or zones. Generally a zoning or planning commission proposes the map and recommends changes or rezoning. A board of appeals hears appeals from enforcement decisions and interpretations of the regulations by the zoning officials as well as requests for variances and special exceptions.

***Requirements.*** A zoning ordinance typically establishes, for each district or zone, requirements such as these:

- Allowable uses (it may be possible to build a residence in a commercial district but not vice versa)
- Uses permitted upon issuance of a special permit (for example, adding gasoline pumps within a commercial district)
- Allowable accessory uses, such as a professional office within a residence
- Allowable outbuildings, such as garages and other structures permitted on the site
- Minimum lot sizes and dimensions, such as a minimum amount of street frontage
- Maximum lot coverage, often expressed as a percentage of building footprint coverage
- Maximum enclosed square footage that may be built on the lot, often expressed as a floor-area ratio
- Maximum building height

- Minimum setbacks from front, rear, and side property lines, sometimes described as "yard" requirements
- Minimum open space requirements
- On-site (i.e., off-street) parking and loading facilities

These requirements create a set of possible uses for the site and a specific envelope within which building may take place on the site. Zoning ordinances may also regulate the type, size, and placement of signs. They may include other land use and design controls (such as landmark protection and architectural review requirements), or these may be incorporated into separate regulations.

*Changing zoning requirements.* Once zoning requirements have been enacted, they can be changed by three means:

- *Variances* grant property owners permission to deviate from the specific terms of the zoning ordinance if the deviations are not contrary to the public interest and if conformance to the zoning ordinance would result in "unnecessary hardship." The purpose of variances is to provide a procedure for modifying the application of a zoning ordinance that otherwise would impose undue hardship on a particular landowner. To obtain a variance, the landowner must be able to show that the ordinance creates a hardship because of the existence of special requirements.
- *Special exceptions* (sometimes called *special permits,* special uses, or conditional uses) allow specified uses in a given zone or district as long as the landowner obtains specific approval from the zoning board to apply the special exception. Special exceptions are for uses the ordinance may consider compatible with other uses in the district. These exceptions must be carefully located because of zoning considerations such as noise, traffic, and safety. For example, it may be necessary to obtain a special permit to locate gas pumps and tanks in a commercial zone. Special exceptions provide a means for zoning authorities to allow particular uses but to impose specified conditions on them. In contrast to a variance, the landowner doesn't have to show undue hardship to receive approval.
- *Amendments* can be made to zoning ordinances by the authority that passed the ordinance in the first place and for the same reason, that is, to promote the health, safety, and general welfare of the community.

Applications for appeals and special exceptions are usually made to an appointed or elected board of citizens. Hearings before a zoning board of appeals are publicly advertised; the law often requires that the owners of adjacent property be specifically notified of the time and place of hearings. Since the arguments for variances and special-use permits may have important design and technical components, architects are often involved in preparing presentations and arguing the owner's case before zoning boards.

By its nature, zoning embodies a fundamental conflict between the rights of the individual ("a man's home is his castle") and those of the community—those who feel they shouldn't suffer the injustice of neighboring land use and development that violates their own rights. Zoning disputes can become emotional and protracted.

There is no denying that zoning codes have had major impacts on cities and towns. Changes in codes (e.g., to require larger lot sizes or to provide incentives such as higher floor-area ratios in dense urban settings in return for street-level amenities such as public plazas) can have enormous impacts on the social structure, economy, and form of our communities.

## PLANNING REGULATIONS

While zoning controls land use, communities have relied on other forms of planning regulation to control a wide variety of site planning and design factors that may affect public safety, health, and welfare.

▷ The "unnecessary hardship" standard for granting zoning variances is widely applied but, as might be expected, has different interpretations.

▷ Keep in mind that as owners and developers are dealing with the public approval process, they are attempting to maintain program and scope, financing (and perhaps financial feasibility), and schedule requirements.

▷ The permitting process is, in effect, a negotiation—and it may be a protracted one.

**Subdivision regulations.** When a plot of land is subdivided into multiple parcels, these regulations come into play. They are intended to protect the public interest by ensuring that adequate infrastructure and public services are designed and built into subdivisions from the beginning. As a result, subdivision regulations often control these features:

- Street layout, including location, block sizes, arrangement, intersections, dead ends, and cul-de-sacs
- Street design, including widths, grades, curve radii, construction, curbing, sidewalks, lighting, and drainage
- Street names and building numbering
- Lots, including requirements for sizes, dimensions, configuration, and access from streets
- Requirements for schools, parks, open spaces, and preservation of natural features

Subdivision regulations are generally administered by local planning or building officials. A planning board, which may be combined with (or separate from) the zoning board, reviews subdivision requests in public meetings.

**Site plan review.** In addition to the regulation of subdivisions, many communities have enacted site plan review ordinances. These empower planning boards to review all (or perhaps all but single-family residential) site plans in detail and to approve site layout, topography, drainage, curb cuts and access to highways, open space and plantings, placement of signs and other outdoor structures, view corridors, and similar design features.

It is common for planning boards to have broad powers of review, negotiation, and approval. Like zoning boards, they hold public hearings on projects brought before them, providing neighbors and interested citizens with opportunities to be informed and to raise questions and objections. Architects can figure prominently in these meetings, helping all to understand the design intentions of the project and how it will affect its surroundings.

**Architectural design regulations.** Used extensively since World War II, architectural design regulations may be enacted separately or as part of local zoning or planning ordinances. A design review board may be established to approve the design, particularly the exterior appearance, of new structures.

**Historic preservation regulations.** These regulations protect the appearance of existing structures in historic districts or of individually designated historic buildings. Their purpose is often aesthetic, but they are also intended to preserve community identity and historic culture.

Generally, the local municipality adopts a historic preservation plan for areas of historic significance. Demolition, exterior alteration, or extensive repairs of structures in a historic district are normally not permitted without prior approval. Major changes or new construction are allowed only if the resulting building is compatible with the existing character of the historic district.

## Zoning Innovations

During the past thirty years enlightened localities have introduced a number of innovations in zoning, many of them designed to offer incentives to owners to take actions that will benefit both them and the community at large. In the Urban Land Institute's book *Real Estate Development: Principles and Process* (2000), authors Mike E. Miles, Emil E. Malizia, Marc A. Weiss, Gayle L. Berens, and Ginger Travis provide this overview of selected zoning innovations:

*Planned unit development (PUD):* an optional procedure for project design, usually applied to a fairly large site, that allows more flexible site design than ordinary zoning would allow by relaxing or waiving some requirements and substituting individual plan reviews. Frequently PUDs permit a variety of housing types and sometimes other uses; they usually include an overall general plan that is implemented through specific subdivision plans.

*Cluster zoning:* allows groups of dwellings on small lots on one part of the site to preserve open space and/or natural features on the remainder of the site. Minimum lot and yard sizes are reduced. Like PUDs, site designs are subjected to more detailed reviews.

*Overlay zoning:* a zoning district, applied over one or more districts; may contain provisions for special features or conditions, such as historic buildings, wetlands, steep slopes, and downtown residential uses.

*Floating zones:* zoning districts and provisions for which locations are not identified until enacted for a specific project. Used to anticipate certain uses, such as regional shopping centers, for which locations will not be designated on the zoning map until developers apply for zoning. Usually requires special review procedures.

*Incentive zoning:* zoning provisions that encourage but do not require developers to provide certain amenities or qualities in their projects in return for identified benefits, such as an increase in density or rapid processing of applications. Often used in downtown areas to gain open space, special building features, or public art.

*Flexible zoning:* zoning regulations that establish performance standards and other criteria for determining appropriate uses and requirements for site design rather than prescribing specific uses and building standards. Rarely applied to all zoning districts but often used for selective locations or types of uses (e.g., PUDs).

*Inclusionary zoning:* zoning regulations that require or encourage construction of lower-income housing as a condition of project approval. May provide density or other bonuses in return for commitments to such housing. May require housing on-site or allow location at another site.

*Transferable (or transfer of) development rights (TDRs):* a procedure that permits owners of property restricted from development to recoup some lost value by selling development rights to developers for transfer to another location where increased densities are allowed. Often used to preserve buildings of historic or architectural importance and sometimes used to preserve open space or farmland.

***Other local controls.*** As neighborhoods and communities have become more concerned about the quality of life—and the role of growth and development in sustaining or diminishing that quality—they have enacted additional land use and development controls. These may include regulations affecting the following:

- Special districts, e.g., airports, areas of natural beauty or environmental fragility, floodplains, and the like
- Specific occupancies, especially those involving education, day care, health care, manufacturing, and places of public assembly (sometimes these requirements are incorporated into licensing or taxation regulations)
- Special ordinances for sidewalks, barricades, canopies, signs, billboards, trailer parks, marquees, swimming pools, and a wide variety of physical features

It is important for the architect to understand that these regulations are all overlaid on the project. It is a rare community that has codified them into a single ordinance with a single application, review, approval, and appeals structure.

## ENVIRONMENTAL REGULATIONS

Environmental law is one of the most rapidly expanding areas of law today, and it influences all aspects of our working and personal lives. The most obvious goal behind environmental regulation is protection of land, water, air, and life. Additional objectives include the attainment of efficiency in our systems, national security, preservation of aesthetics and recreation, community stability, sustainability (maintenance of the environment into the future), and intergenerational equity (preservation of the environment for future generations).

The federal government has pursued its environmental objectives through the creation of extensive legislation, including the Clean Air Act; the Noise Control Act; the Solid Waste Disposal Act; the National Environmental Policy Act; the Comprehensive Environmental Response, Compensation, and Liability Act (CERCLA, or "Superfund"); the Resource Conservation and Recovery Act; and the Toxic Substance Control Act. Many states and localities have also passed legislation in these areas.

The list of regulations is seemingly endless. Consequently, environmental regulation is now a fact of life for the construction industry and plays an extensive role throughout the construction process, including design. Environmental regulation is changing so rapidly that it is impossible to provide an in-depth analysis of the subject; however, there are certain broad issues on which the architect may focus.

***Site.*** Site selection and the design of new and renovated structures must take into account zoning and environmental regulations. Many zoning ordinances are for the protection of the environment. For example, open-space zoning is used to protect the environment as well as to control growth. Ordinances aimed at aesthetic appearance and historic sites may also protect the environment. Finally, construction entities are bound by zoning and other regulations that preserve wetlands, coastal zones, specially protected areas, and other natural habitats.

It is important to be aware of any environmental problems at the site and to protect the environment during construction. Owner and architect might consider reviewing any environmental audits or investigations of the area—especially if the site was used for commercial or industrial purpose—and to check the CERCLA list to see if the site is contaminated or within one mile of a contaminated site. Before construction, it is prudent to check for underground storage tanks, spills of petroleum or hazardous substances, and radon. Throughout construction, care must be exercised in removing trash from the site.

***Water.*** Clean water regulations influence methods of construction as well as the use of the final structure. The Clean Water Act contains storm water management requirements that are particularly applicable to construction. There are also regulations regarding sediment control and water and sewer requirements. If the new structure is to have an on-site water and sewer system, it must adhere to discharge requirements. For example, if the structure is industrial, such as a dry cleaner, a pretreatment system must be designed to prevent volatile organic compounds from entering the groundwater.

▶ **Site Analysis (16.2) discusses how the concept of "services" encompasses activities that address regulatory controls in the context of site selection, programming, and design.**

▶ **Architects are sometimes asked to provide certification to the owner that the site is clean. Such a certification may be beyond the architect's capability.**

## The Importance of the Regulatory Environment

While our system of law establishes the basic framework within which an architect lives and practices, the reality is that many of our everyday actions are governed by the regulatory environment.

Regulations are developed and promulgated as part of what is called administrative law. The idea is that individual statutes, however well conceived by the legislative bodies that pass them, cannot possibly include all of the technical and procedural provisions necessary to implement and enforce them. Thus under the concept of administrative law the executive branches of federal, state, and local governments draft and promulgate regulations that apply laws to everyday situations.

Consider, for example, building codes. A state legislature may decide it is time to adopt a uniform statewide building code. It passes a law mandating such a code and requires that the executive branch write it. In drafting the code, a department of the executive branch (which in this case may be a state building code commission) follows the specific directives included in the law, as well as any legislative intent expressed in the law or in the hearings and proceedings leading to its passage. The resulting building code is very specific and very detailed in its technical provisions. It also includes all of the details needed to enforce it. Once promulgated as a regulation, it has the force of law.

Because they address complex subjects, most regulations include ways for users to seek variances, exceptions, or other forms of dispensation from their provisions. Again using a building code as an example, architects may find that the code does not cover their specific situation or, alternatively, that they have a better way to fulfill the intent of the code. Most codes anticipate this by setting up a variance procedure, with decisions on variances made by individuals or panels of people who represent the community and who often have some technical expertise in design and building. This administrative relief from the provisions of regulations is generally easy to access; decisions should be made in a matter of days or weeks rather than months or years. Once a user has exhausted all administrative avenues, judicial relief (going into the courts) is still possible but rarely successful, as courts generally give great deference to administrative agencies, which have developed significant expertise in their realm of regulation.

*Ava J. Abramowitz, Esq*

**Air.** Clean air regulations apply to the inside and outside of buildings. Increasingly, regulations are looking to heating, ventilating, and air-conditioning systems that are energy-efficient, are environmentally sound, and supply sufficient oxygen to all areas of a building. Legislation restricts the ozone-layer-damaging chlorofluorocarbons (CFCs) emitted into the air by air-conditioning systems. Finally, emissions from exhaust systems and stacks must conform to the air regulations.

**Materials.** Various materials are the subject of environmental regulation, and consideration should be given to these in the design of new and renovated buildings. Noxious building materials, including some types of urea formaldehyde foam insulation, may not be used. In renovation projects, designers should be aware of asbestos and industrial chemicals such as polychlorinated biphenyls (PCBs). Another material subject to extensive regulation is lead paint.

> The AIA documents (e.g., B141 paragraph 9.8 and A201 subparagraph 10.1.4) eliminate any liability on the architect's part for damages related to asbestos and PCBs. Lead paint, however, is not addressed.

New as well as recycled materials considered to be environmentally sound are being used on construction projects. Gypsum board can be ground and used as spray insulation, and some glass can be recycled and used in windows. Some masonry, metal, and aluminum can be reused. Not only is such reuse environmentally sound, but it can be economically beneficial as well.

**"Green consciousness."** Clients have become more environmentally attuned and are demanding that buildings not adversely affect the environment. To accommodate this awareness—and sometimes to stimulate it in the first place—architects are developing sustainable or "green" architecture, which is friendly to the environment and focused on preserving it.

The design of many new buildings focuses on energy efficiency. Designs capitalize on the use of natural light. Lights within the building may have sensors so they turn off when people leave the room. Faucets in bathrooms may turn off automatically to conserve water. More-efficient cooling systems are being designed.

Construction entities that don't conduct business in an environmentally sound fashion not only risk losing business but also face substantial fines for violations of environmental regulations. The environmental statutes provide for substantial civil penalties. In some instances, fines are assessed against several entities on a project in which regulations are violated, regardless of whether the entity is liable. Consequently, it is imperative that design and construction firms stay abreast of constantly changing and evolving environmental law.

> Sustainable Building Design (17.11) services describes the environmental aspects and process elements in building design.

# IMPLICATIONS FOR PRACTICE

The growing importance of community planning and environmental regulation offers architects two practice opportunities: providing professional services in support of the permitting process and participating in the process of creating neighborhood and community design regulations.

***Services during the permitting process.*** As communities become more assertive in planning and controlling development and design, the process of gaining the necessary approvals to build—often called permitting because of the multiple permits involved—has become much more complex.

Owners and developers find they must initiate and define their projects in partnership with multiple public agencies. Increasingly, this partnership includes the public, as represented by neighborhood associations, advocacy groups, and other organizations interested in development in general or a specific issue (perhaps the environment, or schools, or "good government"). If the project is large or captures attention in other ways, ad hoc groups may organize to stop or at least redesign it. The media, of course, are happy to join the fray.

For architects, there are opportunities for involvement in the project definition process:

- Architects may help the owner design the most appropriate path through the permitting process. This path should advance the project and avoid regulatory cul-de-sacs (where Board A refuses to review the project until Board B approves it).
- Architects may offer services to support the permitting process, including site selection and analysis, environmental studies and reports, site development studies, on- and off-site utility studies, and zoning and planning processing assistance.
- Architects may provide site planning and conceptual design services. Design is often necessary to address the questions and concerns raised by the community and its regulatory boards and commissions. In some cases (e.g., landmark conservation), the design may need to be well advanced before approvals are forthcoming.
- Architects may help the community analyze and understand the implications of proposed projects, sometimes guiding all involved to a consensus solution.

Involvement in the project definition process may be long and tortuous, with many twists and turns and multiple submissions. One set of approvals may be gained only to find the project must be redesigned to meet the needs of a subsequent set of approvals. Some projects become "footballs" as special interests are played out through the permitting process.

Architects who choose this involvement find it is in their best interest to remain current with local regulations and procedures and to maintain close working relationships with agency officials and staff. These architects also find they become proficient in negotiating design issues and parameters in public—especially in the crucible of public hearings and meetings. A hearing is a dynamic environment, one often punctuated by proposals and counterproposals—and even a little old-fashioned bargaining—as the public authority attempts to reconcile the needs and rights of project owners with those of the community at large. Rarely is there the luxury of taking the project back to the office for study as the hearing produces possible changes in concept or design. In this environment, the architect needs to know the project well, be able to assess proposed modifications, and provide the owner with these assessments quickly.

Because neither the owner nor the architect can control the permitting process and its outcomes, most architects offer services during this period on an hourly basis.

***Designing the design controls.*** As pervasive as they have become, it is worth remembering that zoning, planning, and other community design controls serve a common purpose. They are meant to protect the welfare of all by ensuring that the public is provided with such communal goods as access to light and air (the traditional legal basis for zoning); protection from nuisances caused by odors, sounds, and, perhaps, inappropriate design; and the opportunity to achieve goals such as environmental conservation or protection of architectural heritage. These purposes have been established, and continue to evolve, through a long line of court cases and judicial decisions.

There are, of course, many ways to achieve these purposes. In the last 30 years some architects have chosen to participate in developing appropriate community design controls by working in municipal urban design offices or as part of the planning and design of large-scale projects and communities. New York City, for example, has a history of zoning innovations developed by architects and planners. More recently, planned communities such as Seaside, Florida, are exercises both in sensitive architectural design and in the design of master plans and design controls intended to achieve community goals while encouraging individual owners to develop their own properties.

### For More Information

Many real estate and land development texts provide a good general description of the approaches that communities take to both stimulate and regulate land use and development. The American Planning Association is a source for a variety of publications and research reports on zoning, land use law, and growth management issues. Call (312) 431-9100 or (202) 872-0611or visit www.planning.org.

Integrating ecology and environmental considerations into community planning is a major issue today. This subject in the context of the real estate development process is addressed by Alex Wilson et al. in *Green Development: Integrating Ecology and Real Estate* (1998). Chapter 7 of the book covers the challenges, strategies, and approval processes from the perspective of executing "green" development solutions.

## Approaching a Community Board

Probably the best advice is this: Do your homework. Here are some guidelines to flesh out this simple maxim:

- Understand what it takes to get on the agenda of a zoning hearing, planning board meeting, or other hearing. What applications need to be made? What information is required? Does the owner's request need to be denied before the owner or the owner's representative can appear in person? How much time is required to file an appeal from a negative decision? How long does it take to get on the agenda?

- Sit down with the public official enforcing the regulations or the secretary of the board and learn the process. Get the technical answers (such as to the questions above) as well as an indication of how the board likes to be approached.

- Find out who is on the board, what they do when they are not providing this public service, and whether there are specific personal agendas on the table. Most regulatory boards are appointed citizen boards, intended to represent the community's interests as well as the law. Find out what those interests are.

- Attend a meeting before the one at which you are scheduled to appear. Observe how the board works, how formal or informal the proceedings are, and the types of issues and questions that seem to be of most concern. While boards operate within a carefully defined regulatory framework, they have considerable latitude in how they approach their responsibilities.

- In constructing the case to be made, work with the owner to review the applicable law (for example, the conditions under which a zoning board can vote a special-use permit). Address these points.

- Consider who besides the board will be in the room. By law, hearings and commission meetings are usually open. Public notice is given in the local newspaper, and frequently the law requires that adjacent landowners be notified. Who will come and what will be on their minds? Will the media be interested? It's one thing to present to a five-person zoning board and another to speak to a roomful of angry neighbors.

- For controversial projects, suggest that the owner consider community informational meetings before the hearing is held. In addition to providing information and explanation, these meetings can bring concerns to the surface—concerns the owner may want to address before taking the project to the hearing where a decision will be made.

- Arrive at the hearing on time (yes, they often run late), bring the necessary materials, and make sure that you, the owner, and anyone else involved in the presentation (perhaps the owner's lawyer) understand what roles you each will play.

- Keep your presentation short and professional. Make sure visuals are legible. When discussion begins, listen carefully to what's being said and address concerns as directly as possible. This is no place to go into an offended-artist act.

- Be sure the owner knows, going in, what to fight for and what to give up in negotiation. Don't attempt a contrary position during the discussion without first huddling with the owner. Remember, this is the owner's project, not yours.

*David Haviland, Hon. AIA*

# 14.4 Building Codes and Regulations

## Marvin J. Cantor, FAIA

*Governments at all levels establish and enforce building codes and regulations to protect the public welfare.*

Building codes and regulations create important disciplines for design. It is imperative that architects design in compliance with building codes and regulations unless they obtain variances or specific rulings allowing alternative solutions. Violation of building codes and regulations can cause injury to building users and expose architects to legal liability and the possible revocation of their licenses.

### BUILDING CODES

The primary regulatory instrument for the design of buildings and structures is the building code. Historically, communities developed building regulations to address specific needs. As long ago as 1700 b.c., the Code of Hammurabi dictated that builders responsible for a structural collapse that resulted in loss of life would lose their own lives. As cities grew and became denser, concerned citizens would gather after a fire and ban the use of straw as a roofing material or require spaces between buildings.

> **Like planning and zoning controls, building codes and regulations are developed and promulgated by governments as part of what is called administrative law.**

At the turn of the century, and in response to major urban fires in the United States (most dramatically the Chicago fire of 1871), the insurance industry developed what many consider to be the modern building code. The National Board of Fire Underwriters published its National Building Code in 1905 as a model code, that is, one that could be adopted (with or without modification) by a locality.

The modern building code is a complex document, protecting building occupants, firefighters and other emergency personnel, the building itself, and the community from fire, structural collapse, and a wide range of health and safety hazards.

***Model codes.*** Given the thousands of American municipalities, the idea of model codes developed and published by code officials and experts in design and construction has become fundamental to building regulation in the United States. During the first half of the twentieth century, three major regional model code organizations evolved:

- Building Officials and Code Administrators International (BOCA), publishers of the BOCA National Building Code
- International Conference of Building Officials (ICBO), publishers of the Uniform Building Code
- Southern Building Code Congress International (sbcci), publishers of the Standard Building Code

Each model code group has a regional orientation, with ICBO serving the western states, the BOCA serving many north-central and northeastern states, and SCBBI serving the South.

The most recent activity in U.S. building code development is a merging of the three major model building codes into a single code, the International Building Code. The new, single code supplants the three model codes, becoming the prime building code regulation for the United States.

---

**Marvin Cantor** *has more than forty years of experience in architecture practice within the Washington, D.C. metropolitan area. He has worked with the Building Codes and Standards PIA for over 15 years and served as chair of the 1991 AIA Building Performance and Regulations Steering Committee. Cantor currently serves on the Virginia building code board of appeals.*

*This topic is adapted from "Building Codes and Regulations," by Henry J. Lawrence Jr., Esq., which appeared in the 12th edition of the* Architect's Handbook of Professional Practice.

# The Model Code Organizations

*Purposes.* The purpose of the model code organizations is to produce model building codes that contain the requirements necessary to protect public health, safety, and welfare. The codes are continuously developed through a consensus process involving members of the building community. Model codes become law only after they are adopted by a state or local government.

*Membership.* Membership in model code organizations is composed primarily of building officials and inspectors from local government building departments. Traditionally, the right to vote on code-change proposals is granted only to code-administering officials, based on their jurisdictions' population.

*Amending codes.* The code organization annually amends its code through a series of public hearings. New editions of the codes are published on three-year cycles, with annual supplements. All members and the public are encouraged to submit proposed changes and to testify at public hearings when code changes are considered. Some architects are employed by government units as building officials. Other architects submit code-change proposals and serve on committees in model code organizations.

*A unified effort.* The model code organizations, which have all published codes during most of the twentieth century, are now in the process of unifying activities by distributing the International Building Code. Since they approved the international code in 1999, the model code organizations remain active in their respective geographic locales. They distribute the new, single model code, conduct training and education seminars relating to code administration and enforcement, issue publications that complement and assist in the use of the International Building Code, and hold conventions of their members.

Initiation of the single U.S. model code can be effectively traced to a 1990 symposium sponsored by the American Institute of Architects Building Performance and Review Committee in New Orleans. There the question was raised as to whether the time had come for a single building code. The AIA membership felt it had. Code administrators, architects, engineers, public officials, and interested citizens took part in the sessions. Past efforts at raising this issue were revisited, analyzed, and reexamined for their timeliness.

Following this groundbreaking session, the model code groups reviewed the arguments for a single code. Meanwhile, the AIA diplomatically endorsed a concept called the "common code format," intended to make it easier for designers to work in multiple jurisdictions. The code groups agreed, and in the next issues of the model codes appeared with a certain level of uniformity among them.

At that point, each of the model codes had the same number of chapters, each chapter dealt with the same issue (such as egress, fire protection, etc.), and all codes had the chapters listed in a sequence designed to follow the normal course of a design project as it moves through the typical designer's office.

The next steps followed in quick and logical fashion, as subcommittees were formed to study each chapter and reconcile the three codes' treatments of these chapters into a single delineation of the topic. Due to its complexity, the Building Code required the most study. The less complex Mechanical and Plumbing Codes were examined and more quickly formatted into the International Mechanical Code and the International Plumbing Code. The three model code groups quickly approved these documents and stipulated that in the future they would accept compliance with the new international codes as being equivalent to active editions of the model codes' mechanical or plumbing requirements.

The code groups then ceased to publish their own mechanical or plumbing codes. A court action was brought by a private proprietary code group but was dismissed by the court, making use of the international codes an accomplished fact. The Building Code Subcommittees issued the first working draft of the proposed International Building Code in 1997, and following the requisite public hearings, code proposals, revisions, and comments, a draft edition and then a final edition were published. The proposed code in its final format was published in early 1999 for review and was finally approved by the three code groups in the same year.

During development of the international family of codes, the Council of American Building Officials (CABO), which previously worked closely with the three code groups to publish the One- and Two-Family Dwelling Code, was officially dissolved. The new International Code Council (ICC) was formed to work with the three model code groups to produce the International Residential Code for one- and two-family dwellings. The ICC will administer changes to the code process, as some of this work was previously handled by CABO.

In addition to the building, plumbing, and mechanical codes mentioned above, the international family of codes includes the International Private Sewage Disposal Code, the International Fire Code, and the International Property Maintenance Code. Complementing all of this will be a new organization, the National Evaluation Service (NES), which will review new and innovative materials and processes and certify their compliance with the new international codes. This service will provide oversight currently provided by the model code groups. Combining their activities into one organization simplifies the process of getting new materials and methods of construction into the marketplace by providers, and makes it quicker for all concerned.

*David C. Bullen, AIA*

***Adoption.*** Most building codes are adopted and enforced at the local level. Because local jurisdictions are authorized to adopt and enforce building regulations, building codes vary among states and even among cities within the same state. There are an estimated 13,000 building codes in the United States.

Assuming one of their reserved powers, states have generally taken one of three approaches to building codes:

- They enact and require a uniform statewide code.
- They enact a state model code, allowing municipalities to adopt it.
- They delegate the power to enact a building code to the municipality.

Thirty-five states now mandate the use of a statewide code, and most states use one or more of the three model building codes. These three codes will be superseded by the International Building Code.

Where states provide a model code and allow municipal adoption a state code may be a minimum or a maximum code. If the state mandates a minimum code, then local jurisdictions must accept that code as the minimum requirement and may adopt more stringent or additional provisions at their discretion. If a state adopts a maximum code, then local jurisdictions cannot adopt more stringent code provisions.

Localities with the power to adopt building codes may, depending on state statutory requirements, have several options:

- *Adopt a model code.* Most jurisdictions amend the code before adopting it. Sometimes modifications can be found only in the adopting ordinances—not in the code itself. Localities may adopt the latest edition (which means that local requirements change as the model codes are modified each year), or they may adopt a specific edition (which sometimes places the municipality several years behind the current edition of a model code).
- *Develop their own codes.* Jurisdictions with the resources and a strong belief that local conditions require locally developed requirements may take this path. New York City has its own building code (it is one of the nation's oldest), as does the state of New York (which did not adopt a mandatory statewide building code until 1984).
- *Do not adopt a code at all.* There are jurisdictions with no building codes. These are predominantly isolated small municipalities.

In addition to the model building code, a number of other model codes are available for local adoption. Many of these are promulgated by the three major model code organizations, but others have been developed by groups such as the National Fire Protection Association (NFPA) and the International Association of Plumbing and Mechanical Officials (IAPMO).

Once adopted by an enforcing jurisdiction, a building code becomes a document that holds the force of law.

***Coverage.*** Building codes regulate building construction through concepts such as:

- Specific design and construction requirements, based on occupancy, building height, floor area, availability of firefighting capacity, and other factors
- Required fire resistance of structural elements, floors, ceilings, and fire and party walls
- Restrictions on building height
- Requirements for compartmentation (fire areas)
- Fire protection systems
- Flame-spread ratings for finishes
- Egress requirements, such as stairs, corridors, and doors
- Access and egress requirements for disabled persons
- Light, ventilation, and other indoor environment requirements
- Requirements for energy conservation
- Structural requirements for building components
- Materials performance and specifications
- Requirements for building services systems

▶ **Recall that building regulation is a power reserved to the state, not being assigned to the federal government by the U.S. Constitution. Some states write statewide building codes; others have passed enabling legislation that transfers the power to develop and enforce building codes to local municipalities (within rules established by the state).**

▶ **Because of varying adoption patterns, architects have to determine which edition of the model code is being used and whether there are additional building requirements that do not appear in the model code.**

The map represents the spheres of influence of the various model codes prior to 2001. As international codes are adopted, the patterns of influence may change.

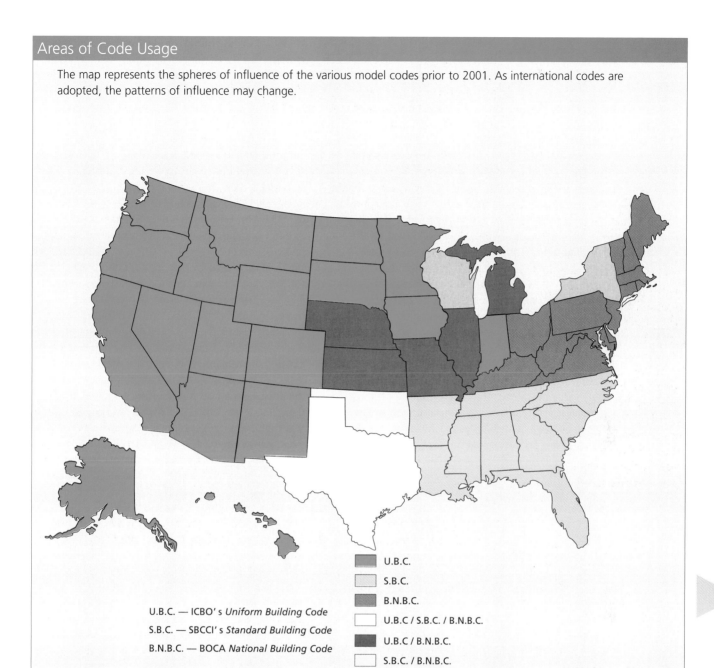

U.B.C.
S.B.C.
B.N.B.C.
U.B.C / S.B.C. / B.N.B.C.
U.B.C / B.N.B.C.
S.B.C. / B.N.B.C.
State-written

U.B.C. — ICBO' s *Uniform Building Code*

S.B.C. — SBCCI' s *Standard Building Code*

B.N.B.C. — BOCA *National Building Code*

Since most local building codes are based, at least in part, on a model code, there are many similarities in overall coverage. Often, however, localities add provisions considered to be unique to local building. In addition, other, more specialized codes govern certain facility types (for example, restaurants and health care facilities) or building products (such as boilers and elevators). Provisions for accessibility for persons with disabilities are incorporated into the building codes, and separate federal regulations exist in response to the Americans with Disabilities Act of 1990.

***Approaches.*** Code provisions may be written in one of two ways: as prescriptive requirements dictating the specific methods and materials that must be used in the building, such as a requirement that 2-by-4 wood studs be located at a minimum of 16 inches on center within a partition or wall, or as performance requirements stating the desired results, such as a wall that will withstand a certain amount of wind load.

Performance requirements are preferred by most architects because they allow some flexibility in meeting the project's overall requirements. For example, either masonry or concrete may be used in a wall as long as the wall is designed to meet the specified load requirements.

▶ **The backgrounder Working with a Building Code (14.4) provides a step-by-step example for using a building code in building design.**

## Building Codes and Regulations: Some Precepts

Here are some key points about building codes and regulations that architects will want to keep in mind:

- A building code is an organized, systematic presentation of a body of law that pertains to all facets of building construction. A building code is a legal document. Building officials are required to enforce it. Participation in the code and regulation process is not optional on the part of any party to the construction project.
- Every project, whether public or private, has an effect on the public and is therefore of concern to the building official.
- Code requirements are based on nationally accepted safety, materials, and testing standards. Necessary building standards are primarily designed to protect a building's occupants.
- Professional registration laws require that design professionals practice in a fully lawful manner, that is, meeting all pertinent laws—including building codes and regulations—involved with their projects and practices. Design professionals must know the codes and apply them appropriately.
- The best interests of the project, the owner, and the design professional are served by the proper and early incorporation of codes and code administration into the various project processes.
- Code administration is an intrinsic part of every owner-architect contract for services regarding a construction project. To meet these contractual obligations, code administration is a continual process from the inception of the owner-architect contract to the final completion of the project.
- The codes and their administration are joint activities of the building officials and the design professionals. Building officials enforce the building code and are not responsible for the design of the building.

*AIA Building Performance and Regulation Committee,*
**An Architect's Guide to Building Codes and Standards** *(1991)*

Building officials frequently prefer more prescriptive codes because they are easier to administer and enforce. Enforcing a prescriptive code by evaluating the material of a wall is easier than enforcing a performance code by evaluating the load-bearing ability of the wall.

***Standards.*** Building codes commonly include a broad range of industry-developed standards by reference. Standards allow private participation in the code-making process and provide consistent approaches to products and processes. One standard (ASTM E 119) ensures that every participant in the industry understands what a two-hour fire-resistance rating is; another (ANSI A 117.1) provides a consensus standard for access for persons with disabilities; a third (ASTM C 94) sets standards for ready-mixed concrete.

***Enforcement.*** Building codes are most commonly enforced at the local level. The central agency is usually a building department that reviews drawings, issues building permits, periodically inspects the project for conformance, and maintains public records.

*Jurisdiction.* A single project may be under the jurisdiction of several agencies. A local health department may enforce its own sanitation regulations. Water and sewer departments often regulate types, sizes, and locations of lines and meters. Street departments may have regulations affecting access drives, loading areas, and turning lanes. Forestry and parks departments may regulate the removal of trees or the use of plantings along roads and walks.

Many times problems arise because of simultaneous and independent enforcement of building and fire codes. The building official is usually responsible for permit enforcement until construction of a new building is complete. Once the building is occupied, the fire marshal assumes authority for continued safety. Sometimes the two codes, and enforcing officials, do not agree on requirements and procedures.

Fire officials may become involved during construction, interpreting the fire code to require changes in the work.

To compensate for confusion caused by jurisdictional overlaps, the most conservative advice is to design according to the most restrictive requirement or to document any permit deviations. Depending on the circumstances, it usually makes sense to keep both fire and building officials informed of a project's progress so that there is a clear understanding of their concerns and roles. Sometimes a single review session with all the applicable code officials allows all concerned parties to communicate more fully and resolve potential conflicts at the earliest possible point in the design process.

*Multiple permits.* A project may require several permits as it proceeds. The building department may issue a building permit (to begin construction), a variety of other permits (to close in a structure or to begin using plumbing or electricity), and finally a certificate of occupancy (before the building may be occupied).

*Variances and appeals.* Recognizing they cannot anticipate all possibilities, most building regulations provide opportunities for seeking relief from requirements through variances, exceptions, and other mechanisms.

These appeals are typically handled as administrative, not judicial, processes. An owner seeking a variance presents a case for an exception to a community board of appeals that may include experts in construction among

**To provide two variance examples, shopping malls and atriums probably would not have been initiated if owners and architects had not had the opportunity to argue, through the code variance process, that these projects were as safe as conventional code-regulated buildings.**

its members. The responsibility falls on the appellant to justify the exception or to document that a proposed alternate solution is at least equal to the existing code requirements. Before making the appeal, owners may want to consider how the appeal process may affect the project schedule.

Once an exception or variance has been granted, it is important to understand that it applies only to the situation at hand; it does not create a precedent for subsequent projects. The experienced architect carefully documents any exceptions, substitutions, or variances gained for the project. (After all, on the face of it, the project now appears to be in violation of the building code or regulation.)

*Judicial relief.* Whether dealing with a local, state, or federal regulation, administrative law requires plaintiffs to seek redress under available administrative procedures before access to the courts is allowed.

Once administrative appeals are exhausted, judicial relief can be sought. Courts, however, normally award the state or municipality the benefit of any doubts, provided the regulation has some rational purpose in protecting public health, safety, and welfare and the procedures used by the state or municipality in developing the regulation were fair and reasonable.

**Penalties.** Various consequences may result from noncompliance with building codes and regulations. Some jurisdictions allow the building official to stop construction for noncompliance, an action that can be very costly to the owner. Failure to comply with regulations can subject an architect to civil liability, and it may also lead to revocation of the license to practice architecture. Continued noncompliance can lead to a fine or a jail sentence.

**Other building regulations.** While building codes are addressed directly to design and construction, other regulations influence design decisions as well:

- Fire prevention codes and ordinances
- Housing codes and ordinances
- Health codes and ordinances (e.g., for restaurants and social clubs)
- Licensing requirements (e.g., for hospitals, nursing homes, dry cleaners, day care centers)

Although many of these regulations do not appear to address design and construction directly, they influence how build-

## SAMPLE MODEL CODES AND STANDARDS

| Building codes | International Building Code (IBC) | ICC |
| | BOCA National Building Code | BOCA |
| | Standard Building Code | SBCCI |
| | Uniform Building Code | ICBO |
| Fire codes | International Fire Code (IFC) | ICC |
| | National Fire Prevention Code | BOCA |
| | Standard Fire Prevention Code | SBCCI |
| | Uniform Fire Code | ICBO |
| | Fire Prevention Code | NFPA |
| Mechanical codes | International Mechanical Code (IMC) | ICC |
| | National Mechanical Code | BOCA |
| | Standard Mechanical Code | SBCCI |
| | Uniform Mechanical Code | ICBO |
| Plumbing codes | International Plumbing Code (IPC) | ICC |
| | National Plumbing Code | BOCA |
| | Standard Plumbing Code | SBCCI |
| | ICBO Plumbing Code | ICBO |
| | Uniform Plumbing Code | IAMPO |
| Energy conservation codes | International Energy Conservation Code (IECC) | ICC |
| | Model Energy Code | CABO (ICC) |
| Electrical codes | ICC Electrical Code (ICCEC) | ICC |
| | National Electrical Code | NFPA |
| Gas codes | International Fuel Gas Code (IFGC) | ICC |
| | National Fuel Gas Codes | NFPA |
| | Standard Gas Code | SBCCI |
| Performance codes | International Performance Code (ICCPC) | ICC |
| Existing buildings codes | International Existing Buildings Code (IEBC) | ICC |
| | Standard Existing Building Code | SBCCI |
| Security codes | Uniform Building Security Code | ICBO |
| Property maintenance codes | International Property Maintenance Code (IPMC) | ICC |
| | National Property Maintenance Code | BOCA |
| | Standard Housing Code | SBCCI |
| | Uniform Housing Code | ICBO |
| Zoning codes | International Zoning Code (IZC) | ICC |
| | Uniform Zoning Code | ICBO |
| One- and two-family dwelling codes | International Residential Code (IRC) | ICC |
| | One- and Two-Family Dwelling Code | ICC |

*BOCA Building Officials and Code Administrators, Inc.*
*CABO Council of American Building Officials*
*ICBO International Conference of Building Officials*
*ICC International Code Council*
*IAMPO International Association of Plumbing and Mechanical Officials*
*NFPA National Fire Protection Association*
*SBCCI Southern Building Code Congress International*

Community Planning Controls (14.3) covers administrative law applied to the regulation of local community development.

## COMMON CODE FORMAT

One way to understand a building code's coverage quickly is to review its table of contents. Starting in 1993, the model codes adopted a "uniform common code format" which will be continued in the International Building Code.

**ADMINISTRATION AND TERMS**

1 Administration
2 Definitions

**BUILDING PLANNING**

3 Use or occupancy
4 Special use and occupancy
5 General building limitations
6 Types of construction

**FIRE PROTECTION**

7 Fire-resistant materials and construction
8 Interior finishes
9 Fire protection systems

**OCCUPANT NEEDS**

10 Means of egress
11 Accessibility
12 Interior environment

**BUILDING ENVELOPE**

13 Energy conservation
14 Exterior wall coverings
15 Roofs and roof structures

**STRUCTURAL SYSTEMS**

16 Structural loads
17 Structural tests and inspections
18 Foundations and retaining walls

**STRUCTURAL MATERIALS**

19 Concrete
20 Lightweight metals
21 Masonry
22 Steel
23 Wood

**NONSTRUCTURAL MATERIALS**

24 Glass and glazing
25 Gypsum board and plaster
26 Plastic

**BUILDING SERVICES**

27 Electrical wiring, equipment, and systems
28 Mechanical systems
29 Plumbing systems
30 Elevators and conveyor systems

**SPECIAL SERVICES AND CONDITIONS**

31 Special construction
32 Construction in the public right-of-way
33 Site work, demolition, and construction
34 Existing structures

**STANDARDS**

35 Referenced standards

Federal licensing, subsidy, insurance, or other assistance programs almost always include some requirements for building use, design, construction, or operation.

ings are used and operated. A hospital or nursing home code, for example, routinely specifies conditions for temperature control and housekeeping. A fire prevention code may regulate exit signs, access for firefighters and equipment, posting requirements for occupant loads, and a variety of other in-use requirements.

## FEDERAL BUILDING REGULATIONS

There is no federal building code, yet the trend over the last several decades has been toward increased federal regulation of design and building:

OSHA has promulgated many regulations affecting health and safety at the construction site. AIA Document A201 places responsibility for construction site safety in the hands of the contractor, but this can become a construction contract administration issue for the architect.

- The federal government regulates the building of its own facilities—federal buildings, military installations, Veterans Administration hospitals, and the like.
- The federal government's power to regulate interstate commerce enables it to regulate commercial trade between citizens of different states. This power has been used, for example, to regulate mobile home construction.

- The federal government can preempt states' rights if it decides its constitutional responsibilities require it to regulate an area of conduct. Examples include Environmental Protection Agency (EPA) and Occupational Safety and Health Act (OSHA) standards.
- Federal aid to states may carry requirements for regulation. For example, states were required to enact energy conservation standards to receive federal energy assistance monies in the 1970s.
- Federal assistance and insurance programs bring federal regulation to many highway, housing, urban development, agricultural, aviation, waterway, and other projects done by states and localities as well as by the private sector.

***Occupational Safety and Health Act (OSHA).*** Although states generally hold the power to regulate public health, safety, and welfare, the federal government may regulate local conduct based on other constitutional provisions. For example, OSHA (passed in 1970) regulates the design of buildings and projects where people are employed. OSHA regulations are specific about items such as the location and design of toilet facilities for employees as well as a wide variety of conditions at construction sites, including:

- Protection of floor and wall openings
- Radiation
- Design of stairs and ladders
- Sanitation
- Means of egress
- Fire protection
- Lifts
- Explosives and blasting
- Air contaminants
- Handling and storage of gases and flammable and combustible liquids
- Ventilation
- Occupational noise exposure

OSHA is enforced by the U.S. Department of Labor. Given the very broad scope of the law's regulations, OSHA inspectors often do not become involved with a specific project or building unless violations produce an injury. At that point, a comprehensive inspection may identify all outstanding violations, and fines may be severe.

***Americans with Disabilities Act (ADA).*** In 1990 Congress passed the Americans with Disabilities Act, requiring operators of commercial facilities and "places of public accommodation" to make reasonable efforts to provide access to persons with disabilities in employment, facilities, and state and local government services. The ADA applies to both new construction and existing commercial facilities and places of public accommodation, requiring that owners make "readily achievable" reasonable efforts to provide access.

The constitutional basis for the ADA lies in the Fourteenth Amendment's protections against discrimination. Thus the ADA is a piece of civil rights legislation, giving persons who feel they have been discriminated against because of a disability an opportunity to sue for redress but not personal gain. Private parties may bring lawsuits or file complaints with the U.S. attorney general (who then may bring a lawsuit).

To provide guidance in designing facilities—

▶ **Government agencies and departments at all levels may be involved. For example, the Environmental Protection Agency may seek to enforce federal environmental protection regulations, and the state health department may regulate hospital construction. Local jurisdictions do not enforce state and federal regulations unless mandated by a higher authority. Therefore it should not be assumed that a local permit covers matters under state or federal jurisdiction.**

## Standards and Certification

The regulatory process also includes the use of standards—acceptable practices as recognized by experts in the area. A wide variety of building standards covers topics as diverse as housing layouts, plumbing, accessibility, amusement devices, and the design of concrete mixes.

Standards alone do not possess the force of law, but they are frequently incorporated by reference in various codes or regulations. Many organizations—including private and public organizations, trade groups, professional societies, and government departments and agencies—have developed standards.

Writing standards generally involves a consensus process employing committees of volunteer experts in the subject at hand. Nonprofit organizations that have participated in standards development include the American National Standards Institute (ANSI), the American Society for Testing and Materials (ASTM), and the National Fire Protection Association (NFPA). Some of these standards are widely used; as an example, NFPA's Life Safety Code has been wholly incorporated into many state and local building codes. Trade and professional groups such as the American Iron and Steel Institute (AISI), the American Concrete Institute (ACI), the American Society of Mechanical Engineers (ASME), and the American Society of Civil Engineers (ASCE) write standards, as do federal agencies for projects under their jurisdictions.

Once product standards have been written, manufacturers and suppliers want to offer some certification that their products meet the standards. Product certification occurs in several ways. For a fee, the Council of American Building Officials (CABO) will verify whether a product conforms to one of the model codes. Another common example involves the use of a seal such as the Underwriters Laboratories (UL) label, which signifies a product has been subjected to UL's testing process. Through these means, testing organizations certify that specific materials and products meet standards.

It is important for everyone to understand, however, that a building is an assembly of elements, components, and subsystems. Even though each of the materials and products in a building assembly may meet specified standards, the assembly itself may not comply with the building code.

*Henry J. Lawrence Jr., Esq.*

part 3 DELIVERY

and retrofitting existing ones—the Department of Justice has developed the ADA Accessibility Guidelines (ADAAG). The Guidelines establish design requirements for a wide variety of building and site features. They include scoping requirements intended to provide accessibility through some, but not all, building features. There are many scoping requirements; here are a few examples:

- Fifty percent of public entrances must be accessible.
- Wheelchair seating is to be dispersed in theaters of more than 300 seats.
- In dining areas with fixed seats, at least 5 percent (with a minimum of one) must be accessible.
- In medical care facilities, 10 percent of patient bedrooms and toilets must be accessible.
- In libraries, at least one lane of stacks, catalogs, and checkout counters must be accessible.

The model codes, and many state and local codes, incorporate ANSI Standard A117.1, Providing Accessibility and Usability for Physically Handicapped People. Their requirements differ somewhat from those in the ADA Accessibility Guidelines.

From the architect's standpoint, the difficulty with state and federal regulations is that they act as overlays, that is, it is unlikely the regulations will be part of (or even referred to by) local codes and regulations. Some, such as OSHA standards and ADA requirements, apply to a wide spectrum of projects; most, however, are invoked only in special circumstances.

## CODES IN DESIGN PRACTICE

Architects relate to the regulatory environment in two fundamental ways: Their actions as designers are governed by its rules, and they have opportunities to change the rules.

***The architect's duty.*** When a building code that has been adopted by a local jurisdiction or a regulation issued by a state or the federal government applies to the project, it creates a legal duty for the architect. Without a variance, an architect failing to design in compliance with the code or regulation may be subject to an allegation of negligence. Neither an owner's requirement to disobey the code nor a building official's unknowing or unreasonable approval of a noncompliant project relieves the architect of this duty.

Codes and regulations set forth only the requirements necessary to protect public health, safety, and welfare. Architects are required to use reasonable care in providing services, and there are times when this requirement may call for a design solution in excess of that mandated by code.

***Using building codes in practice.*** The best results occur when the architect thoroughly understands the regulatory process and makes it an inherent part of the design and construction process. In doing this, the architect is challenged to fulfill the code's requirements while considering how best to meet the client's economic and functional needs.

An architecture firm can respond to this challenge in several ways:

- Acknowledging and asserting that codes are factors in and set parameters for every project.
- Implementing a code search process (and, commonly, a checklist) for each project. Some local jurisdictions have their own checklists, which may capture key code design information and present it as part of the design submission to building officials.
- Teaching staff about code intentions, approach, and procedures.
- Encouraging staff consultation with local building officials to ascertain or clarify code issues.
- Including instructions in specifications requiring contractor compliance with applicable codes.
- Developing code-related procedures—for example, materials approvals, specification text, and recommendations for text and procedural changes.
- Including a code data sheet as part of the documents (some jurisdictions require this).

► **A building code is built on a logic that ties together—often invisibly—its many pages of fine print. The approach to reviewing code requirements included here is one effort to make this logic more apparent to designers.**

**Code search.** An in-depth code search is usually required to identify applicable codes, regulations, and standards for the project. As part of the project definition and programming process, code provisions should be perceived as "ingredients" and not an optional layer of information for design. The code provisions are parameters set upon the project in a mandatory context, but normally they allow multiple solutions.

**Schematic design.** Building codes provide fundamental design parameters—for site placement, building size, height, and interior layout—as well as for a great many design and construction details. Responding to the code is a progression from general requirements (the building requires three exits) to more detailed requirements (the location, size, configuration, and construction of these exits).

**Construction documents.** As the project progresses through design development into construction documents, it is essential that all code requirements be checked and incorporated into the project. Code features used or incorporated in design development must be refined and detailed properly to reflect precisely what is required by the code and what the architect has chosen as a response to the requirements. Fire-rated assemblies, for example, must reflect the specific assembly that was used to establish the rating; any changes may cause the rating to be nullified.

Codes are likely to include specific requirements indicating information that must be included, and called out, in the construction documents. For example, the BOCA National Building Code (1999 edition) requires that for most occupancies the construction documents designate the number of occupants (as determined using procedures embodied in the code) to be accommodated on every floor and in all rooms and spaces as required by the code official. Local code officials may require a summary of code-related design information as the first sheet in a submission for a building permit.

**Standards.** Codes typically refer to (and thus incorporate) standards that may introduce hundreds of pages of data that may affect the project. While the complete information is not written directly into the building code, the requirements are bona fide code provisions and must be met.

**Specifications.** Specifications should be written with a clear delineation of the code environment, clarifying responsibilities and establishing exactly what codes and standards were used as the basis for the design and the depicted construction.

**Substitutions.** Once the code official has approved the construction documents, new or substitute materials should not be introduced directly in the field; the inspector may not allow it and may stop work until proper information and test data are submitted and approved. The field inspector is required to check actual construction against the approved documents. Therefore, solutions or options must be resolved with the plans examiner and the building official before the project is approved and the permit issued.

**Code revisions.** Codes are revised periodically; the widely used model codes are revised on a continuing cycle. Design professionals are responsible for complying with the code provisions as of the date the application for the building permit is submitted; therefore, architects must be aware of the latest code changes.

**Working with code officials.** While codes and regulations may be written in precise terms, interpretations can vary. The power to interpret building codes is often vested in the local building official. The latitude given code officials by the codes and regulations they enforce allows opportunities for discussion and negotiation; sometimes these opportunities are considerable. Thus it is valuable to maintain an open dialogue and a good working relationship with these officials.

Like all others in the building enterprise, code officials vary in their experience and competence. It is in the best interest of the project for the architect to get to know the code officials who will be involved, assess their approaches to interpretation and negotiation, and sense the points at which formal variances may

## Architects, Building Codes, and the Law

Compliance with the building code generally is a duty that cannot be delegated, and code violations in drawings and specifications may be considered evidence of negligence on the architect's part. Often it is not sufficient that the architect has complied with local custom or practice if such conformance is not in accord with the applicable building code.

The design professional should seek to be well informed of applicable code requirements, although this may be a difficult and sometimes impossible task in light of rapidly changing requirements. New regulations are frequently issued, and amendments are regularly passed. A design may be affected by a new requirement or interpretation issued by a code official or a court. Additional existing requirements may become applicable during the course of the project based on some action of the owner. If a number of different regulations apply to the same project, the architect may be faced with conflicting requirements.

Another challenge faced by architects is the application of codes to new or innovative designs. Some aspect of such a design may not be specifically covered by a building code. The architect may be able to elicit guidance from a code official but may have to make a judgment call as to whether the particular design or design aspect complies with the policies underlying the code provisions.

Some clients will want to include a specific provision in the owner-architect agreement requiring the architect to satisfy the applicable codes. Such a requirement may be unrealistic, since codes may change after design is complete and many code provisions may be interpreted subjectively by local building officials. For these reasons, AIA Document B141 does not specifically state that the architect must comply with all building code requirements, although it is assumed the architect will exercise reasonable care in endeavoring to do so.

Pursuant to subparagraph 3.3.1.2 of AIA Document B141, the architect may receive additional compensation for making revisions to drawings, specifications, or other documents when the revisions are made necessary because of codes, regulations, or other laws passed subsequent to the original preparation of the drawings.

*Howard G. Goldberg, Esq.*

## Determining Regulatory Requirements

It is the responsibility of the architect to read and understand the building code. The most effective way to approach code compliance is to meet with local officials before schematic design development to determine which codes and standards apply to the building in question. Local officials often include the responsible building official and the fire marshal. In small communities, the duties of these two officials may be carried out by the same person.

The architect should not expect a full code review at an initial meeting but rather a discussion of general code issues. Items not discussed at this meeting may not comply with the code. Therefore it is helpful for the architect to make notes of what exactly was covered.

Early input by regulatory officials may eliminate costly design

changes later in the project, resulting in a better professional service to the client. Many officials have specialized expertise, and open communication with them can make the architect's job easier.

On complicated or special-purpose projects, it may make sense to engage a code consultant to assist in identifying applicable code requirements and developing strategies for integrating the requirements into the building design.

Once the regulatory requirements have been identified, the architect can proceed with design and develop the documents necessary for the building department to review plans. A complete set of construction documents is usually a prerequisite to obtaining a building permit.

*Henry J. Lawrence Jr., Esq.*

---

> **While code officials are not "public clients," they are subjected to many of the same expectations for accountability as public agencies that act as architects' clients.**

become necessary. Often it is helpful to meet with code officials early in the process, to discuss key issues and clarify review schedules and requirements.

***Seeking variances and exceptions.*** When project requirements and solutions fit neatly within the rules—or within the code official's scope of interpretation—there is little difficulty in carrying out the architect's duty. There is no way, however, that codes and regulations can keep pace with changes in technology and practice or with the scope of owner requirements and the architect's imagination in responding to those requirements. Because these factors are dynamic and codes are less so, it is reasonable for architects to seek variances or exceptions and to propose substitutions. Building officials may not place an interpretation in writing; it is a good idea for architects to document meetings and send the official a copy.

In states or localities that have adopted one of the model codes, it is possible to seek a written interpretation from the model code organization. Such interpretations are advisory to the building official enforcing the code, but they add credibility to a variance request. It's good advice to work with the local officials when you seek an interpretation; no one likes to be blindsided.

***Participating in code enforcement and development.*** Some architects seek appointments to planning, zoning, and code variance boards. As a service to the public, these architects participate in the process of reviewing plans, hearing appeals, and granting exceptions. Their participation adds to the level of professionalism in the regulation of planning, design, and construction.

A smaller number of architects choose to become part of the process of writing codes and regulations or developing the standards that are incorporated into them. This often requires a long-term commitment to sit on a state or local building code commission, become active in a model code organization, or sit on technical committees as part of the consensus process. By their nature, however, codes and regulations address highly technical issues; the participation of design professionals in code making can only enhance the possibility that the resulting codes will accomplish what they set out to do.

### For More Information

The AIA Building Codes and Standards PIA maintains a current listing of major code organizations and reports on performance, technological, and regulatory issues. See the professional interests section at the AIA Web site (www.aia.org).

# Working with a Building Code

Procedures for applying code requirements in the building design process vary from firm to firm. This illustration presents one approach to working with a building code when designing a building. The left-hand column contains a series of steps in building design that are affected by specific code considerations. The right-hand column presents some isolated illustrations using the International Building Code (IBC), 2000 edition.

Please keep these things in mind in using this example:

- IBC is a model code and may be modified in adoption for specific local use.
- All codes contain many specific requirements and exceptions; therefore, reference must be made to the specific code text.
- The illustrations isolate a single code provision in practice; other circumstances or design decisions may modify the requirements listed here.
- There may be other codes, regulations, licensing issues, or state or federal standards at work in a given project. These may require different and possibly more restrictive design practices.

## STEP 1
### Establish building occupancy or use.

Codes establish occupancy classifications. Make the selection that most accurately fits the use of the building you are designing.

Codes present strategies for mixed uses, such as separating uses with fire walls of specified fire resistance or designing the entire building to the requirements of the most restrictive use.

Typically, high-hazard uses have special requirements.

The concept is that use establishes the types and levels of hazards involved in a building and also provides some indication of the nature and capabilities of the occupants.

IBC (Chapter 3) includes these use groups:

A Assembly
B Business
E Educational
F Factory
H High-hazard
I Institutional
M Mercantile
R Residential
S Storage
U Utility and miscellaneous

Several of these are subdivided, e.g.,

A-1 Assembly uses intended for the production and viewing of the performing arts or motion pictures
A-2 Assembly uses intended for food and/or drink consumption
A-3 Assembly uses intended for worship, recreation, or amusement and other assembly uses not classified elsewhere in Group A
A-4 Assembly uses intended for viewing of indoor sporting events and activities with spectator seating
A-5 Assembly uses intended for participation in or viewing outdoor activities

## STEP 2
### Establish type of construction and building height and area.

These three major design parameters are related, and codes typically offer the designer a series of choices.

*Construction type*
Codes establish a number of construction types, each characterized by decreasing fire resistance of building components.

*Building height and fire areas*
For each occupancy or use group and for each construction type, the code stipulates a maximum building height and a maximum building area. Height cannot be exceeded; to increase area, it is necessary to create fully fire-resistant compartments made of building elements that have the fire resistance rating specified for the construction type.

This approach allows the designer to "trade" fire resistance in the building elements for building height and area. An extra investment in fire resistance—made by choosing a more restrictive (and expensive) construction type—allows increases in height and area.

Typically, including automatic sprinkler systems allows additional height and area.

*Fire district provisions*
Some codes reduce these requirements if the structure is within specified "fire limits." Rapid-response firefighting capability can speed extinguishing of a fire as well as escape by building occupants.

IBC (Chapter 6) outlines five major construction classifications: In Types 1 and 2, walls, partitions, structural elements, floors, ceilings, roofs, and exits are constructed of noncombustible materials. Type 3 buildings are constructed of noncombustible exterior elements, but interior structure, walls, floors, ceilings, and roofs may be constructed of any approved material. Type 4 buildings are heavy timber, and Type 5 buildings are constructed of combustible materials. Some types are further divided.

The variation in fire resistance can be seen by looking at the fire resistance ratings (FRRs) required of exterior load-bearing walls:

3 hours  Type 1A
2 hours  Type 1B
1 hour   Types 2A, 3A, 3B, 4, and 5A
0 hours  Types 2B and 5B

IBC (Chapter 5) outlines building limitations. The 2000 edition offers these choices to the designer of an elementary school (Use Group E):

| Construction type | Maximum height (stories) | (feet) | Maximum area (sq. ft.) |
|---|---|---|---|
| Type 1A | Unlimited height and area | | |
| Type 1B | 5 | 160 | Unlimited |
| Type 2A | 3 | 65 | 26,500 |
| Type 2B | 2 | 55 | 14,500 |
| Type 3A | 3 | 65 | 23,500 |
| Type 3B | 2 | 55 | 14,500 |
| Type 4 | 3 | 65 | 25,500 |
| Type 5A | 1 | 50 | 18,500 |
| Type 5B | 1 | 40 | 9,500 |

## STEP 3
### Determine the location on the property.
Building codes require that the structure be separated from the property line—or that additional fire resistance and protection of openings be built into exterior walls that are close to property lines.

Remember that one of the historic purposes of a building code is to help prevent conflagration—the spread of fire to your neighbor's property.

IBC (Chapter 6) outlines this relationship. As an example, a building with a high-hazard occupancy (Use Group H) must have an exterior wall with an FRR of 3 hours for all types of construction if the fire separation distance is less than 5 feet. For distances from 5 feet to less than 10 feet, the required FRR drops to 2 hours, except for Type 1A construction, which still requires 3 hours. From 10 feet to less than 30 feet, the FRR is either 2 hours or 1 hour depending on the type of construction. For a separation of 30 feet and above, the FRR is 0.

## STEP 4
### Determine whether a fire suppression system is required.
Codes often mandate the use of automatic fire suppression systems, including sprinklers, for some occupancy groups. An early determination of whether one is required—or will be installed anyway—is valuable because many decisions can be modified if automatic fire suppression is to be installed.

According to the IBC (Chapter 9), automatic fire suppression systems are required in the elementary school described in Step 2 (except in fire areas less than 20,000 square feet). If sprinklers are installed throughout the school building, the IBC (Chapter 5) allows the maximum height to be increased by 20 feet and permits an additional story. It also permits the building area limitation to be increased by 200 percent in multistory buildings and by 300 percent in single-story buildings.

## STEP 5
### Establish parameters for the egress system.
The building's egress system includes the paths of travel from any point in the building to a public way. It includes interior exit doors, corridors, hallways, stairways, passageways, and horizontal exits within the building.

Except in special circumstances, the challenge is to create two continuous, unobstructed, and protected paths of travel from any point in the building to a public way. Design for egress is a multistep process.

*a. Calculate occupant loads.*
Codes provide tables that allow the designer to calculate occupant loads (based on the square footage of the floor area) for rooms and floors.

IBC (Chapter 10) establishes, for example, one occupant for each 20 square feet in classrooms. A school with 10,000 square feet of classroom space on a floor has an occupant load of 500 students on that floor.

*b. Calculate required exit capacities.*
The code sets standards in inches of exit width per occupant. The total exit width from a floor must be accommodated in the exits from that floor.

If sprinklers are installed in the school example, IBC requires 0.2 inches per occupant for stairs and 0.15 inches for doors, ramps, and corridors. The stairs from the 10,000-square-foot floor being designed must total 100 inches (8' 4") in width.

*c. Determine the number and location of exits.*
Most floors of most buildings must be served by at least two exits that meet the code's "test of remoteness." Floors with high occupancy loads may require three or four exits.

Our floor requires two exits. If the floor is 200 feet by 50 feet in plan dimension, IBC requires that the exits be at least 69 feet apart (one-third of the diagonal dimension). For buildings without sprinklers, the "test of remoteness" is one-half of the diagonal.

*d. Design the exit access.*
Codes regulate access to corridors (door dimensions, fire resistance ratings, and direction of swing), length of travel path, dead-end corridors, and corridor width and finishes.

For Use Group E and when the load exceeds 100 occupants, IBC (Chapter 10) requires that corridors be 72 inches wide. The longest path to an approved exit cannot exceed 250 feet (200 feet if the building does not have sprinklers).

*e. Design the exit.*
Codes establish many requirements for approved exits, including stair enclosures; doors and other openings into exit stairs; headroom; vertical rise; roof access; and the width, risers, treads, landings, and handrails of the stairs themselves. Codes typically limit the use of curved, winder, and spiral stairs. Smokeproof enclosures may be required for high-rise buildings. "Horizontal exits" allowing refuge into an adjoining fire area are permitted under described circumstances.

For our example, two exits will be required from the second floor of the elementary school. Each must be a minimum of 44 inches wide—but recall from step 5b that the total width of the two exits must be 100 inches. There can be no more than a 12-foot vertical rise between landings or platforms. Handrails are required on both sides of each stair. Vertical exit enclosures of 4 stories or more shall have a FFR of 2 hours. Enclosures less than 4 stories shall be 1-hour rated.

*f. Design the exit discharge.*
The final step is to continue the path of egress from the foot of the exit stair to the outdoors. There are limits on exit passageways, discharge through a foyer or lobby, and the use of revolving doors.

One of the fire stairs from the second floor may exit through areas on the level of discharge or through a vestibule as long as specific design criteria are met for construction type, travel distances, etc.

*g. Provide access to persons with disabilities.*
Most of the egress system just designed will also provide access to the building. A review for accessible routes, widths, protruding objects, ramps, elevators, and other features is appropriate at this point.

IBC (Chapter 11) requires that the building meet the standards established in ICC/ANSI 117.1 (1998). It also establishes requirements for accessible parking, routes within the site, and entrances. Finally, it includes "scoping" requirements similar to those in the Department of Justice's Americans with Disabilities Act Accessibility Guidelines.

## STEP 6
### Check detailed fire performance requirements that apply to the specific occupancy and construction type.
The steps taken so far establish the major building design parameters. Codes also offer a wide variety of detailed design requirements. Occupancy-related requirements include, e.g.,

- Covered mall buildings
- High-rise buildings
- Mezzanines and atriums
- Parking structures and garages
- Swimming pools
- Special areas such as projection rooms, stages, areas for hazardous materials

Construction-related requirements include, e.g.,

- Fire walls, partitions, and separations
- Fire doors, glass, windows, and shutters
- Insulation and firestopping
- Vertical shafts
- Interior finishes

Fire protection system requirements establish the need for:

- Heat and smoke detectors
- Alarm systems
- Special fire suppression systems

IBC includes these details in chapters on special use and occupancy (Chapter 4), general building limitations (Chapter 5), types of construction (Chapter 6), fire-resistant materials and construction (Chapter 7), interior finishes (Chapter 8), and fire protection systems (Chapter 9).

Behind the details there is a strategy at work in these sections of the code: The code is attempting to create a margin of safety for the occupants of the building (and also for firefighters) in case of fire.

The margin of safety is provided by some combination of these two goals:

1. Shortening the time it takes occupants to react to the fact of fire and achieve safety. Key code strategies are:

- Early detection of fire
- Rapid notification of occupants (and firefighters)
- Escape or refuge to a safe place

2. Lengthening the time it takes for the fire to produce intolerable conditions. Key code strategies are

- Confinement of fire and its products
- Extinguishing of the fire

## STEP 7
### Determine compliance with interior environment requirements.
Codes look beyond fire protection in providing for public health and welfare. They include requirements for room dimensions, access to light, ventilation, sound control, and for making structures safe from pests.

IBC (Chapter 12) mandates minimum ceiling heights of 7 feet 6 inches in exit access and spaces to be occupied in educational buildings. Natural or artificial light must be capable of producing an average illumination of 10 foot-candles (107 lux) over the area of the room at a height of 30 inches (762 mm) above the floor level.

## STEP 8
### Determine compliance with energy efficiency requirements.
Codes establish requirements for the exterior envelope and for building support services including hot water, heating, air-conditioning, and electrical distribution systems.

IBC (Chapter 13) requires that buildings be designed in accordance with the International Energy Conservation Code.
There are requirements for exterior cladding and veneers (Chapter 14) and for rooftop structures (Chapter 15).

## STEP 9
### Determine compliance with requirements for structure and materials.
Codes establish requirements for design loads as well as roof, snow, wind, earthquake, and impact loads. There are requirements for foundations and retaining walls and for structural tests and inspections. Specific requirements are offered for construction materials, such as:
- Concrete
- Lightweight metals
- Masonry
- Steel
- Wood
- Glass and glazing
- Gypsum board and plaster
- Plastics

A few examples:
IBC (Chapter 16) requires that schools be designed to accommodate minimum uniformly distributed live loads of 40 pounds per square foot (psf) in classrooms, 80 psf in corridors above the first floor, and 100 psf for first-floor corridors.

The code (Chapter 19) requires that concrete slabs supported directly on the ground be not less than 3? inches thick. A vapor-retarding polyethylene sheet is required in most conditions.

The code (Chapter 24) requires that glass sloped more than 15 degrees from vertical in skylights, sun spaces, sloped roofs, and other exterior applications be designed to resist the code-specified combination of wind and snow loads as well as the dead load of the glass. Maximum allowable sizes are specified.

## STEP 10
### Determine compliance with building services systems requirements.
Codes establish design criteria and detail requirements for plumbing, mechanical, electrical, and conveying systems. They may include lighting standards as well.

IBC (Chapter 29) requires that plumbing systems comply with the requirements of the IBC International Plumbing Code. The latter requires, for example, that toilet rooms in educational buildings include one water closet and one lavatory for each 50 occupants and one drinking fountain for each 100 occupants. Note that, as in all situations, there may be a state or local school buildings code with more restrictive requirements.

*This backgrounder is adapted from "One Approach to Using a Building Code in Design Practice" by David Haviland, Hon. AIA. The original appeared in the 12th edition of the Architect's Handbook of Professional Practice.*

# part 4

# SERVICES

*The facility-related concerns and needs of clients occur throughout the building life cycle stages of planning, design and construction, and operation. By the nature of their core knowledge and expertise, architects are in a unique position to address client needs that go beyond the creation of physical space. By selectively expanding their knowledge base and skills, architects can position their firms to offer a broader range of services that are responsive to client facility needs and consistent with the strategic aims of their practices.*

# 15 Defining Services

## Robin Ellerthorpe, FAIA

*Part 1 of the Handbook, which focuses on the client, strives to help us better understand who it is we work for. Parts 2 and 3, on business and delivery, address operational issues on a firm-wide and project level. This part addresses the what and how of providing services to our clients.*

A fundamental concept of the 13th edition of the *Architect's Handbook of Professional Practice* is expansion of architectural services in recognition of the concept of the facility life cycle and the potential of long-term client relationships. To accomplish this, architects must "think outside the box" of traditional design and construction services. The *Handbook* thus presents services in the spirit of *adding to* versus *taking away from* the architect's strong tradition of design and construction service capabilities. Architects can leverage their core capabilities by adding new skills, and present themselves to clients as professionals interested in opportunities that go beyond design and construction.

With the information provided in Part 4, a firm can begin to enhance the services it already provides, create a set of new capabilities, or both. Although the services included are diverse in nature, each is presented on an equal basis, without predilection toward any particular capability or set of capabilities.

> **"The concept of architectural services now extends through the conception, financing, design, construction, and lifetime operation of a facility to include every facility-related aspect that makes the client's life better and more productive."**
> *AIA Project/Service Delivery Think Tank, July 1999*

## THOUGHTS ON EXPANDING SERVICES

To use Part 4 effectively, you should have a definitive grasp of the markets your firm serves and who your potential clients should be. Give considerable thought to the impact a new service will have on the firm as a whole and on the people serving individual markets and clients in particular. For example, what happens when facility management services are introduced to a firm providing interior services? When is a move plan that is part of move management services and includes some space planning distinct from space planning alone? Who does what? The addition of a seemingly innocuous capability can have significant firm-wide impacts, from marketing through client retention.

Before a firm selects a new service or line of services for implementation, it is advisable to understand what the firm's present capabilities and capacities are. This way you can develop implementation costs and time frames that will help you determine potential cost/benefit scenarios before making an investment. Internal staff can be polled for interest in learning new skills, technology can be assessed to determine new requirements, and the firm's organization can be assessed to determine where the new service would fit in. Once these issues have been addressed, undertake a strategic thinking process that includes SWOT analysis (assessment of strengths, weaknesses, opportunities,

*ROBIN ELLERTHORPE is with the Chicago-based firm of OWP&P Architects, Inc. Ellerthorpe directs the firm's facilities consulting group, which he started in 1997 to provide services in strategic planning, change management, and operations and maintenance tool development for facility owners.*

and threats) to determine where you would be in the marketplace. This study will allow you to make a fair determination of market value and return on investment.

Be honest with yourself and admit what you do not know. The *Handbook* is, after all, about the practice of architecture, and architects characteristically believe they can do just about anything. Recognize that certain processes and technologies have become specialties in this profession of generalists. Leading-edge thinkers and doers in the industry have already spent years practicing many "new" services discussed here and possess the mind-set (and battle scars) to hit the ground running. When developing a business plan to implement a new service, consider learning from these professionals or hiring one to leapfrog the competition. One caveat (of many) in establishing a new service within a firm: Allow it to grow and flourish within the organization. Easy to say, hard to do.

***A work in progress.*** This Services section is intended to be a work in progress. A study performed several years ago by the American Institute of Architecture Students resulted in a list of more than 600 possible services that could be performed by individuals trained in architecture. Here we present a small number of service processes that are most generally accepted. As the concepts involved in expanding architectural services through the redefinition of architecture are better understood, many additional services will be issued in later releases of the *Handbook*. Sources for these services include practitioners, professional interest areas (PIAs), and previous *Handbook* authors. Each service supports the basis for the redefinition of architecture and is intended to enable firms of any size to expand their client relationships, capabilities, markets, and profitability.

***The B141 document.*** The current B141 Document, Standard Form of Agreement Between Owner and Architect with Standard Form of Architect's Services, was created to enable architects to respond to client needs without having to use a multitude of contracting instruments. The format of each service description is therefore intended to help architects develop modular inserts for the B141. This document makes it possible to view services discretely as adding value and to have them on the table during the discussion of fees. For example, tradition has often relegated programming to a low-margin or free service in order to gain entree for providing design services. This approach runs counter to sound business practices. By using the modular format of the new B141, architects identify and exclude all services that will not be covered by fees, making it clear that such services are outside the overall scope of work if the client elects them.

**Firm Identity and Expertise (5.1)** looks at how firms can identify their true driving forces and expertise.

---

## *Projects: A Broader Context*

Architects tend to think of projects principally in the construction realm, but projects have now become a common feature of business and government activity, and all kinds of business change are now considered as projects. For example, researching biomedical and pharmaceutical innovation is frequently undertaken on a project basis, as is software development, moving office, or the implementation of new equipment systems.

Projects are unique goal-oriented events, set up in order to get a client from A to B, from a less preferred set of conditions to a more preferred set of conditions. They are mediums for realizing change and vehicles for realizing ambitions. Projects have specific goals and criteria for success.

Projects are unrehearsed events happening in real time. They have start and end points, without which they lose definition and cannot be meaningfully managed except as ongoing programs.

Projects have specific budget allocations, without which, again, they cannot be meaningfully and economically managed or feature as components of larger programs.

*Adapted from Kenneth Allinson,* Getting There by Design: An Architect's Guide to Design and Project Management *(1997)*

---

## SERVICE CATEGORIES

Architects, through training and experience, possess a fundamental understanding of space, massing, and materiality. On the basis of this understanding, architects can make decisions for a client along a broad continuum, beginning with the identification of the need for a facility and through its planning, design and construction, use, renovation, and eventual disposition. Against this continuum, this section presents services under the following categories:

- Planning
- Design and construction
- Operations and maintenance

***Planning services.*** The overarching goal of services in the planning category is to assist the client in defining what the problem is and to begin to set facility-related constraints to craft a statement regarding function, form, economy, and time. The creation of this statement—typically taken into the design process—is considered programming from an architect's perspective. From the client's viewpoint, however, elements of this process may be found in such activities as strategic planning, visioning, scenario planning, master planning, project definition, program management, and myriad other activities that occur before design.

Additional skills can enable architects to lead project feasibility analysis efforts that include financial considerations (both funding and revenue generation) to assist the client in development of return on investment calculations, lease versus buy decisions, or even bond issues. Organizational development skills can be added to facility management and programming skills to create facility management organization definition, outsourcing, performance, or evaluation services.

By creatively assessing client needs and offering additional skills in processes led by the architect, architects can become trusted advisors to their clients. We are there for the right reason: We add value through our fundamental strengths and the ability to access and facilitate multidisciplinary professional services to meet comprehensive facility needs.

***Design and construction services.*** With regard to design and construction services, most firms practice the way they did 30 years ago (albeit with a more efficient pencil). Today, technological change in our industry has progressed to the point where architects can begin to take advantage of integrative tools in their work. While efforts to tie computer-aided design drawings to specification information and material lists are maturing, professionals have also begun to recognize the value of capturing and maintaining project information—for programming, team communications, requests for information, and the like—that is accessible to the entire project team. Services described in this section show a progression (or at least a first step) along the path of integration and responsiveness that will increase our ability to lead the process.

Today changes in project delivery cover every building sector, from residences to houses of worship, institutions to corporations, service sector to industry. All this activity points to industry-wide change in client expectations regarding how they hire architects. Service delivery methods in this section present a number of tested alternatives available today. An effort has been made to make individual services and delivery methods as generic as possible so that architects considering implementation of these methods can evaluate whether introducing them into their firms will differentiate them and increase their ability to compete in the marketplace.

Adoption of services and project delivery methods addressed in this section may have a significant impact on how your firm operates and should be carefully considered and planned for before full-scale implementation. For example, the level of detail provided in construction drawings can vary from traditional design-bid-build to design-build approaches. Operational changes such as these are not minor and should be tested on pilot projects, evaluated against expected return, and modified to meet expectations.

***Operation and maintenance services.*** At this time, operation and maintenance services are perhaps the services least understood by architects. However, they are understood all too well by new competitors who are entering our markets in this area because of our inattention. When asked about operation-based services, most architects suggest postoccupancy evaluation and little else.

Competitors in the operations services arena include building controls equipment manufacturers, accounting and consulting firms, food service firms, and outsourced service vendors. While they provide some services that architects do not or should not provide, they are with the client on a day-to-day basis as a result of providing these services and therefore can fill leadership positions in making facility-based decisions.

> **"Owners . . . want design and construction information to be delivered electronically so they can link operations and facility information. Owners perceive this as a cost-effective way to reduce operational costs. This is the essence behind the life-cycle approach to project information that our industry needs to adopt."**
> *AIA Project/Service Delivery Think Tank, July 1999*

Why should architects be interested in operations-based services? Monetarily—over and above costs for day-to-day operations of utilities and maintenance—owners can spend as much as three times the original cost of a building over a 50-year building life cycle. Technically, operations-based services fall within our core competency. Marketwise, the square footage of existing buildings significantly exceeds the combined square footage of new buildings being created at any point in time or during any market cycle.

Building owners and operators seek stasis in the building operating environment as quickly after move-in as possible. The less that goes wrong and the lower the operating costs, the better. A false sense of security arises after an owner occupies a new facility. Building warranties are in effect for a period of time, and contractors generally will resolve component and finish failures for a specified time after construction. This period ends quickly —usually between budget cycles if planning for new equipment replacement, disaster planning, and other facility churn issues have not been fully thought out.

The opportunity exists for architects to step in and assist in planning for these events, and to take leadership in facilitating and managing the disciplines required for them. The operations section presents services that have been used to help clients address building life cycle issues as they occur. Some services are low-level and do not require journeyman architects to perform.

By managing appropriate resources across many facilities, firms can gain an advantage over their competitors by knowing a particular market better. Applying that knowledge, whether through statistical analysis or publishing proprietary building operations guidelines, is how architects can lead clients through their building operation issues. This will result in expansion of the trusted-advisor role and help establish long-term relationships with clients.

## CONTENT OF SERVICE DESCRIPTIONS

Each service description in this section organizes the discussion in a consistent manner, beginning with an introductory statement that defines or describes the service, recounts significant aspects of its history, and identifies trends in the marketplace for the service. The introduction is followed by three parts: client needs, skills, and process.

***Client needs.*** This part describes why clients may need the service and what the potential benefits and risks are to a client. It also identifies which types of clients typically need this service and, if known, the market value for the service. Major providers of the service are described and other services usually associated with this service are listed.

***Skills.*** In this portion of the service profile, the author discusses the knowledge, skills, and resources needed to provide the service. Related disciplines that may be involved and the kinds of specialists that may be required are identified, along with any special equipment and tools.

***Process.*** This part identifies factors affecting the scope of the service, generic steps to perform the service (sometimes with a sample work plan), typical steps or phases in the service, and the deliverables generally included. The kinds and levels of staffing required are described, and regulatory approvals are noted where they would be expected.

# 16 Planning–Predesign Services

## 16.1 Programming

### Robert G. Hershberger, Ph.D., FAIA

*Architectural programming is the thorough and systematic evaluation of the interrelated values, goals, facts, and needs of a client's organization, facility users, and the surrounding community. A well-conceived program leads to high-quality design.*

Architectural programming has developed as an activity related to, but distinct from, architectural design. It is considered an optional pre-design service under AIA Document B141, Standard Form of Agreement Between Owner and Architect. Document B141 states that under "basic services," the architect is required only "to provide a preliminary evaluation of the Owner's program." Presumably after this preliminary evaluation the architect is expected to proceed with normal design services.

An increasing number of architects have found the above approach unsatisfactory and have elected to offer architectural programming as an integral part of their services. In this context, programming has evolved into a far more thorough and systematic endeavor than when it was offered as an incidental part of the architectural design process or when it was conducted by the owner.

The need for programming services is likely to expand owing to the increasing complexity of buildings and building systems. As well, many clients are becoming much more sophisticated and thus more interested in understanding and managing their physical resources.

Programming led by architects can provide clients with a systematic process for decision making about organizational and project values, goals, and requirements. Many clients have a limited view of the range of physical possibilities for accommodating their operations; architects have the ideal professional background to help them visualize options during programming. The programming process as led by architecture firms can expose clients to a wide range of alternative approaches and help them choose appropriate directions.

### CLIENT NEEDS

All types of clients need programming services. Institutional, government, and corporate clients are most likely to recognize this need and be willing to pay for programming

## Summary

### PROGRAMMING SERVICES

#### Why a Client May Need These Services
▷ To clarify project goals and design issues
▷ To provide a rational basis for design decision making
▷ To ensure that the project reflects the client's values

#### Knowledge and Skills Required
▷ Knowledge of architectural design
▷ Knowledge of construction methods and timelines
▷ Investigative and information-gathering skills
▷ Familiarity with construction costs
▷ Knowledge of space standards
▷ Analytical skills
▷ Strong verbal, writing, and management skills

#### Representative Process Tasks
▷ Assemble programming team
▷ Identify and prioritize client and user values
▷ Determine project goals
▷ Identify project constraints and opportunities
▷ Gather and analyze data
▷ Document project requirements

**ROBERT HERSHBERGER** *is professor and dean emeritus of the College of Architecture at the University of Arizona. He is also a partner in Hershberger and Nickels Architects/Planners of Tucson and Tempe, Arizona. He is the author of* Architectural Programming and Predesign Manager.

services, although in some cases these clients may produce programs in-house or by using other programming consultants before engaging the services of an architect.

Government agencies use programming services extensively because they often base procurement of design services on fully developed programs. Owners of complex institutional facilities such as hospitals and hotels easily recognize the need for careful up-front analysis of design issues and will often employ architecture firms to develop their programs. Owners of owner-occupied office facilities usually want quality programming in order to achieve facilities management objectives. Clients with little experience with the building industry generally appreciate the guidance an architect can provide through the programming process. Developers are the least likely to recognize the need for architectural programming services because many believe they know precisely what is needed in the market and thus see no reason to explore alternatives and weigh potential trade-offs. While some residential clients may not want to pay extra for programming, they need the service, even when they are just remodeling a few rooms.

Discussing the benefits of programming during initial interviews sometimes broadens the vision of resistant clients and helps them understand why they need to contract for these services.

***Preliminary studies.*** Some clients will need financial feasibility, site suitability, and/or master planning services prior to architectural programming. Financial feasibility studies explore market conditions in relation to specific sites and development plans in order to show whether a particular project will be viable. These studies can be led by architects but often require the expertise of other professionals. Site suitability studies may also be required prior to purchase of a particular property to make certain that the site is properly zoned, has needed services, and is appropriately sized and configured for a proposed project.

▶ **Community Planning Controls (14.3)** considers how regulating land use, building development, and environmental quality can be factors in programming services for buildings.

Architects are ideally trained to conduct site suitability studies because of their design skills and knowledge of applicable land use and building codes and regulations. Where geotechnical issues are involved, civil engineering consultants may be brought in. Landscape architects should be consulted on projects where there are significant site planning issues.

Clients with a large site and an extensive program that will develop over time should develop a master plan before programming for any particular building or facility. Architects who provide master planning services followed by complete architectural programming services are in an excellent position to prove their value to the client and thus to be assured of obtaining the commission for design services for each phase of master plan implementation.

▶ **Code Compliance (17.3)** discusses considerations that may come into play in programming services.

***Architectural programming.*** Architectural programming can include all of the above studies but generally commences after they are complete. It tends to focus on specific facilities identified in the master plan and includes all of the areas mentioned in the previous sections: value identification, goal setting, discovery of related facts, and development of specific project requirements. These are all developed in collaboration with the client, user, and community, but depending on the nature of the project, specialists may be required to develop some of the information. Specialists may include kitchen consultants, laboratory consultants, security consultants, data and communications specialists, and transportation and parking specialists.

Some architects specialize in offering programming services, and other professionals, including social and behavioral scientists, systems analysts, interior designers, and building management and operations specialists, have entered the field. Some programming consultants, including architects, specialize in particular building types or functions, such as hospitals, sports complexes, hotels, justice facilities, laboratories, security systems, clean rooms, and kitchens.

***Costs of services.*** Architects who offer programming services have had increasing success in negotiating fees to cover the cost of these services because owners recognize that the resulting buildings better serve their needs. Indeed, architecture firms that offer programming as a primary service are often recognized by their peers as producing quality architecture. Fees for programming vary. Highly technical buildings such as hospitals or laboratories can command higher figures than commercial and moderate-size institutional buildings. Fees for master planning also vary depending on the expected deliverables and project types.

---

### *Values in Architectural Programming*

*Human:* functional, social, physical, physiological, psychological

*Environmental:* site, climate, context, resources, waste

*Cultural:* historical, institutional, political, legal

*Technological:* materials, systems, processes

*Temporal:* growth, change, permanence

*Economic:* finance, construction, operations, maintenance, energy

*Aesthetic:* form, space, color, meaning

*Safety:* structural, fire, chemical, personal, criminal

*Robert Hershberger,* Architectural Programming and Predesign Manager *(1999)*

## VALUE-BASED PROGRAMMING MATRIX

| VALUES | GOALS | FACTS | NEEDS | IDEAS |
|---|---|---|---|---|
| Human | | | | |
| Environmental | | | | |
| Cultural | | | | |
| Technological | | | | |
| Temporal | | | | |
| Economic | | | | |
| Aesthetic | | | | |
| Safety | | | | |
| Other | | | | |

## SKILLS

On smaller projects, one person from the programming firm can usually handle all of the programming tasks. On larger projects, the programming team will generally include a senior architect, who handles sensitive client interviews and work session presentations (or at least introductions); a project programmer, who conducts interviews with key personnel, develops questionnaires (if needed), analyzes data, and oversees development of the programming document; and junior programmers, who do literature searches, conduct user interviews, conduct observational studies including site analysis, and assist the project programmer in developing the program document.

Specialized consultants are used to develop the criteria and parameters for particular spaces or facility types, such as laboratories, airports, prisons, kitchens, and hospitality/entertainment complexes. The involvement of specific personnel should be carefully developed in a programming work plan.

Programmers must be familiar with the fundamentals of the architectural design and building processes and be alert to the design and construction implications of program statements. But they must also have specific knowledge and skill to be effective at programming.

Expertise in information gathering is the heart of the programmer's domain and requires the ability to

- Conduct efficient literature searches
- Employ active listening skills to conduct diagnostic interviews
- Record meaningful data during a walk-through study
- Develop comprehensive space inventories
- Obtain trace evidence
- Conduct systematic observations
- Know when and how to develop and administer questionnaires

Strong verbal and management skills are necessary for group interviewing and work session leadership. Here again, active listening skills are vital, but the ability to direct the course of the session and to lead people of diverse opinions to consensus is even more important.

Data analysis skills are equally important. Knowing what to collect and then how to convert the raw data to useful information is essential to effective programming. Skilled programmers learn how to avoid "data clog," a favorite term of programming pioneer Willie Peña. The programmer must learn to collect only the needed data and then know how to convert them into meaningful (reliable and valid) information that can influence design of the project.

Knowledge of space size standards for various building types is a fundamental requirement for programmers. Before going into the work session, they must know what the standards are for a building type as well as what space the client actually has, so they can guide the client to agreement on appropriate net space needs for a particular facility. They must also be aware of appropriate efficiencies for various building types and quality levels to be able to apply them to net totals to arrive at gross square footage requirements. Efficiency factors are often less than 70 percent for many building types. But clients rarely understand how much of a building area is consumed by such space as halls, walls, utility chases, and closets. The programmer must have the knowledge and skill to guide the client through this part of program development.

The programmer must be familiar with current construction cost information and with general project delivery timelines. In some cases it may be necessary to consult general contractors or cost estimators in order to develop realistic preliminary costing and project schedules. Where clients require full financial feasibility studies, consultants with backgrounds in real estate development and banking often are used. At this early stage, it is common to provide a contingency budget of 20 or 30 percent of the expected building cost because so many factors (land cost, soils, easements, etc.) are unknown. This percentage will be reduced as the project progresses and more is known, so that a common contingency in the master planning would be 15 percent, dropping to 10 or 12 percent in programming and 5 to 7 percent for construction.

Finally, writing skills are needed to capture and delineate the qualitative and quantitative aspects of the client requirements. An architectural programmer must be able to communicate programming information verbally and visually to the client, the users, the community, and the architect who will design the project.

*Equipment.* Given that virtually all architects will have a computer that can produce finished drawings and a word-processed report, the only special equipment needed for architectural programming would be a digital or Polaroid camera. No other special equipment is necessary.

## PROCESS

Architectural programming is inherently a team process. At a minimum, the programmer and client determine the program, but more often several persons from the programming firm, an array of users, and sometimes community participants are involved. The scale of the project (e.g., a building interior, one building, a building complex) will have a strong effect on team size and composition. Other factors include the type of facilities and level of specialized functions that will be required and possibly constraints on interaction with the client and users.

### Client and User Values

Programming is the time to identify, consider, debate, reject, accept, and prioritize values such as institutional purposes, functional efficiency, user comfort, building economics, safety, environmental sustainability, and visual quality. These identified values and concerns can have a profound effect on the ultimate form of a building. If the program is driven primarily by concerns for functional efficiency, as is the case in many owner-produced programs, organizational decisions made during programming will significantly affect the form of the building.

If the program evolves more from the social and psychological needs of the users, prescriptions for form will also be inherent in the identified spaces and their sizes, characteristics, and relationships. If the program responds primarily to economic concerns, it is possible that numerous material and system opportunities as well as potentially unique spaces and places will be eliminated from design consideration during programming. A carefully conceived and comprehensive architectural programming process will help to ensure that all of the appropriate values have been identified and prioritized.

The values identification portion of architectural programming offers the client an opportunity to resolve important questions or make critical decisions about how the client's organization relates to the built environment. As well, consideration should be given to how the client's values relate to the values of the community, the values of the users of the facility, and the values of the design professionals with whom the client is working. Considering these value relationships can help the programmer manage potential conflicts of values and identify opportunities for a fuller expression of common values.

### Project Goals

Once the primary values have been identified and prioritized, it is possible to develop specific project goals. What organizational objectives should be accomplished by providing a new, expanded, or renovated facility? Should the resulting building be a statement of the organization's desired image? Should it be a model of efficiency? Or should it be more loosely organized, allowing for serendipitous events or even changes in how operations are conducted? Should it be environmentally sensitive, a showpiece of "green" architecture? What is the target for overall project cost? When should the facility be ready for operation? Goals in these and many other areas need to be set during programming.

## Constraints and Opportunities

Achievement of the goals will be made easy or difficult by the characteristics of the organization's operations as well as those of the site. Information must be gathered that identifies the specific nature of the constraints and opportunities. Is there enough land on which to locate the proposed facility? Is it in the right location in terms of visibility, access, service, and the like? Can the existing facilities be easily converted to new uses? Are the organization's cash flow and/or reserves sufficient to ensure that the construction and start-up costs can be managed? Questions of fact must be considered before realistic projections for new and renovated spaces can be made.

▶ Site Analysis (16.2) discusses programming considerations for a proposed or an existing site.

## Facility Requirements

When the important values and goals of the client, user group, and community and any related facts have been identified, then and only then should the identification of specific space needs begin. Unfortunately, many client-provided programs are developed without adequate consideration of important institutional values and goals. Personnel assigned to prepare the program tend to proceed directly to identification of user needs and space requirements. Those preparing the program may be unaware that their personal value systems are influencing the decisions they are making and that a more conscious identification of institutional values and the setting of specific project goals would have a profound effect on how the specific needs of the project are developed. Often a few known and pressing facts tend to dominate the decision process, while other facts remain uncovered, even though they may be more important relative to the organization's mission.

Steps for identifying the space needs of a specific facility include the following:

- Identify required spaces
- Establish the size and relationships of these spaces
- Develop appropriate factors for estimating efficiency
- Project budget and schedule requirements

When determining factors for estimating efficiency, allow for nonprogrammed areas such as halls, walls, restrooms, service areas, two-story spaces, and the like. Base budget and schedule requirements on previously identified values, goals, and facts in order to get the most accurate guide for the design of proposed new facilities.

## Information Gathering

Five types of information gathering are used in architectural programming: literature search/review, interviewing, observation, questionnaire/survey, and group sessions.

*Literature search/review.* This task comes first in the programming process, beginning even before the commission is awarded, to give the programmer background knowledge of similar facilities and a general familiarity with the client's mission and language. The literature search includes gathering reports on existing facilities along with site surveys, construction documents, and other relevant documents that the client may possess. It also involves obtaining relevant government documents, including applicable codes and ordinances, as well as recognized building and planning standards, historical documents and archival materials, trade publications, research literature, professional publications, manufacturers' publications, and even sources in popular literature and on the Internet.

*Interviewing.* In most cases this is the core activity in programming. It begins with the client interview. At this interview, the programmer can learn more about the client's values and goals, refine a work plan and schedule, and ascertain whom to contact within the client organization. Interviews with key personnel, other users (clients, patrons, customers, etc.), and interested community members follow. Successful interviews are carefully planned. The programmer first tries to identify the basic values that will affect the design of the facility—human, cultural, environmental, technological, temporal, economic, aesthetic, and safety-related. In planning interviews, the programmer should consider what data could make a design difference, who could provide the most useful information, who has the authority to make decisions and establish priorities, the amount of time and the size of the budget that are available, and how interviewing will relate to other information-gathering techniques that may be used, such as observations or surveys.

For larger organizations, the programmer usually reviews the organizational chart with the client to identify the key officers, department heads, and other persons likely to be knowledgeable about facility needs or in decision-making positions. Others within the organization who might be interviewed include department managers, members of special committees, maintenance people, a sampling of typical employees, and employees with special needs. Those who use or visit the building but do not work for the client organization, such as suppliers, service people, fire officials, or customers, also may have important input. Interviews may take place in an individual or group setting.

Whomever is interviewed and however the interviews take place, the objective is to obtain complete and reliable information. It helps to conduct the interviews in or near the client's or user's existing environment. This setting tends to make interviewees more comfortable in answering questions, and also makes it easier for them to focus on their own architectural environment. Interviewing techniques vary widely and should match the data-gathering objectives.

***Observation.*** This task is another information-gathering technique that programmers should use. A walk-through observation of the existing facility with the property or facility manager is an excellent way to orient yourself to obvious programming requirements. A space inventory, including plans and annotated photographs of existing spaces, equipment, and furnishings, can provide important baseline information. The programmer photographs and measures existing spaces and documents existing furniture and equipment to better understand the space requirements. Trace observation documents wear and tear on existing facilities (surfaces, furniture, fixtures, and equipment) and may tell an important story about traffic and circulation patterns, use levels, and other factors that should be accounted for in the program. Behavioral observation (time-and-motion studies) can document the functions that the building occupants perform and the adequacy of the space accommodating them. For example, the programmer may observe that a hospital room has an inadequate turning radius for a wheelchair when a visitor chair is placed in the room. Quite often the programmer will be told during client or user interviews that a particular space is a problem, prompting subsequent observational study of the space to determine the cause of the problem.

***Questionnaires and surveys.*** These are yet another information-gathering tool used in programming. Surveys are an efficient way to gather facts and quantitative details in a large organization. Furniture and equipment needs of individual users, for example, can be ascertained through a written survey form. The questions must be carefully developed using a systematic process that includes pretesting, or there is a good chance that the resulting data will be meaningless or at least difficult to analyze.

***Group sessions.*** These are the final way to obtain needed information in architectural programming. It is important to conduct at least one group work session (usually several) as a feedback mechanism to allow the client and users to consider, debate, and eventually resolve and agree upon the true nature of the architecture problem—to reach a consensus as to which values, goals, facts, needs, and ideas should influence the design of the facility. This is a type of group interviewing process that typically involves feedback of information obtained from the other information-gathering methods. Techniques include brainstorming new ideas and rejecting as inappropriate some of the information collected earlier, concluding with prioritizing the goals and needs for the project. It is not only a way of gathering information but also a method of obtaining agreement.

## Data Analysis

Throughout the data-gathering process it is important to organize data so that they can be retrieved and analyzed quickly and easily. A key technique is to seek and record only information that will be vital in making design decisions. Based on analysis of all information gathered, the programmer will develop performance and design criteria for the facility. Space requirements, space relationships, circulation, ambient environment, safety and security, needed surfaces, furnishings, flexibility, and site information are among the issues usually addressed. Graphics such as matrices showing space allocations and relationships and bubble diagrams showing adjacency relationships are also developed.

During analysis, the programmer will identify major unresolved programming issues and begin to develop some preliminary ideas about options for their resolution in the final building program. Some writers have referred to these ideas as "precepts" (a term implying a combination of *preliminary* and *concepts,* yet still clearly preliminary to conceptual design). Here the programmer's task is to develop options (precepts) for solutions, to help with their evaluation, and to recommend the most effective alternatives. For example, in a residential facility such as a nursing home or a juvenile justice institution, there might be a trade-off between privacy and isolation in residents' bedrooms. Options might be single, double, or multiple-occupancy bedrooms. A recommendation might be to have a mixture of rooms to allow for occupant or staff choice. The programming team presents the various options or precepts to the client and guides the client through evaluation of the alternatives. As with interviewing, there are many different ways to structure these presentations, and the approach should be tailored to the needs of the client organization and the particular project.

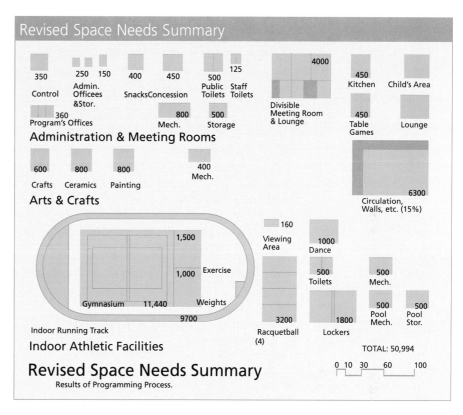

Revised Space Needs Summary
Results of Programming Process.

## Deliverables

The usual deliverable is a written architectural program, which is a comprehensive report that includes documentation of the methodology used, an executive summary, value and goal statements, the relevant facts, data analysis conclusions, and the program requirements, including space listings by function and size, relationship diagrams, space program sheets, stacking plans, precept drawings, and flow diagrams. Photographs or even videos may be used to illustrate space planning requirements. A comprehensive program will also include project cost estimates and a project schedule.

### For More Information

The following titles represent a bookshelf of publications about architectural programming that architects will find useful: Edith Cherry, *Programming for Design* (1998); Donna P. Duerk, *Architectural Programming: Information Management for Design* (1993); Robert Hershberger, *Architectural Programming and Predesign Manager* (1999); Robert R. Kumlin, *Architectural Programming: Creative Techniques for Design Professionals* (1995); Mickey Palmer, ed., *The Architect's Guide to Facility Programming* (1981); William Peña, Steven Parshall, and Kevin Kelly, *Problem Seeking: An Architectural Programming Primer,* 4th ed. (1987); Wolfgang F. E. Preiser, ed., *Facility Programming* (1978); Preiser, ed., *Programming the Built Environment* (1985); Preiser, ed., *Professional Practice in Facility Programming* (1993).

# 16.2 Site Analysis

## Floyd Zimmerman, FASLA

*Sensitive owners and designers understand that from the facility user's perspective, the site and the structures constructed on it are one. Good building design responds to the inherent qualities of the site and at the same time transforms the site into a place that accommodates human enterprise and satisfaction.*

## Summary

### SITE ANALYSIS SERVICES

#### Why a Client May Need These Services
▹ To evaluate development constraints and opportunities for a site
▹ To assess one or more sites as a basis for purchase
▹ To assess the infrastructure characteristics of a site
▹ To gain information as a basis for a zoning variance

#### Knowledge and Skills Required
▹ Knowledge of climate, topography, soils, and natural features
▹ Knowledge of site utility distribution systems
▹ Ability to evaluate site access and circulation factors
▹ Understanding of building siting considerations
▹ Familiarity with planning and zoning ordinances
▹ Ability to analyze multiple factors objectively
▹ Ability to work with related or specialty disciplines

#### Representative Process Tasks
▹ Program investigation
▹ Site inventory and analysis
▹ Site evaluation
▹ Report development

Site analysis is a vital step in the design process. It involves the evaluation of an existing or potential site in relation to the development program, environmental impact, impacts on the community and adjacent properties, project budget, and schedule. The site analysis identifies environmental, program, and development constraints and opportunities. A well-executed site analysis forms the essential foundation for a cost-effective, environmentally sensitive, and rational approach to project development.

In recent years parking requirements have become a key issue in site feasibility analysis and the site planning process for many projects in urban and suburban areas throughout the world. Almost every jurisdiction has requirements for parking counts in relation to site density. Many communities have experienced parking capacity problems and are increasing parking requirements in their zoning requirements for new developments. In some areas market forces rather than regulations are driving the increase in demand for parking. A few cities have taken the opposite approach and are deliberately restricting parking in downtown areas to encourage use of mass transit. In these cases, the municipal code may not allow enough parking on a site to meet user requirements. Where larger facilities are being planned in congested urban areas, traffic issues can be even more troublesome than parking issues. Limits on increases in traffic generated by new facilities often restrict size and use more stringently than parking requirements.

Comprehensive environmental assessment of a site has become more important as clients become more environmentally aware and regulatory oversight increases. Clients want to avoid the expense and health risks that accompany environmental contamination on a site, as well as the cost of preventing any adverse impact on community environmental resources that could be caused by their activities. State and local governments, in turn, are becoming more uniform and effective in enforcing environmental controls on development.

Analysis of a building program and the capability of a site to accommodate it, combined with an assessment of political, environmental, and regulatory issues, reveals the development value of a parcel of land.

## CLIENT NEEDS

Site analyses vary greatly depending on the owner's situation, the project size, program complexity, and the site. One client may have defined a building program and be in search of a site. Another may have selected a site and be interested in fitting a development program to it. Yet another may have both site and program in hand and be seeking the most efficient, economical, and environmentally sensitive approach to site development.

**FLOYD ZIMMERMAN** *is an international planning and design consultant specializing in new towns and large-area planning. Formerly senior vice president and director of international planning for HOK, he is currently a principal in the offices of Tegeler Associates and the Porterfield Group.*

**Site selection.** Often a client has a development program in mind and is looking for the best site for it. It may be necessary to survey the region, town, or neighborhood for available sites and then to evaluate potential sites in terms of the requirements of the development program. The objective of site analysis during the site selection process is to identify the best site based on the physical, cultural, and regulatory characteristics of the site and its surroundings, as well as the site's adaptability to and compatibility with the proposed program.

**Program definition.** Here the client may have control of a site and perhaps have a general idea—from experience, intuition, or formal market research—of how to develop it. The focus in site analysis will be on determining the development capacity of the site so the program can be further defined in terms of density, open space, and environmental quality. The resulting site program will set the stage for site design.

**Site accommodation.** When a client has both a defined program and a selected site, the site analysis objective will be to maximize the potential of the site for its intended use by developing a thorough understanding of the opportunities and limitations it offers.

**Development potential evaluation.** In some cases a client already owns or is considering the purchase of an undeveloped or underdeveloped property and seeks site analysis to accurately define the general development potential and market value of the property.

**Special site studies.** Each site will present a unique set of issues and concerns. As part of site analysis, special studies may be required. Examples are utilities studies, environmental impact studies, historic resources inventories, and studies of special opportunities, such as the construction of co-generation plants or solid waste disposal systems.

Many clients require the architect to provide assistance with planning and zoning approvals in conjunction with site analysis services. Increasingly, local authorities are engaging design consultants of their own (sometimes at the owner's expense) to review project proposals. (See Zoning Process Assistance, topic 17.5).

Architects should emphasize the value that quality site analysis services add when they make compensation proposals to clients. Some clients want architects to provide assistance with initial site analysis and/or planning and zoning assistance on a speculative basis. They promise that the architect's costs will be recovered later through compensation for other services if the project goes forward. The architect should emphasize that effective site analysis services can significantly preserve or add to the economic value of a project for the owner and definitely deserve compensation. As noted above, a good site analysis will enable the client to exploit the full development potential of a site. Effective planning and zoning assistance can maximize the potential for regulatory approvals and significantly reduce the owner's risk of economic loss.

Related services include site design, geotechnical services, real estate evaluation, programming, site surveys, market studies, economic evaluations, and land use studies.

## SKILLS

Site analysis services may be performed by an interdisciplinary team or by an individual capable of directing the work of others. For the designer, skill in the initial evaluation of the physical features and quality of a site is fundamental. The designer leading a site analysis effort must be able to evaluate the site in terms of climate, topography, geotechnical and soil characteristics, utilities, natural features and surroundings, transportation and access, and historic preservation and landmarks. Familiarity with planning and zoning requirements such as parking, building density, use, open space, and design controls also is essential.

Accurate assessment of the political climate surrounding new development in a particular neighborhood or community is increasingly important. Good market analysis consultants can provide this assessment along with assistance in evaluating real estate value. Consultants with a planning or real estate background are frequently part of the site analysis team. Other disciplines normally involved include landscape architects and civil, power, and geotechnical engineers.

Depending on the project, other specialists may be required. These might include traffic engineers or traffic planners, hydrologists, economic analysts, environmental or wildlife scientists, archaeologists, historians, real estate attorneys, or programming specialists.

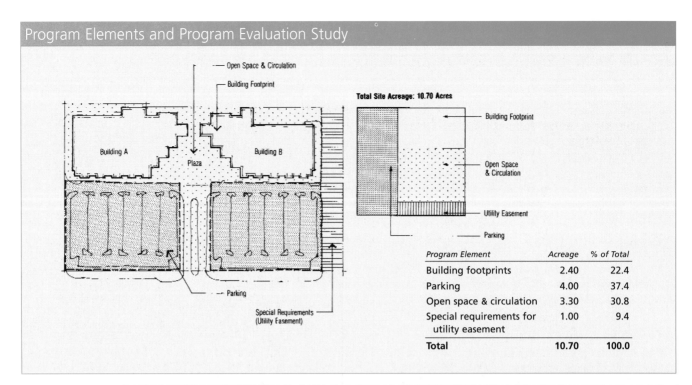

Total Site Acreage: 10.70 Acres

| Program Element | Acreage | % of Total |
|---|---|---|
| Building footprints | 2.40 | 22.4 |
| Parking | 4.00 | 37.4 |
| Open space & circulation | 3.30 | 30.8 |
| Special requirements for utility easement | 1.00 | 9.4 |
| **Total** | **10.70** | **100.0** |

## Sample Site Selection Study

This study examines a series of possible sites for a corporation seeking to relocate its headquarters within a few miles of the interchange of two interstate highways.

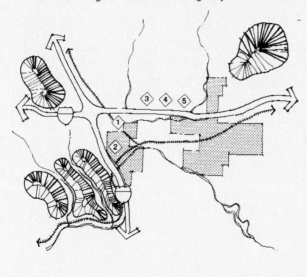

| EVALUATION FACTORS Excellent (+), Good (¤), Poor (–) | Site 1 | Site 2 | Site 3 | Site 4 | Site 5 |
|---|---|---|---|---|---|
| **Traffic factors** | | | | | |
| Restrictions due to traffic congestion | + | + | + | + | + |
| Cost of necessary traffic improvements and method of payment | ¤ | + | ¤ | ¤ | ¤ |
| Mass transit accessibility | + | – | ¤ | ¤ | ¤ |
| **Geotechnical factors** | | | | | |
| Foundation conditions | ¤ | ¤ | + | + | + |
| Earthwork | + | + | – | ¤ | ¤ |
| Expansion or collapse potential of upper soils | ¤ | + | ¤ | ¤ | ¤ |
| Seismic shaking | ¤ | ¤ | + | + | + |
| Faulting | + | ¤ | + | + | + |
| Seismic liquefaction potential | + | + | + | + | + |
| Slope stability problems | + | ¤ | ¤ | ¤ | ¤ |
| Groundwater problems | ¤ | + | ¤ | + | + |
| Environmental hazards | ¤ | ¤ | ¤ | ¤ | ¤ |
| **Utilities** | | | | | |
| Availability of water costs for added water capacity | + | + | + | + | + |
| Availability of sewer costs for added sewer capacity | + | + | ¤ | ¤ | ¤ |
| **Development factors** | | | | | |
| Height limitations | + | – | + | ¤ | + |
| Other zoning requirements | + | + | ¤ | + | + |
| Planning review process | ¤ | + | ¤ | ¤ | ¤ |
| Neighboring uses | + | ¤ | – | – | – |
| Available acreage | + | + | + | + | + |
| **Economic factors** | | | | | |
| Land price per square foot | ¤ | – | + | | – |

Michael D. Knisely, AIA, WBDC Group, Grand Rapids, Michigan
Reprinted from The IDP

Here are some of the results from an analysis of a main street in a small city in Washington. Sketches and drawings examine the spatial sequence while passing through the street (1), contextual qualities (2, 3, and 4), and key neighborhood features and activities (5).

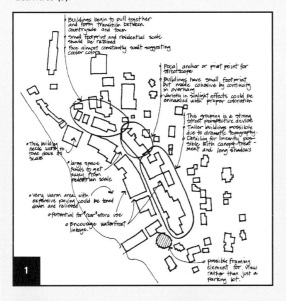

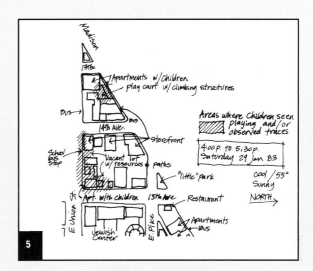

## PROCESS

The size of the site, its anticipated use, and the programming requirements will have a major effect on the scope of work for site analysis services. The site location, configuration, topography, and access and the complexity of adjacency, utility, and environmental issues related to the site are other key factors. Sites associated with controversial development issues may require more involvement, more related services, and more time.

When assembling the project team, a prime consideration is the level of investigation that each site factor requires in relation to the skills of the project manager. The consultant's familiarity with local conditions should be considered, especially when working in foreign countries or in areas in the United States with distinctive regional cultures. During site analysis, an architect often explores the potential for a client to become an accepted part of a community. The site analysis team should be fully capable of making a good impression on a community and dealing effectively with its representatives.

▶ **Community Planning Controls (14.3) discusses community approaches and regulations for planning, design, and construction.**

These are two of many drawings analyzing a large plantation located near a major metropolitan community as the site for a new residential community.

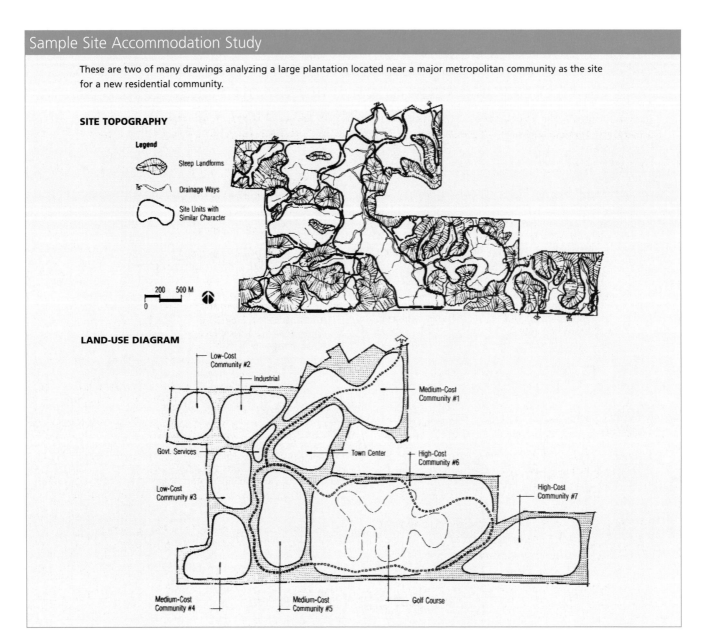

**SITE TOPOGRAPHY**

Legend

Steep Landforms

Drainage Ways

Site Units with Similar Character

200    500 M

0

**LAND-USE DIAGRAM**

Low-Cost Community #2

Industrial

Medium-Cost Community #1

Govt. Services

Town Center

High-Cost Community #6

Low-Cost Community #3

High-Cost Community #7

Medium-Cost Community #4

Medium-Cost Community #5

Golf Course

## Generic Steps to Perform the Service

The typical phases in site analysis are program investigation, site investigation and analysis, site evaluation, and report development.

***Program investigation.*** The building program is investigated with respect to the selected or optional building footprints; area required for parking, circulation, open space, and other program elements; and any special constraints or requirements such as security, easements, preserving natural habitat, wetlands, and the like.

***Site inventory and analysis.*** The physical, cultural, and regulatory characteristics of the site are initially explored. The site evaluation checklist identifies factors that may be considered. Some of these factors can be assessed by collecting and analyzing information; others are best addressed by walking the site and traversing its environs. A preliminary assessment of whether a location and site have the potential to accommodate the building program is made. Priority issues—those (such as environmental contamination) that may preempt further investigation—are identified. A site analysis plan is developed. When this has been approved by the client, consultants may be hired to further explore issues that require analysis beyond the capabilities of the core project team.

***Site evaluation.*** At this point, thorough assessments are conducted when necessary to develop the site analysis plan. These may include physical testing of aspects of the site, its improvements, and adjoining properties.

*Floyd Zimmerman, FASLA, et al.*

This is a checklist of the factors that may be involved in evaluating a site. Although lengthy, this list is not all-inclusive; new factors are added from time to time. Information is usually collected only for those items that are pertinent to the project.

## PHYSICAL FACTORS
### Climate
A. Prevailing winds
 1. Direction
 2. Maximum, minimum, and average velocities
 3. Special forces (e.g., tornadoes, hurricanes)

B. Solar orientation
 1. Sun angles
 2. Days of sunlight
 3. Cloud cover
 4. Shading of (or from) adjacent structures, natural features, and vegetation

C. Temperature
 1. Ranges of variation
 2. Maximums and minimums

D. Humidity
 1. Ranges of variation
 2. Maximums and minimums

E. Precipitation
 1. Peak period totals
 2. Annual and seasonal totals

### Topography
A. Legal property description including limits of property, easement, rights of way, and north indication

B. Topographic maps and aerial photos
 1. Contours and spot elevations
 2. Slopes: percentage, aspect, orientation
 3. Escarpments
 4. Erosion channels
 5. Extent, location, and general configuration of rocks, ledges, outcrops, ridges, drainage lines, and other unique features
 6. Visual characteristics
 7. Potential problem areas during construction: siltation, erosion, etc.

C. Analysis of physical features, including major focal and vantage points and their relationships within, into, and out from the site

D. Existing access and circulation
 1. Vehicular
 2. Pedestrian

E. Vegetation

F. Existing water bodies
 1. Location, size, depth, direction of flow
 2. Water quality: clean, polluted, anaerobic conditions, etc.
 3. Use: seasonal, year-round
 4. Wetlands: ecological features
 5. Variations: expected water levels, tides, wave action
 6. Coastal features

G. Drainage canals: rivers, streams, marshes, lakes, ponds, etc.
 1. Natural and built
 2. Alignments and gradients
 3. Pattern and direction

H. Existing waterway easements
 1. Surface
 2. Subsurface

I. Surface drainage
 1. Patterns on and off the site (location of streams and washes)
 2. Proximity to floodplains
  a. Maximum flood levels
  b. Frequently flooded areas
 3. Local watershed areas, amount of runoff collected, and location of outfalls
 4. Swampy and concave areas of land without positive drainage and other obstacles that may interrupt or obstruct natural surface drainage
 5. Potential areas for impoundments, detention/retention ponds

J. Unique site features

### Geotechnical/soils
A. Basic surface soil type: sand, clay, silt, rock, shale, gravel, loam, limestone, etc.

B. Rock and soil type: character/formation and origin
 1. Geologic formation process and parent material
 2. Inclination
 3. Bearing capacity

C. Bedrock
 1. Depth to bedrock
 2. Bedrock classification

D. Seismic conditions

E. Environmental hazards

### Utilities
A. Potable water
B. Electricity
C. Gas
D. Telephone
E. Cable television
F. Sanitary sewer service
G. Storm drainage (surface, subsurface)
H. Fire protection

### Immediate Surroundings
A. Neighborhood structures: buildings, satellite dishes, etc.
B. Shading and solar access
C. Noise from streets, emergency services, aircraft, etc.
D. Odors
E. Views and vistas

**General Services**

A. Fire and police protection

B. Trash/refuse removal services

C. Snow removal, including on-site storage

**CULTURAL FACTORS**

**Site History**

A. Former site uses

   1. Hazardous dumping

   2. Landfill

   3. Old foundations

   4. Archaeological grounds

B. History of existing structures

   1. Historic worth

   2. Affiliations

   3. Outline

   4. Location

   5. Floor elevations

   6. Type

   7. Condition

   8. Use or service

**Land Use, Ownership, and Control**

A. Present zoning of site and adjacent property

B. Adjacent (surrounding) land uses

   1. Present

   2. Projected

   3. Probable effects on the development of this site

C. Type of land ownership

D. Function and pattern of land use: public domain, farm type, grazing, urbanized

   1. Present

   2. Former

E. Location, type, and size of pertinent community services

   1. Schools and churches

   2. Shopping centers

   3. Parks

   4. Municipal services

   5. Recreational facilities

   6. Banks

   7. Food services

   8. Health services

   9. Access to highways, public transportation

**Economic Value**

A. Political jurisdictions and land costs

B. Accepted "territories"

C. Future potential

D. Size of surrounding lots and approximate price ranges

**REGULATORY FACTORS**

**Zoning Codes**

A. Permitted uses

   1. By variance

   2. By special use permits

   3. Accessory structures

B. Minimum site area requirements

C. Building height limits

D. Yard (setback) requirements

E. Lot coverage

   1. Floor area ratio (FAR)

   2. Percentage of coverage

   3. Open space requirements

F. Off-street parking requirements

G. Landscaping requirements

H. Sign requirements

**Subdivision, Site Plan Review, and Other Local Requirements**

A. Lot requirements

   1. Size

   2. Configuration

   3. Setbacks and coverage

B. Street requirements

   1. Widths

   2. Geometry: grades, curves

   3. Curbs and curb cuts

   4. Road construction standards

   5. Placement of utilities

   6. Dead-end streets

   7. Intersection geometry

   8. Sidewalks

   9. Names

C. Drainage requirements

   1. Removal of spring and surface water

   2. Stream courses

   3. Land subject to flooding

   4. Detention/retention ponds

D. Parks

   1. Open space requirements

   2. Park and playground requirements

   3. Screening from adjacent uses

**Environmental Regulations**

A. Water, sewer, recycling, solid waste disposal

B. Clean air requirements

C. Soil conservation

D. Protected areas, wetlands, floodplains, coastal zones, wild and scenic areas

E. Fish and wildlife protection

F. Protection of archaeological resources

**Other Codes and Requirements**

A. Historic preservation and landmarks

B. Architectural (design) controls

C. Special districts

D. Miscellaneous, e.g., mobile homes, billboards, noise

E. Site-related items in building codes

   1. Building separation

   2. Parking and access for persons with disabilities

   3. Service and emergency vehicle access and parking

***Report development.*** The site analysis report normally includes property maps, geotechnical maps and findings, site analysis recommendations, and a clear statement of the impact of the findings and recommendations on the proposed building program.

Regulatory approvals normally required during or immediately following the site analysis phase include zoning, environmental impact, and highway/transportation.

### For More Information

*Site Planning* (1984), by Kevin Lynch, provides a comprehensive treatment of site planning and design. Other works address site analysis and design from a strong ecological perspective. Ian McHarg's *Design with Nature* (1995) is a classic. *Design with Climate: A Bioclimatic Approach to Architectural Regionalism* (1992), by Victor Olgyay, another classic, establishes a climate-responsive design foundation for both site and buildings.

Other ecologically based texts include *Regenerative Design for Sustainable Development* (1994), by John Tillman Lyle; *Gray World, Green Heart: Technology, Nature, and Sustainability in the Landscape* (1994), by Robert L. Thayer Jr.; and *Ecological Design* (1997), by Sym Van Der Ryn.

Site engineering topics such as mapping, engineering analysis, earthwork, roadways, storm drainage, water supply, and sewers are covered in B. C. Colley's *Practical Manual of Land Development,* 3rd ed. (1998).

*Architectural Graphic Standards,* 10th ed. (2000), and *Time-Saver Standards for Landscape Architecture: Design and Construction Data,* 2nd ed. (1998), contain information and provide technical guidance and standards for drawing, detailing, and documenting site elements.

Associations maintaining Web sites with information relevant to planning and site design include the American Society of Landscape Architects at www.asla.org and the American Society of Civil Engineers at www.asce.org.

# 16.3 Strategic Facility Planning

## Thomas O. McCune, AIA

*Strategic facility planning is the process of translating an organization's strategic business plans into medium- or long-range facility plans and alternatives. Traditional architectural space planning skills play a role but must be supplemented by skills in forecasting, financial analysis, scheduling, real estate transactions, hedging, and site selection.*

## Summary

### STRATEGIC FACILITY PLANNING SERVICES

#### Why a Client May Need These Services
- To maximize facility contributions to business objectives
- To forecast future space needs (type, quantity, location)
- To ensure adequate lead time for project delivery
- To provide a basis for annual capital and operating budgets
- To obtain buy-in from top management
- To identify possible responses to unexpected changes in space needs

#### Knowledge and Skills Required
- Knowledge of architectural programming and space planning
- Ability to analyze strategic business plans
- Skill in financial analysis, forecasting, and budgeting
- Understanding of sequential scheduling
- Familiarity with permitting and other legal issues
- Understanding of site analysis, selection, and planning issues
- Familiarity with real estate transactions and hedges

#### Representative Process Tasks
- Analyze business plans
- Research industry competitors to develop trends and benchmarks
- Research or prepare staffing and production plans
- Develop alternative scenarios for the demand for space
- Develop options for supplying needed space
- Choose an option and create a plan to implement it

Architectural design was traditionally approached as a process of arranging physical form to fulfill one or more functions. Later, architectural programming emerged as a formal process for analyzing owner needs, concepts, and goals and merging them with known facts and constraints to form a rational basis for a design. Architects even provided cost estimating services as part of their basic expertise. Aspects of these traditional processes, such as determining the size of a building, its probable cost, and the proximity of various related functions, play a role in strategic planning. However, the process of converting strategic business plans into facility plans involves much more.

A strategic facility plan answers the following questions about a corporation's real estate portfolio for the foreseeable future:

- How much space will the corporation need? (quantity)
- What kinds of space will the corporation need? (type)
- During what time period will the corporation need it? (timing)
- How will the corporation procure it? (portfolio mix and duration—buy, build, or lease)
- What will it cost? (budget)
- What will be the "big-picture" sequence of moving into it? (migration)
- Where does the space need to be located? (location)
- Which groups need to be located near each others? (affinity and allocation)
- How will the corporation deal with unplanned changes in demand for space? (hedging and exit strategy)

It may also deal with some or all of the following issues:

- What mechanisms will the corporation employ to let users see the actual costs of their occupancy, forecast their future needs accurately, honor their promises concerning occupancy, and use space efficiently? (internal business model, including items such as internal leases and transfer charges)
- How will the facilities contribute to the core business of the corporation through their effect on marketing, employee recruiting, and employee retention? (corporate identity, location, and amenities)
- Can the corporation reduce total real estate costs per person? (density, design standards, and alternative officing)
- Can the corporation affect employee productivity and rate of production throughput by the design of the facilities? (effectiveness and productivity)

**TOM MCCUNE** *is CEO and senior consultant with AE Pragmatics, Inc., a multidisciplinary consulting and outsourcing firm serving Silicon Valley technology companies. McCune serves as the chair of the AIA Corporate Architects PIA Steering Committee.*

# CLIENT NEEDS

Most corporations do not exist for the primary purpose of building, owning, and operating buildings. Exceptions include organizations such as hotel chains and real estate developers, for whom real estate is a revenue-generating asset. Most corporations use buildings to support the pursuit of their core business.

Corporations develop *strategic business plans* that describe the future the corporation sees for itself. Many strategic planning models have been developed, but some of the most widely accepted are those published by Eliot Porter. Porter's methods include analyzing a corporation's strengths, weaknesses, opportunities, and threats relative to four external market factors: competitors, suppliers, customers, and substitute products. Future strategic plans focus on using the corporation's present resources to fund strategic thrusts into areas of future business opportunity.

Strategic business plans drive *tactical business plans,* which describe sales forecasts, manufacturing plans, staffing levels, geographic location, and budgets. It is these tactical business plans that directly affect facility plans. While it is rare for facility planners to be directly involved in the strategic business planning process, they frequently participate in the tactical side of business planning. Facility planners use tactical business planning information as input to strategic facility plans and provide feedback that contributes to future tactical and strategic business plans.

It is currently fashionable for managers of almost every business function to claim that their particular group is of life-and-death importance to the corporation's strategic business plans. Facility planning is no exception. However, as a practical matter, major corporations rarely use facilities as their primary strategic basis for acquiring other companies, diversifying into global markets, or developing major new product lines. Instead, the usual role of strategic facility planning is to support these strategic business decisions.

Acquiring real estate and building facilities are long-lead-time processes. In the case of a large new facility, the process traditionally took three to four years or longer from site selection to occupancy. Even with expedited approvals and fast-track construction, the process now commonly takes more than two years. Corporations need to develop strategic facility plans well in advance of actual needs to ensure that the right types and quantities of land, buildings, and services exist in the right places at the right times to house the corporation's employees and equipment.

If a corporation fails to procure adequate space in the best locations at the right time, this can impair the corporation's ability to hire the quantity and quality of personnel necessary to develop new products and market existing ones. At the most basic level, it can restrict a corporation's ability to produce enough product to meet market demand. Over the long term, this can lead to erosion of the corporation's market share and a decrease in its competitiveness. In the case of a shrinking corporation, the inability to quickly divest non-performing real estate can also decrease the corporation's competitiveness.

Many corporations have their own employees develop long-range facility plans.

▶ **Large management and accounting firms such as Arthur Andersen, Trammel Crow, and KPMG are dipping into the architectural arena, offering real estate planning and management consulting services to mid- and large-size clients. These services almost always involve building facility considerations and evaluations that architects can perform at a more rigorous and substantive level. How are the Andersens and others achieving these commissions? By "thinking like the client." Strategic facility management and planning is a service that requires the provider to think like a member of the client's board of directors and executive staff.**

## Strategic Facility Planning for the Nonprofit and Government Sectors

Although this topic is focused on planning for corporations, nonprofit and government organizations face many of the same challenges and occasionally contract with architects to provide strategic facility planning services. Many of the basic planning techniques are similar for all organizations, but the basic business drivers are different. While corporations are profit-driven, the others are expense-driven. Other differences in planning for these organizations are summarized in the matrix shown here.

### Comparison of Issues in Facility Planning for Different Organizational Types

| PLANNING ISSUES | CORPORATIONS | NONPROFITS | GOVERNMENT |
|---|---|---|---|
| Financial drivers | Revenue, profit | Expenses | Annual budget |
| Volatility | Potentially high | Moderate or low | Usually low |
| Exit strategy | Important | Usually unimportant | Usually unimportant |
| Tax consequences | Very important | Unimportant | Unimportant |
| Politics | Important | Very important | Extremely important |

part 4 SERVICES

However, some engage design or consulting firms on either a project basis or an ongoing partnering basis. Architects who develop the necessary processes and hire staff with the right skills are well positioned to serve this client need. Once a firm has begun offering strategic planning services, it can also offer related services such as design standards programs, workplace effectiveness studies, computer-aided drafting (CAD), computer-aided facility management (CAFM), and move coordination.

## SKILLS

**Information about offering facility management services can be found in Facility Management (18.1).**

Many of the traditional architectural programming and design skills apply to strategic facility planning. The most pertinent of these abilities are analyzing client goals and needs, identifying facts and constraints, generating concepts, and developing space plans. Architecture firms that offer strategic facility planning services supplement these traditional architectural skills with skills and training from other fields, including the following:

- Finance: financial analysis, forecasting, benchmarking competing companies, demographics
- Law: permits, entitlements, restrictions
- Industrial engineering: materials handling, plant layout, throughput analysis, capacity planning
- Civil engineering: transportation planning, site analysis, drainage, utilities
- Landscape architecture: site planning, site selection
- Real estate: site selection, costs, demographics
- MEP engineering: utilities, network telecommunications

**Forecasting** is the process of translating historical correlations, industry trends, economic indicators, and company goals into forward-looking estimates of business drivers and space needs. The simplest form of forecasting is *extrapolation,* which consists of naively extending past trends into the future. In the case of simple trends, *linear regression* can determine the mathematical equation that best fits a line to the existing data points. Extending this linear equation into the future provides an exact mathematical extrapolation of the trend. *Regression analysis* can also fit exponential and higher-order mathematical trends to existing data and extend these trends into the future. Exponential trends are often used to forecast high-growth industries. *Prediction intervals* provide mathematical "probability brackets" around future predictions created by regression analysis. These basic forecasting skills are taught in any good college statistics course, and modern computer spreadsheet programs perform all of the basic operations with ease.

**Financial analysis.** In complex business situations, simple extrapolation of mathematical trends is usually inadequate for meaningful planning. Analysis of company plans and industry forecasts requires skills in financial analysis. Analysis of competing companies with similar organizational structures and product lines can yield useful ratios and benchmarks to use in forecasting the performance of the company in question.

**Space planning.** Macro-level space planning skills are the most relevant to strategic planning. These skills include

- Developing gross planning densities based on prototypical facilities or theoretical test fit studies
- Analyzing affinities between user groups and arranging large blocks of space to accommodate these affinities
- Analyzing shell building designs (either existing buildings or proposed designs) for suitability

**Site selection.** Site selection, a service widely offered by commercial real estate brokers and their consulting subsidiaries, can also be offered by architects. In any case, site selection needs to be built into the strategic facility plan as part of the overall process. Most experienced architects have adequate training and background to assess the physical aspects of a site, at least in the "big picture." However, selection of a major site also involves

- Economic skills, for analyzing demographic elements such as proximity to the workforce

- Financial skills, for analyzing costs
- Negotiation skills, for negotiating tax incentive packages offered by competing communities
- Political skills, for negotiating with competing sellers and communities for the fewest restrictions and the most services at the least cost
- Engineering skills, to analyze site access, transportation, utilities, and drainage
- Site planning skills, to determine how efficiently any particular site can be used

***Scheduling and sequential migration planning.*** Although taught in only a few architecture schools, this skill is essential to getting user groups into their desired locations at the right time without wasted moves, redundant moves, or excessive swing space. CPM (critical path method) scheduling, a powerful tool used by construction managers, is adaptable to planning a complex sequences of moves.

***Budgeting.*** Some architects are trained in construction cost estimating. Traditionally this was unit-price estimating involving detailed quantity take-offs, material costs, and labor rates. Budgeting for strategic facility plans involves higher-level estimating of a wider range of items. This may involve construction loan financing, raw land costs, A/E fees, FF&E costs, real estate commissions, utility connections, move costs, commissioning, temporary facilities, and network telecommunications in addition to construction costs. The owner's internal project management labor costs may even be included in the total project cost. The strategic facility plan must separate capital investments from operating expenses. For example, many architects do not realize that most owners treat architectural fees as capital investments, since they are essential ingredients of capital construction projects.

Strategic facility planners must first be able gather information about the gross costs of comparable facilities. These costs must be adjusted for location, market conditions, and inflation over time. The planner may establish trends and confidence intervals using linear regression analysis. Planners must be able to spread budgets over several fiscal years using cash-flow forecasting. Finally, planners must be able to analyze the relative advantages of alternative financing methods such as synthetic leasing and nonrecourse financing. Specific techniques for these analyses include net present value, internal rate of return, and equivalent annual cost. Any basic course in finance, such as those taught in most MBA programs, teach these basic skills.

***Research in economics.*** The ability to research companies that compete with your client is necessary to develop or confirm the basic business drivers for a strategic facility plan. (We will call the basic business statistics—such as revenue, head count, and unit sales—"drivers" or "business drivers" for lack of a better term.) In the case of public companies, information about their past revenues, head counts, and even real estate portfolios can be found in their annual reports and related documents such as 10-K reports. This information can be downloaded from the Web site maintained by the Securities and Exchange Commission or, in some cases, from the company's own Web site. Industry analysts are another source of information. This admittedly large category includes journalists, trade association officials, academic experts, government officials, and financial analysts employed by a variety of financial institutions.

You can gather two fundamentally different types of information—historic (actual) data and future forecasts. In rare cases it may even be possible to assess the accuracy of past forecasts by measuring the difference between past forecasts and actual performance.

For purposes of facility planning, historical analysis of competing companies is valuable in establishing trends and correlations between variables. *Elasticity* measures the change in one variable in relation to another variable. For example, if over time a 9 percent change in employee head count correlates to a 10 percent change in revenue, the elasticity of head count to revenue is 0.9 (90 percent).

***Written communications.*** Architects have always been trained to draw. The design studio system has also trained us to speak persuasively about our designs, whether we realize it or not. However, architects typically receive little formal training in technical writing.

Strategic facility plans are written documents accompanied by charts, graphs, and diagrams. The written narrative is the part that describes what the planners are trying to achieve and persuades executive management to provide the resources necessary to carry out the plan. Written communications need not be elaborate, but they do need to be clear, simple, grammatically correct, and convincing.

For a description of CPM and other scheduling methods, see the backgrounder Project Scheduling (13.3).

# PROCESS

Strategic facility planning frequently consists of two cyclical processes that come together on a regular basis. The demand cycle comprises those forces that drive the demand for space. The supply cycle comprises those forces that affect the supply of space. The two cycles come together annually in small and slow-growth companies but quarterly in large and fast-growth companies. Once the demand and supply cycles have merged, the steps shown below as 8–11 are taken:

| DEMAND CYCLE | SUPPLY CYCLE |
|---|---|
| 1. Strategic forecasts of revenue, product mix, geographic markets, mergers and acquisitions | 1. Portfolio additions and deletions (construction, leases, divestitures, etc.) |
| 2. Tactical forecasts of head counts, unit sales, R&D projects | 2. Occupancy/vacancy inventory |
| 3. Geographic location drivers | 3. Future additions and deletions (forecast) |
| 4. Workplace research, standards | 4. Budgets, financial constraints |
| 5. Translation into square feet and features | 5. Compare past forecasts to actual supply and demand |
| 6. Affinity relationships | 6. Identification of possible new sites |
| 7. Demand scenarios | 7. Supply scenarios |

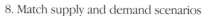

8. Match supply and demand scenarios
9. Determine sequential migration alternatives
10. Select the scenario that seems most likely to happen
11. Develop implementation and hedging techniques for the selected scenario

## Demand Cycle

The demand cycle represents the users' view of the portfolio. Forecasts from the strategic and tactical business plans are converted into forecasts of demand for space over time. While there is no perfect way of doing this, benchmarking various measures of elasticity is sometimes the best that can be done. If the elasticity of head count to revenue is high for both the company in question and its competitors, then revenue is a relatively good predictor of head count. (For example, if benchmarking studies show a 0.9 elasticity of head count to revenue, then a 100 percent increase in revenue can be expected to correspond to a 90 percent increase in head count.)

In extreme cases a corporation may lack credible projections of some or all of its basic business drivers. If this is so, the planner may need to develop independent forecasts of the corporation's basic business performance before developing the strategic facility plan. In some situations planners need to be able to go to executive management and say, "If you don't give us anything better to go on, here's what we will plan for."

Geographic location decisions are determined by a variety of factors. Retail and certain types of industrial businesses may be driven by proximity to customers. Bulk commodity businesses may be driven by proximity to suppliers or raw materials. High-tech businesses may want to locate near population centers with highly educated workers. Low-tech but labor-intensive businesses may want to locate facilities near population centers with inexpensive labor. The task of the planner is to determine which factors are most important to the corporation in question and to identify communities that best match those factors.

One of the most visible aspects of demand-side planning is the translation of all of the foregoing factors into square footage and required features. Head count is a reasonably good predictor of office space, although the recent trend seems to be toward greater density. Benchmarking similar office facilities can yield gross planning densities per seat, but don't forget two items: churn seats and workers without assigned seats. At any given time, roughly 10 percent of seats need to be empty "churn" seats. However, workers without assigned

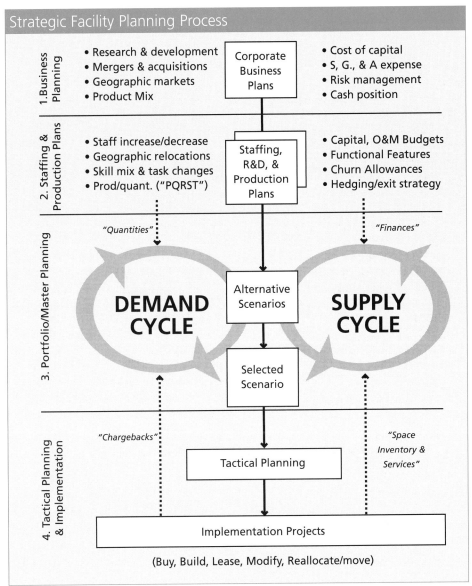

## Strategic Facility Planning Process

**1. Business Planning**

- Research & development
- Mergers & acquisitions
- Geographic markets
- Product Mix

**Corporate Business Plans**

- Cost of capital
- S, G., & A expense
- Risk management
- Cash position

**2. Staffing & Production Plans**

- Staff increase/decrease
- Geographic relocations
- Skill mix & task changes
- Prod/quant. ("PQRST")

**Staffing, R&D, & Production Plans**

- Capital, O&M Budgets
- Functional Features
- Churn Allowances
- Hedging/exit strategy

**3. Portfolio/Master Planning**

*"Quantities"*     *"Finances"*

**DEMAND CYCLE**     **Alternative Scenarios**     **SUPPLY CYCLE**

**Selected Scenario**

**4. Tactical Planning & Implementation**

*"Chargebacks"*     *"Space Inventory & Services"*

**Tactical Planning**

**Implementation Projects**

(Buy, Build, Lease, Modify, Reallocate/move)

seats can account for ratios of more than one worker per seat. Both factors need to be accommodated in planning density. Workplace research can lead to office planning standards that offer greater densities due to more compact designs and more unassigned seating.

In the case of manufacturing space, units of annual throughput may be the best high-level predictor of space required. For example, an engineering analysis may suggest that 110 square feet of manufacturing space will be needed per unit produced. When a detailed manufacturing and materials-handling analysis is not available, or when the manufacturing process has not yet been developed, benchmarking similar facilities for square feet per unit can be helpful.

The culmination of the demand cycle is one or more demand scenarios, which describe the future state of the portfolio as viewed by the demand side of the equation (i.e., the users).

The following items outline key information that is needed during the demand cycle, giving suggestions for where to find the information.

*Corporate strategic business plans for revenue, geographic locations, and markets.* Possible sources for this information include corporate planning or finance staff members or the CEO. Ideally, you would also like information on proposed mergers, acquisitions, and divestitures; however, it is extremely unlikely the CEO will release this information to you.

*Head count forecasts by division and worker type.* Possible sources for this are the human resources department, the finance department, or the operating units. However, different sources tend to make different forecasts, and it is unlikely that any of

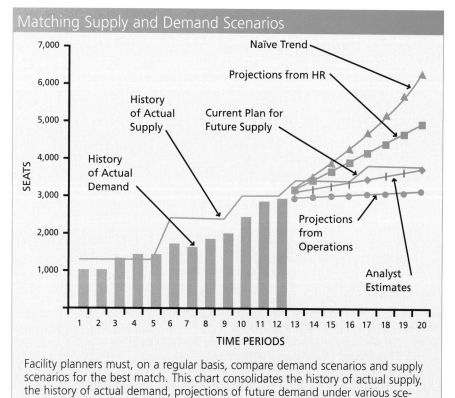

## Matching Supply and Demand Scenarios

**SEATS** (y-axis: 1,000 to 7,000)

**TIME PERIODS** (x-axis: 1 to 20)

- Naïve Trend
- Projections from HR
- History of Actual Supply
- Current Plan for Future Supply
- History of Actual Demand
- Projections from Operations
- Analyst Estimates

Facility planners must, on a regular basis, compare demand scenarios and supply scenarios for the best match. This chart consolidates the history of actual supply, the history of actual demand, projections of future demand under various scenarios, and projections of future supply under at least one scenario.

Copyright 2000 Thomas McCune

them will credibly predict three years out, which is the minimum time frame necessary for strategic facility planning.

*Units of sales and production by product type.* Possible sources for this would be marketing or manufacturing divisions. While one of the best predictors of office space requirements is head count, one of the best predictors of manufacturing space is units of throughput.

*Affinity relationships between major user groups.* Possible sources for this material are line managers of the groups.

*Alternative officing strategies.* These strategies are generally proposed by the real estate, human resources, or operating groups. They can improve the traditional ratio of "one person, one office" used in most traditional planning.

*Forecasts of industry growth, unit sales, and trends.* Possible sources are industry analysts, trade groups, and government agencies.

## Supply Cycle

While the demand cycle effectively represents the user's view of the portfolio, the supply cycle represents the landlord's view.

The first step in the supply cycle is to document changes in the portfolio during the reporting period. New properties that have entered the portfolio increase the supply of available space, while divestitures decrease the supply. Planners inventory the space to determine how much is actually occupied. (For example, there may have been no additions or divestitures, but a detailed inventory could reveal that 35 percent of the seats are unoccupied.) When future planned additions and divestitures to the portfolio are noted, the description of the space available over time becomes complete.

Budgets as financial constraints are largely a function of the supply side of the equation, since it is the landlord part of most corporate real estate organizations that provides the resources to build or otherwise acquire property.

Finally, while the users on the demand side of the equation state their requirements for space, it is frequently the landlord function on the supply side that actually locates and procures new property. Steps that are part of the site selection process include the following:

- Determine allowable site density based on governing regulations and good practice.
- Assess proximity to workforce population centers (demographics).
- Analyze proximity to transportation, utilities, and other infrastructure.
- Evaluate physical aspects of alternative sites, including topography, geology, and geometry.
- Understand financial attributes of various sites, including initial cost, tax incentives, and resale value.
- Assess the liabilities of various sites, including environmental problems, undesirable neighboring properties, covenants, easements, deed restrictions, archaeological impediments, and other entitlement restrictions.
- Confirm adequate on-site circulation and parking.
- Determine if there are similar businesses already in the area.

When the aforementioned information has been assembled, describing the future of the portfolio from the point of view of the supply side of the equation, the supply scenario is complete and it is time to begin melding the demand and supply scenarios into a single, selected portfolio scenario.

The following items suggest key information that is needed during the supply cycle and gives ideas about where to find that information.

*Occupancy of existing buildings.* Possible sources are human resources reports, previous move packages, network addresses, physical inventory of existing buildings by the planning staff, or a CAFM system if it has been maintained accurately.

*Real estate market conditions.* This includes vacancy rates, lease rates, available square footage, and building sizes in the vicinity.

*Alternative officing strategies proposed by the real estate group, human resources department, or operating groups.* These strategies can improve the traditional ratio of "one person, one office" used in most traditional planning.

## Selected Scenario

We now have one or more demand scenarios and one or more supply scenarios. The challenge is to select which supply scenario to implement. Selection strategies include these:

- *The stop-loss strategy.* This minimizes the downside risk of loss but may also limit the upside potential for gain. An example might include leasing space in small chunks with short-term leases so that space could be divested quickly if demand declines. Unfortunately, this would be an expensive strategy if the company grows and requires much additional space.
- *The swing-for-the-fences strategy.* This maximizes upside gain but does little to minimize downside risk. An example would be building a lot of space well ahead of the time when it might be needed, in the expectation of rapid growth. This would work well if the growth occurred as planned but would be very expensive if it did not.
- *The probabilistic strategy.* This attempts to assess the probability of occurrence of various future demand scenarios and to select the supply scenario that works best with the scenario most likely to occur.
- *The goodness-of-fit strategy.* This attempts to select the supply scenario that works acceptably with the widest range of future demand scenarios. The scenario that is finally chosen may not work perfectly with any demand scenario but rather works adequately with many.

Regardless of the technique used, the selected scenario must accommodate common problems and issues. These include lack of credible business plans and forecasts, the ups and downs of the business cycle, and hedging against failure.

*Lack of reliable business plans and forecasts on which to base strategic facility plans.* Strategic facility planners need to interact at the highest levels of the corporation to ensure they have access to current strategic and tactical planning information. Such interaction creates an opportunity to enhance the visibility and value of the facility planning function.

*The need to accommodate the cyclical nature of business in the long term.* The long-term lesson of business is that sooner or later all companies experience a downturn. No trend continues forever.

*The risk that big bets on unproven products will fail.* In industries with very rapid product cycles, corporations must always be developing new generations of product. In some cases they need to think several product cycles ahead of the current market. It is frequently better to bet on success than to promote failure by failing to have adequate facilities to support the core business.

## Strategic Facility Planning Terms

**Affinity:** Any form of working relationship that creates a need for physical proximity between two or more groups of workers.

**Alternative officing:** Any form of telecommuting, hoteling, unassigned seating, or other strategy that moves away from the traditional arrangement of "one person, one office."

**Duration:** The weighted average length of leases remaining in a portfolio.

**Hedge:** Any strategy intended to reduce future adverse consequences associated with a course of action or to provide additional future alternative courses of action.

**Migration:** A sequential process of several moves intended to move multiple user groups from their current locations to a desired future set of locations and proximities.

**Shareholder primacy doctrine:** he name for the legal principle that states that a corporation's primary duty is to maximize shareholder value and wealth.

**Supply-constrained:** Unable to supply the volume of product demanded by customers.

**Synthetic lease:** A special type of lease with option to buy that is treated as an operating lease for tax purposes instead of as a capital lease.

**Throughput:** The number of units that can be produced by a manufacturing plant during a given unit of time (40 automobiles per hour, for example).

**Transfer charges:** Any financial charges within a corporation from one internal group to another.

**Variable labor:** Temps or workers paid for piecework.

**Workplace effectiveness:** Any study of workplace productivity, employee satisfaction or retention, or any other factor that ultimately justifies improving or modifying the workplace to meet the business needs of a corporation.

### For More Information

Mahlon Apgar IV, "The Alternative Workplace: Changing Where and How People Work," *Harvard Business Review* (May-June 1998), is a review of alternative officing strategies. Used wisely, these strategies have the potential to increase density, reduce costs, improve employee recruiting and retention, and enhance productivity.

An overview of site selection processes can be found in Zvi Drezner, ed., *Facility Location: A Survey of Applications and Methods* (1996). Peter F. Drucker's *Innovation and Entrepreneurship: Practice and Principles* (1993) is a modern classic business strategy book. It helps you learn to think like a CEO. A good overview of simple financial analysis techniques using standard computer spreadsheets appears in Michael Hoots, "Dr. Spreadsheet or How I Learned to Stop Worrying and Love Financial Analysis," *Facility Management Journal* (January-February 1998). Classic space planning methods are presented by Richard Muther and J. D. Wheeler in *Simplified Systematic Layout Planning*, 3rd ed. (1994). Comprehensive methods for planning manufacturing facilities can be found in Richard Muther, *Systematic Planning of Industrial Facilities* (2000). Michael E. Porter's *Competitive Strategy: Techniques for Analyzing Industries and Competitors* (1998) is the standard text on strategic business planning.

The International Development Research Council publishes books and research documents for the corporate real estate market. The IDRC Foundation publishes research bulletin, papers, and surveys. *Infrastructure Delivery for Fast-Growth Companies*, IDRC Bulletin 21, compares project delivery methods for emerging companies. It is published in cooperation with ENR, a division of the McGraw-Hill Companies. *Scenario Planning for Corporate Real Estate Managers: Strategic Implications for a Changing Business Environment*, IDRC Bulletin 15, provides a good review of scenario planning methods, although it doesn't offer information about how to select which scenario(s) to pursue.

# 17 Design–Construction Services

## 17.1 Accessibility Compliance

### John P. S. Salmen, AIA

*Lawsuits stemming from accusations that ADA standards have not been followed are proliferating. Building owners and architects want to comply with ADA regulations but find them vague and inconsistent. Interpretations vary from state to state and case to case. Helping clients to navigate this maze can be a profitable service for architects who feel comfortable with the issues.*

According to the U.S. Census Bureau, more than 54 million Americans have disabilities, and more than half of these individuals are deaf. In other words, about two out of every ten people in the United States live with physical and mental impairments. To respond to the needs of this segment of the population, Congress passed the Americans with Disabilities Act (ADA) in 1990 and subsequently the related Americans with Disabilities Act Accessibility Guidelines (ADAAG).

Architects were among the original proponents of ADA legislation because they recognized that nationally consistent building codes were important for meeting the needs of persons with disabilities. The disabled community pushed for civil rights legislation, which is more broadly applicable than building regulations. The disadvantage of the civil rights approach is that there is no clear process for ensuring compliance, making it a challenge to respond appropriately to ADA regulations. The AIA continues to advocate clearer guidelines for ADA compliance and more uniformity in enforcement nationwide.

Consultants and firms that offer ADA compliance as a service assist other designers, building owners, and building operators in matters related to the accessibility of a facility and the ease with which diverse populations can use it. In general, this means determining how to apply the complex requirements of the ADA and ADAAG to a particular project.

Lawsuits have proliferated since the ADA was enacted. Anyone involved in making decisions related to a facility—building owners, designers, constructors, or operators—may be sued, either by individuals when a violation of the ADA is alleged in new or existing construction or by the Department of Justice when a pattern of practice in violation of the ADA is alleged. Initially lawsuits revolved around failure to implement so-called readily achievable measures, but then more complex cases involving alteration and new construction became more prevalent. Architecture firms familiar with the intricacies of the law and its applications can help their clients navigate these complicated issues.

## Summary

### ACCESSIBILITY COMPLIANCE SERVICES

#### Why a Client May Need These Services
▷ To determine if a project design complies with ADA requirements
▷ To survey ADA compatibility of an existing facility
▷ To check ADA compatibility after occupancy
▷ To provide expert witness testimony
▷ To plan space use to conform to ADA requirements

#### Knowledge and Skills Required
▷ Familiarity with the needs of the disabled population
▷ Knowledge of ADA and other accessibility laws
▷ Knowledge of barrier-free technologies

#### Representative Process Tasks
▷ Determine client's general ADA needs
▷ Identify client's potential accessibility problem areas and desired outcomes
▷ Compile plan review matrices
▷ Identify strategies for correcting problem areas
▷ Prepare implementation schedule with cost analysis
▷ Develop prototype design details for implementation

**JOHN P. S. SALMEN** *is president of Universal Designers & Consultants, Inc., a Takoma Park, Maryland, firm that specializes in accessibility compliance.*

## ADA—Protection for Americans with Disabilities

The ADA requires access to public places for individuals with mental and physical disabilities. It protects against discrimination in state and local government, telecommunications, employment, transportation, public accommodations, and private commercial facilities. The ADA includes five main sections. Architects are concerned primarily with titles II and III, which cover state, local, and privately owned commercial facilities and require that new, altered, and renovated facilities be designed and constructed so they are accessible to people with disabilities.

The U.S. Department of Justice (DOJ) is authorized by the ADA to enforce the ADA and its standards. The Architectural and Transportation Barriers Compliance Board (commonly known as the Access Board) develops the Americans with Disabilities Act Accessibility Guidelines (ADAAG). The Access Board serves in an advisory role to the DOJ, and ADAAG is intended for adoption as DOJ regulations. Unfortunately, ADAAG is sometimes unclear, and interpretations continue to evolve. Owners and architects are left frustrated by the lack of clear compliance guidance.

The DOJ may certify that accessibility provisions in state and local building codes are equivalent to ADA. The states of Washington, Florida, Maine, and Texas have received state ADA building code certification. However, designs that meet certified building codes still are not protected from ADA lawsuits, and the number of lawsuits against architects is growing.

The great majority of clients seeking accessibility services do so out of fear of lawsuits. Accessibility analysis can help clients understand current interpretations of ADA requirements to give them some assurance they have met the legal requirements and will not be subject to legal action. Specific accessibility services include provision of project-specific information about ADA compliance in both design and operations phases, existing facility surveys, postoccupancy evaluation surveys, expert witness testimony, space planning, and interior design.

**ADA compliance in design.** ADA protects the civil rights of disabled persons regarding access to public facilities by requiring building owners to make readily achievable modifications to existing facilities. Exactly what is needed to accomplish this goal is subject to shifting interpretation, particularly in complex facilities and in facilities owned by organizations with deep pockets (the latter are expected to spend more to make their facilities accessible).

The Department of Justice publishes a list of readily achievable modifications that can be considered to constitute compliance. These measures include such familiar items as changing doorknobs to levers, painting handicapped designations on parking spaces, and installing grab bars and wider stalls in restrooms. Lawsuits regarding failure to implement measures such as these have leveled off as building owners comply with these simple requirements. Further information about how to implement readily achievable measures for smaller, less complex facilities has been described in a technical update from the Department of Justice and a growing body of settlements and agreements.

More recently, highly visible suits have emerged in which the defendants are charged with improperly interpreting vague performance criteria set forth in the ADA legislation. Building owners and designers have found that ADA features formerly considered adequate for compliance are now being adjudged noncompliant. Often the plaintiffs charge that a building does not meet basic ADA criteria in letter or spirit. For example, a recent case involving the design of an arena addressed the requirement to provide persons in wheelchairs with "comparable lines of sight." In the past this requirement had been interpreted to mean that wheelchair-accessible seats must be provided in every section of an arena (from exclusive, high-priced areas to economy seating). In this case, however, the plaintiffs charged that wheelchair seats should be elevated or designed in some other way to prevent standing spectators from obstructing the view of the wheelchair occupants. One court agreed; two disagreed. The architects admitted no guilt but agreed to design so in the future.

As case law continues to evolve, there is a growing need to interpret ADA requirements. Architects and accessibility specialists must be able to provide insight into the intent of ADA provisions and a wide range of compliance recommendations and ensure that the ADA provisions in a building design meet or exceed currently prevailing interpretations of the federal requirements as well as applicable state and local building codes.

**ADA compliance in operations.** An important aspect of the ADA compliance process is to ensure that ongoing building operations procedures do not render ADA features ineffective. Many clients may not be aware of the operations requirements of the ADA. (For example, when maintenance personnel move a waste bin in a restroom so it blocks the accessible route to the accessible stall, is it the owner who has violated the law, or is the architect responsible for not designing a space large enough to accommodate adequate waste bins?) Accessibility services can also help owners and building operators establish operations procedures and train personnel so that accessibility, and ADA compliance, is maintained. In stadiums, theaters, and concert halls, operations procedures for ticket sales must comply with acceptable practice. Reservation procedures for lodging facilities also must address ADA issues. Accessibility services may include the preparation of ADA operations manuals.

**Facility and postoccupancy surveys.** Facility surveys and postoccupancy surveys are commonly performed to help an owner identify physical or operational issues in an existing facility that should be addressed in order to achieve or maintain ADA compliance. Periodic facility survey services may be offered so clients have some continuing assurance

| PROJECT DESCRIPTION* | FEDERAL LAWS | BUILDING CODES |
| --- | --- | --- |
| Federally owned project of any type | 1968 Architectural Barriers Act<br>1973 Rehabilitation Act<br>Other standards as described by the agency | Building codes may or may not be applicable |
| Project that utilizes federal funds or is built by the recipient of federal funds (private or government) | 1968 Architectural Barriers Act<br>1973 Rehabilitation Act, UFAS<br>Other standards appropriate to ownership use and type | State and/or local building codes may apply |
| Local government-owned commercial or public facility | ADA Title II<br>1973 Rehabilitation Act | State and/or local building codes may apply |
| Local government-owned multifamily housing | ADA Title II<br>1973 Rehabilitation Act<br>1988 Fair Housing Amendments Act | State and/or local building codes may apply |
| Privately owned public accommodation or commercial facility | ADA Title III | State and/or local building codes may apply |
| Privately owned multifamily housing | 1988 Fair Housing Amendments Act (public accommodation spaces must meet ADA) | State and/or local building codes may apply |
| Privately leased, government-owned public accommodation | ADA Title III (tenant)<br>ADA Title II (owner) | State and/or local building codes may apply |
| Government-leased, privately owned public accommodation | 1973 Rehabilitation Act (tenant)<br>ADA Title II (tenant)<br>ADA Title III (owner) | State and/or local building codes may apply |
| Church-operated, church-owned facility | None | Sate and/or local building codes may apply |
| Privately operated, church-owned facility | ADA Title III (tenant) | State and/or local building codes may apply |
| Church-operated, privately owned facility | ADA Title III (owner) | State and/or local building codes may apply |

*Temporary facilities must meet the same federal standards as similar permanent facilities.

Source: AIA, *Architectural Graphic Standards,* 10th ed. (2000).

that their maintenance and operations procedures will not compromise their ADA compliance status. There is a growing market for periodic facility surveys.

**Other services.** Accessibility services may include supporting either the plaintiffs or the defendants as an expert witness when there is a dispute about ADA compliance.

A much smaller (although increasing) number of clients seek "universal" design services to capture a greater market share. Particularly in housing markets in regions with growing elderly populations, owners understand that consumers with disabilities represent a growing market.

Services closely related to accessibility analysis include programming, site analysis, space planning, interior design, code compliance, and environmental graphic design. Some firms help government agencies comply with regulations requiring them to provide accessible "programs, services, and activities," which often (though not always) involves building accessibility.

▶ **Topics that discuss services related to accessibility issues and considerations include Programming (16.1), Site Analysis (16.2), and Code Compliance (17.3).**

## SKILLS

Architecture firms wanting to offer ADA consultation as a service either need to have someone on staff familiar with accessibility issues or contract with a firm with ADA expertise. Independent ADA consultants may practice alone or with a few employees.

Many accessibility compliance services are particularly suited to the talents of architects. For instance, these services often require review of building plans to evaluate conformance to ADA requirements. Building owners are increasingly aware of their liability exposure and use these plan reviews to protect themselves from ADA suits. Some accessibility consultants provide prototype designs for typical ADA-compliant spaces (e.g., restrooms, classrooms, hotel rooms). Helping in product selection and supplying information on barrier-free technologies are other services. Many specific types of equipment allow people with disabilities to use a facility.

***Familiarity with the disabled and accessibility laws.*** The first requirement for a firm or consultant offering accessibility services is familiarity with disabilities and the disabled community. The best way to gain this is to participate in organizations involved in disability advocacy, such as volunteering to serve on a local appeals board for disabled access.

The second major requirement for providing accessibility compliance services is a thorough and up-to-date knowledge of federal, state, and local laws, regulations, and case law. A good understanding of the civil rights nature of the federal law and its implications is also important. Some ADA consultants work with civil rights attorneys who are active in ADA issues.

Technically, an understanding of how people with disabilities operate in their spatial environment is essential. Familiarity with ergonomic design principles, awareness of space planning fundamentals, and product and equipment knowledge contribute to this overall understanding.

***Professional and other staffing needs.*** In delivering accessibility services, a firm or its consultants may work with building designers, landscape architects, and environmental graphic designers. A competent clerical staff is required. Some firms have communications staff to support publications work and report generation.

Health professionals—doctors who specialize in particular diseases or occupational and physical therapists—may also be consulted when designing for occupants with specific disabilities. Employing people with disabilities as consultants can reveal issues that otherwise might not be considered from their point of view. Human factor researchers, trainers, and software developers are other specialists often involved in ADA projects.

Special equipment used by accessibility specialists includes digital slope meters, force gauges, decibel meters, light meters, survey documents, and digital cameras.

## PROCESS

Factors that can affect the scope of accessibility services include the size and visibility of the client organization and the size and complexity of their facility and its uses. As already noted, organizations with greater resources often are expected to do more for ADA compliance than clients with smaller resources. Name recognition also matters—large, publicly visible organizations are more vulnerable to lawsuits. For high-profile clients, a corporate ADA program may be required. Small clients with small facilities may need only a walk-through to ensure that all compliance issues have been addressed.

***Generic steps to perform the service.*** During an initial meeting, the client's perceived ADA needs are determined. At that time clients may also be given basic information about ADA compliance as it relates to their organization.

In order to design an ADA program, the client's potential accessibility problem areas and desired outcomes must be identified. This step results in a set of plan review matrices.

Based on the matrices, strategies for correcting problem areas are identified, including a proposed implementation schedule. A cost analysis for phased implementation of the compliance plan is also prepared.

The next step is to develop prototype design details for project implementation. If surveys are required to assess the population using the building, the survey instrument is prepared and administered.

part 4  SERVICES

In some instances, client training programs and ongoing facility monitoring may be required as part of the ADA plan. These would include presentations for client training and preparation of operations manuals.

### For More Information

Information about the Americans with Disabilities Act and ADA accessibility guidelines is available from many sources, including printed materials and Web sites. Software has also been developed to help those trying to comply with ADA regulations.

The Architectural and Transportation Barriers Compliance Board (also called the Access Board) ADAAG manual *ADA Accessibility Guidelines for Buildings and Facilities* offers the best guidance for architects, as the actual ADA Standards for Accessible Design (28 CFR Part 36) are not particularly readable. The Access Board's Web site can be found at www.access-board.gov. Copies of all their publications are available on or from the site.

The Department of Justice has posted an ADA home page, which can be found at www.usdoj.gov/crt/ada/adahom1.htm. This includes links to technical assistance materials, an ADA information line, enforcement and status report information, settlement information, new or proposed regulations, and ADA mediation. The DOJ also has a hotline that offers help and information on both general and technical ADA questions: (800) 514-0301.

Icon Publishing offers the ADA and FMLA Reference Library CD-ROM. To find out more, visit their Web site at www.iconpublishing.com or call (360) 757-1770.

The *Universal Design Newsletter* covers late-breaking developments in ADA regulation. It is published by Universal Designers & Consultants, Inc., 6 Grant Avenue, Takoma Park, MD 20912, (301) 270-2470 (www.universaldesign.com/newsletter.html).

The Center for Universal Design (formerly the Center for Accessible Housing) evaluates, develops, and promotes accessible housing and universal design in buildings and related projects. The center is based at the North Carolina State University School of Design, Box 8613, Raleigh, NC 27695-8613, (919) 515-3082. The center has an InfoLine at (800) 647-6777 and a Web site at www.ncsu.edu/ncsu/design/cud/.

The software autoBOOK: USADA can help designers maneuver through the ADAAG. The program is published by Intermedia Design Systems, Inc., 950 New Loudon Road, Latham, NY 12110, (800) 320-4043 or (518) 783-1661. Their Web address is www.autobook-ids.com/disability.html.).

# 17.2 Building Design

## Richard McElhiney, AIA, and Joseph A. Demkin, AIA

*In building design, the architect integrates multidisciplinary knowledge to create building form responsive to client values, user needs, and public concerns.*

### Summary

### BUILDING DESIGN SERVICES

#### Why a Client May Need These Services

▷ To respond to rapid or sudden growth
▷ To move to a new location
▷ To update or replace older facilities
▷ To improve productivity in operations
▷ To implement major organizational restructuring
▷ To bring an existing facility up to current regulatory standards
▷ To transform or create a new image or brand identity

#### Knowledge and Skills Required

▷ Ability to evaluate program requirements critically
▷ Ability to create concepts that respond to program requirements
▷ Ability to delineate concepts and design solutions
▷ Understanding of building materials, components, and systems
▷ Understanding of building codes, standards, and regulations
▷ Familiarity with contracts and construction documentation
▷ Ability to communicate concepts to the client and consultants
▷ Knowledge of construction costs

#### Representative Process Tasks

▷ Develop project understanding
▷ Develop schematic design documents
▷ Develop design development documents

Architects don't *make* buildings per se. Using professional knowledge and skills, architects translate abstract ideas into building form expressed by the architect in sketches, plans, models, and specifications. Together these instruments of service provide the instructions for transforming design solutions into the reality of bricks and mortar.

The design process is difficult to map. It is nonlinear and highly interactive, embracing a mix of rational and intuitive decision making. Despite the lack of cookbook-style directions and definitive step-by-step procedures, architects successfully apply design thinking every day in providing building design services to their clients.

Contracts between clients and architects identify types of building design services (e.g., schematic documents, design development documents, construction documents, etc.) and the tasks contained in each. This topic focuses on what is generally addressed in schematic and design development documents. Construction documentation is profiled separately in Construction Documentation— Drawings (18.5) and Construction Documentation—Specifications (18.6).

Several trends are affecting how architects approach and carry out building design. First is the fact that clients continue to seek greater value from design services. Clients who are more sophisticated and better informed increasingly expect their building facilities to fulfill a range of needs beyond those mandated in health and safety regulations. This expectation challenges architects to be cognizant of those client needs and to respond to them creatively.

Other trends present opportunities for architects to increase their design capabilities and expand their range of creativity. In the technology arena, software advances are giving architects more powerful tools to shape and evaluate design solutions. In the regulatory arena, the growing use of performance-based building codes promises to provide architects with more freedom in meeting regulatory requirements.

## CLIENT NEEDS

The need for building design services is rooted in the forces of change that constantly affect the client's world. These forces are reflected in the exponentially increasing power of technology, changing public values and tastes, significant demographic shifts, fluctuating economic conditions, and other societal transformations at different levels and magnitudes. In response, clients implement change within the spheres of interest they can control, including their organizational structures, products and services, processes and technologies, physical and human resources, and facilities.

RICHARD MCELHINEY *is a partner with the New York–based firm R. M. Kliment & Frances Halsband Architects. He has lectured and has served as a critic in design at Columbia University and Rensselaer Polytechnic Institute.* JOSEPH A. DEMKIN *is the executive editor of the 13th edition of the* Architect's Handbook of Professional Practice.

Within this context, building design services become part of a broader decision-making process related to the client's mission and philosophies, business and marketing goals, production needs, and staffing needs. Supply and demand for space, production processes to be housed, when and how long initiatives will occur, and the cost ramifications for facility design and operation are among the factors that determine facility design requirements.

Although no single factor or decision drives the need for design services, some of the more compelling ones occur when a client or potential client does any of the following:

- Decides to launch a new business venture
- Determines that existing building facilities cannot accommodate actual or planned growth
- Finds that a facility has become too costly to operate and maintain
- Decides to relocate to another geographic location
- Desires to improve or create a different public image
- Seeks building investment credits and other tax incentives
- Is compelled to make existing facilities comply with new or updated building codes

***Scope of design services.*** The breadth and depth of building design services is different for each project. To tailor the services required, the architect works with the client to identify needed knowledge and skills and balances them with the project resources that are available. Examples of the types of services that architects may provide can be found in the following:

- Instructions section of AIA B141, Standard Form of Agreement Between Owner and Architect with Standard Form of Architect's Services
- AIA B163, Standard Form of Agreement Between Owner and Architect for Designated Services
- Part 4 (Services) of this *Handbook*

Some predesign services that provide a foundation for building design will be initiated and completed before the start of schematic design. Examples include strategic facility planning, feasibility studies, site selection analyses, programming, and establishment of project budget. Sometimes—depending on the project delivery method used—these services may overlap the building design increments of service. Other services, however, need to be integrated into the building design process if meaningful and effective results are to be achieved. Examples of these design-linked services include sustainable design, energy analysis and design, lighting design, architectural acoustics, and seismic analysis and design.

***Markets for design services.*** The architectural profession serves diverse client groups in different market sectors. Nonetheless, the AIA Firm Survey 2000 reports that most architecture firms tend to concentrate on a single client type, most commonly private businesses and state and local governments. Together, these two client types account for half of all AIA member firm billings. Other clients—in descending order of billings—include developers and construction companies, nonprofit institutions, private individuals, and finally other architects, engineers, and design professionals. Predictably, private individuals represent the largest client base for smaller firms and the smallest base for larger firms.

Most clients have their architects provide all of their required building design services. However, some clients engage architects only for selected portions of design and hire needed consultants and specialists under separate contracts. Clients with internal design capability may elect to do selected design tasks themselves. The client's organizational structure and approval authority determine how much the client will participate in the design process. The client's level of participation and approach to making approvals influence the way the architect will structure and carry out the design process.

## SKILLS

In *How Designers Think* (1990) architect and author Bryan Lawson states that design—in the generic sense—involves "a highly organized mental process capable of manipulating many kinds of information, blending them into a coherent set of ideas and finally generating some realization of those ideas." Lawson notes that although the realization is often in the form of a drawing, it could equally well be a schedule, chart, or other product.

In building design, architects manipulate a spectrum of scientific, artistic, and technological information. To blend this information requires the designer to work in a balanced and creative manner. Some individuals have a more natural, innate feel for design. However, it is generally held that design skills can be acquired and developed through a combination of rigorous formal education, mentoring, on-the-job training, and continuing education. The most significant and fundamental areas of knowledge and skills required for building design include:

- Research skills for the collection of data that can inform and support decision making
- Critical thinking to analyze program requirements and evaluate design choices
- Understanding of how clients think and the nature of users
- Ability to integrate a wide range of knowledge
- Knowledge of building materials, components, and systems and how they work together
- Proficiency in thinking spatially in two and three dimensions
- Ability to depict design concepts and solutions in graphic form
- Ability to collaborate and work in team settings
- Knowledge of and facility with available design tools and technologies
- Understanding of building codes, standards, and regulations
- Knowledge of building economics and cost control
- Ability to communicate orally and in writing

In smaller firms, design capabilities may reside with individuals who also have business and management responsibilities. In larger firms, design capabilities are more likely to be the sole responsibility of one or more individuals, while others handle administrative, business, and management assignments.

***Multidisciplinary knowledge.*** At a minimum, every building design solution integrates architectural knowledge with structural, mechanical, and electrical engineering knowledge. Depending on the nature of the project, however, a greater depth of knowledge may be required from these allied fields or from the consultants for a particular building type, such as hospitals, laboratories, court facilities, and theaters.

Project needs may require the use of specialists in telecommunications, hazardous materials abatement, geotechnical investigations, security, vertical transportation, or curtain wall systems. Other disciplines may include civil engineering, landscape design, acoustical design, lighting design, energy analysis, environmental graphic design, historic preservation, indoor air quality analysis, code compliance, accessibility compliance, cost estimating, materials research, anthropology, and industrial hygiene.

Beyond the ability to integrate a wide range of knowledge, the building design professional is called upon to do three things:

- Determine the areas of knowledge needed for a given initiative
- Assemble and organize the providers of the required knowledge
- Communicate with individuals from many disciplines

***Design tools and techniques.*** Rapidly advancing digital technology is providing architects and other designers with increasing capability and power for addressing design tasks. Examples include 3-D modeling for massing studies; programs for diagramming of adjacencies and developing space plans, sun and shadow analysis or preliminary energy analysis; programs for designing structural, lighting, and acoustical systems; and software for determining the impact of materials on indoor environmental quality. For design delineation and presentations, CAD still represents the most widely used drawing application. Associated delineation software includes specialized rendering programs, animation programs, and programs capable of creating three-dimensional tours and walk-throughs.

The emergence of intelligent parametric building design computer applications, in which building information is stored as objects rather than as a collection of lines and arcs, is likely to integrate a broad range of currently available design and analysis functions. In parametric applications, building objects or components are defined by their parameters, which

**Computer Technology in Architectural Practice (12.1) covers current and emerging automated applications.**

Using the Internet in Practice (12.2) discusses Web applications for architectural practice.

may include the ways in which the object or component interacts with other building components, as well as its performance characteristics.

The Internet continues to grow as a collaboration tool among project team members. Its uses encompass the exchange of project information via e-mail and videoconferencing and the electronic transfer of drawing files.

Models, mock-ups, and special equipment are sometimes used in the course of building design. Three-dimensional models can depict a proposed building form at various scales. Mock-ups can replicate selected building spaces and furnishings such as a cluster of workstations. Using models and mock-ups, a design team can analyze and evaluate spatial quality, ergonomic issues, lighting quality, and other characteristics. When such analyses are critical—as in medical or research facilities—models and mock-ups may be used in controlled laboratory settings to better simulate and evaluate the performance of design options.

Perhaps a lesser known and less widely used design tool is the Heliodon, a device used to simulate sunlight on a building model for various solar azimuths and angles at any given site location for any time of the year. Sometimes time-lapse videos are used in conjunction with the Heliodon to dynamically record and evaluate solar and daylighting effects.

## PROCESS

Architect Francis Duffy describes building design as an "imaginative" process that "is also highly practical, involving an inventive grasp of user requirements so that they can be given—by the clever allocation of always too scarce resources—popular and appropriate spatial expression" (*Architectural Knowledge,* 1998). To help us look deeper into the design process, conceptual models attempt to identify and describe the fundamental components of design and the relationships between them.

One widely cited design model depicts the design process as one that continuously alternates between the steps of analysis and synthesis. In the analysis cycle, facts are gathered, objectives are defined, relationships are explored, and design influences are identified, organized, and prioritized. In the synthesis cycle, concepts are developed and evaluated against objectives set in the analysis cycle. As these steps are repeated over and over, solutions take on increasing depth of detail until a final one is selected.

Another model structures the design process in the major steps of assimilation, general study, development, and communication. In assimilation, general information and information specific to the problem are gathered and organized. In the general study increment, the nature of the problem is investigated along with possible solutions or means of solution. In development, one or more tentative solutions are developed and refined. In communication, one or more solutions are communicated to people inside and outside the design team. As in most design processes, these steps are not necessarily sequential.

A hybrid of the two models described above expands the analysis-synthesis cycle to include appraisal and decision steps. The resulting analysis/synthesis/appraisal/decision sequence is accomplished in increments of outline proposal, schematic design, and detailed design.

***Design influences.*** Regardless of the conceptual approach taken and methods used in building design, each project presents a different combination of opportunities and constraints, and contains a unique set of cultural, environmental, technological, and aesthetic considerations. In the process of understanding a problem and creating solutions, many of these considerations will emerge as inherent to the situation, giving each project its own unique set of design influences.

***Contractual framework.*** Agreements between the client and architect provide a

### Nature of Design

The list below views design within the context of problems, solutions, and process. Although not meant to be a comprehensive list of discrete design properties, the descriptions are intended to provide an overall picture about the *nature* of design.

**Design Problems**
- Design problems cannot be comprehensively stated.
- Design problems require subjective interpretation.
- Design problems tend to be organized hierarchically.

**Design Solutions**
- There are an inexhaustible number of different solutions.
- There are no optimal solutions, with several sometimes yielding equally beneficial results.

**Design Process**
- The process is endless.
- There is no infallibly correct process.
- The process involves identifying problems as well as solving them.
- Design inevitably involves subjective value judgment.
- Design is a prescriptive activity.
- Designers work within the context of a need for action.

*Adapted from Bryan Lawson,* How Designers Think: The Design Process Demystified, *2nd Ed. (1990)*

## Design Influences

Every project situation is different. Each presents a different set of requirements and limitations. Each presents a unique set of cultural, environmental, technological, and aesthetic contexts to be considered. Each presents its own set of challenges and opportunities. Design brings to the surface the major considerations inherent in a situation. It is a process that is both problem-seeking and problem-solving. While every project has a unique combination of design influences, some of the more important ones are discussed here:

**Client.** Some clients have a clear idea of program, budget, and other project objectives, including the final appearance of the building. Others look to their architect to help them define the project objectives and to design a building that meets those objectives. In both cases the effectiveness of the relationship between client and architect is a major factor in making design decisions throughout the project.

**Program.** All clients have a series of aspirations, requirements, and limitations to be met in design. The program provides a place for identifying and delineating these factors and any number of related considerations. The program may be short or long, general or specific, descriptive of needs or suggestive of solutions.

**Community concerns.** Clients and their architects must adjust their designs to satisfy community groups, neighbors, and public officials. These design adjustments are often ad hoc efforts to meet objections or to gain support rather than direct responses to codified requirements.

**Codes and regulations.** Regulatory constraints on design have increased steadily. Beginning with simple safety requirements and minimal land use and light-and-air zoning, building codes and regulations have grown into a major force in design that regulates every aspect of design and construction.

**Context and climate.** Contextual factors include the nature of the surrounding fabric of natural and built elements. Existing patterns and characteristics of this fabric can provide clues or starting points for approaching site development as well as the building design, influencing its configuration and use of materials, colors, and textures. Climatic factors include the nature of regional micro-climates defined by solar radiation, temperatures, humidity, wind, and precipitation.

**Site.** These factors include site size; configuration; topography; geotechnical characteristics; ecological features including vegetation, wildlife habitats, water elements and drainage; and accessibility to the property.

**Building technology.** Building configuration, materials, and systems are rarely arbitrarily chosen and are only partially based on aesthetic criteria. For example, the floor-to-floor height required to accommodate structural, mechanical, lighting, and ceiling systems in a cost-effective manner varies significantly from an apartment house to an office building to a research facility. Similarly, office fenestration may be based on one module and housing on another module. In still other cases, these dimensions may be dictated largely by mechanical systems or even by the knowledge and preferences of the local construction industry.

**Sustainability.** In its broadest scope, sustainability refers to the ability of a society, ecosystem, or any such ongoing system to continue functioning into the indefinite future, without being forced into decline through exhaustion or overloading of the key resources on which that system depends. For architecture, this means design that delivers buildings and communities with lower environmental impacts while enhancing health, productivity, community, and quality of life.

**Cost.** In most cases there is a limit to the funds available for construction. Once defined, this limit has a major influence on subsequent design decisions, from building size and configuration to material selection and detailing. Although most budgets are fixed (often by the amount of financing available), others may be flexible. For example, some owners are willing to increase initial budgets to achieve overall life cycle cost savings.

**Schedule.** The demands and constraints set by the project schedule may influence how specific issues are explored and considered. For example, an alternative requiring a time-consuming zoning variance may be discarded in favor of one that can keep the project on schedule. Another example may include committing to a final site plan early in the process—before the building footprint drawn on the site plan is fully designed.

*Adapted from Bradford Perkins, FAIA, AICP, "Design Phases," Architect's Handbook of Professional Practice, 12th Edition (1994)*

contractual framework for describing what will be done but not the means and methods to be used, which will be left to the discretion of the architect. Within this framework, the contract identifies specific responsibilities, including those of the architect, owner, and possible third parties; establishes a schedule, including starting and completion dates; and defines milestone dates for submittals and approvals.

The agreement may describe design activities in detail or, in the case of small or limited-scope projects, in a few sentences. AIA Document B141, the most commonly used form of owner-architect agreement in the United States, establishes the scope and types of design services organized in the increments of schematic design documents, design development documents, and construction documents. Brief summaries for each of these increments are given below.

Services in the *schematic design* increment establish the general scope and conceptual design of a project, and the scale and relationships among the proposed building components. The primary objective is to arrive at a clearly defined, feasible concept and to present it in a form that results in client understanding and acceptance. To achieve this objective, the architect must understand and verify the project program, explore alternative solutions, and provide a reasonable basis for analyzing the cost of the project. Deliverables at the end of schematic design may include a conceptual site plan, preliminary building plans with elevations and sections, perspective sketches, study models, electronic visualizations, and a statistical summary of the design area and other characteristics in comparison to the program requirements. The final step in schematic design is to obtain client approval—preferably in writing.

Services in the *design development* increment strive to achieve the refinement and coordination necessary for a polished work of architecture. Here decisions made in schematic design are worked out at a more detailed level to minimize the possibility of major modifications being needed during the development of construction contract documents. In design development the design team works out a clear, coordinated description of all aspects of the design, including architectural, mechanical, electrical, plumbing, and fire protection systems. Deliverables are similar to those of schematic design but are more detailed. They include drawings and specifications, an updated cost estimate, and, if required, the preparation of estimated schedules for construction. Again, written client approval provides a basis for subsequent work. The approved design development documents provide the basis for the *construction documents* increment, which sets forth in detail the requirements for construction. Depending on the project delivery method, the design development increment could be significantly minimized or even skipped over.

**Design as an ongoing process.** Design thinking as used by architects can be applied at many points within the facility life cycle. Design doesn't necessarily begin with schematic design and end with design development. In pre-design initiatives, design thinking can help conceptualize and anticipate the physical implications of strategic decisions, also serving to connect the processes of planning and design. In construction documentation, design thinking can help ensure that what is drawn and written is as responsive as possible to the design intent and other project objectives. During construction, design judgment is extremely valuable in making decisions—for example, when an unforeseen condition requires choices that vary from the construction documents.

**Design potential.** The core competencies and capabilities of architects—rooted in building design—represent the unique contribution the architectural profession brings to the construction industry and to the public at large. In the emerging global economy, the currency of knowledge and design thinking—coupled with the integrative and facilitative skills of architects—can play an increasingly expanded and valued role in addressing the needs of clients.

## For More Information

The AIA Design PIA maintains a Web page on the AIA Web site at www.aia.org. The site contains information about the mission, policies, initiatives, and special reports of the AIA Committee on Design.

A vast number of publications address the many facets of architectural design including theory, philosophy, history, and styles. The titles profiled below, however, focus on the nature of the design process and on delineation methods and techniques used in building design.

In *How Designers Think: The Design Process Demystified, 3rd Ed.* (1999), architect and psychologist Bryan Lawson delivers a readable discourse on what design thinking entails and how to understand and apply it. Many architectural examples are used;

▶ **Agreements with Clients (10.1) provides guidance on developing contracts with clients.**

## Discovery and Understanding

Prior to undertaking schematic design tasks, the architect reviews information provided by the owner, which may include program requirements, project schedule, and project budget. The architect also performs an evaluation of the site based on information provided by the owner and reviews the owner's proposed method for construction services to verify if it will affect the scope, schedule, and budget. (These tasks are part of the project administration services, supporting services, and evaluation and planning services described in detail in articles 2.1, 2.2, and 2.3 of the AIA B141 document.)

This preliminary aspect of design is important, even critical, to the eventual success of a project. At this point there is opportunity to discover whether

- Additional information is needed
- There is adequate expertise for the project type
- Constraints may be imposed by incomplete or inadequate information

As the design process unfolds, the architect may turn up new information or discover that the information in hand is not complete or perhaps no longer relevant. Thus, like design itself, the understanding of the project is an ongoing process that requires an ample degree of vigilance and monitoring by the designer.

▶ **The related services of construction documentation are described in Construction Documentation—Drawings (17.4) and Construction Documentation—Specifications (17.5).**

part 4 SERVICES

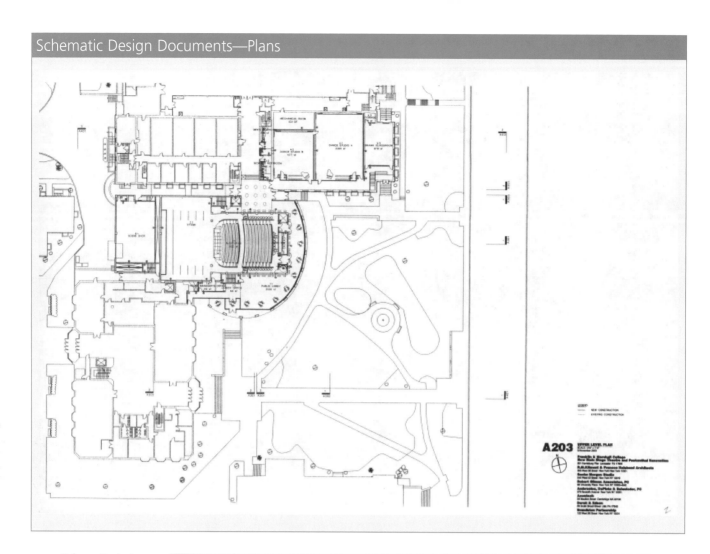

Schematic design documents provide a level of information that establishes and delineates the building design concept.

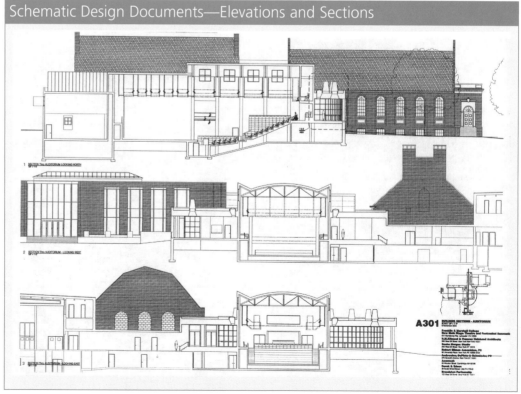

F.M.Kliment & Frances Halsband Architects, New York, New York

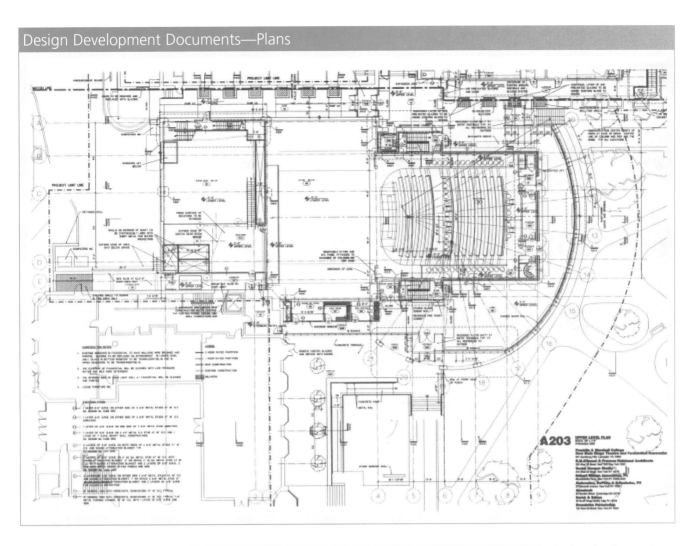

## Design Development Documents—Elevations and Sections

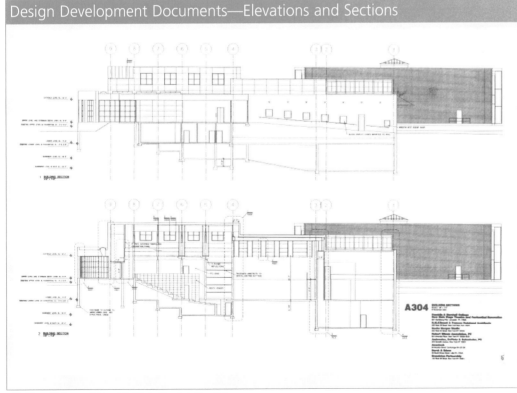

Design development documents augment information contained in schematic design documents to further refine, illustrate, and describe the building design.

F.M.Kliment & Frances Halsband Architects, New York, New York

however, the thrust of the book is about generic aspects of design rather than about building design per se. As noted by the publisher, this book is intended not as an authoritative description of how designers should think but to provide helpful advice on how to develop an understanding of design.

Architect Kenneth Allison meshes the subjects of design and project management into a single discussion in *Getting There by Design: An Architect's Guide to Design and Project Management* (1997). Allison describes fundamental principles for both of these dimensions of practice in four major parts: project context, decisions and techniques, managing costs and fees, and cultures as action systems.

C. Thomas Mitchell's *Redefining Designing: From Form to Experience* (1993) contains a provocative discussion about why architects and designers need to elevate the importance of client and user needs in building design. In a later work, *New Thinking in Design* (1996), Mitchell presents a series of interviews with thirteen leading international designers committed to client- and user-centered design approaches.

James Marston Fitch's classic *American Building: The Environmental Forces That Shape It* (originally published in 1947, now available in an updated and expanded 1999 edition) examines how buildings respond to and control environmental forces through building and system design. William Bobenhausen provides a new discussion about "green" architecture and its connection to meaningful design solutions in the 1999 edition.

Stewart Brand's *How Buildings Learn: What Happens After They're Built* (1994) calls for rethinking the way buildings are designed so that they may be more readily adapted to ever-changing user needs. Brand's thesis is that buildings adapt best when constantly refined and reshaped by their occupants and that architects can mature from being artists of space to becoming artists of time.

Christopher Alexander's mathematically based *Notes on the Synthesis of Form*, which appeared in the 1960s, provided the basis for two subsequent works of a more qualitative bent. These still-in-print titles are *A Timeless Way of Building* (1977) and *A Pattern Language* (1977). Both deal with design approaches intended to let users participate in the design process. In each of 253 patterns, Alexander explicitly links what takes place in various kinds of spaces to the physical layouts of the spaces themselves. Collectively, these patterns represent a "pattern language" that allows designers and non-designers to communicate and to participate in creating an infinite variety of new and unique buildings.

In *Design Drawing* (1997) Frank Ching and colleagues describe delineation from several perspectives: drawing from observation, drawing systems, and drawing from imagination. A supplemental CD-ROM contains information and instruction to elucidate a broad range of design drawing concepts through animation, video, and three-dimensional models.

Paul Laseau's *Architectural Representation Handbook: Traditional and Digital Techniques for Graphic Communication* (2000) provides a guide to traditional, new, hybrid, and emerging representational techniques along with the roles of each in the design process. The illustrations are organized in relation to an architectural drawing "vocabulary" that includes the design activities of seeing, thinking, and communicating.

*Color Drawing: Design Drawing Skills and Techniques for Architects, Landscape Architects, and Interior Designers,* 2nd ed. (1999), by Michael E. Dole, is an extensively updated and reorganized work. It covers drawing techniques, color theory, and presentation drawings with step-by-step instructions and in-depth guidance. Included are innovative ways to create design drawings with color copiers and the latest computer techniques.

*The Art of Architectural Illustration 3* (1999), by architect-illustrator Gordon Grice, showcases the works of forty-three international illustrators. Most of the rendering techniques in use today are represented, including digitally produced drawings.

# 17.3 Code Compliance

## Ralph Gerdes, AIA

*As codes become more complex, the demand for experts in code compliance expands. Architects who combine the necessary technical knowledge with communications and leadership skills will find abundant opportunities to offer this service.*

The most basic code compliance service is review of the project design (from schematic design through design development) to provide advice on code issues. When alternative methods or materials are introduced and must be judged on a performance basis, code compliance services may include assistance with code interpretation. Increasingly, the scope of these services is broadening to include review of construction documents for code-related issues, field reviews during construction, and construction testing.

Code compliance consulting services first emerged in the 1970s with the trend toward design of unique and nontraditional structures such as atriums because these structural types were not specifically addressed in the building codes of the time. The field has seen a steady, progressive growth over the years, with demand for code compliance services increasing as building codes become more complex. The emerging performance-based building codes are expected to further stimulate the market for these services.

## CLIENT NEEDS

Building owners or architects involved in innovative projects with nontraditional architectural elements or building materials often find their designs raise issues not explicitly addressed by the codes. Highly complex facilities (e.g., medical and laboratory facilities; stadiums, arenas, convention centers, and other large assembly areas; airports; large schools; assisted-living complexes; and warehouse facilities) often involve complex code issues. These building types also may involve regulatory integration issues generated by special concerns such as proper ventilation and storage of hazardous materials or accessibility to the disabled.

Many clients will need a code compliance determination in order to show that an alternative method or material meets the intent of a code. Such a determination may be supported by design analysis services that document the projected performance of various design options. Other clients use code compliance consultants only for assistance with controversial code issues.

Clients who need buildings designed in a jurisdiction without a building code often seek the services of a code compliance expert to evaluate the life safety and fire safety aspects of a design. In these cases nationally adopted building code standards can be applied, supplemented by judgment calls based on experience when necessary. Recently some states (e.g., Indiana) where uniform statewide building codes are in effect have discontinued review of building plans by state code officials, creating another market for code compliance services.

Government agency clients are more likely to require a full range of code compli-

### Summary

## CODE COMPLIANCE SERVICES

### Why a Client May Need These Services
- To evaluate code issues for facilities of a complex nature
- To determine whether alternative methods or materials meet code requirements
- To assist in interpreting controversial code issues
- To assist clients in jurisdictions without a building code

### Knowledge and Skills Required
- In-depth knowledge of building codes
- Knowledge of building service systems
- Knowledge of fire safety concepts and technologies
- Experience in the code review and approval process

### Representative Process Tasks
- Analyze preliminary design
- Prepare preliminary report, including code summary and potential code-related design issues
- Obtain review of design development documents by code officials
- Submit request (if needed) for discretionary action before local code officials
- Review construction documents
- Prepare final report

**RALPH GERDES** *is a building code and fire safety consultant with Ralph Gerdes Consultants, LLC. He serves as AIA liaison to the International Code Council and the National Fire Protection Association. Gerdes consults on projects throughout the United States and abroad, lectures on fire safety at universities, and participates in code-writing groups.*

Building Codes and Regulations (14.4) provides an overview of how building codes are established and enforced.

The client needs, skills required, and processes involved in complying with accessibility laws, an important area of code compliance, are described in Accessibility Compliance (17.1).

ance services, extending through the entire design and construction process and including review of construction documents, field review during construction, and construction testing. In these cases, code compliance services may overlap with provision of construction documents and construction administration services. Related services include accessibility compliance, indoor air quality consulting, construction defect analysis, egress studies, energy analysis, materials research and/or specifications, preliminary project programming for code compliance, seismic analysis and design, service as a code change proponent for manufacturers and industry or professional organizations, and zoning process assistance.

The code compliance services field traditionally has been dominated by fire protection engineers. Many firms that began by offering fire code consulting services have broadened their scope to include consulting on building codes and ADA. For example, Rolf Jensen & Associates, a fire protection engineering firm in Chicago, first offered code consulting services in the late 1960s and has grown to be one of four or five very large (50- to 200-person) code consulting firms in the country. These large firms have national and international branch offices and tend to serve clients with large projects.

Dozens of smaller consulting firms also offer code compliance services. These firms, generally staffed by one to five professionals, tend to cluster around engineering schools that offer strong fire protection engineering programs, such as the Illinois Institute of Technology, the University of Maryland, Worcester (Massachusetts) Polytechnic Institute, and Oklahoma State University.

While only a handful of architects currently specialize in code compliance consulting, the growing demand offers abundant opportunities for architects.

## SKILLS

The architect's ability to read drawings and understand architectural intent adds immeasurable value to code-consulting services. The architect's communication skills and ability to understand the integrative aspects of design adds a dimension most engineers are not equipped to deliver.

Much of the core knowledge required of someone offering code compliance services may be obtained by careful study of the model codes. The code development process is public and consensus-based; anyone with an interest can follow current code issues and stay abreast of changes and controversies in the codes arena. Participating in the code development process by serving on one of the committees responsible for recommending changes in the codes is an excellent way to network with the leaders of the code community. (See the For More Information section at the end of this topic.)

People skills are especially important for those offering code compliance services. After all, they are employed not only to provide advice on technical concerns but to resolve potential conflicts in order to keep their clients out of trouble. The ability to establish a good working rapport with state and local code officials is essential to success. Depending on the geographic area of practice, the work may require repeated negotiations with a single set of code officials. In these cases, the ability to earn the respect and trust of the code officials is doubly important.

## PROCESS

Code compliance review must begin early in a project so that any conflicts with applicable codes can be ironed out before they become difficult or expensive to correct. Likewise, it is best to get any specialty consultants required for the project on board early so there are no surprises later in the process.

***Teaming approach.*** Depending on the scope of a project, specialties in structural, electrical, HVAC, fire, seismic, and ADA services are most likely to be pertinent for code compliance review. When computer analysis is required to document the projected performance of various design options, mastery of the relevant modeling program will also be needed. An architecture firm offering code compliance services may have some of these skills in-house but may have to contract for others. The model codes community provides a good nationwide network for locating consultants with expertise in various specialty areas.

## Architects Will Benefit from U.S. Building Code Consolidation

Ever since the development of the first American building codes early in the twentieth century, building codes have varied significantly from region to region. With the publication of the first editions of the International Building Code (IBC) and the International Residential Code (IRC), the fragmentation of American building codes effectively ceased. The international codes were virtually assured of adoption because the three U.S. model code groups—BOCA (Building Officials and Code Administrators), ICBO (International Conference of Building Officials), and SBCCI (Southern Building Code Congress International)—worked together through the International Code Council (ICC) to develop and publish them. At the same time, the three groups are maintaining their separate, regionally based organizations to service the building code community.

**To what extent will the international building codes be used internationally?** The codes are not really international, but there is hope they will become more widely used. "Calling it 'international' keeps it from being called the 'U.S. Building Code,'" explains Bill Tangye, SBCCI chief executive officer. "Some U.S. model codes are already used outside the United States. Bermuda uses BOCA, and Western Samoa uses ICBO." There is also the hope that consolidation of the three U.S. codes will increase the chances of their adoption by developing countries.

**How many international codes are there?** The ICC has published the following codes:

- International Building Code (for non-residential properties)
- ICC Electrical Code
- International Energy Conservation Code
- International Existing Buildings Code
- International Fire Code
- International Fuel Gas Code
- International Mechanical Code
- International Performance Code
- International Plumbing Code
- International Private Sewage Disposal Code
- International Property Maintenance Code
- International Residential Code (covers hotels and motels, apartments, townhouses, and single-family dwellings)
- International Zoning Code

The American Institute of Architects has been promoting a single building code since the 1970s. The benefits to the design profession are great. The design process is simplified and the cost of producing design and construction drawings is often reduced. Companies that build in more than one region of the country or in foreign countries benefit from using a coordinated set of building codes.

The model building code groups finally embraced the idea of a unified building code in the early 1990s, motivated by fear of federal government action. In the wake of the Americans with Disabilities Act (ADA) and the North American Free Trade Agreement, it seemed plausible that the federal government might intrude into the building code promulgation business to call for a unified code in order to maintain competitiveness in the increasingly global construction market. In defense of the voluntary code development process, the code groups embraced the single-code concept.

**What are the benefits of the international building codes?** For architects, the family of international building codes offers a number of benefits and opportunities:

*Streamlined implementation of the Americans with Disabilities Act (ADA).* One of the frustrations with the ADA has been that the Department of Justice (DOJ) hasn't certified local codes. With adoption of the International Building Codes, the DOJ could certify one model code, effectively ending the confusion about what is required for compliance with ADA.

*State-of-the art hazard mitigation.* The most current wind, seismic, and flood criteria have been incorporated into the IBC and IRC. One of the biggest changes is the adoption of the more stringent Southern Building Code wind provisions for low-rise buildings (up to four stories). Previously the one- and two-family dwelling code didn't have seismic and wind requirements, preventing its adoption in certain areas. The new residential code, which results from an effort to reach national consensus, has provisions for wind and seismic conditions and will qualify for the National Flood Insurance Program.

*Performance code.* The International Performance Code provides additional guidance on the "alternate materials and methods" sections of the building and fire codes and ultimately could be the most significant element of the international building codes package.

**Work increments.** Code compliance review typically begins during schematic design or possibly at the end of that project phase. The schematic design is analyzed and a preliminary report prepared that includes a code summary and identifies potential code-related design issues. A code summary contains basic information such as occupancy classification, minimum construction requirements, exiting and materials requirements, and so on. The discussion of code-related design issues typically includes recommendations for resolving each of the issues, for example, through design modification or by seeking a code variance.

During design development, a preliminary review by the local authorities (fire, building code, etc.) is desirable so that any potential compliance concerns can be resolved early in the design process. Jurisdictions and agencies vary in their receptivity to this approach. Some will not perform such reviews, while others encourage it; some charge for the service, and some do not. When a firm staff member or consultant has a good working relationship with local officials, he or she may be able to facilitate this valuable early communication. When it is not possible to meet with officials during design development, a staff member's or consultant's judgment on emerging issues is even more critical.

When code compliance problems do arise, a submittal may be prepared and the case for discretionary action argued before the relevant officials. A staff member or consultant's rapport with the officials and in-depth knowledge of code requirements often is critical to achieving a decision that is positive for a project's success.

In some cases, the scope of code compliance services includes review of construction documents, often at 75–80 percent completion and again at 90 percent. The deliverables would be a letter detailing the findings of the document review, written documentation of relevant phone calls, and copies of all relevant correspondence.

### For More Information

BOCA International, Inc. (Building Officials and Code Administrators) is the code organization for the eastern and midwestern regions of the United States. They can be reached at 4051 W. Flossmoor Road, Country Club Hills, IL 60478, (708) 799-2300 (www.bocai.org).

ICBO (International Conference of Building Officials) is the code organization for the western region of the United States. Their address is 5360 Workman Mill Road, Whittier, CA 90601-2298. They can be reached by dialing (800) 423-6587 or viewing their Web site at www.icbo.org.

SBCCI (Southern Building Code Congress International) is the code organization for the southern region of the United States. They can be reached at 900 Montclair Road, Birmingham, AL 35213-1206 or by dialing (205) 591-1853. Their Web address is www.sbcci.org.

The International Code Council (ICC) is the entity through which the three U.S. code groups—BOCA, ICBO, and SBCCI—worked to develop and publish the international building codes. The groups are maintaining their separate regionally based organizations to better serve the building code community. Information about the ICC can be found at www.intlcode.org or http://codes.icbo.org.

The National Fire Protection Association (NFPA) publishes model fire codes. Their address is 1 Batterymarch Park, P.O. Box 9101, Quincy, MA 02269-9101, (617) 770-3000 or, for orders, (800) 344-3555. The Web address is www.nfpa.org.

The Standards Division of Factory Mutual Research develops property loss guidelines. Their FM Global data sheets present current technical data that can be used to design for loss prevention from fire, earthquakes, and other hazards. Visit their Web site at www.fmglobal.com or contact their headquarters at 1301 Atwood Avenue, Johnston, RI 02919, (401) 275-3000

The faculty and staff in the University of Maryland Department of Fire Protection Engineering are actively involved in a variety of research topics, including topics such as the structural response of composite materials to fire and the legal implications of performance-based codes and standards. Visit their Web site at www.enfp.umd.edu to find out more about their research.

Research conducted at the Worcester Polytechnic Institute Center for Firesafety Studies has covered subjects such as fire safety evaluation methods for buildings and methods for modeling the fire performance of building structures. For more information, see www.wpi.edu/Academics/Depts/Fire/.

# 17.4 Construction Documentation–Drawings

### Ernest L. Grigsby, AIA

*Construction documentation is the bridge between building design and physical building form. A key element of documentation services, construction drawings provide the instructions for transforming design solutions into bricks and mortar.*

By definition, construction documentation encompasses the preparation of drawings and specifications that set forth the detailed requirements for the construction of a building project. Drawings thus represent the illustrative dimension of construction documentation, while specifications represent the written. The two are complementary, with neither having precedence over the other.

Because the creation of drawings and the development of specifications use different sets of knowledge and skills, they are presented in separate profiles in this section of the *Handbook*. In addition, the topic Construction Documents Production (13.4) includes a detailed discussion of the methods and procedures used in preparing drawings and specifications.

Within the context of design and construction documentation, design represents an expression of the desired solution, while construction drawings control—to the extent possible—the eventual physical outcome of that expression. To achieve this, construction drawings depict the components of the intended building design in such a way that construction personnel can clearly understand what results are desired.

Although construction drawings for a given building project are normally done by the firm that provides the design services, there are exceptions to the same firm doing both. For example, two firms may team to take advantage of their respective capabilities. One may take responsibility for design—possibly up through design development. The other might have responsibility for the construction documents along with services for construction procurement and construction contract administration. In other instances, a commercial enterprise may seek documentation services when one of their prototypical facilities must be adapted to a specific site.

In the above scenarios, the documentation may be carried out under separate owner-architect contracts, depending on the project's contractual arrangement. In either case, when design and construction documentation services are carried out by different firms, ensuring that the design intent is adequately interpreted within the construction documentation can become a greater challenge.

Several current and emerging factors affect construction drawings. Foremost are the benefits offered by state-of-the-art computer-assisted design and drafting (CADD) programs, which make it possible to create complex documents faster, to easily delineate repetitive elements, and to readily manipulate data and information to make changes. Also, the power of emerging software is allowing for greater integration between separate software applications.

Building delivery is another factor that can affect construction documentation, espe-

## Summary

### CONSTRUCTION DOCUMENTATION SERVICES– DRAWINGS

#### Why a Client May Need These Services
▷ To provide graphic documentation for bidding and execution of construction services

#### Knowledge and Skills Required
▷ Knowledge of construction materials, components, and assemblies
▷ Ability to develop construction details consistent with design, performance, and budget objectives
▷ Ability to develop specifications to the level of detail required
▷ Knowledge of code review processes and procedures
▷ Familiarity with procurement of construction services
▷ Knowledge of manual and/or computer drawing standards and systems
▷ Skill with CAD programs

#### Representative Process Tasks
▷ Assemble team for drafting, specifications writing, and cost estimating
▷ Confirm client expectations for content, detail level, and packaging of construction documents
▷ Coordinate specs and drawings from all disciplines
▷ Prepare construction drawings based on design development drawings
▷ Prepare specifications to accompany drawings
▷ Submit documents to building code officials
▷ Prepare bid packages
▷ Prepare sketches and specifications for change orders during construction

▷ **Construction documentation services typically represent 2.4 to 4 percent of construction cost.**

**ERNEST L. GRIGSBY** *is a principal for the Zimmer Gunsul Frasca Partnership. He is responsible for providing project management and quality assurance for the Portland-based architecture firm.*

cially from the vantage point of quality. For example, negotiated construction contracts and design-build approaches allow for greater contractor involvement during the development of drawings and specifications. This participation can contribute to the creation of clearer and more integrated documents to help minimize conflicts and misunderstandings among the building trades.

## CLIENT NEEDS

Clients developing new buildings or renovating existing buildings need construction documentation in order to obtain building permits. As mandated by law, construction documents must be prepared by licensed architects for most building types. (Some buildings, such as single-family residences and other designated structures, may not require architect-generated drawings. The specific requirements will depend on the laws of the jurisdiction in which the building project is located.)

*Client need for construction drawings.* Most clients use construction documents on a one-time basis for a single building project. In certain market sectors, some clients may want to use construction documents on a repetitive basis. For example, nationally or regionally based commercial clients may want to build in multiple locations using a prototypical design (e.g., stores, restaurants, car wash facilities, or other retail building types). A school district may wish to adapt a single school design to several locations. A developer or builder may look to construct multiple single-family houses from a given set of plans. In all of these and similar cases, the original construction drawings will require varying degrees of change to adapt the plans for site conditions, orientation issues, code requirements, and other related design considerations.

*Client use of construction drawings.* Construction documents—regardless of the media in which they exist—are the property of the architect. Contractually, they are considered to be *instruments of service,* which means they are among the many products the architect may prepare in conjunction with services for a given building project. AIA Document B141, however, does allow instruments of service to be used for the purposes of "using and maintaining the project." This may include using construction documents as a basis for future modifications or facility expansion, for maintaining and operating a building, or in conjunction with facility management initiatives.

*Client expectations.* Clients expect construction documentation to communicate—as clearly as possible—the components of the structure and the level of quality needed for those components to fulfill the building's intended use. In doing this, construction drawings are detailed to a level that allows the contractor or builder to price the construction with a reasonable degree of confidence. Although clients would prefer to have no or only a few change orders during construction, the reality and possibility of unforeseen conditions or events may create the need for change orders in which further drawing documentation may be required.

*Related needs and services.* In addition to building design and interior design, documentation skills can be applied to facility surveys for preparing architectural drawings that delineate existing conditions. Construction procurement and construction contract administration are natural follow-on services for architects who have provided construction documentation for their clients. Who can better interpret construction documents than those who produced them?

Construction documentation skills can also be applied to postconstruction services such as the preparation of record drawings. In buildings with rented or leased spaces, clients or individual tenants seeking space planning or interior design services will understand the advantages of working with a firm that has produced the construction documents for the shell and core of the building. Likewise, architects who have prepared construction documentation can leverage their experience and knowledge of the facility to provide move-in assistance or move management services.

## SKILLS

The preparation of architectural working drawings represents one of the major core competencies of architects. The work requires knowledge of principles, conventions, standards, applications, and restrictions pertaining to the manufacture and use of

**Building Design (17.2) covers the services generally included in schematic design and design development.**

**Construction Procurement (17.7) covers services used to obtain quotations for building construction.**

**Construction Documents Production (12.3) provides an in-depth look at methods and processes used to produce construction drawings and specifications.**

construction materials, components, and assemblies. In the documentation process, the architect must be able to make technically concise descriptions and execute drawings and other documentation for the proposed design. This knowledge and sets of skills include the following:

- *Detailing.* This is perhaps one of the most crucial skills used in construction documentation. This is because the nature and quality of architectural detailing contributes to how the building is built, what it will look like, what it will cost, and how long it may take to build. For these reasons, staff involved in the documentation process should have a thorough understanding of the methods and techniques used in building construction. This includes knowing how various materials are connected or attached and how they interact when brought together. An understanding of how air, water, and other elements interact with buildings is also crucial to effective detailing.

- *Delineation.* The production of construction drawings is rooted in manual methods that require a facility with pencil or pen. Although CAD systems have replaced manual methods, most of the concepts and principles of effective delineation are still applicable to automated drawing methods. This means that documentation staff should have an understanding of how line weights, lettering, proportionality of drawn objects, and relationships between drawing elements individually and collectively contribute to the overall clarity of a drawing.

- *Drawing systems and standards.* An understanding of drafting conventions and drawing systems for organizing graphical information is important. This includes issues such as sheet naming, drawing sequence, sizes, and layout. For electronically produced documents, knowledge of CAD guidelines and standards is important for producing documents and exchanging them between project team members.

- *Communication and coordination.* The production staff may work with the project designer, project manager, and specifications staff in order to coordinate production issues and decisions. In this process, the ability to communicate verbally as well as in writing is important.

- *Architectural knowledge.* Drafters, CAD operators, and other documentation staff must interpret and make design decisions as they develop detailed working drawings based on design documentation. In doing this, knowledge of design principles and concepts is important. Such decisions balancing functionality, code requirements, and aesthetics constantly come into play in deciding such issues as where to position a clock or a thermostat on a wall or how to proportion and detail a built-in shelving unit.

Equipment used by architectural staff for construction documentation include computer workstations, scanners, plotters, cameras (digital cameras are popular), light meters, and sound meters. Construction documentation teams are increasingly working with electronic transfer of information by e-mail and the Internet. Many teams also use file transfer protocol (FTP) sites to post and retrieve shared information such as drawings.

▶ **The preparation of construction specifications is closely aligned with the preparation of construction drawings. Construction Documentation—Specifications (17.5) profiles the skills and knowledge used in this service increment.**

▶ **Computer Technology in Architectural Practice (12.1) addresses issues in producing drawings with computers.**

## PROCESS

The scope of construction documentation services will depend on the size and complexity of a project and the number of disciplines involved. However, size itself may not always be a driver. Some small projects containing highly specialized spaces and the need for highly customized design may require a higher ratio of drawings per square foot than a larger project that has many repetitive elements (e.g., high-rises, multiple building units).

The scope can also be affected by client requirements and the project delivery approach used. Some clients have their own requirements for the presentation or hierarchy of construction drawing details. Some may expect standard details to be used, while others may require customized details. Fast-tracking and delivery techniques involving phased delivery and preparation of multiple bid packages may also affect the scope of construction documentation.

## Team Considerations

When assembling a construction documentation team, it is prudent to consider the work approaches of the various firms involved. Everyone must agree on the process by which work will be reviewed and approved. All the team members must understand and accept the lead firm's management methods. Also consider whether the team members have compatible equipment and software to ensure interoperability issues and good communication.

Specifications writers and estimators are integral construction documentation team members. The specifications writer brings detailed technical knowledge of available construction products and how they are appropriately used. Specifications writers have expertise in preparing specifications so that product information is conveyed clearly to the contractor.

The project cost estimator helps track the cost of the project and assists the team in budget control. Estimators contribute knowledge of prevailing contractor costs for the project location and the ability to analyze the drawings for cost factors. Some firms separately subcontract specifications writing and bid estimating services. In fast-track or design-build projects where the contractor is brought on board early, it can be productive to have the contractor provide parallel estimating on construction documents before they are bid. As previously noted, contractor involvement in the production process can help the team produce a more complete and effective set of documents.

Usually the designer or project architect will take the lead responsibility for the production of architectural drawings. In small firms the designer may also prepare the construction drawings. In larger firms and on larger projects a team is usually assigned responsibility for producing the drawings. On certain large projects the project architect may have one or more management assistants as well as accounting support.

The documentation team works with all involved disciplines. These may include surveyors; geotechnical and civil engineers; landscape architects; structural, mechanical, and electrical engineers; architects; interior designers; and telecommunications specialists. Depending on the project, other specialists may include acoustical engineers, wind tunnel engineers, environmental specialists, audiovisual specialists, lighting designers, computer specialists, or designers who specialize in particular types of buildings or spaces (e.g., laboratories, detention facilities, auditoriums or sports arenas).

## Producing the Drawings

Construction drawings are normally prepared based on the drawings produced in design development. Each discipline involved will prepare a "discipline package" of construction drawings.

***Preproduction.*** There are several important points to address before starting the production process. These include:

- Confirming that the client has approved the design development documents and the preliminary project budget
- Verifying the project delivery approach and project schedule
- Communicating the client's requirements for the content, detail level, and packaging of the construction documents
- Identifying and confirming client-required formats or standards (e.g., sheet sizes, layouts, sequence, numbering, symbols, and abbreviations)
- Confirming that the proposed CADD software is acceptable to the client

***Development of drawings.*** The preparation of construction documents requires a systematic review process to ensure that all discipline packages (e.g., structural, mechanical, electrical, lighting, audiovisual, interiors, etc.) are coordinated and properly integrated. When the documents—including both drawings and specifications—are completed and approved, they provide a basis for preparing an estimated cost of construction. Based on this estimate, the bid packages can be prepared.

During the development of drawings, coordination and review of the drawing packages requires an ongoing process of checking and rechecking. Each discipline will regularly review its own drawings for adherence to the documentation standards and will coordinate with the work

**Contract Administration (17.8)** profiles services required to administer the contract between the owner and the contractor.

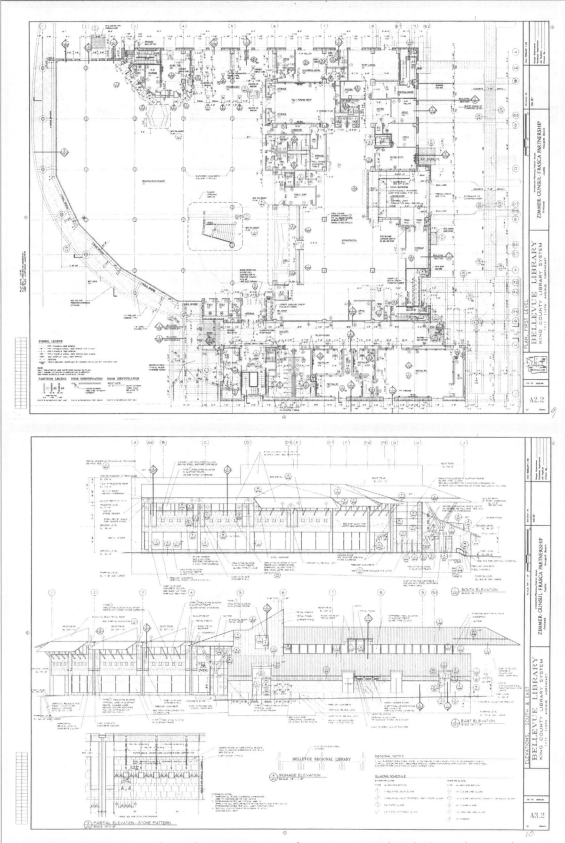

Construction drawings—together with construction specifications—are used to obtain regulatory and financial approvals, to determine cost of construction through bidding or negotiation, and finally to carry out the construction process.

Zimmer Grunsul Frasca Partnership, Portland, Oregon

**During the production of construction documents, cost control is an important factor. For a detailed discussion of cost control, see Construction Cost Management (13.4).**

of other disciplines. Project participants meet with each other and with independent peer consultants to review and coordinate work. Additionally, the entire project team may meet at key points in the process for the same purpose. These review and coordination initiatives are repeated through each step of development, and again when the final documents package is assembled.

Independent peer reviewers are required for document review and checking before documents are released for bidding. Senior staff not involved in the project can be assigned this task, or the client may employ independent consultants for this purpose. The construction drawings must be reviewed and approved by building code officials for compliance with zoning and planning requirements in order for a building permit to be issued. In some jurisdictions design review also is required.

During the bidding and negotiation process, the team that prepared the construction drawings and specifications may provide support to the client by reviewing or confirming cost estimates and perhaps preparing contract modifications, which may involve drawing changes. The team also remains available for consultation during the construction administration phase to assist with preparing revised sketches for addendums and change orders.

### For More Information

Fred Nashed addresses the planning of construction documentation and provides drawing standards in *Time-Saving Techniques for Architectural Construction Drawings* (1997). Richard M. Linde and Osamu A. Wakita cover skills, concepts, and fundamentals for working drawings in *The Professional Practice of Architectural Working Drawings* (1994). In the fourth edition of *Architectural Working Drawings* (1999) Ralph W. Liebing updates the older text with new material, including information on CAD-generated drawings.

Several publications focus on construction drawing standards. These include the *Uniform Drawing System* (1998), which contains standards for sheet types, sheet organization, and schedules; and *AIA CAD Layer Guidelines* (2001), which establishes standard naming of data file layers. These two publications, together with plotting standards developed by the U.S. Coast Guard, have been incorporated into the *U.S. National CAD Standard*.

A useful related resource is the *Uniform Location of Subject Matter*, a joint publication of the American Consulting Engineers Council, the AIA, and the National Society of Professional Engineers. The Redicheck overlay checking and interdisciplinary coordination manual offers a tool for achieving more accurate and thorough construction documents. For information, call Redicheck Associates at (877) 733-4243.

# 17.5 Construction Documentation–Specifications

## Gary Betts, FCSI, CCS, AIA

*Specification services comprise the research, analysis, and evaluation that lead up to preparation of written requirements for building materials, equipment, and construction systems. The scope of the research in this process depends on specific project needs and requirements.*

The goal of construction documents is to communicate the needs of the owner as represented by a design in a form easily understood by those responsible for construction. Specifications, an integral component of construction documentation, outline the levels of quality and the standards to be met in construction of a project. Written specifications were first produced separately from drawings to cut down on the clutter caused by lengthy descriptions. In addition, placing descriptions together in one place avoided the contradictions and errors often caused when specifications are repeated in many places.

Specifications define the qualitative requirements of materials and products to ensure that everyone understands the product requirements. The numbering and titling format used to organize construction information in specifications, the Construction Specifications Institute's (CSI's) MasterFormat, provides a means of coordinating that information with a contractor's submittals, cost accounting systems, material filing, and requests for interpretation.

As defined in the AIA General Conditions of the Contract, drawings and specifications are meant to complement one another rather than one having precedence over the other. It is important for drawings and specifications to be developed concurrently, with both increasing in level of detail as the project moves through the design development and contract document phases. Specification sections are organized into 16 divisions. Division 1, the general requirements, outlines the procedural and administrative requirements for a project. The specification sections for materials, products, and systems are placed in Divisions 2 through 16.

Firms prepare specifications in a variety of ways. Some choose to prepare specifications in-house, either hiring a specifications specialist or relying on a member of the project team. Other firms use the services of an independent specifications consultant. In some instances firms may employ a combined approach, for example, using a specifications consultant for specialized or complex products and systems and relying on in-house staff to document typical construction materials. It is not uncommon for a firm to employ a hardware consultant to develop hardware specifications for a project or a curtain wall consultant to produce specifications for the exterior wall system. Whether specifications are developed in-house or with the assistance of a consultant, they are based either on a unique office master specification system or a commercially available master guide specification system such as MASTERSPEC, a product of the American Institute of Architects (AIA)

Ten to fifteen years ago, a group of specifiers from a number of large firms around

## Summary

### CONSTRUCTION DOCUMENTATION SERVICES— SPECIFICATIONS

#### Why a Client May Need These Services
▷ When engaging architectural services to prepare documentation for new construction

#### Knowledge and Skills Required
▷ In-depth knowledge of building materials and products
▷ Knowledge of material standards and testing methods
▷ Knowledge of construction methods and techniques
▷ Detail oriented with creative problem-solving ability
▷ Strong investigative skills
▷ Ability to communicate complex issues in writing

#### Representative Process Tasks
▷ Establish need or desired level of performance*
▷ Define evaluation criteria*
▷ Prioritize criteria*
▷ Investigate options*
▷ Evaluate options against established criteria*
▷ Document research findings and recommendations*
▷ Prepare specification documents

* These activities and tasks may be expanded in projects for which material performance is highly critical, for which materials do not yet exist to satisfy a specific need, when the client seeks a broader range of material options, or when the client desires to qualify new or untested materials.

**GARY BETTS** *is a principal and director of specifications at Chicago-based Loebl Schlossman & Hackl. He is a nationally recognized expert in the field of specifications, a member of the American Institute of Architects, and a Fellow of the Construction Specifications Institute.*

part 4 SERVICES

the country began meeting informally. An informal survey they conducted indicated that larger firms employed an average of one specifier or specifications specialist for every 20 to 25 design professionals. Today the group's research shows that number is about one specifier for every 100 design professionals. As a result, instead of the specifier developing project manuals for every project, he or she concentrates on maintaining a master set of specifications and supporting the development of project specifications by the project team.

Automation of the process has made specification writing more efficient. CADD programs and the development of object-oriented documentation provide opportunities to assign attributes to objects in the drawings that support links between the drawings and the specifications. This linkage results in better-coordinated documents and supports the concurrent development of drawings and specifications. It is not hard to visualize a future in which construction information will be included in a single database or a series of linked databases and the paper-based drawings and specifications we now produce independently are reports formatted to present information in a way that is familiar.

## CLIENT NEEDS

Product evaluation and development of specifications offers an agreed-upon format for recording and communicating decisions made during the design process. The intent is to develop an accurate match between the needs of a project and the products selected.

At the outset the architect and the owner must come to an agreement about the goals and expectations for a project. Their understanding will have a major impact on the performance characteristics of products selected for use in a project. Reaching a clear understanding of project requirements prevents the tendency to overspecify a product or to identify performance characteristics that go beyond the stated project requirements, either of which can add unnecessarily to the cost of a project.

Accurate documentation of selected materials and products can ensure owners will get what they have agreed to pay for and that the expected level of quality will be met. The specifications process is particularly critical when an owner has identified special performance requirements.

## SKILLS

Product selection is an analytical process, requiring an aptitude for investigation and an eye for detail. It also requires an understanding of how buildings are put together that is gained from years of practical experience. A creative approach to problem solving and an understanding of the application of test procedures is also important. Products being evaluated don't stand alone in a project but must interface with adjacent materials. Therefore knowledge of construction sequence and compatibility of materials improves the evaluation process. Access to multiple information sources and an extensive network of people with varied experience are necessary supports for those writing specifications.

Because material selection and installation involves complex issues and concepts, those writing specifications must be able to communicate well. Specifications should be composed in a concise and comprehensible manner so that they can be understood by individuals with varying levels of experience in the construction industry.

Knowledge of specification principles is basic for writing specifications, and the primary resource is CSI's *Manual of Practice.* It is also important to understand the formats used to organize information in specifications, MasterFormat and SectionFormat. Basic computer skills, which include using word processing, database, and spreadsheet applications, are essential, and being CADD-literate is a big advantage.

Manufacturers and material suppliers play an important role in the process of material research and product evaluation. For established materials, they often represent the primary information resource, although many materials are represented by trade associations that develop standards for them and/or products made from them. For verification of manufacturers' claims, specifiers refer to the work of testing agencies, insurance underwriters, and product certification agencies that evaluate the performance of many materials and products.

► Construction specifications are generally combined with services for construction drawings, as covered in Construction Documentation—Drawings (17.4).

► For more about the use of computer technology to prepare construction specifications, see Computer Technology in Architectural Practice (12.1) and Using the Internet in Practice (12.2).

# PROCESS

Specifications development is concurrent with the design process, which continuously yields performance or specific material or product requirements. The specifier must research products and materials that will meet the designer's requirements. The final specifications reflect decisions made by the owner and designer throughout the process and serve as a record of those decisions. The specifications, assembled into a project manual in combination with the construction drawings, are then used by the constructor to bid and build the project.

## Research Materials and Products

Material research is basic problem solving. A problem, or need, is defined; evaluation criteria are established; possible solutions are identified; potential solutions are evaluated against the established criteria; and the final selection is made.

***Establish a need.*** The first step in the process is to establish the need for a material or product or the level of performance desired for it. What does this material or product need to do? What essential role does it play in the design?

***Define evaluation criteria.*** In order to effectively evaluate the performance of various alternatives, project-specific evaluation criteria must be defined. Each material has many characteristics or attributes that contribute to its overall performance and to its applicability to a particular project. These attributes can be grouped by category. The list of categories below was derived from *Construction Materials Evaluation and Selection: A Systematic Approach,* by Harold J. Rosen, PE, FCSI, and Philip M. Bennett, RA, and from a list of attributes contained in CSI's *Manual of Practice.* Examples of attributes are also provided for each category.

- Structural serviceability: natural forces, strength properties
- Fire safety: fire resistance, flame spread, smoke development, toxicity, fuel load, combustibility
- Habitability: thermal properties, acoustical properties, water permeability, optical properties, hygiene, comfort, safety
- Durability: resistance to wear, weathering, adhesion of coatings, dimensional stability, mechanical properties, rheological properties.
- Practicability: transport, storage at the site, handling at installation, field tolerances, connections
- Compatibility: jointing materials, coatings, galvanic interaction or corrosion resistance
- Maintainability: compatibility of coatings, indention and puncture (patching), chemical or graffiti attack
- Environmental impact: resource consumption at production, life cycle impact
- Cost: installed cost, maintenance cost
- Aesthetics: visual impact, customizing options, color selection

Refer to CSI's *Manual of Practice* for detailed discussions of the material attributes that would be included in the groups listed above.

Based on the project goals and the design concept, attribute categories are used to list the requirements for the material being evaluated. Each material will have its own profile of applicable categories, as some may not be needed while others are critical to the performance of the material. The goal is to define the level of performance required of the material for the particular project. The list of desired attributes and performance criteria becomes the evaluation criteria for each material.

The process of developing evaluation criteria is a great opportunity to involve the client in a project. Clients can help determine and establish the priority of the criteria. Everyone involved in the process has a different point of view regarding which criteria are the most important. From the specifier's technical point of view, the durability of a material may be most important. To the designer, aesthetics may be most important. To the client, cost may be the driving force in terms of material selection. It is important that all parties reach an understanding that results in the establishment and documentation of priorities.

***Identify options.*** Once the criteria have been developed and prioritized, possible

# PRODUCT EVALUATION SUMMARY SHEET

Section number: _07550 Protected Membrane Roof_     Project: _66504_     Date: _6/12/97_

| CRITERIA | TEST RESULTS | SUBJECTIVE EVALUATION | COMMENTS |
|---|---|---|---|
| Structural serviceability | | | |
| Fire safety | Class A? | | |
| Habitability | Water resistant; perm rate: <.027; elongation: 1000% | Ins. properties not affected by water | |
| Durability | Penetration: 110 @ 77°F Flow: none @ 120°F | Sees no thermal stress, protected from foot traffic | On the interior of building insulation, protected from elements and abuse |
| Practicability | | Fluid applied, kettle required | Can be installed w/o slope |
| Compatibility | | Transitions made with neoprene | |
| Maintainability | | Roof membrane not visible, move pavers and insulation to find leak | Adhered to deck, no migration of water if leak develops |
| Environmental impact | Insulation contains no CFC blowing agents | | |
| Cost | | | |
| Aesthetics | | Pavers or other ballast provide an attractive finished appearance | |

## Definitions

_Structural serviceability:_ Natural forces, strength properties
_Fire safety:_ Fire resistance, flame spread, smoke development, toxicity, fuel load, combustibility
_Habitability:_ Thermal properties, acoustic properties, water permeability, optical properties, hygiene, comfort, safety
_Durability:_ Resistance to wear, weathering, adhesion of coatings, dimensional stability, mechanical properties, rheological properties
_Practicability:_ Transport, storage on site, handling at installation, field tolerances, connections
_Compatibility:_ Jointing materials, coatings, galvanic interaction or corrosion resistance
_Maintainability:_ Compatibility of coatings, indention and puncture (patching), chemical or graffiti attack
_Environmental impact:_ Resource consumption at production, life cycle impact
_Cost:_ Installed cost, maintenance cost
_Aesthetics:_ Visual impact, customizing options, color selection

_Definitions from Harold Rosen and Philip Bennett,_ Construction Materials Evaluation and Selection: A Systematic Approach _(1979)_

material or product options are identified. Information about a material or product is collected and organized. In some cases a manufacturer's product literature, product representative, or other information source may not be able to provide information about a specific performance characteristic of a product or material. This product or material should not be considered for a project, then, unless the material manufacturer or a testing authority will conduct the required tests and provide the missing information.

***Evaluate materials and products.*** After material and product information has been compiled, it is compared to the evaluation criteria for the project. A system of pluses for criteria that meet project requirements and minuses for criteria that don't meet them can be used to determine if a material is acceptable. Another method involves developing a rating system of 1 to 10 based on how well a material matches the criteria for a project. Each material is evaluated on each criterion, the scores are added up, and the materials are compared. The higher the score, the better a material satisfies the evaluation criteria. To take the process a step further, the evaluating criteria can be given a weight factor based on its assigned priority. The scores are multiplied by the weight factor and then added to get the total score. This is a simple explanation of the process used in a software package developed by Expert Choice, Inc. The software supports ASTM E1765, "Analytical Hierarchy Process: Standard Practice for Performing Multi-Attribute Decision Analysis in the Evaluation of Buildings and Building Systems."

It is helpful to create a matrix to record the evaluation and rating process. This provides a useful document that can be referred to during bidding and construction if requests for substitute materials are submitted. A record of the criteria used to make your decision can also be helpful during submittal review if a manufacturer has changed its documentation and claims related to the performance of a material.

# Prepare Specifications

Specifications writing is a continuous process. The first draft specifications for a project define qualitative requirements of materials, products, and workmanship. Once product selections have been made, a definition of the salient qualities of each product that make it meet the project requirements should be added to the specifications.

There are four basic types of specifications—descriptive, proprietary, performance, and reference standard. The first three can be used to specify the essential qualities of materials for a project. Reference standard specifications are published by standards organizations or organizations that represent manufacturers of specific building elements and are typically referenced without customization.

*Descriptive specifications* require written descriptions for each material or product to be used in a project. These descriptions should include the attributes that are essential in order for a material or product to meet project requirements.

Care must be taken when drafting a description. If a specification is based on information provided by the manufacturer, include only those attributes required for your project. For example, literature from a manufacturer of clad windows may include the thickness of the cladding as a way to differentiate its product from that of other manufacturers. If the level of performance required for a project does not depend on the thickness of the cladding, the thickness should not be included in the description. If the thickness is included and the specification strictly enforced, only products with the specified skin thickness would qualify, limiting the options to the one manufacturer or forcing other manufacturers to customize their window to meet the specified requirements.

*Proprietary specifications* list only the products and manufacturers that are acceptable for use on a project. They are the most concise form of specification.

If a product model number is identified and includes any options that may be applicable to the product, no lengthy description of the product is required. However, it is important to leave no salient option unidentified. If a specification does not mention an option that is essential to an acceptable product, a claim could result for additional cost if the desired option is not standard, or a contractor could select an alternative product without consulting the architect. A proprietary specification may include only one manufacturer or as many as meet the project requirements.

Including model numbers for all manufacturers selected is the best way to ensure a contractor will select an appropriate product. Another popular method, basis of design, is to list the desired product and manufacturer but allow for comparable products from other specified or approved manufacturers. Note, though, that this degree of latitude can require additional time when reviewing a submittal to determine whether the submitted product meets the requirements and is truly comparable to the specified product.

It is often tempting to combine proprietary specifications and descriptive specifications. Construction administrators complain that they need the description to ensure that the product submitted actually meets the requirements of the specification. However, if there is a slight discrepancy between the description of a generic product and an actual product identified by model number, this can be a problem. As well, the greater the number of manufacturers and products identified, the greater the risk of creating a conflict. Careful coordination is required when proprietary and descriptive methods are combined.

*Performance specifications* identify the performance characteristics that a product, assembly, or system must satisfy. Creating a true performance specification is difficult.

A performance specification has two important components—the intended performance characteristics and a means by which that performance can be verified. The performance specification must include every aspect of desired performance. Missing performance criteria or an assumption that such criteria are understood can cause a contractor to propose a solution that meets all the stated criteria and yet completely misses the intent.

It is also important for performance criteria to be realistic and achievable. In some circumstances there may not be a product that can provide the required performance. Writing a performance specification that stipulates a particular performance won't make a product that can offer that performance available. However, if a firm begins working with manufacturers of similar products as soon as a need is identified, this may be enough incentive for a manufacturer to do the research, development, and

> **The backgrounder AIA MASTERSPEC in Construction Documents Production (12.3) provides information on the AIA-developed specifications product published and supported by ARCOM.**

testing required to bring a product with the desired level of performance to market. Few projects are able to bear the cost of new-product development. Getting a manufacturer involved early may also result in an alternative design for which a product with the desired performance already exists.

*Reference standard specifications* are published standard specifications that are incorporated into project specifications by reference. According to CSI's *Manual of Practice,* reference standards are requirements set by authority, custom, or general consensus and are established as accepted criteria.

Specifying by using reference standards is very concise because a reference standard number can be cited in lieu of a lengthy description of a product. For example, portland cement can be specified by referencing ASTM C150 instead of including a description of the physical properties, chemical composition, and fabrication process of the cement. When using reference standards, it is important to have a copy of the standard and understand its content. Standards may sometimes include options or additional responsibilities for the design professional that should not be included in a project or that, if included, create contradictions or duplications of requirements specified elsewhere. When using a reference standard, make sure that all choices have been identified. For example, the standard for glass includes choices for type, class, quality, finish, and pattern. The reference for clear transparent flat glass would be ASTM C1036, Type I, Class 1, q3. Wire glass would be Type II, Class 1, Form 1, q8, m1.

## File Research Information for Future Reference

The continually expanding library of construction information and data yielded by the design process can be used in different ways and for different purposes. Material and product data compiled while writing specifications for a project can be used both for other projects and later in the life cycle of the project for which they were first researched.

To make use of all the research performed during the specifications preparation process, an architecture firm will want to have a means of storing this information so that it can be retrieved again, both as general information and as project-specific information. For example, an architect can use programming information to establish criteria or rules against which preliminary design solutions can be evaluated. After a project has been completed and occupied, facility managers may find value in this programming information, which often has been discarded after design or occupancy. Along with the record documents, facility managers can use documented design performance criteria so that they will know if contemplated modifications violate any of the original criteria.

As the need expands to access this kind of information, it is important to document final decisions about materials and products and to describe the evaluation and selection process. This is especially important when systems are critical to the function of a project or when the project incorporates new materials or materials used in new and untested ways. However, not every material or product that goes into a project needs to be documented in this manner. Some materials have become commodities, and their use and performance is generally understood (e.g., portland cement, steel door frames, etc.). These, then, do not require extensive material or product research.

In most cases it is important to keep this documentation with the project. Prior to the explosion of electronic information, a folder was created in the main project file and product selection documentation was filed by MasterFormat 16-division specification number. Today the information can be appended electronically to the specification file or a separate folder created for this information. Whatever filing system is used, it is important for the information to be archived with the project when the project is closed out.

If a specifier feels the information would be of value for future projects, the information can be incorporated into a firm's master guide specification system. The information can be integrated as notes in the text of the section, appended to the end of the section, or included in a separate evaluations folder tied to the specification section by the same file name. Most word processing applications provide for the use of hyperlinks. This gives the person accessing the specification section the option to activate the link from the text and jump to the evaluation sheets. This process is automated in MASTERSPEC.

### For More Information

Architectural Computer Services, Inc. (ARCOM) publishes and licenses the MASTER-SPEC Master Specification System, a product of the American Institute of Architects). MASTERSPEC sections are edited by construction specifiers to select products and produce project specifications. MASTERSPEC is endorsed or recommended by major design organizations, including the AIA, ACEC, ASID, ASLA, CASE, IIDA, NLA, and NSPE. ARCOM is located in Salt Lake City, Utah, and Alexandria, Virginia. Information is available at (800) 424-5080 and www.arcomnet.com.

The Construction Specifications Institute (CSI) is a national professional association dedicated to enhancing communication among the disciplines involved in the non-residential building design and construction industry and meeting the industry's need for a common system of organizing and presenting construction documents. CSI provides a variety of resources to its members, who include architects, engineers, contractors, building owners, facility managers, and product manufacturers in addition to construction specifiers. CSI is located at 99 Canal Center Plaza, Suite 300, Alexandria, VA 22314, (800) 689-2900 or (703) 684-0300, and on the Internet at www.csinet.org.

CSI publishes the bible of the construction specifier, the CSI *Manual of Practice,* as well as the monthly magazine *Construction Specifier.* It also offers a certification program whereby individuals pass an exam to demonstrate their competence in preparing specifications and contract documents; those who have passed the exam may carry the letters CCS, for "Certified Construction Specifier," after their names.

The American Society for Testing and Materials (ASTM) is a not-for-profit organization whose members develop and publish voluntary consensus standards for materials, products, systems, and services. ASTM develops standard test methods, specifications, practices, guides, classifications, and terminology for such subjects as metals, paints, construction, energy, and the environment. The organization can be found at 100 Barr Harbor Drive, West Conshohocken, PA 19428-2959, (610) 832-9585, or on the Internet at www.astm.org.

The ASTM document "Analytical Hierarchy Process, Standard Practice for Performing Multi-Attribute Decision Analysis in the Evaluation of Buildings and Building Systems" (ASTM E1765) provides the framework for an objective analysis of building materials and systems based on stated evaluation criteria.

Two additional ASTM standards may be helpful, depending on the type of product evaluation being performed: ASTM E1991, "Standard Guide for Environmental Life-Cycle Assessment of Building Materials/Products," and ASTM E1699, "Standard Practice for Performing Value Analysis of Buildings and Building Systems."

The American National Standards Institute (ANSI) is a private, nonprofit membership organization that administers and coordinates a voluntary private sector U.S. standardization system. ANSI promotes and facilitates the development of voluntary consensus standards and conformity assessment systems by organizations it has accredited. ANSI can be contacted at 1819 L Street, NW, 6th floor, Washington, DC, 20036, (202) 293-8020, http://web.ansi.org.

As mentioned in this topic, many materials used in construction are represented by trade associations that support manufacturers of these products. For example, the American Concrete Institute (ACI) and the Architectural Woodwork Institute (AWI), among many others, provide standards related to the use and installation of the product or trade they represent. Section 01317 of Sweet's Catalog File provides a comprehensive listing of these information sources.

Additional product information can be found in publications by testing agencies such as Underwriters Laboratories (UL) and Intertec Testing Services (ITS). Factory Mutual's Approval Guide includes certifications of products and assemblies approved for use in FM-insured properties. MASTERSPEC evaluations also provide valuable product information.

In the fourth edition of *Construction Specifications Writing: Principles and Procedures,* 4th ed. (1998), Harold J. Rosen describes the relationship between drawings and specifications, the different types of specifications, bidding procedures, and contract issues. The book also covers systems building and performance specifications and computerized specifications, among many other details, as well as information about legal requirements, contract forms, and warranty provisions. A reference source list and sample specification forms are provided.

# 17.6 Construction Management

### Robert C. Mutchler, FAIA, and Christopher R. Widener, AIA

*The construction manager is responsible for coordinating the work of multiple prime construction contracts and for overseeing quality control. Construction management services may be handled by the architect of record or as a professional service by another architect.*

## Summary

### CONSTRUCTION MANAGEMENT SERVICES

#### Why a Client May Need These Services
▶ To have single-point accountability
▶ To maximize return on capital investment
▶ To save time and money
▶ To increase project quality

#### Knowledge and Skills Required
▶ Strong administrative and management skills
▶ Knowledge of business and contracts
▶ Knowledge of construction materials and methods
▶ Field supervisory experience
▶ Good communication and negotiation skills
▶ Ability to prepare detailed cost estimates
▶ Ability to develop detailed schedules

#### Representative Process Tasks
▶ Review of project program
▶ Advising project architect on pertinent project issues
▶ Preparing time schedules
▶ Preparing budgets and cost estimates
▶ Oversee bidding and preparation of construction contracts
▶ Supervising construction phase of work
▶ Overseeing project closeout
▶ Coordinating work of project participants

For architects seeking a way to control the construction process in order to maintain their professional relationships with their clients, providing construction management (CM) as an architectural service is a viable project delivery method. Between 1990 and 1996, according to the 1997 AIA Firm Survey, the number of firms that performed CM services increased from 5 to 17 percent. In the 2000 edition of the survey, 36 percent of the firms reported that they offer CM services.

When architects offer CM services, there are a number of potential benefits for both owner and architect. These include better control of the project construction schedule, improved integration between design and construction, and daily on-site representation by the architect, all of which result in savings in project costs for the owner and increased profitability for the architect. CM services can be integrated into both the design and construction phases of a project or provided during construction only. Construction managers give advice on the time and cost consequences of design and construction decisions, scheduling, and cost control; coordinate contract negotiations and awards; make timely purchases of critical materials and long-lead-time items; and coordinate construction activities.

The beginnings of construction management are rooted in the 1950s with the advent of computerized scheduling methods such as PERT (project evaluation review technique) and CPM (critical path method) for managing complex projects. During the '60s and '70s CM services became institutionalized as public sector clients divided general contracts into multiple packages, which require more coordination. Today construction management is a widely accepted delivery technique. CM services can be provided using different contractual arrangements that engender different degrees of risk (and reward). Architects, designers, building contractors, and other third-party entities offer CM services to clients.

## CLIENT NEEDS

Clients are showing an increased interest in CM services because this delivery method can save them time and money, increase project quality, and, perhaps most importantly, offer single-point accountability. For them, the primary objective of designer-led construction management is maximization of the owner's return on capital investment.

***Possible complications of constructor-led CM services.*** When a client engages a third-party construction manager or other constructor-led CM services, the fee involved increases the cost of the project but does not ensure that the construction manager will

---

**ROBERT MUTCHLER** *expanded his practice in 1980 to include construction management services and has spoken and written extensively on construction management as an architectural service. He is a past member of the AIA board of directors.* **CHRISTOPHER R. WIDENER** *is a managing partner of the Widener Posey Group and a past chairman of the AIA Construction Management PIA.*

operate in the best interest of the client. As well, architects can encounter difficulties in this project delivery process. Third-party construction managers may not attempt to obtain the best bids for the work and may have more allegiance to construction subcontractors than to the owner. In the name of value engineering, a construction manager can also cause difficulties by reducing the project scope and revising the specified materials proposed by the architect; this can interfere with achievement of the client's objectives. Architects may have to perform duties assigned to the construction manager contractually—for example, researching materials, methods, and trades—if the construction manager does not conduct the work in a timely manner. Other problems can arise when CM firms are staffed with people who lack adequate training in scheduling and budgeting or do not possess the communication skills necessary to complete the services in the best interest of the client or the project.

Precipitated by excessive design restrictions and time-consuming design reviews, such problems can create an adversarial relationship between a third-party construction manager and an architect. By comparison, when construction management is performed as an additional service by the design architect, adversarial relationships (and the attendant change orders, cost escalation, schedule delays, and poor design execution) are significantly reduced.

In a traditional design-bid-build project, the architecture firm carries out design and prepares the construction documents necessary to obtain bids from general contractors and perhaps a select group of specialty trade contractors. If the client holds multiple prime contracts, the architect often is responsible for coordinating the prime contractors, with neither contractual obligation nor financial compensation.

During construction, AIA Contract Document B141, the Standard Form of Agreement Between Owner and Architect with Standard Form of Architect's Service, requires the architect to observe the contractor's activities throughout the construction period to ensure that the contractor complies with minimum standards and the agreed-upon scope and completion of work. Within this context, the architect has limited authority on the job site and reports deficiencies directly to the owner. Often the owner is caught between the designer and contractor when problems occur, as each blames the other for construction-related problems. In this arrangement the architect has no control over the construction schedule, and with a fixed design fee, the architect's profits are reduced should any difficulties or delays in construction occur.

**Advantages of designer-led construction management.** When construction management is provided by an architecture firm, the client benefits from project leadership that is focused on ensuring the quality of the entire design and construction process. The goal of designer-led construction management is seamless integration of the steps and processes that must occur to complete a project on time and within budget.

In a designer-led CM practice, the architecture firm designs a project, prepares construction documents, and, acting as the owner's advisor, actively solicits bids from a select group of contractors. Contractors are chosen based on past performance and a demonstrated ability to comprehend the project scope, perform the work contracted for, and minimize requests for additional information or increased compensation.

Rather than a single or a few prime contractors, a CM project generally employs 10 to 15 prime contractors who ordinarily are subcontractors (e.g., concrete, structural steel, masonry, drywall, painting, etc.). The architecture firm provides a construction manager to coordinate the work of prime contractors, while the project architect continues to provide architectural services, including construction-phase observation. The construction contractors remain under contract to the owner, and the architect–construction manager works as the owner's advisor and contract administrator. The client benefits from daily on-site representation and single-point accountability, and the architect benefits from increased compensation and responsibilities that result in higher-quality projects completed on time and on budget.

The strongest selling point for designer-led CM services is that it can save the client money. Many firms have documented that clients save from 7 to 15 percent of project construction cost by eliminating a general contractor's overhead and profit and the cost of a project superintendent employed by the general contractor. A portion of a general contractor's overhead and profit serves as a project management fee. When the architect provides CM services, much of the money that would have gone to pay that project management fee can be paid to the architect as compensation for performing the CM services.

**Client concerns regarding architect-supplied CM services.** Clients may have several concerns about CM services supplied by the architect.

> "In the late 1970s, the rise of construction managers paralleled the unwillingness of architects to take on responsibility for construction. This led to a loss of perceived value and a loss of potential compensation. Owners still had to pay to ensure their buildings were constructed properly, but increasingly they were not paying architects for this. Only in recent years has the architectural profession begun to learn to benefit from risk instead of running from it."
> *AIA Project/Service Delivery Think Tank, July 1999*

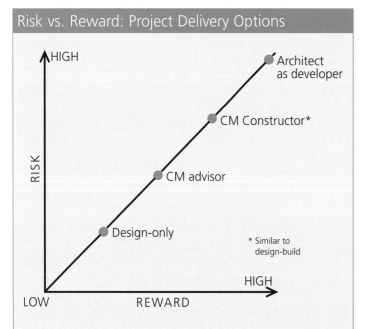

HIGH

Architect
as developer

CM Constructor*

RISK

CM advisor

Design-only

* Similar to
design-build

HIGH

LOW          REWARD

Different levels of risk and reward are associated with various project delivery options. Design-only services have the lowest level of risk and reward, while the architect-as-developer option carries the highest. In between are the CM-as-advisor and CM-as-constructor options. In the former, the architect may provide CM services only or in combination with design services. CM-as-constructor services (which are practically the same as design-build services) fall outside the scope of standard architectural services. In this approach, the architect has higher risk but also more profit opportunity. The CM-as-constructor option is just a step away from the architect becoming a developer.

**In assessing their CM skills, firms should examine the CM services they have performed without obligation or compensation to maintain a professional relationship with clients.**

Administratively, providing CM services as an owner's advisor is essentially the same as providing standard design services. Client concerns about conflict of interest (that the construction manager might try to protect the architect regarding design responsibilities) can be alleviated by involving the client's representative in job meetings and construction decisions. Experience shows that the client will quickly determine that the architect–construction manager as advisor is providing a professional service, that is, acting as the client's representative with an obligation to work in the best interest of the client.

Clients with a great deal of expertise in managing construction may prefer a construction manager–constructor method of project delivery. In this contractual relationship, the individual serving as construction manager–constructor holds the contracts with subcontractors. If this individual is an architect, then this arrangement is similar in risk and reward to the design-build delivery approach, where there is one contract for both design and construction. Firms that frequently use the construction manager-constructor approach like it because it emphasizes both design and construction as professional services.

## SKILLS

A firm offering CM services for the first time must undergo a cultural transformation. To lay the groundwork for this change, it is advisable for a firm to prepare a strategic business plan that addresses the risks, rewards, and financial management of offering CM services. To prepare this, the firm would have to do the following:

- Assess the skills needed to perform competent CM services
- Determine what would be needed in a risk management plan
- Research the legal requirements for construction management in the states where the firm practices
- Determine the forms of contract and agreement the firm will use
- Review insurance requirements
- Consider possible changes in the firm's organization
- Identify strategies for marketing the value these services provide to clients

A traditional architecture practice might begin to add CM-advisor services in one of three ways. The firm could contract to perform the services described in AIA Document B801/CMa, Standard Form of Agreement Between Owner and Construction Manager–Adviser Where the Construction Manager Is Not a Constructor, and use in-house expertise to perform the services.

Alternatively, the firm could hire a consultant to perform the services included in B801/CMa. In this case the consultant could be another architect with expertise in CM services or a trusted contractor who subcontracts to perform on-site duties while the architecture firm continues to perform the administrative duties (similar to hiring an engineering consultant when complete architectural engineering services have been contracted for and in-house engineering is not available).

A third option is for the firm to hire a new employee with the expertise necessary to complete the services. If this option is undertaken, the architect must select the new employee carefully, to avoid introducing differences in cultural attitudes that might negate all the potential positive features.

***Skills required for construction management.*** Administrative acumen is the primary skill a construction manager should possess. Managing dozens of separate contracts requires good business sense, people skills, and organizational talent. Coordinating the efforts of contractors to complete project work on time and within budget is the single most important task of a construction manager.

Estimating, specification writing, scheduling, monitoring, and documenting are also important CM activities. Because these professional skills are so important, it is strongly recommended that firms wanting to offer CM services hire a construction manager with a professional degree in architecture, engineering, or construction management. In addition to having professional expertise, a construction manager must be a natural listener and marketer, have keen negotiation skills, and be comfortable serving as a crisis manager. This combination of abilities requires a special personality with an even temperament.

The construction manager must be familiar enough with the design and construction processes to be able to coordinate the work. Someone with field experience should be able to understand task coordination and be able to answer a contractor's questions without hesitation. Individuals who were trained with general contracting companies may not have the skills necessary to manage a professional service relationship with a client and may tend to favor contractors' interests.

Firms that are successful with designer-led CM services are able to integrate the work of their design and CM staffs to encourage true collaboration. Locating project architects and construction managers in close physical proximity helps develop a collaborative spirit.

A firm offering CM services must have competent and adequate administrative support. The major challenge of construction management is the amount of paperwork involved in tracking progress and administering contracts in a timely manner. Normal duties in construction management include preparing construction contracts, reviewing contractor requests for payment on a monthly basis, keeping accurate documentation, and preparing construction progress reports. A good administrative assistant, or an intern architect or construction manager in training, can help an experienced construction manager manage more work.

*Tools and resources.* Assuming the architect's office has standard word processing and spreadsheet computer programs, little else is needed to add construction management as a basic service. However, Internet and information technology hardware and software are emerging as tools for performing comprehensive CM services for some clients. Sophisticated clients may require their construction managers to use project Web sites and digital information to speed communication between client, architects, consultants, and contractors. The sites can be used to track daily progress and construction-related issues needing immediate attention.

> ▶ **In an architecture firm offering CM services, it is important to instill in the staff the rule that the design architect is in charge throughout all phases of the project. Many construction decisions may be delegated to the construction manager, and the construction manager must actively participate in preparing plans and specifications. Nonetheless, best results are achieved when the design architect remains in control of the scope and quality of a project.**

> ▶ **Using the Internet in Practice (12.2) discusses the use of project Web sites during construction.**

## PROCESS

Construction management services are aligned with the activities and tasks associated with building design, construction documentation, construction procurement, and construction. The scope and approach to construction management is largely determined by the contractual arrangement established between the firm providing construction management services and the client. These relationships are described and expressed in the different forms of agreement in three families of AIA construction management documents.

## AIA Documents

The AIA contract documents address three arrangements an architect's clients can use to contract for CM services: construction manager as advisor, construction manager as constructor, and architect offering CM services along with design services.

*Construction manager as advisor.* This project delivery method closely resembles the traditional relationship between owner and architect, in which the duty of the architect is to act as an advisor to the owner and on behalf of and in the best interest of the owner in all instances. Architects are familiar with the B141, A101, and A201 AIA documents. The CMa designation appended to one of these reflects the provisions added to recognize the responsibilities and duties of a construction manager–advisor. The construction manager–advisor can be either an

## Why Offer CM Services?

There are some pros and cons to consider when an architecture firm is deciding whether to offer construction management as a service of the firm. Generally the positive aspects are many and the concerns few.

### Advantages of Offering CM Services

An architecture firm can gain many benefits from offering CM services to their clients. The most obvious are increased profitability; a comfortable fit with services the firm already offers; improved documentation, estimating, and scheduling skills; improved relationships with clients and employees; an expansion of marketable services; and more attention to risk management issues.

***Increased profitability***. A prime incentive for offering construction management (CM) as an architectural service is the possibility of increased profits. CM services offer great profit potential for many reasons. Expanding the scope of services for an existing client increases the firm's billings with a minimum of marketing effort. Providing broader services without expanding the volume of active projects enables the firm to be more efficient and productive. When the architect controls the construction schedule a CM project can be completed much faster than a conventional project—in most cases at least 25 percent faster. Because there is a construction manager on the project daily, and projects are completed faster, the project architect is relieved of many time-consuming construction problems and can move on to the next project sooner. The efficiency and profitability of design services increases. Finally, CM services are inherently profitable. A single construction manager with about one-third of an administrative assistant's time can administer $4 million to $6 million in construction. While fees for CM services vary across the world, profitability can be as high as 50 percent of gross income, depending on the size and complexity of the projects.

***Natural transition for clients and staff.*** Another reason to consider CM services is the ease of incorporation into a conventional practice. The primary change from a conventional service is that the construction work is divided into multiple bid packages rather than a single prime contract and the architect replaces the prime contractor's construction superintendent with a construction manager to coordinate the efforts of multiple contractors. This transition is not difficult to make. To some degree the architect is already providing much of the service connected with CM without additional compensation.

***Sharpen the firm's documentation, estimating, and scheduling skills.*** Offering CM services can sharpen a firm's skills. CM experience increases the design staff's knowledge of bidding conditions, field problems, and construction means and methods. It can also improve the quality of project drawings and specifications and the accuracy of construction cost estimates.

***Return to master builder.*** CM offers an opportunity to restore the broad scope of services traditionally provided by the architect as master builder. Planners, engineers, interior designers, developers, kitchen and bath specialists, specifications writers, project managers, and construction managers all provide services to clients in areas that used to be the architect's domain. Providing CM services can renew the client's confidence in the architect's ability to provide comprehensive services and open the door for provision of specialty services that have been delivered by others in recent decades. Firms have also reported that offering construction-related opportunities

architect or an independent nonarchitect such as a contractor. Thus a nonarchitect construction manager can also use this series of documents. The B801/CMa carefully outlines the duties and responsibilities of the construction manager as advisor. The use of two contracts for service— one for architectural services and a second for construction management—enables the architect to clearly demonstrate the two types of service to an owner and to formulate proper and adequate charges for each. As well, the use of a second contract for CM services allows an architecture firm to provide CM services on a project for which it is not providing design services.

***Construction manager as constructor.*** The prime document of this series, the A121/CMc, Standard Form of Agreement Between Owner and Construction Manager Where the Construction Manager Is Also the Constructor, was written jointly by the AIA and the Associated General Contractors of America (AGC) and is intended for use if the construction manager provides a guaranteed maximum price (GMP). A131/CMc is the contract for construction manager as constructor when there is no GMP. One of the AIA's goals in writing these documents was to influence the owner-contractor relationship when contractors offer CM services directly to the owner.

Architects also may wish to offer CM services with a GMP, either for a project they have designed or for a project designed by another architect. However, if architects use the A121/CMc document, some very important and serious changes in responsibility will be introduced into the owner-architect relationship. Architects must consider seriously whether they are willing to accept these differences. First, the document incorporates the same responsibilities for means and methods of construction as are found in the standard owner-contractor agreement described in the A101 and A201 documents. Once an architecture firm accepts this responsibility, insurance for professional liability may be voided. Insurance coverage may still be possible, however, using something like the general liability insurance that is available for general contractors.

for employees has helped them find new employees in a tight job market.

***Enhanced marketing of architecture services.*** Marketing might be considered both a reason for adding CM as a service and, at the same time, a concern. First, it is fairly easy to "sell" CM services to an owner looking for a single source of accountability, lower construction costs, and faster project delivery. Even if an owner is not interested in CM services, the architect's experience with CM can only strengthen a proposal to provide design services.

One concern with marketing CM services is reflected in some architects' fears of alienating developers and large general contractors who might also be clients. Initially it may be a good idea to keep a low profile with these "old friends"; however, once a CM service has been established, the profitability and increased income to the architect should soon overshadow any income realized from developer- or contractor-led projects.

***Enhanced risk management.*** Firms can improve their ability to manage professional liability risks by providing CM services. There is no better way to manage professional liability than to have a firm's representative on site every day to document activities in the field, coordinate the work flow, and, most importantly, resolve issues before disputes arise. These techniques do more to reduce professional liability than one can imagine. Many firms report that since the addition of CM services, fees have doubled and even tripled. While the professional liability policies are underwritten primarily on fees, these firms report their premiums have stayed the same. This fact indicates that the professional liability insurance companies recognize the positive effects of a design firm offering CM services. Their documentation improves, and they are better at resolving conflict early, before claims are made or formal dispute resolution methods employed.

## Common Concerns

Of the concerns commonly expressed by firms deciding whether to add construction management as a service, the biggest is the risk involved. The three areas of most concern are professional and general liability (or insurable risks), job site safety, and uninsurable risks, including fixed-cost contracts when acting as a constructor or fines from regulatory agencies for failure to comply with laws and regulations.

Both professional liability and general liability can be covered with adequate insurance. Professionally, CM is an architectural service just like design and can be insured under a standard professional practice liability policy. General liability can be covered with a standard general contractor's general liability policy. (Firms should ask their insurance agents to be sure their activities are properly underwritten. Most insurance companies offer a supervisory constructor category, which can save substantial premium dollars but provide similar coverage.)

Job site safety can pose some added risk, although by contract, the responsibility for job site safety still rests with the construction contractors if the architecture firm has contracted for CM-as-agent responsibilities. (While recent OSHA rulings have been contrary to this philosophy, designers should still strive to remove themselves contractually from job site safety when acting as an agent.) If the firms have contracted for CM as constructor responsibilities, then job site safety is a primary concern, and the firm's business plan must address this new risk. In all cases, the astute firm will consult with legal and insurance counsel for advice on management of the risks associated with offering CM services, for the rewards are likely to outweigh the risks. Firms seeking to provide CM services will become innovative facilitators of the built environment and will be rewarded, professionally and financially.

Another responsibility assumed by an architect who uses the A121/CMc document is job site safety. Professional liability insurance offers no coverage for this risk, but a general (contractor) liability type of insurance policy could provide coverage. Other contractor-type duties and responsibilities normally and readily accepted by contractors are also included in the A121/CMc, but these are easily provided by an architect. Thus architects should carefully study the A121/CMc, the owner–construction manager agreement in which the construction manager is also the constructor, along with the A201, General Conditions of the Contract for Construction (as modified by A121/CMc), to ensure they clearly understand the risks an architecture firm assumes in offering construction management services as a constructor.

***Architect provides CM services along with design services.*** The B144/ARCH-CM is a document intended to make it easier for architects to contract with an owner for construction management as part of normal architectural services. The B144/ARCH-CM document is to be used as an amendment to the B141, Standard Form of Agreement Between Owner and Architect. The items included in the B144/ARCH-CM are very similar to those in the B801/CMa agreement between the owner and construction manager–advisor, but in a slightly abbreviated form. Since this amendment is only a modification of the standard B141, all the other construction administration documents utilized for conventional (design-bid-build) work can be used. The obvious advantage here is that a modification to an existing and familiar document is all that is required for an architecture firm to provide CM services.

On the other hand, the very simplicity of this amendment to the B141 could lead an owner to question the value of the service. In response, the architect may compromise and provide CM-advisor services for a below-market rate of compensation. Some firms have found that using two separate contracts as described above—one for architectural services and

| DOCUMENT TITLE (SHORT) | CM-ADVISOR | CM-CONSTRUCTOR | ARCH-CM |
|---|---|---|---|
| Owner–Contractor Agreement | A101/CMa | See Owner–Construction Manager Agreement | A101 |
| Owner–Architect Agreement | B141/CMa | B141 with modifications (see A511)* | B141 amended by B144/ARCH-CM |
| Owner–Construction Manager Agreement | B801/CMa | A121/CMc or A131/CMc | See Owner–Architect Agreement |
| General Conditions | A201/CMa | A201 as modified by A121/CMc or A131/CMc | A201 |
| Guide to Supplementary Conditions | A511 | A511 | A511 |
| Instructions to Bidders | A701 | A701 | A701 |
| Change Order | G701/CMa | See instructions for A121/CMc or A131/CMc | G701 |
| Application for Payment | G702/Cma G703 | See instructions for A121/CMc or A131/CMc | G702/G703 |
| Certificate of Substantial Completion | G704/CMa | See instructions for A121/CMc or A131/CMc | G704 |
| Construction Change Directive | G714/CMa | See instructions for A121/CMc or A131/CMc | G714 |
| Project Payment Application | G722/CMa G723/CMa | See instructions for A121/CMc or A131/CMc | None |

*Cost estimating services will be performed by the construction manager–constructor. Generally, an owner may not want the architect to duplicate those efforts, although there may be occasions when the owner wants a second opinion to check the CM–constructor's work.

another for CM services—makes it more apparent that a total service is being provided for each discipline, rather than construction management being added on to the architect's standard contract. This distinction makes it easier to negotiate fair compensation for each service.

Finally, it must be noted that once a method of contracting for CM services has been selected, it is important to use only the documents from that family for the project. Serious legal consequences can result when documents for different types of services from unrelated families of documents are mixed.

## Process Activities and Steps

> **Architects and construction managers should carefully review the requirements of the specific form of agreement signed by the architect and the owner.**

The accompanying construction management checklist shows the activities and steps involved in performing competent CM services. The checklist is not intended to replace the duties and requirements noted in B801/CMc, Owner–Construction Manager Agreement, or B144/ARCH-CM, amendment to B141. Rather, the checklist shows activities and steps in project development. Activities are organized within the two major project phases, preconstruction and construction. The preconstruction phase typically accounts for about 20 percent of CM services and the construction phase for the remainder.

### For More Information

Case studies of successful designer-led CM projects can be found in back issues of the Project Delivery Reports issued by the AIA Construction Management and Design Build PIAs. The reports are available on the AIA Web site at www.e-architect.com and can be accessed through the PIA Knowledge Center directory under "Professional Interests."

AIA Ohio has produced a white paper entitled "Managing Public Construction Projects in Ohio," which can be found on their Web site at www.aiaohio.org. Subtitled "A Primer on Methods for Effectively Managing the Process from Beginning to End," the paper discusses what types of projects can benefit from hiring an architect for construction-related services in addition to their design contracts and how to go about defining the CM responsibilities. Goals are to minimize overlapping responsibilities, reduce time delays, and keep costs down.

# CONSTRUCTION MANAGEMENT CHECKLIST

## Preconstruction Phase

- [ ] Check overall CM responsibilities:
  - [ ] Read B801/CMa, Standard Form of Agreement Between Owner and Construction Manager–Adviser Where the CM Is Not a Constructor
  - [ ] Read B144/ARCH-CM, Standard Form of Amendment for the Agreement Between Owner and Architect Where the Architect Provides Construction Management Services as Adviser to the Owner
  - [ ] Read A201/CMa AIA, General Conditions of the Contract for Construction—Construction Manager–Adviser Edition
- [ ] Review project program.
- [ ] Provide preliminary evaluation (for project architect and owner):
  - [ ] Owner's program
  - [ ] Project schedule
  - [ ] Construction budget
- [ ] Prepare or assist in preparing a preliminary cost estimate.
- [ ] Provide cost evaluations for alternative materials and systems.
- [ ] Advise project architect on following (upon request):
  - [ ] Proposed site use
  - [ ] Selections of materials
  - [ ] Building systems and equipment
  - [ ] Availability of materials and labor
  - [ ] Time requirements for procurement, installation, and construction
  - [ ] Possible economies
- [ ] Update project schedule.
- [ ] Update cost estimates:
  - [ ] Schematic design phase
  - [ ] Design development phase
  - [ ] Construction document phase
- [ ] Advise project architect regarding design details that might affect constructability, cost, and schedule.
- [ ] Temporary project facilities—make recommendations to project architect.
- [ ] Safety programs—provide owner with information regarding allocation of responsibilities, i.e., each contractor is responsible for safety.
- [ ] Prepare list of bid packages.
- [ ] Prepare construction schedule (include in specifications).
- [ ] Assist owner in selecting consultants and testing laboratories, if necessary.
- [ ] Analyze labor availability and make recommendations.
- [ ] Check requirements for equal opportunity employment and advise specifier.
- [ ] Review specifications (assist in writing if needed).
- [ ] Prepare list of prospective bidders for project architect's review.
- [ ] Develop bidder's interest.
- [ ] Conduct pre-bid conference, if necessary.
- [ ] Receive bids (with project architect).
- [ ] Prepare bid tab.
- [ ] With project architect, make recommendations to owner regarding acceptance or rejection of bids.
- [ ] Prepare construction contracts and obtain contractor's and owner's signatures.
- [ ] Obtain building permit.

## Construction Phase

- [ ] Return each contractor's copy of the construction contract with notice to proceed. Remind contractors of safety responsibilities.
- [ ] Hold preconstruction conference.
- [ ] Introduce owner, project architect, CM, contractors to project requirements:
  - [ ] Project description by project architect
  - [ ] Project goals by owner
  - [ ] Importance of construction schedule
  - [ ] Site conditions—materials storage, etc.
  - [ ] Temporary facilities—job shack, telephone, power, water, etc.
  - [ ] Applications for payments
    - Number of copies: _____
    - Submittal date: _____
    - Expect payment by: _____
    - One approved copy will be returned to contractor
  - [ ] Contractor safety programs
  - [ ] Weekly progress meetings (set time and day)
  - [ ] Other items
- [ ] Prepare and distribute preconstruction meeting minutes to the owner, the project architect, and all contractors.
- [ ] Materials and equipment delivery:
  - All items needed in next 4 to 8 weeks
  - Check each Monday
- [ ] Conduct weekly progress meetings:
  - [ ] Request presence of present on-site contractors.
  - [ ] Encourage contractors scheduled 2 to 4 weeks ahead to attend.
  - [ ] Project architect should attend.
  - [ ] Invite owner's representative to attend.
  - [ ] Agenda:
    - Record day and date and length of meeting.
    - Record names of attendees.
    - Provide brief update on progress.
    - Review work schedule for next week or two.
    - Check coordination problems.
    - Check construction problems.
    - Identify potential change orders.
    - Other items
    - Remind contractors of safety responsibilities (monthly)
- [ ] Prepare and send copies of progress meeting notes to owner, project architect, and each contractor.
- [ ] Maintain daily log.
- [ ] Process monthly applications for payment.
- [ ] Check shop drawings and monitor processing.
- [ ] Record actual progress on construction schedule.
- [ ] Ascertain whether contractors maintain a clean and orderly job site.
- [ ] Maintain a set of construction documents at the job site.
- [ ] Mark up a set of construction documents for as-built documents.
- [ ] Assist owner with receiving, storage, and installation of owner-purchased equipment and/or furnishings.
- [ ] Observe on-site tests and testing of material, equipment, systems, etc.
- [ ] Prepare pre-final punch list.
- [ ] With project architect, conduct final inspection.
- [ ] Secure copies of warranties and guarantees for the owner.
- [ ] Review final applications for payments.
- [ ] Turn over set of as-built documents to the owner.

# 17.7 Construction Procurement

## William C. Charvat, AIA, CSI

*The procurement of construction services brings together the team and resources needed to translate building plans into physical reality.*

### Summary

**CONSTRUCTION PROCUREMENT SERVICES**

#### Why a Client May Need These Services

▷ To coordinate construction procurement without tying up in-house resources

▷ To obtain expert advice about selecting an appropriate project delivery method

▷ To obtain help in identifying qualified contractors

▷ To ensure that reasonable prices are obtained for construction work

▷ To assist in awarding and preparing contracts for construction

#### Knowledge and Skills Required

▷ Experience with managing construction procurement processes

▷ Knowledge of construction contracting approaches and procedures

▷ Understanding of project design intent, budget, and schedule

▷ Knowledge of construction drawings and specifications

▷ Strong communication and negotiation skills

#### Representative Process Tasks

▷ Assist client in selection of project delivery method

▷ Assemble construction procurement team, including cost estimator and attorney

▷ Identify prospective bidders

▷ Organize or participate in pre-bid conference

▷ Assist in preparation of bidding documents

▷ Review and evaluate competitive bids

▷ Assist client in contractor interviews for obtaining negotiated proposals

▷ Award contract for construction

Construction procurement activities assist the client in obtaining competent construction services. The architect will prepare bid packages or requests for proposal or qualifications and support the selection, negotiation, and contract award processes.

In most projects construction procurement services are packaged with other architectural services such as design, construction documents, or construction contract administration. Clients sometimes choose to treat construction procurement as a discrete service, however. Traditionally this choice depended on the project, but today the demand for construction procurement services is increasing with the trend toward alternative delivery methods such as construction management and design-build.

The increase in construction claims and litigation and the related trends toward increased control of cost and quality have placed more emphasis on the construction procurement process. Clients want to ensure that construction contractors are well qualified, that services are obtained for reasonable cost, and that their projects are well organized contractually to minimize the potential for costly changes and delays.

## CLIENT NEEDS

Clients are motivate to seek construction procurement services when they do not have the experience or resources to do the task in-house or do not wish to devote in-house resources to the task. Large, complex projects may require contracting with a number of different prime contractors, which requires a great deal of coordination of the bid packages or requests for proposal (RFPs) and requests for quotes (RFQs). Often such projects are on tight time schedules with phased, fast-track work plans, necessitating even greater coordination of the procurement process and a higher level of effort for the construction procurement team.

Many clients look to architects for advice regarding the best delivery method for a project, recognizing that delivery method affects risk, schedule, and cost. The architect also may assist in locating qualified contractors, either by prequalifying a bidders list or recommending firms for negotiated procurements.

Clients often want maximum control of the procurement process and will preapprove a bidders list and want to be involved in contractor selection in order to ensure selection of qualified contractors and subcontractors. Clients constructing complex facilities such as laboratories and clients who will be long-term owner-occupants are usually most interested in quality control.

**WILLIAM C. CHARVAT** *is senior vice president of Helman Hurley Charvat Peacock/Architects, Inc, an international architecture, planning, and interior design firm in Maitland, Florida. His practice focuses on project management, construction, and problem-solving for large and complex projects.*

On projects that are publicly funded or for some other reason heavily regulated (e.g., health care facilities that require state inspections or government procurements with minority-owned or women-owned business enterprise participation requirements), the need to comply with regulations motivates some clients to seek outside help with procurements. These clients are concerned about maintaining the quality of construction and complying with regulatory requirements while maintaining cost control.

Clients recognize the relationships between clear bid or proposal request documents, well-executed construction contracts, and a smoother and more effective construction administration process. The architect who designs the building and prepares the construction documents is especially well qualified to prepare bid/proposal packages and legal contracts, since the drawings and specifications are an integral part of both types of documents.

On the other hand, competitors in the market for construction procurement services argue that architects are not capable of independently reviewing their own work when they serve in the construction procurement or construction administration roles.

Firms specializing in program management or owner's project representation are capturing an increasing share of the construction procurement market. These firms position themselves as third-party neutral players who will manage and monitor the project on behalf of the owner, with the owner retaining the construction contract. The services of a program management firm often include project feasibility analyses, programming, design management, and advice on project delivery approach, as well as construction procurement, construction administration, and facility management. Typically these firms are staffed by a mix of design and construction professionals.

Besides architect-engineer and engineer-architect firms, other major providers of construction procurement services include firms specializing in construction management or design-build. Construction management firms manage construction contracts held by the owner. Design-build firms contract directly with the owner to provide design and construction services.

The market value of construction procurement services depends on the type of package offered. Adding construction procurement services to a traditional design contract generally adds 1 to 2 percent to the architect's fees for a project.

## SKILLS

Construction procurement services require a range of knowledge and skills, some of which are developed through practical experience in managing building design and construction and through previous experience in managing procurement processes. Senior architects with project management experience are most likely to have developed the negotiation skills and the knowledge of construction procedures required to negotiate procurements and draft construction contracts. Most architects possess other, more fundamental skills, including the ability to understand the design intent expressed in construction drawings and specifications and the ability to communicate with vendors and construction contractors.

Cost estimators usually work with the procurement team to assist with budget estimation. A good attorney well versed in construction law is another essential member of the construction procurement team.

The construction procurement team usually will coordinate closely with other professionals involved in the project—including site planners, landscape architects, architects, and civil, structural, mechanical, and electrical engineers—in order to be certain the procurement procedures and documents facilitate the design intent.

## PROCESS

Factors that can affect the scope of work for construction procurement include the contract structure (e.g., design-bid-build, design-build, etc.), the number of construction contracts, the timing for contract awards, and the use and extent of fast-tracking.

▶ For discussion of two services closely related to construction procurement, see Construction Documentation—Drawings (17.4) and Construction Documentation—Specifications (17.5).

### Bidding Assumptions

In preparing bids, certain assumptions are made in the building industry:

- The owner can expect that the architect has exercised reasonable diligence, skill, and judgment in preparing the contract documents—so that the contractor complying with them will deliver a project adequate for its intended purpose.

- The contractor can expect that the information given in the construction documents is reliable and adequate to permit comprehensive and accurate bids.

- The contractor can expect that the architect knows local regulations concerning design and construction of the project and has indicated in the contract documents any known unusual conditions that are reasonably likely to affect cost.

- The architect is entitled to the owner's confidence that the architect is acting in the best interest of the project during selection of bidders and taking of bids.

- The owner can expect that a bidder will notify the architect immediately if submission of a bid will not be possible at the designated time and place and will withdraw from the bidding if necessary.

- The owner can expect that every contractor has bid in good faith and has available qualified supervisors to coordinate the work.

- Contractors can expect that the owner is soliciting, receiving, and evaluating all bids in good faith.

*Walter Rosenfeld, AIA, CSI*

**Project Delivery Options (9.1)** addresses several options by which building design and construction services can be structured and provided.

The basic steps involved in contract procurement include preparatory steps, prequalification of bidders, preparation of bidding documents, receipt of bids, and contract award.

## Preparatory Steps

Preparation for bidding and negotiation ideally starts at the very beginning of the project—in selecting the project delivery approach and in deciding how construction contracts will be structured, awarded, and paid.

*Contract structure.* Key preparatory decisions for contract structure include the following:

- Will construction be contracted separately or together with design services? If the latter approach (design-build) is selected, the construction contract includes design and usually is awarded early in project development.
- How many construction contracts will there be? Will there be a single general construction contract or multiple prime contracts? If there are to be multiple prime contracts, who will coordinate or manage them—the architect, the owner, a construction manager, or one of the contractors?
- When will the construction contract(s) be awarded—at one time, based on one set of construction documents, or at several times, with the project divided into a few, several, or even many bid packages?
- If the project is to be divided into bid packages, will it also be fast-tracked—that is, with early packages awarded before design of the later packages is complete?
- What will serve as the basis for establishing the contract sum for construction: a full set of construction documents or a less-developed set of documents, for example, scope documents or 50-percent-construction documents?
- What will be the architect's role during bidding, negotiation, and construction? Is the architect to administer the construction contract for the owner? Will there be a separate construction manager or program manager? Will the architect also serve as construction manager?

*Award system.* Related to delivery approach decisions is the issue of contract award. Will construction contracts be awarded directly (that is, by negotiation) or through competitive bidding? If there is competitive bidding, will it be open to all or restricted to an invited list?

*Contractor compensation.* Will compensation be fixed price, cost plus fee, unit prices, or some form of guaranteed maximum or incentive compensation?

*Timing.* If contracts will be negotiated, and if the owner is prepared to select a builder, it often makes sense to have that builder in place during the design phases. If bids are to be solicited from a restricted list, this list should be prepared as early as possible. It is sensible to assess the availability of the contractors on the list and the degree of competition the owner may foresee. If the project is to be openly bid, an assessment of probable market response may help establish the most appropriate timing of advertisement and bidding.

## Prequalification of Bidders

Prequalifying bidders by investigating their general reputation, financial integrity, demonstrated ability, quality of performance, and prior project experience can help ensure that appropriate standards are met. This option usually is open when there will be a restricted bidders list or open bidding for a project that does not include public funding. Depending on applicable law, it may be possible to prequalify contractors on public projects as well.

## Preparation of Bidding Documents

Having advised the owner on the types of contracts and on prospective bidders, the architect assembles bidding documents for the owner. These documents describe the project in detail and indicate the conditions under which it will be bid and built. The bidding documents usually include the following:

## Prequalification Checklist

Based on AIA Document A305, this checklist can aid in collecting the kind of information that should prove helpful in prequalifying contractors. Be sure to consider the questions carefully—especially in terms of what you plan to do with the answers. Will you be in a position to evaluate what you receive? Are you prepared to follow up with phone calls or reference checks to verify information?

1. Basic information: name, address, principal office, and type of business (corporation, partnership, individual, joint venture, other). A Dun & Bradstreet report may be desirable.
2. Length of time the organization has been in business as a general contractor and whether it has operated under other names. Businesses come and go, and rapid name changes may indicate instability.
3. For corporations: date of incorporation, state of incorporation, and officers' names. Is the corporation registered in the state in which the project is located?
4. For sole proprietorships and partnerships: date of organization and names and addresses of general and limited partners.
5. States and categories in which the organization is legally qualified to do business, indicating registration or license numbers, if applicable, and states in which the partnership or trade name is filed.
6. Types and percentages of work normally performed with the contractor's own forces. Low percentages suggest a smaller vested interest in the project.
7. Whether the organization—or one of its partners or officers as a partner or officer of another organization—has ever failed to complete any work awarded. Details are usually sought, and follow-up may be necessary.
8. List of major construction projects in progress, giving name of project, owner, architect, contract amount, percentage completed, and scheduled completion date. Following up with the architects of these projects may provide valuable insights.
9. List of construction projects completed in the last five years, giving name of project, owner, architect, initial and final contract amounts, date of completion, percentage of the cost of the work completed with the contractor's own forces, and number of requests for information and change orders. Visits to some of these projects may be in order.
10. Construction experience of the individuals being proposed to manage this project.
11. Trade and bank references. Follow-up may be in order.
12. Bonding company and name and address of agent. What is the organization's bonding capacity? How much of it is currently engaged? How much is tentatively outstanding? How much of the organization's current and committed work is not bonded?
13. Litigation history, including complaints, claims, demands for arbitration, and lawsuits brought by (and against) the organization in, say, the last five years.
14. Experience in partnering and alternative dispute resolution methods in, say, the past five years.
15. Lien history, including liens placed on projects as well as liens placed on the contractor by others.
16. Financial statement, audited if available, including the contractor's latest balance sheet and income statement.

---

- Advertisement or invitation to bid
- Instructions to bidders
- Bid forms
- Information on bid security or bond, if required
- Form of owner-contractor agreement
- Performance bond and labor and material payment bond, if required
- General and any supplementary conditions of the contract
- Drawings and specifications
- Any addenda issued prior to the receipt of bids

*Advertisement for bids.* For public work, the law usually requires an invitation to bidding to be announced in one or more newspapers. The client may choose supplemental advertisement in contractors' newsletters, magazines, or other media.

*Instruction to bidders.* AIA Document A701, Instructions to Bidders, contains provisions concerning definitions, bidder's representations, bidding procedures, examination of bidding documents, substitutions, qualifications of bidders, rejection of bids, and submission of post-bid information, including performance and payment bonds.

*Bid form.* The architect should be prepared to help the owner prepare the bid form so that all bids will be submitted in an identical format. Some owners require the use of their own forms.

*Bid documents.* Each bidder, including those bidding on only a portion of the work, should have access to at least one complete set of drawings and specifications. The number of sets furnished to general contractors bidding on the entire project generally depends on the size of the project. To ensure the return of bid documents by unsuccessful bidders, each bidder can be required to provide a security deposit to be refunded (in whole or in part) upon return of the documents in good condition within a stated period.

**Registration of bidders.** The architect should maintain a master list with the name, address, and phone and fax numbers of contractors receiving bidding documents. This list is necessary for issuing addenda, tracking returned sets, and refunding deposits.

**Bid security.** Bid security—usually about 1 percent of the bid—warrants that the selected bidder will execute the construction contract and furnish a performance bond, if required, within a stipulated period.

**Owner-contractor agreement form.** The owner-contractor agreement sets forth the respective rights, duties, and obligations of these principals to the agreement and of the architect (and possibly a construction manager) acting to administer the construction contract. For bidders' information, the agreement form, as well as the general conditions and supplementary conditions of the contract for construction, are included in the project manual. This ensures that all the contract requirements are immediately available to each bidder.

Performance bond. A performance bond binds a surety company to complete the construction contract if the contractor defaults. Performance bonds are usually required for all public work and often for private work, except for small projects.

**Labor and material payment bond.** The performance bond and the labor and material payment bonds are usually written at the same time.

**Addenda.** During the bidding period, reviews of the drawings and specifications by prime bidders, sub-bidders, and material suppliers inevitably reveal items that must be clarified, corrected, or explained. Sometimes the owner or architect will initiate revisions in the bidding documents in response to changes in circumstances or requirements. Written addenda, including drawings or other graphic documents issued before execution of the contract, modify or interpret the bidding documents. Addenda become part of the contract documents when they are first issued; they are sent to all those who have received bidding documents. Addenda issued after bids are received are intended only for the selected bidder and may result in changes to the proposed contract price.

## Receipt of Bids

The construction procurement consultant usually conducts any public bid opening, unless the client prefers to do so. Observing proper protocol is important to avoid bid protests.

**Bidding results.** Final selection of the contractor is the owner's decision, made with the architect's assistance. When the qualifications and financial responsibility of the bidders have been determined in the prequalification process, the expectation is that the contract will be awarded to the lowest bidder. When bidders have not been prequalified, the expectation is that the contract will be awarded to the lowest *responsible* bidder.

**Errors, withdrawals, and revocations.** The bidding documents generally set a date after which bidders cannot withdraw bids. This date should allow sufficient time after submission of bids for accurate bid evaluation and authorization of an award.

**Evaluation of bids.** The architect will, in all likelihood, assist the owner in the selection decision by evaluating the bids or proposals received. This assistance usually includes review and recommendation on any alternatives and substitutions that the owner has solicited. This evaluation takes on special significance if all bids exceed the owner's budget. The owner's options at that point include increasing the budget, rebidding, renegotiating, revising the scope, or abandoning the project.

Rebidding without design changes should be approached carefully. It is of value only where market conditions are changing, so that a second round is likely to produce a significantly lower price. Redesign should be approached even more carefully. Design decisions usually are so intricately interwoven that it may be difficult to make a "few changes" and still maintain the integrity of the project design.

**Negotiation of bids.** Even in competitive bidding situations, it is not uncommon to engage in some negotiation after bids have been received. Minor changes required before the contract is signed should be negotiated only with the selected bidder, and then only when permitted by the owner or the awarding authority's regulations.

If major changes are necessary, they can be negotiated with the selected bidder, if authorized, or the original bids can be rejected and new bids requested based on revised drawings and specifications. Rebidding should occur only when other solutions are not practical.

**Rejection of bids.** The owner customarily includes in the bidding documents the right to reject any or all bids.

**Notification of bidders.** After the owner has selected the contractor(s), all bidders should be informed of the results, as a matter of courtesy.

## Contract Award

The construction procurement consultant prepares a contract reflecting modifications resulting from negotiations and changes. The owner and contractor(s) sign the agreement(s).

**Letter of intent.** When the owner wants to move forward immediately before assembling and executing a formal agreement, a written letter of intent may be used to give the successful contractor interim authorization to begin work. Such orders to proceed, while common, have legal implications and should be drafted by the owner's attorney for the owner's signature.

Usual documents and deliverables for construction procurement services are reports of bidding or proposal results; recommended actions; and construction contracts.

### For More Information

Two AIA contract documents provide both a general and a specific overview of competitive bidding for building construction projects. AIA Document A501, Recommended Guide for Competitive Bidding Procedures and Contract Awards for Building Construction, outlines appropriate procedures when competitive lump sum bids are sought. AIA Document A701, Instructions to Bidders, which is coordinated with A201 and its related documents, contains instructions and procedures to be followed by bidders in preparing and submitting their bids.

---

## Representations on the Bid Form

To underscore the importance of the contractor's representations as outlined in the bidding documents, some architects include these representations on the bid form. This is the language from the 1987 edition of AIA Document A701, Instructions to Bidders:

The bidder by making a bid represents that the following have taken place:

- The bidder has read and understands the bidding documents and the bid is made in accordance therewith.
- The bidder has read and understands the bidding or contract documents, to the extent that such documentation relates to the work for which the bid is submitted and to other portions of the project, if any, being bid concurrently or presently under construction.
- The bidder has visited the site, become familiar with local conditions under which the work is to be performed, and has correlated the bidder's personal observations with the requirements of the proposed contract documents.
- The bid is based upon the materials, equipment, and systems required by the bidding documents without exception.
- The bidder has studied and compared the bidding documents with each other and has reported to the architect any errors, inconsistencies, or ambiguities discovered.

*Walter Rosenfeld, AIA, CSI*

# 17.8 Contract Administration

Patrick Mays, AIA

*As construction administrators, architects interpret construction contract documents, track the progress of the work, and reconcile the sometimes conflicting interests of owners and builders.*

## Summary

### CONTRACT ADMINISTRATION SERVICES

#### Why a Client May Need These Services
▷ To ensure construction conforms to construction documents
▷ To support the design intent
▷ To lessen project risks
▷ To identify and resolve construction problems early
▷ To supplement the client's construction knowledge

#### Knowledge and Skills Required
▷ Substantial design and construction experience
▷ Understanding of construction techniques and methods
▷ Ability to understand and interpret the design intent
▷ Understanding of building codes and standards
▷ Ability to communicate, negotiate, and resolve disputes
▷ Keen observational skills
▷ Ability to document observations and decisions
▷ Ability to organize and manage project records

#### Representative Process Tasks
▷ Establish lines of communication
▷ Establish record-keeping system
▷ Respond to contractor's requests for information
▷ Track changes in construction documents
▷ Review contractor's requests for payment
▷ Review shop drawings and product information
▷ Prepare field reports and records
▷ Supervise completion and closeout

The architect serving as a construction administrator observes construction for conformity to construction drawings and specifications. These documents are part of the legal contract between the owner and general contractor. When interpreting these legal documents, the architect's role shifts. The architect serves not as the owner's direct agent but in a quasi-judicial capacity, showing partiality to neither owner nor contractor. At other times during the construction phase the architect acts as the owner's representative and agent

In the 1970s and early 1980s, in an effort to save money and fast-track construction, many developers started using nonarchitect construction managers for construction administration services. This placed architects in an awkward position, as they retained risk for the completed structure while not being compensated for their site observation services and other duties. Architects have strong incentives to serve as construction administrators. Through construction administration, the architect can support the continuity, quality, and intent of the design. The architect serving as a construction administrator can better manage and limit project risks by facilitating project communications and maintaining clear project records. Serving as construction administrator also enables t he architect to identify and correct problems in time to eliminate or minimize negative impact on construction costs.

## CLIENT NEEDS

The continuing involvement of the architect during the construction phase helps assure the client that the completed building will reflect the design intent, and further ensures the quality of materials and workmanship. When the architect is retained by the owner to administer the construction contract, the architect is the owner's representative in dealing with the contractor. The architect will be available for advice and consultation with the owner. In monitoring the construction, the architect will be alert to whether the contractor has carried out the design intent and the contract requirements relating to quality of workmanship and materials. The architect will endeavor to guard the owner against defects and deficiencies in the work.

Clients who are building or renovating small commercial buildings or single-family residences are good markets for this service because they often lack experience with the building process and do not have the ability to oversee construction themselves. These clients should readily recognize the benefit of having the architect interact with building contractors and code inspectors on their behalf. Developers of multifamily residential or larger commercial facilities generally do not see the need for these services, as they prefer to use their own personnel. Architects who are not retained for services during the construction

**PATRICK MAYS** *is a principal and chief information officer at NBBJ Architecture Design & Planning. He is a co-author of* Construction Administration: An Architect's Guide to Surviving Information Overload *(1997).*

SERVICES   part 4

stage should refrain from visiting the site or volunteering uncompensated services. The standard of care requires design professionals to render the same quality of service whether properly compensated or not. In these cases, the architect might seek indemnification for lack of involvement mandated by the client.

Among owners of owner-occupied buildings, concern for quality is a major motivator. Institutional and public owners of complex facilities such as sports arenas, hospitals, and schools are usually more than willing to pay for the architect's oversight and administration services. Most federal, state, and local government agencies are interested in architect-provided construction administration services, regardless of the type of facility involved. On the other hand, corporate clients who are constantly in the building market may be more confident of their ability to administer the construction phase, since they are more likely to have on-staff experts who are competent to handle it.

A general rule of thumb is that about 25 percent of the architect's total compensation for services accounts for construction administration. This fee percentage is generally sufficient to compensate the architect for the following services during construction:

- Spending one day per week on site, attending a meeting and observing the progress of construction
- Responding to questions from the contractors and material suppliers
- Reviewing shop drawings and submittals
- Reviewing and certifying monthly applications for payment
- Authoring clarifications and minor changes to the documents
- Assisting consultants with construction administration duties
- Record keeping
- Project closeout responsibilities

One successful strategy for negotiating adequate fees for construction administration is to agree on a base fee for general services and then go through a construction administration checklist with the client and add each construction administration task as a supplemental service. This provides an opportunity to explain the value of each task to the client.

Knowledgeable owners realize that the architect can often save them money through proper construction administration practices—that, in effect, quality construction administration can pay for itself in risk reduction and in savings on time, materials, and change orders during the construction process.

In most cases the architect who developed the drawings and specifications is in the best position to interpret them. Some architects make an analogy: If an attorney writes a contract, wouldn't you return to the same attorney when it came time to interpret the contract? The drawings and specifications written by the architect become part of the legal contract between the builder and the owner—and that part of the contract is best interpreted by the professional who wrote it.

No set of drawings and specifications is so tightly written that everything will be built exactly as designed. When the design architect is involved in contract administration, appropriate adjustments can be made as necessary to maintain quality, economy, and design integrity. This point can be a double-edged sword, however. Clients who perceive the architect as preoccupied with aesthetics may lack confidence in the architect's ability to recommend appropriate trade-offs. The architect must achieve credibility with the owner as a professional who will be attentive to cost and performance concerns.

Construction administration is a traditional service that many architects provide within the scope of services defined in AIA Document B141-1997, Standard Form of Agreement Between Owner and Architect, and AIA Document B163, Owner–Architect Agreement for Designated Services.

The services grouped under "Contract Administration Services" in Document B141 include a mixture of tasks, some of which clearly fall under construction administration as discussed here (e.g., general administration, submittals, site visitation, administration of testing and inspection, supplemental documentation, administration of changes in the work, interpretations and decisions), and some of which are more in the realm of construction management (e.g., on-site project representation, payment certification, project closeout, construction management).

The trend toward the design-build method of project delivery strongly influences

▶ **Design-Build Services (17.9)** covers the activities and tasks that provide the client with design and construction services through a single entity.

## The Architect Wears Three Hats

Legally, the architect occupies three different positions as the professional service phases progress from inception of design to completion of construction contract administration.

In 1977 a California appellate court clarified the tripartite legal position of an architect (*Huber, Hunt & Nichols, Inc. v. Moore*, 67 Cal App 3d 278, 136 Cal Reptr 603). The three separate and distinct roles recognized in law are:

- As an independent contractor
- As an agent of the owner
- As a quasi-judicial officer

All of the standard AIA documents are based on these principles.

### As Independent Contractor

An independent contractor is one who contracts to do something for another according to its own means and methods and not under control of the employer except as to the end result.

During the time the architect is conferring with the owner, designing the project, preparing the contract documents, and administering the contract, the architect's relationship to the owner is as an independent contractor. The architect contracts with the owner to furnish architectural services for which the owner agrees to pay a fee. The architect's and owner's duties are spelled out in the owner-architect agreement.

### As Agent of the Owner

An agent is one who has the authority to act for another, called the principal.

After a contract has been entered into between the owner and the contractor, the architect's position changes. During the construction period, when the architect deals with the contractor and others in behalf of the owner, the architect is serving as the owner's agent. This is provided for in the owner-architect agreement (B141-1997, subparagraph 2.6.1.3) and in the general conditions (A201-1997, subparagraph 4.2.1). However, the architect's powers to obligate the owner are restricted to the extent provided in the owner-architect agreement.

When dealing with the contractor, the architect acts in a fiduciary capacity for the owner and in this position of trust must represent the owner's best interests. As a fiduciary, the architect has the duty to disclose to the owner all information that is material to the owner's interests.

Some architects are inclined to shield the owner from some of the unpleasant technical details that plague the construction process. This could very well be a mistake, as some owners or their legal counsel might interpret this to be a violation of the architect's duty, as an agent, to disclose. Concealment of relevant information from the owner could be construed as fraud when there is a duty to disclose. Silence is often interpreted as concealment. Keeping the owner informed is also required by the general conditions (A201-1997, subparagraph 4.2.2), which state, in part, "On the basis of on-site observations as an architect, the Architect will keep the Owner informed of progress of the Work."

> **Construction Management (17.6) describes CM activities and tasks in detail.**

the demand for construction administration. As already noted, the initial introduction of fast-track construction reduced the architect's market for construction administration services, particularly among developers. Now the demand for design-build continues to grow, but owners in the corporate, institutional, and governmental markets more readily understand the benefits of architect-led design-build teams, providing architects with growing opportunities to offer construction administration services as part of more comprehensive construction management or design-build project delivery.

It is useful to distinguish between construction management and construction administration. Construction managers oversee the field operations: administering construction contracts, scheduling materials shipments, and coordinating construction processes. The construction administrator does not oversee construction contracts and has no authority over or legal relationship with construction contractors. The construction administrator has only one way to assert control over construction rules, procedures, or requirements: to write them into the specifications.

Other related services include construction documentation, commissioning, facility management and operations, and postoccupancy review.

## SKILLS

A construction administrator needs substantial design and construction experience, a thorough understanding of construction techniques and methods, and the ability to interpret the intent of construction documents. The construction administrator also needs a thorough understanding of building codes, standards, and regulations as well as the ability to communicate, negotiate, and resolve disputes with trade personnel.

Much of the work of construction administration involves recording decisions that

The architect is not in control of or in charge of the contractor but is authorized to reject work that does not conform to the contract documents. Although the owner is allowed to accept nonconforming work, the architect does not have this power, even as the owner's agent. If the owner wishes to confer this power on the architect, it should be done in writing.

The architect's duty to represent the owner in dealing with the contractor should not be confused with the vigorous partisan advocacy commonly practiced by lawyers, since this would conflict with the third position of the architect.

### As Quasi-Judicial Officer

The architect's third position is one of judge of the performance of the owner and the contractor under terms of the contract. Some have termed this position of the architect as being a "friend of the contract."

All claims by the owner or contractor against each other should be referred to the architect for initial decision as a condition precedent to more formal procedures such as mediation and arbitration. Some claims will be those alleging errors or omissions in the architect's own actions or work product.

The architect must make even-handed, fair decisions strictly in accordance with the contract, not siding with either party.

The architect also must be a fair interpreter of the documents. This can be difficult when the documents are imperfect and the architect's fair ruling will expose the documents to be at fault. When decisions on the "intent of the documents" are made, they must be based on some tangible evidence within the docu-

ments as to what is reasonably inferable and not merely on what is in the architect's mind.

The architect's decisions must be formulated pursuant to procedural due process. This means that the architect must give reasonable notice to each party to allow its position to be made known before the architect makes a final decision.

Arbitration tribunals and courts are inclined to look with suspicion on contracts where final decisions on the performance of the parties are made by a person under the control of one of the parties. Thus an architect's decision that is not fair, and is not seen to be fair, will be easily overturned by arbitrators and judges on appeal.

### The Architect's Liability

The architect can be sued for negligence and breach of duty as an independent contractor and as an agent of the owner. These suits might be brought by the architect's client or by a third party such as the contractor, subcontractors, later owners, tenants, or passers-by. Third-party claims may be made even though the architect's client is satisfied with the professional service and has no complaint.

However, the architect has immunity from suit for decisions made in the quasi-judicial capacity, provided they are made in good faith. The architect is liable only when acting fraudulently or with willful or malicious intent to injure the owner or contractor.

*Adapted from Arthur F. O'Leary, FAIA,* A Guide to Successful Construction: Effective Contract Administration, 3rd Ed. *(1999)*

are made and events that take place on the job site. Keen observational skills are important. Perhaps most important of all is the ability to thoroughly document observations and decisions and to effectively manage the flow and retrieval of project records.

For a typical project, the construction administration team would include the following:

- Construction administrator—a senior person who possesses the necessary management and technical skills. This usually is a registered architect.
- Project architect—someone with intimate knowledge of the project drawings. Often this is the same person as the construction administrator on smaller projects.
- Project assistant—may be a college graduate but not necessarily a registered professional
- Administrative assistant—someone who can handle word processing, organizing, and filing

As always, the key to success is to organize the work so that time-consuming and routine tasks can be assigned to the lower-paid team members, freeing senior professionals to concentrate on matters that require their judgment and expertise.

An architect administering a construction contract will be called upon first to resolve claims by the owner or contractor against the other. The architect must be diplomatic, fair, and studious in all decision making, since the decisions will be final and binding if not appealed in accordance with the contract.

Cost estimators and specifications writers are very important resources for the construction administration team. Cost estimators know how to determine the prevailing market value of various services for a given area, and specifications writers can contribute detailed knowledge about the characteristics and performance of building products. On complex pro-

## AIA Standard Forms Used in Construction Contract Administration

| | |
|---|---|
| G701 | Change Order |
| G701/CMa | Change Order, Construction Manager–Adviser Edition |
| G702 | Application and Certificate for Payment |
| G702/CMa | Application and Certificate for Payment—Construction Manager–Adviser Edition |
| G703 | Continuation Sheet for G702 |
| G704 | Certificate of Substantial Completion |
| G704/CMa | Certificate of Substantial Completion, Construction Manager–Adviser Edition |
| G706 | Contractor's Affidavit of Payment of Debts and Claims |
| G706A | Contractor's Affidavit of Release of Liens |
| G707 | Consent of Surety to Final Payment |
| G707A | Consent of Surety to Reduction in or Partial Release of Retainage |
| G709 | Proposal Request |
| G710 | Architect's Supplemental Instructions |
| G711 | Architect's Field Report |
| G712 | Shop Drawing and Sample Record |
| G714 | Construction Change Directive |
| G714/CMa | Construction Change Directive, Construction Manager–Adviser Edition |
| G722/CMa | Project Application and Project Certificate, Construction Manager–Adviser Edition |
| G723/CMa | Project Application Summary–Construction Manager–Adviser Edition |
| G805 | List of Subcontractors |

jects, the team will benefit from the inclusion of a project management specialist who is familiar with techniques and computer software for managing project resources and costs in real time.

The construction administration team works closely with other disciplines involved in the project, including structural, mechanical, electrical, and civil engineers; landscape architects; and other special consultants.

Special equipment used for construction administration includes hard hats, steel-toed nonskid boots, tape measure, camera with date stamp, carpenter's level, portable tape recorder, a rip-proof jacket and gloves (good inspection involves crawling in some tight spaces), a utility knife, a pocket compass, field glasses, a laptop computer, and a cellular phone.

## PROCESS

The scope of services as stated in the owner-architect agreement will depend on the delivery approach being used (e.g., fast-tracking, design-build), which in turn will affect the expected turnaround times for shop drawings and requests for information (RFIs). The project scope will depend on the size and number of buildings in the project, the phasing of construction, and the distance from the construction site to the architecture firm's location.

The contract administration service is heavily oriented toward the legal rights of the owner and contractor. Therefore the architect must be careful and meticulous in all actions, decisions, and record keeping.

***Communications.*** The contract administrator is responsible for two types of communications: reporting to the client and facilitating communications among the owner, constructors, and design professionals.

A preconstruction meeting is a valuable first step toward good communications in the contract administration process. Here the project work plan and schedule are reviewed. The relationships among the participants are clarified, including the processes for submitting RFIs and change orders.

Subcontractors ordinarily are not allowed to communicate directly with the architect but must submit queries through the prime contractor.

***Record keeping.*** Clear record keeping plays an important role in communications and conflict avoidance. If all events and decisions are clearly recorded, it is easier to talk matters through when issues arise. Good record keeping is also of enormous value should the owner or contractor make legal claims.

Establishing an effective filing system is another fundamental to success. One tip is to organize files by anticipating how contract administration materials will be searched. For example, some sample headings would be communications; meeting minutes; contracts for construction, including change orders and change directives; reports/program data; photographs; specifications and addenda; drawings; accounting records; and construction administration forms.

Accurate telephone records are important in establishing complete project records

## Getting Started in Field Administration

Professional work in an architect's office should be performed under the direct control and supervision of qualified architects. All offices are organized around this elementary principle. How can it be otherwise? Clients have the right to expect that the architect's services will be performed with professional skill and care.

Experienced architects must direct, supervise, and check the work of the less qualified until the latter are able to work without such close control and guidance. This is the usual method by which recent university graduates can make the transition from the academic phase of their professional education through the practical experience phase and ultimately into professional competence and licensing.

Work on clients' projects is the medium through which all this educational and professional development in architects' offices takes place. We cannot subject our clients to the possibility of substandard design, defective construction documentation, or incompetent contract administration. These negative prospects not only would be injurious to our clients but would also expose us to professional liability lawsuits.

All office work should be reviewed in process and on completion by qualified personnel who are capable of recognizing errors, both of commission and of omission. Senior people must always be available to make the decisions that require professional judgment.

### Getting onto the Job Site

All developing architects want to see how their office work looks on the construction site. The transition from office activities to field duties raises the problem of how to provide effective supervision of trainees. The client's project must not be allowed to deteriorate at any stage, least of all during the construction period. In addition, the contractor must not be deprived of the expected administration, advice, and judgment of a competent architect, as promised in the construction contract.

Some of the architect's duties during the construction period will be carried out in the office, where competent supervision is generally available, while others must occur at the construction site.

Common sense dictates that the first few site visits in the career of a trainee architect be in the presence of a fully qualified architect experienced in contract administration. The qualified architect will carry the main burden of responsibility, with the trainee observing, assisting, and learning. The trainee should take the notes in the field and write the reports in the office. Gradually, as the trainee is exposed to more of the process, the senior person can fall back to a position of monitoring and mentoring.

### Preparing for the First Field Trip

Before assuming any duties in the field, the trainee should review the files of similar projects to get an idea of the general scope of documentation and administration, and to learn the language and procedures of contract administration.

In preparation for the first field administration assignment, the trainee must become fully familiar with the requirements of the contract at hand. This means thorough review of the project's contract documents sufficient to gain a comprehensive understanding of their requirements.

The trainee must also have an accurate understanding of the architect's duties and authority, as well as any limitations. In addition, the trainee should review the design file, and possibly interview the designer, to become acquainted with the design objectives and to find out what is important.

### The Architect's Duties and Responsibilities

A good description of the architect's contract administration duties in the field and in the office will be found in the owner-architect agreement. The architect's duties, promised by the owner to the contractor, are in the general conditions.

The main purposes of the architect's site visits are

- To become generally familiar with the progress and quality of the work completed
- To determine in general if the work is being performed in a manner indicating that the work, when completed, will be in accordance with the contract documents

The architect's site observation should not be confused with the direct and constant supervision of workers exercised by contractors and subcontractors. The architect should not get involved in the details of how the work is being performed, but rather focus on whether the work will result in the specified outcome.

The architect's principal duties on the job site are to observe, evaluate, and report; the contractor is responsible for controlling and directing the work.

### Frequency of Architect's Site Visits

There is no specific frequency of site visits necessary to satisfy the contract or the standard of care. It is left up to the architect's professional judgment. Both B141 and A201 specify that the visits should be appropriate to the stage of construction. This implies that the frequency would vary depending on the character of the contractor's work on the site. Some architectural contracts specify the number, duration, or frequency of site visits.

Some architects prefer to visit the site at the same time and day each week, biweekly, or monthly, so the contractor and subcontractors can be on hand to answer specific questions. Others prefer to appear at the site unannounced. In any event, the architect should conduct the site visit in the company of the contractor's representative—usually the superintendent—who can facilitate access to all parts of the work and receive instructions on behalf of the contractor.

### Defective Work

The hope is that the architect on the site will recognize defective work. Defective work is anything that fails to meet some applicable criteria, such as the contract documents, the building code, or specified building standards. The architect does not have the power to

*(continued)*

accept nonconforming work unilaterally. However, the owner may allow nonconforming work to remain, with the contract sum reduced accordingly. The architect should advise the owner when such acceptance would be advantageous or inadvisable.

### Contractor's Responsibilities

While on the construction site, the architect must not interfere in any way with the contractor's responsibility for job site safety and other safety programs. It is the contractor's sole responsibility to determine and control construction means, methods, techniques, sequences, and procedures. The contractor is in charge of the job site and is responsible for coordination of all portions of the work. The architect's prime interest should be to determine that the work, when finished, will conform with the contract documents.

*Adapted from Arthur F. O'Leary, FAIA,* A Guide to Successful Construction: Effective Contract Administration, *3rd Ed. (1999)*

---

because so many decisions are made over the telephone. A log of calls made and notes recording the time, date, results of all telephone conversations are recommended. In addition, all correspondence (letters, faxes, and e-mails) must be logged and filed. Written records of conversations usually are distributed in order to confirm understandings reached verbally.

***Requests for information.*** Responding to RFIs from the contractor is an important duty of the construction administrator, and keeping up with RFIs and submittals can be challenging. A critical point is usually about one-third of the way into the job schedule, when submittals often peak. To avoid misunderstandings, it is important that the contract administrator answer questions from the job site through proper communication channels, in writing, and within a specified time frame. Requests for information are generally handled by an RFI form, which usually is provided by the general contractor and submitted to the construction administrator. As with telephone and correspondence records, it is necessary to keep a log that summarizes the status of all the RFIs.

***Document changes.*** The construction administrator tracks all changes in the construction documents. An addendum is a change made to the construction documents after they have been released for bidding but before the owner and contractor have signed a contract. A modification can take one of four forms:

- A written amendment to the contract signed by both parties
- A change order
- A construction change directive
- A written order for a minor change in the work issued by the architect

A common sequence of steps toward implementing a change order—a change in the drawings or specifications with cost and/or time implications—would usually include a contractor's RFIs, the architect's proposal request (PR) describing what is being changed and why, the contractor's cost proposal, and the architect's change order (CO). An additional important inclusion is a revision sketch or revised specification issued by the architect. A change order becomes part of the owner-contractor agreement when it is signed by the owner and contractor.

***Contractor's payments.*** As the owner's representative, the construction administrator is expected to review the contractor's requests for payment, sometimes known as "requisitions" or "applications for payment." Upon receipt of the contractor's application for payment, the contract administrator should visit the job site, observe the quantity and quality of the work and materials suitably stored on the site, and compare them, item by item, with the contractor's request. Often contractors include the value of work that is expected to be completed by the time the payment is made. The architect cannot approve any work that is not in place at the time of the inspection. If the application includes the value of materials stored off the site or work in process in off-site workshops,

---

### Record Keeping Required by the Owner–Architect Agreement

The B141-1997 owner-architect agreement requires the architect, during the bidding or negotiation phase, to

- Maintain a log of distribution and retrieval of the bidding documents and the amounts of deposits received from and returned to prospective bidders (2.5.4.3)
- Document and distribute the bidding results (2.5.4.7)

In addition to whatever records an architect may keep in the normal process of performing contract administration duties, the owner-architect agreement specifically requires these three records to be maintained:

- Record of the contractor's applications for payment (2.6.3.3)
- Record of submittals and copies of submittals supplied by the contractor (2.6.4.2)
- Records relative to changes in the work (2.6.5.4)

Although the agreement does not specify the ultimate disposition of these records, presumably they are kept for the benefit of the owner. Thus it seems reasonable to provide copies at any time the owner requests them and at completion of the work.

# Agenda for Preconstruction Conference

The specific agenda, of course, depends on the needs of the project. Some topics for discussion may include the following:

- *Notice to proceed.* The owner may issue written notice to proceed to the contractor; any questions should be discussed.
- *Explanation of chain of command.* Included are routing of shop drawings, catalogs, samples, project reports, scheduling reports, test reports, maintenance instructions, and so on.
- *Communications channels.* This is a reminder of the contractually mandated paths for communications among the participants.
- *Project meetings.* Scheduling, agenda, and attendance at project meetings are discussed.
- *Duties of the owner and contractor.* The general conditions and how the contract is intended to work are briefly reviewed.
- *Insurance.* Requirements for amounts and types of coverage and submittal of insurance certificates are reviewed.
- *Financing.* Evidence of the owner's ability to meet financial obligations is given.
- *Submittals.* Schedules are outlined for submittal of engineering data, shop drawings and operation and maintenance manuals, tests and inspections, and other submittals (including items required, procedures, number of copies, and distribution). Contractors are asked to send project representatives an unofficial preliminary copy and to identify specification section with each submittal. Contractors are reminded of their obligations with respect to shop drawing review and submittal as well as the language of the contractor's approval stamp.
- *Progress payments.* A schedule of values is established for the work of all trades, as well as procedures for progress payments. These procedures cover the handling of retainage and partial lien waivers; payment for materials on hand and materials stored off site; inspection, insurance, and title for stored materials; any special requirements for government agencies (e.g., the Department of Housing and Urban Development or the Federal Housing Administration) or the construction lender; scheduling of consultant's site visits; and submission of payroll records if required with requisitions for payment.
- *List of subcontractors.* A reminder is given that the general conditions may require the contractor, after award of the contract, to notify the architect in writing of the names of subcontractors or other persons or organizations proposed for portions of the work designated in the bidding requirements. Further is the requirement that the contractor shall not employ any subcontractor about whom the architect or owner has any reasonable objection.
- *Employment practices.* Any requirements regarding wage rates or similar issues are clarified.

- *Utilities.* Local regulations vary. Applications for temporary and permanent electric, gas, water, and telephone services must usually be made directly by the owner to the utility furnishing the service; the owner should be notified in sufficient time for the services to be in place when they are required.
- *Scheduling.* Job progress scheduling requirements include frequency of updates, times for submittals and approvals, and dates when owner-furnished equipment and furnishings are required.
- *Contract changes and clarification.* Procedures are set up for handling proposals, requests for backup information for change proposals, change orders, and construction change directives. Supplemental instructions are developed, such as procedures for obtaining interpretations of the contract documents (no changes should be made without appropriate authorization in writing).
- *Security.* Job site security during nonworking hours is determined.
- *Parking.* Parking areas are designated.
- *Storage.* Areas are assigned for temporary storage of equipment and materials; special protection is required for stored materials and equipment.
- *Permits.* Licenses, permits, and inspections required by local building authorities are reviewed.
- *Right-of-way.* Restrictions are reviewed on use of the site, access, or availability of rights-of-way, as are special requirements or cautions regarding adjacent property, protection of trees, and similar issues.
- *Testing.* The extent of testing laboratory and inspection services is decided, as well as who will be responsible for coordinating and scheduling their services. Routing of reports is also established.
- *Overtime.* Notice and scheduling necessary for overtime work are arranged.
- *Cleanup.* Responsibilities for cleanup and trash removal are assigned.
- *Owner-furnished equipment and furnishings.* Responsibilities for receipt, unloading, handling, storage, and security information on mechanical and electrical connections are clarified.
- *Closeout.* Procedures for closing out the project are delineated, including record drawings and other required submissions.
- *Public relations.* Policies regarding statements to the media, anticipated public interest in the project, and restrictions on construction operations and other public relations activities are discussed. Construction sign requirements are determined.
- *Separate contracts.* Their impact on the work of the project is evaluated. Requirements for coordination with other contractors on the site are discussed.

## Communications

Although the communication system among the parties during the construction period is defined in the AIA General Conditions, it is advisable to review the requirements so that all may understand and abide by them in practice.

- All communications between the owner and contractor should be channeled through the architect.
- All communications by and with the architect's consultants should be through the architect.
- All communications to or from the subcontractors and suppliers should be through the contractor.
- All communications with separate contractors should be through the owner (A201, 4.2.4).
- The superintendent on the job site is a representative of the contractor, and communications given to the superintendent are as binding as if given to the contractor. (A201, 3.9.1)
- All important communications should be in writing, or if given orally should be confirmed in writing.

the architect cannot approve payment unless the owner and contractor have so agreed in writing.

In signing the requisition form or application and certification for payment, the construction administrator certifies that he or she has reviewed the work at the site, has found it in accordance with the schedule, and approves the release of money for that work. This is not to be taken lightly. All those who rely on the integrity of the architect's certificate, including the owner, contractor, subcontractors, suppliers, and lenders, expect that the architect will perform this function carefully, honestly, and with due diligence.

***Submittal review.*** Submittals are prepared by the contractor and include shop drawings, product literature, or actual samples of specific products to be installed; reports from independent testing agencies; operating instructions and maintenance manuals for installed equipment; and warranties from product suppliers and equipment manufacturers. The submittals are reviewed by the construction administrator, or the appropriate consultant, and become part of the permanent record of the project. Some or all of them are eventually given to the building owner for operations purposes.

***Field reports and records.*** Field reporting is a core activity for the construction administrator. The effective professional knows both how to conduct a thorough field observation and how to properly report relevant information to the owner. When on site it is important to be accompanied by a contractor's representative to facilitate communication with the contractor and to avoid any appearance that the construction administrator is providing supervision or instruction to contractor personnel. Ideally the field report will include notation of the date, time, weather, and temperature; notes about conditions, especially potential problems; a plan of the site that is annotated and keyed to the written report; and photographs to document the condition of the work in progress and to show its degree of completion. It is useful to have a system in place to track the status of issues from field reports until they are resolved.

***Completion and closeout.*** The construction administrator's role becomes especially important during the construction closeout. As the project nears completion, typically the owner is anxious to move in and the contractor is anxious to move on. Both are inclined to want to ignore small details that may cause performance problems later. The construction administrator is in a position to maintain the focus on quality construction through the contract requirements that require the architect to prepare the certificate of substantial completion for submission to the lender. When the contractor considers the work substantially complete, usually the contract administrator will be asked to perform an inspection. The lender often holds a 10 percent retainer until the construction administrator prepares a punch list that includes all the work that the contractor needs to address before the project is complete. Once completed, the punch list is sent to the contractor and owner along with a certificate of substantial completion. This acknowledges that the job is substantially complete and that the contractor can begin billing for monies retained from the construction fee. In signing the certificate, the contractor acknowledges that it will complete all the work on the punch list. A portion of the monies will continue to be retained until the punch list items are completed.

### For More Information

General reference publications include Fred A. Stitt, *Construction Administration and Inspection Checklists: A Complete Guide for Exterior and Interior Practices* (1992); Arthur F. O'Leary, *A Guide to Successful Construction—Effective Contract Administration* (1999); and Ralph W. Liebing, *Construction Contract Administration* (1997).

Architects wanting more detailed information on how to coordinate and manage information generated during the construction process should refer to the author's *Construction Administration: An Architect's Guide to Surviving Information Overload* (1997).

Publications offering advice to building contractors on the contracting process can be invaluable sources of information to architects. An example is *Complete Contracting: A-Z Guide to Controlling Projects* (1997) by Andrew M. Civitello.

# 17.9 Design-Build

## Ron Gupta, AIA, and Paul Doherty, AIA

*The design-build approach returns American architects to their pre–World War II role, in which they oversaw construction as well as design. Of the design-led project delivery methods, it offers the greatest opportunities but also carries the greatest risk.*

If your firm is experienced and talented in construction management, you may want to consider adopting the design-build delivery approach. Potential rewards of taking this step include the ability to offer better client service; increased cash flow, assets, and net worth; and new teaming opportunities that can lead to development of the firm's own projects. The risks of the approach can be controlled through appropriate contract and insurance arrangements.

Project delivery methods appropriate for design-build are the same as those for construction management, except that in design-build the architect signs a contract with the owner for both design and project construction services, usually for a guaranteed maximum price. Engaging in design-build requires the assumption of additional risks, such as responsibility for job site safety and for the means and methods of construction, which can be covered by a higher monetary return and by proper insurance.

Design-build is a rapidly growing market for architecture firms. A spate of litigation between designers and contractors in the early 1990s resulted in soaring liability premiums. In response, clients began to turn away from arrangements that divide design and construction to arrangements that combine them. For the architect, the design-build approach can make possible delivery of superior products and services to clients.

## CLIENT NEEDS

Clients like design-build because it offers single-point accountability and prevents the situation in which the client must referee conflicts between the contractor and the design team. Also attractive to clients are full-time on-site representation by the architect and the seamless integration of design and construction and of cost and schedule control.

In a word, design-build reduces the owner's risk. The architect can ensure the quality of an entire project, both design and construction, and services based on a fixed fee eliminate hidden profit incentives. The only goal should be to provide the client with the highest possible quality of design and construction—on time and within budget.

With the architect as leader of the project delivery process or a member of the lead team, adversarial relationships are dramatically reduced, as are miscommunications, which can lead to costly change orders, scheduling delays, and poor design execution. The design-build approach fosters collaboration between designers and trade contractors and craftspeople from the beginning of conceptual design through project completion.

Another major advantage shared by all design-led project delivery approaches (design-build and various types of CM arrangements) is that they can shorten the project schedule when a fast-track process is used. A maximum cost and schedule can be guaranteed.

## Summary

### DESIGN-BUILD SERVICES

#### Why a Client May Need These Services
- To have single-point responsibility for design and construction
- To achieve better integration between design and construction
- To combine cost and schedule controls
- To increase architect's presence on construction site
- To expedite project timetable

#### Knowledge and Skills Required
- Entrepreneurial outlook
- Excellent negotiation skills
- Expertise in business, management, and construction supervision
- Knowledge of the market, including competitors

#### Representative Process Tasks
- Define project requirements, scope, and goals
- Assemble design-build team
- Determine concept and pricing
- Award contract
- Complete design and construction

**RON GUPTA** *is a an architect and program manager for Parsons, one of the world's largest constructors. Gupta has extensive design-build experience and chaired the 1999 AIA Design-Build PIA.* **PAUL DOHERTY** *is the principal partner of the Digit Group, a company of the Greenway Group, an international management consulting and information technology services firm.*

Designs for components of the project, such as foundations and roofing, can be completed, publicly advertised, and bid in the sequence in which they will be constructed. This allows construction to start very early in the process, trimming the overall project schedule. Because the entire project team of architects, engineers, and constructors truly works together as a team under a single-source contract, it is possible to achieve more aggressive timelines than when these project roles are performed under separate contracts.

From 1987 to 1998 the value of projects delivered by design-build grew from $6 billion to $56 billion. Forecasters say the design-build market will continue to grow rapidly. Design-build is used increasingly for public sector (federal, state, and local government) projects because it allows for a fixed fee for both CM and design professional services as well as a maximum level of competitive bidding of trade services. Industrial clients and private developers also often use this project delivery method.

Not every client or project is suitable for design-build. The design professional must match the client's needs to the delivery process. In general, design-build works best for clients who have a good knowledge of and experience with the design and construction process, have a tight timeline for delivery of the project, and are willing to nurture a trust relationship with a design build team.

▶ **See Construction Management (17.6) for information about offering construction management as a service of an architecture firm.**

---

## Cultural Values Checklist for Design-Build Team Selection

Design-build team members should take the time to determine whether the cultural values and corporate philosophies of their companies are compatible. In many cases, the answer to this rests with the instincts and intuitive feelings of the principals in the companies. Therefore the firms' partners should make sure there are no conflicts of interest and that clear, defined problem-solving techniques and criteria for dispute resolution are in place. As well, they should engage in formal or informal partnering sessions, as necessary, to ensure a compatible, cohesive joint existence.

### Considerations

- Is this the right team?
- Will a teaming agreement be prepared?
- Who will sign the teaming agreement?
- Have all necessary parties been included in the teaming discussions?
- Who will be the team leader?
- What questions should the parties ask of each other prior to entering into any written agreement?
- Why does each member of the design-build team need the other members?
- Are there mutually beneficial levels of experience by size and category?
- Are the groups technologically compatible?
- Are both members competent to compete?
- Do the members have any previous history with the client or with each other?
- Are there other agendas the individual team members need to discuss?

*From the AIA/AGC* Design-Build Teaming Checklist *(1999)*

---

## SKILLS

The decision to offer design-build services for the first time should be made in the context of a firm's overall strategic planning, including consideration of both the firm's culture and organization and its resources and skills. Firms with strong capability and experience in construction management are more readily poised to consider the move to design-build.

***Firm culture.*** Design-build is for entrepreneurial types. If the leaders of your firm are not energized by the challenge of market risks and rewards, design-build is not for you. Political acumen, people skills, and the ability to develop strategic alliances are also important characteristics for principals of firms moving into design-build.

The psychological makeup of the staff is important as well. Design-build requires people who like change and are comfortable instituting new systems and processes. Staff members must enjoy problem solving, be good team players, and be willing to try new things.

***Staffing and skills.*** Project staffing for design-build is very similar to that for construction management. Administrative staffing for a typical design-build project includes a project manager (often the project architect), an accountant, an expediter, and a procurement person.

Business skills become more crucial in design-build projects. Principals and project managers need excellent negotiation skills to reach appropriate agreements with clients, subcontractors, product distributors, and vendors. Consultants, strategic allies, partners, or in-house staff with expertise in budgets, estimating, scheduling, bidding, negotiating, design, documentation, and construction supervision are a necessity. Good information management systems are essential, as information technology has emerged as the key element to achieving better communications on all design-build projects. Use of the Internet allows partners in design-build teams to communicate project data in more cost-effective and efficient ways.

***Team building.*** Staff talents and diversity can benefit the firm. Some staff members will naturally tend toward designer, builder, or general manager roles, and these abilities should be considered as teams are formed. It is important to integrate design-oriented, construction-oriented, or management-oriented employees into a project as soon as possible.

***Subcontractors.*** Good subcontractors are the backbone of successful design-build. To succeed with this delivery method, a firm must have developed a list of well-qualified, dependable subcontractors.

***Market knowledge.*** Design-build contractors must know who their competitors are, whether general contractors or other design firms. In particular, it is important to assess the strengths and weaknesses of potential teaming partners. Other necessary information includes the prevailing subcontractor prices in the market area and the standard markups general contractors charge for overhead and profit.

***Insurance.*** The support of an expert insurance broker or agent and an attorney with expertise in construction contracts is essential. The insurance expert will identify areas of overlap and gaps in coverage. The business owners' package or policy (BOP) that architecture firms typically carry will not cover the additional risks assumed in design-build. The commercial general liability coverage typically held by general contracting firms will be required, even if the construction work is entirely subcontracted. This coverage becomes particularly important when more of the construction-related work is carried out by the architecture firm.

When new employees are hired, a firm takes on all the hiring and employment issues of a general contractor. The firm will need an insurance carrier willing to write workers' compensation policies for the construction trades, which will result in an increase in workers' compensation rates. Employee policy manuals also may require revision. Other types of insurance coverage to consider include builder's risk (which covers damage to the project during construction), commercial auto (for vehicles), and inland marine (for equipment, computers, and tools not fixed to property).

***Bonding.*** Firms engaging in design-build need to consider whether to become bonded. A bond is a third-party guarantee to the client or creditors. Common types of bonds are bid or payment bonds, which guarantee the bidder will enter into a contract with the client; performance bonds, which guarantee completion of a project; and labor and materials bonds, which will pay subcontractors, laborers, and material suppliers should the contractor default.

Many firms offering CM and design-build services are not bonded. Their private clients do not require it and do not want to pay the additional cost (1 to 2.5 percent of the total construction cost) for that extra margin of security. However, architecture firms that are not bonded still require bonds of the key contractors and subcontractors they employ. If a client or a client's financial institution requires a bond, there may be options for how it can be provided. When an architecture firm operates as a joint venture partner with a general contractor, the contractor may provide the bonding. In some cases a general contractor that has subcontracted with an architecture firm may provide sufficient bonding. Or an architecture firm may rely solely on a key subcontractor's bonds. If you require bonds for subcontractors, it may be redundant and not cost-effective for you to have a bond.

## PROCESS

Design-build services may be provided by a single firm, an association of firms, or a joint venture.

The architect often serves as a subcontractor to a contractor-led design-build enterprise. However, the architect also may lead or be a partner in the design-build enterprise, and in some cases owners require that architects take this more active role in the design-build entity. The AIA design-build documents are neutral with regard to the "designer-builder," in contrast to the AGC documents, which explicitly equate the "contractor" with the design-build entity.

Sometimes construction management services may be combined with design-build. However, it should be noted that the construction management approach does not contain the unique and integrated combination of design *and* construction included in the design-build approach.

The design-build process involves the interaction of several participants, including the client, the design-build entity, the designer, and the builder. The basic activities can be described in three increments: project definition, team selection, and design-construction.

***Project definition.*** In this increment the client defines the project requirements and scope and sets forth the project goals. The client may also acquire a site and obtain pro-

See Project Delivery Options (9.1) for further discussion of design-build and other delivery methods.

## Checklist for Definition of Design-Build Team Roles

The integration of the design and construction processes provides tremendous opportunities for greater value and better solutions; however, this very integration can cause confusion in defining the roles of team members. Extensive discussion regarding potential scenarios will benefit the entire team. The items listed below are critical to consider during these discussions.

### Considerations
- Marketing
- Site analysis
- Soft cost management
- Schematic design
- Design development
- Construction documentation
- Construction administration
- Bidding and negotiation
- Interiors
- Fixture, furniture, and equipment specification
- Contingency management
- Pricing package definition
- Bid package definition
- Design phase cost control
- Permitting
- Construction phase cost control
- Information management

- Project scheduling
- Owner communication
- Planning, zoning, and regulatory agency processes
- Quality assurance and quality control
- Correction of work responsibilities for both design and construction
- Level of documentation and specification
- Level of flexibility within the documents and specifications
- Definition of the project budget
- Change orders (who originates, how, and who pays)
- Definition of architectural additional services
- Schedule definition
- Notice to proceed
- Milestone dates
- Date of substantial completion
- Force majeure, including delay claims and costs
- Payment processes, draw requests, and associated timelines
- Tests and inspections
- Intellectual property issues and ownership of documents
- Press releases and press communications
- Claims and litigation
- Safety

ject financing at this time. Depending on staff capabilities and expertise, a client may carry out these activities internally or use an architect to provide assistance (e.g., feasibility analyses, site analysis and selection, master planning, programming. etc.). In defining the scope, a project is usually carried to a conceptual or schematic level. Preliminary and schematic design concepts in combination with budget and schedule criteria establish the performance parameters and project expectations.

*Design-build team selection.* Clients may carry out the selection of the design-build team in a variety of ways. They may engage in direct negotiation with a known or approved design-build entity, receive bids from several teams, employ a competition process, or use a combination of any or all of these methods. Once a design-build team is selected and a price is fixed for the project, the contract is awarded.

*Design-construction.* During the initial phase of this increment, the design-build team completes the design, prepares construction documents, obtains necessary regulatory approvals, determines probable construction costs and preliminary schedules, and obtains construction pricing. During the construction phase, the design-build team obtains building permits, maintains construction schedules, coordinates bids, and oversees the work of subcontractors and tradespeople. This involvement during construction fulfills the requirements of the construction documents, which include guaranteeing the construction quality and actual cost of the project.

### For More Information

The booklet AIA/AGC *Design-Build: Teaming Checklist* (1999) provides multiple checklists for team selection, legal considerations, getting the job, risk management, financial considerations, and related aspects of the design-build approach. The checklists can be applied to other delivery methods, including construction management, construction manager as advisor, and construction manager as general contractor. The booklet is available through the American Institute of Architects or the Associated General Contractors of America.

The AIA and DPIC Companies are sponsoring Designer-Led Project Delivery workshops that address several delivery methods, including design-build. Check the Design-Build PIA page on the AIA Web site (www.aia.org) for current availability and schedules.

# 17.10 Historic Preservation

### Robert Burley, FAIA, and Dan L. Peterson, AIA

*As a growing number of communities seek to preserve and enhance their historic structures and districts to stimulate tourism and economic growth, historic preservation services are in increasing demand.*

Historic preservation services embrace a range of activities that include preservation, rehabilitation, restoration, and reconstruction. Although portions of each service overlap with others, the following are the accepted definitions:

- *Preservation* applies the measures necessary to sustain the existing form, integrity, and materials of a historic property. Preservation work generally focuses on the ongoing maintenance and repair of historic features and materials rather than extensive replacement and new construction.
- *Rehabilitation* adapts a property for a compatible use through repair, alteration, and addition while preserving those portions or features that convey its historical, cultural, or architectural values.
- *Restoration* accurately depicts the form, materials, features, and character of a property as it appeared at a particular period in time. Restoration retains as much of the fabric from the historic period as possible. Inconsistent features may be removed and missing features faithfully reconstructed in accordance with the restoration period.
- *Reconstruction* depicts, with new construction, the form, materials, features, and character of a property that no longer exists, as it appeared at a particular period of time, usually in its historic location.

In the last few decades public recognition of the cultural and economic value of historic preservation has increased dramatically. As a result, the number of architects involved in preservation projects is steadily growing.

## CLIENT NEEDS

With increased public interest, more and more jurisdictions are adopting historic preservation regulations. These generally protect the appearance of existing structures in historic districts or of individually designated historic buildings. The purpose of such regulations is often aesthetic, but they are also intended to preserve community identity and historic culture. In some areas of the country, a property rights backlash is developing as property owners oppose such regulations, which they consider uncompensated "takings."

## Summary

### HISTORIC PRESERVATION SERVICES

#### Why a Client May Need These Services
- To conform to local historic preservation regulations
- To qualify for tax incentive programs for historic properties
- To promote community revitalization or tourism
- To demonstrate support for historic preservation interests

#### Knowledge and Skills Required
- Fundamental architectural knowledge and skills
- Knowledge of historic building styles, interiors, and landscapes
- Knowledge of historic construction methods and materials
- Familiarity with preservation technologies and techniques
- Research and investigative skills*
- Knowledge of government historic preservation tax and grant programs

#### Representative Process Tasks
- Define project goals
- Assemble project team
- Determine significance and condition of property
- Determine applicable regulations
- Research history of property and document existing conditions
- Develop design concept and cost estimate
- Develop final design
- Participate in construction procurement and construction phases

\* Special archaeological expertise may be required for certain sites.

ROBERT BURLEY *is principal of the Burley Partnership in Waitsfield, Vermont. He served on the AIA Task Force for the West Front of the U.S. Capitol, and his firm has completed numerous historic preservation and restoration projects.* DAN PETERSON *has practiced as a historical architect since 1975. He has served as chairman of the AIA Historic Resources Committee and the AIA Historic American Buildings Survey Advisory Committee.*

Tax incentive and grant programs at the federal, state, and local levels directly stimulate the market for preservation services. Owners of historic houses already qualify for federal rehabilitation tax credits, and it appears likely that even stronger federal tax incentives for homeowners will be passed. For business owners and community groups, the federal government and many states offer an array of tax incentive and grant programs. Many of these programs link historic preservation to urban revitalization and economic development objectives.

The resources available to those working on historic properties make them attractive to many different types of clients for a variety of reasons. Architects offering historic preservation services must be familiar with the government programs that support preservation activities as well as knowledgeable about historic architecture.

***Compliance with preservation regulations.*** Many clients—homeowners as well as institutional and corporate clients—seek historic preservation services because their properties are in a location subject to historic preservation regulations. A key service historic preservation architects can provide for these clients is guiding a project through the approval process administered by increasingly overburdened state and local preservation offices.

***Qualification for funding and tax credits***. An architect who is well versed in tax credit and grant programs for historic preservation can be of great value to clients who may not even realize their property has historical significance. Buildings need only be 50 years old to qualify for listing in the National Register of Historic Places, which is a prerequisite for many funding incentive programs. Many modern buildings are now reaching the age of eligibility. As well, the criteria for landmark status have widened considerably in recent years to include buildings that are significant largely in terms of cultural history rather than architectural value; an example might be the first McDonald's restaurant. Because the availability of tax credits or grants can make the critical difference in the financial feasibility of a project, architects familiar with the process and eligibility requirements for taking advantage of tax credits and incentives offer a valuable service.

***Determination of architectural significance and development of a preservation plan.*** Architects who offer historic preservation services advise their clients on preservation, rehabilitation, restoration, or reconstruction approaches appropriate for a project. The architect determines which parts of a building(s) are original and which are later additions, interprets findings for the client, and coordinates the work of other specialists required for a project. The historical importance of the persons or events related to the project and the project's aesthetic value, architectural character, existing condition, and future function are some of the factors considered in the development of a preservation approach.

In some cases a client may discover during site analysis that a property has historical significance. The architect may then be required to oversee archaeological activity and make recommendations for proper handling of historic structures or resources found on the site. Depending on the locale, these activities can be regulated by state or local historic preservation regulations.

Government clients hire historic preservation architects for urban and regional planning projects (the majority of which now contain a historic preservation element), for community revitalization projects that encourage tourism and/or economic growth, and for work on public parks and historic sites. Public agencies upgrading their historic buildings for continued or adaptive reuse sometimes require design teams to include an architect with expertise in historic preservation.

Government agencies face increasing public opposition to construction of new transportation facilities due to concerns about destruction of cultural and natural resources. In order to gain approval for these projects, agencies often package historic preservation programs with civil engineering projects. For this reason civil engineering firms often engage in subcontracts with architects who have historic preservation expertise.

***Correct handling of historic materials.*** Many architecture firms specialize in building preservation, historic reconstruction, and preservation planning. These firms offer services that help other architecture and planning firms with issues related to archaic materials, systems, and elements that are the character-defining features of historic buildings. Many architecture firms may consider themselves capable of working on historic buildings because of their experience with rehabilitation work. However, unless they are true specialists, they often are not aware that improper treatment of archaic materials and systems will accelerate the deterioration or failure of buildings rehabilitated using contemporary approaches.

The burgeoning of historic preservation work has fostered the emergence of sophisticated methodologies and technologies. Architects frequently consult with historians or with a growing cadre of consultants who specialize in preservation technology. These experts use new scientific technologies for dating and identifying the exact type of building materials originally used. They also help locate supply sources. The Internet has helped information flow, making sources of specialized services and products easier to locate.

Services related to historic preservation include master planning, urban planning, site analysis, research and assessments, programming, building design, construction documents, construction procurement, construction contract administration, and landscape design.

## SKILLS

Providing preservation services requires well-developed abilities in analysis, recognition, and restoration of buildings and other historic resources. The practitioner needs knowledge of historic building techniques and materials; expertise in architectural history; specialized experience in research, fieldwork, and analysis of historic artifacts; an understanding of techniques for conserving architectural materials; and the skills and experience to investigate, document, research, and analyze finishes, lighting, furnishings, and decorative arts in building interiors.

*Training and experience.* Some clients have defined training and experience requirements. The U.S. Department of the Interior, for example, requires that professionals providing "historic architecture" services for its projects must meet the department's guidelines for rehabilitating historic structures. At minimum, these individuals must have a professional degree in architecture or a state license to practice architecture plus either at least one year of graduate study in historic preservation, American architectural history, preservation planning, or a closely related field or at least one year of full-time professional experience on historic preservation projects. The Interior Department's professional qualifications standards further specify that the year of graduate study or experience must include detailed investigations of historic structures, preparation of historic structure research reports, and preparation of plans and specifications for preservation projects.

*Specialized skills*. The architect who practices historic preservation must keep abreast of government programs that affect projects with historical significance. Networking is important so that the firm can locate appropriate consultants and identify suppliers of services and building products that may no longer be available in the mainstream.

Specialists that may be required include historians, archaeologists, architecture conservators, and historic interiors specialists. Other related disciplines include structural, mechanical, and electrical engineers and landscape architects.

## PROCESS

Often historic preservation projects require quite a lot of predesign and research time. Coordination with regulatory agencies is also a step that should be initiated early in the process to be certain the work that is planned will be found acceptable by zoning agencies or agencies managing grant or tax incentive programs.

*Factors affecting the scope of services.* Among the factors that can affect the scope of services for a historic preservation project are the basic nature of the effort (to preserve, rehabilitate, restore, or reconstruct), the applicable historic preservation regulations, the significance of the property and facility, and the condition and integrity of the structure.

*Teaming approach.* When possible, it is best to team with structural, mechanical, and electrical engineers and landscape architects who have experience in the special procedures required for preservation of historic structures. Architects who have minimal or no experience with historic preservation projects should include a historic preservation architect on the team. The role of this specialist would be to perform research and assessments, prepare the necessary preservation documents, and provide technical expertise for the proper treatment of archaic materials and systems.

## Steps in a Historic Preservation Project

***Predesign and research.*** To accomplish the items listed here generally requires the participation of a few specialists in historic architecture, historical research, and archaeology as well as someone familiar with the applicable codes and regulations.

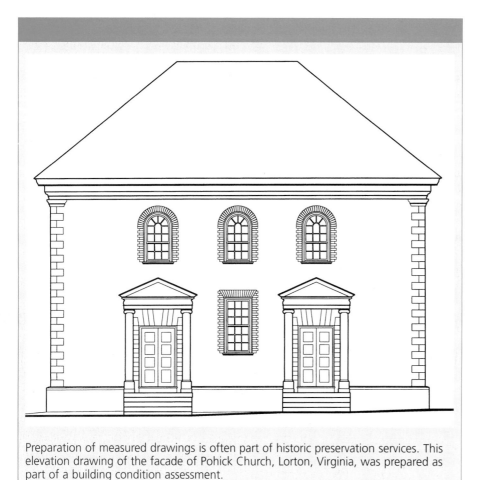

Preparation of measured drawings is often part of historic preservation services. This elevation drawing of the facade of Pohick Church, Lorton, Virginia, was prepared as part of a building condition assessment.

John Milner Associates, Inc., Alexandria, Virginia

- Preliminary analysis and evaluation of existing conditions.
- Programming to determine the intended function and contemporary use of the site, structure, and building.
- Feasibility study to investigate code requirements and regulations and to evaluate the technical and economic feasibility of the proposed work.
- Documentation of existing conditions with photographs and measured drawings and, when possible, comparison of original contract documents with as-built conditions.
- Preparation of Historic American Buildings Survey/Historic American Engineering Record (HABS/HAER) documentation, which includes large-format photographs and measured drawings that record the original construction. (Such documentation can be placed in the Library of Congress.)
- Historical research to study and prepare a report of documents, old photographs, and other data concerning the project, its architectural and construction history, and the people associated with it.

- Archaeological research to investigate the prehistoric, historic, or industrial nature of the project area and, particularly on historically important sites, to recover, restore, and evaluate artifacts.
- Architectural and engineering investigation to determine which elements of the structure are original and which are not, together with a sequence and dates of construction.
- Development of design concept or preliminary design to illustrate proposed development, materials, engineering concepts, alternatives, and other relevant elements of the work.
- Preliminary cost estimate to identify probable costs to help the client establish a project budget.
- Preliminary report that compiles written data, drawings, photographs, and other information into what is commonly called a historic structures report. This may also include assistance in preparing applications for inclusion in federal, state, and local inventories such as the National Register of Historic Places or for funding through federal or state agencies.

▶ **See Building Design (17.2) and Construction Documentation— Specifications (17.5) for discussions of providing these services to clients.**

***Design phase.*** Issues related to working on a historic structure must be coordinated with the standard steps of the building design process throughout design and construction.

- Coordination of preservation issues with architectural design and engineering development for the building
- Coordination of preservation issues with the preparation of outline specifications
- Coordination of preservation issues with the preparation of a probable statement of costs for the work

***Construction documents phase.*** Issues that must be considered in this phase include the following:

- Coordination of preservation issues with the preparation of construction documents, including working drawings and specifications
- Coordination of preservation issues with the preparation of a final cost estimate for the work
- Coordination of preservation issues with bidding or negotiations for procurement of construction services
- Construction contract administration
- Coordination of preservation issues with construction observation and construction contract administration services

Deliverables may include a historic structures report and/or an assessment and conditions report. At the completion of a significant historic project, a cycle maintenance report often is completed. Other types of reports, such as a determination of eligibility and a statement of effects, may be required by authorities having jurisdiction over a project, such as local historic landmark and historic district review boards and the state historic preservation officer.

> **More details about preparing construction documents and offering procurement and construction contract administration services can be found in Construction Documentation—Drawings (17.4), Construction Procurement (17.7), and Contract Administration (17.8).**

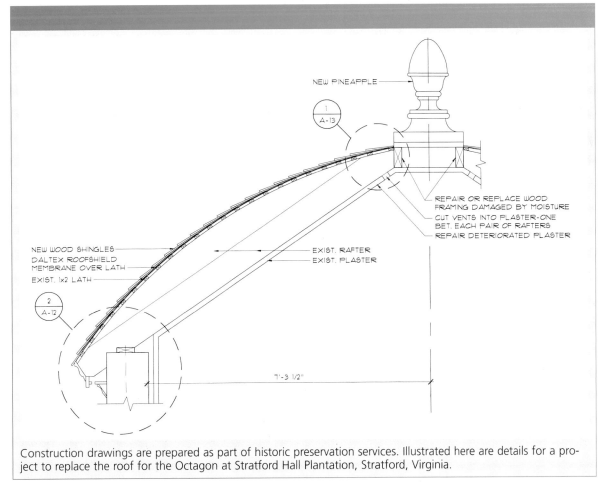

Construction drawings are prepared as part of historic preservation services. Illustrated here are details for a project to replace the roof for the Octagon at Stratford Hall Plantation, Stratford, Virginia.

John Milner Associates, Inc., Alexandria, Virginia

### For More Information

A number of organizations offer detailed information about the historic preservation field. The oldest committee of the American Institute of Architects is the AIA Historic Resources Professional Interest Area, which posts information on the AIA Web site(www.aia.org).

The National Park Service (NPS) is the home of federal government preservation programs. NPS Web sites offer a lot of information and links to other pertinent sites:

- The Technical Preservation Services site (www2.cr.nps.gov/tps) provides access to two sources vital to those working in historic preservation architecture—the "Secretary of the Interior's 'Standards for Rehabilitation' and 'Guidelines for Rehabilitating Historic Buildings'" and the Preservation Briefs series—as well as to information about historic preservation tax incentives. The full text of 41 Preservation Briefs is available on the Web site; these give detailed information about specific aspects of repairing and restoring historic structures (e.g., seismic retrofit, accessibility, and detailed material reports).
- The National Center for Preservation Technology and Training provides research, training, and information on preservation technology (www.ncptt.nps.gov).
- The Historic American Buildings Survey/Historic American Engineering Record Web site includes information about how to fill out HABS/HAER documents (www.cr.nps.gov/habshaer).
- The National Register of Historic Places site gives the criteria for listing a property as well as links to state historic preservation offices (www.cr.nps.gov/nr).

The National Preservation Institute in Alexandria, Virginia, offers seminars in historic preservation and cultural resources management; their programs are registered with the AIA Continuing Education Program. NPI also offers technical preservation assistance. More information about this nonprofit organization is available at their Web site (www.npi.org).

The Association for Preservation Technology International, headquartered in Fredericksburg, Virginia, offers up-to-date technical publications and specialized training and education in preservation and conservation skills and issues. The APT Web site address is www.apti.org.

Many books are available about historic architecture, historic preservation, and the techniques for maintaining old buildings. Still the single best overview of the preservation field is James Marston Fitch's *Historic Preservation: Curatorial Management of the Built World* (reprint, 1990). Here are a few other suggested references:

Martin E. Weaver with F. G. Matero, *Conserving Buildings: Guide to Techniques and Materials,* rev. ed. (1997), covers materials and procedures for maintenance, restoration, and rehabilitation of historic buildings. It combines practical information on the characteristics, composition, and deterioration of building materials with detailed coverage of state-of-the-art conservation methods.

Past editions of *Architectural Graphic Standards* (AGS) may be useful for those working on older buildings. The first edition is available in a facsimile edition as *Architectural Graphic Standards for Architects, Engineers, Decorators, Builders and Draftsmen,* 1st facsimile ed. (1990). A book of excerpts from the 1932–51 editions of AGS, billed as a "source of traditional architectural details for anyone working with old structures," is *Traditional Details: For Building Restoration, Renovation, and Rehabilitation* (1998).

*Historic Building Facades: The Manual for Maintenance and Rehabilitation,* edited by William G. Foulks (1997), is a complete reference manual in which recognized experts provide state-of-the-art information and methodologies for the inspection, maintenance, and restoration of historic buildings of virtually every period, style, and material.

A new work of interest to architects practicing in historic preservation is *Historic Preservation: Project Planning and Estimating,* by Swanke Hayden Connell Architects (2000). The reference is aimed at those preserving and rehabilitating historic structures, particularly architects, contractors, owners, facility mangers, developers, and city planners. The authors offer guidance on budgeting for historic preservation projects, creating detailed estimates, and selecting qualified contractors.

# 17.11 Sustainable Building Design

## Muscoe Martin, AIA

*Sustainable building design requires multidisciplinary consideration of environmental factors throughout the building design process. Areas of major concern include energy efficiency, indoor air quality, and resource efficiency.*

In its broadest context, sustainability refers to the ability of a society, ecosystem, or other system to continue functioning into the indefinite future without being forced into decline through exhaustion or overloading of the resources on which the system depends. Sustainable building design, then, defines a process that strives to preserve, protect, and improve the quality of the environment; protect human health; and achieve a prudent and rational use of natural resources.

Among the issues considered in sustainable building design—sometimes called "green design"—are site selection and site design, energy efficiency, resource efficiency, indoor air quality, water conservation, solid waste management and recycling, and building operations and maintenance. Sustainable design professionals emphasize the importance of an integrated design process that considers multiple environmental and resource issues simultaneously with other aspects of design.

Sustainable design emerged in the late 1980s as an extension and integration of the environmental and energy-efficiency movements. Environmentally conscious designers wanted to more fully integrate their approaches with a wide range of environmental issues, including energy efficiency, indoor air quality, and resource efficiency.

According to the U.S. Green Buildings Council, a coalition of organizations and professionals with an interest in green building practices, the market outlook for these services is quite positive because public interest in environmental issues and corporate responsibility is on the rise. The 1997 Cone Roper Cause-Related Marketing report ranks the environment as one of the top societal problems that businesses should work to solve. Indoor air quality design services for both new and retrofit projects are a particularly rapidly expanding area of opportunity for architects with the required expertise.

## Summary

### SUSTAINABLE DESIGN AND ANALYSIS SERVICES

#### Why a Client May Need These Services
▷ To create healthful and more productive habitats
▷ To promote or show commitment to an environmental ethic
▷ To meet legislated environmental requirements

#### Knowledge and Skills Required
▷ Knowledge of environmental performance of building materials, components, and systems
▷ Understanding of ecological and biological processes
▷ Familiarity with life cycle assessment methodologies
▷ Familiarity with environmental regulations

#### Representative Process Tasks
▷ Define sustainability goals
▷ Establish targets for environmental performance
▷ Gather relevant data for environmental considerations
▷ Identify appropriate technologies
▷ Participate in design team effort throughout the design process
▷ Participate in commissioning to verify environmental performance
▷ Educate facility staff about operational issues to maintain environmental performance

## CLIENT NEEDS

Clients look for sustainable design services for many of the same reasons they seek energy analysis and design. Common goals include reducing operating costs, improving design quality, enhancing public image, fulfilling and demonstrating an organizational commitment to the environment, or responding to a remote site where resource availability is unreliable or there are stringent environmental restrictions on development. Large government, institutional, and corporate clients that own and occupy buildings throughout their life cycle are most likely to take a long-term view and be willing to invest extra time, effort, and money up front to

**MUSCOE MARTIN** *is a principal with the Philadelphia firm of Susan Maxman & Partners. Martin is past chairman of the AIA Committee on the Environment (COTE). He has lectured and written on green architecture, sustainable communities, ethics and sustainable design, and energy-efficient design.*

part 4 SERVICES

achieve sustainability goals. Green buildings have good resale value and attributes that may encourage buyers, and banks should be encouraged to make loans to green building projects because of their long-term value and quality and their reduced life cycle operating costs.

Some clients use a "green" facilities label as a marketing or recruitment tool. Companies competing for scarce computer programming personnel, for example, promote their healthy, energy-efficient work facilities as an incentive to potential employees. As with energy analysis, government agencies at the local, state, and federal level may require analysis of sustainability issues as part of the design process for government facilities. Federal agencies are required to reduce energy consumption by executive order and are encouraged to invest in other cost-effective measures that will reduce environmental impacts and increase the productivity, comfort, and health of building occupants. Many state and city agencies are required to reduce landfill and thus actively promote the use of recycled and recyclable materials.

More environmentally conscious landscaping, materials selection, indoor air quality, recycling, and water conservation are among the issues federal facility managers are encouraged to consider in addition to energy conservation. Some Department of Defense agencies, such as the U.S. Navy, have been particularly proactive in responding to these policies, requiring any firms seeking design work to demonstrate experience in sustainable design.

Some clients seek the services of designers with expertise in sustainable design because of specific concerns. The potential for reducing operating costs through enhanced energy efficiency continues to be a dominant market driver. Clients who have facilities with recognized air quality problems seek expert help in achieving a healthier building environment. Storm water control and water conservation are rapidly emerging as areas of interest, not just in the historically water-scarce western states but elsewhere as well. Erosion and discharge are growing concerns in agricultural, industrial, and urbanized areas alike. Some consultants specialize in designing for chemically sensitive and allergic individuals, many of whom cannot tolerate the chemical compounds from dyes, adhesives, sealers, sealants, finishes, and molds that are emitted into the air from many building products, including carpets, insulation, paint, fabrics, and built-in and movable furniture.

Opinions vary as to whether sustainable design takes more time or costs more money. Some practitioners say sustainable buildings don't have to cost more or take longer to design and build. Others say that any specialized design involving use of specialty products will affect design and construction costs and project schedule. As with any emerging or new design consideration, there is a learning curve. As designers, builders, and clients gain experience with sustainable design, efficiency increases. Costs and benefits for sustainable design are difficult to quantify. Costs include design fees, construction costs, and life cycle operations and maintenance costs. Benefits include operations and maintenance savings as well as environmental, economic, and social benefits.

Sustainable design is a design approach that encompasses many specialized services or areas of expertise such as energy-efficient design and consulting, indoor air quality, lighting design, landscaping, storm water management, and facility management, to name a few. This breadth in relevant subject matter suggests a pragmatic approach for architects or firms interested in offering sustainable design services. Acquire expertise in the constituent areas a few at a time and gradually take on more complex projects.

## SKILLS

Because sustainable design requires varied expertise, the project manager ideally will have a broad knowledge base and an understanding of basic environmental concepts, supplemented as necessary by other team members. Special expertise essential to sustainable design includes the capacity to perform various levels of energy analysis, evaluate energy technologies (including passive solar and daylighting concepts), and assess the environmental attributes, cost, and availability of building materials. Some projects may require more rigorous environmental life cycle assessments to develop comparisons between material choices.

Depending on the project, expertise may also be required in the areas of site and landscape design, storm water management and water conservation, recycling, indoor air quality, and economic analysis. On some projects biologists, botanists, industrial hygienists, or experts offering more specialized services such as design for the chemically sensitive may be needed.

▶ **The AIA Committee on the Environment (COTE) offers workshops and conferences on the subject of sustainable design. Information about upcoming events and reports of past ones, including technical papers, can be found by accessing the COTE page on the AIA Web site (www.aia.org).**

▶ **AIA Continuing Education System (AIA/CES) programs are periodically offered on sustainable design. Check the AIA Web site at www.aia.org for current information.**

# PROCESS

The sustainable design process requires that sustainable parameters be considered, analyzed, and synthesized with other parameters throughout the building planning and design process. To do this, several important items must be incorporated into the process. First, there is often a special preplanning step to determine sustainability goals. Second, the design team effort is "front loaded," which means it occurs earlier in the building design process. Finally, the design process must be fully integrated. The architect serves as the team leader to ensure an integrated design.

In order to determine the project scope and fee, it is best to develop a task list of services to be provided and allocate resources to them. Sustainable or green building projects often have three major components:

1. Energy efficiency criteria are applied to building envelope design, lighting and equipment design and selection, HVAC system design, and landscape design.
2. Indoor air quality criteria are applied to ventilation system source control, materials selection, building commissioning, and building maintenance.
3. Resource efficiency criteria are applied to building materials, site and landscape maintenance efficiency, and water issues.

A determination of the task list of services will be an outcome of the preplanning step.

***Preplanning.*** This stage of the sustainable building design process is a group brainstorming activity (or charrette) with client representatives intended to define the objectives of the sustainable design effort. The results of the session serve as input to the overall programming process. Each preplanning activity is different, depending on the type of project addressed. When programming is provided as a discrete or separate service, sustainable issues must be integrated into the programming process.

To begin the brainstorming session, the designers usually ask the clients to discuss any relevant organizational mission statements. Next, general project objectives (for example, cost savings; energy savings; health, comfort and productivity; resource preservation and management; pollution prevention) are explored and prioritized. Important project parameters can be defined. For example, parameters could include practicality, conventional appearance, ease of implementation, need for uninterrupted operations, or minimal risk.

The next step is to gather baseline information. For example, for a retrofit project with a goal of decreasing energy and water consumption, the designers would look at existing energy and water consumption and costs. For new buildings, average consumption and costs for comparable new (but conventional) facilities would be considered. A number of building assessment tools are being developed (such as the LEED rating system, under development by the U.S. Green Building Council) that can help in comparing environmental performance. The rating system provides credits for including various green features in a project.

▶ To achieve higher levels of environmental performance in building design, environmental issues should be considered throughout building planning, design, documentation, and construction. Related services in which environmental issues may come into play include Programming (16.1), Building Design (17.2), Construction Documentation—Drawings (17.4), and Construction Documentation—Specifications (17.5).

Finally, targets for environmental performance can be established by referencing the performance of other projects with similar goals. For example, a comprehensive sustainable design program might include quantitative performance targets for energy use, water use, indoor air quality, building and transportation emissions, solid waste, recycling, and the water, botanical, and/or wildlife quality on the site. Other building performance improvement targets are more difficult to quantify, such as quality of light, productivity, and user satisfaction. Worker absentee, illness, and productivity rates are sometimes used as measures because these rates have been shown to improve when the building environment improves.

Life cycle cost analysis of potential savings should be a factor in setting the performance goals and in determining project budget. While the preplanning effort requires extra design time, the client should be able to quickly recover the cost of the extra design effort in operations cost savings and other benefits.

***Front-loading.*** Well-executed sustainable design requires consultants to be brought in as early as possible in the process in the interest of optimizing design integration. Overall design fees for a sustainable design team may increase somewhat, due to the preplanning

## Facility and Material Life Cycles

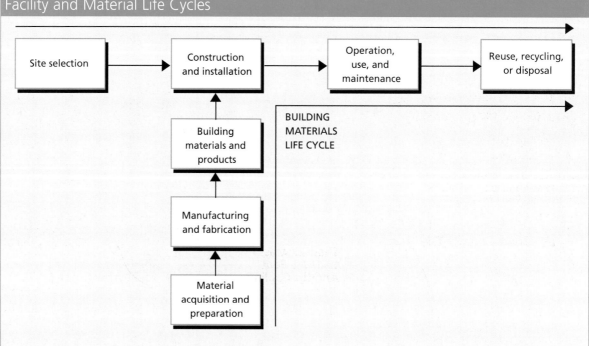

Environmental impacts occur in the life cycle of building construction materials and products during their acquisition, manufacture, and installation in the building. After installation, further impacts may occur during the operation and use of the building.

AIA, *Environmental Resource Guide* (1996)

## Environmental Project Team Organization

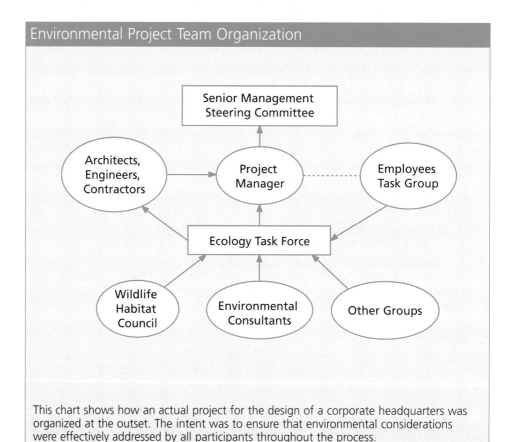

This chart shows how an actual project for the design of a corporate headquarters was organized at the outset. The intent was to ensure that environmental considerations were effectively addressed by all participants throughout the process.

Adapted from AIA, Environmental Resource Guide (Wiley, 1997)

**Operable Clerestory Windows for Night Venting**

**Reflective Roof Membrane**

**Roof Steps to East for Morning Sun**

**Certified Sustainably Harvested Glued Laminate Roof Beams**

**Straw Bale Walls with Soil Cement Finish**

**Direct Sunlight**

**Reflected Sunlight**

**Ventilated Air Cavity Above Radiant Barrier**

**Overhang Sized for Solar Gain Control**

**Movable Insulated Translucent Light Shelves**

**Direct Sunlight**

**Thermal Mass to Store Heat And for Cooling**

**South-Facing Glazing for Passive Gain in Winter**

**Shade Trellis Made From Reclaimed Redwood**

**Cool-Air Intake Vents with Fan Assist**

**Curved White Ceiling Distributes Daylight Evenly**

**Wood-burning Stoves for Backup Heating**

**Shaded, Evaporatively Cooled Oasis Entry**

The design of the Real Goods Solar Living Center in Hopland, California, embodies restorative approaches, climate-responsive design, and renewable energy systems.

AIA, *Architectural Graphic Standards* (2000)

process and the earlier participation of engineering consultants. However, added up-front costs should be balanced by improved coordination of the design documents and, particularly, lower life cycle costs and other benefits to the owner and society.

*Design integration.* All of the members of a design team need to work interactively and often simultaneously in a sustainable design project to ensure that the effects of individual design decisions on the entire building environment are adequately assessed. Designers, consultants, and clients must be involved and stay involved. Energy simulation and other green building design software packages can be tremendous tools for quantifying life cycle costs and environmental impacts and optimizing a design. It is important to draw a distinction between green building products that are recycled and recyclable and those that provide indoor air quality. For example, a 100 percent postconsumer recycled product may emit volatile organic compounds that cause health problems.

*Commissioning and operations.* Commissioning is an especially important component of a sustainable design project, vital to ensuring that installed systems are operating properly. Just as important, user education can be an important determinant of the long-term performance of some resource-conserving design features. User controls and consumption monitoring programs can help ensure long-term performance.

### For More Information

The *Sustainable Building Technical Manual: Green Building Practices for Design, Construction, and Operations,* (1999) offers step-by-step guidelines for energy- and resource-efficient building. The manual is available online from the U.S. Green Building Council (www.usgbc.org).

Firms seeking an overview of sustainable principles or those desiring to introduce such principles to clients may want to refer to *A Primer on Sustainable Building* (1995), by Dianna Barnett and William Browning, and to *Guiding Principles of Sustainable Design* (1993).

The connection between ecology and sustainability in building design is covered by

Sym Van Der Ryn and Stuart Cowan in *Ecological Design* (1996). Brian Edwards covers major components of sustainable building design (from a European perspective) in Towards Sustainable Architecture (1996). Donald Watson, FAIA, articulates the principles of bioclimatic design in Chapter 3 of *Time-Saver Standards for Architectural Design Data, 7th Ed.* (1997).

For information about sustainability at scales beyond the individual building, see Robert L. Thayer Jr.'s *Grey World, Green Heart: Technology, Nature, and the Sustainable Landscape* (1994) and Peter Newman's and Jeffrey Kenworthy's *Sustainability and Cities (1999).* The former presents a framework for achieving a sustainable future, and the latter discusses the role that reduced automobile dependence can play in attaining sustainability on a city scale.

Sustainability in the building development process is addressed by the Rocky Mountain Institute in *Green Development: Integrating Ecology and Real Estate* (1998). This work covers development issues such as planning, zoning, financing, marketing, design, and construction from an environmental perspective.

The *AIA Environmental Resource Guide* (1998) contains detailed and comparative information on the use and performance of building materials. The information is presented in a series of project, application, and material reports based on a "streamlined" environmental life cycle assessment methodology. The ERG is available in CD-ROM format from the publisher, John Wiley & Sons (www.wiley.com).

*Environmental Building News* is a bimonthly newsletter on environmentally sustainable design and construction. Each year a special issue titled "Selected Readings" identifies books, periodicals, and directories that focus on green buildings and related topics. Contact Environmental Building News, 122 Birge Street, Suite 30, Brattleboro, VT 05301, (802) 257-7300, fax (802) 257-7304 (www.ebuild.com).

The U.S. Department of Energy's Center of Excellence for Sustainable Development provides information and resources on green buildings (www.sustainable.doe.gov). The Green Design Network also provides a host of useful resources on green design and construction. The site includes a searchable database and an online green building advisor, Global Environmental Options (www.geonetwork.org).

# 18 Operations–Maintenance Services

## 18.1 Facility Management

### Robin Ellerthorpe, FAIA

*As more clients recognize the benefits of integrating facility planning with corporate strategic planning, architecture firms that have the appropriate skills can vastly expand their facility management services.*

Facility management services can be defined to include many related functions, ranging from strategic planning and asset management to planning and design, construction management, operations, maintenance, and general administrative services. As client needs change, the potential for facility management services expands, offering significant new market opportunities for architecture firms that have or wish to develop the appropriate abilities.

### CLIENT NEEDS

Most companies that own their buildings have facility management (FM) or corporate real estate (CRE) departments. Companies that lease space but retain responsibility for physical plant maintenance and operations are also likely to have an FM or CRE group. Because facility management involves such a broad range of functions, many companies outsource skills and expertise they do not have in-house. The most typical FM clients manage office or multiuse facilities.

In the past, client organizations were relatively stable, manufacturing the same product or providing the same service for twenty years or more. In that environment the role of the design and construction industry was to respond to change as it related to space. Facility management consulting services most often addressed planning new space or reconfiguring existing space, as well as tactical assistance with building operations and maintenance and general office services. Most companies viewed their facilities and their FM/CRE departments as an expense.

In the past 10 to 15 years business cycles have shortened, the pace of business has rapidly accelerated, and real estate values have cycled up and down dramatically. More clients have come to understand the need to manage their facilities as an asset or a means to an end. In-house facility managers are challenged to respond instantly to continual company change, whether it stems from innovation, restructuring, or reorganization.

## Summary

### FACILITY MANAGEMENT SERVICES

**Why a Client May Need These Services**
▷ To profile physical assets
▷ To optimize use of assets in facilities
▷ To provide a system for facility financial tracking
▷ To provide a tool for maintenance management
▷ To provide a basis for budget forecasting

**Knowledge and Skills Required**
▷ Understanding of building operations
▷ Knowledge of finance and accounting methods
▷ Ability to think strategically
▷ Surveying and inventorying capabilities
▷ Ability to create and manage databases

**Representative Process Tasks**
▷ Identify client goals
▷ Identify constraints
▷ Develop strategies for achieving goals
▷ Make recommendations to management
▷ Capture facility data in a database program

**ROBIN ELLERTHORPE** *directs facilities consulting for OWP&P Architects, Inc., a group he began in 1997. His diverse team specializes in strategic planning, change management, and operations and maintenance tool development for facility owners.*

## Providing Information Technology Services

American corporations find that facility management and real estate costs are their second largest expense after personnel. As more clients recognize the benefits of integrating facility planning with corporate strategic planning, there is more call for facility management services that provide information technology support. An architecture firm that has employees with the right skills may be able to provide such services.

Strategic facility planning requires the ability to predict future space needs and costs and to relate projected facility costs to their impact on future profitability. Unfortunately, the information necessary to make such predictions is not readily available in most organizations, and when it is available, it is almost never integrated into a single, easily accessible database. In most organizations facility operations data are maintained separately from design and construction data, which in turn are separate from overall business finance information. Even if all the data are computerized and up-to-date, typically the databases are stored in different software formats and maintained by separate departments within the organization.

Advances such as open database connectivity (ODBC) and object linking and embedding (OLE) technologies make it possible to retrieve data in a relational environment, which greatly assists the integration of information previously stored in separate, vertically organized formats. For example, it is now possible to create a database in which the user can call up the floor plan for an office space and click on a piece of office equipment to retrieve information on the cost of the equipment, its age, and its depreciation rate.

Opportunities for consultants include provision of the initial service of integrating client data into an easily usable facility information system and provision of an ongoing data management service. In some instances the consultant's services may include continuing data analysis support as well. However, in many organizations significant institutional barriers must be overcome and a certain level of trust achieved before consultants will be allowed to maintain proprietary information. Adequate security systems are essential.

Computer-aided facility management is evolving rapidly, and good decision-making software is currently on the market. Information storage and retrieval is the most significant challenge in the field at present, and the market will reward consultants who help their clients meet this challenge.

In the current business environment, client organizations must manage change effectively through strategic facility planning. There is a growing need for FM services to help develop facility strategies that can contribute to the achievement of corporate objectives. As an example, the facility objectives of many organizations now include maximizing productivity and flexibility and attracting and retaining personnel, as well as minimizing operations expenses. Flexibility is particularly important, as it permits organizations to respond more efficiently and economically to future demands.

Many clients today are moving away from hiring a number of different consultants for short-term projects. Instead, they are seeking to lower costs and increase efficiency through long-term relationships with consultants who can help them manage their space over time. In this climate, architects have the opportunity to reestablish themselves as integrators and trusted advisors—roles they played in many companies before the demise of the corporate architect and the emergence of predominantly leased business space in the 1980s.

The market for consultants providing strategic facility planning as part of FM services has enormous potential for growth because of the value it can add to client organizations. Architects and architecture firms that offer such planning services will be in a good position to provide clients with related FM services, as they will have an unusually thorough understanding of clients' needs. Related information management services can provide a client with continually updated data that assist in ongoing management decision making.

At the same time this new version of facility management is developing, the more traditional market for facility management services is continuing to expand. Opportunities abound for architecture firms offering real estate, building design and construction, building operations, maintenance, and general office services to clients that may or may not have made the transition to strategic FM practices.

Due to high rates of churn (movement of people over time), clients continue to have a strong need for work space planning and design, a forte of architecture and interior design consultants. The FM field traces its origins to the increased need for interior space planning that came with office automation in the early 1980s. Now the trend toward team-based work processes, and the fact that teams tend to shift with each new project, is driving office planning in many organizations. As one facility manager explained, "Our job is to make it as easy as possible to form teams." According to a 1996 International Facility Management Association survey, other issues of client concern include ergonomics, sustainability, recycling, emergency response, telecommunications, smart buildings, and sick building syndrome.

Services to help a client minimize operating expenses continue to be of great

## THE WORLD OF FACILITY MANAGEMENT

Today's facility manager may be involved in a wide range of organizational functions, including strategic planning and management of the physical plant and interior operations, as well as day-to-day tactical operations of the facility and facility staff (or contractors).

|  | PLANNING AND MANAGEMENT | TACTICAL OPERATIONS |
|---|---|---|
| **PHYSICAL PLANT** | **Real Estate Management**<br>• Property inventories<br>• Property acquisition, leasing, and disposal<br>• Feasibility studies<br>• Environmental studies<br><br>**Building Design and Construction**<br>• Master site planning<br>• Architecture<br>• Engineering | **Building Operations and Maintenance**<br>• Operations • Grounds<br>• Plant operations • Utilities<br>• Maintenance • Property engineering<br>• FF&E • Space planning<br>• Rentals • Relocation coordination<br>• Office equipment • Telecommunications/<br>• Signage   data distribution |
| **INTERIOR OPERATIONS** | **Facility Planning**<br>• Strategic planning and budgeting<br>• Information management<br><br>**Tactical Planning** | **General Office Services**<br>• Security • Mailroom<br>• Housekeeping • Shuttle<br>• Solid waste • Food service<br>• Pest control • Fitness center<br>• Reception • Printing services<br>• Switchboard • Fleet management<br>• Plant rental • Procurement<br>• Receiving/distribution |

value and in demand. Benchmarking is a service provided by many FM consultants, including both business management and design consultants. Benchmarking evaluates people, processes, systems, and information flow and makes comparisons to industry benchmarks or to goals set by a particular client. For example, one firm moved its accounting department out of the headquarters complex when it found the cost of headquarters space was more than twice the industry benchmark for an accounting function. Many A/E firms provide building engineering services to help facility managers minimize maintenance and operations expenses.

Because FM services are a high-value market, fees are often as high or higher than fees for traditional design services. Of course, this higher fee level attracts other service providers to the FM field, including accounting firms, real estate development firms, and others.

## SKILLS

As is the case with many markets that offer new opportunities to use the skills of an architect, it is important to develop sound capability before offering a service for the first time. Be sure you can deliver a strong product. Team with more experienced providers if necessary.

In analyzing your own organization's ability to provide FM services, consider the skills and background of available staff in relation to the specific tasks involved in the potential work.

As the range of services broadens, there is a greater need for generalists who can develop facility planning strategies and manage the implementation process. This involves the ability to evaluate organizational and management situations, define constraints, and develop options for achieving stated objectives. Architects often develop the necessary organizational development and management skills through their experience in project or contract management or in interior or architectural design. In addition to architectural or other professional design training, a background in business administration, property management, and/or behavioral science is helpful.

Space planning expertise is always in demand for FM projects. Both architects and interior designers have a good background for the work. For the space programming tasks, consider use of junior-level generalists with good communications skills teamed with design professionals for interviewing tasks.

Benchmarking is a financial accounting or business management function and can be performed by any generalist. Indeed, design firms face competition from business management consulting firms in this area. Design firms can gain a competitive edge in this area by offering benchmarking data with more context and analysis.

Information technology services—including data capture, retrieval, analysis, and maintenance—are an emerging component of the FM field. Software programmers who can help integrate data into an information system the client can use for ongoing decision making are an enormous asset to the project team. Information technology skills are in high demand in today's market, and this can be a challenging resource to develop and maintain.

Larger A/E firms may provide a range of building operations and maintenance or general office services to support the FM operations of their clients. In addition to architects and engineers, these services may require personnel skilled in strategic planning, market analysis, building assessment, site evaluation, asset (FF&E) evaluation, construction, office management, property management, and institution/hotel management.

## PROCESS

The process involved in providing facility management services naturally depends on the specific service or group of services being provided. Much also depends on a client's specific needs, organizational style, and competitive environment.

An approach to preparing a facility management plan would include the following: identification of goals and constraints, strategy development, management recommendations, and data capture.

**Goal identification.** A firm providing facility management services works with the client's management team to develop overall goals for the strategic facility plan. The client's mission and vision statements are connected with facility outcomes. For example, are the client's physical facilities an important part of the corporate image program? Is exceptional employee health and comfort part of the organization's human resources strategy? Is minimizing the operations budget a management priority?

**Constraints identification.** Goals analysis is translated into more quantified parameters, such as building and operations budgets, building performance limits, and so on. This often results in a document called a "needs analysis," which carefully outlines the needed outcome and becomes the backbone of the scope document.

**Strategy development.** The consulting team develops specific facility strategies to achieve the goals within the constraints. For example, to develop strategies for managing interior office space, the team would perform interior space programming and planning.

The first step would be to determine the specific amounts and types of space needed in the client organization and the client's space use patterns (such as rate of churn). The consultants would analyze potential trade-off options, for example, strategies for reducing the operations budget or increasing the efficiency of the work process.

Another step would be to identify the work style of the organization so that the space could be planned to facilitate the work process. For example, a current trend in many organizations is to develop interdisciplinary teams to carry out specific work requirements. To accommodate this arrangement, work space must be flexible so that team members can work in close proximity for the duration of a project and then perhaps reconfigure the space for another project. A team-based organization also needs comfortable meeting rooms, since many employees spend most of their working hours in group situations. Organizations with a more linear or hierarchical functional style may not require such levels of flexibility but rather may need more commodious individual workspaces. The design professional's ability to generate creative options that meet the specific needs of an organization's work style adds value to this phase of the work.

To develop more specific strategies for planning work space, in-depth interviews are conducted with division managers to determine precise space requirements. What is currently working well in the space? What doesn't work? This information is translated into both qualitative and quantitative terms. For example, a division manager may report that workers are too crowded; an effort would be made to determine exactly how many additional workspaces are needed and what their size should be. The work style of the organization is taken into account as specific interior planning recommendations are developed.

**Management recommendations.** A facility management plan prepared for presentation to a client assembles and analyzes all of the information that has been gathered

▶ **Programming (16.1) includes a discussion about interviewing techniques applicable to the programming process.**

about space use in the organization and the options that would meet organizational needs. The plan also recommends facility strategies that can achieve corporate objectives at the same time they minimize cost and maximize flexibility. For example, a plan might recommend that the accounting function, which can be accomplished in a space that costs $8 to $10 per square foot, be relocated away from the headquarters office, where it currently occupies a space costing $21 a square foot. Another example might be an organization that is evolving from a linear work style toward a more team-based functional organization. In this case the plan might recommend a gradual transition toward office spaces with larger, more comfortable meeting rooms and movable partitions.

*Data capture.* One of the greatest values an FM consultant can offer to a client is the ability to capture and maintain a facility database that can continue to be used to evaluate strategic facility options. Analyses that in the past took months to perform can now be accomplished within a few minutes with FM software. To use this decision-making software (which involves what-if gaming strategy), a client must have an up-to-date database of its current space requirements.

An architecture firm offering facility management services can produce a database and obtain software for a client on a fee basis or offer to maintain the database and provide an analysis service for a monthly retainer. Not only does this arrangement provide a valuable service for the client, but it also establishes an ongoing working relationship between the client and the firm providing the service.

> **Strategic facility planning services may be the next step for firms already providing facility management services. See Strategic Facility Planning (16.3).**

### For More Information

David G. Cotts discusses facility management, from strategic facility business to cost savings/avoidance, in *The Facility Management Handbook* (1998).

*Facility Maintenance: The Manager's Practical Guide and Handbook* (1996), by Donn W. Brown, offers easy-to-follow guidelines for creating top-quality maintenance programs for organizations. Included are sample forms, checklists, and diagnostic charts.

*Facilities Maintenance Standards* (1991), by Roger W. Liska, is a guide to comprehending and solving maintenance problems. The book contains forms, checklists, and worksheets as well as information on how to predict and estimate the cost of maintenance and repair tasks. *Means Facilities Maintenance and Repair Cost Data* (2000) is a cost-estimating tool that includes information on preventive maintenance and life cycle costing.

*The Facilities Manager's Reference: Management, Planning, Building Audits, Estimating* (1989), by Harvey H. Kaiser, presents the functional activities, organizational responsibilities, and relationships of a facilities department. It contains guidelines for assessing maintenance and capital needs, projecting labor and material costs, and analyzing building conditions. A ready-to-use 24-page building audit form is included.

The *Facilities Operations and Engineering Reference* (1999) presents technical data needed to address essential design, construction, operations, and maintenance issues.

The *Facilities Evaluation Handbook: Safety, Fire Protection and Environmental Compliance, 2nd Ed.* (1999), is designed for on-the-job use by those responsible for keeping facilities operating smoothly, efficiently, and safely. Provided are information and tools for carrying out a comprehensive facility evaluation and identifying problems, as well as self-evaluation checklists for assessing how a facility is functioning.

James E. Piper's *Handbook of Facility Management: Tools and Techniques, Formulas and Tables* (1995) provides straightforward techniques for solving problems and saving money in mechanical, electrical, building, and grounds maintenance as well as in energy use. Included are scores of ready-to-use approaches that work in all types of facilities.

# 18.2 Postoccupancy Evaluation

## Larry Lord, FAIA, and Margaret Serrato, AIA, ASID

*Clients seeking to use their space more cost-effectively, increase the productivity of collaborative work groups, or gain a competitive edge in attracting creative employees are fueling a growing market for postoccupancy evaluations.*

## Summary

### POSTOCCUPANCY EVALUATION SERVICES

#### Why a Client May Need These Services

▷ To reduce costs and enhance building quality in future projects
▷ To discover and correct functional concerns early
▷ To evaluate the effectiveness of design or delivery decisions
▷ To respond to complaints of building users
▷ To identify efficient, cost-effective solutions to space use issues

#### Knowledge and Skills Required

▷ Background in behavioral, environmental, or organizational psychology
▷ Experience with interior space planning
▷ Understanding of the building program, design, and technology
▷ Excellent communication and interview skills
▷ Expertise in data-gathering techniques and tools
▷ Specialized knowledge for particular facility type

#### Representative Process Tasks

▷ Determine the goals of the evaluation
▷ Identify members of the postoccupancy evaluation team
▷ Research effect of physical environment on organizational goals and objectives
▷ Collect and analyze current performance data
▷ Prepare final report, including recommendations for change

Postoccupancy evaluation services address how well a facility contributes to the productivity, satisfaction, and well-being of the occupants and the goals of the organization. Emphasis is on evaluating the functional quality and efficient use of living and working environments. In the case of new construction or renovation projects, actual functions are compared to the program objectives of the project. Sometimes occupancy studies are conducted as a prelude to the proposal of new construction or renovation and are very much like predesign programming. When they compare previous occupancy conditions to new ones, the studies are called pre- and postoccupancy evaluations.

The growing interest in occupancy studies stems from an overall concern for optimizing building performance that has developed in conjunction with the maturation of the facility management profession. Within the area of building performance, there are two distinct focuses: the performance of building materials and systems and the performance of the building in functional, behavioral, economic, and social or cultural context. The latter view is the focus of the postoccupancy evaluation services discussed here.

A growing body of knowledge developing in the environmental design field addresses how the physical environment affects behavior, learning, performance, satisfaction, human productivity, and well-being. As awareness of the effects of environmental factors expands, the market for environmental design services is likely to continue to grow.

## CLIENT NEEDS

From the client's perspective, postoccupancy evaluation can serve many purposes. Especially for repeat builders, postoccupancy evaluation can provide "lessons learned" that can be applied to future projects to reduce cost and enhance building quality. Regardless of whether a client intends to build again, a postoccupancy evaluation study can provide input for facility management and renovation.

***New facilities.*** By including postoccupancy evaluation services as part of the owner-architect agreement for building design and documentation, the designer is able to discover and correct any functional concerns before complaints emerge. Classically, this type of postoccupancy evaluation focuses on comparison of the initial project program with the facility in actual use. The postconstruction study also may evaluate the effectiveness of specific ideas and innovations used in the design or delivery of the project. Results can be used to fine-tune the building to respond to actual conditions.

**LARRY LORD** *is a founding principal with the Atlanta architecture firm of Lord, Aeck & Sargent and is also with Working Buildings, LLC, a firm offering total building commissioning services.* **MARGARET SERRATO** *is an architect and interior designer with Brito Serrato, LLC. Her specialties include environmental and behavioral research, programming, and evaluation.*

In new facilities postoccupancy evaluation studies often are requested when there are complaints. Quite often these complaints stem from inadequate communication between those who designed the building and those who are occupying it. Many of the problems encountered by occupants in new facilities could be avoided by thoroughly researching occupant needs during the programming of new facilities. The research should then be followed by adequate occupant information as part of a commissioning program. If a new facility is dramatically different from the old one, occupants may need a formal support program to enable them to adjust to the new facility. For example, if employees formerly had private offices but now must work in open and collaborative team space, it is normal for them initially to have negative feelings about the new work environment. Some firms that offer postoccupancy evaluations also offer move-in assistance or a change management service to work with occupants before and after a move to orient them to the new space.

*Existing facilities.* Owners of existing buildings may seek postoccupancy evaluations because of a perceived problem with the space. Managers of organizations who want their buildings to work for them and owners interested in ensuring a continued market for the space will seek postoccupancy evaluation services to identify potential solutions. In condominiums, apartment buildings, dormitories, and office buildings, for example, occupants may complain about noise, lighting, adjacencies, or other factors. Commercial, institutional, and government clients may recognize problems with work space in existing facilities and be interested in ways to improve the existing space or to determine whether new facilities are required.

*Impact of technology.* With rapidly changing technology in the workplace, many facility owners feel the need to transform space and make it more flexible to meet changing user demands. Computers, fax machines, and e-mail have altered the way people do business and the way space is configured to accommodate people and machines.

*Change in work processes.* The social structure of work also is changing rapidly, affecting how work is organized and managed and how decisions are made. Change in work processes requires change in workspace organization. In today's knowledge-based economy, the success of many organizations depends on the productivity of creative professionals who work collaboratively. Progressive corporate and academic research and development organizations, for example, are keenly interested in applying environmental design principles to their facilities. They understand that well-designed facilities can make their workers healthier and more productive, support both individual and collaborative work, and help attract the best talent. For such clients, the postoccupancy evaluation will include assessment of the occupants' work processes (by someone trained in behavioral psychology or a related discipline) to determine how the space can best accommodate the size and style of the work team and its type of output (e.g., theories, books, marketing concepts).

*Bottom-line concerns.* Clients are more interested than ever in realizing the full potential of their facilities. They want to enhance the operations that take place within them and to use the space more cost-effectively. Colleges and universities, for example, are very interested in expanding the hours of effective facility utilization in order to increase revenues, and thus they frequently requisition space utilization studies to address that issue. College dormitories, residential health care facilities, and the lodging industry want to maximize the number of units available while maintaining consumer comfort. In the late 1990s there was a perceptible increase in the number of organizations requesting evaluation of current occupancy patterns in existing space, and this trend is likely to continue.

Unfortunately, when clients seek postoccupancy evaluation services for purely economic reasons, they often turn to professional management consulting firms, major accounting firms, or developers. Architects facing these competitors can point out to clients that their comprehensive knowledge of building design makes them better qualified to evaluate all factors that go into effective space use, but they must counter the perception that they are not sufficiently attuned to the client's need for bottom-line return.

*The architect's perspective.* Architecture firms may face many competitors in the market for postoccupancy evaluation services, including management consulting firms, accounting firms, developers, space planning firms, and behavioral or environmental psychologists. Depending on the project, an architecture firm may choose to team with these potential competitors.

There is some controversy regarding whether it is a conflict of interest for the design architect to perform postoccupancy evaluations. Some are concerned the designer will lack the detachment necessary to perform an unbiased assessment, while others maintain that the original designer is best qualified to perform the service because of unmatched knowledge of the facility and its programming goals. Postoccupancy evaluation expresses a long-term commitment to quality control and customer satisfaction when conducted responsibly on projects the architect has designed. Because organizations are dynamic, many changes may occur between programming and occupancy that will require fine-tuning of the building design. Postoccupancy evaluation identifies problems that may be easily corrected. If not corrected, problems could lead to conditions that would be attributed to poor design. Architects can learn much from postoccupancy evaluations that they can apply to future projects.

Postoccupancy evaluation services are closely related to a number of other services that can be marketed as a package. Related services include programming, space planning, systems performance assurance, commissioning, move management, the move-in assistance or change management services noted above, warranty review, energy monitoring, indoor air quality monitoring, the making of record documents, preparation of operations manuals, and operations and maintenance training. The best marketing strategy is to position the designer as a partner with the client over a longer term in order to optimize the client's investment over time and optimize the designer's knowledge.

## SKILLS

The postoccupancy evaluation team should include people with a variety of skills. Someone with a good background in behavioral, environmental, or organizational psychology and interior space planning will be a key team member. Depending on the focus or goal of the organization, an architect may be a good choice for project manager, offering a solid understanding of the building program, building design, and building technology. The project manager should have excellent communication and personal interaction skills, including the ability to facilitate discussions and conduct interviews. Depending on the project, an engineer with additional expertise in building systems operation may be required. The team's collective knowledge should include expertise in data-gathering techniques and tools. Generally, senior staff is required for postoccupancy evaluation work, particularly the portions of the work involving client contact or data analysis. Junior professionals or administrative staff may do administrative and data entry work.

Those listed above are the core team members for most projects. Depending on the project, others may be added as consultants or team members. Sociologists, anthropologists, management consultants, environmental psychologists, or other professionals concerned with human needs, attitudes, and behaviors may be needed to supplement the services of the core team members. Many postoccupancy efforts may require mechanical, electrical, and civil engineers as well as interior designers. Other specialists may include acoustical engineers, networking and telecommunications consultants, energy specialists, environmental and air quality specialists, industrial hygienists, and landscape architects. Depending on the nature of the project, consultants who specialize in particular types of buildings or spaces (e.g., kitchen, justice, entertainment) also may be required.

Equipment and resources required include computers, Web pages where project users can provide information and respond to questionnaires, a camera, a tape recorder, bias-free survey instruments, and software for space syntax analysis.

## PROCESS

The scope of service depends on the type of information the client needs, the size and complexity of the facility involved, the number of functions it houses, and the number of occupant interviews the client requests.

***Goal identification.*** The first step is to identify the people in the client's organization who need information and to clarify how the information is to be used—where it will be applied and by whom. Obtaining buy-in from top-level management (e.g., a chief executive officer or a senior vice president for finance and administration) for the study is advisable to ensure that the recommendations will be implemented. The anticipated benefits (or desired outcomes) from the postoccupancy evaluation study should be explicitly identified at the outset.

***Team formation.*** At this point, with the goals of the postoccupancy evaluation established, the team members for the evaluation effort can be identified. In assembling a postoccupancy evaluation team, prime consideration is given to the client's information needs, each team member's ability to understand the program requirements for the particular facility, and their competency in their respective disciplines. The team should include representatives of the client's organization who will oversee the team's work. The team must take the time to establish rapport with the people who occupy the setting to be evaluated. It is important that the team not be perceived as threatening to the occupants, who may fear the consultants will report negative findings about their work performance to management.

***Preliminary research.*** Working with those identified by in-house team members, the consulting team reviews building programming documentation and conducts interviews with the goal of gaining a preliminary understanding of the following:

- The goals and objectives of the organization and the role the physical environment is asked to play in helping achieve those goals
- The behaviors and tasks needed to achieve those organizational goals
- How the building must perform to support those behaviors and tasks

***Data collection.*** The team will then need to gather data to better understand the factors listed above and to collect evidence regarding how well or poorly the building supports the desired behaviors and tasks. Data collection methods that are appropriate to the setting and to the information needs are then selected. Methods fall into three general levels. The most common and least complex level of data collection is the postoccupancy evaluation questionnaire or interview, which documents what the occupants have to say about the space. The second is sampling and observation, which provide verification of the survey data as well as additional texture and detail. Many clients feel that sampling and observation are not necessary, but they should be conducted to ensure data quality. The third and most complex level of data collection is a longer-term postoccupancy evaluation, which might include diagnostic studies that probe more deeply into problem areas. The team also must decide whether it is appropriate to gather data from just a few respondents or many and over what time period (e.g., a day, month, or year).

***Findings and recommendations.*** After the data are collected and analyzed, findings and recommendations are presented in a draft postoccupancy evaluation report. The report may recommend strategies for improving the building's ability to support desired behaviors and tasks, or it may recommend modification of behaviors and tasks in order to realize the building's potential to contribute to the mission of the organization. The draft report is shared with the appropriate representatives of the client's organization. Report findings and recommendations sometimes have personnel implications. For example, a work group's performance problems may be more relat-

## The POE Process: Major Steps to Be Taken

**1 Entry and Initial Data Collection**

*Documenting history of the project*
*Gaining support of multiple levels throughout organization*

**2 Designing the Research**

*Responding to research goals*
*Developing strategies*
*Sampling*
*Choosing and developing research methods*
*Pre-testing*
*Refining POE budget*

**3 Collecting Data**

*Establishing and pre-testing data collection procedures*
*Evaluating adequacy of data collection methods*
*Obtaining informed consent and considering ethical issues*

**4 Analyzing Data**

*Selecting the appropriate tests*
*Understanding the results*
*Visualizing the data*
*Maintaining contact with client organization*

**5 Presenting Information**

*Targeting the audience*
*Illustrating the major findings*
*Using multiple modes of presentations*

Adapted from Craig Zimring, "Evaluation of Designed Environments: Methods for Post-Occupancy Review" in Robert B. Bechtel, Robert W. Marans, and William Michelson, *Methods in Environmental and Behavioral Research* (1987)

ed to the manager's style than to space configuration. For this reason, it is best that no promises be made in advance regarding widespread circulation of the report.

Based on the client's comments, the postoccupancy evaluation report is revised and clarified for final delivery. A good report has clear recommendations or statements.

***Follow-up.*** The final step is to follow up to learn the outcome of the recommendations.

### For More Information

The book *Post-Occupancy Evaluation* (1990), by Wolfgang F. E. Preiser, Harvey Z. Rabinowitz, and Edward T. White, remains one of the most comprehensive treatments of the subject.

Chapter 20 of *Time-Saver Standards for Architectural Design Data, 7th Edition* (1997), provides an excellent overview and discussion of building performance evaluation.

part 5

# RESOURCES

# Appendix A: SOURCES

## AIA AND RELATED ORGANIZATIONS

**The American Institute of Architects**
1735 New York Avenue, N.W.
Washington, DC 20006-5292
(202) 626-7300

**AIA Advantage Programs**
(202) 626-7438

**AIA Publications and Information**
(800) 365-ARCH

Books, professional development publications, and AIA Documents, as well as books, gifts, posters, and videos sold through the AIA Bookstore, can be ordered with a credit card 24 hours a day, 7 days a week, by calling (800) 365-ARCH (2724).

Information about architects, architecture, and professional practice can be obtained from the AIA Library by calling (202) 626-7492.

**AIA Trust** (insurance information)
(800) 552-1093

**American Architectural Foundation**
(202) 626-7318

**Association Members Retirement Program**
(800) 532-1125

**Electronic Documents** (AIA Contract Documents: Electronic Format)
(800) 246-5030

**MasterSpec and SpecSystems**
(800) 424-5080

**AIA/ACSA Council on Architectural Research**
c/o Association of Collegiate Schools of Architecture
1735 New York Avenue, N.W.
Washington, DC 20006
(202) 785-2324

**The American Architectural Foundation (AAF)**
1735 New York Avenue, N.W.
Washington, DC 20006
(202) 626-7318

**Council of Architecture Component Executives (CACE)**
1735 New York Avenue, N.W.
Washington, DC 20006
(202) 626-7377

**Society of Architectural Administrators (SAA)**
1735 New York Avenue, N.W.
Washington, DC 20006
(202) 626-7300

For the names of AIA state and regional components, call the AIA at
(202) 626-7351

## COLLATERAL ORGANIZATIONS

**The American Institute of Architecture Students (AIAS)**
1735 New York Avenue, N.W.
Washington, DC 20006
(202) 626-7472
(202) 626-7414 fax
www.aiasnatl.org

**Association of Collegiate Schools of Architecture (ACSA)**
1735 New York Avenue, N.W.
Washington, DC 20006
(202) 785-2324
(202) 628-0448 fax
www.acsa-arch.org

**National Architectural Accrediting Board (NAAB)**
1735 New York Avenue, N.W.
Washington, DC 20006
(202) 783-2007
(202) 783-2822 fax
www.naab.org

**National Council of Architectural Registration Boards (NCARB)**
1801 K Street, N.W., Suite 1100
Washington, DC 20006
(202) 783-6500
(202) 783-0290 fax
www.ncarb.org

## STATE REGISTRATION BOARDS

**Alabama Board for Registration of Architects**
770 Washington Avenue, Suite150
Montgomery, AL 36104
(334) 242-4179
(334) 242-4531 fax
www.alarchbd.state.al.us

**Board of Registration for Architects, Engineers, and Land Surveyors**
P.O. Box 110806
Juneau, AK 99811-0806
(907) 465-1676
(907) 465-2974 fax
www.dced.state.ak.us/

**Arizona Board of Technical Registration of Architects**
1990 West Camelback Road, Suite 406
Phoenix, AZ 85015-3465
(602) 255-4053 ext. 210
(602) 255-4051 fax
www.btr.state.az.us

**Arkansas State Board of Architects**
101 East Capitol Street, Suite 208
Little Rock, AR 72201
(501) 682-3171
(501) 682-3172 fax
www.state.ar.us/

**California Architects Board**
400 R Street, Suite 4000
Sacramento, CA 95814
(916) 445-3394
(916) 445-8524 fax
www.cab.ca.gov/

**Colorado Board of Examiners of Architects**
1560 Broadway, Suite 1340
Denver, CO 80202
(303) 894-7801
(303) 894-7802 fax
www.dora.state.co.us/Architects/

**Department of Consumer Protection Occupational and Professional Licensing Division**
Architectural Licensing Board
165 Capitol Avenue
Hartford, CT 06106
(860) 713-6145
(860) 713-7239 fax
www.state.ct.us/dcp/

**Delaware Board of Architects**
861 Silver Lake Boulevard, Suite 203
Dover, DE 19904
(302) 739-4522
(302) 739-2711 fax

**D.C. Department of Consumer and Regulatory Affairs**
941 North Capitol Street, N.E.,
Room 7200
Washington, DC 20002
(202) 442-4461
(202) 442-4528 fax

**Florida Board of Architecture and Interior Design**
1940 North Monroe Street, NW Center
Tallahassee, FL 32399-0751
(850) 488-6685
(850) 922-2918 fax
www4.myflorida.com/dbpr/myflorida/business/learn/bureaus/arch/arc_index.html

**Georgia State Board of Architects**
237 Coliseum Drive
Macon, GA 31217
(912) 207-1400
(912) 207-1410 fax
www.sos.state.ga.us/ebd-architects

**Board of Registration for Engineers, Architects and Land Surveyors**
Government of Guam
718 N. Marine Drive, Unit D, Suite 308
Upper Tumon, GU 96911
(671) 646-3138
(671) 649-9533 fax

**Board of Professional Engineers, Architects, Surveyors and Landscape Architects**
P.O. Box 3469
Honolulu, HI 96801
(808) 586-2702
(808) 586-2874 fax

**Bureau of Occupational Licenses**
Owyhee Plaza
1109 Main Street, Suite 220
Boise, ID 83702
(208) 334-3233
(208) 334-3945 fax
www2.state.id.us/ibol/arc.htm

**Illinois Department of Professional Regulation**
320 W. Washington Street, 3rd Floor
Springfield, IL 62786
(217) 785-0877
(217) 782-7645 fax
www.state.il.us/dpr

**Indiana Professional Licensing Agency**
Indiana Government Center South
Room E034, 302 West Washington Street
Indianapolis, IN 46204
(317) 233-6223
(317) 232-2312 fax
http://www.state.in.us/pla/architect

**Iowa Architectural Examining Board**
1918 S.E. Hulsizer Road
Ankeny, IA 50021
(515) 281-4126
(515) 281-7411 fax
www.state.ia.us/iarch

**Kansas State Board of Technical Professions**
900 South West Jackson Street, Suite 507
Topeka, KS 66612-1257
(785) 296-3053
www.ink.org/public/

**State Board of Examiners and Registration of Architects**
841 Corporate Drive, Suite 200
Lexington, KY 40503
(606) 246-2069
(606) 246-2431 fax
www.kybera.com

**Louisiana State Board of Architectural Examiners**
8017 Jefferson Highway, Suite B2
Baton Rouge, LA 70809
(225) 925-4802
(225) 925-4804 fax
www.lastbdarchs.com

**Board of Architects, Landscape Architects, and InteriorDesigners**
Office of Licensing and Registration
Maine Department of Professional and Financial Regulation
35 State House Station
Augusta, ME 04333
(207) 624-8522
(207) 624-8637 fax
www.state.me.us/pfr/led/architect/

**Maryland Board of Architects**
Department of Labor, Licensing and Regulation
500 North Calvert Street, Room 308
Baltimore, MD 21202-3651
(410) 333-6322
(410) 333-6314 fax
www.dllr.state.md.us/

**Massachusetts Board of Registration of Architects**
239 Causeway Street, Suite 400
Boston, MA 02114
(617) 727-3072
(617) 727-1627 fax
www.state.ma.us/reg/boards/ar

**Michigan Board of Architects**
P.O. Box 30018
Lansing, MI 48909
(517) 241-9253
(517) 241-9280 fax
www.cis.state.mi.us/bcs/arch

**Board of Architecture, Engineering, Land Surveying**
85 East 7th Place, Suite 160
St. Paul, MN 55101
(651) 296-2388
(651) 297-5310 fax
www.state.mn.us/ebranch/aelsla

**Mississippi State Board of Architecture**
239 North Lamar Street, Suite 502
Jackson, MS 39201-1311
(601) 359-6020
(888) 272-2627
(601) 359-6011 fax
www.archbd.state.ms.us

**Board for Architects, Professional Engineers and Land Surveyors**
P.O. Box 184
Jefferson City, MO 65102
(573) 751-0047
(573) 751-8046 fax
www.ecodev.state.mo.us/pr/moapels

**Montana Board of Architects**
Arcade Building, Lower Level
P.O. Box 200513
Helena, MT 59620-0513
(406) 841-2390
(406) 841-2305 fax
www.com.state.mt.us/license/pol/index.htm

**Board of Professional Licensing**
P.O. Box 502078

**Saipan, MP 96950**
(670) 234-5897
(670) 234-6040 fax

**Nebraska Board of Examiners for Engineers and Architects**
P.O. Box 95165
Lincoln, NE 68509-5165
(402) 471-2021
(402) 471-0787 fax
www.nol.org/home/

**State Board of Architecture Interior Design and Residential Design**
2080 E. Flamingo Road, #225
Las Vegas, NV 89119
(702) 486-7300
(702) 486-7304 fax
www.state.nv.us/nsbaidrd

**Board of Engineers, Architects, Land Surveyors, Natural Scientists and Forestors**
57 Regional Drive
Concord, NH 03301-8518
(603) 271-2219
(603) 271-6990 fax
www.state.nh.us/jtboard/home.ht

**NJ Board of Architects and Certified Landscape Architects**
P.O. Box 45001
Newark, NJ 07101
(973) 504-6385
(973) 504-6458 fax
www.state.nj.us/lps/ca/arch/arch.htm

**Board of Examiners for Architects**
P.O. Box 509
Santa Fe, NM 87504
(505) 827-6375
(505) 827-6373 fax
www.nmbea.org

**New York State Board for Architecture**
State Education Department
Cultural Education Center, Room 3019
Albany, NY 12230
(518) 474-3930
(518) 474-6375 fax
www.op.nysed.gov/arch.htm

**North Carolina Board of Architecture**
127 West Hargett Street
Raleigh, NC 27601
(919) 733-9544
(919) 733-1272 fax
www.ncbarch.org

**North Dakota State Board of Architecture**
419 E. Brandon Drive
Bismarck, ND 58501-0410
(701) 223-3184
(701) 223-8154 fax
http://www.governor.state.nd.us/boards/boards_query.asp?Board_ID=10

**State of Ohio Board of Examiners of Architects**
77 S. High Street, 16th Floor
Columbus, OH 43266-0303
(614) 466-2316
(614) 644-9048 fax
www.state.oh.us/arc

**Board of Governors of Licensed Architects and Landscape Architects**
11212 N. May Avenue, Suite 110
Oklahoma City, OK 73120-6335
(405) 751-6512
(405) 755-6391 fax

**Oregon Board of Architect Examiners**
750 Front Street, N.E., Suite 260
Salem, OR 97310
(503) 378-4270
(503) 378-6091 fax
www.architect-board.state.or.us

**Pennsylvania State Architects Licensure Board**
P.O. Box 2649
124 Pine Street, PA 17101
Harrisburg, PA 17105-2649
(717) 783-3397
(717) 705-5540 fax
www.dos.state.pa.us/bpoa/arcbd/main-page.htm

**Board of Engineers, Architects, Landscape Architects and LandGovernment of Puerto Rico, Department of State**
P.O. Box 9023271
San Juan, PR 00902-3271
(787) 722-4816
(787) 722-4818 fax
vargasnunezj@microjuris.com

**Boards for Design Professionals**
One Capitol Hill, 3rd Floor
Providence, RI 02908
(401) 222-2565
(401) 331-8691 fax

**State Board of Architectural Examiners**
P.O. Box 11419
(110 Centerview Drive, 29210)
Columbia, SC 29211-1419
(803) 896-4408
(803) 896-4410 fax
www.llr.state.sc.us/bae1.htm

**South Dakota State Board of Technical Professions**
2040 W. Main Street, Suite 304
Rapid City, SD 57702-2447
(605) 394-2510
(605) 394-2509 fax
www.state.sd.us/dcr/engineer

**Tennessee State Board of Architectural and Engineering Examiners**
500 James Robertson Parkway
Nashville, TN 37243-1142
(615) 741-3221
(615) 532-9410 fax
www.state.tn.us/commerce/ae.html

**Texas Board of Architectural Examiners**
P.O. Box 12337
Austin, TX 78711-2337
(512) 305-9000
(512) 305-8900 fax
www.tbae.state.tx.us

**Utah Department of Commerce**
Division of Occupational and
Professional Licensing
P.O. Box 146741
Salt Lake City, UT 84114-6741
(801) 530-6551
(801) 530-6511 fax
www.commerce.state.ut.us/dopl/dopl1.htm

**Vermont State Board of Architects**
26 Terrace Street, Drawer 09
Montpelier, VT 05609-1106
(802) 828-2373
(802) 828-2465 fax
http://170.222.200.71/architects

**Department of Licensing and Consumer Affairs**
Golden Rock Shopping Center
Christiansted, St. Croix, VI 00820
(340) 773-2226
(340) 778-8250 fax

**Board for Architects, Professional Engineers, Land Surveyors, Certified Interior Designers and Landscape Architects**
Department of Professional and
Occupational Regulation
3600 West Broad Street
Richmond, VA 23230-4917
(804) 367-8511
(804) 367-2475 fax
www.state.va.us/dpor

**Washington State Board of Registration for Architects**
P.O. Box 9045
Olympia, WA 98507-9045
(360) 664-1388
(360) 664-2551 fax
www.wa.gov/dol/bpd/arcfront.htm

**Lexa C. Lewis**
West Virginia Board of Architects
P.O. Box 589
Huntington, WV 25710-0589
(304) 528-5825
(304) 528-5826 fax
www.wvbrdarch.org

**Alfred J. Hall Jr.**
Wisconsin Bureau of Business and
Design Professions
P.O. Box 8935
1400 East Washington Avenue,
Room 1424
Madison, WI 53708-8935
(608) 266-5511
(608) 267-3816 fax
www.state.wi.us/agencies/drl

**Veronica Skoranski**
Wyoming State Board of Architects and
Landscape Architects
2020 Carey Avenue, Suite 201
Cheyenne, WY 82002
(307) 777-7788
(307) 777-3508 fax
soswy.state.wy.us/director/boards/arch.htm

## OTHER PROFESSIONAL ORGANIZATIONS

**Accreditation Board for Engineering and Technology (ABET)**
111 Market Place, Suite 1050
Baltimore, MD 21202-4012
(410) 347-7700
(410) 625-2238 fax
www.abet.org

**Acoustical Society of America (ASA)**
2 Huntington Quadrangle, Suite 1N01
Melville, NY 11747-4502
(516) 576-2360
(516) 576-2377 fax
asa.aip.org

**Alliance to Save Energy (ASE)**
1200 18th Street, N.W., Suite 900
Washington, DC 20036-1401
(202) 857-0666
(202) 331-9588 fax

**American Arbitration Association (AAA)**
335 Madison Avenue
New York, NY 10017-4605
(212) 716-5800
(800) 778-7879
(212) 716-5905 fax
www.adr.org

**American Association of Engineering Societies (AAES)**
1111 19th Street, N.W., Suite 403
Washington, DC 20036
(202) 296-2237
(202) 296-1151 fax
www.aaes.org

**American Association of Homes and Services for the Aging (AAHSA)**
2519 Connecticut Avenue, N.W.
Washington, DC 20008-1520
(202) 783-2242
(202) 783-2255 fax
www.aahsa.org

**American Association of Housing Educators (AAHE)**
Illinois State University
Department of Family and
Consumer Sciences
Normal, IL 61790-5060
(309) 438-5802
(309) 438-6559 fax
www.cast.ilstu.edu/aahe/

**American Bar Association (ABA)**
750 North Lake Shore Drive
Chicago, IL 60611
(312) 988-5000
(800) 285-2221
(312) 988-5528 fax
www.abanet.org

**American Congress on Surveying and Mapping (ACSM)**
5410 Grosvenor Lane, Suite100
Bethesda, MD 20814-2144
(301) 493-0200
(301) 493-8245 fax
www.survmap.com

**American Consulting Engineers Council (ACEC)**
1015 15th Street, N.W., Suite 802
Washington, DC 20005
(202) 347-7474
(202) 898-0068 fax
www.acec.org

**American Council for Construction Education (ACCE)**
1300 Hudson Lane, Suite 3
Monroe, LA 71201-6054
(318) 323-2816
(318) 323-2413 fax
www.acce-hq.org/

**American Council for an Energy Efficient Economy (ACEEE)**
1001 Connecticut Avenue N.W., Suite 801
Washington, DC 20036
(202) 429-8873
(202) 429-2248 fax
www.aceee.org

**American Hospital Association (AHA)**
1 North Franklin
Chicago, IL 60606
(312) 422-3000
(312) 422-4796 fax
www.aha.org

**American Institute for Conservation of Historic and Artistic Works (AIC)**
1717 K Street, N.W., Suite 200
Washington, DC 20006
(202) 452-9545
(202) 452-9328 fax
aic.stanford.edu

**American National Standards Institute (ANSI)**
11 West 42nd Street, 13th Floor
New York, NY 10036
(212) 642-4900
(212) 398-0023 fax
Telex: 424296 ANSI UI
www.ansi.org

**American Planning Association (APA)**
122 S. Michigan Avenue, Suite 1600
Chicago, IL 60603-6107
(312) 431-9100
(312) 431-9985 fax
www.planning.org

**American Society of Civil Engineers (ASCE)**
1801 Alexander Bell Drive
Reston, VA 20191-4400
(703) 295-6300
(800) 548-2723
(703) 295-6222 fax
www.asce.org

**American Planning Association of Chicago**
122 South Michigan Avenue, Suite 1600
Chicago, IL 60603
(312) 431-9100
(312) 431-9985 fax
www.planning.org

**American Society for Engineering Education (ASEE)**
1818 N Street, N.W., Suite 600
Washington, DC 20036
(202) 331-3500
(202) 265-8504 fax
www.asee.org

**American Society of Golf Course Architects (ASGCA)**
221 North LaSalle Street
Chicago, IL 60601
(312) 372-7090
(312) 372-6160 fax
www.golfdesign.org

**American Society of Heating, Refrigerating and Air-Conditioning Engineers (ASHRAE)**
1791 Tullie Circle N.E.
Atlanta, GA 30329
(404) 636-8400
(800) 527-4723
(404) 321-5478 fax
www.ashrae.org

**American Society of Landscape Architects (ASLA)**
636 I Street, N.W.
Washington, DC 20001-3736
(202) 898-2444
(202) 898-1185 fax
www.asla.org

**American Society of Mechanical Engineers (ASME)**
3 Park Avenue
New York, NY 10016-5990
(212) 705-7722
(800) 843-2763
(212) 705-7674 fax
www.asme.org

**American Society for Quality (ASQ)**
P.O. Box 3005
Milwaukee, WI 53201-3005
(414) 272-8575
(800) 248-1946
(414) 272-1734 fax
www.asq.org

**American Society for Testing and Materials (ASTM)**
100 Barr Harbor Drive
West Conshohocken, PA 19428-2959
(610) 832-9500
(610) 832-9555 fax
www.astm.org

**American Solar Energy Society (ASES)**
2400 Central Avenue, Suite G-1
Boulder, CO 80301
(303) 443-3130
(303) 443-3212 fax
www.ases.org

**American Subcontractors Association (ASA)**
1004 Duke Street
Alexandria, VA 22314
(703) 684-3450
(703) 836-3482 fax
www.asaonline.com

**Architects/Designers/Planners for Social Responsibility (ADPSR)**
175 Fifth Avenue, Suite 2210
New York, NY 10010
(212) 941-9679
(212) 924-7893 fax
www.adpsr.org

**Architectural Research Centers Consortium (ARCC)**
c/o Walter Grondzik
School of Architecture
Florida A&M University
Tallahassee, FL 32307-4200
(850) 599-8782
(850) 599-8466 fax
gzik@polaris.net

**ASFE/Association of Engineering Firms Practicing in the Geosciences**
8811 Colesville Road, Suite G106
Silver Spring, MD 20910
(301) 565-2733
(301) 589-2017 fax
www.asfe.org

**Associated Builders and Contractors (ABC)**
1300 North 17th Street, Suite 80
Rosslyn, VA 22209
(703) 812-2000
(703) 812-8200 fax
www.abc.org

**Associated General Contractors of America (AGC)**
333 John Carlyle Street, Suite 200
Alexandria, VA 22314
(703) 548-3118
(703) 548-3119 fax
www.agc.org

**Associated Specialty Contractors (ASC)**
3 Bethesda Metro Center, Suite 1100
Bethesda, MD 20814
(301) 657-3110
(301) 215-4500 fax

**Association for Computer-Aided Design in Architecture (ACADIA)**
c/o Anton C. Harfmann
P.O. Box 210016
Cincinnati, OH 45221-0016
(513) 556-0487
www.acadia.org

**Association of Energy Engineers (AEE)**
4025 Pleasantdale Road, Suite 420
Atlanta, GA 30340
(770) 447-5083
(770) 446-3969 fax
www.aeecenter.org

**The Association of Higher Education Facilities Officers (APPA)**
1643 Prince Street
Alexandria, VA 22314-2818
(703) 684-1446
(703) 549-2772 fax
www.appa.org

**Association for Preservation Technology International (APTI)**
4513 Lincoln Avenue, Suite 213
Lisle, IL 60532-1290
(630) 968-6400
(888) 723-4242 fax
www.apti.org

**Association for Quality and Participation (AQP)**
Executive Building #200
2368 Victory Parkway
Cincinnati, OH 45206
(513) 381-1959
(800) 733-3310
(513) 381-0070 fax
www.aqp.org

**Association of University Architects (AUA)**
Facilities Building, Florida Gulf Coast University
10501 FGCU Boulevard South
Fort Myers, FL 33965-6565
(813) 590-1000
(813) 590-1010 fax

**Building Officials and Code Administrators International (BOCA)**
4051 West Flossmoor Road
Country Club Hills, IL 60478-5795
(708) 799-4981
(708) 799-4981 fax
www.bocai.org

**Building Owners and Managers Association International (BOMA)**
1201 New York Avenue, N.W., Suite 300
Washington, DC 20005
(202) 408-2662
(202) 371-0181 fax
www.boma.org

**Canadian Home Builders' Association (CHBA)**
150 Laurier Avenue West, Suite 500
Ottawa, ON, Canada K1P 5J4
(613) 230-3060
(613) 232-8214 fax
www.chba.ca

**Canadian Institute of Planners (CIP)**
Institut Canadien des Urbanistes (ICU)
116 Albert Street, Suite 801
Ottawa, ON, Canada K1P 5G3
(613) 237-2138
(613) 237-7526 fax
www.cip-icu.ca

**Canadian Society of Landscape Architecture (CSLA)**
P.O. Box 870, Station B
Ottawa, ON K1P 5P9
(604) 437-3942
csla@escape.ca

**Canadian Standards Association (CSA)**
178 Rexdale Boulevard
Toronto, ON, M9W 1R3
Canada
(416) 747-4000
(416) 747-4149 fax
Telex: 06989344
www.csa.ca

**Construction Specifications Institute (CSI)**
99 Canal Center Plaza, Suite 300
Alexandria, VA 22314
(703) 684-0300
(800) 689-2900
(703) 684-0465 fax
www.csinet.org

**Council of Educational Facility Planners, International (CEFPI)**
9180 E. Desert Cove Drive, No. 104
Scottsdale, AZ 85260-6231
(480) 391-0840
(480) 391-0940 fax
www.cefpi.com

**Council of Landscape Architectural Registration Boards (CLARB)**
12700 Fair Lakes Circle, Suite 110
Fairfax, VA 22033
(703) 818-1300
(703) 818-1309 fax
www.clarb.org

**Edison Electric Institute (EEI)**
701 Pennsylvania Aveue, N.W.
Washington, DC 20004-2696
(202) 508-5000
(202) 508-5360 fax
www.eei.org

**EPRI (Electric Power Research Institute)**
3412 Hillview Avenue
Palo Alto, CA 94304-1395
(650) 855-2000
(800) 313-3774
(650) 855-2900 fax
www.epri.com

**Energy Efficient Building Association (EEBA)**
10740 Lyndale Avenue South, Suite 10W
Bloomington, MN 55420-5614
(952) 881-1098
(952) 881-3048 fax
www.eeba.org

**Environmental Design Research Association (EDRA)**
P.O. Box 7146
Edmond, OK 73083-7146
(405) 330-4863
(405) 330-4150 fax
www.telepath.com/edra/home.html

**Foundation for Interior Design Education Research (FIDER)**
60 Monroe Center N.W., Suite 300
Grand Rapids, MI 49503-2920
(616) 458-0400
(616) 458-0460 fax
www.fider.org

**Gas Technology Institute (GTI)**
1700 South Mount Prospect Road
Des Plaines, IL 60018-1804
(773) 399-8100
(773) 399-8170 fax
www.gti.org

**Heritage Canada Foundation (HCF)**
Observatory Crescent
Box 1358, StationB
Ottawa, ON, Canada K1P 5R4
(613) 237-1066
(613) 237-5987 fax
www.heritagecanada.org

**Illuminating Engineering Society of North America (IESNA)**
120 Wall Street, 17th Floor
New York, NY 10005-4001
(212) 248-5000
(212) 248-5017 fax
www.iesna.org

**Industrial Designers Society of America (IDSA)**
1142 East Walker Road, Suite E
Great Falls, VA 22066
(703) 759-0100
(703) 759-7679 fax
www.idsa.org

**International Development Research Council (IDRC)**
35 Technology Park, Suite 150
Norcross, GA 30092-2901
(770) 446-8955
(770) 263-8825 fax
Telex: 804468 ATL
www.idrc.org

**Institute of Electrical and Electronics Engineers (IEEE)**
3 Park Avenue, 17th Floor
New York, NY 10016-5997
(212) 419-7900
(212) 752-4929 fax
www.ieee.org

**Interior Design Educators Council (IDEC)**
9202 North Meridian Street, Suite 200
Indianapolis, IN 46260-1810
(317) 816-6261
(317) 561-5603
www.idec.org

**International Association of Lighting Designers (IALD)**
The Merchandise Mart
200 World Trade Center, Suite 11-114A
Chicago, IL 60654
(312) 527-3677
(312) 527-3680 fax
www.iald.org

**International Conference of Building Officials (ICBO)**
5360 Workman Mill Road
Whittier, CA 90601-2298
(562) 699-0541
(800) 284-4406
(562) 695-4694 fax
www.icbo.org

**International Council for Building Research, Studies, and Documentation (CIB)**
Conseil International du Batiment pour la Recherche, l'Etude et la Documentation (CIB)
Kruisplein 25-G
Postbus 1837
NL-3000 BV Rotterdam, Netherlands
31 10 4110240
31 10 4334372 fax
www.cibworld.nl

**International Facility Management Association (IFMA)**
c/o Diana Steinman
1 E. Greenway Plaza, Suite 1100
Houston, TX 77046-0194
(713) 623-4362
(800) 359-4362
(713) 623-6124 fax
www.ifma.org

**International Institute for Energy Conservation (IIEC)**
750 First Street, N.E., Suite 940
Washington, DC 20002
(202) 842-3388
(202) 842-1565 fax

**International Union of Architects (UIA)**
Union Internationale des Architects
51, rue Raynouard
F-75016 Paris, France
33 1 45243688
33 1 45240278 fax
www.uia-architectes.org

**Junior Engineering Technical Society (JETS)**
1420 King Street, Suite 405
Alexandria, VA 22314-2794
(703) 548-5387
(703) 548-0769 fax
www.jets.org

**Lighting Research Institute (LRI)**
P.O. Box 1550
Hendersonville, NC 28793-1550
(704) 692-7388
(704) 692-6820 fax

**National Association of Home Builders of the United States (NAHB)**
1201 15th Street, N.W.
Washington, DC 20005
(202) 822-0200
(202) 822-0559 fax
Telex(s): 89-2600
www.nahb.com

**National Association of Housing and Redevelopment Officials (NAHRO)**
630 I Street, N.W.
Washington, DC 20001
(202) 289-3500
(202) 289-8181 fax
www.nahro.org

**National Association of Surety Bond Producers (NASBP)**
5225 Wisconsin Avenue, N.W., Suite 600
Washington, DC 20015-2015
(202) 686-3700
(202) 686-3656 fax
www.nasbp.org

**National Conference of State Historic Preservation Officers (NCSHPO)**
Hall of States
444 North Capitol Street, N.W., Suite 342
Washington, DC 20001
(202) 624-5465
(202) 624-5419 fax

**National Conference of States on Building Codes and Standards (NCS-BCS)**
505 Huntmar Park Drive, Suite 210
Herndon, VA 20170
(703) 437-0100
(800) 362- 2633
(703) 481-3596 fax
www.ncsbcs.org

**National Council of Acoustical Consultants (NCAC)**
66 Morris Avenue, Suite 1A
Springfield, NJ 07081-1409
(973) 564-5859
(973) 564-7480 fax
www.ncac.com

**National Council for Interior Design Qualification (NCIDQ)**
1200 18th Street N.W., No. 1001
Washington, DC 20036-2506
(202) 721-0220
www.ncidq.org

**National Fire Protection Association (NFPA)**
1 Batterymarch Park
Quincy, MA 02269-9101
(617) 770-3000
(617) 770-0700 fax
www.nfpa.org

**National Institute of Building Sciences (NIBS)**
1090 Vermont Avenue, N.W., Suite 700
Washington, DC 20005-4905
(202) 289-7800
(202) 289-1092 fax
www.nibs.org

**National Organization of Minority Architects (NOMA)**
5530 Wisconsin Avenue, Suite 1210
Chevy Chase, MD 20815-4301
(301) 941-1065
www.noma.net

**National Research Council of Canada**
Ottawa, ON, Canada K1A 0R6
(613) 990-6091
(613) 952-9907 fax
www.nrc.ca

**National Society of Professional Engineers (NSPE)**
1420 King Street
Alexandria, VA 22314
(703) 684-2800
(888) 285-6773
(703) 836-4875 fax
www.nspe.org

**Sustainable Buildings Industry Council**
1331 H Street, N.W., Suite 1000
Washington, DC 20005
(202) 628-7400
(202) 393-5043 fax
www.sbicouncil.org

**Professional Photographers of America (PP of A)**
229 Peachtree Street N.E., Suite 2200
Atlanta, GA 30303
(404) 876-6277
(800) 786-6277
(404) 614-6400 fax
www.ppa.com

**Professional Services Management Association (PSMA)**
4101 Lake Boone Trail, Suite 201
Raleigh, NC 27607
(919) 571-2562
(919) 787-4916 fax
www.psma.org

**Project Management Institute (PMI)**
4 Campus Boulevard
Newtown Square, PA 19073-3299
(610) 356-4600
(610) 356-4647 fax
www.pmi.org

**Society of Architectural Historians (SAH)**
1365 North Astor Street
Chicago, IL 60610-2144
(312) 573-1365
(312) 573-1141 fax
www.sah.org

**Society for College and University Planning (SCUP)**
311 Maynard Street
Ann Arbor, MI 48104-2211
(734) 998-7832
(734) 998-6532 fax
www.scup.org

**Society for Environmental Graphic Design (SEGD)**
401 F Street, N.W., Suite 333
Washington, DC 20001-2728
(202) 638-5555
(202) 638-0891 fax
www.segd.org

**Society of Fire Protection Engineers (SFPE)**
7315 Wisconsin Avenue, Suite 1225W
Bethesda, MD 20814-3202
(301) 718-2910
(301) 718-2242 fax
www.sfpe.org

**Society for Marketing Professional Services (SMPS)**
99 Canal Center Plaza, Suite 250
Alexandria, VA 22314
(703) 549-6117
(800) 292-7677
(703) 549-2498 fax
www.smps.org

**Surety Association of America (SAA)**
1101 Connecticut Avenue, N.W., Suite 800
Washington, DC 20036
(202) 463-0600
(202) 463-0606 fax
www.surety.org

**Underwriters Laboratories (UL)**
333 Pfingsten Road
Northbrook, IL 60062
(847) 272-8800
(847) 272-8129 fax
Telex: 6502543343
www.ul.com

**United States Committee of the International Council on Monuments and Sites (US/ICOMOS)**
401 F Street, N.W., Room 331
Washington, DC 20001
(202) 842-1866
(202) 842-1861 fax
www.icomos.org/usicomos/

**U.S. Metric Association (USMA)**
10245 Andasol Avenue
Northridge, CA 91325-1504
(818) 368-7443
lamar.colostate.edu/~hillger/

**Urban Land Institute (ULI)**
1025 Thomas Jefferson Street, N.W.,
Suite 500W
Washington, DC 20007-5201
(202) 624-7000
(800) 321-5011
(202) 624-7140 fax
www.uli.org

**Volunteers in Technical Assistance (VITA)**
1600 Wilson Boulevard, Suite 710
Arlington, VA 22209
(703) 276-1800
(703) 243-1865 fax
Telex: 440192 VITAUI
www.vita.org

## FEDERAL GOVERNMENT

**Advisory Council on Historic Preservation**
1100 Pennsylvania Avenue, N.W.,
Suite 809
Washington, DC 20004
(202) 606-8503
achp@.achp.gov

**Americans with Disabilities Act Information Office**
U.S. Department of Justice
Civil Rights Division
P.O. Box 66738
Washington, DC 20035
(202) 514-0301
www.usdoj.gov/crt/ada/adahoml.htm

**Architectural and Transportation Barriers Compliance Board**
1331 F Street, N.W., Suite 1000
Washington, DC 20004
(202) 272-5434
www.access-board.gov

**The Board on Infrastructure and the Constructed Environment**
Harris Building, Room 274
2101 Constitution Avenue, N.W.
Washington, DC 20418
(202) 334-3376
(202) 334-3370 fax
www.nas.edu

**Department of Energy (DOE)**
Forrestal Building
1000 Independence Avenue, S.W..
Washington, DC 20585
(202) 586-5000
www.energy.gov

**Department of Energy Conservation and Renewable Energy Inquiry and Referral Service**
P.O. Box 3048
Marrisfield, VA 22116
1-(800) 363-3732

**Department of Energy Office of Scientific and Technical Information**
Box 62
Oak Ridge, TN 37831
(865) 576-1188
www.osti.gov

**Department of Health and Human Services (HHS)**
Real Property Branch
Parklawn Building, Room 5B17
5600 Fishers Lane
Rockville, MD 20857
(301) 443-2265
www.os.dhhs.gov

**Department of Housing and Urban Development (HUD)**
451 7th Street, S.W.
Washington, DC 20410
(202) 708-1112
www.hud.gov

**Environmental Protection Agency (EPA)**
401 M Street, S.W.
Washington, DC 20460
(202) 260-7751 Public Information Center
(202) 233-9030 Indoor Air Division
(202) 233-9370 Radon Division
(202) 554-1404 Toxic Materials Hotline
www.epa.gov

**Federal Bureau of Prisons**
Facilities Development Division
320 First Street, N.W., Room 5008
Washington, DC 20534
(202) 514-6652
www.bop.gov

**Federal Emergency Management Agency (FEMA)**
500 C Street, S.W.
Washington, DC 20472
(202) 646-4600
www.fema.gov

**General Services Administration (GSA)**
18th and F Streets, N.W.
Washington, DC 20405
(202) 708-5334
www.gsa.gov

**Lawrence Berkeley Laboratory (LBL)**
1 Cyclotron Road
Berkeley, CA 94720
(510) 486-5388 Lighting Systems Group
(510) 486-5605 Windows and Daylighting Group
(510) 486-6940 fax
www.lbl.gov

**National Center for Appropriate Technology**
U.S. Department of Energy
3040 Continental Drive
Butte, MT 59702
(800)-275-6228
(496)-494-2905
www.ncat.org

**National Endowment for the Arts (NEA)**
1100 Pennsylvania Avenue, N.W.
Room 624
Washington, DC 20506
(202) 682-5400
www.arts.endow.gov

**National Institute of Corrections**
U.S. Department of Justice
1860 Industrial Circle, Suite A
Longmont, CO 80501
(303) 682-0213
www.nicic.org

**National Institute of Standards and Technology (NIST)**
100 Bureau Drive
Gaithersburg, MD 20899
(301) 975-6478
(301) 976-1630 fax
www.nist.gov

**National Renewable Energy Laboratory (NREL)**
1617 Cole Boulevard
Golden, CO 80401
(303) 275-3000
(303) 231-1199 fax
www.nrel.gov

**National Technical Information Service (NTIS)**
5285 Port Royal Road
Springfield, VA 22161
(703) 605-6000
www.ntis.gov

**Occupational Safety and Health Administration (OSHA)**
200 Constitution Avenue, N.W., Suite 440
Washington, DC 20210
(202) 693-2000
www.osha.gov

**Veterans Administration Architectural Service (VA)**
Construction Management Office
Department of Veterans Affairs
811 Vermont Avenue, N.W.
Washington, DC 20020
(202) 233-2688

## ARCHITECTURE SCHOOLS
(with NAAB-accredited professional degree programs)

**Andrews University**
Division of Architecture
Berrien Springs, MI 49104-0450
(616) 471-6003
(616) 471-6261 fax
www.andrews.edu/ARCH

**University of Arizona**
College of Architecture, Planning and Landscape
Tucson, AZ 85721
(520) 621-6754
(520) 621-8700 fax
www.architecture.arizona.edu

**Arizona State University**
School of Architecture
Tempe, AZ 85287-1605
(602) 965-3536
www.asu.edu/caed/architecture

**University of Arkansas**
School of Architecture
120 Vol Walker Hall
Fayetteville, AR 72701
(501) 575-4945
(501) 575-7099 fax
comp.uark.edu/~archhome/school.html

**Auburn University**
College of Architecture, Design and Construction
202 Dudley Commons
Auburn, AL 36849-5313
(334) 844-4524
(334) 844-2735 fax
www.auburn.edu/academic/architecture/arch

**Ball State University**
College of Architecture and Planning
Muncie, IN 47306-0305
(765) 285-5861
(765) 285-3726 fax
www.bsu.edu/cap

**Boston Architectural Center**
320 Newbury Street
Boston, MA 02115
(617) 262-5000, ext. 221
(617) 536-5829 fax
www.the-bac.edu

**University of California at Berkeley**
Department of Architecture and Urban Design
232 Wurster Hall
Berkeley, CA 94720
(510) 642-4942
(510) 643-5607 fax
www.ced.berkeley.edu:80/arch

**University of California at Los Angeles**
Department of Architecture and Urban Design
1317 Perloff Hall
Los Angeles, CA 90095-1467
(310) 825-7857
(310) 825-8959 fax
www.aud.ucla.edu

**California College of Arts and Crafts**
School of Architectural Studies
450 Irwin Street
San Francisco, CA 94107
(415) 703-9516
(415) 703-9524 fax
www.ccac-art.edu

**California Polytechnic State University, San Luis Obispo**
College of Architecture and Environmental Design
San Luis Obispo, CA 93407
(805) 756-1316
(805) 756-1500 fax
www.calpoly.edu/~arch

**California State Polytechnic University, Pomona**
Department of Architecture
3801 West Temple Avenue
Pomona, CA 91768-4048
(909) 869-2683
(909) 869-4331 fax
www.csupomona.edu/~arc/

**Carnegie Mellon University**
School of Architecture
201 College of Fine Arts
Pittsburgh, PA 15213-3890
(412) 268-2355
(412) 268-7819 fax
www.arc.cmu.edu

**Catholic University of America**
620 Michigan Avenue, N.E.
Washington, DC 20064
(202) 319-5188
(202) 319-5728 fax
www.acad.cua.edu/apu

**University of Cincinnati**
School of Architecture and Interior Design
Cincinnati, OH 45221-0016
(513) 556-6426
(513) 556-1230 fax
www.daap.uc.edu

**City College of the City University of New York**
School of Architecture and Environmental Studies
Shepard Hall 103
138th Street at Convent Avenue
New York, NY 10031
(212) 650-6889
(212) 650-5388 fax
www.ccny.cuny.edu

**Clemson University**
College of Architecture, Arts and Humanities
Clemson, SC 29634-0503
(864) 656-3938
(864) 656-1810 fax
hubcap.clemson.edu/aah

**University of Colorado at Denver/Boulder**
College of Architecture and Planning
Campus Box 126
P.O. Box 173364
Denver, CO 80217-3364
(303) 556-3382
(303) 556-3687 fax
www.cudenver.edu/public/AandP

**Columbia University**
Graduate School of Architecture, Planning and Preservation
New York, NY 10027
(212) 854-3510
(212) 864-0410 fax
www.arch.columbia.edu/

**Cooper Union**
The Irwin S. Chanin School of Architecture
Cooper Square
New York, NY 10003-7183
(212) 353-4220
(212) 353-4009 fax
www.cooper.edu/architecture/arch.text.html

**Cornell University**
Department of Architecture
143 East Sibley
Ithaca, NY 14853-6701
(607) 255-5236
(607) 255-0291 fax
www.aap.cornell.edu/index.htm

**University of Detroit, Mercy**
School of Architecture
P.O. Box 19900
Detroit, MI 48219-0900
(313) 993-1532
(313) 993-1512 fax
www.udmercy.edu

**Drexel University**
Department of Architecture
Philadelphia, PA 19104
(215) 895-2409
(215) 895-4921 fax
www.coda.drexel.edu/departments/architecture

**Drury College**
Hammons School of Architecture
Springfield, MI 65802
(417) 873-7288
(417) 873-7446 fax
www.drury.edu

**University of Florida**
Department of Architecture
P.O. Box 115702
Gainesville, FL 32611-5702
(352) 392-0205
(352) 392-4606 fax
www.arch.ufl.edu/

**Florida A&M University**
School of Architecture
1936 S. Martin Luther King Jr. Boulevard
Tallahassee, FL 32307
(850) 599-3244
(850) 599-3436 fax
http://168.223.36.3/acad/colleges/soa/

**Florida Atlantic University**
School of Architecture
220 South East Second Avenue, Room 616M
Fort Lauderdale, FL 33301
(954) 762-5654
(954) 762-5673 fax
www.fau.edu/divdept/cupa/

**Florida International University**
School of Architecture
University Park
Miami, FL 33199
(305) 348-3181
(305) 348-2650 fax
www.fiu.edu/index.htm

**Frank Lloyd Wright School of Architecture**
Taliesin West
Scottsdale, AZ 85261-4430
(602) 860-2700
(602) 391-4009 fax
www.taliesin.edu

**Georgia Institute of Technology**
College of Architecture
Atlanta, GA 30332-0155
(404) 894-4053
(404) 894-0572 fax
www.arch.gatech.edu

**Hampton University**
Department of Architecture
Hampton, VA 23668
(757) 727-5440
(757) 728-6680 fax
www.hamptonu.edu

**Harvard University**
Department of Architecture
48 Quincy Street
Cambridge, MA 02138
(617) 495-2591
(617) 495-8916 fax
www.gsd.harvard.edu

**University of Hawaii at Manoa**
School of Architecture
2410 Campus Road
Honolulu, HI 96822
(808) 956-7225
(808) 956-7778 fax
web1.arch.hawaii.edu

**University of Houston**
Gerald D. Hines College of Architecture
Houston, TX 77204-4431
(713) 743-2400
(713) 743-2358 fax
www.arch.uh.edu

**Howard University**
School of Architecture and Design
2366 6th Street, N.W.
Washington, DC 20059
(202) 806-7420
(202) 462-2158 fax
www.imappl.org/CEACS/Departments/Architecture/index.html

**University of Idaho**
Department of Architecture
Moscow, ID 83844-2451
(208) 885-6781
(208) 885-9428 fax
www.aa.uidaho.edu/arch

**University of Illinois at Chicago**
School of Architecture
845 West Harrison Street, M/C 030
Chicago, IL 60607-7024
(312) 996-3335
(312) 413-4488 fax
www.uic.edu:80/depts/arch/homepage.html

**University of Illinois at Urbana-Champaign**
School of Architecture
Temple Hoyne Buell Hall
611 Taft Drive
Champaign, IL 61820-6921
(217) 333-1330
(217) 244-2900 fax
www.arch.uiuc.edu

**Illinois Institute of Technology**
College of Architecture
S. R. Crown Hall
3360 South State Street
Chicago, IL 60616
(312) 567-3230
(312) 567-5820 fax
www.iit.edu/~arch

**Iowa State University**
Department of Architecture
156 College of Design
Ames, IA 50011-3093
(515) 294-4717
(515) 294-1440 fax
www.arch.iastate.edu

**University of Kansas**
School of Architecture and Urban Design
206 Marvin Hall
Lawrence, KS 66045
(785) 864-4281
(785) 864-5393 fax
www.arce.ukans.edu/scharch/scharch.htm

**Kansas State University**
College of Architecture, Planning
and Design
Manhattan, KS 66506-2901
(913) 532-5953
(913) 532-6722 fax
aalto.arch.ksu.edu

**Kent State University**
School of Architecture and
Environmental Design
200 Taylor Hall
Kent, OH 44242
(330) 672-2917
(330) 672-3809 fax
www.saed.kent.edu/SAED

**University of Kentucky**
College of Architecture
Pence Hall
Lexington, KY 40506-0041
(606) 257-7619
(606) 323-9966 fax
www.uky.edu/Architecture

**Lawrence Technological University**
College of Architecture and Design
21000 West Ten Mile Road
Southfield, MI 48075
(810) 204-2805
(810) 204-2900 fax
www.ltu.edu/architecture/

**University of Louisiana at Lafayette**
School of Architecture
Lafayette, LA 70504-3850
(318) 482-6225
(318) 482-5907 fax
arts.louisiana.edu/depts/architecture

**Louisiana State University**
College of Design
136 Atkinson Hall
Baton Rouge, LA 70803-5710
(225) 388-6885
(225) 388-2168 fax
www.cadgis.lsu.edu/design/index.html

**Louisiana Tech University**
School of Architecture
P.O. Box 3147
Ruston, LA 71272
(318) 257-2816
(318) 257-4687 fax
www.latech.edu/tech/arch/

**University of Maryland**
School of Architecture
College Park, MD 20742-1411
(301) 405-6284
(301) 314-9583 fax
www.inform.umd.edu/arch

**Massachusetts Institute of Technology**
Department of Architecture
77 Massachusetts Avenue, Room 7-337
Cambridge, MA 02139
(617) 253-7791
(617) 253-8993 fax
sap.mit.edu

**University of Miami**
School of Architecture
P.O. Box 249178
Coral Gables, FL 33124
(305) 284-5000
(305) 284-5245 fax
www.arc.miami.edu

**Miami University**
Department of Architecture
101 Alumni Hall
Oxford, OH 45056
(513) 529-7210
(513) 529-7009 fax
www.muohio.edu

**University of Michigan**
College of Architecture and
Urban Planning
Ann Arbor, MI 48109-2069
(734) 764-1300
(734) 763-2322 fax
www.caup.umich.edu

**University of Minnesota**
Department of Architecture
89 Church Street, SE
Minneapolis, MN 55455
(612) 624-7866
(612) 624-5743 fax
www.gumby.arch.umn.edu

**Mississippi State University**
School of Architecture
P.O. Drawer AQ
Mississippi State, MS 39762
(601) 325-2202
(601) 325-8872 fax
www.sarc.msstate.edu

**Montana State University**
School of Architecture
Bozeman, MT 59717
(406) 994-4256
(406) 994-4257 fax
www.montana.edu/wwwarch

**Institute of Architecture and Planning**
Morgan State University
Baltimore, MD 21239
(443) 885-3225
(410) 319-3786 fax
www.morgan.edu/academic/schools/
archit/archit.htm

**University of Nebraska**
College of Architecture
210 Architecture Hall
Lincoln, NE 68588-0106
(402) 472-9212
(402) 472-3806 fax
www.unl.edu/archcoll/index.html

**University of Nevada, Las Vegas**
School of Architecture
4505 Maryland Parkway
Las Vegas, NV 89154-4018
(702) 895-3031
(702) 895-1119 fax
www.nscee.edu/unlv/Colleges/Fine_Arts/
Architecture

**New Jersey Institute of Technology**
School of Architecture
University Heights
Newark, NJ 07102
(973) 596-3080
(973) 596-8296 fax
www.njit.edu/Directory/Academic/SOA

**University of New Mexico**
School of Architecture and Planning
2414 Central Southeast
Albuquerque, NM 87131
(505) 277-3133
(505) 277-0076 fax
www.unm.edu/~saap

**New York Institute of Technology**
School of Architecture and Design
Education Hall
Old Westbury, NY 11568
(516) 686-7593
(516) 686-7921 fax
www.nyit.edu/schools/architecture/
welcome.html

**The Newschool of Architecture**
1249 F Street
San Diego, CA 92101-6634
(619) 235-4100 ext. 101
(619) 235-4651 fax
www.newschoolarch.edu

**University of North Carolina at Charlotte**
College of Architecture
Charlotte, NC 28223
(704) 547-2358
(704) 547-3353 fax
www.coa.uncc.edu

**North Carolina State University**
College of Design
Department of Architecture
Box 7701
Raleigh, NC 27695-7701
(919) 515-8350
(919) 515-7330 fax
www.ncsu.edu/design

**North Dakota State University**
Department of Architecture and
Landscape Architecture
SU Station, P.O. Box 5285
Fargo, ND 58105
(701) 231-8614
(701) 231-7342 fax
www.ndsu.nodak.edu/arch

**Norwich University**
Division of Architecture and Art
Northfield, VT 05663
(802) 485-2620
(802) 485-2623 fax
www.norwich.edu

**University of Notre Dame**
School of Architecture
110 Bond Hall
Notre Dame, IN 46556-5652
(219) 631-6137
(219) 631-8486 fax
www.nd.edu/~arch/

**Ohio State University**
Austin E. Knowlton School of
Architecture
Columbus, OH 43210
(614) /292-1012
(614) 292-7106 fax
www.arch.ohio-state.edu/

**University of Oklahoma**
Division of Architecture
Norman, OK 73019-0265
(405) 325-3990
(405) 325-0108 fax
www.ou.edu/architecture/darch

**Oklahoma State University**
School of Architecture
Stillwater, OK 74078-5051
(405) 744-6043
(405) 744-6491 fax
www.master.ceat.okstate.edu

**University of Oregon**
School of Architecture and Allied Arts
Eugene, OR 97403
(541) 346-3656
(541) 346-3626 fax
www.architecture.uoregon.edu/windex.html

**Parsons School of Design**
Department of Architecture
66 Fifth Avenue
New York, NY 10011
(212) 229-8955
(212) 229-8937 fax
www.parsons.edu

**University of Pennsylvania**
Graduate School of Fine Arts
207 Meyerson Hall
Philadelphia, PA 19104-6311
(215) 898-5728
(215) 573-2192 fax
www.upenn.edu/gsfa/arch/index.htm

**Pennsylvania State University**
Department of Architecture
College of Arts and Architecture
206 Engineering Unit C
University Park, PA 16802-1425
(814) 865-9535
(814) 865-3289 fax
www.arch.psu.edu

**Philadelphia University**
(formerly Philadelphia College
of Textiles and Science)
School of Architecture and Design
School House Lane and Henry Avenue
Philadelphia, PA 19144-5497
(215) 951-2896
(215) 951-2110 fax
www.philacol.edu/archdes/ad.htm

**Polytechnic University of Puerto Rico**
New School of Architecture
P.O. Box 192017
San Juan, PR 00919-2017
(787) 754-8000 ext. 451
(787) 281-8342 fax

**Prairie View A&M University**
School of Architecture
P.O. Box 4207
Prairie View, TX 77446-4207
(409) 857-2014
(409) 857-2350 fax
www.pvamu.edu/

**Pratt Institute**
School of Architecture
200 Willoughby Avenue
Brooklyn, NY 11205
(718) 399-4304
(718) 399-4332 fax
www.pratt.edu/arch/index.html

**Princeton University**
School of Architecture
Princeton, NJ 08544
(609) 258-3741
(609) 258-4740 fax
www.princeton.edu

**University of Puerto Rico**
School of Architecture
P.O. Box 21909
San Juan, PR 00931-1909
(787) 250-8581
(787) 763-5377 fax

**Rensselaer Polytechnic Institute**
110 8th Street
Troy, NY 12180-3590
(518) 276-6460
(518) 276-3034 fax
www.rpi.edu/dept/arch/

**Rhode Island School of Design**
Department of Architecture
2 College Street
Providence, RI 02903
(401) 454-6281
(401) 454-6299 fax
www.risd.edu

**Rice University**
School of Architecture
6100 Main Street, MS #50
Houston, TX 77005-1892
(713) 527-4044
(713) 285-5277 fax
www.arch.rice.edu

**Roger Williams University**
School of Architecture
One Old Ferry Road
Bristol, RI 02809
(401) 254-3605
(401) 254-3565 fax
www.arch.rwu.edu/

**Savannah College of Art and Design**
201 W. Charlton Street
Savannah, GA 31401
(912) 238-2450
(912) 238-2428 fax
www.scad.edu

**University of South Florida**
School of Architecture and
Community Design
3702 Spectrum Boulevard, Suite 180
Tampa, FL 33612-9421
(813) 974-4031
(813) 974-2557 fax
www.arch.usf.edu

**University of Southern California**
School of Architecture
Los Angeles, CA 90089-0291
(213) 740-2723
(213) 740-8884 fax
www.usc.edu/dept/architecture

**Southern California Institute of Architecture**
5454 Beethoven Street
Los Angeles, CA 90066
(310) 574-1123, ext. 318
(310) 574-3801 fax
www.sciarc.edu

**Southern Polytechnic State University**
School of Architecture
1100 S. Marietta Parkway
Marietta, GA 30060-2896
(770) 528-7253
(770) 528-5484 fax
www2.spsu.edu/architecture/index.htm

**Southern University and A&M College**
School of Architecture
Baton Rouge, LA 70813
(225) 771-3015
(225) 771-4709 fax
www.subr.edu

**State University of New York at Buffalo**
School of Architecture and Planning
112 Hayes Hall
3435 Main Street, Building 1
Buffalo, NY 14214-3087
(716) 829-3483
(716) 829-3256 fax
www.ap.buffalo.edu

**Syracuse University**
School of Architecture
103 Slocum Hall
Syracuse, NY 13244-1250
(315) 443-2256
(315) 443-5082 fax
mirror.syr.edu/soa.html

**Temple University**
Architecture Program
12th and Norris Streets
Philadelphia, PA 19122-1803
(215) 204-8813
(215) 204-5418 fax
www.temple.edu/architecture

**University of Tennessee, Knoxville**
College of Architecture and Design
Knoxville, TN 37996-2400
(423) 974-5265
(423) 974-0656 fax
www.arch.utk.edu/

**University of Texas at Arlington**
School of Architecture
Box 19108
Arlington, TX 76019
(817) 272-2801
(817) 272-5098 fax
www.uta.edu/architecture

**University of Texas at Austin**
School of Architecture
Goldsmith Hall 2.308
Austin, TX 78712
(512) 471-1922
(512) 471-0716 fax
www.ar.utexas.edu

**University of Texas at San Antonio**
Division of Architecture and
Interior Design
6900 North Loop 1604 West
San Antonio, TX 78249-0642
(210) 458-4299
(210) 458-4760 fax
cofah.utsa.edu/cofah/

**Texas A&M University**
Department of Architecture
College Station, TX 77843-3137
(409) 845-0129
(409) 862-1571 fax
archone.tamu.edu

**Texas Tech University**
College of Architecture
P.O. Box 42091
Lubbock, TX 79409-2091
(806) 742-3136
(806) 742-4017 fax
www.arch.ttu.edu/Architecture/

**Tulane University**
School of Architecture
Richardson Memorial Hall
New Orleans, LA 70118-5671
(504) 865-5389
(504) 862-8798 fax
www.tulane.edu/~tsahome

**Tuskegee University**
School of Engineering, Architecture and
Physical Sciences
Tuskegee, AL 36088
(334) 727-8329
(334) 724-4198 fax
www.tusk.edu/colleges/CEAPS/index.html

**University of Utah**
Graduate School of Architecture
375 South 1530 East, Room 235
Salt Lake City, UT 84112-0370
(801) 581-8254
(801) 581-8217 fax
www.arch.utah.edu

**University of Virginia**
School of Architecture
Campbell Hall
Charlottesville, VA 22903
(804) 924-3715
(804) 982-2678 fax
www.virginia.edu/~arch

**Virginia Polytechnic Institute and
State University**
College of Architecture and Urban
Studies
Blacksburg, VA 24061-0205
(540) 231-6416
(540) 231-9938 fax
www.caus.vt.edu

**University of Washington**
Department of Architecture
Box 355720
Seattle, WA 98195-5720
(206) 543-4180
(206) 616-4992 fax
www.caup.washington.edu/HTML/ARCH

**Washington State University**
School of Architecture
P.O. Box 642220
Pullman, WA 99164-2220
(509) 335-5539
(509) 335-6132 fax
www.arch.wsu.edu

**Washington University**
School of Architecture
One Brookings Drive
St. Louis, MO 63130
(314) 935-6200
(314) 935-7656 fax
www.arch.wustl.edu

**Wentworth Institute of Technology**
Department of Architecture
550 Huntington Avenue
Boston, MA 02115-5998
(617) 989-4450
(617) 989-4571 fax
www.wit.edu

**University of Wisconsin, Milwaukee**
Department of Architecture
P.O. Box 413
Milwaukee, WI 53201
(414) 229-4016
(414) 229-6976 fax
www.sarup.uwm.edu

**Woodbury University**
Department of Architecture
7500 Glenoaks Boulevard
Burbank, CA 91510-7846
(818) 767-0888
(818) 504-9320 fax
www.woodburyu.edu

**Yale University**
School of Architecture
180 York Street
New Haven, CT 06520-8242
(203) 432-2296
(203) 432-7175 fax
www.yale.edu

TRADE PRESS

*Architectural Record*
Two Penn Plaza
New York, NY 10121-2298
(212) 904-2594
(212) 904-4256
www.architecturalrecord.com

*Architecture*
1515 Broadway
New York, NY 10036
www.architecturemag.com

*Building Design and Construction*
1350 E. Touhy Avenue
Des Plaines, IL 60018-3358
(847) 390-2120
(847) 390-2152 fax
www.bdcmag.com

*Construction Specifier*
Construction Specifications Institute
(CSI)
99 Canal Center Plaza, Suite 300
Alexandria, VA 22314
(800) 689-2900
(703) 684-0300
(703) 684-0465 fax
www.csinet.org

*CRIT: The Journal of the American
Institute of Architecture Students*
1735 New York Avenue, N.W.
Washington, DC 20006
(202) 626-7472

*ENR: Engineering News-Record*
Two Penn Plaza, 9th Floor
New York, NY 10120
(212) 904-3249
(212) 904-3150 fax
www.enr.com

*Journal of Architectural Education*
Association of Collegiate Schools
of Architecture
1735 New York Avenue, N.W.
Washington, DC 20006
(202) 785-2324
(202) 628-0448 fax
www.acsa-arch.org

# Appendix B: DEFINITIONS

**Account:** a tabular record of financial transactions related to a particular item or class of items; used to classify and record financial details of business transactions of the firm.

**Account balance:** the difference between the total debit entries and credit entries in a single account or class of accounts. If the debits exceed the credits, the balance is a debit balance; if the credits exceed the debits, the balance is a credit balance. When revenue and expense accounts are closed, the balance is brought to zero by equalizing debits and credits and transferring the excess to one of the balance sheet accounts.

**Accounting period:** the time that elapses between the preparation of financial statements.

**Accounts payable:** money owed by the firm to vendors, consultants, or others for merchandise or services that have been provided to the firm on open account or short-term credit.

**Accounts receivable:** money owed by clients to the firm for services rendered or for reimbursement of expenses. Accounts receivable are aged until they are collected or until it becomes apparent they will not be collectible, at which time they are written off.

**Accrual accounting:** a method of keeping accounting records in which revenue is recognized as having been earned when services are performed and expenses are recognized when incurred, without regard to when cash payments are received or made. See also *cash accounting.*

**Addendum (pl. addenda):** a written or graphic instrument issued by the architect before execution of the construction contract that modifies or interprets the bidding documents by additions, deletions, clarifications, or corrections.

**Additional services (of the architect):** professional services that may, if authorized or confirmed in writing by the owner, be rendered by the architect in addition to the basic services or designated services identified in the owner-architect agreement. See also *designated services.*

**Additive (or add) alternate:** see *alternate bid.*

**Admonition:** a private reprimand issued by a jurisdictional registration board (or other administrative agency) for violation of professional conduct rules in that jurisdiction, or by the AIA for violation of its Code of Ethics and Professional Conduct. See also *censure.*

**Advertisement for bids:** published public notice soliciting bids for a construction project or designated portion thereof, included as part of the bidding documents; most frequently used to conform to legal requirements pertaining to public projects and usually published in newspapers of general circulation in those political subdivisions from which the public funds are derived or in which the project is located.

**Aged accounts receivable:** accounts receivable classified according to the length of time each invoice has been outstanding. The age analysis highlights which accounts are falling past due.

**Agent:** a person or entity who acts for or in place of another. See also *attorney-in-fact.*

**Agreement:** (1) a meeting of minds; (2) a legally enforceable promise or promises between two or several persons; (3) the document stating the terms of the contract between the parties, as between owner and architect, architect and consultants, or owner and contractor. "Agreement" and "contract" are frequently used interchangeably without any intended change in meaning.

**Allowance:** see *cash allowance, contingency allowance.*

**All-risk insurance:** see *causes of loss—special form.*

**Alternate bid:** amount stated in the bid to be added to or deducted from the amount of the base bid if the corresponding change in work, as described in the bidding documents, is accepted. An alternate bid resulting in an addition to the bidder's base bid is an additive (or "add") alternate, and an alternate bid resulting in a deduction from the base bid is a deductive ("deduct") alternate.

**Alternate:** a proposed possible change in the work described in the contract documents; provides the owner with an option to select between alternative materials, products, or systems or to add or delete portions of work.

**Alternative dispute resolution (ADR):** a method of resolving disputes (such as mediation, mini-trial, or dispute review board) by other than arbitration or litigation.

**Anti-indemnification statutes:** state laws that invalidate contract clauses related to a party being indemnified or held harmless for damages or that limit the ways such contract clauses can be utilized.

**Antitrust:** laws to protect trade and commerce from unlawful restraints and monopolies or unfair business practices.

**Application for payment:** contractor's certified request for payment for completed portions of the work and, if the contract so provides, for materials or equipment suitably stored pending their incorporation into the work.

**Approved equal:** material, equipment, or method proposed by the contractor and approved by the architect for incorporation in or use in the work as equivalent in essential attributes to the material, equipment, or method specified in the contract documents.

**Arbitration:** method of dispute resolution in which an arbitrator or panel of arbitrators evaluates the merits of the positions of the respective parties and renders a decision.

**Architect:** designation reserved, usually by law, for a person or organization professionally qualified and duly licensed to perform architectural services.

**Architect of record:** the architect whose name appears on the building permit issued by the regulatory authority having jurisdiction for the construction of the project. The building contractor generally submits the application for the permit with the drawings and specifications. In some jurisdictions, however, the architect submits the plans for the permit. (Note: More than one permit may exist for a given building, reflecting the fact that several architects have rendered services for the building. For example, if one architect designs the core and shell and another designs the tenant improvements, there are two architects of record.)

**Architect–consultant agreement:** contract between an architect and another firm (e.g., engineer, specialist, another architect, or other consultant) for professional services.

**As-built drawings:** Drawings based on field measurements for an existing building. Generally, these drawings record only visible building elements. The level and detail of measurements included in the drawings will depend on how the drawings will be used. As-built drawings should not be confused with record drawings. See *record drawings.*

**Asset:** a resource owned by the firm, either tangible or intangible, on which a monetary value can be placed.

**Associate (or associated) architect:** an architect who has an arrangement with another architect to collaborate in the performance of services for a project or series of projects.

**Attorney-in-fact:** a person authorized to act for or on behalf of another person or entity to the extent usually prescribed in a written instrument known as a *power of attorney*.

**Audit:** a formal method of verifying the firm's statement of assets, liabilities, and capital, and the firm's financial transactions, during a fiscal period. The examination should be in enough detail to permit the auditor to state that the financial transactions are substantially correct and that they have been recorded following generally accepted accounting principles. The audit may also suggest improved or alternative procedures in accounting practices to increase efficiency, safeguard assets, or improve financial operations.

**Average collection period:** accounts receivable divided by an average day's billings; the number of days on average between issuing an invoice and receiving payment.

**Award:** see *contract award*.

**Backlog:** dollar value of anticipated revenues from projects contracted but as yet unearned (i.e., the work is contracted but has not been performed). Backlog is reduced by the value of revenue earned and increased by the value of new commissions acquired in a period.

**Bad debt:** a debt owed to the firm that is uncollectable (e.g., losses on accounts receivable due to clients' failure to pay).

**Balance sheet:** a statement of the firm's financial condition as of a specific date. It is a statement of the balance between the assets accounts, on one hand, and the liabilities and net worth (owners' equity) accounts, on the other.

**Bankruptcy:** a state of insolvency in which the property of the debtor is placed under the control of a receiver or trustee in bankruptcy for the benefit of creditors.

**Base bid:** amount of money stated in the bid as the sum for which the bidder offers to perform the work described in the bidding documents, exclusive of adjustments for alternate bids.

**Beneficial occupancy:** use of a project or portion thereof for the purpose intended.

**Benefits, employee:** personnel benefits required by law (such as employment taxes and other statutory employee benefits) and by custom (such as insurance, sick leave, holidays, vacations, pensions, and similar contributions and benefits). Sometimes called "customary and mandatory benefits."

**Bid:** a complete and properly signed proposal, submitted in accordance with the bidding requirements, to perform the work or a designated portion thereof for the amount or amounts stipulated therein.

**Bid bond:** a form of bid security executed by the bidder as principal and by a surety to guarantee that the bidder will enter into a contract within a specified time and furnish any required bond. See *bid security*.

**Bid date:** see *bid time*.

**Bid form:** a form prescribed by the bidding requirements to be completed, signed, and submitted as the bidder's bid.

**Bid opening:** the physical opening and tabulation of sealed bids following the time specified in the bidding requirements. This term is preferable to "bid letting."

**Bid price:** the amount stated in the bid.

**Bid security:** a deposit of cash, certified check, cashier's check, bank draft, stocks or bonds, money order, or bid bond submitted with a bid; provides that the bidder, if awarded the contract, will execute such contract in accordance with the requirements of the bidding documents.

**Bid time:** the date and hour established by the owner or the architect for the receipt of bids.

**Bidder:** a person or entity who submits a bid for a prime contract with the owner; in contrast to a sub-bidder, who submits a bid to a prime bidder.

**Bidding documents:** collectively, the bidding requirements and the proposed contract documents, including any addenda issued prior to receipt of bids.

**Bidding period:** the calendar period beginning when bidding documents are issued and ending at the prescribed bid time.

**Bidding requirements:** collectively, the advertisement or invitation to bid, instructions to bidders, sample forms, the bid form, and portions of addenda relating to bidding requirements.

**Bill of quantities:** see *quantity survey*.

**Bill of sale:** a document executed by the seller or other transferor of property by which the transferor's ownership or other interest in the property is transferred to the buyer or other transferee.

**Billable time:** time that is charged to projects (direct time) and is ultimately invoiced to the client. Time may be charged to projects but not be billable, i.e., the time is necessary to produce the services contracted but will not result in revenue.

**Billing rate:** the price per unit of time (hour, day, week) for staff (principal or employee) billed to a client for work under a contract for a project.

**Bodily injury (insurance terminology):** physical injury, sickness, disease, or resulting death sustained by a person.

**Bona fide bid:** bid submitted in good faith, complete and in accordance with the bidding documents, and properly signed by a person legally authorized to sign such bid.

**Bond:** in suretyship, an obligation by which one party (surety) agrees to guarantee performance by another (principal) of a specified obligation for the benefit of a third person or entity (obligee). See *bid bond, completion bond, dual obligee bond, fidelity bond, payment bond, performance bond, statutory bond,* and *supply bond.*

**Bonus clause:** a provision in the construction contract for additional payment to the contractor as a reward for completing the work prior to a stipulated date.

**Book value:** (1) the net amount at which an asset is carried on the books of the firm (e.g., a building would be carried at cost, plus improvements, minus deprecia-

tion); this may not resemble the market or intrinsic value of the item; (2) the owners' equity accounts, representing the net worth of the firm.

**Bookkeeping:** the procedures by which financial transactions are systematically analyzed, classified, and recorded in the firm's books of account.

**Borrowed capital:** the portion of total capital that has been furnished by long-term creditors of the firm. See also *equity capital.*

**Breach of contract:** the failure, without legal justification, to fulfill obligations that are the whole or part of an agreement, written or oral. The breach of a contract can be intentional, inadvertent, or caused by the negligence of the party breaching the contract.

**Breach of duty:** a failure to perform an obligation created by law or by contract.

**Break-even:** (1) the point in dollars of revenue at which there is neither profit nor loss, i.e., revenue equals fixed and variable costs; (2) in life cycle cost analysis, the point in time at which two mutually exclusive design alternatives have the same life cycle cost.

**Break-even multiplier:** the relevant factor by which an architect's direct personnel expense, direct salary expense, reimbursable expense, or consultant expense is multiplied to determine compensation required to cover direct salary expenses and indirect expenses—but not profit. See also *multiplier* and *net multiplier.*

**Brief:** a written argument, usually prepared by a lawyer, setting forth facts, legal points, and authorities to persuade a court about the merits of or defenses against a claim.

**Budget:** the sum established as available for a given purpose. See *construction budget, project budget* and (for the architecture firm) *internal project budget.*

**Budgeting:** (1) forecasting future business activities of the firm, usually for fiscal periods or for specific projects in terms of revenues, expenses, and income (profit); (2) developing a plan for achieving future desired activities; (3) planning expenditures of time or money. These definitions can also be applied to budgeting construction or project costs or the firm's costs of providing professional services.

**Builder's risk insurance:** a specialized form of property insurance that provides coverage for loss or damage to the work during the course of construction.

**Building code:** see *codes*.

**Building inspector:** see *code enforcement official*.

**Building permit:** a permit issued by appropriate governmental authority allowing construction of a project in accordance with approved construction documents.

**Burden:** another term for overhead or indirect expense. The efforts of the firm that directly produce revenue are "burdened" with or must carry the indirect expenses of the firm.

**Burden of proof:** the duty of a party to substantiate an allegation or issue in order to convince a trier of fact of the merits of the party's claim; necessary in order to prevail in a claim.

**Business income coverage:** insurance protecting against financial loss during the time required to repair or replace property damaged or destroyed by an insured peril.

**Business plan:** Plan that describes the strategic and tactical goals of a business entity. Strategic issues include mergers and acquisitions, geographic locations, research and development, market penetration, forecasts, new product introduction, and business integration. Tactical considerations include product and quantity information, head counts, subcontracting, logistics, and processes. Business plans form the basis for strategic facilities planning. See *strategic facilities plan*.

**CAD (or CADD):** see *computer-aided design*.

**Capital:** (1) in the broadest sense, the value of total assets of the firm carried on the balance sheet; (2) in the narrowest sense, the net worth or value of owners' equity accounts; (3) typically, the firm's funding that is expected to be provided for periods beyond one year. Includes *equity capital* and *borrowed capital*.

**Capital accounts:** (1) in a partnership, the accounts showing each partner's equity in the firm as well as any transactions other than salary draws that they may have with the firm; (2) in a corporation, the accounts recording the shareholders' investment in the firm represented by three accounts: capital (common or preferred stock at par), paid-in capital (capital contributions in excess of the stated value, or par value, of the shares), and retained earnings.

**Capital expenditure:** an expenditure made for fixed (long-term) assets such as land, buildings, furnishings, equipment, and automobiles.

**Care, custody, or control (insurance terminology):** a standard exclusion in liability insurance policies that provides that the liability insurance does not apply to damage to property over which the insured is for any purpose exercising physical control.

**Cash accounting:** a method of keeping accounting records in which revenue is not considered earned unless received in cash and expenses are not recognized unless disbursed in cash. See also *accrual accounting*.

**Cash allowance:** an amount established in the contract documents for inclusion in the contract sum to cover the cost of prescribed items not specified in detail, with provision that variations between such amount and the finally determined cost of the prescribed items will be reflected in change orders appropriately adjusting the contract sum.

**Cash budget:** a plan for cash that will be needed for future operations. Usually forecast monthly for several months ahead; the beginning cash balance, anticipated cash receipts, and anticipated cash disbursements are evaluated to determine timing and magnitude of cash surpluses and cash deficits.

**Cash cycle:** the use of cash to pay for salaries and other goods and services in delivering professional services (work in process), rendering to the client an invoice for the value of those services (accounts receivable), and collecting the invoice, which returns the value earned back into cash ready to be used again for payment of salaries, goods, and services.

**Cash flow:** the change in the firm's cash account during a given period. Positive cash flow (more cash received than disbursed) results in an increase in the cash account; conversely, negative cash flow decreases the cash account.

**Cash flow statement:** a statement prepared in order to analyze the sources and applications of a firm's cash during a period.

**Cash journals:** the cash receipts journal and the cash disbursements journal. These are books of "original entry" because transactions are first recorded in them, in chronological order, as money is received or paid out.

**Cash projection worksheet:** a form on which cash at the beginning of a period is shown, together with estimated cash inflows and outflows during the period and the resulting cash balance at the end of the period.

**Causes of loss—broad form:** a method of writing a contract of insurance that specifies those perils that are covered. Sometimes referred to as "named perils insurance." See also *causes of loss—special form.*

**Causes of loss—special form:** a form of insurance coverage that protects against losses arising from any cause other than specifically excluded perils; sometimes referred to as "all-risk insurance." See also *causes of loss—broad form.*

**Censure:** a public reprimand issued by a jurisdictional registration board (or other administrative agency) for violation of professional conduct rules in that jurisdiction or by the AIA for violation of its Code of Ethics and Professional Conduct. See also *admonition.*

**Certificate for payment:** a statement from the architect to the owner confirming the amount of money due the contractor for work accomplished or materials and equipment suitably stored or both during a specified period.

**Certificate of insurance:** a document issued by an authorized representative of an insurance company stating the types, amounts, and effective dates of insurance for a designated insured.

**Certificate of occupancy:** document issued by a governmental authority certifying that all or a designated portion of a building is approved for its designated use.

**Certificate of substantial completion:** a certificate prepared by the architect on the basis of an inspection (a) stating that the work or a designated portion thereof is substantially complete; (b) establishing the date of substantial completion; (c) stating the responsibilities of the owner and the contractor for security, maintenance, heat, utilities, damage to the work, and insurance; and (d) fixing the time within which the contractor shall complete the items listed therein.

**Change order:** an amendment to the construction contract signed by the owner, architect, and contractor that authorizes a change in the work, an adjustment in the contract sum or the contract time, or both.

**Chart of accounts:** a list of accounts used by the firm in keeping its books, usually classified as assets, liabilities, owners' equity, revenue, and expense.

**Civil action:** a lawsuit in court seeking enforcement or protection of private rights.

**Claim:** a demand or assertion by a party to the contract who is seeking, as a matter of right, adjustment or interpretation of contract terms, payment of money, extension of time, or other relief with respect to the terms of the contract.

**Claim expense:** as defined in the insurance policy, the costs associated with the handling of a claim. This often includes defense attorney fees, investigation costs, and expert witnesses. The salaries of insurance company employees and direct expenses that they may incur in performing their duties are normally not included.

**Claims-made policy:** an insurance policy that provides coverage only (a) if the claim is first made during the term of the policy and (b) if the services from which the claim arose were performed during the period specified by the policy.

**Clarification drawing:** a graphic interpretation of the drawings or other contract documents issued by the architect.

**Clerk of the works:** variously used to refer to the owner's inspector or owner's site representative.

**Client:** An individual or group of individuals being provided professional services by the architect. The client includes those who own or lease assets relevant to the services being provided and can include individuals who use, operate, and maintain those assets. In the contractual context, the term "Owner" is used to signify the person or entity entering into the agreement with the architect. See *owner.*

**Closed bidders list:** see *invited bidders.*

**Closed specifications:** specifications stipulating the use of specific or proprietary products or processes without provision for substitution.

**Code enforcement official:** a representative of a governmental authority employed to inspect construction for compliance with applicable codes, regulations, ordinances, and permit requirements.

**Codes:** regulations, ordinances, or statutory requirements of a government unit relating to building construction and occupancy, generally adopted and administered for the protection of public health, safety, and welfare.

**Coinsurance:** an insurance policy provision that requires the insured to carry insurance equal to a named percentage of the value of the property covered by the policy or suffer a penalty in the event of a loss. This penalty reduces the amount paid by the insurance company in direct proportion to the amount by which the property is underinsured.

**Commercial general liability insurance:** a broad form of liability insurance covering claims for bodily injury and property damage that combines, under one policy, coverage for business liability exposures (except those specifically excluded) and new and unknown hazards that may develop. Commercial general liability insurance automatically includes contractual liability coverage for certain types of contracts and personal injury coverage. Products liability, completed operations liability, and broader contractual liability coverage may be available on an optional

basis. This policy may be written on either an occurrence form or a claims-made form. See also *occurrence* and *claims-made policy.*

**Commissioning:** a process for achieving, validating, and documenting that the performance of the completed building and its systems meet the design needs and requirements of the owner. (Traditionally, "commissioning" has referred to the process by which the heating, ventilation, and air-conditioning systems of a building were tested and balanced according to established standards prior to acceptance by the building owner. However, the scope of commissioning is being broadened to encompass other systems.)

**Comparative negligence:** the proportional sharing of liability between a plaintiff and defendant for damages based on the percentage of negligence of each. Not all states allow a sharing of liability based on comparative negligence. See also *contributory negligence.*

**Compensation:** (1) payment for services rendered or products or materials furnished or delivered; (2) payment in satisfaction of claims for damages incurred; (3) salary, bonus, profit sharing, and other income received by a firm owner or employee.

**Compensatory damages:** damages awarded to compensate a plaintiff for his or her injuries; includes direct out-of-pocket losses as well as compensation for pain and suffering.

**Completed operations insurance:** liability insurance coverage for injuries to persons or damage to property occurring after an operation is completed (a) when all operations under the contract have been completed or abandoned, (b) when all operations at one project site are completed, or (c) when the portion of the work out of which the injury or damage arises has been put to its intended use by the person or organization for whom that portion of the work was done. Completed operations insurance does not apply to damage to the completed work itself.

**Completion bond:** bond guaranteeing the lender that the project will be completed free of liens.

**Completion date:** see *substantial completion.*

**Computer-aided design (commonly abbreviated as CAD, or CADD, for "computer-aided design and drafting"):** a term applied to systems or techniques for design and drafting that utilize integrated computer hardware and software systems to produce graphic images.

**Conditions of the contract:** those portions of the contract documents that define the rights and responsibilities of the contracting parties and of others involved in the work. The conditions of the contract include general conditions, supplementary conditions, and other conditions.

**Consent of surety:** written consent of the surety on a performance bond, payment bond, or both to changes in the contract, reductions in the contractor's retainage, transfer of final payment to the contractor, or waiver of notification of contract changes. The term is also used with respect to an extension of time in a bid bond.

**Consequential loss:** loss not directly caused by damage to property but which may arise as a result of such damage— e.g., damage to other portions of a building or its contents due to roof leaks.

**Construction budget:** the sum established by the owner as available for construction of the project, including contingencies for bidding and for changes during construction. See also *project budget.*

**Construction change directive:** a written order prepared by the architect and signed by the owner and architect that directs a change in the work and states a proposed basis for adjustment, if any, in the contract sum or contract time.

**Construction cost:** as used for calculating the architect's compensation, or as a fixed limit in the owner-architect agreement, this is the total cost or estimated cost to the owner of all elements of the project designed or specified by the architect, including the cost at current market rates of labor and materials furnished by the owner and equipment specified, selected, designed, or specially provided for by the architect (plus a reasonable allowance for the contractor's overhead and profit).

Construction cost also includes a reasonable allowance for contingencies for market conditions at the time of bidding and for changes in the work during construction; however, it doesn't include compensation of the architect and the architect's consultants or the costs of the land, rights-of-way, financing, or other costs that remain the responsibility of the owner.

**Construction documents:** drawings and specifications that set forth in detail requirements for the construction of the project.

**Construction documents services:** the architect's services in which the architect prepares the construction documents from the approved design development documents and assists the owner in the preparation of the bidding documents.

**Construction management:** management services provided to an owner of a project during the design phase, construction phase, or both by a person or entity possessing the requisite training and experience. Such management services may include advice on the time and cost consequences of design and construction decisions, scheduling, cost control, coordination of contract negotiations and awards, timely purchasing of critical materials and long-lead-time items, and coordination of construction activities.

**Construction manager:** an individual or entity who provides construction management services. This entity may remain as advisor (CMa) during construction or become the construction contractor (CMc).

**Construction procurement services:** services in which the architect assists the owner in obtaining either competitive or negotiated proposals and assists the owner in awarding and preparing contracts for construction.

**Consultant:** a person or entity who provides advice or services.

**Contingency allowance:** a sum included in the project budget to cover unpredictable or unforeseen items of work or changes in the work.

**Contingent agreement:** an agreement,

generally between an owner and an architect, in which some portion of the architect's compensation is contingent upon some specially prescribed condition such as government approvals or the owner's success in obtaining funds for the project.

**Contingent liability:** liability that is not absolute and fixed but dependent on the occurrence of some uncertain future event or the existence of an uncertain specified condition.

**Contract:** a legally enforceable agreement between two or several parties. See also *agreement.*

**Contract administration services:** services that includes the architect's general administration of the construction contract(s). This includes reviewing and certifying amounts due the contractor, approving the contractor's submittals, preparing change orders, and conducting site inspections to determine dates of substantial completion and final completion.

**Contract award:** a communication from an owner accepting a bid or negotiated proposal. An award creates legal obligations between parties.

**Contract date:** see *date of agreement.*

**Contract documents:** these include the agreement between owner and contractor; conditions of the contract (general, supplementary, and other conditions); drawings, specifications, and addenda issued prior to execution of the contract; other documents listed in the agreement; and modifications issued after execution of the contract.

**Contract limit:** (1) a limit line or perimeter line established on the drawings or elsewhere in the contract documents defining the physical boundaries of the site available to the contractor for construction; (2) a monetary limit established by contract.

**Contract sum:** the sum stated in the owner-contractor agreement that is the total amount payable by the owner to the contractor for the performance of the work under the contract documents.

**Contract time:** the period of time allotted in the contract documents for substantial completion of the work, including authorized adjustments thereto. If a number of days is specified, calendar or working days should be stipulated.

**Contracting officer:** the person designated as the official representative of the owner with specific authority to act on the owner's behalf in connection with a project.

**Contractor:** (1) one who enters into a contract; (2) in construction terminology, the person or entity responsible for performing the work under the contract for construction.

**Contractor's affidavit:** a certified statement of the contractor, properly notarized or otherwise subject to prosecution for perjury if false, relating to such items as payment of debts and claims, release of liens, or similar matters requiring specific evidence for the protection of the owner.

**Contractor's liability insurance:** insurance purchased and maintained by the contractor that insures the contractor for claims for property damage, bodily injury, or death.

**Contractor's option:** the provision of the contract documents under which the contractor may select certain specified materials, methods, or systems at the contractor's option without change in the contract sum.

**Contractual liability:** liability assumed by a person or entity under a contract. Indemnification or hold-harmless clauses are examples of contractual liability.

**Contribution:** the extent to which revenues remaining after payment of direct expenses will offset the firm's indirect expenses and add to income (profit); may be expressed in dollars or as a percentage of revenue.

**Contributory negligence:** the plaintiff or claimant, by not exercising ordinary care, contributed to the injury; in some states, a plaintiff's contributory negligence will bar the plaintiff from recovering damages. See also *comparative negligence.*

**Copyright:** exclusive right to control the making of copies of a work of authorship, such as design plans, granted by federal statute to the author for a limited period of time.

**Corporation:** a legal entity organized under the laws of a particular jurisdiction. The entity has a legal identity separate from the stockholders, owners, managers, officers, directors, or employees of the enterprise. A corporation is "domestic" to the state of its incorporation and "foreign" to all other states.

**Cost-plus-fee agreement:** an agreement under which the contractor (in an agreement between owner and contractor) or the architect (in an agreement between owner and architect) is reimbursed for stipulated direct and indirect costs of performance of the agreement and, in addition, is paid a fee for services.

**Counterclaim:** an independent cause of action or demand made by a defendant against a plaintiff. This occurs when a defendant in a case files a claim against the plaintiff.

**Covenant:** a written, signed agreement between two or more parties pledging that something is done, shall be done, or shall not be done (e.g., a covenant not to sue).

**Credit:** (1) the right-hand entry of a double-entry bookkeeping system—abbreviated CR and distinguished from a debit; (2) the firm's reputation for solvency (ability to pay debts in a timely fashion), which enables the firm to purchase goods and services with time allowed for payment.

**Critical path method (CPM):** a schedule or diagram of all events expected to occur and operations to be performed in completing a given process, rendered in a form permitting determination of the optimum sequence and duration of each operation.

**Current assets:** cash or assets that are readily convertible into cash, usually within one year; examples include cash, accounts receivable, notes receivable, work in process, or unbilled revenue and short-term prepaid expenses. See also *fixed assets.*

**Current liability:** see *liabilities.*

**Current ratio:** current assets divided by current liabilities; regarded as a measure of liquidity.

**Customary and mandatory benefits:** see *benefits, employee.*

**Daily billing rate:** a rate established for billing for services of identified personnel on a per day basis.

**Damages:** the amount claimed or allowed as compensation for injuries sustained or property damaged through the wrongful acts, negligence, or breach of contract of another.

**Date of agreement:** the date stated in the agreement. If no date is stated, it is the date on which the agreement is signed by the last person or entity required to make it an enforceable agreement.

**Date of commencement of the work:** the date established in a notice to the contractor to proceed or, in the absence of such notice, the date of the contract for construction or such other date as may be established therein.

**Date of substantial completion:** see *substantial completion.*

**Debit:** the left-hand entry of a double-entry bookkeeping system—abbreviated DR and distinguished from a credit. Debit entries decrease assets and increase liabilities and owners' equity. For every debit, there must be a corresponding credit or series of credits totaling the same amount.

**Debt:** an obligation of one party to pay money, goods, or services to another party as the result of some prior agreement. In an architecture firm, debt usually consists of current liabilities and long-term debt (notes and mortgages).

**Declaratory judgment:** the order of a court that establishes the rights of parties on a question of law or on a contract.

**Deductive (or deduct) alternate:** see *alternate bid.*

**Default:** substantive failure to fulfill a material obligation under a contract.

**Defective work:** see *nonconforming work*.

**Deferred revenue:** the value of revenue that has been billed but not yet earned.

**Demurrage:** a charge for time exceeding that allowed for loading, unloading, or removing goods shipped or delivered from a railroad car or similar vehicle or location.

**Deposit for bidding documents:** monetary deposit required to obtain a set of bidding documents.

**Deposition:** pretrial testimony in the form of oral questions and answers by a party or witness. Depositions are taken under oath and may be used during a trial or arbitration proceeding.

**Depreciation:** the reduction in value of a long-term (fixed) asset that occurs over a stated period of time known as the "useful life" of the asset, after which the asset retains only a salvage value. This reduction in value may result from lapse of time, obsolescence, deterioration, wear, or consumption and is recorded periodically as an expense to the firm. The amount of depreciation that may be taken as a deduction for tax purposes may have no relation to any actual decrease in value or usefulness; consequently, depreciation rates vary depending on whether they are being used for income tax purposes, other types of taxes, or management in planning capital expenditures or establishing credit.

**Design development documents:** drawings and other documents that fix and describe the size and character of the entire project as to architectural, structural, mechanical, and electrical systems; materials; and such other elements as may be appropriate.

**Design development services:** services in which the architect prepares the design development documents, from the approved schematic design studies, for submission to the owner for the owner's approval.

**Design professions:** see *environmental design professions*.

**Design-build:** a method of project delivery in which the owner contracts directly with a single entity that is responsible for both design and construction services for a construction project.

**Designated services (of the architect):** those services agreed to be performed by the architect either directly or through consultants. Used specifically in some AIA documents where services are designated from an established list.

**Detail:** a drawing, explanatory of another drawing, indicating in detail and at a larger scale the design, location, composition, and correlation of elements and materials.

**Detailed estimate of construction cost:** a forecast of construction cost prepared on the basis of a detailed analysis of materials and labor for all items of work, as distinguished from a preliminary estimate of construction cost based on current area, volume, or similar conceptual estimating techniques.

**Direct expense:** all items of expense directly incurred for or specifically attributable to a particular project, assignment, or task.

**Direct personnel expense (DPE):** direct salaries of all the architect's personnel engaged on the project and the portion of the cost of their employee benefits related thereto.

**Direct salary expense (DSE):** direct salaries of all the architect's personnel engaged on the project, excluding the cost of fringe benefits (payroll burden).

**Discovery:** the process by which parties to a lawsuit are required before trial to disclose to the other side all evidence they expect to use as part of their presentations in court or that they possess in relation to the other party's claims or defenses.

**Dividend:** in an ongoing corporation, a payment to shareholders out of net income (profits). Payment is in proportion to the number of shares held and is usually made either in cash or in stock.

**Division:** one of the 16 basic organizational divisions of the project specifications when MasterFormat is used.

**Double-entry bookkeeping:** a system of keeping books of an account in which there are always two entries, a debit and a credit, for every transaction.

**DPE factor:** see *indirect expense factor.*

**Draw:** (1) the amount of cash that a proprietor or partner withdraws from the business. It can be considered the amount the proprietor or partner should earn for personal professional services to the firm on a weekly, semimonthly, or monthly basis. There may be an "added" draw made at the end of a fiscal period to distribute the balance of income (profits) earned by the business during the year. (2) a partial distribution of a construction loan to the borrower.

**Drawings:** graphic and pictorial documents depicting the design, location, and dimensions of the elements of a project. Drawings generally include plans, elevations, sections, details, schedules, and diagrams. When capitalized, the term refers to the graphic and pictorial portions of the contract documents.

**DSE factor:** see *indirect expense factor.*

**Dual obligee bond:** a bond in which two obligees are identified, either of whom may enforce the bonded obligation. For example, a performance bond furnished by a contractor in which the entity providing the financing is named as an additional obligee along with the owner.

**Due care:** a term indicating the requirement to exercise reasonable care, skill, ability, and judgment under the circumstances. Performance of duties and services by a professional must be consistent with the level of reasonable care, skill, ability, and judgment provided by reputable professionals in the same geographic area at the same period of time.

**Duty:** an obligation imposed by law or by contract.

**Earned revenue:** revenue for which services have been rendered by the architect and for which payment from the client may be rightfully claimed. Earned revenue may be unbilled, billed but uncollected, or billed and collected.

**Earned surplus:** retained earnings, accumulated earnings, or retained income (profit) in a corporate accounting system; part of the shareholders' equity, together with capital stock and paid-in capital.

**Earnings per share:** net income (earnings) divided by the number of shares outstanding.

**Easement:** a legally created restriction on the unlimited use of all or part of one's land.

**Employers' liability insurance:** insurance protection purchased by an employer to cover the employer against claims arising out of bodily injury to an employee who is not covered by a workers' compensation statute. This is usually provided on the same policy form as the employer's workers' compensation insurance.

**Entity:** a person, partnership, corporation, estate, trustee, government unit, or other organization.

**Environmental design professions:** the professions collectively responsible for the design of the human physical environment, including architecture, urban planning, and similar environment-related professions.

**Equity:** value of the firm's assets in excess of its liabilities; the total claims the owners would have to the value of the business if all assets were liquidated at the values shown on the balance sheet and all liabilities were paid as reflected on the balance sheet.

**Equity capital:** that portion of funding of the business supplied by the proprietor, partners, or shareholders; the balance is borrowed capital and is furnished by creditors.

**Erratum (pl. errata):** correction of a printing, typographical, or editorial error.

**Errors and omissions insurance:** see *professional liability insurance.*

**Estimate of construction cost:** a forecast of construction cost. See *preliminary estimate of construction cost* and *detailed estimate of construction cost.*

**Estoppel:** a legal bar preventing a person from asserting a legal position because of his or her own conduct or for some other reason created by operation of law.

**Ethics:** see *professional ethics.*

**Excess liability insurance:** a separate insurance policy that provides higher limits of liability than the coverage provided by a scheduled list of underlying insurance policies. The terms of the excess liability insurance are never broader than the underlying policy.

**Exclusions:** a list in an insurance policy or bond of losses, hazards, or circumstances not included within the scope of coverage of the policy or bond.

**Execution of the contract (or agreement):** (1) performance of a contract or agreement according to its terms; (2) the acts of signing and delivering (to the parties) the document or documents constituting the contract or agreement.

**Expenditure:** a commitment by the firm to incur a cost on behalf of the firm. Capital expenditures result in the cost being capitalized—established as an asset. Expenditures that are not to be capitalized become expenses in the period in which they generate revenue.

**Expense:** (1) as a noun: in cash accounting, actual cash disbursements made for goods or services that do not result in the acquisition of an asset, distribution of profit, or reduction of a liability. In accrual accounting, expenses may be recognized when they are incurred without regard to the date of payment. (2) as a verb: to transfer an amount previously regarded as an asset (e.g., an account receivable) to an expense account or to the profit-and-loss account. The amount is said to be "expensed."

**Expense-only claim:** a claim that results only in claim expenses being incurred by the insurance company; no indemnity payment is made.

**Expert witness:** a witness who, by virtue of experience, training, skill, or knowledge of a particular field or subject, is recognized as qualified to render an informed opinion on matters relating to that field or subject.

**Exposure:** estimate of the probability of loss from some hazard, contingency, or circumstance; also used to signify the estimate of an insurer's liability under a policy from any one loss or accident or group or class thereof.

**Express warranty:** an affirmation of fact or promise expressly made by the warrantor. Any description of materials or equipment, or a sample or model, furnished by or agreed to by the warrantor can create an express warranty.

**Extended coverage insurance:** property insurance that extends the perils covered beyond basic causes such as fire and lightning to include windstorm, hail, riot, civil commotion, explosion (except steam boiler), aircraft, vehicles, and smoke.

**Extended reporting period:** the time period beyond the expiration of the original policy term during which an insured may report claims from acts that occur within the original policy term and thereby obtain coverage for such claims.

**Extra:** a term sometimes used to denote an item of work involving additional cost.

**Facilities planning:** planning for the long-term use of a building or buildings, which may include furnishings, equipment, operations, maintenance, renovation, expansion, and life cycle planning.

**Facility life cycle:** the series of stages or increments through which a building facility passes during its lifetime. Stages can be structured in various ways. One example includes planning, entitlement, design, construction, move-in, use and operation, and disposal.

**Faithful performance:** performance of contractual duties with reasonable skill and diligence.

**Fast track:** a process in which certain portions of the architect's design services overlap with construction activities in order to expedite the owner's occupancy of all or a portion of the project.

**Feasibility study:** a detailed investigation and analysis conducted to determine the financial, economic, technical, or other advisability of a proposed project.

**Fee:** a term used to denote the amount of compensation to be paid to a person who provides a specific service; sometimes used to denote compensation of any kind for services rendered. The fee may be the entire compensation or a portion thereof.

**Fidelity bond:** a surety bond that reimburses an obligee named in the bond for loss sustained by reason of the dishonest acts of an individual or entity covered by the conditions of the bond.

**Final acceptance:** the owner's acceptance of the project from the contractor upon certification by the architect of final completion. Final acceptance is confirmed by the making of final payment unless otherwise stipulated at the time such payment is made.

**Final completion:** term denoting that the work has been completed in accordance with the terms and conditions of the contract documents.

**Final design (design-build):** the services of final design for a design-build project using AIA agreement forms, performed after completion of the preliminary design services.

**Final inspection:** final review of the construction by the architect to determine whether final completion has been achieved; performed prior to issuance of the final certificate for payment.

**Final payment:** payment made by the owner to the contractor, upon issuance by the architect of the final certificate for payment, of the entire unpaid balance of the contract sum as adjusted by change orders.

**Fiscal year:** any period of 12 consecutive months that is used as the basis for budgeting or for reporting financial activity. The period may coincide with the calendar year or it may begin on any day of the year and close on the last day of the succeeding 12-month period.

**Fixed assets:** assets of a tangible, physical, and relatively permanent nature (such as furniture, equipment, buildings, and automobiles) that are used in the operation of a business and that will not be consumed within one year. See also *current assets*.

**Fixed fee:** compensation for professional services or construction services on a lump-sum basis, not affected by project scope or other variables except as may be specifically designated.

**Fixed limit of construction cost:** the maximum construction cost established in the agreement between the owner and the architect.

**Force account:** term used when work is ordered, often under urgent circumstances, to be performed by the contractor without prior agreement as to lump sum or unit price cost thereof and is to be billed at the cost of labor, material, and equipment, insurance, taxes, etc., plus an agreed percentage for overhead and profit; sometimes used to describe work performed by the owner's own forces in a similar manner.

**Form of agreement:** a document setting forth in printed form the general provisions of an agreement, with spaces provided for insertion of specific data relating to a particular project.

**Fringe benefits:** benefits paid for by an employer on behalf of an employee in addition to direct compensation; frequently includes health care, retirement, and disability insurance.

**Frivolous suit:** a suit that is so totally without merit on its face as to show bad faith or other improper motive on the part of the plaintiff.

**General conditions (of the contract for construction):** that part of the contract documents that sets forth many of the rights, responsibilities, and relationships of the parties, particularly those provisions that are common to many construction projects.

**General contract:** (1) under the single contract system, the contract between the owner and the contractor for construction of the entire work, which can be accomplished by the contractor with its own forces and through subcontractors; (2) under the separate contract system, a contract between the owner and a contractor for general construction consisting of architectural and structural work.

**General journal:** in accounting, a book of original entry. Adjusting and closing entries and transactions that are not recorded in the cash journals or payroll journal are first recorded here.

**General ledger:** a book of accounts used in complete accounting systems. It is a book of "final entry," containing a summary of all transactions in separate accounts.

**General requirements:** title of Division 1 of the specifications when MasterFormat is used.

**Geotechnical investigation (or subsurface investigation):** the soil boring and sampling process, together with associated laboratory tests, necessary to establish subsurface profiles and the relative strengths, compressibility, and other characteristics of the various strata encountered within depths likely to have an influence on the design of the building.

**Goodwill:** an asset, representing the excess of the value paid or to be paid for a firm over and above its net worth. It usually arises when one firm, or an interest in that firm, is purchased by a second firm for more than its book value. A purchased firm cannot create goodwill for itself. Goodwill may be carried on the books of the purchasing firm as an asset, but it cannot be amortized for tax purposes.

**Gross income from projects:** revenue remaining after direct (project) expenses are subtracted from project revenues.

**Guarantee:** see *warranty.*

**Guaranteed maximum price (GMP):** a sum established in an agreement between owner and contractor as the maximum compensation to be paid by the owner to the contractor for performing specified work on the basis of the cost of labor and materials plus overhead expenses and profit.

**Hold harmless:** see *indemnification.*

**Hourly billing rate:** a rate established for billing for services of identified personnel on a per hour basis.

**Implied warranty:** an affirmation of fact or promise imposed on a party by law, even without an express warranty, as a result of that party's relationship with another. See also *express warranty.*

**Incentive clause:** a term used to describe savings that are shared proportionally in an agreed manner between an owner and a contractor and that are derived from the difference between the guaranteed maximum price and the actual cost of a project when the work is performed on the basis of cost plus a fee with a guaranteed maximum price. The terms of an incentive clause are normally included in the agreement between the owner and the contractor.

**Income:** profits remaining after expenses have been subtracted from revenues.

**Income statement:** the basic operating financial statement showing the activity of the firm for the accounting period specified; shows revenues, expenses, and the resulting income (profit). Also called "profit-and-loss statement" or "revenue-and-expense statement."

**Indemnification:** a contractual obligation by which one person or entity agrees to reimburse others for loss or damage arising from specified liabilities.

**Indemnification, implied:** an indemnification that is implied by law rather than arising out of an expressed contract to provide indemnification.

**Indemnify:** to protect against loss or damage or to promise compensation for loss or damage. The duty to indemnify may be created by rule of common law, by statute, or by contract. The party who is to be indemnified from loss or damage is the indemnitee; the party providing the indemnification is the indemnitor.

**Indemnity payment:** a payment to a third party by an insurance company and/or the insured in satisfaction of a claim made against the insured.

**Indirect expense:** an expense indirectly incurred and not directly related to a specific project. Also called "overhead expense."

**Indirect expense allocation:** the process of allocating or prorating to projects on some consistent basis the indirect expenses of the firm.

**Indirect expense factor:** the ratio of all indirect expenses to either direct salary expense (DSE) or direct personnel expense (DPE), depending on how the firm applies the expense of benefits in project accounting. The ratio can be expressed either as a percentage of DSE or DPE (e.g., 250%) or as a multiple of DSE or DPE (2.50).

**Insolvency:** inability of the firm to meet (pay) financial obligations as they come due. The firm may have assets that exceed the value of its liabilities but be temporarily unable to meet maturing obligations because its assets cannot be easily converted into cash; or the firm may have liabilities greater than its assets, which may lead to bankruptcy.

**Inspection:** (1) examination of work completed or in progress to determine its conformance with the requirements of the contract documents. Distinguished from the more general observations made by the architect from time to time on visits to the site during the progress of the work; (2) examination of the work by a public official, owner's representative, or others.

**Inspection list:** a list of items of work to be completed or corrected by the contractor after substantial completion; sometimes referred to as a "punch list."

**Instructions to bidders:** instructions contained in the bidding documents for preparing and submitting bids for a construction project or designated portion thereof.

**Instruments of service:** drawings, specifications, and other documents prepared by the architect as part of the design process. In addition to drawings and specifications comprising the construction documents, instruments of service may be in any medium and include sketches, preliminary drawings, outline specifications, calculations, studies, analyses, models, and renderings.

**Insurable interest:** any interest in property or relation thereto of such nature that damage to the property will cause pecuniary loss to the insured. If an insured party does not have an insurable interest, the insurance agreement may be treated as an unlawful gambling transaction contrary to public policy.

**Interest:** an amount of money paid for the use of capital, usually expressed as a rate (a percentage). Simple interest is calculated on the principal amount borrowed; compound interest is calculated on the principal amount plus interest added from prior periods.

**Intern:** an individual in the process of satisfying a registration board's training requirements; includes graduates from recognized architecture programs, architecture students who acquire acceptable training prior to graduation, and other qualified individuals identified by a registration board.

**Internal project budget:** resources allocated by a design firm for performance of its obligations with respect to a particular project.

**Interrogatories:** a set or series of formal written questions used in the judicial examination of a party or a witness before the actual trial; a series of written questions exchanged between parties to a lawsuit, which must be answered under oath.

**Investment credit:** federal tax legislation allowing businesses a specified percentage of new capital expenditures as credits against tax liabilities. The IRS defines rules for the percentages, applicability to various expenditures, and recapture in the event of early disposal of the asset before the end of its assumed useful life.

**Invitation to bid:** a portion of the bidding documents soliciting bids for a construction project.

**Invited bidders:** the bidders selected by the owner, after consultation with the architect, as the only persons or entities from whom bids will be received.

**Invoice:** a bill, usually itemized, received or sent for goods or services.

**Job captain:** a term frequently used for an individual within the architect's office responsible for preparation of the construction documents.

**Job site:** see *site*.

**Joinder:** uniting two or more elements into one, such as the joinder of parties as coplaintiffs or codefendants in a suit or as parties to an arbitration.

**Joint and several liability:** a legal concept under which defendants can be held both collectively and individually liable for all damages, regardless of their degree of fault.

**Joint venture:** a business relationship consisting of two or more persons or entities that has legal characteristics similar to those of a partnership.

**Journal:** any book of original entry in accounting. A journal records financial transactions in the order in which they occur day to day. Periodically, the journal entries, which were entered randomly with regard to the accounts involved, are "posted" to the ledger. See *cash journals* and *payroll journal*.

**Judgment:** the final decision of a court with respect to the rights of the parties in a suit. A summary judgment is a decision of a court before the actual trial, made in suits in which there are no disputes about material issues of fact.

**Jury:** (1) a committee for evaluating design work and, in connection with a design competition, for designating awards; (2) a panel convened by a court and sworn to give a verdict in a civil or criminal matter.

**Labor and material payment bond:** see *payment bond*.

**Latent defect:** a defect in materials, equipment, or completed work that reasonably careful observation would not detect; distinguished from a patent defect, which would ordinarily be detected by reasonably careful observation.

**Legal liability:** a legal obligation that arises out of contract or by operation of law.

**Letter form of agreement (or letter agreement):** a letter stating all material terms of an agreement between addressor and addressee. When the letter is countersigned without change by the addressee it becomes a contract.

**Letter of intent:** a letter signifying an intention to enter into a formal agreement, usually setting forth the material terms of the proposed agreement.

**Liabilities:** debts or obligations of the firm owed to others. They may be subdivided as current liabilities (due within one year) and long-term liabilities (due beyond one year). See also *contingent liabilities*.

**Liability insurance:** a contract under which an insurance company agrees to protect a person or entity against claims arising from a real or alleged failure to fulfill an obligation or duty to a third party who is an incidental beneficiary. See also *commercial general liability insurance; completed operations insurance; contractor's liability insurance; employer's liability insurance; owner's liability insurance; professional liability insurance; property damage insurance; public liability insurance;* and *special hazards insurance*.

**Licensed architect:** see *architect*.

**Licensed contractor:** a person or entity authorized by governmental authority to engage in construction contracting for others.

**Licensed engineer:** see *professional engineer*.

**Lien:** see *mechanic's lien*.

**Life cycle cost:** the capital and operational cost of a construction item or system during the estimated useful life of the building.

**Limit of liability:** the maximum amount an insurance company is obligated to pay in case of loss.

**Limitation of liability:** monetary limit of the legal liability of a person or entity to another based on an agreement or established by statute.

**Line of credit:** an agreement between a bank and a firm whereby the bank agrees to lend the firm funds up to a maximum amount. The firm may borrow, as needed, as much as it requires up to the maximum and pays interest only on the amount borrowed and outstanding.

**Liquid assets:** items that have a readily ascertainable market value and can be relatively easily converted to cash without significant loss of value. Items such as cash, notes receivable, marketable securities, and certificates of deposit are typical liquid assets.

**Liquidated damages:** a sum established in a construction contract, usually as a fixed sum per day, as the predetermined measure of damages to be paid to the owner because of the contractor's failure to complete the work within a stipulated time; not enforceable as a penalty.

**Liquidity:** the ability to convert an asset into cash with relative speed and ease and without significant loss in value.

**Long-term:** beyond one year (e.g., long-term liabilities are those liabilities or portions of liabilities that will come due beyond 12 months of the date of the statement).

**Loss:** excess of expense over revenues during an accounting period.

**Loss of use insurance:** see *business income coverage.*

**Low bid:** bid stating the lowest price proposed by two or more bidders for performance of the work, including selected alternates, conforming with the bidding documents.

**Lowest responsible bidder:** bidder who submits the lowest bona fide bid and is considered by the owner and the architect to be fully responsible and qualified to perform the work for which the bid is submitted.

**Lowest responsive bid:** the lowest bid that is responsive to and complies with the requirements of the bidding documents.

**Lump sum agreement:** see *stipulated sum agreement.*

**Malpractice:** breach of a professional duty by one rendering professional services, where the breach is the proximate cause of injury, loss, or damage to other people.

**Margin:** the degree of difference; in financial reporting, the profit margin is the difference between revenues and expenses. ("Margin" has a different meaning in the commodities and securities markets.)

**MasterFormat:** a system for classifying building products and systems by materials and trades, e.g., concrete, masonry, thermal and moisture protection, etc. See also *UniFormat.*

**Mechanic's lien:** a claim on real property, to be satisfied by sale of the real property, created by statute in favor of a person supplying labor, materials, or services for nongovernmental improvements to real property for the value of labor, materials, or services supplied by the claimant. In some jurisdictions an architect or engineer may be entitled to assert a mechanic's lien. Clear title to the property cannot be obtained until the claim is settled.

**Mediation:** effort by an independent party to help others reach settlement of a controversy or claim. The mediator participates impartially in the proceedings, advising and consulting the various parties involved. A mediator cannot impose a settlement but can seek to guide the parties to achieve their own settlement voluntarily.

**Memorandum of insurance:** see *certificate of insurance.*

**Merger:** the combination of two businesses in which one company survives and the other loses all or part of its identity. ("Consolidation" is the complete fusion of two companies to form one entirely new company. "Acquisition" is a general term used to indicate the combining of one business enterprise with another.)

**Meritless claim:** a claim that is so obviously insufficient that it should be rejected on its face without argument or proof.

**Minor changes in the work:** changes in the construction work that do not involve an adjustment in the contract sum or an extension of the contract time and that are not inconsistent with the intent of the contract documents. Minor changes are effected by written order issued by the architect.

**Modification (to the contract documents):** (1) a written amendment to the contract signed by both parties; (2) a change order; (3) a construction change directive; (4) a written order for a minor change in the work issued by the architect.

**Mortgage:** a pledge of property to a creditor as security against a loan; the contract specifying the terms of the pledge to repay the loan. The lender or creditor of a note or loan secured by a mortgage is the mortgagee; the one who borrows on a note or loan secured with a mortgage is the mortgagor.

**Moving average:** a series of averages, each of which excludes the first unit of the preceding average and includes the next unit in the series. Used by some financial managers in calculating statistics or ratios such as average collection period.

**Multiple of direct personnel expense (or DPE multiple):** a method of compensation for professional services based on direct personnel expense multiplied by an agreed DPE factor to cover indirect expenses, other direct expense, and profit.

**Multiple of direct salary expense (or DSE multiple):** a method of compensation for professional services based on direct salary expense multiplied by an agreed DSE factor to cover the cost of payroll burden related to direct salary expense, indirect expenses, other direct expense, and profit.

**Multiplier:** the relevant factor by which an architect's direct personnel expense, direct salary expense, reimbursable expense, or consultant expense is multiplied to determine compensation for professional services or designated portions thereof or for other project expenses. See also *break-even multiplier.*

**Named insured:** any person or entity specifically designated by name in an insurance policy, as distinguished from others who, although unnamed, are afforded coverage under some circumstances.

**Negligence:** failure to exercise due care under the circumstances. Legal liability is imposed on a person or entity that is negligent when such negligence causes damage to some other person to whom the negligent actor owes a duty recognized by law.

**Negligence per se:** an act or omission regarded as negligence without argument or proof because it violates a standard of care defined by statute or is so obviously contrary to common prudence.

**Negligent act or omission:** in law, an act or failure to act involving a failure to exercise due care.

**Net:** (1) as a noun, the amount remaining after some or all specified deductions. Net income is the income (profit) remaining after all expenses are deducted from revenue; value of an asset net of depreciation means the cost of the asset less the amount reserved for depreciation; (2) as a verb, to subtract one value from another to arrive at the net figure.

**Net working capital:** current assets less current liabilities (this definition is used by some financial managers as "working capital").

**Net worth:** the value of the owners' equity (investment) in the firm—basically, book value (assets minus liabilities); in a proprietorship, the proprietor's capital account; in a partnership, the total of the partners' capital accounts; in a corporation, the total of capital stock (par value paid) plus paid-in capital (capital contributed in excess of par value) plus retained earnings.

**Noncollusion affidavit:** statement by a bidder under oath that the bid was prepared without collusion of any kind.

**Nonconforming work:** work that does not fulfill the requirements of the contract documents. Sometimes called "defective work."

**Nonexpense items:** expenditures affecting only the assets, liabilities, or net worth of the firm, including all those that cannot be charged to a reimbursable, direct, or indirect expense account. Most often these expenditures are for the purchase of a capital asset.

**Notice to bidders:** a notice contained in the bidding documents informing prospective bidders of the opportunity to submit bids on a project and setting forth the procedures for doing so.

**Notice to proceed:** written communication that may be issued by the owner to the contractor authorizing the contractor to proceed with the work and establishing the date for commencement of the work.

**Observation of the work:** observation by the architect of the partially completed work during periodic visits to the site, to become generally familiar with the progress and quality of the completed work and to determine in general if the work is being performed in a manner indicating that, when complete, the work will be in accordance with the contract documents.

**Occupancy permit:** see *certificate of occupancy.*

**Occupational accident:** accident occurring in the course of one's employment and caused by inherent or related hazards.

**Occurrence (insurance terminology):** an accident (an unexpected and unintended event, identifiable as to time and place, resulting in bodily injury or property damage) or a continuous or repeated exposure to conditions that result in injury or damage.

**Occurrence policy:** an insurance policy that covers acts or omissions occurring during the policy term, regardless of when a claim against the insured is first asserted, even if the policy is no longer in existence; usually relates to general liability insurance. See also *claims-made policy.*

**On-site observation:** see *observation of the work.*

**Open bidding:** method of soliciting bids in which a public notice inviting bids is published and bids are accepted from all who submit them; most frequently used to conform to legal requirements pertaining to public projects and usually published in newspapers of general circulation in those political subdivisions from which the public funds are derived or where the project is located. See also *invited bidders.*

**Opening of bids:** see *bid opening.*

**Or equal:** see *approved equal.*

**Organizational expense:** expenses incurred in organizing a corporation (e.g., attorney's and accountant's fees, incorporation taxes and fees, printing of stock certificates). These expenses are accounted for as another asset and are amortized over a period of years because it is generally felt that benefits of the expenses are felt over the life of the corporation.

**Other conditions (of the contract for construction):** see *special conditions.*

**Outline specifications:** an abbreviated set of specification requirements normally included with schematic design or design development documents.

**Outstanding stock:** the total shares of a corporation fully paid for and held by shareholders.

**Overhead expense:** see *indirect expense.*

**Owner:** a person or entity who retains services for building design and contracts for construction or acquisition of furniture, furnishings, and equipment; so called because this person or entity typically owns or is the lessee of the site or building premises.

**Owner's and contractor's protective liability coverage:** third-party legal liability insurance coverage protecting a contractor or owner from claims arising from the construction process.

**Owner's inspector:** a person employed by the owner to inspect construction on the owner's behalf; sometimes called "clerk of the works."

**Owner's liability insurance:** insurance to protect the owner against claims arising from its ownership of property. See also *commercial general liability insurance* and *owner's and contractor's protective liability coverage.*

**Owner's representative:** the person designated as the official representative of the owner in connection with a project.

**Owner-architect agreement:** contract between owner and architect for professional services.

**Owner-contractor agreement:** contract between owner and contractor for performance of the work for construction of the project or portion thereof.

**Paid-in capital:** one of the owners' equity accounts, in a corporation, representing the amount of capital contributed by shareholders in excess of the stated par value. Also known as capital surplus.

**Par value:** the minimum dollar value that must be paid for capital stock issued by a corporation. The amount is fixed by the corporation and remains the same regardless of the trading price of the stock. There is no necessary relation between the par value and the real value of the stock.

**Partial occupancy:** occupancy by the owner of a portion of a building facility or facilities prior to its completion.

**Partial payment:** see *progress payment.*

**Partnership:** an association in which two or more persons or entities conduct an enterprise as co-owners.

**Patent defect:** a defect in materials, equipment, or completed work that reasonably careful observation could have discovered. See also *latent defect.*

**Payment bond:** a bond in which the contractor and the contractor's surety guarantee to the owner that the contractor will pay for labor and materials furnished for use in the performance of the contract. Persons entitled to the benefits of the bond are defined as claimants in the bond. A payment bond is sometimes referred to as a "labor and material payment bond."

**Payment request:** see *application for payment.*

**Payroll journal:** a book of "original entry" similar to cash journals, used to record the details of the firm's payroll expenses.

**Payroll taxes:** taxes, such as Social Security taxes, that are based on the payroll.

**Payroll utilization:** see *utilization ratio.*

**Penal sum:** the amount named in a contract or bond as the pecuniary limit of liability to be paid by a signatory thereto in the event the contractual obligations are not performed.

**Penalty clause:** a provision in a contract for a charge against the contractor for failure to complete the work by a stipulated date or to fulfill some other condition. If the penalty is excessive, it may be unenforceable.

**Pension plan:** a plan established and maintained by an employer for the benefit of the firm's employees by which contributions are systematically accumulated and invested during the employment of personnel; pension benefits are payable to its member employees over a period of years after retirement. Funding of a pension plan is not discretionary based on profits, as are profit-sharing plans. Pension plans are subject to regulatory control.

**Percentage fee:** compensation based on a percentage of construction cost; applicable to either construction contracts or professional service agreements.

**Performance:** the fulfillment of a contract.

**Performance bond:** a bond in which the contractor and the contractor's surety guarantee to the owner that the work will be performed in accordance with the contract documents. A performance bond may be included in the same form with a payment bond.

**Permit:** see *building permit, occupancy permit,* and *zoning permit.*

**Personal injury liability coverage:** personal injury insurance includes coverage for injuries or damage to others caused by specified actions of the insured, such as false arrest, malicious prosecution, willful detention or imprisonment, libel, slander, defamation of character, wrongful eviction, invasion of privacy, or wrongful entry. Occasionally the term "personal injury" will include bodily injury by definition in an insurance policy.

**Personal injury:** physical or mental injury to a human being.

**Petty cash:** an amount of cash on hand for disbursements that are too small to justify the use of checks.

**Phase (of professional services):** An increment or stage of development established by the architect for professional services.

**Plan deposit:** see *deposit for bidding documents.*

**Postoccupancy evaluation:** an evaluation by an architect of the performance of a building. Application varies widely in scope, as an evaluation may take place at any time after the building is occupied and may address one or more aspects of the performance of a building.

**Postoccupancy services:** (1) under traditional forms of agreement between owner and architect, services rendered by the architect after issuance of the final certificate for payment or, in the absence of a final certificate for payment, more than 60 days after the date of substantial completion of the work; (2) under designated services forms of agreement, services necessary to assist the owner in the use and occupancy of the facility.

**Power of attorney:** a document authorizing a person or entity to act as another's agent.

**Preconstruction** *(design-build):* preliminary design and budgeting phases of a design-build project.

**Predesign services:** services of the architect provided prior to the customary basic services, including services to assist the owner in establishing the program, financial and time requirements, and limitations for the project.

**Preliminary design (design-build):** architect's services performed under the Part I agreement of a design-build project, including program review, preliminary program evaluation, review of alternative approaches to design and construction, and preliminary design documents. See also *final design.*

**Preliminary design documents (design-build):** preliminary design drawings, outline specifications, and other documents that fix and describe the size, quality, and character of a design-build project, including architectural, structural, mechanical, and electrical systems, as well as materials and such other elements of the project as may be appropriate.

**Preliminary drawings:** drawings prepared during the early stages of the design of a project.

**Preliminary estimate of construction cost:** cost forecasts prepared by the architect as part of schematic design, design development, and construction documents services. In AIA Document B141, these are based on current area, volume, or similar conceptual estimating techniques. See also *detailed estimates of construction cost.*

**Premium:** the amount paid by an insured for the coverage to be provided by the insurance company.

**Prequalification of bidders:** the process of investigating the qualifications of prospective bidders on the basis of their experience, availability, and capability for the contemplated project, and then approving qualified bidders.

**Prime contract:** contract between owner and contractor for performance of the work or designated portion thereof. See also *subcontract.*

**Prime contractor:** any contractor on a project having a contract directly with the owner. See also *subcontractor.*

**Prime professional:** any person or entity having a contract directly with the owner for professional services.

**Principal:** in architecture firms, most often a proprietor or any individual who has an equity position in the firm (owns shares in a corporation or is a partner in a partnership). Sometimes limited to owners holding a certain percent of the business; sometimes expanded to include anyone in a significant leadership role in the firm.

**Principal-in-charge:** the architect charged with the responsibility for the firm's services in connection with a given project.

**Prior acts:** see *retroactive coverage*.

**Privity:** the direct relationship between two parties to a contract. Privity continues when certain subsequent parties succeed to the rights of a contract.

**Pro forma:** provided in advance in prescribed form. For example, a pro forma income statement is a projected or budgeted income statement (profit plan), which shows the effects of planned financial activity during a planning period as if the events had taken place as forecast. Pro formas are also commonly developed as part of real estate financial feasibility studies.

**Pro rata:** in proportion. For example, if three partners owned 30 percent, 30 percent, and 40 percent of a partnership and profits were distributed pro rata based on ownership, the profits would be distributed according to these percentages.

**Product data:** illustrations, standard schedules, performance charts, instructions, brochures, diagrams, and other information furnished by the contractor to illustrate a material, product, or system for some portion of the work.

**Products liability insurance:** insurance for liability imposed for damages caused by an occurrence arising out of goods or products manufactured, sold, handled, or distributed by the insured or others trading under the insured's name. Occurrence must occur after possession of the product has been relinquished to others and after the product has been removed from the possession of the insured.

**Professional:** a person who is deemed to have specialized knowledge and skills acquired through education and experience to be used in advising or providing services to others.

**Professional advisor:** (1) an architect engaged by the owner to direct a design competition for the selection of an architect; (2) in the Intern Development Program, a registered architect, usually outside the intern's firm, who meets periodically with the intern to discuss career objectives and review training progress.

**Professional engineer:** a designation reserved, usually by law, for a person professionally qualified and duly licensed to perform engineering services such as structural, mechanical, electrical, sanitary, civil, etc.

**Professional ethics:** statements of principles promulgated by professional societies or public agencies governing professional practice in order to guide members or licensees in their professional conduct.

**Professional fee plus expenses:** a method of compensation for professional services separating the services from identified costs for reimbursable expenses, consultant services, and similar items.

**Professional fee:** see *fee*.

**Professional liability insurance:** insurance coverage for the insured professional's legal liability for claims arising out of damages sustained by others allegedly as a result of negligent acts, errors, or omissions in the performance of professional services.

**Professional sponsor:** in the Intern Development Program, an individual within the firm or organization who supervises the intern on a daily basis, regularly assesses the quality of his or her effort, and periodically certifies documentation of the intern's training activity.

**Profit:** excess of revenues over expenses during an accounting period. In cash accounting, profit is the excess of cash received (revenue) over cash disbursements (expenses); in accrual accounting, profit is the excess of earned revenue (irrespective of when received) over accrued expenses (irrespective of when paid). Also called "income."

**Profit margin:** see *margin*.

**Profitability:** the quality or state of being able to produce profits (income) from revenues generated in delivering the firm's services.

**Profit-sharing plan:** a mechanism for distributing a portion of the firm's profits to employees during or soon after the period in which they are earned (current profit-sharing plan) or to provide a later benefit to the employees (deferred profit-sharing plan). One of the prime purposes of a profit-sharing plan is to increase interest in current profitable performance since contributions are made only if there are profits.

**Program (architectural or facilities):** a written statement setting forth design objectives, constraints, and criteria for a project, including space requirements and relationships, flexibility and expandability, special equipment and systems, and site requirements.

**Program management:** the science and practice of managing large private and public projects.

**Progress payment:** partial payment made during progress of the work.

**Progress schedule:** a diagram, graph, or other pictorial or written schedule showing proposed or actual times of commencement and completion of the various elements of the work.

**Project:** a planned undertaking in which the architect provides a service or set of services to achieve a desired objective or set of objectives for the client. A project may or may not ultimately result in the creation of physical space. (The term is capitalized in AIA contract documents.)

**Project architect:** see *project manager*.

**Project budget:** the sum established by the owner as available for the entire project, which for building projects includes the construction budget; land costs; costs of furniture, furnishings, and equipment; financing costs; compensation for professional services; costs of owner-furnished goods and services; contingency allowance; and similar established or estimated costs.

See also *construction budget* and *internal project budget*.

**Project checklist:** a list used to record the actions taken by the architect, beginning before the agreement with the owner has been signed, continuing with the range of services to be provided to the owner. For building design and construction services, AIA Document D-200 lists actions for pre-design, design, and construction increments of work.

**Project closeout:** requirements established in the contract documents for final inspection, submittal of necessary documentation, acceptance, and final payment on a construction project.

**Project cost:** total cost of the project, including construction cost, professional compensation, land costs, furnishings and equipment, financing, and other charges.

**Project delivery system:** the method selected to allocate roles, responsibilities, risks, and rewards among the parties accomplishing the design, preparation of construction documents, construction, and management of a construction project.

**Project expense:** see *direct expense*.

**Project gross margin:** the percentage of revenue using gross income from projects (profit after direct expenses have been deducted from revenues but before indirect expenses have been deducted).

**Project manager:** (1) a term frequently used interchangeably with "project architect" to identify the individual designated to manage the firm's services related to a given project. Normally these services include administrative responsibilities as well as technical responsibilities. There may also be a designated principal-in-charge; (2) as to the contractor or construction manager, the term may refer to the individual designated by that entity to manage that entity's activities.

**Project manual:** the volume usually assembled for the construction work, which may include the bidding requirements, sample forms, conditions of the contract, and the specifications.

**Project representative:** the architect's representative at the project site, who assists in the administration of the construction contract.

**Project revenues:** the value received (or anticipated to be received) from the client for services rendered (or to be rendered). Excludes reimbursable revenues, which are offset by reimbursable expenses.

**Project work plan:** (1) a strategy by which the firm intends to produce a project on time, within the client's budget, and within the firm's project budget; (2) the document spelling out the details of the strategy.

**Property damage insurance:** insurance coverage for the insured's legal liability for claims for injury to or destruction of tangible property, including loss of use resulting therefrom but usually not including coverage for injury to or destruction of property in the care, custody, or control of the insured.

**Property insurance:** coverage for loss or damage to property. See also *builder's risk insurance, causes of loss—broad form, causes of loss—special form, extended coverage insurance,* and *special hazards insurance.*

**Proposal, contractor's:** see *bid* and *bid form.*

**Proposal request:** a document issued by the architect after contract award that may include drawings and other information used to solicit a proposal for a change in the work; sometimes called "request for a change" or "bulletin."

**Proprietorship:** a form of business organization that is owned entirely by one person.

**Proximate cause:** the cause of an injury or of damages that, in natural and continuous sequence, unbroken by any legally recognized intervening cause, produces the injury and without which the result would not have occurred. Existence of proximate cause involves both (a) causation in fact, i.e., that the wrongdoer actually produced an injury or damages, and (b) a public policy determination that the wrongdoer should be held responsible.

**Public authority:** local, state, or federal government body having jurisdiction over the work or project.

**Public liability insurance:** insurance covering liability of the insured for negligent acts resulting in bodily injury, disease, or death of persons other than employees of the insured and/or damage to property other than that owned by or within the care, custody, or control of the insured. See also *commercial general liability insurance* and *contractor's liability insurance.*

**Punch list:** see *inspection list.*

**Punitive damages:** damages in addition to proven loss (compensatory damages) that may be assessed against a defendant as punishment or as a deterrent to others.

**Qualified bid:** a bid the bidder has conditioned or restricted in some manner.

**Quantity survey:** detailed listing and quantities (bill of quantities) of all items of material and equipment necessary to construct a project.

**Quotation:** a price quoted by a contractor, subcontractor, materials supplier, or vendor to furnish materials, labor, or both.

**Reasonable care and skill:** see *due care.*

**Record drawings:** construction drawings revised to show significant changes made during the construction process, usually based on marked-up prints, drawings, and other data furnished by the contractor to the architect. This term is preferable to "as-built drawings."

**Registered architect:** see *architect.*

**Reimbursable expenses:** amounts expended for or on account of the project that, in accordance with the terms of the appropriate agreement, are to be reimbursed by the owner.

**Reinsurance:** an arrangement between two insurance companies whereby one assumes all or part of the risk of loss under the terms of a policy issued by the other.

**Rejection of work (by the architect):** the act of rejecting construction work that does not conform to the requirements of the contract documents.

**Release of lien:** an instrument executed by a person or entity supplying labor, materials, or professional services on a project that releases that person's or entity's mechanic's lien or right to assert a mechanic's lien against the project property.

**Remedies:** the legal means a party may have to obtain redress for a loss or injury or to prevent the occurrence of a loss or injury.

**Request for a change:** see *proposal request.*

**Request for payment:** see *application for payment.*

**Responsible bidder:** see *lowest responsible bidder.*

**Restricted bid:** see *qualified bid.*

**Restricted list of bidders:** see *invited bidders.*

**Retainage:** a sum withheld from the progress payments to the contractor and later paid in accordance with the terms of the agreement between owner and contractor.

**Retained earnings:** the portion of net income (income after income taxes) that is accumulated in a corporation and is not distributed as dividends.

**Retroactive coverage:** in an insurance policy, coverage for claims made during the policy period related to occurrences prior to the date of the policy; also referred to as "prior acts coverage." Sometimes the retroactive coverage commences at a specific date referred to as the "retroactive date," which is either the inception date of a claims-made policy or an agreed-upon date set earlier than the inception date.

**Revenue:** the value received from clients as a result of the firm rendering its services (operating revenues); the value received as capital gains from the sale of long-term (fixed) assets or from aspects of the business not central to the primary purpose, such as rents from rental properties or royalties from designs (nonoperating revenues).

**Salary:** regular payments to staff for services; also used to designate the regular withdrawals by a proprietor or by partners to pay for the value of the professional services they render to the firm.

**Samples:** physical examples that illustrate materials, equipment, or workmanship and establish standards by which the work will be judged.

**Schedule:** (1) of drawings: a supplemental list, usually in chart form, of a project system, subsystem, or portion thereof; (2) of specifications: a detailed written list included in the specifications; (3) of tasks and deadlines.

**Schedule of values:** a statement furnished by the contractor to the architect reflecting the portions of the contract sum allocated to the various portions of the work and used as the basis for reviewing the contractor's applications for payment. This term is preferable to "contractor's breakdown."

**Schematic design:** services in which the architect consults with the owner to ascertain the requirements of the building project and prepares schematic design studies consisting of drawings and other documents illustrating the scale and relationships of the building components for approval by the owner. The architect also submits to the owner a preliminary estimate of construction cost based on current area, volume, or similar conceptual estimating techniques.

**Schematic design documents:** drawings and other documents illustrating the scale and relationship of project components.

**Seal:** (1) an embossing device, stamp, or other device used by a design professional on drawings and specifications as evidence of registration in the state where the work is to be performed; (2) a device formerly consisting of an impression upon wax or paper, or a wafer, which is used in the execution of a formal legal document such as a deed or contract. The statute of limitations applicable to a contract under

**seal** may be longer than for a contract not under seal.

**Selected bidder:** the bidder selected by the owner for discussions relative to the possible award of a construction contract.

**Separate contract:** one of several prime contracts for design or the construction of the project.

**Separate contractor:** a contractor on a construction project, other than the contractor identified in the agreement between owner and contractor, who has a contract with the owner.

**Settlement:** voluntary agreement to resolve a claim. It is not an admission of liability.

**Share:** see *stock*.

**Shop drawings:** drawings, diagrams, schedules, and other data specially prepared for the work by the contractor or a subcontractor, sub-subcontractor, manufacturer, supplier, or distributor to illustrate some portion of the work.

**Short-term (in financial management):** within one year; e.g., a short-term loan would come due within 12 months.

**Single contract:** contract for construction of the project under which a single prime contractor is responsible for all of the work.

**Site:** geographic location of the project, usually defined by legal boundary lines.

**Site analysis services (of the architect):** services described in the schedule of designated services in some AIA documents necessary to establish site-related limitations and requirements for a building project.

**Site observation:** see *observation of the work*.

**Soil survey:** see *geotechnical investigation*.

**Solvency:** the ability of the firm to meet its financial obligations as they mature.

**Sovereign immunity:** a long-standing doctrine to the effect that government enti-

ties cannot be sued without their consent. Federal and state laws allow suits against government agencies under certain circumstances.

**Special conditions:** a section of the conditions of the contract, other than general conditions and supplementary conditions, that may be prepared to describe conditions unique to a particular project.

**Special hazards insurance:** insurance coverage for damage caused by additional perils or risks to be included in the property insurance (at the request of the contractor or at the option of the owner). Examples often included are sprinkler leakage, collapse, water damage, and coverage for materials in transit to the site or stored off the site.

**Specifications:** a part of the contract documents contained in the project manual consisting of written requirements for materials, equipment, construction systems, standards, and workmanship.

**Staff leveling:** the process by which needs for staff generated by project services are matched to available sources or staff in an attempt to minimize either the unmet demand for services or the underutilization of staff.

**Standard of care:** the ordinary and reasonable degree of care required of a prudent professional under the circumstances. Defined as what a reasonably prudent architect, in the same community at the same time, facing the same or similar circumstances, would do. It is the measure by which behavior is judged in determining legal duties and rights.

**Statement of account:** a summary of outstanding invoices (rendered to but not paid by the client); usually shows total earned revenue, total paid, and total due. Outstanding invoices sometimes are listed by number, date, and amount.

**Statute of limitations:** a statute specifying the period of time within which legal action must be brought for alleged damage or injury or other legal relief. The lengths of the periods vary from state to state and depend upon the type of legal action.

**Statute of repose:** a statute limiting the time within which an action may be brought, without relation to whether injury has yet occurred or been discovered. The time begins when a specific event occurs, such as substantial completion of a project, and the statute of repose may extinguish the remedy even before a cause of action has accrued.

**Statutory bond:** a bond, the form or content of which is prescribed by statute.

**Stipulated sum agreement:** contract in which a specific amount is set forth as the total payment for performance of the contract. Also called *lump-sum agreement*.

**Stock:** (1) the capital that a corporation raises through the sale of shares entitling the holder of the shares to rights of ownership; (2) the certificate evidencing ownership in a corporation.

**Strategic facilities plan:** Plan that integrates facilities into the organization's strategic business plan and forecasts the supply and demand for physical space, options for acquiring space, location of the space, and budgets and schedules. Strategic facilities plans are based on goals set in business plans. See *business plan*.

**Strict liability:** liability without proof of negligence but based on one or more conditional requirements.

**Sub-bidder:** a person or entity who submits a bid to a bidder for materials or labor for a portion of the work.

**Subcontract:** agreement between a prime contractor and a subcontractor for performance of a portion of the work at the site. See also *prime contract*.

**Subcontractor:** a person or entity who has a direct contract with the contractor to perform any of the work at the site. See also *prime contractor*.

**Subpoena:** a writ issued under the authority of a court or arbitrator to compel the appearance of a witness for deposition, trial, or arbitration hearing.

**Subrogation:** the substitution of one person for another with respect to legal rights such as a right of recovery. Subrogation occurs when a third person, such as an insurance company, has paid a debt of another or claim against another and succeeds to all legal rights that the debtor or person against whom the claim was asserted may have against other persons.

**Substantial completion:** the stage in the progress of the work when the work or designated portion thereof is sufficiently complete in accordance with the contract documents that the owner can occupy or utilize the work for its intended use.

**Substitution:** a material, product, or item of equipment in place of that specified.

**Sub-subcontractor:** a person or entity who has a direct or indirect contract with a subcontractor to perform any of the work at the site.

**Subsurface investigation:** see *geotechnical investigation*.

**Successful bidder:** the bidder chosen by the owner for the award of a construction contract. Also called "selected bidder."

**Successor:** a person or entity who succeeds to a title, estate, or office.

**Summons:** a legal paper to be served on a person named as a defendant in a legal action notifying him or her to answer the complaint or be in default; also used to require nonparty witnesses to appear for depositions or at the trial or arbitration hearings.

**Superintendent:** the contractor's representative at the site who is responsible for continuous field supervision, coordination, completion of the work, and, unless another person is designated in writing by the contractor to the owner and the architect, for the prevention of accidents.

**Supervision (during construction):** direction of the work by the contractor's personnel.

**Supplemental authorization (professional services):** a written agreement authorizing a modification to a professional services agreement.

**Supplemental services (of the architect):** services described in the schedule of designated services in some AIA documents that are in addition to the generally sequential services (from predesign through postconstruction) of the architect, including such items of service as renderings, value analyses, energy studies, project promotion, expert testimony, and the like.

**Supplementary conditions:** a part of the contract documents that supplements and may also modify, change, add to, or delete provisions of the general conditions.

**Supplier:** a person or entity who supplies materials or equipment for the work, including that fabricated to a special design, but who does not perform labor at the site.

**Supply bond:** a bond by which a surety guarantees that goods or materials will be furnished by a supplier.

**Surety:** a person or entity who guarantees, in writing, the performance of an obligation by another.

**Surety bond:** see *bond.*

**Survey:** (1) mapping the boundary, topographic, and/or utility features of a site; (2) measuring an existing building; (3) analyzing a building for use of space; (4) determining owner's requirements for a project; (5) investigating and reporting required data for a project.

**Termination:** the abrogation of a contract by one party, with notice to the other party; depending upon the terms of the contract, governing law, and the actual circumstances, such abrogation may or may not be within the rights of the terminating party.

**Termination expenses (professional services):** expenses directly attributable to the termination of a professional services agreement, including an amount allowing for compensation earned to the time of termination.

**Testimony:** oral evidence given by a witness.

**Third party:** someone other than the original parties involved in a contract, claim, or action.

**Third-party beneficiary:** someone who is not a party to a contract but has a direct interest in some or all of the terms and conditions of the contract.

**Time (as the essence of a construction contract):** time limits or periods stated in the contract. A provision in a construction contract that "time is of the essence of the contract" signifies that the parties consider punctual performance within the time limits or periods in the contract to be a material part of the performance, and failure to perform on time is a breach for which the injured party is entitled to damages in the amount of loss sustained.

**Time of completion:** date established in the contract, by calendar date or by number of calendar or working days, for substantial completion of the work.

**Time utilization:** see *utilization ratio.*

**Timely completion:** completion of the work or designated portion thereof on or before the date required.

**Timely notice:** notice given within time limits prescribed by contract or in sufficient time to allow the party receiving notice to take appropriate action.

**Tort:** a violation of a right created by operation of law; a private or civil wrong or injury.

**Trade discount:** the difference between the seller's list price and the purchaser's actual cost, excluding discounts for prompt payment.

**Trial balance:** a list of the debit and credit balances of accounts maintained in the general ledger. The purpose of the trial balance is to see if the total debit balances equal the total credit balances.

**Turnkey:** a construction process in which one party agrees to deliver to another party a fully completed project, ready for the other party's use and occupancy by "turning the key."

**Umbrella liability insurance:** insurance providing coverage in an amount above existing liability policies and sometimes providing direct coverage for losses not insured under existing policies; frequently specified deductible amounts are required.

**Unbilled revenue:** revenue that has been earned but for which the client has not been given an invoice. See also work in process.

**Unearned revenue:** backlog. Revenue from services the firm has a signed commitment to render but which the firm has not yet rendered.

**Uniform commercial code (UCC):** a model statute dealing with commercial transactions that has been adopted by every state except Louisiana. UCC provisions do not normally apply to professional services.

**UniFormat:** a system for classifying building products and systems by functional subsystem, e.g., substructure, superstructure, exterior closure, etc. Illustrated on page 688 in Volume 2. See also *MasterFormat*.

**Unit price:** amount stated in the bid as a price per unit of measurement for materials or services as described in the bidding documents or in the proposed contract documents.

**Unit price contract:** a contract based on acceptance and incorporation of unit price quotations for the various portions of the project.

**Unjust enrichment:** a legal concept that prevents a party from receiving a monetary benefit to which he or she is not entitled.

**Upset price:** see *guaranteed maximum price*.

**Utilization ratio:** (1) time utilization is a ratio of direct hours billed to projects to the total hours reported; (2) payroll utilization is the ratio of direct salary expense to total salary expense. Can be calculated for an individual, a group of individuals, or the entire firm.

**Value-enhanced design:** the process of analyzing the elements of a building design in terms of its cost-effectiveness, including the proposed substitution of less expensive materials or systems for those initially suggested (this is also referred to as "value engineering").

**Vandalism and malicious mischief insurance:** insurance against loss or damage to the insured's property caused by willful and malicious damage or destruction.

**Variance:** an actual value less a budgeted or planned value.

**Vicarious liability:** indirect liability imposed on a party resulting from the acts or omissions of another person for whom the party is responsible.

**Vouchers:** forms of receipt or statements used to recognize the existence of an expense and to justify a cash outlay, serving as evidence of an obligation owed by the firm.

**Waiver of lien:** a document by which a person or entity who has or may have a right of mechanic's lien against the property of another relinquishes such right.

**Waiver of subrogation:** the relinquishment by an insured of the right of its insurance carrier to collect damages paid on behalf of the policyholder.

**Warranty:** legally enforceable assurance of quality or performance of a product or work or of the duration of satisfactory performance.

**Work (in the AIA documents):** the construction and services required by the contract documents—whether completed or partially completed—including all labor, materials, equipment, and services provided or to be provided by the contractor to fulfill the contractor's obligations. The work may constitute the whole or a part of the project.

**Work in process:** work the firm has under way for a client that is not far enough along to be billed. Work in process is a current asset and may be carried at cost or at the value of expected revenue, in which case it can also be called "unbilled revenue."

**Workers' compensation insurance:** insurance covering the liability of an employer to employees for compensation and other benefits required by workers' compensation laws with respect to injury, sickness, disease, or death arising from their employment. Previously referred to as "workmen's compensation insurance."

**Working capital:** the minimum amount of liquid capital needed to maintain the flow of capital from cash to work in process (unbilled revenue) to accounts receivable and again to cash, plus an amount as contingency.

**Working drawings:** see *drawings*.

**Write off:** to transfer an amount previously regarded as an asset (e.g., an account receivable) to an expense account or to the profit-and-loss account. The amount is said to be "expensed."

**Zoning permit:** a permit issued by appropriate government authority authorizing land to be used for a specific purpose.

# Appendix C: DOCUMENTS FINDER

Architecture projects and the relationships they entail can be structured in a number of different ways. Given a spectrum of delivery options, AIA documents can be grouped into "families" that may be applied to particular delivery methods. Within each family, the documents provide a consistent structure—and consistent text and definitions—to support the major relationships on a design and construction project.

The first choice facing an owner or architect seeking the most appropriate AIA documents for a given project is the selection of the family to which the project belongs. Six families of documents, some of which contain variations, are available:

1. A201 family
   - Cost-plus variation
   - Abbreviated variation
   - Architect-CM variation
   - Project representative variation
   - Designated services variation
   - Housing variation
   - Special services variation

2. Small project family

3. Interiors family
   - Abbreviated variation

4. Construction management–advisor (CMa) family
   - CMa project forms

5. Construction management–constructor (CMc) family

6. Design-build family

In addition, there are general agreements and forms that can be used with all the families.

AIA documents also are grouped alphanumerically by series. A sample of each document is provided for reference in the CD-ROM included with the *Handbook.* AIA documents are available for purchase through the AIA Bookstore as well as from local, full-service distributors. To receive all new and revised documents when they are issued, you can subscribe to the Documents Supplement Service by calling (800) 365-ARCH (2724) or by faxing (800) 246-5030.

Since AIA documents undergo revision cycles on a basis more or less frequent than this *Handbook,* it is wise to obtain a current AIA Documents Price List or Document Synopses from the AIA before using an AIA document.

When the owner's project is divided into separate contracts for design (with the architect) and for construction (with one or more builders), it may be appropriate to use the *A201 family* or one of its variations. This is the most commonly used family of documents since it is suitable for the conventional delivery approach of linearly sequential design-bid-build.

When the owner's project is (1) small, such as a residential renovation or addition; (2) straightforward in design; (3) blessed with established and good working relationships among the project team; (4) of short duration—less than one year from start of design to completion of construction; and (5) without delivery complications such as competitive bidding, it may be appropriate to use the *small project family.* This family of documents was introduced in 1993 to meet the growing need for standard agreements for small projects such as residential renovations, additions and other projects of relatively low cost and brief duration.

When the owner's project is divided into separate contracts for design and for the purchase of commercial or institutional furniture, furnishings, and equipment (FF&E), it may be appropriate to use the *interiors family* or one of its abbreviated variations. Similar in concept to the A201 family, the interiors documents procure FF&E under a contract separate from the design services, thereby preserving the architect's independence from any monetary interest in the sale of those goods. Unlike the A201 family, the interiors documents are not suitable for construction work, such as major tenant improvements.

When the owner's project incorporates a fourth prime player on the construction team (the other players are the owner, architect, and contractor) to act as an independent advisor on construction management matters throughout the course of both design and construction, it may be appropriate to use the *CM-advisor (CMa) family.* The CM-advisor, in theory, enhances the level of expertise applied to managing the project from start to finish. In its purest form, the CM-advisor approach preserves the construction manager's independent judgment, keeping that individual from being influenced by any monetary interest in the actual labor and materials incorporated into the construction work.

When the owner's project employs a construction manager who will go beyond purely giving advice and take on the financial risk of the construction, such as by giving a guaranteed maximum price or signing subcontracts, it may be appropriate to use the *CM-constructor (CMc) family.* Under the CM-constructor arrangement, the functions of contractor and construction manager are merged and assigned to one entity who may or may not give a GMP, but who typically assumes control over the construction work by direct contracts with the subcontractors.

When the owner's project consolidates the design and construction responsibilities into a single contract, it may be appropriate to utilize the *design-build family.* Licensing and ethical matters complicate this apparently simplified mode of delivery because the otherwise independent judgment of professionals may be clouded by influences from financial risk-taking found on the "build" side of the design-build process.

## THE A201 FAMILY: A CONVENTIONAL APPROACH

The most commonly used family of AIA documents centers on AIA Document A201, General Conditions of the Contract for Construction. This document sets forth the duties, responsibilities, and interrelationships among the principal participants in a construction project: owner, architect, and contractor, as well as subcontractors, sureties, and insurance companies.

AIA Document A201 presents industry-wide practices for projects delivered using a design-bid-build approach. The following statements generally apply to this type of project:

- The owner executes two prime contracts, one with an architect and another with a contractor.
- The architect develops the design into a set of construction documents that serve as a basis for bidding or negotiation of the construction contract(s).
- One or more contractors constructs the project for a stipulated sum or on a cost-plus-a-fee basis (with or without a guaranteed maximum price).
- The architect administers the construction contract for the owner.

The design-bid-build delivery approach is described and analyzed in Project Delivery Options (10.1). There are, of course, many variations in these "rules." The A201 family offers a number of possible forms of agreement, and each can be modified to suit the circumstances at hand. It is important to note that the various agreements in the A201 family incorporate the A201 by reference; that is to say, the general conditions are legally part of the various agreements as if written in or attached to them.

## A201 Family: Owner–Contractor Relationships

### A101 Owner-Contractor Agreement Form—Stipulated Sum

This is a standard form of agreement between owner and contractor for use when the basis of payment is a stipulated sum (fixed price). The A101 document adopts by reference and is designed for use with AIA Document A201, General Conditions of the Contract for Construction, thus providing an integrated pair of legal documents. When used together, they are appropriate for most projects. For projects of limited scope, however, use of AIA Document A107 might be considered.

### A201 General Conditions of the Contract for Construction

The general conditions are an integral part of the contract for construction in that they set forth the rights, responsibilities, and relationships of the owner, contractor, and architect. While not a party to the contract for construction between owner and contractor, the architect does participate in the preparation of the contract documents and performs certain duties and responsibilities described in detail in the general conditions. This document is typically adopted by reference into certain other AIA documents, such as owner-architect agreements, owner-contractor agreements, and contractor-subcontractor agreements. When a document is adopted by reference into another document, it is treated as fully binding under the law just as if it were written into that other document. A201's central role as a reference document for the major contracts makes it the glue that binds these contractual relationships. Therefore it is often called the "keystone" document. Since conditions vary by locality and by project, supplementary conditions are usually added to amend or supplement portions of the general conditions as required by the individual project. See A511 for a compatible guide in creating supplementary conditions for A201.

### A201/SC Federal Supplementary Conditions of the Contract for Construction

A201/SC is intended for use on certain federally assisted construction projects. For such projects, A201/SC adapts A201 by providing (1) necessary modifications of the general conditions, (2) additional conditions, and (3) insurance requirements for federally assisted construction projects.

### A401 Standard Form of Agreement Between Contractor and Subcontractor

This document is intended for use in establishing the contractual relationship between the contractor and subcontractor. It spells out the responsibilities of both parties and lists their respective obligations, which are written to parallel AIA Document A201. Blank spaces are provided where the parties can supplement the details of their agreement. A401 may be modified for use as a subcontractor–sub-subcontractor agreement.

### A511 Guide for Supplementary Conditions

The A511 is a guide containing model provisions with explanatory notes for supplementing A201 in order to adapt the conditions of the contract for construction to local circumstances. Similarly, the numbering used in this guide follows the numbering of A201. Most of the suggested language in A511 can also be adapted for use in modifying A201/CMa, A271, and the abbreviated general conditions contained in A107 and A177. The AIA permits excerption of the model text under a limited license for reproduction granted for drafting the supplementary conditions of a particular project.

### A701 Instructions to Bidders

This document is used when competitive bids are to be solicited for construction of the project. Coordinated with A201 and its related documents, A701 contains instructions on procedures to be followed by bidders in preparing and submitting their bids. Specific instructions or special requirements, such as the amount and type of bonding, are to be attached to A701 as supplementary conditions.

### *Variations*

### A107 Abbreviated Owner–Contractor Agreement Form—Stipulated Sum—for Construction Projects of Limited Scope

As an abbreviated form of agreement between owner and contractor, this document is intended for use when the basis of payment is a stipulated sum (fixed price). It is appropriate for construction projects of limited scope that do not require the complexity and length of the combination of AIA Documents A101 and A201. A107 contains abbreviated general conditions based on AIA Document A201. It may be used when the owner and contractor have established a prior working relationship (e.g., a previous project of like or similar nature) or when the project is relatively simple in detail or short in duration.

### A111 Owner–Contractor Agreement Form—Cost of the Work Plus a Fee with or Without a Guaranteed Maximum Price

This standard form of agreement between owner and contractor is appropriate for use when the basis of payment to the contractor is the cost of the work plus a fee, which in turn may be either a stipulated amount or a percentage of the construction cost. A guaranteed maximum price may be designated, with provisions, if any, for distribution of any savings below the guaranteed maximum price. A111 adopts by reference and is intended for use with AIA Document A201, thus providing an integrated pair of legal documents.

## A201 Family: Owner–Architect Relationships

### B141 Standard Form of Agreement Between Owner and Architect with Standard Form of Architect's Services

B141 is a flexible contracting package that allows architects to offer a broad range of services to clients spanning the life of a project, from conception to completion and beyond. It is structured in a multipart format consisting of an agreement form, Standard Form of Agreement, that contains initial information, terms and conditions, compensation, and a service form, Standard Form of Architect's Services: Design and Contract Administration, that defines the architect's scope of services. The separation of the scope of services from the rest of the owner-architect agreement allows users the freedom to choose alternative scopes of services. The AIA intends to publish additional scopes of services that correlate to the terms and conditions of B141.

### B511 Guide to Amendments to AIA Document B141

This document contains model text for optional provisions that may be appropriate to adapt B141 to the specific circumstances of an individual project but are not necessarily applicable to every project as standard provisions.

### *Variations*

### B144/ARCH-CM Standard Form of Amendment for the Agreement Between the Owner and Architect—Construction Management Services

B144/ARCH-CM is an amendment for use in circumstances in which the architect agrees to provide the owner with a package of construction management services to expand upon, blend with, and supplement the architect's design and other construction administration services as described in AIA Document B141, Standard Form of Agreement Between Owner and Architect. This amendment maintains and elaborates upon the architect's normal role as an advisor to the owner as set forth in both B141 and AIA Document A201, General Conditions of the Contract for Construction. Under this amendment, it is not intended that the architect provide the owner with a guaranteed maximum price (GMP) or dictate the methods and means of, or safety requirements for, the construction.

Although this document is philosophically similar to AIA's construction manager–advisor (CMa) documents, it should not be used in conjunction with any CMa documents because the underlying premise of B144/ARCH-CM is that there are only three primary players on the project: the owner, the architect (who is providing construction management services), and the contractor. In contrast, the CMa documents envision a fourth player: an independent construction manager–advisor.

### B151 Abbreviated Owner–Architect Agreement

This abbreviated owner-architect agreement is intended for use on projects of limited scope when a concise, readable contract is needed but when the services and detail of B141 may not be required. B151 provides for three phases of services, while B141 provides for five. It is also appropriate to use B151 when the owner and architect have established a prior working relationship (e.g., a previous project of like or similar nature) or where the project is relatively simple in detail or short in duration.

### B163 Standard Form of Agreement Between Owner and Architect for Designated Services

B163 is the most comprehensive AIA owner-architect agreement. This three-part document contains, among other things, a very thorough list of services divided into nine phases covering pre-design through supplemental services. By breaking the tasks of the architect into fine detail, B163 permits the architect to estimate more accurately the time and personnel costs required to do a particular project. The architect's compensation may then be calculated on a time/cost basis through use of the worksheet provided in the instructions to B163. Part one of the document deals with the typical variables of an owner-architect agreement, such as compensation and scope of services. The scope of services is delimited through use of a matrix that allows the parties to designate their agreed-upon services and responsibilities. Part two contains detailed descriptions of the specific services found in part one's matrix. Part three contains general descriptions of the parties' duties and responsibilities. The list of services in B163 has been expanded beyond any of its predecessor documents through inclusion of construction management and interiors services.

### B181 Standard Form of Agreement Between Owner and Architect for Housing Services

This document has been developed with the assistance of the U.S. Department of Housing and Urban Development and other federal housing agencies. Similar to AIA Document B151, an abbreviated owner-architect agreement, this document has some unique features, such as the requirement that the owner, and not the architect, furnish cost estimating services. B181 is coordinated with and adopts by reference AIA Document A201, General Conditions of the Contract for Construction.

### B188 Standard Form of Agreement Between Owner and Architect for Limited Architectural Services for Housing Projects

B188 is a unique addition to the AIA Contract Documents collection. Unlike its distant cousin B181, B188 is intended for use in situations where the architect will provide limited architectural services in connection with a development housing project. It anticipates that the owner will have extensive control over management of the project, acting in capacity similar to that of a developer or speculative builder of a housing project. As a result, the owner or separate consultants retained by the owner likely will provide the engineering services, specify the brand names of materials and equipment, and administer payments to contractors, among other project responsibilities. *B188 is not coordinated for use with any other AIA standard form contract.*

### B352 Duties, Responsibilities, and Limitations of Authority of the Architect's Project Representative

When and if the owner wants additional project representation at the construction site on a full- or part-time basis, B141 and other AIA owner-architect agreements reference B352 to establish the project representative's duties, responsibilities, and limitations of authority. The project representative is employed and supervised by the architect. Up until the early 1950s, B352 predecessor documents called the representative "the Clerk of the Works" because such persons were hired by the owner but supervised by the architect. The split between hiring and supervising caused numerous problems that have been resolved under B352 with the architect acting as both employer and supervisor. B352 is fully coordinated with both B141 and A201.

### B727 Standard Form of Agreement Between Owner and Architect for Special Services

B727 is the most open-ended of any AIA owner-architect agreement in that the description of services is left completely up to the ingenuity of the parties. Otherwise, many of the terms and conditions are very similar to those found in AIA Document B141. B727 is often used for planning, feasibility studies, and other services (such as construction administration) that do not follow the complete phasing sequence of services set forth in B141 and other AIA documents. If construction administration services are to be provided, care must be taken to coordinate B727 with the appropriate general conditions of the contract for construction.

## A201 Family: Architect–Consultant Relationships

Although the C series documents (architect-consultant agreements) are classified under the A201 family, they may also be used with the other families of documents—except for the Small Project family because they do not meet the simplified circumstances assumed for small projects. Care must be taken with C series documents to insert the appropriate cross-references to the specific general conditions and prime agreement used on the project.

### C141 Standard Form of Agreement Between Architect and Consultant

This is a standard form of agreement between architect and consultant establishing their respective responsibilities and mutual rights. C141 is most applicable to engineers but may also be used by consultants in other disciplines providing services for architects engaged in five phases of service as described in AIA Document B141. Its provisions are in accord with those of B141 and AIA Document A201, General Conditions of the Contract for Construction.

### *Variations*

### C142 Abbreviated Architect–Consultant Agreement

This is an abbreviated form of agreement between architect and consultant and adopts the terms of a prime agreement between owner and architect by reference. It is intended that the prime agreement be based on AIA Document B141.

### C727 Standard Form of Agreement Between Architect and Consultant for Special Services

This is a standard form of agreement between architect and consultant for special services, and is intended for use when other C series documents are inappropriate. It is often used for planning, feasibility studies, postoccupancy studies, and other services that require specialized descriptions.

### C801 Joint Venture Agreement for Professional Services

This document may be used by two or more parties to provide for their mutual rights and obligations. It is intended that the joint venture, once established, will enter into a project agreement with the owner to provide professional services. The parties may be all architects, all engineers, a combination of architects and engineers, or another combination of professionals. The document provides a choice between two methods of joint venture operation. The "division of compensation" method assumes that services provided and compensation received will be divided among the parties in the proportions agreed to at the outset of the project. Each party's profitability then depends on individual performance of preassigned tasks and is not directly tied to that of the other parties. The "division of profit and loss" method is based on each party performing work and billing the joint venture at cost plus a nominal amount for overhead. The ultimate profit or loss of the joint venture is thus divided between the parties at completion of the project, based on their respective interests.

## SMALL PROJECT FAMILY

The small project documents are primarily for use on projects with straightforward designs when these three conditions are satisfied:

- A single contractor will be employed on a negotiated basis rather than through competitive bidding.
- Modest changes are to be effected to a structure such as a residence or small commercial office.
- The total project duration will not exceed one year.

To achieve brevity, many provisions commonly found in the AIA's longer form documents have been removed, resulting in concomitant reductions in the levels of protection afforded to the parties. It is therefore necessary to make good working relationships among all participants an important requisite at the outset of the project.

It is particularly important to note that dispute resolution procedures have not been included in this family of documents. If claims and disputes are to be resolved through arbitration, mediation, or other alternative dispute resolution methods, the documents must be modified to add the appropriate terms.

The small project documents have been written in a plain language format and are suitable for use in circumstances in which the complexity and thoroughness of the AIA's more in-depth agreements is not required. On the other hand, when circumstances call for the thoroughness and detail found in other AIA documents, the small project documents may prove to be inappropriate substitutes.

### A105 Standard Form of Agreement Between Owner and Contractor for a Small Project

This is a standard form of agreement between owner and contractor employing the stipulated sum or fixed price method of compensation. It is intended for use in conjunction with the A205 general conditions document and the B155 owner-architect agreement.

### A205 General Conditions of the Contract for Construction of a Small Project

Like the A201 general conditions on which it is modeled, A205 sets forth the rights, responsibilities, and relationships of the owner, architect, and contractor, but it does so in an abridged, plain language format. A205 is adopted by reference into both the A105 and B155 agreements, and thus is treated under the law as though it were written directly into those documents.

### B155 Standard Form of Agreement Between Owner and Architect for a Small Project

The small project owner-architect agreement is also based on the stipulated sum (fixed price) method of compensation and, like A105 and A205, is an abridged form written in plain language. Like the A105 owner-contractor agreement, B155 incorporates the A205 general conditions by reference, so it is as though A205 was written directly into the owner-architect agreement.

# INTERIORS FAMILY

The interiors family is published for use in the design and procurement of furniture, furnishings, and equipment (FF&E).

Conceptually similar in part to the A201 family, the interiors family centers around a general conditions document—AIA Document A271. Through its incorporation by reference into various agreements in the family, A271 becomes a coordinating device for the responsibilities and relationships on an interiors project.

Unlike the A201 family, this family is not intended for use in significant construction, such as the renovation or addition of structural components. For such interior construction, it is assumed a separate contract will be awarded based on the A201 family of documents.

Unique to the interiors family is the assumption that, because FF&E

constitutes most of the work under the contract, the Uniform Commercial Code (UCC) applies to the transaction. Most states have adopted a version of the UCC, Article 2 of which applies to the sale of goods that are not fixed to real property. The UCC supplies, by statute, any terms that may be missing from a written contract to complete the sales transaction. Because some implied terms of the UCC may not match existing practices of the profession or the industry—such as the concept of substantial completion—A271 has been drafted to supplement the UCC by adopting those familiar practices. Users of the interiors family should become familiar with the provisions of UCC's Article 2 that may apply to the procurement of FF&E. Copies of the UCC are generally available from law bookstores or state departments of commerce or by calling West Publishing Company at (800) 328-9352.

## Interiors Family: Owner–Contractor Relationships

### A171 Owner–Contractor Agreement Form—Stipulated Sum—for Furniture, Furnishings, and Equipment

This is a standard form of agreement between owner and contractor for furniture, furnishings, and equipment (FF&E) when the basis of payment is a stipulated sum (fixed price). A171 adopts by reference and is intended for use with AIA Document A271, General Conditions of the Contract for Furniture, Furnishings, and Equipment. It may be used in any arrangement between the owner and the contractor in which the cost of FF&E has been determined in advance, either through bidding or through negotiation.

### A271 General Conditions of the Contract for Furniture, Furnishings, and Equipment

When the scope of a contract is limited to furniture, furnishings, and equipment (FF&E), A271 is intended for use in a manner similar to the way in which A201 is used for construction projects. Because the Uniform Commercial Code (UCC) has been adopted in virtually every jurisdiction, A271 has been drafted to recognize the commercial standards set forth in Article 2 of the UCC and uses certain standard UCC terminology. Except for minor works, A271 should not be used for construction involving life safety systems or structural components.

### A571 Guide for Interiors Supplementary Conditions

Similar to A511, AIA Document A571 is intended to aid practitioners in preparing supplementary conditions on interiors projects. AIA Document A571 provides additional information to address local variations in project requirements when A271, General Conditions of the Contract for Furniture, Furnishings, and Equipment, is used.

### A771 Instructions to Interiors Bidders

Similar to A701, A771 is used for competitive bidding but contains minor changes to maintain consistency with A271 and its related FF&E documents.

#### *Variations*

### A177 Abbreviated Owner–Contractor Agreement Form—Stipulated Sum—for Furniture, Furnishings, and Equipment

A177 is an abbreviated document that philosophically derives much of its content from a combination of the more complex and lengthy

A171 and A271 documents. Its abbreviated terms and conditions may be used when the contractor for furniture, furnishings, and equipment (FF&E) has a prior working relationship with the owner or when the project is relatively simple in detail or short in duration. *Caution:* This document is not intended for use on major construction work that may involve life safety systems or structural components.

## Interiors Family: Owner-Architect Relationships

### B171 Standard Form of Agreement Between Owner and Architect for Interior Services

B171 is intended for use when the architect agrees to provide an owner with design and administrative services for the procurement of interior furniture, furnishings, and equipment (FF&E). Unlike B141, which is used for building design, this document includes programming of the interior spaces and requirements as part of the package of basic services. The authority to reject goods is also left in the hands of the owner instead of the architect, because the procurement of goods is governed by the Uniform Commercial Code (UCC), which would make the architect's mistaken rejection or acceptance of goods binding upon the owner. B171 is coordinated with and adopts by reference AIA Document A271, General Conditions of the Contract for Furniture, Furnishings, and Equipment. When B171 is used, it is anticipated that A271 will form part of the contract between the owner and the contractor for FF&E.

### *Variation*

### B177 Abbreviated Form of Agreement Between Owner and Architect for Interior Services

B177 is an abbreviated document that is similar to B171 but has less complexity and detail. This document might be used when the owner and architect have a continuing relationship from previous work together or when the project is relatively simple in detail or short in duration.

## CM-ADVISER FAMILY

The CM-adviser documents are predicated upon the construction management services being provided by an independent professional who acts purely as an advisor to the owner from the start of design through the completion of construction and who does not take a monetary interest in the means and methods of construction. Under the CM-adviser arrangement, it is assumed the construction manager does not give the owner a guaranteed maximum price (GMP) or contract for any construction labor or materials. Instead, the owner contracts directly with one or more contractors for the construction work.

The result of this arrangement is the introduction of a fourth prime player—the construction manager—on the project team. This feature makes the CM-adviser family unique among AIA documents. Because of their uniqueness, the CM-adviser family should not be mixed with any of the other families of documents, especially the CM-constructor family.

A variation on the CM-adviser approach is found in the A201 fam-

ily with the new standard amendment, AIA Document B144/ARCH-CM. With this amendment, the construction management services may be integrated with the architect's typical basic services, thus eliminating the need for a fourth party on the project team.

## CM-Adviser Family: Owner–Contractor Relationships

### A101/CMa Owner–Contractor Agreement Stipulated Sum—Construction Manager–Adviser Edition

A101/CMa is a standard form of agreement between owner and contractor for use on projects when the basis of payment is a stipulated sum (fixed price) and when, in addition to the contractor and the architect, a construction manager assists the owner in an advisory capacity during design and construction. The document has been prepared for use with AIA document A201/CMa, General Conditions of the Contract for Construction—Construction Manager–Adviser Edition. This integrated set of documents is appropriate for use on projects when the construction manager serves only in the capacity of an advisor to the owner, rather than as constructor (the latter relationship being represented in AIA Document A121/CMc). A101/CMa is suitable for any arrangement between the owner and the contractor for projects when the construction cost has been predetermined, either by bidding or by negotiation.

### A201/CMa General Conditions of the Contract for Construction—Construction Manager–Adviser Edition

A201/CMa is an adaptation of AIA Document A201 and has been developed for construction management projects when a fourth player, a construction manager, has been added to the team of owner, architect, and contractor. Under A201/CMa, the construction manager has the role of an independent adviser to the owner. A major difference between A201 and A201/CMa occurs in Article 2, Administration of the Contract, which deals with the duties and responsibilities of both the architect and the construction manager–adviser. Another major difference implicit in A201/CMa is the use of multiple construction contracts directly with trade contractors.

*Caution:* It is also important to note that A201/CMa should not be used in combination with documents when it is assumed the construction manager takes on the role of constructor, gives the owner a guaranteed maximum price, or contracts directly with those who supply labor and materials for the project.

### A511/CMa Guide for Supplementary Conditions—Construction Manager-Adviser Edition

Similar to A511, the A511/CMa document is a guide to model provisions for supplementing the general conditions of the contract for construction, construction manager-adviser edition (AIA Document A201/CMa). A511/CMa should only be employed—as should A201/CMa—on projects where the construction manager is serving in the capacity of adviser to the owner (as represented by the CMa document designation), and not in situations where the Construction Manager is also the constructor (CMc document-based relationships).

Like A511, this document contains suggested language for supplementary conditions, along with notes on appropriate usage. However, many important distinctions are made to ensure consistency with other construction manager-adviser documents.

## CM-Adviser Family: Owner–Architect Relationship

### B141/CMa Standard Form of Agreement Between Owner and Architect, Construction Manager–Adviser Edition

B141/CMa is a standard form of agreement between owner and architect for use on building projects when construction management services are to be provided under separate contract with the owner. It is coordinated with AIA Document B801/CMa, an agreement between owner and construction manager–adviser in which the construction manager is an independent, professional adviser to the owner throughout the course of the project. Both B141/CMa and B801/CMa are based on the premise that a separate construction contractor will also contract with the owner. The owner-contractor contract is jointly administered by the architect and the construction manager under AIA Document A201/CMa, General Conditions of the Contract for Construction—Construction Manager–Adviser Edition. B141/CMa is not coordinated with and should not be used with documents in which the construction manager acts as the constructor (i.e., contractor) depicted in AIA Document A121/CMc. For situations in which the architect provides both design and extended construction management services, see AIA Document B144/ARCH-CM in the A201 family.

## CM-Adviser Family: Owner–Construction Manager Relationship

### B801/CMa Standard Form of Agreement Between Owner and Construction Manager–Adviser

This standard form of agreement is intended for use on projects when construction management services are assumed by a single entity who is separate and independent from the architect and the contractor and who acts solely as an adviser (CMa) to the owner throughout the course of the project. B801/CMa is coordinated with AIA Document B141/CMa, Standard Form of Agreement Between Owner and Architect—Construction Manager–Adviser Edition. Both B801/CMa and B141/CMa are based on the premise that there will be a separate construction contractor (and possibly multiple contractors) whose contracts with the owner are jointly administered by the architect and the construction manager under AIA Document A201/CMa, General Conditions of the Contract for Construction—Construction Manager–Adviser Edition. B801/CMa is not coordinated with and should not be used with documents when the construction manager acts as the constructor (i.e., contractor) for the project, such as under AIA Document A121/CMc. For situations in which the architect provides both design and extended construction management services, see AIA Document B144/ARCH-CM in the A201 family.

## CMa Project Forms

### G701/CMa Change Order—Construction Manager–Adviser Edition

The purpose of this document is essentially the same as that of G701. The major difference is that the signature of the construction manager–adviser, along with those of the owner, architect, and contractor, is required to validate a change order.

### G702/CMa Application and Certificate for Payment—Construction Manager–Adviser Edition; AIA Document G703, Continuation Sheet

Though the use and purpose of G702/CMa is substantially similar to that of G702, the construction manager–adviser edition expands responsibility for certification of payment to include both architect and construction manager. Similarly, both architect and construction manager may certify a different amount than that applied for, with each initialing the figures that have been changed and providing written explanation(s) accordingly. The standard G703 continuation sheet is appropriate for use with G702/CMa.

### G714/CMa Construction Change Directive, Construction Manager–Adviser Edition

G714/CMa is designed to effect the same type of substantive changes in the work described in the synopsis of G714. The difference between the two lies not in purpose but in execution: Whereas the owner and architect must both sign the G714 in order for the directive to become a valid contractual instrument, G714/CMa requires execution by owner, architect, and construction manager.

### G722/CMa G723/CMa Project Application and Project Certificate for Payment and Project Application Summary

These documents are similar in purpose to the combination of G702 and G703 but are for use on construction management projects. Each contractor submits separate G702CMa/G703CMa documents to the construction manager, who collects and compiles them to complete G723CMa, which serves as a summary of the contractors' applications. Project totals are then transferred to a G722CMa. The construction manager can then sign the form, have it notarized, and submit it along with the G723CMa (which has all of the separate contractors' G702 forms attached) to the architect for review and appropriate action.

## CM-CONSTRUCTOR FAMILY

The CM-constructor (CMc) documents are intended for use on projects when the construction management services are integrated with the risk-taking functions of a construction contractor, including the subcontracting and purchase of labor and materials for incorporation into the construction work.

In both CMc documents described below, the construction manager's compensation is split into two parts: Under the preconstruction phase, the CM may be compensated on a lump sum, percentage, or hourly basis, whereas under the construction phase, the CM is compensated on a cost-plus-fee basis similar to A111.

Although the responsibilities of the CM-constructor are similar to those of the CM-adviser (CMa) during a project's preconstruction phase, the CM-constructor switches into an entrepreneurial position when the design is sufficiently defined so that a guaranteed maximum price (GMP) or a firm control estimate can be proposed for the owner's approval. If the owner does not approve the GMP proposal or control estimate, the parties part ways and the owner finds another method for delivering the project. If the parties do agree, the CM-constructor proceeds to build the project and takes responsibility for the means and methods of construction.

It is important to note that the CM-constructor documents are based on significantly different parameters from those assumed for the CM-adviser family. Under no circumstances should CMc documents be used with CMa documents.

## CM-Constructor Family: Owner–Construction Manager Relationships

**A121/CMc Standard Form of Agreement Between Owner and Construction Manager Where the Construction Manager Is Also the Constructor**

This document represents the collaborative efforts of the American Institute of Architects and the Associated General Contractors of America. The AIA designates this document as A121/CMc, and the AGC as AGC 565. The construction manager provides the owner with a guaranteed maximum price proposal, which the owner may accept, reject, or negotiate. Upon the owner's acceptance of the proposal by execution of an amendment, the construction manager becomes contractually bound to provide labor and materials for the project. The document divides the construction manager's services into two phases: the preconstruction phase and the construction phase, portions of which may proceed concurrently in order to fast-track the process. A121/CMc is coordinated for use with AIA Document A201, General Conditions of the Contract for Construction, and B141, Standard Form of Agreement Between Owner and Architect. *Caution:* To avoid confusion and ambiguity, do not use this construction management document with any other AIA or AGC construction management document.

**A121/CMc-a—Amendment to the Standard Form of Agreement Between Owner and Construction Manager Where the Construction Manager Is Also the Constructor**

This document is included with A121/CMc and is intended to amend the 1991 editions of A121/CMc and AGC Document 565. Use of this document will ensure that the 1991 editions of A121/CMc and AGC Document 565 comport with A201-1997 and B141-1997.

**A131/CMc Standard Form of Agreement Between Owner and Construction Manager Where the Construction Manager Is Also the Constructor; and Where the Basis of Payment Is the Cost of the Work Plus a Fee and There Is No Guarantee of Cost**

Similar to A121/CMc, this standard form of agreement is based on the integration of construction management services with the typical construction contractor's responsibility for construction means and methods. Unlike A121/CMc, because the owner does not receive a guaranteed maximum price (GMP) as a cap on the construction costs, the owner is given the power to terminate the construction phase portion of the contract for convenience (i.e., without showing cause).

**A131/CMc-a—Amendment to the Standard Form of Agreement between Owner and Construction Manager Where the Construction Manager Is Also the Constructor— Cost Plus a Fee, No Guarantee of Cost**

This document is included with A131/CMc and is intended to amend the 1994 editions of A131/CMc and AGC Document 566. Use of this document will ensure that the 1991 editions of A131/CMc and AGC Document 566 comport with A201-1997 and B141-1997.

## DESIGN-BUILD FAMILY

Design-build documents are appropriate for use when the owner desires to place single-point responsibility for both design and construction on one entity—the design-builder.

In design-build, the owner signs one contract, A191, for both design and construction services. The designer-builder may be an architect, contractor, developer, or any other person or entity legally capable of entering into such an agreement. The designer-builder may perform all the services itself or may choose to contract separately with an architect for design services or a contractor for construction services or both. The design-build family is flexible enough to permit many of these arrangements.

It is important to note that the design-build delivery method recasts some of the traditional roles and responsibilities of the construction team. For example, unlike the conventional approach found in the A201 family, the contractual obligations of the architect in design-build are undertaken in the interest of the designer-builder, not the owner. In addition, some jurisdictions prohibit or place restrictions on the use of the design-build delivery method. It would be prudent for parties contemplating involvement in a design-build arrangement to seek professional advice regarding legal and insurance considerations associated with this method.

**A191 Standard Form of Agreements Between Owner and Design/Builder**

This document contains two agreements to be used in sequence by an owner contracting with one entity as a single point of responsibility for both design and construction services. The first agreement covers preliminary design and budgeting services, while the second deals with final design and construction. Although it is anticipated that an owner and a designer-builder entering into the first agreement will later enter into the second, the parties are not obligated to do so and may conclude their relationship after the terms of the first agreement have been fulfilled.

**A491 Standard Form of Agreements Between Design/Builder and Contractor**

This document contains two agreements to be used in sequence by a designer-builder and a construction contractor. The first agreement covers management consulting services to be provided during the preliminary design and budgeting phase of the project, while the second covers construction. It is presumed that the designer-builder has contracted with an owner to provide design and construction services under the agreements contained in AIA Document A191. Although it is anticipated that a designer-builder and a contractor entering into the first agreement will later enter into the second, the parties are not obligated to do so and may conclude their relationship after the terms of the first agreement have been fulfilled. It is also possible that the parties may forgo entering into the first agreement and proceed directly to the second.

### B901 Standard Form of Agreements Between Design/Builder and Architect

This document contains two agreements to be used in sequence by a designer-builder and an architect. The first covers preliminary design, and the second covers final design. It is presumed that the designer-builder has previously contracted with an owner to provide design and construction services under the agreements contained in AIA Document A191. Although it is anticipated that a designer-builder and an architect entering into the first agreement will later enter into the second, the parties are not obligated to do so and may conclude their relationship after the terms of the first agreement have been fulfilled. Prior to entering into either agreement in this document with a designer-builder, architects are advised to contact their legal, insurance, and management advisors.

## OFFICE AND PROJECT AGREEMENTS AND FORMS

Some AIA documents are not tied to any particular family and can be more or less applied to a variety of project delivery methods. For instance, many methods of project delivery have similarities when the owner needs to select a contractor or architect based on qualifications or other factors. Several forms from the A, B, and G series can help in this regard. In addition, when the architect merely acts as a facilitator to help the owner contract directly with surveyors or geotechnical engineers, special agreement forms have been created in the G series for that purpose. Finally, numerous forms needed by an architect's office to administer the construction process are available for use in a variety of delivery methods.

### A305 Contractor's Qualification Statement

An owner preparing to request bids or to award a contract for a construction project needs a vehicle for verifying the background, history, references and financial stability of contractors being considered. The time frame for construction and the contractor's performance, history, previous experience, and financial stability are important factors for an owner to investigate. This form provides a sworn, notarized statement with appropriate attachments to elaborate on important aspects of the contractor's qualifications.

### A310 Bid Bond

A bid bond establishes the maximum penal amount that may be due the owner if the selected bidder fails to execute the contract and provide any required performance and payment bonds. This simple one-page form was drafted with input from the major surety companies to ensure its legality and acceptability.

### A312 Performance Bond and Payment Bond

This form incorporates two bonds covering the contractor's performance and the contractor's obligations to pay subcontractors and others for material and labor. The A312 document obligates the surety to act responsively to the owner's requests for discussions aimed at preventing or anticipating a contractor's default. Prior to executing the document for a public project, a user of A312 should check with legal counsel to determine whether A312 meets local legal requirements.

### A501 Recommended Guide for Competitive Bidding Procedures and Contract Awards for Building Construction

This guide is intended to outline appropriate procedures in the bidding and award of contracts when competitive lump sum bids are requested in connection with building and related construction. This guide is a joint publication of the AIA and the Associated General Contractors of America (AGC).

### A521 Uniform Location of Subject Matter

A521 is a tabulation to guide the user in determining the proper placement and phrasing of information customarily used on a construction project. This document shows the importance of maintaining uniformity in location and language from document to document with respect to subject matter. Inconsistencies in either area may cause confusion or unanticipated legal problems. A521 is a joint publication of the AIA and the Engineers Joint Contract Documents Committee (EJCDC), which is composed of the National Society of Engineers, American Consulting Engineers Council, and American Society of Civil Engineers. By consensus of these organizations, the AIA and EJCDC documents follow A521's tabular guide with regard to the placement of subject matter among the various contract and bidding documents.

### B431 Architect's Qualification Statement

This is a standardized outline of information that a client may wish to review prior to selecting an architect for a particular project. It may be used as part of a request for proposals (RFP) or as a final check on the credentials of an architect. Under some circumstances, B431 may also be attached to the owner-architect agreement to show, for example, the team of professionals and consultants expected to be employed on the owner's project.

### D101 The Architectural Area and Volume of Buildings

This document defines methods for calculating the architectural area and volume of buildings. D101 also covers interstitial space, single-occupant-net-assignable area, and store-net-assignable area.

### D200 Project Checklist

The project checklist is a convenient list of tasks a practitioner is likely to perform on a given project. This checklist will help the architect recognize the tasks required and locate the data necessary to fulfill assigned responsibilities. By providing space to note the date of actions taken, D200 may also serve as a permanent record of the owner's, the contractor's, and the architect's actions and decisions.

### G601 Land Survey Agreement

This document is intended for use by an owner in requesting a proposal and in subsequently executing an agreement for surveying services. The form should be used in accordance with the owner-architect agreement provisions establishing the owner's responsibility for providing a certified survey of the site. G601 enables the owner, in consultation with the architect, to establish survey requirements for the site and to evaluate the proposal prior to executing the agreement.

### G602 Geotechnical Services Agreement

This document is intended for use by an owner in requesting a proposal and in subsequently executing an agreement for geotechnical services. The document should be used in accordance with the owner-architect agreement provisions establishing the owner's responsibility for furnishing the services of geotechnical engineers. G602 enables the owner, in consultation with the architect and the structural engineer, to establish the geotechnical services required for the project and to evaluate the proposal prior to executing the agreement.

### G605 Notification of Amendment to the Professional Services Agreement

This document is intended to be used by an architect when notifying an owner of a proposed amendment to most of the AIA's owner-architect agreements, such as B141 and B151.

### G606 Amendment to the Professional Services Agreement

This document is intended to be used by an architect when amending the professional services provisions in most of the AIA's owner-architect agreements, such as B141 and B151.

### G607 Amendment to the Consultant Services Agreement

This document is intended to be used by an architect or consultant when amending the professional services provisions in most of the AIA's architect-consultant agreements, such as C141 and C142.

### G701 Change Order

G701 may be used as the written documentation of changes in the work and the contract sum or contract time that are mutually agreed to by the owner and contractor. G701 provides space for the signatures of the owner, architect, and contractor and for a complete description of the change.

### G702/G703 Application and Certificate for Payment and Continuation Sheet

These documents provide convenient and complete forms on which the contractor can apply for payment and the architect can certify that payment is due. The forms require the contractor to show the status of the contract sum to date, including the total dollar amount of the work completed and stored to date, the amount of retainage, the total of previous payments, a summary of change orders, and the amount of current payment requested. G703, Continuation Sheet, breaks the contract sum into portions of the work in accordance with a schedule of values required by the general conditions. The form serves as both the contractor's application and the architect's certification. Its use can expedite payment and reduce the possibility of error. If the application is properly completed and acceptable to the architect, the architect's signature certifies to the owner that a payment in the amount indicated is due to the contractor. The form also allows the architect to certify an amount different than the amount applied for, with explanation by the architect.

### G704 Certificate of Substantial Completion

G704 is a standard form for recording the date of substantial completion of the work or a designated portion. The contractor prepares a list of items to be completed or corrected, and the architect verifies and amends this list. If the architect finds that the work is substantially complete, the form is prepared for acceptance by the contractor and the owner. Appended thereto is the list of items to be completed or corrected. The form provides for agreement as to the time allowed for completion or correction of the items, the date upon which the owner will occupy the work or designated portion thereof, and a description of responsibilities for maintenance, heat, utilities, and insurance.

### G704/CMa Certificate of Substantial Completion, Construction Manager-Adviser Edition

This document expands responsibility for certification of substantial completion to include both the architect and the construction manager.

### G706 Contractor's Affidavit of Payment of Debts and Claims

The contractor submits this affidavit with the final request for payment, stating that all payrolls, bills for materials and equipment, and other indebtedness connected with the work for which the owner might be responsible have been paid or otherwise satisfied. G706 requires the contractor to list any indebtedness or known claims in connection with the construction contract that have not been paid or otherwise satisfied and to furnish a lien bond or indemnity bond to protect the owner with respect to each exception.

### G706A Contractor's Affidavit of Release of Liens

This document is useful in support of AIA Document G706 when the owner requires a sworn statement of the contractor that all releases or waivers of liens have been received. In such event, it is normal for the contractor to submit G706 and G706A, along with attached releases or waivers of liens for the contractor, all subcontractors, and others who may have lien rights against the owner's property. The contractor is required to list any exceptions to the sworn statement provided in G706A and to furnish a lien bond or indemnity bond to protect the owner with respect to such exceptions.

### G707 Consent of Surety to Final Payment

By obtaining the surety's approval of final payment to the contractor and its agreement that final payment will not relieve the surety of any of its obligations, the owner may preserve its rights under the bonds.

### G707A Consent of Surety to Reduction in or Partial Release of Retainage

This is a standard form for use when a surety company is involved and the owner-contractor agreement contains a clause whereby retainage is reduced during the course of the construction project. When duly executed, the form assures the owner that such reduction or partial release of retainage does not relieve the surety of its obligations.

### G709 Proposal Request

This form is used to obtain price quotations required in the negotiation of change orders. G709 is not a change order or a direction to proceed with the work; it is simply a request to the contractor for information related to a proposed change in the construction contract.

## G710 Architect's Supplemental Instructions

Supplemental instructions are used by the architect to issue additional instructions or interpretations or to order minor changes in the work. The form is intended to assist the architect in performing obligations as interpreter of the contract document requirements in accordance with the owner-architect agreement and the general conditions. This form should not be used to change the contract sum or contract time. If the contractor believes a change in the contract sum or contract time is involved, other G series documents must be used.

## G711 Architect's Field Report

This is a standard form for the architect's project representative to use in maintaining a concise record of site visits or, in the case of a full-time project representative, a daily log of construction activities.

## G712 Shop Drawing and Sample Record

This is a standard form by which the architect can schedule and monitor shop drawings and samples. Since the shop drawing process tends to be complex, this schedule, which shows the progress of a submittal, contributes to the orderly processing of work and serves as a permanent record of the chronology of the process.

## G714 Construction Change Directive

This document replaces AIA Document G713, Construction Change Authorization. G714 was developed as a directive for changes in the work that, if not expeditiously implemented, might delay the project. In contrast to a change order (AIA Document G701), G714 is to be used when the owner and contractor, for whatever reason, have not reached agreement on proposed changes in the contract sum or contract time. Upon receipt of a completed G714, the contractor must promptly proceed with the change in the work described therein.

## G715 Instruction Sheet and Attachment for ACORD Certificate of Insurance

The ACORD form certificate is widely used to certify the coverage required of contractors under the terms of A201 and other AIA documents. Since the ACORD certificate does not have space to show all the coverages required by such AIA documents, the Supplement Attachment is used to add that information to the ACORD certificate.

## G805   List of Subcontractors

AIA Document G805 is a form for listing subcontractors and others proposed to be employed on a project as required by the bidding documents. It is to be filled out by the contractor and returned to the architect.

# Index

# AIA Documents on CD-ROM

**DOCUMENT SYNOPSES**

**COMMENTARIES**

A201 Commentary

B141 Commentary

**A SERIES DOCUMENTS**

**A101** Standard Form of Agreement Between Owner and Contractor—Stipulated Sum

**A101/CMa** Standard Form of Agreement Between Owner and Contractor—Stipulated Sum, Construction Manager-Adviser Edition

**A105** Standard Form of Agreement Between Owner and Contractor for a Small Project—Stipulated Sum

**A205** General Conditions of the Contract for Construction of a Small Project

**A107** Abbreviated Standard Form of Agreement Between Owner and Contractor for Construction Projects of Limited Scope—Stipulated Sum

**A111** Standard Form of Agreement Between Owner and Contractor—Cost of the Work Plus a Fee, Guaranteed Maximum Price

**A121/CMc** Standard Form of Agreement Between Owner and Construction Manager Where the Construction Manager Is Also the Constructor (AGC Document 565)

**A121/CMc-a** Amendment to A121/CMc

**A131/CMc** Standard Form of Agreement Between Owner and Construction Manager Where the Construction Manager Is Also the Constructor—Cost Plus a Fee, No Guarantee of Cost (AGC Document 566)

**A131/CMc-a** Amendment to Al3l/CMc

**A171** Standard Form of Agreement Between Owner and Contractor for Furniture, Furnishings, and Equipment—Stipulated Sum

**A177** Abbreviated Form of Agreement Between Owner and Contractor for Furniture, Furnishings, and Equipment—Stipulated Sum

**A191** Standard Form of Agreements Between Owner and Design/Builder

**A201** General Conditions of the Contract for Construction

**A201/CMa** General Conditions of the Contract for Construction Where the Construction Manager Is Not a Constructor, Construction Manager–Adviser Edition

**A201/SC** Federal Supplementary Conditions of the Contract for Construction

**A271** General Conditions of the Contract for Furniture, Furnishings, and Equipment

**A305** Contractor's Qualification Statement

**A310** Bid Bond

**A312** Performance Bond and Payment Bond

**A401** Standard Form of Agreement Between Contractor and Subcontractor

**A491** Standard Form of Agreements Between Design/Builder and Contractor

**A501** Recommended Guide for Competitive Bidding Procedures and Contract Awards for Building Construction

**A511** Guide for Supplementary Conditions

**A511/CMa** Guide for Supplementary Conditions, Construction Manager–Adviser Edition

**A521** Uniform Location of Subject Matter

**A571** Guide for Interiors Supplementary Conditions

**A701** Instructions to Bidders

**A771** Instructions to Interiors Bidders

## B SERIES DOCUMENTS

**B141** Standard Form of Agreement Between Owner and Architect with Standard Form of Architect's Services

**B141/CMa** Standard Form of Agreement Between Owner and Architect Where the Construction Manager Is Not a Constructor, Construction Manager–Adviser Edition

**B144/ARCH-CM** Standard Form of Amendment for the Agreement Between Owner and Architect Where the Architect Provides Construction Management Services as an Adviser to the Owner

**B151** Abbreviated Standard Form of Agreement Between Owner and Architect

**B155** Standard Form of Agreement Between Owner and Architect for a Small Project

**B163** Standard Form of Agreement Between Owner and Architect with Descriptions of Designated Services and Terms and Conditions

**B171** Standard Form of Agreement for Interior Design Services

**B177** Abbreviated Form of Agreement for Interior Design Services

**B181** Standard Form of Agreement Between Owner and Architect for Housing Services

**B188** Standard Form of Agreement Between Owner and Architect for Limited Architectural Services for Housing Projects

**B352** Duties, Responsibilities and Limitations of Authority of the Architect's Project Representative

**B431** Architect's Qualification Statement

**B511** Guide for Amendments to AIA Owner–Architect Agreements

**B727** Standard Form of Agreement Between Owner and Architect for Special Services

**B801/CMa** Standard Form of Agreement Between Owner and Construction Manager Where the Construction Manager Is Not a Constructor

**B901** Standard Form of Agreement Between Design/Builder and Architect

## C SERIES DOCUMENTS

**C141** Standard Form of Agreement Between Architect and Consultant

**C142** Abbreviated Standard Form of Agreement Between Architect and Consultant to Be Used in Conjunction with Standard Form of Agreement Between Owner and Architect

**C727** Standard Form of Agreement Between Architect and Consultant for Special Services

**C801** Joint Venture Agreement for Professional Services

## D SERIES DOCUMENTS

**D101** The Architectural Area and Volume of Buildings

**D200** Project Checklist

## G SERIES DOCUMENTS

**G601** Request for Proposal–Land Survey

**G602** Request for Proposal–Geotechnical Services

**G605** Notification of Amendment to the Professional Services Agreement

**G606** Amendment to the Professional Services Agreement

**G607** Amendment to the Consultant Services Agreement

**G701** Change Order

**G701/CMa** Change Order, Construction Manager–Adviser Edition

**G702** Application and Certificate for Payment

**G702/CMa** Application and Certificate for Payment, Construction Manager–Adviser Edition

**G703** Continuation Sheet

**G704** Certificate of Substantial Completion

**G704/CMa** Certificate of Substantial Completion, Construction Manager–Adviser Edition

**G706** Contractor's Affidavit of Payment of Debts and Claims

**G706A** Contractor's Affidavit of Release of Liens

**G707** Consent of Surety to Final Payment

**G707A** Consent of Surety to Reduction in or Partial Release of Retainage

**G709** Proposal Request

**G710** Architect's Supplemental Instructions

**G711** Architect's Field Report

**G712** Shop Drawing and Sample Record

**G714** Construction Change Directive

**G714/CMa** Construction Change Directive, Construction Manager–Adviser Edition

**G715** Supplemental Attachment for ACORD Certificate of Insurance

**G722/CMa** Project Application and Project Certificate for Payment

**G723/CMa** Project Application Summary

**G805** List of Subcontractors

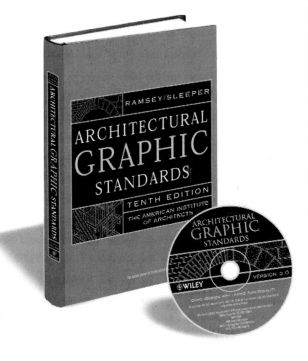

# About the Handbook CD-ROM

## Contents of the CD-ROM

The CD accompanying the 13th edition of the *Architect's Handbook of Professional Practice Student Edition* contains *samples* of all the AIA contract documents (series A, B, C, D, and G) in Adobe Acrobat PDF format. These files, current when this edition went to press, are for reference purposes only.

## To view the documents

On a Windows operating system, insert the CD-ROM and wait for the introductory screen to appear. If this does not occur automatically, launch the setup.exe file. On a Macintosh platform, launch the AIAsetup file and wait for the introductory screen to appear. To open and view the documents, Adobe Acrobat Reader® 4 or higher is required. Acrobat Reader for PC, Macintosh, and other platforms can be downloaded free from the Adobe Web site at www.adobe.com.

## To Purchase AIA contract documents

AIA contract documents are available in print and in the AIA Contract Documents: Electronic Format 3.0, which allows users to digitally customize and create contract documents for all types and sizes of projects. For information on how to purchase these products and how to keep current on document updates, call 800-365-2724 or 301-987-1683.

## For technical support

For basic installation or operation of the CD-ROM, or if your CD-ROM is defective, contact John Wiley & Sons via e-mail at: techhelp@wiley.com. If technical problems are experienced with the CD, please contact AIA technical support by phone, fax, or e-mail:

*Tel:* 800-942-7732          *Fax:* 410-964-9098
*Tel:* 410-964-1583          *E-mail:* elecdoc@aia.org